Third Canadian Edition

Marketing

Charles W. Lamb, Jr.
M.J. Neeley Professor of Marketing
M.J. Neeley School of Business
Texas Christian University

Joseph F. Hair, Jr.
Alvin C. Copeland Endowed Chair of Franchising and Director, Entrepreneurship Institute
Louisiana State University

Carl McDaniel
Chair, Department of Marketing
College of Business Administration
University of Texas at Arlington

A. J. Faria
University of Windsor

William J. Wellington
Associate Professor of Marketing at the Odette School of Business, University of Windsor

THOMSON
NELSON

Australia Canada Mexico Singapore Spain United Kingdom United States

Marketing, Third Canadian Edition

by Charles W. Lamb, Jr., Joseph F. Hair, Jr., Carl McDaniel, Anthony J. Faria, and William J. Wellington

Associate Vice-President, Editorial Director
Evelyn Veitch

Executive Editors:
Veronica Visentin
Ric Kitowski

Senior Executive Marketing Manager:
Don Thompson

Senior Developmental Editor:
Katherine Goodes

Photo Researcher and Permissions Coordinator:
Kristiina Bowering

Production Editor:
Julie van Veen

Copy Editor:
Erin Moore

Proofreader:
Matthew Kudelka

Indexer:
Belle Wong

Senior Production Coordinator:
Hedy Sellers

Creative Director:
Angela Cluer

Interior Design:
Liz Harasymczuk

Cover Design:
Rocket Design

Cover Image:
www.firstlight.ca

Compositor:
Doris Chan

Printer:
Transcontinental

Adapted from *Marketing* 7e, by Lamb, Hair & McDaniel, published by SOUTH-WESTERN, © 2004.

Printed and bound in Canada
1 2 3 4 08 07 06 05

For more information contact Nelson, 1120 Birchmount Road, Toronto, Ontario, M1K 5G4. Or you can visit our Internet site at http://www.nelson.com

Library and Archives Canada Cataloguing in Publication

Marketing / Charles W. Lamb, Jr ... [et al.]. — 3rd Canadian ed.

First ed. published 1997 had edition statement: Canadian 3rd ed.; 2nd ed. published as: The subject is marketing.

Includes bibliographical references and index.

ISBN 0-17-641649-8

1. Marketing—Textbooks.
2. Marketing—Management—Textbooks. I. Lamb, Charles W. II. Title: Subject is marketing.

HF5415.M29325 2005 658.8
C2004-906275-1

>> BRIEF CONTENTS

>> TABLE OF CONTENTS

Part 5 Closing 470

>> PART 6
Pricing Decisions 473

15 Pricing Concepts 474

16 Setting the Right Price 504

>> YOUR GUIDE TO FEATURES

Opening Vignettes

Global Perspectives boxes

Ethics in Marketing boxes

Try It

Watch It: video cases

Marketing Miscues

Critical Thinking Cases

>> PREFACE

>> ABOUT THIS EDITION

You are holding a textbook that has experienced a dramatic increase in the number of college and university student-users with each edition. We are very grateful to the many professors who have selected our text to give students their first exposure to the dynamic world of marketing. We are pleased that so many professors stayed with our text when we brought out the second edition. Our research gives us an indication why this is true. Students find *Marketing*, by Lamb, Hair, McDaniel, Faria, and Wellington, the most exciting, readable, and enjoyable text of their college/university career.

chapter 3

The Marketing Environment and Marketing Ethics

>> LEARNING OBJECTIVES

1 Discuss the external environment of marketing and explain how it affects a firm

2 Describe the social factors that affect marketing

3 Explain the importance to marketing managers of current demographic trends

4 Explain the importance to marketing managers of multiculturalism and growing ethnic markets

5 Identify consumer and marketer reactions to the state of the economy

6 Identify the impact of technology on a firm

7 Discuss the political and legal environment of marketing

8 Explain the basics of foreign and domestic competition

9 Describe the role of ethics and ethical decisions in business

10 Discuss corporate social responsibility

NEL

>> WHAT MAKES *MARKETING*, THIRD CANADIAN EDITION, SO POPULAR WITH INSTRUCTORS?

Our Integrated Learning System

All of our new and exciting content is anchored by the cornerstone of our text, our **Integrated Learning System**. The text and all major supplements are organized around the learning objectives that appear at the beginning of each chapter, so *Marketing*, Third Canadian Edition, is both easy to teach from, for you, the instructor, and to learn from for your students.

1 A numbered icon like the one shown in the margin identifies each learning objective in each chapter and appears next to its related material throughout the text, Instructor's Manual, Test Bank, and Study Guide. In other words, every learning objective links the text, Study Guide, Test Bank, and all components of the Instructor's Manual.

Chapter learning objectives are the linchpin of the Integrated Learning System. They provide a structure for your lesson plans—everything you need to ensure complete coverage of each objective icon. Do you want to stress learning objective 2, Chapter 12, "Describe the nature of retail operations?" No problem. Go to the Instructor's Manual, objective 2, Chapter 12, and you'll find supplemental material. Do you want to emphasize the same objective on an exam? In every chapter in the Test Bank, questions are organized by type and level of difficulty. Now you can test on objective 2 by type of question and degree of difficulty. This value-driven system for you, the instructor, delivers what it promises—full integration.

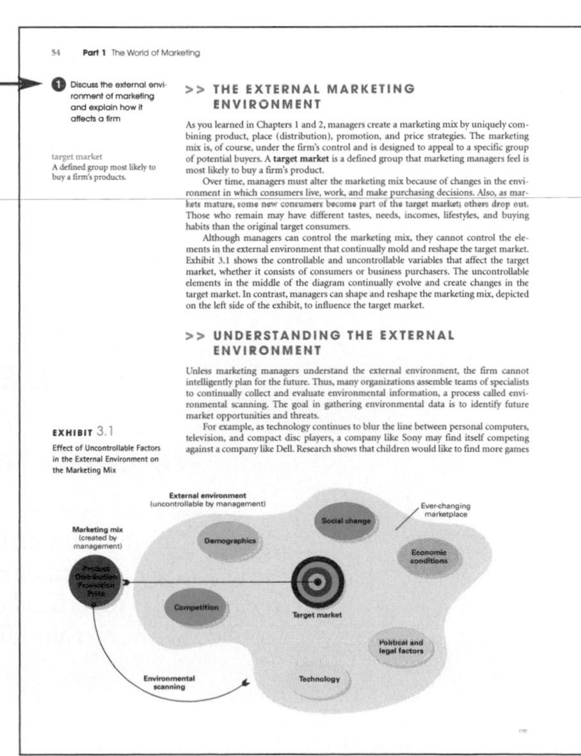

54 **Part 1** The World of Marketing

1 Discuss the external environment of marketing and explain how it affects a firm

>> THE EXTERNAL MARKETING ENVIRONMENT

As you learned in Chapters 1 and 2, managers create a marketing mix by uniquely combining product, place (distribution), promotion, and price strategies. The marketing mix is, of course, under the firm's control and is designed to appeal to a specific group of potential buyers. A **target market** is a defined group that marketing managers feel is most likely to buy a firm's product.

target market
A defined group most likely to buy a firm's products.

Over time, managers must alter the marketing mix because of changes in the environment in which consumers live, work, and make purchasing decisions. Also, as markets mature, some new consumers become part of the target market; others drop out. Those who remain may have different tastes, needs, incomes, lifestyles, and buying habits than the original target consumers.

Although managers can control the marketing mix, they cannot control the elements in the external environment that continually mold and reshape the target market. Exhibit 3.1 shows the controllable and uncontrollable variables that affect the target market, whether it consists of consumers or business purchasers. The uncontrollable elements in the middle of the diagram continually evolve and create changes in the target market. In contrast, managers can shape and reshape the marketing mix, depicted on the left side of the exhibit, to influence the target market.

>> UNDERSTANDING THE EXTERNAL ENVIRONMENT

Unless marketing managers understand the external environment, the firm cannot intelligently plan for the future. Thus, many organizations assemble teams of specialists to continually collect and evaluate environmental information, a process called environmental scanning. The goal in gathering environmental data is to identify future market opportunities and threats.

For example, as technology continues to blur the line between personal computers, television, and compact disc players, a company like Sony may find itself competing against a company like Dell. Research shows that children would like to find more games

EXHIBIT 3.1
Effect of Uncontrollable Factors in the External Environment on the Marketing Mix

Our Text Pedagogy Excites and Reinforces Learning

Pedagogical features are meant to reinforce learning, but that doesn't mean that they have to be boring. We have created teaching tools within the text itself that will excite student interest as well as teach.

- Opening Vignettes, revisited at chapter conclusions: each chapter begins with a new, current, real-world story about a marketing decision or situation facing a predominantly Canadian company. A special section called Connect It answers the teaser questions posed in the opening vignette and helps illustrate how the chapter material relates to the real world of marketing.
- Review It: each chapter ends with Review It, a summary that distills the main points of the chapter. Chapter summaries are organized around the learning objectives so that students can use them as a quick check on their achievement of learning objectives. Discussion questions and activities are listed under the learning objective to which they pertain.

- Writing Questions: to help students improve their writing skills, we have included writing exercises with the Review It questions at the end of each chapter. These exercises are marked with the icon shown here. The writing questions are designed to be brief so that students can accomplish writing assignments in a short time and so that grading time is minimized.

- End-of-Chapter Team Activities: the ability to work collaboratively is key to success in today's business world. End-of-chapter team activities, identified by the icon shown here, give students opportunities to learn to work together by engaging in consensus building and problem solving.
- Define It: key terms appear in boldface in the text, with definitions in the margins, making it easy for students to check their understanding of key definitions. A complete alphabetical list of key terms with page references appears at the end of each chapter as a study checklist called Define It.
- Apply It: these short scenarios prompt students to apply marketing concepts to small business and entrepreneurial settings. Each scenario ends with provocative questions to aid student analysis and comprehension.
- Think About It: students are often heard to comment, "Yes, I can use this information when I graduate and get into my career, but what take-away value can I get right now?" Think About It addresses this concern by covering a topic related to the chapter that the student could put to work today.
- Try It: all chapters contain Try It, a case with questions to help students work through problems facing real companies today.

>> WHAT MAKES *MARKETING*, THIRD CANADIAN EDITION, SO POPULAR WITH STUDENTS?

We Grab Their Attention

We have done extensive research to provide a comprehensive, up-to-the-minute introduction to the field of marketing. Because we weave hundreds of real-world examples into our discussions, our text is lively and interesting. You should know that this never means superficial or shallow. Important concepts are covered in detail in a lucid manner with numerous illustrations.

It's Easy to Learn

The **Integrated Learning System** delivers value for students as they prepare for exams. The learning objective icons identify all the material in the text and Study Guide that relates to each specific learning objective. Students can easily check their grasp of each objective by reading the list at the beginning of each chapter, reading the text sections, reviewing the corresponding summary section (Review It), answering the Study Guide questions for that objective, and returning to the appropriate text sections for further review when they have difficulty with any of the questions. Students can quickly identify all material relating to an objective by simply looking for the learning objective icon.

We Integrate Technology in a Meaningful Way

Fresh Internet Activities and Real-Time Examples

Despite the technology bust of the last few years, the Internet is here to stay and continues to be a powerful resource for teaching and learning. Each chapter of *Marketing* contains numerous examples of the Internet's role in marketing, designated throughout the text by the icon in the margin. On Line icons appear in the margins throughout each chapter and are tied to either organizations mentioned in the text or the concepts being discussed. Links to all URLs in the book are located on the text's Internet site at **http://www.lamb3e.nelson.com.**

Technology Exercises that Reinforce the Chapter Concepts

Nearly every chapter has multiple technology assignments in the Review It section. Questions that contain a technology component are identified with the On Line icon.

In addition to the numerous Internet assignments throughout the book, students also have access to the InfoTrac® College Edition database. InfoTrac® College Edition contains over 11 million articles from over 3,800 sources, including many Canadian publications, dating back to 1980. InfoTrac® College Edition exercises can be found throughout the text to either guide an original research project or provide a structured reading exercise.

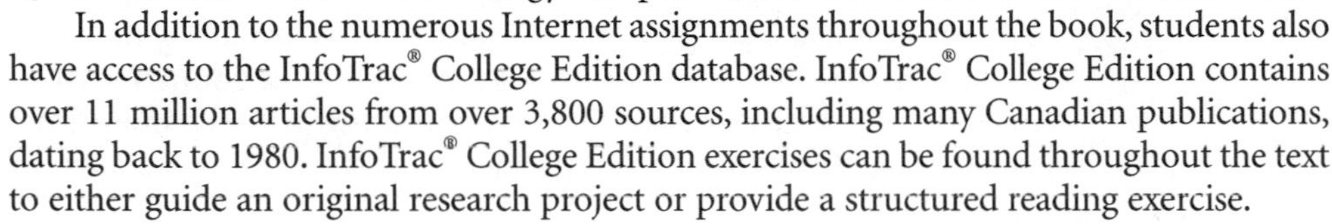

Who Wants to Be a Marketer?

Who Wants to Be a Marketer? is a fun and exciting way to review terminology and concepts with students. This easy-to-use game only requires Microsoft® PowerPoint® software and a method to display the screen to the entire class (such as a data projector). Who Wants to Be a Marketer? has two rounds of 50 original questions per chapter and can be found on the text's website at **http://www.lamb3e.nelson.com**!

We Offer a Robust Comprehensive Website

The text's website is dedicated to students' needs and geared toward helping them succeed. It is organized around and integrated with the learning objectives found in the text. The abundant student materials include:

- chapter summary points;
- crossword puzzles of marketing terminology;
- Internet applications that contain on-line margin activities, plus Think About It and Review It items from the text that have an Internet component;
- interactive quizzes with a self-assessment for each chapter;
- the order form for the *Grademaker Study Guide and Workbook*, plus an abridged sample chapter from the study guide;
- Your Marketing Career, a valuable tool that presents information on a variety of marketing careers and includes helpful advice and a multitude of resources for starting a marketing career; and
- Career *Exersites*, unique Internet activities designed to help students use the Web as a career research tool. Developed specifically for each chapter, the exersites give students resources for researching a marketing career in a field related to the chapter content.

>> SO WHAT'S NEW?

chapter 6

Segmenting and Targeting Markets

>> LEARNING OBJECTIVES

1. Describe the characteristics of markets and market segments
2. Explain the importance of market segmentation
3. Discuss criteria for successful market segmentation
4. Describe the bases commonly used to segment consumer markets
5. Describe the bases for segmenting business markets
6. List the steps involved in segmenting markets
7. Discuss alternative strategies for selecting target markets
8. Explain how and why firms implement positioning strategies and how product differentiation plays a role
9. Discuss global market segmentation and targeting issues

>> OPENING VIGNETTES

Carefully prepared opening vignettes stimulate student interest in the chapter topics. Canadian companies like the Toronto Blue Jays, Grocery Gateway, Krave's Candy Company of Winnipeg, Pet Valu, Spin Master Ltd., H.J. Heinz (Leamington, Ontario), Maple Leaf Sports & Entertainment Ltd., and Canada Post are discussed.

14 **Part 1** The World of Marketing

GLOBAL PERSPECTIVES

Powering into Europe

The Coca-Cola Company sees the fragmented and fast-growing European sports-drink market as an important opportunity, which is why the company is investing over $50 million to launch Powerade in Europe. It is Coke's biggest marketing push in Europe in a number of years. "There is an open field in Europe," says Keith Pardy, director of strategic marketing for Coca-Cola West Europe.

Sports drinks command a higher premium in Europe than in Canada or the United States, where the market is well established. A 500-millilitre bottle of a sports drink costs between 90 pence and £1 ($2.20 and $2.45) in Britain, for example, compared with about 75 pence ($1.85) for the same size bottle of Coke or Pepsi.

Moreover, Coke believes Europeans aged 13 to 29, the target market for Powerade, increasingly are making sports a bigger part of their lives. Coke says its new Powerade drink increases endurance during exercise by combining the benefits of a sports drink with the energy boost of drinks such as Red Bull, made by a closely held Austrian company. The formula in Europe is the same as in the new vitamin-B–enhanced Powerade sold in Canada, but the taste is slightly different because of certain European regulations on ingredients, Mr. Pardy says. The look is the same as in Canada, with a futuristic letter "P" logo.

As in Canada, Coke is marketing Powerade to the likes of roller bladers and skateboarders. Posters to be placed in gyms across Europe as part of the advertising campaign for Powerade will allude to "extreme sports" challenges, for example. But the company hopes the drink will eventually transcend its original use and that European youths will begin drinking sports beverages more generally, as youths do in North America.

"We want to grow the market in Europe to the point where you'll use it whenever you need endurance, beyond sports occasions," Mr. Pardy says.

Powerade will be launched in Britain, Ireland, France, Germany, Spain, Sweden, Turkey, Italy, Poland, Hungary, and Greece. The drink, which will be sold in citrus, orange, and vivid-blueberry flavours, will be distributed first through vending machines in gyms, sports centres, and soccer stadiums before moving to convenience stores and supermarkets.

Advertising for the drink will span billboards, television commercials, sponsorships with sports figures, the Internet, and direct mail. Most of the advertising will be directed at a male audience, because in Europe the sports-drink market is generally skewed more toward men.[24]

Describe Coke's target market strategy for Powerade in Europe. Explain the marketing mix that the company plans to employ.

ETHICS IN MARKETING

The Marketing of Gambling?

With the recent opening of three casinos in Detroit, Michigan (just across the Ambassador Bridge from Windsor, Ontario), and the possibility of a smoke-free workplace and consumer environment in Windsor and Essex County, the Ontario Lottery and Gaming Corporation has become increasingly concerned about the prospect of Casino Windsor losing revenue. "It will never retrench on my watch," said Stanley Sadinsky, chairman of the Ontario Lottery and Gaming Corporation. With those words, Mr. Sadinsky announced the hiring of a group of marketing experts to identify ways to ensure that gamblers keep coming back to Casino Windsor.

Casino Windsor has contributed significantly to the billions of dollars generated by the Ontario Government from gambling revenues. In 2003, Casino Windsor grossed in excess of $600 million. An average of nearly 14,000 people a day visit, and lose some of their money, at Casino Windsor. The profitability of Casino Windsor makes it a valuable asset to the province, according to Mr. Sadinsky: "It's very worthwhile and we're paying a lot of attention to it. There is no thought of doing anything but moving the casino forward. We'll develop the best strategy for it that we can."

The new competition from the Detroit casinos, the SARS problem of 2003 in Windsor and the rest of Ontario, and delays at the border since heightened terrorists alerts in the U.S. were put into effect have all caused problems for Casino Windsor. In 2003, Casino ... enues were down 30 perc... keting experts will be explo... to bring these customers b... Sadinsky. Expanding the ... option being explored.

The Liberal governm... create a smoke-free prov... some, and the OLGC is making its concerns on this matter known to the government. Mr. Sadinsky said that this could have a big impact and cites a drop in revenue of up to 20 percent at two racetrack slot operations that went smoke-free. While all local governments in Essex County, outside of the City of Windsor, have made all workplaces smoke-free, Windsor allows smoking in all places where food and beverages are served. Mr. Sadinsky is scheduled to meet with the mayor of Windsor to ensure that Casino Windsor does not become smoke-free.[25]

Chapter 5 Business Marketing 151

customer service. The survey indicated that 65 percent of the firms took 24 hours to respond to e-mail; another 29 percent did not respond at all. In addition, although 65 percent of the firms reported having on-line service available for customers, only 2 percent of the firms had capabilities beyond answering FAQs (frequently asked questions).[31]

>> CONNECT IT

Look back at the story about Canada Post at the beginning of the chapter. You now know that business firms and organizations are the highest-spending customers in the Canadian market.

Canada Post has recognized the importance of its business customers and has also realized that in the future, its services will be in more demand from business customers rather than consumers, who will communicate more and more through electronic channels and less and less via the mail.

Canada Post provides a wide array of business services as part of its B2B (business-to-business) marketing strategy through its "Canada Post Group" of companies, which include Purolator Courier, Progistix-Solutions, Intelcom Courier, epost, Innovapost, and Canada Post International Ltd. Finally, Canada Post offers its business customers access to its On-line Business Centre, which offers business services, such as on-line ordering, electronic shipping tools, account management, postal code lookup, postal outlet locator, a rate calculator, and shipment tracking.

REVIEW IT

1. **Describe business marketing.** Business marketing provides goods and services that are bought for use in business rather than for personal consumption. Intended use, not physical characteristics, distinguishes a business product from a consumer product.

   1.1 As the marketing manager for Huggies diapers made by Kimberly-Clark, you are constantly going head-to-head with Pampers, produced by rival Procter & Gamble. You are considering unlocking the potential of the business market to increase your share of the disposable diaper market, but how? Write an outline of several ways you could transform this quintessentially consumer product into a successful business product as well.

2. **Describe the role of the Internet in business marketing.** The rapid expansion and adoption of the Internet have made business markets more competitive than ever before. The number of business buyers and sellers using the Internet is rapidly increasing. Firms are seeking new and better ways to expand markets and sources of supply, increase sales and decrease costs, and better serve customers. With the Internet, every business in the world is potentially a local competitor.

   2.1 How could you use the website http://strategis.ic.gc.ca to help define a target market and develop a marketing plan?

   2.2 Reconsider question 1.1. How could you use the Internet in your business marketing of Huggies diapers?

3. **Discuss the role of relationship marketing and strategic alliances in business marketing.** Relationship marketing entails seeking and establishing long-term alliances or partnerships with customers. A strategic alliance is a cooperative agreement among business firms. Firms form alliances to leverage what they do well by partnering with others who have complementary skills.

   3.1 Why is relationship or personal selling the best way to promote in business marketing?

NEL

>> GLOBAL PERSPECTIVES BOXES

GLOBAL

Global Perspectives boxes, which appear in all chapters, provide expanded global examples of the marketing issues facing not only Canadian companies but companies operating in countries from Asia to Africa to Europe. Global marketing is fully integrated throughout the book. Those in the text are identified with the icon shown in the margin.

>> ETHICS IN MARKETING BOXES

ETHICS

The Ethics in Marketing boxes, complete with questions focusing on ethical decision making, have been revised in each chapter. This feature offers provocative examples of how ethics come into play in many marketing decisions.

>> CONNECT IT

NEW

The Connect It section helps illustrate how the chapter relates to real-world situations, and it answers the questions posed in the Opening Vignettes.

>> REVIEW IT

NEW

The Review It section follows the **Integrated Learning System**, providing end-of-chapter discussion and writing questions within each chapter summary.

>> DEFINE IT

The Define It section lists the key terms introduced in each chapter. Page references are included for easy-to-find definitions.

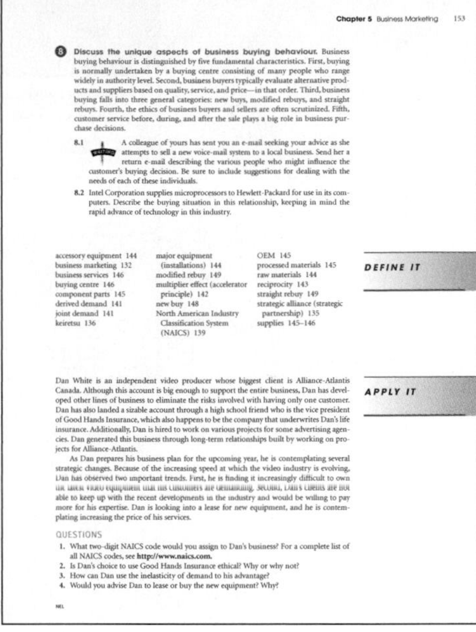

Chapter 5 Business Marketing 153

8 **Discuss the unique aspects of business buying behaviour.** Business buying behaviour is distinguished by five fundamental characteristics. First, buying is normally undertaken by a buying centre consisting of many people who range widely in authority level. Second, business buyers typically evaluate alternative products and suppliers based on quality, service, and price—in that order. Third, business buying falls into three general categories: new buys, modified rebuys, and straight rebuys. Fourth, the ethics of business buyers and sellers are often scrutinized. Fifth, customer service before, during, and after the sale plays a big role in business purchase decisions.

8.1 A colleague of yours has sent you an e-mail seeking your advice as she attempts to sell a new voice-mail system to a local business. Send her a return e-mail describing the various people who might influence the customer's buying decision. Be sure to include suggestions for dealing with the needs of each of these individuals.

8.2 Intel Corporation supplies microprocessors to Hewlett-Packard for use in its computers. Describe the buying situation in this relationship, keeping in mind the rapid advance of technology in this industry.

DEFINE IT

accessory equipment 144
business marketing 132
business services 146
buying centre 146
component parts 145
derived demand 141
joint demand 141
keiretsu 136
major equipment (installations) 144
modified rebuy 149
multiplier effect (accelerator principle) 142
new buy 148
North American Industry Classification System (NAICS) 139
OEM 145
processed materials 145
raw materials 144
reciprocity 143
straight rebuy 149
strategic alliance (strategic partnership) 135
supplies 145–146

APPLY IT

Dan White is an independent video producer whose biggest client is Alliance-Atlantis Canada. Although this account is big enough to support the entire business, Dan has developed other lines of business to eliminate the risks involved with having only one customer. Dan has also landed a sizable account through a high school friend who is the vice president of Good Hands Insurance, which also happens to be the company that underwrites Dan's life insurance. Additionally, Dan is hired to work on various projects for some advertising agencies. Dan generated this business through long-term relationships built by working on projects for Alliance-Atlantis.

As Dan prepares his business plan for the upcoming year, he is contemplating several strategic changes. Because of the increasing speed at which the video industry is evolving, Dan has observed two important trends. First, he is finding it increasingly difficult to own the latest video equipment that his customers are demanding. Second, Dan's clients are not able to keep up with the recent developments in the industry and would be willing to pay more for his expertise. Dan is looking into a lease for new equipment, and he is contemplating increasing the price of his services.

QUESTIONS

1. What two-digit NAICS code would you assign to Dan's business? For a complete list of all NAICS codes, see **http://www.naics.com.**
2. Is Dan's choice to use Good Hands Insurance ethical? Why or why not?
3. How can Dan use the inelasticity of demand to his advantage?
4. Would you advise Dan to lease or buy the new equipment? Why?

NEL

>> APPLY IT

Apply It exercises at the end of each chapter are mini-cases designed to illustrate how small businesses can create strategies and tactics using the material in the chapter.

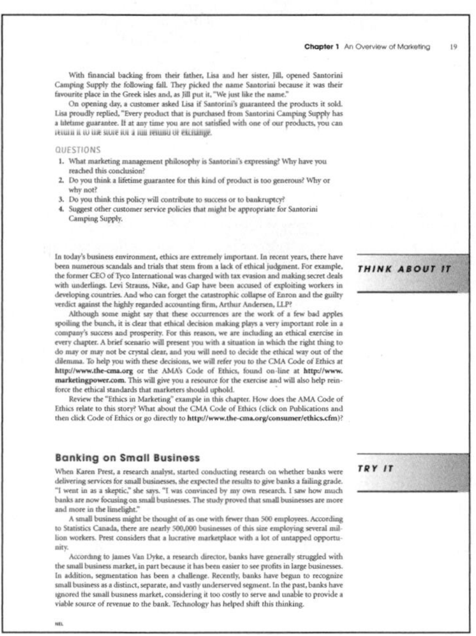

Chapter 1 An Overview of Marketing 19

With financial backing from their father, Lisa and her sister, Jill, opened Santorini Camping Supply the following fall. They picked the name Santorini because it was their favourite place in the Greek isles and, as Jill put it, "We just like the name."

On opening day, a customer asked Lisa if Santorini's guaranteed the products it sold. Lisa proudly replied, "Every product that is purchased from Santorini Camping Supply has a lifetime guarantee. If at any time you are not satisfied with one of our products, you can return it to the store for a full refund or exchange."

QUESTIONS

1. What marketing management philosophy is Santorini's expressing? Why have you reached this conclusion?
2. Do you think a lifetime guarantee for this kind of product is too generous? Why or why not?
3. Do you think this policy will contribute to success or to bankruptcy?
4. Suggest other customer service policies that might be appropriate for Santorini Camping Supply.

THINK ABOUT IT

In today's business environment, ethics are extremely important. In recent years, there have been numerous scandals and trials that stem from a lack of ethical judgment. For example, the former CEO of Tyco International was charged with tax evasion and making secret deals with underlings. Levi Strauss, Nike, and Gap have been accused of exploiting workers in developing countries. And who can forget the catastrophic collapse of Enron and the guilty verdict against the highly regarded accounting firm, Arthur Andersen, LLP?

Although some might say that these occurrences are the work of a few bad apples spoiling the bunch, it is clear that ethical decision making plays a very important role in a company's success and prosperity. For this reason, we are including an ethical exercise in every chapter. A brief scenario will present you with a situation in which the right thing to do may or may not be crystal clear, and you will need to decide the ethical way out of the dilemma. To help you with these decisions, we will refer you to the CMA Code of Ethics at **http://www.the-cma.org** or the AMA's Code of Ethics, found on-line at **http://www.marketingpower.com.** This will give you a resource for the exercise and will also help reinforce the ethical standards that marketers should uphold.

Review the "Ethics in Marketing" example in this chapter. How does the AMA Code of Ethics relate to this story? What about the CMA Code of Ethics (click on Publications and then click Code of Ethics or go directly to **http://www.the-cma.org/consumer/ethics.cfm**)?

TRY IT

Banking on Small Business

When Karen Prest, a research analyst, started conducting research on whether banks were delivering services for small businesses, she expected the results to give banks a failing grade. "I went in as a skeptic," she says. "I was convinced by my own research. I saw how much banks are now focusing on small businesses. The study proved that small businesses are more and more in the limelight."

A small business might be thought of as one with fewer than 500 employees. According to Statistics Canada, there are nearly 500,000 businesses of this size employing several million workers. Prest considers that a lucrative marketplace with a lot of untapped opportunity.

According to James Van Dyke, a research director, banks have generally struggled with the small business market, in part because it has been easier to see profits in large businesses. In addition, segmentation has been a challenge. Recently, banks have begun to recognize small business as a distinct, separate, and vastly underserved segment. In the past, banks have ignored the small business market, considering it too costly to serve and unable to provide a viable source of revenue to the bank. Technology has helped shift this thinking.

NEL

>> THINK ABOUT IT

NEW

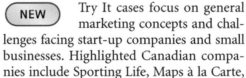

Think About It is a new ethical/moral exercise appearing in every chapter. It reinforces Canadian ethical standards that marketers should uphold. Students are always referred back to the Canadian Marketing Association's Code of Ethics, found on-line at http://www.the-cma.org/consumer/ethics.cfm.

>> TRY IT

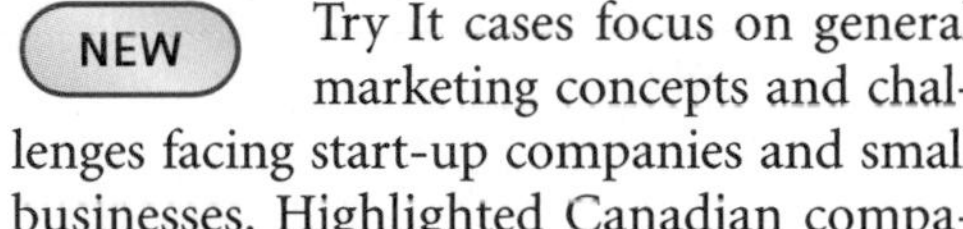

NEW

Try It cases focus on general marketing concepts and challenges facing start-up companies and small businesses. Highlighted Canadian companies include Sporting Life, Maps à la Carte, United Way of Greater Toronto, HMV, The Chippery, eBay.ca, and Taco Time Canada.

>> FLIP IT AND CLICK IT

NEW

The third Canadian edition includes two new sections at the end of each chapter to help students identify the study aids that are right for them. Flip It describes learning opportunities in the *Grademaker Study Guide and Workbook,* and Click It reminds students of the many resources at their disposal found on the text's website at http://www.lamb3e.nelson.com.

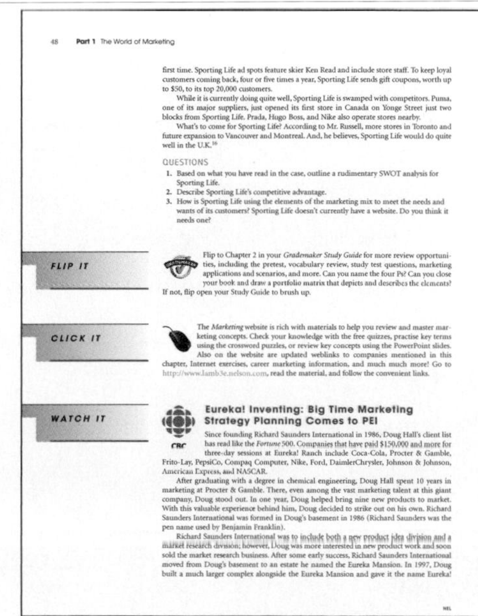

48 Part 1 The World of Marketing

first time. Sporting Life ad spots feature skier Ken Read and include store staff. To keep loyal customers coming back, four or five times a year, Sporting Life sends gift coupons, worth up to $50, to its top 20,000 customers.

While it is currently doing quite well, Sporting Life is swamped with competitors. Puma, one of its major suppliers, just opened its first store in Canada on Yonge Street just two blocks from Sporting Life. Prada, Hugo Boss, and Nike also operate stores nearby.

What's to come for Sporting Life? According to Mr. Russell, more stores in Toronto and future expansion to Vancouver and Montreal. And, he believes, Sporting Life would do quite well in the U.K.[16]

QUESTIONS

1. Based on what you have read in the case, outline a rudimentary SWOT analysis for Sporting Life.
2. Describe Sporting Life's competitive advantage.
3. How is Sporting Life using the elements of the marketing mix to meet the needs and wants of its customers? Sporting Life doesn't currently have a website. Do you think it needs one?

FLIP IT

Flip to Chapter 2 in your *Grademaker Study Guide* for more review opportunities, including the pretest, vocabulary review, study test questions, marketing applications and scenarios, and more. Can you name the four Ps? Can you close your book and draw a portfolio matrix that depicts and describes the elements? If not, flip open your Study Guide to brush up.

CLICK IT

The *Marketing* website is rich with materials to help you review and master marketing concepts. Check your knowledge with the free quizzes, practise key terms using the crossword puzzles, or review key concepts using the PowerPoint slides. Also on the website are updated weblinks to companies mentioned in this chapter, Internet exercises, career marketing information, and much much more! Go to http://www.lamb3e.nelson.com, read the material, and follow the convenient links.

WATCH IT

CBC

Eureka! Inventing: Big Time Marketing Strategy Planning Comes to PEI

Since founding Richard Saunders International in 1986, Doug Hall's client list has read like the *Fortune* 500. Companies that have paid $150,000 and more for three-day sessions at Eureka! Ranch include Coca-Cola, Procter & Gamble, Frito-Lay, PepsiCo, Compaq Computer, Nike, Ford, DaimlerChrysler, Johnson & Johnson, American Express, and NASCAR.

After graduating with a degree in chemical engineering, Doug Hall spent 10 years in marketing at Procter & Gamble. There, even among the vast marketing talent at this giant company, Doug stood out. In one year, Doug helped bring nine new products to market. With this valuable experience behind him, Doug decided to strike out on his own. Richard Saunders International was formed in Doug's basement in 1986 (Richard Saunders was the pen name used by Benjamin Franklin).

Richard Saunders International was to include both a new product idea division and a market research division; however, Doug was more interested in new product work and soon sold the market research business. After some early success, Richard Saunders International moved from Doug's basement to an estate he named the Eureka Mansion. In 1997, Doug built a much larger complex alongside the Eureka Mansion and gave it the name Eureka!

NEL

>> WATCH IT

Videos are a valuable teaching tool, so this edition has a video package that is coupled to a video case from CBC or Thomson South-Western at the end of each chapter.

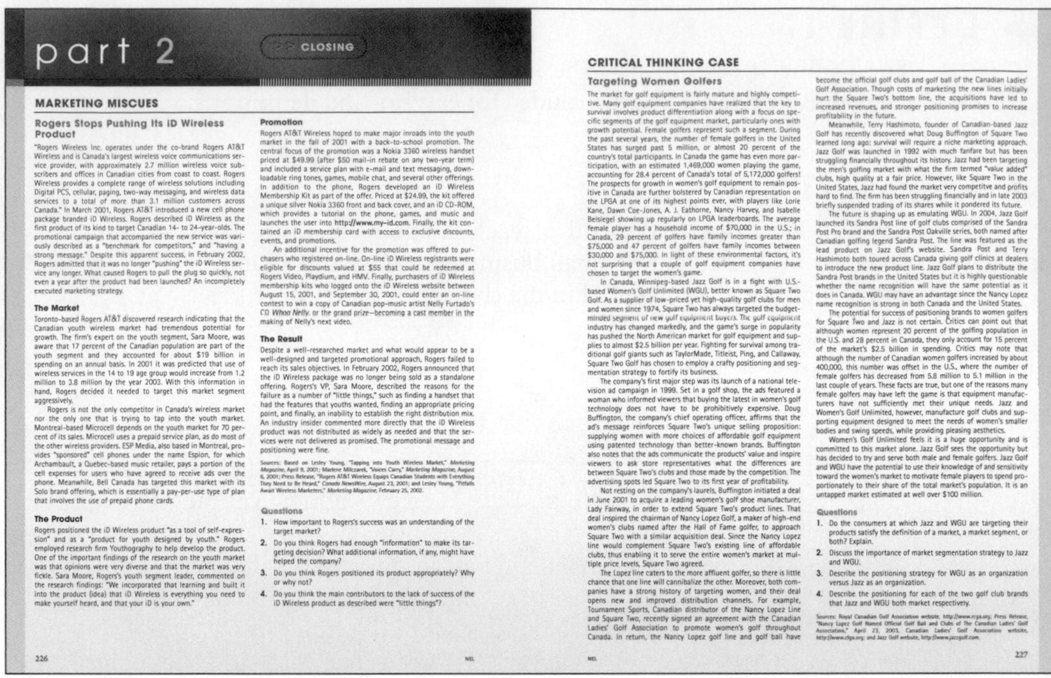

part 2

>> CLOSING

MARKETING MISCUES

Rogers Stops Pushing Its iD Wireless Product

"Rogers Wireless Inc. operates under the co-brand Rogers AT&T Wireless and is Canada's largest wireless voice communications service provider, with approximately 2.7 million wireless voice subscribers and offices in Canadian cities from coast to coast. Rogers Wireless provides a complete range of wireless solutions including Digital PCS, cellular, paging, two-way messaging, and wireless data services to a total of more than 3.1 million customers across Canada." In March 2001, Rogers AT&T introduced a new cell phone package branded iD Wireless. Rogers described iD Wireless as the first product of its kind to target Canadian 14- to 24-year-olds. The promotional campaign that accompanied the new service was variously described as a "benchmark for competitors," and "having a strong message." Despite this apparent success, in February 2002, Rogers admitted that it was no longer "pushing" the iD Wireless service any longer. What caused Rogers to pull the plug so quickly, not even a year after the product had been launched? An incompletely executed marketing strategy.

The Market

Toronto-based Rogers AT&T discovered research indicating that the Canadian youth wireless market had tremendous potential for growth. The firm's expert on the youth segment, Sara Moore, was aware that 17 percent of the Canadian population are part of the youth segment and they accounted for about $19 billion in spending on an annual basis. In 2001 it was predicted that use of wireless services in the 14 to 19 age group would increase from 1.2 million to 3.8 million by the year 2003. With this information in hand, Rogers decided it needed to target this market segment aggressively.

Rogers is not the only competitor in Canada's wireless market nor the only one that is trying to tap into the youth market. Montreal-based Microcell depends on the youth market for 70 percent of its sales. Microcell uses a prepaid service plan, as do most of the other wireless providers. ESP Media, also based in Montreal, provides "sponsored" cell phones under the name Espion, for which Archambault, a Quebec-based music retailer, pays a portion of the cell expenses for users who have agreed to receive ads over the phone. Meanwhile, Bell Canada has targeted this market with its Solo brand offering, which is essentially a pay-per-use type of plan that involves the use of prepaid phone cards.

The Product

Rogers positioned the iD Wireless product "as a tool of self-expression" and as a "product for youth designed by youth." Rogers employed research firm Youthography to help develop the product. One of the important findings of the research on the youth market was that opinions were very diverse and that the market was very fickle. Sara Moore, Rogers's youth segment leader, commented on the research findings: "We incorporated that learning and built it into the product (idea) that iD Wireless is everything you need to make yourself heard, and that your iD is your own."

Promotion

Rogers AT&T Wireless hoped to make major inroads into the youth market in the fall of 2001 with a back-to-school promotion. The central focus of the promotion was a Nokia 3360 wireless handset priced at $49.99 (after $50 mail-in rebate on any two-year term) and included a service plan with e-mail and text messaging, downloadable ring tones, games, mobile chat, and several other offerings. In addition to the phone, Rogers developed an iD Wireless Membership Kit as part of the offer. Priced at $24.99, the kit offered a unique silver Nokia 3360 front and back cover, and an iD CD-ROM, which provides a tutorial on the phone, games, and music and launches the user into **http://www.my-id.com**. Finally, the kit contained an iD membership card with access to exclusive discounts, events, and promotions.

An additional incentive for the promotion was offered to purchasers who registered on-line. On-line iD Wireless registrants were eligible for discounts valued at $55 that could be redeemed at Rogers Video, Playdium, and HMV. Finally, purchasers of iD Wireless membership kits who logged onto the iD Wireless website between August 15, 2001, and September 30, 2001, could enter an on-line contest to win a copy of Canadian pop-music artist Nelly Furtado's CD *Whoa Nelly*, or the grand prize—becoming a cast member in the making of Nelly's next video.

The Result

Despite a well-researched market and what would appear to be a well-designed and targeted promotional approach, Rogers failed to reach its sales objectives. In February 2002, Rogers announced that the iD Wireless package was no longer being sold as a standalone offering. Rogers's VP, Sara Moore, described the reasons for the failure as a number of "little things," such as finding a handset that had the features that youths wanted, finding an appropriate pricing point, and finally, an inability to establish the right distribution mix. An industry insider commented more directly that the iD Wireless product was not distributed as widely as needed and that the services were not delivered as promised. The promotional message and positioning were fine.

Sources: Based on Lesley Young, "Tapping into Youth Wireless Market," *Marketing Magazine*, April 9, 2001; Marlene Milczarek, "Voices Carry," *Marketing Magazine*, August 6, 2001; Press Release, "Rogers AT&T Wireless Equips Canadian Students with Everything They Need to Be Heard," *Canada NewsWire*, August 23, 2001; and Lesley Young, "Pitfalls Await Wireless Marketers," *Marketing Magazine*, February 25, 2002.

Questions

1. How important to Rogers's success was an understanding of the target market?
2. Do you think Rogers had enough "information" to make its targeting decision? What additional information, if any, might have helped the company?
3. Do you think Rogers positioned its product appropriately? Why or why not?
4. Do you think the main contributors to the lack of success of the iD Wireless product as described were "little things"?

226 NEL

CRITICAL THINKING CASE

Targeting Women Golfers

The market for golf equipment is fairly mature and highly competitive. Many golf equipment companies have realized that the key to survival involves product differentiation along with a focus on specific segments of the golf equipment market, particularly ones with growth potential. Female golfers represent such a segment. During the past several years, the number of female golfers in the United States has surged past 5 million, or almost 20 percent of the country's total participants. In Canada the game has even more participation, with an estimated 1,469,000 women playing the game, accounting for 28.4 percent of Canada's total of 5,172,000 golfers! The prospects for growth in women's golf equipment to remain positive in Canada are further bolstered by Canadian representation on the LPGA at one of its highest points ever, with players like Lorie Kane, Dawn Coe-Jones, A. J. Eathorne, Nancy Harvey, and Isabelle Beisiegel showing up regularly on LPGA leaderboards. The average female player has a household income of $70,000 in the U.S.; in Canada, 29 percent of golfers have family incomes greater than $75,000 and 47 percent of golfers have family incomes between $30,000 and $75,000. In light of these environmental factors, it's not surprising that a couple of golf equipment companies have chosen to target the women's game.

In Canada, Winnipeg-based Jazz Golf is in a fight with U.S.-based Women's Golf Unlimited (WGU), better known as Square Two Golf. As a supplier of low-priced yet high-quality golf clubs for men and women since 1974, Square Two has always targeted the budget-minded segment of new golf equipment buyers. The golf equipment industry has changed markedly, and the game's surge in popularity has pushed the North American market for golf equipment and supplies to almost $2.5 billion per year. Fighting for survival among traditional golf giants such as TaylorMade, Titleist, Ping, and Callaway, Square Two Golf has chosen to employ a crafty positioning and segmentation strategy to fortify its business.

The company's first major step was its launch of a national television ad campaign in 1999. Set in a golf shop, the ads featured a woman who informed viewers that buying the latest in women's golf technology does not have to be prohibitively expensive. Doug Buffington, the company's chief operating officer, affirms that the ad's message reinforces Square Two's unique selling proposition: supplying women with more choices of affordable golf equipment using patented technology than better-known brands. Buffington also notes that the ads communicate the products' value and inspire viewers to ask store representatives what the differences are between Square Two's clubs and those made by the competition. The advertising spots led Square Two to its first year of profitability.

Not resting on the company's laurels, Buffington initiated a deal in June 2001 to acquire a leading women's golf shoe manufacturer, Lady Fairway, in order to extend Square Two's product lines. That deal inspired the chairman of Nancy Lopez Golf, a maker of high-end women's clubs named after the Hall of Fame golfer, to approach Square Two with a similar acquisition deal. Since the Nancy Lopez line would complement Square Two's existing line of affordable clubs, thus enabling it to serve the entire women's market at multiple price levels, Square Two agreed.

The Lopez line caters to the more affluent golfer, so there is little chance that one line will cannibalize the other. Moreover, both companies have a strong history of targeting women, and their deal opens new and improved distribution channels. For example, Tournament Sports, Canadian distributor of the Nancy Lopez Line and Square Two, recently signed an agreement with the Canadian Ladies' Golf Association to promote women's golf throughout Canada. In return, the Nancy Lopez golf line and golf ball have become the official golf clubs and golf ball of the Canadian Ladies' Golf Association. Though costs of marketing the new lines initially hurt the Square Two's bottom line, the acquisitions have led to increased revenues, and stronger positioning promises to increase profitability in the future.

Meanwhile, Terry Hashimoto, founder of Canadian-based Jazz Golf has recently discovered what Doug Buffington of Square Two learned long ago: survival will require a niche marketing approach. Jazz Golf was launched in 1992 with much fanfare but has been struggling financially throughout its history. Jazz had been targeting the men's golfing market with what the firm termed "value added" clubs, high quality at a fair price. However, like Square Two in the United States, Jazz had found the market very competitve and profits hard to find. The firm has been struggling financially and in late 2003 briefly suspended trading of its shares while it pondered its future.

The future is shaping up as emulating WGU. In 2004, Jazz Golf launched its Sandra Post line of golf clubs comprised of the Sandra Post Pro brand and the Sandra Post Oakville series, both named after Canadian golfing legend Sandra Post. The line was featured as the lead product on Jazz Golf's website. Sandra Post and Terry Hashimoto both toured across Canada giving golf clinics at dealers to introduce the new product line. Jazz Golf plans to distribute the Sandra Post brands in the United States but it is highly questionable whether the name recognition will have the same potential as it does in Canada. WGU may have an advantage since the Nancy Lopez name recognition is strong in both Canada and the United States.

The potential for success of positioning brands to women golfers for Square Two and Jazz is not certain. Critics can point out that although women represent 20 percent of the golfing population in the U.S. and 28 percent in Canada, they only account for 15 percent of the market's $2.5 billion in spending. Critics may note that although the number of Canadian women golfers increased by about 400,000, this number was offset in the U.S., where the number of female golfers has decreased from 5.8 million to 5.1 million in the last couple of years. These facts are true, but one of the reasons many female golfers may have left the game is that equipment manufacturers have not sufficiently met their unique needs. Jazz and Women's Golf Unlimited, however, manufacture golf clubs and supporting equipment designed to meet the needs of women's smaller bodies and swing speeds, while providing pleasing aesthetics.

Women's Golf Unlimited feels it is a huge opportunity and is committed to this market alone. Jazz Golf sees the opportunity but has decided to try and serve both male and female golfers. Jazz Golf and WGU have the potential to use their knowledge of and sensitivity toward the women's market to motivate female players to spend proportionately to their share of the total market's population. It is an untapped market estimated at well over $100 million.

Questions

1. Do the consumers at which Jazz and WGU are targeting their products satisfy the definition of a market, a market segment, or both? Explain.
2. Discuss the importance of market segmentation strategy to Jazz and WGU.
3. Describe the positioning strategy for WGU as an organization versus Jazz as an organization.
4. Describe the positioning for each of the two golf club brands that Jazz and WGU both market respectively.

Sources: Royal Canadian Golf Association website, http://www.rcga.org; Press Release, "Nancy Lopez Golf Named Official Golf Ball and Clubs of The Canadian Ladies' Golf Association," April 23, 2003, Canadian Ladies' Golf Association website, http://www.clga.org; and Jazz Golf website, http://www.jazzgolf.com.

NEL 227

>> MARKETING MISCUES

NEW Mistakes can have tough consequences, but they also offer great lessons. Often amusing and always interesting, Marketing Miscues cases at the end of each part are intended to help your students understand marketing mistakes and learn to avoid them.

>> CRITICAL THINKING CASES

NEW Critical Thinking Cases at the end of each part put your students in the role of decision maker. They will evaluate the marketing planning activities of well-known organizations like Hewlett-Packard, Segway, Jazz Golf, Square Two Golf, Morpheus, Nokia, Shoppers Drug Mart, Unilever Canada, and Kraft Canada.

>> SO WHAT ELSE IS NEW?

If you are already familiar with *Marketing*, you may be asking, "So what else is new?" The answer is: quite a bit. In addition to the dozens of new examples in each chapter, we have added new content and revised and updated existing material throughout the book.

>> BRAND NEW CONTENT AND ORGANIZATION

The text has been reorganized from five parts to seven parts, reflecting the traditional functional approach to marketing. The number of chapters has been reduced from 20 to 18 and the Internet chapter content, which was formerly only available electronically, has been directly included in the text in Chapter 17.

Part 1: The World of Marketing

Chapter 1 (An Overview of Marketing) has been completely revised to provide the reader with a view of marketing from the perspectives of marketing managers in the twenty-first century. We have streamlined Chapter 2 (Strategic Planning for Competitive Advantage) to make the discussion of strategy more relevant for today's marketing environment. Chapter 3 (The Marketing Environment and Marketing Ethics) has a new section on consumer values and new content on demographics, including material on women as principal economic decision makers. We have revised the section on older consumers and included a completely new section on multicultural marketing.

Part 2: Analyzing Marketing Opportunities

Chapter 4 (Consumer Decision Making) has new material on trends in gender marketing, and Chapter 5 (Business Marketing) has a completely revised section on business marketing on the Internet. Chapter 6 (Segmenting and Targeting Markets) now includes updated information based on the most recent Statistics Canada data, plus a thoroughly revised section on bases for segmenting business markets. Chapter 7 (Decision Support Systems and Marketing Research) has been updated and further Canadianized.

Part 3: Product Decisions

Part 3 begins with Chapter 8 (Product Concepts), which has a new section on global brands. Chapter 9 (Developing and Managing Products) follows with new exhibits on the history of new product introductions and the diffusion process, plus a completely new section on on-line test marketing. We have revised the discussion on how services differ from goods in Chapter 10 (Services and Nonprofit Organization Marketing).

Part 4: Distribution Decisions

Distribution concepts can be difficult, so we have revised Chapter 11 (Marketing Channels and Supply Chain Management) to give students an introduction to supply chain management that sticks to the basics while providing just enough detail on the marketing channel system. We have condensed the chapter in several areas to make it more readable. In Chapter 12 (Retailing and Wholesaling) we describe the two major types of supply chain intermediaries available to marketers in the channel of distribution and the functions these intermediaries perform. We provide a look at the rapidly changing retail landscape in Canada and highlight the many different forms of retailing in use today. We have included a wholesaling section in the retailing chapter to emphasize the important role that wholesaling plays in the distribution channel.

Part 5: Promotion Decisions

Chapter 13 (Marketing Communication and Personal Selling) has a new section on Internet advertising; also, it describes new and innovative ways of advertising. Chapter 14 (Advertising, Sales Promotion, and Public Relations) has an expanded discussion of point-of-purchase promotion.

Part 6: Pricing Decisions

Chapter 15 (Pricing Concepts) opens Part 6 with more examples of elastic and inelastic demand, a thoroughly revised and expanded section on the impact of Internet and extranets on pricing, and a revised section on Internet auctions. Chapter 16 (Setting the Right Price) follows with expanded discussions of choosing a pricing strategy, predatory pricing, and bundling and services. The chapter also has a new section on the implications of zero-percent financing and a revised section on value pricing, with a new section on the dangers of pricing products too low.

NEW

Part 7: Managing Marketing-Created Relationships

Much is revised in Part 7. Chapter 17 (One-to-One and Internet Marketing) combines the topics of database marketing with Internet marketing, the technology application that is enabling virtually any business to undertake one-to-one marketing. The material on one-to-one marketing simplifies the introduction to database marketing and abridges the discussion of data mining, now covered in depth in Chapter 18. As is the case with every edition of *Marketing*, the Internet content is completely revised to reflect the constantly evolving world of Internet marketing and e-commerce. Finally, Chapter 18 (Customer Relationship Management) is a new chapter that introduces a company-wide business strategy—customer relationship management (CRM)—designed to optimize profitability, revenue, and customer satisfaction by focusing on highly defined and precise customer groups.

>> INNOVATIVE AND VALUABLE INSTRUCTOR SUPPLEMENTS

All components of our comprehensive support package have been developed to help you prepare lectures and tests as quickly and easily as possible. We provide a wealth of information and activities beyond the text to supplement your lectures, as well as teaching aids in a variety of formats to fit your own teaching style.

Instructor's Manual (0176407669)

by Lynne Ricker, University of Calgary, and Bill Wellington, University of Windsor

Our Instructor's Manual is the core of our **Integrated Learning System**. For the third Canadian edition of *Marketing,* we have made our popular Instructor's Manual even more valuable for new and experienced instructors alike. Here is a list of the new features that will reduce class preparation time:

- Suggested syllabi for 12- and 16-week terms.
- A pedagogy grid for each chapter briefly laying out (1) all the options the professor has in the chapter and (2) what key points in the chapter each feature addresses. The features included on the grid are the opening vignette, the boxed features, **Use It**, **Apply It**, **Try It**, and each video option.
- Three suggested lesson plans for each chapter: a lecture lesson plan, a small-group-work lesson plan, and a video lesson plan.

We have retained the proven features such as the detailed chapter outline, lists of support material, supplemental articles, additional class activities, and solutions for all **Review It**, **Apply It**, **Try It,** and part-ending cases in the book. Our manual is truly "one-stop shopping" for instructors teaching any size of marketing course.

Microsoft® PowerPoint® CD-ROM (017640788X)

by Miguel Morales, Saint Mary's University

To take full advantage of the new features of the *Marketing* PowerPoint® presentation, you'll want to use the customizable PowerPoint® CD-ROM. Many of the 1,000 full-colour images provided with *Marketing* contain valuable teaching notes to help guide you through your lecture. In addition, hyperlinks to the On Line activities in the chapter margins are embedded in each chapter of slides so that you can maximize your use of these activities during class time. Short, 30-second television ads from recent Super Bowl broadcasts are embedded in the slide presentation and are only viewable through the PowerPoint® CD-ROM. All you need is the Windows® operating system to run the PowerPoint® viewer and an LCD panel for classroom display.

JoinIn™ on TurningPoint®

JoinIn™ on TurningPoint® is simply the easiest, most powerful, completely interactive Microsoft® PowerPoint® tool on the market today. This unique tool transforms PowerPoint® presentation files into an easy-to-use, graphically enhanced system for delivering interactive content in the classroom. By using JoinIn™ on TurningPoint®, instructors can pose questions to a large group, gather results, compare percentages to the class average, and display them to the class in "real time" while using PowerPoint® presentation slides. Ask your Thomson Nelson sales rep about JoinIn™ on TurningPoint®!

Four Video Packages (0176407871)

The video packages to accompany *Marketing* are the most comprehensive in our history. We provide you with four options for video use: each chapter has a Canadian-based CBC video case or a Thomson South-Western video case and accompanying video clip; there are also 30-second clips (short) embedded in the instructor's PowerPoint® CD-ROM presentation, 2- to 4-minute clips (medium) for classroom viewing, and 10- to 15-minute clips (long) for both classroom viewing and home viewing via the new U.S. video CD-ROM. In total there are 40 short clips, 21 medium clips, and 17 long segments for *Marketing*, Third Canadian Edition.

Mostly drawn from the CBC *Venture* or CBC *Marketplace* programs, the **CBC** video clips are coupled with the chapter video cases (**Watch It**). The short clips consist of television ads that were originally broadcast during the **Super Bowl** games. The medium clips have been pulled from **CNN**'s news footage archives and show how marketing principles operate in the world of big business. And the long clips are excerpted footage from various episodes of the 30-minute **Small Business School** (**SBS**) program broadcast nationwide on PBS.

Computerized Test Bank

by Craig Dyer, Red River College

To complete the **Integrated Learning System**, our Computerized Test Bank runs on ExamView® software, which allows instructors to prepare tests that cover all learning objectives, or emphasize those you feel are most important. This updated Computerized Test Bank is one of the most comprehensive on the market, with over 3,300 true/false, multiple-choice, scenario, and essay questions. Our testing database, combined with the ease of ExamView®, takes the pain out of exam preparation. The CTB is only available on the Instructor Resource CD-ROM.

Comprehensive Printed Test Bank (0176407898)

Based on the enhanced Computerized Test Bank, the printed Test Bank is also organized around the learning objectives. This print version is available in electronic Word format as well.

Instructor Resource CD-ROM (0176407650)

Managing your classroom resources is now easier than ever. The new Instructor Resource CD-ROM contains all key instructor supplements—Instructor's Manual, Test Bank, Computerized Test Bank, and Microsoft® PowerPoint® slides.

>> OTHER OUTSTANDING SUPPLEMENTS

Great Ideas in Teaching Marketing

This exciting booklet is now available on our instructor's resource page of the *Marketing*, Third Canadian Edition, website. In this way, we can regularly add to our collection of teaching ideas without having to wait for the next edition of *Marketing*. Submissions will be collected, organized, and presented on-line to keep Great Ideas a dynamic and up-to-date teaching resource. For Great Ideas, go to http://www.lamb3e.nelson.com.

>> VALUABLE STUDENT SUPPLEMENTS

The *Grademaker Study Guide and Workbook* (0176407642)

by Diana Serafini, Dawson College

Make the grades with the ***Grademaker Study Guide and Workbook***! As part of the **Integrated Learning System**, the study guide questions are linked to the learning objectives by numbered icons. Every chapter includes application questions in a variety of formats to help students to master concepts. Study guide questions are designed to be similar in type and difficulty level to the Test Bank questions. By careful review of the *Grademaker*, students can dramatically improve their test scores. Each *Grademaker* chapter opens with a self-assessment pre-test to help students identify areas where they need the most review, followed by chapter outlines with definitions, vocabulary practice, and true/false, multiple choice, agree/disagree, and essay questions. Two new sections have been created for this edition of the *Grademaker:* marketing scenarios and marketing applications. Each scenario presents a marketing situation and is followed by a series of questions that ask students to evaluate the situation presented.

Marketing Student Resources Website

http://www.lamb3e.nelson.com

Organized around the learning objectives and available free to students, this powerful web-based supplement provides:

- Chapter-related true/false questions
- Chapter-related multiple-choice questions
- Chapter-related short questions
- Chapter-related Internet activities
- Chapter-related summaries
- Career-related exercises
- Crossword puzzles
- Marketing Plan assignments and templates
- Glossary of key terms
- Chapter weblinks
- CBC Videos
- And much, much more!

>> ACKNOWLEDGMENTS

There are many individuals to whom we owe gratitude for their help in making *Marketing,* Third Canadian Edition, a reality. In particular, we would like to thank the team at Thomson Nelson, including our Executive Editors, Veronica Visentin and Ric Kitowski, and a special thanks to our Developmental Editor, Katherine Goodes. This project could not have been realized without Katherine's outstanding commitment and expertise. We would also like to thank our local representative, Blaine Prentice of Thomson Nelson, a former student of ours, who encouraged us to affiliate ourselves as authors with Thomson Nelson.

We are especially indebted to the reviewers who took the time to comment on the Table of Contents and to review the manuscript of *Marketing,* Third Canadian Edition. We would like to extend our gratitude to the following reviewers:

Denton Anthony,
Saint Francis Xavier University

Pat Browne,
Kwantlen University College

Gary Dover,
Georgian College

Gordon Fullerton,
Saint Mary's University

Ashwin Joshi,
York University

Rajesh V. Manchanda,
University of Manitoba

Miguel Morales,
Saint Mary's University

Keith Murray,
Langara College

Paul Myers,
St. Clair College

Lynne Ricker,
University of Calgary

Shelley Rinehart,
University of New Brunswick

Christopher Ross,
Concordia University

Ted Seath,
Durham College

Diana Serafini,
Dawson College

Dilip Soman,
University of Toronto

Rae Varity,
Southern Alberta Institute of Technology

Maria Vincenten,
Red River College

Anne-Marie Webb-Hughes,
British Columbia Institute of Technology

>> MEET THE AUTHORS

>> CHARLES W. LAMB, JR.
TEXAS CHRISTIAN UNIVERSITY

Charles W. Lamb, Jr., is the M.J. Neeley Professor of Marketing, M.J. Neeley School of Business, Texas Christian University. He served as chair of the department of marketing from 1982 to 1988 and again from 1997 to the present. He is currently serving as president-elect of the Academy of Marketing Science.

Lamb has authored or co-authored more than a dozen books and anthologies on marketing topics and over 150 articles that have appeared in academic journals and conference proceedings. In 1997, he was awarded the prestigious Chancellor's Award for Distinguished Research and Creative Activity at TCU. This is the highest honour that the university bestows on its faculty. Other key honours he has received include the M.J. Neeley School of Business Research Award, selection as a Distinguished Fellow of the Academy of Marketing Science, and a Fellow of the Southwestern Marketing Association.

>> JOSEPH F. HAIR, JR.
LOUISIANA STATE UNIVERSITY

Joseph Hair is Alvin C. Copeland Endowed Chair of Franchising and Director, Entrepreneurship Institute, Louisiana State University. Previously, Hair held the Phil B. Hardin Chair of Marketing at the University of Mississippi. He has taught graduate and undergraduate marketing and marketing research courses.

A member of the American Marketing Association, Academy of Marketing Science, Southern Marketing Association, and Southwestern Marketing Association, Hair has authored 27 books, monographs, and cases and over 60 articles in scholarly journals. He also has participated on many university committees and has chaired numerous departmental task forces. He serves on the editorial review boards of several journals.

>> CARL McDANIEL
UNIVERSITY OF TEXAS, ARLINGTON

Carl McDaniel is a professor of marketing at the University of Texas–Arlington, where he has been chairman of the marketing department since 1976. He has been an instructor for more than 20 years and is the recipient of several awards for outstanding teaching. McDaniel has also been a district sales manager for Southwestern Bell Telephone Company. Currently, he serves as a board member of the North Texas Higher Education Authority, and is a member of the American Marketing Association, Academy of Marketing Science, Southern Marketing Association, Southwestern Marketing Association, and Western Marketing Association.

>> A.J. FARIA
UNIVERSITY OF WINDSOR

A.J. Faria is professor of marketing and chairman of the Department of Marketing and Management Science in the Odette School of Business at the University of Windsor. He has taught for 30 years at five different universities. He has also worked in industry in sales and marketing management positions and has served as a consultant to more than 50 corporations, industry trade associations, and government departments. Dr. Faria has run marketing strategy seminars across North America as well as in Russia, China, Estonia, France, the Netherlands, Singapore, and Hong Kong.

In addition to *Marketing,* Dr. Faria has authored seven other texts, 12 chapters for others' texts, and more than 150 refereed journal articles and conference papers. Dr. Faria has won eight conference best paper awards and is currently the business editor for *Simulation & Gaming.* He serves as Dean of Fellows of the Association for Business Simulation and Experiential Learning.

>> WILLIAM J. WELLINGTON
UNIVERSITY OF WINDSOR

William J. Wellington is an associate professor in the Department of Marketing and Management Science in the Odette School of Business at the University of Windsor, where he has held an appointment since 1986. He also held an administrative appointment as Associate Dean of the Odette School of Business from 1999 through 2002. Dr. Wellington has an Honours Bachelor of Science from the University of Western Ontario, an MBA from the University of Windsor, and a PhD in Marketing and Transportation from Michigan State University. His teaching interests lie in the areas of introductory marketing, advertising and promotion, sales management, marketing management, and strategic marketing management.

Dr. Wellington's research interests lie in the areas of marketing education and strategic marketing management. In addition to *Marketing,* Dr. Wellington has authored seven other books, two chapters for others' books, five journal articles, and 20 refereed conference proceedings. He has edited one book, published three abstracts, and delivered six papers as well as five invited addresses to professional associations.

>> The World of Marketing

part 1

ON LINE

Check It Out

For articles and exercises on the material in this part, and for other great study aids, visit the *Marketing* website at

www.lamb3e.nelson.com

chapter 1

An Overview of Marketing

>> LEARNING OBJECTIVES

1. Define the term *marketing*
2. Describe four marketing management philosophies
3. Discuss the differences between sales and market orientations
4. Describe the marketing process
5. Describe several reasons for studying marketing

>> "Highly addictive" is the warning printed on packages of Clodhoppers Candy—and anyone familiar with the product knows that this is not false advertising. Winnipeggers Chris Emery and Larry Finnson are the founders of Krave's Candy Company, which produces Clodhoppers in the original vanilla and the newly created chocolate and peanut butter flavours. Since its founding in 1996, Krave's Candy has been listed as Winnipeg's fastest-growing company by *Winnipeg Business Magazine* and one of the 10 fastest-growing food companies in Canada by *Food in Canada Magazine*. Chris and Larry want Krave's to become Canada's premier candy company, eventually competing on a level with Hershey's and Nestlé's.

Krave's began with Chris's grandmother's recipe for a cashew-graham wafer-and-white-chocolate candy. Chris says he knew the product was a winner when, every time his grandmother sent him a box of the candy, his college roommates and friends kept stealing his supply. Everyone who tried the candy, loved it. Chris saw a marketing opportunity.

As Chris had always dreamed of becoming a millionaire business tycoon, the next step was to start a company. In 1996, Chris enlisted his high school friend, Larry Finnson, who was a graduate of the electronics program at Red River Community College, to go into business with him. Chris's father supplied the initial $20,000 funding for the business. Chris and Larry selected the names Krave's for the company (it comes from craves) and Clodhoppers for the product. No special reason for Clodhoppers—Chris just thought it would be a good name for a candy.

Initially, Chris and Larry contracted out the making of the candy with a company that already was producing other candies. Chris and Larry personally sold the candy to local stores in the Winnipeg area and at trade shows they attended. Eventually, Larry, with his technical ability, was able to transform an old packaging machine into one that made candy and Chris and Larry began manufacturing Clodhoppers themselves.

Sales grew slowly but picked up, with Clodhoppers's first national sales coming as a fundraising product used by Fundrite. The company's big break came in 1998 when Wal-Mart, after much selling effort by Chris and Larry, agreed to stock Clodhoppers in its Canadian stores for the Christmas selling season. To ensure good sales of the product, Chris and Larry personally visited as many Wal-Mart outlets as they could to push Clodhoppers through in-store demonstrations and sampling. Clodhoppers sold well enough that Wal-Mart agreed to take on the product again for the 1999 Christmas selling season and Zellers also signed on. In three short years, through a lot of hard work by Chris and Larry, Clodhoppers's sales had passed $1 million.

In December 1999, Krave's Candy Co. and Clodhoppers were featured on CBC's *Venture* TV show. In January 2000, *The Globe and Mail* featured Clodhoppers in a full-page story. In June 2000, Wal-Mart U.S. began to stock Clodhoppers and in August of that year Dairy Queen Canada created a Clodhoppers Blizzard. Today, Clodhoppers can be found in Safeway, Costco, FoodFare, Giant Tiger, IGA, Loblaws, London Drugs, Overwaitea, Provigo, Save-On-Foods, Shoppers Drug Mart, Sobeys, The Bay, 7-Eleven, and Nicholby's convenience outlets on major highways across the country.

Beyond the good-tasting candy, much of the success of Clodhoppers belongs to the personal efforts of Chris and Larry. Based on customer feedback, they added chocolate and peanut butter flavours to their original product and created more appealing packaging. Continuing their selling efforts, Chris and Larry participated in a deal with Rogers Video stores and Blockbuster video outlets across Canada to package two videos, a bottle of Coca-Cola, and a bag of Clodhoppers for sale in 274 Rogers outlets and 400 Blockbuster outlets. While already in Dairy Queen outlets in Canada, Clodhoppers weren't in Dairy Queen outlets in the U.S. What did Chris and Larry do? They attended a franchise convention in Nashville, Tennessee, where a day with Chuck Mooty, the president of Dairy Queen U.S., was available in a charity auction. Of course, Chris and Larry submitted the highest bid ($6,500 U.S.) and had Chuck Mooty visit their facilities in Winnipeg and visit a local Dairy Queen to taste a Clodhoppers Blizzard. Will Clodhoppers get into Dairy Queen U.S.? Don't bet against it.

With sales ready to pass $10 million in 2004, there seems to be no end in sight for Krave's Candy. What about Chris's grandmother, who originated the Clodhoppers recipe? She's 87 now and very happy with the success of her concoction.[1]

Chris and Larry's initial motivation to go into the candy business was based on a product developed by Chris's grandmother that everyone seemed to like. Describe Chris and Larry's original philosophy of business. How has this philosophy of business changed over time? Can you identify the types of marketing efforts undertaken by Chris and Larry?

ON LINE 

Krave's Candy Co.

How does Krave's Candy use its website to connect with its market? What indications do you have that this is a customer-oriented company?

http://www.kraves.com

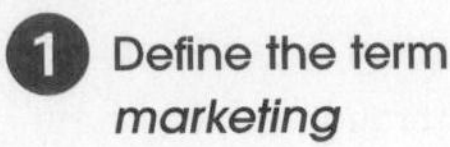
Define the term *marketing*

marketing
The process of planning and executing the conception, pricing, promotion, and distribution of ideas, goods, and services to create exchanges that satisfy individual and organizational goals.

>> WHAT IS MARKETING?

What does the term *marketing* mean to you? Many people think it means the same as personal selling. Others think that marketing is the same as advertising and promotion. Still others believe that marketing has something to do with making products available in stores, arranging displays, and maintaining inventories of products for future sales. Actually, marketing includes all of these activities and many more.

Marketing has two facets. First, it is a philosophy, an attitude, a perspective, or a management orientation that stresses customer satisfaction. Second, marketing is a set of activities used to implement this philosophy. The definition of marketing adopted for this text encompasses both perspectives: "**Marketing** is the process of planning and executing the conception, pricing, promotion, and distribution of ideas, goods, and services to create exchanges that satisfy individual and organizational goals."[2]

>> THE CONCEPT OF EXCHANGE

exchange
The idea that people give up something to receive something they would rather have.

Exchange is the key term in the definition of marketing. The concept of **exchange** is quite simple. It means that people give up something to receive something they would rather have. Normally, we think of money as the medium of exchange. We "give up" money to "get" the goods and services we want. Exchange does not require money, however. Two persons may barter or trade such items as hockey cards, books, or oil paintings.

Five conditions must normally exist for an exchange to take place:

1. There are at least two parties.
2. Each party has something that might be of value to the other party.
3. Each party is capable of communication and delivery.
4. Each party is free to accept or reject the exchange offer.
5. Each party believes it is appropriate or desirable to deal with the other party.[3]

Exchange will not necessarily take place even if all these conditions exist. They are, however, necessary for exchange to be possible. For example, you may place an advertisement in your local newspaper stating that your used automobile is for sale at a certain price. Several people may call you to ask about the car, some may test-drive it, and one or more may even make an offer. All five conditions are necessary for an exchange to exist. But unless you reach an agreement with a buyer and actually sell the car, an exchange will not take place. Notice that marketing can occur even if an exchange does not occur. In the example just discussed, you would have engaged in marketing activities even if no one bought your used automobile.

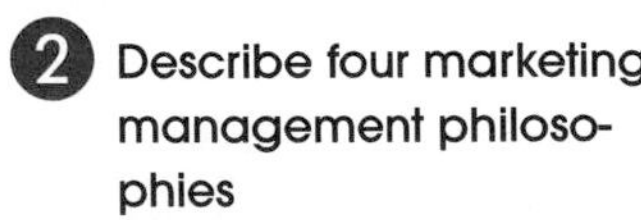
Describe four marketing management philosophies

>> MARKETING MANAGEMENT PHILOSOPHIES

Four competing philosophies strongly influence an organization's marketing activities. These philosophies are commonly referred to as the production, sales, market, and societal marketing orientations.

Production Orientation

production orientation
A philosophy that focuses on the internal capabilities of the firm rather than on the desires and needs of the marketplace.

A **production orientation** is a philosophy that focuses on the internal capabilities of the firm rather than on the desires and needs of the marketplace. A production orientation means that management assesses its resources and asks these questions: "What can we do best?" "What can our engineers design?" "What is easy to produce, given our equipment?" In the case of a service organization, managers ask, "What services are most convenient for the firm to offer?" and "Where do our talents lie?" Some have referred to this orientation as a *Field of Dreams* orientation, referring to the movie line, "If we build it, they will come." The furniture industry is infamous for its disregard of customers and for its slow cycle times. This has always been a production-oriented industry.

There is nothing wrong with assessing a firm's capabilities; in fact, such assessments are major considerations in strategic marketing planning (see Chapter 2). A production orientation falls short because it does not consider whether the goods and services the firm produces most efficiently also meet the needs of the marketplace. Some-times what a firm can best produce is exactly what the market wants. For example, the research and development department of 3M's commercial tape division developed and patented the adhesive component of Post-it Notes a year before a commercial application was identified. Clodhoppers candy, as our opening example showed, was also a product accepted by the market. In yet other situations, as when competition is weak or demand exceeds supply, a production-oriented firm can survive and even prosper. More often, however, firms that succeed in competitive markets have a clear understanding that they must first determine what customers want and then produce it, rather than focus on what company management thinks should be produced.

A Webvan sign is seen behind an auctioneer October 31, 2001, as he takes bids during an auction of Webvan's assets. After churning through $830 million in two years, Webvan was forced into bankruptcy. Despite having mastered its supply chain and supplying great service, Webvan was not able to generate enough revenue to stay in business.

Sales Orientation

A **sales orientation** is based on two ideas: people will buy more goods and services if aggressive sales techniques are used, and high sales result in high profits. Sales to the final buyer are emphasized, and intermediaries are encouraged to push manufacturers' products more aggressively. To sales-oriented firms, marketing means selling things and collecting money.

sales orientation
The idea that people will buy more goods and services if aggressive sales techniques are used and that high sales result in high profits.

The fundamental problem with a sales orientation, as with a production orientation, is a lack of understanding of the needs and wants of the marketplace. Sales-oriented companies often find that, despite the quality of their sales personnel, they cannot convince people to buy goods or services that they don't want or need.

Some sales-oriented firms simply lack understanding of what is important to their customers. Many so-called dot.com businesses that came into existence in the late 1990s are no longer around. Some experts have predicted that 95 to 98 percent of the dot.coms will go out of business.[4] Most of the dot.coms that failed focused on the technology rather than the customer.

Market Orientation

The **marketing concept** is a simple and intuitively appealing philosophy. It states that the social and economic justification for an organization's existence is the satisfaction of customer wants and needs while meeting organizational objectives. It is based on an understanding that a sale does not depend on an aggressive sales force, but rather on a customer's decision to purchase a product. What a business thinks it produces is not of primary importance to its success. Instead, what customers think they are buying—the perceived value—defines a business. The marketing concept includes the following:

marketing concept
The idea that the social and economic justification for an organization's existence is the satisfaction of customer wants and needs while meeting organizational objectives.

- Focusing on customer wants and needs so that the organization can distinguish its product(s) from competitors' offerings.
- Integrating all of the organization's activities, including production, to satisfy these wants.

- Achieving long-term goals for the organization by satisfying customer wants and needs legally and responsibly.

The marketing concept recognizes that there is no reason why customers should buy one organization's offerings unless they are in some way better at serving the customers' wants and needs than those offered by competing organizations.

ON LINE

Customers have higher expectations and more choices than ever before. This means that marketers have to listen more closely than ever before.[5] They also have to anticipate needs, to solve problems before they start, to provide service that wows, and to offer responses to mistakes that more than make up for the original error.[6] For example, Netpulse Communications provides Internet connections to health clubs allowing exercisers to surf the Web or check their e-mail while they are working out. Netpulse uses a monitoring system to diagnose problems remotely. So, if a janitor accidentally disconnects a power cord, a service representative can call the club and ask it to plug the machine back in. Nine times out of ten, Netpulse reports a problem to the club before anyone there is even aware of it.[7]

BILL GREENBLATT/UPI/LANDOV

Adopting a market orientation requires top-management leadership and involvement. Bill Marriott knows this, so each year he travels widely, visiting the company's hotels to ensure that every Marriott delivers superior customer value.

Firms that adopt and implement the marketing concept are said to be market oriented. Achieving a **market orientation** involves obtaining information about customers, competitors, and markets; examining the information from a total business perspective; determining how to deliver superior customer value; and implementing actions to provide value to customers.[8] It also entails establishing and maintaining mutually rewarding relationships with customers.

market orientation
A philosophy that assumes that a sale does not depend on an aggressive sales force but rather on a customer's decision to purchase a product.

Today, companies of all types are adopting a market orientation. Bill Marriott, Marriott International's CEO, logs an average of 250,000 kilometres every year visiting the company's hotels, inspecting them, and talking to employees at all levels in the organization. Burton Snowboards became the best-known brand in one of the world's fastest-growing sports by identifying its most important customers, figuring out the product that those customers want, and then designing it. Almost every day Burton staffers visit with some of the 300 professional riders worldwide who advise the company. These conversations take place on the slopes and on the phone. If one of them has a suggestion or a problem, a Burton employee calls back within 24 hours. Riders help develop virtually every Burton product.[9]

Understanding your competitive arena and competitors' strengths and weaknesses is a critical component of a market orientation. This includes assessing what existing or potential competitors might be intending to do tomorrow as well as what they are doing today. Western Union failed to define its competitive arena as telecommunications, concentrating instead on telegraph services, and was eventually outflanked by fax technology. Had Western Union been a market-oriented company, its management might have better understood the changes taking place, seen the competitive threat, and developed strategies to counter the threat.[10]

ON LINE

Western Union

Has Western Union rebounded from its failure to define its competitive arena as telecommunications? Evaluate the company's website to find out. Against whom does Western Union seem to be competing in the twenty-first century?

http://www.westernunioncanada.ca

Societal Marketing Orientation

One reason a market-oriented organization may choose not to deliver the benefits sought by customers is that these benefits may not be good for individuals or society. This philosophy, called a **societal marketing orientation,** states that an organization exists not only to satisfy customer wants and needs and to meet organizational objectives but also to preserve or enhance individuals' and society's long-term best interests. Marketing products and containers that are less toxic than normal, are more durable, contain reusable materials, or are made of recyclable materials is consistent with a societal marketing orientation. For example, Duracell and Eveready battery companies have reduced the levels of mercury in their batteries and will eventually market mercury-free products. Turtle Wax car wash products and detergents are biodegradable and can be "digested" by waste treatment plants. The company's plastic containers are made of recyclable plastic, and its spray products do not use propellants that damage the ozone layer in the earth's upper atmosphere.

societal marketing orientation
The idea that an organization exists not only to satisfy customer wants and needs and to meet organizational objectives but also to preserve or enhance individuals' and society's long-term best interests.

>> DIFFERENCES BETWEEN SALES AND MARKET ORIENTATIONS

3 Discuss the differences between sales and market orientations

The differences between sales and market orientations are substantial. Exhibit 1.1 compares the two orientations in terms of five characteristics: the organization's focus, the firm's business, those to whom the product is directed, the firm's primary goal, and the tools used to achieve those goals.

The Organization's Focus

Personnel in sales-oriented firms tend to be "inward looking," focusing on selling what the organization makes rather than making what the market wants. Many of the historic sources of competitive advantage—technology, innovation, and economies of scale—allowed companies to focus their efforts internally and prosper. Today, many successful firms derive their competitive advantage from an external, market-oriented focus. A market orientation has helped companies such as Bombardier, Dell Computer, Hewlett-Packard, and WestJet outperform their competitors. A sales orientation has led to the decline or demise of many firms, including General Motors and Eaton's. As one technology industry analyst put it, "no one has ever gone to a website because they heard there was great Java running."[11] Former Kmart Corporation CEO Charles Conaway adds that "anyone who loses their focus on the customer is in for ruin … It's just a matter of when it catches up with you."[12] Kmart, of course, failed in Canada a number of years ago and exited the market. What was Kmart's biggest problem? It focused on trying to match Zellers' products and prices rather than on determining what its customers wanted.[13] Today, key issues in developing competitive advantage include creating customer value, maintaining customer satisfaction, and building long-term relationships.

COURTESY OF TURTLE WAX, INC.

Although Turtle Wax is not founded on a societal marketing orientation in the same way as, say, the Sierra Club, the company still communicates to its customers that it is concerned about the environment. This placement on the Turtle Wax website reminds customers that the company includes societal concerns in its corporate philosophy.

EXHIBIT 1.1

Differences Between Sales and Market Orientations

	WHAT IS THE ORGANIZATION'S FOCUS?	WHAT BUSINESS ARE YOU IN?	TO WHOM IS THE PRODUCT DIRECTED?	WHAT IS YOUR PRIMARY GOAL?	HOW DO YOU SEEK TO ACHIEVE YOUR GOAL?
Sales Orientation	Inward, upon the organization's needs	Selling goods and services	Everybody	Profit through maximum sales volume	Primarily through intensive promotion
Market Orientation	Outward, upon the wants and preferences of customers	Satisfying customer wants and needs and delivering superior value	Specific groups of people	Profit through customer satisfaction	Through coordinated marketing and interfunctional activities

Customer Value

customer value
The ratio of benefits to the sacrifice necessary to obtain those benefits.

Customer value is the ratio of benefits to the sacrifice necessary to obtain those benefits. The automobile industry illustrates the importance of creating customer value. To penetrate the fiercely competitive luxury automobile market, Lexus adopted a customer-driven approach, with particular emphasis on service. Lexus stresses product quality with a standard of zero defects in manufacturing. The service quality goal is to treat each customer as one would treat a guest in one's home, to pursue the perfect person-to-person relationship, and to strive to improve continually. This pursuit has enabled Lexus to establish a clear quality image and capture a significant share of the luxury car market in Canada.

Customer value is not simply a matter of high quality. A high-quality product that is available only at a high price will not be perceived as a good value, nor will bare-bones service or low-quality goods selling for a low price. Instead, customers value goods and services that are of the quality they expect and that are sold at prices they are willing to pay. Value can be used to sell a $189,000 Porsche 911 Turbo Cabriolet as well as a $4.99 package of President's Choice chocolate chip cookies.

Value also stretches beyond quality and price to include customized options and fast delivery. Dell Computer Corporation encourages shoppers to customize products to their liking on its websites. By one count, customers can choose from among more than 25,000 different computer configurations. Toyota has announced a build-to-order system that allows customers to custom design cars on-line for delivery to a dealership nearest to them in less than 14 days.[14]

Marketers interested in customer value:

- *Offer products that perform:* This is the bare minimum requirement. Consumers have lost patience with shoddy merchandise.

- *Give consumers more than they expect:* For more than 40 years, MTD Canada has been intent on raising the customer service bar. For many of its well-known Yard-Man and McCulloch products, the company offers lifetime parts warranties and 90-day price protection. The price protection and service plans are intended to demonstrate the extent to which the company stands behind all of its products.[15]

- *Avoid unrealistic pricing:* E-marketers are leveraging Internet technology to redefine how prices are set and negotiated. With lower costs, e-marketers can often offer lower prices than their bricks-and-mortar counterparts. The enormous popularity of auction sites such as eBay and Amazon.com and the customer-bid model used by Priceline illustrate that on-line customers are interested in bargain prices. Many are not willing to pay a premium for the convenience of examining the merchandise and taking it home with them.

ON LINE

MTD Canada

What evidence of a market orientation do you see on MTD Canada's website? How does the company demonstrate its commitment to the customer?

http://www.mtdcanada.com/home.asp

- *Give the buyer facts:* Today's sophisticated consumer wants informative advertising and knowledgeable salespeople. A study by Andersen Consulting (now Accenture) revealed that websites that don't provide enough information are among the top 10 things that "irk" Internet shoppers most.[16]

- *Offer organization-wide commitment in service and after-sales support:* People fly WestJet Airlines because the airline offers superior value. Passengers do not always get preassigned seats or meals (just peanuts or crackers) when they use the airline, but its service is reliable and friendly and costs less than Air Canada. All WestJet employees are involved in the effort to satisfy customers. Pilots tend the boarding gate when their help is needed, and ticket agents help move luggage.

According to a Datamonitor study, "... online businesses lose more than $6 billion in potential e-commerce sales annually due to lack of customer service at their websites."[17] Another recent report revealed that while 38 percent of studied companies responded to customer e-mails in six hours or less, a whopping 24 percent sent no response at all![18]

AP/WIDE WORLD PHOTOS

Customer-intimate companies achieve great success by building longtime relationships with their customers. Home Depot is an industry benchmark in customer satisfaction. Here, employee Juan Cruz loads plywood into a customer's car.

Customer Satisfaction

customer satisfaction The feeling that a product has met or exceeded the customer's expectations.

Customer satisfaction is the feeling that a product has met or exceeded the customer's expectations. Keeping current customers satisfied is just as important as attracting new ones and a lot less expensive. Firms that have a reputation for delivering high levels of customer satisfaction do things differently from their competitors. Top management is obsessed with customer satisfaction, and employees throughout the organization understand the link between their job and satisfied customers. The culture of the organization is to focus on delighting customers rather than on selling products. Cisco Systems accomplishes this by directly linking employee compensation programs to customer satisfaction study results.[19]

Staples, the office supply retailer, offers great prices on its paper, pens, fax machines, and other office supplies, but its main strategy is to grow by providing customers with the best solutions to their problems. Its approach is to emulate customer-intimate companies like Home Depot and FedEx. These companies do not pursue one-time transactions; instead, they cultivate relationships.

Building Relationships

Attracting new customers to a business is only the beginning. The best companies view new customer attraction as the launching point for developing and enhancing a long-term relationship. Companies can expand market share in three ways: by attracting new customers, by increasing business with existing customers, and by retaining current customers. Building relationships with existing customers directly addresses two of the three possibilities and indirectly addresses the other.

relationship marketing A strategy that entails forging long-term partnerships with customers.

Relationship marketing is a strategy that entails forging long-term partnerships with customers. It begins with developing a clear understanding of who your customers are, what they value, what they want to buy, and how they prefer to interact with you and be served by you.[20] Companies then build relationships with customers by offering value and providing customer satisfaction. They are rewarded with repeat sales and referrals that lead to increases in sales, market share, and profits. Costs also

ON LINE 

Volvo

How does Volvo use its website to maintain customer relations? Do you think Volvo has a sales or a market orientation? What evidence do you have to support your conclusion?

http://www.volvocanada.com

fall because serving existing customers is less expensive than attracting new ones. Lee Iacocca, former president of both Ford and Chrysler, says that if you "take care of your customers, everything else will fall into place. You have to understand your customers, and you have to follow them. You have to change as your customers' lives change."[21]

The Internet is an effective tool for generating relationships with customers because of its ability to interact with the customer. With the Internet, companies can use e-mail for fast customer service, discussion groups for building a sense of community, and database tracking of buying habits for customizing products.[22]

Customers also benefit from stable relationships with suppliers. Business buyers have found that partnerships with their suppliers are essential to producing high-quality products while cutting costs. Customers remain loyal to firms that provide them with greater value and satisfaction than they expect from competing firms.

Most successful relationship marketing strategies depend on customer-oriented personnel, effective training programs, employees with the authority to make decisions and solve problems, and teamwork.

Customer-Oriented Personnel

For an organization to be focused on building relationships with customers, employees' attitudes and actions must be customer oriented. An employee may be the only contact a particular customer has with the firm. In that customer's eyes, the employee *is* the firm. Any person, department, or division that is not customer oriented weakens the positive image of the entire organization. For example, a potential customer who is greeted discourteously may well assume that the employee's attitude represents that of the whole firm.

The Role of Training

Leading marketers recognize the role of employee training in customer service and relationship building. Of *Fortune*'s 100 best companies to work for, 53 offer on-site university courses and 91 have tuition reimbursement programs.[23] It is no coincidence that the public companies on this list, such as Cisco Systems, perform much better than other firms in their respective industries. All new employees at Disneyland and Walt Disney World must attend Disney University, a special training program for Disney employees. They must first pass Traditions 1, a daylong course focusing on the Disney philosophy and operational procedures. Then they go on to specialized training. Similarly, McDonald's has Hamburger University. At American Express's Quality University, line employees and managers learn how to treat customers. There is an extra payoff for companies that train their employees to be customer oriented. When employees make their customers happy, the employees are more likely to derive satisfaction from their jobs. Having contented workers who are committed to their jobs leads to better customer service and greater employee retention.

empowerment
Delegation of authority to solve customers' problems quickly—usually by the first person the customer notifies regarding the problem.

Empowerment

In addition to training, many marketing-oriented firms are giving employees more authority to solve customer problems on the spot. The term used to describe this delegation of authority is **empowerment.** Employees develop ownership attitudes when they are treated like part-owners of the business and are expected to act the part. These employees manage themselves, are more likely to work hard, account for their own performance and the company's, and take prudent risks to build a stronger business and sustain the company's success. FedEx customer service representatives are trained and empowered to resolve customer problems. Although the average FedEx transaction is for less than $20, the customer service representatives are empowered to spend up to $100 to resolve a customer problem.

After Pierre Derome, general manager of Real's Truck Stop in Lancaster, Ontario, committed to empowering his employees, profit margins increased

ON LINE

Disney

Disney training stretches beyond the bounds of its own organizational structures. Visit the Disney site listed below and search the site for information on the Disney Institute and its professional programs. What are the major themes of these programs? View a sample agenda to find out. What does this tell you about Disney's business philosophy?

http://disney.go.com

significantly. Real's Truck Stop, on Highway 401 just west of the Quebec border, includes gas and service facilities for cars and large trucks, a motel, a restaurant, and a convenience store. Giving employees more responsibility resulted in each taking a greater interest in his or her job and in the performance of the business.

Empowerment gives customers the feeling that their concerns are being addressed and gives employees the feeling that their expertise matters. The result is greater satisfaction for both customers and employees.

Teamwork

Many organizations, such as WestJet Airlines and MTD Canada, which are frequently noted for delivering superior customer value and providing high levels of customer satisfaction, assign employees to teams and teach them team-building skills. **Teamwork** entails the collaborative efforts of people to accomplish common objectives. Job performance, company performance, product value, and customer satisfaction all improve when people in the same department or work group begin supporting and assisting each other and emphasize cooperation instead of competition. Performance is also enhanced when people in different areas of responsibility such as production and sales or sales and service practise teamwork, with the ultimate goal of delivering superior customer value and satisfaction.

teamwork
Collaborative efforts of people to accomplish common objectives.

The Firm's Business

As Exhibit 1.1 illustrates, a sales-oriented firm defines its business (or mission) in terms of goods and services. A market-oriented firm defines its business in terms of the benefits its customers seek. People who spend their money, time, and energy expect to receive benefits, not just goods and services. This distinction has enormous implications.

Because of the limited way it defines its business, a sales-oriented firm often misses opportunities to serve customers whose wants can be met through only a wide range of product offerings instead of specific products. For example, in 1989, 220-year-old Britannica had estimated revenues of $650 million and a worldwide sales force of 7,500. Just five years later, after three consecutive years of losses, the sales force had collapsed to as few as 280 representatives. How did this respected company sink so low? Britannica managers saw that competitors were beginning to use CD-ROM to store huge masses of information but chose to ignore the new computer technology, as well as an offer to team up with Microsoft.

It's not hard to see why parents would rather give their children an encyclopedia on a compact disk instead of a printed one. The CD-ROM versions were either given away or sold by other publishers for under $400. A full 32-volume set of *Encyclopedia Britannica* weighs about 55 kg, costs a minimum of $1,500, and takes up nearly a metre and a half of shelf space. If Britannica had defined its business as providing information instead of publishing books, it might not have suffered such a precipitous fall.

Empowering employees not only boosts job satisfaction, but also boosts customer satisfaction. Each FedEx customer service representative has the authority to spend $100 to resolve a customer's complaint on the spot. FedEx customer service representatives are trained and empowered to resolve customer problems.

Adopting a "better late than never" philosophy, Britannica has made its complete 32-volume set available free on the Internet. The company no longer sells door-to-door and hopes to return to profitability by selling advertising on its website.

Answering the question "What is this firm's business?" in terms of the benefits customers seek, instead of goods and services, has at least three important advantages:

- It ensures that the firm keeps focusing on customers and avoids becoming preoccupied with goods, services, or the organization's internal needs.
- It encourages innovation and creativity by reminding people that there are many ways to satisfy customer wants.

ON LINE

Britannica

Go to Britannica's Web page. What evidence do you see that Britannica has redefined its core business? What do you think its business definition currently is? How has the company met the challenge of CD-ROM technology?

http://www.britannica.com

- It stimulates an awareness of changes in customer desires and preferences so that product offerings are more likely to remain relevant.

A market orientation and the idea of focusing on customer wants do not mean that customers will always receive everything they want. It is not possible, for example, to profitably manufacture and market automobile tires that will last for 100,000 kilometres and sell for $25. Furthermore, customers' preferences must be mediated by sound professional judgment as to how to deliver the benefits they seek. As one adage suggests, "People don't know what they want—they only want what they know." Consumers have a limited set of experiences. They are unlikely to request anything beyond those experiences because they are not aware of benefits they may gain from other potential offerings. For example, before the Internet, many people thought that shopping for some products was boring and time consuming, but could not express their need for electronic shopping.

Those to Whom the Product Is Directed

A sales-oriented organization targets its products at "everybody" or "the average customer." A market-oriented organization aims at specific groups of people (see again Exhibit 1.1). The fallacy of developing products directed at the average user is that relatively few average users actually exist. Typically, populations are characterized by diversity. An average is simply a midpoint in some set of characteristics. Because most potential customers are not "average," they are not likely to be attracted to an average product marketed to the average customer. Consider the market for shampoo as one simple example. There are shampoos for oily hair, dry hair, and dandruff. Some shampoos remove the grey or add colour to hair. Special shampoos are marketed for infants and elderly people. There is even shampoo for people with average or normal hair (whatever that is), but this is a fairly small portion of the total market for shampoo.

A market-oriented organization recognizes that different customer groups want different features or benefits. It may therefore need to develop different goods, services, and promotional appeals. A market-oriented organization carefully analyzes the market and divides it into groups of people who are fairly similar in terms of selected characteristics. Then the organization develops marketing programs that will bring about mutually satisfying exchanges with one or more of those groups.

Paying attention to the customer isn't exactly a new concept. Back in the 1920s, General Motors began designing cars for every lifestyle and pocketbook. This was a breakthrough for an industry that had been largely driven by production needs ever since Henry Ford promised any colour as long as it was black.

AP/WIDE WORLD PHOTOS

A market-oriented organization recognizes that customer groups and their wants vary, so it creates products and services to address these differences. *Grace* magazine embodies the full-fashioned lifestyle with features and columns that highlight relevant fashion, beauty, and style tips for larger women. But while fashion features are definitely geared to the 30 percent of Canadian women size 14 and up, the rest of the magazine is of far more general interest.

The Firm's Primary Goal

As Exhibit 1.1 illustrates, a sales-oriented organization seeks to achieve profitability through sales volume and tries to convince potential customers to buy, even if the seller knows that the customer and product are mismatched. Sales-oriented organizations place a higher premium on making a sale than on developing a long-term relationship with a customer. In contrast, the ultimate goal of most market-oriented organizations is to make a profit by creating customer value, providing customer satisfaction, and building long-term relationships with customers. The exception is so-called nonprofit organizations, which exist to achieve goals other than profits. Nonprofit organizations can and should adopt a market orientation.

Tools the Organization Uses to Achieve Its Goals

Sales-oriented organizations seek to generate sales volume through intensive promotional activities, mainly personal selling and advertising. In contrast, market-oriented organizations recognize that promotion decisions are only one of four basic marketing mix decisions that have to be made: product, place (or distribution), promotion, and pricing decisions. A market-oriented organization recognizes each of these four components as important. Furthermore, market-oriented organizations recognize that marketing is not just a responsibility of the marketing department. Interfunctional coordination means that skills and resources throughout the organization are needed to deliver superior customer service and value.

A Word of Caution

This comparison of sales and market orientations is not meant to belittle the role of promotion, especially personal selling, in the marketing mix. Promotion is the means by which organizations communicate with present and prospective customers about the merits and characteristics of their organization and products. Effective promotion is an essential part of effective marketing. Salespeople who work for market-oriented organizations are generally perceived by their customers to be problem solvers and important links to supply sources and new products.

>> THE MARKETING PROCESS

4 Describe the marketing process

Marketing managers are responsible for a variety of activities that together represent the marketing process. These include the following:

- Understanding the organization's mission and the role marketing plays in fulfilling that mission.
- Setting marketing objectives.
- Gathering, analyzing, and interpreting information about the organization's situation, including its strengths and weaknesses as well as opportunities and threats in the environment.
- Developing a marketing strategy by deciding exactly which wants and whose wants the organization will try to satisfy (target market strategy) and by developing appropriate marketing activities (the marketing mix) to satisfy the desires of selected target markets (the "Global Perspectives" box in this chapter describes an effort to enter a new target market). The marketing mix combines product, distribution, promotion, and pricing strategies in a way that creates exchanges that satisfy individual and organizational goals. The marketing mix is examined in detail in Chapter 2.
- Implementing the marketing strategy.
- Designing performance measures.
- Periodically evaluating marketing efforts, and making changes if needed.

These activities and their relationships form the foundation on which the rest of this book is based. The table of contents on page v of this text shows the order in which the activities are described. Exhibit 2.1 in Chapter 2 illustrates their interrelationships.

>> WHY STUDY MARKETING?

5 Describe several reasons for studying marketing

Now that you understand the meaning of the term *marketing,* the importance of adopting a marketing orientation, and how organizations implement this philosophy, you may be asking, "What's in it for me?" or "Why should I study marketing?" There are several important reasons to study marketing: Marketing plays an important role in society, marketing is important to businesses, marketing offers outstanding career opportunities, and marketing affects your life every day.

GLOBAL PERSPECTIVES

Powering into Europe

The Coca-Cola Company sees the fragmented and fast-growing European sports-drink market as an important opportunity, which is why the company is investing over $50 million to launch Powerade in Europe. It is Coke's biggest marketing push in Europe in a number of years. "There is an open field in Europe," says Keith Pardy, director of strategic marketing for Coca-Cola West Europe.

Sports drinks command a higher premium in Europe than in Canada or the United States, where the market is well established. A 500-millilitre bottle of a sports drink costs between 90 pence and £1 ($2.20 and $2.45) in Britain, for example, compared with about 75 pence ($1.85) for the same size bottle of Coke or Pepsi.

Moreover, Coke believes Europeans aged 13 to 29, the target market for Powerade, increasingly are making sports a bigger part of their lives. Coke says its new Powerade drink increases endurance during exercise by combining the benefits of a sports drink with the energy boost of drinks such as Red Bull, made by a closely held Austrian company. The formula in Europe is the same as in the new vitamin-B-enhanced Powerade sold in Canada, but the taste is slightly different because of certain European regulations on ingredients, Mr. Pardy says. The look is the same as in Canada, with a futuristic letter "P" logo.

As in Canada, Coke is marketing Powerade to the likes of roller bladers and skateboarders. Posters to be placed in gyms across Europe as part of the advertising campaign for Powerade will allude to "extreme sports" challenges, for example. But the company hopes the drink will eventually transcend its original use and that European youths will begin drinking sports beverages more generally, as youths do in North America.

"We want to grow the market in Europe to the point where you'll use it whenever you need endurance, beyond sports occasions," Mr. Pardy says.

Powerade will be launched in Britain, Ireland, France, Germany, Spain, Sweden, Turkey, Italy, Poland, Hungary, and Greece. The drink, which will be sold in citrus, orange, and vivid-blueberry flavours, will be distributed first through vending machines in gyms, sports centres, and soccer stadiums before moving to convenience stores and supermarkets.

Advertising for the drink will span billboards, television commercials, sponsorships with sports figures, the Internet, and direct mail. Most of the advertising will be directed at a male audience, because in Europe the sports-drink market is generally skewed more toward men.[24]

Describe Coke's target market strategy for Powerade in Europe. Explain the marketing mix that the company plans to employ.

ETHICS IN MARKETING

The Marketing of Gambling?

With the recent opening of three casinos in Detroit, Michigan (just across the Ambassador Bridge from Windsor, Ontario), and the possibility of a smoke-free workplace and consumer environment in Windsor and Essex County, the Ontario Lottery and Gaming Corporation has become increasingly concerned about the prospect of Casino Windsor losing revenue. "It will never retrench on my watch," said Stanley Sadinsky, chairman of the Ontario Lottery and Gaming Corporation. With those words, Mr. Sadinsky announced the hiring of a group of marketing experts to identify ways to ensure that gamblers keep coming back to Casino Windsor.

Casino Windsor has contributed significantly to the billions of dollars generated by the Ontario Government from gambling revenues. In 2003, Casino Windsor grossed in excess of $600 million. An average of nearly 14,000 people a day visit, and lose some of their money, at Casino Windsor. The profitability of Casino Windsor makes it a valuable asset to the province, according to Mr. Sadinsky: "It's very worthwhile and we're paying a lot of attention to it. There is no thought of doing anything but moving the casino forward. We'll develop the best strategy for it that we can."

The new competition from the Detroit casinos, the SARS problem of 2003 in Windsor and the rest of Ontario, and delays at the border since heightened terrorists alerts in the U.S. were put into effect have all caused problems for Casino Windsor. In 2003, Casino Windsor revenues were down 30 percent. "The marketing experts will be exploring all options to bring these customers back," stated Mr. Sadinsky. Expanding the casino is one option being explored.

The Liberal government's plan to create a smoke-free province is worrisome, and the OLGC is making its concerns on this matter known to the government. Mr. Sadinsky said that this could have a big impact and cites a drop in revenue of up to 20 percent at two racetrack slot operations that went smoke-free. While all local governments in Essex County, outside of the City of Windsor, have made all workplaces smoke-free, Windsor allows smoking in all places where food and beverages are served. Mr. Sadinsky is scheduled to meet with the mayor of Windsor to ensure that Casino Windsor does not become smoke-free.[25]

Do you think that developing strategies to bring gamblers to Casino Windsor is an appropriate way to use marketing knowledge, principles, and expertise? If yes, why? If no, for what types of products or services is marketing appropriate and for what types of products and services isn't it? Explain your reasons.

Marketing Plays an Important Role in Society

As you read this text, Canada's population will be passing 32 million. Think about how many transactions are needed each day to feed, clothe, and shelter a population of this size. The number is huge. And yet it all works quite well, partly because the well-developed Canadian economic system efficiently distributes the output of farms and factories. A typical Canadian family, for example, consumes 2.5 tonnes of food a year. Marketing makes food available when we want it, in desired quantities, at accessible locations, and in sanitary and convenient packages and forms (such as instant and frozen foods).

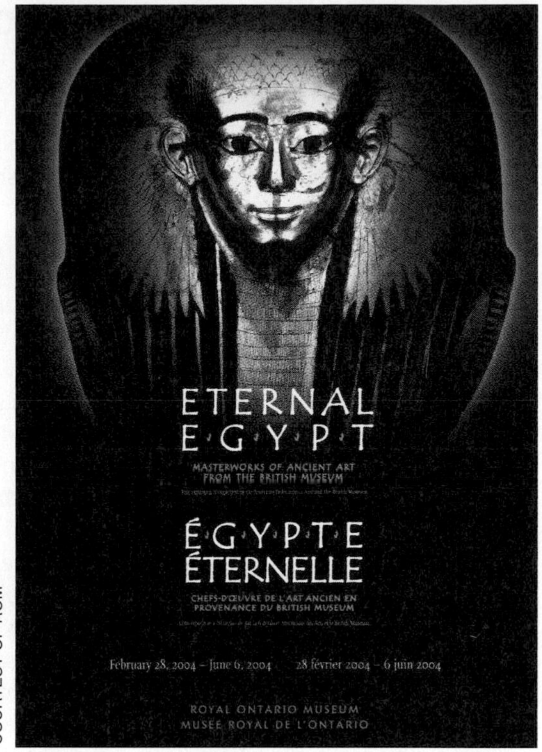

COURTESY OF ROM

Businesses are not the only entities that conduct marketing activities. Not-for-profit organizations like the Royal Ontario Museum in Toronto, Ontario, provide career opportunities in marketing as well.

Marketing Is Important to Businesses

The fundamental objectives of most businesses are survival, profits, and growth. Marketing contributes directly to achieving these objectives. Marketing includes the following activities, which are vital to business organizations: assessing the wants and satisfactions of present and potential customers, designing and managing product offerings, determining prices and pricing policies, developing distribution strategies, and communicating with present and potential customers.

All businesspeople, regardless of specialization or area of responsibility, need to be familiar with the terminology and fundamentals of accounting, finance, management, and marketing. People in all business areas need to be able to communicate with specialists in other areas. Furthermore, marketing is not just a job done by people in a marketing department. Marketing is a part of everyone's job in the organization. As David Packard of Hewlett-Packard put it: "Marketing is far too important to be left only to the marketing department." Marketing is not a department so much as a companywide orientation.[26] Therefore, a basic understanding of marketing is important to all businesspeople.

Marketing Offers Outstanding Career Opportunities

Between one-quarter and one-third of the entire civilian workforce performs marketing activities. Marketing offers great career opportunities in such areas as professional selling, marketing research, advertising, retail and industrial buying, distribution management, product management, product development, and wholesaling. Marketing career opportunities also exist in a variety of nonbusiness organizations, including hospitals, museums, universities, the armed forces, sports organizations, and various government and social service agencies.

As the global marketplace becomes more challenging, companies all over the world and of all sizes are going to have to become better marketers. For a comprehensive look at career opportunities in marketing and a variety of other useful information about careers, visit our website at http://www.lamb3e.nelson.com.

Marketing Affects Your Life Every Day

Marketing plays a major role in your everyday life. You participate in the marketing process as a consumer of goods and services. About half of every dollar you spend pays for marketing costs, such as marketing research, product development, packaging, transportation, storage, advertising, and sales expenses. By developing a better understanding of marketing, you will become a better-informed consumer. You will better understand the buying process and be able to negotiate more effectively with sellers. Moreover, you will be better prepared to demand satisfaction when the goods and services you buy do not meet the standards promised by the manufacturer or the marketer.

>> LOOKING AHEAD

This book is divided into 18 chapters organized into seven parts. The chapters are written from the marketing manager's perspective. Each chapter begins with a brief list of learning objectives followed by a brief story about a marketing situation faced by a firm or industry. At the end of each of these opening vignettes, thought-provoking questions link the story to the subject addressed in the chapter. Your instructor may wish to begin chapter discussions by asking members of your class to share their views about the questions.

The examples of global marketing highlighted in most chapters will help you understand that marketing takes place all over the world, between buyers and sellers in different countries. These and other global marketing examples throughout the book, marked with the icon shown in the margin, are intended to help you develop a global perspective on marketing.

Marketing ethics is another important topic selected for special treatment throughout the book. Chapters include highlighted stories about firms or industries that have faced ethical dilemmas or have engaged in practices that some consider unethical. Questions are posed to focus your thinking on the key ethical issues raised in each story.

End-of-chapter materials begin with a final comment on the chapter-opening vignette called "Connect It." This is followed by a summary of the major topics ("Review It"), with discussion and writing questions (writing questions are identified with the icon in the margin) related to the topics. The questions include specific Internet and team activities, which are identified by appropriate icons. The on-line icon is also placed throughout the text to identify examples relating to technology. Another section, "Apply It," with discussion questions, is next, followed by a detailed exercise called "Think About It." Then comes "Try It," a longer case, and "Flip It" and "Click It," which let you know what additional learning opportunities are available in your study guide and on the *Marketing* website.

Marketing is also supported by InfoTrac® College Edition. Several chapters throughout the book will give you the opportunity to refine your research skills through exercises specifically designed for InfoTrac®. The icon at the left will flag these exercises. All these features are intended to help you develop a more thorough understanding of marketing and enjoy the learning process.

The remaining chapters in Part 1 introduce you to the activities involved in developing a marketing plan and the dynamic environment in which marketing decisions must be made. Part 2 covers consumer decision making and buyer behaviour; business marketing; the concepts of positioning, market segmentation, and targeting; and the nature and uses of marketing research and decision support systems. Parts 3 through 6 examine the elements of the marketing mix—product, place (distribution), promotion, and pricing. Part 7 contains two final chapters. The first examines one-to-one and Internet marketing while the second focuses on customer relationship management and the development of the complete marketing program.

>> CONNECT IT

Look back at the story at the beginning of this chapter about Chris and Larry and Krave's Candy Co. You should now find the assignment at the end of the story fairly easy. Chris and Larry's initial motivation to go into business was based on a candy product concocted by Chris's grandmother. People liked the product and Chris saw a business opportunity. This is a typical product orientation. While the product was well liked, this often isn't enough for business success. Chris and Larry had to work hard to get Clodhoppers onto the shelves of retail stores. This they accomplished primarily through personal selling efforts. In doing so, they moved from a product orientation to a sales orientation. But then Chris and Larry began undertaking customer research to help identify new products and new packaging. This moved Chris and Larry toward a marketing orientation. The long-term success of Krave's Candy Co. will depend on how well Chris and Larry are able to understand the wants of their market and successfully satisfy their customers' needs.

REVIEW IT

1 **Define the term *marketing*.** The ultimate goal of all marketing activity is to facilitate mutually satisfying exchanges between parties. The activities of marketing include the conception, pricing, promotion, and distribution of ideas, goods, and services.

1.1 ON LINE What is the AMA? What does it do? How do its services benefit marketers across North America (see **http://www.marketingpower.com**)? Now check out the CMA (**http://www.the-cma.org**). How does it differ from the AMA and what are the similarities?

1.2 Log on to InfoTrac® at **http://infotrac.thomsonlearning.com** and conduct a keyword search for "marketing." Read a couple of the articles. Based on what you have learned in this chapter, how do these articles describe or relate to marketing?

2 **Describe four marketing management philosophies.** The role of marketing and the character of marketing activities within an organization are strongly influenced by its philosophy and orientation. A production-oriented organization focuses on the internal capabilities of the firm rather than on the desires and needs of the marketplace. A sales orientation is based on two beliefs: that people will buy more products if aggressive sales techniques are used, and that high sales volumes produce high profits. A market-oriented organization focuses on satisfying customer wants and needs while meeting organizational objectives. A societal marketing orientation goes beyond a market orientation to include the preservation or enhancement of individuals' and society's long-term best interests.

2.1 WRITING Your company president has decided to restructure the firm to make it more market oriented. She is going to announce the changes at an upcoming meeting. She has asked you to prepare a short speech outlining the general reasons for the new company orientation.

2.2 Donald E. Petersen, former chairman of the board of Ford Motor Company, remarked, "If we aren't customer driven, our cars won't be either." Explain how this statement reflects the marketing concept.

2.3 Give an example of a company that might be successfully following a production orientation. Why might a firm in this industry be successful following such an orientation?

3 **Discuss the differences between sales and market orientations.** First, sales-oriented firms focus on their own needs; market-oriented firms focus on customers' needs and preferences. Second, sales-oriented companies consider themselves to be deliverers of goods and services, whereas market-oriented companies view themselves as satisfiers of customers. Third, sales-oriented firms direct their products to everyone; market-oriented firms aim at specific segments of the population. Fourth, although the primary goal of both types of firms is profit, sales-oriented businesses pursue maximum sales volume through intensive promotion, whereas market-oriented businesses pursue customer satisfaction through coordinated activities.

3.1 A friend of yours agrees with the adage "People don't know what they want—they only want what they know." Write your friend a letter expressing the extent to which you think marketers shape consumer wants.

3.2 WRITING Your local supermarket's slogan is "It's your store." However, when you asked one of the stockpeople to help you find a bag of chips, he told you it was not his job and that you should look a littler harder. On your way out, you noticed a sign with an address for complaints. Draft a letter explaining why the supermarket's slogan will never be credible unless the employees carry it out.

4 **Describe the marketing process.** The marketing process includes understanding the organization's mission and the role marketing plays in fulfilling that mission, setting marketing objectives, scanning the environment, developing a marketing

strategy by selecting a target market strategy, developing and implementing a marketing mix, implementing the strategy, designing performance measures, and evaluating marketing efforts and making changes if needed. The marketing mix combines product, distribution (place), promotion, and pricing strategies in a way that creates exchanges satisfying to individual and organizational objectives.

4.1 

Form a group of three or four members. Suppose you and your colleagues work for an up-and-coming gourmet coffee company that has several stores, mostly in large cities across the country. Your team has been assigned the task of assessing whether the company should begin marketing on the Internet. Each member has been assigned to visit three or four Internet sites for ideas. Some possibilities are:

- Toys "R" Us at http://www.toysrus.ca
- Wal-Mart at http://www.wal-mart.ca
- Godiva chocolates at http://www.godiva.com
- Levi Strauss at http://www.levi.com

Use your imagination and look up others. As you can see, many companies are easy to find, as long as you can spell their names. Typically, you would use the following: http://www.companyname.ca (for example, http://www.canadiantire.ca or http://www.zellers.ca).

Has Internet marketing helped the companies whose sites you visited? If so, how? What factors should your company consider before committing to Internet activity? Prepare a three- to five-minute presentation to give to your class.

5 **Describe several reasons for studying marketing.** First, marketing affects the allocation of goods and services that influence a nation's economy and standard of living. Second, an understanding of marketing is crucial to understanding most businesses. Third, career opportunities in marketing are diverse, profitable, and expected to increase significantly during the coming decade. Fourth, understanding marketing makes consumers more informed.

5.1 

Write a letter to a friend or family member explaining why you think a course in marketing will help you in your career in some field other than marketing.

DEFINE IT

APPLY IT

Lisa King enjoyed working as a camp counsellor during the summer. She started about the time she entered high school and continued through university. She even took a job at a camp the summer after graduating from university. She rationalized that this "internship," developing the camp yearbook, would help prepare her for a job in advertising.

As the summer passed, Lisa spent more time thinking about "what she was going to do in the years ahead," as she put it. Her thoughts always seemed to return to camping. Lisa finally decided that she would like to open a small retail store specializing in camping supplies. The more she thought about it, the better she liked the idea.

She finally got up enough nerve to call her father, Tom, to discuss the idea. Tom's first response was, "Have you prepared a written plan?" Lisa remembered preparing a marketing plan in her first class in marketing at the University of New Brunswick. She asked her father to FedEx the class text to her.

With financial backing from their father, Lisa and her sister, Jill, opened Santorini Camping Supply the following fall. They picked the name Santorini because it was their favourite place in the Greek isles and, as Jill put it, "We just like the name."

On opening day, a customer asked Lisa if Santorini's guaranteed the products it sold. Lisa proudly replied, "Every product that is purchased from Santorini Camping Supply has a lifetime guarantee. If at any time you are not satisfied with one of our products, you can return it to the store for a full refund or exchange."

QUESTIONS

1. What marketing management philosophy is Santorini's expressing? Why have you reached this conclusion?
2. Do you think a lifetime guarantee for this kind of product is too generous? Why or why not?
3. Do you think this policy will contribute to success or to bankruptcy?
4. Suggest other customer service policies that might be appropriate for Santorini Camping Supply.

THINK ABOUT IT

In today's business environment, ethics are extremely important. In recent years, there have been numerous scandals and trials that stem from a lack of ethical judgment. For example, the former CEO of Tyco International was charged with tax evasion and making secret deals with underlings. Levi Strauss, Nike, and Gap have been accused of exploiting workers in developing countries. And who can forget the catastrophic collapse of Enron and the guilty verdict against the highly regarded accounting firm, Arthur Andersen, LLP?

Although some might say that these occurrences are the work of a few bad apples spoiling the bunch, it is clear that ethical decision making plays a very important role in a company's success and prosperity. For this reason, we are including an ethical exercise in every chapter. A brief scenario will present you with a situation in which the right thing to do may or may not be crystal clear, and you will need to decide the ethical way out of the dilemma. To help you with these decisions, we will refer you to the CMA Code of Ethics at http://www.the-cma.org or the AMA's Code of Ethics, found on-line at http://www.marketingpower.com. This will give you a resource for the exercise and will also help reinforce the ethical standards that marketers should uphold.

Review the "Ethics in Marketing" example in this chapter. How does the AMA Code of Ethics relate to this story? What about the CMA Code of Ethics (click on Publications and then click Code of Ethics or go directly to http://www.the-cma.org/consumer/ethics.cfm)?

TRY IT

Banking on Small Business

When Karen Prest, a research analyst, started conducting research on whether banks were delivering services for small businesses, she expected the results to give banks a failing grade. "I went in as a skeptic," she says. "I was convinced by my own research. I saw how much banks are now focusing on small businesses. The study proved that small businesses are more and more in the limelight."

A small business might be thought of as one with fewer than 500 employees. According to Statistics Canada, there are nearly 500,000 businesses of this size employing several million workers. Prest considers that a lucrative marketplace with a lot of untapped opportunity.

According to James Van Dyke, a research director, banks have generally struggled with the small business market, in part because it has been easier to see profits in large businesses. In addition, segmentation has been a challenge. Recently, banks have begun to recognize small business as a distinct, separate, and vastly underserved segment. In the past, banks have ignored the small business market, considering it too costly to serve and unable to provide a viable source of revenue to the bank. Technology has helped shift this thinking.

When technology proved that services could be accomplished securely over the Internet, the banking industry experienced something of an epiphany. Web-based products have proliferated and enabled banks to target small businesses profitably. Some banks have long provided computer-based banking products. DOS-based cash management products have been used since the late 1980s. Windows-based products were launched in the 1990s and met with less success. But the greatest success in this area has occurred since the creation of Web-based products.

Why have banks had difficulty entering the small business market? One key reason is that banking products have not been tailored to fit the size of small business finances. This made the cash management process too expensive for the banks trying to service small business accounts. The Internet has changed that dramatically, and not only from the perspective of product offerings. The Internet has affected service delivery as well. As one industry consultant states, "With the Internet, the dynamics change. Businesses can go right to the website. There's no cost to place software. There's standard browser technology. The cost of distribution is low, and the vendors have tuned in to this. There are hundreds of options for packaging the products, and we work with banks to help them package our cash management products for their customers."

QUESTIONS

1. Describe the shift in marketing management philosophy that banks have had to make in order to serve small business.
2. Describe at least two steps in the marketing process that have been undertaken in order to help banks better serve potential small business customers.
3. Describe the major change in the marketing environment that has made it possible for banks to profitably serve small business clients.

FLIP IT

To learn more about the study opportunities available in your *Grademaker Study Guide*, read the "Flip It" section at the end of each chapter. Each study guide chapter includes vocabulary review, study test questions, Internet activities, marketing applications and scenarios, and more. To help you determine the concepts you most need to review, you can perform a self-assessment by completing the pretest at the beginning of each study guide chapter. Can you explain the four marketing management philosophies? What about listing the steps in the marketing process? Check out your *Grademaker Study Guide* and find out.

CLICK IT

The *Marketing* website is rich with materials to help you review and master marketing concepts. Check your knowledge with the free quizzes, practise key terms using the crossword puzzles, or review key concepts using the Microsoft® PowerPoint® slides. Also on the website are updated weblinks to companies mentioned in this chapter, Internet exercises, career marketing information, and much much more! Go to http://www.lamb3e.nelson.com, read the material, and follow the convenient links.

WATCH IT

Lord of the Boards

In 1977, Jake Burton, an avid rider, founded Burton Snowboards, the industry leader with a 40 percent market share. Jake's recipe for success has always been simple: "We always focused on the sport and everything else took care of itself." In 1978, working out of a barn, Jake hit on a successful formula (horizontally laminated wood) and was able to sell 300 boards at $88 each. The next 10 years saw Jake spending time and money lobbying ski areas to open their slopes to snowboarders. Today, slopes everywhere are open to snowboarders.

Jake, the businessman, has always kept his eye on the big picture. While campaigning to open slopes to snowboarders, Jake also established a number of snowboard competitions. By the mid-1990s, many sporting magazines were calling snowboarding the fastest-growing sport. Finally, the ultimate—snowboarding made its debut in the 1998 Winter Olympics in Nagano, Japan. At the 2002 Winter Olympics, three Burton pro riders won medals.

Jake didn't let the Olympics go to his head. He kept his company going with product development, R&D, and lots of riding. The company provides free private lessons for newbies (new riders) and Burton employees are all encouraged to ride. The sport draws mainly a young crowd. According to the National Ski & Snowboard Retailers Association, 80.8 percent of active snowboarders are under 24 and 74.1 percent are male—although the fastest-growing segment of the market is female.

Newbies can visit the Burton website (http://www.burton.com) for basic information on equipment and clothing as well as instructions on how to get started. An on-snow demonstration is considered a must, so Burton posts its travel schedule and offers free, local demonstrations and a chance to try on equipment.

Burton continues to stay close to customers by constantly talking with pro and amateur riders, retailers, designers, and others. Burton currently operates facilities in North America, Japan, and Austria. Current brands include Burton snowboards; AK, Radar, and Ronin outerwear; R.E.D. protective gear; Anon opticwear; Gravis footwear; and Analog streetwear.

Jake Burton's strategy for the company seems to be paying off. Jake Burton privately owns Burton Snowboards, and while detailed financial information is not available, sales were estimated to have surpassed $200 million in 2000. As sales have grown, Jake Burton has been trying to give back. In 1994, Burton started the Chill Program to provide free lessons, trips, and equipment to disadvantaged kids. While more competition is entering the snowboard industry, Jake Burton truly remains the Lord of the Boards.

QUESTIONS

1. Describe the exchange process at Burton.
2. How has Jake Burton's entrepreneurial philosophy made his company successful?
3. Does Burton use a sales orientation or a market orientation?
4. How does Burton Snowboards achieve customer satisfaction?

SUGGESTED INFORMATION SOURCES

Reade Bailey, "Jake Burton, King of the Hill," *Ski*, February 1998, 60–67.

www.burton.com

www.nssra.com

http://us.logicalis.com/casestudy/burton.htm

www.vermont.org/gbic/burtonsnow.html

www.wetfeet.com/asp/companyprofiles.asp?companypk=268

chapter 2

Strategic Planning for Competitive Advantage

>> LEARNING OBJECTIVES

1. Understand the importance of strategic marketing and know a basic outline for a marketing plan
2. Develop an appropriate business mission statement
3. Describe the criteria for stating good marketing objectives
4. Explain the components of a situation analysis
5. Identify sources of competitive advantage
6. Identify strategic alternatives and describe tools used to help select alternatives
7. Discuss target market strategies
8. Describe the elements of the marketing mix
9. Explain why implementation, evaluation, and control of the marketing plan are necessary
10. Identify several techniques that help make strategic planning effective

>>Steve Ader was talking with one of his customers about the number of years he had left until retirement when another patron at his Pet Valu store in Toronto broke in. "She said 'Steve, you can't possibly retire. I'm going to forbid you to retire,'" he recalled. "It wasn't really addressed specifically to me. It was about the kind of treatment they get in the store from my staff. They didn't want that to change."

As a franchisee of Pet Valu Canada Inc., Mr. Ader said that his staff must be friendly, courteous, and as knowledgeable as possible since they can't offer all of the pet products to be found in the 15,000 to 25,000 square feet of pet merchandise that much larger big-box retailers such as PetsMart and Petcetera can cram into their mega-stores.

The first Pet Valu store was opened in Scarborough, Ontario, in 1976 by Geoff and Carole Holt. By 1977, Geoff and Carole were operating three stores. Within 10 years, Geoff and Carole were offering franchises and the number of Pet Valu stores had grown to 75. In 1995, the company opened its first outlet in the U.S. Today there are over 250 Pet Valu stores in Canada, from Ontario to Manitoba, and over 100 outlets in the Northeastern U.S. Pet Valu is the largest retailer of pet products in Canada. A typical Pet Valu store is less than 2,500 square feet, is located in or near a neighbourhood shopping plaza, and carries about 7,000 pet products.

The success of the big-box retailers like PetsMart and Petcetera has presented Pet Valu with a challenge. Pet Valu must persuade customers that small and intimate stores can meet their needs as well as, if not better than, their larger competitors. Geoff Holt, who is now president and CEO of Pet Valu Canada Inc., feels that his stores can walk the fine line required to pack a large enough selection of merchandise into an intimate setting. Geoff Holt believes that Pet Valu's hard-working franchisees and their knowledgeable workforces, more intimate locations, and private label products (products found only at Pet Valu) will allow them to successfully compete with PetsMart and Petcetera.

"We are constantly developing ways to provide specialized products and services not offered by big-box stores," Mr. Holt said, citing knowledgeable staff and carryout service as features that set Pet Valu apart from its mega-store competitors. The personalized service seems to be working. Steve Ader's store in Toronto has dozens of regular customers whom he knows by name and who come in to talk to Steve and play with his dog, Amber. The lines of private labels like Performatrin and Feline Cuisine keep many customers coming back as well.

While smaller and more intimate, and even with its emphasis on high customer service, Pet Valu strives to be price competitive with the mega-stores. Costs are partially kept in line through the operation of a fully owned warehousing and distribution company called Peton Distributors Inc., which buys in large volume and services hundreds of independent pet outlets in addition to all of the Pet Valu stores.

Is the combination of neighbourhood locations, intimate store settings, high-quality service, competitive prices, and private labels working? Profits of Pet Valu grew from $1.23 million in 2002 to well over $2 million in 2003, and more Pet Valu franchise locations are being opened across the country each week.[1]

What are the elements of Pet Valu's marketing strategy? What would you describe as Pet Valu's competitive advantage? Describe each element of Pet Valu's marketing mix. Over the long term, will Pet Valu be able to compete with the mega-stores?

ON LINE

Pet Valu

How well do you think Pet Valu uses its website to build competitive advantage? Compare Pet Valu to its competitors, PetsMart and Petcetera.

http://www.petvalu.com

http://www.petsmart.com

http://www.petcetera.ca

1 Understand the importance of strategic marketing and know a basic outline for a marketing plan

strategic planning
The managerial process of creating and maintaining a fit between the organization's objectives and resources and evolving market opportunities.

>> THE NATURE OF STRATEGIC PLANNING

Strategic planning is the managerial process of creating and maintaining a fit between the organization's objectives and resources and the evolving market opportunities. The goal of strategic planning is long-run profitability and growth. Thus, strategic decisions require long-term commitments of resources.

A strategic error can threaten a firm's survival. On the other hand, a good strategic plan can help protect and grow the firm's resources. For instance, if the March of Dimes had decided to focus on fighting polio, the organization would no longer exist. Most of us view polio as a conquered disease. The March of Dimes survived by making the strategic decision to switch to fighting birth defects.

Strategic marketing management addresses two questions: What is the organization's main activity at a particular time? And how will it reach its goals? Here are some examples of strategic decisions:

AP/WIDE WORLD PHOTOS

Strategic planning is critical to business success. Coca-Cola rolled out Vanilla Coke on the soft drink's 116th birthday. The new flavour was launched, appropriately, at the Vanilla Bean Café. The café's owner, Barry Jessurun, is pictured unloading the truck carrying the first order of Vanilla Coke.

- The decision of Sears to buy Lands' End, a successful clothing catalogue and on-line retail business, for $1.9 billion. This move could upgrade Sears's image and increase its presence in the catalogue business and on the Internet. Lands' End clothing will enjoy greater retail distribution in Sears stores.[2]
- Bombardier's decision to invest $2 billion to develop a new line of regional jets for this fast-growing segment of the airline industry.[3]
- After its successful penetration of the Western Canadian market, using Hamilton as its hub, WestJet began offering flights to airports in Eastern Canada, including Toronto's Pearson Airport.[4] More recently still, WestJet has moved its hub of operations to Toronto.
- Molson Inc. has developed a major new promotional campaign to introduce the "Bubba" mini-keg. The Bubba mini-keg is a party-sized container of Molson Canadian featuring some of the most outlandish suits worn by Don Cherry during *Hockey Night in Canada.*[5]

All of these decisions have affected or will affect each organization's long-run course, its allocation of resources, and ultimately its financial success. In contrast, an operating decision, such as changing the package design for Post's cornflakes or altering the sweetness of a Kraft salad dressing, probably won't have a big impact on the long-run profitability of each company.

How do companies go about strategic marketing planning? How do employees know how to implement the long-term goals of the firm? The answer is the marketing plan.

planning
The process of anticipating future events and determining strategies to achieve organizational objectives in the future.

marketing planning
Designing activities relating to marketing objectives and the changing marketing environment.

marketing plan
A written document that acts as a guidebook of marketing activities for the marketing manager.

>> WHAT IS A MARKETING PLAN?

Planning is the process of anticipating future events and determining strategies to achieve organizational objectives in the future. **Marketing planning** involves designing activities relating to marketing objectives and the changing marketing environment. Marketing planning is the basis for all marketing strategies and decisions. Issues such as product lines, distribution channels, marketing communications, and pricing are all delineated in the **marketing plan.** The marketing plan is a written document that acts as a guidebook of marketing activities for the marketing manager. In this chapter, you will learn the importance of writing a marketing plan and the types of information contained in a marketing plan.

Why Write a Marketing Plan?

By specifying objectives and defining the actions required to attain them, a marketing plan provides the basis by which actual and expected performance can be compared. Marketing can be one of the most expensive and complicated business components; it is also one of the most important business activities. The written marketing plan provides clearly stated activities that help employees and managers understand and work toward common goals.

Writing a marketing plan allows you to examine the marketing environment in conjunction with the inner workings of the business. Once the marketing plan is written, it serves as a reference point for the success of future activities. Finally, the marketing plan allows the marketing manager to enter the marketplace with an awareness of possibilities and problems.

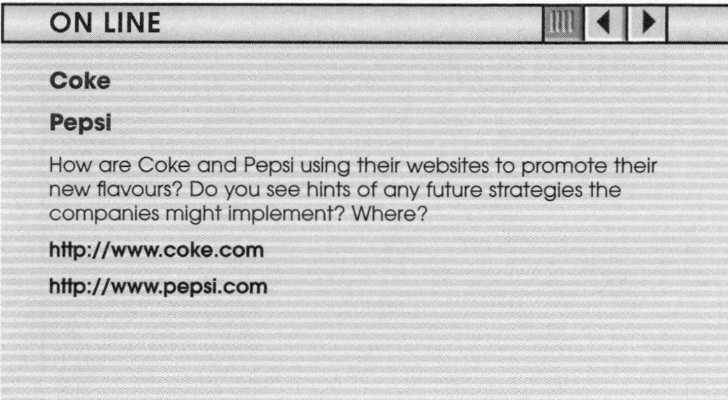

ON LINE
Coke
Pepsi
How are Coke and Pepsi using their websites to promote their new flavours? Do you see hints of any future strategies the companies might implement? Where?
http://www.coke.com
http://www.pepsi.com

Marketing Plan Elements

Marketing plans can be presented in many different ways. Most businesses need a written marketing plan because the scope of a marketing plan is large and can be complex. Details about tasks and activity assignments may be lost if communicated orally. Regardless of the way a marketing plan is presented, some elements are common to all marketing plans. These include defining the business mission and objectives, performing a situation analysis, delineating a target market, and establishing components of the marketing mix. Exhibit 2.1 shows these elements, which are also described further below. Other elements that may be included in a plan are budgets, implementation timetables, required marketing research efforts, and evaluation of plan outcomes. An example of a thumbnail marketing plan sketch appears in Exhibit 2.2.

>> WRITING THE MARKETING PLAN

The creation and implementation of a complete marketing plan will allow the organization to achieve marketing objectives and succeed. However, the marketing plan is only as good as the information it contains and the effort, creativity, and thought that went into its creation. Having a good marketing information system and a wealth of competitive intelligence is critical to a thorough and accurate situation analysis. The role of managerial intuition is also important in the creation and selection of marketing strategies. Managers must weigh any information against its accuracy and their own judgment when making a marketing decision.

Note that the overall structure of the marketing plan (Exhibit 2.1) should not be viewed as a series of sequential planning steps. Many of the marketing plan elements are decided on in conjunction with one another. Similarly, the summary sample marketing plan (Exhibit 2.2) does not begin to cover the intricacies and detail of a full marketing plan. Further, every marketing plan has a different content, depending on the organization, its mission, objectives, targets, and marketing mix components. Visualize how the marketing plan in Exhibit 2.2 would differ if the firm offered only wireless communication connectivity services (not the physical products). How would the plan differ if the target market consisted of *Fortune* 500 firms with large sales forces instead of executives?

The marketing plan outline shown later in Exhibit 2.7 is an expanded set of questions that can guide the formulation of a marketing plan. However, this outline should not be regarded as the only correct format for a marketing plan. Many organizations have their own distinctive format or terminology for creating a marketing plan. Every marketing plan should be unique to the firm for which it was created. Remember that, although the format and order of presentation should be flexible, the same types of questions and topic areas should be covered in any marketing plan.

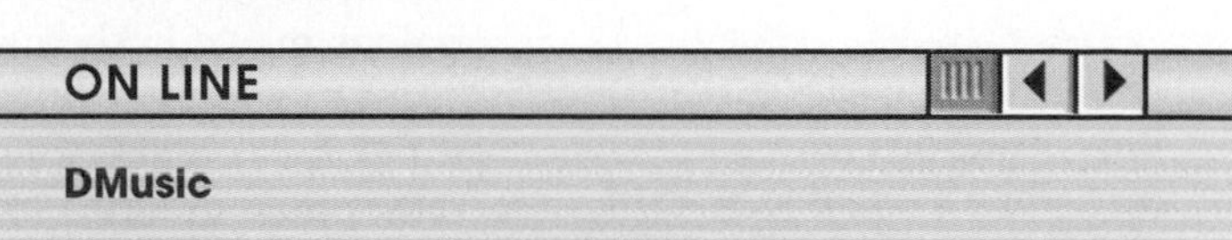

ON LINE
DMusic
Use Exhibit 2.2 to create a sample summary marketing plan for Dmusic.com, an Internet start-up created by a teenage entrepreneur.
http://www.dmusic.com

EXHIBIT 2.1

Elements of a Marketing Plan

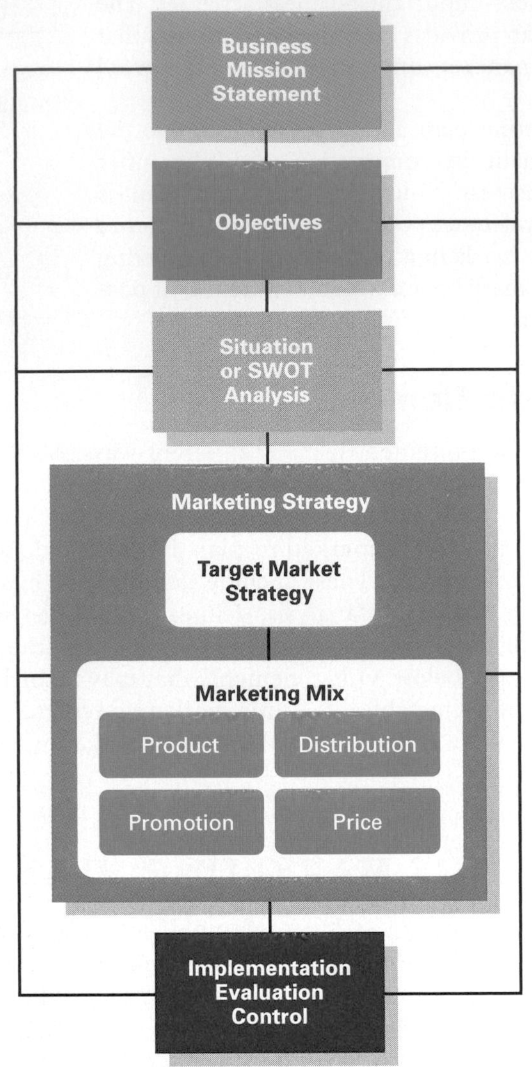

2 Develop an appropriate business mission statement

mission statement
The firm's long-term vision based on a careful analysis of benefits sought by present and potential customers and analysis of existing and anticipated environmental conditions.

marketing myopia
Defining a business in terms of goods and services rather than in terms of the benefits that customers seek.

>> DEFINING THE BUSINESS MISSION

The foundation of any marketing plan is the firm's **mission statement,** which answers the question, "What business are we in and where are we going?" Business mission definition profoundly affects the firm's long-run resource allocation, profitability, and survival. The mission statement is based on a careful analysis of benefits sought by present and potential customers and analysis of existing and anticipated environmental conditions. The firm's long-term vision, embodied in the mission statement, establishes boundaries for all subsequent decisions, objectives, and strategies. Canadian Tire's mission statement is shown in Exhibit 2.3 on page 29.

A mission statement should focus on the market or markets the organization is attempting to serve rather than on the good or service offered. Otherwise, a new technology may quickly make the good or service obsolete and the mission statement irrelevant to company functions. Business mission statements that are stated too narrowly suffer from **marketing myopia**—defining a business in terms of goods and services rather than in terms of the benefits that customers seek. In this context, *myopia* means narrow, short-term thinking. For example, Frito-Lay defines its mission as being in the snack-food business rather than in the corn chip business. The mission of sports teams is not just to play games but also to serve the interests of the fans. Telus does not sell only camera telephones or long-distance services; it markets communications technology.

EXHIBIT 2.2

Sample Summary Marketing Plan

Business Mission	Ultracel is in the business of providing advanced communications technology and communications convenience to mobile users.
Marketing Objective	To achieve 20 percent, in dollar volume, of the wireless telephone market by year-end, 2006.
Situation Analysis	
Strengths	Well-funded organization, highly skilled workforce with low turnover, excellent relationships with suppliers, product differential and sustainable competitive advantage of patented colour screen and Internet connectivity.
Weaknesses	Company name not well-known, small firm with no manufacturing cost advantages, no long-term contracts with distributors, inexperience in the wireless communications market.
Opportunities	Explosive growth of wireless phone users, worldwide acceptance of cellular technology, newly expanded digital networks.
Threats	Heavy competition; technology is incompatible with current analog systems; not everyone can afford the systems, potential governmental regulation.
Target Market Selection	Young, mobile executives in North America and Europe, with incomes over $200,000 per year; frequent travellers; computer-dependent individuals.
Marketing Mix	
Product	Personal digital telephone. Brand name: Ultracel-4000. Features: simultaneous voice/data communication, Internet access, operation within buildings, linkups to data subscription and e-mail services, computer data storage, colour screen, lightweight, 500-hour battery, three-year unlimited warranty on parts and labour, 24-hour technical support, leather or titanium carrying case.
Place	Available through electronics retailers, upscale computer retailers, or via Web order company direct; products transported via airplane and temperature-controlled motor carrier.
Promotion	Fifty manufacturer's representatives for selling force, with 25 percent commissions; advertising in print media, Internet websites, cable television, and outdoor billboards; sales promotion in the form of introductory product rebates, technology trade shows; public relations efforts to news media and sponsorship of world-championship sporting events.
Price	Retail price of $299; assuming mild price sensitivity and future price wars. Lease option available; corporate discounts of 20 percent for volume purchases.
Implementation	First quarter: Complete marketing research on price, design promotional campaign, sign contracts with manufacturer's reps. Second quarter: Public relations campaign, product introduction at trade shows, rollout of advertising. Third quarter: Test market international markets.

Alternatively, business missions may be stated too broadly. "To provide products of superior quality and value that improve the lives of the world's consumers" is probably too broad a mission statement for any firm except Procter & Gamble. Care must be taken when stating what business a firm is in. The mission statement of Norco, a British Columbia manufacturer of performance bikes, states: "We are dedicated to building rewarding, long-term relationships with our Customers, our Employees, and our Suppliers. We are driven by our customers to supply innovative cycle products and outstanding service and marketing support that will promote their growth and success."[6] Once a firm correctly states its business mission in terms of the benefits that customers seek, the

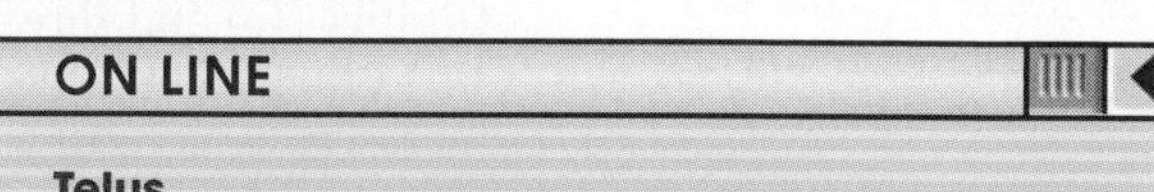

Telus

How does Telus use its website to market its communication technology? What range of products and services does Telus offer? What specific new product is Telus promoting on its website right now?

http://www.telus.com

foundation for its marketing plan is set. Many companies are focusing on designing more appropriate mission statements because these statements are frequently displayed on the World Wide Web.

strategic business unit (SBU)
A subgroup of a single business or collection of related businesses within the larger organization.

The organization may need to define a mission statement and objectives for a **strategic business unit (SBU),** which is a subgroup of a single business or collection of related businesses within the larger organization. A properly defined SBU should have a distinct mission and specific target market, control over its resources, its own competitors, and plans independent of the other SBUs in the organization. Thus, a large firm such as Kraft General Foods may have marketing plans for each of its SBUs, which include breakfast foods, desserts, pet foods, and beverages.

3 Describe the criteria for stating good marketing objectives

>> SETTING MARKETING PLAN OBJECTIVES

Before the details of a marketing plan can be developed, goals and objectives for the plan must be stated. Without objectives, there is no basis for measuring the success of marketing plan activities. For example, in one recent year, Hewlett-Packard's net income was $408 million—an 89 percent one-year growth rate. Sales and the number of employees also grew during this period. Sounds great, doesn't it? Actually, these figures failed to meet company objectives for that year and H-P executives were denied their bonuses.[7]

marketing objective
A statement of what is to be accomplished through marketing activities.

A **marketing objective** is a statement of what is to be accomplished through marketing activities. To be useful, stated objectives should meet several criteria. First, objectives should be realistic, measurable, and time specific. It is tempting to state that the objective is "to be the best marketer of ferret food." However, what is "best" for one firm might be sales of one million packages of ferret food per year, whereas to another firm, "best" might mean dominant market share. It may be unrealistic for start-up firms or new products to plan to command dominant market share, given other competitors in the marketplace. Finally, by what time should the goal be met? A more realistic objective would be: "To achieve 10 percent dollar market share in the specialty pet food market within 12 months of product introduction."

Second, objectives must be consistent and indicate the priorities of the organization. Specifically, objectives flow from the business mission statement to the rest of the marketing plan. Exhibit 2.4 shows some well-stated and poorly stated objectives. Notice how well they do or do not meet the preceding criteria.

Carefully specified objectives serve several functions. First, they communicate marketing management philosophies and provide direction for lower-level marketing managers so that marketing efforts are integrated and pointed in a consistent direction. Objectives also serve as motivators by creating something for which employees strive to reach. When objectives are attainable and challenging, they motivate those charged with achieving the objectives. Additionally, the process of writing specific objectives forces executives to clarify their thinking. Finally, objectives form a basis for control; the effectiveness of a plan can be gauged in light of the stated goals.

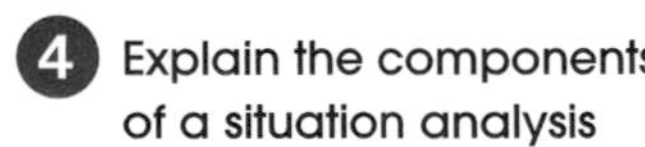
4 Explain the components of a situation analysis

>> CONDUCTING A SITUATION ANALYSIS

SWOT analysis
Identifying internal strengths (S) and weaknesses (W) and also examining external opportunities (O) and threats (T).

Before specific marketing activities can be defined, marketers must understand the current and potential environment that the product or service will be marketed in. A situation analysis is sometimes referred to as a **SWOT analysis;** that is, the firm should identify its internal strengths (S) and weaknesses (W) and also examine external opportunities (O) and threats (T).

When examining internal strengths and weaknesses, the marketing manager should focus on organizational resources such as production costs, marketing skills, financial resources, company or brand image, employee capabilities, and available technology. For example, a potential weakness for Algoma Steel is that it is the smallest of Canada's major steel companies; this means that it may lack economies of scale in comparison with other steel makers. Other weaknesses include high labour rates and high management turnover. A potential strength is the low operating costs of its newest mill in Sault Ste. Marie, Ontario, which incorporates the latest technology in the industry.

EXHIBIT 2.3

Canadian Tire's Mission Statement

Canadian Tire is a growing network of interrelated businesses, each one leveraging the core capabilities and privileged assets of the others. Canadian Tire continuously strives to meet the needs of its customers for total value by offering a unique package of location, price, service, and assortment. The 45,000 employees of Canadian Tire and its Associate Dealers, franchisees, and agents all contribute to the Corporation's objective to deliver top-quartile total return to shareholders among North American retailers.

SOURCE: © Canadian Tire Corporation, Limited.

EXHIBIT 2.4

Examples of Marketing Objectives

POORLY STATED OBJECTIVES	WELL-STATED OBJECTIVES
Our objective is to be a leader in the industry in terms of new-product development.	Our objective is to spend 12 percent of sales revenue between 2005 and 2006 on research and development in an effort to introduce at least five new products in 2006.
Our objective is to maximize profits.	Our objective is to achieve a 10 percent return on investment during 2006, with a payback on new investments of no longer than four years.
Our objective is to better serve customers.	Our objective is to obtain customer satisfaction ratings of at least 90 percent on the 2005 annual customer satisfaction survey, and to retain at least 85 percent of our 2005 customers as repeat purchasers in 2006.
Our objective is to be the best that we can be.	Our objective is to increase market share from 30 percent to 40 percent in 2006 by increasing promotional expenditures by 14 percent.

When examining external opportunities and threats, marketing managers must analyze aspects of the marketing environment. This process is called **environmental scanning**—the collection and interpretation of information about forces, events, and relationships in the external environment that may affect the future of the organization or the implementation of the marketing plan. Environmental scanning helps identify market opportunities and threats and provides guidelines for the design of marketing strategy. The six most often-studied macroenvironmental forces are social, demographic, economic, technological, political and legal, and competitive. These forces are examined in detail in Chapter 3.

environmental scanning
Collection and interpretation of information about forces, events, and relationships in the external environment that may affect the future of the organization or the implementation of the marketing plan.

>> COMPETITIVE ADVANTAGE

5 Identify sources of competitive advantage

Performing a SWOT analysis allows firms to identify their competitive advantage. A **competitive advantage** is a set of unique features of a company and its products that are perceived by the target market as significant and superior to the competition. It is the factor or factors that cause customers to patronize a firm and not the competition. There are three types of competitive advantages: cost, product/service, and niche.

competitive advantage
The set of unique features of a company and its products that are perceived by the target market as significant and superior to the competition.

Cost Competitive Advantage

Cost leadership can result from obtaining inexpensive raw materials, creating an efficient scale of plant operations, designing products for ease of manufacture, controlling overhead costs, and avoiding marginal customers. DuPont, for example, has an exceptional cost competitive advantage in the production of titanium dioxide. Technicians created a production process using low-cost feedstock, giving DuPont a 20 percent cost advantage over its competitors. Having a **cost competitive advantage** means being the low-cost competitor in an industry while maintaining satisfactory profit margins.

cost competitive advantage
Being the low-cost competitor in an industry while maintaining satisfactory profit margins.

A cost competitive advantage enables a firm to deliver superior customer value. By closely watching costs, WestJet has been able to operate over its routes at a lower cost than Air Canada. Thus it has been able to offer lower ticket prices and take passengers from its larger competitor.

Sources of Cost Competitive Advantage

Costs can be reduced in a variety of ways.

experience curves
Curves that show costs declining at a predictable rate as experience with a product increases.

- *Experience curves:* **Experience curves** tell us that costs decline at a predictable rate as experience with a product increases. The experience curve effect encompasses a broad range of manufacturing, marketing, and administrative costs. Experience curves reflect learning by doing, technological advances, and economies of scale. Firms like Bombardier and MTD Canada use historical experience curves as a basis for predicting and setting prices. Experience curves allow management to forecast costs and set prices based on anticipated costs as opposed to current costs.
- *Efficient labour:* Labour costs can be an important component of total costs in low-skill, labour-intensive industries such as product assembly and apparel manufacturing. Many manufacturers such as Nike, Levi Strauss, and Liz Claiborne have gone offshore to achieve cheaper manufacturing costs. Many automotive parts companies are also moving production to countries with lower labour costs, such as Mexico, Argentina, and China.
- *No-frills goods and services:* Marketers can lower costs by removing frills and options from a product or service. This is true of airlines, like WestJet, grocery stores, like No Frills and Price Chopper, and retailers, like A Buck or Two.

- *Product design:* Cutting-edge design technology can help offset high labour costs. BMW is a world leader in designing cars for ease of manufacture and assembly. Reverse engineering—the process of disassembling a product piece by piece to learn its components and clues as to the manufacturing process—can also mean savings. Japanese engineers have reversed many products, such as computer chips, and have been able to build them at lower cost.
- *Re-engineering:* Re-engineering to make firms more efficient often leads to downsizing or layoffs of employees, pruning product lines, closing obsolete factories, and renegotiating contracts with suppliers. General Motors, for example, demanded a 15 percent average price reduction from suppliers during its re-engineering.
- *Production innovations:* Production innovations such as new technology and simplified production techniques help lower the average cost of production. Technologies such as computer-aided design and computer-aided manufacturing (CAD/CAM) and increasingly sophisticated robots help companies like Bombardier, Ford, and General Electric reduce their manufacturing costs.
- *New methods of service delivery:* Medical expenses have been substantially lowered by the use of outpatient surgery and walk-in clinics. Airlines are lowering reservation and ticketing costs by encouraging passengers to use the Internet to book flights and by promoting "ticketless travel."

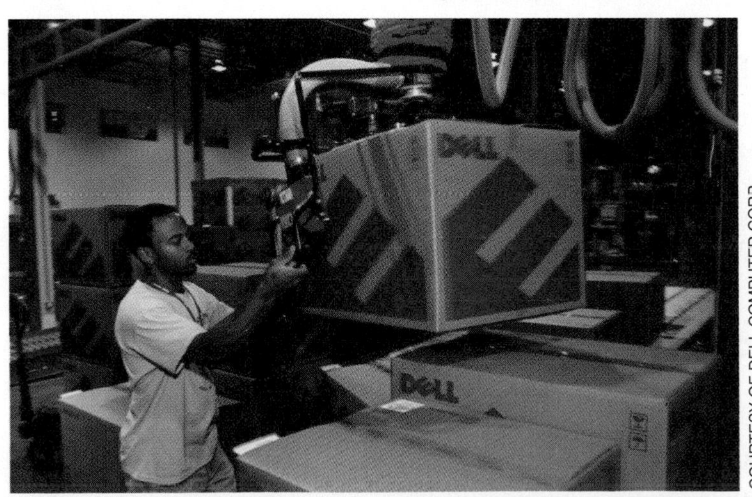

COURTESY OF DELL COMPUTER CORP.

Dell Computer blends production innovation, efficient labour, and product design into a cost-competitive advantage that fully supports the build-to-order business model it follows. A strong, long-lasting product and service competitive advantage is the outcome that provides the company with superior performance results.

Product/Service Differentiation

Because cost competitive advantages are subject to continual erosion, product/service differentiation tends to provide a longer-lasting competitive advantage. The durability of this strategy tends to make it more attractive to many top managers.

Product/service differentiation exists when a firm provides something unique that is valuable to buyers besides simply offering a low price. Examples include brand names (Lexus), a strong dealer network (Caterpillar Tractor for construction work), product reliability (Maytag appliances), image (Calvin Klein), or service (FedEx). A great example of a company that has a strong product/service competitive advantage is Dell Computer. Dell takes orders straight from customers and builds each customer's personal computer to demand. This means that customers get exactly what they want. Dell also gives its customers fast, convenient service that other companies can't match, including three-day delivery of PCs with all custom software preloaded. No other computer company can do what Dell does.[8]

product/service differentiation The provision of something that is unique and valuable to buyers beyond simply offering a lower price than the competition's.

Niche Competitive Advantage

A **niche competitive advantage** seeks to target and effectively serve a single segment of the market. For small companies with limited resources that potentially face giant competitors, niching may be the only viable option. A market segment that has good growth potential but is not crucial to the success of major competitors is a good candidate for developing a niche strategy.

niche competitive advantage The advantage achieved when a firm seeks to target and effectively serve a small segment of the market.

Many companies using a niche strategy serve only a limited geographic market. TBQ is a very successful restaurant chain but is found only in the Windsor market. Migros is the dominant grocery chain in Switzerland but it has no stores outside that small country.

Block Drug Company uses niching by focusing its product line on tooth products. It markets Polident to clean false teeth, Poligrip to hold false teeth, and Sensodyne toothpaste for people to polish sensitive teeth. The Orvis Company, a very successful nicher, manufactures and sells everything that anyone might ever need for fly-fishing.

Building Tomorrow's Competitive Advantage

The key to having a competitive advantage is the ability to sustain that advantage. A **sustainable competitive advantage** is one that cannot be copied by the competition. Dell Computer, discussed earlier, is a good example of a company that has a sustainable competitive advantage. Others include Rolex (high-quality watches), Caterpillar Tractor (service), and Magna (patented hydroforming technology for shaping automotive parts). In contrast, when Datril was introduced into the pain-reliever market, it was touted as being exactly like Tylenol, only cheaper. Tylenol responded by lowering its price, thus destroying Datril's competitive advantage and ability to remain on the market. In this case, low price was not a sustainable competitive advantage. Without a competitive advantage, target customers don't perceive any reason to patronize an organization instead of its competitors.

sustainable competitive advantage An advantage that cannot be copied by the competition.

The notion of competitive advantage means that a successful firm will stake out a position unique in some way from its rivals. Imitation of competitors indicates a lack of competitive advantage and almost ensures mediocre performance. Moreover, competitors rarely stand still, so it is not surprising that imitation causes managers to feel trapped in a seemingly endless game of catch-up. They are regularly surprised by the new accomplishments of their rivals. The "Ethics in Marketing" box describes a new promotion campaign used by Labatt. Is this type of campaign likely to result in a sustainable competitive advantage?

Companies need to build their own competitive advantages rather than copy a competitor. The sources of tomorrow's competitive advantages are the skills and assets of the organization. Assets include patents, copyrights, locations, and equipment and technology that are superior to those of the competition. Skills are functions such as customer service and promotion that the firm performs better than its competitors. Travelocity, for example, is known for the ease of its on-line travel reservations. Marketing managers should constantly focus the firm's skills and assets on sustaining and creating competitive advantages.

ON LINE

Travelocity

How would you characterize Travelocity's competitive advantage based on the company's website? Does it have a sustainable competitive advantage? Why or why not?

http://www.travelocity.ca

ETHICS IN MARKETING

Labatt Uses Free Long-Distance to Promote Beer

With beer sales flat in Canada over the past few years, and imports grabbing market share from Labatt and Molson, Canada's beer companies are looking for better ways to promote and sell their products. In the summer of 2003, Labatt Brewing Co. Ltd. unveiled a new tool in the beer marketing wars: the telephone.

Labatt teamed up with Onlinetel Corp., a Kitchener, Ontario, provider of over-the-Internet telephone services, to offer free long-distance telephone calls. The catch? To get your free long-distance call, you first had to listen to a Labatt Blue commercial. After listening to the sales pitch, callers could make a free long-distance call. Of course, callers had to declare that they were 19 years of age or older.

"It's a unique way to communicate with our customers," Labatt spokeswoman Kathy Murphy said at the launch. "We expect to facilitate millions of calls." Labatt promoted the free calls on a website, **http://www.labattblueline.com**, as well as through brochures inserted into cases of beer.

A sample Labatt message: "Hey, how's it going? You know something? I like you. You stay in touch with people. That's good. Friends are important. We all have fond memories of good times over a nice cold Labatt Blue. Well, thanks for supporting Labatt Blue. Let's make your call."

One marketing consultant, Andrew Stodart, president of Brand Builders in Toronto, questioned whether giving away long-distance is a sound way to promote a beer brand. "It seems rather cheesy," he said of the Labatt effort.[9]

Do you think that Labatt's offering of free long-distance telephone calls to potential customers is an ethical way to promote a beer brand? How does Labatt know that listeners to its sales pitches are 19 years of age or over?

Remember, a sustainable competitive advantage is a function of the speed with which competitors can imitate a leading company's strategy and plans. Imitation requires a competitor to identify the leader's competitive advantage, determine how it is achieved, and then learn how to duplicate it.

6 Identify strategic alternatives and describe tools used to help select alternatives

>> STRATEGIC DIRECTION

The purpose of the SWOT analysis and of identifying a competitive advantage is to evaluate the strategic direction of the firm. Selecting a strategic alternative is the next step in marketing planning.

Strategic Alternatives

To discover a marketing opportunity, management must know how to identify the alternatives. One method for developing alternatives is Ansoff's strategic opportunity matrix (see Exhibit 2.5), which matches products with markets. Firms can explore these four options:

market penetration
A marketing strategy that tries to increase market share among existing customers.

- *Market penetration:* A firm using the **market penetration** alternative would try to increase market share among existing customers. If Kraft General Foods started a major campaign for Maxwell House coffee, with aggressive advertising and cents-off coupons to existing customers, it would be following a penetration strategy. McDonald's sold the most Happy Meals in its history with a promotion that included Ty's Teeny Beanie Babies.

market development
A marketing strategy that entails attracting new customers to existing products.

- *Market development:* **Market development** means attracting new customers to existing products. Ideally, new uses for old products stimulate additional sales among existing customers while also bringing in new buyers. McDonald's, for example, has opened restaurants in Russia, China, and Italy and is eagerly expanding into Eastern European countries. At home, WestJet is constantly opening new routes to serve additional Canadian cities. Another example of market development can be found in the "Global Perspectives" box.

product development
A marketing strategy that entails the creation of marketable new products; the process of converting applications for new technologies into marketable products.

- *Product development:* A **product development** strategy entails the creation of new products for present markets. Nike, the famous maker of athletic shoes, has introduced sleek ergonomic running watches, a high-altitude wrist compass, and a portable heart-rate monitor. These new offerings are targeted at athletes who want

EXHIBIT 2.5
Ansoff's Strategic Opportunity Matrix

	PRESENT PRODUCT	NEW PRODUCT
Present Market	**Market penetration:** McDonald's sells more Happy Meals with Disney movie promotions.	**Product development:** McDonald's introduces salad shakers and McWater.
New Market	**Market development:** McDonald's opens restaurants in China.	**Diversification:** McDonald's introduces line of children's clothing.

to time their daily jog and monitor how fast their heart is beating. The company has formed a new division called Techlab to develop sports-technology products, which will have Nike's trademark swoosh and come in shades like "fire warm," "green leaf," and "cool sparkle."[10] Tim Hortons has grown its business significantly by adding soups, sandwiches, bagels, and new desserts.

Managers following the product development strategy can rely on their extensive knowledge of their target audience. They usually have a good feel for what customers like and dislike about current products and what existing needs are not being met. In addition, managers can rely on established distribution channels.

- *Diversification:* **Diversification** is a strategy of increasing sales by introducing new products into new markets. For example, Magna, the largest automotive parts manufacturer in Canada, diversified into the entertainment business with its acquisition of racetracks and amusement parks. Sony practised a diversification strategy when it acquired Columbia Pictures; although motion pictures are not a new product in the marketplace, they were a new product for Sony. Coca-Cola manufactures and markets water-treatment and water-conditioning equipment, which has been a very challenging task for the traditional soft drink company. A diversification strategy can be risky when a firm is entering unfamiliar markets. On the other hand, it can be very profitable when a firm is entering markets with little or no competition.

diversification
A strategy of increasing sales by introducing new products into new markets.

Selecting a Strategic Alternative

Selecting which alternative to pursue depends on the overall company philosophy and culture. The choice also depends on the tool used to make the decision. Companies generally have one of two philosophies about when they expect profits. They either pursue profits right away or first seek to increase market share and then pursue profits. In the long run, market share and profitability are compatible goals. Many companies have long followed this credo: Build market share, and profits will surely follow. Michelin, the tire producer, consistently sacrifices short-term profits to achieve market share. On the other hand, IBM stresses profitability and stock valuation over market share, quality, and customer service. As you can see, different firms may view the same strategic alternative entirely differently.

A number of tools exist to help managers select a strategic alternative. The most common of these tools are in matrix form. Below, the portfolio matrix is described in more detail.

Portfolio Matrix

Recall that large organizations engaged in strategic planning may create strategic business units. Each SBU has its own rate of return on investment, growth potential, and associated risk. Management must find a balance among the SBUs that yields the overall organization's desired growth and profits with an acceptable level of risk. Some SBUs generate large amounts of cash, and others need cash to foster growth. The challenge is to balance the organization's "portfolio" of SBUs for the best long-term performance.

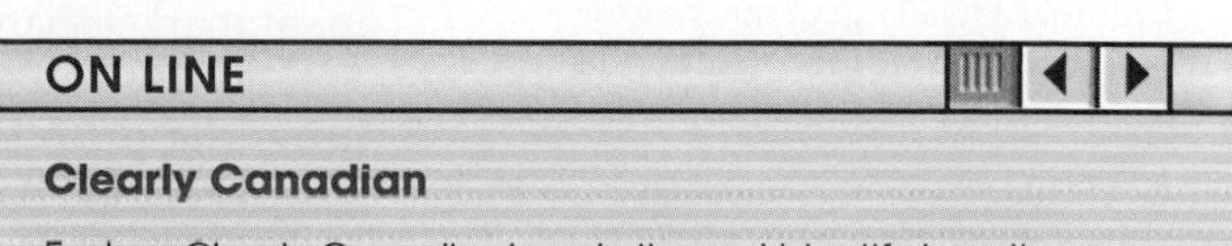

Clearly Canadian

Explore Clearly Canadian's website and identify how it uses each of the four strategic alternatives. Create a portfolio matrix for Clearly Canadian based on the information available on its website.

http://www.clearly.ca

GLOBAL PERSPECTIVES

Designing Products around Customer Needs

Brother Industries, Ltd., in Nagoya, Japan, has just introduced a phone music service that allows Japanese mobile phone users to download one of 4,800 tunes when a call arrives. The service also provides karaoke to be downloaded into cell phones, so that pictures and words come out on the screen.

This new service is an example of how Brother has been devising products for nearly 70 years. Brother's strategy is, simply, to satisfy customers. The result is world-class products to support small businesses—including its first sewing machines, typewriters, printers, and electronic labelling systems. For the past six years, the company has held the top share of the facsimile market. Now, it is aiming to expand beyond its traditional market of small business and home offices and sell more to corporations. Brother has already set up special solution teams in Europe for customers in larger corporations.

Key to Brother's success is its approach to product development. Instead of finding a use for technology developed in its laboratories, the company follows a system it calls Brother Value Chain Management. This system starts with finding out what customers want, a process it calls the "demand chain," and then figures out ways to meet these needs—the "concurrent chain." Finally, it delivers the products in the supply chain. Its customer research focuses on how products feel for users. Once Brother gathers customer data, it designs products to meet the needs of its target market. Often this research leads the company to provide customers with multifunctional equipment—like a cost-saving fax, copier, telephone, scanner, and printer all-in-one unit.

Another key to satisfying customers in the future is through what the company calls "humanware," which is a successor to the hard- and software that have dominated the marketplace over the past century. For example, sewing machines in the past were all manual; now they have microchip "brains" that make them more efficient and more pleasurable to use. By exchanging computerized embroidery patterns over the Internet, people on different sides of an ocean can share the same pattern and get their machines to stitch it automatically.[11]

What is Brother's competitive advantage? If you were to write a mission statement for Brother, what would it be?

portfolio matrix
A tool for allocating resources among products or strategic business units on the basis of relative market share and market growth rate.

To determine the future cash contributions and cash requirements expected for each SBU, managers could use the Boston Consulting Group's portfolio matrix. This **portfolio matrix** classifies each SBU by its present or forecasted growth and market share. The underlying assumption is that market share and profitability are strongly linked. The measure of market share used in the portfolio approach is *relative market share,* the ratio between the company's share and the share of the largest competitor. For example, if firm A has a 50 percent share and the competitor has 5 percent, the ratio is 10 to 1 (or 10x). If firm A has a 10 percent market share and the largest competitor has 20 percent, the ratio is 0.5 to 1 (or 0.5x).

Exhibit 2.6 is a hypothetical portfolio matrix for a large computer manufacturer. The size of the circle in each cell of the matrix represents dollar sales of the SBU relative to dollar sales of the company's other SBUs. The following categories are used in the matrix:

star
In the portfolio matrix, a business unit that is a fast-growing market leader.

- *Stars:* A **star** is a market leader and growing fast. For example, computer manufacturers have identified subnotebook and handheld models as stars. Star SBUs usually have large profits but need a lot of cash to finance rapid growth. The best marketing tactic is to protect existing market share by reinvesting earnings in product improvement, better distribution, more promotion, and production efficiency. Management must strive to capture most of the new users as they enter the market.

cash cow
In the portfolio matrix, a business unit that usually generates more cash than it needs to maintain its market share.

- *Cash cows:* A **cash cow** is an SBU that usually generates more cash than it needs to maintain its market share. It is in a low-growth market, but the product has a dominant market share. Personal computers and laptops are categorized as cash cows in Exhibit 2.6. The basic strategy for a cash cow is to maintain market dominance by being the price leader and making technological improvements in the product. Managers should resist pressure to extend the basic line unless they can dramatically increase demand. Instead, they should allocate excess cash to the product categories where growth prospects are the greatest. For instance, the Clorox Company owns KINGSFORD® charcoal, the GLAD® brand of products, FRESH STEP®, SCOOP AWAY® and other pet litters, BLACK FLAG® pest control products, BRITA® water filtration systems, and K.C. MASTERPIECE® barbecue sauce, among others.

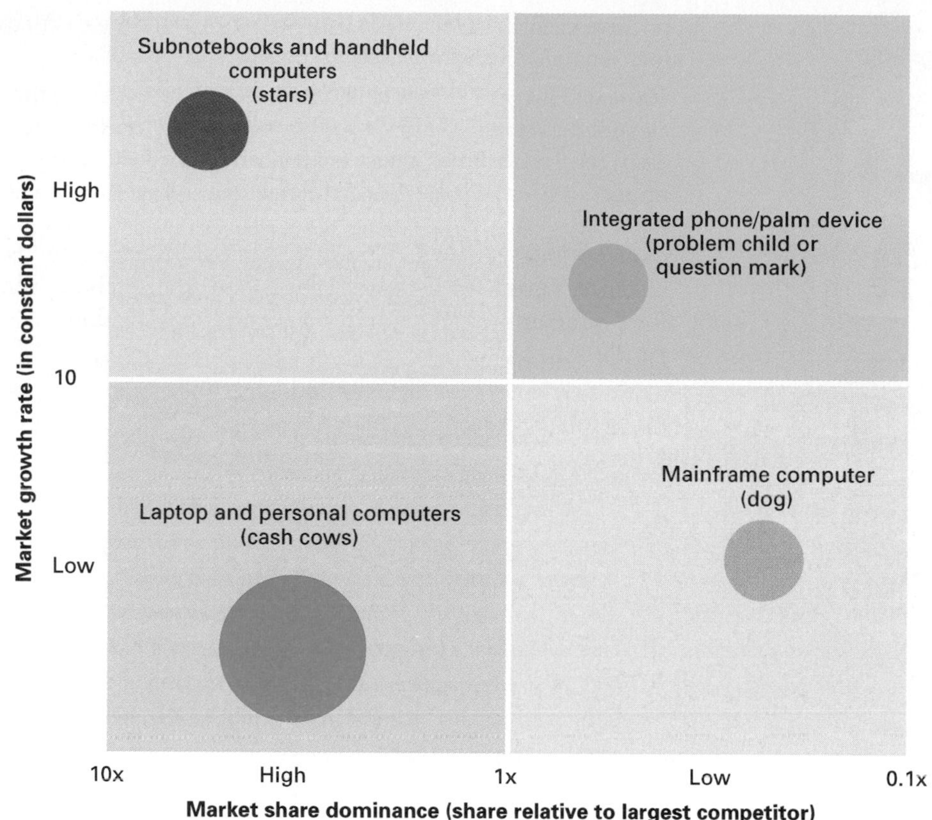

EXHIBIT 2.6

Portfolio Matrix for a Large Computer Manufacturer

NOTE: The size of the circle represents the dollar sales relative to sales of other SBUs on the matrix.

Traditionally, the company's cash cow has been CLOROX® bleach, which owns the lion's share of a low-growth market. The Clorox Company has been highly successful in stretching the CLOROX® line to include scented chlorine bleach, as well as CLOROX 2®, a chlorine-free bleach for coloured clothing.

- *Problem children:* A **problem child,** also called a **question mark,** shows rapid growth but poor profit margins. It has a low market share in a high-growth industry. Problem children need a great deal of cash. Without cash support, they eventually become dogs. The strategy options are to invest heavily to gain better market share, acquire competitors to get the necessary market share, or drop the SBU. Sometimes a firm can reposition the products of the SBU to move them into the star category.

problem child (question mark)
In the portfolio matrix, a business unit that shows rapid growth but poor profit margins.

- *Dogs:* A **dog** has low growth potential and a small market share. Most dogs eventually leave the marketplace. In the computer manufacturer example, the mainframe computer has become a dog. Two other examples of dogs include Warner-Lambert's Reef mouthwash and Campbell's Red Kettle soups. Frito-Lay has produced several dogs, including Stuffers cheese-filled snacks, Rumbles granola nuggets, and Toppels cheese-topped crackers—a trio irreverently known as Stumbles, Tumbles, and Twofers. The strategy options for dogs are to harvest or divest.

dog
In the portfolio matrix, a business unit that has low growth potential and a small market share.

After classifying the company's SBUs or products in the matrix, the next step is to allocate future resources for each. The four basic strategy options are to

- *Build:* If an organization has an SBU that it believes has the potential to be a star (probably a problem child at present), building would be an appropriate goal. The organization may decide to give up short-term profits and use its financial resources to achieve this goal. Procter & Gamble built Pringles from a money loser to a record profit maker.
- *Hold:* If an SBU is a very successful cash cow, a key goal would surely be to hold or preserve market share so that the organization can take advantage of the very

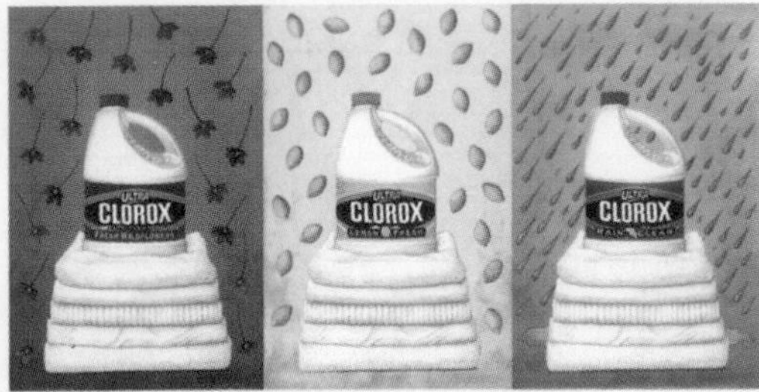

What Clorox® Bleach does for whites...

Clorox 2® does for colors.
CLOROX
CLOROX
CLOROX
Now in three wonderful scents.

Cash cows generate more cash than they need to maintain their market share. Clorox® is a cash cow. It has a 60 percent market share and has successfully introduced numerous scents as well as a chlorine-free bleach for coloured clothes.

positive cash flow. Bisquick has been a prosperous cash cow for General Mills for over two decades.

- *Harvest:* This strategy is appropriate for all SBUs except those classified as stars. The basic goal is to increase the short-term cash return without too much concern for the long-run impact. It is especially worthwhile when more cash is needed from a cash cow with long-run prospects that are unfavourable because of a low market growth rate. For instance, Lever Brothers has been harvesting Lifebuoy soap for a number of years with little promotional backing.
- *Divest:* Getting rid of SBUs with low shares of low-growth markets is often appropriate. Problem children and dogs are most suitable for this strategy. Procter & Gamble dropped Cincaprin, a coated aspirin, because of its low growth potential.

>> DESCRIBING THE MARKETING STRATEGY

A **marketing strategy** involves the activities of selecting and describing one or more target markets and developing and maintaining a marketing mix that will produce mutually satisfying exchanges with target markets.

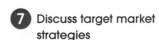

marketing strategy
The activities of selecting and describing one or more target markets and developing and maintaining a marketing mix that will produce mutually satisfying exchanges with target markets.

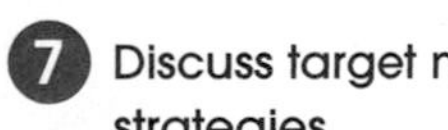
7 Discuss target market strategies

market opportunity analysis (MOA)
The description and estimation of the size and sales potential of market segments that are of interest to the firm and the assessment of key competitors in these market segments.

Target Market Strategy

A market segment is a group of individuals or organizations that share one or more characteristics. They therefore may have relatively similar product needs. For example, parents of newborn babies need products such as formula, diapers, and special foods. A target market strategy identifies the market segment or segments on which to focus. This process begins with a **market opportunity analysis (MOA)**—the description and estimation of the size and sales potential of market segments that are of interest to the firm and the assessment of key competitors in these market segments. After the firm describes the market segments, it may target one or more of them. There are three general strategies for selecting target markets. Target market(s) can be selected by appealing to the entire market with one marketing mix, concentrating on one segment, or appealing to multiple market segments using multiple marketing mixes.

Any market segment that is targeted must be fully described. Demographics, psychographics, and buyer behaviour should be assessed. Buyer behaviour is covered in Chapters 4 and 5. If segments are differentiated by ethnicity, multicultural aspects of the marketing mix should be examined. If the target market is international, it is especially important to describe differences in culture, economic and technological development, and political structure that may affect the marketing plan.

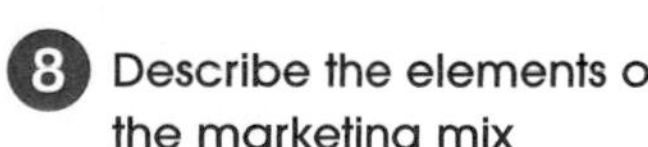
8 Describe the elements of the marketing mix

marketing mix
A unique blend of product, distribution, promotion, and pricing strategies designed to produce mutually satisfying exchanges with a target market.

four Ps
Product, place, promotion, and price, which together make up the marketing mix.

The Marketing Mix

The term **marketing mix** refers to a unique blend of product, distribution, promotion, and pricing strategies designed to produce mutually satisfying exchanges with a target market. Distribution is sometimes referred to as place, thus giving us the **four Ps** of the marketing mix: product, place, promotion, and price. The marketing manager can control each component of the marketing mix, but the strategies for all four components must be blended to achieve optimal results. Any marketing mix is only as good as its weakest component. For example, the first pump toothpastes were distributed over cosmetic counters and failed. Not until pump toothpastes were distributed the same way as tube toothpastes did the products succeed. The best promotion and the lowest price cannot save a poor product. Similarly, excellent products with poor distribution, pricing, or promotion cannot expect success.

Successful marketing mixes have been carefully designed to satisfy target markets. At first glance, McDonald's and Wendy's may appear to have roughly identical marketing mixes because they are both in the fast-food hamburger business. However, McDonald's has been most successful with targeting parents with young children for lunchtime meals, whereas Wendy's targets the adult crowd for lunches and dinner. McDonald's has playgrounds, Ronald McDonald the clown, and children's Happy Meals. Wendy's has salad bars, carpeted restaurants, and no playgrounds.

Variations in marketing mixes do not occur by chance. Astute marketing managers devise marketing strategies to gain advantages over competitors and best serve the needs and wants of a particular target market segment. By manipulating elements of the marketing mix, marketing managers can fine-tune the customer offering and achieve competitive success.

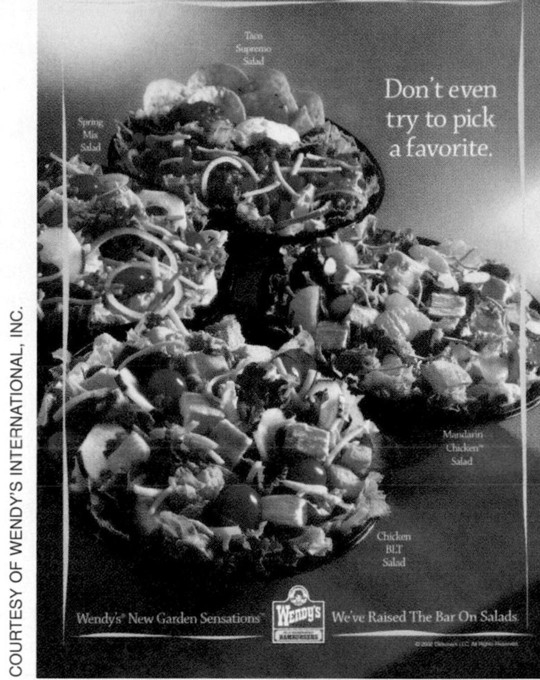

Although competing in the saturated fast-food industry, Wendy's does an excellent job of differentiating itself through its product mix. Rather than cater to families with young children, Wendy's tailors its offerings to meet the needs and wants of the adult lunch crowd. Its salad offerings are part of this strategy.

Product Strategies

Typically, the marketing mix starts with the product "P." The heart of the marketing mix is the product offering and product strategy. It is hard to design a distribution strategy, decide on a promotion campaign, or set a price without knowing the product to be marketed.

The product includes not only the physical unit but also its package, warranty, after-sale service, brand name, company image, value, and many other factors. A Godiva chocolate has many product elements: the chocolate itself, a fancy gold wrapper, a customer satisfaction guarantee, and the prestige of the Godiva brand name. We buy things not only for what they do (benefits) but also for what they mean to us (status, quality, or reputation).

Products can be tangible goods such as computers, ideas like those offered by a consultant, or services such as medical care. Products should also offer customer value. Product decisions are covered in Chapters 8 and 9; services marketing is detailed in Chapter 10.

Distribution (Place) Strategies

Distribution strategies are concerned with making products available when and where customers want them and providing the means for buyers to take ownership. Would you rather buy a kiwi fruit at the 24-hour grocery store within walking distance or fly to Australia to pick your own? A part of this place "P" is physical distribution, which involves all the business activities concerned with storing and transporting raw materials or finished products. The goal of distribution is to make sure products arrive in usable condition at designated places when needed. Distribution strategies are covered in Chapters 11 and 12.

Promotion Strategies

Promotion includes personal selling, advertising, sales promotion, and public relations. Promotion's role in the marketing mix is to bring about mutually satisfying exchanges with target markets by informing, educating, persuading, and reminding them of the benefits of an organization or a product. A good promotion strategy, like using the Dilbert character in a national promotion strategy for Office Depot, can dramatically increase sales. Good promotion strategies do not guarantee success, however. Despite massive promotional campaigns, the movies *Titan A.E.* and *Pearl Harbor* had disappointing box-office returns. Each element of the promotion "P" is coordinated and managed with the others to create a promotional blend or mix. These integrated marketing communications activities are described in Chapters 13 and 14. Technology-driven aspects of promotional marketing are covered in Chapters 17 and 18.

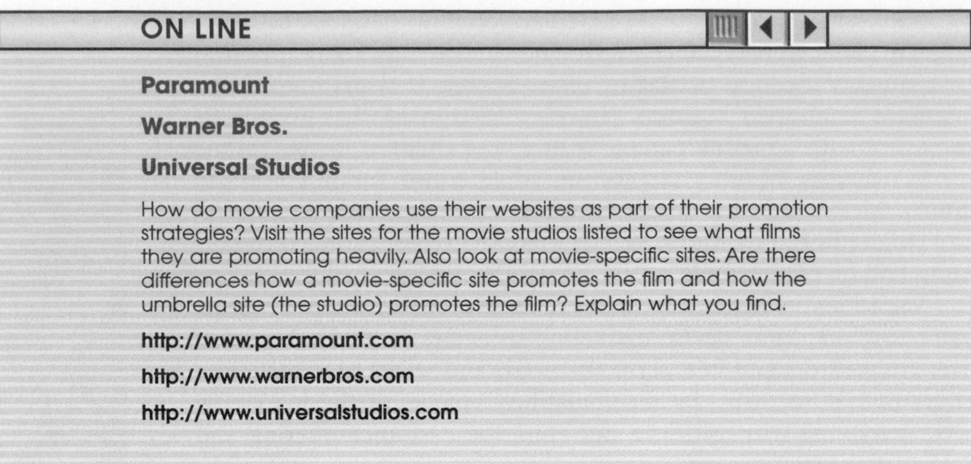

Pricing Strategies

Price is what a buyer must give up to obtain a product. It is often the most flexible of the four marketing mix elements—the quickest element to change. Marketers can raise or lower prices more frequently and easily than they can change other marketing mix variables. Price is an important competitive weapon and is very important to the organization because price multiplied by the number of units sold equals total revenue for the firm. Pricing decisions are covered in Chapters 15 and 16.

9 Explain why implementation, evaluation, and control of the marketing plan are necessary

>> FOLLOWING UP THE MARKETING PLAN

Implementation

implementation
The process that turns marketing plans into action assignments and ensures that these assignments are executed in a way that accomplishes the plan's objectives.

Implementation is the process that turns marketing plans into action assignments and ensures that these assignments are executed in a way that accomplishes the plan's objectives. Implementation activities may involve detailed job assignments, activity descriptions, timelines, budgets, and lots of communication. Although implementation is essentially "doing what you said you were going to do," many organizations repeatedly experience failures in strategy implementation. Brilliant marketing plans are doomed to fail if they are not properly implemented.

Evaluation and Control

evaluation
Gauging the extent to which the marketing objectives have been achieved during the specified time period.

control
Provides the mechanisms for evaluating marketing results in light of the plan's goals and for correcting actions that do not help the organization reach those goals within budget guidelines.

marketing audit
A thorough, systematic, periodic evaluation of the goals, strategies, structure, and performance of the marketing organization.

After a marketing plan is implemented, it should be evaluated. **Evaluation** entails gauging the extent to which marketing objectives have been achieved during the specified time period. Four common reasons for failing to achieve a marketing objective are unrealistic marketing objectives, inappropriate marketing strategies in the plan, poor implementation, and changes in the environment after the objective was specified and the strategy was implemented. Actual marketing performance must be monitored on an ongoing basis to ensure that corrective action is taken immediately if plan objectives are not being met.

Once a plan is chosen and implemented, its effectiveness must be monitored. **Control** provides the mechanisms for evaluating marketing results in light of the plan's goals and for correcting actions that do not help the organization reach those goals within budget guidelines. Firms need to establish formal and informal control programs to make the entire operation more efficient.

Perhaps the broadest control device available to marketing managers is the **marketing audit**—a thorough, systematic, periodic evaluation of the goals, strategies, structure, and performance of the marketing organization. A marketing audit helps management allocate marketing resources efficiently. It has four characteristics:

- *Comprehensive:* The marketing audit covers all of the major marketing issues facing an organization and not just trouble spots.
- *Systematic:* The marketing audit takes place in an orderly sequence and covers the organization's marketing environment, internal marketing system, and specific marketing activities. The diagnosis is followed by an action plan with both short-run and long-run proposals for improving overall marketing effectiveness.
- *Independent:* The marketing audit is normally conducted by an inside or outside party who is independent enough to have top management's confidence and to be objective.
- *Periodic:* The marketing audit should be carried out on a regular schedule instead of only in a crisis. Whether it seems successful or is in deep trouble, any organization can benefit greatly from such an audit.

Although the main purpose of the marketing audit is to develop a full profile of the organization's marketing effort and to provide a basis for developing and revising the marketing plan, it is also an excellent way to improve communication and raise the level of marketing consciousness within the organization. It is a useful vehicle for selling the philosophy and techniques of strategic marketing to other members of the organization.

>> EFFECTIVE STRATEGIC PLANNING

10 Identify several techniques that help make strategic planning effective

Effective strategic planning requires constant attention, creativity, and management commitment:

- Strategic planning is not an annual exercise, in which managers go through the motions and forget about strategic planning until the next year. It should be an ongoing process because the environment is constantly changing and the firm's resources and capabilities are constantly evolving.
- Sound strategic planning is based on creativity. Managers should challenge assumptions about the firm and the environment and establish new strategies. For example, major oil companies developed the concept of the gasoline service station in an age when cars needed frequent and rather elaborate servicing. They held on to the full-service approach, but independents were quick to respond to new realities and moved to lower-cost self-service and convenience-store operations. The majors took several decades to catch up.
- Perhaps the most critical element in successful strategic planning is top management's support and participation. For example, Pete Mateja, president of Home & Park Motorhomes, the largest manufacturer of camper vans in Canada, takes direct leadership responsibility in the development of the short and long-term marketing plans at Home & Park. Pete works directly with the heads of all departments in the company to ensure that input is received from everyone. All employees are assured that their concerns will be addressed so that there will be complete company buy-in to the plan. Pete then racks up hundreds of hours of travel time visiting Home & Park distributors to include them in the development of the plan and to make sure that they come on board.

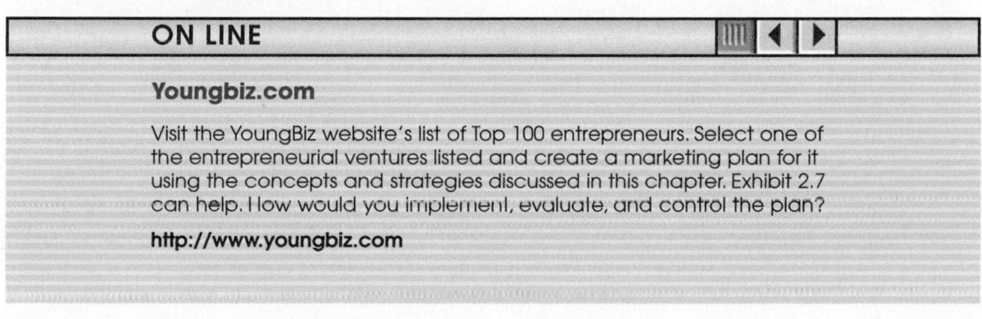

ON LINE

Youngbiz.com

Visit the YoungBiz website's list of Top 100 entrepreneurs. Select one of the entrepreneurial ventures listed and create a marketing plan for it using the concepts and strategies discussed in this chapter. Exhibit 2.7 can help. How would you implement, evaluate, and control the plan?

http://www.youngbiz.com

EXHIBIT 2.7

Marketing Plan Outline

I. BUSINESS MISSION

- What is the mission of the firm? What business is it in? How well is its mission understood throughout the organization? Five years from now, what business does it wish to be in?
- Does the firm define its business in terms of benefits its customers want rather than in terms of goods and services?

II. OBJECTIVES

- Is the firm's mission statement able to be translated into operational terms regarding the firm's objectives?
- What are the stated objectives of the organization? Are they formally written down? Do they lead logically to clearly stated marketing objectives? Are objectives based on sales, profits, or customers?
- Are the organization's marketing objectives stated in hierarchical order? Are they specific so that progress toward achievement can be measured? Are the objectives reasonable in light of the organization's resources? Are the objectives ambiguous? Do the objectives specify a time frame?
- Is the firm's main goal to maximize customer satisfaction or to get as many customers as possible?

III. SITUATION ANALYSIS (SWOT ANALYSIS)

- Have one or more competitive advantages been identified in the SWOT analysis?
- Are these advantages sustainable against the competition?

A. Internal Strengths and Weaknesses

- What is the history of the firm, including sales, profits, and organizational philosophy?
- What is the nature of the firm and its current situation?
- What resources does the firm have (financial, human, time, experience, asset, skill)?
- What policies inhibit the achievement of the firm's objectives with respect to organization, resource allocation, operations, hiring, training, and so on?

B. External Opportunities and Threats

- *Social:* What major social and lifestyle trends will have an impact on the firm? What action has the firm been taking in response to these trends?
- *Demographics:* What impact will forecasted trends in the size, age, profile, and distribution of population have on the firm? How will the changing nature of the family, the increase in the proportion of women in the workforce, and changes in the ethnic composition of the population affect the firm? What action has the firm taken in response to these developments and trends? Has the firm re-evaluated its traditional products and expanded the range of specialized offerings to respond to these changes?
- *Economic:* What major trends in taxation and income sources will have an impact on the firm? What action has the firm taken in response to these trends?
- *Political, Legal, and Financial:* What laws are now being proposed at international, federal, provincial, and municipal levels that could affect marketing strategy and tactics? What recent changes in regulations and court decisions affect the firm? What political changes are taking place at each government level? What action has the firm taken in response to these legal and political changes?
- *Competition:* Which organizations are competing with the firm directly by offering a similar product? Which organizations are competing with the firm indirectly by securing its prime prospects' time, money, energy, or commitment? What new competitive trends seem likely to emerge? How effective is the competition? What benefits do competitors offer that the firm does not? Is it appropriate for the firm to compete?
- *Technological:* What major technological changes are occurring that affect the firm?
- *Ecological:* What is the outlook for the cost and availability of natural resources and energy needed by the firm? Are the firm's products, services, and operations environmentally friendly?

IV. MARKETING STRATEGY

A. Target Market Strategy

- Are the members of each market homogeneous or heterogeneous with respect to geographic, sociodemographic, and behavioural characteristics?
- What are the size, growth rate, and national and regional trends in each of the organization's market segments?
- Is the size of each market segment sufficiently large or important enough to warrant a unique marketing mix?
- Are market segments measurable and accessible to distribution and communication efforts?

- Which are the high- or low-opportunity segments?
- What are the evolving needs and satisfactions being sought by target markets?
- What benefits does the organization offer to each segment? How do these benefits compare with benefits offered by competitors?
- Is the firm positioning itself with a unique product? Is the product needed?
- How much of the firm's business is repeat versus new business? What percentage of the public can be classified as nonusers, light users, or heavy users?
- How do current target markets rate the firm and its competitors with respect to reputation, quality, and price? What is the firm's image with the specific market segments it seeks to serve?
- Does the firm try to direct its products only to specific groups of people or to everybody?
- Who buys the firm's products? How does a potential customer find out about the organization? When and how does a person become a customer?
- What are the major objections given by potential customers as to why they do not buy the firm's products?
- How do customers find out about and decide to purchase the product? When and where?
- Should the firm seek to expand, contract, or change the emphasis of its selected target markets? If so, in which target markets, and how vigorously?
- Could the firm more usefully withdraw from some areas where there are alternative suppliers and use its resources to entice new, unserved customer groups?
- Which publics other than target markets (financial, media, government, citizen, local, general, and internal) represent opportunities or problems for the firm?

B. Marketing Mix

- Does the firm seek to achieve its goals chiefly through coordinated use of all marketing activities (product, distribution, promotion, and pricing) or only through intensive promotion?
- Are the objectives and roles of each element of the marketing mix clearly specified?

1. Product
    - What are the major product/service offerings of the firm? Do they complement one another, or is there unnecessary duplication?
    - What are the features and benefits of each product offering?
    - Where are the firm and each major product in the life cycle?
    - What are the pressures among various target markets to increase or decrease the range and quality of products?
    - What are the major weaknesses in each product area? What are the major complaints? What goes wrong most often?
    - Is the product name easy to pronounce? Spell? Recall? Is it descriptive and does it communicate the benefits the product offers? Does the name distinguish the firm or product from all others?
    - What warranties are offered with the product? Are there other ways to guarantee customer satisfaction?
    - Does the product offer good customer value?
    - How is customer service handled? How is service quality assessed?
2. Place/Distribution
    - Should the firm try to deliver its offerings directly to customers, or can it better deliver selected offerings by involving other organizations? What channel(s) should be used in distributing product offerings?
    - What physical distribution facilities should be used? Where should they be located? What should be their major characteristics?
    - Are members of the target market willing and able to travel some distance to buy the product?
    - How good is access to facilities? Can access be improved? Which facilities need priority attention?
    - How are facility locations chosen? Is the site accessible to target markets? Is it visible to target markets?
    - What are the location and atmosphere of retail establishments? Do these retailers satisfy customers?
    - When are products made available to users (season of year, day of week, time of day)? Are these times most appropriate?
3. Promotion
    - How does a typical customer find out about the firm's products?
    - Does the message the firm delivers gain the attention of the intended target audience? Does it address the wants and needs of the target market, and does it suggest benefits or a means for satisfying these wants? Is the message appropriately positioned?

- Does the promotion effort effectively inform, persuade, educate, and remind customers about the firm's products?
- Does the firm establish budgets and measure the effectiveness of promotional efforts?

a. Advertising
  - Which media are currently being used? Has the firm chosen the types of media that will best reach its target markets?
  - Are the types of media used the most cost-effective and do they contribute positively to the firm's image?
  - Are the dates and times the ads will appear the most appropriate? Has the firm prepared several versions of its advertisements?
  - Does the organization use an outside advertising agency? What functions does the ad agency perform for the organization?
  - What system is used to handle consumer inquiries resulting from advertising and promotions? What follow-up is done?

b. Public Relations
  - Is there a well-conceived public relations and publicity program? Does the program have the ability to respond to bad publicity?
  - How is public relations normally handled by the firm? By whom? Have those responsible nurtured working relationships with media outlets?
  - Is the firm using all available public relations avenues? Is an effort made to understand each publicity outlet's needs and to provide each with story types that will appeal to its audience in readily usable forms?
  - What does the annual report say about the firm and its products? Who is being effectively reached by this vehicle? Does the benefit of the publication justify the cost?

c. Personal Selling
  - How much of a typical salesperson's time is spent soliciting new customers as compared to serving existing customers?
  - How does the sales force determine which prospect will be called on and by whom? How is the frequency of contacts determined?
  - How is the sales force compensated? Are there incentives for encouraging more business?
  - How is the sales force organized and managed?
  - Has the sales force prepared an approach tailored to each prospect?
  - Has the firm matched sales personnel with target market characteristics?
  - Is there appropriate follow-up to the initial personal selling effort? Are customers made to feel appreciated?
  - Can database or direct marketing be used to replace or supplement the sales force?

d. Sales Promotion
  - What is the specific purpose of each sales promotion activity? Why is it offered? What does it try to achieve?
  - What categories of sales promotion are being used? Is sales promotion directed to the trade, the final consumer, or both?
  - Is the effort directed at all of the firm's key publics or restricted to only potential customers?

4. Price
  - What levels of pricing and specific prices should be used?
  - What mechanisms does the firm have to ensure that the prices charged are acceptable to customers?
  - How price sensitive are customers?
  - If a price change is put into effect, how will the number of customers change? Will total revenue increase or decrease?
  - Which method is used for establishing a price: going rate, demand oriented, or cost based?
  - What discounts are offered and with what rationale?
  - Has the firm considered the psychological dimensions of price?
  - Have price increases kept pace with cost increases, inflation, or competitive levels?
  - How are price promotions used?
  - Do interested prospects have opportunities to sample products at an introductory price?
  - What methods of payment are accepted? Is it in the firm's best interest to use these various payment methods?

V. IMPLEMENTATION, EVALUATION, AND CONTROL

- Is the marketing organization structured appropriately to implement the marketing plan?
- What specific activities must take place? Who is responsible for these activities?

- What is the implementation timetable?
- What other marketing research is necessary?
- What will be the financial impact of this plan on a one-year projected income statement? How does projected income compare with expected revenue if the plan is not implemented?
- What are the performance standards?
- What monitoring procedures (audits) will take place and when?
- Does the firm seem to be trying to do too much or not enough?
- Are the core marketing strategies for achieving objectives sound? Are the objectives being met, and are the objectives appropriate?
- Are enough resources (or too many resources) budgeted to accomplish the marketing objectives?

>> CONNECT IT

Look back at the story about Pet Valu. Pet Valu has used several marketing strategy elements to grow over the past 30 years. Product strategies include private labels and nearly 7,000 items offered in an intimate store setting. Distribution strategies include the operation of a fully owned warehousing and distribution company that achieves further economies through servicing outlets beyond just those of Pet Valu. Place strategies also include remaining close to customers in neighbourhood plaza locations. Price strategies include remaining very competitive with the low-price mega-stores.

The foundation of Pet Valu's competitive advantage, though, is maintaining knowledgeable staff and providing a high level of customer service. The strategic alternative that most closely describes Pet Valu's strategy is market penetration—the company continues to strive to do a better job with its existing customers to more deeply penetrate its existing markets. Secondarily, the company is also following a market development strategy as it continues to penetrate new geographic markets in Canada and has, in addition, moved into the U.S. market. As long as Pet Valu continues to do what it has been doing, there is every reason to believe that it will continue to compete effectively with the mega-stores.

REVIEW IT

1 **Understand the importance of strategic marketing and know a basic outline for a marketing plan.** Strategic marketing planning is the basis for all marketing strategies and decisions. The marketing plan is a written document that acts as a guidebook of marketing activities for the marketing manager. By specifying objectives and defining the actions required to attain them, a marketing plan provides the basis on which actual and expected performance can be compared.

Although there is no set formula for a marketing plan or a single correct outline, basic factors that should be covered include stating the business mission, setting objectives, performing a situation analysis of internal and external environmental forces, selecting target market(s), delineating a marketing mix (product, place, promotion, and price), and establishing ways to implement, evaluate, and control the plan.

1.1 Your cousin wants to start his own business and he is in a hurry. He has decided not to write a marketing plan because he thinks that preparing such a document would take too long. He says he doesn't need a formal proposal because he has already received funding from your uncle. Explain why it is important for him to write a plan anyway.

1.2 WRITING After graduation, you decide to take a position as the marketing manager for a small snack-food manufacturer. The company, Shur Snak, is growing and this is the first time that the company has ever employed a marketing manager. Consequently, there is no marketing plan in place for you to follow. Outline a basic marketing plan for your boss to give her an idea of the direction you want to take the company.

2 **Develop an appropriate business mission statement.** The mission statement is based on a careful analysis of benefits sought by present and potential customers and an analysis of existing and anticipated environmental conditions. The

firm's long-term vision, embodied in the mission statement, establishes boundaries for all subsequent decisions, objectives, and strategies. A mission statement should focus on the market or markets the organization is attempting to serve rather than on the good or service offered.

2.1 ON LINE How can a new company best define its business mission statement? Can you find examples of good and bad mission statements on the Internet? How might you improve the bad ones?

2.2 Thinking back to question 1.2, write a business mission statement for Shur Snak. What elements should you include? Evaluate the mission statement you wrote against some of those you found on-line in question 2.1.

3 **Describe the criteria for stating good marketing objectives.** Objectives should be realistic, measurable, and time specific. Objectives must also be consistent and indicate the priorities of the organization.

3.1 Building on our Shur Snak example, imagine that your boss has stated that the marketing objective of the company is to do the best job of satisfying the needs and wants of the customer. Explain that although this objective is admirable, it does not meet the criteria for good objectives. What are these criteria? What is a specific example of a better objective for Shur Snak?

4 **Explain the components of a situation analysis.** In the situation (or SWOT) analysis, the firm should identify its internal strengths (S) and weaknesses (W) and also examine external opportunities (O) and threats (T). When examining external opportunities and threats, marketing managers must analyze aspects of the marketing environment through a process called environmental scanning. The six most often-studied macroenvironmental forces are social, demographic, economic, technological, political and legal, and competitive. During the situation analysis, it is crucial for the marketer to identify a competitive advantage and establish that it is a sustainable competitive advantage.

4.1 WRITING ON LINE Competition in the private courier sector is fierce. UPS and FedEx dominate, but other companies, such as DHL, Emery, and even Canada Post, still have a decent chunk of the express package delivery market. Perform a mini–situation analysis on one of the companies listed below by stating one strength, one weakness, one opportunity, and one threat. You may want to consult the following websites as you build your grid:

United Parcel Service (UPS) **http://www.ups.com**

FedEx **http://www.fedex.com**

DHL **http://www.dhl=usa.com/home/home.asp**

Emery **http://www.emeryworldwide.com**

Canada Post **http://www.canadapost.ca**

5 **Identify sources of competitive advantage.** A competitive advantage is a set of unique features of a company and its products that are perceived by the target market as significant and superior to the competition. There are three types of competitive advantages: cost, product/service, and niche. Sources of cost competitive advantages include experience curves, efficient labour, no-frills goods and services, government subsidies, product design, re-engineering, product innovations, and new methods of service delivery. Product/service differentiation exists when a firm provides something unique that is valuable to buyers besides just low price. Niche competitive advantages come from targeting unique segments with specific needs and wants. The goal of all these sources of competitive advantage is to be sustainable.

5.1 

Break into small groups and discuss examples (at least two per person) of the last few products you have purchased. What specific strategies were used to achieve competitive advantage? Is that advantage sustainable against the competitors?

6 **Identify strategic alternatives and describe tools used to help select alternatives.** The strategic opportunity matrix can be used to help management develop strategic alternatives. The four options are market penetration, product development, market development, and diversification. The portfolio matrix is a method of determining the profit potential and investment requirements of a firm's SBUs by classifying them as stars, cash cows, problem children, or dogs and then determining appropriate resource allocations for each.

6.1 Based on your SWOT analysis, decide what the strategic growth options are for the company you chose in question 4.1. Also, decide where your company's products fit in the Boston Consulting Group matrix (scc Exhibit 2.6).

7 **Discuss target market strategies.** The target market strategy identifies which market segment or segments to focus on. This process begins with a market opportunity analysis (MOA), which describes and estimates the size and sales potential of market segments that are of interest to the firm. In addition, an assessment of key competitors in these market segments is performed. After the market segments are described, the firm may target one or more of them. The three strategies for selecting target markets are appealing to the entire market with one marketing mix, concentrating on one segment, or appealing to multiple market segments using multiple marketing mixes.

7.1 You are given the task of deciding the marketing strategy for a transportation company. How do the marketing mix elements change when the target market is (a) low-income workers without personal transportation, (b) corporate international business travellers, or (c) companies with urgent documents or perishable materials to get to customers?

8 **Describe the elements of the marketing mix.** The marketing mix (or four Ps) is a blend of product, distribution (place), promotion, and pricing strategies designed to produce mutually satisfying exchanges with a target market. The starting point of the marketing mix is the product offering. Products can be tangible goods, ideas, or services. Distribution strategies are concerned with making products available when and where customers want them and providing for the transfer of ownership. Promotion includes personal selling, advertising, sales promotion, and public relations. Price is what a buyer must give up to obtain a product and is often the easiest to change of the four marketing mix elements.

8.1 

Choose three or four other students and make up a team. Create a marketing plan to increase enrollment in your school. Describe the four marketing mix elements that make up the plan.

9 **Explain why implementation, evaluation, and control of the marketing plan are necessary.** Before a marketing plan can work, it must be implemented; that is, people must perform the actions in the plan. The plan should also be evaluated to see if it has achieved its objectives. Poor implementation can be a major factor in a plan's failure. Control provides the mechanisms for evaluating marketing results in light of the plan's goals and for correcting actions that do not help the organization reach those goals within budget guidelines.

9.1 Have your school enrollment marketing plan team (from question 8.1) develop a plan to implement, evaluate, and control the marketing strategy.

9.2  Using InfoTrac® College Edition and *The Wall Street Journal's* archive at http://wsj.com, trace the history of Kimberly-Clark's marketing plan and strategy for Cottonelle Fresh Rollwipes (premoistened toilet paper). Once you have a basic understanding of the product development and launch history, evaluate the plan set in motion by Kimberly-Clark. Does the company consider the product (and hence the plan) a success? Has the product been well received in the market? Are competitors moving in to take away market share with their own versions? Write a brief report giving a short synopsis of the product history and then describing what went right with the plan and what went wrong (if anything). If you identify flaws in the plan, identify what the company could have done to avoid those problems.

⑩ **Identify several techniques that help make strategic planning effective.** First, management must realize that strategic planning is an ongoing process and not a once-a-year exercise. Second, good strategic planning involves a high level of creativity. The last requirement is top management's support and cooperation.

10.1 What techniques can make your school enrollment marketing plan more effective?

DEFINE IT

cash cow 34
competitive advantage 29
control 38
cost competitive advantage 29
diversification 33
dog 35
environmental scanning 29
evaluation 38
experience curves 30
four Ps 36
implementation 38
market development 32
market opportunity analysis (MOA) 36
market penetration 32
marketing audit 38
marketing mix 36
marketing myopia 26
marketing objective 28
marketing plan 24
marketing planning 24
marketing strategy 36
mission statement 26
niche competitive advantage 31
planning 24
portfolio matrix 34
problem child (question mark) 35
product development 32
product/service differentiation 31
star 34
strategic business unit (SBU) 28
strategic planning 24
sustainable competitive advantage 31
SWOT analysis 28

APPLY IT

Providing security for VIPs—ranging from government officials to movie stars—when they appear in public, typically means deploying protective barriers such as concrete walls or Plexiglas shields. A new product aims to replace those obstructive protection devices. Ibis Technology, a three-year-old company, has developed an Instantaneous Personal Protection System (IPPS). The IPPS is a cross between an aircraft ejection seat and a car air bag. In less time than the ear can register the sound of gunfire, the IPPS surrounds the intended victim with a bulletproof shield. This new security device can sit on the floor next to a VIP or terrorist target, or it can be used as a security guard in a busy lobby, disguised as a set of decorative planters.[12]

How does the IPPS work? A radar-sensor detects incoming objects (such as bullets or knives) and triggers an inflating air bag. The bulletproof material traps the projectile like a baseball glove folding around a ball. In demonstrations, the shield has deployed quickly enough to survive assaults from .22-calibre through .44-calibre magnum rounds, submachine guns, shotgun blasts at close range, and knife-wielding attackers. Its detection range is about 50 metres. The device can also be fired by radio control.[13] The fully installed system weighs less than 175 kilograms.

The IPPS technology can be extended to other applications, such as protecting vehicles and securing windows on buildings. A key challenge will be to find ways to ensure that the system will not be set off accidentally by electronic signals such as from cellular phones and aircraft radar. Hedge fund manager Jeffrey Puglisi has selected Ibis Technology Corporation as a top technology stock pick.[14]

QUESTIONS

1. What is an appropriate mission statement for Ibis Technology?
2. What specific objective would you suggest the company try to achieve?
3. What are the strengths, weaknesses, opportunities, and threats in this situation?
4. Does Ibis Technology have a competitive advantage? Is it sustainable?
5. What strategic growth options can Ibis Technology pursue?
6. Where do Ibis Technology and its IPPS fit on strategic matrix tools?
7. What should the target market for the company be? Why?
8. What are the elements of the marketing mix? Describe a brief strategy for each of the four Ps.

THINK ABOUT IT

Britney Spears brought her raunchy show to Toronto for the first Canadian date of her cross-Canada tour. The show was complete with scenes of simulated sex that sent some parents and their young children home early. Most of the teen and 20-something audience, though, cheered for more.

"Disgusting," was the opinion of nine-year-old Carly Woodcox of Collingwood, Ontario. Emerging from under a white robe during one part of the show to reveal a transparent, sequin-covered bodysuit, Spears thrashed about in a bathtub while dancers simulated sex acts on the stage. "A little too much for this age group," said Lucy Triagiai, who left with her three young girls moments after the simulated sex act began.[15]

QUESTIONS

1. Is marketing adult-styled entertainment to a younger audience appropriate? What views might there be on both sides of this issue?
2. What does the CMA Code of Ethics have to say about using sex to market to younger consumers? Read the code at **http://www.the-cma.org/consumer/ethics.cfm** and then write a brief paragraph on how the code relates to this situation.

TRY IT

High-End Fashions and Sporting Goods for the Sporting Life

The SARS crisis in the spring of 2003 wasn't the best of times to open a new store on Bloor Street in Toronto, but that's exactly what Sporting Life did. "It was a tough beginning," acknowledged David Russell, president of Sporting Life. There were no tourists on the streets of Toronto for quite a while. In spite of such problems, over the past year, Sporting Life has doubled the number of outlets it operates in Ontario to six.

While exact sales of Sporting Life are unknown, as it is a privately owned company, estimates are that the six outlets gross about $100 million, averaging about $500 per square foot. That can be compared to an average of $440 per square foot for mighty Wal-Mart. Sporting Life's formula for success combines high-end fashions with sporting goods. Rivals have picked up on the theme. "They're very unique," says Bill Gregson, president of the Forzani Group. "It's not very often that you can buy a snowboard and Hugo Boss or Prada in the same store."

What has contributed to Sporting Life's growth in the past year? It keeps on top of the hottest trends in sports and in fashions but doesn't forget mainstream products. You can find ultra-hip Triple Five Soul and Juicy Couture alongside Lacoste and Fred Perry. And customer service is strongly emphasized. The staff at Sporting Life, generally teenagers and young adults, are told to treat the store like home and look at customers as guests.

Sporting Life sticks to only core sporting goods including skis, snowboards, racquets, and running equipment. To get its message out, Sporting Life has turned to television for the first time. Sporting Life ad spots feature skier Ken Read and include store staff. To keep loyal customers coming back, four or five times a year Sporting Life sends gift coupons, worth up to $50, to its top 20,000 customers.

While it is currently doing quite well, Sporting Life is swamped with competitors. Puma, one of its major suppliers, just opened its first store in Canada on Yonge Street just two blocks from Sporting Life. Prada, Hugo Boss, and Nike also operate stores nearby.

What's to come for Sporting Life? According to Mr. Russell, more stores in Toronto and future expansion to Vancouver and Montreal. And, he believes, Sporting Life would do quite well in the U.K.[16]

QUESTIONS

1. Based on what you have read in the case, outline a rudimentary SWOT analysis for Sporting Life.
2. Describe Sporting Life's competitive advantage.
3. How is Sporting Life using the elements of the marketing mix to meet the needs and wants of its customers? Sporting Life doesn't currently have a website. Do you think it needs one?

FLIP IT

Flip to Chapter 2 in your *Grademaker Study Guide* for more review opportunities, including the pretest, vocabulary review, study test questions, marketing applications and scenarios, and more. Can you name the four Ps? Can you close your book and draw a portfolio matrix that depicts and describes the elements? If not, flip open your Study Guide to brush up.

CLICK IT

The *Marketing* website is rich with materials to help you review and master marketing concepts. Check your knowledge with the free quizzes, practise key terms using the crossword puzzles, or review key concepts using the Microsoft® PowerPoint® slides. Also on the website are updated weblinks to companies mentioned in this chapter, Internet exercises, career marketing information, and much much more! Go to http://www.lamb3e.nelson.com, read the material, and follow the convenient links.

WATCH IT

Eureka! Inventing: Big-Time Marketing Strategy Planning Comes to PEI

Since founding Richard Saunders International in 1986, Doug Hall's client list has read like the *Fortune* 500. Companies that have paid $150,000 and more for three-day sessions at Eureka! Ranch include Coca-Cola, Procter & Gamble, Frito-Lay, PepsiCo, Compaq Computer, Nike, Ford, DaimlerChrysler, Johnson & Johnson, American Express, and NASCAR.

After graduating with a degree in chemical engineering, Doug Hall spent 10 years in marketing at Procter & Gamble. There, even among the vast marketing talent at this giant company, Doug stood out. In one year, Doug helped bring nine new products to market. With this valuable experience behind him, Doug decided to strike out on his own. Richard Saunders International was formed in Doug's basement in 1986 (Richard Saunders was the pen name used by Benjamin Franklin).

Richard Saunders International was to include both a new product idea division and a market research division; however, Doug was more interested in new product work and soon sold the market research business. After some early success, Richard Saunders International moved from Doug's basement to an estate he named the Eureka Mansion. In 1997, Doug built a much larger complex alongside the Eureka Mansion and gave it the name Eureka!

Ranch. The seminars and training programs conducted by Doug's company are held at the Eureka! Ranch; Doug and his family now live in the Eureka Mansion.

Doug's company, which is now divided into three strategic business units (SBUs), undertakes a full range of marketing planning and marketing strategy activities for its clients. Sessions at Eureka! Ranch take place in large "play" rooms filled with video games, jukeboxes, and toys. It is not unusual for a Eureka! Ranch session to begin with a Nerf gunfight. Doug feels that fun leads to more creative output.

Eureka! Inventing is the largest of the three company SBUs. Eureka! Inventing sessions generally run for three days at the Eureka! Ranch and include the client's top marketing people and a team from Doug's company. The unorthodox and highly creative sessions might be geared toward generating new product ideas, new line extensions, new advertising campaigns, programs to reposition existing products, turnaround strategies for failing products, or entire marketing plans. TrailBlazer Training, a second SBU, is an on-client site portion of the business that runs training sessions for $50,000 a day or more. The final SBU is Merwyn Technology. Merwyn is a computer simulation test marketing and expert coaching software program. Merwyn assists clients in forecasting the probability for success for new product concepts and makes recommendations for improving the concepts' chances for success.

The success of Richard Saunders International has made Doug Hall rich and famous. He now commands over $20,000 for talks to business groups. Doug is still young (mid-40s) and is searching for more to do. Among other things, he has decided to provide the expertise of Eureka! Inventing to small businesses that would not otherwise be able to afford these services. As a start, he has decided to offer his services, at no charge, to four small businesses on Prince Edward Island. Why there? Doug's mother is from New Brunswick and Doug has a vacation home on PEI.

A one-day creativity seminar was arranged for four small PEI businesses: Cavendish Figurines, Wooly Wares, Island Winds, and Mic Mac Productions. Cavendish Figurines creates and sells heirloom-quality figurines based on characters from great literary classics (*Anne of Green Gables* is a leading seller). The company has been in business since 1989 and has 13 employees. Wooly Wares is a retail store operated on John and Carol MacLeod's sheep farm. Wooly Wares sells handmade wool felt products. Island Winds is a one-man operation. Peter Baker makes and sells hand-tuned wind chimes. Mic Mac Productions sells handmade native crafts such as beadwork, carvings, drums, pipes, masks, pottery, rattles, headdresses, and moccasins.

After the one-day creativity seminar with the owners of each of the four businesses, Doug arranged to meet with each owner for a two-hour session. Inside of two hours at Cavendish Figurines, Doug and his crew had developed a new promotional brochure for the business, recommended a new display for the lead-selling figurines, developed a new promotional message, and recommended a new product assortment. Wooly Wares was persuaded to concentrate on several product offerings that were clearly superior to others that John and Carol MacLeod crafted, and Doug and his group came up with some catchy brand names for the products. Peter Baker at Island Winds was advised to stay with top-of-the-line chimes, where he had an advantage over the competition, and not get into low-priced products. As well, new product ideas were developed, along with new brand names and a new promotional campaign. Mic Mac Productions was advised to change its name to Mic Mac Legends, build a new promotional campaign around the legends associated with its products, expand its product lines, develop a new pricing strategy, and organize product combination packages.

QUESTIONS

1. What do you think Doug Hall's corporate mission statement might have been in 1986 when he founded Richard Saunders International, and what do you think that it might be today?
2. What do you think is the major competitive advantage of Richard Saunders International?

3. Into which cell of the portfolio matrix do you feel that each SBU of Richard Saunders International would fall?
4. Can the marketing strategies used for large clients of Doug Hall work for small businesses?
5. Do you feel that Doug Hall might learn something from his work with small businesses that he can successfully incorporate into his marketing programs for large clients?

SUGGESTED INFORMATION SOURCES

CBC, *Venture*, "PEI Meets Doug Hall," Broadcast: March 13, 2001.
http://www.cavendishfigurines.com
http://www.eurekaranch.com/eureka/history.asp
http://www.gov.pe.ca/business/onebusiness.php3?number=18717
http://www.islandwindcraft.com
http://www.sun-sea.pe.ca/tynevalley.htm

chapter 3

The Marketing Environment and Marketing Ethics

>> LEARNING OBJECTIVES

1. Discuss the external environment of marketing and explain how it affects a firm
2. Describe the social factors that affect marketing
3. Explain the importance to marketing managers of current demographic trends
4. Explain the importance to marketing managers of multiculturalism and growing ethnic markets
5. Identify consumer and marketer reactions to the state of the economy
6. Identify the impact of technology on a firm
7. Discuss the political and legal environment of marketing
8. Explain the basics of foreign and domestic competition
9. Describe the role of ethics and ethical decisions in business
10. Discuss corporate social responsibility

>>Some things go out of fashion. That has been a hard lesson for Levi Strauss & Co. (Canada) of Richmond Hill, Ontario, a company whose 501 blue jeans became famous in 1984 when a hunky model stripped them off in a laundromat for millions of admiring young women in Levi's television ads of the time.

"In the mid-80s, Levi's transformed the denim sector with that ad," says Sean Pillot de Chenecey, a youth-trend specialist at forecasting firm Captain Crikey in London. "But Levi's then committed the cardinal sin of becoming self-referential" by focusing too much on the 501 and not paying attention to changing tastes in threads. And while Levi's was stagnating, competitors such as Earl Jean and Diesel crowded the market with new products that seemed hipper to a generation stricken with chronic brand-attention-deficit disorder.

A sales decline at the closely held apparel maker began after a peak in 1996, when Levi's reported global sales of $7.1 billion, and has persisted ever since. Now the company speaks of "slowing the decline" rather than boosting sales. In Canada, Levi's market share has dropped from 28.4 percent in 2000 to 20.1 percent in 2003.

Levi's management readily admits it has made some mistakes. And instead of sloughing off the blame on a decline in the denim market, Levi's delivers a mea culpa: "We weren't selling in stores where young people shop. We weren't making the products they were interested in. We weren't branding our products in a famous way, and we weren't serving our customers well," says Robert Hanson, president of the Levi's brand in Europe, ticking off the four main reasons for Levi's recent hard times in Europe. "We were responsible for the decline in the denim market," he adds.

Levi's is indeed the classic jeans maker, with brands such as Levi's®, Dockers ®, and GWG®, which can be found in stores like Zellers and The Bay. Most industry executives aren't as hard on the company as Robert Hanson and doubt it single-handedly brought on a decline in demand for denim. "Sometimes your products go out of fashion," says Alex Batchelor, managing director for Interbrand, a brand consultancy that is part of the Omnicom Group.

But Levi's is making a concerted effort to come back. The company is in the midst of a massive restructuring during which it has already laid off thousands of workers (1,180 in Canada) and closed plants in both North America and Europe, including plants in Edmonton, Alberta, and Stoney Creek and Brantford, Ontario. At the same time, Levi's is trying to put its best foot forward with new products and promotions.

In Levi's latest ad campaign in Europe, it promotes its "engineered" jeans, those with twisted seams designed to ergonomically fit both men and women. This product will be on Canadian store shelves this year.

After pushing the 501 for years, Levi's has developed a range of jeans in a bid to create a trickle-down effect. The company produces several high-end products, known as its red line and vintage lines, and also manufactures more basic models for mass consumption.

The company's retail plans mirror its product diversification in Europe. In what the company calls its "Icon" stores, the Levi's brand name is nowhere to be seen. Instead, the stores sell expensive vintage Levi's products alongside secondhand books, vinyl albums, and custom-made shoes designed by local artisans.

In contrast, the company's heavily branded flagship stores offer themselves to the middle market and often adopt a more youthful approach. In department stores, Levi's has introduced what it calls the advanced retail concept, which drapes jeans like spaghetti and displays Levi's products like fresh pasta and produce in a grocery store. "Some we hang like spaghetti, others lie down like lasagna," Mr. Hanson says. He hopes the new presentation will have the jeans selling—as in the brand's glory days—like hot cakes.

To get at the four million Canadians who purchase their apparel at the nearly 240 Wal-Mart Canada and Sam's Club Canada stores, Levi has launched a new apparel brand, Levi Strauss Signature®, which will be available initially only in Wal-Mart stores. How are things going? Preliminary sales data show Levi's market share holding steady in Canada in 2004.[1]

Changing tastes, fashion trends, and demographics all represent threats and/or opportunities to marketing managers. These are only a few factors in the external environment that can have an impact on a firm. Does the external environment affect the marketing mix of most companies? What other uncontrollable factors in the external environment might affect Levi's?

ON LINE 

Levi Strauss

Has Levi's recovered from its failure to see changes in its external environment? How is the company using its website to rebuild its brand among the younger age groups?

http://www.levi.com

1 Discuss the external environment of marketing and explain how it affects a firm

>> THE EXTERNAL MARKETING ENVIRONMENT

target market
A defined group most likely to buy a firm's products.

As you learned in Chapters 1 and 2, managers create a marketing mix by uniquely combining product, place (distribution), promotion, and price strategies. The marketing mix is, of course, under the firm's control and is designed to appeal to a specific group of potential buyers. A **target market** is a defined group that marketing managers feel is most likely to buy a firm's product.

Over time, managers must alter the marketing mix because of changes in the environment in which consumers live, work, and make purchasing decisions. Also, as markets mature, some new consumers become part of the target market; others drop out. Those who remain may have different tastes, needs, incomes, lifestyles, and buying habits than the original target consumers.

Although managers can control the marketing mix, they cannot control the elements in the external environment that continually mold and reshape the target market. Exhibit 3.1 shows the controllable and uncontrollable variables that affect the target market, whether it consists of consumers or business purchasers. The uncontrollable elements in the middle of the diagram continually evolve and create changes in the target market. In contrast, managers can shape and reshape the marketing mix, depicted on the left side of the exhibit, to influence the target market.

>> UNDERSTANDING THE EXTERNAL ENVIRONMENT

Unless marketing managers understand the external environment, the firm cannot intelligently plan for the future. Thus, many organizations assemble teams of specialists to continually collect and evaluate environmental information, a process called environmental scanning. The goal in gathering environmental data is to identify future market opportunities and threats.

For example, as technology continues to blur the line between personal computers, television, and compact disc players, a company like Sony may find itself competing against a company like Dell. Research shows that children would like to find more games

EXHIBIT 3.1
Effect of Uncontrollable Factors in the External Environment on the Marketing Mix

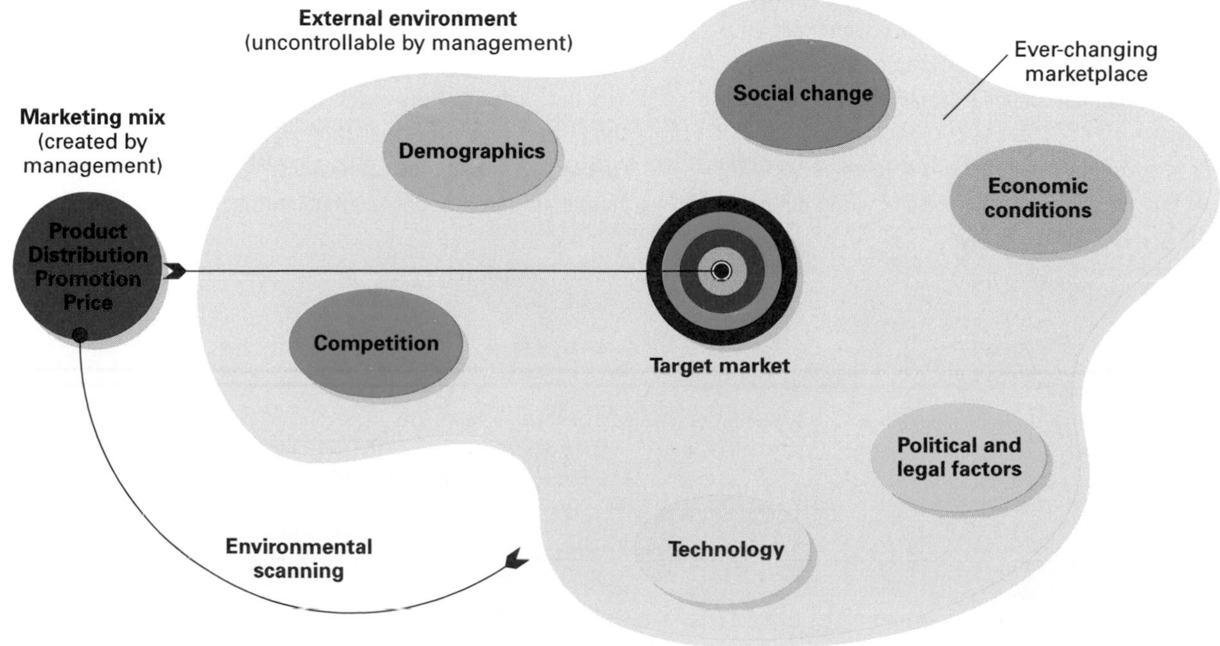

bundled with computer software, while adults are more likely to desire various word-processing and business-related software. Is this information an opportunity or a threat to Dell marketing managers?

Environmental Management

No one business is large or powerful enough to create major change in the external environment. Thus, marketing managers are basically adapters rather than agents of change. For example, despite the huge size of General Motors and Ford, these companies are continually challenged to meet the competitive push by the Japanese for an ever-growing share of the Canadian automobile market. Competition is basically an uncontrollable element in the external environment.

A firm is not always completely at the mercy of the external environment, however. Sometimes a firm can influence external events. For example, extensive lobbying by FedEx enabled it to acquire virtually all of the Japanese routes that it had been seeking. Japan had originally opposed new cargo routes for FedEx, but the company's lobbying efforts won out for it over time. When a company implements strategies that attempt to shape the external environment within which it operates, it is engaging in **environmental management.**

environmental management
When a company implements strategies that attempt to shape the external environment within which it operates.

The factors within the external environment that are important to marketing managers can be classified as social, demographic, economic, technological, political and legal, and competitive.

>> SOCIAL FACTORS

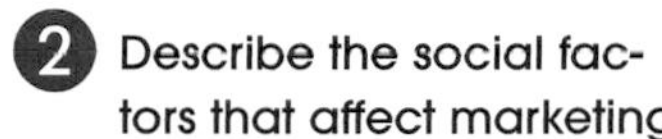

2 Describe the social factors that affect marketing

Social change is perhaps the most difficult external variable for marketing managers to forecast, influence, or integrate into marketing plans. Social factors include our attitudes, values, and lifestyles. Social factors influence the products people buy, the prices they pay for products, the effectiveness of specific promotions, and how, where, and when people expect to purchase products.

Marketing-Oriented Values of Today

A *value* is a strongly held and enduring belief. Four basic values strongly influence Canadian consumers' attitudes and lifestyles:

- *Self-sufficiency:* Every person should stand on his or her own two feet.
- *Upward mobility:* Success should come to anyone who gets an education, works hard, and plays by the rules.
- *Work ethic:* Hard work, dedication to family, and frugality are moral and right.
- *Conformity:* No one should expect to be treated differently from everybody else.

These core values still hold for a majority of Canadians today. A person's values are key determinants of what is important and not important, what actions to take or not to take, and how one behaves in social situations.

A person's values are typically formed through interaction with family, friends, and other influencers such as teachers, religious leaders, and politicians. The environment can also play a key role in shaping one's values. For example, people born during the Great Depression tend to be very conservative with money. People who came of age in the "hippie revolution" of the 1960s tend to be much less conservative with money.[2]

Values also influence our buying habits. Today's consumers are demanding, inquisitive, and discriminating. No longer willing to tolerate products that break down, they are insisting on high-quality goods that save time, energy, and often calories. Consumers rank the characteristics of product quality as (1) reliability, (2) durability, (3) easy maintenance, (4) ease of use, (5) a trusted brand name, and (6) a low price. Shoppers are also concerned about nutrition and want to know what's in their food, and many are also environmentalists.

The Poverty of Time

poverty of time
A lack of time to do anything but work, commute to work, handle family situations, do housework, shop, sleep, and eat.

Today, fewer consumers say that expensive cars, designer clothes, pleasure trips, and "platinum" credit cards are necessary components of a happy life. Instead, they place value on nonmaterial accomplishments, such as having control of their lives and being able to take a day off when they want. Dual-career families have a **poverty of time,** with few hours to do anything but work and commute to work, handle family situations, do housework, shop, sleep, and eat.

A poverty of time means that people will decrease the amount of time spent doing things they dislike. That means doing less housework and home maintenance, and doing more dining out. It also means paying more attention to brand names—not in search of status, but to make buying decisions quicker and easier. Consumers on a constrained time budget will likely favour small shops over large ones, spend less time comparing prices, use technology to reduce transaction time, and patronize businesses that make life easier.

No company has learned this better than Kinko's, the copy-shop empire. A few years ago, Kinko's noticed that busy customers in its stores didn't just want to do their photocopying and head home. They wanted to pop into a store, create a computer document, print it out, staple it, glue it, hole-punch it, and put it in a three-ring binder. In response, Kinko's has added computer workstations to many of its stores, along with sophisticated technical support and basic supplies that turn each of its copy centres into home offices away from home.

Today, 39 percent of adults spend leisure time getting ready for work.[3] Casual Fridays and home offices seem to be further blurring the boundaries between work and leisure. A recent survey noted that the leisure activity undertaken most often was to spend time with family.[4] There is little doubt that the value employees place on time versus money will continue to shift in favour of time. More employers will offer time off as an incentive. Aladdin Equipment, a maker of pool and spa replacement parts, achieved a 50 percent reduction in absenteeism and a 10 percent increase in worker productivity after it launched a four-and-a-half-day-a-week production schedule.[5] Perhaps the growth in home-based self-employment is a backlash against the lack of quality family time.

component lifestyles
The practice of choosing goods and services that meet one's diverse needs and interests rather than conforming to a single, traditional lifestyle.

The Growth of Component Lifestyles

Many of today's consumers are piecing together **component lifestyles.** A lifestyle is a mode of living; it is the way people decide to live their lives. In other words, they are choosing products and services that meet diverse needs and interests rather than conforming to traditional stereotypes.

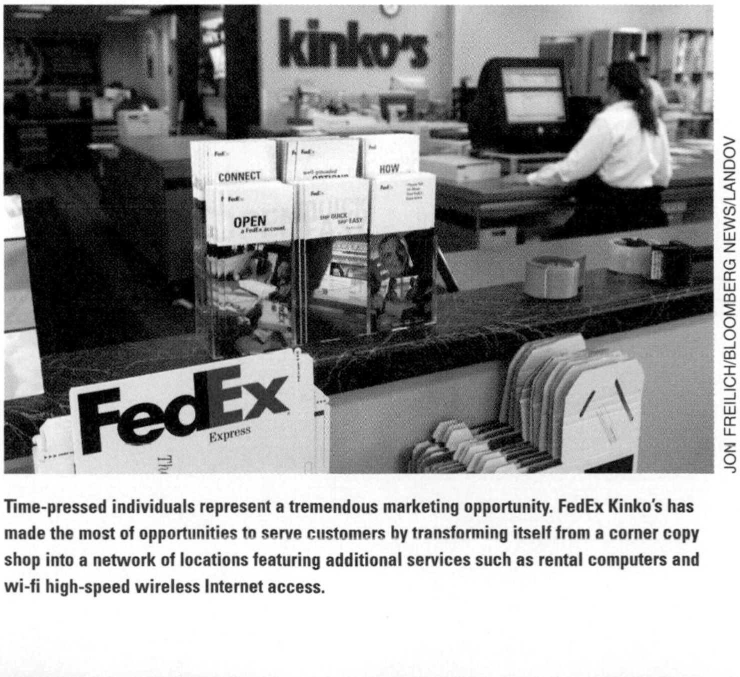

In the past, a person's profession—for instance, banker—defined his or her lifestyle. Today, a person can be a banker and also a gourmet, fitness enthusiast, dedicated single parent, and Internet guru. Each of these lifestyles is associated with different goods and services and represents a target audience. For example, for the gourmet, marketers offer cooking utensils, wines, and exotic foods through magazines like *Bon Appetit* and *Gourmet.* The fitness enthusiast buys Adidas equipment and special jogging outfits and reads *Runner* magazine. Component lifestyles increase the complexity of consumers' buying habits. The banker may own a BMW but change the oil himself or herself. He or she may buy fast food for lunch but French wine for dinner, own sophisticated photographic equipment and a low-priced home stereo, and shop for socks at Zellers and suits or dresses at Harry Rosen or high-priced boutiques.

JON FREILICH/BLOOMBERG NEWS/LANDOV

Time-pressed individuals represent a tremendous marketing opportunity. FedEx Kinko's has made the most of opportunities to serve customers by transforming itself from a corner copy shop into a network of locations featuring additional services such as rental computers and wi-fi high-speed wireless Internet access.

The unique lifestyles of every consumer can require a different marketing mix. Sometimes blending products for a single target market can result in failure. To the bright young founders of WebTV, it looked like a home run: hook televisions up to the Net and tap into the vast market of couch potatoes curious about the World Wide Web. After burning through an estimated $50 million to advertise the new service, however, WebTV and partners Sony and Philips Electronics counted a disappointing 50,000 subscribers. The problem was the wrong marketing message. Couch potatoes want to be better entertained, whereas computer users are content to explore the Internet using small PC screens.

The Changing Role of Families and Working Women

Component lifestyles have evolved because consumers can choose from a growing number of goods and services, and most have the money to exercise more options. The growth of dual-income families has resulted in increased purchasing power. Nearly two-thirds of all women between 18 and 65 are now in the workforce, and women's participation in the labour force will continue to grow. The phenomenon of working women has probably had a greater effect on marketing than has any other social change.

As women's earnings grow, so do their levels of expertise, experience, and authority. Working-age women are not the same group that businesses targeted 30 years ago. They expect different things in life—from their jobs, from their spouses, and from the products and services they buy. More males are actively involved in cooking and housework today. More women are involved in home repairs as evidenced by Mag Ruffman, the tool-savvy host of WTN's *A Repair to Remember.*

The automotive industry has finally begun to realize the power of women in vehicle purchase decisions. Women are the principal buyers for over 40 percent of all cars and trucks sold. Saturn's advertising aims not only to attract women as customers, but also to woo them into the business. In an industry with a woefully small representation of women in sales, 16 percent of Saturn's sales staff are women, compared with 7 percent industry-wide. This has had a visible impact on sales to women. Saturn claims that women buy 64 percent of its cars.[6]

The growth in the number of working women has meant an increase in dual-career families. Although dual-career families typically have greater household incomes, they have less time for family activities (poverty of time). Their purchasing roles (which define the items traditionally bought by the man or the woman) are changing, as are their purchasing patterns. With the growth in the number of working women, Calgary-based Mark's Work Wearhouse, which traditionally carried only men's work and casual clothes, has launched an advertising campaign in national magazines including *Canadian Living* and *Chatelaine* to target female buyers. Sales of women's clothing now account for 15 percent of Mark's sales at its 280 stores across Canada.[7]

Importantly, cost is more prominent in decisions made by women, whereas quality is relatively more important to men. When it comes to big-ticket, long-term items, women remain active in the decision-making process, although a plurality say they are more likely to make these decisions with a spouse.[8]

More working women has meant an ever-increasing demand for timesaving devices and products, particularly for the kitchen. An increasingly popular way to preserve foods is irradiation. Irradiation, however, evokes the notion of nuclear weapons in the minds of some consumers. The "Ethics in Marketing" box explores this new technology and its expanded use in Canada.

>> DEMOGRAPHIC FACTORS

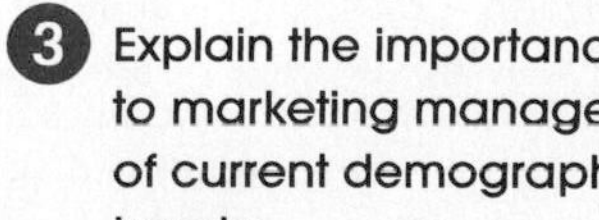

3
Explain the importance to marketing managers of current demographic trends

Another uncontrollable variable in the external environment—also extremely important to marketing managers—is **demography,** the study of people's vital statistics, such as their age, race and ethnicity, and location. Demographics are significant because the basis for any market is people. Demographic characteristics are strongly related to consumers' buying behaviour in the marketplace. Some demographic characteristics of

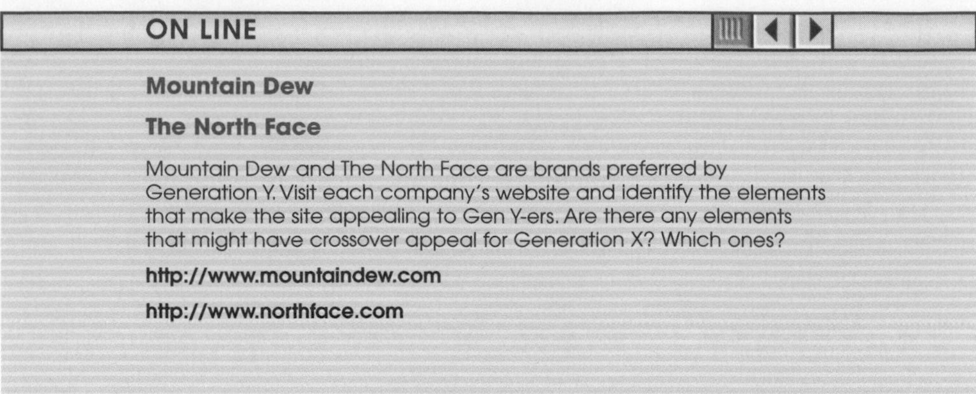

demography
The study of people's vital statistics, such as their age, race and ethnicity, and location.

Canada and the rest of the world are shown in Exhibit 3.2. This exhibit tells marketers many things. For example, Canada is growing much more slowly than the rest of the world. Faster growth, if it is coupled with rising incomes, means expanding markets. The longer life span of Canadians suggests a growing market for products and services targeted toward the elderly. Read through the table and see what other implications for marketers you can identify.

We turn our attention now to age groups, their impact, and the opportunities they present for marketers. The cohorts have been given the names of Generation Y, Generation X, and baby boomers. You will find that each cohort group has its own needs, values, and consumption patterns.

ETHICS IN MARKETING

Irradiated Food by Any Other Name Might Be a Winner

The scene in the television commercial is straight out of Norman Rockwell, with a grey-haired woman pedalling her bicycle through quaint, sun-dappled streets.

This could be a spot for aspirin, or for orange juice, or for any other product. But as the woman makes her way home, to a barbecue with elderly friends and children, it becomes apparent that she isn't pushing a specific product. Instead, the ad is asking consumers to look for packages with the international radiation symbol—a symbol used on foods that have been irradiated.

Irradiation involves exposing foods to controlled levels of ionizing radiation, such as gamma rays, electron beams, and X-rays. The decades-old process kills most pathogens, including potentially deadly strains of *E. coli* bacteria and *Salmonella*. Irradiation also allows foods to safely be stored longer. The World Health Organization and the UN Food and Agricultural Organization have endorsed food irradiation, and some 42 countries have approved its use. In Canada, foods approved for irradiation, include herbs, spices, wheat flour, onions, vegetable seasonings, potatoes, and wheat. Soon to be added to this list in Canada are mangoes, fresh and frozen poultry, fresh and prepared prawns, frozen shrimp and prawns, and fresh and frozen ground beef.

Irradiated foods are not radioactive. Still, consumer groups are divided as to their safety. The National Consumers League, for instance, lauds irradiation as a valuable safety net as does the Food Safety Network of Canada; Public Citizen, on the other hand, contends that health-related issues loom. Extensive research undertaken by Health Canada has concluded that the consumption of irradiated foods will not result in any health risk to consumers and that the use of irradiation would improve food safety.

Not all consumers are convinced of the safety of irradiated foods, however. An Angus Reid poll of Canadians showed that 51 percent thought irradiation was a good idea but 42 percent thought it was not; 54 percent would not buy irradiated food whereas 43 percent would; and 93 percent of Canadians thought more information on irradiation was needed. Most Canadians were surprised that irradiated foods are already being sold.

According to Health Canada, there are approximately 7.6 million cases of food-borne illnesses in Canada each year, resulting in 32,000 hospitalizations and 500 deaths. Proponents of irradiation suggest that much of this could be eliminated by irradiating more foods, as has been done for years in the United States. Some U.S. supermarket chains, like Publix, report that beef products labelled as irradiated outsell those which don't have the label. Did you know that every hamburger you buy at a Dairy Queen in the U.S. is cooked using an irradiated beef patty? If this worries you, hamburgers cooked at Dairy Queens in Canada do not yet use irradiated beef patties.[9]

Would you mind eating irradiated foods? Why or why not? Do you think that the list of foods approved for irradiation by Health Canada should be expanded? Should foods that have been irradiated be conspicuously labelled as such? Is labelling food products as being irradiated a good marketing tool? Why or why not? Because of their supposed benefits, should Canadian companies actively lobby to sell more irradiated food products?

EXHIBIT 3.2

The Demographic Facts of Life*

	CANADA	PLANET EARTH
Population	31,414,000	6.1 billion
Area, in square kilometres	9,984,670	84,900,846
Births per 1,000	11	22
Deaths per 1,000	7	9
Doubling time in years at current rate	150	51
Projected population, 2025	36,190,600	7.8 billion
Infant deaths per 1,000 live births	5	57
Life expectancy	79	66
Percentage of population under age 19	25	39
Percentage of population over 65	13	7
Population per square km	3.1	71
Percentage urban population	72	45
Percentage of labour force in agriculture	2.2	49
Percentage of labour force in industry	21.7	20
Percentage of labour force in services	76.1	31

SOURCE: Population Connection (http://www.populationconnection.org). Reprinted with permission.

*Data are for 2002. How much more information can you find about Canada and the world at this website?

Generation Y

Those designated by demographics as **Generation Y** were born between 1979 and 1994. They are about 6.4 million strong in Canada, about the same size as Generation X. If this group of consumers does not like the mature brands of the baby boomers or Generation X, marketers will be in trouble. Why? Simply because of the size of the Gen-Y market. For example, baby boomers are into Lexus, Esteé Lauder, L.L. Bean, and Coke. Gen Y-ers like Jeep Wrangler, Hard Candy, The North Face, and Mountain Dew.

Generation Y — People born between 1979 and 1994.

Gen Y-ers, having grown up in an even more media-saturated, brand-conscious world than their parents, respond to ads differently and prefer to encounter those ads in different places. The marketers that capture Gen-Y's attention do so by bringing their messages to the places where these kids and young adults congregate, whether it's the Internet, a snowboarding tournament, or cable TV. The ads may be funny or disarmingly direct. What they don't do is suggest that the advertiser knows Gen Y better than these savvy consumers know themselves.

Generation Y is already driving the educational software and snowboard industries and soon will drive many others. Apparel manufacturers from Ralph Lauren to The Gap are targeting the Generation-Y crowd, which prefers jeans, sports jerseys, and baseball caps to dressier clothes. A recent survey by Ipsos-Reid indicated that 84 percent of Generation-Y Canadians currently do not own a home but that 37 percent expect to buy a home within two years.[10]

For Generation Y, anyone can be a star. Everyone deserves to have his or her say. For young people, getting heard and becoming well-known are not only easy, but natural. You can create your own website; make a movie with your own webcam or digital camera; post your thoughts, pictures, and writings on-line; even be on television. Part of the draw of reality TV shows like *Survivor* is that "real people" can become stars.

Generation Y also loves customized products and services. The product categories in which Generation-Y consumers most want customized goods and services are clothes, shoes, travel planning, and computers and electronics.

Companies are learning that they have to provide something unique and deeply personal to win loyalty from this audience. Winning consumer loyalty and repeat business is

ON LINE

Generation Y

Compare the two sites below, which are designed to reach members of Generation Y. Which site does this more successfully? Explain. Can you find a similar site for Generation X?

http://www.generation-y.com

http://www.y-generation.com

exactly what Wyndham Hotels seems to be doing with its mass customized guest-recognition program, Wyndham By Request. Guests can join the free program by filling out a detailed preference form: Do you prefer foam or feather pillows? Sweet or salty snacks? A glass of Merlot or a cold Labatt in the minifridge? Requests are automatically filled each time a customer reserves a room at any Wyndham property.

Generation X

Generation X
People born between 1965 and 1978.

Generation X—people born between 1965 and 1978—consists of over 7 million consumers across Canada. It is the first generation of latchkey children—products of dual-career households or, in roughly half of the cases, of divorced or separated parents. Generation X began entering the workforce in the era of downsizing and downturn, so its members are likelier than the previous generation to be unemployed, underemployed, and living at home with Mom and Dad. Yet, as a generation that's been bombarded by multiple media since their cradle days, Gen X-ers are savvy and cynical consumers.

The members of Generation X don't mind indulging themselves. Among the young women of Generation X, 38 percent go to the movies in a given month, compared with 19 percent of women 45 and older. The members of Generation X devote a larger-than-average share of their spending dollars to restaurant meals, alcoholic beverages, clothing, and electronic items such as televisions and stereos. They are more materialistic than past generations but have less hope of achieving their goals.

COURTESY OF LETTWEEN MARKETING GROUP INC./HOUSE DESIGN + FILM, CALIFORNIA

Generation X is not nearly as large as the baby-boom generation. Still, it represents a lucrative market as its members spend a larger-than-average share of their incomes on restaurant meals, clothing, and electronics.

Travel companies, such as hotels, airlines, and car rental companies, which have spent the last 30 years marketing to baby boomers, have discovered that Gen X-ers have vastly different preferences and interests from the older generation. To woo them, travel companies are creating unusual perks and unconventional gags in TV commercials. They're affixing airfare promos to pizza boxes, teaching kick-boxing classes in hotel fitness centres, and replacing buttoned-down restaurants with sweatshirt-casual bistros.

Starwood created an entire hotel chain for Gen X-ers, giving it the name W. Each hotel, where rooms go for about $300 a night, features contemporary designs, hip bars, and whimsical amenities such as gumball machines with Hot Tamale candies. All of these features make W hotels magnets for Gen-X travellers. And if they outgrow W's, Starwood hopes they'll switch to its more traditional Sheratons and Westins. "If we catch hold of the Generation-X crowd now, they'll stay with us forever," says Starwood's vice president, Guy Hensley[11]

Another example of creating a product specifically for Gen X-ers comes from Harley-Davidson. Harley-Davidson/Buell targeted the Buell "Blast" directly to Gen X-ers. This new model is a smaller, lighter, easier-handling, one-cylinder motorcycle, selling for under $6,000. It was designed specifically for the male or female new rider or novice rider who is not yet ready for the heavier Harley-Davidson cruising or touring bikes.[12]

Baby Boomers: A Mass Market

baby boomers
People born between 1946 and 1964.

Almost 9 million **baby boomers** were born in Canada between 1946 and 1964. This created a huge market. The oldest are now over 55, but they cling to their youth. One study found that baby boomers see themselves as continuing to be very active after they turn 50. Many won't think of themselves as being senior citizens until after they turn 70.[13]

This group cherishes convenience, which has resulted in a growing demand for home delivery of items like large appliances, furniture, and groceries. The spreading culture of convenience also explains the tremendous appeal of prepared take-out foods and the necessity of DVD players and cell phones.

Baby boomers' parents raised their children to think for and of themselves. Postwar affluence also allowed parents to indulge their children as never before. They invested in their children's skills by sending them to university. They encouraged their children to succeed in a job market that rewarded competitive drive more than cooperative spirit and individual skills more than teamwork.

In turn, the sheer size of the generation encouraged businesses to promote the emerging individuality of baby boomers. Even before the oldest baby boomers started earning their own living more than three decades ago, astute businesspeople saw the profits that come from giving millions of young people what they want. Businesses offered individualistic baby boomers a growing array of customized products and services—houses, cars, furniture, appliances, clothes, vacations, jobs, leisure time, and even beliefs.

The importance of individualism among baby boomers led to a **personalized economy**—a system that delivers customized goods and services at a good value on demand. Successful businesses in a personalized economy give customers what they want when they want it. To do this, they must know their customers extremely well. In fact, the intimacy between producer and consumer is exactly what makes an economy personalized.

personalized economy
Delivering customized goods and services at a good value on demand.

As the age of today's average consumer moves toward 40, average consumption patterns are changing. People in their early 40s tend to focus on their families and finances. As this group grows in number, its members will buy more furniture from manufacturers like La-Z-Boy, Baker, and Drexel-Heritage to replace the furniture they bought early in their marriages. The demand for family counsellors and wellness programs should also increase. Additionally, discount investment brokers like Charles Schwab and E-trade and mutual funds like Fidelity and Dreyfus should profit. Because middle-aged consumers buy more reading materials than any other age group, the market for books and magazines should remain strong throughout the late 2000s. Women aged 40 to 64 will be the largest age demographic group by the year 2010. *More* magazine has been created to target this market. *More* promises features about fashion, beauty, and health, as well as pieces on married life after three decades. And all the models in *More*'s editorial pages are 40-plus.

Baby boomers are now in the nesting stage of their lives. Secure in their careers and generally stable, boomers are in their low-migration years. Leisure time, vacations, and spending money as they please are important to the boomers. According to one source, "baby boomers are driving into the sunset behind the wheel of a 40-foot diesel van with flat-screen television and a queen-sized bed."[14]

Older Consumers: Not Just Grandparents

As mentioned above, the oldest baby boomers have already crossed the 55-threshold that many demographers use to define the "mature market." Today's mature consumers are wealthier, healthier, and better educated than those of earlier generations. Over 9 million Canadians are now 50 or older, making up nearly 30 percent of the population. Consumers in the mature market keep up with the times, are quite definite about their wants and needs, and have a series of unique behaviour patterns. To summarize:

- They take frequent vacations.
- They eat out often—in both high-end and fast-food restaurants.
- They have specific needs with regard to banking and investment services, with definite differences between boomers and older consumers (those over 60 years old).
- They own computers and utilize them for a broad range of purposes.
- They are heavily into the Internet, including on-line shopping.

ON LINE 

Grand Circle Travel

Maupintour

How does Grand Circle Travel dispel the stereotypes about seniors on its Web page? Compare it to Maupintour's website. Given that both companies target seniors, which company does this more effectively? Why do you think this is so?

http://www.gct.com

http://www.maupintour.com

- They are somewhat light viewers of television (watching the major networks for news and entertainment, cable for education).

Mature consumers are not happy with the way they are treated by marketers and advertisers. For the most part, they believe marketers and advertisers do not have their interests or needs in mind when developing products, designing packaging, and preparing advertising.

- More than half feel marketers do only a fair to poor job in considering their needs when they develop new products.
- Two out of five say marketers do only a fair to poor job in considering their needs when they develop packaging (as opposed to the 4 percent who feel they do an excellent job).
- And, most damaging to advertisers, almost half of all mature consumers feel that advertisers and their agencies ignore them in preparing their campaigns (only 4 percent are satisfied).[15]

Marketers who want to actively pursue the mature market must understand it. Aging consumers create some obvious opportunities. Easy Dressing brand clothes feature Velcro-fastened clothing for women with arthritis or other ailments, who may have difficulty with zippers or buttons. Windex now comes in a bottle with an indented neck that is easier to grip. Cadaco offers a line of games with easy-to-read big print and larger game pieces. The series focuses on nostalgia by including rummy, hearts, poker, and bingo. Trivia buffs more familiar with Mitch Miller than Guns 'n' Roses can play Parker Brothers' "The Vintage Years" edition of *Trivial Pursuit.* The game, aimed at the 60-plus crowd, poses questions covering the era from Arthur Conan Doyle to Rocket Richard.

To persuade active retirees to move, the housing industry first renamed retirement developments, which are now often called "active-adult communities." Builders are also piling on amenities, adding restaurants, concierge services, computer labs, and gyms. Other products companies are providing to attract older consumers include laundry detergents with snap-on lids that are easier to open than perforated flaps; pill bottles with battery-operated clocks to indicate when the bottle was last opened; and Grandparents Clubs that offer discounts on toy purchases for grandchildren.

4 Explain the importance to marketing managers of multiculturalism and growing ethnic markets

>> GROWING ETHNIC MARKETS

Canada is undergoing a demographic transition: it is becoming a truly multicultural society. According to the 2001 Census, 3 in 10 Canadians are not of French or British descent. Over the next decade, Canada will become even more diverse. Over two-thirds of immigrants to Canada are now classified as "visible minorities," and 13.4 percent of Canadians are "visible minorities." The largest groups of visible minorities now coming to Canada are from China, South and Southeast Asia, Hong Kong, India, and Africa. Furthermore, nearly 25 percent of all visible minorities in Canada are under 14 and, as such, will become an even bigger force in our economy in the years ahead.[16]

Ethnic and Cultural Diversity

multiculturalism
When all major ethnic groups in an area—such as a city, county, or census metropolitan area—are roughly equally represented.

Multiculturalism occurs when all major ethnic groups in an area—such as a city, county, or census metropolitan area—are roughly equally represented. Because of its current demographic transition, the trend in Canada is toward greater multiculturalism.

The greatest degree of multiculturalism is found in the largest census metropolitan areas across the country, metropolitan areas such as Toronto, Vancouver, Calgary, Edmonton, and Montreal. In the 2001 Census, nearly 20 percent of the people in these cities listed neither English nor French as their first language. In recognition of this, a number of companies are now including visible minorities in their

ON LINE

Multicultural Marketing Resources

As a marketer, what does MMR have to help you with multicultural marketing? Consider attending events posted to the MMR calendar that will take place in your area.

http://www.multiculturalmarketingresources.com

advertising. Air Canada, Nabisco, and the TD Bank are among the companies advertising in languages other than English and French. Radio stations such as CHIN in Toronto and Ottawa broadcast in as many as 20 languages.

Across provinces, visible minorities range from less than 1 percent of the population in Newfoundland and Prince Edward Island to 19.1 percent of the population in Ontario and 21.6 percent of the population in British Columbia. Toronto, Montreal, and Vancouver account for 33.7 percent of Canada's total population but are home to 72.7 percent of Canada's visible minorities. The visible minority population of Toronto (1,712,535), by itself, would rank as the fourth-largest city in Canada! Exhibit 3.3 shows the visible minority populations in 10 CMAs across Canada and compares the 2001 Census figures to 1996. Look at the growth in all 10 CMAs over a short five-year period.

Marketing Implications of Multiculturalism

The marketer's task is more challenging in a diverse society because of differences among consumers and varying demand for goods and services. What's more, ethnic markets are not homogeneous. There is not an Asian market or an Indian market, any more than there is a single French market. Instead, there are many niches within ethnic markets that require micromarketing strategies.

Providing service to customers who do not speak English or French could be a problem, but not for the Habib family, who own Global Quality Market in Windsor, Ontario. Each staff member hired at Global Quality Market speaks at least two languages; these languages include Italian, Lebanese, Chinese, and Hindi. Why? "Because we are in the centre of a European, Middle East, Egyptian, and Pakistani population of over 20,000 people," says Sam Habib, one of the family members running the successful $3 million store.[17]

Not all ethnic marketing is successful. The Vancouver Grizzlies basketball team regularly targeted Vancouver's growing Asian market with its advertising and promotional programs. The Grizzlies were sold and moved to an American city, so it would seem that the ethnic marketing program didn't attract enough ticket buyers. Slightly more successful has been Air Canada's advertising to the Asian market.

COURTESY OF CITIZENSHIP AND IMMIGRATION CANADA, www.cic.gc.ca

Multicultural marketing has found great success on the Internet. Numerous sites provide information and services targeted toward a variety of minority groups. This site, from Citizenship and Immigration Canada (http://www.cic.gc.ca) provides links for immigrants and members of visible minorities.

Another large company that has increased its emphasis on multicultural marketing is Sears, Roebuck and Company. Sears has a number of stores located in urban areas with large Asian populations. Recently, the company recognized an opportunity to boost fall sales in those stores by forging a connection with the Asian Moon Festival.

EXHIBIT 3.3

Visible Minority Population in Selected Major Canadian Cities

	2001	1996
Vancouver	36.9%	31.1%
Toronto	36.8	31.6
Calgary	17.5	15.6
Edmonton	14.6	13.5
Ottawa–Hull	14.1	11.5
Montreal	13.6	12.2
Windsor	12.9	10.0
Winnipeg	12.5	11.1
Kitchener	10.7	8.9
Hamilton	9.8	7.9

SOURCE: Statistics Canada, *Visible Minority Population, Census Metropolitan Areas*, 2001 Census, www.statcan.ca. Used with the permission of the Minister of Industry, as Minister responsible for Statistics Canada.

The September holiday is a harvest-time celebration, similar to Thanksgiving, which is celebrated in many Asian countries. It coincides with the kickoff of retail's fall selling season (when Sears would be staging promotions, anyway), so a Moon Festival tie-in made sense. "We've had great success with it," says Gilbert Davila, Sears's vice president of multicultural and relationship marketing. "It's a good way for us to connect with the community."[18] Sears also does promotions tied to Black History Month in February.

The Asian market is a particular challenge for marketers because of the many different languages. Depending on the makeup of the surrounding communities, Sears advertises the Moon Festival in Mandarin, Cantonese, Vietnamese, or Korean. The programs staged in the stores are conducted in English, however. The ads run mainly in local Asian-language newspapers.

If Sears is looking for a new place to advertise to the Asian community, *Jasmine* magazine, a glossy lifestyle magazine, hit the newsstands in Canada in August 2003. *Jasmine* is targeted to Asian-Canadian women aged 18 to 34. It will be published four times a year and will feature many of the same sections as other women's magazines—health, beauty, travel, and careers—but with a distinct Asian focus. *Jasmine* will address such topics as Asian-specific illnesses (like osteoporosis and lupus), interracial dating, and workplace barriers.[19]

The Internet Goes Multicultural

Since 1995, non-English-speaking Internet users have gone from less than 10 percent to as high as 50 percent, according to research firm Wired Digital. Growth in Internet usage within many ethnic markets is outpacing growth among the general public, according to Forrester Research.[20]

The huge growth in the multicultural on-line market has resulted in a proliferation of websites targeted to specific ethnic groups. Examples include AsianAvenue.com, a site for the Asian market; StarMedia Network, which focuses on Latinos; and iMinorities.com, a job site for minorities. One of the more popular sites for the Black market is BlackPlanet.com, which averages 300 million page views per month across Canada and the U.S.[21]

5 Identify consumer and marketer reactions to the state of the economy

>> ECONOMIC FACTORS

In addition to social and demographic factors, marketing managers must understand and react to the economic environment. The three economic areas of greatest concern to most marketers are the distribution of consumer income, inflation, and recession.

Rising Incomes

As disposable (or after-tax) incomes rise, more families and individuals can afford the "good life." Fortunately, Canadian incomes have continued to rise, although at a rather slow pace. After adjustment for inflation, average disposable incomes in Canada rose less than 3 percent per year between 2001 and 2003.[22]

Today, about 55 percent of all Canadian households earn a "middle-class" income. The rough boundaries for a middle-class income are $30,000 (well above poverty) to $75,000 (short of wealth). In 2003, about half of all households were in the upper end of this range. More than 14 percent of households now earn above $75,000.[23] As a result, Canadians are buying more goods and services than ever before. For example, in raising a child to age 17, a middle-class family will spend over $180,000 in 2001 dollars. This new level of affluence is not limited to professionals or even individuals within specific age or education brackets. Rather, it cuts across all household types, well beyond

ON LINE

Multiculturalism in Canada

Want to learn more about the wide range of cultures and subcultures in Canada? Check out the information on the Culture Canada website. What can marketers learn from the information on this site? Can you find other websites devoted to the wide range of cultures found in Canada?

http://www.culturecanada.gc.ca

EXHIBIT 3.4

Median Family Income for Selected Canadian Cities (2001)

CITY	MEDIAN FAMILY INCOME
Ottawa	$72,300
Windsor	65,600
Victoria	58,500
Toronto	57,900
Sudbury	56,800
St. Catharines-Niagara	55,200
Vancouver	54,800
Regina	54,600
Saskatoon	54,300
Montreal	52,100

SOURCE: Eric Beauchesne, "Ottawa Records Highest Income," *The Windsor Star*, September 5, 2003, C1. Reprinted with permission.

what businesses traditionally consider to be markets for high-priced goods and services. This rising affluence stems primarily from the increasing number of dual-income families.

In the 2000s, many marketing managers are focusing on families with incomes over $50,000, because this group has the most discretionary income. The middle, or median, income for all Canadian families in 2001 was $50,100. Median family income for selected Canadian cities is shown in Exhibit 3.4. The average Canadian household has over $16,000 in discretionary income to spend each year. Some marketers are concentrating their efforts on higher-quality, higher-priced goods and services, such as the Lexus automobile, Breitling watches, and five-star resort hotels.

Inflation

inflation
A general rise in prices without a corresponding increase in wages that results in decreased purchasing power.

Inflation is a general rise in prices without a corresponding increase in wages, which results in decreased purchasing power. Fortunately, Canada has had a low rate of inflation for over a decade. The late 1990s and early 2000s have been marked by an inflation rate under 4 percent. By 2003, the inflation rate in Canada had dropped to 2.2 percent.[24] The low rate of inflation is due to the tremendous productivity of the high-tech sector of the economy and the stability of the price of services. Both education and healthcare costs are rising more slowly than in the past. The other good news is that the economy grew at an annual rate of over 4.8 percent from 2001 to 2003.[25] These economic conditions benefit marketers, because real wages, and hence purchasing power, go up when inflation stays down. A significant increase in inflation almost always depresses real wages and the ability to buy more goods and services.

In times of low inflation, businesses seeking to increase their profit margins can do so only by increasing their efficiency. If they significantly increase prices, no one will purchase their goods or services.

In more inflationary times, marketers use a number of pricing strategies to cope. But in general, marketers must be aware that inflation causes consumers to either build up or diminish their brand loyalty. In one research session, a consumer panelist noted, "I used to use just Betty Crocker mixes, but now I think of either Betty Crocker or Duncan Hines, depending on which is on sale." Another participant said, "Pennies count now, and so I look at the whole shelf, and I read the ingredients. I don't really understand, but I can tell if it's exactly the same. So now I use this cheaper brand, and honestly, it works just as well." Inflation pressures consumers to make more economical purchases. Nevertheless, most consumers try hard to maintain their standard of living.

In creating marketing strategies to cope with inflation, managers must realize that, despite what happens to the seller's cost, the buyer is not going to pay more for a product than the subjective value he or she places on it. No matter how compelling the justification might be for a 10 percent price increase, marketers must always examine its impact on demand. Many marketers try to hold prices level as long as is practical.

Recession

recession
A period of economic activity when income, production, and employment tend to fall—all of which reduce demand for goods and services.

A **recession** is a period of economic activity when income, production, and employment tend to fall—all of which reduce demand for goods and services. The slowdown in the high-tech sector, overextended consumer credit, and the terrorist attacks on the United States, Canada's largest trading partner, resulted in the economy slowing down in 2001. The problems of inflation and recession go hand in hand, yet recession requires different marketing strategies:

- *Improve existing products and introduce new ones:* The goal is to reduce production hours, waste, and the cost of materials. Recessions increase the demand for goods and services that are economical and efficient, offer value, help organizations streamline practices and procedures, and improve customer service.
- *Maintain and expand customer services:* In a recession, many organizations postpone purchases of new equipment and materials. Sales of replacement parts and other services may become an important source of income.
- *Emphasize top-of-the-line products and promote product value:* Customers with less to spend will seek demonstrated quality, durability, satisfaction, and capacity to save time and money. Well-priced, high-value items consistently fare well during recessions.

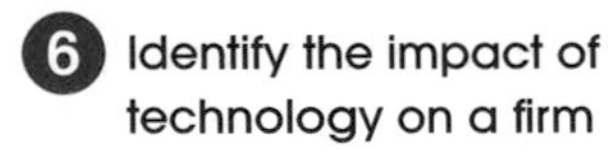

6 Identify the impact of technology on a firm

>> TECHNOLOGICAL AND RESOURCE FACTORS

Sometimes new technology is an effective weapon against inflation and recession. New machines that reduce production costs can be one of a firm's most valuable assets. The power of a personal-computer microchip doubles about every 18 months. The Pentium Pro, for example, introduced in 1995, contained 5.3 million transistors and performed 300 million instructions per second (MIPS). The 886 chip, introduced in 2000, has 15 million transistors and performs 1,000 MIPS. Our ability, as a nation, to maintain and build wealth depends in large part on the speed and effectiveness with which we invent and adopt machines that lift productivity. For example, coal mining is typically thought of as unskilled, backbreaking labour. But visit a coal mine today and you will find workers with push-button controls who walk along massive machines that shear metre-long slices from the mine walls. Laptop computers help miners track equipment breakdowns and water quality.

basic research
Pure research that aims to confirm an existing theory or to learn more about a concept or phenomenon.

applied research
An attempt to develop new or improved products.

Canada excels at both basic and applied research. **Basic research** (or *pure research*) attempts to expand the frontiers of knowledge but is not aimed at a specific, pragmatic problem. Basic research aims to confirm an existing theory or to learn more about a concept or phenomenon. For example, basic research might focus on high-energy physics. **Applied research,** in contrast, attempts to develop new or improved products. Canada is improving its track record in applied research. Many Canadian companies spend heavily on R&D, as shown in Exhibit 3.5.

The huge investment in information technology in this country has helped hold down inflation and maintain economic growth and has allowed Canadian companies to compete in world markets. Business purchases of information technology have been rising by 25 percent a year since the 1970s.

Information technology and the Internet have been the innovations driving increased productivity for the past decade. They will continue to do so in the foreseeable future. When Oracle wanted to boost operating margins, it automated such functions as office supply purchasing. That helped keep the company workforce stable even

EXHIBIT 3.5

Canada's Top Corporate R&D Spenders for 2003

COMPANY	R&D SPENDING
Nortel Networks Corp.	$3,501,992,000
Magna International Inc.	574,766,000
Pratt & Whitney Canada	428,000,000
JDS Uniphase Corp.	400,138,000
IBM Canada	315,300,000
Bell Canada	300,000,000
ATI Technologies	286,361,000
Bombardier Inc.	233,500,000
Ericsson Canada	201,000,000
Alcan Inc.	180,596,000

SOURCE: Research Infosource Inc., http://www.researchinfosource.com. Reprinted with permission of The Impact Group.

as sales soared 30 percent. The company saved about $1 billion, and margins jumped from 20 percent to 33 percent.[26] Dell uses WebMethods software to act as a type of translator enabling instant communication between Dell's order management system and customers' procurement systems. By making it easier for corporate customers to use the Internet to place orders, Dell has dramatically reduced procurement errors and shaved approximately $5 million a year off its costs. Dell also uses TradeMatrix software to run its plants. This system allows Dell to see deep inside suppliers' business processes and vice versa. It tells suppliers which parts to get to which plant and when. TradeMatrix has saved Dell millions of dollars and has become a major competitive advantage. Dell's inventory averages one-tenth the average level of its rivals.[27] For more examples of how information technology and the Internet are boosting productivity, see Exhibit 3.6.

Sometimes, even though new technology is available, its effective utilization can be stymied by the external environment. Our "Global Perspectives" box details how culture and tradition in Japan have slowed the use of the Internet and information technology.

>> POLITICAL AND LEGAL FACTORS

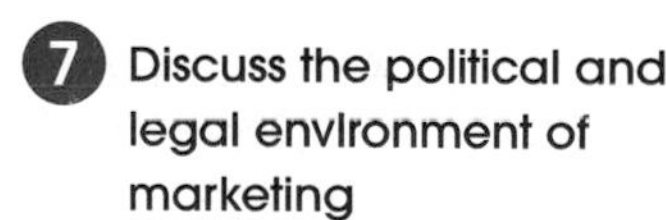

7
Discuss the political and legal environment of marketing

Business needs government regulation to protect innovators of new technology, the interests of society in general, one business from another, and consumers. In turn, government needs business, because the marketplace generates taxes that support public efforts to educate our youth, protect healthcare, and so on. The private sector also serves as a counterweight to government. The decentralization of power inherent in a private-enterprise system supplies the limitation on government that is essential for the survival of democracy.

Every aspect of the marketing mix is subject to laws and restrictions. It is the duty of marketing managers or their legal assistants to understand these laws and conform to them, because failure to comply with regulations can have major consequences for a firm. Sometimes just sensing trends and taking corrective action before a government agency acts can help avoid regulation. This didn't happen in the case of the tobacco industry. As a result, it is facing tougher and tougher restrictions on its promotional activities.

The challenge is not simply to keep the marketing department out of trouble, however, but to help it implement creative new programs to accomplish marketing objectives. It is all too easy for a marketing manager or sometimes a lawyer to say no to a marketing innovation that actually entails little risk. For example, an overly cautious lawyer could hold up sales of a desirable new product by warning that the package design could prompt a copyright infringement suit. Thus, it is important to have a thorough understanding of the laws established by the federal government, provincial governments, municipal governments, and regulatory agencies to control marketing-related issues.

EXHIBIT 3.6

How Companies Are Using the Internet and Information Technology to Boost Productivity throughout the Organization

PROCESS	EXAMPLE	PAYOFF
Innovation	Royal Dutch/Shell's "Game-Changer" teams use the Net to generate new business ideas.	New "Light Touch" oil discovery method found 30 million barrels.
Collaboration	Ocean Spray's Extranet assesses cranberry quality immediately and helps growers get better prices.	Growers get higher profits; Ocean Spray cuts waste and boosts productivity.
Design	Honeywell uses the Net to help fashion customized prototypes of anything from a fan blade to a golf club head.	Design time cut from six months to 24 hours.
Purchasing	Ford's AutoXchange creates massive on-line trading bazaar for its 30,000 suppliers.	Could save as much as $8 billion in first few years.
Manufacturing	BP Amoco, using Net technology from Honey-well, can quickly identify plant inefficiencies.	Stems 2 percent per day productivity loss in Grangemouth, Scotland, refinery.
Logistics	Cement maker Cemex uses Net-based truck dispatch system to speed deliveries to customers.	Cement delivered within 20 minutes, down from three hours.
Marketing	Weyerhaeuser uses the Net to weed out its least valuable customers.	Boosted return on net assets from –2 percent to 27 percent in a five-year period.
Service	GE Power Systems lets customers use the Net to compare the performance of its turbines against other GE turbines in the market.	Turbine productivity expected to rise by 1 percent to 2 percent annually.

SOURCE: "Working the Web," reprinted from February 14, 2000, issue of *Business Week*, p.116, by special permission, copyright ©2000 by The McGraw-Hill Companies, Inc.

Federal Legislation

In Canada, the Combines Investigation Commission was established in 1888 to protect small businesses that were suffering as a result of collusive practices by larger businesses. In 1923, the Combines Investigation Act was passed to prevent anticompetitive conduct among businesses. Until 1975 this was the most important act affecting the legal environment of business.

Dissatisfaction with the Combines Investigation Act led to the passage in 1975 of Bill C-2, known as the Competition Act. At first, the Bureau of Competition Policy, which was part of Consumer and Corporate Affairs Canada, administered this act. Bill C-2 was updated in 1986 and is now administered by the Competition Bureau of Industry Canada.

Criminal offences under the Competition Act include the following: price fixing, bid rigging, price maintenance (i.e., manufacturers requiring retailers to charge a specific price), price discrimination, predatory pricing, misleading advertising, refusal to deal, and deceptive practices (such as bait-and-switch selling, certain forms of pyramid selling, and double-ticketing). Noncriminal matters dealt with by the act include mergers, exclusive dealing, consignment selling, and tied selling.

Most of the consumer and business protection legislation in Canada—the Competition Act, the Consumer Packaging and Labelling Act, the National Trade Mark and True Labelling Act, the Motor Vehicle Safety Act, the Food and Drug Act, the Textile Labelling Act, the Precious Metals Marking Act, and the Personal Information Protection and Electronic Documents Act—is enforced by the **Competition Bureau** of Industry Canada. This bureau has several agencies (e.g., the Fair Business Practices Branch) and is responsible for enforcing the laws covering bankruptcy, trade practices, competition, credit, labelling and packaging, copyrights, hazardous products, patents, pensions, precious metals, trademarks, and food inspection. The bureau's website, http://www.strategis.ic.gc.ca, lists the full range of responsibilities of the Competition Bureau.

Competition Bureau
The federal department charged with administering most marketplace laws.

ON LINE

The Competition Bureau

As a marketing manager, how could you use the Competition Bureau's website for help when designing a new marketing campaign?

http://strategis.ic.gc.ca

GLOBAL PERSPECTIVES

The Internet Runs Headlong into Japan's Cultural Traditions

Japan's electronics manufacturers are rushing to capitalize on the popularity of the Internet, rolling out everything from Internet music players to digital cameras to Web-friendly computers. There's just one problem: Very little of the gear can be bought on-line in Japan.

The few exceptions come mostly from Sony Corporation. When it launched its PlayStation 2 video-game machine in Japan, enthusiastic buyers not only lined up for blocks in Akihabara, Tokyo's electronics district, but also mobbed Sony's website. The site sold 380,000 PlayStation 2 units—nearly 40 percent of the total.

In North America, electronic goods are readily sold on-line: Dell Computer Corporation says its dell.com website generates nearly 50 percent of its total sales, an average of $40 million a day. But it is going to be harder in Japan. That's partly for cultural reasons, industry insiders say: the Japanese tend to be pickier about what they buy and are reluctant to deal with merchants at a distance.

An even bigger obstacle is a major fortress of Old Japan: each of the top electronics makers has a nationwide network of exclusive dealers, usually mom-and-pop stores long on the personal touch but short on information about up-to-date products.

Take a look at a typical store on Tokyo's Shinobazu Avenue, an outlet that is part of the 22,000-member Panasonic/National retail network. The dusty shelves are filled with 1950s hits—AM radios and space heaters, for example. Asked about Will PC, a heavily advertised Panasonic computer, the aged owner says: "I'm sorry, is that a new product? I don't know anything about computers, since we don't stock any."

Manufacturers are reluctant to compete with these merchants, with whom they have long relationships. And small stores and big discounters would object to price cutting on direct sales via the Net.

All this explains an apparent paradox: many electronics executives, who stand to win big on sales of Web-related products, dismiss Internet sales as a nonstarter. "We can't do it," says Akiyoshi Takano, president of Sanyo Electric Company's multimedia company, which sells such popular Web-related products as digital cameras.

But what about the success of PlayStation 2 on the Internet? Skeptics note that game fans knew all about the new PlayStation from advance publicity, so they had no need to test it out in the store. Still, many retailers are worried. "This sort of thing would have been unthinkable before now," says Takeo Higashikawa, the manager of a Sony-affiliated store. He thinks Sony was too "dry" in elbowing aside longtime retailers in favour of Internet sales. "What about the people who worked so hard over the years selling Sony's?" he wonders. Koichiro Katsurayama, a spokesman for Sony Computer Entertainment, says Sony gave retailers and its website equal treatment.

Many Japanese retailers are hoping the Internet will end up as a vehicle for only such specialty items. But a Sony managing director, Sunobu Horigome, says that's wishful thinking.[28]

Do you think e-commerce will ever be as popular in Japan as it is in Canada and the United States? What might Japanese manufacturers do to avoid clashes with Japanese retailers? Can you think of other countries where culture and tradition might hinder the development of e-commerce? What about in Canada?

Provincial Laws

For national companies, provincial legislation often poses difficulties because laws vary from province to province. Quebec's Bill 101 requires that French be the primary (and sometimes exclusive) language in all promotional and advertising activities in that province. Also, advertisers in Quebec are forbidden to target children directly. There are many provincial laws regulating pricing, business start-ups, door-to-door selling, and the sale of alcoholic beverages. As well, there are provincial laws that apply to certain types of businesses (e.g., travel agents, car dealers, realtors) and to certain types of business activities (e.g., billboards and direct mail advertising). Marketing managers must be aware of any legislation that directly affects their businesses. For example, Wal-Mart stores in Ontario can sell wine, but the Liquor Control Board of Ontario sets the minimum price that Wal-Mart can charge for each bottle of wine.

Self-Regulation

Some business groups make efforts to police themselves. This is referred to as **self-regulation.** The Canadian Code of Advertising Standards, for example, was established by Canada's largest advertising agencies to monitor honesty and fairness in advertising. The Canadian Broadcasting Association, whose members include Canada's major television and radio stations, has developed its own code of ethics. The Canadian Marketing Association, whose members do over 80 percent of all telemarketing in Canada, has established guidelines for its members with regard to protecting consumers' privacy and right to not be contacted. Businesses that belong to the Better Business Bureau voluntarily agree to maintain fair business practices.

self-regulation
Programs voluntarily adopted by business groups to regulate the activities of their members.

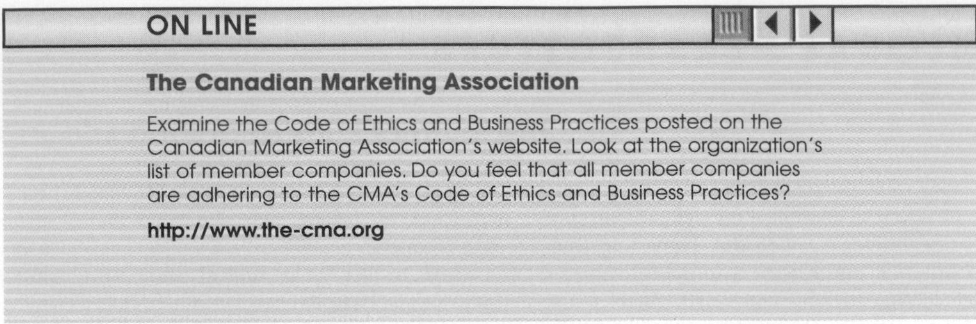

ON LINE
The Canadian Marketing Association
Examine the Code of Ethics and Business Practices posted on the Canadian Marketing Association's website. Look at the organization's list of member companies. Do you feel that all member companies are adhering to the CMA's Code of Ethics and Business Practices?
http://www.the-cma.org

NAFTA

North American Free Trade Agreement (NAFTA)
An agreement among Canada, the United States, and Mexico that created the world's largest free trade zone.

Canada has had a free trade agreement with its largest trading partner, the United States, since 1988. This was expanded by the **North American Free Trade Agreement (NAFTA),** which created the world's largest free trade zone by bringing Mexico into the free trade agreement. Canada, the United States, and Mexico combined have a population of nearly 400 million people and an economy in excess of $10 trillion.

NAFTA has brought about new business opportunities for Canadian companies by lowering the trade barriers between the NAFTA countries. The opening of Mexico's borders has meant expanded markets for exporting companies. NAFTA has also forced Canadian businesses to become more efficient to compete with Mexico, which has lower wage rates and less restrictive environmental regulations. Efforts are underway to expand NAFTA so that it includes the countries of Central and South America. The result would be a Western Hemisphere Free Trade Zone.

8 Explain the basics of foreign and domestic competition

>> COMPETITIVE FACTORS

The competitive environment encompasses the number of competitors a firm must face, the relative sizes of the competitors, the specific target markets and marketing strategies each competitor is pursuing, and the degree of interdependence within the industry. Management has little control over the competitive environment confronting a firm.

Competition for Market Share and Profits

As population growth slows, costs rise, and available resources tighten, firms find that they must work harder to maintain their profits and market share regardless of the form of the competitive market. Take, for example, the competition among warehouse stores. Wal-Mart Stores Inc., the world's largest retailer, opened its first Sam's Club warehouse store in Canada during the week of October 27, 2003, promising to significantly change the face of retailing in Canada. Even before the first Sam's Club store opened, a number of food retailers, such as Loblaws, anticipating stronger competition, lowered employee wages and cut prices.

With the coming of Sam's Club, Costco Wholesale Canada will have its first direct competition in the low-priced, buy-in-bulk, wholesale-club market. Sam's Club entered Canada with four stores opening the same week in the Toronto area; a fifth store opened in February 2004 in London, Ontario. Wal-Mart expects to open as many as 60 warehouse stores across Canada. Costco, which currently has 61 warehouse stores across the country, was planning on eventually expanding to 90 stores. Most analysts do not believe that there is room in Canada for 150 warehouse outlets.[29]

One of the greatest competitive battles is occurring in consumer package goods, and the two giants going toe-to-toe are Procter & Gamble and Unilever. Between 1996 and 2003, $52 billion Unilever and $45 billion P&G have been living in a parallel slow-growth universe. Since 1996, Unilever's sales have declined an average of 3.6 percent a year. P&G's have inched up 3.6 percent a year. Every market these companies compete in is barely growing, flat, or declining.

In this kind of environment, "it's a death struggle to incrementally gain share," says Burt Flickinger, a former P&G brand manager who now works as a consumer products consultant. P&G and Unilever have to slog it out for every fraction of market share in every category in every market where they compete. And that's a lot of slogging. Both companies own hundreds of the world's best-known brands—Crest, Pampers, Ivory (Procter & Gamble); Dove, Vaseline, Lipton (Unilever)—competing in some 140 countries. But perhaps the fiercest competition is taking place in the market for laundry detergent, where P&G's Tide and Unilever's Wisk have been locked in battle for nearly 40 years.

In recent years, nobody has played the competition game better than Tide. While the rest of the industry stagnated, Tide's sales climbed by 41 percent, to $1.8 billion over the past five years. It now owns 40 percent of the laundry detergent market. Its strategy? First, it spends more than $100 million a year promoting the Tide brand name through advertising on TV, billboards, subways, buses, magazines, and the Internet. Tide is the sponsor of a NASCAR race car and youth soccer leagues. It holds nationwide publicity stunts. Tide has made itself a brand icon—right up there with Coke and McDonald's.

Competition is a driving force in the marketing environment, including laundry detergent. Tide has become one of the best-known brands in the market, in part by continually improving its product and increasing its market share. How competitive is the world of detergents? The formula for Tide is covered by 44 patents.

But the real genius of Tide's strategy is its relentless stream of new and improved products. Each year, P&G spends close to $2 billion on R&D, a large portion of which goes toward developing new formulations of Tide. There's Tide With Bleach, Tide Free (which has no fragrance), Tide WearCare (which purports to keep fabrics vibrant longer), and Tide Kick (whose package includes a nozzle to rub detergent directly into fabrics). In all, Tide has spawned more than 60 variations of itself.[30]

Global Competition

Wal-Mart, Costco, Unilever, and Procter & Gamble are savvy international competitors conducting business throughout the world. Many foreign competitors consider Canada a ripe target market. Thus, Canadian marketing managers can no longer worry about only domestic competitors. In automobiles, automotive parts, textiles, pharmaceuticals, retailing, steel, and many other areas, foreign competition has been strong. In the past, foreign firms penetrated Canadian markets by concentrating on price; today the emphasis has switched to product quality. Nestlé, Sony, Rolls-Royce, and premium imported wine and beer are noted for quality, not cheap prices.

 Describe the role of ethics and ethical decisions in business

>> ETHICAL BEHAVIOUR IN BUSINESS

ethics
The moral principles or values that generally govern the conduct of an individual.

Regardless of the intensity of the competition or the shifting external environment, firms must compete in an ethical manner. **Ethics** refers to the moral principles or values that generally govern the conduct of an individual or a group. Ethics can also be viewed as the standard of behaviour by which conduct is judged. Standards that are legal may not always be ethical, and vice versa. Laws are the values and standards enforceable by the courts. Ethics consists of personal moral principles and values rather than societal prescriptions.

Defining the boundaries of ethicality and legality can be difficult. Often, judgment is needed to determine whether an action that may be legal is indeed ethical. For example, advertising two-for-one drink nights in local pubs, nude dancing, and X-rated movies in campus newspapers is not illegal, but is it ethical?

morals
The rules people develop as a result of cultural values and norms.

Morals are the rules people develop as a result of cultural values and norms. Culture is a socializing force that dictates what is right and wrong. Moral standards may also reflect the laws and regulations that affect social and economic behaviour. Thus, morals can be considered the foundation of ethical behaviour.

Morals are usually characterized as good or bad. "Good" and "bad" have different connotations, including "effective" and "ineffective." A good salesperson makes or exceeds the assigned quota. If the salesperson sells a new stereo or television set to a disadvantaged consumer—knowing full well that the person can't keep up the monthly payments—is the salesperson still a good one? What if the sale enables the salesperson to exceed his or her quota?

Other connotations of "good" and "bad" relate to "conforming" and "deviant" behaviours. A lawyer who advertises that he or she will get drunk drivers their licences back may be engaged in legal behaviour but might not conform to the norms of the general public. "Bad" and "good" are also used to express the distinction between criminal and law-abiding behaviour. And finally, the distinctions between "good" and "bad" as defined by different religions differ markedly. A Muslim who eats pork would be considered bad, as would a fundamentalist Christian who drinks whiskey.

Morality and Business Ethics

Today's business ethics actually consist of a subset of major life values learned since birth. The values businesspeople use to make decisions have been acquired through family as well as through educational and religious institutions.

Ethical values are situation specific and time oriented. Nevertheless, everyone must have an ethical base that applies to conduct in the business world and in personal life. One approach to developing a personal set of ethics is to examine the consequences of a particular act. Who is helped or hurt? How long-lasting are the consequences? What actions produce the greatest good for the greatest number of people? A second approach stresses the importance of rules. Rules come in the form of customs, laws, professional standards, and common sense. Consider these examples of rules:

- Always treat others as you would like to be treated.
- Copying copyrighted computer software is against the law.
- It is wrong to lie, bribe, or exploit.

The last approach emphasizes the development of moral character within individuals. Ethical development can be thought of as having three levels:[31]

- *Preconventional morality,* the most basic level, is childlike. It is calculating, self-centred, and even selfish, and is based on what will be immediately punished or rewarded. Fortunately, most businesspeople have progressed beyond the self-centred and manipulative actions of preconventional morality.
- *Conventional morality* moves from an egocentric viewpoint toward the expectations of society. Loyalty and obedience to the organization (or society) become paramount. At the level of conventional morality, an ethical marketing decision would be

concerned only with whether it is legal and how others will view it. This type of morality could be likened to the adage "When in Rome, do as the Romans do."

- *Postconventional morality* represents the morality of the mature adult. At this level, people are less concerned about how others might see them and more concerned about how they see and judge themselves over the long run. A marketing decision maker who has attained a postconventional level of morality might ask, "Even though it is legal and will increase company profits, is it right in the long run? Might it do more harm than good in the end?"

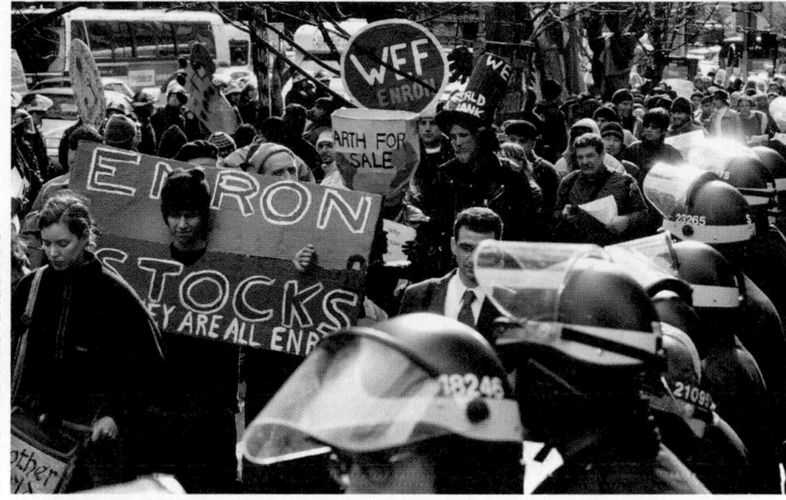

BRIAN SNYDER/REUTERS/LANDOV

Perhaps the most egregious example of unethical business practices in recent memory was the Enron scandal, which extended to the company's auditing firm, the venerable Arthur Andersen. Thousands of employees were negatively affected by the scandal.

>> ETHICAL DECISION MAKING

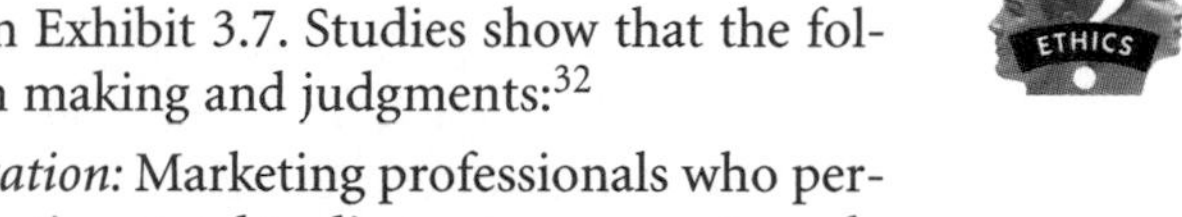

How do businesspeople make ethical decisions? There is no cut-and-dried answer. Some of the ethical issues managers face are shown in Exhibit 3.7. Studies show that the following factors tend to influence ethical decision making and judgments:[32]

- *Extent of ethical problems within the organization:* Marketing professionals who perceive fewer ethical problems in their organizations tend to disapprove more strongly of "unethical" or questionable practices than those who perceive more ethical problems. Apparently, the healthier the ethical environment, the greater is the likelihood that marketers will take a strong stand against questionable practices.
- *Top-management actions on ethics:* Top managers can influence the behaviour of marketing professionals by encouraging ethical behaviour and discouraging unethical behaviour.
- *Potential magnitude of the consequences:* The greater the harm done to victims, the more likely it is that marketing professionals will recognize the behaviour as unethical.
- *Social consensus:* The greater the degree of agreement among managerial peers that an action is harmful, the more likely it is that marketers will recognize the behaviour as unethical.
- *Probability of a harmful outcome:* The greater the likelihood that an action will result in a harmful outcome, the more likely it is that marketers will recognize the behaviour as unethical.
- *Length of time between the decision and the onset of consequences:* The shorter the length of time between the action and the onset of negative consequences, the more likely it is that marketers will perceive the behaviour as unethical.
- *Number of people to be affected:* The greater the number of persons affected by a negative outcome, the more likely it is that marketers will recognize the behaviour as unethical.

Ethical Guidelines

Many organizations have become more interested in ethical issues. One sign of this interest is the increase in the number of large companies that appoint ethics officers—from virtually none five years ago to almost 25 percent of large corporations now. In addition, many companies of various sizes have developed a **code of ethics** as a guideline to help marketing managers and other employees make better decisions. In fact, a study found that 60 percent of the companies surveyed maintained a code of ethics,

code of ethics
A guideline to help marketing managers and other employees make better decisions.

EXHIBIT 3.7

Unethical Practices Marketing Managers May Have to Deal With

- Entertainment and gift giving
- False or misleading advertising
- Misrepresentation of goods, services, and company capabilities
- Lies told to customers in order to get the sale
- Manipulation of data (falsifying or misusing statistics or information)
- Misleading product or service warranties
- Unfair manipulation of customers
- Exploitation of children and/or disadvantaged groups
- Stereotypical portrayals of women, minority groups, and senior citizens
- Invasion of customer privacy
- Sex-oriented advertising appeals
- Product or service deception
- Unsafe products or services
- Price deception
- Price discrimination
- Unfair remarks and inaccurate statements about competitors
- Smaller amounts of product in the same-size packages

33 percent offered ethics training, and 33 percent employed an ethics officer.[33] Some of the most highly praised codes of ethics are those of Boeing, Hewlett-Packard, Johnson & Johnson, and Norton Company.

Creating ethics guidelines has several advantages:

- It helps employees identify what their firm recognizes as acceptable business practices.
- A code of ethics can be an effective internal control on behaviour, which is more desirable than external controls like government regulation.
- A written code helps employees avoid confusion when determining whether their decisions are ethical.
- The process of formulating the code of ethics facilitates discussion among employees about what is right and wrong and ultimately leads to better decisions.

Businesses, however, must be careful not to make their code of ethics too vague or too detailed. Codes that are too vague give little or no guidance to employees in their day-to-day activities. Codes that are too detailed encourage employees to substitute rules for judgment. For instance, if employees are involved in questionable behaviour, they may use the absence of a written rule as a reason to continue behaving that way, even though their conscience may be saying no. The checklist in Exhibit 3.8 is an example of a simple but helpful set of ethical guidelines. Following the checklist will not guarantee the "rightness" of a decision, but it will improve the chances that the decision will be ethical.

Although many companies have issued policies on ethical behaviour, marketing managers must still put the policies into effect. They must address the classic "matter of degree" issue. For example, marketing researchers must often resort to deception to obtain unbiased answers to their research questions. Asking for a few minutes of a respondent's time is dishonest if the researcher knows the interview will last 45 minutes. Not only must management post a code of ethics, but it must also give examples of what is ethical and unethical for each item in the code. Moreover, top management must stress to all employees the importance of adhering to the company's code of ethics. Without a detailed code of ethics and top management's

ON LINE

University of British Columbia Centre for Applied Ethics

Research corporate codes of ethics through the Applied Ethics Resources page. Compare the codes of three companies. What common themes do you find?

http://www.ethics.ubc.ca/resources/business

EXHIBIT 3.8

Ethics Checklist

- Does the decision benefit one person or group but hurt or not benefit other individuals or groups? In other words, is my decision fair to all concerned?
- Would individuals or groups, particularly customers, be upset if they knew about my decision?
- Has important information been overlooked because my decision was made without input from other knowledgeable individuals or groups?
- Does my decision presume that my company is an exception to a common practice in this industry and that I, therefore, have the authority to break a rule?
- Would my decision offend or upset qualified job applicants?
- Will my decision create conflict between individuals or groups within the company?
- Will I have to pull rank or use coercion to implement my decision?
- Would I prefer to avoid the consequences of my decision?
- Did I avoid truthfully answering any of the above questions by telling myself that the risks of getting caught are low or that I could get away with the potentially unethical behaviour?

support, creating ethical guidelines becomes an empty exercise. A recent survey of 2,300 employees of large corporations found that 75 percent had observed violations of the law or company standards in the previous 12 months.

Among other things, workers noted sexual harassment, conflicts of interest, employment discrimination, deceptive sales practices, unsafe working conditions, and environmental breaches. "People are not reporting misconduct because they are not encouraged to do so," says Richard Girgenti, a KPMG executive. The study found that nearly 75 percent of workers believed cynicism, low morale, and indifference were to blame for misconduct.[34] Many of these concerns have been addressed by the Professional Standards Committee of the Canadian Marketing Association (see http://www.the-cma.org).

>> CORPORATE SOCIAL RESPONSIBILITY

Discuss corporate social responsibility

Ethics and social responsibility are closely intertwined. Besides questioning tobacco companies' ethics, one might ask whether they are acting in a socially responsible manner when they promote tobacco. Are companies that produce low-cost handguns socially responsible in light of the fact that these guns are used in the majority of inner-city crimes? **Corporate social responsibility** is a business's concern for society's welfare. This concern is demonstrated by managers who consider both the long-range best interests of the company and the company's relationship to the society within which it operates.

corporate social responsibility
Business's concern for society's welfare.

pyramid of corporate social responsibility
A model that suggests that corporate social responsibility is composed of economic, legal, ethical, and philanthropic responsibilities and that the firm's economic performance supports the entire structure.

One theorist suggests that total corporate social responsibility has four components: economic, legal, ethical, and philanthropic.[35] The **pyramid of corporate social responsibility,** shown in Exhibit 3.9, portrays economic performance as the foundation for the other three responsibilities. At the same time that it pursues profits (economic responsibility), however, a business is expected to obey the law (legal responsibility); to do what is right, just, and fair (ethical responsibilities); and to be a good corporate citizen (philanthropic responsibility). These four components are distinct but together constitute the whole. Still, if the company doesn't make a profit, then the other three responsibilities are moot.

Many companies are already working to make the world a better place to live. Consider these examples:

- The LeBlanc Estate Winery in Harrow, Ontario, grows grapes organically, relying on natural pest control.
- Ben & Jerry's Ice Cream uses unbleached paper in its cartons and purchases only steroid-free milk.[36]
- Talisman Energy, a Calgary-based oil company, has developed a code of conduct to govern its activities with regard to how people and the environment are treated (see www.talisman-energy.com).[37]

ON LINE

Consumers' Association of Canada

Privacy Commissioner of Canada

What can companies learn from visiting the websites for the Consumers' Association of Canada and the Privacy Commissioner of Canada? Can these sites help companies to be more ethical and moral in their business operations?

http://www.consumer.ca

http://www.privcom.gc.ca

EXHIBIT 3.9
Pyramid of Corporate Social Responsibility

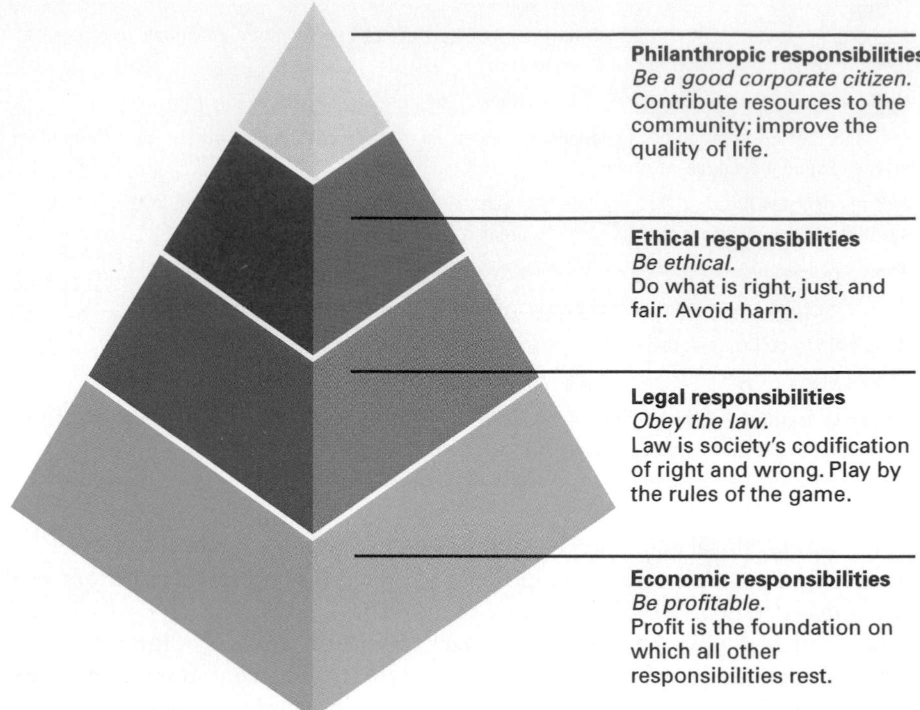

Contribute resources to the community; improve the quality of life.

Law is society's codification of right and wrong. Play by the rules of the game.

Bob Nardelli, CEO of The Home Depot, working with associates on Habitat for Humanity build, Atlanta 2002
"Roll Up Your Sleeves and Join Me"
Volunteerism is something all of us at The Home Depot understand and embrace. It's been a part of our culture from the beginning. Collectively and individually, we have always returned to our communities a fair measure of what we have earned. We are 250,000 strong. We know we can make a difference. So can you. Volunteer in your community today.

TEAMDEPOT

© 2002, Homer TLC, Inc.

COURTESY OF THE HOME DEPOT

Corporate social responsibility has become a part of Canadian expectations. Bob Nardelli's Home Depot was ranked as having the highest level of social responsibility. Nardelli is pictured here working on a Habitat for Humanity house with Home Depot associates.

- Abbott Laboratories funds free hearing examinations for the elderly at EarCare Clinics.[38]
- Burger King has donated millions of dollars to assist the victims of natural disasters around the world.[39]

A study conducted recently ranked Home Depot, Johnson & Johnson, DaimlerChrysler, and McDonald's as companies exhibiting the highest levels of social responsibility.[40] But does being socially responsible create additional demand for a firm's products or services? The answer is not always easy. In some cases it may be "yes" while in others it may be "no." For example, one factor is the issue on which the company focuses, such as health, education, or charitable giving, and how the issue is perceived by the company's target market. Other factors are product/service quality and how the target market perceives the importance of social responsibility.[41]

Multinational companies have important social responsibilities. Often a corporation can be a dynamic force for social change in host countries. Multinational companies played a major role in breaking down apartheid in South Africa through the economic pressure they exerted on the South African government. Over 300 apartheid laws had been enacted in South Africa based purely on the colour of one's skin. Mixed marriages were banned, schools were segregated, and Blacks were forced to live in the most arid regions of the country. To protest apartheid, many multinational companies closed their South African operations. Other companies refused to trade with South

Africa. These actions seriously impeded South Africa's economy, causing the government to undertake major social reforms. After apartheid officially ended, the multinational companies resumed their operations in South Africa.

>> CONNECT IT

Look back at the story about Levi's. You should now understand that the external environment affects all firms and their marketing mixes. All of the other external variables, in addition to demographics and social factors, can influence Levi's sales. Political and legal factors may block the importation of Levi's into some countries. Changing labour laws can increase production costs. Boom periods and recessions can also affect sales. And, of course, competition is the single biggest factor affecting Levi's performance in Canada.

REVIEW IT

1 **Discuss the external environment of marketing and explain how it affects a firm.** The external marketing environment consists of social, demographic, economic, technological, political and legal, and competitive variables. Marketers generally cannot control the elements of the external environment. Instead, they must understand how the external environment is changing and the impact of that change on the target market. Then marketing managers can create a marketing mix to effectively meet the needs of target customers.

1.1 What is the purpose of environmental scanning? Give an example.

1.2 TEAM Form six teams and make each one responsible for one of the uncontrollable elements in the marketing environment. Your boss, the company president, has asked each team to provide one-year and five-year forecasts of the major trends the firm will face. The firm is in the telecommunications equipment industry. It has no plans to become a telecommunications service provider like, for example, MCI. Each team should use the library, the Internet, and other data sources to make its forecasts. Each team member should examine a minimum of one data source. The team should then pool its data and prepare its recommendation. A spokesperson for each team should present the findings to the class.

2 **Describe the social factors that affect marketing.** Within the external environment, social factors are perhaps the most difficult for marketers to anticipate. Several major social trends are currently shaping marketing strategies. First, people of all ages have a broader range of interests, defying traditional consumer profiles. Second, changing gender roles are bringing more women into the workforce and increasing the number of men who shop. Third, a greater number of dual-career families has led to a poverty of time, creating a demand for timesaving goods and services.

2.1 Every country has a set of core values and beliefs. These values may vary somewhat from region to region of the nation. Identify five core values for your area of the country. Clip magazine advertisements that reflect these values and bring them to class.

3 **Explain the importance to marketing managers of current demographic trends.** Today, several basic demographic patterns are influencing marketing mixes. Because the population is growing at a slower rate, marketers can no longer rely on profits from generally expanding markets. Marketers are also faced with increasingly experienced consumers among the younger generations, many of whom are "turned off" by traditional marketing mixes. And because the population is also growing older, marketers are offering more products that appeal to middle-aged and elderly markets.

3.1 Baby boomers in Canada are aging. Describe how this might affect the marketing mix for the following:

a. Health clubs
b. McDonald's
c. Whirlpool Corporation
d. Niagara Falls
e. Zellers

3.2 WRITING You have been asked to address a local Chamber of Commerce on the subject of "Generation Y." Prepare an outline for your talk.

3.3 How should Ford Motor Company market differently to Generation Y, Generation X, and baby boomers?

4 **Explain the importance to marketing managers of multiculturalism and growing ethnic markets.** Multiculturalism occurs when all major ethnic groups in an area are roughly equally represented. Growing multiculturalism makes the marketer's task more challenging. Canada is not a melting pot but numerous mini-melting pots. Ethnic minorities are the fastest-growing segment of the population. Many companies are now creating departments and committees to effectively target multicultural market segments. The heavy use of the Internet by minorities has resulted in the creation of many websites and portals tailored specifically for the needs of each group.

4.1 Explain how the Internet is having an impact on multicultural marketing.

4.2 WRITING Go to the library and look up a minority market such as the Asian or Indian market. Write a memo to your boss that details the many sub-markets within the minority segment.

5 **Identify consumer and marketer reactions to the state of the economy.** Marketers are currently targeting the increasing number of consumers with higher discretionary income by offering higher-quality, higher-priced goods and services. During a time of inflation, marketers generally attempt to maintain level pricing to avoid losing customer brand loyalty. During times of recession, many marketers maintain or reduce prices to counter the effects of decreased demand; they also concentrate on increasing production efficiency and improving customer service.

5.1 Explain how consumers' buying habits may change during a recessionary period.

5.2 WRITING Periods of inflation require firms to alter their marketing mix. Suppose a recent economic forecast predicts inflation to be almost 10 percent during the next 18 months. Your company manufactures hand tools for the home gardener. Write a memo to the company president explaining how the firm may have to alter its marketing mix.

6 **Identify the impact of technology on a firm.** Monitoring new technology is essential to keeping up with competitors in today's marketing environment. Information technology and the Internet have been driving increased productivity for the past decade. Without innovation, companies can't compete in global markets.

6.1 Give three examples of how technology has benefited marketers. Also, give several examples of how firms have been hurt by not keeping up with technological changes.

7 **Discuss the political and legal environment of marketing.** All marketing activities are subject to municipal, provincial, and federal laws and the rulings of

regulatory agencies. Marketers are responsible for remaining aware of and abiding by such regulations.

7.1 Governments have been both praised and criticized for their regulation of marketing activities. To what degree do you think the government should regulate marketing? Explain your position.

8 **Explain the basics of foreign and domestic competition.** The competitive environment encompasses the number of competitors a firm must face, the relative sizes of the competitors, how the companies compete, and the degree of interdependence within the industry. Declining population growth, rising costs, and shortages of resources have heightened domestic competition. Yet small firms that have an effective marketing mix continue to be able to compete with the giants. Meanwhile, dwindling international barriers are bringing in more foreign competitors and offering expanding opportunities for Canadian companies abroad.

8.1 Explain how the nature of competition is changing in Canada.

8.2 Might there be times when a company becomes too competitive? If so, what could be the consequences?

9 **Describe the role of ethics and ethical decisions in business.** Business ethics may be viewed as a subset of the values of society as a whole. The ethical conduct of businesspeople is shaped by societal elements, including family, education, religion, and social movements. As members of society, businesspeople are morally obligated to consider the ethical implications of their decisions.

Ethical decision making is approached in three basic ways. The first approach examines the consequences of decisions. The second approach relies on rules and laws to guide decision making. The third approach is based on a theory of moral development that places individuals or groups in one of three developmental stages: preconventional morality, conventional morality, or postconventional morality.

Many companies develop a code of ethics to help their employees make ethical decisions. A code of ethics can help employees identify acceptable business practices, can be an effective internal control on behaviour, can help employees avoid confusion when determining whether decisions are ethical, and can facilitate discussion about what is right and wrong.

9.1 WRITING Write a paragraph discussing the ethical dilemma in the following situation and identifying possible solutions: An insurance agent forgets to get the required signature from one of her clients who is buying an automobile insurance policy. The client acknowledges the purchase by giving the agent a signed personal cheque for the full amount. To avoid embarrassment and inconvenience, the agent forges the client's signature on the insurance application and sends it to the insurance company for processing.

10 **Discuss corporate social responsibility.** Responsibility in business refers to a firm's concern for the way its decisions affect society. Social responsibility has four components: economic, legal, ethical, and philanthropic. These are intertwined, yet the most fundamental is earning a profit. If a firm does not earn a profit, the other three responsibilities are moot. Most businesspeople believe they should do more than pursue profits. Although a company must consider its economic needs first, it must also operate within the law, do what is ethical and fair, and be a good corporate citizen.

10.1 Describe at least three situations in which you would not purchase the products of a firm even though it is very socially responsible.

10.2 A firm's only responsibility to society is to earn a fair profit. Comment.

DEFINE IT

applied research 66
baby boomers 60
basic research 66
code of ethics 73
Competition Bureau 68
component lifestyles 56
corporate social responsibility 75
demography 57–58
environmental management 55
ethics 72
Generation X 60
Generation Y 59
inflation 65
morals 72
multiculturalism 62
North American Free Trade Agreement (NAFTA) 70
personalized economy 61
poverty of time 56
pyramid of corporate social responsibility 75
recession 66
self-regulation 69
target market 54

APPLY IT

Jeanette and Jeff Horowitz just inherited $175,000 from Jeanette's late uncle, David Forski. The couple had always wanted to own a franchise and, after some initial investigation, have narrowed their choices down to two. The first is FASTSIGNS, the original retail sign franchise that has hundreds of locations and is found in virtually every province. Its advantages are business customers; standard business hours; a clean, attractive retail environment; national advertising support; and operational and marketing support.

Jeanette and Jeff's other opportunity is a Subway sandwich franchise, a highly rated sandwich system with over 13,000 restaurants. Its key advantages are a simple system with no cooking, low initial investment, quality products, and complete training and support.

QUESTIONS

1. What are some of the threats in the external environment that Jeanette and Jeff may face?
2. What factors in the external environment may create an opportunity for Jeff and Jeanette?
3. Go to **http://www.subway.ca** and **http://www.fastsigns.ca** and determine which franchise is more appealing to you. Why?

THINK ABOUT IT

Jane Barksdale has designed a line of clothing targeted toward the Asian market. The items are sold only by catalogue and on the Internet. She thinks that she can increase sales by publicizing that an Asian Canadian owns the firm and that all the employees are Asian. Jane is not Asian and neither are most of the employees. She needs a high level of sales to pay her bank loan and remain in business.

QUESTIONS

1. Should Jane claim that she is Asian?
2. Does the CMA Code of Ethics address this issue? Go to **http://www.the-cma.org/consumer/ethics.cfm** and review the code. Then write a brief paragraph on what the CMA Code of Ethics contains that relates to Jane Barksdale's dilemma.

TRY IT

Sunday Shopping in Nova Scotia

During the six weeks leading up to Christmas in 2003, for the first time in over 10 years, retail stores in Nova Scotia were open on Sunday. Retailers in communities bordering New Brunswick, which has Sunday shopping, were losing some weekend trade, so the decision by the Tory government to experiment for six weeks with Sunday shopping was welcome news to a number of businesses.

Armed with results from a $98,000 market research survey indicating that 54.4 percent of Nova Scotians were in favour of Sunday shopping, the government determined that a six-week Sunday shopping trial period would be undertaken in November and December 2003, and that a plebiscite on eliminating the ban on Sunday shopping would be held in October 2004.

The news of Sunday shopping in Nova Scotia was greeted with mixed feelings. "Totally against it," stated Bruce Roberts, owner of Hub Cycle in Truro. "My employees are against it as well." Sandy Murray of Sandy's Fashions for Men was also dismayed: "It's just going to cost us more to operate." Greg Johnson of Inglis Jewellers said: "From a moral standpoint I'm not in favour of Sunday shopping."

Most retailers in Nova Scotia, however, intended to be open on the Sundays leading up to Christmas. "We're definitely excited about it," said Toys "R" Us manager Patty Sampson. "The public wants it, so it can only be beneficial."

For those retailers who opened Sundays during the trial period, results looked quite positive. Karen Cormier of Margolians, a popular department store in Amherst, Nova Scotia, said that the stove didn't have enough staff on hand for all the business it got on the first Sunday. Paul Hawkes, president of the Amherst and Area Chamber of Commerce, was pleased with the number of retailers who opened and indicated that Sundays in downtown Amherst were as busy as Saturdays.[42]

QUESTIONS

1. Should the government or businesses decide whether they should open on Sundays? Explain your answer.
2. How big a role should government play in business operation?
3. If a majority of Nova Scotians wants to shop on Sunday, shouldn't all retailers open on Sunday?
4. If a business owner and the employees want to remain closed on Sundays, but that business starts losing sales to competitors who are open, what should that business do?

FLIP IT

GRADEMAKER

Flip to Chapter 3 in your *Grademaker Study Guide* for more review opportunities, including the pretest, vocabulary review, study test questions, marketing applications and scenarios, and more. Can you draw the marketing environment? Can you close your book and list the uncontrollable factors in the external environment? Open your Study Guide to find out how much you know—or don't know.

CLICK IT

The *Marketing* website is rich with materials to help you review and master marketing concepts. Check your knowledge with the free quizzes, practise key terms using the crossword puzzles, or review key concepts using the Microsoft® PowerPoint® slides. Also on the website are updated weblinks to companies mentioned in this chapter, Internet exercises, career marketing information, and much much more! Go to http://www.lamb3e.nelson.com, read the material, and follow the convenient links.

WATCH IT

Ben & Jerry's: "We Do Good by Doing Good"

In addition to making a quality product, Ben & Jerry's is trying to make the world a better place. The gourmet ice cream manufacturer makes premium ice cream with catchy names like Cherry Garcia (after the Grateful Dead icon) and specialty ice cream like Mummy's Tomb at Halloween, and uses only top-quality ingredients in all of its products. But besides making ice cream, the company founders, Ben Cohen and Jerry Greenfield, are trying to get everyone to recognize that we have a responsibility to improve the world we all share. Ben and Jerry like to refer to this philosophy as "caring capitalism."

Caring capitalism goes beyond simply writing cheques to good causes, as many large corporations do. Ben & Jerry's links the company to others that wish to improve the quality of life for everyone and actively support many social and environmental causes. For example, on the Ben & Jerry's website (http://www.benjerry.com) you will find pleas to help fight global warming and a listing of 50 ways in which you can support global peace. The site includes suggestions about how to get involved in the causes, and links to other organizations promoting the cause. By the way, the Ben & Jerry Foundation also writes cheques, donating over $1.5 million every year to various causes.

Another way in which Ben & Jerry's is involved is through a program called PartnerShops, which are Ben & Jerry's franchises that are owned by charitable and nonprofit organizations. There are now over 450 PartnerShop franchises all around the world (check the Ben & Jerry's website for locations in Canada near you that you may want to support).

Another way to tie together social and business values is to buy products from "socially aligned" suppliers. The brownies in the Ben & Jerry Chocolate Fudge Brownie Frozen Yogurt are made by Greyston Bakery, a nonprofit firm that trains homeless and low-income people for better-paying jobs. As part of the minority supplier program of the company, Ben & Jerry's encourages its pecan processor to use a farm co-op dedicated to employing minorities. About one-third of Ben & Jerry's purchases reflect this social mission.

Caring for the planet is another company concern. The only milk and cream that go into the ice cream comes from the St. Alban's co-op of family farmers. These dairies do not use rBGH, a growth hormone believed to be bad for cows and bad for the future of small-scale family dairies. Another bold, and costly, step was the elimination of bleach in the company packaging. The industry standard container was tested and found to be environmentally poor. The company invested large sums of money to perfect chlorine-free packaging. While the more environmentally friendly packaging is more costly to manufacture, it is what Ben & Jerry's uses.

Still, from time to time, the company makes decisions that do not reflect a social conscience. Ben & Jerry's discontinued the purchase of organic fruits and cancelled its line of organic ice cream. The organic fruit was too costly, resulting in prices for the organic ice cream that were too high. In this case, were social mission values being sacrificed for short-term economic considerations?

In other cases, some of the social causes advocated by Ben & Jerry's are not to everyone's liking. Several websites advocate a boycott of Ben & Jerry's due to disagreements with social positions taken by the company (see, for example, http://www.officer.com/faulkner/boycott.htm).

Where should Ben & Jerry's loyalties be placed? Should the company always promote social causes? If so, who is to decide which causes? What does Ben & Jerry's owe to its shareholders? These people have invested in the company to earn a return on their investment. Should Ben & Jerry's accept losses on organic ice cream because it is the right thing to do, even though it decreases the value of shareholder investments? It is not always easy to answer these questions. Can a company continue to "do good" if it loses money and goes out of business? This isn't likely to happen to Ben & Jerry's in the near future, by the way, as company sales have now surpassed $300 million.

QUESTIONS

1. What do you think of the Ben & Jerry's philosophy of "caring capitalism"? Can Ben & Jerry's truly follow its social mission if there is always an economic argument that leads to a different conclusion?
2. Do you think that it is in the shareholders' best interests to select minority and disadvantaged suppliers when there may be other, lower-cost suppliers?
3. What do you think of Ben & Jerry's decision to drop the line of organic ice creams?
4. Do you think that Ben & Jerry's could grow faster, or be more profitable, if it dropped its social mission?

SUGGESTED INFORMATION SOURCES

Ben & Jerry's 2003 Annual Report.
http://www.benjerry.com
http://www.officer.com/faulkner/boycott.htm

MARKETING MISCUES

Is the Competitive Environment Too Competitive for Air Canada?

Air Canada, established by the Parliament of Canada in 1937, has long been Canada's largest airline. Globally, Air Canada serves over 700 destinations in 128 countries. In 2003, Air Canada generated $8.368 billion in revenue but suffered a loss of $1.867 billion. On April 1, 2003, Air Canada obtained an order from the Ontario Superior Court, providing creditor protection under the Companies' Creditors Arrangement Act (CCAA).

Air Canada's losses are not due to Canadians flying less. In fact, Canadians are flying more. It's just that Air Canada is carrying fewer of us. After taking over Canadian Airlines, Air Canada's share of the domestic market was well in excess of 90 percent. As recently as the first quarter of 2002, Air Canada still held 82 percent of the domestic market. By the first quarter of 2003, Air Canada's share had fallen to 69.6 percent; this fell further to 59.2 percent in the first quarter of 2004.

Air Canada's major rivals, Calgary-based WestJet Airlines Ltd. and Jetsgo Corp. of Montreal, are garnering growing shares of the air passenger market. Competition in the Canadian airline market is certainly having a major impact on Canada's largest air carrier. For the first quarter of 2004, WestJet's market share had grown to 29.4 percent from 25.6 percent in 2003, while Jetsgo's share grew to 11.3 percent from just 4.7 percent in 2003.

And the competitive environment continues to get tougher for Air Canada. Traditionally, the Toronto-Montreal-Ottawa triangle has been one of the most profitable markets for Air Canada. However, WestJet has recently boosted the number of flights it operates in this triangle and Jetsgo has just launched a new hourly shuttle between Montreal and Toronto.

What has been the problem with Air Canada? First, of course, originally being a Crown corporation, without a clear profit incentive, Air Canada added too many employees and built too high a cost base. In addition, even with privatization, Air Canada was, at first, a near monopoly in the Canadian market and was little concerned with taking on the efficiencies necessary in a competitive marketplace.

When competition, in the form of start-up airlines like WestJet, entered the market, Air Canada at first ignored it as no threat and then was very slow to react. As WestJet, and others, began to grow, entering more and more markets served by Air Canada, offering no frills service with lower fares, Air Canada began to lose passengers in greater numbers to the start-ups.

It is estimated that operating costs of airlines like WestJet and Jetsgo are approximately 50 percent lower than Air Canada's. This fact allows these airlines to charge lower fares and still make a profit.

What is Air Canada doing? Air Canada has initiated its own discount airlines, Zip and Jazz, to compete on a fare basis with WestJet and Jetsgo. Air Canada is seeking new investment to improve its facilities while it remains under creditor protection. Air Canada is adding more international routes. Air Canada is extracting lower wage agreements from its pilots and other unions to reduce costs. Air Canada has expanded its reward seat program to offer better selections for Air Canada frequent flyers. And Air Canada has initiated a lawsuit against WestJet, alleging the theft of confidential data on passenger seats sold on Air Canada flights, by a former Air Canada employee now working for WestJet. The confidential information, according to Air Canada, allowed WestJet to determine the most profitable routes operated by Air Canada. WestJet, allegedly, would then add new flights on these routes.

Questions

1. What do you think of the competitive environment in the Canadian airline industry?
2. Are airfares alone the key to success in the airline industry?
3. Does Air Canada seem to have a marketing strategy?
4. What else does Air Canada need to do to become competitive?

Source: Keith McArthur, "Rivals Grab Bigger Piece of Air Canada's Market Share," *The Globe and Mail*, April 21, 2004, B1, B6; Keith McArthur, "Air Canada Boosting Reward Seat Program," *The Globe and Mail*, April 23, 2004, B1, B2; Paul Waldie and John Partridge, "Allegations of Espionage, Moles Fly in Air Canada-WestJet Spat," *The Globe and Mail*, April 8, 2004, B1, B24; and http://www.aircanada.ca.

CRITICAL THINKING CASE

Hewlett-Packard's CoolTown Puts Everyone and Everything on the Web

While much of the business press focused on the merger between computer giants Hewlett-Packard and Compaq Computer, the techno wizards at Hewlett-Packard were spending their time on a new experiment. Called "CoolTown," the experiment attempts to bridge the physical and virtual worlds and showcases HP's product offerings in building this bridge. Given HP's complex product line, which has led to an unclear image in the marketplace, the jury is still out as to whether CoolTown will succeed at conveying the company's vision for the future in the wireless era.

The Company

In 1939, Bill Hewlett and David Packard founded Hewlett-Packard. Hewlett and Packard believed that HP existed to invent the "useful and significant." To them, the term *useful* meant contributions that would free businesses and consumers to focus on what mattered most. The term *significant* was indicative of HP's vow not only to make a profit but to also make a difference. The bottom line is that HP will help create a world where technology works for consumers and not vice versa. Consistent with this vision is the set of corporate objectives, referred to as "The HP Way." The company's objectives focus on seven major areas: profit, customers, fields of interest, growth, company people, management, and citizenship.

At the beginning of this century, HP was listed by *Fortune* magazine as one of the 20 largest corporations in the world. Carly Fiorina is CEO. The company has almost 90,000 employees and revenues approaching $75 billion. Hewlett-Packard operates a major manufacturing and research centre in Toronto and is the largest seller of PCs in Canada. Product offerings include printers, personal computers, servers, wireless devices, software, and consulting services. The company refers to its vision as service-centric computing, meaning that information technologies are delivered, managed, and purchased as services. To fulfil this vision, HP focuses on three key areas of invention: (1) enabling intelligent, connected devices and environment, (2) enabling an always-on Internet infrastructure, and (3) enabling a new generation of applications delivered as e-services.

When Fiorina took the helm of the company in 1999, she envisioned a reinvention of HP. At that time, HP had a major market niche with its printers but was lacklustre in the remainder of its markets. Many felt that the company was not only old-fashioned but also resistant to change. In a major move to reinvent HP, Fiorina spearheaded the merger with Compaq Computer. The merger would be a first step toward HP becoming a technology solutions provider.

Marketing Deficiencies

Although the merger between HP and Compaq may take the company in the technology solutions direction, some are concerned about the longer-term implications of HP's weak marketing. HP is not known for its ability to tell a compelling story in the marketplace. Its image as a stodgy, old company is not expected to fare well in the new-age economy. While boasting a strong product line, the company has not been able to excite the marketplace. With expectations of significant growth and sales reaching $100 billion by 2006, the company will have to improve its marketing efforts.

CoolTown

In June 2001, HP launched CoolTown. This project is a mock city that allows users to experience life in a technological environment. The goal of CoolTown is to make this futuristic environment transparent to the user. CoolTown visitors can experience how wireless technologies will change their lives.

Four components work in sync to make CoolTown functional: the Internet, handheld electronics, wireless networks, and computer intelligence. Combining these ingredients, users can see what a typical wireless day would be like. Examples include a CoolTown bookstore that recognizes customers and recommends new books, a CoolTown bus line that pinpoints bus locations so that the rider does not get to the bus stop too early or too late, a CoolTown conference room where the speaker can control the projector remotely, and the CoolTown museum where a visitor can purchase products on-line as they are being viewed at the exhibit. Basically, CoolTown allows smart devices to link to other smart devices that are using the same language.

Of course, all of the technology employed in CoolTown is HP technology. The Coolbase Appliance Server is an embedded server from HP, Coolkit enables developers to build applications to run on Cool-base, E-Squirt allows mobile phones or PDAs to direct e-services to other devices, and Beacons are handheld devices that broadcast to other wireless units (for example, PDAs and phones). Naturally, when HP customers are touring the CoolTown showroom, HP's Jornada handheld computers are used to navigate through the experience.

CoolTown, in conjunction with HP's Mobile E-Services Bazaar, has allowed HP to tap into new markets. Rather than focus on internal uses for CoolTown products, HP now can partner with wireless application engineers, who can use HP products when they develop e-services for their customers. The hope is that the CoolTown experience will interest customers in purchasing HP's consulting services to help with the wireless integration process.

HP as Net Innovator

While the Hewlett-Packard Company of this century sees itself as an innovator, this image is very different from the stodgy company it became during the late twentieth century. It is unlikely that today's marketplace would identify HP on it short list of Internet innovators. Can HP compete with the likes of Microsoft, Oracle, and Sun Microsystems? How can HP merge its engineering expertise with a marketing message that will change its image in the customer's mind?

Questions

1. What is HP's core business? How did the company build on this core business?
2. Does HP's success depend on its engineering prowess or its marketing expertise?
3. Describe the component parts of CoolTown and explain how these integrated parts could be used in everyday life. How does CoolTown help HP change its image in the marketplace?
4. Is the "new" HP consistent with the company's original reason for being in existence (to invent the "useful and significant")? Why or why not?

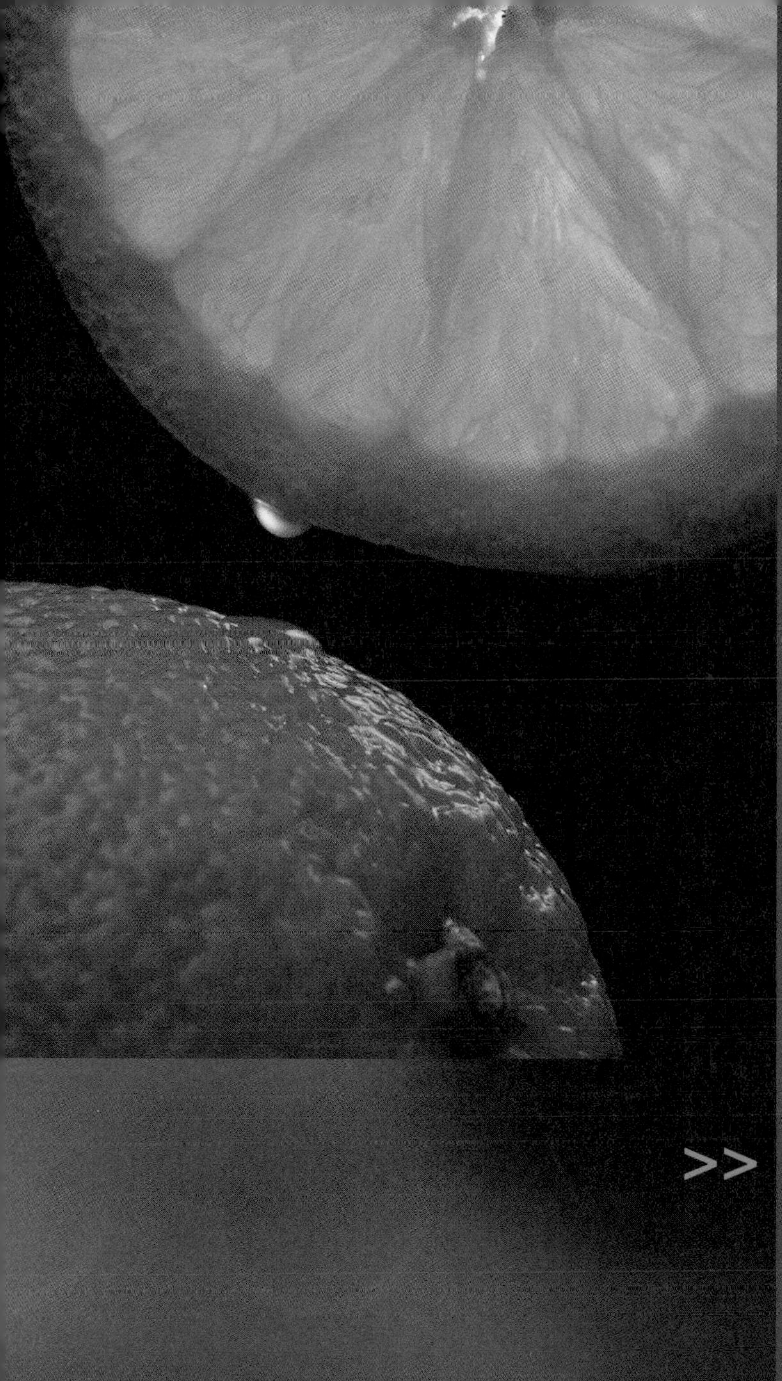

>> Analyzing Marketing Opportunities

part 2

chapter 4

Consumer Decision Making

>> LEARNING OBJECTIVES

1. Explain why marketing managers should understand consumer behaviour
2. Analyze the components of the consumer decision-making process
3. Explain the consumer's postpurchase evaluation process
4. Identify the types of consumer buying decisions and discuss the significance of consumer involvement
5. Identify and understand the cultural factors that affect consumer buying decisions
6. Identify and understand the social factors that affect consumer buying decisions
7. Identify and understand the individual factors that affect consumer buying decisions
8. Identify and understand the psychological factors that affect consumer buying decisions

>> Observing changes in consumer behaviour is often a risky task involving picking up on a small blip on a marketer's radar that over time becomes more and more obvious. But sometimes marketers decide to respond to change by resisting it, or even counterattacking it. This is how Harvey's Restaurants has decided to respond to the "Healthy Trend" in fast food. While Wendy's trumpets its line of healthy garden salads and McDonald's Restaurants promotes its "light menu" choices, Harvey's is promoting "Long Live the Grill."

The trend in fast food these days has been to respond to the "poor nutrition" image that is characteristic of the industry. The World Health Organization has gone so far as to state that there is an obesity epidemic in the developed world. Statistics Canada supports this contention by reporting that 14.9 percent of Canadians aged 20 to 64 were considered obese in the years 2000 and 2001.

Foods with excessive empty calories, high fat and low vitamin and mineral counts, and just plain unhealthy ingredients, describe a few of the offerings of fast-food restaurants. In New York, class action suits were launched in 2002 against McDonald's, Wendy's, KFC, and Burger King citing them for responsibility for their patrons' unhealthy eating. Although these suits were dismissed, this kind of legal attack does not portend well for fast-food retailing.

The response of McDonald's and its competitors to this consumer environment has been to make subtle changes to food ingredients and food preparation methods combined with healthier menu choices and low-fat offerings. McCain Foods of Canada, a major producer of French fries, has developed a non-hydrogenated French fry. A further response by food marketers is to provide more detailed labelling and nutrition information. It is even possible that food marketers may go so far as to give actual "warning labels" on their food products!

Despite all of this, Harvey's has decided to tilt the other way based on market research that says there is a market among men for the "old style hamburger." The result is the Big Harv, a six-ounce hamburger that is being promoted on the positioning statement of "Long Live the Grill." Harvey's has always catered to a segment of customers that want a grilled burger with custom garnishing. Harvey's wants to continue to serve this market with a taste and quality approach as opposed to competing on price the way McDonald's and Burger King do. In addition, despite the vocalization about health concerns, the reality is that a large number of consumers simply "love" junk food.[1]

What do you think? Should Harvey's swim upstream and ignore the "healthy" trend? What motivates fast food consumers today? What factors affect their buying decisions? Questions like these will be considered as you read this chapter on the consumer decision-making process and its influences.

ON LINE 

How concerned are health authorities about obesity? Visit the World Health Organization and Health Canada to find out. How are fast-food marketers responding to this trend? Visit the McDonald's, Wendy's, and Harvey's websites and see.

http://www.who.int

http://www.hc-sc.gc.ca

http://www.mcdonalds.ca

http://www.wendys.com

http://www.harveys.ca

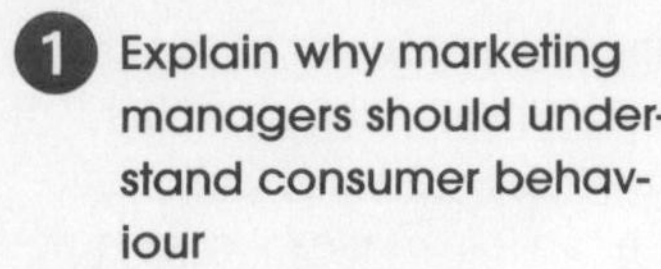

1 Explain why marketing managers should understand consumer behaviour

>> THE IMPORTANCE OF UNDERSTANDING CONSUMER BEHAVIOUR

consumer behaviour
Processes a consumer uses to make purchase decisions, as well as to use and dispose of purchased goods or services; also includes factors that influence purchase decisions and product use.

Consumers' product and service preferences are constantly changing. In order to address this constant state of flux and to create a proper marketing mix for a well-defined market, marketing managers must have a thorough knowledge of consumer behaviour. **Consumer behaviour** describes how consumers make purchase decisions and how they use and dispose of the purchased goods or services. The study of consumer behaviour also includes an analysis of factors that influence purchase decisions and product use.

Understanding how consumers make purchase decisions can help marketing managers in several ways. For example, if a manager knows through research that gas mileage is the most important attribute for a certain target market, the manufacturer can redesign the product to meet that criterion. If the firm cannot change the design in the short run, it can use promotion in an effort to change consumers' decision-making criteria. For example, an automobile manufacturer can advertise a car's maintenance-free features and sporty European style while downplaying gas mileage.

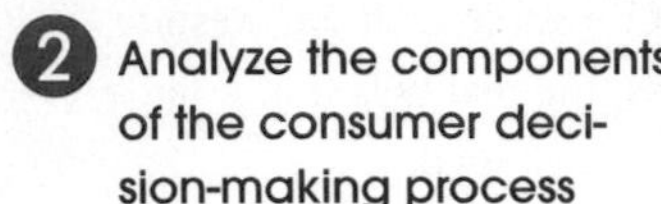

2 Analyze the components of the consumer decision-making process

>> THE CONSUMER DECISION-MAKING PROCESS

consumer decision-making process
A five-step process used by consumers when buying goods or services.

When buying products, consumers generally follow the **consumer decision-making process** shown in Exhibit 4.1: (1) need recognition, (2) information search, (3) evaluation of alternatives, (4) purchase, and (5) postpurchase behaviour. These five steps represent a general process that moves the consumer from recognition of a product or service need to the evaluation of a purchase. This process is a guideline for studying how consumers make decisions. It is important to note that this guideline does not assume that consumers' decisions will proceed in order through all of the steps of the process. In fact, the consumer may end the process at any time; he or she may not even make a purchase. Explanations as to why a consumer's progression through these steps may vary are offered at the end of the chapter in the section on the types of consumer buying decisions. Before addressing this issue, we will describe each step in the process in greater detail.

Need Recognition

need recognition
Result of an imbalance between actual and desired states.

stimulus
Any unit of input affecting one or more of the five senses: sight, smell, taste, touch, hearing.

The first stage in the consumer decision-making process is need recognition. **Need recognition** occurs when consumers are faced with an imbalance between actual and desired states. For example, do you often feel thirsty after strenuous exercise? Has a television commercial for a new sports car ever made you wish you could buy it? Need recognition is triggered when a consumer is exposed to either an internal or an external **stimulus.** Hunger and thirst are *internal stimuli;* the colour of an automobile, the design of a package, a brand name mentioned by a friend, an advertisement on television, or cologne worn by a stranger are considered *external stimuli.*

A marketing manager's objective is to get consumers to recognize an imbalance between their present status and their preferred state. Advertising and sales promotion often provide this stimulus. Surveying buyer preferences provides marketers with information about consumer wants and needs that can be used to tailor products and services. For example, Procter & Gamble frequently surveys consumers regarding their wants and needs. P&G recently used the Internet to test market its new Crest Whitestrips home-bleaching kit. The test revealed that 80 percent of potential buyers were women between the ages of 35 and 54, identifying the best target market for the product. The company was then able to fine-tune its marketing plan before launching the product in North America.[2] In another example of how far P&G will go to learn about market trends, the company recently began videotaping consumers at home in its own version of reality TV to learn more about them than surveys could reveal.[3]

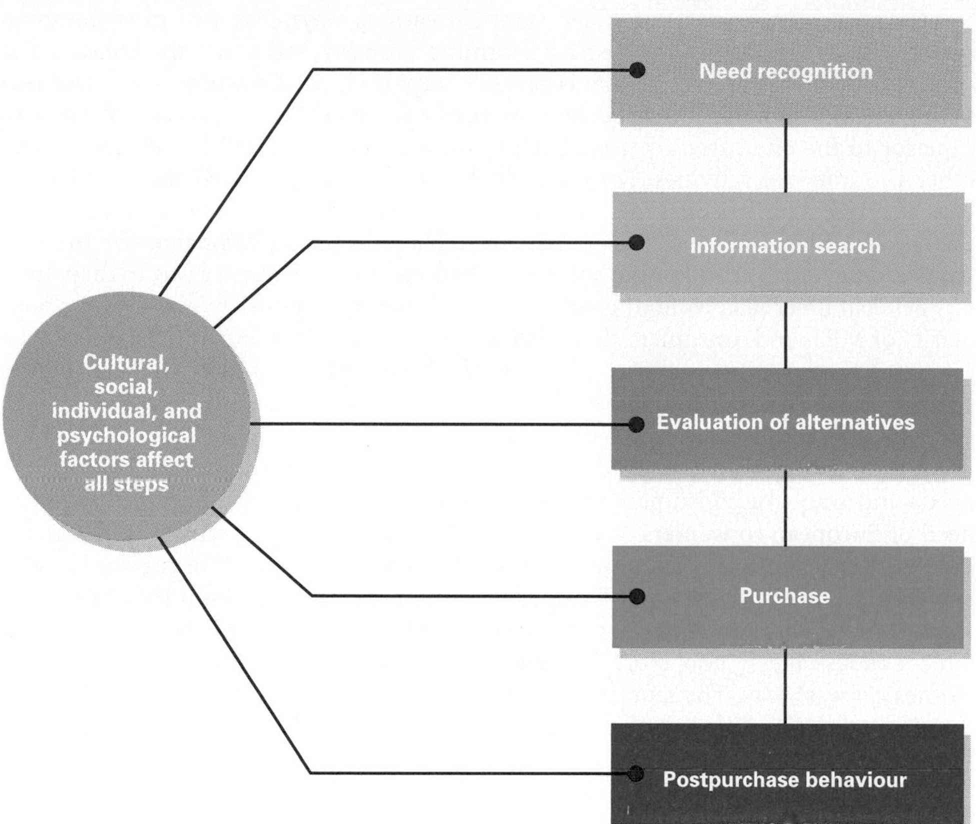

EXHIBIT 4.1
Consumer Decision-Making Process

Marketing managers can create wants on the part of the consumer. A **want** exists when someone has an unfulfilled need and has determined that a particular good or service will satisfy it. Young children may want toys, video games, and baseball equipment to meet their innate need to play and learn new skills. Teenagers may want compact discs, fashionable sneakers, and wide-leg jeans to fulfill their need of belonging. A want can be for a specific product or it can be for a certain attribute or feature of a product. For instance, adults may want ready-to-eat meals, drive-through dry cleaning service, and catalogue shopping to fulfill their need for convenience. Older consumers may want goods and services that offer convenience, comfort, and security. Remote-controlled appliances, home deliveries, speaker phones, and motorized carts are all designed for comfort and convenience. A personal transmitter that can signal an ambulance or the police in an emergency offers security for older consumers.

want
Recognition of an unfulfilled need and a product that will satisfy it.

Another way that marketers create new products and services is by observing trends in the marketplace. For example, today's youth are very conscious of popular culture and highly interested in movies and entertainment products. The Royal Canadian Mint has developed a strategy to tap into this interest by developing retail products associated with highly successful films targeted to 6- to 12-year-olds. It has developed a product line referred to as "Reel Coinz," which involves offering coin collections that feature characters and events from hit movies. Aside from coin medallions, the products have stickers and sticker booklets as well. The Royal Canadian Mint started its product line with the movie *Shrek,* which featured the voice of Canadian actor Mike Myers as the lead character Shrek. The mint followed up this offering with medallion collections associated with the films *Harry Potter and the Philosopher's Stone, The Lord of the Rings: The Fellowship of the Ring, Jurassic Park III,* and *How the Grinch Stole Christmas.* The mint has taken part in a number of joint promotions with movie studios and other retailers such as Toys "R" Us, Zellers, The Bay, and Burger King to promote and distribute their offerings. The Royal Canadian Mint is hoping to develop the ReelCoinz brand so it can tie it into the never-ending cycle of new movie releases.[4]

Consumers recognize unfulfilled wants in various ways. The two most common occur when a current product isn't performing properly and when the consumer is about to run out of something that is generally kept on hand. Consumers may also recognize unfulfilled wants if they become aware of a product whose features make it seem superior to the one currently used. Such wants are usually created by advertising and other promotional activities. For example, Dockers recently created the new Mobile Pant that offers professional men seven invisible pockets to carry their wallet, keys, cell phone, and PDA (personal digital assistant). The advertising campaign for the new pants is designed to create a need among professional men for a better way to carry their business paraphernalia without giving up their casual style. Similarly, aware of the popularity of MP3s and consumers' desire to take their music with them, more than a dozen car stereo manufacturers such as Sonicblue and Kenwood have added MP3 capabilities to their products. Other companies are also hoping to fulfill consumer needs with small portable MP3 players such as the iPod from Apple Computers.[5]

Marketers selling their products in global markets must carefully observe the needs and wants of consumers in various regions. Unilever hit on an unrecognized need of European consumers when it introduced Persil Tablets, premeasured laundry detergent in tablet form. Though the tablets are more expensive than regular laundry detergents, Unilever found that European consumers considered laundry a chore and wanted the process as simple and uncomplicated as possible. Unilever launched the tablets as less messy and more convenient to consumers tackling the pile of dirty clothes on wash day. The laundry tablets proved so popular in the United Kingdom that Unilever's Persil brand edged ahead of rival Procter & Gamble's best-selling Ariel powder detergent.[6]

Information Search

internal information search The process of recalling past information stored in the memory.

After recognizing a need or want, consumers search for information about the various alternatives available to satisfy it. An information search can occur internally, externally, or both. An **internal information search** is the process of recalling information stored in the memory. This stored information stems largely from previous experience with a product. For instance, while travelling you encounter a restaurant belonging to a chain that you tried somewhere else. By searching your memory, you can probably remember whether the food was good and in your price range.

external information search The process of seeking information in the outside environment.

nonmarketing-controlled information source A product information source that is not associated with advertising or promotion.

In contrast, an **external information search** seeks information in the outside environment. There are two basic types of external information sources: nonmarketing-controlled and marketing-controlled. A **nonmarketing-controlled information source** is not associated with marketers promoting a product. A friend might recommend an IBM personal computer because he or she bought one and likes it. Nonmarketing-controlled information sources include personal experience (trying or observing a new product); personal sources (family, friends, acquaintances, and coworkers); and public sources, such as the Canadian Standards Association (CSA), *Consumer Reports,* and other rating organizations. For instance, consumers rely heavily on doctor and pharmacist recommendations when buying over-the-counter medications, and many consumers buy an OTC drug for the first time because their pharmacist recommends it. A recent survey on new car purchases by Generation Y found these car buyers were almost twice as likely as older buyers to get information about new cars from friends and relatives. Car manufacturers would therefore be likely to focus their marketing strategy on generating enthusiasm for their models via word of mouth.[7]

marketing-controlled information source A product information source that originates with marketers promoting the product.

On the other hand, a **marketing-controlled information source** is biased toward a specific product because it originates with marketers promoting that product. Marketing-controlled information sources include mass-media advertising (radio, newspaper, television, and magazine advertising), sales promotion (contests, displays, premiums, and so forth), salespeople, product labels and packaging, and the Internet. A recent survey found that "Today's advertising is a non-stop barrage ... to 73 percent of Canadians ... But 56 percent of them are totally okay with that ... only 31 percent ... call the ceaseless bombardment of advertising unacceptable."[8] Many consumers, however, are wary about the information they receive from marketing-controlled sources, arguing that most marketing campaigns stress the attributes of the product and don't mention the faults. These sentiments tend to be stronger among better-educated and higher-income consumers. For instance, surveys showed that consumers were skeptical about quality assurance advertisements made by Bridgestone's Firestone Tires in the wake of the company's massive tire recall.[9]

Consumers rely on external nonmarketing-controlled information when buying a variety of products. For example, consumers rely heavily on the recommendations of doctors and pharmacists before buying an over-the-counter medication.

The extent to which an individual conducts an external search depends on his or her perceived risk, knowledge, prior experience, and level of interest in the good or service. Generally, as the perceived risk of the purchase increases, the consumer enlarges the search and considers more alternative brands. For instance, assume you want to buy a digital camera. The decision is a relatively risky one due to the expense and the technical nature of the camera's features, so you are motivated to search for information about models, options, and capabilities. You may decide to compare attributes of many cameras because the value of the time expended in finding data will be less than the cost of buying the wrong camera.[10] In contrast, more than 60 percent of bar patrons don't know what they will drink until seconds before they place their order, challenging the marketers of alcoholic beverages to find ways of "educating" potential customers on the spot.[11]

A consumer's knowledge about the product or service will also affect the extent of an external information search. If the consumer is knowledgeable and well informed about a potential purchase, he or she is less likely to search for additional information. In addition, the more knowledgeable the consumer is, the more efficiently he or she will conduct the search process, thereby requiring less time to search.

Another closely related factor that affects the extent of a consumer's external search is confidence in one's decision-making ability. A confident consumer not only has sufficient stored information about the product but also feels self-assured about making the right decision. People lacking this confidence will continue an information search even when they know a great deal about the product. Consumers with prior experience in buying a certain product will have less perceived risk than inexperienced consumers. Therefore, they will spend less time searching and limit the number of products that they consider.

A third factor influencing the external information search is product experience. Consumers who have had a positive prior experience with a product are more likely to limit their search to only those items related to the positive experience. For example, many consumers are loyal to Honda automobiles, which enjoy low repair rates and consequently high customer satisfaction, and they often own more than one.

Product experience can also play a major role in a consumer's decision to make a high-risk purchase. For example, TiVo, the maker of personal video recorders, found that due to the expensive and complex nature of its product, advertising was only moderately effective in generating sales. Instead, personal experience is the most important factor in the decision to purchase a PVR.[12]

Finally, the extent of the search undertaken is positively related to the amount of interest a consumer has in a product. A consumer who is more interested in a product will spend more time searching for information and alternatives. For example, suppose you are a dedicated runner who reads jogging and fitness magazines and catalogues. In searching for a new pair of running shoes, you may enjoy reading about the new brands available and spend more time and effort than other buyers in deciding on the right shoe.

evoked set (consideration set) Group of brands, resulting from an information search, from which a buyer can choose.

The consumer's information search should yield a group of brands, sometimes called the buyer's **evoked set** (or **consideration set**), which are the consumer's most preferred alternatives. From this set, the buyer will further evaluate the alternatives and make a choice. Consumers do not consider all the brands available in a product category, but they do seriously consider a much smaller set. For example, there are dozens of brands of shampoos and over 200 different models of automobiles available in Canada, yet most consumers seriously contemplate only about four shampoos and no more than five automobiles when faced with a purchase decision. Having too many choices can, in fact, confuse consumers and affect their decision to buy. In a recent survey, only 3 percent of customers who were presented with 30 varieties of jam made the decision to purchase. In contrast, 30 percent of shoppers who had only six choices made a purchase.[13]

Evaluation of Alternatives and Purchase

After getting information and constructing an evoked set of alternative products, the consumer is ready to make a decision. A consumer will use the information stored in memory and obtained from outside sources to develop a set of criteria. These standards help the consumer evaluate and compare alternatives. One way to begin narrowing the number of choices in the evoked set is to pick a product attribute and then exclude all products in the set that don't have that attribute. For instance, assume that Pam is thinking about buying a new notebook computer to replace her current desktop machine. She is interested in one with a large colour active-matrix display, a gigabyte of RAM, DVD-RW drive, and a hyperthreading processor with a speed of at least 3.8 gigahertz, so she excludes all notebooks without these features.

Another way to narrow the number of choices is to use cutoffs, or minimum or maximum levels of an attribute that an alternative must pass to be considered. Suppose Pam still must choose from a wide array of notebook computers that have active-matrix screens, 1 gigabyte of RAM, DVD-RW drives, and hyperthreading processors with 3.8-plus processor speeds. She then names another product attribute: price. Given the amount of money she has set aside for a new computer, Pam decides she cannot spend more than $2,500. Therefore, she can exclude all notebook computers priced above $2,500. A final way to narrow the choices is to rank the attributes under consideration in order of importance and evaluate the products based on how well they perform on the most important attributes. To reach a final decision, Pam would pick the most important attributes, such as processor speed and active display, weigh the merits of each, and then evaluate alternative notebook computers on those criteria.

If new brands are added to an evoked set, the consumer's evaluation of the existing brands in that set changes. As a result, certain brands in the original set may become more desirable. Suppose Pam sees two notebook computers priced at $1,999 and $2,199. At the time, she may judge the $2,199 notebook computer as too expensive and choose not to purchase it. However, if she then adds to her list of alternatives another notebook computer that is priced at $2,499, she may view the $2,199 one as less expensive and decide to purchase it.

The goal of the marketing manager is to determine which attributes have the most influence on a consumer's choice. Several attributes may collectively affect a consumer's evaluation of products. A single attribute, such as price, may not adequately explain how consumers form their evoked set. Moreover, attributes that the marketer thinks are important may not be very important to the consumer. For example, if you are buying a new car, you will first have to determine which cars are in your price range. But then you would also likely consider size, styling, and the reputation of the car manufacturer before making a final decision.

A brand name can also have a significant impact on a consumer's ultimate choice. In a recent on-line survey, Johnson & Johnson was found to have the best corporate reputation among North American companies, benefiting from its heritage as the premier maker of baby powder and shampoo. Respondents uniformly cited the familiarity and comfort they feel in using J&J products on their children. When faced with dozens of products on the drugstore shelf, consumers naturally gravitate toward J&J products. By providing consumers with a certain set of promises, brands in essence simplify the consumer decision-making process so that consumers do not have to rethink their options every time they need something.[14]

Following the evaluation of alternatives, the consumer decides which product to buy or decides not to buy a product at all. If he or she decides to make a purchase, the next step in the process is an evaluation of the product after the purchase.

Postpurchase Behaviour

3 Explain the consumer's postpurchase evaluation process

When buying products, consumers expect certain outcomes from the purchase. How well these expectations are met determines whether the consumer is satisfied or dissatisfied with the purchase. For example, a person buys a used car with somewhat low expectations for the car's actual performance. Surprisingly, the car turns out to be one of the best cars she has ever owned. Thus, the buyer's satisfaction is high, because her fairly low expectations were exceeded. On the other hand, a consumer who buys a brand-new car would expect it to perform especially well. But if the car turns out to be a lemon, she will be very dissatisfied because her high expectations have not been met. Price often creates high expectations.

For the marketer, an important element of any postpurchase evaluation is reducing any lingering doubts that the decision was sound. This is particularly important because 75 percent of all consumers say they had a bad experience in the previous year with a product or service they purchased.[15] When people recognize inconsistency between their values or opinions and their behaviour, they tend to feel an inner tension called **cognitive dissonance.** For example, suppose a consumer spends half his monthly salary on a new TV entertainment system. If he stops to think how much he has spent, he will probably feel dissonance. Dissonance occurs because the person knows the purchased product has some disadvantages as well as some advantages. In the case of the entertainment system, the disadvantage of cost battles the advantage of technological superiority.

cognitive dissonance
Inner tension that a consumer experiences after recognizing an inconsistency between behaviour and values or opinions.

Consumers try to reduce dissonance by justifying their decision. They might seek new information that reinforces positive ideas about the purchase, avoid information that contradicts their decision, or revoke the original decision by returning the product. People who have just bought a new car often read more advertisements for the newly purchased car than for other cars in order to reduce dissonance. In some instances, people deliberately seek contrary information in order to refute it and reduce dissonance. Dissatisfied customers sometimes rely on word of mouth to reduce cognitive dissonance, by letting friends and family know they are displeased.

Marketing managers can help reduce dissonance through effective communication with purchasers. For example, a customer service manager may slip a note inside the package congratulating the buyer on making a wise decision. Postpurchase letters sent by manufacturers and dissonance-reducing statements in instruction booklets may help customers feel at ease with their purchase. Advertising that displays the product's superiority over competing brands or guarantees can also help relieve the possible dissonance of someone who has already bought the product. Hyundai Auto Canada promotes "Canada's Best Warranty," which includes a five-year/100,000 km limited "Bumper to Bumper" plus 24-hour roadside assistance and a seven-year/120,000 km powertrain warranty and no deductibles. The warranty is transferable, so if the car is sold before the warranty expires, the car remains under warranty with the new owner.[16]

One way companies reduce the effects of cognitive dissonance is by offering comprehensive money-back guarantees or refund policies. Future Shop's on-line retail division offers a lowest-price guarantee and promises guaranteed safe shopping to its on-line buyers.

 Identify the types of consumer buying decisions and discuss the significance of consumer involvement

>> TYPES OF CONSUMER BUYING DECISIONS AND CONSUMER INVOLVEMENT

involvement
The amount of time and effort a buyer invests in the search, evaluation, and decision processes of consumer behaviour.

All consumer buying decisions generally fall along a continuum of three broad categories: routine response behaviour, limited decision making, and extensive decision making (see Exhibit 4.2). Goods and services in these three categories can best be described in terms of five factors: level of consumer involvement, length of time to make a decision, cost of the good or service, degree of information search, and the number of alternatives considered. The level of consumer involvement is perhaps the most significant determinant in classifying buying decisions. **Involvement** is the amount of time and effort a buyer invests in the search, evaluation, and decision processes of consumer behaviour.

routine response behaviour
The type of decision making exhibited by consumers buying frequently purchased, low-cost goods and services; requires little search and decision time.

Frequently purchased, low-cost goods and services are generally associated with **routine response behaviour.** These goods and services can also be called low-involvement products because consumers spend little time on search and decision before making the purchase. Usually, buyers are familiar with several different brands in the product category but stick with one brand. Consumers engaged in routine response behaviour normally don't experience need recognition until they are exposed to advertising or see the product displayed on a store shelf. Consumers buy first and evaluate later, whereas the reverse is true for extensive decision making. A parent, for example, will not stand at the cereal shelf in the grocery store for 20 minutes thinking about which brand of cereal to buy for the children. Instead, he or she will walk by the shelf, find the family's usual brand, and put it into the cart.

limited decision making
The type of decision making that requires a moderate amount of time for gathering information and deliberating about an unfamiliar brand in a familiar product category.

Limited decision making typically occurs when a consumer has previous product experience but is unfamiliar with the current brands available. Limited decision making is also associated with lower levels of involvement (although higher than routine decisions) because consumers do expend moderate effort in searching for information or in considering various alternatives. Suppose the children's usual brand of cereal, Kellogg's Frosted Flakes, is unavailable in the grocery store. Completely out of cereal at home, the parent now must select another brand. Before making a final selection, he or she may pull from the shelf several brands similar to Kellogg's Frosted Flakes, such as Quaker Oats Cap'n Crunch Cereal and Honey Nut Cheerios, to compare their nutritional value and calories and to decide whether the children will like the new cereal.

extensive decision making
The most complex type of consumer decision making, used when buying an unfamiliar, expensive product or an infrequently bought item; requires use of several criteria for evaluating options and much time for seeking information.

Consumers practise **extensive decision making** when buying an unfamiliar, expensive product or an infrequently bought item. This process is the most complex type of consumer buying decision and is associated with high involvement on the part of the consumer. This process resembles the model outlined earlier in Exhibit 4.1. These consumers want to make the right decision, so they want to know as much as they can about the product category and available brands. People usually experience cognitive dissonance only when buying high-involvement products. Buyers use several criteria for evaluating their options and spend much time seeking information. Buying a home or a car, for example, requires extensive decision making.

EXHIBIT 4.2
Continuum of Consumer Buying Decisions

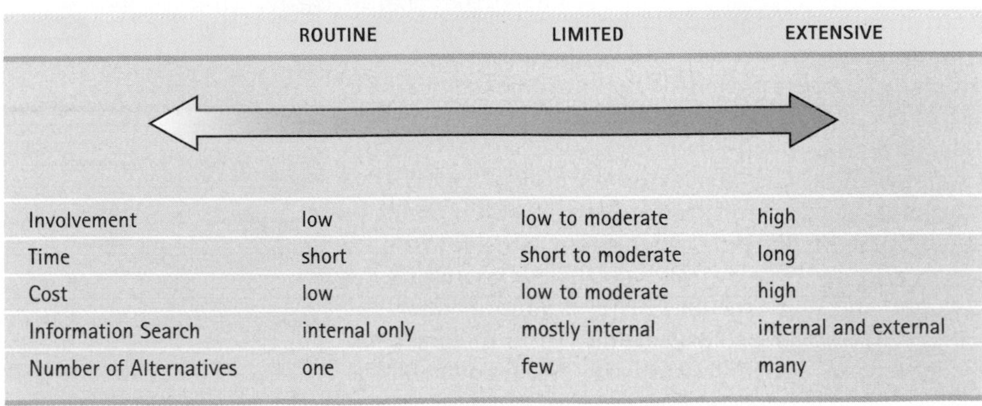

	ROUTINE	LIMITED	EXTENSIVE
Involvement	low	low to moderate	high
Time	short	short to moderate	long
Cost	low	low to moderate	high
Information Search	internal only	mostly internal	internal and external
Number of Alternatives	one	few	many

The type of decision making that consumers use to purchase a product does not necessarily remain constant. For instance, if a routinely purchased product no longer satisfies, consumers may practise limited or extensive decision making to switch to another brand. And people who first use extensive decision making may then use limited or routine decision making for future purchases. For example, a new mother may first extensively evaluate several brands of disposable diapers before selecting one. Subsequent purchases of diapers will then become routine.

ON LINE 

Heart and Stroke Foundation: HealthCheck.org

Does the Heart and Stroke Foundation's Health Check website seem more health oriented or commercially oriented? What makes you think so? Is the emphasis what you expected it would be?

http://www.healthcheck.org

Factors Determining the Level of Consumer Involvement

The level of involvement in the purchase depends on five factors: previous experience, interest, perceived risk, situation, and social visibility.

- *Previous experience:* When consumers have had previous experience with a good or service, the level of involvement typically decreases. After repeated product trials, consumers learn to make quick choices. Because consumers are familiar with the product and know whether it will satisfy their needs, they become less involved in the purchase. For example, consumers with pollen allergies typically buy the sinus medicine that has relieved their symptoms in the past.
- *Interest:* Involvement is directly related to consumer interests, as in cars, music, movies, bicycling, or electronics. Naturally, these areas of interest vary from one individual to another. Although some people have little interest in nursing homes, a person with elderly parents in poor health may be highly interested.
- *Perceived risk of negative consequences:* As the perceived risk in purchasing a product increases, so does a consumer's level of involvement. The types of risks that concern consumers include financial risk, social risk, and psychological risk. First, financial risk is exposure to loss of wealth or purchasing power. Because high risk is associated with high-priced purchases, consumers tend to become extremely involved. Therefore, price and involvement are usually directly related: As price increases, so does the level of involvement. For example, someone who is thinking of buying a home will normally spend much time and effort to find the right one. Second, consumers take social risks when they buy products that can affect people's social opinions of them (for example, driving an old, beat-up car or wearing unstylish clothes). Third, buyers undergo psychological risk if they feel that making the wrong decision might cause some concern or anxiety. For example, should a working parent hire a baby sitter or enroll the child in a daycare centre?
- *Situation:* The circumstances of a purchase may temporarily transform a low-involvement decision into a high-involvement one. High involvement comes into play when the consumer perceives risk in a specific situation. For example, an individual might routinely stay at limited service low-budget hotels when travelling alone. When travelling with a partner, however, the consumer might make a high-involvement decision and stay at more prestigious and expensive hotels with far more services.
- *Social visibility:* Involvement also increases as the social visibility of a product increases. Products often on social display include clothing (especially designer labels), jewellery, cars, and furniture. All these items make a statement about the purchaser and, therefore, carry a social risk.

Marketing Implications of Involvement

Marketing strategy varies according to the level of involvement associated with the product. For high-involvement product purchases, marketing managers have several responsibilities. First, promotion to the target market should be extensive and

© KRISTIINA PAUL

Although food products are generally considered low-involvement purchases, marketers can increase sales by linking high-involvement issues to their products. In this ad for Maple Leaf's Nature's Gourmet brand, the issue of healthy eating is identified by the Health Check logo from the Canadian Heart and Stroke Foundation.

informative. A good ad gives consumers the information they need for making the purchase decision, as well as specifying the benefits and unique advantages of owning the product. For example, manufacturers of high-tech computers and peripheral equipment like scanners, printers, and modems run lengthy ads that detail technical information about such attributes as performance, resolution, and speed. To make the purchase decision easier, major automobile manufacturers now enable their customers to use virtual reality to test different combinations of colours, fabrics, hubcaps, and so forth. Customers can see the effect of different options using a touch screen to generate an image of the car after making their selections. They can even hear different configurations of stereo sound systems to select the one they like best.

Purchasing on-line involves added risk for many consumers, even in limited decision-making situations. To overcome the challenges of getting shoppers to complete purchases on-line, Landsend.com created a virtual three-dimensional model that customers can use to try on clothes. It also offers an on-line "personal shopper" to help customers identify items they might like. Purchase rates have been 26 percent higher among on-line shoppers who use the model and 80 percent higher among customers who use the personal shopper.[17]

For low-involvement product purchases, consumers may not recognize their wants until they are in the store. Therefore, in-store promotion is an important tool when promoting low-involvement products. Marketing managers have to focus on package design so the product will be eye-catching and easily recognized on the shelf. Examples of products that take this approach are Campbell's soups, Tide detergent, Velveeta cheese, and Heinz ketchup. In-store displays also stimulate sales of low-involvement products. A good display can explain the product's purpose and prompt recognition of a want. Displays of health and beauty aid items in supermarkets have been known to increase sales many times above normal. Coupons, cents-off deals, and two-for-one offers also effectively promote low-involvement items.

Linking a product to a higher-involvement issue is another tactic that marketing managers can use to increase the sales of a low-involvement product. For example, many food products are no longer just nutritious but also low in fat or cholesterol. Although packaged food may normally be a low-involvement product, reference to health issues raises the involvement level. To take advantage of aging baby boomers' interest in healthier foods, a recent advertisement from H.J. Heinz Company linked its ketchup with a growing body of research that suggests lycopene, an antioxidant found in tomatoes, can reduce the risk of prostate and cervical cancer.[18] Similarly, food products, such as SoyaWorld's So Good Omega soy milk and Maple Leaf's Nature's Gourmet soy-based frozen entrees among many other brands, tout their health benefits in reducing the risk of coronary heart disease, preventing certain cancers, and reducing the symptoms of menopause. Manufacturers of soy-based products, which have long been shunned in Canada for their strong taste, are planning to tap into strong consumer interest in nutritional eating as a result of these health claims.[19]

>> FACTORS INFLUENCING CONSUMER BUYING DECISIONS

The consumer decision-making process does not occur in a vacuum. On the contrary, underlying cultural, social, individual, and psychological factors strongly influence the decision process. They have an effect from the time a consumer perceives a stimulus through postpurchase behaviour. Cultural factors, which include culture and values, subculture, and social class, exert the broadest influence over consumer decision making. Social factors sum up the social interactions between a consumer and influential groups of people, such as reference groups, opinion leaders, and family members. Individual factors, which include gender, age, family life-cycle stage, personality, self-concept, and lifestyle, are unique to each individual and play a major role in the types of products and services consumers want. Psychological factors determine how consumers perceive and interact with their environments and influence the ultimate decisions consumers make. They include perception, motivation, learning, beliefs, and attitudes. Exhibit 4.3 summarizes these influences.

>> CULTURAL INFLUENCES ON CONSUMER BUYING DECISIONS

5 Identify and understand the cultural factors that affect consumer buying decisions

The first major group of factors that influence consumer decision making are cultural factors, which exert the broadest and deepest influences over individual consumer behaviour and decision making. Marketers must understand the way a people's culture and its accompanying values, as well as their subculture and social class, influence their buying behaviour.

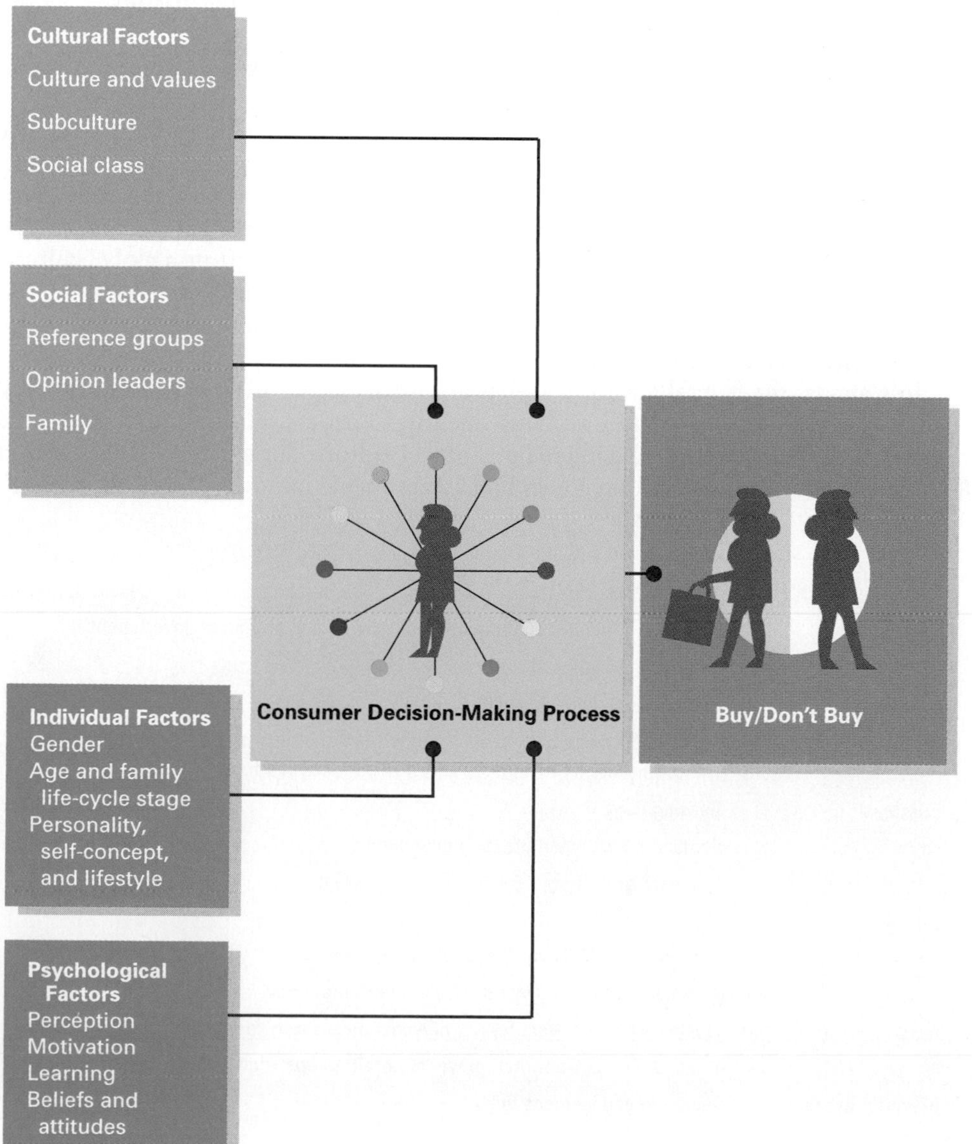

EXHIBIT 4.3

Factors That Affect the Consumer Decision-Making Process

Culture and Values

culture
The set of values, norms, attitudes, and other meaningful symbols that shape human behaviour and the artifacts, or products, of that behaviour as they are transmitted from one generation to the next.

Culture is the essential character of a society that distinguishes it from other cultural groups. The underlying elements of every culture are the values, language, myths, customs, rituals, and laws that shape the behaviour of the culture, as well as the material artifacts, or products, of that behaviour as they are transmitted from one generation to the next. Exhibit 4.4 lists some defining components of Canadian culture.

Culture is pervasive. Cultural values and influences are the ocean in which individuals swim, and yet most are completely unaware that it is there. What people eat, how they dress, what they think and feel, and what languages they speak are all dimensions of culture. It encompasses all the things consumers do without conscious choice because their culture's values, customs, and rituals are ingrained in their daily habits.

Culture is functional. Human interaction creates values and prescribes acceptable behaviour for each culture. By establishing common expectations, culture gives order to society. Sometimes these expectations are coded into laws. For example, drivers in our culture must stop at a red light. Other times these expectations are taken for granted. For example, convenience stores and hospitals are open 24 hours whereas bank lobbies are open only during bankers' hours.

Culture is learned. Consumers are not born knowing the values and norms of their society. Instead, they must learn what is acceptable from family and friends. Children learn the values that will govern their behaviour from parents, teachers, and peers. As members of our society, they learn to shake hands when they greet someone, to drive on the right-hand side of the road, and to eat pizza and drink coffee.

Culture is dynamic. It adapts to changing needs and an evolving environment. The rapid growth of technology in today's world has accelerated the rate of cultural change. In the twentieth century, television changed entertainment patterns and family communication and heightened public awareness of political and other news events. In the twenty-first century, the Internet promises to be a force that will create a global culture. Automation has increased the amount of leisure time we have and, in some ways, has changed the traditional work ethic. Cultural norms will continue to evolve because of our need for social patterns that solve problems.

In Canada, the federal government has an official policy of multiculturalism and encourages large-scale immigration. Consequently, Canada has been undergoing rapid changes in diversity that are causing major shifts in culture. For example, there are over 80 different ethnic groups in Canada and many are visible minorities. In 1991 approxi-

EXHIBIT 4.4
Components of Canadian Culture

COMPONENT	EXAMPLES
Values	Founding principles of Confederation: law, order, and good government Emphasis on personal freedom
Language	Bilingualism—English and French official languages
Myths	Santa Claus delivers presents to good boys and girls on Christmas Eve. The tooth fairy leaves money in return for baby teeth.
Customs	Bathing daily Shaking hands when greeting new people Standard gratuity of 15 percent at restaurants
Rituals	Victoria Day fireworks Standing for "O Canada" before hockey games Attending religious services on the appropriate day
Laws	Quebec's Child Protection Act prevents advertising to children Bill C-2, Competition Act, prevents unfair competition
Material artifacts	Diamond engagement rings Eskimo carvings

SOURCE: Adapted from *Consumer Behavior* by William D. Wells and David Prensky.

mately 10 percent of Canada's population was classified as visible minorities; the 2001 Census indicated this percentage had grown to 17.7 percent, and it is projected that by 2016 almost 25 percent of Canadians will be classified as visible minorities. The rapid growth of these ethnic groups will have dramatic influences on the food, music, clothing, and entertainment industries in Canada. For example, Canadian brewers have been very careful to have multicultural representation in their promotional campaigns. In fact, when Mississauga-based Premium Beer wanted to promote its Caffrey's Irish Ale brand with a radio ad, the company featured three different people talking about the beer with French, German, and Jamaican ethnic accents. The performers were actually French, German, and Jamaican and the tag line in the ad was: "Caffrey's Irish Ale. It's from Ireland, but you don't have to be." [20]

The most defining element of a culture is its **values**—the enduring beliefs shared by a society that a specific mode of conduct is personally or socially preferable to another mode of conduct. People's value systems have a great effect on their consumer behaviour. Consumers with similar value systems tend to react alike to prices and other marketing-related inducements. Values also correspond to consumption patterns. For example, Canadians are actually brand disloyal.[21] This value has created highly competitive markets for generic and private label products such as Loblaw's No Name and President's Choice brands. Values can also influence consumers' TV viewing habits or the magazines they read. For instance, people who strongly object to violence avoid crime shows, and those who oppose pornography do not buy *Hustler.* A number of examples of core values—those considered central to the way of life in North America—are presented in Exhibit 4.5.

value
The enduring belief that a specific mode of conduct is personally or socially preferable to another mode of conduct.

The personal values of target consumers have important implications for marketing managers. When marketers understand the core values that underlie the attitudes that shape the buying patterns of Canadian consumers and how these values were moulded by experiences, they can target their message more effectively. For example, the personal value systems of matures, baby boomers, Generation X-ers, and Generation Y-ers are quite different. The key to understanding *matures,* or everyone born before 1945, is recognizing the impact of the Great Depression and World War II on their lives. Facing these two immense challenges shaped a generation characterized by discipline, self-denial, financial and social conservatism, and a sense of obligation. Boomers, those individuals nurtured in the bountiful postwar period between 1945 and 1964, believe they are entitled to the wealth and opportunity that seemed endless in their youth. Generation X-ers are very accepting of diversity and individuality. They are also a very entrepreneurial-driven generation, ready to tackle life's challenges for themselves rather than as part of a crowd.[22] Gen Y-ers are more serious and socially conscious than Gen X-ers. Some of the defining events in the lives of Canadian Gen Y-ers include the death of Princess Diana, the terrorist attacks in New York and Washington on September 11, 2001, and the gold medal wins by the Canadian men's and women's Olympic hockey teams in 2002. They grew up with cable television, computers, debit cards, and cell phones, making them the most well connected generation to date—a fact that has important implications for word-of-mouth influence.[23]

Values represent what is most important in people's lives. Therefore, marketers are very aware that they must have an understanding of their consumers' values. Canadian values that marketers and social commentators have identified include the following: support for collective responsibility; confidence in social institutions (e.g. education, health care, and the police); tolerance for diversity and differences; pessimism and skepticism; value driven; frugality; brand disloyalty; health consciousness; freedom of choice; democracy; and fiscal responsibility. [24]

Understanding Culture Differences

Underlying core values can vary across cultures. Most Canadians and Americans are more concerned about their health than their weight. But for many Brazilian women, being thin is more important than being healthy. In fact, a recent survey found that 75 percent of Brazilian women over the age of 20 who wanted to lose weight had taken

EXHIBIT 4.5

Core North American Values

Success	North Americans admire hard work, entrepreneurship, achievement, and success. Those achieving success in society are rewarded with money, status, and prestige. For example, Bill Gates, once a nerdy computer buff, built Microsoft Computers into an internationally known giant. Gates is now one of the richest people in the world today.
Materialism	North Americans value owning tangible goods. Our society encourages consumption, ownership, and possession. We judge others based on their material possessions; for example, the type of car they own, where they live, and what type of clothes they wear.
Freedom	North American culture was founded on the principle of religious and political freedom. The founding of Confederation in Canada and the Canadian Charter of Rights and Freedoms are based on the notions of law, order, and good government. These freedoms are fundamental to the legal systems and the moral fibre of North American culture. The Internet, for example, is built on the principle of the right to free speech. Lawmakers who have attempted to limit the material available on the Internet have met with tough free-speech opponents.
Progress	Technological advances, as well as advances in medicine, science, health, and the quality of products and services, are important to North Americans. Each year, for example, more than 25,000 new or improved consumer products are introduced on supermarket shelves.*
Youth	North Americans are obsessed with youth and spend a good deal of time on products and procedures that make them feel and look younger. We spend millions each year on health and beauty aids, health clubs, and healthy foods. Media and advertising encourage the quest for youth by using young, attractive, slim models, such as those in ads from fashion designer Calvin Klein.
Capitalism	North Americans believe in a free enterprise system characterized by competition and the chance for monetary success. Capitalism creates choices, quality, and value. Laws like Canada's Competition Act prohibit monopolistic control of a market, and NAFTA was designed to encourage and regulate free trade. Small business success leading to international recognition, such as that found by Seagram's, Wal-Mart, and McDonald's, all of which started as small enterprises that topped their competition.

*Data obtained from the New Products Showcase and Learning Center, Ithaca, New York, website at http://www.showlearn.com, 1998.

SOURCE: Adapted from *Consumer Behavior* by William D. Wells and David Prensky. Copyright © 1996 John Wiley & Sons, Inc. This material is used by permission of John Wiley & Sons, Inc.

prescription diet drugs for obesity even though less than one-third of the women were obese and the drugs presented the risk of side effects such as heart and lung damage. In contrast, most Chinese women do not place a high value on thinness and show little concern about being overweight.[25]

GLOBAL

Without understanding a culture, a firm has little chance of selling products in it. Like people, products have cultural values and rules that influence their perception and use. Culture, therefore, must be understood before the behaviour of individuals within the cultural context can be understood. Colours, for example, may have different meanings in global markets than they do at home. In China, white is the colour of mourning and brides wear red. In the United States, black is for mourning and brides wear white. The importance of understanding culture was not lost on American designers from Universal Studios who found they had much to learn about Japanese culture while planning a new theme park for Japan. Surveys showed that many of their original ideas to create Japanese attractions would not appeal to Japanese consumers, who were hoping for an authentic American theme park that catered to their cultural differences. After extensive surveying and product testing, the result was a Universal Studios theme park with a more orderly clockwise layout, Japanese-style American food, and a Jurassic Park water slide designed to prevent riders from getting wet.[26]

AP/WIDE WORLD PHOTOS

McDonald's has responded to cultural differences like no other company. Its website boasts: "If meeting the demands of local culture means adding to our regular menu, we'll do it." In Japan, the company introduced the Teriyaki McBurger, and in India, McDonald's serves meatless sandwiches.

Language is another important aspect of culture that global marketers must deal with. They must take care in translating product names, slogans, and promotional messages into foreign languages so as not to convey the wrong message. Consider the following examples of blunders made by marketers when delivering their message to Spanish-speaking consumers: General Motors discovered too late that Nova (the name of an economical car) literally means "doesn't go" in Spanish; Coors encouraged its English-speaking customers to "Turn it loose," but the phrase in Spanish means "Suffer from diarrhea"; and when Frank Perdue said, "It takes a tough man to make a tender chicken," Spanish speakers heard "It takes a sexually stimulated man to make a chicken affectionate."

As more companies expand their operations globally, the need to understand the cultures of foreign countries becomes more important. While marketers expanding into global markets generally adapt their products and business formats to the local culture, some fear that increasing globalization, as well as the proliferation of the Internet, will result in a homogeneous world culture of the future. Canadians have long worried about being submerged by U.S. culture and U.S. companies but it's not just Canada that is being Americanized. U.S. companies are Americanizing the world by exporting bastions of American culture, such as McDonald's fast-food restaurants, Starbucks coffeehouses, Microsoft software, and American movies and entertainment. Read more about this issue in the "Global Perspectives" box.

Subculture

A culture can be divided into subcultures on the basis of demographic characteristics, geographic regions, national and ethnic background, political beliefs, and religious beliefs. A **subculture** is a homogeneous group of people who share elements of the overall culture as well as cultural elements unique to their own group. Within subcultures, people's attitudes, values, and purchase decisions are even more similar than they are within the broader culture. Subcultural differences may result in considerable variation within a culture in what, how, when, and where people buy goods and services.

subculture
A homogeneous group of people who share elements of the overall culture as well as unique elements of their own group.

Canada is a multicultural society with French Canadian being the dominant subculture in the country. Most French Canadians reside in the province of Quebec, but Canada being a bilingual nation, the French-Canadian culture is found on a national scale too. Language is a critical factor for marketers designing campaigns for French Canadians but language is not the only distinguishing feature of Canada's largest subculture. In comparison to Anglo Canadians, French Canadians concern themselves more with their quality of life. Time is not as important to them and they don't worry as much about deadlines. French Canadians are more comfortable with authority and they place more importance on a person's status since there is less room for social mobility.[27]

Aside from French Canadians, however, there are estimated to be more than 80 other ethnic groups in Canada. In the past most of Canada's immigrants were from Europe but the most recent Canadian immigrants tend to come from visible-minority groups such as Chinese (23 percent), Blacks (19 percent), South Asians (Pakistani and Indian) (19 percent), Arabs and West Asians (13 percent), Filipinos and Other Pacific Islanders (8 percent), Latin Americans (6 percent), Southeast Asians (5 percent), and others (7 percent). For the most part ethnic Canadians have chosen to live in the largest census metropolitan areas of the country. More than 75 percent of ethnic Canadians live in the four major metropolitan areas of Toronto (37 percent), Vancouver (15 percent), Montreal (15 percent), and Calgary/Edmonton (9 percent).[28]

Other subcultures are geographically dispersed. For example, computer hackers, people who are hearing or visually impaired, Harley-Davidson bikers, military families,

ON LINE

Grateful Dead

What kind of marketing program could you design to attract the subculture of Grateful Dead followers? Visit the GD on-line store to see how marketers are currently doing this. What other elements of the site could help you design a successful program?

http://www.dead.net

OMNI Television

What evidence can you find on the OMNI Television website that the company has a multicultural marketing campaign? Explain what you find.

http://www.omni1.ca

GLOBAL **PERSPECTIVES**

Will Cultural Differences Survive a Global Economy?

> Modern industry has established the world market. ... All old-established national industries ... are dislodged by new industries whose ... products are consumed, not only at home, but in every quarter of the globe. In place of old wants ... we find new wants, requiring for their satisfaction the products of distant lands and climes.
>
> —Karl Marx and Friedrich Engels
> *The Communist Manifesto*

Although Karl Marx and Friedrich Engels wrote these words more than 150 years ago, this passage describes a present-day phenomenon in the world's cultures called *globalization.* Thirty years ago, most Chinese did not own televisions, refrigerators, or washing machines. But as economic reforms allowed more Western companies to offer their goods in China, ordinary people demanded these products. Today, 97 percent of Chinese in cities have televisions, and 88 percent have refrigerators and washing machines.

Globalization is not a new concept. Humans have been weaving commercial and cultural connections since the beginning of civilization. Today, computers, the Internet, cellular phones, cable television, and cheaper air transportation have accelerated and complicated these connections. Yet the basic dynamic remains the same: As people cross borders and oceans moving goods and services, their ideas move with them. And cultures change. The difference today is the speed at which these changes take place. Case in point: It took television 13 years to acquire 50 million users; it took the Internet only five.

Everywhere, it seems, people are experiencing the fusion of cultures. London coffeehouses sell Italian espresso served by Algerian waiters while strains of the Beach Boys singing: "I wish they all could be California girls . . ." can be heard in the background. The classic American Barbie doll, once only available as a blond, now comes in some 30 national varieties, including, most recently, Austrian and Moroccan. At Hollywood High School in Los Angeles, the student body represents 32 different languages. Computer games fanatics in the United States play mah jong, an ancient Chinese game of strategy and luck, over the Internet against players from all over the world. Some 260,000 Chinese women read *Cosmopolitan* magazine, the racy American fashion publication, every month. Adventurous diners in the midst of south Louisiana savour authentic Japanese sushi and join in karaoke singing. For about 100 rupees a month—about $2.34—slum-dwelling families in Mumbai (formerly Bombay) can surf more than 50 cable channels including Western imports such as TNT, MTV, CNN, and ESPN. McDonald's now has some 25,000 restaurants worldwide, making the Golden Arches perhaps the most widely recognized trademark on the planet.

Not everyone is happy about the blending of cultures. Sociologists and anthropologists fear cultural cloning will result from what they regard as the "cultural assault" of ubiquitous Western multinationals such as McDonald's, Coca-Cola, Disney, Nike, MTV, and even the English language itself. Globalization has become a worrisome issue for many cultures. France worries about American films and television elbowing out French entertainment. People in India agonize that American junk food, television, films, blue jeans, pornography, and Christian missionaries will ruin traditional Indian values. Australians, in particular, have been phobically fearful of what they refer to as the remorseless march of American "cultural imperialism." In China, a recent book entitled *China Can Say No* became a bestseller by admonishing Chinese who believe blindly in anything foreign. Critics of globalization are convinced that Western, especially American, influences will pervade every culture, producing, as one observer terms it, one big "McWorld."

But not everyone is paranoid about cultural cloning. Proponents of globalization feel cultural change is inevitable and part of national evolution. For the most part, they believe, cultures take what they want from other cultures and adapt it to their needs. Tom Freston, CEO of MTV, contends that "kids today, outside of the U.S. in particular, travel with two passports. They have the international passport . . . that plugs them into what is going on with their peers around the world. So when you talk about action movies, sports stars, certain music stars like a Mariah Carey, certain kinds of clothing and styles, there is homogeneity. But while that trend is going on, they have their other passport that is about their local world, which increasingly is more important to them." Hence, multinationals consistently adapt products and services to meet the needs of peoples in other lands. MTV tailors its music offerings in different countries to include local stars who sing in their own language. McDonald's outlets in India, where there are more than 400 local languages and several very strict religions, serve mutton instead of beef and offer vegetarian menus acceptable to orthodox Hindus. Similarly, Revlon adapted the colour palette and composition of its cosmetics to suit the Indian skin and climate.

Cultural change, supporters say, is a reality, not a choice. They believe that cultures won't become more uniform, but instead both old and new will tend to transform each other. Globalization won't mean just more television sets or Nike shoes, but rather a common destiny shaped by humanity.[29]

university professors, and gays may be found throughout the country. Yet they have identifiable attitudes, values, and needs that distinguish them from the larger culture. For instance, Vancouver's VanCity Credit Union targeted gay consumers with an outdoor campaign in the West End of Vancouver, an area that is popular with gays and lesbians. It developed a print campaign to go with billboards featuring a photograph of two men embracing affectionately with the headline: "I want to bank with people who value all partnerships."[30]

If marketers can identify subcultures, they can then design special marketing programs to serve their needs. However, one problem for Canadian firms is that the cost of research is extremely large while many of the subcultures are relatively small in numbers. In addition, there is considerable sensitivity among many people when asked to respond to market research questioning about their race or ethnicity. Ford of Canada ran into this issue when it asked about ethnicity in a survey of customers. Several customers complained about the question and the media got wind of the complaints and Ford of Canada received negative publicity. It responded by pulling the question from all of its surveys. Still, even though research on ethnicity is difficult to do, Canadian marketers have a wide choice of media vehicles to reach out to ethnic marketers including: 18 television stations/networks, 49 radio stations that provide programming for 75 different ethnic groups, and 190 different newspapers designed for 43 different ethnic groups.[31]

Social Class

Canada, like other societies, does have a social class system. A **social class** is a group of people who are considered nearly equal in status or community esteem, who regularly socialize among themselves both formally and informally, and who share behavioural norms.

social class
A group of people in a society who are considered nearly equal in status or community esteem, who regularly socialize among themselves both formally and informally, and who share behavioural norms.

A number of techniques have been used to measure social class, and a number of criteria have been used to define it. One view of Canadian status structure is shown in Exhibit 4.6.

As you can see from Exhibit 4.6, the capitalist/executive class comprises the small segment of affluent and wealthy Canadians. The capitalist/executive class is more likely than other classes to contribute something to society—for example, by volunteer work or active participation in civic affairs. In terms of consumer buying patterns, the affluent are more likely to own their own home and purchase new cars and trucks and are less likely to smoke. The very rich flex their financial muscles by spending more on owned vacation homes, vacations and cruises, and housekeeping and gardening services. The most affluent consumers are more likely to attend art auctions and galleries, dance performances, opera, the theatre, museums, concerts, and sporting events.[32]

The majority of Canadians today define themselves as middle class, regardless of their actual income or educational attainment. This phenomenon is most likely due to the fact that working-class Canadians tend to aspire to the middle-class lifestyle while some of those who do achieve affluence may downwardly aspire to respectable middle-class status as a matter of principle.[33] Attaining goals and achieving status and prestige are important to middle-class consumers. People falling into the middle class live in the gap between the haves and the have-nots. They aspire to the lifestyle of the more affluent but are constrained by the economic realities and cautious attitudes they share with the working class.

The working class perceives itself to be middle class. Interest in organized labour is one of the attributes most common among the working class. This group is more likely to rate job security as the most important reason for taking a job.[34] The working-class person depends heavily on relatives and the community for economic and emotional support. The emphasis on family ties is one sign of the group's intensely local view of the world. They like the local news far more than do middle-class audiences who favour national and world coverage. They are also more likely to vacation closer to home.

Social class is typically measured as a combination of occupation, income, education, wealth, and other variables. For instance, affluent capitalist/executive consumers are more likely to be salaried executives or self-employed professionals with at least an undergraduate degree. New middle-class consumers are also likely to have an undergraduate degree or college diploma and work in salaried and professional occupations. Old middle-class and working-class consumers are more likely to be hourly service workers or blue-collar employees with only a high school education. Educational attainment, however, seems to be the most reliable indicator of a person's social and economic

EXHIBIT 4.6
Canadian Social Classes by Sex

	MEN	WOMEN	POPULATION TOTAL
Capitalist/executive	8.8%	2.7%	6.2%
New middle class	25.3	24.4	24.9
Old middle class	15.7	5.1	11.3
Working class	50.3	67.9	57.6
Total	100.0	100.0	100.0

SOURCE: Adapted from Simon Langlois, "Empirical Studies on Social Stratification in Quebec and Canada," in Yannick Lemel and Heinz-Herbert Noll, eds., *Changing Structures of Inequality: A Comparative Perspective* (Montreal: McGill-Queen's University Press, © 2002), p. 83. Reprinted with permission.

status. Those with college degrees or graduate degrees are more likely to fall into the capitalist/executive or new middle class, while those people with some college experience but no degree fall closest to the old middle class.

Marketers are interested in social class for two main reasons. First, social class often indicates which medium to use for advertising. If an insurance company is seeking to sell its policies to middle-class families, it might advertise during the local evening news because middle-class families tend to watch more television than other classes do. If the company wants to sell more policies to upscale individuals, it might place a print ad in a business publication like the *Financial Post.* The Internet, long the domain of more educated and affluent families, is becoming an important advertising outlet for advertisers hoping to reach blue-collar workers and homemakers. As the middle class rapidly adopts the medium, marketers are having to do more research to find out which websites will reach their audience.[35]

Second, knowing what products appeal to which social classes can help marketers determine where to best distribute their products. For example, in Toronto, The Hospital for Sick Children Foundation has developed a direct response television video to raise funds. The video presents the compelling stories of several hospital patients. The video is designed to appeal very strongly to the emotions of its viewers and, of course, to solicit donations so the hospital can continue to help children and their families cope with illness. Media research on these video spots indicated that they strongly appealed to 35–50 year old new middle-class people who had children. According to Cheryl Hicks, a direct marketing specialist with the foundation, the video spots were reaching a completely different group from those reached by other fundraising efforts.[36]

6 Identify and understand the social factors that affect consumer buying decisions

>> SOCIAL INFLUENCES ON CONSUMER BUYING DECISIONS

Most consumers are likely to seek out the opinions of others to reduce their search and evaluation effort or uncertainty, especially as the perceived risk of the decision increases. Consumers may also seek out others' opinions for guidance on new products or services, products with image-related attributes, or products where attribute information is lacking or uninformative. Specifically, consumers interact socially with reference groups, opinion leaders, and family members to obtain product information and decision approval.

Reference Groups

reference group
A group in society that influences an individual's purchasing behaviour.

All the formal and informal groups that influence the buying behaviour of an individual are that person's **reference groups.** Consumers may use products or brands to identify with or become a member of a group. They learn from observing how members of their reference groups consume, and they use the same criteria to make their own consumer decisions.

Reference groups can be categorized very broadly as either direct or indirect (see Exhibit 4.7). Direct reference groups are face-to-face membership groups that touch people's lives directly. They can be either primary or secondary. **Primary membership**

groups include all groups with which people interact regularly in an informal, face-to-face manner, such as family, friends, and coworkers. In contrast, people associate with **secondary membership groups** less consistently and more formally. These groups might include clubs, professional groups, and religious groups.

Consumers also are influenced by many indirect, nonmembership reference groups to which they do not belong. **Aspirational reference groups** are those that a person would like to join. To join an aspirational group, a person must at least conform to the norms of that group. (**Norms** are the values and attitudes deemed acceptable by the group.) Thus, a person who wants to be elected to public office may begin to dress more conservatively, as other politicians do. He or she may go to many of the restaurants and social engagements that city and business leaders attend and try to play a role that is acceptable to voters and other influential people. Similarly, teenagers today may dye their hair, experiment with body piercing and tattoos, and carry around copies of "in" books so that their peers will perceive them as well read.[37]

Nonaspirational reference groups, or dissociative groups, influence our behaviour when we try to maintain distance from them. In order to avoid being associated with a particular group, consumers may reject certain styles and brands of clothing and automobiles. They will not patronize particular stores or restaurants and will even refuse to consider a home purchase in particular neighbourhoods if they feel it will associate them with an undesirable reference group.

The activities, values, and goals of reference groups directly influence consumer behaviour. For marketers, reference groups have three important implications: (1) they serve as information sources and influence perceptions; (2) they affect an individual's aspiration levels; and (3) their norms either constrain or stimulate consumer behaviour. For example, Youth Culture Group, a Toronto-based research firm regularly interviews over 1,200 Canadian teens and asks them questions about their social values, behaviours, and attitudes. Using this information, the firm publishes an annual report entitled *Trendscan: The Report on Teenage Lifestyles*. *Trendscan* reports the following attitudes among Canadian teens: 12- to 15-year-olds aspire to be like 18-year-olds while 16- to 18-year-olds would like to be at least 19; teens agree that one of the best things about Canada is "how we welcome people of different races and ethnic groups"; Canadian teens feel freedom is one of the things they like most about being a teen; and finally, teens say their parents can improve their lives the most by buying them a car. Finally, for marketers interested in trend setters, *Trendscan* has identified "Early Style Adopters" as teens "who have purchased non-mainstream or cool clothing brands—brands that are authentic and niche."[38]

primary membership group
A reference group with which people interact regularly in an informal, face-to-face manner, such as family, friends, or fellow employees.

secondary membership group
A reference group with which people associate less consistently and more formally than a primary membership group, such as a club, professional group, or religious group.

aspirational reference group
A group that someone would like to join.

norm
A value or attitude deemed acceptable by a group.

nonaspirational reference group
A group with which an individual does not want to associate.

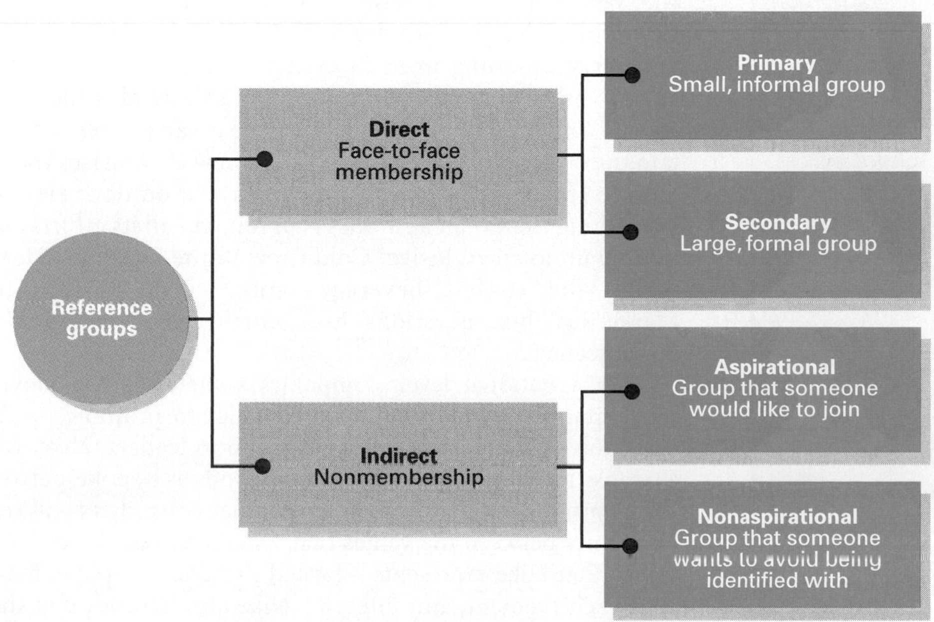

EXHIBIT 4.7
Types of Reference Groups

Understanding the effect of reference groups on a product is important for marketers as they track the life cycles of their products. In Japan, companies have long relied on the nation's high school girls to give them advice during product testing. Fads that catch on among teenage girls often become big trends throughout the country and among Japanese consumers in general. Food manufacturers frequently recruit Tokyo schoolgirls to sample potato chip recipes or chocolate bars. Television networks survey high school girls to fine-tune story lines for higher ratings on prime-time shows. Other companies pay girls to keep diaries of what they buy. For example, Warner-Lambert, maker of Adams brands chewing gums, hired high school girls to help choose a new gum flavour. After extensive chewing and comparing, the girls settled on a flavour that became Trickle, now Japan's best-selling bubble gum.[39]

Opinion Leaders

opinion leader
An individual who influences the opinions of others.

Reference groups frequently include individuals known as group leaders, or **opinion leaders**—those who influence others. Obviously, it is important for marketing managers to persuade such people to purchase their goods or services. Many products and services that are integral parts of Canadian's lives today got their initial boost from opinion leaders. For example, opinion leaders embraced VCRs and sport utility vehicles well ahead of the general public.

Opinion leaders are often the first to try new products and services out of pure curiosity. They are typically self-indulgent, which makes them more likely to explore unproven but intriguing products and services. Technology companies have found that teenagers, because of their willingness to experiment, are key opinion leaders for the success of new technologies. For example, text messaging, which first appealed to teenagers, has gained widespread popularity. Thus, many technology companies see creating a buzz among teens as a critical part of their marketing programs.[40]

© PETER M. WILSON/CORBIS

Japanese teenage girls have long provided the marketing litmus test companies need before launching new products. Perhaps their success in this area is due to the fact they are caught in a pivotal clash between a tradition of collectivism and a growing sense of individualism.

Opinion leadership is a casual, face-to-face phenomenon and usually inconspicuous, so locating opinion leaders can be a challenge. Thus, marketers often try to create opinion leaders. They may use high school cheerleaders to model new fall fashions or civic leaders to promote insurance, new cars, and other merchandise. The B.C. Dairy Foundation is trying to encourage teens to drink more milk by using "Cold Crew" street teams who dress in white. The "Cold Crew" is a group of young, sexy urban girls and guys who visit major events designed for teens throughout British Columbia. The girls are dressed in Lara Croft-style outfits and carry branding irons at events, where they stamp the crowd with Cold Crew logos. The Cold Crew also includes an MC who talks to the audiences while break dancers entertain the crowds that gather. The Cold Crew also carries water guns to spray the crowds during hot days at outdoor events. Everything the Cold Crew does is in fun and all its efforts are leading up to an exclusive "Cold Crew White Out Party" featuring the coolest beverage, milk.[41] The "Ethics in Marketing" box questions how much marketers should target teenagers.

On a national level, companies sometimes use movie stars, sports figures, and other celebrities to promote products, hoping they are appropriate opinion leaders. Nike, for example, signed golf superstar Tiger Woods as a spokesperson for its products. The company hopes that consumers will see an affinity between the values that Woods represents and the values that Nike represents—earned success, discipline, hard work, achievement, and integrity. Nike also believes that the

ETHICS IN MARKETING

Targeting Teens at School

As we have discussed in this chapter, marketers study consumers, identify unmet needs, develop products and services to meet those needs, and find a way to sell the products to those consumers. That sounds simple, but the process is not always without critics.

For example, soft drink manufacturers know that teenagers are the biggest consumers of their products. They also know that most soft drink consumers develop brand loyalty in their teen years, so it is critical to the manufacturers' long-term success to convince teens to choose their brand. Therefore, Coca-Cola and PepsiCo spend millions of dollars marketing their products to teens. To this point, the behaviour of Coca-Cola and PepsiCo is no different from that of any other successful marketing company.

But what happens when soft drink companies target high schools for product distribution? Given the amount of time teens spend at school, it is a logical choice. But parents, teachers, and politicians are becoming increasingly concerned over the practice.

Here are a few reasons why. First, according to Statistics Canada's *National Longitudinal Survey of Children and Youth: Childhood Obesity*, 37 percent of Canadian youths were classified as being overweight in 1998/99 compared to 34 percent in 1994/1995. And according to the Centers for Disease Control in Atlanta, American high school students are three times as likely to be overweight now than they were 20 years ago. Looking to explain the increases in weight, some people point to the greater availability of soft drinks and junk foods on school campuses. Others say the increase cannot be blamed on soft drinks and junk food alone and that the increased consumption of all types of food and the decline in exercise are to blame. Still other critics blame soft drinks for tooth decay, and one study even linked soft drink consumption to fractured bones in high school girls.

Second, other critics are concerned about the commercialization of our schools. In most cases, soft drinks are sold in schools through exclusive agreements, which give the soft drink company high visibility. In return, the schools are able to use profits from a percentage of the sales to fund student programs. Because so many schools need the funding, critics say, the schools are unable to turn down the offers and, in some cases, feel the need to promote soft drink sales in spite of health concerns.

In response to criticism, the Coca-Cola Company recently announced that it would no longer encourage the exclusive agreements and would look for less commercial ways to benefit the schools. But the contracts are made not by the Coca-Cola Company, but by its bottlers, many of which have continued the practice in spite of Coca-Cola's announcement because they are proud of their relationships with the schools and because of increased competition from PepsiCo. PepsiCo says it doesn't encourage the practice of exclusive contracts but that it will bid on them when asked.[42]

So what do you think? Should Coca-Cola and PepsiCo be able to target teens at school? What if the companies reduced the number of soft drinks in machines and added more water and juice options since both companies offer those products? What are the advantages and disadvantages of targeting teens in school?

quality of Woods's golf game will be associated with the quality and value of its products. One year after Woods began appearing in ads and on the fairway with Nike's new line of golf balls, the company's market share tripled.[43]

The effectiveness of celebrity endorsements depends largely on how credible and attractive the spokesperson is and how familiar people are with him or her. Endorsements are most likely to succeed if an association between the spokesperson and the product can be reasonably established. This leads to what are called "equity style endorsements." Equity style endorsements involve deals where the celebrities either become part owners or take a form of equity in the programs they endorse. For example, former NHL superstar Wayne Gretzky "has equity partnerships in a new production company, Take 99 Productions, the Wayne Gretzky Roller Hockey Centres, restaurants such as the All Star Cafes and Wayne Gretzky's, Toronto's Hespeler Hockey, and a new Internet venture."[44]

A marketing manager can also try to use opinion leaders through group sanctioning or referrals. Consider the earlier example of Maple Leaf's Nature's Gourmet products, which have the seal of approval of the Canadian Heart and Stroke Association. In the United States the Arthritis Foundation and McNeil Consumer Products formed an alliance to launch the Arthritis Foundation line of pain relievers, which quickly jumped to the number one selling position in the over-the-counter arthritis segment. Marketers also seek endorsements from schools, churches, cities, and fraternal organizations as a form of group opinion leadership. Salespeople often ask to use opinion leaders' names as a means of achieving greater personal influence in a sales presentation.

Family

socialization process
How cultural values and norms are passed down to children.

The family is the most important social institution for many consumers, strongly influencing values, attitudes, self-concept—and buying behaviour. For example, a family that strongly values good health will have a grocery list distinctly different from that of a family that views every dinner as a gourmet event. Moreover, the family is responsible for the **socialization process,** the passing down of cultural values and norms to children. Children learn by observing their parents' consumption patterns, and so they will tend to shop in a similar pattern.

Decision-making roles among family members tend to vary significantly, depending on the type of item purchased. Family members assume a variety of roles in the purchase process. *Initiators* are the ones who suggest, initiate, or plant the seed for the purchase process. The initiator can be any member of the family. For example, Sister might initiate the product search by asking for a new bicycle as a birthday present. *Influencers* are those members of the family whose opinions are valued. In our example, Mom might function as a price-range watchdog, an influencer whose main role is to veto or approve price ranges. Brother may give his opinion on certain makes of bicycles. The *decision maker* is the member of the family who actually makes the decision to buy or not to buy. For example, Dad or Mom is likely to choose the final brand and model of bicycle to buy after seeking further information from Sister about cosmetic features such as colour and imposing additional criteria of his or her own, such as durability and safety. The *purchaser* (probably Dad or Mom) is the one who actually exchanges money for the product. Finally, the *consumer* is the actual user—Sister, in the case of the bicycle.

Marketers should consider family purchase situations along with the distribution of consumer and decision-maker roles among family members. Ordinary marketing views the individual as both decision maker and consumer. Family marketing adds several other possibilities: Sometimes more than one family member or all family members are involved in the decision; sometimes only children are involved in the decision; sometimes more than one consumer is involved; and sometimes the decision maker and the consumer are different people. Exhibit 4.8 represents the patterns of family purchasing relationships that are possible.

Children can have great influence over the purchase decisions of their parents. In many families, with both parents working and short on time, children are encouraged to participate. In addition, children in single-parent households become more involved in family decisions at an earlier age. Children are especially influential in decisions about food and eating out. Therefore, food companies listen closely to what children want. Children also are more interested in entertainment than food. Therefore, McDonald's and Burger King spend about $US4 billion annually on toys for their kid meals; Quaker

EXHIBIT 4.8

Relationships among Purchasers and Consumers in the Family

Consumer	Purchase Decision Maker: Parent(s) Only	Purchase Decision Maker: Child/Children Only	Purchase Decision Maker: Some or All Family Members
Parent(s)	golf clubs cosmetics wine	Mother's Day card	Christmas gifts minivan
Child/ Children	diapers breakfast cereal	candy small toys	bicycle
Some Family Members	videos long-distance phone service	children's movies	computers sports events
All Family Members	clothing life insurance	fast-food restaurant	swim club membership vacations

SOURCE: From "Pulling the Family's Strings" by Robert Boutillier, *American Demographics*, August 1993.

Oatmeal now features hidden treasures; Heinz ketchup is available in funky purple; and Parkay margarine comes in shocking pink and electric blue. Both the ketchup and the margarine come in squeezable bottles designed to allow small hands to design pictures. Promotions for food products aimed at children include a website that illustrates how to build a fort with French fries and books that teach children to count using Cheerios, M&Ms, and Oreos.[45] Children influence purchase decisions for many more products and services than food. Even though they are usually not the actual purchasers of such items, children often participate in decisions about toys, clothes, vacations, recreation, automobiles, and many other products.

ON LINE 

GameGirlz

What kinds of games are available at the GameGirlz website? How do the games "for" girls differ from the games "for" boys at GameSpot?

http://www.gamegirlz.com

http://www.gamespot.com

>> INDIVIDUAL INFLUENCES ON CONSUMER BUYING DECISIONS

7 Identify and understand the individual factors that affect consumer buying decisions

A person's buying decisions are also influenced by personal characteristics that are unique to each individual, such as gender; age and life-cycle stage; and personality, self-concept, and lifestyle. Individual characteristics are generally stable over the course of one's life. For instance, most people do not change their gender, and the act of changing personality or lifestyle requires a complete reorientation of one's life. In the case of age and life-cycle stage, these changes occur gradually over time.

Gender

Physiological differences between men and women result in different needs, such as health and beauty products. Just as important are the distinct cultural, social, and economic roles played by men and women and the effects that these have on their decision-making processes. For instance, when asked what features they would want on their next vehicle, Generation Y men yearn for more gadget and performance-oriented options, such as turbo-diesel or turbo-charged gas engines, run-flat tires, and high-intensity headlights. Generation Y women, on the other hand, prefer features that provide organization, practicality, and convenience, such as a wet storage area, power rear seats, cargo area dividers, and heated/cooled cup holders.[46]

Men and women also shop differently. Studies show that men and women share similar motivations in terms of where to shop—that is, seeking reasonable prices, merchandise quality, and a friendly, low-pressure environment—but they don't necessarily feel the same about shopping in general. Most women enjoy shopping; their male counterparts claim to dislike the experience and shop only out of necessity. Further, men desire simple shopping experiences, stores with less variety, and convenience. Stores that are easy to shop in, are near home or office, or have knowledgeable personnel appeal more to men than to women.[47] The Internet appeals to men who find it's an easier and more enjoyable way to shop for clothing and gifts. Many Internet retailers are designing their sites to attract male gift buyers. Find Gift.com's website is designed to take the worry out of gift buying. The site has a gift registry so that you can choose a gift from your special person's wish list. If you find the perfect gift idea while browsing their website, but the occasion is still months away, you can bookmark the gift and return at a later date to purchase it. Finally, there is an e-mail service that will remind you about upcoming special occasions. To help out its male shoppers, intimate apparel retailer Victoria's Secret lets women create password-protected wish lists and then zap them to their significant others to ensure there's no mistaking colours or sizes.[48]

AP/WIDE WORLD PHOTOS

As the proportion of children in the Canadian population swells, this market segment is becoming increasingly important to marketers wanting to influence the kids that influence their parents' purchasing habits. Heinz's coloured ketchups in the E-Z Squirt bottles are designed to do just that.

Trends in gender marketing are influenced by the changing roles of men and women in society. For instance, as women around the world are working and earning more, many industries are attracting new customers by marketing to women. The video game industry, which has traditionally targeted 18- to 22-year-old men with games featuring guns and explosions, is beginning to develop new games based on popular female characters like Barbie and Nancy Drew aimed at capturing female customers. In South Korea, major credit card companies are now targeting working women by offering credit card benefits attractive to women such as discounts at department and bridal stores and disfigurement insurance for plastic surgery.[49]

The changing roles of women are also forcing companies that have traditionally targeted women to develop new strategies. Revlon stopped using glamorous supermodels to promote its products because it felt traditional "Cindy Crawford" ads "conveyed a man's view of women, not a woman's."[50] The company attempted to modernize its image by using new unknown models in ads highlighting universal truths about being a woman, such as a woman checking her reflection in the frozen food section of the grocery store. But the campaign did not work, and after seven months Revlon began using well-known models again with the new positioning statement "Be Unforgettable." The focus of the new campaign was on product benefits and promoting the Revlon brand name. It is often difficult for marketers to know how to respond as gender roles evolve and change.

Age and Family Life-Cycle Stage

The age and family life-cycle stage of a consumer can have a significant impact on consumer behaviour. How old a consumer is generally indicates what products he or she may be interested in purchasing. Consumer tastes in food, clothing, cars, furniture, and recreation are often age related; therefore, Toronto magazine publisher Bayard Canada targets children ages 3–6 with *Chirp* Magazine, ages 6–9 with *Chickadee* Magazine, and ages 9–13 with *Owl* Magazine. But as these children become teenagers their tastes in magazines diverge in favour of sports titles for boys and fashion/lifestyle titles for girls.[51]

Related to a person's age is his or her place in the family life cycle. As Chapter 6 explains in more detail, the *family life cycle* is an orderly series of stages through which consumers' attitudes and behavioural tendencies evolve through maturity, experience, and changing income and status. Marketers often define their target markets in terms of family life cycle, such as "young singles," "young married with children," and "middle-aged married without children." For instance, young singles spend more than average on alcoholic beverages, education, and entertainment. New parents typically increase their spending on health care, clothing, housing, and food and decrease their spending on alcohol, education, and transportation. Households with older children spend more on food, entertainment, personal care products, and education, as well as cars and gasoline. After their children leave home, spending by older couples on vehicles, women's clothing, health care, and long-distance calls typically increases. For instance, the presence of children in the home is the most significant determinant of the type of vehicle that's driven off the new car lot. Parents are the ultimate need-driven car consumers, requiring larger cars and trucks to haul their children and all their belongings. It comes as no surprise then that for all households with children, sport utility vehicles rank either first or second among new-vehicle purchases, followed by minivans.[52]

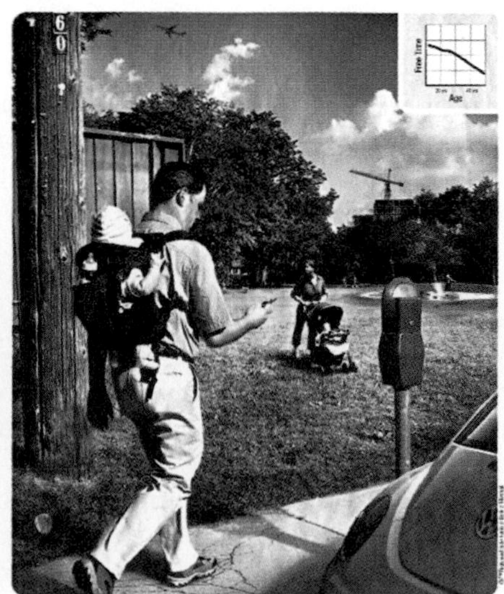

COURTESY OF THE BMO.

Bank Of Montreal Financial Group Recognizes the many different lifestyles that people have today with its "For the world you live in" campaign.

Marketers should also be aware of the many nontraditional life-cycle paths that are common today and provide insights into the needs and wants of such consumers as divorced parents, lifelong singles, and childless couples. Four decades ago, the majority of Canadian families were traditional families comprised of married couples with children under 18 with an average size of 3.9 persons. According to Statistics Canada's Census of Canada, in 2001 there were 8,371,020 Canadian families with an average size of 3.0 persons. In 2001, 63.4 percent of Canadian families had children at home; 41.4 percent of families with children were married couples, 6.4 percent were common-law couples, and 15.6 percent were single-parent families, the majority of which were headed by a female (12.7 percent of all Canadian families). Single-parent households headed by women represent over 20 percent of all households with children and are part of a broader societal change that has put more women on the career track. In addition, the sanctioning of gay marriages by Canadian courts in 2003 means a further change in the definition of family for marketers. Although many marketers continue to be wary of targeting nontraditional families, Bank of Montreal Financial Group targeted single fathers in a recent advertising campaign, which featured a split screen shot of two men, each walking and talking on a cell phone. One of the men was middle-aged and carrying a set of golf clubs on his back while the second man was a younger man walking with a baby strapped to his back in a carryall. The tag line was: "For the world you live in," and the idea was to let people know they would be treated as individuals.[53]

ON LINE 

Goodlife Fitness Clubs

Does Goodlife Fitness use its website as a means to connect with consumers via their body image? Do the content and design of the site surprise you? Why or why not?

http://www.goodlifefitness.com

Personality, Self-Concept, and Lifestyle

Each consumer has a unique personality. **Personality** is a broad concept that can be thought of as a way of organizing and grouping how an individual typically reacts to situations. Thus, personality combines psychological makeup and environmental forces. It includes people's underlying dispositions, especially their most dominant characteristics. Although personality is one of the least useful concepts in the study of consumer behaviour, some marketers believe that personality influences the types and brands of products purchased. For instance, the type of car, clothes, or jewellery a consumer buys may reflect one or more personality traits. Personality traits like those listed in Exhibit 4.9 may be used to describe a consumer's personality.

personality
A way of organizing and grouping the consistencies of an individual's reactions to situations.

Self-concept, or self-perception, is how consumers perceive themselves. Self-concept includes attitudes, perceptions, beliefs, and self-evaluations. Although self-concept may change, the change is often gradual. Through self-concept, people define their identity, which in turn provides for consistent and coherent behaviour.

self-concept
How consumers perceive themselves in terms of attitudes, perceptions, beliefs, and self-evaluations.

Self-concept combines the **ideal self-image** (the way an individual would like to be) and the **real self-image** (how an individual actually perceives himself or herself). Generally, we try to raise our real self-image toward our ideal (or at least narrow the gap). Consumers seldom buy products that jeopardize their self-image. For example, someone who sees herself as a trendsetter wouldn't buy clothing that doesn't project a contemporary image.

ideal self-image
The way an individual would like to be.

real self-image
The way an individual actually perceives himself or herself.

Human behaviour depends largely on self-concept. Because consumers want to protect their identity as individuals, the products they buy, the stores they patronize, and the credit cards they carry support their self-image. No other product quite reflects a person's self-image as much as the car he or she drives. For example, in a consumer survey conducted by Nissan, many consumers expressed dislike for family sedans like the Honda Accord and Toyota Camry, stating that "they would buy one for their mothers, but not for themselves."[54] Likewise, Mitsubishi found that car buyers did not want to sacrifice their youthful self-image just because they have new responsibilities in life. Thus, advertising for the Montero sport utility vehicle and the Eclipse Spyder positions these vehicles as "spirited cars for spirited people" and encourages would-be car buyers to experience the exhilaration of driving stylish, exciting cars.

EXHIBIT 4.9

Some Common Personality Traits

• Adaptability	• Deference
• Need for affiliation	• Defensiveness
• Aggressiveness	• Emotionalism
• Need for achievement	• Orderliness
• Ascendancy	• Sociability
• Autonomy	• Stability
• Dominance	• Self-confidence

By influencing the degree to which consumers perceive a good or service to be self-relevant, marketers can affect consumers' motivation to learn about, shop for, and buy a certain brand. Marketers also consider self-concept important because it helps explain the relationship between individuals' perceptions of themselves and their consumer behaviour.

An important component of self-concept is *body image,* the perception of the attractiveness of one's own physical features. For example, individuals who have cosmetic surgery often experience significant improvement in their overall body image and self-concept. Moreover, a person's perception of body image can be a stronger reason for weight loss than either good health or other social factors.[55] With the median age of Canadians rising, many companies are introducing products and services aimed at aging baby boomers who are concerned about their age and physical appearance. Sales of hair-colouring products for men, for instance, have more than doubled over the last decade, and television and print advertisements aimed at getting men to dye the grey out of their hair have tripled. Similarly, many companies, including PepsiCo with its Tropicana juices and Pfizer with Viagra, are repositioning their products to focus on lifestyle. Les Rotisseries St-Hubert is targeting baby boomers with sentimental ads to bring them back to dining in restaurants instead of buying chicken at fast-food restaurants or in the supermarket.[56]

lifestyle
A mode of living as identified by a person's activities, interests, and opinions.

Personality and self-concept are reflected in **lifestyle.** A lifestyle is a mode of living, as identified by a person's activities, interests, and opinions. *Psychographics* is the analytical technique used to examine consumer lifestyles and to categorize consumers. Unlike personality characteristics, which are hard to describe and measure, lifestyle characteristics are useful in segmenting and targeting consumers. Lifestyle and psychographic analysis explicitly addresses how consumers outwardly express their inner selves in their social and cultural environment.

Many companies now use psychographics to better understand their market segments. For many years, marketers selling products to mothers conveniently assumed that all moms were fairly homogeneous and concerned about the same things—the health and well-being of their children—and that they could all be reached with a similar message. But recent lifestyle research has shown that there are traditional, blended, and nontraditional moms, and companies like Procter & Gamble and Pillsbury are using strategies to reach these different types of mothers. Psychographics is also effective with other segments. General Motors of Canada targeted women car buyers in Quebec with a French-only advertising campaign. GM's research indicated that women represent 40 percent of actual car buyers in Canada and that they influenced 80 percent of all car purchases. GM was looking to promote its Pontiac Sunfire Cabriolet model. The buyer profile it was interested in was "defined by psychographics, which are active, youthful, fashion-sensitive. In this case, female, fairly good income, white collar, young, but not high executive." GM also knew that there was high fashion awareness in Quebec among women. It decided to use a print campaign targeting women through magazines such as *Elle Québec, Clin d'Oeil, Femmes Plus* and *Magazine les Ailes de la Mode.*[57] Psychographics and lifestyle segmentation are discussed in more detail in Chapter 6.

Although fitness is categorized most closely as a physiological need, it can also be considered a self-esteem need, particularly the prestigious health club memberships that it often entails. Even during recession, members will not sacrifice expensive memberships because to do so would be a subtle admission of financial difficulties.

>> PSYCHOLOGICAL INFLUENCES ON CONSUMER BUYING DECISIONS

8 Identify and understand the psychological factors that affect consumer buying decisions

An individual's buying decisions are further influenced by psychological factors: perception, motivation, learning, and beliefs and attitudes. These factors are what consumers use to interact with their world. They are the tools consumers use to recognize their feelings, gather and analyze information, formulate thoughts and opinions, and take action. Unlike the other three influences on consumer behaviour, psychological influences can be affected by a person's environment because they are applied on specific occasions. For example, you will perceive different stimuli and process these stimuli in different ways depending on whether you are sitting in class concentrating on the instructor, sitting outside of class talking to friends, or sitting in your dorm room watching television.

Perception

The world is full of stimuli. A stimulus is any unit of input affecting one or more of the five senses: sight, smell, taste, touch, and hearing. The process by which we select, organize, and interpret these stimuli to form a meaningful and coherent picture is called **perception.** In essence, perception is how we see the world around us and how we recognize that we need some help in making a purchasing decision.

perception
The process by which people select, organize, and interpret stimuli into a meaningful and coherent picture.

People cannot perceive every stimulus in their environment. Therefore, they use **selective exposure** to decide which stimuli to notice and which to ignore. A typical consumer is exposed to more than 250 advertising messages a day but notices only between 11 and 20.

selective exposure
The process whereby a consumer notices certain stimuli and ignores others.

The familiarity of an object, contrast, movement, intensity (such as increased volume), and smell are cues that influence perception. Consumers use these cues to identify and define products and brands. The shape of a product's packaging, such as Coca-Cola's signature contour bottle, for instance, can influence perception. Colour is another cue, and it plays a key role in consumers' perceptions. Packaged foods manufacturers use colour to trigger unconscious associations for grocery shoppers, who typically make their shopping decisions in the blink of an eye. Red, for instance, used on packages of Campbell's soups and SunMaid raisins, is associated with prolonged and increased eating. Green is associated with environmental goodness and healthy, low-fat foods.[58]

What consumers perceive may also depend on the stimuli's vividness or shock value. Graphic warnings of the hazards associated with a product's use are perceived more readily and remembered more accurately than less vivid warnings or warnings that are written in text. "Sexier" ads excel at attracting the attention of younger consumers. Companies like Calvin Klein and Guess use sensuous ads to "cut through the clutter" of competing ads and other stimuli to capture the attention of the target audience. Similarly, Benetton ads use shock value by portraying taboo social issues, from racism to homosexuality.

Two other concepts closely related to selective exposure are selective distortion and selective retention. **Selective distortion** occurs when consumers change or distort information that conflicts with their feelings or beliefs. For example, people who smoke and have no plans to quit may distort information from medical reports about the links between smoking and cancer and ignore the strong Health Canada warnings like "Smoking Can Kill You" that are prominently displayed on cigarette packages.

selective distortion
A process whereby a consumer changes or distorts information that conflicts with his or her feelings or beliefs.

Selective retention is remembering only information that supports personal feelings or beliefs. The consumer forgets all information that may be inconsistent. After reading a pamphlet that contradicts one's political beliefs, for instance, a person may forget many of the points outlined in it.

selective retention
A process whereby a consumer remembers only that information which supports his or her personal beliefs.

Which stimuli will be perceived often depends on the individual. People can be exposed to the same stimuli under identical conditions but perceive them very differently. For example, two people viewing a TV commercial may have different interpretations of the advertising message. One person may be thoroughly engrossed by the message and become highly motivated to buy the product. Thirty seconds after the ad ends, the second person may not be able to recall the content of the message or even the product advertised.

Marketing Implications of Perception

Marketers must recognize the importance of cues, or signals, in consumers' perception of products. Marketing managers first identify the important attributes, such as price or quality, that the targeted consumers want in a product and then design signals to communicate these attributes. For example, consumers will pay more for candy wrapped in expensive-looking foil packages. But shiny labels on wine bottles signify less expensive wines; dull labels indicate more expensive wines. Marketers also often use price as a signal to consumers that the product is of higher quality than competing products. Gibson Guitar Corporation briefly cut prices on many of its guitars to compete with Japanese rivals Yamaha and Ibanez but found instead that it sold more guitars when it charged more for them. Consumers perceived that the higher price indicated a better quality instrument.[59]

Of course, brand names send signals to consumers. The brand names of Close-Up toothpaste, DieHard batteries, and Caress moisturizing soap, for example, identify important product qualities. Names chosen for search engines and sites on the Internet, such as Yahoo!, Amazon.ca, CDNow, and Excite, are intended to convey excitement, intensity, and vastness. Companies might even change their names to send a message to consumers. As today's electric utility companies increasingly enter nonregulated markets to sell power, natural gas, and other energy-related products and services, they are finding their old company names may hold some negative perceptions with consumers. Consequently, many are shaking their stodgy "Power & Light & Electric" names in favour of those that let consumers know they are not just about electricity anymore. Examples include Alberta-based Enmax and Ontario-based Direct Energy.

Consumers also associate quality and reliability with certain brand names. Companies watch their brand identity closely, in large part because a strong link has been established between perceived brand value and customer loyalty. Canadian brand names that consistently enjoy high perceived value from consumers include Kraft, Seagram's, Molson, Weston, Tim Hortons, Schick, and President's Choice. Naming a product after a place can also add perceived value by association. Brand names using the words Banff, Whistler, and Yukon convey a sense of openness, freedom, and youth; products named after other locations might conjure up images of pollution and crime.

Marketing managers are also interested in the *threshold level of perception:* the minimum difference in a stimulus that the consumer will notice. This concept is sometimes referred to as the "just-noticeable difference." For example, how much would Sony have to drop the price of a home theatre system before consumers recognized it as a bargain—$25? $50? or more? One study found that the just-noticeable difference in a stimulus is about a 20 percent change. For example, consumers will likely notice a 20 percent price decrease more quickly than a 15 percent decrease. This marketing principle can be applied to other marketing variables as well, such as package size or loudness of a broadcast advertisement.[60]

Besides changing such stimuli as price, package size, and volume, marketers can change the product or attempt to reposition its image. Listerine is a well-known brand of mouthwash that has been on retailer's shelves for over 125 years! A very strong-tasting mouthwash, for nearly a century it was positioned as a brand that "kills germs that cause bad breath." In the 1970s and 1980s sweet tasting mouthwashes took hold and Listerine lost market share. In addition, the cosmetic-focused "bad breath" appeal was losing strength and consumers were becoming more concerned with plaque, tartar, and gingivitis, which were health-related appeals. Listerine's image had been health-related and medicinal as a bad breath fighter so it would seem natural to use this for a health appeal. However, Listerine decided to take the opportunity to break out of the old image. The brand decided to launch a new product, Listerine PocketPaks, and use a campaign where Listerine was an "Action Hero" battling the "Evil Gingivitis." The result was that Listerine's dollar market share jumped from 38 percent in 1999 to 45 percent in 2002.[61] But marketers must be careful when adding features. How many new services will discounter Zellers need to add before consumers perceive it as a full-service department store? How many sporty features will DaimlerChrysler have to add to a basic two-door sedan before consumers start perceiving it as a sports car?

Marketing managers who intend to do business in global markets should be aware of how foreign consumers perceive their products. For instance, in Japan, product labels are often written in English or French, even though they may not translate into anything meaningful. But many Japanese associate foreign words on product labels with the exotic, the expensive, and high quality.

Marketers have often been suspected of sending advertising messages subconsciously to consumers in what is known as *subliminal perception.* The controversy began in 1957 when a researcher claimed to have increased popcorn and Coca-Cola sales at a movie theatre after flashing "Eat popcorn" and "Drink Coca-Cola" on the screen every five seconds for 1/300th of a second, although the audience did not consciously recognize the messages. Almost immediately consumer protection groups became concerned that advertisers were brainwashing consumers, and this practice was promptly made illegal in Canada and California. Although the researcher later admitted to making up the data and scientists have been unable to replicate the study since, consumers are still wary of hidden messages that advertisers may be sending.

Motivation

By studying motivation, marketers can analyze the major forces influencing consumers to buy or not buy products. When you buy a product, you usually do so to fulfill some kind of need. These needs become motives when aroused sufficiently. For instance, suppose this morning you were so hungry before class that you needed to eat something. In response to that need, you stopped at Tim Hortons for a breakfast muffin. In other words, you were motivated by hunger to stop at Tim Hortons. **Motives** are the driving forces that cause a person to take action to satisfy specific needs.

motive
A driving force that causes a person to take action to satisfy specific needs.

Maslow's hierarchy of needs
A method of classifying human needs and motivations into five categories in ascending order of importance: physiological, safety, social, esteem, and self-actualization.

Why are people driven by particular needs at particular times? One popular theory is **Maslow's hierarchy of needs,** shown in Exhibit 4.10, which arranges needs in ascending order of importance: physiological, safety, social, esteem, and self-actualization. As a person fulfills one need, a higher-level need becomes more important.

The most basic human needs are *physiological*—that is the needs for food, water, and shelter. Because they are essential to survival, these needs must be satisfied first. Ads showing a juicy hamburger or a runner gulping down Gatorade after a marathon are examples of appeals to satisfy the physiological needs of hunger and thirst.

Safety needs include security and freedom from pain and discomfort. Marketers often exploit consumers' fears and anxieties about safety to sell their products. Michelin has long positioned its products on an appeal to safety. In a recent media campaign, the Michelin Man—his name is Bibendum, by the way—lies in the snow making snow angels. Several consumers wrote letters to Michelin expressing how nice it was to think of Michelin tires as "guardian angels." Michelin was please to discover consumers were getting the point of the campaign, which was "to make consumers feel warm and safe with Michelin."[62] On the other hand, some companies or industries advertise to allay consumer fears. For example, in the wake of the 2003 Alberta mad cow disease discovery, the beef industry found itself having to conduct an image campaign to reassure consumers about the safety of eating beef.[63]

After physiological and safety needs have been fulfilled, *social needs*—especially love and a sense of belonging—become the focus. Love includes acceptance by one's peers, as well as sex and romantic love. Marketing managers probably appeal more to this need than to any other. Ads for clothes, cosmetics, and vacation packages suggest that buying the product can bring love. The need to belong is also a favourite of

EXHIBIT 4.10

Maslow's Hierarchy of Needs

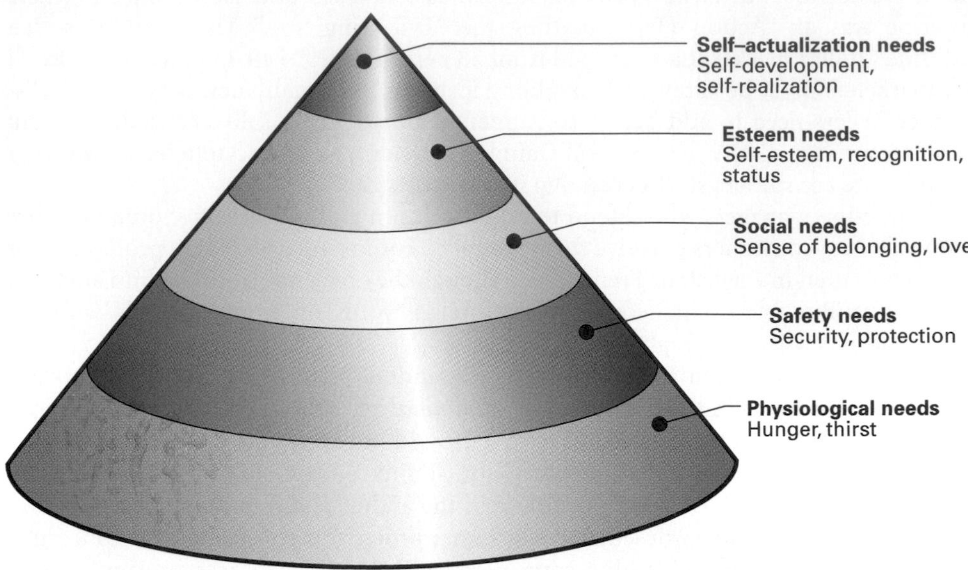

marketers, especially those marketing products to teens. Shoes and clothing brands such as Nike, Adidas, Old Navy, Gap, West 49, Hurley, and Guess score high with Canadian teenagers as "cool" brands. Teens who wear these labels feel and look like they belong to the in-crowd.[64]

Love is acceptance without regard to one's contribution. Esteem is acceptance based on one's contribution to the group. *Self-esteem needs* include self-respect and a sense of accomplishment. Esteem needs also include prestige, fame, and recognition of one's accomplishments. Mont Blanc pens, Mercedes-Benz automobiles, and Holt Renfrew stores all appeal to esteem needs. As an international cosmetics retailer, The Body Shop embarked on an international poster campaign to challenge societal notions of beauty. Designed to appeal to average female consumers, the campaign featured "Ruby," a computer generated spokesperson with normal body dimensions posing on a couch with the headline: "There are 3 billion women who don't look like supermodels and only 8 who do." The Body Shop communicates its aims with the following profile of Ruby: "measuring 43-36-40, Ruby's ambitions are to help everyone develop more positive self-esteem, so they can find inner contentedness and realize their full potential within society." Her turnoffs are "people who think you can never be too rich or too thin."[65]

Asian consumers, in particular, are strongly motivated by status and appearance. Asians are always conscious of their place in a group, institution, or society as a whole. The importance of gaining social recognition turns Asians into some of the most image-conscious consumers in the world. Status-conscious Asians will not hesitate to spend freely on premium brands, such as BMW, Mercedes-Benz, and the best Scotch whiskey and French cognac. Indeed, marketers of luxury products such as Gucci, Louis Vuitton, and Prada find that demand for their products is so strong among image-conscious consumers that their sales are generally unaffected by economic downturns. In some cases, companies have been able to make up for sluggish European and North American sales by raising prices and volume in Asia.[66]

The highest human need is *self-actualization.* It refers to finding self-fulfillment and self-expression, reaching the point in life at which "people are what they feel they should be." Maslow felt that very few people ever attain this level. Even so, advertisements may focus on this type of need. For example, American Express ads convey the message that acquiring its card is one of the highest attainments in life. Similarly, Microsoft appealed to consumers' needs for self-actualization when it chose "Yes, You Can" as the Windows XP slogan.[67] And the Canadian Armed Forces' slogan tells young people "There's no life like it."

Learning

Almost all consumer behaviour results from **learning,** which is the process that creates changes in behaviour through experience and practice. It is not possible to observe learning directly, but we can infer when it has occurred by a person's actions. For example, suppose you see an advertisement for a new and improved cold medicine. If you go to the store that day and buy that remedy, we infer that you have learned something about the cold medicine.

learning
A process that creates changes in behaviour, immediate or expected, through experience and practice.

There are two types of learning: experiential and conceptual. *Experiential learning* occurs when an experience changes your behaviour. For example, if you try the new cold medicine when you get home and it does not relieve your symptoms, you may not buy that brand again. *Conceptual learning,* which is not learned through direct experience, is the second type of learning. Assume, for example, that you are standing at a soft drink machine and notice a new diet flavour with an artificial sweetener. Because someone has told you that diet beverages leave an aftertaste, you choose a different drink. You have learned that you would not like this new diet drink without ever trying it.

Reinforcement and repetition boost learning. Reinforcement can be positive or negative. If you see a vendor selling frozen yogurt (stimulus), buy it (response), and find the yogurt to be quite refreshing (reward), your behaviour has been positively reinforced. On the other hand, if you buy a new flavour of yogurt and it does not taste good (negative reinforcement), you will not buy that flavour of yogurt again (response). Without positive or negative reinforcement, a person will not be motivated to repeat the behaviour pattern or to avoid it. Thus, if a new brand evokes neutral feelings, some marketing activity, such as a price change or an increase in promotion, may be required to induce further consumption. Learning theory is helpful in reminding marketers that concrete and timely actions are what reinforce desired consumer behaviour.

Repetition is a key strategy in promotional campaigns because it can lead to increased learning. Most marketers use repetitious advertising so that consumers will learn what their unique advantage is over the competition. Generally, to heighten learning, advertising messages should be spread over time rather than clustered together.

A related learning concept useful to marketing managers is stimulus generalization. In theory, **stimulus generalization** occurs when one response is extended to a second stimulus similar to the first. Marketers often use a successful, well-known brand name for a family of products because it gives consumers familiarity with and knowledge about each product in the family. Such brand-name families spur the introduction of new products and facilitate the sale of existing items. Microsoft recently entered the video game industry, hoping that the Microsoft brand would guarantee sales for the Xbox. Initial response to the Xbox has been strong based on Microsoft's reputation, but the company will have to work hard to make real progress in an industry dominated by other brand giants Sony and Nintendo.[68] Branding is examined in more detail in Chapter 8.

stimulus generalization
A form of learning that occurs when one response is extended to a second stimulus similar to the first.

Another form of stimulus generalization occurs when retailers or wholesalers design their packages to resemble well-known manufacturers' brands. Such imitation often confuses consumers, who buy the imitator thinking it's the original. Canadian manufacturers in foreign markets have sometimes found little, if any, brand protection. The Cowichan First Nations people found a market for their hand-knit sweaters among Japanese tourists in British Columbia. Hoping to capitalize on this interest by selling in Japan, they were shocked to find machine-made Cowichan knockoffs that were being imported from New Zealand![69] In South Korea, Procter & Gamble's Ivory soap competes head-on with the Korean brand Bory, which has an almost identical logo on the package. Consumers dissatisfied with Bory may attribute their dissatisfaction to Ivory, never realizing that Bory is an imitator. Counterfeit products are also manufactured to look exactly like the original. For

ON LINE

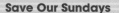

Save Our Sundays

Identify the beliefs and attitudes of the supporters of Save Our Sundays. Check the links to the Canada Family Action Coalition organization and the Canadian Christian Business Federation. What are the values of these organizations? Can you think of any way for Nova Scotia Tourism to respond to these beliefs?

http://members.tripod.com/saveoursundays

http://www.familyaction.org

http://www.ccbf.org

example, counterfeit Levi's jeans made in China are hot items in Europe, where Levi Strauss has had trouble keeping up with demand. The knockoffs look so much like the real thing that unsuspecting consumers don't know the difference—until after a few washes, when the belt loops fall off and the rivets begin to rust.

stimulus discrimination
A learned ability to differentiate among similar products.

The opposite of stimulus generalization is **stimulus discrimination,** which means learning to differentiate among similar products. Consumers usually prefer one product as more rewarding or stimulating. For example, some consumers prefer Coca-Cola and others prefer Pepsi; many insist they can taste a difference between the two brands.

With some types of products—such as aspirin, gasoline, bleach, and paper towels—marketers rely on promotion to point out brand differences that consumers would otherwise not recognize. This process, called *product differentiation,* is discussed in more detail in Chapter 6. Usually, product differentiation is based on superficial differences. For example, Bayer tells consumers that it's the aspirin "doctors recommend most."

Beliefs and Attitudes

belief
An organized pattern of knowledge that an individual holds as true about his or her world.

attitude
A learned tendency to respond consistently toward a given object.

Beliefs and attitudes are closely linked to values. A **belief** is an organized pattern of knowledge that an individual holds as true about his or her world. A consumer may believe that Sony's camcorder makes the best home videos, tolerates hard use, and is reasonably priced. These beliefs may be based on knowledge, faith, or hearsay. Consumers tend to develop a set of beliefs about a product's attributes and then, through these beliefs, form a *brand image*—a set of beliefs about a particular brand. In turn, the brand image shapes consumers' attitudes toward the product.

An **attitude** is a learned tendency to respond consistently toward a given object, such as a brand. Attitudes rest on an individual's value system, which represents personal standards of good and bad, right and wrong, and so forth; therefore, attitudes tend to be more enduring and complex than beliefs.

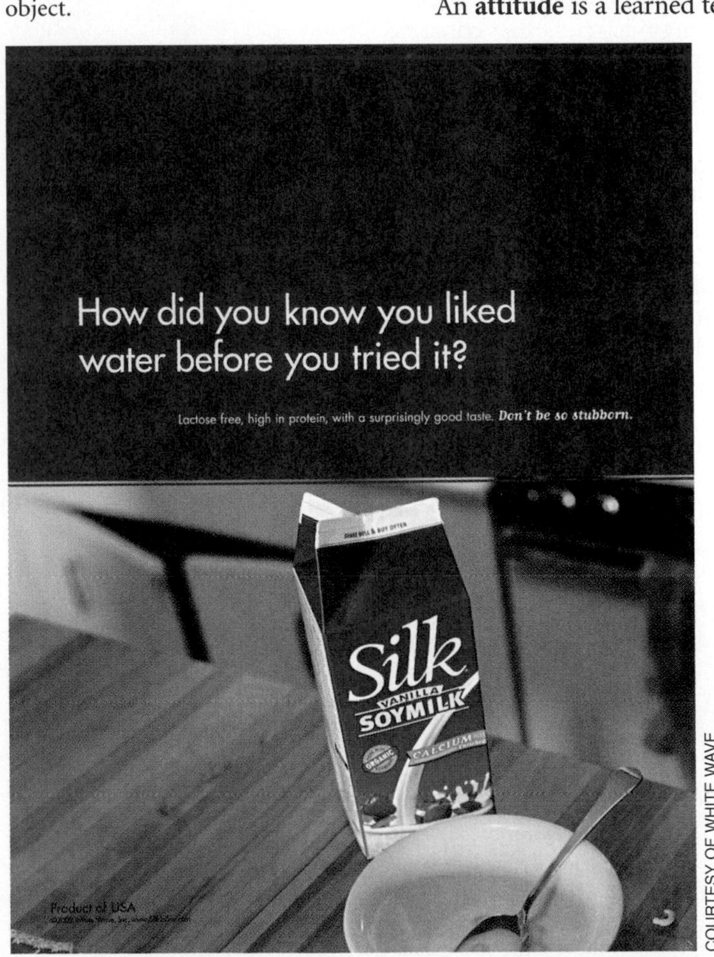

How did you know you liked water before you tried it?
Lactose free, high in protein, with a surprisingly good taste. Don't be so stubborn.
Silk
VANILLA
SOYMILK
CALCIUM
Product of USA
COURTESY OF WHITE WAVE

In order to increase sales, a company must change negative attitudes about its product held by those who are not buying it. One way to accomplish this is to change the beliefs about the product's attributes, such as taste. This ad for Silk soymilk does just that with its catchy question, and the follow-up, "Don't be so stubborn."

GLOBAL

For an example of the nature of attitudes, consider the differing attitudes of consumers around the world toward the practice of purchasing on credit. Canadians and Americans are known to be enthusiastic about charging goods and services and are willing to pay high interest rates for the privilege of postponing payment. To many European consumers, doing what amounts to taking out a loan—even a small one—to pay for anything seems absurd. Germans especially are reluctant to buy on credit. Italy has a sophisticated credit and banking system well suited to handling credit cards, but Italians prefer to carry cash, often huge wads of it. Although most Japanese consumers have credit cards, card purchases amount to less than 1 percent of all consumer transactions. The Japanese have long looked down on credit purchases but will acquire cards to use while travelling abroad.[70]

If a good or service is meeting its profit goals, positive attitudes toward the product merely need to be reinforced. If the brand is not succeeding, however, the marketing manager must strive to change target consumers' attitudes toward it. Changes in attitude tend to grow out of an individual's attempt to reconcile long-held values with a constant stream of new information. This change can be accomplished in three ways: changing beliefs about the brand's attributes, changing the relative importance of these beliefs, and adding new beliefs.

Changing Beliefs about Attributes

The first technique is to turn neutral or negative beliefs about product attributes into positive ones. For example, Quebec-based Canadelle, maker of Wonderbra, wants to reach more youthful customers. The firm is trying to change young women's beliefs about Wonderbra products with its new "Design" brand bra. Research indicated that young women viewed the Wonderbra brand as "their grandmother's bra" and were not receptive to purchasing it. The new "Design" brand was developed as a fashion style bra targeted at young women and contrasts with the moulded functional style bras associated with the Wonderbra brand.[71]

Changing beliefs about a service can be more difficult because service attributes are intangible. Convincing consumers to switch hairstylists or lawyers or to go to a mall dental clinic can be much more difficult than getting them to change brands of razor blades. Image, which is also largely intangible, significantly determines service patronage. For example, the Bank of Montreal in Quebec noticed a decline in its brand image and employee motivation between 1996 and 2000. Research showed that Quebeckers viewed money as not only something to be saved for retirement but also as a means to enjoy life. The Bank of Montreal decided to appeal to this attitude and establish a new image with a new marketing approach called "Profitez." The word *profitez* "means not only to profit in a financial sense, but also to enjoy, to take advantage of life." The campaign features humorous and memorable commercials such as one showing a proud father giving a speech at his daughter's wedding during which he blurts out "the cost." The campaign has raised awareness for the Bank of Montreal by 18.2 percent and revenue, profitability, and employee morale have increased as well.[72] Service marketing is explored in detail in Chapter 10.

Changing the Importance of Beliefs

The second approach to modifying attitudes is to change the relative importance of beliefs about an attribute. For years, consumers have known that bran cereals are high in natural fibre. The primary belief associated with this attribute is that the fibre tends to act as a mild, natural laxative. Today, however, cereal marketers promote the high fibre content of bran cereals as a possible factor in preventing certain types of cancer, vastly increasing the importance of this attribute in the minds of consumers.

Marketers can also emphasize the importance of some beliefs over others. For example, DaimlerChrysler's Jeep unit positions it as being rugged but promotes its luxury features. The newest Grand Cherokees have even more off-road capability, but very few owners ever take them off-road. Luxury features include a climate-control system with infrared beams that track drivers' and passengers' skin temperature to automatically adjust air conditioning and heat, his and her key rings that remember settings for power seats and mirrors, a system to reprogram radio stations for different drivers, and many other comforts.

Adding New Beliefs

The third approach to transforming attitudes is to add new beliefs. Although changes in consumption patterns often come slowly, cereal marketers are betting that consumers will eventually warm up to the idea of cereal as a snack. A print ad for Cookie-Crisp cereal features a boy popping the sugary nuggets into his mouth while he does his homework. Boxes of Kellogg's Cracklin' Oat Bran boast that the cereal tastes like oatmeal cookies and makes "a great snack ... anytime." Similarly, commercials for Quaker Oats 100 percent Natural cereal promote eating it straight from the box. James River Corporation, the manufacturer of Dixie paper products, is also attempting to add new beliefs about the uses of its paper plates and cups with an advertising campaign aimed at positioning its product as a "home cleanup replacement." New commercials pitch Dixie paper plates as an alternative to washing dishes after everyday meals.[73]

North American companies attempting to market their goods overseas may need to help consumers add new beliefs about a product in general. For example, both Coca-Cola and PepsiCo have both found it challenging to sell their diet cola brands to consumers in India partly because diet foods of any kind are a new concept there. Until recently, malnutrition was widespread in India. Indians also have deep-rooted attitudes that anything labelled "diet" is meant for a sick person, such as a diabetic. As a general rule, most Indians are not diet-conscious, preferring food prepared in the traditional manner that tastes good. Indians are also suspicious of the artificial sweeteners used in diet colas. India's Health Ministry has required labels warning "Not Recommended for Children" on cans and bottles of Diet Coke and Diet Pepsi.[74]

>> CONNECT IT

Reflecting on the chapter material, you should now be able to see how cultural, social, individual, and psychological factors affect the consumer decision-making process. Purchase decisions are influenced by many factors, from opinion leaders to peer groups. Individuals have unique values and opinions based upon the environment in which they have grown up. Marketers hoping to reach different segments must understand each segment's needs and wants, as well as how the influences that shape them vary. Consumer behaviour is a fascinating and often intricate process. An appreciation of consumer behaviour and the factors that influence it will help you identify target markets and design effective marketing mixes. Harvey's Restaurants believes it has a good understanding of the needs and wants of its target market with respect to eating. It has based its "Long Live the Grill" positioning on this understanding, and its success or failure will depend on how well Harvey's Restaurants has applied its knowledge of consumer decision making.

REVIEW IT

1 Explain why marketing managers should understand consumer behaviour. Consumer behaviour describes how consumers make purchase decisions and how they use and dispose of the products they buy. An understanding of consumer behaviour reduces marketing managers' uncertainty when they are defining a target market and designing a marketing mix.

1.1 The type of decision making a consumer uses for a product does not necessarily remain constant. Why? Support your answer with an example from your own experience.

2 Analyze the components of the consumer decision-making process. The consumer decision-making process begins with need recognition, when stimuli trigger awareness of an unfulfilled want. If additional information is required to make a purchase decision, the consumer may engage in an internal or external information search. The consumer then evaluates the additional information and establishes purchase guidelines. Finally, a purchase decision is made.

2.1 ON LINE Visit Canada.com's car website at http://autos.canada.com/national/buying. How does the site assist consumers in the evaluation stage of choosing a new car? Develop your own hypothetical evoked set of three or four car models and present your comparisons. Which vehicle attributes would be most important in your purchase decision?

3 Explain the consumer's postpurchase evaluation process. Consumer postpurchase evaluation is influenced by prepurchase expectations, the prepurchase information search, and the consumer's general level of self-confidence. Cognitive dissonance is the inner tension that a consumer experiences after recognizing a purchased product's disadvantages. When a purchase creates cognitive dissonance, consumers tend to react by seeking positive reinforcement for the purchase decision, avoiding negative information about the purchase decision, or revoking the purchase decision by returning the product.

3.1 WRITING Recall an occasion when you experienced cognitive dissonance about a purchase. In a letter to a friend, describe the event and explain what you did about it.

4 **Identify the types of consumer buying decisions and discuss the significance of consumer involvement.** Consumer decision making falls into three broad categories. First, consumers exhibit routine response behaviour for frequently purchased, low-cost items that require very little decision effort; routine response behaviour is typically characterized by brand loyalty. Second, consumers engage in limited decision making for occasional purchases or for unfamiliar brands in familiar product categories. Third, consumers practise extensive decision making when making unfamiliar, expensive, or infrequent purchases. High-involvement decisions usually include an extensive information search and a thorough evaluation of alternatives. In contrast, low-involvement decisions are characterized by brand loyalty and a lack of personal identification with the product. The main factors affecting the level of consumer involvement are previous experience, interest, perceived risk of negative consequences (financial, social, and psychological), situation, and social visibility.

4.1 Describe the three categories of consumer decision-making behaviour. Name typical products for which each type of consumer behaviour is used.

5 **Identify and understand the cultural factors that affect consumer buying decisions.** Cultural influences on consumer buying decisions include culture and values, subculture, and social class. Culture is the essential character of a society that distinguishes it from other cultural groups. The underlying elements of every culture are the values, language, myths, customs, rituals, laws, and the artifacts, or products, which are transmitted from one generation to the next. The most defining element of a culture is its values—the enduring beliefs shared by a society that a specific mode of conduct is personally or socially preferable to another mode of conduct. A culture can be divided into subcultures on the basis of demographic characteristics, geographic regions, national and ethnic background, political beliefs, and religious beliefs. Subcultures share elements of the overall culture as well as cultural elements unique to their own group. A social class is a group of people who are considered nearly equal in status or community esteem, who regularly socialize among themselves both formally and informally, and who share behavioural norms.

5.1 WRITING You are a new marketing manager for a firm that produces a line of athletic shoes to be targeted to the college/university student subculture. In a memo to your boss, list some product attributes that might appeal to this subculture and the steps in your customers' purchase processes, and recommend some marketing strategies that can influence their decision.

6 **Identify and understand the social factors that affect consumer buying decisions.** Social factors include such external influences as reference groups, opinion leaders, and family. Consumers seek out others' opinions for guidance on new products or services and products with image-related attributes or because attribute information is lacking or uninformative. Consumers may use products or brands to identify with or become a member of a reference group. Opinion leaders are members of reference groups who influence others' purchase decisions. Family members also influence purchase decisions; children tend to shop in patterns similar to their parents'.

6.1 Family members play many different roles in the buying process: initiator, influencer, decision maker, purchaser, and consumer. In your family, name who might play each of these roles in the purchase of a dinner at Pizza Hut, a summer vacation, Froot Loops breakfast cereal, a Roots Canadian Olympic team jacket, golf clubs, an Internet service provider, and a new car.

7 **Identify and understand the individual factors that affect consumer buying decisions.** Individual factors that affect consumer buying decisions include gender; age and family life-cycle stage; and personality, self-concept, and lifestyle. Beyond obvious physiological differences, men and women differ in their social and economic roles that affect consumer buying decisions. How old a consumer is generally indicates what products he or she may be interested in purchasing. Marketers often define their target markets in terms of consumers' life-cycle stage, and then follow changes in consumers' attitudes and behavioural tendencies as they mature. Finally, certain products and brands reflect consumers' personality, self-concept, and lifestyle.

7.1 Assume that you are involved in the following consumer decision situations: (a) renting a video to watch with your roommates, (b) choosing a fast-food restaurant to go to with a new friend, (c) buying a popular music compact disc, (d) buying jeans to wear to class. List the individual factors that would influence your decision in each situation and explain your responses.

8 **Identify and understand the psychological factors that affect consumer buying decisions.** Psychological factors include perception, motivation, learning, values, beliefs, and attitudes. These factors allow consumers to interact with the world around them, recognize their feelings, gather and analyze information, formulate thoughts and opinions, and take action. Perception allows consumers to recognize their consumption problems. Motivation is what drives consumers to take action to satisfy specific consumption needs. Almost all consumer behaviour results from learning, which is the process that creates changes in behaviour through experience. Consumers with similar beliefs and attitudes tend to react alike to marketing-related inducements.

8.1 ON LINE How do beliefs and attitudes influence consumer behaviour? How can negative attitudes toward a product be changed? How can marketers alter beliefs about a product? Give some examples of how marketers have changed negative attitudes about a product or added or altered beliefs about a product.

8.2 How can nonmarketing periodicals help you understand consumer behaviour? Using InfoTrac® College Edition (**http://infotrac.thomsonlearning.com**), research articles from such publications as the *Journal of Psychology, Psychology Today, Race and Class, Working Women, Society,* and others. Select and read three articles that explore different topics (i.e., do not select three articles on psychology). Then make a list of factors you think could affect consumer purchasing behaviour. Include with each factor a way marketers could use this information to their benefit.

DEFINE IT

aspirational reference group 107
attitude 120
belief 120
cognitive dissonance 95
consumer behaviour 90
consumer decision-making process 90
culture 100
evoked set (consideration set) 94
extensive decision making 96
external information search 92
ideal self-image 113
internal information search 92
involvement 96
learning 119
lifestyle 114
limited decision making 96
marketing-controlled information source 92
Maslow's hierarchy of needs 117
motive 117
need recognition 90
nonaspirational reference group 107
nonmarketing-controlled information source 92
norm 107
opinion leader 108
perception 115
personality 113
primary membership group 106–107
real self-image 113

APPLY IT

Quiznos Canada, based in Mississauga, Ontario, is one of Canada's newest franchise opportunities offering gourmet toasted sub sandwiches, fresh salads, hearty soups, and specialty desserts. It is positioned to compete with Mr. Sub, Subway, and similar sandwich restaurants. Quiznos is trying to distinguish itself from its competitors by offering a premium-quality menu of gourmet toasted submarine sandwiches, made with the highest-quality ingredients. According to Charlotte Russell, executive vice president of Quiznos Canada Corporation, "People are trying to live healthier and a big part of that is eating better quality food. Quiznos offers only the finest-quality ingredients. We make our sandwiches with real Canadian cheese, and you will never find fillers in any of our meats."

Because this is a new franchise, potential customers must first be made aware of Quiznos and then be convinced to try it. Over the long run, a loyal customer base must be established to make each Quiznos location a success. As such, Quiznos decided to use well-known Canadian personality and *Hockey Night in Canada*'s "Coaches Corner" host, Don Cherry, to promote its product. "Take it from me, forget about the bagged lunches, and come on over to Quiznos today for the best-tasting sandwich in Canada," Cherry says. "If there were a Stanley Cup for subs, it would go to Quiznos, 'cause toasted tastes better!"

In addition to commercials featuring Don Cherry, Quiznos also developed a special coupon promotion to encourage Canadians to try the product. In honour of the opening of its 200th store in June 2003, Quiznos distributed $2.00 sandwich coupons to more than 1.5 million Canadians. The result was that Quiznos Canada produced approximately $100 million in sales in Canada in 2003.

However, in its boldest move yet, Quiznos decided to take on its competition with a direct taste test it promoted as the Quiznos "Eat Me" Sub Challenge. The firm promoted the taste test well before undertaking it so there was some risk if the results were not in its favour. Regardless, the firm undertook a national survey of more than 2,500 Canadians, who each taste-tested one-inch cheese-and-steak sandwich samples from Quiznos, Subway, and Mr. Sub. The results were that 88 percent of the participants rated the Quiznos Philly Cheesesteak as the best-tasting sub. Greg MacDonald, vice president of marketing for Quiznos Sub, commented on the taste test: "Canada has wowed us with an overwhelming 88 percent voting the Quiznos Philly Cheesesteak Canada's best tasting beef sub sandwich!" Quiznos Sub had been experiencing strong levels of sales for its Philly Cheesesteak Sub and is expecting sales to increase further based on a promotion of its test results.

Based on: Press Release, "Don Cherry Toasts Quiznos Sub Sandwiches to Mark Chain's 200th Store Opening Celebration," *Canada NewsWire*, June 23, 2003; Press Release, "Quiznos Sub Shows Canada Who's Got the Beef!" *Canada NewsWire*, March 11, 2004; and Quiznos website, **http://www.quiznos.com**.

QUESTIONS

1. Are Quiznos Canada's unique advantages strong enough to attract customers from Mr. Sub and other sandwich competitors? Why or why not?
2. Discuss the approaches that Quiznos Canada has used to make potential customers aware of Quiznos locations and menu selections. Do you think they are effective? Why or why not?
3. How can Quiznos Canada convince individuals who try Quiznos to become regular customers?

THINK ABOUT IT

EyeOnU operates a Web filter service for public schools and libraries to protect students from inappropriate material on the Internet. Like the industry as a whole, the company's market share has been stagnant for the past two years. Looking for new sources of revenue, the company is considering selling the data it has collected about student surfing habits to marketers trying to learn more about students' behaviour on the Web. The data is anonymous but privacy advocates are concerned about the precedent of selling information about children to marketers.

QUESTIONS

1. What should EyeOnU do? Should it protect the student's data, or should it take the opportunity to create new revenues?
2. Does the CMA Code of Ethics for marketing on the Internet address this issue? Go to **http://www.the-cma.org/consumer/ethics.cfm** and review the code of ethics. Then write a brief paragraph on how the CMA Code of Ethics for marketing on the Internet relates to EyeOnU's dilemma.

TRY IT

Consumer Behaviour Case: Mexican Food and Canadian Flavour

Ken Pattenden wants to bring "authentic Mexican food" to all of Canada with a new chain of TacoTime restaurants and he wants to challenge Taco Bell for first place in doing so. TacoTime is a Western Canadian-based "Quick Service Restaurant." It was founded 25 years ago in Lethbridge, Alberta, with a single store. By 2003, it had grown into a chain of 112 stores located between Victoria, British Columbia, and Thunder Bay, Ontario. TacoTime has been competing with McDonald's and Burger King all along and now, of course, it competes with Taco Bell, although Taco Bell has not been a strong force in Western Canada up to now. In 2000, Ken Pattenden realized that competing against these fast-food giants was going to become more and more difficult for TacoTime. He decided that the company needed to consider repositioning.

Pattenden commissioned a series of focus group studies so that he could get a handle on the market for Mexican food. When asked about what they associated with Mexico, focus group participants said, "sunshine, beaches, tequila, and food." When asked about presentation of Mexican food, the focus groups said that food served on a plate was more authentic than food served on wax paper. TacoTime decided to test out the focus group findings by promoting its Casita Platter product, which was a marginal seller with one or two being sold per day in an average store. Using in-store posters of the platter, TacoTime saw an increase from one or two per day to an average of 15 platters per day.

Based on the focus group findings, TacoTime has decided to embark on a major repositioning move from being a "Quick Service Restaurant" (known more commonly as a fast-food restaurant) to a "Fast Casual Dining" restaurant that serves authentic Mexican food. The first stroke in this campaign involved developing a new line of Mexican Fiesta Platters composed of salad, rice, and beans and priced at $6.00. The second step in the repositioning involved aggressive advertising of the new Fiesta Platters. The ads feature the promotional line, "Mexico from about $6," to sound more like travel ads than fast-food menus. The next move was to open new "Fast Casual" cantina-like restaurants, which would offer Mexican beer and sangria as beverages to go with the food. This means higher-end food, table service, and bigger food cheques than "Quick Service Restaurants."

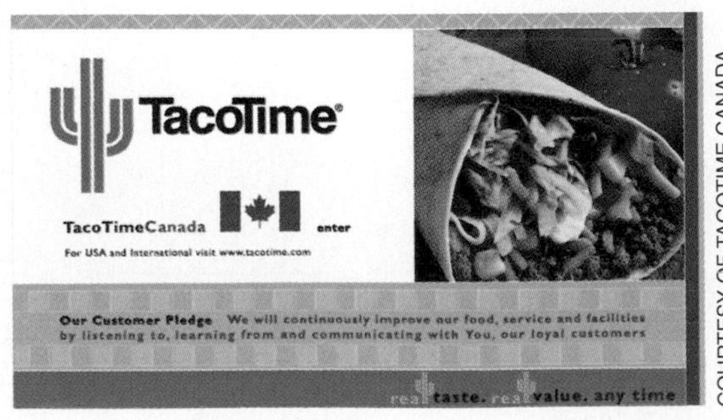

COURTESY OF TACOTIME CANADA.

Fast Casual restaurants are the newest trend in the restaurant business. Statistics indicate tremendous potential with a growth rate of about 16 percent per year in the United States. Despite their tremendous growth, Fast Casual restaurants only have about 2 percent of the restaurant business. By comparison, Quick Service Restaurants like Taco Bell have seen their growth slow to about 2 percent per year, which means TacoTime is planning to ride the "highest wave" at the moment. In addition, although there are some Fast Casual Mexican food outlets in the U.S., there were none known to be operating in Canada. TacoTime plans to begin its initial repositioning in British Columbia, where it already has a presence. Cantinas are planned for Nanaimo, Cranbrook, and Kelowna, British Columbia. The positioning statement for the new cantinas is: "The TacoTime Cantina is a fast casual restaurant featuring authentic Mexican food, music, liquor, and decor." The operating business philosophy is "TacoTime prides itself on preparing authentic Mexican food in a friendly environment that provides outstanding customer service and value."

TacoTime's longer term plans are to move into Eastern Canada, but at the moment Ken Pattenden says it does not have sufficient financial backing for a move into these markets. Even more daunting than the need for cash to move east will be having to take on Taco Bell head-to-head when it does. Although at the moment, TacoTime is the "Fastest Gun in the West" when it comes to Mexican food in Canada, Taco Bell is the "Beast of the East."

Sources: Norma Ramage, "TacoTime Dreams Grande," *Marketing Magazine*, March 3, 2003; TacoTime Corporate website, http://www.tacotimecanada.ca, accessed October 28, 2003.

QUESTIONS

1. What type of consumer buying decision best describes dining at TacoTime's new authentic Mexican Cantina restaurants? Is it different from the decision made to dine at the current TacoTime or a Taco Bell restaurant? Is it different from deciding to dine at a McDonald's restaurant? How?
2. List the factors that would influence a consumer to spend his or her dining budget at a TacoTime restaurant. Include cultural, social, individual, and psychological factors on your list.
3. Given the health concerns people have with restaurant food these days, what issues do you think TacoTime will have to consider on this front? Based on the factors you identify, what advice would you give TacoTime with respect to its menu?
4. Vist the TacoTime website at **http://www.tacotimecanada.com**. Does the website communicate the image of "authentic" Mexican food? Why or why not? Make some suggestions to TacoTime management for reinforcing the company's authentic Mexican food positioning on its website.

FLIP IT

GRADEMAKER

Flip to Chapter 4 in your *Grademaker Study Guide* for more review opportunities, including the pretest, vocabulary review, Internet activities, study test questions, and consumer behaviour scenarios. Do you know the major factors that influence consumer behaviour? Can you close your book and diagram the consumer decision-making process? Open you Study Guide to find out how much you know—or don't know.

CLICK IT

The *Marketing* website is rich with materials to help you review and master marketing concepts. Check your knowledge with the free quizzes, practise key terms using the crossword puzzles, or review key concepts using the Microsoft® PowerPoint® slides. Also on the website are updated weblinks to companies mentioned in this chapter, Internet exercises, career marketing information, and much much more! Go to http://www.lamb3e.nelson.com, read the material, and follow the convenient links.

WATCH IT

Quest for a Vegetarian "Happy Meal"

Neil Wadhvana is a motivated consumer who is on a quest to lobby the fast-food industry. Neil is not your typical lobbyist. For starters, he is only seven years old, but he is a highly energetic, motivated, and precocious seven-year old with an amazing singing voice, and he wants to be a "singing brain surgeon" when he grows up. Neil is also a celebrity who has sung "O Canada" at over 180 events, including five performances for former Canadian Prime Minister Jean Chrétien and one for Queen Elizabeth II of England. Also known as "Mr. O Canada," Neil is still a kid, and he likes child-oriented fast-food restaurant meals that come with collectible toys. Neil has a major problem with the fast-food burger chains, though: he is a vegetarian, and the burger chains do not cater to vegetarians. In particular, Neil is upset that he is unable to order a McDonald's "Happy Meal" with a veggie burger.

Most seven-year-olds just give up when an adult tells them they just can't have what they want, but not Neil. He believed he could convince McDonald's and the other fast-food burger chains—Burger King, Harvey's, and Wendy's—to offer a veggie burger option with their kids' meals. Neil's problem was how to go about doing so. He took the problem to his grade one class. His teacher, Carolyn Cosburn, was taken aback at first because of the extent of the project. After all, Neil was proposing to lobby four major corporations. However, rather than try and talk him out of it, she decided to involve the class in the project and help him by turning the situation into a learning experience.

Neil began by undertaking a consumer survey of his class to see how they felt about the issue. Not surprisingly, his classmates supported him and his point of view. They also informed him that each and every one of them patronized his targeted restaurant, McDonald's. However, Neil realized that simply having a single class of grade one kids on his side was only a start. He realized that he needed more support for his cause. The problem for Neil, and for any consumer lobbyist for that matter, is that marketers seek to serve customer needs and wants at a profit. The most recent information on the Canadian market indicates that only 4 percent of the population, about 1.3 million people, are actually vegetarian. In addition, the vast majority of vegans are adults, not children. The profit potential of a strictly vegan child's meal is not great. Fast-food marketers would be clearly aware of these statistics and thus one complaint from one child would be as likely to be ignored as anything else.

Neil realized he needed support from the general community, so he got permission to lobby the audience at a soccer game where he sang the national anthem. He handed out 1,000 surveys to the soccer fans and got back 427, with 247 of the respondents saying they favoured a veggie meal offering. He used this information along with his own personal arguments in letters and e-mails to McDonald's, Harvey's, Burger King, and Wendy's to ask them to provide a "kids' veggie burger meal." McDonald's, Harvey's and Wendy's all responded to Neil. They sent him coupons to use in their restaurants, but none of them committed to a kids' veggie burger meal. All of them indicated that they had food choices for vegetarians but not kids' meals.

The fact is, the fast-food industry was already responding indirectly to Neil Wadhvana and people like him. The desire for healthy food choices and less meat has prompted all fast-food restaurants to create meatless offerings that satisfy lower-cholesterol and fat-free diets as well as vegetarian diets. Virtually all fast-food restaurants have been offering some form of veggie burger meal, but these have been targeted to adults. Despite this, Leslie Root, a marketing manager at Burger King, responded to Neil by agreeing to add a veggie burger to the kids' menu. To quote Leslie Root, "We thought it was quite a good idea and something we really hadn't thought about before. It was just sort of 'eureka' – yeah, surprise. Obviously we should be offering this item." Leslie's response also fits very well with Burger King's "Have It Your Way" business motto.

The response from McDonald's was to reply that the restaurants would be offering a grilled cheese Happy Meal, but this was not what Neil was shooting for. He wanted a veggie burger offering. So Neil didn't get what he wanted from McDonald's. In addition, McDonald's may not have hit the market it was shooting for either. You see, cheese is still an animal product and this won't satisfy strict vegans.

QUESTIONS

1. What do you think motivates consumers like Neil Wadhvana to lobby businesses to meet their needs? What, if anything, do you think Neil's age had to do with the manner in which the fast-food firms responded to him?
2. Evaluate the respective responses of McDonald's, Harvey's, and Wendy's. Do you think the responses were appropriate? Why or why not? Evaluate Burger King's response to Neil. Why do you think Burger King responded the way it did?

3. Given that vegans represent 4 percent of the general population and that burger chains were created to sell hamburgers, how do you think these restaurants should respond to the needs of vegans?
4. Evaluate Neil's lobbying approach. What do you think he did well? Do you have any suggestions for Neil that might help him to win his case with McDonald's?

Sources: CBC, *Marketplace*, "One Kid's Quest for a Vegetarian 'Happy Meal'", Broadcast: November 18, 2003; Hattie Klotz, "Meatless Meals on the Rise," *Calgary Herald* [Final Edition], November 28, 2002, S11.

chapter 5

Business Marketing

>> LEARNING OBJECTIVES

1. Describe business marketing
2. Describe the role of the Internet in business marketing
3. Discuss the role of relationship marketing and strategic alliances in business marketing
4. Identify the four major categories of business market customers
5. Explain the North American Industry Classification System
6. Explain the major differences between business and consumer markets
7. Describe the seven types of business goods and services
8. Discuss the unique aspects of business buying behaviour

>> When Canadians think of Canada Post they have an image of a postal carrier delivering mail to their homes. This is certainly one of the most visible and tangible functions of Canada Post, which delivers 37 million pieces of mail each day, much of which is sent to the households of 31 million Canadians. However, Canada Post also delivers daily mail to over 1 million organizations. To quote from Canada Post's on-line brochure: "Our ongoing quest for evolution and change has transformed Canada Post from a singularly-focused service into a multi-faceted enterprise with a more global outlook." Part of this transformation includes offering business services, which are promoted with the motto, "Helping you to stay connected."

How does Canada Post help businesses stay connected? The company created the "Canada Post Group," which is comprised of Purolator Courier, Progistix-Solutions, Intelcom Courier, epost, Innovapost, and Canada Post International Ltd. Purolator Courier is billed as Canada's leading overnight courier; it offers 24-hour pickup and delivery. Progistix-Solutions is a logistics company that specializes in consolidation of order management, order fulfillment, and order delivery. Intelcom Courier duplicates some of Purolator's activities but focuses on same-day delivery instead of overnight. Canada Post has recognized electronic communication as a threat to its mail delivery business but also as an opportunity for growth. As such, the firm created epost, promoted as "the world's first electronic post office, delivering the mail online for Canada Post." Canada Post states that "epost is leading the evolution of mail in Canada by providing an expanding electronic document delivery network that connects Canadian businesses and consumers at a range of relevant online locations." Finally, Canada Post created Innovapost to leverage its knowledge and expertise by providing "IS/IT services and eBusiness solutions" for use by its internal companies and to market them "to postal administrations around the world."

Canada Post describes its business services as follows: "Whether you're a large multinational corporation or a budding family business with big ambitions, our one goal remains the same: to deliver your products efficiently and cost-effectively. Since our inception, Canada Post has played an essential role in delivering the last mile of customer order fulfilment. Today, with the addition of the expertise of Progistix-Solutions and the speed of Purolator, we can take care of your supply chain every step of the way. Our geographic reach and breadth of services provide the leadership that retailers are demanding in this expanding and competitive market. The beauty of this one-stop, seamless solution lies in its simplicity. When a consumer places an order with a company, whether it's by telephone, mail order or over the Internet, it can be routed directly to one of our warehouses. There, we keep the company's inventory on hand, and the purchase is immediately picked, packed and shipped—without the business owner ever having to lift a finger. In major centres, online customers can also choose to receive deliveries in the evening or on Saturdays. Depending on your needs, your supply chain solution can even manage product returns, ship parts to your suppliers, and provide sales reports.

"Our Online Business Centre is a prime destination for Canada Post commercial customers, offering a secure electronic site for simple, accurate and fast solutions to business transactions. Always open for business, the centre offers online ordering, electronic shipping tools, account management and other useful online tools. Our Website also includes a postal code look-up, a postal outlet locator, a rate calculator, and shipment tracking.

"Technically adept and well positioned for the international eBusiness market, Canada Post continues to take advantage of emerging opportunities. By offering a spectrum of solutions that go far beyond our traditional services, we're broadening the ability of companies to manage their business locally, domestically and globally."[1]

What do you think motivated Canada Post to develop business services and to go on-line? What kinds of relationships does Canada Post have with its customers? What kinds of business services does it offer?

ON LINE

Canada Post

Visit the Canada Post website and find out about the company's various business products and services. How well are the business services promoted on Canada Post's website?

http://www.canadapost.ca

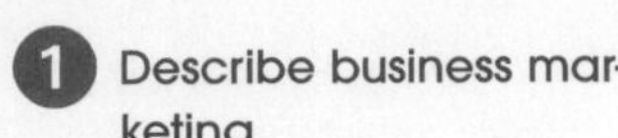
1 Describe business marketing

business marketing
The marketing of goods and services to individuals and organizations for purposes other than personal consumption. Often referred to as B2B.

>> WHAT IS BUSINESS MARKETING?

Business marketing is the marketing of goods and services to individuals and organizations for purposes other than personal consumption. It is commonly referred to as business-to-business marketing or B2B. The sale of a digital data projector to your college or university is an example of business marketing. Business products include those that are used to manufacture other products, become part of another product, or aid the normal operations of an organization, or that are acquired for resale without any substantial change in form. The key characteristic distinguishing business products from consumer products is intended use, not physical characteristics. Hence, this activity is called business-to-business marketing (B2B) when the intended product use is for business and business-to-consumers marketing (B2C) when the intended product use is for consumers. A product that is purchased for personal or family consumption or as a gift is a consumer good. If that same product, such as a microcomputer or a cellular telephone, is bought for use in a business, it is a business product.

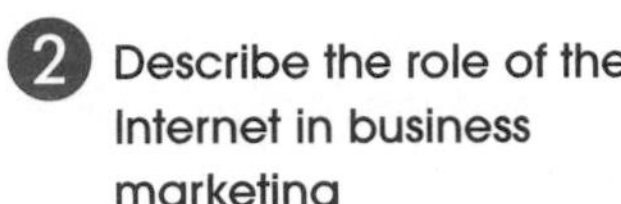
2 Describe the role of the Internet in business marketing

ON LINE

>> BUSINESS MARKETING ON THE INTERNET

It is hard to imagine that commercial use of the Internet began as recently as the mid-1990s.[2] In 1995, those commercial websites that did exist were static. Only a few had data-retrieval capabilities. Frames, tables, and styles were not available. Security of any sort was rare, and streaming video did not exist. In early 1995, the entire Internet could have been stored on fewer than 50 compact disks.[3]

What a difference a few years have made! The worldwide purchase of business goods and services runs into the trillions of dollars annually. Cost savings just from purchasing goods and services on-line are estimated to exceed $2 trillion annually. In Canada, on-line transactions were valued at $13.7 billion in 2002, a growth rate of 46 percent over 2001. Of this amount, $9.7 billion was business-to business sales, which represented a 19.8 percent increase over 2001. This trend in growth is expected to continue. A survey by Forrester Research indicated that in 2003 approximately 12 percent of all business-to-business transactions were made on-line; another study reports that in 2005 approximately 18 percent of business-to-business transactions will be on-line.[4]

Business marketing on the Internet offers tremendous opportunities for firms to increase efficiency, reduce costs, improve customer service, create one-to-one relationships, introduce new products, and expand markets. However, the e-commerce market has been volatile and continues to be. A Statistics Canada survey on electronic commerce reported that among businesses that responded that they sold on-line in 2001, 43 percent said they stopped doing so in 2002; additionally, in 2002, seven firms stopped selling over the Internet for every 10 that started.[5]

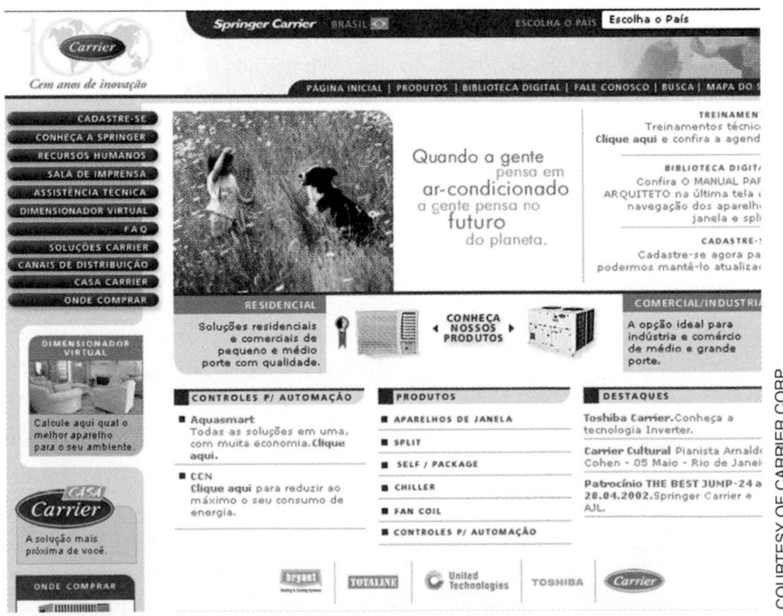

COURTESY OF CARRIER CORP.

One company that has successfully deployed its e-business initiative is Carrier, maker of air conditioners. Particularly noteworthy is how the company's Brazilian division used the Internet to increase sales, inventory turns, and customer satisfaction, all while decreasing delivery times.

Two Success Stories

Carrier Corporation and BellZinc.ca illustrate the opportunities for businesses to use the Internet to reduce costs, streamline order processing, and enhance customer service and satisfaction.

At Carrier, the world's largest manufacturer of air conditioners, company officials claim to have reduced costs by $100 million annually by buying and selling on the Internet.[6] Carrier now sells over $1 billion worth of products through the company's website. International sales and service results have been particularly remarkable.

The time required for Brazilian customers to place an order with Carrier and get confirmation has gone from six days to six minutes. Inventory turnover has increased from 17 to 24 times per year. And 77 percent of the Brazilian customers report that they are "satisfied" or "highly satisfied" with the service they are receiving.[7] A similar initiative in Korea has resulted in 50 percent of all sales passing through the website and orders being delivered in 18 days compared to 33 days in the past.[8]

ON LINE

B2B in Canada with BellZinc.ca

Business to business marketing on the Internet represents the vast majority of business done through this medium. Visit BellZinc.ca and see what this website has to offer marketers who are interested in doing business through the Internet.

http:// www.bellzinc.ca

Montreal-based BCE, parent company of Bell Canada, has developed a specialized business-to-business portal called BellZinc.ca that is designed to provide small and medium businesses with a virtual marketplace. BellZinc estimates there are about 1 million small- and medium-sized businesses in Canada, and it wants to sign up between 60 and 70 percent of these businesses to the BellZinc portal. Membership on BellZinc is free and includes a listing in a business directory. BellZinc had 60,000 members signed up even before officially launching its website in January 2001.[9]

BellZinc promotes itself as "Canada's leading Web destination for businesses, you can take advantage of a host of products and services designed to help you save time, save money, and increase sales." BellZinc states it has an "online Business Directory of more than 65,000 suppliers from industries across Canada and around the globe." The website hosts a library of information designed for small- and medium-sized business owners and provides services its subscribers can pay for, such as Bell ActiMedia, which distributes print and electronic Yellow Pages™ products and provides Internet access and e-commerce solutions to Canadian small- and medium-sized businesses; and Bell Canada, which provides "connectivity to residential and business customers through wired and wireless voice and data communications, high speed and wireless Internet access, IP-broadband services, e-business solutions, local and long distance phone and directory services."[10]

Potential Unrealized

Carrier was a successful marketer before it created an easy-to-use website. Putting the operations on-line didn't require changing fundamental business relationships: the website was just a way to make the firm more efficient. BellZinc.ca wants to enable all businesses in Canada to take advantage of the Web; it also wants to profit from the chargeable e-services it offers.

Most business buying and selling is done off-line. As one person put it: "If you are buying a stapler, you have no problems clicking around on-line. If you're buying 15,000 staplers, you want to talk to someone."[11] A study by Statistics Canada reports that 68 percent of small firms had Internet access in 2001 in comparison to 91 percent of medium-sized firms and 94 percent of large firms. "About 74 percent of large firms had a website in 2001, compared with 57 percent of medium-sized firms and only 24 percent of small firms. The percentage of firms that made purchases on-line was higher than the percentage of firms selling over the Internet. Moreover, this percentage increased from 18 percent in 2000 to 22 percent in 2001. About 20 percent of small firms, 33 percent of medium-sized firms, and 52 percent of large firms purchased on-line, again emphasizing the gap between large and small."[12]

What are the business marketers that have websites on the Internet but are not selling goods and services offering? Most provide product information and promotion. Some answer questions. Others provide contact and ordering information. Worldwide, business Internet marketing represents trillions of dollars of sales potential per year. It has currently reached only a fraction of its potential.

Benefits of Business Marketing on the Internet

As many examples in this book demonstrate, companies that use the Internet effectively gain clear advantages. These include:

1. *Lower prices:* Competition among on-line vendors leads to lower prices for business buyers.
2. *Greater selection of products and vendors:* The Web makes it possible for corporate purchasing agents to find numerous vendors for almost any product.
3. *Access to customer and product sales data:* Companies can develop customer lists and learn their buying characteristics. They can also immediately learn which products are selling best.
4. *Around-the-clock ordering and customer service:* Company websites provide extensive product information for prospective customers around the world on a "24/7" basis, thereby expanding markets and facilitating more transactions—without hiring additional personnel. Customers themselves decide how much information they require by clicking on website links. Well-designed sites offer solutions to customer problems and make product suggestions.
5. *Lower costs:* Cost savings are a major benefit of e-commerce. These can take many forms, from distribution savings to staff reductions and lower costs of purchasing supplies. Carrier used the Web to cut costs by $100 million.
6. *Customized products:* The Internet is revolutionizing product design and manufacturing. No longer do companies have to design and build products well in advance of the sale, basing product decisions on market research. They can use the Internet to take orders for products tailored to customer specifications. Dell Computers was one of the first to allow Canadian computer buyers to configure their ideal computer from menus at Dell's Canadian website. Even though Dell's build-to-order procedures were remarkably efficient when customers phoned in all their orders, the Web has increased its efficiency and profitability. Warehouses receive supply orders via Internet messages every two hours instead of daily faxes. Suppliers know about the company's inventory and production plans and get feedback on their performance in meeting shipping deadlines. Finally, buyers can track their computer orders through Dell Canada's website at http://www.dell.ca.

Many business marketers now realize that the Internet is a valuable tool for expanding markets and better serving customers. Exhibit 5.1 identifies eight Internet sites that contain important information for Canadian firms interested in competing in foreign markets. Exhibit 5.2 provides examples of popular Internet sites that cater to small businesses.

3 Discuss the role of relationship marketing and strategic alliances in business marketing

>> RELATIONSHIP MARKETING AND STRATEGIC ALLIANCES

As Chapter 1 explained, relationship marketing is the strategy that entails seeking and establishing ongoing partnerships with customers. Relationship marketing has become an important business marketing strategy as customers have become more demanding and competition has become more intense. Building long-term relationships with customers offers companies a way to build competitive advantage. For example, IFS of Canada is a company that develops and supplies component-based business applications for medium and large enterprises and organizations. Bridor Inc. of Boucherville, Quebec, a manufacturer of frozen breads and Viennese pastries for grocery and food service markets, recently signed with IFS. Bridor wants IFS to provide business software that will help the firm improve demand planning, cost control, inventory management, and customer relationship management. Francine Fontaine, VP of Finance for Bridor comments, "We have been

ON LINE

Bombardier

How many different divisions and international offices does Bombardier have? Check the website to find out.

http://www.bombardier.com

EXHIBIT 5.1

An Internet Guide to Small-Business Exporting

One of the easiest ways to delve into exporting is to utilize the Internet. Visit these sites, which offer valuable resources as well as links to additional information.

http://strategis.ic.gc.ca Strategis is Industry Canada's information website, which was launched on March 27, 1996, in order to harness the power of the Internet to provide business and consumer information to all Canadians without the constraints of time and geography.

http://exportsource.gc.ca Team Canada Inc. is a network of more than 20 federal departments and agencies working with the provinces, territories, and other partners to help Canadian businesses prepare for the global marketplace.

http://www.ccc.ca The Canadian Commercial Corporation is a Crown corporation established in 1946 whose mandate is "to assist in the development of trade between Canada and other nations." CCC does so as a prime contractor and guarantor for sales by Canadian exporters to foreign governments and international organizations, as well as private-sector buyers.

http://www.fitt.ca The Forum for International Trade Training (FITT) is a not-for-profit organization providing export/import training to Canadian business and individuals.

http://www.dfait-maeci.gc.ca The Department of Foreign Affairs and International Trade advances Canada's trade interests in two key ways—through the work of the Trade Commissioner Service and through efforts to negotiate and administer trade agreements and rules.

http://www.ustr.gov The Office of the U.S. Trade Representative (USTR) is responsible for developing and coordinating U.S. international trade and direct investment policy, and for leading or directing negotiations with other countries on such matters.

http://www.wto.org The World Trade Organization is the legal and institutional foundation of the multilateral trading system. It is the platform on which trade relations among countries evolve through collective debate, negotiation, and adjudication.

http://www.fita.org Trade associations are invaluable resources for exporters. Visit the Federation of International Trade Associations' website to take advantage of all of its resources, which include a network of 300,000 companies belonging to 300 international trade associations in North America.

SOURCES: Based on information accessed from http://strategis.ic.gc.ca.

using an old system that is becoming hard to maintain. IFS Applications™ is a single integrated system that will increase access to information, help us with production planning, and provide more flexible and timely reporting."[13]

Strategic Alliances

strategic alliance (strategic partnership)
A cooperative agreement between business firms.

A **strategic alliance,** sometimes called a *strategic partnership*, is a cooperative agreement between business firms. Strategic alliances can take the form of licensing or distribution agreements, joint ventures, research and development consortia, and partnerships. They can be between manufacturers, manufacturers and customers, manufacturers and suppliers, and manufacturers and channel intermediaries.

Business marketers form strategic alliances to leverage what they have (technology, financial resources, access to markets) by combining these assets with those of other firms. Sometimes the alliance partners' assets are complementary. For example, Canada Post's epost developed a strategic alliance with Derivion "to work together as eBusiness Solution Partners to accelerate the growth of e-billing in Canada." Epost is a secure Web-based service (http://www.epost.ca) where customers and businesses can receive and process their mail, including e-bills. Derivion is Canada's leading e-billing application service provider (ASP); it believes that its partnership with epost will contribute to the growth of electronic bill payment by offering businesses greater options on where to send bills and by giving consumers more choices on where they receive and pay them.[14]

Some strategic alliances are formed to achieve economies of scale. General Motors, Ford, DaimlerChrysler, Nissan Motor Company, and Renault SA created an Internet automobile parts exchange, called Covisint, that is expected to account for $300 billion in sales per year.[15] Covisint officials claim that the exchange will benefit small suppliers because they will have access to advanced technology that will provide them with faster and better access to buyers. Covisint officials also say that smaller firms will be able to improve profit margins by reducing inventory and saving time.[16]

EXHIBIT 5.2

Internet Sites Specifically for Small Businesses

http://strategis.ic.gc.ca Strategis is Industry Canada's information website, which was launched on March 27, 1996, in order to harness the power of the Internet to provide business and consumer information to all Canadians without the constraints of time and geography.
http://www.cbsc.org The Canada Business Service Centres (CBSCs) are a network of centres representing each provincial/territorial jurisdiction in Canada. They are a gateway to government information for business. The CBSCs provide a wide range of information on government services, programs, and regulations and are there to answer questions about starting a new business or improving an existing one.
http://www.bellzinc.ca Billed as Canada's leading Web destination for businesses, it is an "online Business Directory of more than 65,000 suppliers from industries across Canada and around the globe."
http://sbinfocanada.about.com If you're a Canadian running your own small business or thinking of starting an enterprise, Small Business: Canada offers you all the business resources, such as indexes, articles on particular topics, and one-stop resource pages.
http://www.smallbusinessbc.ca The Canada/British Columbia Business Services Society (the "Society") is a non-profit organization that delivers high-quality, single-window, business information services in Vancouver and Victoria, and throughout B.C. via community partnership sites. The Society offers business information and advice to a full range of business types, including existing businesses, start-up ventures, and would-be entrepreneurs.
http://www.canadaone.com The CanadaOne website includes an on-line magazine, a Canadian business directory, Canadian-specific business resources, a technology centre, and several other promotional tools designed to help Canadians grow their businesses.
http://www.cfib.ca The Canadian Federation of Independent Business (CFIB) is an advocacy group that started in 1971 as a political action organization for small- and medium-sized enterprises.
http://www.microsoft.com/canada/smallbiz Discover Microsoft® Windows® Small Business Server 2003. Learn how small business owners can increase return on their information technology investment. Information on Microsoft operating systems and business productivity software is provided.
http://www.quicken.com/small_business This site offers information on starting, running, and growing a small business. It also provides links to a variety of other Quicken sites that are useful to small business owners and managers.

Relationships in Other Cultures

keiretsu
A network of interlocking corporate affiliates.

Although the terms "relationship marketing" and "strategic alliances" are fairly new, and popularized mostly by North American business executives and educators, the concepts have long been familiar in other cultures. Businesses in countries such as Mexico, China, Japan, Korea, and much of Europe rely heavily on personal relationships. Chapter 18 explores customer relationship management in detail.

In Japan, for example, the basis of exchange between firms is personal relationships that are developed through what is called *amae*, or indulgent dependency. *Amae* is the feeling of nurturing concern for, and dependence upon, another. Reciprocity and personal relationships contribute to *amae*. Relationships between companies can develop into a **keiretsu**—a network of interlocking corporate affiliates. Within a keiretsu, executives may sit on the boards of their customers or their suppliers. Members of a keiretsu trade with one another whenever possible and often engage in joint product development, finance, and marketing activity. For example, the Toyota Group keiretsu includes fourteen core companies and another 170 that receive preferential treatment. Toyota holds an equity position in many of these 170 member firms and is represented on many of their boards of directors.

Many Canadian firms have found that the best way to compete in Asian countries is to form relationships with Asian firms. For example, Inco Asia Holdings, a subsidiary of Toronto-based Inco Ltd., has partnered with Liaoning Wanzhong Real Property Development of Dalian and the Korea Nickel Corporation. The joint venture, called Inco Wanzhong Advanced Technology Materials (Dalian) Ltd., will construct a new nickel foam production plant in Dalian, China to produce large volumes of high-quality nickel foam for the world market.[17] The "Global Perspectives" box in this chapter describes a strategic alliance between General Motors and Shanghai Automotive to create a "Farmer Car" for rural residents of China.

www.epost.ca
Online Access To Your Bills
Manage your bills conveniently and securely
Delivering the mail online for Canada Post, epost™ is a free online service that helps you organize your bills and other important household mail.
With epost, your bills and other mail documents are sent to a personal electronic mailbox (epost box), where you can pay, organize and store them anytime, using any computer with Internet access.
Sign up today for a free, private and secure epost box.™ Next, select the bills you would like to receive in your epost box from over 65 leading Canadian companies including: Rogers, Canadian Tire, Future Shop and more.
WIN your epost bills paid for a year!*
Sign up today and you will automatically receive a chance to WIN your epost bills paid for a year!
The more Mailers you add, the better your chances of winning.
If you're already an epost user, just add another Mailer for a chance to WIN.

COURTESY OF EPOST

Strategic alliances are at the heart of business marketing. Nobody knows this better than epost. Its alliance with Derivion makes electronic bill payment services available to the multitude of businesspeople who want to engage in e-commerce.

>> MAJOR CATEGORIES OF BUSINESS CUSTOMERS

4 Identify the four major categories of business market customers

The business market consists of four major categories of customers: producers, resellers, governments, and institutions.

Producers

The producer segment of the business market includes profit-oriented individuals and organizations that use purchased goods and services to produce other products, to incorporate into other products, or to facilitate the daily operations of the organization. Examples of producers include construction, manufacturing, transportation, finance, real estate, and food service firms.

In Canada during 2002, producers shipped $518.5 billion worth of goods. Some of these firms are small; others such as Bombardier (US$15.1 billion in sales), Magna International (US$13 billion in sales), and Alcan (US$12.5 billion in sales) are in the top 500 of the world's largest businesses. Individual producers often buy large quantities of goods and services. Consider that General Motors, which had annual sales of US$186.7 billlion in 2002, spends more than US$70 billion annually—more than the gross domestic product of Ireland, Portugal, Turkey, or Greece—on such business products as steel, metal components, and tires.[18]

Resellers

The reseller market includes retail and wholesale businesses that buy finished goods and resell them for a profit. A retailer sells mainly to final consumers; wholesalers sell mostly to retailers and other organizational customers.

GLOBAL PERSPECTIVES

Shanghai Auto and GM to Market Farmer's Car

Under a new agreement, Shanghai Automotive, one of China's biggest auto companies, will license GM technology to build a cheap, bare-bones combination pickup-delivery truck designed specifically for the country's farmers.

With nearly 1 billion consumers and a fast-growing network of national highways, China boasts an auto market expected to be the biggest in the world someday. The rural focus, however, is a major shift for GM and Shanghai Automotive, which so far have focused on catering to the country's white-collar urban workers. The two already make Buick sedans, which sell for around $40,000, and will soon begin regular production of a new, more affordable compact car, the Sail, priced around $10,000.

But with almost every major automaker in the world competing to sell cars to the few Chinese urbanites who can afford them, sales of the Buicks haven't lived up to expectations, and some auto analysts say the new compact car could also face a lukewarm reception. In fact, total car sales in Chinese cities grew just 6 percent last year, less than half the rate of rural auto sales, initial figures show.

The new Farmer's Car, as it is currently called, is based on GM's Corsa Combo and will be sold under Shanghai Auto's brand, retailing for about $7,000. Shanghai Auto and GM are betting the car will be a hit among China's 800 million rural inhabitants, a huge group of consumers mostly overlooked by foreign investors because of their skimpy earnings and frugal lifestyle.

For now, that is the biggest stumbling block the new car faces. Though living standards in the countryside have leapt in the past decade, rural dwellers remain the country's lowest earners, making less than $300 a year on average. And with grain and some produce prices falling, that figure is unlikely to rise significantly during the next few years.

Shanghai Auto is so confident in the rural car that it recently bought an unprofitable government auto company in coastal Jiangsu province, where it will produce the new Combo. Already, dozens of executives from Shanghai GM, the joint venture, are being lent to the Combo factory, where they plan to retool the outdated plant using GM's Corsa platform. Plans call for the car to use some existing parts, possibly including the engine made at Shanghai GM's plant here, a $1.5 billion facility that now makes Buicks, family wagons, and, soon, the new Sail compact car.

Though China has a handful of auto companies that make simple pickup trucks for farmers, Shanghai Auto and GM are the first two major concerns to step into the vast countryside market. If the Combo proves successful, auto analysts say, that could change quickly. "This is a part of the market that hasn't registered on most companies' radar screens, but given the sheer number of farmers out there, these vehicles could end up dominating the market," says Yale Zhang, a Beijing executive with industry consultant Automotive Resources Asia.[19]

Do you think the first product of the Shanghai Auto/GM alliance, the Farmer's Car, will be successful? What are the benefits to each company in establishing such a partnership? The disadvantages?

There were approximately 235,000 retail outlets in Canada with combined sales of about $306 billion in 2002, and $67 billion of these sales were for food. Food retailing is a key sector in Canada, accounting for 22 percent of all retail sales. Chain retailers such as Loblaws and Sobeys dominate the Canadian food retailing market, but Wal-Mart and Costco are also important competitors. The Retail Council of Canada is an industry association that keeps track of retailing in Canada.

The Canadian wholesale sector has approximately 123,000 outlets that had sales of $419 billion in 2002. Wholesale inventories were valued at nearly $44 billion in 2002. The sales revenue of wholesalers is split up among its customers in the following proportions: retailers (43 percent), industry (31 percent), other wholesalers (17 percent), exporters (11 percent), household consumers (4 percent), and farmers (4 percent).

Canadian consumer-product firms like George Weston Ltd, McCain Foods, Maple Leaf Foods, and Parmalat sell directly to large food retailers and retail chains; they also sell to smaller food retailers through wholesalers like MacDonalds Consolidated and Lanzarotta Wholesale Grocers. Retailing and wholesaling are explored in detail in Chapter 12.[20]

Business product distributors are wholesalers that buy business products and resell them to business customers. They often carry thousands of items in stock and employ sales forces to call on business customers. Businesses that wish to buy a gross of pencils or a hundred pounds of fertilizer typically purchase these items from local distributors rather than directly from manufacturers such as Empire Pencil or Dow Chemical.

Governments

A third major segment of the business market is government. Senior government organizations are represented by one federal, ten provincial, and three territorial units. The next grouping is the MASH sector (Municipal, Academic, Social, and Hospitals) and is compromised of approximately 6,000 municipal buying units as well as thousands more Academic, Social, and Hospital purchasing units. Together, these government buyers make up the largest single market for goods and services in Canada, with expenditures in 2002–03 of $440 billion.

"In government procurement, public institutions seek to achieve value-for-money through open tendering. Open tendering allows purchasers to predetermine the terms of engagement with potential suppliers, set out requirements and terms of the potential deal and bind competing suppliers to their offers for a predetermined amount of time while competing offers are compared. This process can result in an organization getting a deal tailored to its needs, on its terms, and at potentially lower costs."[21]

Government purchasing by the federal, provincial, and territorial governments of Canada is subject to the Agreement on Internal Trade (AIT), which came into effect during the 1990s. The specific rules for procurement are set out in Chapter 5 of the AIT. One of the key provisions stipulates that purchases of $100,000 for goods and $250,000 for services and construction are to be procured "by way of open tender call accessible equally to all Canadian suppliers."[22]

© ANDY SACKS/TONY STONE IMAGES

The producer segment of the business market includes manufacturing, like this globe production line, as well as construction, finance, transportation, and real estate.

Senior Government

Name just about any good or service and chances are that someone in the federal government uses it. The Canadian federal government is the nation's largest customer, spending about $187 billion in 2003. The provincial and territorial governments spent $242 billion in 2003, with health, social services, and education expenses representing the lion's share of these expenditures.

Much of the federal government's buying is centralized. However, no single federal agency contracts for all the government's requirements, and no single buyer in any agency purchases all that the agency needs. We can view the federal government as a combination of several large purchasing agencies and Crown corporations with overlapping responsibilities and thousands of small, independent units. Major purchases (expenditures exceeding $100,000 for goods and $250,000 for services and construction) must go through Supply and Services Canada and Public Works and Government Services.

One popular source of information about government procurement is Contracts Canada (http://www.contractscanada. gc.ca). Information about bidding for federal, provincial, and even MASH contracts can be obtained directly from http://www.contractscanada.gc.org or from http://www.merx.com.

Municipal, Academic, Social, and Hospitals (MASH)

Municipal governments in Canada spent $82 billion in 2003, colleges and universities spent $22.2 billion, schools spent $35 billion, healthcare organizations spent $49 billion, and social services spent $5 billion. For both small and large vendors, selling to the MASH sector can be less frustrating than selling to the federal and provincial governments. Many contracts are valued at levels below the AIT agreement threshold so the paperwork is typically simpler and more manageable. On the other hand, vendors must decide which of these diverse sectors to serve. For example, there are over 6,000 municipal clients alone that are available to buy their wares.

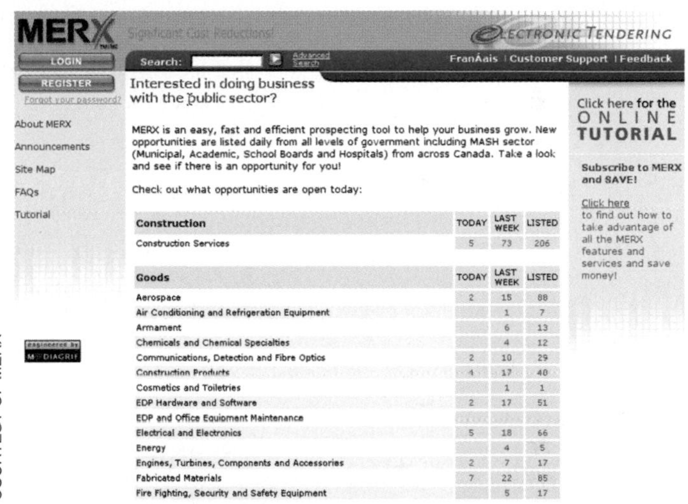

For doing business with buyers from all levels of Canadian governments, there is no better on-line resource than http://www.merx.com. Users can access government public tenders and order tender documents through MERX.

Institutions

The fourth major segment of the business market is institutions that seek to achieve goals other than the standard business goals of profit, market share, and return on investment. Excluding the MASH sector, this segment includes churches, labour unions, fraternal organizations, civic clubs, foundations, not-for-profit organizations, and other so-called nonbusiness organizations. There are an estimated 78,000 registered not-for-profit organizations in Canada with total of $100 billion in annual revenues.[23]

>> THE NORTH AMERICAN INDUSTRY CLASSIFICATION SYSTEM

5 Explain the North American Industry Classification System

The **North American Industry Classification System (NAICS)** is an industry classification system introduced in 1997 to replace the standard industrial classification system (SIC). Updated in 2002, the NAICS (pronounced *nakes*) is a system for classifying North American business establishments. The system, developed jointly by Canada, the United States, and Mexico, provides a common industry classification system for the North American Free Trade Association (NAFTA) partners. Goods- or service-producing firms that use identical or similar production processes are grouped together.

North American Industry Classification System (NAICS)
A detailed numbering system developed by Canada, the United States, and Mexico to classify North American business establishments by their main production processes.

NAICS is an extremely valuable tool for business marketers engaged in analyzing, segmenting, and targeting markets. It classifies Canada's economic activity into 20 different sectors and 928 industries. Each classification group is relatively homogeneous in terms of raw materials required, components used, manufacturing processes employed, and problems faced. The more digits in a code, the more homogenous is the group. Therefore, if a supplier understands the needs and requirements of a few firms within a classification, requirements can be projected for all firms in that category. The number, size, and geographic dispersion of firms can also be identified. This information can be converted to market potential estimates, market share estimates, and sales forecasts. It can also be used for identifying potential new customers. NAICS codes can help identify firms that may be prospective users of a supplier's goods and services.

Exhibit 5.3 provides an overview of the 20 NAICS economic sectors. Exhibit 5.4 illustrates the six-digit classification system for two of these sectors: manufacturing and information. The hierarchical structure of NAICS allows industry data to be summarized at several levels of detail. To illustrate:

- The first two digits designate a major economic sector such as agriculture (11) or manufacturing (31–33).
- The third digit designates an economic subsector such as crop production or apparel manufacturing.
- The fourth digit designates an industry group, such as grain and oil seed farming or fibre, yarn, and thread mills.
- The fifth digit designates the NAICS industry, such as wheat farming or broadwoven fabric mills.
- The sixth digit, when used, identifies subdivisions of NAICS industries that accommodate user needs in individual countries.[24]

For a complete listing of all 2002 NAICS codes, see the NAICS Association website http://www.naics.com or visit Statistics Canada's website, http://www.statcan.ca.

6 Explain the major differences between business and consumer markets

>> BUSINESS VERSUS CONSUMER MARKETS

The basic philosophy and practice of marketing are the same whether the customer is a business organization or a consumer. Business markets do, however, have characteristics different from consumer markets. Exhibit 5.5 on page 142 summarizes the main differences between business and consumer markets.

EXHIBIT 5.3

2002 NAICS Two-Digit Codes and Corresponding Economic Sectors

NAICS CODE	ECONOMIC SECTOR
11	Agriculture, forestry, fishing, and hunting
21	Mining and oil and gas extraction
22	Utilities
23	Construction
31–33	Manufacturing
41	Wholesale trade
44–45	Retail trade
48–49	Transportation and warehousing
51	Information and cultural industries
52	Finance and insurance
53	Real estate and rental and leasing
54	Professional, scientific, and technical services
55	Management of companies and enterprises
56	Administrative and support, waste management and remediation services
61	Educational services
62	Health care and social assistance
71	Arts, entertainment, and recreation
72	Accommodation and food services
81	Other services (except public administration)
91	Public administration

EXHIBIT 5.4

Examples of 2002 NAICS Hierarchy

	EXAMPLE 1		EXAMPLE 2	
NAICS Level	NAICS Code	Description	NAICS Code	Description
Sector	31–33	Manufacturing	51	Information
Subsector	334	Computer and electronic product manufacturing	517	Broadcasting and telecommunications
Industry group	3346	Magnetic and optical recording media manufacturing	5172	Telecommunications
Industry media	33461	Manufacturing and reproduction of magnetic and optical	51721	Cellular and other wireless telecommunications
U.S. industry services	334611	Software reproducing	517211	Paging services

SOURCES: Statistics Canada, "North American Industrial Classification System–NAICS–Canada," http://www.statcan.ca/ and NAICS Association website, http://www.naics.com.

Demand

Consumer demand for products is quite different from demand in the business market. Unlike consumer demand, business demand is derived, inelastic, joint, and fluctuating.

Derived Demand

The demand for business products is called **derived demand** because organizations buy products to be used in producing their customers' products. For example, the market for CPUs, hard drives, and CD-ROMs is derived from the demand for personal computers. These items are only valuable as components of computers. Demand for these items rises and falls with the demand for PCs.

derived demand
The demand for business products.

Because demand is derived, business marketers must carefully monitor demand patterns and changing preferences in final consumer markets, even though their customers are not in those markets. Moreover, business marketers must carefully monitor their customers' forecasts, because derived demand is based on expectations of future demand for those customers' products.

Some business marketers not only monitor final consumer demand and customer forecasts but also try to influence final consumer demand. Aluminum producers use television and magazine advertisements to point out the convenience and recycling opportunities that aluminum offers to consumers, who can choose to purchase soft drinks in either aluminum or plastic containers.

Inelastic Demand

The demand for many business products is inelastic with regard to price. *Inelastic demand* means that an increase or decrease in the price of the product will not significantly affect demand for the product. This idea will be discussed further in Chapter 15.

The price of a product used in the production of or as part of a final product is often a minor portion of the final product's total price. Therefore, demand for the final consumer product is not affected. If the price of automobile paint or spark plugs rose significantly—say, 200 percent in one year—do you think the number of new automobiles sold that year would be affected? Probably not.

Joint Demand

Joint demand occurs when two or more items are used together in a final product. For example, a decline in the availability of memory chips will slow production of microcomputers, which will in turn reduce the demand for disk drives. One of the largest markets for Caterpillar diesel engines is over-the-road, heavy-duty truck manufacturers. A recent decline in sales of the behemoth trucks has led to fewer engines being purchased.[25]

joint demand
The demand for two or more items used together in a final product.

EXHIBIT 5.5

Major Characteristics of Business Markets Compared to Consumer Markets

CHARACTERISTIC	BUSINESS MARKET	CONSUMER MARKET
Demand	Organizational	Individual
Purchase volume	Larger	Smaller
Number of customers	Fewer	Many
Location of buyers	Geographically concentrated	Dispersed
Distribution structure	More direct	More indirect
Nature of buying	More professional	More personal
Nature of buying influence	Multiple	Single
Type of negotiations	More complex	Simpler
Use of reciprocity	Yes	No
Use of leasing	Greater	Lesser
Primary promotional	Personal selling	Advertising method

Fluctuating Demand

The demand for business products—particularly new plants and equipment—tends to be more unstable than the demand for consumer products. A small increase or decrease in consumer demand can produce a much larger change in demand for the facilities and equipment needed to make the consumer product. Economists refer to this phenomenon as the **multiplier effect** (or **accelerator principle**).

multiplier effect (accelerator principle)
Phenomenon in which a small increase or decrease in consumer demand can produce a much larger change in demand for the facilities and equipment needed to make the consumer product.

Cummins Engine Company, a producer of heavy-duty diesel engines, uses sophisticated surface grinders to make parts. Suppose Cummins is using 20 surface grinders. Each machine lasts about 10 years. Purchases have been timed so two machines will wear out and be replaced annually. If the demand for engine parts does not change, two grinders will be bought this year. If the demand for parts declines slightly, only 18 grinders may be needed and Cummins won't replace the worn ones. However, suppose in the next year demand returns to previous levels plus a little more. To meet the new level of demand, Cummins will need to replace the two machines that wore out in the first year, and the two that wore out in the second year, plus one or more additional machines. The multiplier effect works this way in many industries, producing highly fluctuating demand for business products.

Purchase Volume

Business customers buy in much larger quantities than consumers. Just think how large an order Kellogg typically places for the wheat bran and raisins used to manufacture Raisin Bran. Imagine the number of tires that DaimlerChrysler buys for its new Pacifica SUV line manufactured in Windsor, Ontario.

Number of Customers

Business marketers usually have far fewer customers than consumer marketers. The advantage is that it is a lot easier to identify prospective buyers, monitor current customers' needs and levels of satisfaction, and personally attend to existing customers. The main disadvantage is that each customer becomes crucial—especially for those manufacturers that have only one or two customers. For example, suppliers of secret military equipment and systems may have one customer, such as NATO (North Atlantic Treaty Organization). The success or failure of one bid can make the difference between prosperity and bankruptcy. CAE Inc. of Montreal, Quebec, has experienced both immediate ups and immediate downs in its stock price as a result of market reaction to contract bids. CAE Inc. provides aviation military training services to NATO countries. In the fall of 2003, CAE's share price dropped in value by 18 percent when it was announced that a $1 billion contract bid to provide training services to the U.S. Army had been lost to a rival bidder. Only a scant 18 months earlier, CAE's share price shot up by 400 percent on the announcement that it was bidding for this contract in partnership with Boeing Corporation of Seattle, Washington.[26]

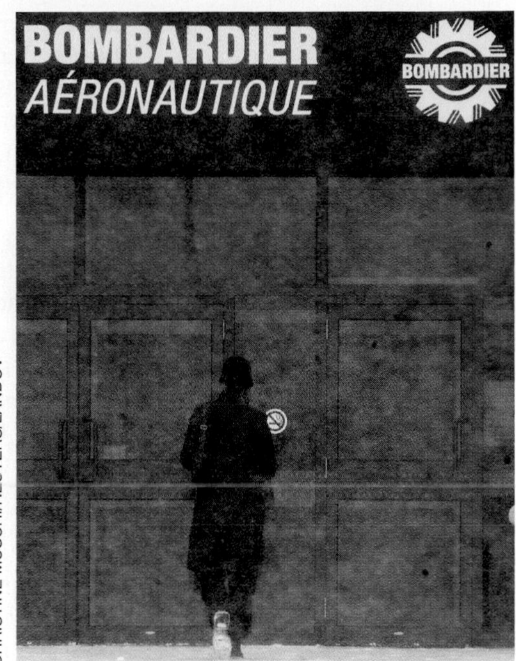

CHRISTINE MUSCHI/REUTERS/LANDOV

Bombardier is the leading Canadian aerospace firm. Business customers tend to be much more geographically concentrated than consumers. The Canadian aircraft industry is concentrated in Quebec and Ontario.

Location of Buyers

Business customers tend to be much more geographically concentrated than consumers. For instance, most of Canada's buyers are located in the major metropolitan urban areas of Toronto, Montreal, and Vancouver. The oil and gas industry is centred in Alberta, the shoe industry in Quebec, the aircraft industry is concentrated in Quebec and Ontario, and many of the firms that supply the automobile manufacturing industry are located in southwestern Ontario.

Distribution Structure

Many consumer products pass through a distribution system that includes the producer, one or more wholesalers, and a retailer. However, because of many of the characteristics already mentioned, channels of distribution are typically shorter in business marketing. Direct channels, where manufacturers market directly to users, are much more common.

Many businesses that market directly to users are discovering that the Internet offers great potential for reaching new and existing customers domestically and around the world, while reducing costs to both buyers and sellers. Several examples of the expanding potential of the Internet are cited in this chapter.

Nature of Buying

Unlike consumers, business buyers usually approach purchasing rather formally. Businesses use professionally trained purchasing agents or buyers who spend their entire careers purchasing a limited number of items. They get to know the items and the sellers well. Some professional purchasers earn the designation of Certified Purchasing Manager (CPM) after participating in a rigorous certification program.

Nature of Buying Influence

Typically, more people are involved in a single business purchase decision than in a consumer purchase. Experts from fields as varied as quality control, marketing, and finance, as well as professional buyers and users, may be grouped in a buying centre (discussed later in this chapter).

Type of Negotiations

Consumers are used to negotiating price on automobiles and real estate. However, in most cases consumers expect sellers to set the price and other conditions of sale, such as time of delivery and credit terms. In contrast, negotiating is common in business marketing. Buyers and sellers negotiate product specifications, delivery dates, payment terms, and other pricing matters. Sometimes these negotiations occur during many meetings over several months. Final contracts are often very long and detailed.

Use of Reciprocity

Business purchasers often choose to buy from their own customers, a practice known as **reciprocity.** For example, General Motors buys engines for use in its automobiles and trucks from Borg Warner, which in turn buys many of the automobiles and trucks it

reciprocity
A practice where business purchasers choose to buy from their own customers.

needs from GM. This practice is neither unethical nor illegal unless one party coerces the other and the result is unfair competition. Reciprocity is generally considered a reasonable business practice. If all possible suppliers sell a similar product for about the same price, doesn't it make sense to buy from those firms that buy from you?

Use of Leasing

Consumers normally buy products rather than lease them. But businesses commonly lease expensive equipment such as computers, construction equipment and vehicles, and automobiles. Leasing allows firms to reduce capital outflow, acquire a seller's latest products, receive better service, and gain tax advantages.

The lessor, the firm providing the product, may be either the manufacturer or an independent firm. The benefits to the lessor include greater total revenue from leasing compared to selling and an opportunity to do business with customers who cannot afford to buy.

Primary Promotional Method

Business marketers tend to emphasize personal selling in their promotion efforts, especially for expensive items, custom-designed products, large-volume purchases, and situations requiring negotiations. The sale of many business products requires a great deal of personal contact. Personal selling is discussed in more detail in Chapter 13.

7 Describe the seven types of business goods and services

>> TYPES OF BUSINESS PRODUCTS

Business products generally fall into one of the following seven categories, depending on their use: major equipment, accessory equipment, raw materials, component parts, processed materials, supplies, and business services.

Major Equipment

major equipment (installations)
Capital goods such as large or expensive machines, mainframe computers, blast furnaces, generators, airplanes, and buildings.

Major equipment includes such capital goods as large or expensive machines, mainframe computers, blast furnaces, generators, airplanes, and buildings. (These items are also commonly called **installations.**) Major equipment is depreciated over time rather than charged as an expense in the year it is purchased. In addition, major equipment is often custom-designed for each customer. Personal selling is an important part of the marketing strategy for major equipment because distribution channels are almost always direct from the producer to the business user.

Accessory Equipment

accessory equipment
Goods, such as portable tools and office equipment, that are less expensive and shorter-lived than major equipment.

Accessory equipment is generally less expensive and shorter-lived than major equipment. Examples include portable drills, power tools, microcomputers, and fax machines. Accessory equipment is often charged as an expense in the year it is bought rather than depreciated over its useful life. In contrast to major equipment, accessories are more often standardized and are usually bought by more customers. These customers tend to be widely dispersed. For example, all types of businesses buy microcomputers.

Local industrial distributors (wholesalers) play an important role in the marketing of accessory equipment because business buyers often purchase accessories from them. Regardless of where accessories are bought, advertising is a more vital promotional tool for accessory equipment than for major equipment.

Raw Materials

raw materials
Unprocessed extractive or agricultural products, such as mineral ore, lumber, wheat, corn, fruits, vegetables, and fish.

Raw materials are unprocessed extractive or agricultural products—for example, mineral ore, lumber, wheat, corn, fruits, vegetables, and fish. Raw materials become part of finished products. Extensive users, such as steel or lumber mills and food canners, generally buy huge quantities of raw materials. Because there is often a large number of relatively small sellers of raw materials, none can greatly influence price or supply. Thus, the market tends to set the price of raw materials, and individual producers have little pricing flexibility. Promotion is almost always via personal selling, and distribution channels are usually direct from producer to business user.

Magna International of Aurora, Ontario, produces and ships automotive parts to original equipment manufacturers (OEMs) of cars and trucks in Canada, the United States, Mexico, Europe, Asia, and South America.

Component Parts

Component parts are either finished items ready for assembly or products that need very little processing before becoming part of some other product. The Caterpillar diesel engines used in heavy-duty trucks that were mentioned earlier in this chapter are component parts. Other examples include spark plugs, tires, and electric motors for automobiles. A special feature of component parts is that they can retain their identity after becoming part of the final product. For example, automobile tires are clearly recognizable as part of a car. Moreover, because component parts often wear out, they may need to be replaced several times during the life of the final product. Thus, there are two important markets for many component parts: the original equipment manufacturer (OEM) market and the replacement market.

component parts
Either finished items ready for assembly or products that need very little processing before becoming part of some other product.

Many of the business features listed in Exhibit 5.5 characterize the **OEM** market. The difference between unit costs and selling prices in the OEM market is often small, but profits can be substantial because of volume buying.

OEM
The acronym OEM stands for original equipment manufacturer. OEMs buy business goods, which they incorporate into the products they produce for eventual sale to other producers or to consumers.

The replacement market is composed of organizations and individuals buying component parts to replace worn-out parts. Because components often retain their identity in final products, users may choose to replace a component part with the same brand used by the manufacturer—for example, the same brand of automobile tires or battery. The replacement market operates differently from the OEM market, however. Whether replacement buyers are organizations or individuals, they tend to demonstrate the characteristics of consumer markets that were shown in Exhibit 5.5. Consider, for example, an automobile replacement part. Purchase volume is usually small and there are many customers, geographically dispersed, who typically buy from car dealers or parts stores. Negotiations do not occur, and neither reciprocity nor leasing is usually an issue. Manufacturers of component parts often direct their advertising toward replacement buyers.

Processed Materials

Processed materials are products used directly in manufacturing other products. Unlike raw materials, they have had some processing. Examples include sheet metal, chemicals, specialty steel, lumber, corn syrup, and plastics. Unlike component parts, processed materials do not retain their identity in final products.

processed materials
Products used directly in manufacturing other products.

Most processed materials are marketed to OEMs or to distributors servicing the OEM market. Processed materials are generally bought according to customer specifications or to some industry standard, as is the case with steel and lumber. Price and service are important factors in choosing a vendor.

Supplies

Supplies are consumable items that do not become part of the final product for example, lubricants, detergents, paper towels, pencils, and paper. Supplies are normally standardized items that purchasing agents routinely buy.

ON LINE  

Precision Machined Products Association

Read about history's oldest component part industry at the PMPA website. Does the PMPA participate in any global organizations? If so, what are they? Surf the site to find out.

http://www.pmpa.org

supplies
Consumable items that do not become part of the final product.

Supplies typically have relatively short lives and are inexpensive compared to other business goods. Because supplies generally fall into one of three categories—maintenance, repair, or operating supplies—this category is often referred to as MRO.

Competition in the MRO market is intense. Office product retailers Staples and Grand and Toy battle each other constantly for the office supply purchases of Canadian businesses.

Business Services

business services
Expense items that do not become part of a final product.

Business services are expense items that do not become part of a final product. Businesses often retain outside providers to perform janitorial, advertising, legal, management consulting, marketing research, maintenance, and other services. Hiring an outside provider makes sense when it costs less than hiring or assigning an employee to perform the task and when an outside provider is needed for particular expertise.

8 Discuss the unique aspects of business buying behaviour

>> BUSINESS BUYING BEHAVIOUR

As you probably have already concluded, business buyers behave differently from consumers. Understanding how purchase decisions are made in organizations is a first step in developing a business selling strategy. Business buying behaviour has five important aspects: buying centres, evaluative criteria, buying situations, business ethics, and customer service.

Buying Centres

buying centre
All those persons in an organization who become involved in the purchase decision.

A **buying centre** includes all those persons in an organization who become involved in the purchase decision. Membership and influence vary from company to company. For instance, in engineering-dominated firms like Bell Helicopter of Mirabel, Quebec, the buying centre may consist almost entirely of engineers. In marketing-oriented firms like Toyota and IBM, marketing and engineering have almost equal authority. In consumer goods firms like Procter & Gamble, product managers and other marketing decision makers may dominate the buying centre. University Hospital in London, Ontario, uses acquisition/disbursement teams composed of buyers and support staff who have been cross-trained as customer service representatives for the hospital's many departments.[27] In a small manufacturing company, almost everyone may be a member.

The number of people involved in a buying centre varies with the complexity and importance of a purchase decision. The composition of the buying group will usually change from one purchase to another and sometimes even during various stages of the buying process. To make matters more complicated, buying centres do not appear on formal organization charts.

For example, even though a formal committee may have been set up to choose a new plant site, it is only part of the buying centre. Other people, like the company president, often play informal yet powerful roles. In a lengthy decision-making process, such as finding a new plant location, some members may drop out of the buying centre when they can no longer play a useful role. Others whose talents are needed then become part of the centre. No formal announcement of "who is in" and "who is out" is ever made.

Roles in the Buying Centre

As in family purchasing decisions, several people may play a role in the business purchase process:

- *Initiator:* the person who first suggests making a purchase.
- *Influencers/evaluators:* people who influence the buying decision. They often help define specifications and provide information for evaluating options. Technical personnel are especially important as influencers.

- *Gatekeepers:* group members who regulate the flow of information. Frequently, the purchasing agent views the gatekeeping role as a source of his or her power. A secretary may also act as a gatekeeper by determining which vendors get an appointment with a buyer.
- *Decider:* the person who has the formal or informal power to choose or approve the selection of the supplier or brand. In complex situations, it is often difficult to determine who makes the final decision.
- *Purchaser:* the person who actually negotiates the purchase. It could be anyone from the president of the company to the purchasing agent, depending on the importance of the decision.
- *Users:* members of the organization who will actually use the product. Users often initiate the buying process and help define product specifications.

An example illustrating these basic roles is shown in Exhibit 5.6.

Implications of Buying Centres for the Marketing Manager

Successful vendors realize the importance of identifying who is in the decision-making unit, each member's relative influence in the buying decision, and each member's evaluative criteria. Successful selling strategies often focus on determining the most important buying influences and tailoring sales presentations to the evaluative criteria most important to these buying-centre members.

For example, Amex Canada Inc., provider of Corporate Credit Cards used for business travel, found that in order to control travel costs, many firms had travel managers who were corporate procurement professionals. Amex noted that these managers "increasingly have a role to play in controlling these costs as policies become more consistent and companies adopt the same approach to travel buying that they already employ in more 'traditional' purchases."[28]

Evaluative Criteria

Business buyers evaluate products and suppliers against three important criteria: quality, service, and price—in that order.

Quality

In this case, quality refers to technical suitability. A superior tool can do a better job in the production process, and superior packaging can increase dealer and consumer acceptance of a brand. Evaluation of quality also applies to the salesperson and the salesperson's firm. Business buyers want to deal with reputable salespeople and with companies that are financially responsible. Quality improvement should be part of every organization's marketing strategy.

EXHIBIT 5.6

Buying-Centre Roles for Computer Purchases

ROLE	ILLUSTRATION
Initiator	Division general manager proposes to replace company's computer network.
Influencers/evaluators	Corporate controller's office and vice president of data processing have an important say about which system and vendor the company will deal with.
Gatekeepers	Corporate departments for purchasing and data processing analyze company's needs and recommend likely matches with potential vendors.
Decider	Vice president of administration, with advice from others, selects vendor the company will deal with and system it will buy.
Purchaser	Purchasing agent negotiates terms of sale.
Users	All division employees use the computers.

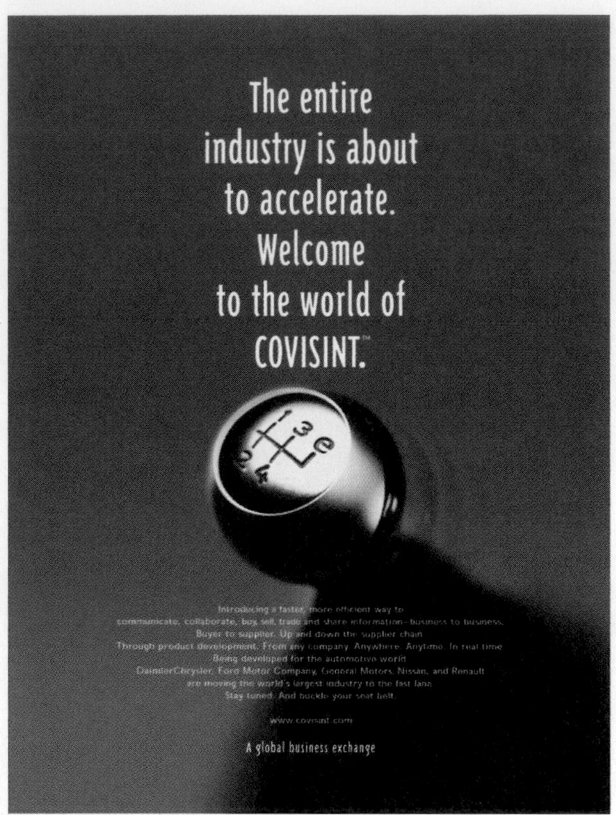

© COURTESY OF COVISINT

One way that business buyers evaluate products and suppliers is by looking at the service the prospect provides. Covisint advertises itself as a more efficient way to conduct business with other businesses.

Service

Almost as much as they want satisfactory products, business buyers want satisfactory service. A purchase offers several opportunities for service. Suppose a vendor is selling heavy equipment. Prepurchase service could include a survey of the buyer's needs. After thorough analysis of the survey findings, the vendor could prepare a report and recommendations in the form of a purchasing proposal. If a purchase results, postpurchase service might consist of installing the equipment and training those who will be using it. Postsale services may also include maintenance and repairs. Another service that business buyers seek is dependability of supply—they must be able to count on scheduled delivery of what was ordered. Buyers also welcome services that help them sell their finished products. Services of this sort are especially appropriate when the seller's product is an identifiable part of the buyer's end product.

Price

Business buyers want to buy at low prices—at the lowest prices, under most circumstances. However, a buyer who pressures a supplier to cut prices to a point where the supplier loses money on the sale almost forces shortcuts on quality. The buyer also may, in effect, force the supplier to quit selling to him or her. Then a new source of supply will have to be found.

Buying Situations

Often business firms, especially manufacturers, must decide whether to make something or buy it from an outside supplier. The decision is essentially one of economics. Can an item of similar quality be bought at a lower price elsewhere? If not, is manufacturing it in-house the best use of limited company resources? For example, Briggs & Stratton Corporation, a major manufacturer of four-cycle engines, might be able to save $150,000 annually on outside purchases by spending $500,000 on the equipment needed to produce gas throttles internally. Yet Briggs & Stratton could also use that $500,000 to upgrade its carburetor assembly line, which would save $225,000 annually. If a firm does decide to buy a product instead of making it, the purchase will be a new buy, a modified rebuy, or a straight rebuy.

New Buy

new buy
A situation requiring the purchase of a product for the first time.

A **new buy** is a situation requiring the purchase of a product for the first time. For example, suppose a manufacturing company needs a better way to page managers while they are working on the shop floor. Currently, each of the several managers has a distinct ring, for example, two short and one long, which sounds over the plant intercom whenever he or she is being paged by anyone in the factory. The company decides to replace its buzzer system of paging with handheld wireless radio technology that will allow managers to communicate immediately with the department initiating the page. This situation represents the greatest opportunity for new vendors. No long-term relationship has been established for this product, specifications may be somewhat fluid, and buyers are generally more open to new vendors.

If the new item is a raw material or a critical component part, the buyer cannot afford to run out of supply. The seller must be able to convince the buyer that the seller's firm can consistently deliver a high-quality product on time.

Purchasing Management Association of Canada

Familiarize yourself with the Purchasing Management Association of Canada by reading about the organization on its website. Based on what you read, do you think a purchasing manager can be effective without being certified by PMAC? Evaluate PMAC's Code of Ethics, which is presented in the "Ethics in Marketing" box.

http://www.pmac.ca

Modified Rebuy

A **modified rebuy** is normally less critical and less time-consuming than a new buy. In a modified-rebuy situation, the purchaser wants some change in the original good or service. It may be a new colour, greater tensile strength in a component part, more respondents in a marketing research study, or additional services in a janitorial contract.

modified rebuy
A situation where the purchaser wants some change in the original good or service.

Because the two parties are familiar with each other and credibility has been established, buyer and seller can concentrate on the specifics of the modification. But in some cases, modified rebuys are open to outside bidders. The purchaser uses this strategy to ensure that the new terms are competitive. An example would be the manufacturing company buying radios with a vibrating feature for managers who have trouble hearing the ring over the factory noise. The firm may open the bidding to examine the price/quality offerings of several suppliers.

Straight Rebuy

A **straight rebuy** is a situation vendors prefer. The purchaser is not looking for new information or other suppliers. An order is placed and the product is provided as in previous orders. Usually, a straight rebuy is routine because the terms of the purchase have been agreed to in earlier negotiations. In this case the manufacturing company we have been discussing wants to supply its new managers with radios. The company decides to purchase additional radios from the same supplier on a regular basis.

straight rebuy
A situation in which the purchaser reorders the same goods or services without looking for new information or investigating other suppliers.

One common instrument used in straight-rebuy situations is the purchasing contract. Purchasing contracts are used with products that are bought often and in high volume. In essence, the purchasing contract makes the buyer's decision-making routine and promises the salesperson a sure sale. The advantage to the buyer is a quick, confident decision and, to the salesperson, reduced or eliminated competition.

Suppliers must remember not to take straight-rebuy relationships for granted. Retaining existing customers is much easier than attracting new ones.

Business Ethics

The ethics of business buyer and seller relationships are often scrutinized and sometimes criticized by superiors, associates, other prospective suppliers, the general public, and the news media. The Purchasing Management Association of Canada has developed a code of ethics to guide purchasing agents in their dealings with vendors, as shown in the "Ethics in Marketing" box.

Customer Service

Business marketers need to recognize the benefits of developing a formal system to monitor customer opinions and perceptions of the quality of customer service. Consumer-oriented firms like McDonald's and Lexus build their strategies not only around products but also around a few highly developed service skills. Business marketers are leading the way in adoption of new media technologies such as on-line services and CD-ROMs.

For example, Grand and Toy, a leading office products supplier in Canada, has experienced continuous double-digit growth rates in its B2B e-commerce business. The firm boasts an "award winning Internet ordering system," which it adapts to its customers' purchasing systems. Pete Vanexan, president of Grand and Toy comments: "Each bill payment method that we have implemented is the result of us working in partnership with individual customers to create a process that brings measurable cost savings to their business. We're not sourcing 'off-the-shelf' solutions here." Besides integrating with its customers' purchasing systems, Grand and Toy offers interactive customer service technologies, such as *LiveHelp*, an interactive on-line chat feature that allows customer service representatives to manage site navigation or product queries instantaneously by troubleshooting live with the customer, and *Screen Sharing*, a

ETHICS IN MARKETING

The Code of Ethics of the Purchasing Management Association of Canada

Values and Norms of Ethical Behaviour

A. Values

Members will operate and conduct their decisions and actions based on the following values:

1. Honesty/Integrity
   Maintaining an unimpeachable standard of integrity in all their business relationships both inside and outside the organizations in which they are employed;
2. Professionalism
   Fostering the highest standards of professional competence amongst those for whom they are responsible;
3. Responsible Management
   Optimizing the use of resources for which they are responsible so as to provide the maximum benefit to their employers;
4. Serving the Public Interest
   Not using their authority of office for personal benefit, rejecting and denouncing any business practice that is improper;
5. Conformity to the Laws
   In Terms of:
   A. The laws of the country in which they practice;
   B. The Institute's or Corporation's Rules and Regulations;
   C. Contractual obligations.

B. Norms of Ethical Behaviour

1. To consid.er first, the interest of one's organization in all transactions and to carry out and believe in its established policies.
2. To be receptive to competent counsel from one's colleagues and be guided by such counsel without impairing the responsibility of one's office.
3. To buy without prejudice, seeking to obtain the maximum value for each dollar of expenditure.
4. To strive for increased knowledge of the materials and processes of manufacture, and to establish practical procedures for the performance of one's responsibilities.
5. To participate in professional development programs so that one's purchasing knowledge and performance are enhanced.
6. To subscribe to and work for honesty in buying and selling and to denounce all forms of improper business practice.
7. To accord a prompt and courteous reception to all who call on a legitimate business mission.
8. To abide by and to encourage others to practice the Professional Code of Ethics of the Purchasing Management Association of Canada and its affiliated Institutes and Corporation.
9. To counsel and assist fellow purchasers in the performance of their duties.
10. To cooperate with all organizations and individuals engaged in activities which enhance the development and standing of purchasing and materials management.

Rules of Conduct

In applying these rules of conduct, members should follow guidance set out below:

A. Declaration of Interest.
   Any personal interest which may impinge or might reasonably be deemed by others to impinge on a member's impartiality in any matter relevant to his or her duties should be immediately declared to his or her employer.

B. Confidentiality and Accuracy of Information.
   The confidentiality of information received in the course of duty must be respected and should not be used for personal gain; information given in the course of duty should be true and fair and not designed to mislead.

C. Competition.
   While considering the advantages to the member's employer of maintaining a continuing relationship with a supplier, any arrangement which might prevent the effective operation of fair competition should be avoided.

D. Business Gifts and Hospitality
   To preserve the image and integrity of the member, employer and the profession, business gifts other than items of small intrinsic value should not be accepted. Reasonable hospitality is an accepted courtesy of a business relationship. The frequency and nature of gifts or hospitality accepted should not be allowed whereby the recipient might be or might be deemed by others to have been influenced in making a business decision as a consequence of accepting such hospitality or gifts.

E. Discrimination and Harassment
   No member shall knowingly participate in acts of discrimination or harassment towards any person that he or she has business relations with

F. Environmental Issues
   Members shall recognize their responsibility to environmental issues consistent with their corporate goals or missions.

G. Interpretation
   When in doubt on the interpretation of these rules of conduct, members should refer to the Ethics Committee of their Institute or Corporation.[29]

technology that enables Grand and Toy's customer service representatives to lead the customer through grandandtoy.com and its features by controlling the customer's desktop mouse movement.[30]

Although many firms are finding new ways to enhance customer service through technology, it is important that the technology be used effectively. One recent survey reported that business-to-business marketers were not using e-mail effectively for customer service. The survey indicated that 65 percent of the firms took 24 hours to respond to e-mail; another 29 percent did not respond at all. In addition, although 65 percent of the firms reported having on-line service available for customers, only 2 percent of the firms had capabilities beyond answering FAQs (frequently asked questions).[31]

>> CONNECT IT

Look back at the story about Canada Post at the beginning of the chapter. You now know that business firms and organizations are the highest-spending customers in the Canadian market.

Canada Post has recognized the importance of its business customers and has also realized that in the future, its services will be in more demand from business customers rather than consumers, who will communicate more and more through electronic channels and less and less via the mail.

Canada Post provides a wide array of business services as part of its B2B (business-to-business) marketing strategy through its "Canada Post Group" of companies, which include Purolator Courier, Progistix-Solutions, Intelcom Courier, epost, Innovapost, and Canada Post International Ltd. Finally, Canada Post offers its business customers access to its On-line Business Centre, which offers business services, such as on-line ordering, electronic shipping tools, account management, postal code lookup, postal outlet locator, a rate calculator, and shipment tracking.

REVIEW IT

1 Describe business marketing. Business marketing provides goods and services that are bought for use in business rather than for personal consumption. Intended use, not physical characteristics, distinguishes a business product from a consumer product.

1.1 WRITING As the marketing manager for Huggies diapers made by Kimberly-Clark, you are constantly going head-to-head with Pampers, produced by rival Procter & Gamble. You are considering unlocking the potential of the business market to increase your share of the disposable diaper market, but how? Write an outline of several ways you could transform this quintessentially consumer product into a successful business product as well.

2 Describe the role of the Internet in business marketing. The rapid expansion and adoption of the Internet have made business markets more competitive than ever before. The number of business buyers and sellers using the Internet is rapidly increasing. Firms are seeking new and better ways to expand markets and sources of supply, increase sales and decrease costs, and better serve customers. With the Internet, every business in the world is potentially a local competitor.

2.1 ON LINE How could you use the website http://strategis.ic.gc.ca to help define a target market and develop a marketing plan?

2.2 ON LINE Reconsider question 1.1. How could you use the Internet in your business marketing of Huggies diapers?

3 Discuss the role of relationship marketing and strategic alliances in business marketing. Relationship marketing entails seeking and establishing long-term alliances or partnerships with customers. A strategic alliance is a cooperative agreement among business firms. Firms form alliances to leverage what they do well by partnering with others who have complementary skills.

3.1 Why is relationship or personal selling the best way to promote in business marketing?

4 Identify the four major categories of business market customers. Producer markets consist of for-profit organizations and individuals that buy products to use in producing other products, as components of other products, or in facilitating business operations. Reseller markets consist of wholesalers and retailers that buy finished products to resell for profit. Government markets include federal, provincial, territorial, and municipal governments that buy goods and services to support their own operations and serve the needs of citizens. Institutional markets consist of very diverse nonbusiness institutions whose main goals do not include profit.

4.1 WRITING Understanding businesses is key to business marketing. Use Business Gateway (http://businessgateway.ca) to learn about all the government services and information available to help you start a business. Examine the sources of business statistics available to you. Read about e-business and describe some of the issues that you would have to deal with to set up an e-business. Access the information on selling to government. What kinds of contracts are listed?

5 Explain the North American Industry Classification System. The 2002 NAICS provides a way to identify, analyze, segment, and target business and government markets. Organizations can be identified and compared by a numeric code indicating business sector, subsector, industry group, industry, and country industry. NAICS is a valuable tool for analyzing, segmenting, and targeting business markets.

5.1 ON LINE Explain how a marketer can use the website http://www.naics.com to convert SIC data to the 2002 NAICS.

6 Explain the major differences between business and consumer markets. In business markets, demand is derived, price-inelastic, joint, and fluctuating. Purchase volume is much larger than in consumer markets, customers are fewer in number and more geographically concentrated, and distribution channels are more direct. Buying is approached more formally using professional purchasing agents, more people are involved in the buying process, negotiation is more complex, and reciprocity and leasing are more common. And, finally, selling strategy in business markets normally focuses on personal contact rather than on advertising.

6.1 How might derived demand affect the manufacturing of an automobile?

6.2 You are the company's purchasing manager and your boss has asked you to buy new computers for an entire department. Since you have just recently purchased a new home computer, you are well educated about the various products available. How will your buying process for the company differ from your recent purchase for yourself?

7 Describe the seven types of business goods and services. Major equipment includes capital goods, such as heavy machinery. Accessory equipment is typically less expensive and shorter-lived than major equipment. Raw materials are extractive or agricultural products that have not been processed. Component parts are finished or near-finished items to be used as parts of other products. Processed materials are used to manufacture other products. Supplies are consumable and not used as part of a final product. Business services are intangible products that many companies use in their operations.

7.1 WRITING TEAM In small groups, brainstorm examples of companies that feature the products in different business categories. (Avoid examples already listed in the chapter.) Compile a list of 10 specific business products, including at least one in each category. Then match up with another group. Have each group take turns naming a product and have the other group identify its appropriate category. Try to resolve all discrepancies by discussion. Some identified products might appropriately fit into more than one category.

8 **Discuss the unique aspects of business buying behaviour.** Business buying behaviour is distinguished by five fundamental characteristics. First, buying is normally undertaken by a buying centre consisting of many people who range widely in authority level. Second, business buyers typically evaluate alternative products and suppliers based on quality, service, and price—in that order. Third, business buying falls into three general categories: new buys, modified rebuys, and straight rebuys. Fourth, the ethics of business buyers and sellers are often scrutinized. Fifth, customer service before, during, and after the sale plays a big role in business purchase decisions.

8.1 WRITING A colleague of yours has sent you an e-mail seeking your advice as she attempts to sell a new voice-mail system to a local business. Send her a return e-mail describing the various people who might influence the customer's buying decision. Be sure to include suggestions for dealing with the needs of each of these individuals.

8.2 Intel Corporation supplies microprocessors to Hewlett-Packard for use in its computers. Describe the buying situation in this relationship, keeping in mind the rapid advance of technology in this industry.

DEFINE IT

accessory equipment 144
business marketing 132
business services 146
buying centre 146
component parts 145
derived demand 141
joint demand 141
keiretsu 136
major equipment (installations) 144
modified rebuy 149
multiplier effect (accelerator principle) 142
new buy 148
North American Industry Classification System (NAICS) 139
OEM 145
processed materials 145
raw materials 144
reciprocity 143
straight rebuy 149
strategic alliance (strategic partnership) 135
supplies 145–146

APPLY IT

Dan White is an independent video producer whose biggest client is Alliance-Atlantis Canada. Although this account is big enough to support the entire business, Dan has developed other lines of business to eliminate the risks involved with having only one customer. Dan has also landed a sizable account through a high school friend who is the vice president of Good Hands Insurance, which also happens to be the company that underwrites Dan's life insurance. Additionally, Dan is hired to work on various projects for some advertising agencies. Dan generated this business through long-term relationships built by working on projects for Alliance-Atlantis.

As Dan prepares his business plan for the upcoming year, he is contemplating several strategic changes. Because of the increasing speed at which the video industry is evolving, Dan has observed two important trends. First, he is finding it increasingly difficult to own the latest video equipment that his customers are demanding. Second, Dan's clients are not able to keep up with the recent developments in the industry and would be willing to pay more for his expertise. Dan is looking into a lease for new equipment, and he is contemplating increasing the price of his services.

QUESTIONS

1. What two-digit NAICS code would you assign to Dan's business? For a complete list of all NAICS codes, see **http://www.naics.com.**
2. Is Dan's choice to use Good Hands Insurance ethical? Why or why not?
3. How can Dan use the inelasticity of demand to his advantage?
4. Would you advise Dan to lease or buy the new equipment? Why?

THINK ABOUT IT

Cameron Stock, purchasing manager for Goalie Keepaway, a sports equipment manufacturer, is responsible for buying $5 million of component parts and supplies every year. He has a preferred list of certified suppliers, many of which are awarded a large percentage of this business annually. Cameron has been offered an all-expense paid weekend for two in Las Vegas as a Christmas present from a major supplier with whom he has done business for close to a decade. Over this time, Cameron has built a very good relationship with the vendor.

QUESTIONS

1. Would it be legal and ethical for Cameron Stock to accept this gift?
2. How is this situation addressed in the PMAC Code of Ethics? Go to the "Ethics in Marketing" box in the chapter and review the PMAC Code of Ethics. Also visit the CMA website at **http://www.the-cma.org/consumer/ethics.cfm** and reread the Code of Ethics of the CMA. Write a brief paragraph summarizing where PMAC and the CMA stand on the issue of supplier gifts.

TRY IT

Mediagrif Interactive Technologies: An Online B2B Brokerage Firm

Mediagrif Interactive Technologies is a Montreal-based on-line business-to-business brokerage firm that has annual sales in the $40 million range and was recently rated as one of the 50 best-managed companies in Canada. The company was founded in 1996 by Denis Gadbois, a former information technology executive who saw the Internet as a great business opportunity as an exchange forum for businesses. Mediagrif began as "The Broker Forum," a computer-parts network that evolved into an operator of e-business networks and a provider of complete e-business solutions, including content management and e-tendering solutions. Mediagrif currently operates nine networks, including The Broker Forum (**http://www.brokerforum.com**), Power Source Online Inc. (**http://www.powersourceonline.com**), TelecomFinders (**http://www.telecomfinders.com**), and Global Wine & Spirits (**http://www.globalwinespirits.com**).

Mediagrif began its on-line business operations with a different approach. It recruits firms as "members" and charges them a flat "membership fee." Through its networks, Mediagrif currently serves a membership base of more than 8,350 business located in 60 countries. Mediagrif has grown its business via acquisition of specialized on-line B2B services. For example, Mediagrif acquired the MERX e-tendering service from the Bank of Montreal. MERX is the official distributor of tender documents for the federal government of Canada, which allows more than 22,000 Canadian businesses to access government contract opportunities. It followed this up with the acquisition of Governmentbids.com, an Atlanta, Georgia-based firm that allows more than 2,000 business subscribers to access over 250,000 government contract opportunities annually at the federal, state, and local government levels. Governmentbids.com provides bid opportunities from more than 20,000 government-purchasing offices across both Canada and the United States.

To develop business, Mediagrif focuses on customer service. The firm monitors its website activity very carefully to see which customers are using the service and which customers aren't. It gets feedback from both kinds of customers. The firm boasts an annual renewal rate of between 70 and 80 percent. Kevin Lo, a technology analyst at Lightyear Capital in Calgary, made the following comments on Mediagrif's business approach: "Mediagrif's management is very prudent. Instead of having a *Field of Dreams* kind of attitude—build it and they will come—they're very targeted, very focused on certain niches, and very driven to dominate those niches."

The development of on-line brokerage services is not without controversy. For example, Global Wine & Spirits (**www.globalwinespirits. com**) is a joint venture with the Société des alcools du Quebec (SAQ) designed to bring commercial buyers, sellers, and agents in the wine industry together to simplify transactions, expedite logistics, and provide unparalleled product selection. However, a year after its inception only 30 percent of the SAQ's 1,800 suppliers were using it. Also, Global Wine & Spirits' on-line catalogue contained 5,600 products, which was substantially less than the 15,000 the joint venture hoped to have. The SAQ is strongly motivated to make the venture work, as a study of its supply chain revealed the potential for savings of nearly $200 million by reducing delays in shipping by 15 percent through on-line transactions. Consequently, the SAQ sent a notice to all its suppliers indicating they would have to go on-line through Global Wine & Spirits or risk being delisted!

Viewing the notice as a strong ultimatum, some key industry associations such as the Federation of Wine & Spirits Exporters of France and the European Committee of Wine Enterprises indicated they did not want to use the portal. In addition, the EU filed a complaint with the Canadian Department of Foreign Affairs and International Trade, which argued that forcing suppliers to use an exclusive procurement system was a violation of the World Trade Organization agreement. Another major issue is the requirement of a US$1,400 listing fee combined with transactions fees between 0.56 and 2 percent of sales for all SAQ suppliers. Some small suppliers felt they would not be able to transact profitably with the SAQ with these fees in place.

In response to the issue of resistance to the on-line procurement system, Robert Bonneau, Global Wine's chief operating officer, commented: "If the SAQ had told its suppliers, 'We would like to do e-commerce and we'll do it when you're ready,' it would never happen." The SAQ did respond by allowing alternative electronic procurement platforms to be used by suppliers. As for the issue of fees, Mediagrif is used to the concerns. Marc Duhamel, Mediagrif vice president, comments: "In each of the sectors we have developed, there has always been resistance to change. We change not only the way they work electronically, but also their business processes—and pricing is one of those elements. And when that happens, it's destabilizing, and people wonder what the benefits are, so it becomes a matter of proving that it is worthwhile."

Sources: Based on Robin Raizel, "Net Gains," *Canadian Business*, October 14–26, 2003, 107; Mediagrif website, http://www.mediagrif.com; Press Release, "Mediagrif Announces Acquisition of GovernmentBids.com, A Leading US-based Government Bid Aggregation Service," *Canada NewsWire*, February 23, 2004, 1; and Luis. E. Millan, "Over a Barrel: At some Point, The Bigger Industry Players Have to Twist Some Arms to Get Their Smaller Supply Chain Partners On the E-Commerce Bandwagon," *Business Journal*, March 2002, 15.

QUESTIONS

1. Evaluate Mediagrif's growth-through-acquisition approach. What are the strengths and weaknesses of businesses that grow this way?
2. A lot of e-businesses have failed in recent times and more will continue to fail. What is it about Mediagrif's approach to e-business that may allow it to succeed? What are some threats to its approach that could lead to a risk of failure?
3. How would you classify the types of on-line services that Mediagrif provides? What business markets does it serve?
4. How do you think going on-line would be "worthwhile" for the wine suppliers of the SAQ?

FLIP IT

Flip to Chapter 5 in your *Grademaker Study Guide* for more review opportunities, including the pretest, vocabulary review, Internet activities, study test questions, and business marketing scenarios. Do you know what distinguishes consumer products from business products? And can you list the four major categories of business market customers? Close your book and describe the seven types of business goods and services. You can't? Then flip open your Study Guide to brush up.

CLICK IT

The *Marketing* website is rich with materials to help you review and master marketing concepts. Check your knowledge with the free quizzes, practise key terms using the crossword puzzles, or review key concepts using the Microsoft® PowerPoint® slides. Also on the website are updated weblinks to companies mentioned in this chapter, Internet exercises, career marketing information, and much much more! Go to http://www.lamb3e.nelson.com, read the material, and follow the convenient links.

WATCH IT

CBC

Smed: The Falkridge Marketing and Retreat Centre

SMED Office Furniture is a Calgary-based manufacturer of modular office furniture system products with sales in the $250 million range. The firm was founded as a private company in 1983 by Mogens Smed and went public in 1996. It was acquired by Haworth Office furniture in 2000. SMED currently operates a 72,000-square metre manufacturing and office facility in Calgary.

SMED approaches office furniture manufacturing and marketing with a very unique approach. The Calgary production facility is ISO 9001 registered and features modern equipment and innovative work processes that enable SMED to offer one of the shortest lead times in the office furniture business. SMED is environmentally conscious and employs "recycling programs, efficient lighting, processes that minimize material use and waste, carpooling and water conservation" in its factory. The factory itself is also oriented to make employees and visitors feel comfortable. It features "a workout facility and gym, an excellent restaurant called 'The Bridge,' and Lake Smed, which has a path around it for walking and is used for skating in the winter." It is part of SMED's approach to see that every day the employees "work in a landscape of leading-edge technology, efficient space, total flexibility, and aesthetically, ergonomically, and environmentally pleasing surroundings."

As pleasing and innovative as SMED's factory is, the Marketing Centre at Falkridge is even more impressive. SMED refers to it as "our ode to architectural detail. Every sense is indulged in textures, lines and colours, all surrounded by the beautiful scenery of the Canadian Rocky Mountains. Spectacular architecture and design is coupled with superior craftsmanship provided by local trades."

Falkridge is a small resort reserved specifically for SMED clients and employees. It features two main buildings that have 13 guest suites designed for "comfort, amenities, and style." As such, each suite (single or double accommodation) offers its guests Jacuzzi tubs, snack fridges, luxurious beds, automatic blinds, and forest/valley views. In addition to the 13 suites, there is also a three-bedroom apartment with kitchen and laundry facilities available. The accommodations support a 22-seat presentation room and a small eight-seat training room, all of which are equipped with state-of-the art audiovisual equipment. Falkridge has an informal kitchen-dining area that serves for breakfast and a larger dining room designed to offer sit-down service. Both the kitchen and the dining room present exquisite architectural surroundings and a cozy fireplace. Virtually all of the furniture and systems in Falkridge are SMED designs and samples of SMED products.

SMED employs the Falkridge Marketing Centre for four purposes. It serves as a product training centre for SMED's employees. It is also a place where important clients are brought for SMED product demonstrations and to see examples of SMED's design capabilities in practice. It is also a way to "thank" clients for taking time to consider SMED's products and services. In SMED's words: "While visiting us we want clients to have firsthand exposure to our people, our culture, and our company. Falkridge celebrates what we're all about: our style, our commitment to quality and design, and of course our ongoing relationships with our clients." Finally, Falkridge is also available to rent for corporate retreats.

Training aside, the real power of Falkridge lies in its use to appeal to potential clients and purchase influencers. As CBC reporter Colin King states: "A visit to Falkridge closes many deals." When SMED clients come to Falkridge, they live among SMED products for several days. Mogens Smed likens it to fishing. The clients are the "fish" he is hoping to catch, and Falkridge and its attractive and compelling displays are the bait. Clients can enjoy the view and the luxury of the mountain resort while they live and work among SMED's products. After this, if they can say "no" to a deal, they are resistant clients indeed!

SMED is not using Falkridge to impress buyers alone. The company is also aware of the importance of key influencers in the purchase of office furniture. That is why it sponsored a retreat for the Northern Pacific Chapter of the International Interior Design Association. A report on the retreat included the following commentary about Falkridge: "The facility was beautiful with architectural textures, lines, and colours all surrounded by the beautiful scenery of the Canadian Rocky Mountains. Though snowing and chilly outside, we were toasty warm inside and enjoyed some productive and quality time among approximately 20 board members. We were also very privileged to have a special dinner at Mogens Smed's log home with beautiful interior detailing all by local craftsmen."

The only problem for SMED is that Falkridge has only 13 rooms, one apartment, and there are only 365 days in the year and 52 weekends. There are only so many clients and so many retreats that SMED can fit in. Falkridge will have to produce a lot of million-dollar deals to justify its existence, but so far it seems to be up to the task.

Sources: Based on SMED Corporate website, http://www.smed.ca/company/falkridge.asp; CBC, *Venture*, "Turning Smed Around," Broadcast: January 19, 1999; International Interior Design Association, Northern Pacific Chapter, http://www.iida-wa.org/nl_sp03_board_retreat.html.

QUESTIONS

1. How do you think a facility like Falkridge helps SMED improve its business marketing?
2. What kinds of "clients" would mostly likely be interested in a facility like Falkridge for their "corporate retreats?"
3. What kinds of "ethical" issues might arise around the use of Falkridge to entertain and educate SMED's customers? (Review the PMAC Code of Conduct in the "ethics in Marketing" box in the chapter, and review the CMA's Code of Ethics on the CMA website, **http://www.the-cma.org,** to help you answer this question.)
4. The case mentions the four purposes for Falkridge. Advise SMED on how to "ration" the four purposes for Falkridge so it can maximize the centre's impact as a marketing tool.

chapter 6

Segmenting and Targeting Markets

>> LEARNING OBJECTIVES

1. Describe the characteristics of markets and market segments
2. Explain the importance of market segmentation
3. Discuss criteria for successful market segmentation
4. Describe the bases commonly used to segment consumer markets
5. Describe the bases for segmenting business markets
6. List the steps involved in segmenting markets
7. Discuss alternative strategies for selecting target markets
8. Explain how and why firms implement positioning strategies and how product differentiation plays a role
9. Discuss global market segmentation and targeting issues

>> "I don't want to grow up, I'm a Toys "R" Us Kid, they've got games and cosmetics for girls that I can play with?" It may become a new version of an old marketing campaign song, but non-traditional approaches to marketing are called for if you want to serve one of Canada's most significant markets: tweens. Tweens are 9 to 12 years old and they represent a very important market in Canada. Up until now the only marketers who paid serious attention to the tween market were involved in selling mainly snack foods, cereal, fast food, toys, clothing, and back-to-school items. Marketers have long been aware that tweens are important influencers in the purchase decisions of their parents for these kinds of products. However, marketers have discovered that tweens have considerably more personal buying power and buying discretion and indeed, more family purchase influence than previously thought. Marketers are now realizing that tweens are important customers and influencers for cosmetics and Internet services too!

Toys "R" Us Canada has been selling body glitter, manicure sets, hair mascara, and temporary tattoos for a number of years. It saw the tween market as a tremendous opportunity and decided to go after the tween cosmetic market. Toys "R" Us developed its own brand of cosmetics branded "Girl Stuff" to serve this market. The firm has seen double-digit growth rates in this product line so far. Of course Toys "R" Us is not the only firm seeking to provide cosmetics to this market. N.Y.C. is a cosmetic brand that was launched in Canada on the basis of a low price point—all of the products are priced around $2.99. The firm is hoping to introduce tweens to cosmetics and then maintain its brand loyalty as they grow older and trade up to more expensive cosmetic lines. Coty Canada is employing the philosophy of "building brand loyalty" early with its Smiley line of bath products. The Smiley line is part of the firm's Calgon label, and Coty plans to have Calgon bath products that will be used by its customers "for every stage of life."

Internet provider Shaw@home is targeting tweens and teens as key influencers for its high-speed Internet service. It has posted banner ads on websites frequented by tweens and teens such as muchmusic.com, billboard.com, get-music.com, skateboarding.com, cosmogirl.com, and loewscineplex.com. Off-line advertising using radio, transit advertising, and newspapers to reach the tweens' parents also supported the campaign. The ads feature children under 12 discussing how they are more technologically adept than their teenage siblings. One ad includes the line: "Sure I'll slow down. When I'm 15. Until then, I'll need a faster connection."

One source of information on the tween market is "The Web Resource for Marketers to Young People" (**http://www.kidsmarketing.com**). In an article titled "Tweens Today: Teen Wannabes," the tween market was characterized as follows: "they are culturally and brand aware; they define themselves by the friends they have; they are more independent than previous tween generations; thanks to sports, computer technology, and what trend marketers are calling KGOY (Kids Getting Older Younger), tween boys and girls are more comfortable with and accepting of one another; they like advertising but are suspicious of empty and unfulfilled product promotion promises; and they are experimenters."

Recent surveys of Canadian tweens uncovered the following attitudes: Canadian tweens aspire to be older than they are (at least 18 years), 83 percent of tweens say that school is important to their future; 81 percent say that having high marks at school constitutes "cool"; and two-thirds plan to attend college or university after they finish high school (75 percent among girls). Because they watch a lot of television, about 14 hours a week, tweens are a very well-informed market. They also use the Internet often, with 88 percent of tweens reporting that they have Internet access. Canadian tweens represent a market force, spending $1.6 billion on their own purchases. They also influence 87 percent of their parent's purchases![1]

Based on the preceding information, how would you define market segmentation and targeting? What type of targeting strategy are tween cosmetic marketers using? What kinds of issues to you think tween marketers will have to pay attention to in order to market to this segment? Explain your answer. This chapter will help you answer these questions and more.

ON LINE

KIDs Marketing.com

What kind of information is available at Kidsmarketing.com. What kinds of services does Kidsmarketing.com offer? What information or services can it provide that might be of use to Canadian marketers?

http://www.kidsmarketing.com

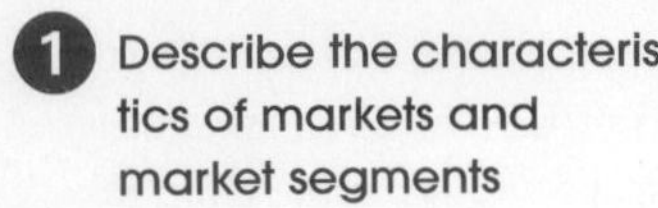

1 Describe the characteristics of markets and market segments

>> MARKET SEGMENTATION

The term *market* means different things to different people. We are all familiar with the supermarket, stock market, labour market, fish market, and flea market. All these types of markets share several characteristics. First, they are composed of people (consumer markets) or organizations (business markets). Second, these people or organizations have wants and needs that can be satisfied by particular product categories. Third, they have the ability to buy the products they seek. Fourth, they are willing to exchange their resources, usually money or credit, for desired products. In sum, a **market** is (1) people or organizations with (2) needs or wants and with (3) the ability and (4) the willingness to buy. A group of people or an organization that lacks any one of these characteristics is not a market.

market
People or organizations with needs or wants and the ability and willingness to buy.

market segment
A subgroup of people or organizations sharing one or more characteristics that cause them to have similar product needs.

Within a market, a **market segment** is a subgroup of people or organizations sharing one or more characteristics that cause them to have similar product needs. At one extreme, we can define every person and every organization in the world as a market segment because each is unique. At the other extreme, we can define the entire consumer market as one large market segment and the business market as another large segment. All people have some similar characteristics and needs, as do all organizations.

market segmentation
The process of dividing a market into meaningful, relatively similar, and identifiable segments or groups.

From a marketing perspective, market segments can be described as somewhere between the two extremes. The process of dividing a market into meaningful, relatively similar, and identifiable segments or groups is called **market segmentation.** The purpose of market segmentation is to enable the marketer to tailor marketing mixes to meet the needs of one or more specific segments.

Exhibit 6.1 illustrates the concept of market segmentation. Each box represents a market consisting of seven persons. This market might vary as follows: one homogeneous market of seven people, a market consisting of seven individual segments, a market composed of two segments based on gender, a market composed of three age segments, or a market composed of five age and gender market segments. Age and gender and many other bases for segmenting markets are examined later in this chapter.

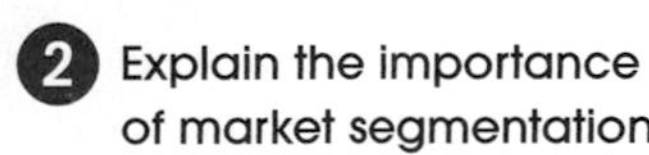

2 Explain the importance of market segmentation

>> THE IMPORTANCE OF MARKET SEGMENTATION

Until the 1960s, few firms practised market segmentation. When they did, it was more likely a haphazard effort than a formal marketing strategy. Before 1960, for example, the Coca-Cola Company produced only one beverage and aimed it at the entire soft drink market. Today, Coca-Cola offers over a dozen different products to market segments based on diverse consumer preferences for flavours and calorie and caffeine content. Coca-Cola offers traditional soft drinks, energy drinks (such as PowerAde), flavoured teas, fruit drinks (Fruitopia), and water (Dasani).

Market segmentation plays a key role in the marketing strategy of almost all successful organizations and is a powerful marketing tool for several reasons. Most importantly, nearly all markets include groups of people or organizations with different product needs and preferences. Market segmentation helps marketers define customer needs and wants more precisely. Because market segments differ in size and potential, segmentation helps decision makers more accurately define marketing objectives and better allocate resources. In turn, performance can be better evaluated when objectives are more precise.

Aliant Telecom, is targeting new cell phone users in Atlantic Canada based on research on purchase intentions. The firm is planning to market to 18- to 25-year-olds, who were reported to be the highest percentage among people intending to purchase a cell phone. The market is described as "tech-savvy" and early adopters. "They understand that pretty soon they're going to be surfing the Internet on their phone." The firm researched people in Atlantic Canada to see what kinds of promotional campaigns would work best for them. Rather than the basic approach of showing local landmarks, Aliant Telecom decided to be more personal and appeal to this group with a promotional campaign based on the theme, "If you're normal, why don't you have a cell phone?"[2]

No market segmentation

Fully segmented market

Market segmentation by gender: M, F

Market segmentation by age group: 1, 2, 3

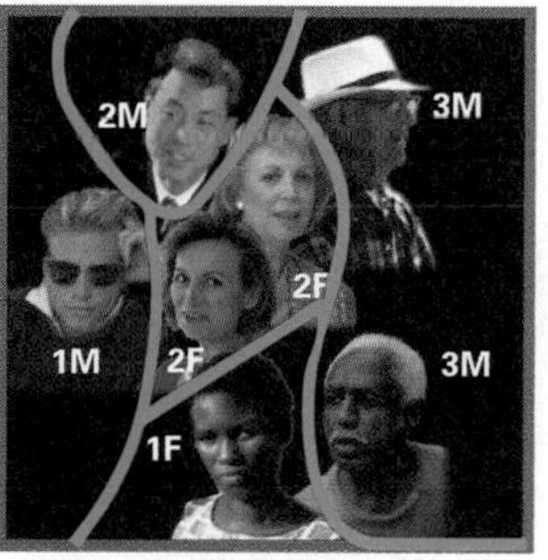

Market segmentation by gender and age group

EXHIBIT 6.1

Concept of Market Segmentation

>> CRITERIA FOR SUCCESSFUL SEGMENTATION

Marketers segment markets for three important reasons. First, segmentation enables marketers to identify groups of customers with similar needs and to analyze the characteristics and buying behaviour of these groups. Second, segmentation provides marketers with information to help them design marketing mixes specifically matched with the characteristics and desires of one or more segments. Third, segmentation is consistent with the marketing concept of satisfying customer wants and needs while meeting the organization's objectives.

3 Discuss criteria for successful market segmentation

To be useful, a segmentation scheme must produce segments that meet four basic criteria:

- *Substantiality*: A segment must be large enough to warrant developing and maintaining a special marketing mix. This criterion does not necessarily mean that a segment must have many potential customers. Marketers of custom-designed homes and business buildings, commercial airplanes, and large computer systems typically develop marketing programs tailored to each potential customer's needs. In most cases, however, a market segment needs many potential customers to make commercial sense. In the 1980s, home banking failed because not enough people owned personal computers. Today, a larger number of people own computers, and home banking is a growing industry.
- *Identifiability and measurability*: Segments must be identifiable and their size measurable. Data about the population within geographic boundaries, the number of people in various age categories, and other social and demographic characteristics are often easy to get, and they provide fairly concrete measures of segment size. Suppose that a social service agency wants to identify segments by their readiness to participate in a drug and alcohol program or in prenatal care. Unless the agency can measure how many people

ON LINE

Too Faced Cosmetics

Visit the various pages on the Too Faced website. What demographic group (age, ethnicity, etc.) do you think this new cosmetic company is targeting? Defend your answer.

http://www.toofaced.com

are willing, indifferent, or unwilling to participate, it will have trouble gauging whether there are enough people to justify setting up the service.

- *Accessibility*: The firm must be able to reach members of targeted segments with customized marketing mixes. Some market segments are hard to reach—for example, senior citizens (especially those with reading or hearing disabilities), individuals who don't speak English, and the illiterate.
- *Responsiveness*: As Exhibit 6.1 illustrates, markets can be segmented using any criteria that seem logical. Unless one market segment responds to a marketing mix differently from other segments, however, that segment need not be treated separately. For instance, if all customers are equally price-conscious about a product, there is no need to offer high-, medium-, and low-priced versions to different segments.

4 Describe the bases commonly used to segment consumer markets

>> BASES FOR SEGMENTING CONSUMER MARKETS

segmentation bases (variables) Characteristics of individuals, groups, or organizations.

Marketers use **segmentation bases,** or **variables,** which are characteristics of individuals, groups, or organizations, to divide a total market into segments. The choice of segmentation bases is crucial because an inappropriate segmentation strategy may lead to lost sales and missed profit opportunities. The key is to identify bases that will produce substantial, measurable, and accessible segments that exhibit different response patterns to marketing mixes.

Markets can be segmented using a single variable, such as age group, or several variables, such as age group, gender, and education. Although it is less precise, single-variable segmentation has the advantage of being simpler and easier to use than multiple-variable segmentation. The disadvantages of multiple-variable segmentation are that it is often harder to use than single-variable segmentation; usable secondary data are less likely to be available; and as the number of segmentation bases increases, the size of individual segments decreases. Nevertheless, the current trend is toward using more rather than fewer variables to segment most markets. Multiple-variable segmentation is clearly more precise than single-variable segmentation.

Consumer goods marketers commonly use one or more of the following characteristics to segment markets: geography, demographics, psychographics, benefits sought, and usage rate.

Geographic Segmentation

geographic segmentation Segmenting markets by region of a country or the world, market size, market density, or climate.

Geographic segmentation refers to segmenting markets by region of a country or the world, market size, market density, or climate. Market density means the number of people within a unit of land, such as a census tract. Climate is commonly used for geographic segmentation because of its dramatic impact on residents' needs and purchasing behaviour. Snowblowers, water and snow skis, clothing, and air-conditioning and heating systems are products with varying appeal, depending on climate.

Consumer goods companies take a regional approach to marketing for four reasons. First, many firms need to find new ways to generate sales because of sluggish and intensely competitive markets. Second, computerized checkout stations with scanners enable retailers to assess accurately which brands sell best in their region. Third, many packaged-goods manufacturers are introducing new regional brands intended to appeal to local preferences. Fourth, a more regional approach allows consumer goods companies to react more quickly to competition. Kokanee Beer, brewed in the Columbia Brewery in Creston, B.C., has taken a regional approach for entering the U.S. market. The company has targeted the states of Washington, Oregon, Idaho, Montana, and Alaska based on their proximity to British Columbia. Kokanee has gone with a very low-key promotional campaign featuring posters and radio ads and has banked on the fact that many of the people living in these states have visited B.C. and have been exposed to "spill-over" promotion from Canada. The campaign focuses on the fact that Kokanee is

GLOBAL **PERSPECTIVES**

Bringing Science to Weight Loss in China

On a recent afternoon, five chubby teenagers, two women of normal build, and a man with a potbelly came to the Sino-Japanese Friendship Hospital. They are asked about their eating habits, then step on a high-tech scale connected to a computer, which calculates body mass and prints out an elaborate diet and exercise regimen. Each person also leaves the hospital with a bottle of a weight-loss drug called Xenical.

"I feel more secure seeing a doctor. At least there's less of a chance of getting cheated," says Cai Shuang, an 18-year-old in baggy denim shorts and high tops who says she has tried several weight-loss pills advertised on television.

This is the kind of customer Roche Holding AG, the Swiss maker of Xenical, is hoping will help it conquer China's booming market in weight-loss products. China has hundreds of weight-loss treatments ranging from "slimming soups" to a traditional herb laxative, *dahuang*, derived from the rhubarb plant. As with the rest of China's pharmaceutical industry, shams and scams abound, piracy is rampant, claims are overblown, and regulation is minimal—a situation that has led many foreign drugmakers to target the country.

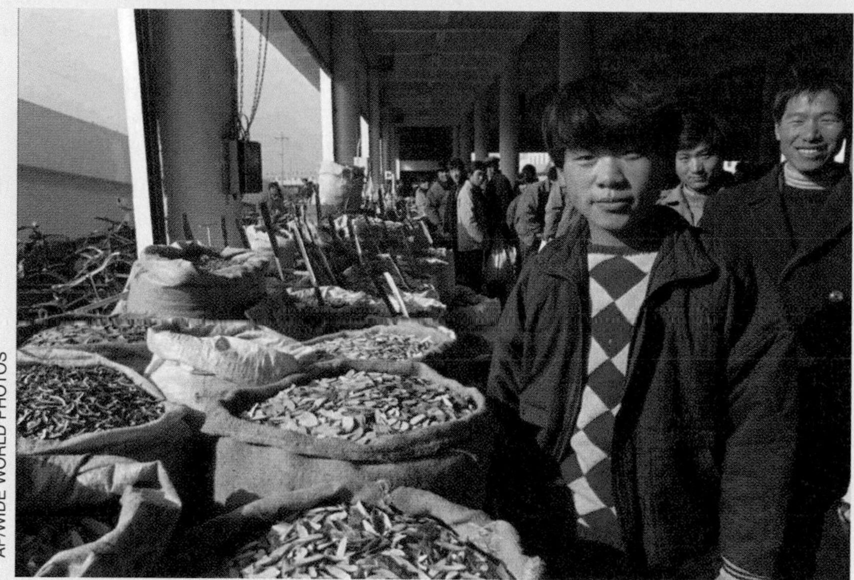

AP/WIDE WORLD PHOTOS

As China's economy is growing, obesity is becoming a serious national health problem. Western pharmaceutical companies are trying to bring science to China's weight-loss market, but they are having difficulty penetrating a market that is comfortable self-prescribing traditional medicines, like those pictured here, without consulting a physician.

Roche is hoping to bring science to the business of weight loss in China. Its patented Xenical, which works by blocking fat absorption and was introduced in China in January 2001, is the first prescription weight-loss drug approved by the Chinese government: all other weight-loss products are labelled "health products" and cannot be sold in hospitals or prescribed by doctors. Roche has set up high-end hospital clinics in major cities and trained doctors at each one. It is counting on the doctors to help sell patients on the benefits of Xenical.

Roche, as well as other drug companies, face cultural hurdles in China. Many Chinese have some knowledge of traditional medicine and feel comfortable self-prescribing instead of seeing a doctor. Also, most Chinese people see weight as more of a cosmetic than a health issue, as do many doctors. Furthermore, it is not clear that Chinese consumers want to go to hospitals for their dieting advice. Many state-run hospitals have outdated facilities and require hours-long waits.

China has 70 million obese people, which ranks them second to the United States in terms of the number of obese people. Over the past 10 years, consumption of meat, fast food, and soft drinks in the country has increased with incomes. A generation that can still remember malnutrition and famine now worries about diseases like diabetes, hypertension, and the obesity that facilitates both. However, unlike in North America, where many people understand basic nutrition and exercise, China is awash in ignorance. And the rapid pace of change in people's lives means that they are still eating as they used to even though they are no longer engaged in the physical labour they once were.

While Roche will not reveal actual numbers, it says sales of Xenical in China are growing between 30 percent and 50 percent a month and that it is targeting $12 million in sales in 2001.[3]

What cultural differences do manufacturers of obesity drugs like Roche have to contend with in China? Do you think China will continue to be a lucrative market segment for makers of obesity drugs to target? Explain your answer.

from Canada and that Americans need to know how to pronounce the brand name. One poster simply reads: "KOE-CAN-EE not KARE-EE-OKEE." One radio commercial features an American customer in the store asking for a case of "cockatoo" or "coconut" or "maybe cookamunga . . . It's that crazy Canadian spelling," he says. An announcer's voice breaks in: "Well you might not be able to pronounce it, but at least now you can enjoy the cool crisp taste of Kokanee beer right here in Washington.[4] The "Global Perspectives" box provides another example of geographic market segmentation.

Demographic Segmentation

demographic segmentation
Segmenting markets by age, gender, income, ethnic background, and family life cycle.

Marketers often segment markets on the basis of demographic information because it is widely available and often related to consumers' buying and consuming behaviour. Some common bases of **demographic segmentation** are age, gender, income, ethnic background, and family life cycle. The discussion here provides some important information about the main demographic segments.

Age Segmentation[5]

Canada's population of 31.6 million people is divided into 19 different age groups for statistical purposes. Marketers use these statistical age groups, often combining them with other information, in order to estimate demand potentials for products that are age related. Attracting children is a popular strategy for many companies hoping to instill brand loyalty early. Furthermore, children influence a great deal of family consumption. There are three subsegments in the children's market: young children (under age 9), tweens (ages 9 to 12), and teens (ages 13 to 19).

Statistics Canada data indicates that there were more than 3.6 million children under age 9 in Canada in 2003; this group represented 11.6 percent of the total population—an important market. Marketers are reaching out with high-end playthings like luxurious playhouses and BMW skateboards.[6] YTV Canada, once simply a television network for kids, now publishes YTV *Whoa!* magazine for this target market and operates a special travelling road show promotion called the *Weird on Wheels Tour.*[7] Older children, dubbed "tweens," number about 2.1 million, represent 6.6 percent of the population, and have an estimated spending power of over $1.6 billion.[8] Tweens desire to be kids, but also want some of the fun and glamour of being a teenager.[9] In the late summer of 2003, Binney & Smith Canada, makers of Crayola crayons, decided to target tweens with back-to-school promotions rather than moms as it had historically done. These days, kids want to shop as a social activity and they want to make their own decisions, even about back-to-school items.[10] Teens, sometimes referred to as Generation Y, number 2.1 million and represent 6.6 percent of the population, like the tweens. Canada's Print Measurement Bureau (PMB) reports: "Canadian teenagers earn an average of $5,255 every year and they spend about 90 percent of it on entertainment and leisure, including clothes, fragrances, hair care and cologne." Marketers are trying very hard to reach out to this market, and a number of specialty magazines have been developed specifically to reach Canadian teens. For example, Transcontinental-Hachette has developed *Elle Quebec Girl* as a specialty magazine targeted specifically at teenage girls who live in Quebec, and Famous Players theatres publishes *Teen Tribute* magazine, which is distributed to 300,000 teenage moviegoers.[11]

COURTESY OF VOLVO CARS OF NORTH AMERICA

Age segmentation can clearly define your target, but it can also be restrictive. Volvo has broken out of its older, family image by launching a new ad campaign with ads like the one pictured. The goal is to attract youthful Gen X-ers to a brand most typically associated with family life.

Other age segments are also appealing targets for marketers. The approximately 6.5 million Canadians classified as young adults between 20 and 34 years of age represent 21 percent of the population. Many beer, wine, and spirits companies are targeting this group. For example, Bacardi Ltd. hired a young marketing team to develop ads for Dewar's Scotch. The team dropped the "mixability" angle stressed in previous ads and revived the famous Dewar's profiles campaign, showing adventure-seeking 25- to 34-year-olds. The campaign appeals to Generation X by focusing on people following their dreams and not just evoking money and success.[12] The computer-literate Gen X-ers also are a large and viable market for the Internet.

The baby-boom generation, born between 1946 and 1964, comprises the largest age segment, with 9.2 million people—about 29 percent of the entire Canadian population. Many in this group are over 50 years of age and are continuing to lead active, fully involved lifestyles. The over-50 boomers are changing the way people look at aging; this presents an opportunity for brands to reposition themselves and to be more lifestyle-oriented. North Vancouver-based A&W is bringing back Chubby Chicken to appeal to the baby-boom generation and their families. Chicken was phased out in the 1980s when boomers were choosing burgers for fast food. Now boomers are abandoning fast-food burgers in favour of fast-food chicken. A&W is hoping to revive the memories and nostalgia associated with the Chubby Chicken name with the campaign line: "It's back! Same recipe. Same taste. New chickens."[13]

Seniors (aged 65 and over) are especially attracted to companies that build relationships by taking the time to get to know them and their preferences. Canadian seniors number about 4 million and represent 12.8 percent of the Canadian population. As an example, older customers say they prefer catalogue shopping over retail outlets because of their dissatisfaction with customer service at retail stores. People of this age group are more likely than most to have the combination of free time, money, and health that lets them pursue leisure-time activities, especially education and travel. However, they do not think of themselves as old or as seniors despite their demands for traditional "senior" products. Mississauga-based Block Drug Company, realizing that today's seniors are "healthier and perceive themselves as younger" than any seniors before, has launched a very different promotional campaign for its Polident brand denture cleansers. In the past, denture ads featured what is described as "grannies in the garden talking about dentures." Polident is breaking with this portrayal drastically by developing an ad that features two unmarried seniors who have just had sex. One of them goes into the other's bathroom and asks to borrow their Polident denture cleanser![14]

Gender Segmentation

Marketers of products such as clothing, cosmetics, personal-care items, magazines, jewellery, and footwear commonly segment markets by gender. The population breakdown by gender in Canada is 49.5 percent males and 50.5 percent females. However, the ratio of males to females is not equal for all of the age distributions. For example, the number of males exceeds the number of females in every age group under age 45. The ratio changes after 45, at which time the number of females in the population exceeds the number of males in every age group.[15] Men aged 18 to 49 are the segment most likely to purchase goods on-line. The Montreal-based owners of the website AskMen.com have been very successful at providing a venue for companies who want to reach out to men 18 to 49 who surf the Net. According to Nielsen/Net ratings, the site ranks 341st in the world for visits and delivers more male readers than *GQ* magazine, *FHM* magazine, *Fitness* magazine, and many others. The site has secured advertising from firms such as Seagram Crown Royal, FTD florists, British Airways, Match.com, Orbitz, and Columbia House and, of course, Viagra.[16] However, brands that have traditionally been marketed to men, such as Gillette razors and Rogaine baldness remedy, are increasing their efforts to attract women. Computer and video game companies have traditionally targeted young men, but Interactive Digital Software Association, a trade group, found that women are buying just as much game software as men. As a result, more game companies and websites are focusing their marketing efforts on girls and women.[17] Conversely, "women's" products such as cosmetics, household products, and furniture are also being marketed to men. About 35 percent of the buyers of Tommy Hilfiger's beauty-care products are young men, who buy items such as Tommy's Remote Control hair gel and Juiced Up orange-scented soap.[18]

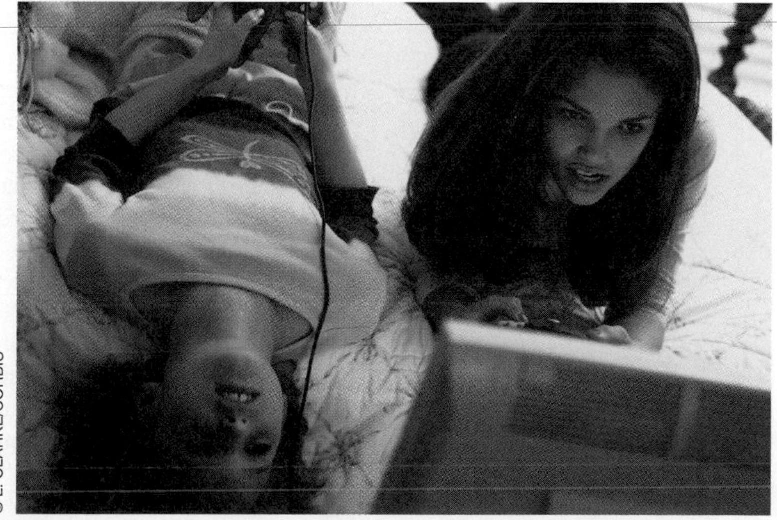

© L. CLARKE/CORBIS

Gender segmentation can be a tricky, yet profitable, form of segmentation, particularly for companies that launch unique product offerings for each gender. One such example is video games. Once marketers discovered that girls and women buy as much game software as boys and men, more companies began to focus marketing efforts on both genders—and with great success.

Income Segmentation

Income is a popular demographic variable for segmenting markets because income level influences consumers' wants and determines their buying power. In Canada, income is measured as "economic family income. An economic family is a group of individuals sharing a common dwelling unit who are related by blood, marriage (including common-law relationships) or adoption." In 2001, the average economic family income for Canadians was $70,814, which represented an increase of 10 percent over 1997. However, marketers can learn more about consumers by looking at their expenditures, which were an average of $57,496 per family in 2001 were assigned to the following key items: 21.3 percent on income taxes, 18.7 percent on shelter, 12.2 percent on transportation, 11.25 percent on food, 6 percent on recreation, 5.4 percent on insurance and pensions, 4.6 percent on household operation, 4.2 percent on clothing, 2.9 percent on household furnishings and equipment, 2.5 percent on health care, 2.3 percent on alcohol and tobacco products, 2.1 percent on charity, 1.7 percent on personal care, 1.6 percent on education, 0.5 percent on reading, and 0.5 percent on gambling.[19]

Many markets are segmented by income, including the markets for housing, clothing, automobiles, and food. Value retailers, like "The Dollar Store," appeal to low- and fixed-income customers with easy access, small stores, and rock-bottom pricing. Wholesale club Costco attracts more upscale customers with warehouse prices for gourmet foods and upscale brands like Waterford crystal, Raymond Weil watches, and Ralph Lauren clothing.[20]

Ethnic and Visible Minority Segmentation

Many companies are segmenting their markets by ethnicity and/or visible minority status. The gathering of this kind of data can raise some sensitivity concerns among respondents. The collection of Canadian statistics on ethnic groups and visible minorities was only recently undertaken as part of the 1996 Census of Canada and has been repeated only once since, for the 2001 Census. An overview of the ethnic and visible minority makeup of the Canadian population is provided in Exhibit 6.2.

Canada is a very culturally diverse country. It begins with the French-Canadian and English-Canadian markets but then goes further than that to target other ethnic populations. The first issue for marketers in reaching out to ethnic markets is to choose a language for communication in addition to or instead of English and French, which are Canada's two official languages. According to the 2001 Census, 62 percent of Canadians speak only English in the home, 20 percent of Canadians speak only French in the home, and 8.3 percent of Canadians speak English and another non-official language, while 0.7 percent of Canadians speak French and another non-official language, 3.4 percent of Canadians speak both English and French in the home, and finally, 5.7 percent of Canadians speak a language other than French and English in the home, including 1.5 percent of Canadians who speak Chinese in the home.[21]

Canadian marketers are strongly aware of the multicultural makeup of the Canadian market and, in particular, the Chinese-Canadian market. A number of marketers are developing unique approaches to appeal to the Chinese market. For example, the Toronto Symphony Orchestra discovered that Chinese families had higher levels of musical literacy than the average for North America. The TSO decided to develop a Chinese-language promotional campaign that included season brochures in Chinese and a Chinese-language page on its website. It also ran advertising in Chinese newspapers and on Chinese radio stations. In addition, the TSO has a customer service hotline with both Cantonese and Mandarin speakers to handle inquiries. At the Aberdeen Centre near Vancouver, B.C., nearly 80 percent of the merchants are Chinese Canadians, as are 80 percent of the customers. The mall offers fashions made in Hong Kong, a shop for traditional Chinese medicines, and a theatre showing Chinese movies. Demonstrations of kung fu martial arts and Chinese folk dances are held in the mall on weekends.[22]

EXHIBIT 6.2

Profile of the Ethnic Origins and Visible Minorities in the Canadian Population for the Year 2001

ETHNIC ORIGIN	TOTAL NUMBER	% OF CANADIAN POPULATION
Canadian	11,682,680	39.4
English	5,978,875	20.2
French	4,668,410	15.8
Scottish	4,157,210	14.0
Irish	3,822,660	12.9
German	2,742,765	9.3
Italian	1,270,370	4.3
Chinese	1,094,700	3.7
Ukrainian	1,071,060	3.6
North American Indian	1,000,890	3.4
Dutch (Netherlands)	923,310	3.1
Polish	817,085	2.8
East Indian	713,330	2.4
Norwegian	363,760	1.2
Portuguese	357,690	1.2
Welsh	350,365	1.2
Jewish	348,605	1.2
Russian	337,960	1.1
Filipino	327,550	1.1
Métis	307,845	1.0
Swedish	282,760	1.0
Hungarian (Magyar)	267,255	0.9
American (USA)	250,005	0.8
Greek	215,105	0.7
Spanish	213,105	0.7
Jamaican	211,720	0.7
Danish	170,780	0.6
Vietnamese	151,410	0.5

	TOTAL NUMBER	% OF CANADIAN POPULATION
Total visible minority	3,983,845	13.4
Chinese	1,029,395	3.5
South Asian	917,075	3.1
Black	662,210	2.2
Filipino	308,575	1.0
Arab/West Asian	303,965	1.0
Latin American	216,975	0.7
Southeast Asian	198,880	0.7
Korean	100,660	0.3
Japanese	73,315	0.2

Note: Total Canadian population was 29,639,035 in 2001.

Sources: Statistics Canada, "Population by Selected Ethnic Origins, 2001," Canadian Statistics: The People, www.statcan.ca, accessed November 7, 2003; Statistics Canada, "Origins and Visible Minorities, 2001," Canadian Statistics: The People, www.statcan.ca, accessed November 7, 2003.

COURTESY OF TSO

This ad for the Toronto Symphony Orchestra targets Asians who enjoy classical music.

Family Life-Cycle Segmentation

The demographic factors of gender, age, and income often do not sufficiently explain why consumer buying behaviour varies. Frequently, consumption patterns among people of the same age and gender differ because they are in different stages of the family life cycle. The **family life cycle (FLC)** is a series of stages determined by a combination of age, marital status, and the presence or absence of children.

family life cycle (FLC)
A series of stages determined by a combination of age, marital status, and the presence or absence of children.

Traditional families—married couples with children younger than 18 years—constituted 41.4 percent of families according to the 2001 Census data. Families have been shrinking in size over the years. In 1961 the average household size was 3.9, by 1971 it had fallen to 3.5, and by 1981 it had fallen to 2.9, then down to 2.7 in 1991; by 2001 household size was at 2.6. Currently, household size seems to be stabilizing.[23] Exhibit 6.3 illustrates both traditional and contemporary FLC patterns and shows how families' needs, incomes, resources, and expenditures differ at each stage. The horizontal flow shows the traditional family life cycle. The lower part of the exhibit gives some of the characteristics and purchase patterns of families in each stage of the traditional life cycle. The exhibit also acknowledges that about half of all first marriages end in divorce. When young marrieds move into the young divorced stage, their consumption patterns often revert back to those of the young single stage of the cycle. About four out of five divorced people remarry by middle age and reenter the traditional life cycle, as indicated by the "recycled flow" in the exhibit. An understanding of the FLC is evident in Sunlight laundry detergent's partnership with the Canadian Parks and Recreation Association and the International Play Association to develop the "Sunlight National PlayDay program." The whole idea came out of Sunlight detergent's campaign theme of "Go Ahead, Get Dirty," which features Sunlight cleaning the dirt from the clothes of children who have played in mud. The PlayDay events are built around fun, discovery, dirt, and family involvement. Sunlight wants "to be the brand that makes parents aware of the importance of play, and helps clean them up when the playing is done."[24]

ON LINE

Reach Advisors

Identify the kinds of services and information that Research Advisors provide to help marketers target families.

http://www.reachadvisors.com

EXHIBIT 6.3 Family Life Cycle

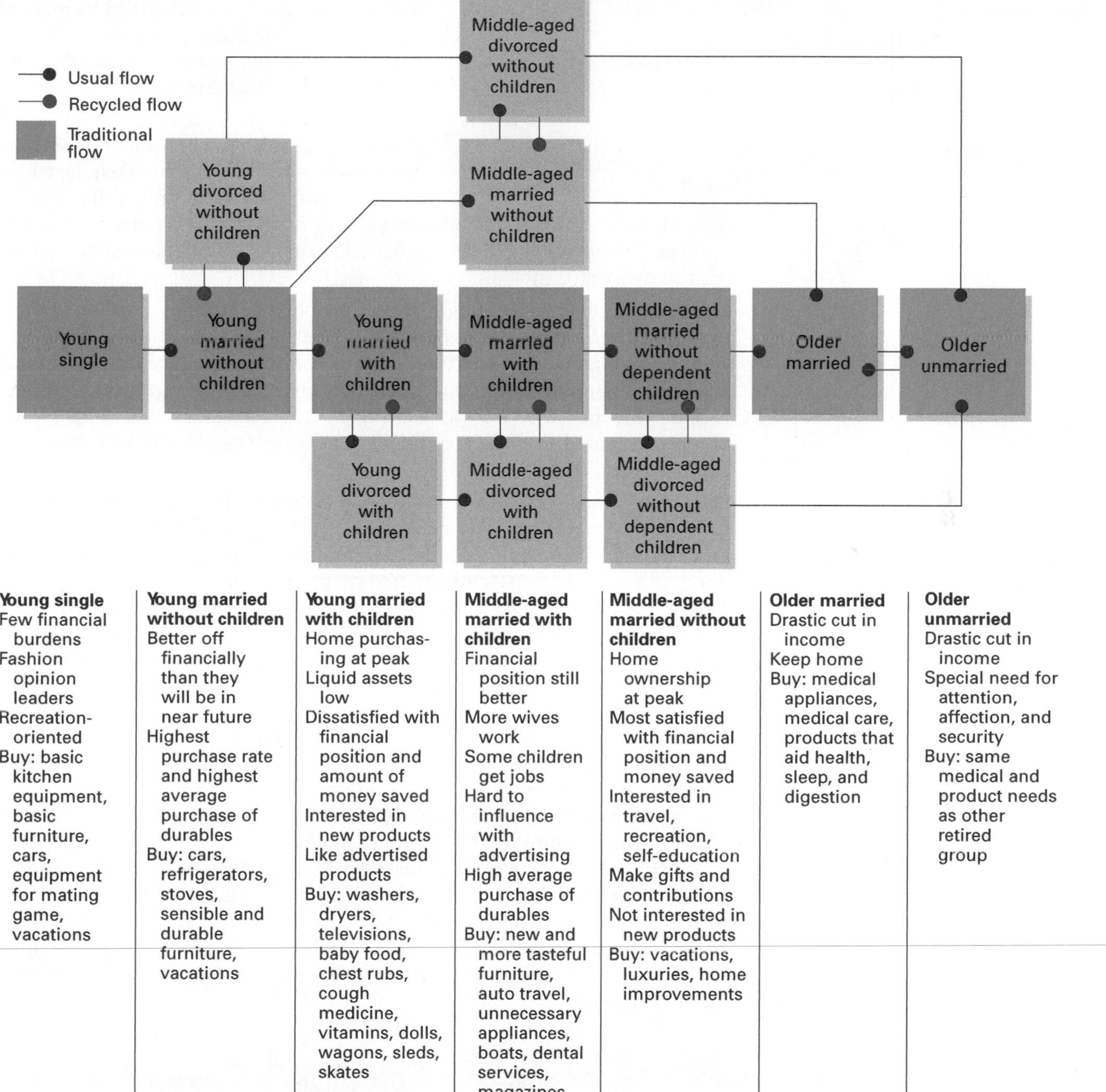

Young single	Young married without children	Young married with children	Middle-aged married with children	Middle-aged married without children	Older married	Older unmarried
Few financial burdens Fashion opinion leaders Recreation-oriented Buy: basic kitchen equipment, basic furniture, cars, equipment for mating game, vacations	Better off financially than they will be in near future Highest purchase rate and highest average purchase of durables Buy: cars, refrigerators, stoves, sensible and durable furniture, vacations	Home purchasing at peak Liquid assets low Dissatisfied with financial position and amount of money saved Interested in new products Like advertised products Buy: washers, dryers, televisions, baby food, chest rubs, cough medicine, vitamins, dolls, wagons, sleds, skates	Financial position still better More wives work Some children get jobs Hard to influence with advertising High average purchase of durables Buy: new and more tasteful furniture, auto travel, unnecessary appliances, boats, dental services, magazines	Home ownership at peak Most satisfied with financial position and money saved Interested in travel, recreation, self-education Make gifts and contributions Not interested in new products Buy: vacations, luxuries, home improvements	Drastic cut in income Keep home Buy: medical appliances, medical care, products that aid health, sleep, and digestion	Drastic cut in income Special need for attention, affection, and security Buy: same medical and product needs as other retired group

Psychographic Segmentation

Age, gender, income, ethnicity, family life-cycle stage, and other demographic variables are usually helpful in developing segmentation strategies, but often they don't paint the entire picture. Demographics provide the skeleton, but psychographics adds the meat to the bones. **Psychographic segmentation** is market segmentation on the basis of the following variables:

psychographic segmentation
Market segmentation on the basis of personality, motives, lifestyles, and geodemographics.

- *Personality*: Personality reflects a person's traits, attitudes, and habits. Porsche Cars North America understood well the demographics of the Porsche owner: a 40-something male college graduate earning over $200,000 per year. However, research discovered that this general demographic category included five

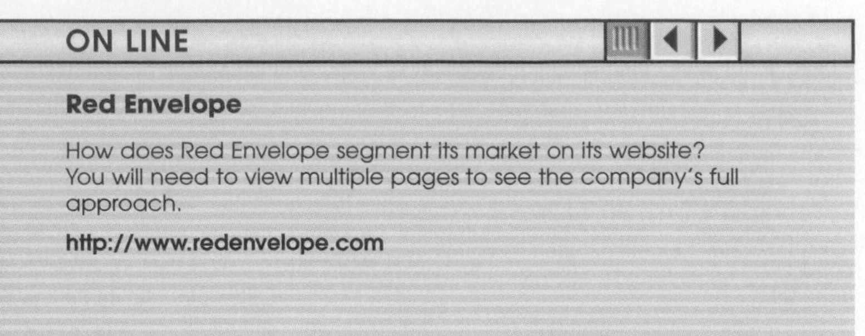
ON LINE

Red Envelope

How does Red Envelope segment its market on its website? You will need to view multiple pages to see the company's full approach.

http://www.redenvelope.com

personality types that more effectively segmented Porsche buyers. Exhibit 6.4 describes the five segments. Porsche refined its marketing as a result of the study, and, after a previous seven-year slump, the company's North American sales rose 48 percent.[25]

- *Motives*: Marketers of baby products and life insurance appeal to consumers' emotional motives—namely, to care for their loved ones. Using appeals to economy, reliability, and dependability, carmakers like Subaru and Suzuki target customers with rational motives. Carmakers like Mercedes-Benz, Jaguar, and Cadillac appeal to customers with status-related motives.
- *Lifestyles*: Lifestyle segmentation divides people into groups according to the way they spend their time, the importance of the things around them, their beliefs, and socioeconomic characteristics such as income and education. For example, Harley-Davidson divides its customers into seven lifestyle segments, from "cocky misfits" who are most likely to be arrogant troublemakers, to "laid-back camper types" committed to cycling and nature, to "classy capitalists" who have wealth and privilege.[26]

geodemographic segmentation Segmenting potential customers into neighbourhood lifestyle categories.

- *Geodemographics:* **Geodemographic segmentation** clusters potential customers into neighbourhood lifestyle categories. It combines geographic, demographic, and lifestyle segmentations. Geodemographic segmentation helps marketers develop marketing programs tailored to prospective buyers who live in small geographic regions, such as neighbourhoods, or who have very specific lifestyle and demographic characteristics. Chain-store retailers have a strong affinity for geodemographic segmentation data because it helps them make physical store location decisions. In addition, database marketers such as magazine publishers, charities, and financial institutions find this form of segmentation very useful for identifying prospective customers.[27] In Canada, geodemographic data are commercially available from census information at the enumeration area level, which involves surveys of 250–300 households (EA); and according to postal code information, which is subdivided into 20,000 assigned Postal Walk levels (PWK), which comprise 200–400 households, or into 1,500 Forward Sortation Areas (FSAs), which are comprised of between 6,000 and 10,000 households. "These three systems are the foundation of the various services that supply data to retailers. For example, Taxfiler data is at the Postal Walk level but not EA, while Compusearch's PSYTE data is available for either the census geography, at the EA levels or, for postal geography, at the FSA unit. Geomedia's system focuses on the FSA level." [28]

EXHIBIT 6.4

Taxonomy of Porsche Buyers

TYPE	% OF ALL	OWNERS' DESCRIPTION
Top Guns	27	Driven, ambitious types. Power and control matter. They expect to be noticed.
Elitists	24	Old-money blue bloods. A car is just a car, no matter how expensive. It is not an extension of personality.
Proud Patrons	23	Ownership is an end in itself. Their car is a trophy earned for hard work, and who cares if anyone sees them in it?
Bon Vivants	17	Worldly jet setters and thrill seekers. Their car heightens the excitement in their already passionate lives.
Fantasists	9	Walter Mitty types. Their car is an escape. Not only are they uninterested in impressing others with it, they also feel a little guilty about owning one.

Psychographic variables can be used individually to segment markets or be combined with other variables to provide more detailed descriptions of market segments. One combination approach is the Claritas PRIZM Lifestyle software program, which divides North Americans into 62 "clusters," or consumer types, all with catchy names. The clusters combine basic demographic data such as age, ethnicity, and income with lifestyle information, such as magazine and sports preferences taken from consumer surveys. For example, the "Kids and Cul-de-Sacs" group are upscale, suburban families with a median household income of $68,900 who tend to shop on-line and visit Disney theme parks. The "Bohemian Mix" cluster are professionals aged 25 to 44 with a median income of $38,500 who are likely to shop at The Gap and read *Elle* magazine. The program also predicts to which neighbourhoods across the country the clusters are likely to gravitate. Using PRIZM, Hyundai chose postal codes with a high percentage of promising clusters and sent test-drive offers only to those areas (instead of blanketing entire cities with the offer). In those markets, Hyundai not only increased the number of people showing up for a test-drive but also increased its sales and halved its costs per vehicle sold.[29]

Benefit Segmentation

Benefit segmentation is the process of grouping customers into market segments according to the benefits they seek from the product. Most types of market segmentation are based on the assumption that this variable and customers' needs are related. Benefit segmentation is different because it groups potential customers on the basis of their needs or wants rather than some other characteristic, such as age or gender. The snack-food market, for example, can be divided into six benefit segments, as shown in Exhibit 6.5.

benefit segmentation
The process of grouping customers into market segments according to the benefits they seek from the product.

Customer profiles can be developed by examining demographic information associated with people seeking certain benefits. This information can be used to match marketing strategies with selected target markets. Advertising agency Vickers & Benson Direct & Interactive developed a unique benefit segmentation appeal for the Bank of Montreal's new invoice-processing automation service for businesses. Chief financial officers were targeted with a promotion involving a transparent acrylic box filled with shredded paper. Inside the shredded paper was a small complimentary paper shredder and a promotional note stating: "Push Profits, Not Paper."[30]

EXHIBIT 6.5

Lifestyle Segmentation of the Snack-Food Market

	NUTRITIONAL SNACKERS	WEIGHT WATCHERS	GUILTY SNACKERS	PARTY SNACKERS	INDISCRIMINATE SNACKERS	ECONOMICAL SNACKERS
Percentage of snackers	22 percent	14 percent	9 percent	15 percent	15 percent	18 percent
Lifestyle characteristics	Self-assured, controlled	Outdoorsy, influential, venturesome	Highly anxious, isolated	Sociable	Hedonistic	Self-assured, price-oriented
Benefits sought	Nutritious, without artificial ingredients, natural	Low in calories, quick energy	Low in calories, good tasting	Good to serve guests, served with pride, go well with beverages	Good tasting, satisfies hunger	Low in price, best value
Consumption level of snacks	Light	Light	Heavy	Average	Heavy	Average
Type of snacks usually eaten	Fruits, vegetables, cheese	Yogurt, vegetables	Yogurt, cookies, crackers, candy	Nuts, potato chips, crackers, pretzels	Candy, ice cream, cookies, potato chips, pretzels, popcorn	No specific products
Demographics	Better educated, have younger children	Younger, single	Younger or older, female, lower socio-economic status	Middle-aged, nonurban	Teenager	Have large family, better educated

Usage-Rate Segmentation

usage-rate segmentation
Dividing a market by the amount of product bought or consumed.

Usage-rate segmentation divides a market by the amount of product bought or consumed. Categories vary with the product, but they are likely to include some combination of the following: former users, potential users, first-time users, light or irregular users, medium users, and heavy users. Segmenting by usage rate enables marketers to focus their efforts on heavy users or to develop multiple marketing mixes aimed at different segments. Because heavy users often account for a sizable portion of all product sales, some marketers focus on the heavy-user segment.

80/20 principle
A principle holding that 20 percent of all customers generate 80 percent of the demand.

The **80/20 principle** holds that 20 percent of all customers generate 80 percent of the demand. Although the percentages usually are not exact, the general idea often holds true. For example, in the fast-food industry, the heavy user accounts for only one of five fast-food patrons, but makes about 60 percent of all visits to fast-food restaurants. Using this definition, the heavy user (who is most often a single male) would account for roughly $1.3 billion of the $2 billion that an Environment Canada report said is spent on hamburgers at Canada's 1,600 fast-food hamburger restaurants.[31]

Developing customers into heavy users is the goal behind many frequency/loyalty programs, such as the airlines' frequent flyer programs. Many supermarkets have also designed loyalty programs that reward the heavy-user segment with deals available only to them, such as in-store coupon dispensing systems, loyalty card programs, and special price deals on selected merchandise.

The "Ethics in Marketing" box describes how the brewing industry's use of the Internet to market beer to heavy users may also attract those who are too young to drink.

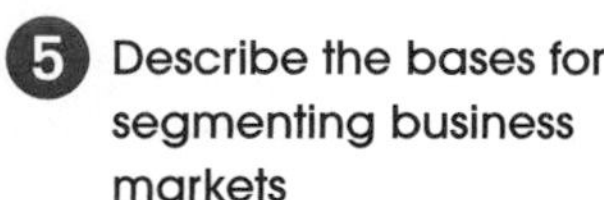

>> BASES FOR SEGMENTING BUSINESS MARKETS

The business market consists of four broad segments: producers, resellers, institutions, and governments (for a detailed discussion of the characteristics of these segments, see Chapter 5). Whether marketers focus on only one or on all four of these segments, they are likely to find diversity among potential customers. Thus, further market segmentation offers just as many benefits to business marketers as it does to consumer-product marketers.

Company Characteristics

Company characteristics, such as geographic location, type of company, company size, and product use, can be important segmentation variables. Some markets tend to be regional because buyers prefer to purchase from local suppliers and distant suppliers may have difficulty competing in terms of price and service. Therefore, firms that sell to geographically concentrated industries benefit by locating close to their markets.

Segmenting by customer type allows business marketers to tailor their marketing mixes to the unique needs of particular types of organizations or industries. Many companies are finding this form of segmentation to be quite effective. For example, RONA/Réno-Dépôt, one of Canada's "Big Box" do-it-yourself retail businesses, has targeted professional repair and remodelling contractors in addition to consumers.

Volume of purchase (heavy, moderate, light) is a commonly used basis for business segmentation. Another is the buying organization's size, which may affect its purchasing procedures, the types and quantities of products it needs, and its responses to different marketing mixes. Banks frequently offer different services, lines of credit, and overall attention to commercial customers based on their size.

Many products, especially raw materials like steel, wood, and petroleum, have diverse applications. How customers use a product may influence the amount

ON LINE

RONA

Does RONA's website reflect the same type of business and consumer segmentation it implements in its physical stores? (Each store has special areas for contractors.) Explain what you find.

http://www.rona.ca

ETHICS IN MARKETING

Are Brewers Using the Internet to Target Underage Drinkers?

Reluctantly nudged into the on-line world, major brewers are finding the Web offers a new way to win brand loyalty—especially among the young adult males who drank more than half of the 2.2 billion litres of beer sold in Canada in 2002. "We want to get that one-on-one time," says Tony Ponturo, vice president of marketing for Anheuser-Busch Companies, the brewer of Budweiser and the firm that has licensed Labatt Breweries of Canada to distribute Budweiser and Bud Light in Canada. "If [consumers] are on the Budweiser.com site and interacting with your site, that is something special and different. They will feel some loyalty to you."

Brewers are also adding features to their sites that have less to do with beer and more to do with the lifestyle of beer drinkers. For example, The Labatt Blue website (**http://www.labattblue.ca**) has features such as "Blue Bomber Beer" in relation to the CFL's Winnipeg Blue Bombers, a "save the bottle caps promotion," and a cell phone promotion called "text blue." The Canadian-based Bud Light Institute (**http://www.budlight.ca**) is one of the most entertaining of all the "Beer" websites, with promotions targeted at men such as "Let Us Make Excuses for You," which offers a bank of excuses or will generate some personalized excuses to get out of the house, get out of work, and get out of the doghouse using a hilarious set of questions and choices. The site also offers "Bud Light Institute Greeting Cards," "Join the Bud Light Institute," and a "Romantic Poetry starter kit" for men. Of course, the Bud Light Institute does not discourage women from entering and finding out what the men are up to and even provides membership for women. The Molson Canadian website (**http://www.iam.ca**) presents a wide variety of features, such as "Molson Canadian Does Campus," concert promotions, Molson Canadian Rocks, a party planner, sports features, a chat room, and a Molson "insider" program. All three websites present the ability to view the latest television commercials associated with their brands.

As the sites try to be more hip and youth-oriented, some public-health advocates worry that the on-line campaigns will increasingly attract underage drinkers. Beer companies, like other manufacturers of consumer products, strive to make a connection with consumers as early as possible. That requires a delicate balancing act of trying not to appeal to underage drinkers while still targeting young people who are of legal drinking age. In Canada, there are different regulations for promotion of alcoholic beverages in virtually every provincial and territorial jurisdiction. As such, the use of websites to promote beer presents a difficulty for provincial regulators because of the interprovincial and indeed, international reach of websites. In addition, since it is a "relatively new medium," a whole new set of regulations probably needs to be designed for websites.

The Labatt website (**http://www.labatt.com**) states that you must be of legal drinking age to enter the site. There is a terms and conditions link that reiterates this position and identifies the legal drinking age in Canada as 19 in all provinces except Quebec, where it is 18 years of age. Both the initial warning and the terms and conditions are presented on the home page in both English and French. The first page of the Labatt Blue brand website asks: "Are you of Legal Drinking Age?" If you click "yes," you're in. However, on virtually every page of the site the statement: "Must be of legal drinking age" is presented at the bottom. The Bud Light Institute simply asks if you are of legal drinking age or not. If you click "yes" you are in. The Molson website (**http://www.molson.com**) does not present a page requesting legal drinking age up front. It presents itself initially as a company information website with links to "brand pages" inside the site. The Molson Canadian website home page asks if you are of "Legal Drinking Age," "yes" or "no." If you answer "yes" you are invited in to view all the promos. All of the websites respond to a "no" answer to the legal drinking age question with an abrupt message: "You must be of legal drinking age to enter."

But skeptics say the warning screen requiring you to be of legal drinking age may actually attract underage drinkers because it suggests the site is taboo. The abrupt response to a "no" answer actually encourages you to hit the back button and choose "yes." Finally, the legal drinking age disclaimer is based on the honour system—there is no way to verify whether the user is of legal drinking age or not.

The addition of games, concert promotions, and other pop culture to beer websites will inevitably lead to an increase in visits from teenagers, believes Kathryn Montgomery, the president of the Center for Media Education, a nonprofit organization that promotes television and Internet safeguards for children. She notes: "The whole nature of the Web creates new opportunities to make the products more fun and exciting and the site more about play than traditional advertising. I think there is an ulterior motive, one that is hard for us to prove, but it appears targeted at young people. [Youths who see the beer sites] connect consuming alcohol with having a lot of fun. It is very playful. There is no discussion of consequences."

George Hacker, director of the U.S.-based Alcohol Policies Project of the Center for Science in the Public Interest, says: "The Internet represents another means for beer to be in young kids' faces. There are so many young people in the [on-line] audience that any standards brewers hold relating to targeting young people are worthless."[32]

Discuss the ethical implications of the Canadian beer industry's design and use of websites to promote alcoholic products. Do you think the beer industry is targeting children with its sites? Explain your answer.

they buy, their buying criteria, and their selection of vendors. For example, a producer of springs may have customers that use the product in applications as diverse as making machine tools, bicycles, surgical devices, office equipment, telephones, and missile systems.

Buying Processes

Many business marketers find it helpful to segment customers and prospective customers on the basis of how they buy. For example, companies can segment some business markets by ranking key purchasing criteria, such as price, quality, technical support, and service. Atlas Corporation developed a commanding position in the industrial door market by providing customized products in just four weeks, which was much faster than the industry average of 12 to 15 weeks. Atlas's primary market is companies with an immediate need for customized doors.

The purchasing strategies of buyers may provide useful segments. Two purchasing profiles that have been identified are satisficers and optimizers. **Satisficers** contact familiar suppliers and place the order with the first one to satisfy product and delivery requirements. **Optimizers** consider numerous suppliers (both familiar and unfamiliar), solicit bids, and study all proposals carefully before selecting one.

satisficers
Business customers who place an order with the first familiar supplier to satisfy product and delivery requirements.

optimizers
Business customers who consider numerous suppliers, both familiar and unfamiliar, solicit bids, and study all proposals carefully before selecting one.

The personal characteristics of the buyers themselves (their demographic characteristics, decision style, tolerance for risk, confidence level, job responsibilities, etc.) influence their buying behaviour and thus offer a viable basis for segmenting some business markets. IBM computer buyers, for example, are sometimes characterized as being more risk averse than buyers of less expensive computers that perform essentially the same functions. In advertising, therefore, IBM has stressed its reputation for high quality and reliability.

Customer Relationship

More and more, companies are going beyond the traditional segmentation variables by focusing on the type of relationship they have with their customers. For example, Cable & Wireless, a British telephone company, had traditionally segmented customers based on size. This meant that a *Fortune* Global 500 organization would have priority over a midsize customer, even if the midsize client accounted for more business. Recently, the company reevaluated this method and began using other factors, such as revenue generated by each customer, and how cost-effective and efficient it is for Cable & Wireless to serve particular customers.[33]

The Chapman Group (http://www.chapmanhq.com), a company that specializes in sales and marketing process improvement, designed a segmentation strategy based on types of relationships companies have with their customers. It developed three segments of relationships: client accounts, customer accounts, and buyer accounts. Clients collaborate with the organization on attaining mutual goals of profitability. They appreciate support, consistently offer profitable revenue, and have reasonable expectations of service for the price they pay. They are willing to work on teams and expand relationships between both organizations. Customers are less interested in building a relationship network, are indifferent about mutual profitability, want most goods and services for lower-than-market prices, and are more costly to service. Buyers focus on price only. Value, relationships, and services typically do not offset pricing differences in this segment. Companies using this segmentation strategy can then offer different service approaches for each segment.[34]

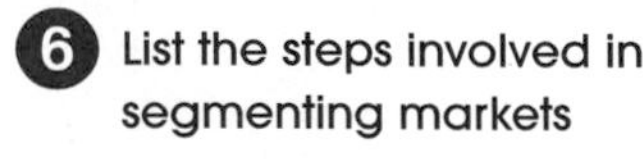

>> STEPS IN SEGMENTING A MARKET

The purpose of market segmentation, in both consumer and business markets, is to identify marketing opportunities. Exhibit 6.6 traces the following steps in segmenting a market. Note that Steps 5 and 6 are actually marketing activities that follow market segmentation (Steps 1 through 4).

1. *Select a market or product category for study:* Define the overall market or product category to be studied. It may be a market in which the firm already competes, a new but related market or product category, or a totally new one. For instance, Rogers AT&T examined the youth market carefully before launching its Totalphone

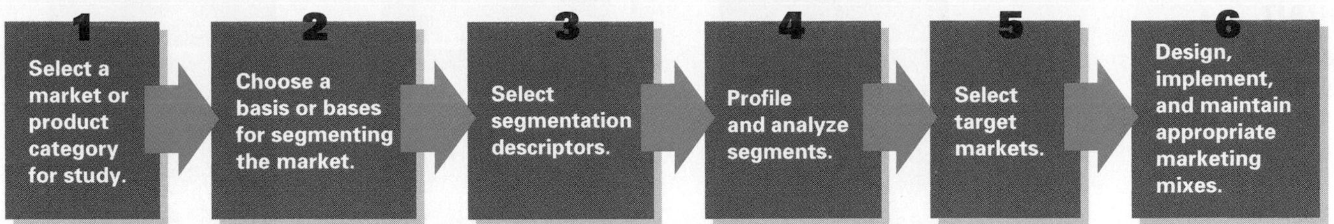

EXHIBIT 6.6
Steps in Segmenting a Market and Subsequent Activities

product, which is a prepaid cell phone that offers postpaid-type rates. Rogers needed a product it could sell to people who were too young to legally sign a phone service contract.

2. *Choose a basis or bases for segmenting the market:* This step requires managerial insight, creativity, and market knowledge. There are no scientific procedures for selecting segmentation variables. However, a successful segmentation scheme must produce segments that meet the four basic criteria discussed earlier in this chapter.
3. *Select segmentation descriptors:* After choosing one or more bases, the marketer must select the segmentation descriptors. Descriptors identify the specific segmentation variables to use. For example, if a company selects demographics as a basis of segmentation, it may use age, occupation, and income as descriptors. A company that selects usage segmentation needs to decide whether to go after heavy users, nonusers, or light users.
4. *Profile and analyze segments:* The profile should include the segments' size, expected growth, purchase frequency, current brand usage, brand loyalty, and long-term sales and profit potential. This information can then be used to rank potential market segments by profit opportunity, risk, consistency with organizational mission and objectives, and other factors important to the firm.
5. *Select target markets:* Selecting target markets is not a part of but a natural outcome of the segmentation process. It is a major decision that influences and often directly determines the firm's marketing mix. This topic is examined in greater detail later in this chapter.
6. *Design, implement, and maintain appropriate marketing mixes:* The marketing mix has been described as product, distribution, promotion, and pricing strategies intended to bring about mutually satisfying exchange relationships with target markets. Chapters 8 through 16 explore these topics in detail.

>> STRATEGIES FOR SELECTING TARGET MARKETS

7 Discuss alternative strategies for selecting target markets

So far this chapter has focused on the market segmentation process, which is only the first step in deciding whom to approach about buying a product. The next task is to choose one or more target markets. A **target market** is a group of people or organizations for which an organization designs, implements, and maintains a marketing mix intended to meet the needs of that group, resulting in mutually satisfying exchanges. The three general strategies for selecting target markets—undifferentiated, concentrated, and multisegment targeting—are illustrated in Exhibit 6.7. Exhibit 6.8 illustrates the advantages and disadvantages of each targeting strategy.

target market
A group of people or organizations for which an organization designs, implements, and maintains a marketing mix intended to meet the needs of that group, resulting in mutually satisfying exchanges.

Undifferentiated Targeting

A firm using an **undifferentiated targeting strategy** essentially adopts a mass-market philosophy, viewing the market as one big market with no individual segments. The firm uses one marketing mix for the entire market. A firm that adopts an undifferentiated targeting strategy assumes that individual customers have similar needs that can be met with a common marketing mix.

undifferentiated targeting strategy
Marketing approach that views the market as one big market with no individual segments and thus requires a single marketing mix.

EXHIBIT 6.7

Three Strategies for Selecting Target Markets

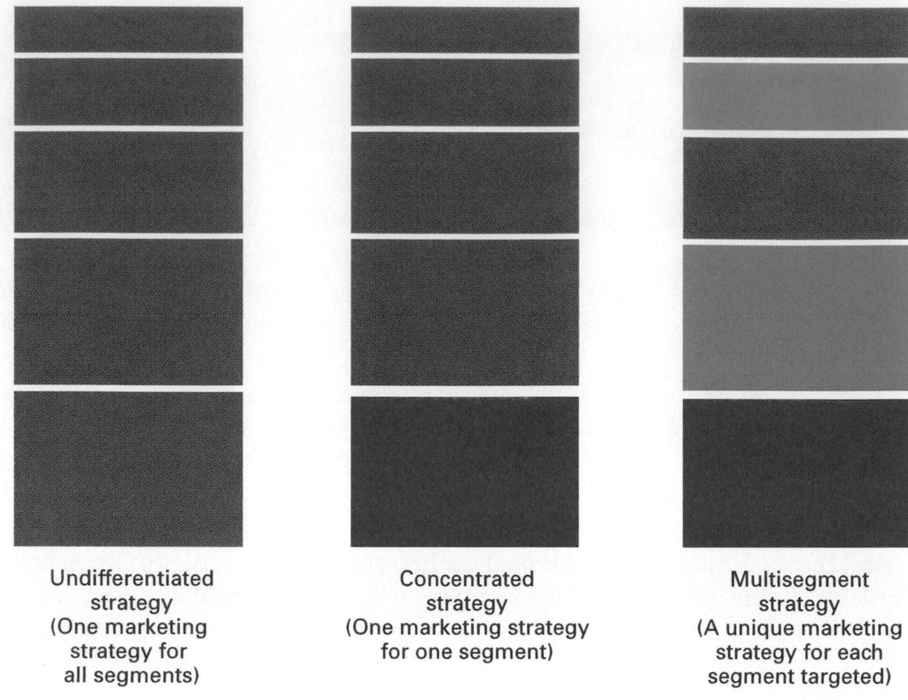

The first firm in an industry sometimes uses an undifferentiated targeting strategy. With no competition, the firm may not need to tailor marketing mixes to the preferences of market segments. Henry Ford's famous comment about the Model T is a classic example of an undifferentiated targeting strategy: "They can have their car in any color they want, as long as it's black." At one time, Coca-Cola used this strategy with a single product and a single size of its familiar green bottle. Marketers of commodity products, such as flour and sugar, are also likely to use an undifferentiated targeting strategy.

One advantage of undifferentiated marketing is the potential for saving on production and marketing. Because only one item is produced, the firm should be able to achieve economies of mass production. Also, marketing costs may be lower when there is only one product to promote and a single channel of distribution. Too often, however, an undifferentiated strategy emerges by default rather than by design, reflecting a failure to consider the advantages of a segmented approach. The result is often sterile, unimaginative product offerings that have little appeal to anyone.

EXHIBIT 6.8

Advantages and Disadvantages of Target Marketing Strategies

TARGETING STRATEGY	ADVANTAGES	DISADVANTAGES
Undifferentiated targeting	• Potential savings on production/marketing costs • Company more susceptible to competition	• Unimaginative product offerings
Concentrated targeting	• Concentration of resources • Can better meet the needs of a narrowly defined segment • Allows some small firms to better compete with larger firms • Strong positioning	• Segments too small, or changing • Large competitors may more effectively market to niche segment
Multisegment targeting	• Greater financial success • Economies of scale in production/marketing	• High costs • Cannibalization

Another problem associated with undifferentiated targeting is that it makes the company more susceptible to competitive inroads. Coca-Cola forfeited its position as the leading seller of cola drinks in supermarkets to Pepsi-Cola in the late 1950s, when Pepsi began offering consumers a choice of several sizes of containers.

ON LINE

M&M Meat Shops

What targeting strategy does M&M Meat Shops employ on its website? Why do you think as you do?

http://www.mmmeatshops.com

You might think a firm producing a standard product like toilet tissue would adopt an undifferentiated strategy. However, this market has industrial segments and consumer segments. Industrial buyers want an economical, single-ply product sold in boxes of a hundred rolls. The consumer market demands a more versatile product in smaller quantities. Within the consumer market, the product is differentiated with designer print or no print, cushioned or noncushioned, and economy priced or luxury priced. Fort Howard Corporation, the market share leader in industrial toilet paper, does not even sell to the consumer market.

Concentrated Targeting

With a **concentrated targeting strategy,** a firm selects a market **niche** (one segment of a market) for targeting its marketing efforts. Because the firm is appealing to a single segment, it can concentrate on understanding the needs, motives, and satisfactions of that segment's members and on developing and maintaining a highly specialized marketing mix. Some firms find that concentrating resources and meeting the needs of a narrowly defined market segment is more profitable than spreading resources over several different segments.

concentrated targeting strategy
A strategy used to select one segment of a market for targeting marketing efforts.

niche
One segment of a market.

For example, Starbucks became successful by focusing on a group of consumers that wanted gourmet coffee products. America Online (AOL) became one of the world's leading Internet providers by targeting Internet newcomers. By making the Internet interface easy to use, AOL was able to attract millions of people who otherwise might not have subscribed to an on-line service.[35] The City University of Hong Kong is restructuring its entire focus and transforming its programs into an e-business curriculum.[36]

Small firms often adopt a concentrated targeting strategy to compete effectively with much larger firms. Fashion retailer Winners was developed to attract working women who wanted to buy designer fashions at discounted prices. On the other hand, some firms use a concentrated strategy to establish a strong position in a desirable market segment. Porsche, for instance, targets an upscale automobile market through "class appeal, not mass appeal."

Concentrated targeting violates the old adage: "Don't put all your eggs in one basket." If the chosen segment is too small or if it shrinks because of environmental changes, the firm may suffer negative consequences. For instance, OshKosh B'Gosh, Inc., was highly successful selling children's wear in the 1980s. It was so successful, however, that the children's line came to define OshKosh's image to the extent that the company could not sell clothes to anyone else. Attempts at marketing older children's clothing, women's casual clothes, and maternity wear were all abandoned. Recognizing it was in the children's-wear business, the company expanded into products such as kids' shoes, children's eyewear, and plush toys.

A concentrated strategy can also be disastrous for a firm that is not successful in its narrowly defined target market. Before Procter & Gamble introduced Head and Shoulders shampoo, several small firms were already selling antidandruff shampoos. Head and Shoulders was introduced with a large promotional campaign, and the new brand captured over half the market immediately. Within a year, several of the firms that had been concentrating on this market segment went out of business.

COURTESY OF MODROBES

Modrobes uses a concentrated marketing strategy by targeting Canadian college and university students. Founder Sal Debus attributes the product concept to his desire for comfortable "exam pants" when he was a student at Brock University. The physical design was loosely based on that of "medical scrub" pants often worn by operating room physicians. Today, Modrobes offers a full line of clothing with over 100 styles.

Multisegment Targeting

multisegment targeting strategy
A strategy that chooses two or more well-defined market segments and develops a distinct marketing mix for each.

A firm that chooses to serve two or more well-defined market segments and develops a distinct marketing mix for each has a **multisegment targeting strategy.** Stouffer's, for example, offers gourmet entrees for one segment of the frozen dinner market and Lean Cuisine for another. Cosmetics companies seek to increase sales and market share by targeting multiple age and ethnic groups. Maybelline and Cover Girl, for example, market different lines to tween girls, teenage women, young adult women, older women, and visible minority women. Mattel targets multiple markets with its Barbie doll. To make Barbie relevant to older girls, the brand has a new logo, new packaging, and an expanded product line of books and trendy apparel. Other new items include an electronic Barbie scrapbook to keep voice-recorded secrets and activity sets for fingernails and make-your-own lip-gloss. To target preteen girls, the company is introducing Barbie dolls with strands of hair studded with rhinestones, street-fashion clothing, and a first-ever Barbie belly button.[37]

AP/WIDE WORLD PHOTOS

Mattel targets multiple markets with its Barbie doll. In an attempt to appeal to today's generation of young girls, the company rolled out "Generation" dolls. Traditional Barbies now share shelf space with the new line, which includes a doll with a nose ring and one with a butterfly tattoo on her stomach.

Sometimes organizations use different promotional appeals, rather than completely different marketing mixes, as the basis for a multisegment strategy. This can lead to mixed results; for example, Labatt has used two completely different approaches to promoting its Labatt 50 beer in Quebec and Ontario over the years. In the early days of promotion for Labatt 50, the advertising themes in Quebec played to Quebec patriotism and used characters and celebrities who were well-known in Quebec. In contrast, Ontario drinkers were exposed to "slice of life with beer" advertising that showed people singing about Labatt 50 and travelling about the country. As a result, in Quebec, beer drinkers think of the product as a Quebec-only brand and the product has a strong customer base, whereas in Ontario, the current drinkers think of Labatt 50 as an Ontario-only brand, but they are a lot fewer in number.[38]

Multisegment targeting offers many potential benefits to firms, including greater sales volume, higher profits, larger market share, and economies of scale in manufacturing and marketing. Yet it may also involve greater costs for product design, production, promotion, inventory, marketing research, and management. Before deciding to use this strategy, firms should compare the benefits and costs of multisegment targeting to those of undifferentiated and concentrated targeting.

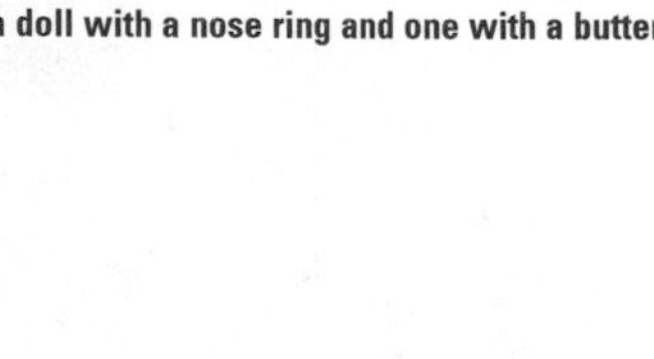

cannibalization
A situation that occurs when sales of a new product cut into sales of a firm's existing products.

Another potential cost of multisegment targeting is **cannibalization,** which occurs when sales of a new product cut into sales of a firm's existing products. In many cases, however, companies prefer to steal sales from their own brands rather than lose sales to a competitor. Also, in today's fast-paced world of Internet business, some companies are willing to cannibalize existing business to build new business. For example, electronic retailer Future Shop launched FutureShop.ca to build business in cities and towns where it didn't have physical locations. However, a lot of the visitors to the website turned out to be customers who had received flyers in the local papers of cities where Future Shop already had bricks-and-mortar locations. This realization has caused Future Shop to start working on a system that will allow customers who order on-line to either pick up their merchandise at the nearest store location or have their purchases shipped to them.

8 Explain how and why firms implement positioning strategies and how product differentiation plays a role

positioning
Developing a specific marketing mix to influence potential customers' overall perception of a brand, product line, or organization in general.

position
The place a product, brand, or group of products occupies in consumers' minds relative to competing offerings.

>> POSITIONING

The development of any marketing mix depends on **positioning,** a process that influences potential customers' overall perception of a brand, product line, or organization in general. **Position** is the place a product, brand, or group of products occupies in consumers' minds relative to competing offerings. Consumer goods marketers are particularly concerned with positioning. Procter & Gamble, for example, markets eleven different laundry detergents, each with a unique position, as illustrated in Exhibit 6.9.

ON LINE 

Use the Internet to see how the positionings of the detergents listed in Exhibit 6.9 are reflected on their websites.

Positioning assumes that consumers compare products on the basis of important features. Marketing efforts that emphasize irrelevant features are therefore likely to misfire. For example, Crystal Pepsi and a clear version of Coca-Cola's Tab failed because consumers perceived the "clear" positioning as more of a marketing gimmick than a benefit.

Effective positioning requires assessing the positions occupied by competing products, determining the important dimensions underlying these positions, and choosing a position in the market where the organization's marketing efforts will have the greatest impact. The best example is that of Seven Up brand's decision to position its clear lemon-lime flavoured soft drink as the "Uncola." The firm assessed the market and decided to position its flavour comparison as an alternative to the leading soft drinks, which were Coke and Pepsi, rather than trying to differentiate its product from similar flavoured brands such as Sprite and Mountain Dew.

As the previous example illustrates, **product differentiation** is a positioning strategy that many firms use to distinguish their products from those of competitors. The distinctions can be either real or perceived. Tandem Computer designed machines with two central processing units and two memories for computer systems that can never afford to be down or lose their databases (for example, an airline reservation system). In this case, Tandem used product differentiation to create a product with very real advantages for the target market. However, many everyday products, such as bleaches, aspirin, unleaded regular gasoline, and some soaps are differentiated by such trivial means as brand names, packaging, colour, smell, or "secret" additives. The marketer attempts to convince consumers that a particular brand is distinctive and that they should demand it over competing brands.

product differentiation
A positioning strategy that some firms use to distinguish their products from those of competitors.

Some firms, instead of using product differentiation, position their products as being similar to competing products or brands. Artificial sweeteners advertised as tasting like sugar and margarine advertised as tasting like butter are two examples.

Perceptual Mapping

Perceptual mapping is a means of displaying or graphing, in two or more dimensions, the locations of products, brands, or groups of products in customers' minds. For example, after several years of decreasing market share and the perception among teenagers that Levi's were not "cool," Levi Strauss has developed a number of youth-oriented fashions, ranging from oddly cut jeans to nylon pants that unzip into shorts. It has also introduced apparel appealing to adults by extending the Dockers and Slates casual-pants brands.[39] The perceptual map in Exhibit 6.10 shows Levi's dozens of brands and subbrands, from cheap basics to high-priced fashion.

perceptual mapping
A means of displaying or graphing, in two or more dimensions, the location of products, brands, or groups of products in customers' minds.

EXHIBIT 6.9
Positioning of Procter & Gamble Detergents

BRAND	POSITIONING	MARKET SHARE
Tide	Tough, powerful cleaning	31.1%
Cheer	Tough cleaning and colour protection	8.2
Bold	Detergent plus fabric softener	2.9
Gain	Sunshine scent and odour-removing formula	2.6
Era	Stain treatment and stain removal	2.2
Dash	Value brand	1.8
Oxydol	Bleach-boosted formula, whitening	1.4
Solo	Detergent and fabric softener in liquid form	1.2
Dreft	Outstanding cleaning for baby clothes, safe for tender skin	1.0
Ivory Snow	Fabric and skin safety on baby clothes and fine washables	0.7
Ariel	Tough cleaner, aimed at U.S. Hispanic market	0.1

Positioning Bases

Firms use a variety of bases for positioning, including the following:

- *Attribute:* A product is associated with an attribute, product feature, or customer benefit. Rockport shoes are positioned as an always comfortable brand that is available in a range of styles, from working shoes to dress shoes.
- *Price and quality:* This positioning base may stress high price as a signal of quality or emphasize low price as an indication of value. Denmark-based Lego Building Blocks uses the high-price strategy, whereas Montreal-based Ritvik's Mega Bloks brand uses a low-price and value strategy.[40]
- *Use or application:* Rogers AT&T cell phones emphasize communicating with friends and family with its "Share the Joy" campaign. Stressing uses or applications can be an effective means of positioning a product with buyers. Kahlua liquor used advertising to point out 228 ways to consume the product.
- *Product user:* This positioning base focuses on a personality or type of user. Canadian Tire is Canada's number-one hardware retailer, in large part because it has positioned itself as a one-stop source for Canadian families while offering its customers discounting practices, such as Canadian Tire Money for cash purchases and Canadian Tire Money on the card for credit card transactions. Forty percent of Canadians make at least one trip a week to a Canadian Tire store.[41]
- *Product class:* The objective here is to position the product as being associated with a particular category of products; for example, positioning a margarine brand with butter.
- *Competitor:* Positioning against competitors is part of any positioning strategy. The Seven Up Uncola campaign mentioned earlier and the classic Avis rental car positioning as number two exemplify positioning against specific competitors.

It is not unusual for a marketer to use more than one of these bases. The Rogers AT&T "Share the Joy" campaign that stresses being able to call all of your friends also emphasizes a range of customized calling plans. Mountain Dew positioned its soft drink to the youth market as a thirst-quenching drink associated with teens having fun outdoors.

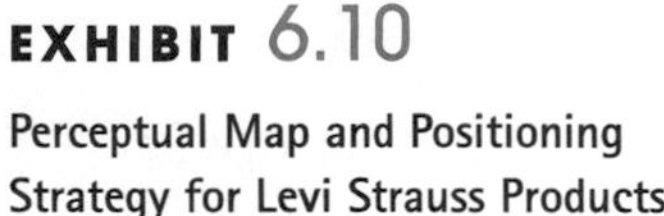

EXHIBIT 6.10

Perceptual Map and Positioning Strategy for Levi Strauss Products

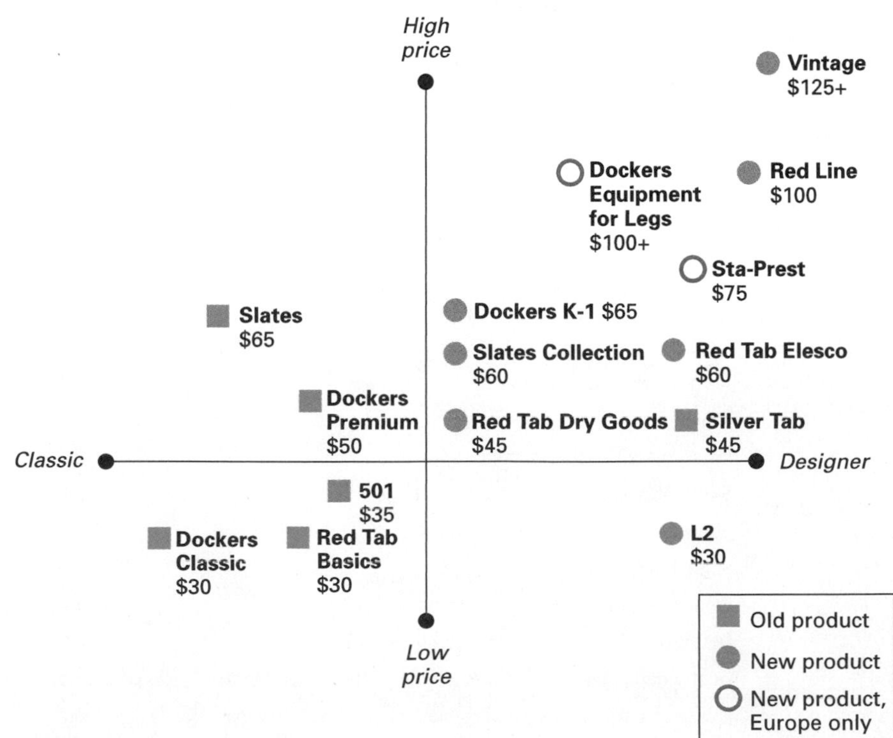

SOURCE: Nina Munk, "How Levi's Trashed a Great American Brand," *Fortune*, April 12, 1999, p. 84.

Repositioning

Sometimes products or companies are repositioned in order to sustain growth in slow markets or to correct positioning mistakes. **Repositioning** is changing consumers' perceptions of a brand in relation to competing brands. Agrinove Dairy, Quebec's third-largest dairy cooperative, found that its Grand Pre' UHT (ultra high temperature) brand of milk was being ignored by consumers. A shelf-stable non-refrigerated milk, consumers perceived Grand Pre' "as a marginal product ... a tide-over product for camping, the cottage or office." Like all shelf-stable milks, consumers were uncertain about the nutritional value and quality of the product. Agrinove decided it had to reposition the product and developed "a five-pronged strategy" to do this. The first step was to broaden the product line to include other shelf-stable dairy products such as cream, flavoured milk (chocolate, strawberry, and cappuccino), and regular milk products that were high-quality, fresh, and creamy in taste. Next, Agrinove decided to position Grand Pre' brand as "a supplier of natural, high quality dairy products" by using distinctive packaging. The packaging was designed to present purity, freshness, and a farm and country type look. The positioning statement was "Grand Pre' maitre laitier" (literally, Grand Pre' master milkman). The firm realized that store shelf locations were also an important element in the brand's presentation and success. Agrinove developed a special display to be placed near the dairy section of foodstores rather than having Grand Pre' sitting with regular packaged foodstuffs. Agrinove also realized that an institutional effort was needed to convince people that shelf-stable milk is a flavourful, nutritious, and healthy product. The firm hired a public relations firm to help it design an advertising campaign; it also designed Web campaigns, undertook sponsorship efforts, and hired a well-known dietitian and spokesperson, Helene Laurendeau, to give credibility to the brand.[42]

Companies often use a mix of positioning bases to reach their target audience. Mountain Dew is one of these products. This ad combines the elements of youth, outdoor fun, and even irreverence.

repositioning
Changing consumers' perceptions of a brand in relation to competing brands.

>> GLOBAL ISSUES IN MARKET SEGMENTATION AND TARGETING

9 Discuss global market segmentation and targeting issues

The most recent trend for businesses is toward global market standardization; thus, multinational firms like Coca-Cola, Colgate-Palmolive, McDonald's, and Nike have chosen to market similar products using similar marketing strategies in many different countries. This chapter has also discussed the trend toward targeting smaller, more precisely defined markets.

The tasks involved in segmenting markets, selecting target markets, and designing, implementing, and maintaining appropriate marketing mixes (described in Exhibit 6.6) are the same whether the marketer has a local perspective or a global vision. The main difference is the segmentation variables commonly used. Countries are commonly grouped using such variables as per capita gross domestic product, geography, religion, culture, and political system.

Some firms have tried to group countries or customer segments around the world using lifestyle or psychographic variables. So-called Asian yuppies in places like Singapore, Hong Kong, Japan, and South Korea have substantial spending power and exhibit purchase and consumption behaviour similar to that of their better-known counterparts in Canada and the United States. In this case, firms may be able to use a global market standardization approach.

ON LINE 

Canadian Egg Marketing Agency

First, write down what your thoughts and opinions are about eggs as a food. What position do they hold in your mind? Now, visit the Canadian Egg Marketing Agency site and review some of the facts and information you find. What position is being promoted? Have you changed your thoughts and opinions about eggs after visiting this site? Why or why not?

http://www.canadaegg.ca

Metabolife International has introduced a line of Chinese herb formulas designed to treat five common ailments, such as the common cold and upset stomach. The line, called Chinac, is being marketed to both North American and Chinese consumers. For North Americans, Chinac offers an easy way to access what is for most consumers an unfamiliar field of medicine. For Chinese, Chinac may offer a welcome change to the numerous and confusing choices they face in a traditional Chinese pharmacy.[43]

>> CONNECT IT

As you read at the beginning of this chapter, market segmentation refers to the process of dividing a market into meaningful, relatively similar, and identifiable segments or groups. Targeting is selecting one or more market segments for which an organization designs, implements, and maintains distinctive marketing mixes. Most of the marketers discussed in the opening story are using a niche targeting strategy. They are attempting to appeal to one segment of the market: children. (One firm in the opening vignette, Coty Canada, also targets parents, so it is using a multisegmentation strategy.) The tweens' market would appear to violate one of the criteria for successful segmentation—substantiality—because it represents only 6.6 percent of the Canadian market. However, if you continually reach this 6.6 percent and retain them as they grow older, as Coty Canada is doing with its Calgon product line, this niche will prove to have long-run profitability.

REVIEW IT

1 Describe the characteristics of markets and market segments. A market is composed of individuals or organizations with the ability and willingness to make purchases to fulfill their needs or wants. A market segment is a group of individuals or organizations with similar product needs as a result of one or more common characteristics.

1.1 Mercedes-Benz is thinking about advertising its cars to college and university students. Do you think these students are a viable potential market for Mercedes? Why or why not?

1.2 

How are visitors to the following website segmented when seeking relevant job openings? Try this search engine and report your results: http://www.monster.ca.

2 Explain the importance of market segmentation. Before the 1960s, few businesses targeted specific market segments. Today, segmentation is a crucial marketing strategy for nearly all successful organizations. Market segmentation enables marketers to tailor marketing mixes to meet the needs of particular population segments. Segmentation helps marketers identify consumer needs and preferences, areas of declining demand, and new marketing opportunities.

2.1 Describe market segmentation in terms of the historical evolution of marketing.

3 Discuss criteria for successful market segmentation. Successful market segmentation depends on four basic criteria: (1) a market segment must be substantial and have enough potential customers to be viable; (2) a market segment must be identifiable and measurable; (3) members of a market segment must be accessible to marketing efforts; and (4) a market segment must respond to particular marketing efforts in a way that distinguishes it from other segments.

3.1 WRITING Refer to the story about tweens at the beginning of the chapter. As a marketing consultant for a chain of hair salons, you have been asked to evaluate the kids' market as a potential segment for the chain to target. Write a memo to your client discussing your evaluation of the kids' segment in terms of the four criteria for successful market segmentation.

4 **Describe the bases commonly used to segment consumer markets.** Five bases are commonly used for segmenting consumer markets. Geographic segmentation is based on region, size, density, and climate characteristics. Demographic segmentation is based on age, gender, income level, ethnicity, and family life-cycle characteristics. Psychographic segmentation includes personality, motives, and lifestyle characteristics. Benefits sought is a type of segmentation that identifies customers according to the benefits they seek in a product. Finally, usage segmentation divides a market by the amount of product purchased or consumed.

4.1 WRITING Choose magazine ads for five different consumer products. For each ad, write a description of what you think the demographic characteristics of the targeted market are.

4.2 ON LINE Investigate how computer retailer Dell Canada (http://www.dell.ca) uses its website to cater to its market segments.

5 **Describe the bases for segmenting business markets.** Business markets can be segmented on three general bases. First, businesses segment markets based on company characteristics, such as customers' geographic location, type of company, company size, and product use. Second, companies may segment customers based on the buying processes those customers use. Third, companies are increasingly basing market segmentation on the type of relationship they have with their customers.

5.1 WRITING Choose five ads from business publications such as *Marketing Magazine, Canadian Business,* the *Financial Post,* and *The Globe and Mail.* For each ad, write a description of how you think the company has segmented its business market.

6 **List the steps involved in segmenting markets.** Six steps are involved when segmenting markets: (1) selecting a market or product category for study; (2) choosing a basis or bases for segmenting the market; (3) selecting segmentation descriptors; (4) profiling and evaluating segments; (5) selecting target markets; and (6) designing, implementing, and maintaining appropriate marketing mixes.

6.1 WRITING Write a letter to the president of your bank or trust company suggesting ideas for increasing profits and enhancing customer service by improving segmentation and targeting strategies.

7 **Discuss alternative strategies for selecting target markets.** Marketers select target markets using three different strategies: undifferentiated targeting, concentrated targeting, and multisegment targeting. An undifferentiated targeting strategy assumes that all members of a market have similar needs that can be met with a single marketing mix. A concentrated targeting strategy focuses all marketing efforts on a single market segment. Multisegment targeting is a strategy that uses two or more marketing mixes to target two or more market segments.

7.1 TEAM Form a team with two or three other students. Create an idea for a new product. Describe the segment (or segments) you are going to target with the product, and explain why you chose the targeting strategy you did.

8 **Explain how and why firms implement positioning strategies and how product differentiation plays a role.** Positioning is used to influence consumer perceptions of a particular brand, product line, or organization in relation to competitors. The term *position* refers to the place that the offering occupies in consumers' minds. To establish a unique position, many firms use product differentiation, emphasizing the real or perceived differences between competing offerings. Products may be differentiated on the basis of attribute, price and quality, use or application, product user, product class, or competitor.

8.1 Choose a product category (e.g., blue jeans), and identify at least three different brands and their respective positioning strategies. How is each position communicated to the target audience?

9 **Discuss global market segmentation and targeting issues.** The key tasks in market segmentation, targeting, and positioning are the same regardless of whether the target market is local, regional, national, or multinational. The main differences are the variables used by marketers in analyzing markets and assessing opportunities and the resources needed to implement strategies.

9.1 Find an article in a business newspaper or magazine that describes how a Canadian company is marketing its products in another country. Create a chart that compares the Canadian marketing mix elements with the same elements for the other country. You may also wish to consult foreign periodicals to see how multinational companies advertise their products in other countries.

DEFINE IT

benefit segmentation 171
cannibalization 178
concentrated targeting strategy 177
demographic segmentation 164
80/20 principle 172
family life cycle (FLC) 168
geodemographic segmentation 170
geographic segmentation 162
market 160
market segment 160
market segmentation 160
multisegment targeting strategy 178
niche 177
optimizers 174
perceptual mapping 179
position 178
positioning 178
product differentiation 179
psychographic segmentation 169
repositioning 181
satisficers 174
segmentation bases (variables) 162
target market 175
undifferentiated targeting strategy 175
usage-rate segmentation 172

APPLY IT

Judy Brown has always loved working with animals. She has experience in pet grooming, boarding, and in-home pet sitting. Judy wants to open a full-service business utilizing her skills that is uniquely positioned in relation to the traditional pet grooming/boarding businesses that operate in the town where she lives. Customers who use these current pet services deliver their pets to the firms and later pick them up. Most are open between 9 a.m. and 6 p.m. from Monday through Friday.

Judy lives in a midsize community that is close to a major airport. Many high-tech companies are located in or near her community, so there are a large number of men and women in managerial and information-technology positions who must travel frequently as part of their work. A lot of families have pets, so Judy thinks there is a market for pet-related services, despite the current competition.

QUESTIONS

1. How should Judy segment the market for pet services?
2. What targeting strategy should Judy use to start her business? Should this strategy change as her business prospers and grows?
3. How should Judy position her pet services business against her competition?

THINK ABOUT IT

Alcoholic beverage marketers including breweries, wineries, and liquor and spirits distillers are frequently criticized for targeting potential customers below the legal drinking age to purchase and use their products. Critics cite the kinds of promotions and contests found on the websites of these firms and the sponsorship of professional sports that interests many younger viewers. If alcoholic beverage marketers were actually following this particular demographic targeting strategy, most would agree that it is unethical if not illegal.

QUESTIONS

1. Is the sponsorship of programs and events that attract younger consumers unethical?
2. Many are beginning to argue that fast-food companies, such as McDonald's and Burger King, are knowingly marketing unhealthy food to consumers. Is it unethical for fast-food companies to market kids' meals to children?
3. What does the CMA Code of Ethics have to say about marketing unhealthy or harmful products to consumers, particularly children and young adults? Go to the CMA website at **http://www.the-cma.org/consumer/ethics.cfm** to review the code. Write a brief paragraph summarizing where the CMA stands on this important issue.

Segmenting the On-line Market: The Case of eBay.ca

TRY IT

When Pam Omidyar dreamed of a place where she could meet, talk, and trade with other collectors of Pez candy dispensers, her computer-programmer and soon-to-be husband, Pierre Omidyar, immediately set to work on developing the software that would enable such interaction on-line. Together, in September 1995, they launched http://www.eBay.com, and within five short years it was one of the most recognizable brand names on the Internet. From its humble beginnings as a niche website, it has become the premier Internet auction showcase. eBay's 4,300 categories include everything from tie-dyed Grateful Dead Beanie Babies to bubblegum cards to nearly new Ferraris and even fine jewellery. Once you find what you're looking for, you can haggle for it in one of the 4 million daily auctions.

eBay positions itself as a folksy and friendly facilitator of an on-line community that caters to traders with varying tastes and preferences, but the original idea was to service one type of collector in a single geographic area—Pam and Pierre's neighbourhood in San Francisco. The Omidyars' customer-focused strategy led to such a high degree of customer satisfaction that awareness of the site quickly spread through the entire Bay area. High customer loyalty, repeat usage, and very strong word-of-mouth advertising (*viral marketing*) fuelled eBay's growth. eBay is unique in that it has equal appeal to the occasional Internet surfer, the nostalgic trader, the fanatic trader, the small business in search of used or inexpensive equipment, and those who simply love the thrill of the deal.

In trying to nurture its growing enterprise, eBay's entrepreneurial management team was faced with many marketing challenges that it still grapples with today:

- Attracting users who are accustomed to trading in traditional venues such as auction houses, estate sales, and flea markets.
- Convincing Internet users to execute transactions on-line.
- Organizing many specific product categories into a much smaller number of broad categories and corresponding market segments.
- Developing a marketing mix to reach multiple targets.

The first step for eBay was to build a killer product. eBay focuses on delivering a first-class user experience by providing frequent content and auction updates. The site's help areas are customized for either experienced or new users, and detailed collector news and information is available. The second step was developing a pricing schedule to satisfy its broad spectrum of users. Transactions can be executed for as little as 25 cents for the seller of a Pez dispenser, but eBay can claim as much as a 5 percent commission on the selling price of an expensive item like a diamond necklace. Under the direction of senior vice president of marketing, Brian Swette, the company rethought its past strategy of restricting on-line promotions to its own website and has accomplished prolific distribution on the World Wide Web. eBay has struck deals to gain presence on major entry portals like AOL, shopping verticals like http://www.mySimon.com, and destination sites like http://www.autotrader.ca.

©KIM KULISH/CORBIS

The final component of the marketing mix, promotion, was the most complex to address. At first glance, eBay has only one product—the on-line auction forum—which it sells to traders and consumers. To that end, eBay has remained faithful to its grassroots marketing effort in the off-line world. It has also maintained its presence at trade and collector shows of all kinds in order to evangelize the benefits of auctioning on-line. A closer look at what transpires at the site, however, reveals that eBay is the auction utility of choice for a range of collectors so stratified that on any one day a browser at eBay can encounter auctions for coins, clothes, model airplanes, or more controversial and hence discouraged items like hate-group materials, used underwear, or a human kidney. The challenge for eBay, therefore, is not so much that it has so many different consumers, but that each one of its consumers has very different needs. With that in mind, eBay has chosen to divide markets using a variety of segmentation strategies. It has employed demographic, psychographic, geodemographic, benefit, and usage-rate segmentation techniques to better understand and serve customer needs across a broad range in each.

In order to promote the site effectively to its eclectic audience, eBay developed a complex and comprehensive print advertising campaign aimed at several targets. Working with the advertising agency of Ogilvy & Mather, eBay decided to avoid mass print media and use niche publications. This way, the company could reach an audience that would be more captive at the point of exposure to the advertisement. Unique messaging and advertising copy was developed for campaigns deployed in 12 different vertical markets. Across those 12 markets, eBay selected 75 specialty magazines for its highly tailored advertisements. eBay still supports this strategy today. Although segmenting its market into multiple niches was a demanding and complex initiative, it has clearly been a successful tactic.

On any given day, there are millions of items across thousands of categories for sale on eBay. Currently, eBay attracts over 68 million registered users worldwide. eBay enables trade on a local, national, and international basis with customized sites in markets around the world. In Canada, more than 6 million Canadians visit eBay in any month. Customers range from infrequent traders to traders who use eBay regularly to generate personal profit streams. eBay has special services such as My eBay and eBay Turbo Lister for frequent users, and currency converters for international customers, and has gone so far as to build a Business Exchange area where it caters to needs of small businesses. Customers can participate in local auctions specific to their geographic region, bid on items whose proceeds go directly to one of many charities, or sign up for the eBay magazine. Chat rooms, an on-line library of articles organized by collection category, and eBay's own newsletter all provide information to enhance and empower the customer's trading experience. eBay's success has inspired a proliferation of copycat auction sites, but none enjoys the customer base or widespread brand recognition of the original.

QUESTIONS

1. What types of segmentation does eBay use?
2. Does eBay use an undifferentiated, a niche, or a multisegment targeting strategy? Discuss the range of tactics eBay uses to reach its target market.
3. Explain the tools eBay has developed for usage-rate segmentation and consider how eBay might use those tools to enhance its profitability.
4. How did eBay tackle the marketing challenges it faced as it grew from an entrepreneurial venture to a multimillion-dollar operation?
5. Describe eBay's target market.

FLIP IT

GRADEMAKER

Flip to Chapter 6 in your *Grademaker Study Guide* for more review opportunities, including the pretest, vocabulary review, Internet activities, study test questions, and segmentation scenarios. Can you explain why market segmentation is important? What are the most common bases that marketers use to segment markets? Don't know? Then you need to review with your Grademaker.

CLICK IT

The *Marketing* website is rich with materials to help you review and master marketing concepts. Check your knowledge with the free quizzes, practise key terms using the crossword puzzles, or review key concepts using the Microsoft® PowerPoint® slides. Also on the website are updated weblinks to companies mentioned in this chapter, Internet exercises, career marketing information, and much much more! Go to http://www.lamb3e.nelson.com, read the material, and follow the convenient links.

WATCH IT

Creating a Craze

Young girls are spending a lot of time on the Internet these days, and many are talking to their favourite heartthrob popstars. Sony Music is aware of the spending power of children 9 to 14, and has launched a meticulously manufactured "boy band" to create a buzz that will ensure that these "tween" girls spend heavily on CDs and concerts.

Sony launched the band B4-4 by encouraging on-line relationships between young girls and the band's members, Dan, Ryan, and Ohad. The New Media team at Sony introduced B4-4 through the Internet and promoted its on-line relationship with 8- to 14-year-old girls, who are anxious to get to know the objects of their desires—the boy band. In a carefully crafted on-line blitz, the girls were introduced to the B4-4 boys. They can chat with them daily and learn intimate details about them and their lives. They know about the boys' upbringing, their pets, and their hobbies, and they have even seen their baby pictures. The boys make time to say a personalized on-line goodnight to their fans almost every night.

The B4-4 website became highly interactive for the girl fans. The site provides on-line trading cards for girls to swap with other fans; it also gives easy, step-by step instructions for the girls to create their own grassroots B4-4 websites, which link to the main corporate site. The B4-4 site even provides craft ideas, prerecorded bandmembers' voice messages for girls to use on their answering machines, and lots of information about the boy band. Word-of-mouth promotion of the band was instantaneous, and the fan base has exploded based on the on-line hype created by Sony and the fans themselves.

Sony's New Media team (most of them in their early 20s) knows that many of these girls spend more time on-line than off-. The girls in the know were happy to circulate information about this great new boy band months before a CD was ever recorded. The New Media team allowed the girls to develop a relationship with the band, as the boys spent time answering sometimes very personal questions in the on-line chat rooms. So much was happening on the B4-4 website that the girls really believed they had made friends with the pop stars, and they were happy to tell others about it.

This type of on-line relationship marketing begins a new era of promoting new bands, especially to young markets that are easily influenced. B4-4 had thousands of dedicated fans long before it had a concert, a CD, or a song on the radio. In terms of number of hits, the B4-4 website was second in Canada only to that of Celine Dion. The result? A number-one song for B4-4 within days of its release, and amazing sales and concert success in a very short time with B4-4's first CD going gold in just six weeks.

Source: CBC, *Undercurrents*, "Creating a Craze," Broadcast: November 4, 2000.

QUESTIONS

1. Is Sony using a niche or multisegment targeting strategy in promoting this new band? Explain why.
2. What communications strategy has Sony adopted to position its new band to its market?
3. What is the common behaviour pattern that Sony has focused on?

chapter 7

Decision Support Systems and Marketing Research

>> LEARNING OBJECTIVES

1. Explain the concept and purpose of a marketing decision support system
2. Define marketing research and explain its importance to marketing decision making
3. Describe the steps involved in conducting a marketing research project
4. Discuss the profound impact of the Internet on marketing research
5. Discuss the growing importance of scanner-based research
6. Explain the concept of competitive intelligence

>> In trying to understand why consumers behave as they do, marketers have realized that they need to undertake research in "natural habitats" and observe their subjects. In the past, researchers felt they could only really learn from observation if consumers didn't know they were being watched. After all, a consumer who knew he or she was being observed probably wouldn't act "naturally." As a result, marketing researchers would use hidden cameras, two-way mirrors, or hidden observation stations called "duck blinds" to observe their subjects. Although apparently unobtrusive, observation in this fashion does bring strong ethical questions into play. Observing "ducks" from a "duck blind" to study their behaviour is a well-accepted research practice, but ducks do not enjoy the rights to privacy that people do. In addition, there is a difference between watching people and watching ducks as far as understanding "why" they do what they can be observed to do. So marketers have turned to "anthropologists" to try and discover approaches to research that can help them "observe" people in their "natural habitat" and find out "why people do what they do."

The usual tools of market research involve focus groups and survey questionnaires. These are important tools that give marketers insights into the marketplace. One of the issues with these research methods is that sometimes consumers cannot really articulate their buying motives and may not fully understand their buying behaviour. Further, actual purchasing behaviour is not done in a focus group or by questionnaire. To truly understand consumers, marketers must literally "go with them" when they shop. But how does one conduct "appropriate" research by "hanging" out with consumers?

This is where the anthropological approach comes in. Anthropologists use research methods such as participant observation, one-on-one interviews, subjects as mentors, and storylines to understand the behaviours, motives, and experiences of people. More importantly, this understanding takes place within the "social context" of the people being researched. In this way the anthropologist is both a participant and an observer in the process. The issue of "affecting" the outcome by virtue of "intrusive" observation is a concern with this approach. Anthropologists take the view that they must obtain informed consent of their subjects and then build up a bond of trust. Anthropologists insinuate themselves with their subjects and become a part of the process and observers at the same time.

Some examples of how anthropologists have helped marketers research consumers include "an anthropologist" who worked directly with Kimberly-Clark analyzing hundreds of hours of diaper changes at a daycare centre in order to help the producer redesign disposable diapers. To help an advertiser pitch a campaign to a financial firm, an anthropologist analyzed the nature and value of the relationship between investors and investment advisors. Other anthropologists working with vendors have demonstrated such things as the fact that many women don't like to shop in confined spaces where they risk being grabbed from behind. Anthropologists have also discovered that men often become embarrassed and angry and leave a clothing store quickly rather than ask: "Where is the men's section?"[1]

What are the various techniques for conducting marketing research? Should managers always do marketing research before they make a decision? How does marketing research relate to decision support systems? We will explore all these topics and others in Chapter 7.

ON LINE

University of Manitoba Anthropology

American Anthropological Association

What kinds of "business" and "marketing" related careers can you discover on these websites? Explore some of the links on the American Anthropological Association website and identify three or four that you believe might be useful for marketers. Explain your reasoning.

http://www.umanitoba.ca/faculties/arts/anthropology

http://www.aaanet.org

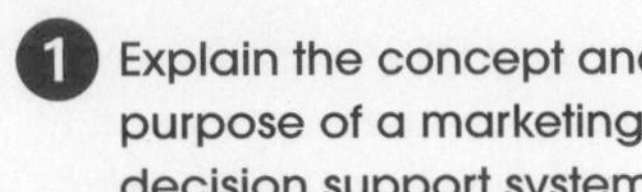
1 Explain the concept and purpose of a marketing decision support system

>> MARKETING DECISION SUPPORT SYSTEMS

marketing information
Everyday information about developments in the marketing environment that managers use to prepare and adjust marketing plans.

decision support system (DSS)
An interactive, flexible computerized information system that enables managers to obtain and manipulate information as they are making decisions.

Accurate and timely information is the lifeblood of marketing decision making. Good information can help maximize an organization's sales and efficiently use scarce company resources. To prepare and adjust marketing plans, managers need a system for gathering everyday information about developments in the marketing environment, that is, for gathering **marketing information**. The system most commonly used these days for gathering marketing information is called a *marketing decision support system.*

A marketing **decision support system (DSS)** is an interactive, flexible computerized information system that enables managers to obtain and manipulate information while they are making decisions. A DSS bypasses the information-processing specialist and gives managers access to useful data from their own desks.

These are the characteristics of a true DSS:

- *Interactive:* Managers give simple instructions and see immediate results. The process is under their direct control; no computer programmer is needed. Managers don't have to wait for scheduled reports.
- *Flexible:* A DSS can sort, regroup, total, average, and manipulate the data in various ways. It will shift gears as the user changes topics, matching information to the problem at hand. For example, the CEO can see highly aggregated figures, and the marketing analyst can view very detailed breakouts.
- *Discovery-oriented:* Managers can probe for trends, isolate problems, and ask "what if" questions.
- *Accessible:* Managers who aren't skilled with computers can easily learn how to use a DSS. Novice users should be able to choose a standard, or default, method of using the system. They can bypass optional features so that they can work with the basic system right away while gradually learning to apply its advanced features.

As a hypothetical example of how a DSS can be used, consider Renee Smith, vice president and manager of new products for Central Corporation. To evaluate sales of a recently introduced product, Renee can "call up" sales by the week, then by the month, breaking them out at her option by, say, customer segments. As she works at her desktop computer, her inquiries can go in several directions, depending on the decision at hand. If her train of thought raises questions about monthly sales last quarter compared to forecasts, she can use her DSS to analyze problems immediately. Renee might see that her new product's sales were significantly below forecasts. Were her forecasts too optimistic? She compares other products' sales to her forecasts and finds that the targets were very accurate. Was something wrong with the product? Is her sales department getting insufficient leads, or is it not putting leads to good use? Thinking a minute about how to examine that question, she checks ratios of leads converted to sales, product by product. The results disturb her. Only 5 percent of the new product's leads generated orders, compared to the company's 12 percent all-product average. Why? Renee guesses that the sales force is not supporting the new product vigorously enough. Quantitative information from the DSS could perhaps provide more evidence to back that suspicion. But already having enough quantitative knowledge to satisfy herself, the VP acts on her intuition and experience and decides to have a chat with her sales manager.

database marketing
The creation of a large computerized file of customers' and potential customers' profiles and purchase patterns.

Perhaps the fastest-growing use of DSSs is for **database marketing**, which is the creation of a large computerized file of customers' and potential customers' profiles and purchase patterns. It is usually the key tool for successful micromarketing, which relies on very specific information about a market (see Chapter 17).

2 Define marketing research and explain its importance to marketing decision making

>> THE ROLE OF MARKETING RESEARCH

marketing research
The process of planning, collecting, and analyzing data relevant to a marketing decision.

Marketing research is the process of planning, collecting, and analyzing data relevant to a marketing decision. The results of this analysis are then communicated to management. Marketing research plays a key role in the marketing system. It provides decision makers with data on the effectiveness of the current marketing mix and also with insights for necessary changes. Furthermore, marketing research is a main data source for both management information systems and DSS.

Marketing research has three roles: descriptive, diagnostic, and predictive. Its *descriptive* role includes gathering and presenting factual statements. For example, what is the historic sales trend in the industry? What are consumers' attitudes toward a product and its advertising? Its *diagnostic* role includes explaining data. For instance, what was the impact on sales of a change in the design of the package? Its *predictive* function is to address "what if" questions. For example, how can the researcher use the descriptive and diagnostic research to predict the results of a planned marketing decision?

CANADIAN PRESS CP

Marketing research can help managers in several ways. For example, research revealed what kinds of activities and amenities were most important to sea cruise passengers. Royal Caribbean Cruise Lines' *Vision of the Sea* cruise ship is shown here docked in Quebec City.

Management Uses of Marketing Research

Marketing research can help managers in several ways. It improves the quality of decision making and helps managers trace problems. Most important, sound marketing research helps managers focus on the paramount importance of keeping existing customers, aids them in better understanding the marketplace, and alerts them to marketplace trends. Marketing research helps managers gauge the perceived value of their goods and services as well as the level of customer satisfaction.

Improving the Quality of Decision Making

Managers can sharpen their decision making by using marketing research to explore the desirability of various marketing alternatives. For example, despite the growing popularity of cruise ships—nearly 6 million North American passengers boarded U.S.-based ships in 2001—cruises still get only a tiny slice of North Americans' vacation time. Just 5 percent of people who take vacations longer than five days and are willing to spend $1,000 per person take cruises.[2] Royal Caribbean Cruise Lines liked the tremendous potential in the cruising market. Its job was to find a way to woo those people who wouldn't be caught dead on a cruise ship. The classic objections that people raise to vacationing on a cruise ship have not changed in nearly 20 years. Marketing research found that people worry about feeling trapped; they'd rather participate in activities than sit in a pool lounge all day long; they don't like having to eat in an elegant dining room, seven nights in a row, and share a table with strangers; and they don't like having to eat at a set time. In other words, they want options.

Royal Caribbean tackled those objections. That's how *Voyager of the Sea* ended up with an in-line skating track, a kids-only pool, a rock-climbing wall, an English pub, a Johnny Rockets restaurant, and a roulette wheel so big that gamblers can ride around its rim as if it were a carousel. To date, the ship has been very successful at attracting first-time cruisers.

ON LINE 

British Airways

How are the changes in British Airways's services reflected by the marketing on its website? Does the company use the site to collect marketing data? If so, how? If not, how would you suggest it do this?

http://www.british-airways.com

Tracing Problems

Another way managers use marketing research is to find out why a plan backfired. Was the initial decision incorrect? Did an unforeseen change in the external environment cause the plan to fail? How can the same mistake be avoided in the future?

Molson Breweries found its once dominant brand, Molson Export, was losing market share rapidly. The company researched the market to discover why and found that it was facing new competitors, its advertising messages were inconsistent, and it wasn't supporting the brand very much. In addition, the brand was becoming viewed as outdated and irrelevant to new beer drinkers in Quebec. Further research was undertaken about the image of the brand and Molson discovered that while beer drinkers considered the brand "old," it was positively viewed as being a traditional brand that was tied to the heritage of Quebeckers. The same research indicated that young Quebeckers considered heritage and tradition to be important attributes. As a result, Molson Breweries decided to tie Molson Ex into heritage and tradition and changed its positioning image from "Ex says it all" to "Molson Ex. Today's beer since 1903." The brewery developed a campaign that tied the drinking of Molson Ex in "classic bar settings" to "classic moments in hockey history," featuring the lines "Bar Epoque" and "Hockey Epoque." The result was not only an arrest of Export's falling market share but also, in fact, three years of growth and a tripling in consumption among young Quebeckers.[3]

Focusing on the Paramount Importance of Keeping Existing Customers

An inextricable link exists between customer satisfaction and customer loyalty. Long-term relationships don't just happen but are grounded in the delivery of service and value by the firm. Customer retention pays big dividends for organizations. Powered by repeat sales and referrals, revenues and market share grow. Costs fall because firms spend less money and energy attempting to replace defectors. Steady customers are easy to serve because they understand the modus operandi and make fewer demands on employees' time. Increased customer retention also drives job satisfaction and pride, which lead to higher employee retention. In turn, the knowledge employees acquire as they stay longer increases productivity. A Bain & Company study estimates that a 5 percent decrease in the customer defection rate can boost profits by 25 to 95 percent.[4]

The ability to retain customers is based on an intimate understanding of their needs. This knowledge comes primarily from marketing research. For example, British Airways recast its first-class transatlantic service based on detailed marketing research. Most airlines stress top-of-the-line service in their transatlantic first-class cabins, but British Air's research found that most first-class passengers simply want to sleep. British Air now gives premium flyers the option of dinner on the ground, before takeoff, in the first-class lounge. Then, once on board, they can slip into British Air pajamas, put their heads on real pillows, slip under blankets, and enjoy an interruption-free flight. On arrival at their destination, first-class passengers can have breakfast, use comfortable dressing rooms and showers, and even have their clothes pressed before they set off. These changes in British Air's first-class service were driven strictly by marketing research.

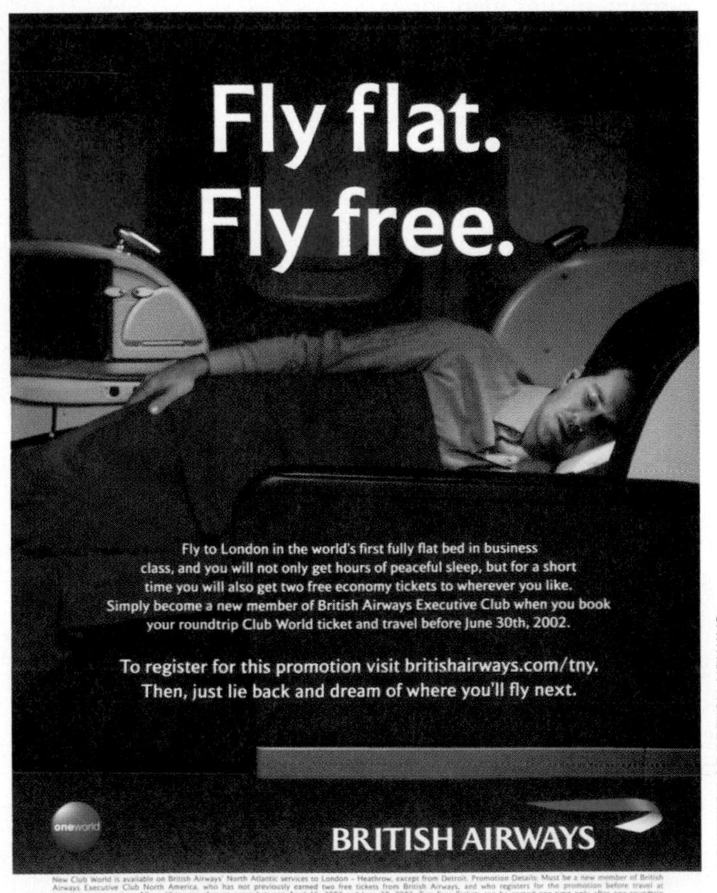

Fly flat.
Fly free.
Fly to London in the world's first fully flat bed in business class, and you will not only get hours of peaceful sleep, but for a short time you will also get two free economy tickets to wherever you like. Simply become a new member of British Airways Executive Club when you book your roundtrip Club World ticket and travel before June 30th, 2002.
To register for this promotion visit britishairways.com/tny. Then, just lie back and dream of where you'll fly next.
oneworld
BRITISH AIRWAYS
COURTESY OF BRITISH AIRWAYS

British Airways refined its First Class service based on marketing research that revealed that travellers often wanted to sleep during long-haul flights. The company further applied this information to create the world's first fully flat bed in business class (Club World) as shown above.

Understanding the Ever-Changing Marketplace

Marketing research also helps managers understand what is going on in the marketplace and take advantage of opportunities. Historically, marketing research has been practised for as long as marketing has existed. The early Phoenicians carried out market demand studies as they traded in the various ports of the Mediterranean Sea. Marco Polo's diary indicates he was performing a marketing research function as he travelled to China. There is even evidence that the Spanish systematically conducted "market surveys" as they explored the New World, and there are examples of marketing research conducted during the Renaissance.

Today, Internet marketing research can help companies quickly and efficiently understand what is happening in the marketplace. For example, Women.com, an on-line community site that offers editorial content and e-commerce services, has surveyed visitors for several years but recently boosted its research efforts. The surveys are designed to discover visitors' demographic and psychographic profiles for the network's internal use, as well as to share with advertisers.

Along with collecting basic demographic data, the site also asks visitors about their e-commerce habits (whether they've shopped for or purchased anything on-line recently, for instance), their feelings about privacy on the Internet, and value and attitudinal questions, such as whether they agree or disagree with statements like: "I'm usually the first in my peer group to try something new." Such information provides a picture of the person on the other side of the computer that goes beyond her average age and income, says Regina Lewis, director of research for Women.com Networks, Inc. Understanding whether visitors are more risk oriented, family focused, or career minded helps Women.com set the right tone when talking to visitors, Lewis says, and has resulted in page redesigns.[5]

>> STEPS IN A MARKETING RESEARCH PROJECT

3 Describe the steps involved in conducting a marketing research project

Virtually all firms that have adopted the marketing concept engage in some marketing research because it offers decision makers many benefits. Some companies spend millions on marketing research; others, particularly smaller firms, conduct informal, limited-scale research studies. For example, George McLeod thought he would try something different by freezing wine on a stick, dipping it in chocolate, and distributing 600 at a "wine and dine" convention in Pendicton, B.C. McLeod says his invention of the "gewurtztsicle" was just a joke when he started. However, the joke has taken hold; a number of wineries have approached George to use their wines in his products. Aside from his "sampling" test market research, George had students at two local universities take on projects to look at the market potential for this product. A test market survey conducted by business students studying at the B.C. Institute of Technology forecasted potential sales of 900,000 frozen treats a year, while students from Kwantlen University College in Vancouver looked at the Japanese market and concluded the frozen treats had the potential to "take 2 percent of that country's $8-billion annual dessert market." Now George is looking for a financial partner to help him turn his "product concept" and his "market potentials" into a "real business."[6]

Whether a research project costs $200 or $2 million, the same general process should be followed. The marketing research process is a scientific approach to decision making that maximizes the chances of getting accurate and meaningful results. Exhibit 7.1 traces the steps: (1) identifying and formulating the problem/opportunity, (2) planning the research design and gathering primary data, (3) specifying the sampling procedures, (4) collecting the data, (5) analyzing the data, (6) preparing and presenting the report, and (7) following up.

The research process begins with the recognition of a marketing problem or opportunity. As changes occur in the firm's external environment, marketing managers are faced with the questions: "Should we change the existing marketing mix?" and, if so, "How?" Marketing research can be used to evaluate product, promotion, distribution, or pricing alternatives. In addition, it is used to find and evaluate new market opportunities.

For example, the four Canadian cell phone companies believe that the major growth potential for cell phone products is in the Canadian youth market. This market is defined as the 14- to 24-year-old age group. Cell phone marketers recognize that these people have more disposable income than their parents, are more willing and able to adopt new technologies than their parents, and are strong influencers on their families. One research and publishing firm, Toronto-based Youth Culture Group, reports that disposable income among youths is about $107 per week, which is more than double the amount for their parents. The statistical story indicates the youth portion of the cell phone market is growing at twice the rate of the rest of the Canadian market. The Canadian market has accepted cell phone usage extremely well, with 10.7 million users in 2001 (34 percent of the Canadian market); the forecast is that by 2006 at least 70 percent of Canadians (22.6 million people) will be users, creating a $9.9-billion market![7]

For savvy marketers, the statistics on the youth market represent opportunity. Marketing research can hone in and clarify where the best opportunities lie. Sometimes research can lead to unexpected results requiring creative uses of the marketing mix. General Motors recently completed an analysis of "backseat consumers," that is, children between 5 and 15. Marketing research discovered that parents often let their children play a tie-breaking role in deciding what car to purchase. Marketing managers, armed with this information, launched several programs. GM purchased the inside cover of *Sports Illustrated for Kids*, a magazine targeted to 8- to 14-year-old boys. The ad featured a brightly coloured two-page spread for the Chevy Venture minivan, a vehicle marketed toward young families. GM also displayed the minivan in malls and showed Disney movies on a video player inside the van.

marketing research problem Determining what information is needed and how that information can be obtained efficiently and effectively.

marketing research objective The specific information needed to solve a marketing research problem; the objective should be to provide insightful decision-making information.

management decision problem A broad-based problem that requires marketing research in order for managers to take proper actions.

The GM story illustrates an important point about problem/opportunity definition. The **marketing research problem** is information oriented. It involves determining what information is needed and how that information can be obtained efficiently and effectively. The **marketing research objective**, then, is to provide insightful decision-making information. This requires specific pieces of information needed to answer the marketing research problem. Managers must combine this

EXHIBIT 7.1

The Marketing Research Process

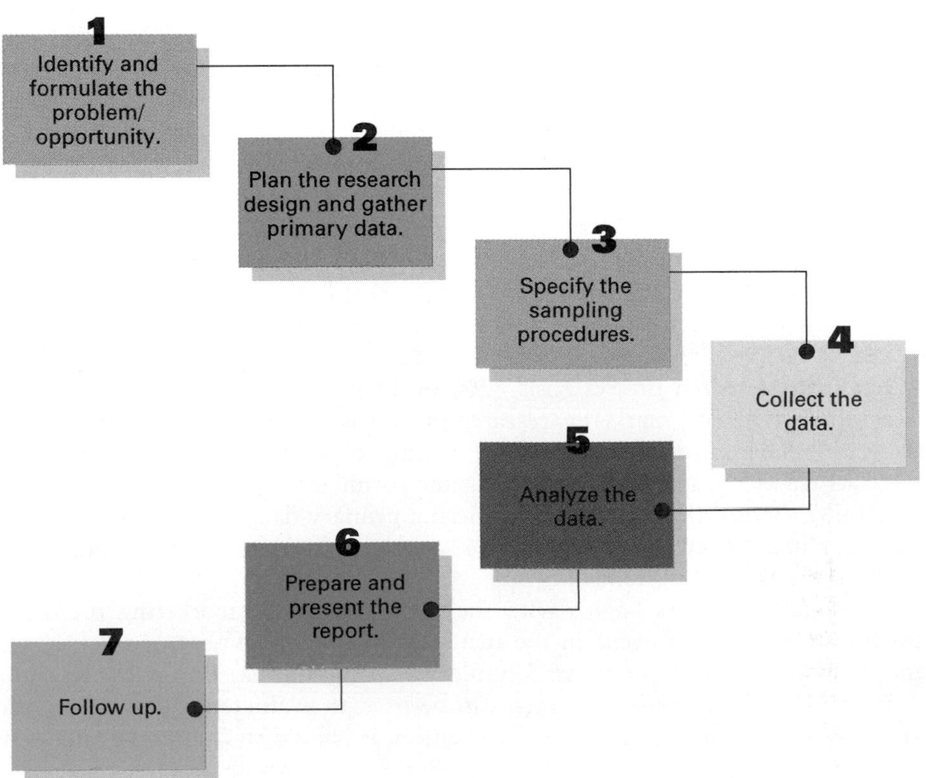

information with their own experience and other information to make a proper decision. In the GM scenario, the marketing research objective was to determine what role, if any, backseat consumers play in a family's decision to purchase an automobile. In contrast, the **management decision problem** is action oriented. Management problems tend to be much broader in scope and far more general, whereas marketing research problems must be more narrowly defined and specific if the research effort is to be successful. Sometimes several research studies must be conducted to solve a broad management problem. Once GM determined that children within this target market played a tie-breaker role, the question became one of what should be done to influence the tie-breakers. GM used marketing research to determine that direct advertising to children in the target market and mall promotions would be the best form of promotion.

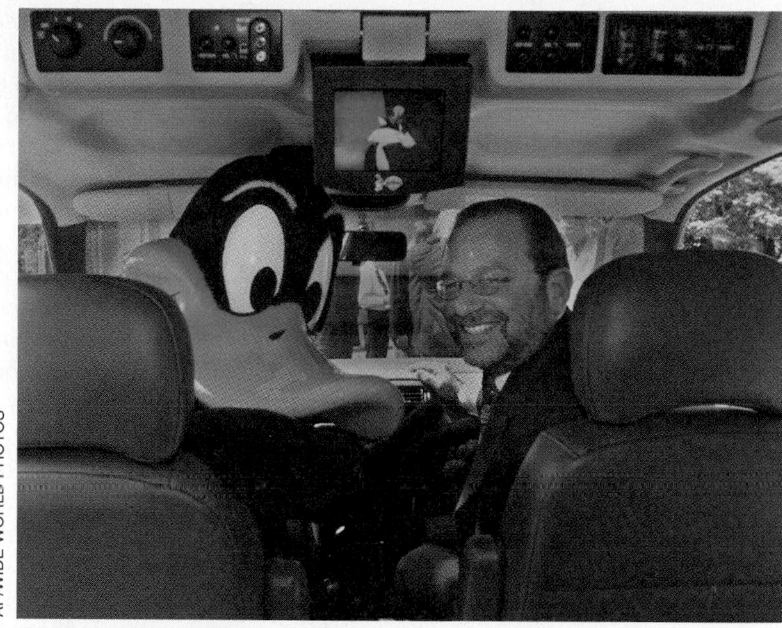

AP/WIDE WORLD PHOTOS

GM continues to reap the benefits of its marketing research revealing how important kids are in the family decision-making process. In 2000, the company introduced the Warner Bros. Edition Chevy Venture minivan. This model includes a built-in child's restraining seat, a video player, and an ongoing package called VentureTainment!

Secondary Data

A valuable tool throughout the research process but particularly in the problem/opportunity identification stage is **secondary data**—data previously collected for any purpose other than the one at hand. Secondary information originating within the company includes documents such as annual reports, reports to stockholders, product testing results perhaps made available to the news media, and house periodicals composed by the company's personnel for communication to employees, customers, or others. Often this information is incorporated into a company's internal database.

secondary data
Data previously collected for any purpose other than the one at hand.

Innumerable outside sources of secondary information also exist, principally in the forms of government (federal, provincial, municipal) departments and agencies that compile and publish summaries of business data. Trade and industry associations also publish secondary data. Still more data are available in business periodicals and other news media that regularly publish studies and articles on the economy, specific industries, and even individual companies. The unpublished summarized secondary information from these sources corresponds to internal reports, memos, or special-purpose analyses with limited circulation. Economic considerations or priorities in the organization may preclude publication of these summaries. Most of the sources listed above can be found on the Internet.

ON LINE

Statistics Canada

Statistics Canada is a federal government source for statistics and has been legislated to serve the function of producing statistics for the whole of Canada and each of the provinces. Statistics Canada's mission is to produce statistics that help Canadians better understand their country—its population, resources, economy, society, and culture. "Objective statistical information provides a solid foundation for informed decisions by elected representatives, businesses, unions, and non-profit organizations, as well as individual Canadians."

Before you visit the Statistics Canada website, consider the kinds of information that you think would be most useful to marketers. Now visit the website and review the information that is available. How well did Statistics Canada meet the information needs you thought were important?

http://www.statcan.ca

Secondary data save time and money if they help solve the researcher's problem. Even if the problem is not solved, secondary data have other advantages. They can aid in formulating the problem statement and suggest research methods and other types of data needed for solving the problem. In addition, secondary data can pinpoint the kinds of people to approach and their locations and serve as a basis of comparison for other data. The disadvantages of secondary data stem mainly from a mismatch between the researcher's unique problem and the purpose for which the secondary data were originally gathered, which are typically different. For example, a major consumer-products manufacturer wanted to determine the market potential for a fireplace log made of coal rather than compressed wood byproducts. The researcher found plenty of secondary data about total wood consumed as fuel, quantities consumed in each province, and types of wood burned. Secondary data were also available about consumer attitudes and purchase patterns of wood byproduct fireplace logs. The wealth of secondary data provided the researcher with many insights into the artificial log market. Yet nowhere was there any information that would tell the firm whether consumers would buy artificial logs made of coal.

The quality of secondary data may also pose a problem. Often secondary data sources do not give detailed information that would enable a researcher to assess their quality or relevance. Whenever possible, a researcher needs to address these important questions: Who gathered the data? Why were the data obtained? What methodology was used? How were classifications (such as heavy users versus light users) developed and defined? When was the information gathered?

The New Age of Secondary Information: The Internet

Gathering secondary data, while necessary in almost any research project, has traditionally been a tedious and boring job. The researcher often had to write to government agencies, trade associations, or other secondary data providers and then wait days or weeks for a reply that might never come. Often, one or more trips to the library were required and the researcher might find that needed reports were checked out or missing. With the rapid development of the Internet and World Wide Web in the last few years, however, much of the drudgery associated with the collection of secondary data has been eliminated.

Finding Secondary Data on the Internet

If you know the address of a particular website that contains the secondary data that you are searching for, you can type a description of what you are looking for directly into your Web browser (Netscape Navigator and Microsoft Internet Explorer are the dominant browsers).

Search Engines

Sites such as AltaVista, Excite, and Google have become popular with researchers looking for information on the Web. These organizations offer *search engines* that scan the Web looking for sites on a designated topic. Each search engine uses its own indexing system to locate relevant information. All of them allow users to enter one or more keywords that will initiate a search of the databases of websites for all occurrences of those words. They then return listings that allow users to go immediately to the sites described.

Remember that the Internet is a self-publishing medium. Your visits to search engines will yield files with a wide range of quality from a variety of sources. Try out multiple sites when you are investigating a topic.

Directories

In addition to search engines, you can use subject directories on the Web to explore a subject. There are two basic types of directories: (1) academic and professional directories, often created and maintained by subject experts to support the needs of researchers, and (2) commercial portals, which cater to the general public and are competing for traffic. Directories depend upon people to compile their listings.

- *Academic and professional directories* are created by librarians or subject experts and tend to be associated with libraries and academic institutions. These collections are created to enhance the research process and help users find high-quality sites of interest. A careful selection process is applied, and links to the selected resources are usually annotated. These collections are often created to serve an institution's constituency but may be useful to any researcher. As a rule, these sites do not generate income or carry advertising. The CBCA (Canadian Business and Current Affairs) is a multidisciplinary database with a Canadian focus. It is an academic directory, and the subjects it covers include current events, business, education, science and medicine, arts, law, academia, and lifestyle.
- *Commercial portals* are created to generate income and serve the general public. These services link to a wide range of topics and often emphasize entertainment, commerce, hobbies, sports, travel, and other interests not necessarily covered by academic directories. These sites seek to draw traffic in order to support advertising. As a part of this goal, the directory is offered in conjunction with a number of additional customer services. Yahoo! is an example of a commercial portal.

> **ON LINE**
>
> **Coca-Cola Store**
>
> When you are asked for your opinion on the Coke Store website, is Coca-Cola doing marketing research or gathering information for a DSS? Read the whole survey before deciding. Which did you pick and why?
>
> **http://www.coca-colastore.com**

The lines between directories and search engines are blurring. Directories are present at some search engine sites, and sometimes their contents are searched along with content from the general Web. For example, AltaVista offers the LookSmart directory; Infoseek shares the screen with the directory at the Go Network; Excite has its own directory; and Lycos offers the directory contents from the Netscape Open Directory. Directory results are sometimes placed before search results to steer users to the directory's content. This can be a useful way of getting at substantive content relating to your query. Most subject directories offer a search engine mechanism to query the database.

Sites of Interest to Marketing Researchers

A number of websites are accessed daily by marketing researchers in search of information. These sites offer an incredible variety of information. A list of those used most often is shown in Exhibit 7.2.

Periodical, Newspaper, and Book Databases

Several excellent periodical, newspaper, and book databases are available to researchers. Some can be directly accessed via the Internet and others through your local library's website. A list of these databases is shown in Exhibit 7.3.

Internet Discussion Groups and Special Interest Groups as Sources of Secondary Data

A primary means of communicating with other professionals and special interest groups on the Internet is through newsgroups. With an Internet connection and newsreader software, you can visit any newsgroup supported by your service provider. If your service provider does not offer newsgroups or does not carry the group in which you are interested, you can find one of the publicly available newsgroup servers that does carry the group you would like to read.

Newsgroups function much like bulletin boards for a particular topic or interest. A newsgroup is established to focus on a particular topic. Readers stop by that newsgroup to read messages left by other people, post responses to others' questions, and send rebuttals to comments with which they disagree. Generally, there is some management of the messages to keep discussions within the topic area and to remove offensive material. However, readers of a newsgroup are free to discuss any issue and communicate with anyone in the world who visits that newsgroup. Images and data files can be exchanged in newsgroups, just as they can be exchanged via e-mail.

newsgroups
Function like bulletin boards on the Internet. They are established to focus on a particular topic.

With over 250,000 newsgroups currently in existence and more being added every day, there is a newsgroup for nearly every hobby, profession, and lifestyle. Newsgroup messages look like e-mail messages. They contain a subject title, author, and a message body. Unlike normal e-mail messages, though, newsgroup messages are threaded discussions. This means that any reply to a previous message will appear linked to that message. Therefore, you can follow a discussion between two or more people by starting at the original message and following the links (or threads) to each successive reply. You can send images, sound files, and video clips attached to your message for anyone to download and examine.

Planning the Research Design and Gathering Primary Data

research design
Specifies which research questions must be answered, how and when the data will be gathered, and how the data will be analyzed.

Good secondary data can help researchers conduct a thorough situation analysis. With that information, researchers can list their unanswered questions and rank them. Researchers must then decide the exact information required to answer the questions. The **research design** specifies which research questions must be answered, how and when the data will be gathered, and how the data will be analyzed. Typically, the project budget is finalized after the research design has been approved.

EXHIBIT 7.2

Some Sources of Secondary Data for Marketing Researchers on the Web

ORGANIZATION	URL	DESCRIPTION
American Demographics/Marketing Tools	http://www.marketingtools.com	Searches the full text of all of *American Demographics* and *Marketing Tools.*
American Marketing Association	http://www.ama.org	Searches all of the AMA's publications by using keywords.
BLS Consumer Expenditure Surveys	http://stats.bls.gov/cex/home.htm	Provides information on the buying habits of consumers, including data on their expenditures, income, and consumer credit.
BuildingBrands	http://www.buildingbrands.com	A resource for anyone interested in brands and how to build them.
BusinessGateway.ca	http://businessgateway.ca	BusinessGateway.ca provides a single access point to all the government services and information needed to start, run, and grow a business.
Canada Business Service Centres (CBSCs)	http://www.cbsc.org	The CBSCs provide a wide range of information on government services, programs, and regulations, and can answer questions about starting a new business or improving an existing one.
CanadaOne	http://www.canadaone.com	The CanadaOne website includes an on-line magazine, a Canadian business directory, Canadian-specific business resources, a technology centre, and several other promotional tools designed to help Canadians grow their businesses.
Canadian Advertising Rates & Data (CARD)	http://www.cardmedia.com	Advertising rates and related data are available on every significant medium in Canada and on selected international media.
Canadian Business	http://www.canadianbusiness.com	Canadian Business magazine appeals to leaders, entrepreneurs, and innovators of corporate Canada by providing them with the insight they need to make the most informed management decisions.
Canadian Institute of Marketing	http://www.cinstmarketing.ca	Members of the institute are accredited professionals who have the qualifications and experience to provide services in marketing, including the following: Advertising, Branding and Corporate Identity; Communications Audits; Corporate Communications; Customer Relations Management; Database Marketing; Direct Mail and Response; Graphics Design; Interactive Marketing—websites, CD-ROM etc.; International Marketing; Marketing Audits; Marketing Plans; Marketing Research; Marketing Training and Seminars; Public Relations and Publicity; Sales Presentations; Sales Promotion/Incentive Programs; Speeches; Telemarketing; Trade Shows and Exhibit Marketing; and website Marketing.

(continued)

(continued)

ORGANIZATION	URL	DESCRIPTION
Canadian Marketing Association	http://www.the-cma.org	The association benefits its members in five key areas: market protection and self-regulation; stakeholder confidence; information and intelligence; education and skills improvement; and networking and business development.
Canadian Trade Index	http://www.ctidirectory.com	This index provides a list of more than 29,000 suppliers of industrial products and services; some 25,000 products and service categories; and the ability to search by company name, product/services description, or trademark.
ClickZ Network	http://www.clickz.com/stats	Viewers can browse the latest research compiled from several reputable firms, including Media Metrix, Greenfield Online, Intelliquest, and Inteco. The geography page fills you in on surveys about on-line populations around the world. There's also a generous section on e-commerce that breaks out research in different markets, such as advertising, finance, and retail. Peek into the stats toolbox for a motherlode of lists on everything from weekly usage data to the Top-10 banner ads.
The Dismal Scientist	http://www.economy.com/dismal	An authoritative site offering timely U.S. economic information, with comprehensive data and analysis at the metro, state, and national levels. There are also data and analyses of global issues, including situations facing Asia, South America, and Europe. Visitors can rank states and metro areas on more than 100 economic, socioeconomic, and demographic categories.
Easy Analytic Software	http://www.easidemographics.com	Easy Analytic Software, a New York City-based developer and marketer of demographic data, offers demographic site reports, or three-ring studies, including current estimates for population and households. Each three-ring study offers census estimates for race, ethnicity, age distribution, and income distribution, as well as weather data. The site also offers 1 million pages of U.S. demographic reports for all zip codes, counties, metropolitan areas, cities, sectional centres, television markets, states, and other geographies.
EconData	http://www.econdata.net	A premier site for researchers interested in economics and demographics. There are a tremendous number of links to government, private, and academic data sources. Check out the Top-10 data sources list.
Encyclopedia Britannica	http://www.britannica.com	Entire 32-volume encyclopedia is available free on-line.
Equifax National Decision Systems	http://www.equifax.com/biz/index.shtml	Provides access to a wide range of secondary data on many topics. Most must be purchased.
ESRI	http://www.esribis.com	On ESRI Business Information Solutions' site, U.S. users can type in their zip codes to get a snapshot of the dominant profile type in their town. Population figures are available for the zips, as are percentages for ethnicity and gender. Median household income, average home values, and average rents are also presented.
Financial Post Data Group	http://www.financialpost.com	Provides a broad range of relevant data to help with key business decisions including the following: over 200 full-text databases, trade journals, magazines and newswires; current financials and company data on over 300,000 Canadian companies.
Frasers Canadian Trade Directory	http://www.frasers.com	A directory that includes more than 40,000 suppliers of industrial products and services; more than 80,000 branch offices; about 30,000 product and service categories; and the ability to search by company, product/service, or brand name.
Government of Canada	http://canada.gc.ca	Provides a listing and links to all major Canadian government agencies and departments.
Industry Canada	http://www.ic.gc.ca	Industry Canada provides programs and services, for the purpose of helping to build a dynamic and innovative economy where all Canadians have the opportunity to benefit from more and better-paying jobs, stronger business growth, and a marketplace that is fair, efficient, and competitive.

(continued)

(continued)

ORGANIZATION	URL	DESCRIPTION
Marketing Magazine	**http://www.marketingmag.ca**	Current articles on marketing and advertising in Canada including an annual Market Research Guide that lists over 50 different Canadian-based market research firms and the Media Digest, a detailed information source on media in Canada.
Marketing Research Association	**http://www.mra-net.org**	Analyzes causes and solutions of "declining respondent cooperation"; links to research suppliers.
Mediamark Research	**http://www.mediamark.com/mri docs/toplinereports.html**	Marketers and researchers looking for demographic data on magazines, cable TV, or 53 different product or service categories can find it at Top-Line Reports site. Top-Line Reports breaks down cable TV networks according to viewers' age, gender, median age, and income. Magazines are listed by total audience, circulation, readers per copy, median age, and income.
Nielsen Media Research	**http://www.nielsen-netratings.com**	Course on Internet audience information. Researchers can find data and Internet growth and user patterns.
Purchasing Management Association of Canada	**http://www.pmac.ca**	PMAC is dedicated to serving the needs of the supply management practitioner and the business community by advancing the strategic value of supply management, through continuous learning, standards of practice, advocacy and promotion, research, partnerships, and networking.
@ResearchInfo.com	**http://www.researchinfo.com**	A source for information on the market research industry.
Scott's Directories	**http://www.scottsinfo.com**	Provides information on 115,000 Canadian manufacturers, wholesalers, distributors, and other businesses including product/service, revenue, year established, square footage, company executives, ISO number, and number of employees.
Small Business Canada	**http://sbinfocanada.about.com**	Provides business resources such as articles on particular topics, indexes, and one-stop resource pages.
Standards Council of Canada	**http://www.scc.ca**	Publishes the Consumer Products Safety Guide and offers a variety of programs and services for organizations and individuals who deal either directly or indirectly with standardization issues. Its programs and services can be divided into three broad areas: standards; conformity assessment; and intergovernmental affairs and trade.
Statistics Canada	**http://www.statcan.ca**	A wealth of Canadian statistical data, including the Census of Canada and other statistics on the economy, communication, transportation and trade, international trade, manufacturing and construction, census of agriculture, finance and services, geography, environment, the population, health, education, families, households and housing, labour, employment and unemployment, culture, leisure and travel, government, justice and crime.
Strategis	**http://strategis.ic.gc.ca**	Strategis is Industry Canada's information website and is a rich source of information including but not limited to the following data of interest to market researchers: trade mark searches, copyrights and patents, market research, technology, innovations, economic analysis and statistics, forecasts, business information by sector and consumer information.
Strategy Magazine	**http://www.strategymag.com**	Current articles on marketing and advertising in Canada.
Transport Canada	**http://www.tc.gc.ca**	Statistics and information on Canada's transportation systems and infrastructure.
USA Data	**http://www.usadata.com**	Provides access to U.S. consumer lifestyle data on a local, regional, or national basis.
World Opinion	**http://www.worldopinion.com**	Perhaps the premier site for the marketing research industry; thousands of marketing research reports available.

EXHIBIT 7.3

Full-Text Periodical, Newspaper, and Book Databases Used by Marketing Researchers

SOURCE	DESCRIPTION
ABI/INFORM	Updated monthly; provides in-depth coverage of journal articles about business conditions, trends, corporate strategies and tactics, management techniques, competitive and product information, and a wide variety of other topics. It gives you citations, substantive abstracts, and recently, full text of articles from more than 1,300 leading business and management publications, including marketing journals such as the *Journal of Marketing, JMR: Journal of Marketing Research*; and *Journal of the Academy of Marketing Science.*
Canadian Encyclopedia	The Canadian Encyclopedia Online "provides a reliable source of Canadian information" ranging from agriculture to zoology.
Canadian Newsstand	Canadian Newsstand provides the fulltext of 13 Canadian newspapers. The database includes full access to the articles, columns, editorials, and features published in each newspaper. Database content is updated daily following a seven-day embargo period.
CBCA: Canadian Business and Current Affairs	This is a multidisciplinary database with a Canadian focus. Subjects covered include: current events, business, education, science and medicine, arts, law, academia, and lifestyle.
CBCA Education	CBCA Fulltext Education is a bibliographic database providing indexing and fulltext access to the principal education literature published in Canada. Materials are collected from across the country to provide current information to teachers, administrators, researchers, and academics. Items of both practical and research value are indexed. Journal articles, government and research reports, monographs, book announcements, curriculum documents, and graduate dissertations in education are included in CBCA Fulltext Education.
CPI.Q	A database containing articles from a comprehensive list of Canadian and international journals, magazines, selected sections of *The Globe and Mail*, Canadian biographies, and other reference content from Gale Group, all with a Canadian focus.
Dow Jones Interactive	Includes full-text news and articles from over 3,400 sources including newspapers from around the world, as well as information on companies, industries, stocks, bonds, mutual funds, and foreign exchange rates; updated daily.
EconLit	Provides bibliographic coverage of a wide range of economics-related literature from 1963 to the present. EconLit indexes journals, books, and dissertations and covers both economic theory and application. It is updated monthly. Virtually all records include abstracts. Also included are the full text of book reviews published in the *Journal of Economic Literature* since 1993. Major areas of coverage include agricultural and natural resource economics, business administration and business, country studies, economic development, technological change, and growth, economic history, financial economics, general economics and teaching, health, education, and welfare, industrial organization, international economics, labour and demographic economics, law and economics, macroeconomics and monetary economics, mathematical and quantitative methods, methodology and history of economic thought, microeconomics, public economics, and urban, rural, and regional economics.
Economist Intelligence Unit: Country Information	The EIU produces objective and timely analysis and forecasts of the political, economic, and business environment in more than 180 countries. It also produces reports on certain strategic industries and on the latest management thinking. Its services are aimed at senior executives, their support staff, and managers responsible for international operations.
Financial Post Reports	Historical Reports, Investor Reports, and Industry Reports on Canada's leading 500 publicly traded companies.
JSTOR	JSTOR, a project begun with a grant from the Mellon Foundation, seeks to digitize the complete back runs of selected journals in the humanities and social sciences, and make them available to subscribers on the Internet. About 120 titles are currently available, from volume 1 of each title (whatever year that may be) to the volume for three to five years ago. The goal of the project is to archive historical data, not compete with publishers who may be providing access to recent volumes of their journal titles. Over 4 million pages are now available. New titles and fields are being added constantly. The capacity for searching across disciplines opens up new possibilities for scholarship and research.
Valueline	The Valueline Investment Survey is one of the most widely used independent investment information services in the world. It includes full-page, individual stock reports (encapsulating the company's past performance, current status, and outlook) and industry reviews. The Valueline Investment Survey is a comprehensive source of information and advice on approximately 1,700 stocks, more than 90 industries, the stock market, and the economy.
World Book Online	World Book Online is "your online route to up-to-date, reliable, authoritative, easy-to-understand information and an array of supplementary search tools and information sources."
World News Digest	FACTS.com brings together complete content from the Facts On File World News Digest database since 1940 and selected content from six other reference databases to answer questions about events, issues, statistics, and people of the last 60 years. Features include maps, photographs, historic documents, and overviews of key issues, newsmakers, and events. All relevant materials are connected using approximately 500,000 Internal hyperlinks. FACTS.com is updated every week and headline news stories from Reuters are updated every hour.

Do convenience polls qualify as bona fide survey research? The woman pictured here is casting a poll vote in a survey asking Australians whether they should cut constitutional ties with Britain (Country) or retain Queen Elizabeth as Australia's constitutional monarch (Queen).

Sometimes research questions can be answered by gathering more secondary data; otherwise, primary data may be needed. **Primary data**, or information collected for the first time, can be used for solving the particular problem under investigation. The main advantage of primary data is that they will answer a specific research question that secondary data cannot answer. For example, suppose Harvey's Hamburgers wants to add a new chicken sandwich to its menu and it has to decide between two different chicken sandwich meals it has developed. Which one will consumers like better? Secondary data will not help answer this question. Instead, targeted consumers must try each sandwich and evaluate the tastes, textures, appearance, and nutritional value of each meal. Another advantage of primary data over secondary data is they are current and researchers know the source. Sometimes researchers gather the data themselves rather than assign projects to outside companies. Researchers also specify the methodology of the research. Secrecy can be maintained because the information is proprietary. In contrast, secondary data are available to all interested parties for relatively small fees.

primary data
Information collected for the first time. Can be used for solving the particular problem under investigation.

Gathering primary data is expensive; costs can range from a few thousand dollars for a limited survey to several million for a nationwide study. For instance, a nationwide, 15-minute telephone interview with 1,000 adult males can cost $50,000 for everything, including a data analysis and report. Because primary data gathering is so expensive, firms commonly cut back on the number of interviews to save money. Larger companies that conduct many research projects use another cost-saving technique. They piggyback studies, or gather data on two different projects using one questionnaire. The drawback is that answering questions about, say, dog food and gourmet coffee may be confusing to respondents. Piggybacking also requires a longer interview (sometimes a half hour or longer), which tires respondents. The quality of the answers typically declines, with people giving curt replies and thinking, "When will this end?!" A lengthy interview also makes people less likely to participate in other research surveys.[8]

Nevertheless, the disadvantages of primary data gathering are usually offset by the advantages. It is often the only way of solving a research problem. And with a variety of techniques available for research—including surveys, observations, and experiments—primary research can address almost any marketing question.

Survey Research

survey research
The most popular technique for gathering primary data. A researcher interacts with people to obtain facts, opinions, and attitudes.

The most popular technique for gathering primary data is **survey research**, in which a researcher interacts with people to obtain facts, opinions, and attitudes. Exhibit 7.4 summarizes the characteristics of traditional forms of research.

In-Home Personal Interviews

Although in-home personal interviews often provide high-quality information, they tend to be very expensive because of the interviewers' travel time and costs. Therefore, they are rapidly disappearing from the marketing researcher's survey toolbox.

Mall Intercept Interviews

mall intercept interview
A survey research method that involves interviewing people in the common areas of shopping malls.

The **mall intercept interview** is conducted in the common areas of shopping malls or in a market research office within the mall. It is the economy version of the door-to-door interview, with personal contact between interviewer and respondent, minus the interviewer's travel time and costs. To conduct this type of interview, the research firm rents office space in the mall or pays a significant daily fee. One drawback is that it is hard to get a representative sample of the population.

EXHIBIT 7.4

Characteristics of Traditional Forms of Survey Research

CHARACTERISTIC	IN-HOME PERSONAL INTERVIEWS	MALL INTERCEPT INTERVIEWS	CENTRAL-LOCATION TELEPHONE INTERVIEWS	SELF-ADMINISTERED AND ONE-TIME MAIL SURVEYS	MALL PANEL SURVEYS	EXECUTIVE INTERVIEWS	FOCUS GROUPS
Cost	High	Moderate	Moderate	Low	Moderate	High	Low
Time span	Moderate	Moderate	Fast	Slow	Relatively slow	Moderate	Fast
Use of interviewer probes	Yes	Yes	Yes	No	Yes	Yes	Yes
Ability to show concepts to respondent	Yes (also taste tests)	Yes (also taste tests)	No	Yes	Yes	Yes	Yes
Management control over interviewer	Low	Moderate	High	n/a	n/a	Moderate	High
General data quality	High	Moderate	High to moderate	Moderate to low	Moderate	High	Moderate
Ability to collect large amounts of data	High	Moderate	Moderate to low	Low to moderate	Moderate	Moderate	Moderate
Ability to handle complex questionnaires	High	Moderate	High if computer-aided	Low	Low	High	Low

However, an interviewer can also probe when necessary—a technique used to clarify a person's response. For example, an interviewer might ask, "What did you like best about the salad dressing you just tried?" The respondent might reply, "Taste." This answer doesn't provide a lot of information, so the interviewer could probe by saying, "Can you tell me a little bit more about taste?" The respondent then elaborates: "Yes, it's not too sweet, it has the right amount of pepper, and I love that hint of garlic."

Mall intercept interviews must be brief. Only the shortest ones are conducted while respondents are standing. Usually, researchers invite respondents to their office for interviews, which are still rarely over 15 minutes long. The researchers often show respondents concepts for new products or a test commercial or have them taste a new food product. The overall quality of mall intercept interviews is about the same as telephone interviews.

Marketing researchers are applying computer technology in mall interviewing. The first technique is **computer-assisted personal interviewing**. The researcher conducts in-person interviews, reads questions to the respondent off a computer screen, and directly keys the respondent's answers into the computer. A second approach is **computer-assisted self-interviewing**. A mall interviewer intercepts and directs willing respondents to nearby computers. Each respondent reads questions off a computer screen and directly keys his or her answers into a computer. The third use of technology is fully automated self-interviewing. Respondents are guided by interviewers or independently approach a centrally located computer station or kiosk, read questions off a screen, and directly key their answers into the station's computer.

computer-assisted personal interviewing
An interviewing method in which the interviewer reads the questions from a computer screen and enters the respondent's data directly into the computer.

computer-assisted self-interviewing
An interviewing method in which a mall interviewer intercepts and directs willing respondents to nearby computers where the respondent reads questions off a computer screen and directly keys his or her answers into a computer.

Telephone Interviews

Compared to the personal interview, the telephone interview costs less and may provide the best sample of any traditional survey procedure. Most telephone interviewing is conducted from a specially designed phone room called a **central-location telephone (CLT) facility**. A phone room has many phone lines, individual interviewing stations, sometimes monitoring equipment, and headsets. The research firm typically will interview people nationwide from a single location.

central-location telephone (CLT) facility
A specially designed phone room used to conduct telephone interviewing.

Many CLT facilities offer computer-assisted interviewing. The interviewer reads the questions from a computer screen and enters the respondent's data directly into the computer. The researcher can stop the survey at any point and immediately print out the survey results. Thus, a researcher can get a sense of the project as it unfolds and fine-tune the research design as necessary. An on-line interviewing system can also save time and money because data entry occurs as the response is recorded rather than as a separate process after the interview. Hallmark Cards found that an interviewer administered a printed questionnaire for its Shoebox Greeting cards in 28 minutes. The same questionnaire administered with computer assistance took only 18 minutes.

Mail Surveys

Mail surveys have several benefits: relatively low cost, elimination of interviewers and field supervisors, centralized control, and actual or promised anonymity for respondents (which may draw more candid responses). Some researchers feel that mail questionnaires give the respondent a chance to reply more thoughtfully and to check records, talk to family members, and so forth. A disadvantage is that mail questionnaires usually produce low response rates.

Low response rates pose a problem because certain elements of the population tend to respond more than others. The resulting sample may therefore not represent the surveyed population. For example, the sample may have too many retired people and too few working people. In this instance, answers to a question about attitudes toward the Canada Pension Plan might indicate a much more favourable overall view of the system than is actually the case. Another serious problem with mail surveys is that no one probes respondents to clarify or elaborate on their answers.

Mail panels like those operated by Toronto-based Ipsos-Reid offer an alternative to the one-shot mail survey. A mail panel consists of a sample of households recruited to participate by mail for a given period. Panel members often receive gifts in return for their participation. Essentially, the panel is a sample used several times. In contrast to one-time mail surveys, the response rates from mail panels are high. Rates of 70 percent (of those who agree to participate) are not uncommon.

Executive Interviews

executive interviews
A type of survey that involves interviewing businesspeople at their offices concerning industrial products or services.

Marketing researchers use **executive interviews** to conduct the industrial equivalent of door-to-door interviewing. This type of survey involves interviewing businesspeople, at their offices, concerning industrial products or services. For example, if Dell wanted information regarding user preferences for different features that might be offered in a new line of computer printers, it would need to interview prospective user-purchasers of the printers. It is appropriate to locate and interview these people at their offices.

This type of interviewing is very expensive. First, individuals involved in the purchase decision for the product in question must be identified and located. Sometimes lists can be obtained from various sources, but more frequently screening must be conducted over the telephone. A particular company is likely to have individuals of the type being sought, but locating those people within a large organization can be expensive and time-consuming. Once a qualified person is located, the next step is to get that person to agree to be interviewed and to set a time for the interview. This is not as hard as it might seem because most professionals seem to enjoy talking about topics related to their work.

Finally, an interviewer must go to the particular place at the appointed time. Long waits are frequently encountered; cancellations are not uncommon. This type of survey requires the very best interviewers because they are frequently interviewing on topics that they know very little about. Executive interviewing has essentially the same advantages and disadvantages as in-home interviewing.

Focus Groups

focus group
Seven to ten people who participate in a group discussion led by a moderator.

A **focus group** is a type of personal interviewing. Often recruited by random telephone screening, seven to ten people with certain desired characteristics form a focus group. These qualified consumers are usually offered an incentive (typically $30 to $50) to participate in a group discussion. The meeting place (sometimes resembling a living room, sometimes featuring a conference table) has audiotaping and perhaps videotaping equipment. It also likely has a viewing room with a one-way mirror so that clients (manufacturers or retailers) can watch the session. During the session, a moderator, hired by the research company, leads the group discussion.

Focus groups are much more than question-and-answer interviews. Market researchers draw a distinction between "group dynamics" and "group interviewing." The interaction provided in **group dynamics** is essential to the success of focus-group research; this interaction is the reason for conducting group rather than individual research. One of the essential postulates of group-session usage is the idea that a response from one person may become a stimulus for another, thereby generating an interplay of responses that may yield more information than if the same number of people had contributed independently.

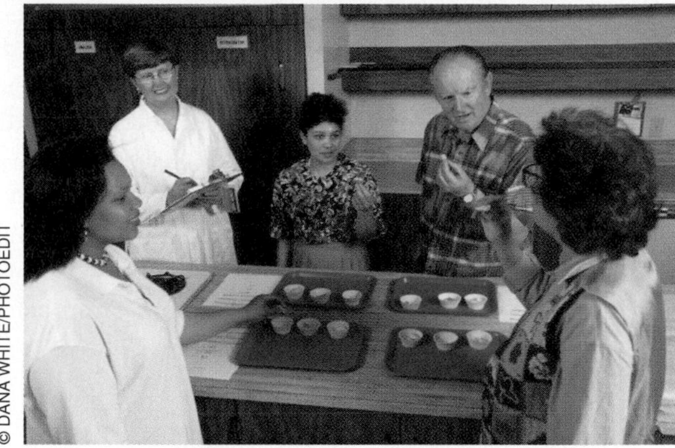

© DANA WHITE/PHOTOEDIT

Because of the group dynamics of focus groups, researchers can uncover more information than in a single interview. Here people are tasting cookies while a food scientist takes notes. Later they will conduct a focus group regarding the cookies.

Focus groups are occasionally used to brainstorm new product ideas or to screen concepts for new products. Ford Motor Company, for example, asked consumers to drive several automobile prototypes. These "test drivers" were then brought together in focus groups. During the discussions, consumers complained that they were scuffing their shoes because the rear seats lacked foot room. In response, Ford sloped the floor underneath the front seats, widened the space between the seat adjustment tracks, and made the tracks in the Taurus and Sable models out of smooth plastic instead of metal.

group dynamics
Group interaction essential to the success of focus-group research.

A new system by FocusVision Network allows client companies and advertising agencies to view live focus groups from distant locations. For example, the private satellite network would allow a researcher in Toronto observe an Edmonton focus group and control two cameras in the viewing room. The researcher can get a full-group view or a close-up, and zoom or pan the participants. The researcher can also communicate directly with the moderator using an ear receiver. Ogilvy Mather, a large advertising agency whose clients include StarKist SeaFoods, Seagram's, MasterCard, and Burger King, has installed this system.

The newest development in qualitative research is the on-line or cyber focus group. A number of organizations are currently offering this new means of conducting focus groups. The process is fairly simple.

- The research firm builds a database of respondents via a screening questionnaire on its website.
- When a client comes to a firm with a need for a particular focus group, the firm goes to its database and identifies individuals who appear to qualify. It sends an e-mail message to these individuals, asking them to log on to a particular site at a particular time scheduled for the group. The firm pays them an incentive for their participation.
- The firm develops a discussion guide similar to the one used for a conventional focus group.
- A moderator runs the group by typing in questions on-line for all to see. The group operates in an environment similar to that of a chat room so that all participants see all questions and all responses.
- The firm captures the complete text of the focus group and makes it available for review after the group has finished.

Many advantages are claimed for cyber groups. Cyber Dialogue, a marketing research company specializing in cyber groups, lists the following benefits of on-line focus groups on its website:

ON LINE

Marketing Magazine

Go to *Marketing Magazine*'s website and participate in its on-line poll. What do you think about the idea of polling "marketers"? How do you think *Marketing Magazine* will use the information?

http://www.marketingmag.ca

- *Speed:* Typically, focus groups can be recruited and conducted, with delivery of results, within five days of client approval.
- *Cost effectiveness:* Off-line focus groups incur costs for facility rental, airfare, hotel, and food. None of these costs is incurred with on-line focus groups.
- *Broad geographic scope:* In a given focus group, you can speak to people in Victoria, B.C., and Hamilton, Ontario, at the same time.
- *Accessibility:* On-line focus groups give you access to individuals who otherwise might be difficult to recruit (e.g., business travellers, doctors, and mothers with infants).
- *Honesty:* From behind their screen names, respondents are anonymous to other respondents and tend to talk more freely about issues that might create inhibitions in a face-to-face group.

Cyber Dialogue charges $3,000 for its focus groups. This cost compares very favourably to a cost in the range of $7,000 without travel costs for conventional focus groups. Unfortunately, no systematic evaluation comparing on-line focus groups and conventional focus groups has been done at this time.

Questionnaire Design

All forms of survey research require a questionnaire. Questionnaires ensure that all respondents will be asked the same series of questions. Questionnaires include three basic types of questions: open-ended, closed-ended, and scaled-response (see

EXHIBIT 7.5

Types of Questions Found on Questionnaires for National Market Research

OPEN-ENDED QUESTIONS	CLOSED-ENDED QUESTIONS	SCALED-RESPONSE QUESTION
1. What advantages, if any, do you think ordering from a mail-order catalogue offers compared to shopping at a local retail outlet? (Probe: What else?) 2. Why do you have one or more of your rugs or carpets professionally cleaned rather than having you or someone else in the household clean them? 3. What is there about the colour of the eye shadow that makes you like it the best?	**Dichotomous** 1. Did you heat the Danish product before serving it? Yes ....1 No ....2 2. The federal government doesn't care what people like me think. Agree ....1 Disagree ....2 **Multiple choice** 1. I'd like you to think back to the last footwear of any kind that you bought. I'll read you a list of descriptions and would like for you to tell me which category they fall into. (*Read list and circle proper category.*) Dress and/or formal ....1 Casual ....2 Canvas/trainer/gym shoes ....3 Specialized athletic shoes ....4 Boots ....5 2. In the last three months, have you used Noxzema skin cream . . . (Circle all that apply.) As a facial wash ....1 For moisturizing the skin ....2 For treating blemishes ....3 For cleansing the skin ....4 For treating dry skin ....5 For softening skin ....6 For sunburn ....7 For making the facial skin smooth 8	Now that you have used the rug cleaner, would you say that you... (*Circle one.*) Would definitely buy it ....1 Would probably buy it ....2 Might or might not buy it ....3 Probably would not buy it ....4 Definitely would not buy it 5

Exhibit 7.5). An **open-ended question** encourages an answer phrased in the respondent's own words. Researchers get a rich array of information based on the respondent's frame of reference. In contrast, a **closed-ended question** asks the respondent to make a selection from a limited list of responses. Traditionally, marketing researchers separate the two-choice question (called *dichotomous*) from the many-item type (often called *multiple choice*). A **scaled-response question** is a closed-ended question designed to measure the intensity of a respondent's answer.

open-ended question
An interview question that encourages an answer phrased in the respondent's own words.

closed-ended question
An interview question that asks the respondent to make a selection from a limited list of responses.

scaled-response question
A closed-ended question designed to measure the intensity of a respondent's answer.

Closed-ended and scaled-response questions are easier to tabulate than open-ended questions because response choices are fixed. On the other hand, unless the researcher designs the closed-ended question very carefully, an important choice may be omitted.

For example, suppose a food study asked this question: "Besides meat, which of the following items do you normally add to a taco that you prepare at home?"

Avocado	1	Olives (black/green)	6
Cheese (Monterey Jack/cheddar)	2	Onions (red/white)	7
Guacamole	3	Peppers (red/green)	8
Lettuce	4	Pimento	9
Mexican hot sauce	5	Sour cream	0

The list seems complete, doesn't it? However, consider the following responses: "I usually add a green, avocado-tasting hot sauce"; "I cut up a mixture of lettuce and spinach"; "I'm a vegetarian; I don't use meat at all. My taco is filled only with guacamole." How would you code these replies? As you can see, the question needs an "other" category.

A good question must also be clear and concise, and ambiguous language must be avoided. Take, for example, the question: "Do you live within 10 minutes of here?" The answer depends on the mode of transportation (maybe the person walks), driving speed, perceived time, and other factors. Instead, respondents should see a map with certain areas highlighted and be asked whether they live in one of those areas.

Designing and interpreting scaled-response questions can be particularly difficult in global marketing research. A researcher must fully understand cultural differences, as the "Global Perspectives" box explains.

Clarity also implies using reasonable terminology. A questionnaire is not a vocabulary test. Jargon should be avoided, and language should be geared to the target audience. A question such as: "What is the level of efficacy of your preponderant dishwasher powder?" would probably be greeted by a lot of blank stares. It would be much simpler to say: "Are you (1) very satisfied, (2) somewhat satisfied, or (3) not satisfied with your current brand of dishwasher powder?"

Stating the survey's purpose at the beginning of the interview also improves clarity. The respondents should understand the study's intentions and the interviewer's expectations. Sometimes, of course, to get an unbiased response, the interviewer must disguise the true purpose of the study. If an interviewer says, "We're conducting an image study for the Bank of Nova Scotia" and then proceeds to ask a series of questions about the bank, chances are the responses will be biased. Many times repondents will try to provide answer that they believe are "correct" or that the interviewer wants to hear.

Finally, to ensure clarity, the interviewer should avoid asking two questions in one; for example, "How did you like the taste and texture of McCain Triple Chill cake?" This question should be divided into two questions, one concerning taste and the other texture.

A question should also be unbiased. A question such as: "Have you purchased any quality Canadian Tire Mastercraft tools in the past six months?" biases respondents to think of the topic in a certain way (in this case, to link quality and Canadian Tire Mastercraft tools). Questions can also be leading: "Weren't you pleased with

ON LINE 

CreateSurvey.com

Design a marketing questionnaire to post on your class website using the tools offered by CreateSurvey. Visit the demo polls at the site for ideas and tips.

http://www.createsurvey.com

Brand Marketing International

Learn more about mystery shopping by requesting a mystery shopper kit from BMI and reading its shopper application.

http://www.bmiltd.com

GLOBAL PERSPECTIVES

Culture Complicates Global Marketing Research

Except in very unusual circumstances, customer interviews should always be conducted in the local language by local interviewers. That would include even those interviews conducted with respondents who speak English or French very well. Few people are as at ease or articulate in a second or third language as they are in their own mother tongue. By forcing respondents to speak a foreign language, you are, from the outset, limiting their ability to express their opinions and needs clearly and articulately.

Even something as straightforward as a scaled-response question should be given careful thought. It is best to utilize rating scales that make the most sense to the given population. For example, Canadians may be very comfortable giving performance ratings using an A–F "school grade" system. That scale, however, is meaningless to Germans, who are more familiar with a 1–6 rating scale, with 1 indicating the best performance and 6 indicating the worst performance. And of course the Japanese wouldn't understand our letter grades at all—they generally use a 100-point scale for these purposes. You may even find that different populations use the same rating scales differently. For example, Germans may consistently give lower grades than Italians, while Italians may consistently rate every attribute as more important than Spaniards. These differences need to be factored in during the analysis phase.

Cultural differences can also surface with an issue like participation incentives. The first question is, "Are cash incentives appropriate in this market?" In Japan, for example, incentives for businesspeople often take the form of a gift, rather than cash. Sometimes it is better to offer gift certificates to major department stores as incentives. Charitable donations might also be an option.[9]

Australia, Canada, the United Kingdom, and the United States have all been part of the British Empire and have all designated English as an official language. Therefore, cultural considerations are not important when designing and interpreting a marketing research study. Do you agree or disagree? Why? Door-to-door interviewing is almost nonexistent anymore in Canada. Do you think this is a worldwide trend? Why or why not? If a person in Regina, Saskatchewan, and another person in Beijing, responding to the same questionnaire (the only difference being that one is in English and one is in Mandarin), both give something a "6" rating, do their responses really mean the same thing? Isn't a "6" always a "6" on a scale of 1–7?

the good service you received last night at the Chateau Laurier Hotel?" (The respondent is all but instructed to say "yes.") These examples are quite obvious; unfortunately, bias is usually subtler. Even an interviewer's clothing or gestures can create bias.

Often getting people to answer a questionnaire is not easy. One innovative approach that ties research to gaming is thriving on the Internet. The "Ethics in Marketing" box discusses this new approach to data gathering.

Observation Research

observation research
A research method that relies on three types of observation: people watching people, people watching an activity, and machines watching people.

In contrast to survey research, **observation research** depends on watching what people do. Specifically, it can be defined as the systematic process of recording the behavioural patterns of people, objects, and occurrences without questioning or communicating with them. A market researcher using the observation technique witnesses and records information as events occur or compiles evidence from records of past events. Carried a step further, observation may involve watching people or phenomena and may be conducted by human observers or machines. Examples of these various observational situations are shown in Exhibit 7.6.

mystery shoppers
Researchers posing as customers who gather observational data about a store.

Two common forms of people-watching-people research are mystery shoppers and one-way mirror observations. **Mystery shoppers** are researchers posing as customers who gather observational data about a store (i.e., are the shelves neatly stocked?) and collect data about customer/employee interactions. In the latter case, of course, there is communication between the mystery shopper and the employee. The mystery shopper may ask, "How much is this item?" "Do you have this in blue?" or "Can you deliver this by Friday?" The interaction is not an interview, and communication occurs only so that the mystery shopper can observe the actions and comments of the employee. Mystery shopping is, therefore, classified as an observational marketing research method even though communication is often involved. Conducted on a continuous basis, mystery shopping can motivate and recognize service performance. Used as a benchmark, mystery shopping can pinpoint strengths and weaknesses for training operations and policy refinements.

ETHICS IN MARKETING

Find the Monkey and You Get to Fill Out a Questionnaire

Not all Internet sites have fallen on hard times. In the United States, sites like FreeLotto.com, Flipside.com, and TreeLoot.com are continuing to grow at a rapid pace. By offering free gifts, prizes, coupons, or big cash winnings, gaming and sweepstakes sites are able to sign up game players and get them to divulge their names, addresses, and, in some cases, hobbies, interests, and buying patterns. The sites then use the information to sell advertisers targeted e-mail lists or space in a daily e-mail message to players.

That is gold to advertisers who want to get better results by targeting their ads to specific users. Ford Motor Company, for example, could put ads in e-mails sent to users who indicated they might buy a car in the next 12 months. Or a credit card company could offer a new card with a bigger limit to someone who plans to buy a computer.

"It's market research disguised as a game," says analyst Jim Magahad of PC Data Corporation, a research firm in Reston, Virginia. "And the information they are getting is very valuable."

To lure players to those games, sites have come up with some pretty catchy campaigns. One of the most memorable approaches is TreeLoot's "Punch the Monkey" banner ad that has run for almost the past two years. The ad invites Web surfers to try to knock out a monkey zooming across a banner at the top of their screens. If you can click on the elusive monkey, you win $20 in credits that can be exchanged for discounts at Web retailers or other prizes—and you get linked to TreeLoot's website, where you can play the site's money-tree game to win more credits.

FreeLotto runs a daily lotto drawing that has $11 million in cash prizes available to be won each day. Players must provide a valid e-mail, postal address, and the name that will be on the cheque if they win. While choosing lottery numbers, users answer questions about interests in travel or any plans to buy a computer, car, or house. Plus, to submit their lotto numbers for the daily drawing, the players must click on one of several featured ads.

"It's direct mail without the postage, and the consumer does your daily entry—what could be better?" asks FreeLotto's chief executive Kevin Aronin.

Further, Jim Magahad of PC Data says the proliferation of Internet use among a broader population has helped boost the use of these sites. Gaming sites were the fastest-growing segment of the Internet last year, according to PC Data, and that is largely due to the willingness of people to give out information about themselves for the chance to win big.

"Now you have Middle America online—it's not just the affluent—and Middle America loves lotto," says Magahad.

Privacy concerns have largely been a moot point for the companies. Most promise not to disclose information without the players' consent, but the players, who volunteer the information, generally agree to let it be used.[10]

Are FreeLotto and TreeLoot really conducting marketing research? Is it ethical to require game participants to answer questions about purchase plans as a requirement to continue in the game? Is it ethical for a marketing research company to sell names, addresses, and question responses to companies? What if the respondent consents? Do you see any privacy issues here?

EXHIBIT 7.6

Observational Situations

SITUATION	EXAMPLE
People watching people	Observers stationed in supermarkets watch consumers select frozen Mexican dinners; the purpose is to see how much comparison shopping people do at the point of purchase.
People watching phenomena	Observer stationed at an intersection counts traffic moving in various directions.
Machines watching people	Movie or videotape cameras record behaviour as in the people-watching-people example above.
Machines watching phenomena	Traffic-counting machines monitor traffic flow.

At the Fisher-Price Play Laboratory, children are invited to spend 12 sessions playing with toys. Toy designers watch through one-way mirrors to see how children react to Fisher-Price's and other makers' toys. Fisher-Price, for example, had difficulty designing a toy lawn mower that children would play with. A designer, observing behind the mirror, noticed the children's fascination with soap bubbles. He then created a lawn mower that spewed soap bubbles. It sold over a million units in the first year.

Experiments

An **experiment** is a method a researcher can use to gather primary data. The researcher alters one or more variables—price, package design, shelf space, advertising theme, advertising expenditures—while observing the effects of those alterations on another

experiment
A method a researcher uses to gather primary data.

© MICHAEL GREENLAR/THE IMAGE WORKS

One interesting observation situation is toy-testing day camp. Pictured here, Fama Ana tries on a pair of "spy glasses" at Duracell Toy Testing Camp. In one week, over 1,000 children in 15 North American cities test 25 different toys while marketers look on.

variable (usually sales). The best experiments are those in which all factors are held constant except the ones being manipulated. The researcher can then observe that changes in sales, for example, result from changes in the amount of money spent on advertising.

Holding all other factors constant in the external environment is a monumental and costly, if not impossible, task. Such factors as competitors' actions, weather, and economic conditions are beyond the researcher's control. Yet market researchers have ways to account for the ever-changing external environment. Mars, the candy company, was losing sales to other candy companies. Traditional surveys showed that the shrinking candy bar was not perceived as a good value. Mars wondered whether a bigger bar sold at the same price would increase sales enough to offset the higher ingredient costs. The company designed an experiment in which the marketing mix stayed the same in different markets but the size of the candy bar varied. The substantial increase in sales of the bigger bar quickly proved that the additional costs would be more than covered by the additional revenue. Mars increased the bar size—and its market share and profits.

Specifying the Sampling Procedures

Once the researchers decide how they will collect primary data, their next step is to select the sampling procedures they will use. A firm can seldom take a census of all possible users of a new product, nor can they all be interviewed. Therefore, a firm must select a sample of the group to be interviewed. A **sample** is a subset from a larger population.

Several questions must be answered before a sampling plan is chosen. First, the population, or **universe**, of interest must be defined. This is the group from which the sample will be drawn. It should include all the people whose opinions, behaviour, preferences, attitudes, and so on are of interest to the marketer. For example, in a study whose purpose is to determine the market for a new canned dog food, the universe might be defined to include all current buyers of canned dog food.

sample
A subset from a large population.

universe
The population from which a sample will be drawn.

After the universe has been defined, the next question is whether the sample must be representative of the population. If the answer is "yes," a probability sample is needed. Otherwise, a nonprobability sample might be considered.

Probability Samples

A **probability sample** is a sample in which every element in the population has a known statistical likelihood of being selected. Its most desirable feature is that scientific rules can be used to ensure that the sample represents the population.

probability sample
A sample in which every element in the population has a known statistical likelihood of being selected.

One type of probability sample is a **random sample**—a sample arranged in such a way that every element of the population has an equal chance of being selected as part of the sample. For example, suppose a university is interested in getting a cross section of student opinions on a proposed sports complex to be built using student activity fees. If the university can acquire an up-to-date list of all the enrolled students, it can draw a random sample by using random numbers from a table (found in most statistics books) to select students from the list.

random sample
A sample arranged in such a way that every element of the population has an equal chance of being selected as part of the sample.

Nonprobability Samples

Any sample in which little or no attempt is made to get a representative cross section of the population can be considered a **nonprobability sample**. A common form of a nonprobability sample is the **convenience sample**, which uses respondents who are convenient or readily accessible to the researcher—for instance, employees, friends, or relatives.

nonprobability sample
Any sample in which little or no attempt is made to get a representative cross section of the population.

convenience sample
A form of nonprobability sample using respondents who are convenient or readily accessible to the researcher—for example, employees, friends, or relatives.

Nonprobability samples are acceptable as long as the researcher understands their nonrepresentative nature. Because of their lower cost, nonprobability samples are the basis of much marketing research.

Types of Errors

Whenever a sample is used in marketing research, two major types of error may occur: measurement error and sampling error. **Measurement error** occurs when there is a difference between the information desired by the researcher and the information provided by the measurement process. For example, people may tell an interviewer that they drink milk daily when they do not. Measurement error generally tends to be larger than sampling error.

measurement error
An error that occurs when there is a difference between the information desired by the researcher and the information provided by the measurement process.

Sampling error occurs when a sample somehow does not represent the target population. Sampling error can be of several types. **Nonresponse error** occurs when the sample actually interviewed differs from the sample drawn. This error happens because the original people selected to be interviewed either refused to cooperate or were inaccessible.

sampling error
An error that occurs when a sample somehow does not represent the target population.

nonresponse error
An error that occurs when the sample that responds is different from the sample that was selected

Frame error, another type of sampling error, arises when the sample drawn from a population differs from the target population. For instance, suppose a telephone survey is conducted to find out Toronto milk drinkers' attitudes toward milk consumption. If a Toronto telephone directory is used as the *frame* (the device or list from which the respondents are selected), the survey will contain a frame error. Not all Toronto milk drinkers have a phone, and many phone numbers are unlisted.

frame error
An error that occurs when a sample drawn from a population differs from the target population.

Random error occurs when the selected sample is an imperfect representation of the overall population. Random error represents how accurately the chosen sample's true average (mean) value reflects the population's true average (mean) value. For example, we might take a random sample of milk drinkers in Toronto and find that 16 percent regularly drink chocolate milk. The next day we might repeat the same sampling procedure and discover that 14 percent regularly drink chocolate milk. The difference is due to random error.

random error
An error that occurs when the selected sample is an imperfect representation of the overall population.

Collecting the Data

Marketing research field service firms collect most primary data. A **field service firm** specializes in interviewing respondents on a subcontracted basis. Many have offices throughout the country. A typical marketing research study involves data collection in several cities, requiring the marketer to work with a comparable number of field service firms. To ensure uniformity among all subcontractors, detailed field instructions should be developed for every job. Nothing should be open to chance; no interpretations of procedures should be left to subcontractors.

field service firm
A firm that specializes in interviewing respondents on a subcontracted basis.

Besides conducting interviews, field service firms provide focus-group facilities, mall intercept locations, test product storage, and kitchen facilities to prepare test food products. They also conduct retail audits (counting the amount of a product sold off retail shelves).

Analyzing the Data

After collecting the data, the marketing researcher proceeds to the next step in the research process: data analysis. The purpose of this analysis is to interpret and draw conclusions from the mass of collected data. The marketing researcher tries to organize and analyze those data by using one or more techniques common to marketing research: one-way frequency counts, cross-tabulations, and more sophisticated statistical analysis. Of these three techniques, one-way frequency counts are the simplest. One-way frequency tables record the responses to a question. For example, the answers to the question "What brand of microwave popcorn do you buy most often?" would provide a one-way frequency distribution. One-way frequency tables are always done in data analysis, at least as a first step, because they provide the researcher with a general picture of the study's results.

A **cross-tabulation**, or "cross-tab," lets the analyst look at the responses to one question in relation to the responses to one or more other questions. For example, what is the association between gender and the brand of microwave popcorn bought most

cross-tabulation
A method of analyzing data that lets the analyst look at the responses to one question in relation to the responses to one or more other questions.

EXHIBIT 7.7

Hypothetical Cross-Tabulation between Gender and Brand of Microwave Popcorn Purchased Most Frequently

BRAND	PURCHASE BY GENDER (%) MALE	FEMALE
Orville Redenbacher	31	48
Act II	12	6
Pop Rite	38	4
President's Choice	7	23
Weight Watchers	4	18
Other	8	0

frequently? Hypothetical answers to this question are shown in Exhibit 7.7. Although the Orville Redenbacher brand was popular with both males and females, it was more popular with females. Compared with women, men strongly preferred Pop Rite, whereas women were more likely than men to buy Weight Watchers popcorn.

Researchers can use many other more powerful and sophisticated statistical techniques, such as hypothesis testing, measures of association, and regression analysis. A description of these techniques goes beyond the scope of this book but can be found in any good marketing research textbook. The use of sophisticated statistical techniques depends on the researchers' objectives and the nature of the data gathered.

Preparing and Presenting the Report

After data analysis has been completed, the researcher must prepare the report and communicate the conclusions and recommendations to management. This is a key step in the process. If the marketing researcher wants managers to carry out the recommendations, he or she must convince them that the results are credible and justified by the data collected.

Researchers are usually required to present both written and oral reports on the project. Today, the written report is no more than a copy of the Microsoft® PowerPoint® slides used in the oral presentation. Both reports should be tailored to the audience. They should begin with a clear, concise statement of the research objectives, followed by a complete, but brief and simple, explanation of the research design or methodology employed. A summary of major findings should come next. The conclusion of the report should also present recommendations to management.

Most people who enter marketing will become research users rather than research suppliers. Thus, they must know what to notice in a report. As with many other items we purchase, quality is not always readily apparent. Nor does a high price guarantee superior quality. The basis for measuring the quality of a marketing research report is the research proposal. Did the report meet the objectives established in the proposal? Was the methodology outlined in the proposal followed? Are the conclusions based on logical deductions from the data analysis? Do the recommendations seem prudent, given the conclusions?

Following Up

The final step in the marketing research process is to follow up. The researcher should determine why management did or did not carry out the recommendations in the report. Was sufficient decision-making information included? What could have been done to make the report more useful to management? A good rapport between the product manager, or whoever authorized the project, and the market researcher is essential. Often they must work together on many studies throughout the year.

>> THE PROFOUND IMPACT OF THE INTERNET ON MARKETING RESEARCH

4 Discuss the profound impact of the Internet on marketing research

In many ways, the Internet has turned the world of marketing research upside-down. Old ways of conducting some types of research may soon seem as quaint as the steam-engine train. New techniques and new ways of conducting traditional marketing research are coming on-line in increasing numbers every day. By 2005, Internet marketing research will account for about 50 percent of all marketing research revenue in North America.[11]

There are several reasons for the success of Internet marketing research:

- It allows for better and faster decision making through much more rapid access to business intelligence.
- It improves the ability to respond quickly to customer needs and market shifts.
- It makes follow-up studies and longitudinal research much easier to conduct and more fruitful.
- It slashes labour- and time-intensive research activities (and associated costs), including mailing, telephone solicitation, data entry, data tabulation, and reporting.[12]

Advantages of Internet Surveys

The huge growth in the popularity of Internet surveys is the result of the many advantages offered by the Internet. The specific advantages of Internet surveys are related to many factors:

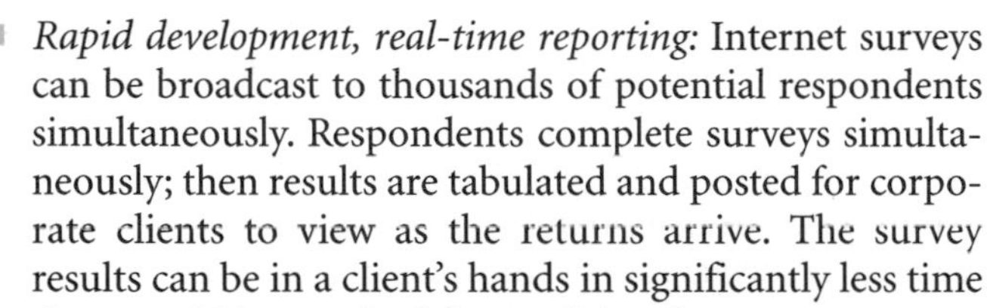

- *Rapid development, real-time reporting:* Internet surveys can be broadcast to thousands of potential respondents simultaneously. Respondents complete surveys simultaneously; then results are tabulated and posted for corporate clients to view as the returns arrive. The survey results can be in a client's hands in significantly less time than would be required for traditional surveys.
- *Dramatically reduced costs:* The Internet can cut costs by 25 to 40 percent and provide results in half the time it takes to do traditional telephone surveys. Data-collection costs account for a large proportion of any traditional market research budget. Telephone surveys are labour-intensive efforts incurring training, telecommunications, and management costs. Electronic methods eliminate these completely. While costs for traditional survey techniques rise proportionally with the number of interviews desired, electronic solicitations can grow in volume with little increase in project costs.

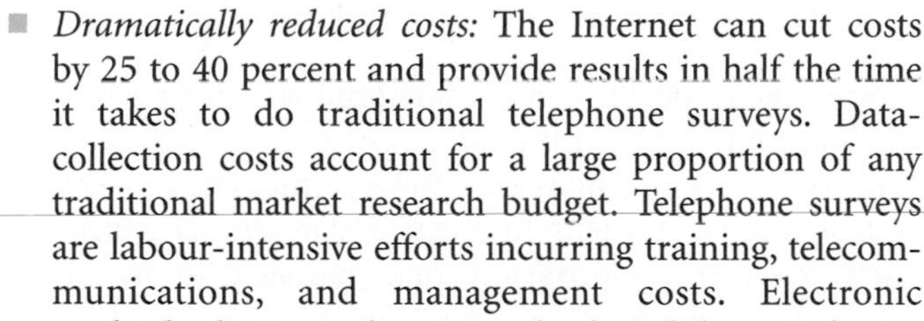

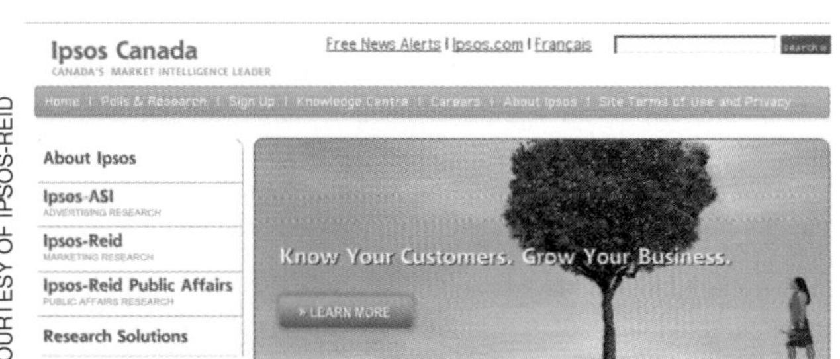

COURTESY OF IPSOS-REID

The Internet is becoming a powerful tool in marketing research with 17.2 million Canadians on-line and 54 percent of Canadians using broadband networks. Ipsos-Reid is a leading Canadian market research firm that uses the Internet to gather data about customers and their opinions.

- *Personalized questions and data:* Internet surveys can be highly personalized for greater relevance to each respondent's own situation, thus speeding the response process. Respondents enjoy a personalized survey because they are asked to answer only pertinent questions, can pause and resume the survey as needed, and can see previous responses and correct inconsistencies.
- *Improved respondent participation:* Busy respondents may be growing increasingly intolerant of "snail mail" or telephone-based surveys. Internet surveys take half as much time to complete as phone interviews, can be accomplished at the respondent's convenience (after work hours), and are much more stimulating and engaging. Graphics, interactivity, links to incentive sites,

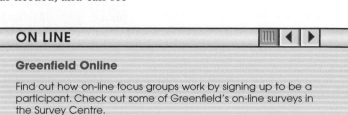

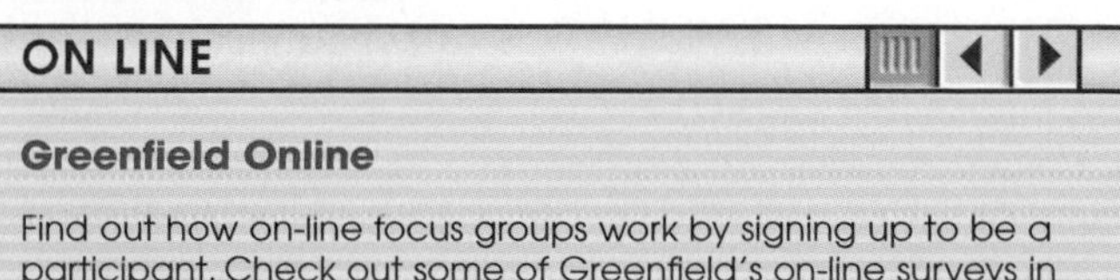

ON LINE

Greenfield Online

Find out how on-line focus groups work by signing up to be a participant. Check out some of Greenfield's on-line surveys in the Survey Centre.

http://www.greenfieldonline.com

and real-time summary reports make the interview enjoyable. The result? Much higher response rates.

- *Contact with the hard-to-reach:* Certain groups—doctors, high-income professionals, top management in Global 2000 firms—are among the most surveyed on the planet and the most difficult to reach. Many of these groups are well represented on-line. Internet surveys provide convenient anytime/anywhere access that makes it easy for busy professionals to participate.[13]

The rapid growth of Internet survey research is a result of the large number of Canadians on-line—the current estimate being about 75 percent, with 54 percent of these using broadband connections. This in turn has meant that researchers are finding that on-line and off-line research results are the same. For example, America Online's (AOL) Digital Marketing Services (DMS), an on-line research organization, has done a number of surveys with both on-line and off-line samples. DMS's clients include IBM, Eastman Kodak, and Procter & Gamble. In well over a hundred side-by-side comparisons of on-line and off-line studies, both techniques led clients to the same business decisions.[14] The guidance from both sets of data was the same.

Internet Samples

unrestricted Internet sample
A survey in which anyone with a computer and modem can fill out the questionnaire.

Internet samples may be classified as unrestricted, screened, or recruited.[15] In an **unrestricted Internet sample**, anyone who desires can complete the questionnaire. It is fully self-selecting and probably representative of nothing except Web surfers. The problem is exacerbated if the same Internet user can access the questionnaire repeatedly. For example, *InfoWorld*, a computer user magazine, decided to conduct its Readers Choice survey for the first time on the Internet. The results were so skewed by repeat voting for one product that the entire survey was publicly abandoned and the editor asked for readers' help to avoid the problem again. A simple solution to repeat respondents is to lock respondents out of the site after they have filled out the questionnaire.

screened Internet sample
An Internet sample with quotas based on desired sample characteristics.

Screened Internet samples adjust for the unrepresentativeness of the self-selected respondents by imposing quotas based on some desired sample characteristics. These are often demographic characteristics such as gender, income, and geographic region, or product-related criteria such as past purchase behaviour, job responsibilities, or current product use. The applications for screened samples are generally similar to those for unrestricted samples.

Screened sample questionnaires typically use a branching or skip pattern for asking screening questions to determine whether the full questionnaire should be presented to a respondent. Some Web survey systems can make immediate market segment calculations that first assign a respondent to a particular segment based on screening questions and then select the appropriate questionnaire to match the respondent's segment.

Alternatively, some Internet research providers maintain a "panel house" that recruits respondents who fill out a preliminary classification questionnaire. This information is used to classify respondents into demographic segments. Clients specify the desired segments, and the respondents who match the desired demographics are permitted to fill out the questionnaires of all clients who specify that segment.

recruited Internet sample
A sample in which respondents are prerecruited and must qualify to participate. They are then e-mailed a questionnaire or directed to a secure website.

Recruited Internet samples are used for targeted populations in surveys that require more control over the makeup of the sample. Respondents are recruited by telephone, mail, or e-mail, or in person. After qualification, they are sent the questionnaire by e-mail or are directed to a website that contains a link to the questionnaire. At websites, passwords are normally used to restrict access to the questionnaire to the recruited sample members. Since the makeup of the sample is known, completions can be monitored, and the participation rate can be improved by sending follow-up messages to those who do not complete the questionnaire.

Recruited samples are ideal in applications that already have a database from which to recruit the sample. For example, a good application would be a survey that used a customer database to recruit respondents for a purchaser satisfaction study.

Other Uses of the Internet by Marketing Researchers

The Internet revolution in marketing research has had an impact on more than just the way surveys are conducted. The management of the research process and the dissemination of information have also been greatly enhanced by the Internet. Several key areas have been affected by the Internet:

- *The distribution of requests for proposals (RFPs) and proposals:* Companies can now quickly and efficiently send RFPs to a select e-mail list of research suppliers. In turn, research suppliers can develop proposals and e-mail them back to clients. A process that used to take days using snail mail now occurs in a matter of hours.
- *Collaboration between the client and the research supplier in the management of a research project:* Now a researcher and client may both be looking at a proposal, RFP, report, or some type of statistical analysis at the same time on their respective computer screens while discussing it over the telephone. This setup is very powerful and efficient. Changes in the sample size, quotas, and other aspects of the research plan can be discussed and made immediately.
- *Data management and on-line analysis:* Clients can access their survey via the research supplier's secure website and monitor the data gathering in real time. The client can use sophisticated tools to actually do data analysis as the survey develops. This real-time analysis may result in changes in the questionnaire, sample size, or the types of respondents being interviewed. The research supplier and the client become partners in "just-in-time" marketing research.
- *Publication and distribution of reports:* Reports can be published to the Web directly from programs such as Microsoft® PowerPoint® and all the latest versions of leading word-processing, spreadsheet, and presentation software packages. This means that results are available to appropriate managers worldwide on an almost instantaneous basis. Reports can be searched for the content of interest using the same Web browser used to view the report.
- *Viewing of oral presentations of marketing research surveys by widely scattered audiences:* By placing oral presentations on password-protected websites, managers throughout the world can see and hear the actual client presentation. This saves time and money by avoiding the need for the managers to travel to a central meeting site.[16]

IRI's BehaviorScan product allows IRI to track individual household purchases over time. Participants in the household panel present an ID card at the checkout of a scanner-equipped grocery store.

>> SCANNER-BASED RESEARCH

5 Discuss the growing importance of scanner-based research

Scanner-based research is a system for gathering information from a single group of respondents by continuously monitoring the advertising, promotion, and pricing they are exposed to and the things they buy. The variables measured are advertising campaigns, coupons, displays, and product prices. The result is a huge database of marketing efforts and consumer behaviour. Scanner-based research is bringing ever closer the Holy Grail of marketing research: an accurate, objective picture of the direct causal relationship between different kinds of marketing efforts and actual sales.

scanner-based research
A system for gathering information from a single group of respondents by continuously monitoring the advertising, promotion, and pricing they are exposed to and the things they buy.

The two major scanner-based suppliers are Information Resources, Inc. (IRI) and the AC Nielsen Company. Each has about half the market. However, IRI is the founder of scanner-based research.

IRI's first product is called **BehaviorScan**. A household panel (a group of 3,000 long-term participants in the research project) has been recruited and maintained in each BehaviorScan town. Panel members shop with an ID card, which is presented at the checkout in scanner-equipped grocery stores and drugstores, allowing IRI to track electronically each household's purchases, item by item, over time. It uses microcomputers to measure TV viewing in each panel household and can send special commercials to

BehaviorScan
A scanner-based research program that tracks the purchases of 3,000 households through store scanners.

panel member television sets. With such a measure of household purchasing, it is possible to manipulate marketing variables, such as TV advertising or consumer promotions, or to introduce a new product and analyze real changes in consumer buying behaviour.

InfoScan
A scanner-based sales-tracking service for the consumer packaged-goods industry.

IRI's most successful product is **InfoScan**—a scanner-based sales-tracking service for the consumer packaged-goods industry. Retail sales, detailed consumer purchasing information (including measurement of store loyalty and total grocery basket expenditures), and promotional activity by manufacturers and retailers are monitored and evaluated for all bar-coded products. Data are collected weekly from more than 31,000 supermarkets, drugstores, and mass merchandisers in North America.[17]

>> WHEN SHOULD MARKETING RESEARCH BE CONDUCTED?

When managers have several possible solutions to a problem, they should not instinctively call for marketing research. In fact, the first decision to make is whether to conduct marketing research at all.

Some companies have been conducting research in certain markets for many years. Such firms understand the characteristics of target customers and their likes and dislikes about existing products. Under these circumstances, further research would be repetitive and waste money. Procter & Gamble, for example, has extensive knowledge of the coffee market. After it conducted initial taste tests with Folgers Instant Coffee, P&G went into national distribution without further research. Sara Lee Bakery followed the same strategy with its frozen croissants, as did Quaker Oats with Chewy Granola Bars. This tactic, however, does not always work. Clairol felt it understood the hair care market very well when it launched "Look of Buttermilk" shampoo only to find consumers rejected the product because of negative perceptions toward buttermilk. Undaunted, Clairol followed up with "Touch of Yogurt" shampoo, which also failed, indicating low acceptance for "dairy-based" shampoos. [18]

Managers rarely have such great trust in their judgment that they would refuse more information if it were available and free. But they might have enough confidence that they would be unwilling to pay very much for the information or to wait a long time to receive it. The willingness to acquire additional decision-making information depends on managers' perceptions of its quality, price, and timing. Of course, if perfect information were available—that is, the data conclusively showed which alternative to choose—decision makers would be willing to pay more for it than for information that still left uncertainty. In summary, research should be undertaken only when the expected value of the information is greater than the cost of obtaining it.

6 Explain the concept of competitive intelligence

>> COMPETITIVE INTELLIGENCE

competitive intelligence (CI)
An intelligence system that helps managers assess their competition and vendors in order to become more efficient and effective competitors.

Derived from military intelligence, competitive intelligence is an important tool for helping a firm overcome a competitor's advantage. Specifically, competitive intelligence can help identify the advantage, play a major role in determining how the advantage was achieved, and then provide insights regarding how it was achieved.

Competitive intelligence (CI) is the creation of a system that helps managers assess their competitors and their vendors in order to become a more efficient and effective competitor. Intelligence is analyzed information. It becomes decision-making intelligence when it has implications for the organization. For example, a primary competitor may have plans to introduce a product with performance standards equal to ours but with a 15-percent cost advantage. The new product will reach the market in eight months. This intelligence has important decision-making and policy consequences for management. Competitive intelligence and environmental scanning (where manage-

Society of Competitive Intelligence Professionals

Find of more about competitive intelligence at the Society for Competitive Intelligence (SCIP) website. Research a career in CI by checking out the job marketplace at SCIP.

http://www.scip.org

ment gathers data about the external environment—see Chapter 2) combine to create marketing intelligence. Marketing intelligence is then used as input into a marketing decision support system.

Advantages of Competitive Intelligence

Competitive intelligence is one of the hottest areas in marketing today. Multinational firms like General Motors, Ford, Motorola, and many others have large, well-established CI units. In Canada, companies such as CAE Electronics Ltd., Labatt Breweries, Alcan, Inc., and Northern Telecom, along with nearly every major telephone company and energy utility, have sophisticated CI systems in place. Further, practitioners of competitive intelligence have been increasing in numbers; however, as recently as five years ago, only 5 percent of Canada's large corporations had competitive intelligence units.[19]

Competitive intelligence helps managers assess their competition and their vendors, which, in turn, means fewer surprises. Competitive intelligence allows managers to predict changes in business relationships, identify marketplace opportunities, guard against threats, forecast a competitor's strategy, discover new or potential competitors, learn from the success or failure of others, learn about new technologies that can affect the company, and learn about the impact of government regulations on the competition. In summary, CI promotes effective and efficient decision making, which should lead to greater profitability. Sheena Sharp, principal of Sharp Market Intelligence, says: "CI gives the company the competitive advantage of foresight and allows it to learn today what will be discovered by others tomorrow."[20]

Several years ago NutraSweet's patent on the artificial sweetener *aspartame* was expiring, and the company faced potential disaster. Management was afraid that chemical and food companies would move into the market. NutraSweet analyzed competitors' prices, customer relations, expansion plans, and advertising campaigns. The company used the information to cut costs, improve service, and preserve most of its market. "We maintained over 80 percent of our market," said NutraSweet's Robert E. Flynn. He said that CI practices are worth $50 million a year to his company.

Sources of Competitive Intelligence

The Internet and its databases are a great source of competitive intelligence. A CI researcher can use Internet databases to answer these and other questions:

ON LINE

- What articles were written about this market?
- What companies are associated with this product group?
- What patents have been filed for this technology?
- What are the major magazines or texts in this industry?
- What are the chances that I will find something in print on the target company?
- How many companies are in the same industry as the target company?
- Who are the reporters studying this industry?
- How can I be updated on industry and company events without having to constantly request the information?
- How can I compile a list of the leading experts in the industry and the key institutions they are associated with?

Non-computer-based sources of CI can be found in a variety of areas:

- A company's salespeople, who can directly observe and ask questions about the competition.
- Experts with in-depth knowledge of a subject or activity.
- CI consultants, who can use their knowledge and experience to gather needed information quickly and efficiently.
- Government agencies, a valuable source of all types of data.

- Uniform Commercial Code (UCC) filings, a system that identifies goods that are leased or pledged as collateral. This is an excellent source for learning about a company's latest additions to plant assets.
- Suppliers, a group that may offer information on products shipped to a competitor.
- Periodicals, a good source for timely articles on successes, failures, opportunities, and threats.
- The Yellow Pages, which often provide data on number of competitors, trading areas, and special offerings.
- Trade shows, official gatherings where competitors display their latest offerings.

This list is not exhaustive but it does provide an idea of how CI can be gathered.

>> CONNECT IT

Look back at the story about the anthropological approach to observational research at the beginning of this chapter. A company can use survey research, observations, or experiments to conduct marketing research.

Unless a company has extensive knowledge, based on research, of the problem at hand, it should probably conduct marketing research. Yet managers should also be reasonably sure that the cost of gathering the information would be less than the value of the data gathered.

Key marketing data often come from a company's own decision support system, which continually gathers data from a variety of sources and funnels the information to decision makers. They then manipulate the data to make better decisions. DSS data are often supplemented by marketing research information.

REVIEW IT

1 Explain the concept and purpose of a marketing decision support system. A decision support system (DSS) makes data instantly available to marketing managers and allows them to manipulate the data themselves to make marketing decisions. Four characteristics make DSSs especially useful to marketing managers: they are interactive, flexible, discovery oriented, and accessible. Decision support systems give managers access to information immediately and without outside assistance. They allow users to manipulate data in a variety of ways and to answer "what if" questions. And, finally, they are accessible to novice computer users.

1.1 In the absence of company problems, is there any reason to develop a marketing DSS?

1.2 Explain the difference between marketing research and a DSS.

2 Define marketing research and explain its importance to marketing decision making. Marketing research is a process of collecting and analyzing data for the purpose of solving specific marketing problems. Marketers use marketing research to explore the profitability of marketing strategies. They can examine why particular strategies failed and analyze characteristics of specific market segments. Managers can use research findings to help keep current customers. Moreover, marketing research allows management to behave proactively, rather than reactively, by identifying newly emerging patterns in society and the economy.

2.1 The task of marketing is to create exchanges. What role might marketing research play in the facilitation of the exchange process?

2.2 Marketing research has traditionally been associated with manufacturers of consumer goods. Today, however, an increasing number of organizations, both profit and nonprofit, are using marketing research. Why do you think this trend exists? Give some examples of specific reasons why organizations might use marketing research.

2.3 WRITING Write a reply to the following statement: "I own a restaurant in the downtown area. I see customers every day whom I know on a first-name basis. I understand their likes and dislikes. If I put something on the menu and it doesn't sell, I know that they didn't like it. I also read the magazine *Modern Restaurants*, so I know what the trends are in the industry. This is all of the marketing research I need to do."

2.4 Give an example of (a) the descriptive role of marketing research, (b) the diagnostic role, and (c) the predictive function of marketing research.

3 **Describe the steps involved in conducting a marketing research project.** The marketing research process involves several basic steps. First, the researcher and the decision maker must agree on a problem statement or set of research objectives. The researcher then creates an overall research design to specify how primary data will be gathered and analyzed. Before collecting data, the researcher decides whether the group to be interviewed will be a probability or nonprobability sample. Field service firms are often hired to carry out data collection. Once data have been collected, the researcher analyzes them using statistical analysis. The researcher then prepares and presents oral and written reports, with conclusions and recommendations, to management. As a final step, the researcher determines whether the recommendations were implemented and what could have been done to make the project more successful.

3.1 Critique the following methodologies and suggest more appropriate alternatives:

a. A supermarket was interested in determining its image. It dropped a short questionnaire into the grocery bag of each customer before putting in the groceries.

b. To assess the extent of its trade area, a shopping mall stationed interviewers in the parking lot every Monday and Friday evening. Interviewers walked up to people after they had parked their cars and asked them for their postal codes.

c. To assess the popularity of a new movie, a major studio invited people to call a 900 number and vote "yes," they would see it again, or "no," they would not. Each caller was billed a $2 charge.

3.2 WRITING You have been charged with determining how to attract more business majors to your school. Write an outline of the steps you would take, including the sampling procedures, to accomplish the task.

3.3 Why are secondary data sometimes preferable to primary data?

3.4 Discuss when focus groups should and should not be used.

3.5 TEAM Divide the class into teams of eight persons. Each group will conduct a focus group on the quality and number of services that your college or university is providing to its students. One person from each group should be chosen to act as moderator. Remember, it is the moderator's job to facilitate discussion, not to lead the discussion. These group discussions should last approximately 45 minutes. If possible, the groups should be videotaped or recorded. Upon completion, each group should write a brief report of its results. Consider offering to meet with the dean of students to share the results of your research.

4 **Discuss the profound impact of the Internet on marketing research.** The Internet has vastly simplified the secondary data search process, placing more sources of information in front of researchers than ever before. Internet survey research is surging in popularity. Internet surveys can be created rapidly and reported in real time. They are also relatively inexpensive and can easily be personalized. Often researchers can use the Internet to contact respondents who are difficult to reach by other means. The Internet can also be used to distribute research proposals and reports and to facilitate collaboration between the client and the research supplier. Clients can access real-time data and analyze the information as the collection process continues.

4.1 

Use the Internet and a Web browser, such as Lycos or Yahoo!, and type "marketing research." You will then have thousands of options. Pick a website that you find interesting and report on its content to the class.

4.2 

Why has the Internet been of such great value to researchers seeking secondary data?

5 **Discuss the growing importance of scanner-based research.** A scanner-based research system enables marketers to monitor a market panel's exposure and reaction to such variables as advertising, coupons, store displays, packaging, and price. By analyzing these variables in relation to the panel's subsequent buying behaviour, marketers gain useful insight into sales and marketing strategies.

5.1 Why has scanner-based research been seen as "the ultimate answer" for marketing researchers? Do you see any disadvantages to this methodology?

5.2 Detractors claim that scanner-based research is like "driving a car down the road looking only in the rearview mirror." What does this mean? Do you agree?

6 **Explain the concept of competitive intelligence.** Competitive intelligence (CI) is the creation of an intelligence system that helps managers assess their competition and their vendors in order to become more efficient and effective competitors. Intelligence is analyzed information, and it becomes decision-making intelligence when it has implications for the organization.

By helping managers assess their competition and vendors, CI leads to fewer surprises. CI allows managers to predict changes in business relationships, guard against threats, forecast a competitor's strategy, and develop a successful marketing plan.

The Internet and databases accessed via the Internet offer excellent sources of CI. Company personnel, particularly sales and service representatives, are usually good sources of CI. Many companies require their salespeople to routinely fill out CI reports. Other external sources of CI include experts, CI consultants, government agencies, suppliers, newspapers and other publications, Yellow Pages, and trade shows.

6.1 Why do you think that CI is so hot in today's environment?

6.2 WRITING Prepare a memo to your boss at TD Canada Trust and outline why the organization needs a CI unit.

6.3 

Form a team with three other students. Each team must choose a firm in the PC manufacturing industry and then go to the website of the firm and acquire as much CI as possible. Each team will then prepare a five-minute oral presentation on its findings.

DEFINE IT

primary data 202
probability sample 210
random error 211
random sample 210
recruited Internet sample 214
research design 198
sample 210
sampling error 211
scaled-response question 207
scanner-based research 215
screened Internet sample 214
secondary data 195
survey research 202
universe 210
unrestricted Internet sample 214

APPLY IT

Bill and Mary Osborn hit it lucky with dot.com stocks. At the age of 39, they have amassed $5.2 million from astutely playing the stock market. They cashed out before the dot.com crash, and now they are ready to pursue their dream.

The Osborns have always wanted to live in the Muskokas and have dreamed of owning a small hotel. Mary hit upon the idea of doing both—that is, building a hotel in the Muskokas that they could manage. Initial research uncovered the following information.

When asked which two or three things are most important in choosing a hotel for a vacation, Canadians put nonsmoking rooms first (40 percent), followed by 24-hour access to food (36 percent), quality in-room amenities such as coffeemakers and hair dryers (34 percent), athletic facilities (31 percent), and "good evening facilities" (26 percent). Vacationers rank supervised activities for children much higher than do business travellers (10 percent versus 3 percent).

In contrast, overnight business travellers who travelled in the past year focus on things that will make their trip more productive. Like vacationers, they rate nonsmoking rooms tops (46 percent), but they put quality in-room amenities (39 percent) and transportation to the airport (32 percent) next. And, while business travellers cite many of the same things that vacationers rank as being important, they also put a much higher priority on other features, particularly in-room connections for computer, fax, and on-line access (21 percent, 17 points higher than vacationers), being able to earn airline miles (15 percent, eight points higher), and frequent guest programs (14 percent, five points higher).

QUESTIONS

Use the Internet to help determine the following:

1. What price range should be offered?
2. Where in the Muskokas should the hotel be built?
3. Should the hotel cater primarily to business or vacation travellers?
4. What amenities and features should the hotel offer?
5. Should Mary and Bill consider becoming a franchisee?

THINK ABOUT IT

John Michael Smythe owns a small marketing research firm in Newmarket, Ontario, which employs 25 people. Most employees are sole breadwinners in their families. John's firm has not fared well for the past two years and is on the verge of bankruptcy. The company recently surveyed over 2,500 people in the Greater Toronto area about new car purchase plans as part of a study on car emissions sponsored by the Ontario Ministry of Transportation. Because the study identified many hot prospects for new cars, a new car dealer has offered John $8,000 for the names and phone numbers of people saying they are "likely" or "very likely" to buy a new car within the next 12 months. John needs the money to avoid laying off a number of employees.

QUESTIONS

1. Should John Smythe sell the names?
2. Does the CMA Code of Ethics address this issue? Go to **http://www.the-cma.org/consumer/ethics.cfm** and review the code. Then write a brief paragraph on what the CMA Code of Ethics contains that relates to John Smythe's dilemma.

TRY IT

Cool Seeking

Marketers can be quickly left behind while trying to keep up in the fast-moving world of youth trends. But there is no need for despair; Canada's Youth Culture Group is a resource that guides marketers in this turbulent market by providing an accurate information resource on Canada's youth culture. Youth Culture Group, founded in 1993, focuses on the youth market. A combination of both a research organization and a media company, the firm serves a wide variety of clients, including beverage firms, youth apparel manufacturers, youth retailers, music distributors, media producers, confectionary firms, and government agencies.

Youth Culture Group provides three different services to its clients. Through its Youth Culture Research services, it provides "strategic consultant services, qualitative research, quantitative research and Trendscan, our annual survey of Canadian Youth." The group's Youth Culture Media includes magazines *Verve* and *Fuel*, which are supported by the websites http://www.vervegirl.com and http://fuelpowered.com. The firm reaches out to hundreds of thousands of Canadian teens on a monthly basis through its media; it also engages in retail and in-school promotions, undertakes one-on-one interviews, and conducts focus groups and quantitative surveys. Youth Culture Group is also developing youth programming; it launched its first show, "Bang!" in the fall of 2003 as part of its "Youth Culture Entertainment" service.

In terms of research services, Trendscan, Youth Culture's annual quantitative study, is of particular interest to marketers. Every year, the Trendscan survey asks approximately 1,200 Canadian youths, ages 12 to 19, about their "media habits, leisure activities, income and spending behaviour, brand loyalties and consumption, and attitudes." The sample is contacted via the telephone using a Random Digit Dialing (RDD) phone methodology. As part of the Trendscan survey, Youth Culture Group identifies Early Style Adopters (ESAs), who are the "style and opinion leaders within the Canadian youth population." They are "the cool kids" who influence their peers, and their attitudes and beliefs are of particular interest to youth marketers.

Youth Culture Research provides research techniques to help marketers with location research, taste-testing/product development, advertising creative testing, package design, Web auditing, branding/logo recognition, personification of brands, and competitive review. With respect to research approaches, it offers qualitative research that involves mini-sessions, family session/cool mom/purchaser vs. consumer, and ideation sessions.

The teens who take part in Youth Culture's research are recruited from across Canada including places as far north as Whitehorse in the Yukon. Youth Culture uses what it calls a "multitiered recruiting approach," which involves personal recruiting from a "countrywide system of teen recruiters and a countrywide group of teen counsellors, teachers, and related-volunteers." It also recruits teens, "who apply through http://www.fuelpowered.com and http://www.vervegirl.com," with "an on-site database that houses teens and their profiles," and with "street-beat, known as 'cool hunting.'" "Each candidate is run through a youth-specific questionnaire and once determined to be a good fit for future projects with Youth Culture Research, their data and picture are entered into our database. The database allows us to recruit for client projects super-fast because we've already done the groundwork."

And how have marketers benefited from the efforts of the Youth Culture Group? Based on Trendscan data, marketers have learned that Canadian teens have more than $19 billion in disposable income. This money comes from a number of sources, including allowances, gifts, and both summer and school-year employment. Almost 50 percent of Canadian teens work during the school year, and this percentage climbs to two-thirds of Canadian teens who work during the summer. They receive an average weekly allowance of $20 during the school year, that climbs to $32 in the summer, with teens in B.C. and the Atlantic provinces having the highest allowances. Canada has an estimated 3.3 million teens, and 19 percent of them are tremendously coddled; they receive 67 percent of all the allowance money that is doled out. They use this money to buy sports equipment, jeans, and electronic equipment. It is clear that educational needs are being well met, with 80 percent of Canadian teens reporting they have their own personal computer.

Finally, cosmetics marketers have discovered new market potential among "teenage" boys. A recent article provided this characterization: "Far from being the shaggy bedheads who once sneered at even basic hygiene habits, more of today's teen boys are becoming grooming gurus, spending nearly as much time in front of the mirror as their sisters. Stylists at cosmetic counters and beauty salons across the country say young men are asking about concealers, moisturizers, and how to accentuate their eyes." Teenage boys want to look good, and this now goes beyond their clothes and shoes to encompass hairstyles, hair dyes, working out, and even depilatories to remove body hair. Youth Culture's Michele Erskine says, "There's a blending of the gender differences—boys being more worried about their appearances and girls being less so. They're not afraid to say they wear hair gel or that looking good is important to them. Suddenly popular music became a forum for cultivated bands of really good-looking guys who clearly had been groomed for the spotlight." Michael Levine, owner of Statik salon in Vancouver's trendy South Granville strip, commented on this trend: "We're literally seeing these guys within four weeks. Before it was almost non-existent unless mom dragged them in."

Sources: Youth Culture Group website, http://www.youthculture.com; Julia Drake, "Teen Purchasing Power [Study]," *Canadian Grocer*, September 2001, G11; and Cassandra Szklarski, "Teen Boys Spend More Time, Money on Their Appearance," *Canadian Press NewsWire*, May 23, 2002.

QUESTIONS

1. What is the Youth Culture Group offering businesses that traditional market research firms cannot offer?
2. Describe the role of the Internet in youth trend spotting. Do you think a research firm can accurately forecast youth trends without an on-line component to its research plan? What kinds of trends have you observed in your city or region, or among your friends and classmates?
3. Go to Youth Culture Group's website at **http://www.youthculture.com** and check out some of the research tools available. How useful to marketers do you find the information?
4. Make a list of products or companies that you think could benefit from Youth Culture Group's market research. Next to each item, write a brief reason why and how you think cool seeking would benefit the company or product.

FLIP IT

Flip to Chapter 7 in your *Grademaker Study Guide* for more review opportunities, including the pretest, vocabulary review, Internet activities, study test questions, and marketing research scenarios. Can you explain why market research is so important? Can you close your book and outline the marketing research process? Can't? Then you need to review with your Grademaker.

CLICK IT

The *Marketing* website is rich with materials to help you review and master marketing concepts. Check your knowledge with the free quizzes, practise key terms using the crossword puzzles, or review key concepts using the Microsoft® PowerPoint® slides. Also on the website are updated weblinks to companies mentioned in this chapter, Internet exercises, career marketing information, and much much more! Go to http://www.lamb3e.nelson.com, read the material, and follow the convenient links.

WATCH IT

Marketing Research: Science or Hocus Pocus?

Accurate and timely information is the lifeblood of marketing decision making. With good information, a company can increase sales and use its resources wisely. But what is the best way to collect good, accurate information?

While marketing is an art, not a science, some aspects of marketing are thought to be more scientific in nature. Marketing research is one of those fields viewed as quite scientific. One of the most important means of gathering marketing research information is consumer surveys. When surveys are used, it is generally assumed by the researcher that survey respondents will give truthful answers to the questions asked. The experience of many researchers suggests, however, that consumers often can't tell or identify their true motivations for purchasing one product over another in the marketplace. As a result, even the most scientifically designed marketing research undertaking may not provide the behavioural information that the study was designed to elicit.

The idea that consumers may not be able to correctly identify purchase motivations has significant implications for marketing managers. If marketing decision makers are misled by the findings from the marketing surveys undertaken, incorrect marketing decisions will be made. Due to the severe consequences of developing and marketing the wrong product, or initiating the wrong promotional campaign, it is important for marketing managers to know what consumers truly feel and think.

To get around the problems inherent in trying to elicit feelings that survey respondents might not be able to give, market researchers have long used approaches other than direct questions. With regard to print advertising, packaging design, and other promotional elements, for example, rather than question people about feelings or interest in different parts of an ad or promotional piece, market research firms have used eye cameras. The eye camera records movements of the eye. It is used to determine which parts of a newspaper or magazine page are read first, or the order and amount of time an individual spends looking at the various parts of an advertisement or package, or which of two competing stimuli receives the most attention.

Another device, the pupilometric camera, photographs eye movements of a different nature and for a different purpose. The dilation and restriction of the pupils has been found to correlate with the degree of interest aroused by visual stimuli. More interesting stimuli result in the dilation of the pupils. An advertisement or a package that is of more interest to the viewer will cause dilation of the pupils, even if the subject is not conscious of this fact.

Yet another device, the psychogalvanometer, is used for measuring an individual's response to a product, package, or advertisement. The principle involved is that the perspiration rate of the body is increased by excitement. The amount of interest or excitement provided by a product or advertisement can, therefore, be measured by recording changes in the perspiration rate. The psychogalvanometer can also be used to measure whether subjects have an emotional reaction to brand names, slogans, or even political candidates.

What else can be done to identify unconscious motivations? Market researchers have long used in-depth interviews. These are long, probing interviews with one question building on another to delve as deeply as possible into the respondent's motivations. Psychologists, trying to delve deeply into patients' thoughts, have used another approach, hypnosis. Hypnosis, an artificially induced state, is now being used in marketing research as well. As consumers aren't always aware of their true feelings and motives, hypnosis might be used to help subjects explain their real reasons for choosing one product over another. It might also be used to uncover those hidden or subconscious emotions that drive our purchasing behaviour.

According to Hypnosis Insights, a marketing research firm that uses hypnosis on their clients, "Hypnosis shows that consumers or business buyers are more than objective, rational problem solvers—they have essential emotional, sensual aspects to their decision making. Often their choices are much more emotional and impulsive than rational. Properly conducted hypnosis focus groups and personal interviews get people to articulate latent, or underlying, motives, revealing powerful themes and benefits for marketing strategies and advertising campaigns."

Many large firms are using hypnosis in their marketing research. Two examples are Shell Oil and Dewar's Scotch. Most companies, however, don't want it known that they're using this form of research.

Source: CBC, *Undercurrents,* "Inside Information," Broadcast: January 21, 2001.

QUESTIONS

1. What do you think of using hypnosis for collecting marketing research on consumer buying motivations?
2. What might be the benefits of using hypnosis over other forms of marketing research?
3. Why do you think that most companies using hypnosis in their research don't want it generally known?
4. Should market researchers be able to use truth serum drugs, as well as hypnosis, in their efforts to get at true consumer motivations?

part 2 >> CLOSING

MARKETING MISCUES

Rogers Stops Pushing Its iD Wireless Product

"Rogers Wireless Inc. operates under the co-brand Rogers AT&T Wireless and is Canada's largest wireless voice communications service provider, with approximately 2.7 million wireless voice subscribers and offices in Canadian cities from coast to coast. Rogers Wireless provides a complete range of wireless solutions including Digital PCS, cellular, paging, two-way messaging, and wireless data services to a total of more than 3.1 million customers across Canada." In March 2001, Rogers AT&T introduced a new cell phone package branded iD Wireless. Rogers described iD Wireless as the first product of its kind to target Canadian 14- to 24-year-olds. The promotional campaign that accompanied the new service was variously described as a "benchmark for competitors," and "having a strong message." Despite this apparent success, in February 2002, Rogers admitted that it was no longer "pushing" the iD Wireless service any longer. What caused Rogers to pull the plug so quickly, not even a year after the product had been launched? An incompletely executed marketing strategy.

The Market

Toronto-based Rogers AT&T discovered research indicating that the Canadian youth wireless market had tremendous potential for growth. The firm's expert on the youth segment, Sara Moore, was aware that 17 percent of the Canadian population are part of the youth segment and they accounted for about $19 billion in spending on an annual basis. In 2001 it was predicted that use of wireless services in the 14 to 19 age group would increase from 1.2 million to 3.8 million by the year 2003. With this information in hand, Rogers decided it needed to target this market segment aggressively.

Rogers is not the only competitor in Canada's wireless market nor the only one that is trying to tap into the youth market. Montreal-based Microcell depends on the youth market for 70 percent of its sales. Microcell uses a prepaid service plan, as do most of the other wireless providers. ESP Media, also based in Montreal, provides "sponsored" cell phones under the name Espion, for which Archambault, a Quebec-based music retailer, pays a portion of the cell expenses for users who have agreed to receive ads over the phone. Meanwhile, Bell Canada has targeted this market with its Solo brand offering, which is essentially a pay-per-use type of plan that involves the use of prepaid phone cards.

The Product

Rogers positioned the iD Wireless product "as a tool of self-expression" and as a "product for youth designed by youth." Rogers employed research firm Youthography to help develop the product. One of the important findings of the research on the youth market was that opinions were very diverse and that the market was very fickle. Sara Moore, Rogers's youth segment leader, commented on the research findings: "We incorporated that learning and built it into the product (idea) that iD Wireless is everything you need to make yourself heard, and that your iD is your own."

Promotion

Rogers AT&T Wireless hoped to make major inroads into the youth market in the fall of 2001 with a back-to-school promotion. The central focus of the promotion was a Nokia 3360 wireless handset priced at $49.99 (after $50 mail-in rebate on any two-year term) and included a service plan with e-mail and text messaging, downloadable ring tones, games, mobile chat, and several other offerings. In addition to the phone, Rogers developed an iD Wireless Membership Kit as part of the offer. Priced at $24.99, the kit offered a unique silver Nokia 3360 front and back cover, and an iD CD-ROM, which provides a tutorial on the phone, games, and music and launches the user into **http://www.my-id.com**. Finally, the kit contained an iD membership card with access to exclusive discounts, events, and promotions.

An additional incentive for the promotion was offered to purchasers who registered on-line. On-line iD Wireless registrants were eligible for discounts valued at $55 that could be redeemed at Rogers Video, Playdium, and HMV. Finally, purchasers of iD Wireless membership kits who logged onto the iD Wireless website between August 15, 2001, and September 30, 2001, could enter an on-line contest to win a copy of Canadian pop-music artist Nelly Furtado's CD *Whoa Nelly*, or the grand prize—becoming a cast member in the making of Nelly's next video.

The Result

Despite a well-researched market and what would appear to be a well-designed and targeted promotional approach, Rogers failed to reach its sales objectives. In February 2002, Rogers announced that the iD Wireless package was no longer being sold as a standalone offering. Rogers's VP, Sara Moore, described the reasons for the failure as a number of "little things," such as finding a handset that had the features that youths wanted, finding an appropriate pricing point, and finally, an inability to establish the right distribution mix. An industry insider commented more directly that the iD Wireless product was not distributed as widely as needed and that the services were not delivered as promised. The promotional message and positioning were fine.

Sources: Based on Lesley Young, "Tapping into Youth Wireless Market," *Marketing Magazine*, April 9, 2001; Marlene Milczarek, "Voices Carry," *Marketing Magazine*, August 6, 2001; Press Release, "Rogers AT&T Wireless Equips Canadian Students with Everything They Need to Be Heard," *Canada NewsWire*, August 23, 2001; and Lesley Young, "Pitfalls Await Wireless Marketers," *Marketing Magazine*, February 25, 2002.

Questions

1. How important to Rogers's success was an understanding of the target market?
2. Do you think Rogers had enough "information" to make its targeting decision? What additional information, if any, might have helped the company?
3. Do you think Rogers positioned its product appropriately? Why or why not?
4. Do you think the main contributors to the lack of success of the iD Wireless product as described were "little things"?

CRITICAL THINKING CASE

Targeting Women Golfers

The market for golf equipment is fairly mature and highly competitive. Many golf equipment companies have realized that the key to survival involves product differentiation along with a focus on specific segments of the golf equipment market, particularly ones with growth potential. Female golfers represent such a segment. During the past several years, the number of female golfers in the United States has surged past 5 million, or almost 20 percent of the country's total participants. In Canada the game has even more participation, with an estimated 1,469,000 women playing the game, accounting for 28.4 percent of Canada's total of 5,172,000 golfers! The prospects for growth in women's golf equipment to remain positive in Canada are further bolstered by Canadian representation on the LPGA at one of its highest points ever, with players like Lorie Kane, Dawn Coe-Jones, A. J. Eathorne, Nancy Harvey, and Isabelle Beisiegel showing up regularly on LPGA leaderboards. The average female player has a household income of $70,000 in the U.S.; in Canada, 29 percent of golfers have family incomes greater than $75,000 and 47 percent of golfers have family incomes between $30,000 and $75,000. In light of these environmental factors, it's not surprising that a couple of golf equipment companies have chosen to target the women's game.

In Canada, Winnipeg-based Jazz Golf is in a fight with U.S.-based Women's Golf Unlimited (WGU), better known as Square Two Golf. As a supplier of low-priced yet high-quality golf clubs for men and women since 1974, Square Two has always targeted the budget-minded segment of new golf equipment buyers. The golf equipment industry has changed markedly, and the game's surge in popularity has pushed the North American market for golf equipment and supplies to almost $2.5 billion per year. Fighting for survival among traditional golf giants such as TaylorMade, Titleist, Ping, and Callaway, Square Two Golf has chosen to employ a crafty positioning and segmentation strategy to fortify its business.

The company's first major step was its launch of a national television ad campaign in 1999. Set in a golf shop, the ads featured a woman who informed viewers that buying the latest in women's golf technology does not have to be prohibitively expensive. Doug Buffington, the company's chief operating officer, affirms that the ad's message reinforces Square Two's unique selling proposition: supplying women with more choices of affordable golf equipment using patented technology than better-known brands. Buffington also notes that the ads communicate the products' value and inspire viewers to ask store representatives what the differences are between Square Two's clubs and those made by the competition. The advertising spots led Square Two to its first year of profitability.

Not resting on the company's laurels, Buffington initiated a deal in June 2001 to acquire a leading women's golf shoe manufacturer, Lady Fairway, in order to extend Square Two's product lines. That deal inspired the chairman of Nancy Lopez Golf, a maker of high-end women's clubs named after the Hall of Fame golfer, to approach Square Two with a similar acquisition deal. Since the Nancy Lopez line would complement Square Two's existing line of affordable clubs, thus enabling it to serve the entire women's market at multiple price levels, Square Two agreed.

The Lopez line caters to the more affluent golfer, so there is little chance that one line will cannibalize the other. Moreover, both companies have a strong history of targeting women, and their deal opens new and improved distribution channels. For example, Tournament Sports, Canadian distributor of the Nancy Lopez Line and Square Two, recently signed an agreement with the Canadian Ladies' Golf Association to promote women's golf throughout Canada. In return, the Nancy Lopez golf line and golf ball have become the official golf clubs and golf ball of the Canadian Ladies' Golf Association. Though costs of marketing the new lines initially hurt the Square Two's bottom line, the acquisitions have led to increased revenues, and stronger positioning promises to increase profitability in the future.

Meanwhile, Terry Hashimoto, founder of Canadian-based Jazz Golf has recently discovered what Doug Buffington of Square Two learned long ago: survival will require a niche marketing approach. Jazz Golf was launched in 1992 with much fanfare but has been struggling financially throughout its history. Jazz had been targeting the men's golfing market with what the firm termed "value added" clubs, high quality at a fair price. However, like Square Two in the United States, Jazz had found the market very competitve and profits hard to find. The firm has been struggling financially and in late 2003 briefly suspended tradinq of its shares while it pondered its future.

The future is shaping up as emulating WGU. In 2004, Jazz Golf launched its Sandra Post line of golf clubs comprised of the Sandra Post Pro brand and the Sandra Post Oakville series, both named after Canadian golfing legend Sandra Post. The line was featured as the lead product on Jazz Golf's website. Sandra Post and Terry Hashimoto both toured across Canada giving golf clinics at dealers to introduce the new product line. Jazz Golf plans to distribute the Sandra Post brands in the United States but it is highly questionable whether the name recognition will have the same potential as it does in Canada. WGU may have an advantage since the Nancy Lopez name recognition is strong in both Canada and the United States.

The potential for success of positioning brands to women golfers for Square Two and Jazz is not certain. Critics can point out that although women represent 20 percent of the golfing population in the U.S. and 28 percent in Canada, they only account for 15 percent of the market's $2.5 billion in spending. Critics may note that although the number of Canadian women golfers increased by about 400,000, this number was offset in the U.S., where the number of female golfers has decreased from 5.8 million to 5.1 million in the last couple of years. These facts are true, but one of the reasons many female golfers may have left the game is that equipment manufacturers have not sufficiently met their unique needs. Jazz and Women's Golf Unlimited, however, manufacture golf clubs and supporting equipment designed to meet the needs of women's smaller bodies and swing speeds, while providing pleasing aesthetics.

Women's Golf Unlimited feels it is a huge opportunity and is committed to this market alone. Jazz Golf sees the opportunity but has decided to try and serve both male and female golfers. Jazz Golf and WGU have the potential to use their knowledge of and sensitivity toward the women's market to motivate female players to spend proportionately to their share of the total market's population. It is an untapped market estimated at well over $100 million.

Questions

1. Do the consumers at which Jazz and WGU are targeting their products satisfy the definition of a market, a market segment, or both? Explain.
2. Discuss the importance of market segmentation strategy to Jazz and WGU.
3. Describe the positioning strategy for WGU as an organization versus Jazz as an organization.
4. Describe the positioning for each of the two golf club brands that Jazz and WGU both market respectively.

Sources: Royal Canadian Golf Association website, http://www.rcga.org; Press Release, "Nancy Lopez Golf Named Official Golf Ball and Clubs of The Canadian Ladies' Golf Association," April 23, 2003, Canadian Ladies' Golf Association website, http://www.clga.org; and Jazz Golf website, http://www.jazzgolf.com.

>> Product Decisions

part 3

chapter 8

Product Concepts

>> LEARNING OBJECTIVES

1. Define the term *product*
2. Classify consumer products
3. Define the terms *product item*, *product line*, and *product mix*
4. Describe marketing uses of branding
5. Describe marketing uses of packaging and labelling
6. Discuss global issues in branding and packaging
7. Describe how and why product warranties are important marketing tools

>> On any given afternoon in the summer of 2003, a marketing group from Spin Master Ltd. might have been found at a playground, baseball field, or any other place where kids gather in Toronto handing out samples of a new toy to the children playing there. The toy samples included a collectors' guide showing additional variations of the toy that might serve to drive further interest in the product. This was the initial marketing effort for Mighty Beanz, the most successful toy for the 2003 Christmas season in Canada and now the biggest-selling product for Spin Master.

Anton Rabie, co-chief executive of Toronto-based Spin Master, first saw the peanut-sized capsules, later to be named Mighty Beanz, at a toymaker show in late 2002. The product was designed and manufactured by a company in Australia. Mr. Rabie liked the product immediately and, before leaving the show, worked out a deal for the North American sales rights for Mighty Beanz. This quick action, which is important in the ever-changing toy market, is typical for Spin Master.

Choosing winners in the fickle toy industry isn't easy, but Mr. Rabie and his partners Ronnen Harary and Ben Varadi have been quite successful with the company they formed 10 years ago. "Marketing toys to kids is like picking stocks," says Mr. Rabie. Spin Master numbers among its past successes Air Hogs planes, Shrinky Dinks, Flick Trix collectibles, and McDonald's McFlurry ice cream maker. Spin Master is already North America's ninth-largest toy company, with sales set to pass $300 million.

Mighty Beanz, a twist on the old Mexican jumping bean, are decorated with a range of cartoon characters. The toy beans retail for $6 to $8 a pack in Canada, with accessories that include a collector's case (about $13) and a track to play on (about $10). The collectible aspect of the toy has contributed to its great success. There are 60 separate Mighty Beanz characters, divided into 12 teams, such as the jungle, wrestling, and circus teams. Each character can jump, dance, and do back flips, and each Mighty Bean is worth Mighty Merit Points (MMPs). Rare beans are worth more MMPs. The rare Mighty Moose Bean is worth a whopping 1,000 MMPs. Are kids eagerly trying to complete Mighty Beanz collections? Just look at the product's Christmas sales and undertake a Web search. You will find hundreds of websites devoted to trading and selling Mighty Beanz—and all of these websites came into existence within four months of the product hitting store shelves in Canada!

"It's really taken off," says Andrew Pelletier of Wal-Mart Canada, one of the country's top toy sellers. "I think it will have a lot of life." Both Wal-Mart and Zellers found that they had great difficulty keeping the product on their shelves during the Christmas season. Spin Master was originally anticipating sales of about $40 million for Mighty Beanz. The Christmas selling season's success of the product makes it look like Mighty Beanz may reach $60 million in sales for 2003 and who knows what for 2004.

Mr. Rabie attributes Spin Master's success to instilling in its people an "obsession with ideas." Each month the company awards a prize to one employee for the best idea. Because Japan is one of the leading markets for new children's ideas, Spin Master moved its director of global licensing to Japan. How many Canadian toy companies, or toy companies in all of North America for that matter, have an employee in Japan looking for ideas?

After graduating from the University of Western Ontario in 1994, the three partners formed Spin Master with $10,000 in startup capital. Their first product was the Earth Buddy, a small novelty head that sprouts hair when set in water. Mr. Rabie expects Spin Master's Bella Ballerina kit, which teaches ballet to young girls, to be a big hit in 2004. "We call ourselves a children's entertainment consumer products company," he says. "We believe the sky is the limit for where we can take this company."[1]

Explain how Mighty Beanz fits into Spin Master's product mix. Why do you think that Mighty Beanz has been so successful? What other new products might Spin Master be successful with besides toys as a "children's entertainment consumer products company"? We will answer these questions and more in Chapter 8.

ON LINE 

Spin Master

Check Spin Master's website to review all the products the company makes. Do you find any products made by Spin Master that surprise you?

http://www.spinmaster.com

http://www.mightybeanz.com

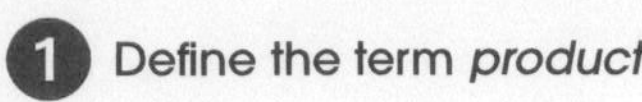
Define the term *product*

>> WHAT IS A PRODUCT?

The product offering, the heart of an organization's marketing program, is usually the starting point in creating a marketing mix. A marketing manager cannot determine a price, design a promotion strategy, or create a distribution channel until the firm has a product to sell. Moreover, an excellent distribution channel, a persuasive promotion campaign, and a fair price have no value with a poor or inadequate product offering.

product
Everything, both favourable and unfavourable, that a person receives in an exchange.

A **product** may be defined as everything, both favourable and unfavourable, that a person receives in an exchange. A product may be a tangible good like a pair of shoes, a service like a haircut, an idea like "don't litter," or any combination of these three. Packaging, style, colour, options, and size are some typical product features. Just as important are intangibles such as service, the seller's image, the manufacturer's reputation, and the way consumers believe others will view the product.

To most people, the term *product* means a tangible good. However, services and ideas are also products. (Chapter 10 focuses specifically on the unique aspects of marketing services.) The marketing process identified in Chapter 1 is the same whether the product marketed is a good, a service, an idea, or some combination of these.

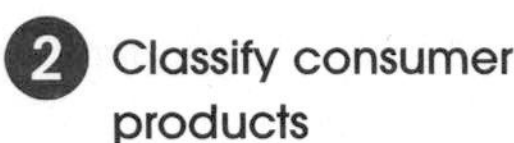
Classify consumer products

>> TYPES OF CONSUMER PRODUCTS

business product (industrial product)
A product used to manufacture other goods or services, to facilitate an organization's operations, or to resell to other customers.

consumer product
A product bought to satisfy an individual's personal wants.

Products can be classified as either business (industrial) or consumer products, depending on the buyer's intentions. The key distinction between the two types of products is their intended use. If the intended use is a business purpose, the product is classified as a business or industrial product. As explained in Chapter 5, a **business product** is used to manufacture other goods or services, to facilitate an organization's operations, or to resell to other customers. A **consumer product** is bought to satisfy an individual's personal wants. Sometimes the same item can be classified as either a business or a consumer product, depending on its intended use. Examples include lightbulbs, pencils and paper, and computers.

We need to know about product classifications because business and consumer products are marketed differently. They are marketed to different target markets and tend to use different distribution, promotion, and pricing strategies.

Chapter 5 examined seven categories of business products: major equipment, accessory equipment, component parts, processed materials, raw materials, supplies, and services. The current chapter examines an effective way of categorizing consumer products. Although there are several ways to classify them, the most popular approach includes these four types: convenience products, shopping products, specialty products, and unsought products (see Exhibit 8.1). This approach classifies products according to how much effort is normally used to shop for them.

Convenience Products

convenience product
A relatively inexpensive item that merits little shopping effort.

A **convenience product** is a relatively inexpensive item that merits little shopping effort—that is, a consumer is unwilling to shop extensively for such an item. Candy, soft drinks, combs, aspirin, bread and milk, small hardware items, dry cleaning, and car washes fall into the convenience product category.

Consumers buy convenience products regularly, usually without much planning. Nevertheless, consumers do know the brand names of popular convenience products, such as Coca-Cola, Bayer aspirin, and Right Guard deodorant. Convenience products normally require wide distribution in order to sell sufficient quantities to meet profit goals.

Shopping Products

shopping product
A product that requires comparison shopping because it is usually more expensive than a convenience product and is found in fewer stores.

A **shopping product** is usually more expensive than a convenience product and is found in fewer stores. Consumers usually buy a shopping product only after comparing several brands or stores on style, practicality, price, and lifestyle compatibility. They are willing to invest some effort into this process to get the desired benefits.

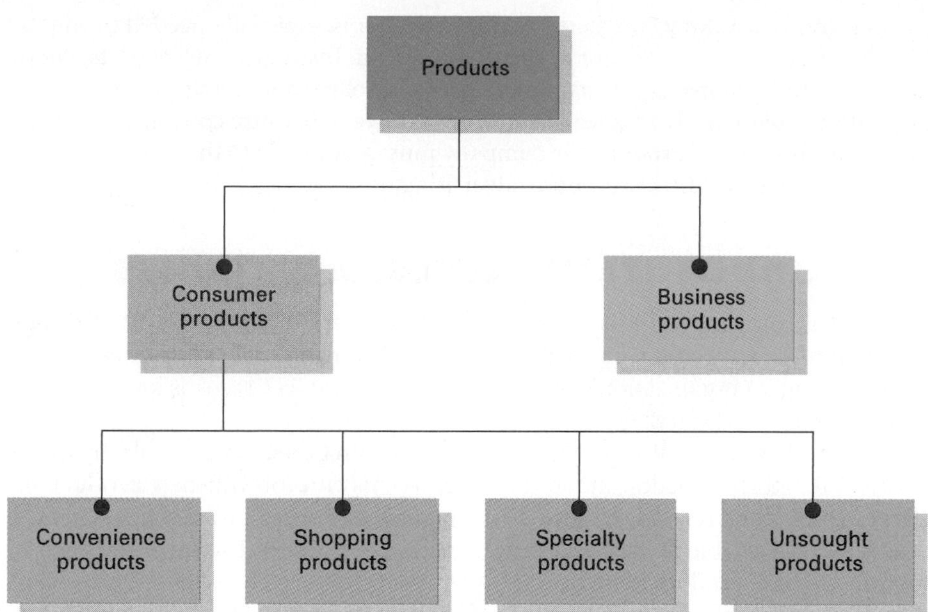

EXHIBIT 8.1

Classification of Consumer Products

There are two types of shopping products: homogeneous and heterogeneous. Consumers perceive *homogeneous* shopping products as basically similar—for example, washers, dryers, refrigerators, and televisions. With homogeneous shopping products, consumers typically look for the lowest-priced brand that has the desired features.

In contrast, consumers perceive *heterogeneous* shopping products as essentially different—for example, furniture, clothing, housing, and universities. Consumers often have trouble comparing heterogeneous shopping products because the prices, quality, and features vary so much. The benefit of comparing heterogeneous shopping products is "finding the best product or brand for me"; this decision is often highly individual.

specialty product
A particular item for which consumers search extensively and for which they are very reluctant to accept substitutes.

unsought product
A product unknown to the potential buyer or a known product that the buyer does not actively seek.

Specialty Products

When consumers search extensively for a particular item and are very reluctant to accept substitutes, that item is a **specialty product**. Breitling watches, Rolls-Royce automobiles, Simaudio stereo equipment, Leica cameras, Laguiole knives, gourmet restaurants, and highly specialized forms of medical care are generally considered specialty products. Guitars made one at a time for rock stars such as Keith Richards, James Taylor, Peter Gabriel, and Sting by George Rizsanyi on his farm in Bridgewater, Nova Scotia, would also qualify as specialty items.[2]

Marketers of specialty products often use selective, status-conscious advertising to maintain their product's exclusive image. Distribution is often limited to one or a very few outlets in a geographic area. Brand names and quality of service are often very important.

Unsought Products

A product unknown to the potential buyer or a known product that the buyer does not actively seek is referred to as an **unsought product**. New products fall into this category until advertising and distribution increase consumer awareness of them.

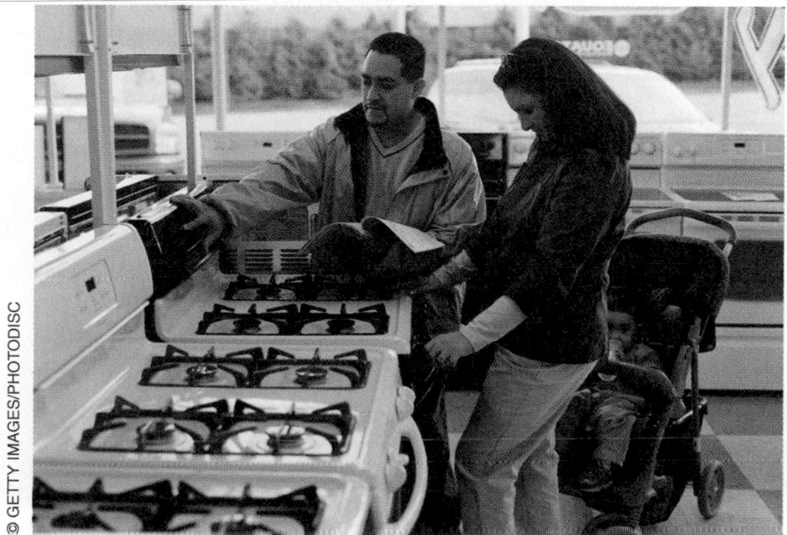

© GETTY IMAGES/PHOTODISC

With homogeneous products such as stoves, consumers typically buy the lowest-priced brand that has the desired features.

Some goods are always marketed as unsought items, especially needed products we do not like to think about or care to spend money on. Insurance, burial plots, encyclopedias, and similar items require aggressive personal selling and highly persuasive advertising. Salespeople actively seek leads to potential buyers. Because consumers usually do not seek out this type of product, the company must go directly to them through a salesperson, direct mail, or direct-response advertising.

3 Define the terms *product item*, *product line*, and *product mix*

product item
A specific version of a product that can be designated as a distinct offering among an organization's products.

product line
A group of closely related product items.

product mix
All products that an organization sells.

>> PRODUCT ITEMS, LINES, AND MIXES

Rarely does a company sell a single product. More often, it sells a variety of things. A **product item** is a specific version of a product that can be designated as a distinct offering among an organization's products. Gillette's MACH3 razor is an example of a product item (see Exhibit 8.2).

A group of closely related product items is a **product line**. For example, the column in Exhibit 8.2 titled "Blades and Razors" represents one of Gillette's product lines. Different container sizes and shapes also distinguish items in a product line. Diet Coke, for example, is available in cans and various plastic containers. Each size and each container are separate product items.

An organization's **product mix** includes all of the products it sells. All Gillette's products—blades and razors, toiletries, writing instruments, and lighters—constitute its product mix. Each product item in the product mix may require a separate marketing strategy. In some cases, however, product lines and even entire product mixes share some marketing strategy components. Nike promoted all of its product items and lines with the theme "Just Do It."

Organizations derive several benefits from organizing related items into product lines, including the following:

- *Advertising economies:* Product lines provide economies of scale in advertising. Several products can be advertised under the umbrella of the line. Campbell's can talk about its soup being "m-m-good" and promote the entire line.
- *Package uniformity:* A product line can benefit from package uniformity. All packages in the line may have a common look and still keep their individual identities. Again, Campbell's soup is a good example.
- *Standardized components:* Product lines allow firms to standardize components, thus reducing manufacturing and inventory costs. For example, many of the components Samsonite uses in its folding tables and chairs are also used in its patio furniture. General Motors and Toyota use the same parts on many automobile makes and models.
- *Efficient sales and distribution:* A product line enables sales personnel for companies like Procter & Gamble to provide a full range of choices to customers.

EXHIBIT 8.2
Gillette's Product Lines and Product Mix

	WIDTH OF THE PRODUCT MIX			
	BLADES AND RAZORS	TOILETRIES	WRITING INSTRUMENTS	LIGHTERS
Depth of the product lines	MACH3	Series	Paper Mate	Cricket
	Sensor	Adorn	Flair	S.T. Dupont
	TracII	Toni		
	Atra	Right Guard		
	Swivel	Silkience		
	Double-Edge	Soft&Dri		
	Lady Gillette	Foamy		
	Super Speed	Dry Look		
	Twin Injector	Dry Idea		
	Techmatic	Brush Plus		

Distributors and retailers are often more inclined to stock the company's products if it offers a full line. Transportation and warehousing costs are likely to be lower for a product line than for a collection of individual items.

- *Equivalent quality:* Purchasers usually expect and believe that all products in a line are about equal in quality. Consumers expect that all Campbell's soups and all President's Choice cookies will be of similar quality.

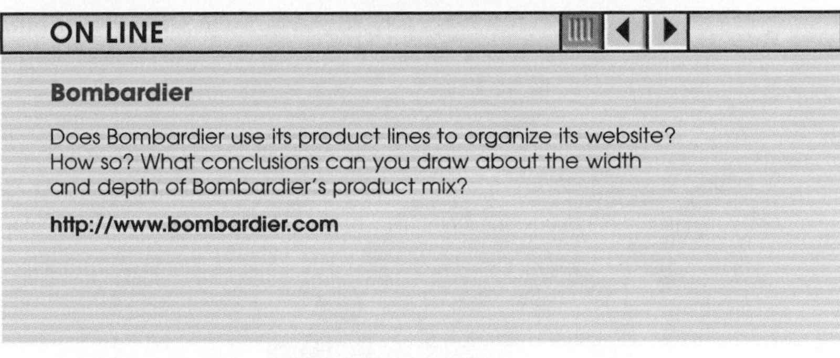

ON LINE
Bombardier
Does Bombardier use its product lines to organize its website? How so? What conclusions can you draw about the width and depth of Bombardier's product mix?
http://www.bombardier.com

Product mix width (or breadth) refers to the number of product lines an organization offers. In Exhibit 8.2, for example, the width of Gillette's product mix is four product lines. **Product line depth** is the number of product items in a product line. As shown in Exhibit 8.2, the blades and razors product line consists of 10 product items; the toiletries product line also includes 10 product items; the writing instrument and lighters lines contain two items each.

product mix width The number of product lines an organization offers.

product line depth The number of product items in a product line.

Firms increase the *width* of their product mix to diversify risk. To generate sales and boost profits, firms spread risk across many product lines rather than depend on only one or two. Firms also widen their product mix to capitalize on established reputations. By introducing new product lines, Kodak capitalized on its image as a leader in photographic products. Kodak's product lines now include film, processing, still cameras, movie cameras, paper, and chemicals. Limited Brands, Inc., a company that mostly comprises women's apparel stores (Limited, Limited Too, Victoria's Secret) developed a line of makeup under the Victoria's Secret brand.

Firms increase the *depth* of product lines to attract buyers with different preferences, to increase sales and profits by further segmenting the market, to capitalize on economies of scale in production and marketing, and to even out seasonal sales patterns. Marriott International has 14 different lodging brands that are divided into three groups. The full-service group includes flagship Marriott, upscale Renaissance Hotels and Resorts, and Marriott Conference Centres. The select service group includes Courtyard, SpringHill Suites, and Fairfield Inn. The extended stay group includes Residence Inn and ExecuStay.

Adjustments to Product Items, Lines, and Mixes

Over time, firms change product items, lines, and mixes to take advantage of new technical or product developments or to respond to changes in the environment. They may adjust by modifying products, repositioning products, or extending or contracting product lines. Visit the Bombardier website highlighted in the On Line example. How many new products have been added to its product mix in recent years?

Product Modification

Marketing managers must decide if and when to modify existing products. **Product modification** changes one or more of a product's characteristics:

product modification Changing one or more of a product's characteristics.

- *Quality modification:* change in a product's dependability or durability. Reducing a product's quality may let the manufacturer lower the price and appeal to target markets unable to afford the original product. On the other hand, increasing quality can help the firm compete with rival firms. Increasing quality can also result in increased brand loyalty, greater ability to raise prices, or new opportunities for market segmentation. Inexpensive ink-jet printers have improved in quality to the point that they produce photo-quality images. These printers are now competing with camera film. Michelin has added a higher-quality, higher-priced "run-flat" tire to its product mix. This tire will travel up to 70 kilometres after suffering total air loss.

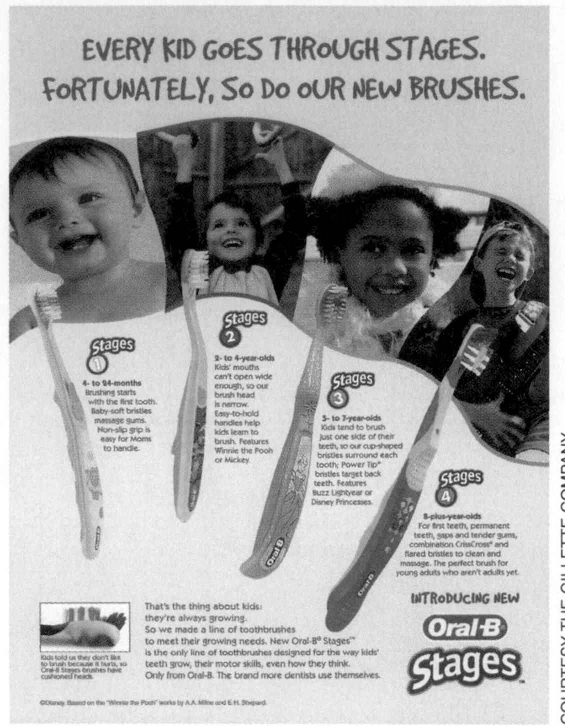

COURTESY THE GILLETTE COMPANY

Oral-B's Stages toothbrushes represent a functional modification to adult toothbrushes. Numerous colours and designs of a single stage toothbrush would be a style modification.

- *Functional modification:* change in a product's versatility, effectiveness, convenience, or safety. Oral-B introduced Stages toothbrushes, a line of toothbrushes for children. For example, Stage 2, designed for toddlers, has an easy-to-grip handle and a narrow brush that makes it easier to reach all teeth.[3] Lea & Perrins offers its steak sauce in a value-priced squeeze bottle with a "no mess, stay clean" cap.
- *Style modification:* aesthetic product change, rather than a quality or functional change. Pontiac modified the style of its Aztec car based on focus-group results after initial sales were weak. The original two-tone colour scheme that featured gray trim was replaced by a monochromatic colour scheme, and the small wheels were replaced with 16-inch cast aluminum wheels. A spoiler was also added to soften some of the car's sharp lines.[4] Clothing and auto manufacturers also commonly use style modifications to motivate customers to replace products before they are worn out. **Planned obsolescence** is a term commonly used to describe the practice of modifying products so those that have already been sold become obsolete before they actually need replacement. Some argue that planned obsolescence is wasteful; some claim it is unethical. Marketers respond that consumers favour style modifications because they like changes in the appearance of goods like clothing and cars. Marketers also contend that consumers, not manufacturers and marketers, decide when styles are obsolete.

planned obsolescence
The practice of modifying products so those that have already been sold become obsolete before they actually need replacement.

Repositioning

Repositioning involves changing consumers' perceptions of a brand. For example, Tommy Hilfiger started out as a company offering classic, preppy clothing. During the 1990s, Hilfiger was repositioned as a hipper, more urban brand to appeal to a younger audience. During 2001, to combat decreasing sales and to regain its core market, Hilfiger once again repositioned itself and returned to its clean-cut image.[5]

Changing demographics, declining sales, or changes in the social environment often motivate firms to reposition established brands. The Japanese cosmetics company Shiseido changed the positioning of its cosmetics from masking products to products that enhance women's inner beauty. Based on this repositioning, the company introduced a new skin-care line that has helped to attract a younger audience (25- to 30-year-olds) than its traditional market of women aged 30 to 45.[6]

Product Line Extensions

product line extension
Adding additional products to an existing product line in order to compete more broadly in the industry.

A **product line extension** occurs when a company's management decides to add products to an existing product line in order to compete more broadly in the industry. Minute Maid has added two calcium-fortified juices—Premium HomeSqueezed Style orange juice and Ruby Red Grapefruit Blend—to attract health-conscious baby boomers.[7] Jolly Rancher launched Fruit Chews to compete in the chewy candy product category.[8] Procter & Gamble has developed numerous extensions of its Tide laundry detergent, including Tide with Bleach, Tide Free (which has no fragrance), Tide WearCare (which claims to keep fabrics brighter longer), and Tide Kick (whose package has a nozzle to rub detergent directly into fabrics).[9] Harvey's recently added a monster-size burger to its menu to appeal to Canadian males who love a large burger. The Big Harv weighs 170 grams compared with 64 grams in a regular burger.[10]

ON LINE

Unilever

Can Unilever delete anything from its product lines? Visit the company's product category pages on its "Brands" Web page to see the number of existing products and new products planned. Write a proposal for contracting one of Unilever's product lines.

http://www.unilever.ca

The story in the "Global Perspectives" box illustrates how Coca-Cola and Procter & Gamble expanded their beverage lines to respond to consumer needs in developing countries. Sometimes, though, we have to watch out for new products, or at least the claims made for new products, as the "Ethics in Marketing" box warns.

Product extensions enable a company to compete more broadly in an industry. Coca-Cola's Minute Maid was successful building upon its original Premium orange juice brand with Premium Blends, which mix orange juice with cranberry, passion fruit, strawberry and banana, or tangerine juice. Other product extensions include Minute Maid Coolers, Minute Maid Smoothies, and Minute Maid Frozen Fruit Bars.

Product Line Contraction

Does the world really need 31 varieties of Head & Shoulders shampoo? Or 52 versions of Crest? Black & Decker has decided that sometimes too many varieties can be offered. The company has deleted a number of household products—Dustbusters, SnakeLight flashlights, and toaster ovens—and is concentrating on power tools. Symptoms of product line overextension include the following:

- Some products in the line do not contribute to profits because of low sales or they cannibalize sales of other items in the line.
- Manufacturing or marketing resources are disproportionately allocated to slow-moving products.
- Some items in the line are obsolete because of new product entries in the line or new products offered by competitors.

Three major benefits are likely when a firm contracts overextended product lines. First, resources become concentrated on the most important products. Second, managers no longer waste resources trying to improve the sales and profits of poorly performing products. Third, new product items have a greater chance of being successful because more financial and human resources are available to manage them.

>> BRANDING

4 Describe marketing uses of branding

The success of any business or consumer product depends in part on the target market's ability to distinguish one product from another. Branding is the main tool marketers use to distinguish their products from the competition's.

A **brand** is a name, term, symbol, design, or combination thereof that identifies a seller's products and differentiates them from competitors' products. A **brand name** is that part of a brand that can be spoken, including letters (GM, YMCA), words (Mastercraft and MotoMaster), and numbers (WD-40, 7-Eleven, Ford F-150). The elements of a brand that cannot be spoken are called the **brand mark**—for example, the well-known Mercedes-Benz, Nike, and McDonald's symbols.

brand
A name, term, symbol, design, or combination thereof that identifies a seller's products and differentiates them from competitors' products.

brand name
That part of a brand that can be spoken, including letters, words, and numbers.

brand mark
The elements of a brand that cannot be spoken.

Benefits of Branding

Branding has three main purposes: product identification, repeat sales, and new-product sales. The most important purpose is *product identification*. Branding allows marketers to distinguish their products from all others. Many brand names are familiar to consumers and indicate quality.

The term **brand equity** refers to the value of company and brand names. A brand that has high awareness, perceived quality, and brand loyalty among customers has high brand equity. A brand with strong brand equity is a valuable asset.

brand equity
The value of company and brand names.

The term **global brand** has been used to refer to brands where at least 20 percent of the product is sold outside the home country or region. "A strong global brand acts as an ambassador when companies enter new markets or offer new products." It also helps guide corporate strategy decisions by indicating which new ideas fit within the brand concept and which do not.[11] Yum! Brands (formerly Tricon Global Restaurants), which owns Pizza Hut, KFC, and Taco Bell, is a good example of a company that has developed strong global brands. Yum! believes that it has to adapt its restaurants to local tastes and different cultural and political climates. In Japan, for instance, KFC sells tempura crispy

global brand
A brand where at least 20 percent of the product is sold outside its home country or region.

GLOBAL PERSPECTIVES

Drinks for Developing Countries

The Coca-Cola Company recently conducted a clinical test of a special drink on children in Gabarone, Botswana. The beverage looked and tasted like the company's Hi-C orange-flavoured drink, but this drink contained 12 vitamins and minerals chronically lacking in the diets of people in developing countries. The test was part of "Project Mission," a continuing research and development effort aimed at creating a drink to help fight diseases like anemia, blindness, and other afflictions that are common in poorer parts of the world. At the end of eight weeks, results of the test showed that levels of iron and zinc in the children's blood had grown. Some parents said their children, whose diets consist mostly of cornmeal and rice, had more energy and had become more attentive at school. The new drink, to be called Vitango, could help Coke increase sales at a time when growth for carbonated beverages is slowing.

After its launch, Vitango will put Coca-Cola in direct competition with Procter & Gamble Company, which has a similar drink that is already being sold. P&G launched its product, Nutristar, in late 2001 in Venezuela after years of research and development and clinical tests. A powdered drink that contains eight vitamins and five minerals, Nutristar is sold at most food stores in flavours like mango and passion fruit. So far, the drink is doing well. Available also at McDonald's, Nutristar is the chosen beverage with about half the Happy Meals the restaurants sell. Nutristar is also being sampled in schools.

While the market for such drinks is limited, they are meant to offer Coke and P&G a chance to attempt the role of good corporate citizen at a time when being perceived as such is increasingly important for multinational firms. Coke has high hopes for Vitango in Africa and Latin America, where its products already reach some of the most remote areas. A second clinical test, to determine how well Vitango's nutrients are absorbed into the bloodstream, was just finished in Peru.

"Micronutrient" deficiencies, or a lack of vitamins and minerals such as vitamin A, iron, and zinc, are believed to afflict about 2 billion children around the world. With vitamin pills costly to distribute and pill-taking regimes hard to enforce, fortification of foods offers the most promising prospects for combating some deficiencies.

Coke's Project Mission began in April 2000, when a group of marketing and innovation executives visited the company's operations in Ecuador. Local managers there were looking for a less obtrusive way to advance the Coca-Cola name in secondary schools than through bottle-cap contests that promoted sales of cola. With economic conditions in the country deteriorating, children were poorly nourished and inattentive in class. In developing the beverage, Coke found out that a powdered version of Hi-C sold to restaurants appealed to consumer groups tested in South Africa. With that information, the company put together a "worldwide nutrition advisory board" to create a combination of vitamins and minerals that would be absorbed well and whose taste would not be too strong. Powder, liquid, and even carbonated forms of the beverage were developed. Concerned with water quality in Africa, Coke wants to sell the beverage there in a ready-to-drink form. The beverage is not intended to replace drinking milk or juice, but as a supplement that augments a healthy diet.[12]

Would you consider Vitango to be a product modification for Coca-Cola? If so, what type of modification does it represent? What type of branding strategy does Coca-Cola appear to be using with Vitango? Do you think that this brand name would be successful in other countries? Support your answer.

strips. In northern England, KFC focuses on gravy and potatoes, while in Thailand it offers rice with soy or sweet chili sauce. In China, the company recruits employees who balance an understanding of the Chinese mindset with Western business training.[13] Exhibit 8.3 lists the world's 10 most valuable brands as reported in *The Globe and Mail.*

What constitutes a good brand name? Most effective brand names have several of the following features:

- Is easy to pronounce (by both domestic and foreign buyers)
- Is easy to recognize
- Is easy to remember
- Is short
- Is distinctive, unique
- Describes the product
- Describes the product use
- Describes product benefits
- Has a positive connotation
- Reinforces the desired product image
- Is legally protectable in home and foreign markets of interest

ETHICS IN MARKETING

Herbal Diet Pills or All Natural Placebos?

Most Canadians want to lose weight, but most Canadians do not want to put in the effort needed to lose weight. We're always looking for an easy solution. This situation probably opens the door for some questionable products to find their way onto the market. One such easy solution advertised for dieters is a product called Weightralight.

Weightralight is being advertised in health food magazines and claims to contain "All Natural Super Fat Burners." The product is a mixture of 20 different herbs and spices which, according to the ads, will suppress the user's appetite, boost the user's metabolism, and even tone your muscles! The miracle drug is priced at $25 per bottle.

To test out the claims for this product, CBC television, for its show *Marketplace Microscope*, had a volunteer try it. Georgia Spyracopoulos of Toronto had never tried diet pills before. "I feel better knowing it's not chemicals or drugs," Georgia told *Marketplace*. For the test, Georgia first weighed in with a dietitian and then took two pills a day for four weeks as prescribed in the Weightralight directions.

Like most Canadians, Georgia thought that diet pills had to be tested and approved before their miracle weight loss claims could be advertised. This is not true. Health Canada does not monitor non-prescription diet pills unless there are complaints or the product offers a serious health threat. Health Canada says that it doesn't know of any herbs or spices, in any combinations, that are proven to burn fat.

Corine Bezemer, who formulated and sells Weightralight, is not a dietitian and has no training in this field. She claims to simply have used the known properties of the herbs used to make the pills. Corine also claims that 90 percent of 50 volunteers who used the product lost weight but won't provide the names of any of the volunteers. Corine also says that, "the pill doesn't work for everyone."

Georgia Spyracopoulos is one of those for whom the pill didn't work. Over the four weeks Georgia took the pill, she put on some weight, even though she claims to have eaten less and consumed seven glasses of water a day. Corine Bezemer says that Georgia would have lost weight had she taken the pills for three months instead of one.

To read more about Weightralight and to view the CBC *Marketplace* television show on this product visit **http://www.cbc.ca/consumers/market/microscope/micro_2000/dietpills.html.** What do you think about the claims being made for this product? Should consumers be protected from such unfounded claims? Should we be smart enough to recognize when product claims are "too good to be true"? Should Health Canada be more actively involved with diet pills and dietary supplements?

EXHIBIT 8.3

The World's 10 Most Valuable Brands

RANK	BRAND	2003 BRAND VALUE ($ BILLIONS)
1	Coca-Cola	70.5
2	Microsoft	65.2
3	IBM	51.8
4	GE	42.4
5	Nokia	35.0
6	Intel	34.7
7	Disney	32.6
8	Ford	30.1
9	McDonald's	25.3
10	Mercedes	21.4

SOURCE: *INTER BRAND*, reported in *The Globe and Mail*, July 25, 2003, B9. Reprinted with permission from *The Globe and Mail*.

Obviously, no brand exhibits all of these characteristics. The most important issue is whether its owner can protect the brand for exclusive use.

The best generator of *repeat sales* is a satisfied customer. Branding helps consumers identify products they wish to buy again and avoid those they do not. **Brand loyalty**, a consistent preference for one brand over all others, is quite high in some product categories. Over half the users in product categories such as cigarettes, mayonnaise, toothpaste, coffee, headache remedies, photographic film, bath soap, and ketchup are loyal to one brand. Brand identity is essential to developing brand loyalty.

brand loyalty
A consistent preference for one brand over all others.

ON LINE

Tide

How does Tide use its website to maintain customer relationships? To build its brand?

http://www.tide.com

The third main purpose of branding is to *facilitate new-product sales.* Company and brand names like those listed in Exhibit 8.3 are extremely useful when introducing new products.

ON LINE

The Internet has provided firms with a new alternative for generating brand awareness, promoting a desired brand image, stimulating new and repeat brand sales, enhancing brand loyalty, and building brand equity. A number of packaged-goods firms, such as Procter & Gamble, Campbell's soup, and Gerber, have a presence on-line. Tide.com offers a useful feature called Stain Detective, a digital tip sheet on how to remove almost any substance from almost any fabric. Reflect.com lets women mix and match various options to create their own "brands" of makeup, perfume, and other beauty-care products.[14]

Procter & Gamble has an extensive Web presence to support its complete slate of brands. P&G has launched the pg.com network, touting it as "the one place where all our brands hang out together."

Branding Strategies

Firms face complex branding decisions. As Exhibit 8.4 illustrates, the first decision is whether to brand at all. Some firms actually use the lack of a brand name as a selling point. These unbranded products are called generic products. Firms that decide to brand their products may choose to follow a policy of using manufacturers' brands, private (distributor) brands, or both. In either case, they must then choose among individual branding (different brands for different products) or family branding (common names for different products) or a combination of the two.

Generic Products versus Branded Products

generic product
A no-frills, no-brand-name, low-cost product that is simply identified by its product category.

A **generic product** is typically a no-frills, no-brand-name, low-cost product that is simply identified by its product category. (Note that a generic product and a brand name that becomes generic, such as cellophane, are not the same thing.) Generic products have captured significant market shares in some product categories, such as canned fruits, canned vegetables, and paper products. These unbranded products are frequently identified only by black stenciled lettering on white packages.

The main appeal of generics is their low price. Generic grocery products are usually 30 to 40 percent less expensive than manufacturers' brands in the same product category and 20 to 25 percent less expensive than retailer-owned brands.

Pharmaceuticals are another product category where generics have made inroads. When patents on successful pharmaceutical products expire, low-cost generics rapidly appear on the market. For example, when the patent on Merck's popular antiarthritis drug Clinoril expired, sales declined by 50 percent almost immediately.

EXHIBIT 8.4
Major Branding Decisions

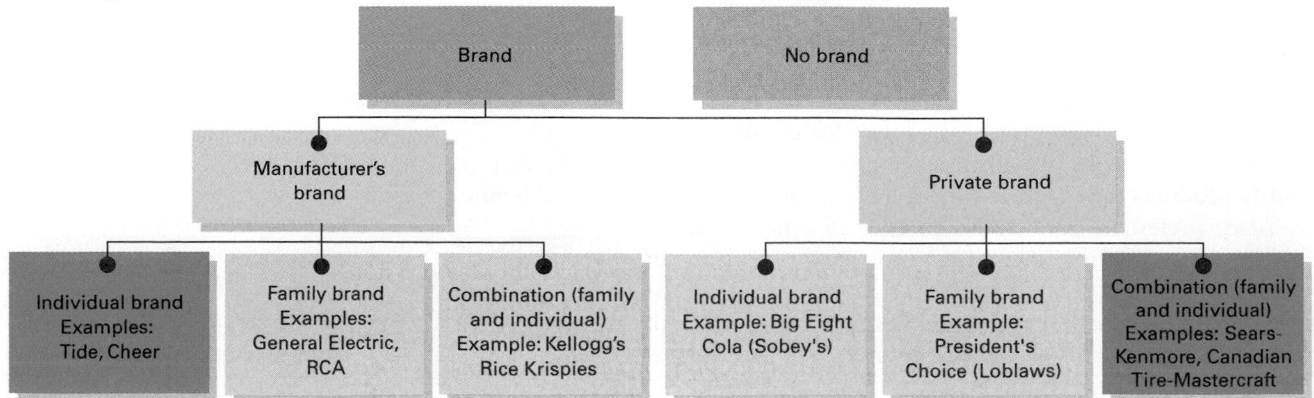

Manufacturers' Brands versus Private Brands

The brand name of a manufacturer—such as Kodak, Nike, or Fruit of the Loom—is called a **manufacturer's brand**. Sometimes "national brand" is used as a synonym for "manufacturer's brand." This term is not always accurate, however, because many manufacturers serve only regional markets. Using "manufacturer's brand" more precisely defines the brand's owner.

manufacturer's brand
The brand name of a manufacturer.

A **private brand**, also known as a private label or store brand, is a brand name owned by a wholesaler or a retailer. Craftsman (a Sears brand), President's Choice (Loblaws), Mastercraft (Canadian Tire), Beaumark (The Bay), Big Eight (Sobeys), Select (Safeway), Kirkland (Costco Canada), and Life Brand (Shoppers Drug Mart) are all private brands. Private brands now account for over 20 percent of sales at all mass merchandisers, drugstores, and supermarkets across the country. At some stores, such as Canadian Tire and Wal-Mart, the penetration is much higher, exceeding 40 percent. Ol' Roy, Wal-Mart's private brand of dog food, is not only the largest-selling dog food in Canada but also the largest-selling brand of dog food in the world. Private-label sales are higher in Ontario (25.2 percent of sales) and lower in Quebec (11.4 percent of sales). And across the board, store brands are growing faster than national brands.[15] Marketing experts predict that private labels will make up as much as 30 percent of grocery sales within the next few years—particularly as big supermarkets continue to consolidate and mass merchandisers such as Wal-Mart expand grocery offerings.[16]

private brand
A brand name owned by a wholesaler or a retailer.

Exhibit 8.5 illustrates key issues that wholesalers and retailers should consider in deciding whether to sell manufacturers' brands or private brands. Many firms, such as Zellers, Wal-Mart, and Loblaws, offer a combination of both. In fact, Wal-Mart and Sears have turned their low-priced, private-label jeans into some of the most popular brands around, thanks to hip marketing campaigns that feature rock bands, websites, and imagery targeted at teens. Loblaws, on the other hand, has moved some of its private labels upmarket by emphasizing the quality of the product (e.g., President's Choice Decadent Chocolate Chip Cookies). As an in-between strategy, Zellers carries many brands that are exclusive to Zellers in Canada but carried by other retailers in other countries. Examples include Cherokee (casual clothes), Mossimo (designer clothes and home decor), Sportek (sports clothing), and Wabasso (linens and home accessories).[17]

EXHIBIT 8.5
Comparing Manufacturers' and Private Brands from the Reseller's Perspective

KEY ADVANTAGES OF CARRYING MANUFACTURERS' BRANDS	KEY ADVANTAGES OF CARRYING PRIVATE BRANDS
• Heavy advertising to the consumer by manufacturers like Procter & Gamble helps develop strong consumer loyalties.	• A wholesaler or retailer can usually earn higher profits on its own brand. In addition, because the private brand is exclusive, there is less pressure to mark the price down to meet competition.
• Well-known manufacturers' brands, such as Kodak and Fisher-Price, can attract new customers and enhance the dealer's (wholesaler's or retailer's) prestige.	• A manufacturer can decide to drop a brand or a reseller at any time or even to become a direct competitor to its dealers.
• Many manufacturers offer rapid delivery, enabling the dealer to carry less inventory.	• A private brand ties the customer to the wholesaler or retailer. A person who wants a DieHard battery must go to Sears.
• If a dealer happens to sell a manufacturer's brand of poor quality, the customer may simply switch brands and remain loyal to the dealer.	• Wholesalers and retailers have no control over the intensity of distribution of manufacturers' brands. Canadian Tire store managers don't have to worry about competing with other sellers of Mastercraft or MotoMaster products. They know that these brands are sold only in Canadian Tire stores.

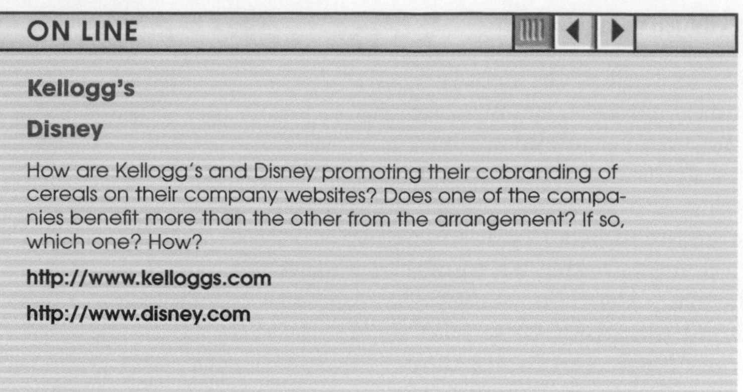

Individual Brands versus Family Brands

individual branding
Using different brand names for different products.

family brand
Marketing several different products under the same brand name.

Many companies use different brand names for different products, a practice referred to as **individual branding**. Companies use individual brands when their products vary greatly in use or performance. For instance, it would not make sense to use the same brand name for a pair of dress socks and a hockey stick. Canada Packers sells its food products under the names Maple Leaf, York, Domestic, Dial, and Devon. Procter & Gamble targets different segments of the laundry-detergent market with Bold, Cheer, Dash, Dreft, Era, Gain, Ivory Snow, and Tide. Marriott International also targets different market segments with Courtyard by Marriott, Residence Inn, and Fairfield Inn.

In contrast, a company that markets several different products under the same brand name is using a **family brand**. Sony's family brand includes radios, television sets, stereos, and other electronic products. Roots is another family brand, applied to a wide range of clothing items. A brand name can only be stretched so far, however. Do you know the differences among Holiday Inn, Holiday Inn Express, Holiday Inn Select, Holiday Inn Sun Spree Resort, Holiday Inn Garden Court, and Holiday Inn Hotel & Suites? Neither do most travellers.

Cobranding

cobranding
Placing two or more brand names on a product or its package.

Cobranding entails placing two or more brand names on a product or its package. There are three types of cobranding. *Ingredient branding* identifies the brand of a part that makes up the product. Examples of ingredient branding are a microprocessor (Intel) in a personal computer (Dell), a premium leather interior (Coach) in an automobile (Lincoln), and the Clodhoppers (candy) Blizzard that can be purchased at Dairy Queen Canada. *Cooperative branding* occurs when two brands receiving equal treatment (in the context of an advertisement) borrow on each other's brand equity. An example would be Air Canada promoting the Second Cup coffee that is served on its planes. Another example of cooperative branding was a promotional contest jointly sponsored by Ramada Inns and American Express. Guests at Ramada who paid with an American Express card were automatically entered in the contest and were eligible to win more than a hundred getaways for two at any Ramada Inn.[18] Finally, there is *complementary branding*, where products are advertised or marketed together to suggest usage, such as a spirits brand (Seagram's) and a compatible mixer (Seven Up).

Cobranding is a useful strategy when a combination of brand names enhances the prestige or perceived value of a product or when it benefits brand owners and users. Toyota Motor's luxury division has introduced a Platinum version of its Lexus brand. For a premium of as much as 10 percent above the base sticker prices, buyers get upgraded paint, leathers, and accessories and a free two-year subscription to the $300-a-year American Express Platinum Card. Both companies say that the Platinum Series models will reinforce their brands while delivering added value.[19] American Express also cobranded with Costco outlets in Canada to allow shoppers to earn dollars off on purchases when they used the American Express card.

Cobranding may be used to increase a company's presence in markets in which it has little or no market share. For example, Disney is attempting to increase its share of the food and beverage market by developing cobranding deals with Minute Maid for an 18-variety line of Disney Xtreme! Coolers based on Mickey and Friends, and with Kellogg for cobranded cereals.[20]

European firms have been slower than Canadian firms to adopt cobranding. One reason is that European customers seem to be more skeptical than Canadian customers about trying new brands. European retailers also typically have less shelf space than their Canadian counterparts and are less willing to give new brands a try.

Trademarks

A **trademark** is the exclusive right to use a brand or part of a brand. Others are prohibited from using the brand without permission. A **service mark** performs the same function for services, such as H&R Block and Weight Watchers. Parts of a brand or other product identification may qualify for trademark protection. Some examples are

- Shapes, such as the Jeep front grille and the Coca-Cola bottle
- Ornamental colour or design, such as the decoration on Nike tennis shoes, the black-and-copper colour combination of a Duracell battery, Levi's small tag on the left side of the rear pocket of its jeans, and the cutoff black cone on the top of Cross pens
- Catchy phrases, such as Prudential's "Own a piece of the rock," Timex's "Takes a licking and keeps on ticking," and Harvey's "Long live the grill"
- Abbreviations, such as Blue, Coke, or CN
- Sounds, such as General Electric Broadcasting Company's ship's bell clock sound and the MGM lion's roar

ON LINE

Post Cereals

Quaker Oats

Ingredient branding can enhance the prestige and value of a brand. Cookies and candies are some common ingredients that appear in other products, like cereal and ice cream. Visit the Post Cereals and Quaker Oats websites to see how each company has incorporated ingredient branding into their marketing strategies. What ingredients is each company using in its products? Do you think the cobranded products you find have increased value over a plain product (i.e., a product without a branded ingredient)?

http://www.kraftfoods.com/postcereals

http://www.quakeroats.com

trademark
The exclusive right to use a brand or part of a brand.

service mark
A trademark for a service.

In Canada, trademarks are registered under the Trademarks Act. Rights to a trademark last as long as the mark is used. Usually, if a firm does not use a trademark for two years, the trademark is considered abandoned. If a new user picks up the abandoned trademark, that new user can claim exclusive ownership of the mark. The Trademarks Act specifies the types of marks that can be protected and the remedies available for trademark violations. Businesses planning to introduce new brands, trademarks, or packages should consider the following:

- Check carefully before adopting a trademark or packaging style to make sure you're not infringing on someone else's.
- After a thorough search, consider registering your trademark.
- Make your packaging as distinctive as possible.
- Police your trademark.

Companies that fail to protect their trademarks face the possibility that their product names will become generic. A **generic product name** identifies a product by class or type and cannot be trademarked. Former brand names that were not sufficiently protected by their owners and subsequently became generic product names include aspirin, cellophane, linoleum, thermos, kerosene, monopoly, cola, and shredded wheat.

generic product name
Identifies a product by class or type and cannot be trademarked.

Companies like Rolls-Royce, Cross, Xerox, Levi Strauss, Frigidaire, and McDonald's aggressively enforce their trademarks. Rolls-Royce, Coca-Cola, and Xerox even run newspaper and magazine ads stating that their names are trademarks and should not be used as descriptive or generic terms. Some ads threaten lawsuits against competitors that violate trademarks. In some cases, it is hard to say whether a trademark has been infringed or not. A few years ago, GolfGear International began marketing the Ti-Gear driver. The company claimed that it had been using the name Titanium Gear since 1990 and simply shortened it to Ti-Gear. Representatives for Tiger Woods, however, felt that this was an unauthorized attempt to play off the Tiger Woods name.[21] What do you think?

Despite severe penalties for trademark violations, trademark infringement lawsuits are not uncommon. One of the major battles is over brand names that closely resemble another brand name. Donna Karan filed a lawsuit against Donnkenny Inc., whose Nasdaq trading symbol—DNKY—was too close to Karan's DKNY trademark.

Companies must also contend with fake or unauthorized brands, such as fake Levi's jeans, Microsoft software, Rolex watches, Reebok and Nike footwear, and Louis Vuitton handbags. Sales of copycat golf clubs, such as Big Bursa, a knockoff of Callaway's popular Big Bertha, are growing.

In Europe, you can sue counterfeiters only if your brand, logo, or trademark is formally registered. Until recently, formal registration was required in each country in which a company sought protection. A company can now register its trademark in all European Union (EU) member countries with one application.

5 Describe marketing uses of packaging and labelling

>> PACKAGING

Packages have always served a practical function—that is, they hold contents together and protect goods as they move through the distribution channel. Today, however, packaging is also a container for promoting the product and making it easier and safer to use.

Packaging Functions

The three most important functions of packaging are to contain and protect products, promote products, and facilitate the storage, use, and convenience of products. A fourth function of packaging that is becoming increasingly important is to facilitate recycling and reduce environmental damage.

Containing and Protecting Products

The most obvious function of packaging is to contain products that are liquid, granular, or otherwise divisible. Packaging also enables manufacturers, wholesalers, and retailers to market products in specific quantities, such as grams.

Physical protection is another obvious function of packaging. Most products are handled several times between the time they are manufactured, harvested, or otherwise produced and the time they are consumed or used. Many products are shipped, stored, and inspected several times between production and consumption. Some, like milk, need to be refrigerated. Others, like beer, are sensitive to light. Still others, like medicines and bandages, need to be kept sterile. Packages protect products from breakage, evaporation, spillage, spoilage, light, heat, cold, infestation, and many other conditions.

Promoting Products

Packaging does more than identify the brand, list the ingredients, specify features, and give directions. A package differentiates a product from competing products and may associate a new product with a family of other products from the same manufacturer. Welch's repackaged its line of grape juice–based jams, jellies, and juices to unify the line and get more impact on the shelf.

Packages use designs, colours, shapes, and materials to try to influence consumers' perceptions and buying behaviour. For example, marketing research shows that health-conscious consumers are likely to think that any food is probably good for them as long as it comes in green packaging. Two top brands of low-fat foods—Snackwell and Healthy Choice—use green packaging. SunSweet Growers, appealing to baby boomers' interest in health foods, used the theme "Be good to yourself" on new packages for its line of prune products.[22]

Packaging may have a measurable effect on sales. Quaker Oats revised the package for Rice-A-Roni without making any other changes in marketing strategy and experienced a 44 percent sales increase in one year.

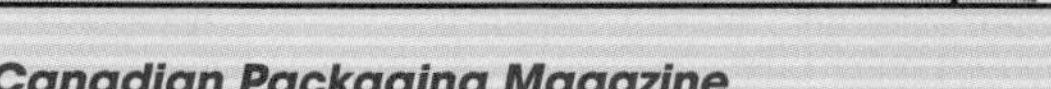

Canadian Packaging Magazine

Packaging Association of Canada

What does it take to design a successful package? Visit the websites of *Canadian Packaging Magazine* and the Packaging Association of Canada to find out. What is the most innovative or eye-catching package you see? Try out the "interactive packaging kit" on the *Canadian Packaging Magazine* site. What do you think of the most recent package design award winners on the Packaging Association of Canada site?

http://www.bizlink.com/canadianpackaging.htm

http://www.pac.ca

Facilitating Storage, Use, and Convenience

Wholesalers and retailers prefer packages that are easy to ship, store, and stock on shelves. They also like packages that protect products, prevent spoilage or breakage, and extend the product's shelf life.

Consumers' requirements for storage, use, and convenience cover many dimensions. Consumers are constantly seeking items that are easy to handle, open, and reclose, although some consumers want packages that are tamperproof or childproof. Consumers also want reusable and disposable packages. Quaker State oil, packaged in easy to open and reseal twist-off tops, makes the product more convenient to customers at self-serve gas stations. Such packaging innovations as zipper tear strips, hinged lids, tab slots, screw-on tops, and pour spouts were introduced to solve these and other problems. H.J. Heinz Company developed a new container for ketchup designed to fit the hands of children and encourage extra squeezing, which facilitates use for this target market.[23] Miracle-Gro's new packages have pictures on the front of the plants for which the products are formulated, so gardeners can more easily identify which product best fits their needs.[24]

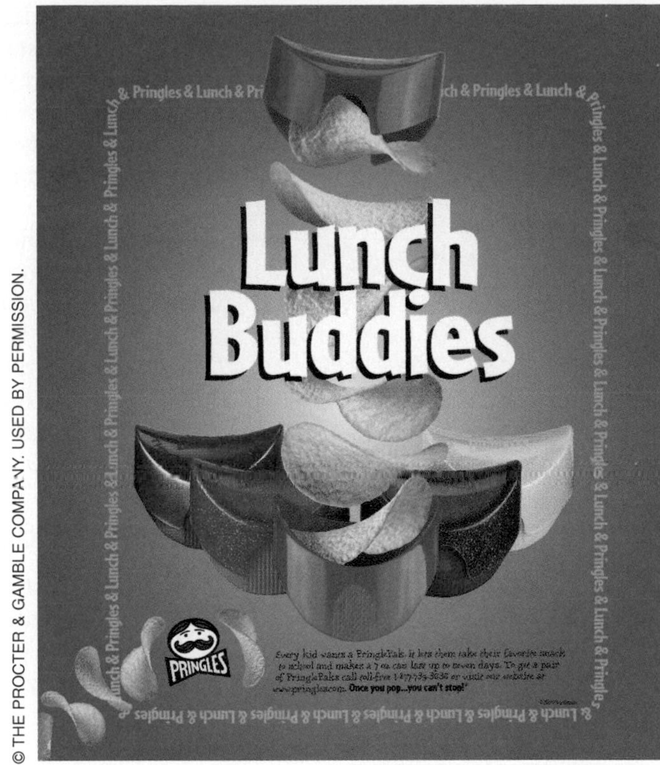

Pringles invented the innovative tube package that has become as much a part of the product as the chip itself. New packaging ideas, however, are crucial to Pringles in the twenty-first century. Why? The patent on the package just expired, and rivals are quickly entering the market with their own versions of the chip tube.

Some firms use packaging to segment markets. For example, a C&H sugar carton with an easy-to-pour, reclosable top is targeted to consumers who don't do a lot of baking and are willing to pay at least 20 cents more for the package. Different-size packages appeal to heavy, moderate, and light users. Salt is sold in package sizes ranging from single serving to picnic size to giant economy size. Campbell's soup is packaged in single-serving cans aimed at the elderly and singles market segments. Beer and soft drinks are similarly marketed in various package sizes and types. Packaging convenience can increase a product's utility and, therefore, its market share and profits. Guinness Bass Import is testing a packaged-draft system that allows consumers to drink nitrogenated Guinness Stout right out of the bottle. This package could win converts among consumers who prefer to drink beer straight from the bottle and in clubs that offer beer only in bottles rather than in a glass or on draft.[25]

The Internet will soon give consumers more packaging options. Indeed, the Internet may significantly change the purpose and appearance of packaging. Packaging for products sold on the Internet will be more under the customer's control and will be customized by consumers to fit their needs. Some designers are already offering to personalize, for a fee, packages such as wine bottle labels.[26] Jones Soda can be purchased over the Internet in any flavour or flavours desired and with any picture desired on the label.

Facilitating Recycling and Reducing Environmental Damage

One of the most important packaging issues today is compatibility with the environment.

Some firms use their packaging to target environmentally concerned market segments. Brocato International markets shampoo and hair conditioner in bottles that are biodegradable in landfills. Procter & Gamble markets Sure Pro and Old Spice in "eco-friendly" pump-spray packages that do not rely on aerosol propellants. Other firms that have introduced pump sprays include SC Johnson (Pledge furniture polish) and Reckitt & Coleman Household Products (Woolite rug cleaner).

Labelling

An integral part of any package is its label. Labelling generally takes one of two forms: persuasive or informational. **Persuasive labelling** focuses on a promotional theme or logo, and consumer information is secondary. Price Pfister developed a new, persuasive label—featuring a picture of a faucet, the brand name, and the logo—with the goal of

persuasive labelling
A type of package labelling that focuses on a promotional theme or logo; consumer information is secondary.

strengthening brand identity and becoming known as a brand instead of as a manufacturer. Note that the standard promotional claims—such as "new," "improved," and "super"—are no longer very persuasive. Consumers have been saturated with "newness" and thus discount these claims.

informational labelling
A type of package labelling designed to help consumers make proper product selections and lower their cognitive dissonance after the purchase.

Informational labelling, in contrast, is designed to help consumers make proper product selections and lower their cognitive dissonance after the purchase. Sears attaches a "label of confidence" to all its floor coverings. This label gives such product information as durability, colour, features, cleanability, care instructions, and construction standards. Most major furniture manufacturers affix labels to their wares that explain the products' construction features, such as type of frame, number of coils, and fabric characteristics. The Consumer Packaging and Labelling Act and the Food and Drug Act state the minimum information that must appear on food products and set the standards for health claims on food packaging. An important outcome of this legislation is that guidelines now exist for using terms like *low fat, light, reduced cholesterol, low sodium, low calorie,* and *fresh.*

Universal Product Codes

universal product codes (UPCs)
Series of thick and thin vertical lines (bar codes), readable by computerized optical scanners, which represent numbers used to track products.

The **universal product codes (UPCs)** that appear on most items in supermarkets and other high-volume outlets were first introduced in 1974. Because the numerical codes appear as a series of thick and thin vertical lines, they are often called *bar codes.* The lines are read by computerized optical scanners that match codes with brand names, package sizes, and prices. They also print information on cash register tapes and help retailers rapidly and accurately prepare records of customer purchases, control inventories, and track sales.

6 Discuss global issues in branding and packaging

>> GLOBAL ISSUES IN BRANDING AND PACKAGING

International marketers must address several concerns regarding branding and packaging.

Branding

When planning to enter a foreign market with an existing product, a firm has three options for handling the brand name:

- *One brand name everywhere:* This strategy is useful when the company markets mainly one product and the brand name does not have negative connotations in any local market. The Coca-Cola Company uses a one-brand-name strategy in 195 countries around the world. The advantages of a one-brand-name strategy are greater identification of the product from market to market and ease of coordinating promotion from market to market.
- *Adaptations and modifications:* A one-brand-name strategy is not possible when the name cannot be pronounced in the local language, when the brand name is owned by someone else, or when the brand name has a negative or vulgar connotation in the local language. The Iranian detergent "Barf," for example, might encounter some problems in the Canadian market, as would a Mexican bread named Bimbo or a Japanese coffee creamer named Creap. Even a name that works in the U.S. market may not work in Canada. The Buick Regal, which was renamed the Buick LaCrosse in the U.S., could not be used in Canada as LaCrosse was found to mean "I just got taken" among some young people in Canada.
- *Different brand names in different markets:* Local brand names are often used when translation or pronunciation problems occur, when the marketer wants the brand to appear to be a local brand, or when regulations require localization. Gillette's Silkience hair conditioner is called Soyance in France and Sientel in Italy. The adaptations were deemed to be more appealing in the local markets. Coca-Cola's Sprite

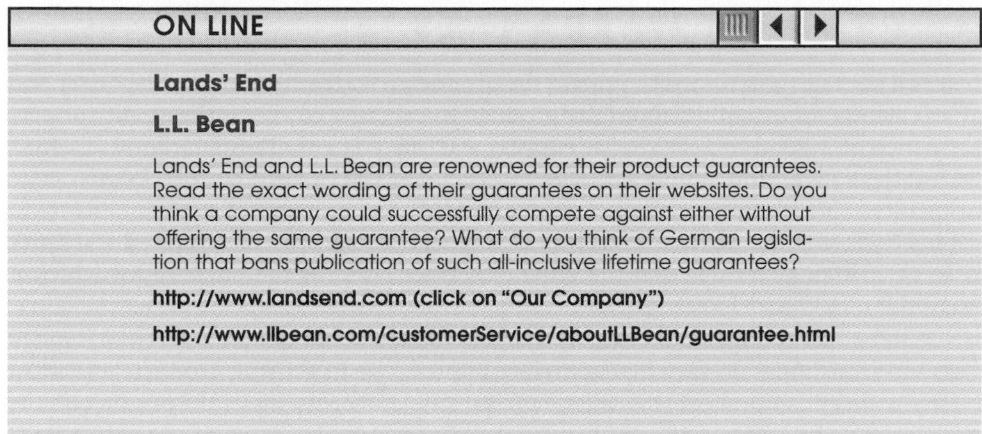

ON LINE

Lands' End

L.L. Bean

Lands' End and L.L. Bean are renowned for their product guarantees. Read the exact wording of their guarantees on their websites. Do you think a company could successfully compete against either without offering the same guarantee? What do you think of German legislation that bans publication of such all-inclusive lifetime guarantees?

http://www.landsend.com (click on "Our Company")

http://www.llbean.com/customerService/aboutLLBean/guarantee.html

brand had to be renamed Kin in Korea to satisfy a government prohibition on the unnecessary use of foreign words. Snuggle fabric softener is called FaFa in Japan, Cajoline in France, and other cuddly names elsewhere in the world.

Packaging

Three aspects of packaging that are especially important in international marketing are labelling, aesthetics, and climate considerations. The major *labelling* concern is properly translating ingredient, promotional, and instructional information on labels. In Eastern Europe, packages of Ariel detergent are printed in 14 languages, from Latvian to Lithuanian. Care must also be employed in meeting all local labelling requirements. Several years ago, an Italian judge ordered that all bottles of Coca-Cola be removed from retail shelves because the ingredients were not properly labelled. Labelling is also harder in countries like Belgium and Finland, which require it to be bilingual, as is the case in Canada.

Package *aesthetics* may also require some attention. The key is to stay attuned to cultural traits in host countries. For example, colours may have different connotations. Red is associated with witchcraft in some countries, green may be a sign of danger, and white may be symbolic of death. Aesthetics also influence package size. Soft drinks are not sold in six-packs in countries that lack refrigeration. In some countries, products like detergent may be bought only in small quantities because of a lack of storage space. Other products, like cigarettes, may be bought in small quantities, and even single units, because of the low purchasing power of buyers.

On the other hand, simple visual elements of the brand, such as a symbol or logo, can be a standardizing element across products and countries. For example, when Scott Paper wanted to establish a global brand identity for its product line, it used a single brand mark for all product lines that had the flexibility to accommodate such variables as country-specific product names.

Extreme *climates* and long-distance shipping necessitate sturdier and more durable packages for goods sold overseas. Spillage, spoilage, and breakage are all more important concerns when products are shipped long distances or frequently handled during shipping and storage. Packages may also have to ensure a longer product life if the time between production and consumption lengthens significantly.

© JEFF GREENBERG/ PHOTOEDIT

Coca-Cola uses a one-brand-name strategy in 195 countries around the world. Its product and positive image are recognizable almost everywhere.

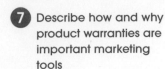

Describe how and why product warranties are important marketing tools

warranty
A confirmation of the quality or performance of a good or service.

express warranty
A written guarantee.

implied warranty
An unwritten guarantee that the good or service is fit for the purpose for which it was sold.

>> PRODUCT WARRANTIES

Just as a package is designed to protect the product, a **warranty** protects the buyer and gives essential information about the product. A warranty confirms the quality or performance of a good or service. An **express warranty** is a written guarantee. Express warranties range from simple statements—such as "100 percent cotton" (a guarantee of quality) and "complete satisfaction guaranteed" (a statement of performance)—to extensive documents written in technical language. In contrast, an **implied warranty** is an unwritten guarantee that the good or service is fit for the purpose for which it was sold.

While court rulings would suggest that all products sold in Canada carry an implied warranty, warranties do vary from province to province. In general, products sold must be free from encumbrances (the seller has clear title), descriptions of the product on the package must be accurate, the product must be fit for its purpose, and the product must be of reasonable durability.

ON LINE

Industry Canada

For more information about warranties and consumers' rights when purchasing new products, visit Industry Canada's Web page on consumer information. This site also contains links to provincial sites with warranty information.

http://www.industrycanada.ca

http://www.strategis.ic.gc.ca/sc_consu/engdoc/homepage.html

>> CONNECT IT

Look back at the chapter-opening story about Mighty Beanz from Spin Master. Mighty Beanz represents a new product item for Spin Master—an addition to the Spin Master product mix. Mighty Beanz would also fit in as part of an existing product line for Spin Master with other toys that have a collectible aspect to them like Shrinky Dinks and Flick Trix collectibles. A number of factors likely led to the success of Mighty Beanz. The product was new and innovative; it was inexpensive; Spin Master's initial marketing program led to good word-of-mouth; and, once sales began, children's desire to collect the complete set took over. Thinking of themselves as a "children's entertainment consumer products company" could lead Spin Master into a number of product categories beyond toys. Videos, books, educational materials, decorations for children's rooms, and clothing would represent just a few possibilities.

REVIEW IT

Define the term *product*. A product is anything, desired or not, that a person or organization receives in an exchange. The basic goal of purchasing decisions is to receive the tangible and intangible benefits associated with a product. Tangible aspects include packaging, style, colour, size, and features. Intangible qualities include service, the retailer's image, the manufacturer's reputation, and the social status associated with a product. An organization's product offering is the crucial element in any marketing mix.

1.1 TEAM Form a team of four or five. Have the team determine what the tangible and intangible benefits are for a computer, a tube of toothpaste, a beauty salon, and a dentist.

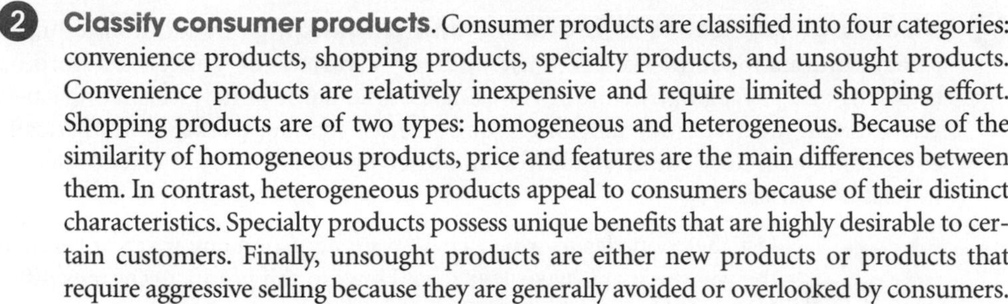

2 **Classify consumer products.** Consumer products are classified into four categories: convenience products, shopping products, specialty products, and unsought products. Convenience products are relatively inexpensive and require limited shopping effort. Shopping products are of two types: homogeneous and heterogeneous. Because of the similarity of homogeneous products, price and features are the main differences between them. In contrast, heterogeneous products appeal to consumers because of their distinct characteristics. Specialty products possess unique benefits that are highly desirable to certain customers. Finally, unsought products are either new products or products that require aggressive selling because they are generally avoided or overlooked by consumers.

2.1 TEAM Break into groups of four or five. Have the members of each group classify each of the following products into the category (convenience, shopping, specialty, unsought) that they think fits best from their perspective as consumers (i.e., if they were buying the product): Coca-Cola (brand), car stereo, winter coat, pair of shoes, life insurance, blue jeans, fast-food hamburgers, shampoo, canned vegetables, and frozen pizza.

3 **Define the terms *product item, product line*, and *product mix*.** A product item is a specific version of a product that can be designated as a distinct offering among an organization's products. A product line is a group of closely related products offered by an organization. An organization's product mix includes all the products it sells. Product mix width refers to the number of product lines an organization offers. Product line depth is the number of product items in a product line. Firms modify existing products by changing their quality, functional characteristics, or style. Product line extension occurs when a firm adds new products to existing product lines.

3.1 WRITING A local civic organization has asked you to give a luncheon presentation about planned obsolescence. Rather than pursuing a negative approach by talking about how businesses exploit customers through planned obsolescence, you have decided to talk about the benefits of producing products that do not last forever. Prepare a one-page outline of your presentation.

3.2 ON LINE What is the product mix offered at website http://www.rubbermaid.com?

4 **Describe marketing uses of branding.** A brand is a name, term, or symbol that identifies and differentiates a firm's products. Established brands encourage customer loyalty and help new products succeed. Branding strategies require decisions about individual, family, manufacturers', and private brands.

4.1 WRITING A local supermarket would like to introduce its own brand of paper goods (i.e., paper towels, facial tissue, etc.) to sell alongside its current inventory. The company has hired you to generate a report outlining the advantages and disadvantages of doing so. Write the report.

5 **Describe marketing uses of packaging and labelling.** Packaging has four functions: containing and protecting products; promoting products; facilitating product storage, use, and convenience; and facilitating recycling and reducing environmental damage. As a tool for promotion, packaging identifies the brand and its features. It also serves the critical function of differentiating a product from competing products and linking it with related products from the same manufacturer. The label is an integral part of the package, with persuasive and informational functions. In essence, the package is the marketer's last chance to influence buyers before they make a purchase decision.

5.1 WRITING Find a product at home that has a distinctive package. Write a paragraph evaluating that package based on the four functions of packaging discussed in the chapter.

6 Discuss global issues in branding and packaging. In addition to brand piracy, international marketers must address a variety of concerns regarding branding and packaging, including choosing a brand name policy, translating labels and meeting host-country labelling requirements, making packages aesthetically compatible with host-country cultures, and offering the sizes of packages preferred in host countries.

6.1 ON LINE List the countries to which Levi Strauss & Company markets through the website http://www.levi.com. How do the product offerings differ between the Canadian and European selections?

7 Describe how and why product warranties are important marketing tools. Product warranties are important tools because they offer consumers protection and help them gauge product quality.

7.1 Learn more about how product warranties are handled worldwide. Using InfoTrac® College Edition (http://infotrac.thomsonlearning.com), run a keyword search for "warranty" or "guarantee" and a country of interest. For example, search for "warranty" and "Germany" or "guarantee" and "Mexico." Write a paragraph about what you discover.

DEFINE IT

brand 237
brand equity 237
brand loyalty 239
brand mark 237
brand name 237
business product (industrial product) 232
cobranding 242
consumer product 232
convenience product 232
express warranty 248
family brand 242
generic product 240
generic product name 243
global brand 237
implied warranty 248
individual branding 242
informational labelling 246
manufacturer's brand 241
persuasive labelling 245
planned obsolescence 236
private brand 241
product 232
product item 234
product line 234
product line depth 235
product line extension 236
product mix 234
product mix width 235
product modification 235
service mark 243
shopping product 232
specialty product 233
trademark 243
universal product code (UPCs) 246
unsought product 233
warranty 248

APPLY IT

The Baker family owns the largest Atlantic salmon farm in Nova Scotia and is known for raising the best-quality salmon in the area. After graduating from the University of Halifax with a degree in marketing, Frank Baker returned to the farm with lots of ideas for new ways to cash in on the farm's reputation. At the time, the family allowed several local supermarkets and restaurants to use the Baker name on the salmon they sold. In the surrounding area, eating Baker Farms salmon was a sign of status. Frank, eager to put his degree to work, convinced his family that they could make money off their name by selling their salmon products already packaged to supermarkets. After hearing the idea, the family quickly met to formulate a plan to begin selling Baker Farms branded products.

QUESTIONS

1. What type of product is the Baker family selling? List your reasons.
2. What type of branding is the Baker family using? List your reasons.
3. How should Baker Farms salmon be packaged?
4. Assuming that the Baker family wishes to reposition its products, what would be an optimal strategy?

A product that a potential buyer knows about but that he or she is not actively seeking is called an unsought product. If a product is unsought, doesn't that suggest that consumers don't want it? Is the marketing of unsought products unethical?

THINK ABOUT IT

Maps à la Carte

TRY IT

A love of maps combined with some computer savvy may have translated into a viable business for two budding entrepreneurs. Ed McNierney and Bill Everett, both former executives with Kodak, launched Maps à la Carte in 1999 and created the Topo Zone website in November of that year.

Topographic maps are used extensively by hikers, hunters, surveyors, and geologists. The maps contain information such as elevation, positioning, and landmarks. Unfortunately, the thousands of different topographic maps do not fit together when users try to move from map to map. For example, some maps are curved at the edges, while others are rectangles, and they may even come in different scales. McNierney and Everett were able to solve such problems with Topozone.com.

PROVIDED COURTESY OF MAPS A LA CARTE, INC. TOPOZONE IS A TRADEMARK OF MAPS A LA CARTE.

Targeting the more than 50 million outdoor recreation enthusiasts across North America (both McNierney and Everett are avid outdoorsmen), the Topozone.com site is the first interactive, seamless topographic map site on the Web. Prior to this on-line capability, outdoor recreation enthusiasts had to use paper and CD-ROM topographic maps to plan their outdoor adventures. Map giant DeLorme Publishing Company offers topographic maps on CD-ROMs, and Maptech, Inc. includes topographic maps on its site. However, DeLorme's CD-ROMs sell for around $100 and Maptech, with its emphasis on nautical areas, has tended to target boaters rather than hikers. These facts led McNierney and Everett to believe that Topozone.com, with its high-quality and extensive site search tools, could become a map industry leader.

Within six months of launch, the Topozone.com site was averaging around 150,000 visitors a month. In addition to outdoor enthusiasts, the site was reaching beyond the intended target market. Visitors included genealogists, hobbyists, and cemetery associations. Additionally, the site won About.com's "1999 Best of the Net" award and was designated as the number one on-line geography site, replacing MapQuest.

While Maps à la Carte's new product offering appeared to be a huge success, company executives were not experiencing overnight wealth. Even with a good product service idea that was lauded by many, the company was not charging consumers to print out screen maps. By June 2000, the company had made only $50,000 in revenue from advertising and licensing fees. Maps à la Carte licensed its Topozone.com topographic map content to leading websites such as MapQuest.com, Trails.com, and GreatLodge.com, and the company was offering banner advertising opportunities.

To make money on this new product venture, McNierney and Everett developed a business model wherein they would give away the topographic map data and sell consumers the software that would allow them to make full use of the better-quality maps available at Topozone.com. To work within this new product development business model, Maps à la Carte sold almost 20 percent of the company to Navitrak, a Canadian mapping company, in June 2000 for approximately $1 million. Navitrak is a wireless navigation technology company specializing in the development and manufacture of personal navigation devices. Along with this 20 percent acquisition, the companies will work together to further develop topographic mapping systems for the outdoor recreation market.

As entrepreneurs, McNierney and Everett developed and introduced a product that satisfied a need of outdoor enthusiasts and others. With a major investment by Navitrak, the two must focus on extending the product concept into new markets and/or product extensions. With the fast pace of change and development in Internet-related offerings and a slew of potential competitors, McNierney and Everett have to move quickly.

QUESTIONS

1. What type of product does Topozone.com offer?
2. Should Maps à la Carte consider a branding strategy?
3. Should Maps à la Carte combine with Navitrak (see **http://www.navitrak.com**) in a cobranding strategy? What would be the benefits of cobranding?

FLIP IT

Flip to Chapter 8 in your *Grademaker Study Guide* for more review opportunities, including the pretest, vocabulary review, Internet activities, study test questions, and a marketing application based on product concepts. Can you describe branding? Do you know the difference between product lines, items, and mixes? If you're not quite sure, then you need to review with your *Grademaker.*

CLICK IT

The *Marketing* website is rich with materials to help you review and master marketing concepts. Check your knowledge with the free quizzes, practise key terms using the crossword puzzles, or review key concepts using the Microsoft® PowerPoint® slides. Also on the website are updated weblinks to companies mentioned in this chapter, Internet exercises, career marketing information, and much much more! Go to http://www.lamb3e.nelson.com, read the material, and follow the convenient links.

WATCH IT

Counterfeit Crusader

In late 2003, six Edmonton men were arrested and pleaded guilty to selling counterfeit merchandise at the Prince Albert Exhibition. The merchandise seized filled 150 garbage bags and included sunglasses, hats, and clothing bearing the names of Tommy Hilfiger, Oakley Eyewear, Disney Enterprises, Molson Canadian, Quiksilver, Versace, Nike, and Fila. The RCMP estimated the seized counterfeit merchandise to have a street value of $200,000. The six men were given fines ranging from $1,500 to $2,500 and were given from one to two years to pay.

In March 2004, RCMP from Toronto and Montreal executed three search warrants against three companies in Montreal (T.O.S.H. Sportswear Inc., Authentique Classique, and Z-Star Embroiderers). Counterfeit merchandise, estimated to be worth in excess of $1 million and bearing the names West Coast Choppers, Orange County Choppers, Playboy Enterprises, Von Dutch, Gap, and Tommy Hilfiger was seized.

These are just two examples of the counterfeiting activity that goes on across Canada every day. Counterfeit products are being brought into Canada and counterfeit merchandise is being produced in Canada, sticking many unsuspecting consumers with counterfeit items. According to the International Chamber of Commerce, counterfeit merchandise accounts for between 5 and 7 percent of all commerce. The problem is particularly acute in Canada.

Why is the problem so big in Canada? Essentially there are two reasons: (1) it is easy and (2) the penalties are light. For example, an owner of four retail stores in Ontario travelled to China where he was able to secure any counterfeit merchandise he wanted with whatever labels he requested, from Chinese manufacturers at very low cost. Importing the merchandise into Canada was also easy since Canada Customs does not have the personnel or resources to closely monitor all the merchandise coming across the border. After four years and sales of an estimated $10 million in counterfeit merchandise at his four stores, the business owner was finally caught. The merchandise was seized and the businessman was fined only $24,000. This businessman left Ontario and is now operating a clothing store in Vancouver.

According to the RCMP, the typical penalty for selling counterfeit merchandise is so minimal that it provides an incentive for criminals to deal in counterfeit goods. The sale of counterfeit goods, however, does much harm to companies that spend millions of dollars to develop new products and well-known brand names, only to lose sales to counterfeiters. Furthermore, the government loses billions in tax revenue. In addition, some counterfeit products, such as batteries that explode in children's toys, are dangerous. Under the Copyright Act, counterfeiters can be fined up to $1 million and sentenced to five years in jail. Sentencing, however, is usually much lighter.

Angry at losing millions of dollars in sales from Chinese companies counterfeiting his products, Garry Peters, owner of Art in Motion of Coquitlam, B.C., spent three years and over $100,000 of his own money to track down the counterfeiters and put them out of business. Lawyers, and others, are tracking down counterfeiters in Canada every day. Of the Bey Blades and Mighty Beanz products that were such big sellers this past Christmas, millions of dollars worth were counterfeits.

QUESTIONS

1. Why is counterfeiting such a big problem in Canada?
2. What should Canada Customs and the RCMP be doing to reduce the size of this problem?
3. What is the current size of this problem in Canada and what laws specifically address this issue?
4. Should business owners like Garry Peters have to spend considerable amounts of time and money policing the counterfeiting of their companies' products?

SUGGESTED INFORMATION SOURCES

Stewart Bell, "'It Was So Easy,' Says Peddler of Knock-Offs," *National Post*, December 13, 2003, A1;

Jim Bronskill, "Phoney Goods Thrive on 'Light Sentences': RCMP Says Global Crooks Endanger Canadian Public," *Edmonton Journal*, March 26, 2001, A5;

CBC, *Venture*, "Counterfeit Crusader," Broadcast: December 21, 2003.

"RCMP Seize an Estimated $1 million of Counterfeit Merchandise," *Canada NewsWire*, March 12, 2004;

"Six Plead Guilty to Sale of Counterfeit Merchandise," *Saskatoon Star-Phoenix*, June 10, 2004, A12.

chapter 9

Developing and Managing Products

>> LEARNING OBJECTIVES

1. Explain the importance of developing new products and describe the six categories of new products
2. Explain the steps in the new-product development process
3. Explain why some products succeed and others fail
4. Discuss global issues in new-product development
5. Explain the diffusion process through which new products are adopted
6. Explain the concept of product life cycles

>> It all started when a 4-year-old asked her mom if she could put coloured cake sprinkles on her favourite ketchup. The intrigued mom said it was okay, and thus came about a new product, later to be named Sparky, from the H.J. Heinz Co. of Canada Ltd.

It happens that the mom works for the H.J. Heinz Co. in Leamington, Ontario. When the mom related the sprinkles story to the marketing people in Leamington, they too were intrigued. The product concept was tested with consumers. The test kitchen crew in Leamington had to invent sprinkles that would not only taste good in ketchup but also withstand sitting in ketchup bottles for months and still look good. The finished product was given to 250 households with children to try. Thus was born Sparky.

Unfortunately, Sparky didn't sell as well as Heinz had hoped and was withdrawn from the market. It was a product failure. For companies like Heinz, and just about every other company, some new products fail. However, for companies that work hard and do their homework, for every product failure, there will be some product successes. Clearly, Heinz, with over $9 billion in worldwide sales, including sales of over 400 million bottles of ketchup each year, has had some successes.

Heinz took what it had learned from the Sparky failure, interviewed hundreds of kids, the biggest consumers of ketchup, and introduced Blastin' Green ketchup to the market. Blastin' Green was an immediate success, reaching sales of over 1 million bottles a month within 90 days of introduction. The success of Blastin' Green increased Heinz's already dominant share of the ketchup market from 55 percent to 59 percent, its highest share ever!

Shortly after the success of Blastin' Green came Funky Purple ketchup. Why purple? For the same reason as the green colour. Interviews with thousands of kids said these were the colours they wanted. Most recently hitting store shelves have been Heinz Kool Blue and Mystery Colour ketchups. And all of the Heinz coloured ketchups come in the "EZ Squirt" plastic bottles with an hourglass shape that are easier for kids to handle. The "EZ Squirt" bottles also have smaller openings that allow kids to write their names and draw pictures on their food with the ketchup—and, of course, use more of it. To keep parents happy, Heinz has added more vitamin C to its coloured ketchups.

With all of the success of coloured ketchups for kids, Heinz hasn't forgotten adults. In addition to the coloured ketchups, Heinz has introduced flavoured ketchups, such as Hot & Spicy, Sweet Basil and Oregano, and Roasted Garlic. These ketchups also come in easy-to-squeeze bottles that are easier to handle, contain a new valve design so that they won't clog, and can be stored on their caps, upside down, to keep remaininq ketchup at the top of the bottle for quick and easy application when next needed.

While coloured ketchups have been a huge success, you can only take a product concept so far. With great anticipation, Heinz launched a line of Funky Fries. For this product line, Heinz tested over 50 flavours, including Fruit Loops-flavoured French fries, before settling on Cocoa Crispers, Crunchy Rings, and Kool Blue. Unfortunately, kids already seemed to like plain French fries and never warmed up to chocolate-flavoured fries. Heinz quickly withdrew this product from the market. Not to fret, though—the 17 people working in the Heinz test kitchen in Leamington have other ideas that you'll be seeing in the months ahead on store shelves.[1]

Why do you think Sparky failed while Blastin' Green, Funky Purple, and Kool Blue ketchups have been huge successes? Why have coloured ketchups succeeded while Funky Fries have failed? Are you surprised at the idea source for Sparky ketchup? Where do new product ideas come from? How are new product ideas tested?

ON LINE

H. J. Heinz

How does Heinz's website support its new products? What can you find out about new products on this website? What can you find out about product testing?

http://www.heinz.com

NewProductWorks

Not all new products are well received in the marketplace. Go to NewProductWorks' website and read the polls for an overview of products the company expects to "hit" and some it expects to "miss." What is your opinion of the products listed?

http://www.newproductworks.com

1 Explain the importance of developing new products and describe the six categories of new products

>> THE IMPORTANCE OF NEW PRODUCTS

New products are important to sustain growth and profits and to replace obsolete items. 3M Company introduces about 500 new products each year. Of the products Corning, Inc. sells, 84 percent have been introduced within the past four years.[2] While continuing at relatively high levels, the number of new-product introductions in recent years has declined from the very high levels of the 1970s and 1980s. In the late 1990s, and continuing through this year, fewer new products have been introduced annually. The decline in new-food-item introductions is particularly dramatic. What accounts for this reversal after 25 years of annual increases? The cost of new-product failures is a contributing factor. Others include the intense competitive pressure and rigorous financial scrutiny that marketers face from financial analysts.[3] The decline in the economy from 2000 through 2002 also left many firms risk averse.

Categories of New Products

new product
A product new to the world, the market, the producer, the seller, or some combination of these.

The term **new product** is somewhat confusing because its meaning varies widely. Actually, the term has several "correct" definitions. A product can be new to the world, to the market, to the producer or seller, or to some combination of these. There are six categories of new products:

- *New-to-the-world products* (also called *discontinuous innovations*): These products create an entirely new market. The telephone, television, computer, and facsimile machine are commonly cited examples of new-to-the-world products. New-to-the-world products represent the smallest category of new products.
- *New product lines:* These products, which the firm has not previously offered, allow it to enter an established market. Bombardier was formed in 1942 to manufacture enclosed multipassenger snowmobiles for military use. In 1959 it introduced the Ski-Doo snowmobile. Later the Sea-Doo, a watercraft product, was introduced. In 1974, Bombardier won a contract to supply cars for the Montreal subway. Since then, the company has added corporate jets, regional jets for the airlines, surface-to-air defence systems, and golf carts, among other products. Each of these additions represents a new product line for Bombardier.
- *Additions to existing product lines:* This category includes new products that supplement a firm's established line. Examples of product line additions include Tide detergent in tablet form, Downy Wrinkle Releaser fabric softener, and Yoplait's Go-GURT, packaged in kid-friendly, Popsicle-style tubes.[4] Kimberly-Clark has added a moistened version of toilet paper to its Cottonelle line.[5] NSF International of Toronto added a new product to its existing lines as a result of *Escherichia coli* outbreak in the drinking water of Walkerton, Ontario, which resulted in seven deaths. The product, called the UVD8.40—Ultra Violet Sterilizing Water Purification & Water Filtration System, is based on the Ultra Light technology that the company already possessed. The product, marketed to builders, attaches to the main water line outside the home and purifies all water before it enters the home.
- *Improvements or revisions of existing products:* The "new and improved" product may be significantly or slightly changed. For example, Breyers Soft 'n Creamy! ice cream "scoops right out without bending the spoon." Anyone who has ever sat around for 15 minutes waiting for an ice cream container to thaw would certainly agree that this is a product improvement. Another type of revision is package improvement. The Heinz EZ Squirt Ketchup bottle is short, is made from easy-to-squeeze plastic, and has a needle-shaped nozzle that lets small hands use it to decorate food.[6] Most new products fit into the revision or improvement category.

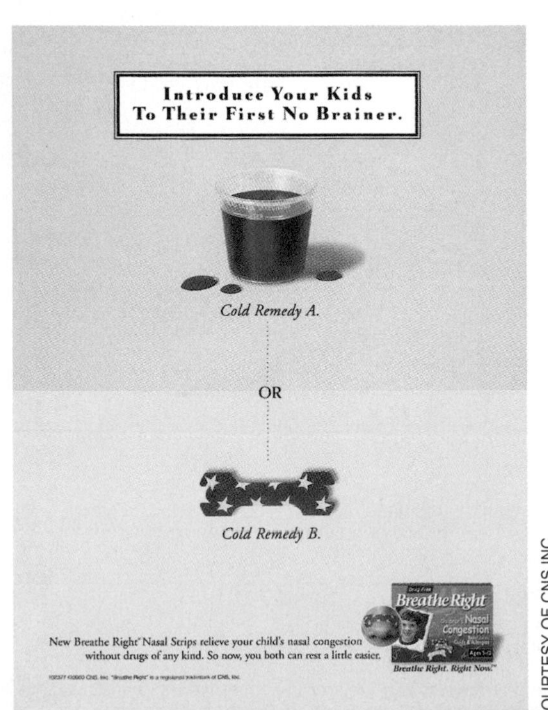

Introduce Your Kids
To Their First No Brainer.
Cold Remedy A.
OR
Cold Remedy B.
New Breathe Right® Nasal Strips relieve your child's nasal congestion without drugs of any kind. So now, you both can rest a little easier.
Breathe Right
Nasal Congestion
Breathe Right. Right Now.™

COURTESY OF CNS INC.

Into what category of new products do you think the Breathe Right Nasal Strip falls? It could possibly fall into more than one: additions to existing product lines and repositioned products. How?

- *Repositioned products:* These are existing products targeted at new markets or market segments. The bottle for Beefeater gin was totally redesigned in an effort to appeal to a younger, more upscale market.[7] Dippity-do, the "green coloured goo" that has been marketed to adult women since 1965, is being repositioned to target teen buyers, according to managers at White Rain, the corporate parent.[8]
- *Lower-priced products:* This category refers to products that provide performance similar to competing brands at a lower price. Hewlett-Packard Laser Jet 3100 is a scanner, copier, printer, and fax machine combined. This new product is priced lower than many conventional colour copiers and much lower than the combined price of the four items purchased separately. The so-called e-machines that have been introduced for under $500 also fit into this category of new product.

©KRISTIINA PAUL

Into what category of new products do you think the Chevrolet Optra falls? The Optra is a new small car introduced at the Montreal Automobile Show. It has been designed for the Canadian market that wants extras in smaller cars. The Optra might be considered an addition to an existing product line, a repositioned product, or a lower-priced product (priced under $16,000).

In some cases, we might question whether some new products being introduced to the market are needed or even desirable, as the "Ethics in Marketing" box discusses.

>> THE NEW-PRODUCT DEVELOPMENT PROCESS

2 Explain the steps in the new-product development process

The management and technology consulting firm Booz Allen Hamilton has studied the new-product development process for over 30 years. Analyzing five major studies undertaken during this period, the firm has concluded that the companies most likely to succeed in developing and introducing new products are those that take the following actions:

ETHICS IN MARKETING

More Beer for More Target Markets

Beer consumption in Canada peaked in 1986. In that year, Canadians drank an average of 76.88 litres of beer. By 1997, that figure had fallen below 65 litres. Canada now ranks 17th in the world in beer consumption. Worse still for the beer companies, the number of Canadians between ages 19 and 34—the biggest beer drinkers—is declining.

In response to the stagnant market, the breweries are chasing all of the beer drinkers that they can get their hands on. Molson and Labatt are targeting 20- to 35-year-olds with imports such as Boddingtons, Leffe, and Belle-Vue Kriek. These beers are sold exclusively through bars catering to the young and are heavily promoted to this audience. Microbreweries have been penetrating this market with specialty products such as Upper Canada's Rebellion. Molson has also opened brew pubs in the Air Canada Centre, home to the Maple Leafs and Raptors, as well as in Vancouver's GM Place.

Since the 1980s, Canadian breweries have been targeting women, not traditionally a beer-drinking audience, by introducing light and ice beers and through trendy advertising of these products.

Are you among the many Canadians who enjoy a glass of wine with dinner? The beer companies want you. With wine growing in popularity, now accounting for 11.9 percent of alcoholic beverage consumption in Canada (beer accounts for 81.3 percent of the market), Molson has brought A Marca Bavaria to Canada from Brazil and Labatt has begun importing Stella Artois from Belgium. These beers are targeted to replace wine at fine dining establishments.

As low-carb diets have become more popular in Canada (an Ipsos-Reid poll shows that eight of 10 Canadians believe that a low-carb diet can lead to weight loss), the breweries have responded to this target audience as well. Labatt has introduced Sterling, which contains 2.5 grams of carbohydrates and 88 calories in a 341 mL bottle; Molson has launched Ultra with 2.5 grams of carbohydrates and less than 100 calories; and Sleeman Breweries Ltd. has introduced Clear with 2.5 grams of carbohydrates. The average regular bottle of beer contains from 11 to 17 grams of carbs.

Have all of these new product introductions worked? Beer consumption is not yet back to 1986 levels but was up again, for the fifth straight year, in 2002.[9]

Are all of the new beer brands new products? If so, into what category of new product do they fit? Should breweries be so aggressively targeting so many different groups of consumers to increase beer consumption? How do the beer companies know that their aggressive targeting of 20-year-olds isn't encouraging middle teens to drink beer?

- Make the long-term commitment needed to support innovation and new-product development
- Use a company-specific approach, driven by corporate objectives and strategies, with a well-defined new-product strategy at its core
- Capitalize on experience to achieve and maintain competitive advantage
- Establish an environment—a management style, organizational structure, and degree of top-management support—conducive to achieving company-specific new-product and corporate objectives

Most companies follow a formal new-product development process, usually starting with a new-product strategy. Exhibit 9.1 traces the seven-step process, which is discussed in detail in this section. The exhibit is funnel-shaped to highlight the fact that each stage acts as a screen. The purpose is to filter out unworkable ideas.

New-Product Strategy

new-product strategy
A plan that links the new-product development process with the objectives of the marketing department, the business unit, and the corporation.

A **new-product strategy** links the new-product development process with the objectives of the marketing department, the business unit, and the corporation. A new-product strategy must be compatible with these objectives, and in turn, all three objectives must be consistent with one another.

A new-product strategy is part of the organization's overall marketing strategy. It sharpens the focus and provides general guidelines for generating, screening, and evaluating new-product ideas. The new-product strategy specifies the roles that new products must play in the organization's overall plan and describes the characteristics of products the organization wants to offer and the markets it wants to serve.

Idea Generation

New-product ideas come from many sources, including customers, employees, distributors, competitors, research and development (R&D), and consultants.

- *Customers:* The marketing concept suggests that customers' wants and needs should be the springboard for developing new products. Thermos, the vacuum bottle manufacturer, provides an interesting example of how companies tap customers for ideas. The company's first step in developing an innovative home barbecue grill was to send 10 members of its interdisciplinary new-product team into the field for about a month. Their assignment was to learn all about people's cookout needs and to invent a product to meet them. In various cities, the team conducted focus groups, visited people's homes, and even videotaped barbecues. In keeping with this marketing concept and in response to millions of Canadians going on low-carbohydrate diets such as the Atkins and South Beach diets, McDonald's added the new Adult Happy Meal, which includes a salad, bottled water, a Stepometer and exercise tips; and brewers have introduced low-carb beer such as Sleeman's Clear, Labatt's Sterling, and Molson's Ultra.
- *Employees:* Marketing personnel—advertising and marketing research employees, as well as salespeople—often create new-product ideas because they analyze and are involved in the marketplace. The very successful introduction of Post-it Notes started with an employee's idea. In 1974, the R&D department of 3M's commercial tape division developed and patented the adhesive component of Post-it Notes. However, it was a year before an employee of the commercial tape division, who sang in a church choir, identified a use for the adhesive. He had been using paper clips and slips of

ON LINE

IDEO

Canada Foundation for Innovation

What can you learn about new product innovations from The Canada Foundation for Innovation? What are some recent innovations to come out of IDEO? Who might be the clients for the Canada Foundation for Innovation and IDEO?

http://www.ideo.com

http://www.innovationcanada.ca/10/en

Canadian Inventions

You might be surprised at the wide range of products and services that have been initiated in Canada or by Canadians. Check out all of the Canadian inventions at this website. Which ones surprise you the most?

http://www3.sympatico.ca/taniah/Canada/things

EXHIBIT 9.1

New-Product Development Process

paper to mark places in hymn books. But the paper clips damaged his books, and the slips of paper fell out. The solution, as we now all know, was to apply the adhesive to small pieces of paper and sell them in packages. The idea for Heinz's coloured ketchups, as the opening example of this chapter showed, came from an employee at the company's Leamington plant. Many companies, like Kindred Industries of Midland, Ontario, routinely offer financial awards to employees who suggest new-product ideas or ideas for product improvements.

- *Distributors:* A well-trained sales force routinely asks distributors about needs that are not being met. Because they are closer to end users, distributors are often more aware of customer needs than are manufacturers. The inspiration for Rubbermaid's litter-free lunch box, named Sidekick, came from a distributor. The distributor suggested that Rubbermaid place some of its plastic containers inside a lunch box and sell the box as an alternative to plastic wrap and paper bags.
- *Competitors:* No firms rely solely on internally generated ideas for new products. A big part of any organization's marketing intelligence system should be monitoring the performance of competitors' products. One purpose of competitive monitoring is to determine which, if any, of the competitors' products should be copied.

There is plenty of information about competitors on the World Wide Web. For example, AltaVista (http://www.altavista.com) is a powerful index tool that can be used to locate information about products and companies. Fuld & Company's competitive intelligence guide provides links to a variety of market intelligence sites.

- *Research and development:* R&D is carried out in four distinct ways. Basic research is scientific research aimed at discovering new technologies. Applied research takes these new technologies and tries to find useful applications for them. **Product development** goes one step further by converting applications into marketable products. *Product modification* makes cosmetic or functional changes in existing products. Many new-product breakthroughs come from R&D activities. Pert Plus, Procter & Gamble's combination shampoo and conditioner, was invented in the laboratory. So was Take Heart, a new product line from Quaker Oats, that includes an ingredient called Reducol, which has been found to lower the level of low-density lipoprotein or LDL cholesterol.[10]

product development
A marketing strategy that entails the creation of marketable new products; the process of converting applications for new technologies into marketable products.

- *Consultants:* Outside consultants are always available to examine a business and recommend product ideas. Examples include the Weston Group; Booz Allen Hamilton; and Management Decisions. Traditionally, consultants determine whether a company has a balanced portfolio of products and, if not, what new-product ideas are needed to offset the imbalance. For instance, an outside consultant conceived Airwick's highly successful Carpet Fresh carpet cleaner.

Creativity is the wellspring of new-product ideas, regardless of who comes up with them. A variety of approaches and techniques have been developed to stimulate creative thinking. The two considered most useful for generating new-product ideas are brainstorming and focus-group exercises. The goal of **brainstorming** is to get a group to think of unlimited ways to vary a product or solve a problem. Group members avoid criticism of an idea, no matter how ridiculous it may seem. Objective evaluation is postponed. The sheer quantity of ideas is what matters. As noted in Chapter 7, an objective of focus-group interviews is to stimulate insightful comments through group interaction. Focus groups usually consist of seven to 10 people. Sometimes consumer focus groups generate excellent new-product ideas—for example, Cycle dog food, Stick-Up room deodorizers, Dustbuster vacuum cleaners, and Wendy's salad bar. In the industrial market, machine tools, keyboard designs, aircraft interiors, and backhoe accessories have evolved from focus groups.

brainstorming
The process of getting a group to think of unlimited ways to vary a product or solve a problem.

Idea Screening

After new ideas have been generated, they pass through the first filter in the product development process. This stage, called **screening**, eliminates ideas that are inconsistent with the organization's new-product strategy or are obviously inappropriate for some other reason. The new-product committee, the new-product department, or some other formally appointed group performs the screening review. General Motors' Advanced Portfolio Exploration Group (APEx) knows that only one out of every 20 new car concepts developed by the group will ever become a reality. That's not a bad percentage. In the pharmaceutical business, one new product out of 5,000 ideas is not uncommon.[11] Most new-product ideas are rejected at the screening stage.

screening
The first filter in the product development process; it eliminates ideas that are inconsistent with the organization's new-product strategy or are obviously inappropriate for some other reason.

Concept tests are often used at the screening stage to rate concept (or product) alternatives. A **concept test** evaluates a new-product idea, usually before any prototype has been created. Typically, researchers get consumer reactions to descriptions and visual representations of a proposed product.

concept test
A test to evaluate a new-product idea, usually before any prototype has been created.

Concept tests are considered fairly good predictors of success for line extensions. They have also been relatively precise predictors of success for new products that are not copycat items, are not easily classified into existing product categories, and do not require major changes in consumer behaviour—such as Betty Crocker Tuna Helper, Cycle dog food, and Libby's Fruit Float. However, concept tests are usually inaccurate in predicting the success of new products that create new consumption patterns and require major changes in consumer behaviour—such as microwave ovens, videocassette recorders, computers, and word processors.

Business Analysis

New-product ideas that survive the initial screening process move to the **business analysis** stage, where preliminary figures for demand, cost, sales, and profitability are calculated. For the first time, costs and revenues are estimated and compared. Depending on the nature of the product and the company, this process may be simple or complex.

business analysis
The second stage of the screening process, where preliminary figures for demand, cost, sales, and profitability are calculated.

The newness of the product, the size of the market, and the nature of the competition all affect the accuracy of revenue projections. In an established market like soft drinks, industry estimates of total market size are available. Forecasting market share for a new entry is a bigger challenge.

Analyzing overall economic trends and their impact on estimated sales is especially important in product categories that are sensitive to fluctuations in the business cycle. If consumers view the economy as uncertain and risky, they will put off buying durable goods like major home appliances, automobiles, and homes. Likewise, business buyers postpone major equipment purchases if they expect a recession.

These questions are commonly asked during the business analysis stage:

- What is the likely demand for the product?
- What impact would the new product probably have on total sales, profits, market share, and return on investment?
- How would the introduction of the product affect existing products? Would the new product cannibalize existing products?
- Would current customers benefit from the product?
- Would the product enhance the image of the company's overall product mix?
- Would the new product affect current employees in any way? Would it lead to hiring more people or reducing the size of the workforce?
- What new facilities, if any, would be needed?
- How might competitors respond?
- What is the risk of failure? Is the company willing to take the risk?

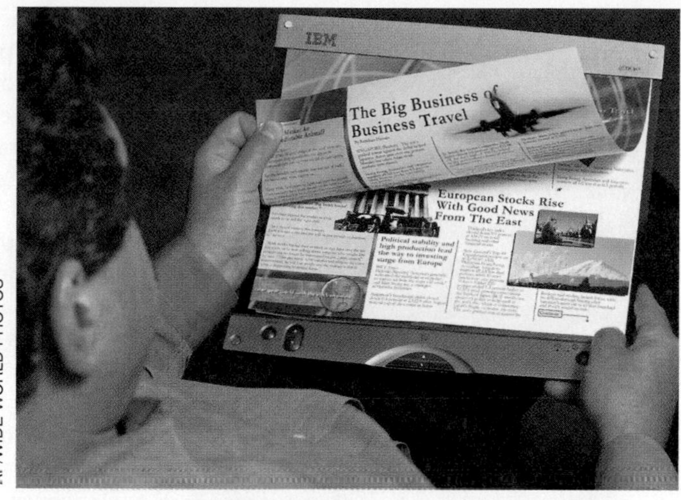

AP/WIDE WORLD PHOTOS

New product development is the lifeblood of many companies. IBM is working on a flexible panel/e-newspaper device that will allow users to download news services through wireless access.

Answering these and related questions may require studies of markets, competition, costs, and technical capabilities. But at the end of this stage, management should have a good understanding of the product's market potential. This full understanding is important because costs increase dramatically once a product idea enters the development stage.

Development

In the early stage of **development**, the R&D department or engineering department may develop a prototype of the product. During this stage, the firm should start sketching a marketing strategy. The marketing department should decide on the product's packaging, branding, labelling, and so forth. In addition, it should map out preliminary promotion, price, and distribution strategies. The technical feasibility of manufacturing the product at an acceptable cost should also be thoroughly examined.

development
The stage in the product development process in which a prototype is developed and a marketing strategy is outlined.

The development stage can last a long time and thus be very expensive. Crest toothpaste was in the development stage for 10 years. It took 18 years to develop Minute Rice, 15 years to develop the Polaroid Colorpack camera, 15 years to develop the Xerox copy machine, and 55 years to develop television. Gillette spent six years developing the MACH3 razor.

The development process works best when all the involved areas (R&D, marketing, engineering, production, and even suppliers) work together rather than sequentially, a process called **simultaneous product development**. This approach allows firms to shorten the development process and reduce costs. With simultaneous product development, all relevant functional areas and outside suppliers participate in all stages of the development process. Rather than proceeding through highly structured stages, the cross-functional team operates in unison. Involving key suppliers early in the process capitalizes on their specialized knowledge and enables them to design and develop critical component parts.

simultaneous product development
A team-oriented approach to new-product development.

The Internet is a useful tool for implementing simultaneous product development. On the Net, multiple partners from a variety of locations can meet regularly to assess new-product ideas, analyze markets and demographics, and review cost information. Ideas judged to be feasible can quickly be converted into new products. For example, Procter & Gamble has created an autonomous idea laboratory called

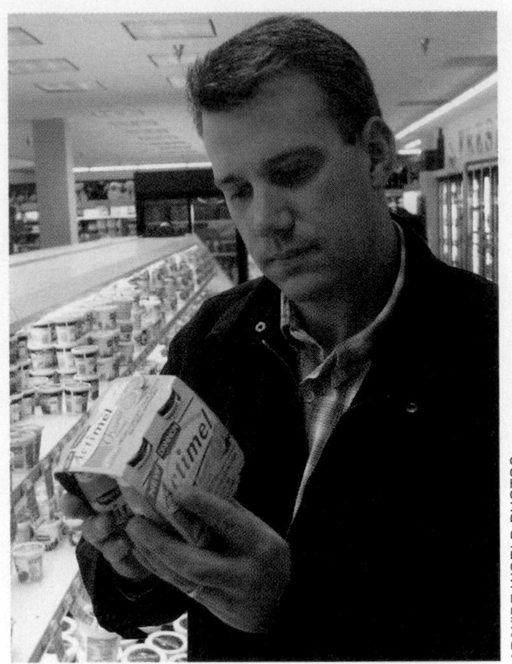

AP/WIDE WORLD PHOTOS

Dannon chose to test market its successful European product Actimel before rolling out the bacteria-loaded dairy product North America-wide. Test marketing for two years allowed the company to refine its marketing strategy and determine customer reaction.

Corporate New Ventures. Its mission is to encourage ideas for products and put the best ideas into speedy production. Corporate New Ventures has $250 million in seed money and reports directly to top management.

Laboratory tests are often conducted on prototype models during the development stage. User safety is an important aspect of laboratory testing, which actually subjects products to much more severe treatment than is expected by end users. Kindred Industries of Midland, Ontario, tests kitchen faucets by running water through them at much higher pressure and for much longer time periods than would ever occur in someone's kitchen.

Many products that test well in the laboratory are also tried out in homes or businesses. Product categories well suited for such use tests include human and pet food products, household cleaning products, and industrial chemicals and supplies. These products are all relatively inexpensive, and their performance characteristics are apparent to users. For example, at the W.K. Kellogg Institute for Food and Nutrition Research, cross-functional teams of employees spend their days cooking, eating, and comparing notes. Management believes that creativity comes from diversity, so researchers with unusual backgrounds are recruited. The institute employs people from 22 different countries. The company is quite pleased with the results produced by the institute. In one month, researchers generated 65 new product ideas and 94 new packaging ideas.[12]

Most products require some refinement based on the results of laboratory and use tests. General Mills tested various package prototypes of Go-GURT with mothers and their children. "If you could squeeze it, push it, pump it, peel it, or sip it, we tried it." [13] A second stage of development often takes place before test marketing.

Test Marketing

test marketing
The limited introduction of a product and a marketing program to determine the reactions of potential customers in a market situation.

After products and marketing programs have been developed, they are usually tested in the marketplace. **Test marketing** is the limited introduction of a product and a marketing program to determine the reactions of potential customers in a market situation. Test marketing allows management to evaluate alternative strategies and to assess how well the various aspects of the marketing mix fit together. Quaker Oats test marketed the Take Heart line of food products including ready-to-eat cereals, snack bars, and fruit juice beverages in selected markets before introducing the line nationwide.[14] Even established products are test marketed to assess new marketing strategies. One-dollar bottles of chocolate, strawberry, and coffee-flavoured milk, distributed through vending machines, were offered in schools to assess this alternative distribution strategy. Initial weekly sales ran about 200 bottles per machine.[15]

The cities chosen as test sites should reflect market conditions in the new product's projected market area. Yet no "magic city" exists that can universally represent market conditions, and a product's success in one city doesn't guarantee that it will be a nationwide hit. When selecting test market cities, researchers should therefore find locations where the demographics and purchasing habits mirror the overall market. The company should also have good distribution in test cities. Moreover, test locations should be isolated from the media. If the TV stations in a particular market reach a very large area outside that market, the advertising used for the test product may pull in many consumers from outside the market. The product may then appear more successful than it really is. Exhibit 9.2 provides a useful checklist of criteria for selecting test markets. As an example, Winnipeg is a popular test market city.

ON LINE

What can you find out on the Internet about current test marketing? Use the Google search engine and type in "Test Marketing."

http://www.google.ca

EXHIBIT 9.2

Checklist for Selecting Test Markets

IN CHOOSING A TEST MARKET, MANY CRITERIA NEED TO BE CONSIDERED, ESPECIALLY THE FOLLOWING:
Similarity to planned distribution outlets
Relative isolation from other cities
Availability of advertising media that will cooperate
Diversified cross section of ages, religions, cultural-societal preferences, etc.
No atypical purchasing habits
Representative population size
Typical per capita income
Good record as a test city, but not overly used
Not easily "jammed" by competitors
Stability of year-round sales
No dominant television station; multiple newspapers, magazines, and radio stations
Availability of research and audit services
Availability of retailers that will cooperate
Freedom from unusual influences, such as one industry's dominance or heavy tourism

The High Costs of Test Marketing

Test marketing frequently takes one year or longer, and costs can exceed $1 million. Some products remain in test markets even longer. McDonald's spent 12 years developing and testing salads before introducing them. Despite the cost, many firms believe it is a lot better to fail in a test market than in a national introduction.

Because test marketing is so expensive, some companies do not test line extensions of well-known brands. For example, because the Folgers brand is well known, Procter & Gamble faced little risk in distributing its instant decaffeinated version nationally. Consolidated Foods Kitchen of Sara Lee followed the same approach with its frozen croissants. Other products introduced without being test marketed include General Foods' International Coffees, Quaker Oats' Chewy Granola Bars and Granola Dipps, and Pillsbury's Milk Break Bars.

The high cost of test marketing is not just financial. One unavoidable problem is that test marketing exposes the new product and its marketing mix to competitors before its introduction. Thus, the element of surprise is lost. Several years ago, for example, Procter & Gamble began testing a ready-to-spread Duncan Hines frosting. General Mills took note and rushed to market with its own Betty Crocker brand, which now is the best-selling brand of ready-to-spread frosting. Also, a competitor can sabotage or "jam" a testing program by introducing its own sales promotion, pricing, or advertising campaign. The purpose is to hide or distort the normal conditions that the testing firm might expect in the market.

Alternatives to Test Marketing

Many firms are looking for cheaper, faster, safer alternatives to traditional test marketing. In the early 1980s, Information Resources, Inc., pioneered one alternative: single-source research using supermarket scanner data. A typical supermarket scanner test costs about $300,000. Another alternative to traditional test marketing is **simulated (laboratory) market testing**. Advertising and other promotional materials for several products, including the test product, are shown to members of the product's target market. These people are then taken to shop at a mock or real store, where their purchases are recorded. Shopper behaviour, including repeat purchasing, is monitored to assess the product's likely performance under true market conditions. Research firms offer simulated market tests for $25,000 to $100,000, compared to $1 million or more for full-scale test marketing.

simulated (laboratory) market testing
The presentation of advertising and other promotion materials for several products, including a test product, to members of the product's target market.

ON LINE

Harvey's

How important are new products in the fast-food market? What new product is Harvey's promoting this month? Go to its website to find out.

http://www.harveys.ca

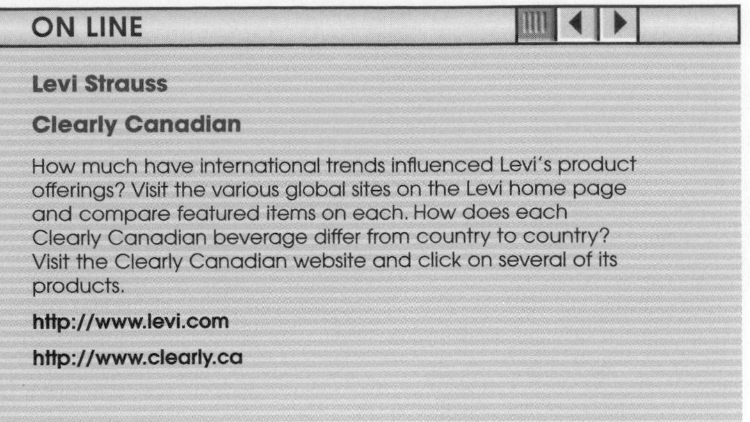

ON LINE

Levi Strauss

Clearly Canadian

How much have international trends influenced Levi's product offerings? Visit the various global sites on the Levi home page and compare featured items on each. How does each Clearly Canadian beverage differ from country to country? Visit the Clearly Canadian website and click on several of its products.

http://www.levi.com

http://www.clearly.ca

On-Line Test Marketing

Despite these alternatives, most firms still consider test marketing essential for most new products. The high price of failure simply prohibits the widespread introduction of most new products without testing. Many firms are finding that the Internet offers a fast, cost-effective way to conduct test marketing.

Procter & Gamble is an avid proponent of using the Internet as a means for gauging customer demand for potential new products. The company reportedly conducts 40 percent of its product tests and other studies on-line and hopes to cut its $140 million annual research budget in half by shifting efforts to the Internet.[16]

Many products that are not available in grocery stores or drugstores can be sampled or purchased from P&G's corporate website (http://PG.com.) Crest Whitestrips provides an illustration.

In August 2000, when P&G brand manager Val Bogdan-Powers was ready to launch Crest Whitestrips, a new home tooth-bleaching kit, management wasn't sure that consumers would be willing to pay the proposed $44 retail price. She then began an eight-month campaign offering the strips exclusively on P&G's http://www.whitestrips.com. TV spots and magazine ads were run to promote the on-line sale. In eight months, 144,000 whitening kits were sold on-line. The product was introduced in retail outlets in 2001, and $50 million worth of kits were sold in the first three months at the $44 per kit price.[17]

Other consumer goods firms that have recently begun on-line test marketing include General Mills and Quaker Oats. Other sites have appeared that offer consumers prototype products developed by all sizes of firms.

Commercialization

commercialization
The decision to market a product.

The final stage in the new-product development process is **commercialization**, the decision to market a product. The decision to commercialize the product sets several tasks in motion: ordering production materials and equipment, starting production, building inventories, shipping the product to field distribution points, training the sales force, announcing the new product to the trade, and advertising to potential customers. Pete Mateja, president of Home & Park Motorhomes in Kitchener, Ontario, the largest builder of camper vans in Canada, says that it is his company's goal to deliver to customers what they want even before they realize they want it.[18]

The time from the initial commercialization decision to the product's actual introduction varies. It can range from a few weeks for simple products that use existing equipment to several years for technical products that require custom manufacturing equipment.

The total cost of development and initial introduction can be staggering. Gillette spent $750 million developing MACH3, and the first-year marketing budget for the new three-bladed razor was $300 million.

For some products, a well-planned Internet campaign can provide new-product information for people who are looking for the solutions that a particular new product offers. Attempting to reach customers at the point in time when they need a product is much more cost-effective and efficient than communicating with a target market that may eventually have a need for the product.

3 Explain why some products succeed and others fail

Despite the high cost of developing and testing new products, a large proportion of all new-product introductions fail. Products fail for a number of reasons. One common reason is that they simply do not offer any discernible benefit compared to existing products. Another commonly cited factor in new-product failures is a poor match between product features and customer desires. For example, there are telephone systems on the market with over 700 different functions, although the average user is happy with just 10 functions. Other reasons for failure include overestimation of market size, incorrect positioning, a price too high or too low, inadequate distribution, poor promotion, or simply an inferior product compared to those of competitors.

Failure can be a matter of degree. Absolute failure occurs when a company cannot recoup its development, marketing, and production costs. The product actually loses money for the company. A relative product failure results when the product returns a profit but fails to achieve sales, profit, or market share goals.

High costs and other risks of developing and testing new products do not stop many companies, such as Rubbermaid, Magna, Nortel, Bombardier, Colgate-Palmolive, Campbell's Soup, 3M Company, and Procter & Gamble, from aggressively developing and introducing new products.

The most important factor in successful new-product introduction is a good match between the product and market needs—as the marketing concept would predict. Successful new products deliver a meaningful and perceivable benefit to a sizable number of people or organizations and are different in some meaningful way from their intended substitutes. Firms that routinely experience success in new-product introductions tend to share the following characteristics:

- A history of carefully listening to customers
- An obsession with producing the best product possible
- A vision of what the market will be like in the future
- Strong leadership
- A commitment to new-product development
- A project-based team approach to new-product development
- Getting every aspect of the product development process right.[19]

>> GLOBAL ISSUES IN NEW-PRODUCT DEVELOPMENT

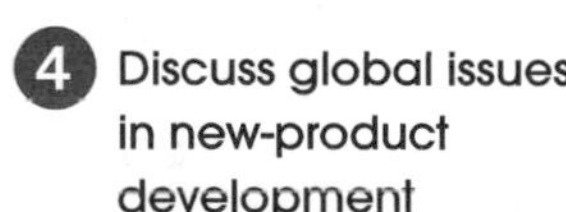
4 Discuss global issues in new-product development

Increasing globalization of markets and of competition provides a reason for multinational firms to consider new-product development from a worldwide perspective. A firm that starts with a global strategy is better able to develop products that are marketable worldwide. In many multinational corporations, every product is developed for potential worldwide distribution, and unique market requirements are built in whenever possible. Procter & Gamble introduced Pampers Phases into global markets within one month of first getting the product on the market. P&G's goal was to have the product on store shelves in 90 countries within one year. The objective was to establish brand loyalty among dealers and consumers before foreign competitors could react.

Some global marketers design their products to meet regulations and other key requirements in their major markets and then, if necessary, meet smaller markets' requirements country by country. Nissan develops lead-country car models that, with minor changes, can be sold in most markets. For the remaining markets, Nissan provides other models that can readily be adapted. With this approach, Nissan has been able to reduce the number of its basic models from 48 to 18.

Some products, however, have little potential for global market penetration without modification. Russia and China represent two huge automobile markets but not at prevailing international prices. General Motors, Ford Motor Company, Fiat, Renault, and others are working with Russian partners to produce cars that can retail for $15,000 or less.[20] GM, Ford, Chrysler, Toyota, and Volkswagen AG are focusing on China.[21] You may recall from Chapter 5 that GM and Shanghai Automotive Industry Corporation have formed a strategic alliance to develop and market a "Farmer's Car" targeted at rural Chinese consumers. Interestingly, in recent years, a number of new car models have been designed specifically for the Canadian market, as the "Global Perspectives" box indicates.

© MICHAEL NEWMAN/PHOTOEDIT

Insights for new products are coming increasingly from around the world. An Argentine success, Häagen-Dazs's *dulce de leche*, is gaining popularity in North America where in-store displays promote the new flavour.

We often hear about how popular North American products are in foreign countries. Recently, companies such as Levi Strauss, Roots, Coca-Cola, RJR Nabisco, and Nike have been finding that products popular in foreign markets can become hits here. An example is Häagen-Dazs's new ice cream flavour *dulce de leche,* originally introduced in Buenos Aires in 1997. The brand is named after a caramelized milk spread that is popular in Argentina. *Dulce de leche* became an instant success in Argentina. The brand has since been introduced in North America, and sales are increasing at over 25 percent per month.

Other companies are applying a new twist on the popular international business aphorism, "think global, act local." Former Coca-Cola CEO Douglas N. Daft used "think local, act local" as a strategy to give country managers more autonomy in new-product development.[22] The idea has resulted in seven new brands of energy drinks, waters, and teas being introduced in various Asian countries recently. More are planned to diversify beyond colas. Results are impressive. Xing Mu (Smart), a Coca-Cola brand, has become the fourth-most-popular carbonated soft drink in China in just four years.[23]

Coca-Cola also follows a one product–one message strategy in some markets. It markets Powerade, a brand of sport drink, the same way in Europe as in Canada. It also markets a popular European rehydrating, after-exercise drink called Aquarius.[24]

>> THE SPREAD OF NEW PRODUCTS

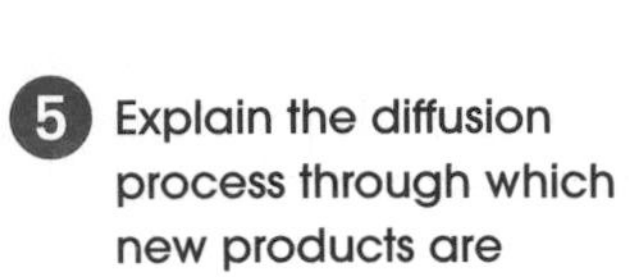

5 Explain the diffusion process through which new products are adopted

adopter
A consumer who was happy enough with his or her trial experience with a product to use it again.

innovation
A product perceived as new by a potential adopter.

diffusion
The process by which the adoption of an innovation spreads.

Managers have a better chance of successfully marketing products if they understand how consumers learn about and adopt products. A person who buys a new product never before tried may ultimately become an **adopter**, a consumer who was happy enough with his or her trial experience with a product to use it again.

Diffusion of Innovation

An **innovation** is a product perceived as new by a potential adopter. It really doesn't matter whether the product is "new to the world" or some other category of new product. If it is new to a potential adopter, it is an innovation in this context. **Diffusion** is the process by which the adoption of an innovation spreads.

Five categories of adopters participate in the diffusion process:

- *Innovators:* the first 2.5 percent of all those who adopt the product. Innovators are eager to try new ideas and products, almost as an obsession. In addition to having higher incomes, they are worldlier and more active outside their community than noninnovators. They rely less on group norms and are more self-confident. Because they are well educated, they are more likely to get their information from scientific sources and experts. Innovators are characterized as being venturesome.
- *Early adopters:* the next 13.5 percent to adopt the product. Although early adopters are not the very first, they do adopt early in the product's life cycle. Compared to innovators, they rely much more on group norms and values. They are also more oriented to the local community, in contrast to the innovators' worldly outlook. Early adopters are more likely than innovators to be opinion leaders because of their closer affiliation with groups. The respect of others is a dominant characteristic of early adopters.
- *Early majority:* the next 34 percent to adopt. The early majority weigh the pros and cons before adopting a new product. They are likely to collect more information and evaluate more brands than early adopters, therefore extending the adoption process. They rely on the group for information but are unlikely to be opinion leaders themselves. Instead, they tend to be opinion leaders' friends and neighbours. The early majority are an important link in the process of diffusing new ideas because they

©WOLFGANG KAEHLER/CORBIS

Coca-Cola is a company that seems to need little help with global penetration of its product. In fact, despite adapting its product formula and product mix to various cultures, Coke is one of the world's most recognized brands.

GLOBAL PERSPECTIVES

Canada—A Unique Segment in the Global Automotive Market

The worldwide light-vehicle market (new cars, minivans, SUVs, and pickup trucks) has grown to 59.5 million units in 2003 and is expected to pass 60 million units for the first time in 2004. A number of companies are players in this worldwide market. For example, General Motors sells over 8.5 million light vehicles around the world, Ford and Toyota nearly 7 million each, and Volkswagen and Daimler Chrysler approximately 5 million each.

North America is the largest light-vehicle market in the world, accounting for nearly 20 million new vehicles sold in 2003. By country, the U.S. represents the largest automotive market with sales of nearly 17 million units, followed by Japan, Germany, and, maybe surprisingly to many, China at over 3 million new light-vehicle sales in 2003. In fact, China will likely pass Germany in 2004 to become the third-largest automotive market in the world. New light-vehicle sales in Canada in 2003 were approximately 1.6 million units, making Canada the 10th largest automotive market in the world.

For years, each of the major automotive assemblers has been trying to develop a "world car," essentially a car that they can assemble and sell in all markets around the globe. Ford, for example, invested $2.5 billion in the development of the Mondeo, a car that was to be Ford's "world car." As it turns out, Mondeo sales have been much better in some markets, such as Europe, and minimal in others, including North America. Economically, it would be much more efficient for automotive assemblers to manufacture a small number of models to be sold around the world than separate models for each market around the globe. In fact, some car models have achieved reasonable sales around the globe, including the Toyota Camry and Corolla models, Honda Accord and Civic, and Ford Focus, although names and features offered on the cars vary from country to country.

More often, the major vehicle assemblers have been designing cars for specific markets. In developing markets like China and Russia, where consumers do not have a lot of money to spend, very basic, very low-priced vehicles are produced and sold. In many countries in Europe, like Italy and France, cars must be designed for the narrow, congested roads and powered by diesel engines because of the high cost of gasoline. The U.S. market likes large vehicles with powerful engines that are not particularly fuel efficient.

In the past, the auto companies tended to produce and sell the same vehicles in Canada as had been designed for the U.S. market. Canada had not been considered a big enough market to merit its own car designs. However, with the growing size of the Canadian market and the growing competition among the major automobile assemblers for every bit of the worldwide market they can attract, Canada now merits its own new vehicle designs.

Cars shown at the 2003 Montreal Auto Show that are sold only in Canada, or will be coming exclusively to the Canadian market, include the Toyota Echo Hatchback and Acura EL, Pontiac Wave, Suzuki Swift, and Subaru Impreza TS. Chevrolet and Nissan each had three unique Canadian designs displayed at the Montreal Auto Show. Chevrolet displayed the Optra, Optra5, and Epica while Nissan unveiled the C-Note, Cube, and X-Trail. These vehicles hit what the Canadian market is looking for: smaller, sensible vehicles that offer some amenities and are priced from $16,000 to $26,000.[25]

As only the tenth-largest light-vehicle market in the world at under 1.7 million units, does Canada really merit unique car designs? Do you think that it is more effective to design and produce for the Canadian market or simply make available in Canada the same light vehicles that are being sold in the much larger U.S. market?

are positioned between earlier and later adopters. A dominant characteristic of the early majority is deliberateness.

- *Late majority:* the next 34 percent to adopt. The late majority adopt a new product because most of their friends have already adopted it. Because they also rely on group norms, their adoption stems from pressure to conform. This group tends to be older and below average in income and education. They depend mainly on word-of-mouth communication rather than on the mass media. The dominant characteristic of the late majority is skepticism.
- *Laggards:* the final 16 percent to adopt. Like innovators, laggards do not rely on group norms. Their independence is rooted in their ties to tradition. Thus, the past heavily influences their decisions. By the time laggards adopt an innovation, it has probably been outmoded and replaced by something else. For example, they may have bought their first black-and-white TV set after colour television was already widely diffused. Laggards have the longest adoption time and the lowest socioeconomic status. They tend to be suspicious of new products and alienated from a rapidly advancing society. The dominant value of laggards is tradition. Marketers typically ignore laggards, who do not seem to be motivated by advertising or personal selling.

ON LINE 

Electronic Gadget Depot

Visit the Electronic Gadget Depot and shop for an Internet appliance. Choose one, and rate it on a scale of 1 to 10 for each of the product characteristics listed in the section below. How quickly do you think this innovation will be adopted based on your perception of its complexity, compatibility, relative advantage, observability, and trialability?

http://www.electronicgadgetdepot.com

Exhibit 9.3 illustrates the diffusion of three familiar products. Virtually every household is equipped with one or more colour televisions. Note that some product categories, such as monochrome televisions, may never be adopted by 100 percent of the population. The adopter categories refer to all of those who will eventually adopt a product, not the entire population.

Product Characteristics and the Rate of Adoption

Five product characteristics can be used to predict and explain the rate of acceptance and diffusion of a new product:

- *Complexity:* the degree of difficulty involved in understanding and using a new product. The more complex the product, the slower is its diffusion. For instance, before many of their functions were automated, 35mm cameras were used primarily by hobbyists and professional photographers. The cameras were just too complex for most people to learn to operate. In quick order, 35mm cameras are now being replaced by digitals but, as with the early 35mm cameras, many people are not yet buying digital cameras, feeling that they are too complex.
- *Compatibility:* the degree to which the new product is consistent with existing values and product knowledge, past experiences, and current needs. Incompatible products diffuse more slowly than compatible products. For example, the introduction of contraceptives is incompatible in countries where religious beliefs discourage the use of birth control.
- *Relative advantage:* the degree to which a product is perceived as superior to existing substitutes. For example, because it reduces cooking time, the microwave oven has a clear relative advantage over a conventional oven.
- *Observability:* the degree to which the benefits or other results of using the product can be observed by others and communicated to target customers. For instance, fashion items and automobiles are highly visible and more observable than personal-care items.
- *"Trialability":* the degree to which a product can be tried on a limited basis. It is much easier to try a new toothpaste or breakfast cereal than a new automobile or microcomputer. Demonstrations in showrooms and test drives are different from in-home trial use. To stimulate trials, marketers use free-sampling programs, tasting displays, and small package sizes.

EXHIBIT 9.3

Consumer Adoption Line Graph

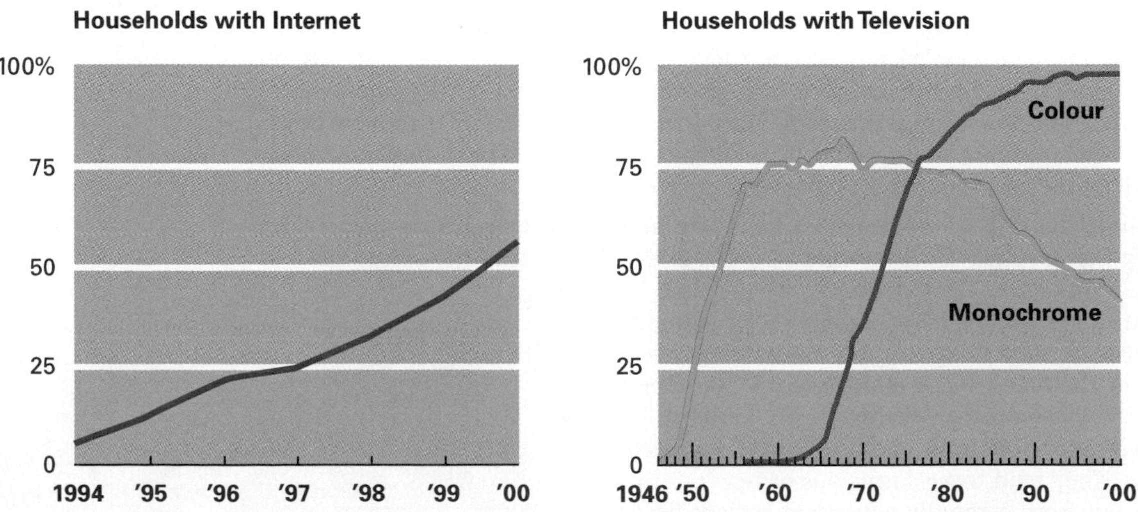

SOURCE: Julia Angwin, "Consumer Adoption Rate Slows in Replay of TV's History; Bad News for Online Firms," *Wall Street Journal*, July 16, 2001, B1. Reprinted by permission of the *Wall Street Journal*. © 2001 Dow Jones & Company, Inc. All rights reserved worldwide. 2001. Dow Jones & Company, Inc. Data supplied by Forrester Research; Consumer Electronics Association.

Marketing Implications of the Adoption Process

Two types of communication aid the diffusion process: *word-of-mouth communication* among consumers and communication from marketers to consumers. Word-of-mouth communication within and across groups speeds diffusion. Opinion leaders discuss new products with their followers and with other opinion leaders. Marketers must therefore ensure that opinion leaders receive the types of information desired in the media that they use. Suppliers of some products, such as professional and healthcare services, rely almost solely on word-of-mouth communication for new business.

The second type of communication aiding the diffusion process is *communication directly from the marketer to potential adopters.* Messages directed toward early adopters should normally use different appeals than messages directed toward the early majority, the late majority, or the laggards. Early adopters are more important than innovators because they make up a larger group, are more socially active, and are usually opinion leaders.

As the focus of a promotional campaign shifts from early adopters to the early majority and the late majority, marketers should study the dominant characteristics, buying behaviour, and media characteristics of these target markets. Then they should revise messages and media strategy to fit. The diffusion model helps guide marketers in developing and implementing promotion strategies.

>> PRODUCT LIFE CYCLES

6 Explain the concept of product life cycles

The **product life cycle (PLC)** is one of the most familiar concepts in marketing. Few other general concepts have been so widely discussed. Although some researchers have challenged the theoretical basis and managerial value of the PLC, most believe it has great potential as a marketing management tool.

product life cycle (PLC)
A concept that provides a way to trace the stages of a product's acceptance, from its introduction (birth) to its decline (death).

The product life cycle provides a way to trace the stages of a product's acceptance, from its introduction (birth) to its decline (death). As Exhibit 9.4 shows, a product progresses through four major stages: introduction, growth, maturity, and decline. Note that the product life cycle illustrated does not refer to any one brand; rather, it refers to the life cycle for a product category or product class. A **product category** includes all brands that satisfy a particular type of need. Product categories include passenger cars, cigarettes, soft drinks, and coffee. When we trace the product life cycle of a product such as DVD players, we are including the aggregate sales of all brands of DVD players, not just a single brand.

product category
All brands that satisfy a particular type of need.

The time a product spends in any one stage of the life cycle may vary dramatically. Some products, such as fad items, move through the entire cycle in weeks. Others, such as electric clothes washers and dryers, stay in the maturity stage for decades. Exhibit 9.4 illustrates the typical life cycle for a consumer durable good, such as a washer or dryer. In contrast, Exhibit 9.5 illustrates typical life cycles for styles (such as formal, business, or casual clothing), fashions (such as miniskirts or stirrup pants), and fads (such as leopard-print clothing). Changes in a product, its uses, its image, or its positioning can extend that product's life cycle.

The product life cycle concept does not tell managers the length of a product's life cycle or its duration in any stage. It does not dictate marketing strategy. It is simply a tool to help marketers forecast future events and suggest appropriate strategies. Look at Exhibit 9.6, which shows DVD unit sales in Canada from 1997 to 2003. What conclusions can you draw about the product life cycle of DVD players based on seven years of sales data?

Introductory Stage

The **introductory stage** of the product life cycle represents the full-scale launch of a new product into the marketplace. Computer databases for personal use, room-deodorizing air-conditioning filters, and wind-powered home electric generators are all product categories that have recently entered the product life cycle. A high failure rate, little competition, frequent product modification, and limited distribution typify the introduction stage of the PLC.

introductory stage
The full-scale launch of a new product into the marketplace.

EXHIBIT 9.4

Four Stages of the Product Life Cycle

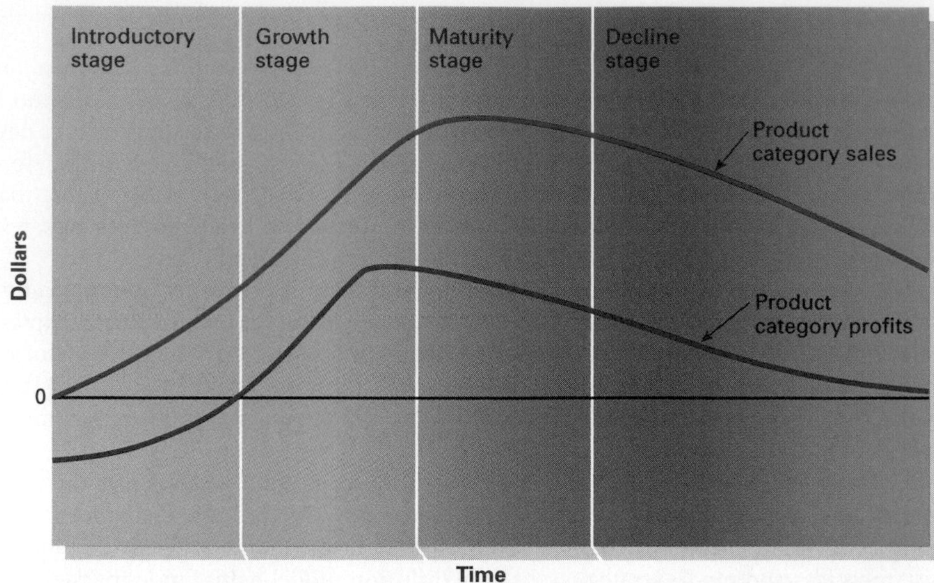

EXHIBIT 9.5

Product Life Cycles for Styles, Fashions, and Fads

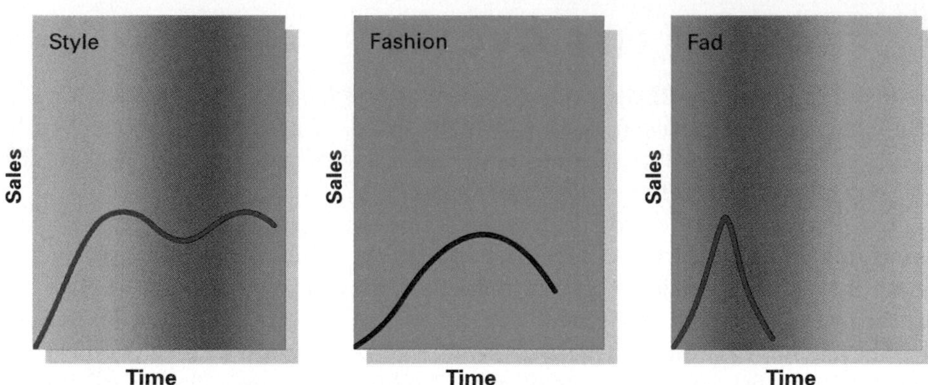

Marketing costs in the introductory stage are normally high for several reasons. High dealer margins are often needed to obtain adequate distribution, and incentives are needed to get consumers to try the new product. Advertising expenses are high because of the need to educate consumers about the new product's benefits. Production costs are also often high in this stage, as product and manufacturing flaws are identified and corrected and efforts are undertaken to develop mass-production economies.

As Exhibit 9.4 illustrates, sales normally increase slowly during the introductory stage. Moreover, profits are usually negative because of R&D costs, factory tooling, and high introduction costs. The length of the introductory phase is largely determined by product characteristics, such as the product's advantages over substitute products, the educational effort required to make the product known, and management's commitment of resources to the new item. A short introductory period is usually preferred to help reduce the impact of negative earnings and cash flows. As soon as the product gets off the ground, the financial burden should begin to diminish. Also, a short introduction helps dispel some of the uncertainty as to whether the new product will be successful.

Promotion strategy in the introductory stage focuses on developing product awareness and informing consumers about the product category's potential benefits. At this stage, the communication challenge is to stimulate primary demand—demand for the product in general rather than for a specific brand. Intensive personal selling is often required to gain acceptance for the product among wholesalers and retailers. Promotion of convenience products often requires heavy consumer sampling and couponing. Shopping and specialty products demand educational advertising and personal selling to the final consumer.

Growth Stage

If a product category survives the introductory stage, it advances to the **growth stage** of the life cycle. In this stage, sales typically grow at an increasing rate, many competitors enter the market, and large companies may start to acquire small pioneering firms. Profits rise rapidly in the growth stage, reach their peak, and begin declining as competition intensifies. Emphasis switches from primary demand promotion (for example, promoting personal digital assistants [PDAs]) to aggressive brand advertising and communication of the differences between brands (for example, promoting Casio versus Palm and Visor).

Distribution becomes a major key to success during the growth stage, as well as in later stages. Manufacturers scramble to sign up dealers and distributors and to build long-term relationships. Without adequate distribution, it is impossible to establish a strong market position.

Styles, fashions, and fads tend to follow different product life cycles. Based on what you see in Exhibits 9.4 and 9.5, what is the life cycle for Vitaballs, a new vitamin-infused bubblegum? Do you think it will be adopted by the mainstream? If so, how quickly?

Maturity Stage

A period during which sales increase at a decreasing rate signals the beginning of the **maturity stage** of the life cycle. New users cannot be added indefinitely, and sooner or later the market approaches saturation. Normally, this is the longest stage of the product life cycle. Many major household appliances are in the maturity stage of their life cycles.

For shopping products and many specialty products, annual models begin to appear during the maturity stage. Product lines are lengthened to appeal to additional market segments. Service and repair assume more important roles as manufacturers strive to distinguish their products from others. Product design changes tend to become stylistic (i.e., how can the product be made different?) rather than functional (i.e., how can the product be made better?).

As prices and profits continue to fall, marginal competitors start dropping out of the market. Dealer margins also shrink, resulting in less shelf space for mature items, lower dealer inventories, and a general reluctance to promote the product. Thus, promotion to dealers often intensifies during this stage in order to retain loyalty.

Heavy consumer promotion by the manufacturer is also required to maintain market share. Consider these well-known examples of competition in the maturity stage: the "cola war" featuring Coke and Pepsi, the "beer war" featuring Molson's and Labatt's, and the "burger wars" pitting leader McDonald's against challengers like Burger King, Wendy's, and Harvey's.

growth stage
The second stage of the product life cycle, when sales typically grow at an increasing rate, many competitors enter the market, large companies may start acquiring small pioneering firms, and profits are healthy.

maturity stage
A period during which sales increase at a decreasing rate.

EXHIBIT 9.6

Sales of DVD Players in Canada

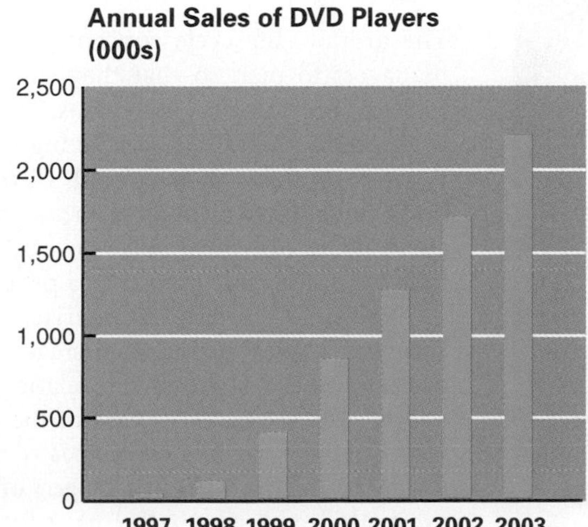

SOURCE: *Marketing Magazine*, Market Shares Report, http://www.marketingmag.ca; and Consumer Electronics Association, DVD Player Sales, http://www.thedigitalbits.com.

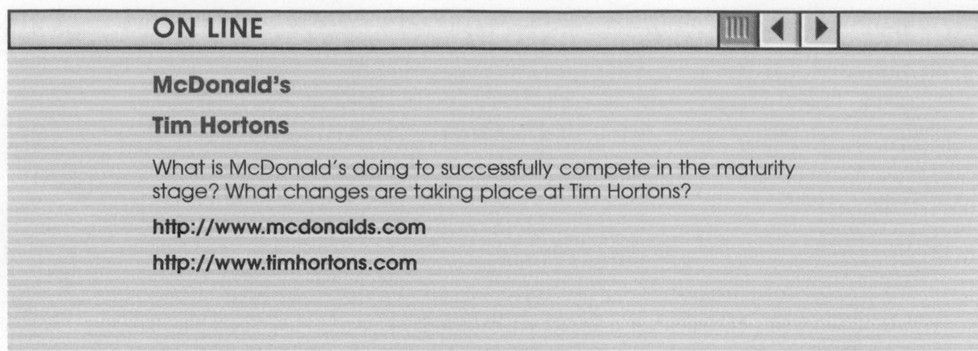

ON LINE

McDonald's

Tim Hortons

What is McDonald's doing to successfully compete in the maturity stage? What changes are taking place at Tim Hortons?

http://www.mcdonalds.com

http://www.timhortons.com

Another characteristic of the maturity stage is the emergence of "niche marketers" that target narrow, well-defined, underserved segments of a market. Starbucks Coffee targets its gourmet line at the only segment of the coffee market that is growing: newer, younger, more affluent coffee drinkers. As the "Global Perspectives" box illustrated earlier, companies in the auto industry, an industry that is in the maturity phase, are targeting smaller and smaller segments of the market.

Decline Stage

decline stage
A long-run drop in sales.

A long-run drop in sales signals the beginning of the **decline stage**. The rate of decline is governed by how rapidly consumer tastes change or substitute products are adopted. Many convenience products and fad items lose their market overnight, leaving large inventories of unsold items, such as designer jeans. Others die more slowly, like citizen band (CB) radios, black-and-white console television sets, and nonelectronic wristwatches.

Some firms have developed successful strategies for marketing products in the decline stage of the product life cycle. They eliminate all nonessential marketing expenses and let sales decline as more and more customers stop purchasing the products. Eventually, the product is withdrawn from the market.

Management sage Peter Drucker says that all companies should practise "organized abandonment," which entails reviewing every product, service, and policy every two or three years and asking the critical question: "If we didn't do this already, would we launch it now?" Would we introduce the product, service, or policy now? If the answer is "no," it's time to begin the abandonment process.[26]

AP/WIDE WORLD PHOTOS

Coffee is an example of a product in the maturity stage where niche marketers have emerged. Starbucks, for example, targets its gourmet products at newer, younger, more affluent coffee drinkers.

Implications for Marketing Management

The product life cycle concept encourages marketing managers to plan so that they can take the initiative instead of reacting to past events. The product life cycle is especially useful as a predicting or forecasting tool. Because products pass through distinctive stages, it is often possible to estimate a product's location on the curve using historical data. Profits, like sales, tend to follow a predictable path over a product's life cycle.

Exhibit 9.7 briefly summarizes some typical marketing strategies during each stage of the product life cycle. Exhibit 9.8 shows the relationship between the adopter categories and stages of the product life cycle. Note that the various categories of adopters first buy products during different stages of the product life cycle. Almost all sales in the maturity and decline stages represent repeat purchasing.

EXHIBIT 9.7

Typical Marketing Strategies during the Product Life Cycle

MARKETING MIX STRATEGY	INTRODUCTION	GROWTH	MATURITY	DECLINE
Product strategy	Limited number of models; frequent product modifications	Expanded number of models; frequent product modifications	Large number of models	Elimination of unprofitable models and brands
Distribution strategy	Distribution usually limited, depending on product; intensive efforts and high margins often needed to attract wholesalers and retailers	Expanded number of dealers; intensive efforts to establish long-term relationships with wholesalers and retailers	Extensive number of dealers; margins declining; intensive efforts to retain distributors and shelf space	Unprofitable outlets phased out
Promotion strategy	Develop product awareness; stimulate primary demand; use intensive personal selling to distributors; use sampling and couponing for consumers	Stimulate selective demand; advertise brand aggressively	Stimulate selective demand; advertise brand aggressively; promote heavily to retain dealers and customers	Phase out all promotion
Pricing strategy	Prices are usually high to recover development costs	Prices begin to fall toward end of growth stage as a result of competitive pressure	Prices continue to fall	Prices stabilize at relatively low level; small price rises are possible if competition is negligible

EXHIBIT 9.8

Relationship between the Diffusion Process and the Product Life Cycle

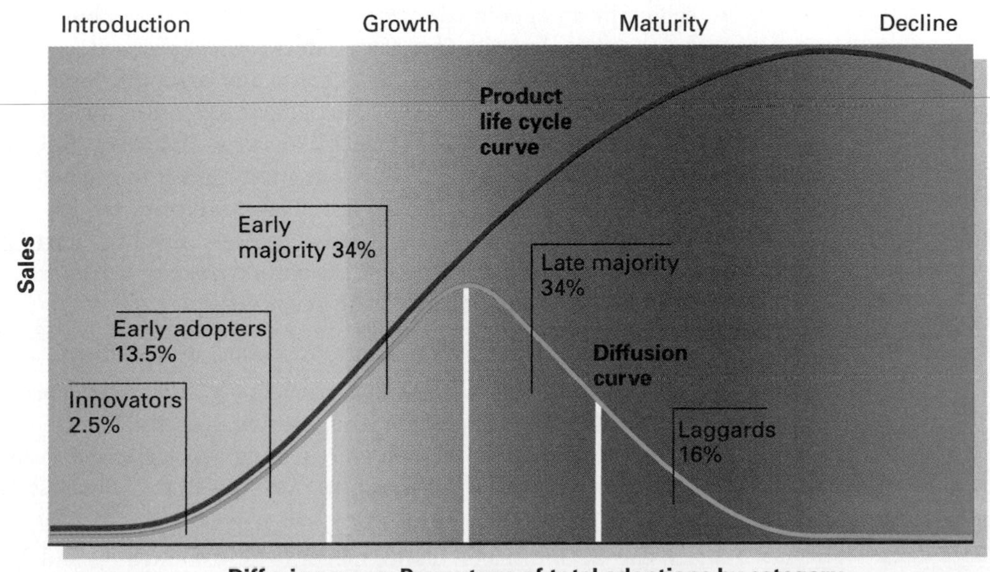

>> CONNECT IT

Look back at the story at the beginning of this chapter about some successful new product introductions and some product failures from the H.J. Heinz Co. It is often hard to say why one product fails and another succeeds. Certainly Blastin' Green and Funky Purple benefited from what was learned from the Sparky failure. As well, Blastin' Green and Funky Purple taste the same as regular red ketchup; they're simply a different colour. Funky Fries failed because the product did not offer a desired benefit to the target market. Kids already liked regular French fries and the flavour of Funky Fries was not the same.

New product ideas come from many sources, both inside and outside the company. It is important that companies be aware of sources for new product ideas and actively encourage these sources to contribute ideas. Without ideas, companies cannot develop new products. Whenever possible, companies will test new product ideas on the customers who are being targeted with the new product—as Heinz has done with its coloured ketchups.

REVIEW IT

1 **Explain the importance of developing new products and describe the six categories of new products.** New products are important to sustain growth and profits and to replace obsolete items. New products can be classified as new-to-the-world products (discontinuous innovations), new product lines, additions to existing product lines, improvements or revisions of existing products, repositioned products, or lower-cost products. To sustain or increase profits, a firm must introduce at least one new successful product before a previous product advances to the maturity stage and profit levels begin to drop. Several factors make it more important than ever for firms to consistently introduce new products: shortened product life cycles, rapidly changing technology and consumer priorities, the high rate of new-product failures, and the length of time needed to implement new-product ideas.

1.1 How many new products can you identify? Visit a supermarket and make a list of at least 15 items with the word "New" on the label. Include on your list anything that looks like a new product. Next to each item on your list, write the category of new product that best describes the item. Share your results with the class.

2 **Explain the steps in the new-product development process.** First, a firm forms a new-product strategy by outlining the characteristics and roles of future products. Then new-product ideas are generated by customers, employees, distributors, competitors, and internal R&D personnel. Once a product idea has survived initial screening by an appointed screening group, it undergoes business analysis to determine its potential profitability. If a product concept seems viable, it progresses into the development phase, in which the technical and economic feasibility of the manufacturing process is evaluated. The development phase also includes laboratory and use testing of a product for performance and safety. Following initial testing and refinement, most products are introduced in a test market to evaluate consumer response and marketing strategies. Finally, test market successes are propelled into full commercialization. The commercialization process involves starting up production, building inventories, shipping to distributors, training a sales force, announcing the product to the trade, and advertising to consumers.

2.1 List the advantages of simultaneous product development.

2.2 WRITING You are a marketing manager for Nike. Your department has come up with the idea of manufacturing a baseball bat for use by amateur teams around the country. Assuming you are in the business analysis stage, write a brief analysis based on the questions in the "Business Analysis" section of this chapter.

2.3 What are the major disadvantages to test marketing, and how might they be avoided?

2.4 ON LINE How could information from customer orders at http://www.pizzahut.ca help the company's marketers plan new-product developments?

2.5  

How is customer input affecting the development of Baked Lay's potato chips? Go to http://www.fritolay.ca to find out.

3 **Explain why some products succeed and others fail.** The most important factor in determining the success of a new product is the extent to which the product matches the needs of the market. Good matches are frequently successful. Poor matches are not.

3.1 

In small groups, brainstorm ideas for a new wet-weather clothing line. What type of product would potential customers want and need? Prepare and deliver a brief presentation to your class.

4 **Discuss global issues in new-product development.** A marketer with global vision seeks to develop products that can easily be adapted to suit local needs. The goal is not simply to develop a standard product that can be sold worldwide. Smart global marketers also look for good product ideas worldwide.

4.1 

Visit http://www.pg.com and look at the brands Procter & Gamble offers around the world. What conclusions can you draw about Procter & Gamble's global new-product development strategy?

5 **Explain the diffusion process through which new products are adopted.** The diffusion process is the spread of a new product from its producer to ultimate adopters. Adopters in the diffusion process belong to one of five categories: innovators, early adopters, the early majority, the late majority, and laggards. Product characteristics that affect the rate of adoption include product complexity, compatibility with existing social values, relative advantage over existing substitutes, visibility, and "trialability." The diffusion process is facilitated by word-of-mouth communication and communication from marketers to consumers.

5.1 Describe some products whose adoption rates have been affected by complexity, compatibility, relative advantage, observability, and/or "trialability."

5.2 What type of adopter behaviour do you typically follow? Explain.

6 **Explain the concept of product life cycles.** All product categories undergo a life cycle with four stages: introduction, growth, maturity, and decline. The rate at which products move through these stages varies dramatically. Marketing managers use the product life cycle concept as an analytical tool to forecast a product's future and devise effective marketing strategies.

6.1 

Place the personal computer on the product life cycle curve, and give reasons for placing it where you did. Use InfoTrac® College Edition (http://www.infotrac.thomsonlearning.com) to consult publications like *Technology Review, Computer World,* and *Computer Weekly* to help support your position.

DEFINE IT

adopter 266
brainstorming 260
business analysis 260
commercialization 264
concept test 260
decline stage 272
development 261
diffusion 266
growth stage 271
innovation 266
introductory stage 269
maturity stage 271
new-product strategy 258
new product 256
product category 269
product development 259
product life cycle (PLC) 269
screening 260
simulated (laboratory) market testing 263
simultaneous product development 261
test marketing 262

APPLY IT

Joyce Strand went to the oven to remove the newest batch of beef jerky, which she would later sell to the Frontenac Central Store. To her surprise, she had turned the oven up too high and the beef jerky had dried to a crisp. Although the texture was much different, the jerky still had its unmistakable taste. Joyce decided to take it to the Central Store anyway and let the customers decide. The new snack became a huge success in the snack-food section of the store. Because of her recent success, Joyce began experimenting with different tastes and textures of snack foods, which she sells at the Central Store. Realizing that innovation can be very profitable, Joyce now actively looks for new ways to please her customers.

QUESTIONS

1. How might Joyce ensure that proper attention is paid to developing new products?
2. What factors should she be aware of that might lead to product failure?

THINK ABOUT IT

One source of new product ideas is competitors. Steven Fischer recently joined Frankie and Alex Specialty Products as a brand manager. His new boss told him, "We don't have a budget for new product development. We just monitor our competitors' new product introductions and offer "knock-offs" or copies of any that look like they will be successful."

QUESTIONS

1. Is this practice ethical?
2. Does the CMA Code of Ethics address this issue? Go to **http://www.the-cma.org/consumer/ethics.cfm** and review the code. Then write a brief paragraph on what the CMA Code of Ethics contains that relates to knock-off products.

TRY IT

Chippery: Fresh, Flavoured Chips

Lee Burnstein never thought that he would find a new business opportunity by watching the Food Network, but the restaurant owner has. He has added freshly made, gourmet potato chips to his restaurant menu.

Featured on the TV show watched by Lee Burnstein was gourmet chip-making equipment offered by Chippery of Toronto. The chip-making equipment cost Mr. Burnstein $55,000. In addition, Lee Burnstein bought licensing rights to open Chippery outlets that would feature hamburgers, sandwiches, soups, salads, and, of course, gourmet potato chips.

Since installing Chippery chip-making equipment in his restaurant, Lee Burnstein has been selling gourmet chips not only to his restaurant customers, but also to institutional customers, parties and gatherings, and to 14 local convenience stores.

Chippery was founded in the mid-1990s after a father and daughter took a tour of a large Canadian potato chip factory. The father, Christopher Smith, was intrigued by the fact that all of the children on the tour were fascinated to see fresh, hot potato chips coming off an assembly line. Furthermore, they all loved the taste of freshly made potato chips that were still warm. With this, Christopher and his brother invested in a new company designed to manufacture and sell fresh, gourmet chips.

Chippery uses potatoes grown especially for chips. The potatoes are placed in a metal chute on the chip-making equipment, where they are peeled, sliced, and rolled into hot sunflower oil. The chips are cooked for three minutes and then loaded into bowls on the side of the machine. The chips can be made in any of 13 flavours, including spicy jalapeno, sour cream and onion, dill pickle, white cheddar, sea salt, and Caribbean banana. If the facility is set up for it, customers can watch their chips being made.

In addition to Chippery outlets in Canada, there are already Chippery franchise holders in the U.S., the Netherlands, and Germany.

QUESTIONS

1. What do you think of Chippery's concept? Do you think this new organization will continue to grow?
2. What, if anything, is unique about Chippery?
3. What kind of marketing strategy is Chippery following?
4. Visit the Chippery websites of various countries to see how the product offerings differ from one country to another.
   http://www.chippery.com (Canada)
   http://www.chipperyamerica.com (U.S.)
   http://www.chippery.nl (Netherlands)
   http://www.chippery.de (Germany)

FLIP IT

Flip to Chapter 9 in your *Grademaker Study Guide* for more review opportunities, including the pretest, vocabulary review, study test questions, and a marketing application based on product concepts. Can you describe the product life cycle? Do you know which marketing mix strategies work best at each point in the product life cycle? What about the diffusion of innovation? If you're unsure, then pick up your *Grademaker* and review.

CLICK IT

The *Marketing* website is rich with materials to help you review and master marketing concepts. Check your knowledge with the free quizzes, practise key terms using the crossword puzzles, or review key concepts using the Microsoft® PowerPoint® slides. Also on the website are updated weblinks to companies mentioned in this chapter, Internet exercises, career marketing information, and much much more! Go to http://www.lamb3e.nelson.com, read the material, and follow the convenient links.

WATCH IT

Kayak Flipper Stew: New Kayak Designs from Two Start-Up Companies in Newfoundland

CBC

You may not be aware of it, particularly if you live in a land-locked area, but kayaking is a very fast-growing sport. Kayak sales have grown by a whopping 150 percent over the past three years. And one of the major kayaking locations in Canada is Newfoundland. Thousands of tourists come to Newfoundland from across Canada, the United States, and other countries around the world to kayak in the beautiful ocean environment surrounding Newfoundland. And a growing number of sea kayak tour operators are bringing more tourists to Newfoundland each year.

Given these facts, it may not be too surprising that two Newfoundlanders, Lindy Rideout and Craig Greenham, have founded start-up kayak manufacturing companies in their home province. Lindy Rideout is founder and president of Seaknife Kayaks; Craig Greenham is founder and president of Eastern Island Kayaks. While both Seaknife and Eastern Island are new, currently small, and located in Newfoundland, they differ profoundly in how they are approaching the marketing of their new products.

Lindy Rideout is a 37-year-old Grade 12 teacher who, among other things, teaches entrepreneurship courses. Following what he preaches, Lindy founded Seaknife Kayaks three years ago. Lindy invested most of his savings to research and design his own kayaks. Seaknife kayaks are manufactured by a two-person workforce in Lindy's garage. Lindy's wife assists by developing the colour schemes for the kayaks. While the business is not yet successful enough to allow him to leave his teaching job, Lindy has sold over 200 kayaks.

Craig Greenham is 28 years old and had worked for Necky (located in British Columbia), one of the largest kayak manufacturers in Canada. Craig, however, wanted to build and sell his own kayak designs. So after three years with Necky, Craig returned to Newfoundland to start Eastern Island Kayaks. Craig has borrowed all that he can to get Eastern Island Kayaks started and is heavily in debt. Craig needs a big sale to get out of debt and ensure the future of the company.

Lindy and Craig have taken very different approaches to marketing their kayaks. Lindy is selling his Seaknife kayaks exclusively over the Internet. Lindy hopes that by using this direct sales approach, he will be able to sell his kayaks at the lowest possible price. In fact, you can buy a SK-17 Pro model fibreglass model kayak for under $2,000. This is a price that is comparable to the less expensive plastic kayaks on the market (fibreglass kayaks are considered to be far superior to plastic). Lindy will ship the kayak to you anywhere in the world.

Craig has chosen to use a different marketing approach. Eastern Island kayaks are being marketed to distributors and large retailers. Rather than selling one (or a few) kayaks at a time over the Internet, Craig is hoping for a few very large orders from large distributors and retailers. In this regard, Craig is trying to compete directly with the largest kayak manufacturers in Canada, companies like Necky, Perception, and Seaward. Craig's kayaks are priced considerably higher than Lindy's. In fact, Craig is quite curious as to how Lindy can price his fibreglass kayaks at plastic prices.

Let's watch as Lindy and Craig meet for the first time at a business trade show in Gander, Newfoundland, to discuss their new companies and products, their unique designs, and their different pricing and distribution plans.

As well, let's watch Craig attempt to secure a large order from Outfitters, the largest retailer of kayaks in Newfoundland. Will Craig get his large sale and get out of debt? What happens when Lindy unexpectedly gets an order for 120 kayaks from a sea kayak tour operator? Can a two-person workforce, normally making a few kayaks at a time, meet this order?

QUESTIONS

1. Which marketing approach will be more successful, the low-price Internet sales approach being used by Seaknife or the higher-price distributor/retailer approach being used by Eastern Island? Why?
2. As a new, small company with a new product, how would you react to the large order that Seaknife suddenly received? Do you think that Seaknife can satisfy this order? How will Seaknife handle normal orders that continue to come in while trying to fulfill the large order?
3. Log on to Seaknife's website (**http://www.seaknife.com**). How easy is it to place an order for a Seaknife kayak?
4. Newfoundland is a wonderful location for kayaking, but is it a good location for a kayak business? Why or why not?

SUGGESTED INFORMATION SOURCES

CBC, *Venture*, "Kayak Flipper Stew," Broadcast: February 29, 2004.
http://www.seaknife.com
http://www.theoutfitters.nf.ca/easternislandkayaks/kayaks.html

chapter 10

Services and Nonprofit Organization Marketing

>> LEARNING OBJECTIVES

1. Discuss the importance of services to the economy
2. Discuss the differences between services and goods
3. Describe the components of service quality and the gap model of service quality
4. Develop marketing mixes for services
5. Discuss relationship marketing in services
6. Explain internal marketing in services
7. Discuss global issues in services marketing
8. Describe nonprofit organization marketing

>> Several years ago, Yellow Freight Systems, now called Yellow Transportation, began implementing a marketing strategy that would help to transform the company from a long-haul carrier into something completely different: a carrier that offered multiple services and that was built around unprecedented customer service. Today, Yellow is a different company. It still transports primarily big, heavy freight (minimum 100 kilograms). But the one-dimensional long-haul approach is gone and so is the complacency that resulted from long years of regulation in the trucking industry. No more telling customers: "Sorry, we can't do that." Instead, the new approach is saying: "Yes, we can."

In an attempt to offer one-stop shopping, Yellow has added a variety of services, including regional and expedited shipping and expedited electronic transmission of Customs documentation for cross-border shipments, to satisfy a broader range of transportation needs. The old Yellow gave customers a rough estimate of when a shipment would arrive. It might show up then, or it might not. The new Yellow is faster, more precise, and more profitable. It has gone from being a company in the trucking business to being a company that recognizes it is in the service business.

For a long time, Yellow's focus was on operational efficiency. Employees monitored how much freight moved through the network daily, how full the trailers were, and other internal measures. While Yellow was a model of efficiency, it had no idea whether its customers were satisfied. The new focus of the company became how to best satisfy customer needs. To that end, the company conducts over 600 surveys with different customers each month to determine what will satisfy customers. For example, the research made a compelling case for dramatically improving reliability: customers who said that they would use Yellow again and recommend it to others had received good service. Those who had not were less loyal. While this was a fairly obvious lesson for a traditional service provider, it was a critical one for a company that was trying to become customer-centric.

Yellow's Exact Express service epitomizes the company's commitment to customers. Exact Express was Yellow's first expedited, time-definite, guaranteed service. Everyone involved, from the customer representative to the driver, is committed to doing what it takes to satisfy the customer's needs—even if that means using an outside air-cargo partner to meet a deadline. Exact Express has a good track record—deliveries arrive when they are supposed to arrive 98 percent of the time. It is Yellow's most expensive and most profitable service, growing with double-digit increases every year.

One of the main reasons Yellow has been able to expand and improve service is its state-of-the-art technology. Over the past 10 years, the company has spent an average of $80 million a year on its highly integrated information systems. The technology has led to significant changes in virtually every stage of the business. For example, it has influenced how orders get processed and relayed from the call centres to the terminals, how the dispatchers assign drivers for pickups and deliveries, and how the dock workers load and unload trailers. When repeat customers call 1-800-GO-YELLOW, the system automatically opens a customer profile that corresponds to the caller's phone number. The representative instantly knows where the customer's company is located; what type of loading dock it has; the size, weight, and contents of previous shipments; previous shipping destinations; and who has signed for deliveries. If a customer calls back in the future with an identical shipping order, the entire process then takes about 15 seconds.

Each dock worker is equipped with a wireless mobile data terminal designed to speed up the loading and unloading process. The dock supervisor also has access to the incoming and outgoing freight at his computer station. If he notices that a truck is running behind, he can dispatch a second employee and a forklift to speed things up. The old system was inflexible: one employee per trailer. The central dispatch office can track the day's shipping activity on a map of Canada, and identify service failures in the making and work with the terminals to devise solutions.

Yellow's defect rate is down from 40 percent in the late 1990s to 5 percent today, and its on-time performance (excluding weather delays) is in the high 90s. The number of customers surveyed who said that they would recommend Yellow has doubled in the last five years. And in an industry where profit margins are typically slim, the company continues to create promising sources of revenue, including Transportation.com, a logistics service for small- and medium-sized businesses.[1]

How does a service, such as trucking, differ from goods—for example, soft drinks, automobiles, or blue jeans? How has Yellow's service mix changed in recent years? Which components of service quality improved as a result of Yellow's concern with satisfying its customers? We will answer these questions and more in Chapter 10.

ON LINE

Yellow Freight

How friendly is Yellow Freight's website? Is the company's concern for the customer obvious?

http://www.myyellow.com

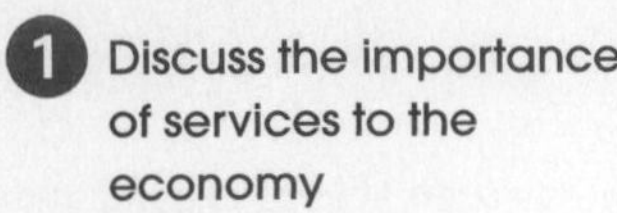

1 Discuss the importance of services to the economy

service
The result of applying human or mechanical efforts to people or objects.

>> THE IMPORTANCE OF SERVICES

A **service** is the result of applying human or mechanical efforts to people or objects. Services involve a deed, a performance, or an effort that cannot be physically possessed. Today, the service sector substantially influences the Canadian economy. The service sector accounts for nearly 70 percent of the Canadian gross domestic product and nearly 75 percent of employment, including 87.2 percent of female employment in Canada.[2] The demand for services is expected to continue to grow. According to Statistics Canada, service occupations will be responsible for most of the net job growth in Canada over the next few years. Over the period from December 2002 to December 2003, manufacturing employment in Canada grew by 0.1 percent while service employment grew by 2.3 percent.[3] As can be seen in Exhibit 10.1, the service labour force continues to grow at a pace well beyond that of the goods sector. Much of this demand results from demographics. An aging population will need nurses, home healthcare, physical therapists, and social workers. Two-earner families need childcare, house cleaning, and lawn care services. Also increasing will be the demand for information managers, such as computer engineers and systems analysts.

The marketing process described in Chapter 1 is the same for all types of products, whether they are goods or services. Many ideas and strategies discussed throughout this book have been illustrated with service examples. In many ways, marketing is marketing, regardless of the product's characteristics. In addition, although a comparison of goods and services marketing can be beneficial, in reality it is hard to distinguish clearly between manufacturing and service firms. Indeed, many manufacturing firms can point to service as a major factor in their success. For example, maintenance and repair services offered by the manufacturer are important to buyers of copy machines. Nevertheless, services have some characteristics that distinguish them from goods, and marketing strategies need to be adjusted for these characteristics.

2 Discuss the differences between services and goods

>> HOW SERVICES DIFFER FROM GOODS

Services have four characteristics that distinguish them from goods. Services are intangible performances, they are produced and consumed simultaneously, they have greater variability in inputs and outputs than goods, and they are perishable.

intangibility
The inability of services to be touched, seen, tasted, heard, or felt in the same manner that goods can be sensed.

Services Are Intangible Performances

The basic difference between services and goods is that services are intangible performances. Because of their **intangibility**, they cannot be touched, seen, tasted, heard, or felt in the same manner as goods. Services cannot be stored and are often easy to duplicate.

EXHIBIT 10.1

The Impact of the Service Sector on Job Growth

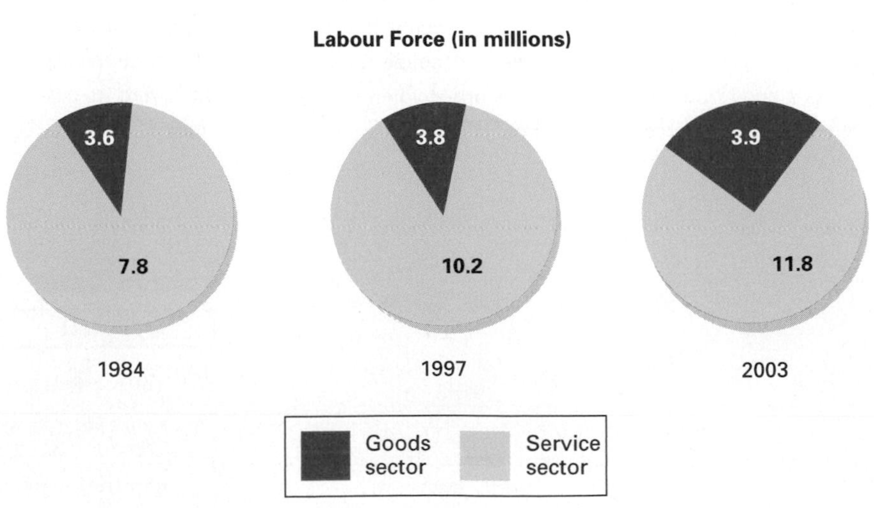

Evaluating the quality of services before or even after making a purchase is harder than evaluating the quality of goods because, compared to goods, services tend to exhibit fewer search qualities. A **search quality** is a characteristic that can be easily assessed before purchase—for instance, the colour of an appliance or automobile. At the same time, services tend to exhibit more experience and credence qualities. An **experience quality** is a characteristic that can be assessed only after use, such as the quality of a meal in a restaurant or the actual experience of a vacation. A **credence quality** is a characteristic that consumers may have difficulty assessing even after purchase because they do not have the necessary knowledge or experience. Medical and consulting services are examples of services that exhibit credence qualities.

ON LINE 

Westin Bayshore Resort & Marina—Vancouver

What elements of Weston's website communicate the search, experience, and credence qualities of the services offered by this hotel?

http://westinbayshore.com/bayshore/main.php

search quality
A characteristic that can be easily assessed before purchase.

experience quality
A characteristic that can be assessed only after use.

credence quality
A characteristic that consumers may have difficulty assessing even after purchase because they do not have the necessary knowledge or experience.

These characteristics also make it harder for marketers to communicate the benefits of an intangible service than to communicate the benefits of tangible goods. Thus, marketers often rely on tangible cues to communicate a service's nature and quality. For example, Travelers Insurance Company's use of the umbrella symbol helps make tangible the benefit of protection that insurance provides.

The facilities that customers visit, or from which services are delivered, are a critical tangible part of the total service offering. Messages about the organization are communicated to customers through such elements as the decor, the clutter or neatness of service areas, and the staff's manners and dress. The Sheraton Hotel chain is replacing its outdated shag carpeting and flowered bedspreads with pin stripes and sleigh beds. Its goal is to restore a reputation for reliability and comfort and to avoid scaring off travellers with tacky accommodations. The new design will feature clubby, library-like furnishings and practical amenities like ergonomic desk chairs and two-line phones. The remodelling is also a part of the strategy followed by Sheraton's parent company, Starwood Hotels & Resorts Worldwide, to differentiate the company's hotel brands aesthetically. For example, it wants its Sheratons to attract conservative business travellers while its Westin Hotels are targeting younger, hipper, and somewhat wealthier overnighters.[4]

Services Are Produced and Consumed Simultaneously

Goods are produced, sold, and then consumed. In contrast, services are often sold, produced, and consumed at the same time. In other words, their production and consumption are inseparable activities. This means that, because consumers must be present during the production of services like haircuts or surgery, they are actually involved in the production of the services they buy. That type of consumer involvement is rare in goods manufacturing.

Simultaneous production and consumption also means that services normally cannot be produced in a centralized location and consumed in decentralized locations, as goods typically are. Services are also inseparable from the perspective of the service provider. Thus, the quality of service that firms are able to deliver depends on the quality of their employees.

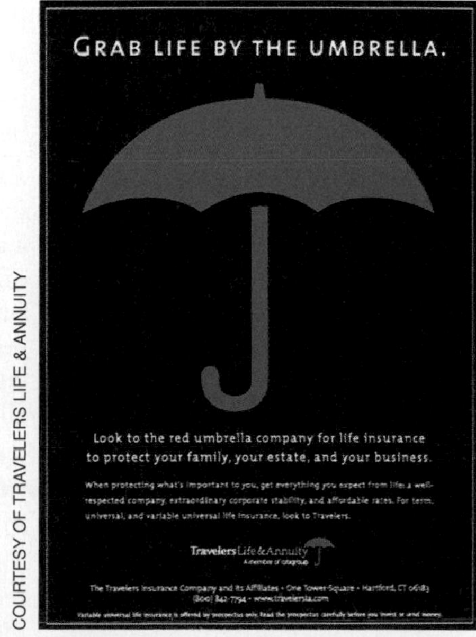

GRAB LIFE BY THE UMBRELLA.
Look to the red umbrella company for life insurance to protect your family, your estate, and your business.
TravelersLife&Annuity

COURTESY OF TRAVELERS LIFE & ANNUITY

To communicate the benefits of intangible services, marketers often rely on concrete symbols. The umbrella symbol used by Travelers Insurance signifies protection. This helps give substance to the company's service.

Services Have Greater Variability

One great strength of McDonald's is consistency. Whether customers are ordering Big Mac and French fries in Halifax, Vancouver, Tokyo, or Moscow, they know exactly what they are going to get. This is not the case with many service providers. Because services have greater variability of inputs and outputs, they tend to be less standardized and uniform than goods. For example, physicians in a group practice or barbers in a barbershop differ within each group in their technical and interpersonal skills. A given physician's or barber's performance may even vary depending on time of day, physical health, or some other factor.

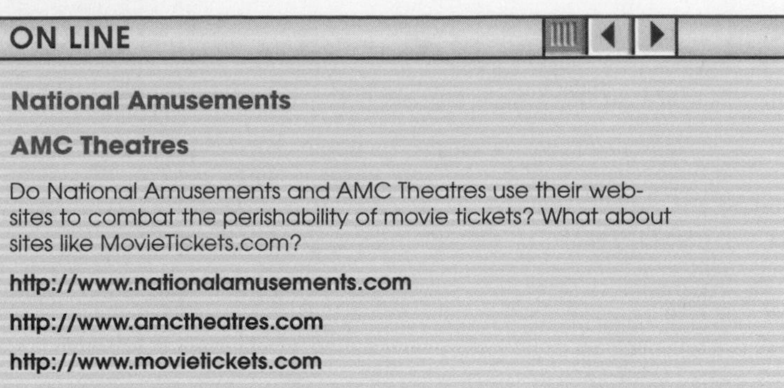

Because services tend to be labour-intensive and production and consumption are inseparable, consistency and quality control can be hard to achieve.

Standardization and training help increase consistency and reliability. Limited-menu restaurants like Harvey's and KFC offer customers high consistency from one visit to the next because of standardized preparation procedures. Another way to increase consistency is to mechanize the process. Banks have reduced the inconsistency of teller services by providing automated teller machines (ATMs). Internet banking, like Mbanx (www.bmo.com/banking) from the Bank of Montreal, also results in greater service consistency.

Services Are Perishable

Services are perishable, which means that they cannot be stored, warehoused, or inventoried. An empty hotel room or airplane seat produces no revenue that day. Yet service organizations are often forced to turn away full-price customers during peak periods.

One of the most important challenges in many service industries is finding ways to synchronize supply and demand. The philosophy that some revenue is better than none has prompted many hotels to offer deep discounts on weekends and during the off-season and has prompted airlines to adopt similar pricing strategies during off-peak hours. Car rental agencies, movie theatres, and restaurants also use discounts to encourage demand during nonpeak periods.

3 Describe the components of service quality and the gap model of service quality

>> SERVICE QUALITY

Because of the four unique characteristics of services, service quality is more difficult to define and measure than is the quality of tangible goods. Business executives rank the improvement of service quality as one of the most critical challenges facing them today.

Research has shown that customers evaluate service quality by the following five components:[5]

reliability
The ability to perform a service dependably, accurately, and consistently.

responsiveness
The ability to provide prompt service.

- ***Reliability:*** the ability to perform the service dependably, accurately, and consistently. Reliability is performing the service right the first time. This component has been found to be the one most important to consumers.
- ***Responsiveness:*** the ability to provide prompt service. Examples of responsiveness include calling the customer back quickly, serving lunch fast to someone who is in a hurry, or mailing a transaction slip immediately. The ultimate in responsiveness is offering service 24/7. For example, customer service representatives answer calls round the clock at Relocation Management Resources, Inc., which arranges all the details of transporting household goods for companies that are relocating their employees. Even the company's president invites customers to call his cell phone at all hours.[6]

assurance
The knowledge and courtesy of employees and their ability to convey trust.

empathy
Caring, individualized attention to customers.

- ***Assurance:*** the knowledge and courtesy of employees and their ability to convey trust. Skilled employees who treat customers with respect and make customers feel that they can trust the firm exemplify assurance.
- ***Empathy:*** caring, individualized attention to customers. Firms whose employees recognize customers, call them by name, and learn their customers' specific requirements are providing empathy. When taking your car in for servicing at Windsor (Ontario) Honda, the Honda dealership personnel will address you by name, drive you to work, call when your car is ready, and come back to your place of employment to drive you back to your car. As well, when you pick up your car, it will be cleaned outside and in.

- ***Tangibles:*** the physical evidence of the service. The tangible parts of a service include the physical facilities, tools, and equipment used to provide the service, such as a doctor's office or an ATM, and the appearance of personnel.

tangibles
The physical evidence of a service, including the physical facilities, tools, and equipment used to provide the service.

Overall service quality is measured by combining customers' evaluations for all five components.

The Gap Model of Service Quality

A model of service quality called the **gap model** identifies five gaps that can cause problems in service delivery and influence customer evaluations of service quality.[7] These gaps are illustrated in Exhibit 10.2.

gap model
A model identifying five gaps that can cause problems in service delivery and influence customer evaluations of service quality.

- *Gap 1*: the gap between what customers want and what management thinks customers want. This gap results from a lack of understanding or a misinterpretation of the customers' needs, wants, or desires. A firm that does little or no customer satisfaction research is likely to experience this gap. An important step in closing Gap 1 is to keep in touch with what customers want by doing research on customer needs and customer satisfaction. Every two years, Kindred Industries of Midland, Ontario, recipient of a 2002 Canadian Business Best Practices Award in the category of

EXHIBIT 10.2
Gap Model of Service Quality

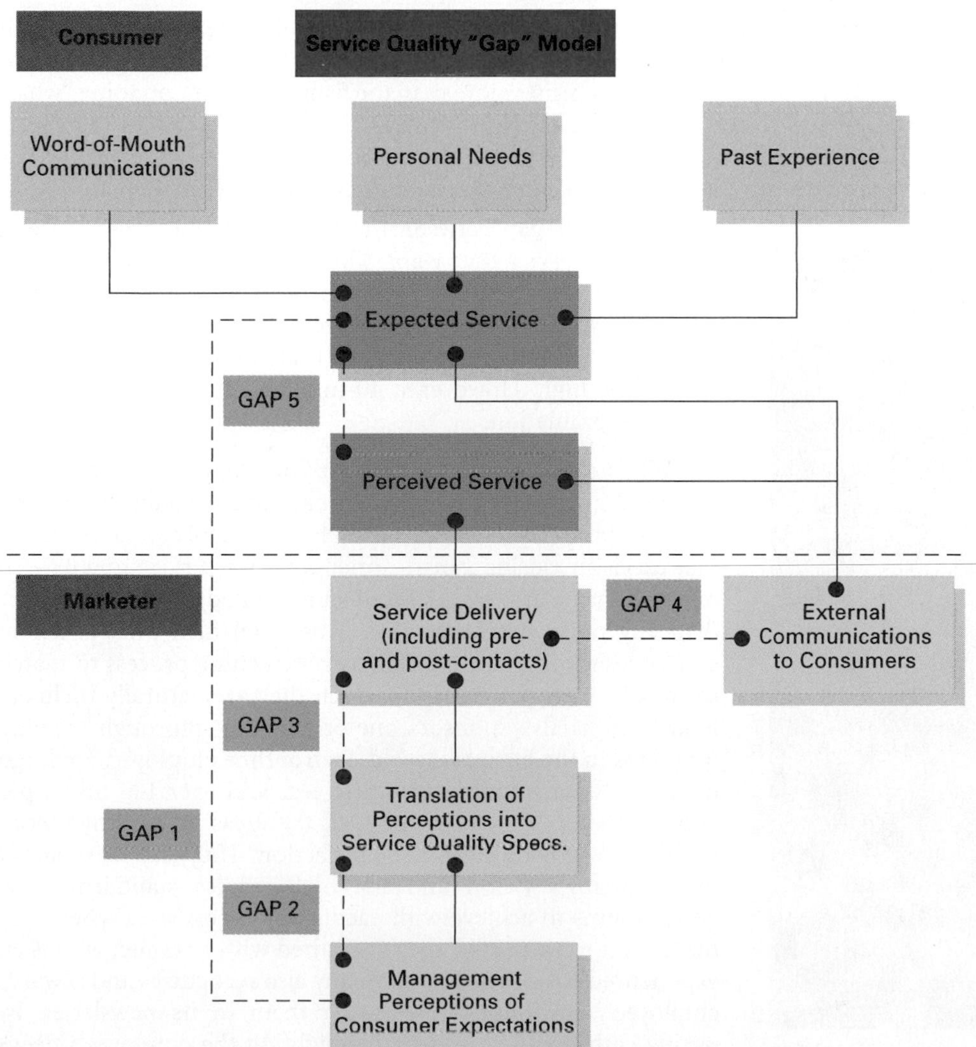

SOURCE: A. Parasuraman, Valarie A. Zeithaml, and Leonard L. Berry, "A Conceptual Model of Service Quality and Its Implications for Future Research," *Journal of Marketing,* 49 (Fall) 1985, 41–50.

ON LINE

Evaluate your last Internet purchase according to Gaps 4 and 5. How could the company bridge those gaps?

Customer Satisfaction, undertakes thousands of interviews with its customers to determine how well Kindred is satisfying their needs.

- *Gap 2:* the gap between what management thinks customers want and the quality specifications that management develops to provide the service. Essentially, this gap is the result of management's inability to translate customers' needs into delivery systems within the firm. For example, KFC once rated its managers' success according to "chicken efficiency," or how much chicken they threw away at the end of the night. Consumers who came in late at night would either have to wait for chicken to be cooked or settle for chicken several hours old. The "chicken efficiency" measurement did not take customers into account.
- *Gap 3:* the gap between the service quality specifications and the service that is actually provided. If both Gaps 1 and 2 have been closed, then Gap 3 is due to the inability of management and employees to do what should be done. Poorly trained or poorly motivated workers can cause this gap. Management needs to ensure that employees have the skills and the proper tools to perform their jobs. Other techniques that help to close Gap 3 are training employees so they know what management expects and encouraging teamwork.
- *Gap 4:* the gap between what the company provides and what the customer is told it provides. This is clearly a communication gap. It may include misleading or deceptive advertising campaigns promising more than the firm can deliver or doing "whatever it takes" to get the business. To close this gap, companies need to create realistic customer expectations through honest, accurate communication about what they can provide. The "Ethics in Marketing" box examines an example of Gap 4.
- *Gap 5:* the gap between the service that customers receive and the service they want. This gap can be positive or negative. For example, if a patient expects to wait 20 minutes in the physician's office before seeing the physician but waits only 10 minutes, the patient's evaluation of service quality will be high. However, a 40-minute wait would result in a lower evaluation.

When one or more of these gaps are large, service quality is perceived as low. As the gaps shrink, service quality improves. Toronto-based Four Seasons Hotels and Resorts is a company that excels in closing gaps to offer superior service quality—so much so that it has won 17 Five Diamond Lodging Awards, more than any other hotel operator. This hotel firm puts potential employees through a comprehensive screening process to match their skills with positions for which they are naturally inclined. Four Seasons also sponsors one of the most thorough training programs in the business world. Its frontline employees undergo many weeks of training their first year and over 100 hours per year thereafter. They learn how all the areas in the hotel work together to provide customer satisfaction. They also learn about the company's vision and the high service standards Four Seasons aims to achieve with each guest experience. When they first report to their jobs, they are paired with a trainer, who is an experienced coworker. The company also recognizes and rewards employee contributions by listing them in its newsletter, by paying cash bonuses, and by highlighting the employee's deeds during staff meetings. What has been the result of this high level of service? The Four Seasons has expanded from 22 hotels in three countries in 1990 to nearly 60 hotels in 23 countries today.[8]

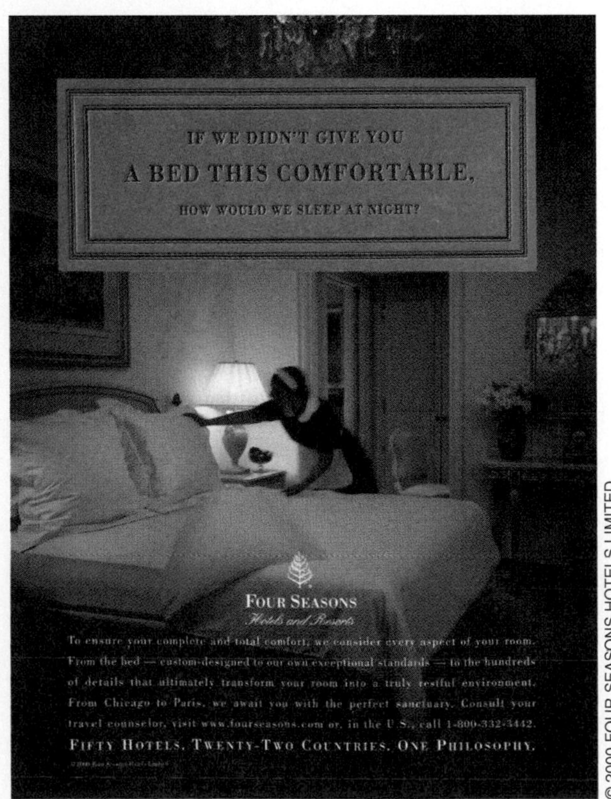

Toronto-based Four Seasons Hotels and Resorts works hard to close any gaps in service its customers might experience. The winner of 17 Five Diamond Lodging Awards trains its employees to give superior service in one of the most thorough training programs in the business world.

ETHICS IN MARKETING

Paying More Than You Bargained For

Canadians are increasingly buying more on the Internet, and Internet sources generally promise convenient service and good prices.

Delores Friesen of Winnipeg likes a good deal and shopped around for some books that she eventually ordered on-line. To keep shipping costs low, she had the books shipped by slower, but less expensive, ground transportation. The books cost $78 and the shipping by UPS was quoted on-line as an additional $15. Naturally, Delores assumed that her total bill would be $93.

When the books arrived, though, Delores found that her total bill was not only the $93 she expected but also an additional $31! The additional fee was for a service called "clearing customs." When goods come across the border, there may be duty and taxes payable on them. Couriers take care of these charges and then collect when they deliver the goods.

Delores was surprised and angry at the additional cost of $31. Initially, she considered refusing to take delivery. However, as Delores wanted the books, she reluctantly paid the additional charges. The books that Delores thought she was getting at a bargain price could have been purchased cheaper elsewhere.

Delores isn't the first customer to be irritated at what appears to be a hidden fee. Many customers have complained about these unexpected charges. CBC shows, such as *Marketplace*, have aired programs on them. Phil Cahly of the Canadian Courier Association says that on-line sellers should inform customers of these "clearing customs" charges but many don't. Delores Friesen says that there was no mention of these charges on the fee quoted when she ordered her books.

Since Delores purchased the books from a U.S. source, shouldn't she expect some sort of customs charges? Who is responsible for informing customers of these hidden costs? When the on-line seller knows that an order is being placed from outside the country, shouldn't the on-line seller warn of possible customs charges? For more information on this issue, and to view a *Marketplace* video on hidden brokerage fees, go to **http://www.cbc.ca/consumers/market/files/home/courierfees/index.html.**

>> MARKETING MIXES FOR SERVICES

Develop marketing mixes for services

Services' unique characteristics—intangibility, simultaneous production and consumption, variability, and perishability—make marketing more challenging. Elements of the marketing mix (product, distribution, promotion, and pricing) need to be adjusted to meet the special needs created by these characteristics.

Product (Service) Strategy

The development of "product" strategy in services marketing requires planning focused on the service process.[9] Four types of processing occur:

- *People processing* takes place when the service is directed at a customer. Examples are transportation services, hairstyling, health clubs, and dental and health care.
- *Possession processing* occurs when the service is directed at customers' physical possessions. Examples are lawn care, car repair, dry cleaning, and veterinary services.
- *Mental stimulus processing* refers to services directed at people's minds. Examples are entertainment, spectator sports events, theatre performances, and education.
- *Information processing* describes services that use technology or brainpower directed at a customer's assets. Examples are insurance, banking, and consulting.

Because customers' experiences and involvement differ for each of these types of services, marketing strategies may also differ. For example, people-processing services require customers to enter the *service factory*, which is a physical location, such as an aircraft, a physician's office, or a hair salon. In contrast, possession-processing services typically do not require the presence of the customer in the service factory; the customer may simply leave the car at the garage for repairs, for example. Marketing strategies for the former would therefore

© SPENCER GRANT/PHOTOEDIT

Dry cleaning is an example of possession-processing services. These types of services require less focus on attractive physical environments and customer service training than people-processing services like hairdressers and airlines.

focus more on an attractive, comfortable physical environment, and employee training more on employee–customer interaction issues, than would strategies for the latter.

Core and Supplementary Services

core service
The most basic benefit the consumer is buying.

supplementary services
A group of services that support or enhance the core service.

The service offering can be viewed as a bundle of activities that includes the **core service**, which is the most basic benefit the customer is buying, and a group of **supplementary services** that support or enhance the core service. Exhibit 10.3 illustrates these concepts for FedEx. The core service is overnight transportation and delivery of packages, which involves possession processing. The supplementary services, some of which involve information processing, include problem solving, advice and information, billing statements, and order taking.

In many service industries, the core service becomes a commodity as competition increases. Thus, firms usually emphasize supplementary services to create a competitive advantage. Virgin Atlantic, Malaysia Airlines, and Japan Airlines provide complimentary limo service to and from the airport. Virgin's chauffeurs check in passengers en route.[10] On the other hand, some firms are positioning themselves in the marketplace by greatly reducing supplementary services. For example, Microtel Inns & Suites is an amenity-free hotel concept known as "fast lodging." These low-cost hotels have one- and two-bedroom accommodations and a swimming pool, but no meeting rooms or other services.

Mass Customization

An important issue in developing the service offering is whether to customize or standardize it. Customized services are more flexible and respond to individual customers' needs. They also usually command a higher price. The traditional law firm, which treats each case differently according to the client's situation, offers customized services. Standardized services are more efficient and cost less. Unlike the traditional law firm, Walk-In LAW FIRM of Canada offers low-cost, standardized service "packages" for those with uncomplicated legal needs, such as drawing up a will or mediating an uncontested divorce.

EXHIBIT 10.3
Core and Supplementary Services for FedEx

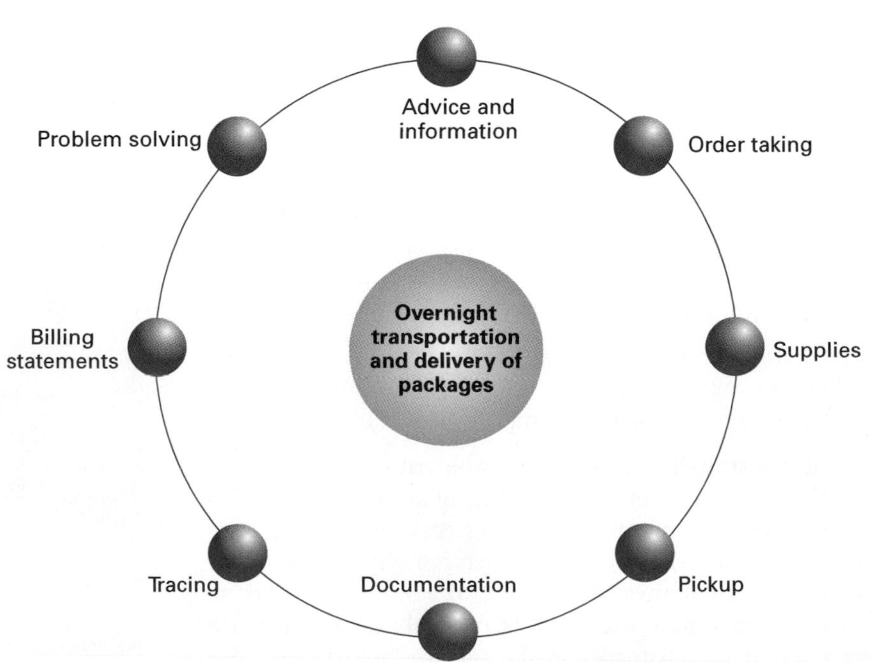

SOURCE: Lovelock, Christopher, *Services Marketing,* 3rd ed., © 1996. Reprinted by permission of Pearson Education, Inc., Upper Saddle River, NJ.

Instead of choosing to either standardize or customize a service, a firm may incorporate elements of both by adopting an emerging strategy called **mass customization.** Mass customization uses technology to deliver customized services on a mass basis; the result is that each customer receives whatever he or she asks for.

mass customization
A strategy that uses technology to deliver customized services on a mass basis.

For example, a feature on the Lands' End website allows women to define their figures on-line, receive advice on what swimsuits will flatter their shapes, and mix and match more than 216 combinations of colours and styles. Several airlines are designing services to cater to travellers' individual needs and preferences. Some will serve dinner to passengers when they want to eat it, rather than when the airline wants to serve it. More airlines are offering video-on-demand systems, which let passengers start or stop their movie anytime they want. British Airways predicts that there will be airline seats that will read passengers' shapes and program their seat-position preferences into smart cards.[11]

The Service Mix

Most service organizations market more than one service. For example, ChemLawn offers lawn care, shrub care, carpet cleaning, and industrial lawn services. Each organization's service mix represents a set of opportunities, risks, and challenges. Each part of the service mix should make a different contribution to achieving the firm's goals. To succeed, each service may also need a different level of financial support.

Designing a service strategy therefore means deciding which new services to introduce to which target market, which existing services to maintain, and which services to eliminate. For example, to increase membership, the CAA added financial services, credit cards, and travel perks. Organic, a company that designs websites for clients, has set up two new service divisions: Organic Communications, a full-service public relations department; and Organic Logistics, which helps clients figure out how to get products ordered on-line into customers' hands.[12]

Distribution Strategy

Distribution strategies for service organizations must focus on such issues as convenience, number of outlets, direct versus indirect distribution, location, and scheduling. A key factor influencing the selection of a service provider is convenience. Therefore, service firms must offer convenience. Many Shoppers Drug Mart outlets, especially those in downtown locations, have late-night hours, and some are even open 24/7, to provide maximum customer convenience.

An important distribution objective for many service firms is the *number of outlets* to use or the number of outlets to open during a certain time. Generally, the intensity of distribution should meet, but not exceed, the target market's needs and preferences. Having too few outlets may inconvenience customers; having too many outlets may boost costs unnecessarily. Intensity of distribution may also depend on the image desired. Having only a few outlets may make the service seem more exclusive or selective.

The next service distribution decision is whether to distribute services to end users *directly* or *indirectly* through other firms. Because of the intangible nature of services, many service firms have to use direct distribution or franchising. Examples include legal, accounting, real estate, and personal-care services. The newest form of direct distribution is the Internet. Most of the major airlines are now using on-line services to sell tickets directly to consumers; this process results in lower distribution costs for the airline companies. Merrill Lynch offers Merrill Lynch OnLine, an Internet-based service that connects clients with company representatives. Most of Canada's retail banks now offer on-line banking services.

© INDEX STOCK IMAGERY/STEWART COHEN

Making services more personalized is the goal of mass customization. Serving passengers when they want to eat, rather than when the airline wants to serve, is an example of this.

The *location* of a service most clearly reveals the relationship between its target market strategy and its distribution strategy. Reportedly, Conrad Hilton claimed that the three most important factors in determining a hotel's success are "location, location, and location." An interesting location trend has started in the banking industry. In the past few years, banks have aggressively directed customers away from branches and toward ATMs and the Internet. In a recent about-face, banks are trying to entice customers back into the branches. For example, CIBC is designing new branches and remodelling old ones to provide a brighter, more open atmosphere.

For time-dependent service providers like airlines, physicians, and dentists, scheduling is often a more important factor. Scheduling is sometimes the most important factor in a customer's choice of airline.

Promotion Strategy

Consumers and business users have more trouble evaluating services than goods because services are less tangible. In turn, marketers have more trouble promoting intangible services than tangible goods. Here are four promotion strategies they can try:

- *Stressing tangible cues:* A tangible cue is a concrete symbol of the service offering. To make their intangible services more tangible, hotels turn down the bedcovers and put mints on the pillows. Insurance companies use symbols like rocks, blankets, umbrellas, and hands to help make their intangible services appear tangible. Merrill Lynch uses a bull to help give substance to its services.
- *Using personal information sources:* A personal information source is someone consumers are familiar with (such as a celebrity) or someone they know or can relate to personally. Celebrity endorsements are sometimes used to reduce customers' perceived risk in choosing a service. Service firms may also seek to simulate positive word-of-mouth communication among present and prospective customers by using real customers in their ads.
- *Creating a strong organizational image:* One way to create an image is to manage the evidence, including the physical environment of the service facility, the appearance of the service employees, and the tangible items associated with a service (like stationery, bills, and business cards). For example, McDonald's has created a strong organizational image with its Golden Arches, relatively standardized interiors, and employee uniforms. Another way to create an image is through branding. MCI Communications has grown by creating and promoting brands in the commodity business of common-carrier long-distance service. An example of an MCI brand is 1-800-COLLECT.
- *Engaging in postpurchase communication:* Postpurchase communication refers to the follow-up activities that a service firm might engage in after a customer transaction. Postcard surveys, telephone calls, brochures, and various other types of follow-up show customers that their feedback matters and that their patronage is appreciated.

AP/WIDE WORLD PHOTOS

Using real customers can be a successful promotion strategy. One of the more successful of recent memory has been Jared Fogle, spokesperson for Subway. When Subway executives heard that Fogle went from 425 pounds to 180 pounds eating their product, they put him in a TV commercial.

Price Strategy

Considerations in pricing a service are similar to the pricing considerations to be discussed in Chapters 15 and 16. However, the unique characteristics of services present two special pricing challenges.

First, in order to price a service, it is important to define the unit of service consumption. For example, should pricing be based on completing a specific service task (cutting a customer's hair), or should it be time based (how long it takes to cut a customer's hair)? Some services include the consumption of goods, such as food and beverages. Restaurants charge customers for food and drink rather than the use of a table and chairs. Some transportation firms charge by distance; others charge a flat rate.

Second, for services that are composed of multiple elements, the issue is whether pricing should be based on a "bundle" of elements or whether each element should be priced separately. A bundled price may be preferable when consumers dislike having

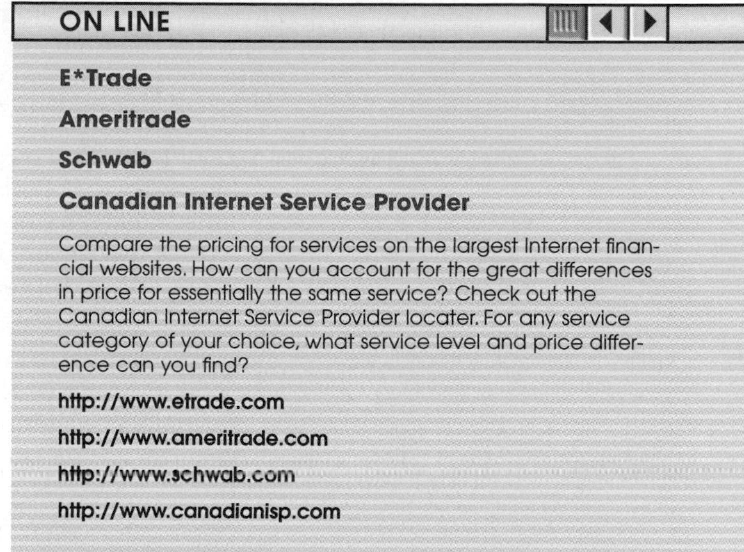

to pay "extra" for every part of the service (for example, paying extra for baggage or food on an airplane), and it is simpler for the firm to administer. For instance, MCI offered a basic communications package that included 30 minutes of telephone time, five hours of Internet access, a personal number that could route calls to several locations, and a calling card all for one price. Alternatively, customers may not want to pay for service elements they do not use. Many furniture stores now have "unbundled" delivery charges from the price of the furniture. Customers who wish to can pick up the furniture at the store, saving on the delivery fee.

Marketers should set performance objectives when pricing each service. Three categories of pricing objectives have been suggested:[13]

- *Revenue oriented pricing* focuses on maximizing the surplus of income over costs. A limitation of this approach is that determining costs can be difficult for many services.
- *Operations-oriented pricing* seeks to match supply and demand by varying prices. For example, matching hotel demand to the number of available rooms can be achieved by raising prices at peak times and decreasing them during slow times.
- *Patronage-oriented pricing* tries to maximize the number of customers using the service. Thus, prices vary with different market segments' ability to pay, and methods of payment (such as credit) are offered that increase the likelihood of a purchase.

A firm may need to use more than one type of pricing objective. In fact, all three objectives probably need to be included to some degree in a pricing strategy, although the importance of each type may vary depending on the type of service provided, the prices that competitors are charging, the differing ability of various customer segments to pay, and the opportunity to negotiate price. For customized services (for example, legal services and construction services), customers may also have the ability to negotiate a price.

>> RELATIONSHIP MARKETING IN SERVICES

5 Discuss relationship marketing in services

Many services involve ongoing interaction between the service organization and the customer. Thus, they can benefit from relationship marketing, the strategy described in Chapter 1, as a means of attracting, developing, and retaining customer relationships. The idea is to develop strong loyalty by creating satisfied customers who will buy additional services from the firm and who are unlikely to switch to a competitor. Satisfied customers are also likely to engage in positive word-of-mouth communication, thereby helping bring in new customers.

Many businesses have found that it is more cost-effective to hang on to the customers they have than to focus only on attracting new ones. A bank executive, for example, found that increasing customer retention by 2 percent could have the same effect on profits as reducing costs by 10 percent.

Services that purchasers receive on a continuing basis (for example, cable TV, banking, insurance) can be considered membership services. This type of service naturally lends itself to relationship marketing. When services involve discrete transactions (for example, a movie theatre, a restaurant, public transportation), it may be more difficult to build membership-type relationships with customers. Nevertheless, services involving discrete transactions can be transformed into membership relationships using marketing tools. For example, the service could be sold in bulk (a theatre series subscription or a commuter ticket on public transportation). Or a service firm could offer special benefits to customers who choose to register with the firm (for example, loyalty programs for hotels, airlines, and car rental firms). The service firm that has a more formalized relationship with its customers has an advantage because it knows who its customers are and how and when they use the services offered.[14]

It has been suggested that relationship marketing can be practised at three levels:[15]

- *Level 1:* The firm uses pricing incentives to encourage customers to continue doing business with it. Examples include the frequent flyer programs offered by many airlines and the free or discounted travel services given to frequent hotel guests. This level of relationship marketing is the least effective in the long term because other firms easily imitate its price-based advantage.

- *Level 2:* This level of relationship marketing also uses pricing incentives but seeks to build social bonds with customers. The firm stays in touch with customers, learns about their needs, and designs services to meet those needs. 1-800-FLOWERS, for example, developed an on-line Gift Reminder Program. Customers who reach the company via its website can register unlimited birthdays, anniversaries, or other special occasions. Five days before each occasion and at their request, 1-800-FLOWERS sends them an e-mail reminder. Level 2 relationship marketing has a higher potential for keeping the firm ahead of the competition than does Level 1 relationship marketing.
- *Level 3:* At this level, the firm again uses financial and social bonds but adds structural bonds to the formula. Structural bonds are developed by offering value-added services that are not readily available from other firms. Hertz #1 Gold Club program allows members to call and reserve a car, board a courtesy bus at the airport, tell the driver their name, and get dropped off in front of their car. Hertz also starts up the car and turns on the air conditioning or heat, depending on the temperature. Marketing programs like this one have the strongest potential for sustaining long-term relationships with customers.

6 Explain internal marketing in services

internal marketing
Treating employees as customers and developing systems and benefits that satisfy their needs.

>> INTERNAL MARKETING IN SERVICE FIRMS

Services are performances, so the quality of a firm's employees is an important part of building long-term relationships with customers. Employees who like their jobs and are satisfied with the firm they work for are more likely to deliver superior service to customers. In other words, a firm that makes its employees happy has a better chance of keeping its customers coming back. Studies show that replacing an employee costs roughly 1.5 times a year's pay. Also, companies with highly committed employees have been found to post sharply higher shareholder returns.[16] Thus, it is critical that service firms practise **internal marketing**, which means treating employees as customers and developing systems and benefits that satisfy their needs. Internal marketing involves the following activities: competing for talent, offering a vision, training employees, stressing teamwork, giving employees more freedom to make decisions, measuring and rewarding good service performance, and knowing employees' needs.[17]

Companies have instituted a wide variety of programs designed to satisfy employees. Some companies are trying to retain happy employees by offering concierges who run errands to help ease the lives of time-strapped, stressed-out workers. Marriott International set up a 24-hour hotline to answer questions from employees having personal and family problems.[18] These examples illustrate how service firms can invest in their most important resource—their employees.

COURTESY LA SALLE BANK N.A., CHICAGO, ILLINOIS

Corporate concierge services are one way companies are beginning to market themselves to their own employees. Internal marketing efforts like this can help employers attract and retain valuable employees.

>> GLOBAL ISSUES IN SERVICES MARKETING

7 Discuss global issues in services marketing

The international marketing of services is a major part of global business, and Canada is a growing exporter of services. Competition in international services is increasing rapidly, however.

To succeed in the global marketplace, service firms must first determine the nature of their core product. Then the marketing mix elements (additional services, pricing, promotion, distribution) should be designed to take into account each country's cultural, technological, and political environment.

Because of their competitive advantages, many Canadian service industries have been able to enter the global marketplace. Canadian banks, for example, have advantages in customer service and collections management. The field of construction and engineering services offers great global potential; Canadian companies have vast experience in this industry, so economies of scale are possible for machinery and materials, human resource management, and project management. The Canadian insurance industry has substantial knowledge about underwriting, risk evaluation, and insurance operations that it can export to other countries. In fact, a current survey of top executives of Canadian companies by Ipsos-Reid indicates that 87 percent of the CEOs feel that their companies have what it takes to compete in the global market.[19] As highlighted in the "Global Perspectives" box, however, failure to respect the local culture can lead to disaster for the service provider.

>> NONPROFIT ORGANIZATION MARKETING

8 Describe nonprofit organization marketing

A **nonprofit organization** is an organization that exists to achieve some goal other than the usual business goals of profit, market share, or return on investment. Nonprofit organizations share important characteristics with private-sector service firms. Both market intangible products. Both often require the customer to be present during the production process. Both for-profit and nonprofit services vary greatly from producer to producer and from day to day, even from the same producer. Neither for-profit nor nonprofit services can be stored in the way that tangible goods can be produced, saved, and sold at a later date.

nonprofit organization
An organization that exists to achieve some goal other than the usual business goals of profit, market share, or return on investment.

Few people realize that nonprofit organizations account for nearly 20 percent of the economic activity in Canada. The cost of government, the predominant form of nonprofit organization, has become the biggest single item in the Canadian family budget—more than housing, food, or transportation. Together, federal, provincial, and local governments collect tax revenues that amount to more than one third of the Canadian gross domestic product. Moreover, they employ one of every five nonagricultural civilian workers.[20] In addition to government entities, nonprofit organizations include thousands of private museums, theatres, schools, churches, and so on.

What Is Nonprofit Organization Marketing?

Nonprofit organization marketing is the effort by nonprofit organizations to bring about mutually satisfying exchanges with target markets. Although these organizations vary substantially in size and purpose and operate in different environments, most perform the following marketing activities:

nonprofit organization marketing
The effort by nonprofit organizations to bring about mutually satisfying exchanges with target markets.

- Identify the customers they wish to serve or attract (although they usually use another term, such as *clients, patients, members,* or *sponsors)*
- Explicitly or implicitly specify objectives
- Develop, manage, and eliminate programs and services
- Decide on prices to charge (although they use other terms, such as *fees, donations, tuition, fares, fines,* or *rates*)
- Schedule events or programs, and determine where they will be held or where services will be offered

ON LINE

PETA

What do you think are the marketing objectives of PETA? Visiting its website may help you find the answers. Are there conflicting objectives? Objectives that surprise you?

http://www.peta.org

GLOBAL PERSPECTIVES

Wal-Mart's Service with a Smile? Not in Germany

In retailing, as well as in other businesses across Canada, the saying "the customer is king" generally applies. This is not the case in Germany, however. The rules of German retailing seem to be "the grumpier the better" and "the customer comes last." Surprisingly, this approach seems to work with German customers. If you don't believe this, just ask executives at Wal-Mart, the world's largest business with sales approaching $300 billion.

Wal-Mart first arrived in Germany in 1998, bubbling with confidence and bringing with it the high level of customer consideration and service provided at Wal-Mart outlets around the world. Staff in all of the German Wal-Mart stores were specially trained before the store openings and were ordered to apply the Wal-Mart golden rules. If a customer approached a store employee, the staff member was to smile and be as helpful as possible. Customers' bags were to be packed at the checkout—a service not present in other German retail outlets.

The result of all this? A huge culture clash! Instead of charming German shoppers, Wal-Mart's policies angered customers and made them suspicious. "German customers cannot handle this kind of service," said Barbara Schnappauf, a researcher at GfK, Germany's biggest research firm. "If someone tries to put things in a bag for them, they say to themselves, 'Hey, I just paid for that. That's mine.' If someone takes hold of their possessions at the checkout, they think they are trying to steal them."

Wal-Mart's unusual service, at least for this market, contributed to the company losing $222 million in its first year in the German market. In an annual survey of customer feelings, Wal-Mart ranked at the bottom of retailers in Germany. And customers weren't the only ones with problems. Wal-Mart employees were hiding in washrooms rather than joining in on the traditional before-store-opening pep rallies and were avoiding customers so that they would not have to smile.[21]

Evaluate Wal-Mart's entry into the German market. What are some of the things that have gone wrong? What lessons has Wal-Mart learned? What marketing elements might Wal-Mart have to adjust in different countries?

- Communicate their availability through brochures, signs, public service announcements, or advertisements

Often, the nonprofit organizations that carry out these functions do not realize they are engaged in marketing.

Unique Aspects of Nonprofit Organization Marketing Strategies

Like their counterparts in business organizations, nonprofit managers develop marketing strategies to bring about mutually satisfying exchanges with target markets. However, marketing in nonprofit organizations is unique in many ways—including the setting of marketing objectives, the selection of target markets, and the development of appropriate marketing mixes.

Objectives

In the private sector, the profit motive is both an objective for guiding decisions and a criterion for evaluating results. Nonprofit organizations do not seek to make a profit for redistribution to owners or shareholders. Rather, their focus is often on generating enough funds to cover expenses. The Methodist Church does not gauge its success by the amount of money collected in offering plates. The Canadian Film Centre does not base its performance evaluations on the dollars of revenue it brings in.

Most nonprofit organizations are expected to provide equitable, effective, and efficient services that respond to the wants and preferences of multiple constituencies. These include users, payers, donors, politicians, appointed officials, the media, and the general public. Nonprofit organizations cannot measure their success or failure in strictly financial terms.

The lack of a financial "bottom line" and the existence of multiple, diverse, intangible, and sometimes vague or conflicting objectives make prioritizing objectives, making decisions, and evaluating performance hard for nonprofit managers. They must often use approaches different from the ones commonly used in the private sector. For example, the Art Gallery of Windsor has devised a system for basing salary increases on how employees perform in relation to the objectives they set each year.

Target Markets

Three issues relating to target markets are unique to nonprofit organizations:

- *Apathetic or strongly opposed targets:* Private-sector organizations usually give priority to developing those market segments that are most likely to respond to particular offerings. In contrast, nonprofit organizations must often target those who are apathetic about or strongly opposed to receiving their services, such as vaccinations, family-planning guidance, help for problems of drug or alcohol abuse, and psychological counselling.
- *Pressure to adopt undifferentiated segmentation strategies:* Nonprofit organizations often adopt undifferentiated strategies by default. Sometimes they fail to recognize the advantages of targeting, or an undifferentiated approach may appear to offer economies of scale and low per capita costs. In other instances, nonprofit organizations are pressured or required to serve the maximum number of people by targeting the average user. The problem with developing services targeted at the average user is that there are few "average" users. Therefore, such strategies typically fail to fully satisfy any market segment.
- *Complementary positioning:* The main role of many nonprofit organizations is to provide services, with available resources, to those who are not adequately served by private-sector organizations. As a result, the nonprofit organization must often complement, rather than compete with, the efforts of others. The positioning task is to identify underserved market segments and to develop marketing programs that match their needs rather than to target the niches that may be most profitable. For example, a university library may see itself as complementing the services of the public library, rather than as competing with it.

Product Decisions

There are three product-related distinctions between business and nonprofit organizations:

- *Benefit complexity:* Rather than simple product concepts, like "Long live the grill" or "We earn money the old-fashioned way," nonprofit organizations often market complex behaviours or ideas. Examples include the need to exercise or eat right, not to drink and drive, and not to smoke tobacco. The benefits that a person receives are complex, long term, and intangible and therefore are more difficult to communicate to consumers.
- *Benefit strength:* The benefit strength of many nonprofit offerings is quite weak or indirect. What are the direct, personal benefits to you of driving under the speed limit, donating blood, or asking your neighbours to contribute money to a charity? In contrast, most private-sector service organizations can offer customers direct, personal benefits in an exchange relationship.
- *Involvement:* Many nonprofit organizations market products that elicit very low involvement ("Prevent forest fires" or "Don't litter") or very high involvement ("Buy only Canadian-made vehicles" or "Stop smoking"). The typical range for private-sector goods is much narrower. Traditional promotional tools may be inadequate to motivate adoption of either low- or high-involvement products.

Distribution Decisions

A nonprofit organization's capacity for distributing its service offerings to potential customer groups when and where they want them is typically a key variable in determining the success of those service offerings. For example, many universities have one or more satellite campus locations to provide easier access for students in other areas. Some educational institutions also offer classes to students at off-campus locations via interactive video technology.

The extent to which a service depends on fixed facilities has important implications for distribution decisions. Obviously, services like rail transit and lake fishing can be delivered only at specific points. Many nonprofit services, however, do not depend on

> **ON LINE**
>
> **Advertising Council**
>
> What are the most compelling PSAs on the Ad Council site at the moment?
>
> **http://www.adcouncil.org**

special facilities. Counselling, for example, need not take place in agency offices; it may occur wherever counsellors and clients can meet. Probation services, outreach youth programs, and educational courses taught on commuter trains are other examples of deliverable services.

Promotion Decisions

Some nonprofit organizations are explicitly or implicitly prohibited from advertising; other nonprofit organizations simply do not have the resources to retain advertising agencies, promotion consultants, or marketing staff. However, nonprofit organizations have a few special promotion resources to call on:

- *Professional volunteers:* Nonprofit organizations often seek out marketing, sales, and advertising professionals to help them develop and implement promotion strategies. In some instances, an advertising agency donates its services in exchange for potential long-term benefits. One advertising agency donated its services to a major symphony because the symphony had a blue-ribbon board of directors. Donated services create goodwill, personal contacts, and general awareness of the donor's organization, reputation, and competency.
- *Sales promotion activities:* Sales promotion activities that make use of existing services or other resources are increasingly being used to draw attention to the offerings of nonprofit organizations. Sometimes nonprofit charities even team up with other companies for promotional activities. For example, Rainbow Cinemas, The Toronto Star, and Cadillac Fairview Shopping Centres all teamed up with United Way to run a Movie Marathon at the Galleria Cinemas. All proceeds during the 12-hour movie marathon at the Toronto theatres went to the United Way.[22]
- *Public service advertising:* A **public service advertisement (PSA)** is an announcement that promotes a program of a federal, provincial, or local government or of a nonprofit organization. Unlike a commercial advertiser, the sponsor of the PSA does not pay for the time or space. Instead, it is donated by the medium.

public service advertisement (PSA)
An announcement that promotes a program of a federal, provincial, or local government or of a nonprofit organization.

Cause-related marketing can be a controversial marketing technique because not all companies are as scrupulous as they should be about their intentions. A company like Newman's Own, however, which donates all after-tax profits to charity, is clear in its mission. By not profiting from using causes as a marketing tool, its motives are beyond reproach.

Pricing Decisions

Five key characteristics distinguish the pricing decisions of nonprofit organizations from those of the profit sector:

- *Pricing objectives:* The main pricing objective in the profit sector is revenue or, more specifically, profit maximization, sales maximization, or target return on sales or investment. Many nonprofit organizations must also be concerned about revenue. Often, however, nonprofit organizations seek to either partially or fully defray costs rather than to achieve a profit for distribution to stockholders. Nonprofit organizations also seek to redistribute income—for instance, through taxation and sliding-scale fees. Moreover, they strive to allocate resources fairly among individuals or households or across geographic or political boundaries.
- *Nonfinancial prices:* In many nonprofit situations, consumers are not charged a monetary price but instead must absorb nonmonetary costs. The importance of those costs is illustrated by the large number of eligible citizens who do not take advantage of so-called free services for the poor. In many public assistance programs, about half the people who are eligible don't participate. Nonmonetary costs consist of the opportunity cost of time, embarrassment costs, and effort costs.

- *Indirect payment:* Indirect payment through taxes is common to marketers of "free" services, such as libraries, fire protection, and police protection. Indirect payment is not a common practice in the profit sector.
- *Separation between payers and users:* By design, the services of many charitable organizations are provided for those who are relatively poor and largely paid for by those who are better off financially. Although examples of separation between payers and users can be found in the profit sector (such as insurance claims), the practice is much less prevalent.
- *Below-cost pricing:* University tuition is an example of below-cost pricing. Virtually all colleges and universities price their services below full cost.

>> CONNECT IT

Look back at the story about Yellow Transportation at the beginning of this chapter. After reading the chapter, you should know the answers to the questions posed at the end of the story. A service, such as trucking, differs from goods in four basic characteristics. Services are intangible performances, are produced and consumed simultaneously, have greater variability, and are perishable. Yellow's service before 1996 was narrowly focused on long-haul trucking. After 1996, it broadened its service mix to offer one-stop shopping for shipping. Yellow's concern with satisfying its customers helped the company to improve the reliability, responsiveness, and assurance components of service quality.

REVIEW IT

1 **Discuss the importance of services to the economy.** The service sector plays a crucial role in the Canadian economy, employing about three-quarters of the workforce and accounting for nearly 70 percent of the gross domestic product.

1.1 

What services does the website http://www.travelweb.com offer? How do visitors use the Special Offer List?

2 **Discuss the differences between services and goods.** Services are distinguished by four characteristics. Services are intangible performances in that they lack clearly identifiable physical characteristics, making it difficult for marketers to communicate their specific benefits to potential customers. The production and consumption of services occur simultaneously. Services are variable because their quality depends on such elements as the service provider, individual consumer, location, and so on. Finally, services are perishable in the sense that they cannot be stored or saved. As a result, synchronizing supply with demand is particularly challenging in the service industry.

2.1 WRITING Assume you are a manager of a bank branch. Write a list of the implications of intangibility for your firm.

3 **Describe the components of service quality and the gap model of service quality.** Service quality has five components: reliability (ability to perform the service dependably, accurately, and consistently), responsiveness (providing prompt service), assurance (knowledge and courtesy of employees and their ability to convey trust), empathy (caring, individualized attention), and tangibles (physical evidence of the service).

The gap model identifies five key discrepancies that can influence customer evaluations of service quality. When the gaps are large, service quality is low. As the gaps shrink, service quality improves. Gap 1 is found between customers' expectations and management's perceptions of those expectations. Gap 2 is found between management's perception of what the customer wants and specifications for service quality. Gap 3 is found between service quality specifications and delivery of the service. Gap 4 is found between service delivery and what the company promises to the customer through external communication. Gap 5 is found between customers' service expectations and their perceptions of service performance.

3.1 Analyze a recent experience that you have had with a service business (for example, hairdresser, movie theatre, dentist, restaurant, car repair) in terms of your expectations and perceptions about each of the five components of service quality.

4 **Develop marketing mixes for services.** "Product" (service) strategy issues include what is being processed (people, possessions, mental stimulus, information), core and supplementary services, customization versus standardization, and the service mix or portfolio. Distribution decisions involve convenience, number of outlets, direct versus indirect distribution, and scheduling. Stressing tangible cues, using personal sources of information, creating strong organizational images, and engaging in postpurchase communication are effective promotion strategies. Pricing objectives for services can be revenue oriented, operations oriented, patronage oriented, or any combination of the three.

4.1 TEAM Form a team with at least two other classmates, and come up with an idea for a new service. Develop a marketing mix strategy for the new service.

5 **Discuss relationship marketing in services.** Relationship marketing in services involves attracting, developing, and retaining customer relationships. There are three levels of relationship marketing: Level 1 focuses on pricing incentives; Level 2 uses pricing incentives and social bonds with customers; and Level 3 uses pricing, social bonds, and structural bonds to build long-term relationships.

5.1 TEAM For the new service developed for question 4.1, have the members of the team discuss how they would implement a relationship marketing strategy.

6 **Explain internal marketing in services.** Internal marketing means treating employees as customers and developing systems and benefits that satisfy their needs. Employees who like their jobs and are happy with the firm they work for are more likely to deliver good service. Internal marketing activities include competing for talent, offering a vision, training employees, stressing teamwork, giving employees freedom to make decisions, measuring and rewarding good service performance, and knowing employees' needs.

6.1 WRITING Choose a service firm with which you do a lot of business. Write a memo to the manager explaining the importance of internal marketing and outlining the factors that internal marketing includes.

7 **Discuss global issues in services marketing.** Canada is a growing exporter of services. Although competition is keen, Canada has a competitive advantage because of its vast experience in many service industries. To be successful globally, service firms must adjust their marketing mix for the environment of each target country.

7.1 What issues would you have to think about in going global with the new service that you developed in the questions above? How would you change your marketing mix to address those issues?

8 **Describe nonprofit organization marketing.** Nonprofit organizations pursue goals other than profit, market share, and return on investment. Nonprofit organization marketing facilitates mutually satisfying exchanges between nonprofit organiza-

tions and their target markets. Several unique characteristics distinguish nonbusiness marketing strategy, including a concern with services and social behaviours rather than manufactured goods and profit; a difficult, undifferentiated, and in some ways marginal target market; a complex product that may have only indirect benefits and elicit very low involvement; a short, direct, immediate distribution channel; a relative lack of resources for promotion; and prices only indirectly related to the exchange between the producer and the consumer of services.

8.1 

Form a team with two or three classmates. Using the promotion strategies discussed in the nonprofit section of this chapter, develop a promotion strategy for your college or university.

DEFINE IT

assurance 284
core service 288
credence quality 283
empathy 284
experience quality 283
gap model 285
intangibility 282
internal marketing 292
mass customization 289
nonprofit organization 293
nonprofit organization marketing 293
public service advertisement (PSA) 296
reliability 284
responsiveness 284
search quality 283
service 282
supplementary services 288
tangibles 285

APPLY IT

Amanda Jacobs has decided she wants to start a marketing consulting business. She has been able to generate solid financial backing for her venture because she has already developed an outstanding reputation as a creative and successful marketer. Thus, start-up resources are not a large problem. Amanda will target small companies with her services. Her business will be located in a medium-sized community not far from a large city.

QUESTIONS

1. How can Amanda make her service tangible for potential clients?
2. What can Amanda do to ensure she will offer a quality service to her clients?
3. What marketing strategies can Amanda use to help her develop long-term relationships with her clients?

THINK ABOUT IT

Websites such as Oncology.com, CancerPage.com, and CancerSource.com offer cancer patients sophisticated medical data and advice in exchange for personal data, which are then sold to advertisers and business partners and used by the websites to create products to sell back to patients. Some argue that cancer patients visiting these sites are willingly exchanging their personal information for the sites' medical information. Others would contend that this kind of exchange is unethical.

QUESTIONS

1. Is this practice ethical?
2. Does the CMA Code of Ethics have anything to say about this issue? Go to **http://www.the-cma.org/consumer/ethics.cfm** and review the code. Then write a brief paragraph on what the CMA Code of Ethics contains that relates to this scenario.

TRY IT

Closing the Digital Divide

As we move into 2005 with many young people looking for better-paying careers, there are tens of thousands of unfilled technology jobs across the country. In an effort to help young people and fill some of these jobs, Walter Manney left his position as a computer consultant at the University of Windsor to form Canadian Computer Schools. Start-up funds were provided by several local businesses.

The goal of Canadian Computer Schools, a not-for-profit organization, is to prepare 18- to 24-year-olds for the technology, telecommunications, and Internet industry workplace. The program will give special emphasis to young people who, otherwise, might not be able to afford to undertake a university or community college degree program. Visible minorities, the poor, and the disabled will be targeted.

The Canadian Computer Schools program is an intensive three-month program that includes a cost-of-living stipend for the participants. The first month of the program focuses on technical training. In the second month of the program, participants develop and execute their own websites. In the third month, participants work with paying clients on Web-related projects. The objective of the program is to place participants in Web-related or IT positions after the third month. If the program is to succeed, Walter needs about $500,000 to be donated from businesses in addition to money raised by projects undertaken during the third month of the program by each participant.

Walter's five-year plan for Canadian Computer Schools includes:

Years 1 and 2: Perfect the three-month training program
Years 2 and 3: Serve the Southern Ontario business community and technology market
Years 3 and 4: Create a Canadian Computer Schools consulting service
Year 5: Attain financial security through training program, consulting services, and participant placement

QUESTIONS:

1. What is Canadian Computer Schools's product?
2. What is Canadian Computer Schools's marketing strategy?
3. What pricing issues face Canadian Computer Schools?
4. What does Walter Manney need to do to generate $500,000 in contributions from businesses?

FLIP IT

Flip to Chapter 10 in your *Grademaker Study Guide* for more review opportunities, including the pretest, vocabulary review, Internet activities, study test questions, and an application exercise based on services marketing. Do services really differ from goods? How do you develop a marketing mix for service businesses? If you don't know, then flip open your *Grademaker* and review.

CLICK IT

The *Marketing* website is rich with materials to help you review and master marketing concepts. Check your knowledge with the free quizzes, practise key terms using the crossword puzzles, or review key concepts using the Microsoft® PowerPoint® slides. Also on the website are updated weblinks to companies mentioned in this chapter, Internet exercises, career marketing information, and much much more! Go to http://www.lamb3e.nelson.com, read the material, and follow the convenient links.

WATCH IT

The Wickaninnish Inn

Cold and stormy winters may not sound enticing for vacationers—but The Wickaninnish Inn has turned this type of weather into a positive. The Inn promotes spectacular views of storms as a major feature of staying at the inn. The Wickaninnish Inn has been designed from the ground up for the specific purpose of providing the most comfortable location on North America's west coast for storm watching. The Wickaninnish Inn is built on a rocky ledge on the rugged west coast of Vancouver Island. With the inn surrounded by water on three sides, every one of the 76 guest rooms has an ocean view, as well as a fireplace and other amenities that you would find only in luxury hotels.

By getting to know its key target audience, generally busy city dwellers, The Wickaninnish Inn has been able to devise a range of service packages to suit different tastes. Those wanting a fast, hassle-free escape are directed to the No Stress Express package, which combines a convenient flight with a weekend stay at the inn. The Nature Lover's package includes guided nature walks, while the Gourmet Trail offers excursions to the finest dining spots around Vancouver Island.

For those guests who do not want to preplan their stay, The Wickaninnish Inn offers dedicated guest services representatives. These concierges act as personal assistants to guests, helping them organize any activity at short notice. Take a look at the two websites that feature The Wickaninnish Inn (http://www.wickinn.com or http://bcadventure.com/wickaninnish) to find out more about how the McDiarmid family has gone about making the inn a huge success.

The Wickaninnish Inn near Tofino, British Columbia, has found a unique positioning for itself as a leading service provider among Canada's resort hotels.

QUESTIONS

1. Services are intangible, inseparable from the provider, perishable, and heterogeneous. How do these characteristics apply to The Wickaninnish Inn?
2. Lodging is a fiercely competitive service business. What are the different elements of Wickaninnish's promotional strategy, and how are they helping it attract customers the whole year around? What else might the inn do?
3. The five components of service quality are reliability, responsiveness, assurance, empathy, and tangibles. What evidence can you cite that The Wickaninnish Inn delivers on these components? What might be done to improve service quality?

Source: CBC, *Venture*, "Stormy Weather," Broadcast: February 3, 1998.

MARKETING MISCUES

Did Moxi Digital Stop to Consider Demand?

A home entertainment revolution was on the horizon if one believed Steve Perlman, the founder of Moxi Digital, Inc. A relatively new company, formerly known as Rearden Steel Technologies, Inc. Moxi Digital was seeking to dominate the home entertainment market by seamlessly integrating a home's television, stereo, and computer. The company's revolutionary product, the Moxi Media Centre, was unveiled in January 2002. At the time, however, there were rumours that potential demand might be uncertain and that the company might not have the cash flow to survive.

The Moxi Media Centre was five products in one: a digital cable/satellite receiver, a digital music jukebox, a personal video recorder, a DVD player, and a cable/DSL modem. With these five products, the Moxi had three main capabilities: (1) a navigation system to reduce the number of clicks to find items, (2) secure multiformatted video and music playback, and (3) storage and organization of music tracks. The Moxi was similar in appearance to a videocassette recorder, sat on the television, and had a remote control. Beyond appearances, the Moxi was a technological breakthrough that allowed any television or personal computer in the house to receive entertainment and data. Interestingly, the product's name was not related to any technological aspect of the product market. "Moxi" came from the word *moxie*, meaning gumption, excitement, and spunk.

Total North American consumer electronics sales were expected to be well in excess of $100 billion in 2003. Included in these estimates were sales of multiuse products such as a cell phone and MP3 combination and a digital voice recorder box combined with direct broadcast satellite, as well as increased sales of DVD players, digital cameras, and mobile electronics. Nevertheless, industry experts were skeptical as to whether a product such as the Moxi that could truly be classified as a disruptive technology would generate much demand. With the Moxi selling to consumers at nearly $500, the company would need to do considerable market education to generate demand at the break-even level.

In fact, market acceptance of the Moxi appeared questionable. Would consumers who were only beginning to adjust to the potential of digital entertainment accept, much less adopt, such state-of-the-art technology? Did consumers see a need to network their televisions, computers, stereos, and MP3 players? Or were consumers happy with their current arrangement of separate entertainment devices? Additionally, did the typical household own the entertainment equipment necessary to make the Moxi useful?

In addition to these market-oriented questions, several company-related concerns had arisen. Moxi Digital would not actually manufacture the product. Rather, it would offer the designs for free to consumer electronics manufacturers. Thus, the company would rely on intermediaries to fulfill the product's offerings. Would Moxi Digital, along with the necessary and numerous intermediaries, be able to deliver what it promised? More important, however, would the company, which had raised almost $70 million in funding, run out of money before the product even hit the market? There were sincere questions as to whether Moxi Digital could turn its dreams into reality. Was the Moxi Media Centre an expensive product idea that was too advanced for the marketplace to adopt quickly enough to warrant funnelling more dollars into the invention?

Questions

1. How is the Moxi a disruptive technology?
2. What can a company do to prevent such elaborate investments that do not result in bringing a product to market?

CRITICAL THINKING CASE

The Segway Human Transporter

A product code-named after Ginger Rogers and a media frenzy about an invention bigger than the Internet set the stage for DEKA Research & Development Corporation's Segway Human Transporter (Segway HT at **http://www.segway.com**). But was the buzz about the product too much? Did it create expectations beyond the product's capabilities? Was it too early? Was the buzz leak really an accident? Will the Segway HT change the transportation marketplace? Just as important, what is the market for this new product?

DEKA Research & Development Corporation

Founded in 1982 by Dean Kamen, DEKA focuses on the product market of radical technologies, with a mission to foster innovations that enhance quality of life. Though technically a research and development group, DEKA has the capabilities to take a product from concept to low-volume manufacturing runs. The company remains relatively small and employs about 200 engineers, technicians, and machinists.

Kamen is a well-known inventor and entrepreneur, holding more than 150 international patents. His innovative, scientific achievements have resulted in numerous awards and public recognition. *Smithsonian* magazine labelled him "the Pied Piper of technology." He is the recipient of the Kilby Award (for extraordinary contributions to society), the Heinz Award in Technology, and the National Medal of Technology.

Innovative healthcare products resulting from Kamen's inventions are numerous. His infusion devices gained immediate and international recognition. The market for these devices was huge, prompting Kamen to found AutoSyringe, Inc., to manufacture and market the products. The company's wearable infusion pump gained rapid acceptance in chemotherapy, neonatology, and endocrinology. AutoSyringe also produced and marketed the first insulin pump for diabetics. Eventually, Kamen sold AutoSyringe, Inc., to Baxter International, Inc. and then went on to start DEKA.

Since its inception, DEKA has worked closely with several large companies in the healthcare industry. Major corporate partners include Baxter Healthcare Corporation, Davol, Inc., and Johnson & Johnson. DEKA designs and develops products for its corporate partners. For Baxter Healthcare Corporation, DEKA developed a relatively small, lightweight peritoneal dialysis machine that allows greater mobility for the user. In conjunction with Davol, Inc., DEKA developed a one-system irrigation pump for common medical procedures such as laparoscopy, arthroscopy, and hysteroscopy. Various companies within Johnson & Johnson (Cordis Corporation, THERAKOS, Inc., and Independence Technology, L.L.C.) have used DEKA's medical innovations. DEKA and Cordis introduced the first intravascular stent to reduce artery blockage, and DEKA and THERAKOS developed the most advanced and innovative technology used to treat cutaneous T-cell lymphoma. DEKA and Independence Technology are working together to develop and market a product similar to a wheelchair that can climb stairs, raise the user to eye level, and traverse uneven terrain.

Introducing the Segway Human Transporter

The Segway HT, referred to as a disruptive technology, could soon hit the sidewalks, streets, and hallways of our cities and businesses. This new-age people mover has been described as a cross between a rotary lawn mower and a scooter or a large weed whacker that a person can stand on. This description is somewhat deceptive, however, in that the Segway HT is not as straightforward as a rotary lawn mower, scooter, or weed whacker. It has three personal computers' worth of computer technology, dual-motored wheels, five solid-state gyroscopes, tubeless and flat-resistant lightweight tires, and handlebars for balance. The product does not have a brake, engine, throttle, gearshift, or steering wheel. It works with human equilibrium by responding to movements. Leaning forward on the Segway HT causes it to accelerate, and leaning backward causes it to stop. Basically, the gyroscopes act like the inner ear, the computer acts like a brain, the motors act like muscles, and the wheels act like feet.

Product specifications include a maximum speed of 8 to 27 kilometres per hour depending upon settings and terrain, a battery charge of 28 kilometres on flat surfaces, one hour of charge for two hours of operation, a passenger load of 115 kilograms, a weight of under 34 kilograms, and a cost of $3,000 for the consumer model and $8,000 for the industrial model.

Bringing the Segway HT to market has not been without obstacles. One obstacle is that the federal government must determine whether the product should be classified as a motor vehicle.

Empowering Pedestrians

DEKA has no mass-market experience, yet it has developed a product that could change the way pedestrians get from point A to point B. Early product-related buzz prompted mixed opinions. While people who had seen or tried the Segway HT were enthusiastic about its potential for success, others were skeptical of its ability to make it to market. The bottom line—would the practicalities of manufacturing and marketing the invention keep it out of consumer hands?[23]

Questions

1. Why is the Segway HT considered a disruptive technology? Is it really just a high-end toy?
2. Can DEKA make the transition from inventing to selling?
3. How can DEKA garner a portion of the $300 billion transportation industry? Who are likely the purchasers of this product?
4. Is the Segway HT a consumer product or a business-to-business product?

>> Distribution Decisions

part 4

ON LINE

For articles and exercises on the material in this part, and for other great study aids, visit the *Marketing* Website at

www.lamb3e.nelson.com

chapter 11

Marketing Channels and Supply Chain Management

>> LEARNING OBJECTIVES

1. Explain what a marketing channel is and why intermediaries are needed
2. Describe the channel structures for consumer and business-to-business products and discuss alternative channel arrangements
3. Define supply chain management and discuss its benefits
4. Discuss the issues that influence channel strategy
5. Explain channel leadership, conflict, and partnering
6. Describe the logistical components of the supply chain
7. Discuss new technology and emerging trends in supply chain management
8. Discuss channels and distribution decisions in global markets
9. Identify the special problems and opportunities associated with distribution in service organizations

>>A green truck pulls up in front of the offices of Home & Park Motorhomes in Kitchener, Ontario. Home & Park Motorhomes is the largest assembler of camper vans in Canada. The driver of the green truck delivers gourmet coffee to be used at all of the coffee machines in the Home & Park offices. As well, the driver delivers a wide range of office supplies ranging from paper, to pens and pencils, to toner, to light bulbs, a new fax machine, and much more. Later that day, a similar green truck arrives at the home of Pete and Pat Mateja (Pete is the president of Home & Park Motorhomes) in Oakville, Ontario. The driver delivers the week's groceries that were ordered earlier in the day through Pat's home computer.

Grocery Gateway, which began by selling only grocery products, is an office supply, home and office furnishing, home and office equipment, gourmet coffee and grocery retailer that sells and delivers directly to business and household customers without the need and investment in bricks-and-mortar stores. Sales are made via the Internet, through a chain of suppliers and a well-designed logistics network, and delivery is made directly to each customer's door. And it's not only groceries, as it was just a few years ago. Grocery Gateway can now deliver wine, beer, books, drugstore products, household items, furniture, home and office supplies, and home and office equipment.

Household shoppers can do their home and grocery shopping and office managers can purchase their office supply needs in about the time it takes to write up a shopping list. Grocery Gateway's website (**http://www.grocerygateway.com**) is organized like the aisles in a traditional store. You select the products and sizes that you need. At any point during your shopping trip, you can view your shopping cart to see what you've selected. A subtotal always appears on the screen to let you know exactly how much you have spent. You can choose from any variety of grocery products, beers and wines, drugstore items, books, office furniture, home and office supplies, and office equipment (and don't forget the gourmet coffee for the office). At "checkout" you choose a window of time within which you wish to have your order delivered.

The Grocery Gateway delivery person will call 15 minutes before arriving and will carry your order into your kitchen or your office supply room. Don't like to give credit card information over the Internet? No problem, the delivery person will accept credit cards, cheques, debit cards, or Interac payments, but won't take a tip.

Grocery Gateway works through partnerships with wholesalers; food retailers like Sobeys; home and office supply outlets like Home Depot and Staples Business Depot; Van Houtte coffees; and many others. These suppliers promise that you will have available to purchase all of your favourite brands at prices competitive with those you will find in the retail outlets you would otherwise visit.

Logistics are handled with special software. Orders and schedules are created and maintained with state-of-the-art technology, and deliveries are made from warehouse distribution centres. Grocery Gateway was founded in 1996 and sales surpassed $70 million in 2003. With on-line sales now in the neighbourhood of $5 billion in Canada, there is a lot more market for Grocery Gateway to capture.[1]

What advantages does Grocery Gateway gain by selling direct and bypassing traditional market intermediaries? What areas of distribution, such as inventory, materials handling, and logistics, could be streamlined to compete yet more effectively? Grocery Gateway has grown by expanding its range of product offerings through supply relationships with Sobeys, Home Depot, Staples Business Depot, Van Houtte coffees, and others. What would be further natural extensions for Grocery Gateway?

ON LINE

Grocery Gateway

What elements of Grocery Gateway's supply chain are evident on the company's website? How easy is it to navigate Grocery Gateway's site? Would you buy groceries and office supplies through this site?

http://www.grocerygateway.com

Explain what a marketing channel is and why intermediaries are needed

>> MARKETING CHANNELS

The term *channel* is derived from the Latin word *canalis*, which means canal. A marketing channel can be viewed as a large canal or pipeline through which products, their ownership, communication, financing, and payment, and the accompanying risk, flow to the consumer. Formally, a **marketing channel** (also called a **channel of distribution**) is a business structure of interdependent organizations that reach from the point of product origin to the consumer with the purpose of moving products to their final consumption destination. Marketing channels facilitate the physical movement of goods through the supply chain, representing the "place" element in the marketing mix (product, price, promotion, and place) and encompassing the processes involved in getting the right product to the right place at the right time.

marketing channel (channel of distribution)
A set of interdependent organizations that ease the transfer of ownership as products move from producer to business user or consumer.

channel members
All parties in the marketing channel that negotiate with one another, buy and sell products, and facilitate the change of ownership between buyer and seller in the course of moving the product from the manufacturer into the hands of the final consumer.

supply chain
The connected chain of all of the business entities, both internal and external to the company, that perform or support the logistics function.

Many different types of organizations participate in marketing channels. **Channel members** (also called *intermediaries*, *resellers*, and *middlemen*) negotiate with one another, buy and sell products, and facilitate the change of ownership between buyer and seller in the course of moving the product from the manufacturer into the hands of the final consumer. An important aspect of marketing channels is the joint effort of all channel members to create a continuous and seamless supply chain. The **supply chain** is the connected chain of all of the business entities, both internal and external to the company, that perform or support the marketing channel functions. As products move through the supply chain, channel members facilitate the distribution process by providing specialization and division of labour, overcoming discrepancies, and providing contact efficiency.

Providing Specialization and Division of Labour

According to the concept of specialization and division of labour, breaking down a complex task into smaller, simpler ones and allocating them to specialists will create greater efficiency and lower average production costs. Manufacturers achieve economies of scale through the use of efficient equipment capable of producing large quantities of a single product.

Marketing channels can also attain economies of scale through specialization and division of labour by aiding producers who lack the motivation, financing, or expertise to market directly to end users or consumers. In some cases, as with most consumer convenience goods, such as soft drinks, the cost of marketing directly to millions of consumers—taking and shipping individual orders—is prohibitive. For this reason, producers hire channel members, such as wholesalers and retailers, to do what the producers are not equipped to do or what channel members are better prepared to do. Channel members can do some things more efficiently than producers because they have built good relationships with their customers. Therefore, their specialized expertise enhances the overall performance of the channel.

Overcoming Discrepancies

Marketing channels also aid in overcoming the discrepancies of quantity, assortment, time, and space created by economies of scale in production. For example, assume that the H.J. Heinz Co. can efficiently produce its Heinz ketchup only at a rate of 20,000 units in a typical day at its Leamington, Ontario, plant. Not even the most ardent ketchup user could consume that amount. The quantity produced to achieve low unit costs has created a **discrepancy of quantity**, which is the difference between the amount of product produced and the amount an end user wants to buy. By storing the product and distributing it in the appropriate amounts, marketing channels overcome quantity discrepancies by making products available in the quantities that consumers desire.

discrepancy of quantity
The difference between the amount of product produced and the amount an end user wants to buy.

discrepancy of assortment
The lack of all the items a customer needs to receive full satisfaction from a product or products.

Mass production creates not only discrepancies of quantity but also discrepancies of assortment. A **discrepancy of assortment** occurs when a consumer does not have all of the items needed to receive full satisfaction from a product. For Heinz ketchup to provide maximum satisfaction, several other products are required to complete the assortment. At the very least, most people want a knife, fork, plate, and various foods to put the ketchup on. Even though Heinz is a large consumer-products company, it does not come close to providing the optimal assortment to go with its ketchup. To overcome discrepancies of assortment, marketing channels assemble in one place many of the products necessary to complete a consumer's needed assortment.

A **temporal discrepancy** is created when a product is produced but a consumer is not ready to buy it. Marketing channels overcome temporal discrepancies by maintaining inventories in anticipation of demand. For example, manufacturers of seasonal merchandise, such as Christmas decorations, are in operation all year even though consumer demand is concentrated during certain months of the year.

temporal discrepancy
A situation that occurs when a product is produced but a customer is not ready to buy it.

Furthermore, because mass production requires many potential buyers, markets are usually scattered over large geographic regions, creating a **spatial discrepancy**. Often global, or at least nationwide, markets are needed to absorb the outputs of mass producers. Marketing channels overcome spatial discrepancies by making products available in locations convenient to consumers. For example, automobile manufacturers overcome spatial discrepancies by franchising dealerships close to consumers.

spatial discrepancy
The difference between the location of the producer and the location of widely scattered markets.

Providing Contact Efficiency

The third need fulfilled by marketing channels is for a way to provide contact efficiency. Consider your extra costs if supermarkets, department stores, and shopping centres or malls did not exist. Suppose you had to buy your milk at a dairy and your meat at a stockyard. Imagine buying your eggs and chicken at a hatchery and your fruits and vegetables at various farms. You would spend a great deal of time, money, and energy just shopping for a few groceries. Supply chains simplify distribution by cutting the number of transactions required to get products from manufacturers to consumers and making an assortment of goods available in one location.

Consider the example illustrated in Exhibit 11.1. Four consumers each want to buy a television set. Without a retail intermediary like Future Shop, television manufacturers JVC, Zenith, Sony, Toshiba, and RCA would each have to make four contacts to reach the four buyers who are in the target market, totaling twenty transactions. However,

EXHIBIT 11.1
Marketing Channels

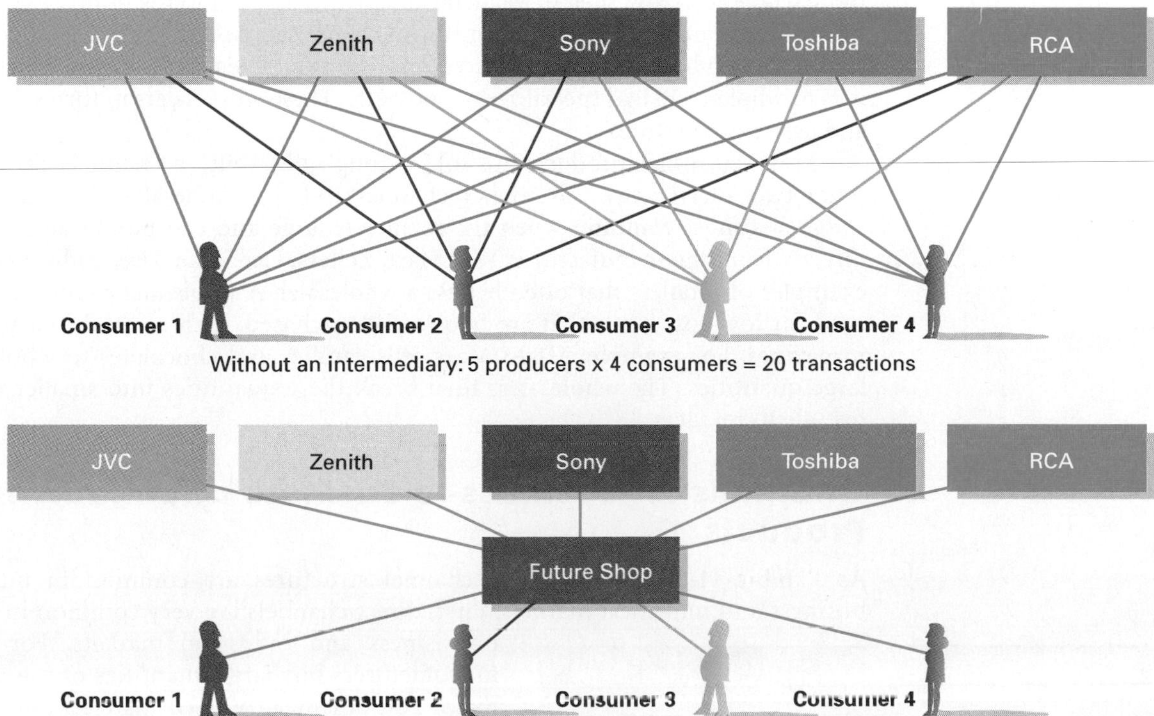

when Future Shop acts as an intermediary between the producer and consumers, each producer only has to make one contact, reducing the number of transactions to nine. Each producer sells to one retailer rather than to four consumers. In turn, consumers buy from one retailer instead of from five producers.

2 Describe the channel structures for consumer and business-to-business products and discuss alternative channel arrangements

>> CHANNEL STRUCTURES

A product can take many routes to reach its final consumer. Marketers search for the most efficient channel from the many alternatives available. Marketing a consumer convenience good like gum or candy differs from marketing a specialty good like a Mercedes-Benz. The two products require very different distribution channels. Likewise, the appropriate channel for a major equipment supplier like Boeing aircraft would be unsuitable for an accessory equipment producer like Black & Decker.

Channels for Consumer Products

direct channel
A distribution channel in which producers sell directly to consumers.

Exhibit 11.2 illustrates the four ways manufacturers can route products to consumers. Producers use the **direct channel** to sell directly to consumers. Direct marketing activities—including telemarketing, mail-order and catalogue shopping, and forms of electronic retailing like on-line shopping and shop-at-home television networks—are good examples of this type of channel structure. For example, home computer users can purchase Dell computers directly over the telephone or directly from Dell's Internet website. There are no intermediaries. Producer-owned stores and factory outlet stores—like Sherwin-Williams, Polo Ralph Lauren, Nike, Club Monaco, and Body Shop—are other examples of direct channels. Farmers' markets are also direct channels.

At the other end of the spectrum, an *agent/broker channel* (see Chapter 12 for a complete discussion of channel intermediaries) involves a fairly complicated process. *Agents* and *brokers* are middlemen who do not take title to goods but simply bring buyers and sellers together. Agent/broker channels are typically used in markets with many small manufacturers and many retailers that lack the resources to find one another. Agents or brokers bring manufacturers and wholesalers together for negotiations, but they do not take title to merchandise. Ownership passes directly to one or more wholesalers and then to retailers. Finally, retailers sell to the ultimate consumer of the product. For example, a food broker may represent sellers of grocery products. The broker acts on behalf of many different producers and negotiates the sale of their products to wholesalers that specialize in foodstuffs. These wholesalers in turn sell to grocers and convenience stores.

Most consumer products are sold through distribution channels similar to the other two alternatives: the retailer channel and the wholesaler channel. A *retailer channel* is most common when the retailer is large and can buy in large quantities directly from the manufacturer. Wal-Mart, Zellers, Canadian Tire, and car dealers are examples of retailers that often bypass a wholesaler. A *wholesaler channel* is generally used for low-cost items that are frequently purchased, such as candy, cigarettes, and magazines. For example, M&M/Mars sells candies and chocolates to wholesalers in large quantities. The wholesalers then break these quantities into smaller quantities for sale to retailers.

Channels for Business-to-Business and Industrial Products

As Exhibit 11.3 illustrates, five channel structures are common in business-to-business and industrial markets. First, direct channels are very common in business-to-business and industrial markets. For example, manufacturers buy large quantities of raw materials, major equipment, processed materials, and supplies directly from other manufacturers. Manufacturers that require suppliers to meet detailed technical spec-

ON LINE 

What kind of marketing channel functions can be performed over the Internet? Why do you think so?

EXHIBIT 11.2

Marketing Channels for Consumer Products

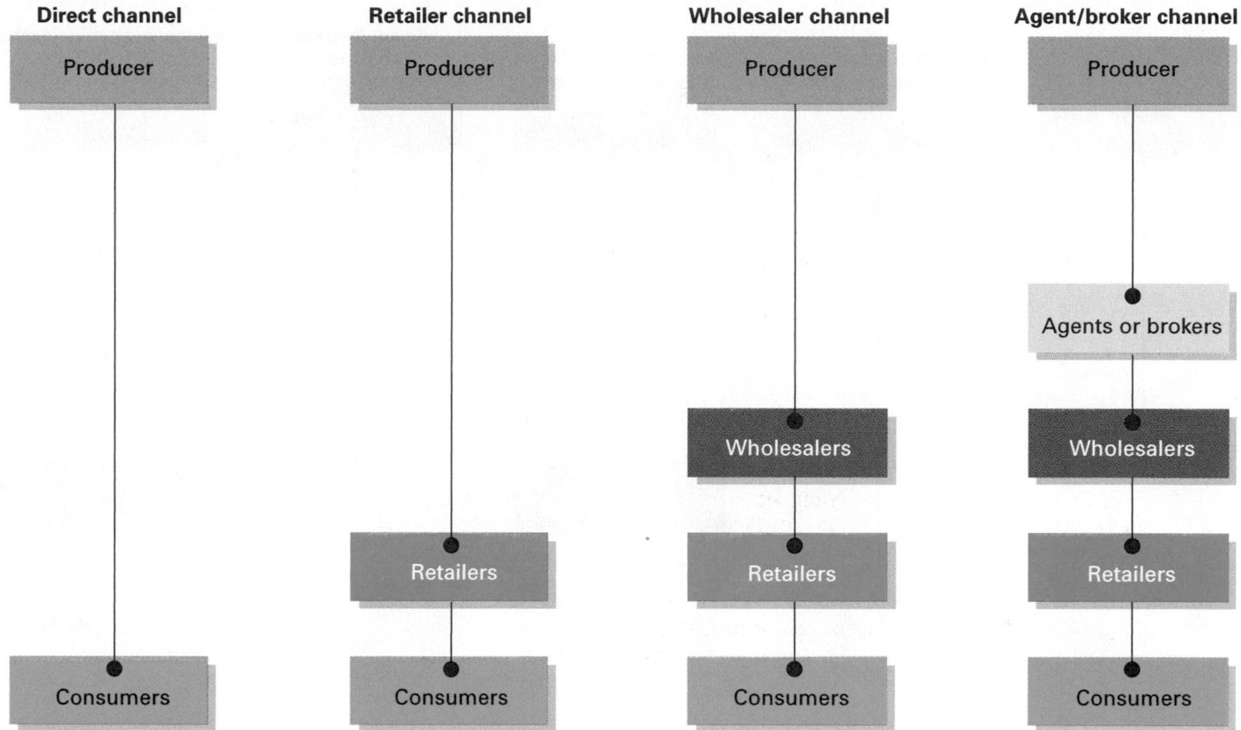

ifications often prefer direct channels. The direct communication required between DaimlerChrysler and its suppliers, for example, along with the tremendous size of the orders, makes anything but a direct channel impractical. The channel from producer to government buyers is also a direct channel. Since much of government buying is done through bidding, a direct channel is attractive. Dell Computer Corporation, for example, a top seller of desktop computers to federal, provincial, and local governments, sells its computers through direct channels.[2]

Companies selling standardized items of moderate or low value often rely on *industrial distributors.* In many ways, an industrial distributor is like a supermarket for organizations. Industrial distributors are wholesalers and channel members that buy and take title to products. Moreover, they usually keep inventories of their products and sell and service them. Often small manufacturers cannot afford to employ their own sales forces. Instead, they rely on manufacturers' representatives or selling agents to sell to either industrial distributors or users.

Increasingly, companies are using the Internet to create more direct and efficient business-to-business channels. Currently, three major forms of business-to-business exchanges are taking place on the Internet. The first and smallest sector is made up of new Internet companies that have been developed to link buyers and sellers. These companies act as agents and charge a service fee. A second form of marketplace has been developed by existing companies looking for ways to drop the intermediary from the supply chain. For example, the WorldWide Retail Exchange is a marketplace created by more than 50 major retailers. Retailers use the exchange to make purchases that in the past would have required telephone, fax, or face-to-face sales calls. Retailers using the exchange estimate they have saved approximately 15 percent in their purchasing costs. Finally, the third type of Internet marketplace is a "private exchange." Private exchanges allow companies to automate their supply chains while sharing information only with select suppliers. Home Hardware and Hewlett-Packard, for example, use private exchanges to manage their inventory supplies.[3]

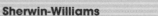

ON LINE

Sherwin-Williams

Visit Sherwin-Williams's home page to see how and where it sells its products. Are there different channels for its consumer products and its business products?

http://www.sherwin-williams.com

EXHIBIT 11.3

Channels for Business-to-Business and Industrial Products

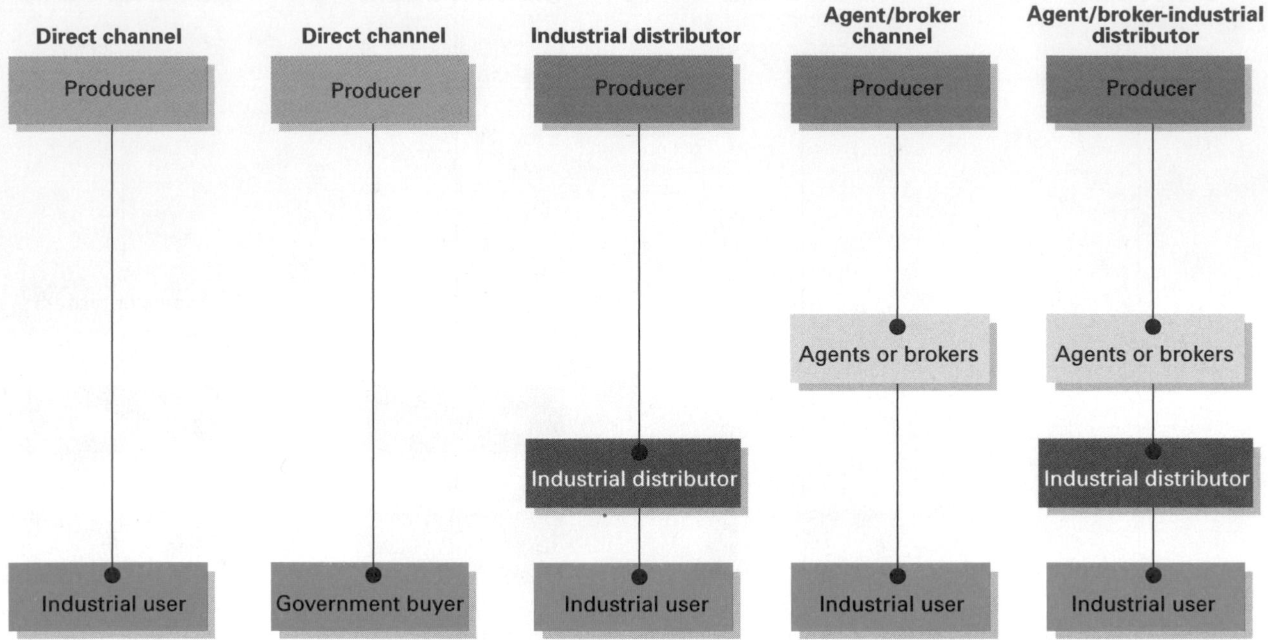

Alternative Channel Arrangements

Rarely does a producer use just one type of channel to move its product. It usually employs several different or alternative channels, which include multiple channels, nontraditional channels, and strategic channel alliances.

Multiple Channels

dual distribution (multiple distribution)
The use of two or more channels to distribute the same product to target markets.

When a producer selects two or more channels to distribute the same product to target markets, this arrangement is called **dual distribution** (or **multiple distribution**). For example, Whirlpool sells its washers, dryers, and refrigerators directly to home and apartment builders and contractors, but it also sells these same appliances to retail stores that sell to consumers. Avon, which has traditionally sold its products only through a company sales force, has launched a new cosmetic line sold in retail outlets.[4] Similarly, Dell Computer Corporation recently made a radical departure from its direct channel sales model by testing retail kiosks in shopping malls as a way to increase its market share of home computers. Dell has also tried selling computers directly to home users through cable shopping channels.[5] Multiple channels may also be employed by producers with unique second brands. For example, the Walt Disney Company routinely releases first-run animated films to movie theatres and then releases a sequel directly to the home-video market. Such sequels as *Aladdin and the King of Thieves* and *Beauty and the Beast: The Enchanted Christmas* follow up Disney theatre blockbusters.

Adding a new supply chain can renew a company's image. Such is the case with Avon, the leading company in direct selling, which broke its own mould with the launch of beComing, the company's first brand distributed exclusively in retail outlets.

Nontraditional Channels

Often nontraditional channel arrangements help differentiate a firm's product from the competition. For example, manufacturers may decide to use nontraditional channels such as the Internet, mail-order channels, or infomercials, to sell products instead of going through traditional retailer channels. Although nontraditional channels may limit a brand's coverage, they can give a producer serving a niche market a way to gain market access and customer attention without having to establish channel intermediaries. Nontraditional channels can also provide another avenue of sales for larger firms. For example, a London publisher has begun selling short stories through a vending machine in the London Underground. Instead of the traditional book format, the stories are printed like folded maps, which makes them an easy-to-read alternative for commuters.[6]

COURTESY OF ROCKWELL AUTOMATION

Supply chain management is the key to competitiveness, and many companies market tools to help other businesses manage their supply chains effectively. Rockwell Automation is one such solutions provider, helping companies share critical production information across the business enterprise.

Strategic Channel Alliances

Producers often form **strategic channel alliances**, which enable the producers to use another manufacturer's already established channel. Alliances are used most often when the creation of marketing channel relationships may be too expensive and time-consuming. Starbucks and Kraft recently announced a long-term licensing arrangement to begin stocking Starbucks coffee on supermarket shelves. Under the arrangement, Starbucks will roast and package the coffee, and Kraft will market and distribute it in supermarkets. The Starbucks coffee will be sold by Kraft's sales force. The alliance will allow Starbucks to distribute its coffee through grocery stores much faster than it could have done on its own.

Strategic channel alliances are proving to be more successful for growing businesses than mergers and acquisitions. This is especially true in global markets, where cultural differences, distance, and other barriers can prove challenging. For example, Heinz has a strategic alliance with Kagome, one of Japan's largest food companies. The companies are working together to find ways to reduce operating costs while expanding both brands' market presence globally.[7]

strategic channel alliance
A cooperative agreement between business firms to use the other's already established distribution channel.

>> SUPPLY CHAIN MANAGEMENT

3 Define supply chain management and discuss its benefits

In today's sophisticated marketplace, many companies are turning to supply chain management for competitive advantage. The goal of **supply chain management** is to coordinate and integrate all of the activities performed by supply chain members into a seamless process from the source to the point of consumption, ultimately giving supply chain managers "total visibility" of the supply chain both inside and outside the firm. The philosophy behind supply chain management is that by visualizing the entire supply chain, supply chain managers can maximize strengths and efficiencies at each level of the process to create a highly competitive, customer-driven supply system that is able to respond immediately to changes in supply and demand.

supply chain management
A management system that coordinates and integrates all of the activities performed by supply chain members into a seamless process, from the source to the point of consumption, resulting in enhanced customer and economic value.

An important element of supply chain management is that it is completely customer driven. In the mass-production era, manufacturers produced standardized products that were "pushed" down through the supply channel to the consumer. In contrast, in today's marketplace, customers, who expect to receive product configurations and services matched to their unique needs, are driving products. For example, Dell only builds computers according to its customers' precise specifications, such as the amount of RAM memory; type of monitor, modem, or CD drive; and amount of hard disk space. Similarly, car companies offer customers the option to customize even economy-priced cars. For less than $25,000, customers can order a Mitsubishi Lancer with spoilers and flashy colours or a Mazda Protegé with a faster engine, special transmission, and 280-watt MP3 sound system. The focus is on pulling products

ON LINE 

George Weston

What is the relationship between George Weston Limited and Loblaw Companies Limited in the supply chain? What would this form of channel relationship be called?

http://www.weston.ca

http://www.loblaws.ca

into the marketplace and partnering with members of the supply chain to enhance customer value. Customizing an automobile is now possible because of new supply chain relationships between the automobile manufacturers and the after-market auto-parts industry.[8]

This reversal of the flow of demand from a "push" to a "pull" has resulted in a radical reformulation of both market expectations and traditional marketing, production, and distribution functions. Through the channel partnership of suppliers, manufacturers, wholesalers, and retailers along the entire supply chain who work together toward the common goal of creating customer value, supply chain management allows companies to respond with the unique product configuration and mix of services demanded by the customer. Today, supply chain management plays a dual role: first, as a *communicator* of customer demand that extends from the point of sale all the way back to the supplier, and second, as a *physical flow process* that engineers the timely and cost-effective movement of goods through the entire supply pipeline.

Accordingly, supply chain managers are responsible for making channel strategy decisions, coordinating the sourcing and procurement of raw materials, scheduling production, processing orders, managing inventory, transporting and storing supplies and finished goods, and coordinating customer service activities. Supply chain managers are also responsible for the management of information that flows through the supply chain. Coordinating the relationships between the company and its external partners, such as vendors, carriers, and third-party companies, is also a critical function of supply chain management. Because supply chain managers play such a major role in both cost control and customer satisfaction, they are more valuable than ever.[9] Exhibit 11.4 depicts the supply chain process.

Benefits of Supply Chain Management

Supply chain management is a key means of differentiation for a firm and a critical component in marketing and corporate strategy. Companies that focus on supply chain management commonly report lower inventory, transportation, warehousing, and packaging costs; greater supply chain flexibility; improved customer service; and higher revenues. Research has shown a clear relationship between supply chain performance and profitability. Leaders in supply chain management report a 5 percent increase in revenue, a 65 percent increase in supply chain flexibility, and an 18 percent improvement in cash flow.[10]

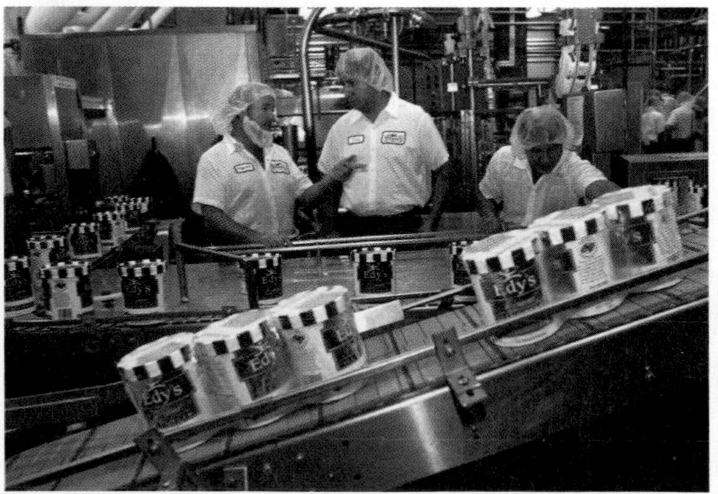

AP/WIDE WORLD PHOTOS

Dreyer's Ice Cream's successful logistics system starts with its state-of-the-art manufacturing facility. The return on investment the company experienced subsequent to its supply chain upgrades was extremely impressive.

Dreyer's ice cream has built its success on its logistics system. The company recently invested $150 million in a new fleet of trucks, manufacturing centres, additional employees, and a computerized delivery system that enables dispatchers to design delivery routes around sales volume, distance, traffic patterns, road conditions, and a store's hours of operation. As a return on its investment, the company has experienced a 33 percent increase in sales accounts, eliminated many unnecessary stops, saved $11 million in gas and labour hours, and increased its net income by 150 percent. In fact, the system provides such strong customer service capability and cost savings that nearly one-third of Dreyer's revenue comes from deals to distribute its competitors' brands such as Häagen-Dazs and Ben & Jerry's.[11]

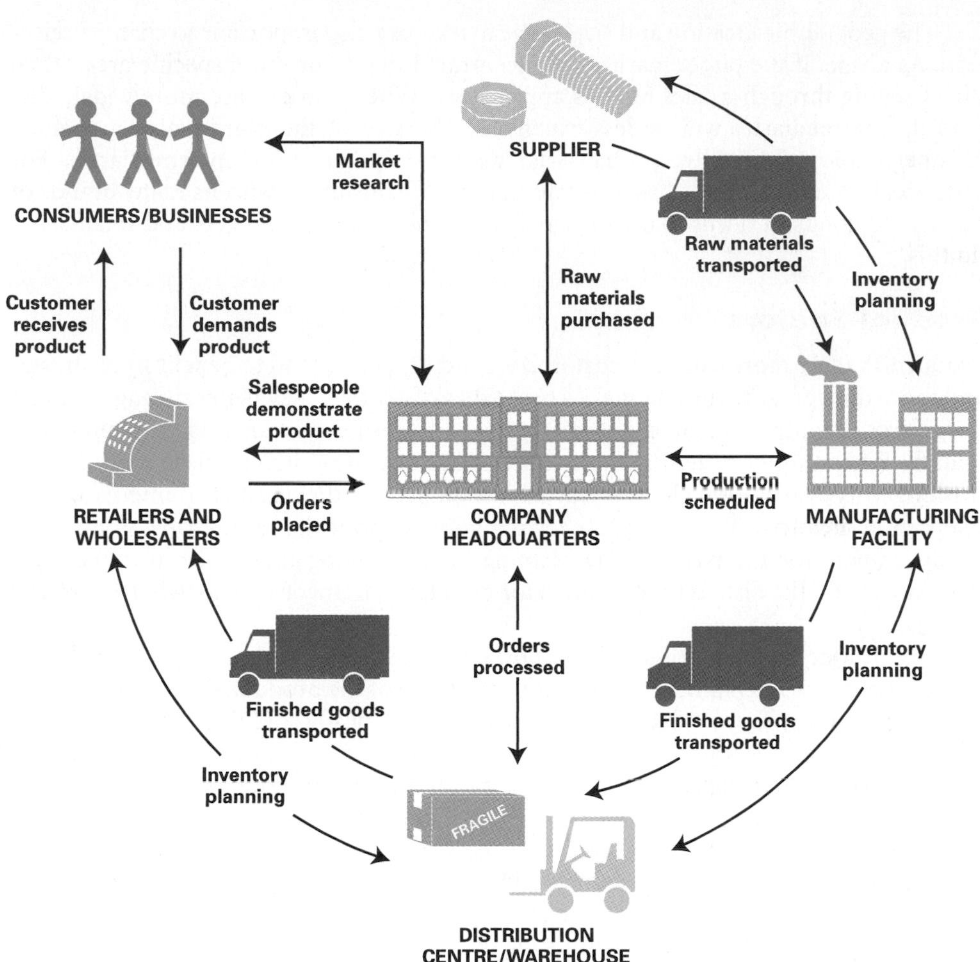

EXHIBIT 11.4

The Supply Chain Process

>> MAKING CHANNEL STRATEGY DECISIONS

4 Discuss the issues that influence channel strategy

Devising a marketing channel strategy requires several critical decisions. Supply chain managers must decide what role distribution will play in the overall marketing strategy. In addition, they must be sure that the channel strategy chosen is consistent with product, promotion, and pricing strategies. In making these decisions, marketing managers must analyze what factors will influence the choice of channel and what level of distribution intensity will be appropriate.

Factors Affecting Channel Choice

Supply chain managers must answer many questions before choosing a marketing channel. The final choice depends on the analysis of several factors, which often interact. These factors can be grouped as market factors, product factors, and producer factors.

Market Factors

Among the most important market factors affecting the choice of distribution channel are target customer considerations. Specifically, supply chain managers should answer the following questions: Who are the potential customers? What do they buy? Where do they buy? When do they buy? How do they buy? Additionally, the choice of channel depends on whether the producer is selling to consumers or to industrial customers. Industrial customers' buying habits are very different from those of consumers. Industrial customers tend to buy in larger quantities and require more customer service. Consumers usually buy in very small quantities and sometimes do not mind if they get no service at all, as in a discount store.

The geographic location and size of the market are also important to channel selection. As a rule, if the target market is concentrated in one or more specific areas, then direct selling through a sales force is appropriate. When markets are more widely dispersed, intermediaries will be less expensive. The size of the market also influences channel choice. Generally, a very large market requires more intermediaries. For instance, Procter & Gamble has to reach millions of consumers with its many brands of household goods. It needs many intermediaries, including wholesalers and retailers, to do this.

Product Factors

Products that are more complex, customized, and expensive tend to benefit from shorter and more direct marketing channels. These types of products sell better through a direct sales force. Examples include pharmaceuticals, scientific instruments, airplanes, and mainframe computer systems. On the other hand, the more standardized a product is, the longer its distribution channel can be and the greater the number of intermediaries that can be involved. For example, chewing gum is about the same from producer to producer, with the exception of flavour and shape. Chewing gum is also very inexpensive. As a result, the distribution channel for gum tends to involve many wholesalers and retailers.

The product's life cycle is also an important factor in choosing a marketing channel. In fact, the choice of channel may change over the life of the product. For example, when photocopiers were first available, a direct sales force typically sold them. Now, however, photocopiers can be found in several places, including warehouse clubs, electronics superstores, and mail-order catalogues. As products become more common and less intimidating to users, producers tend to look for alternative channels. Gatorade was originally sold to sports teams, gyms, and fitness clubs. As the drink became more popular, supermarket channels were added, followed by convenience stores and drugstores. Now Gatorade can be found in vending machines and fast-food restaurants.

Another factor is the delicacy of the product. Perishable products like vegetables and milk have a relatively short life span. Fragile products like china and crystal require a minimum amount of handling. Therefore, both require fairly short marketing channels.

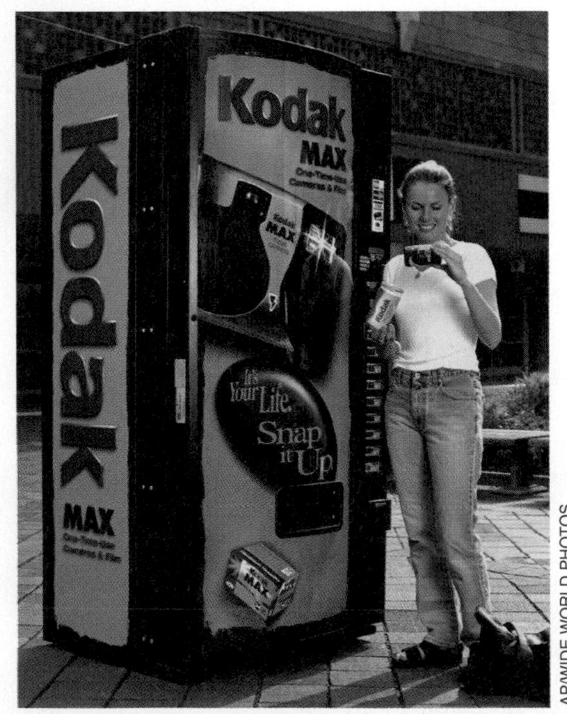

AP/WIDE WORLD PHOTOS

Vending machines are becoming a popular way to sell everything from boxer shorts to cameras. Kodak teamed up with Maytag to roll out thousands of camera-and-film vending machines this past year. Kodak wants to satisfy instant cravings for a must-have snapshot in places like amusement parks, resorts, and the beach.

Producer Factors

Several factors pertaining to the producer are important to the selection of a marketing channel. In general, producers with large financial, managerial, and marketing resources are better able to use more direct channels. These producers have the ability to hire and train their own sales forces, warehouse their own goods, and extend credit to their customers. Smaller or weaker firms, on the other hand, must rely on intermediaries to provide these services for them. Compared to producers with only one or two product lines, producers that sell several products in a related area are able to choose channels that are more direct. Sales expenses then can be spread over more products.

A producer's desire to control pricing, positioning, brand image, and customer support also tends to influence channel selection. For instance, firms that sell products with exclusive brand images, such as designer perfumes and clothing, usually avoid channels in which discount retailers are present. Manufacturers of upscale products, such as Gucci (handbags) and Godiva (chocolates), may sell their wares only in expensive stores in order to maintain an image of exclusivity. Many producers have opted to risk their image, however, and test sales in discount channels. Levi Strauss expanded its distribution to include Zellers, Wal-Mart, and Sears.

Levels of Distribution Intensity

Organizations have three options with regard to intensity of distribution: intensive distribution, selective distribution, or exclusive distribution (see Exhibit 11.5).

Intensive Distribution

Intensive distribution is a form of distribution aimed at maximum market coverage. The manufacturer tries to have the product available in every outlet where potential customers might want to buy it. If buyers are unwilling to search for a product (as is true of convenience goods and operating supplies), the product must be very accessible to buyers. A low-value product that is purchased frequently may require a lengthy channel. For example, candy is found in almost every type of retail store imaginable. It is typically sold to retailers in small quantities by a food or candy wholesaler. The Wrigley Company could not afford to sell its gum directly to every service station, drugstore, supermarket, and discount store. The cost would be too high.

intensive distribution
A form of distribution aimed at having a product available in every outlet where target customers might want to buy it.

Selective Distribution

Selective distribution is achieved by screening dealers and retailers to eliminate all but a few in any single area. Because only a few are chosen, the consumer must seek out the product. For example, when Heeling Sports Ltd. launched Heelys, thick-soled sneakers with a wheel embedded in each heel, the company hired a group of 40 teens to perform Heelys exhibitions in targeted malls, skate parks, and college campuses across the country. Then the company made the decision to avoid large stores and to distribute the shoes only through selected mall retailers and skate and surf shops in order to position the product as "cool and kind of irreverent."[12]

selective distribution
A form of distribution achieved by screening dealers to eliminate all but a few in any single area.

Selective distribution strategies often hinge on a manufacturer's desire to maintain a superior product image so as to be able to charge a premium price. DKNY clothing, for instance, is sold only in select retail outlets, mainly full-price department stores. Likewise, premium pet food brands such as Hill's Pet Nutrition and Ralston-Purina's Pro Plan are distributed chiefly through specialty pet food stores and veterinarians, rather than mass retailers, so that a premium price can be charged. On the other hand,

EXHIBIT 11.5
Intensity of Distribution Levels

INTENSITY LEVEL	DISTRIBUTION INTENSITY OBJECTIVE	NUMBER OF INTERMEDIARIES IN EACH MARKET	EXAMPLES
Intensive	Achieve mass-market selling; popular with health and beauty aids and convenience goods that must be available everywhere	Many	Pepsi-Cola, Frito-Lay potato chips, Huggies diapers, Alpo dog food, Crayola crayons
Selective	Work closely with selected intermediaries who meet certain criteria; typically used for shopping goods and some specialty goods	Several	Donna Karan clothing, Hewlett-Packard printers, Burton snowboards, Aveda aromatherapy products
Exclusive	Work with a single intermediary for products that require special resources or positioning; typically used for specialty goods and major industrial equipment	One	BMW cars, Rolex watches, Rolls-Royce cars

Procter & Gamble recently purchased premium pet food brand Iams and expanded Iams's selective distribution strategy to include mass retailers. Do you think this action could jeopardize Iams's high-price strategy and disenfranchise the breeders and veterinarians who have been the brand's primary source of strength?[13]

Exclusive Distribution

exclusive distribution
A form of distribution that establishes one or a few dealers within a given area.

The most restrictive form of market coverage is **exclusive distribution**, which entails only one or a few dealers within a given area. Because buyers may have to search or travel extensively to buy the product, exclusive distribution is usually confined to consumer specialty goods, a few shopping goods, and major industrial equipment. Products such as Rolls-Royce automobiles, Chris-Craft powerboats, and Pettibone tower cranes are distributed under exclusive arrangements. Sometimes exclusive territories are granted by new companies (such as franchisers) to obtain market coverage in a particular area. Limited distribution may also serve to project an exclusive image for the product.

Retailers and wholesalers may be unwilling to commit the time and money necessary to promote and service a product unless the manufacturer guarantees them an exclusive territory. This arrangement shields the dealer from direct competition and enables it to be the main beneficiary of the manufacturer's promotion efforts in that geographic area.

Exclusive distribution has been part of retailing for years. Toys are often made exclusively for certain retailers and cannot be found elsewhere. Exclusive distribution may also take place within a retailer's store rather than a geographic area—for example, when a retailer agrees not to sell a manufacturer's competing brands. RadioShack, for instance, has prospered in recent years by offering electronics manufacturers exclusivity within its stores. When Sprint was looking for a retail base from which to sell its new wireless phone network, RadioShack offered to make Sprint its exclusive wireless phone. The agreement helped Sprint become the leader in digital personal communications services. RadioShack cut similar exclusive distribution deals with HP Compaq Computers and RCA for audio and video equipment.[14]

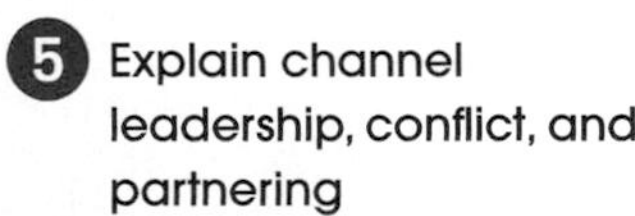
5
Explain channel leadership, conflict, and partnering

>> MANAGING CHANNEL RELATIONSHIPS

A marketing channel is more than a set of institutions linked by economic ties. Social relationships play an important role in building unity among channel members. A critical aspect of supply chain management, therefore, is managing the social relationships among channel members to achieve synergy. The basic social dimensions of channels are power, control, leadership, conflict, and partnering.

Channel Power, Control, and Leadership

channel power
The capacity of a particular marketing channel member to control or influence the behaviour of other channel members.

channel control
A situation that occurs when one marketing channel member intentionally affects another member's behaviour.

channel leader (channel captain)
A member of a marketing channel that exercises authority and power over the activities of other channel members.

Channel power is a channel member's capacity to control or influence the behaviour of other channel members. **Channel control** occurs when one channel member affects another member's behaviour. To achieve control, a channel member assumes channel leadership and exercises authority and power. This member is termed the **channel leader**, or **channel captain.** In one marketing channel, a manufacturer may be the leader because it controls new-product designs and product availability. In another, a retailer may be the channel leader because it wields power and control over the retail price, inventory levels, and postsale service.

Channel Conflict

channel conflict
A clash of goals and methods between distribution channel members.

Inequitable channel relationships often lead to **channel conflict**, which is a clash of goals and methods among the members of a distribution channel. Conflicts among channel members can be due to many different situations and factors. Oftentimes, conflict arises because channel members have conflicting goals. For instance, athletic footwear retailers want to sell as many shoes as possible in order to maximize profits, regardless of whether the shoe is manufactured by Nike, Adidas, or Saucony. But as a manufacturer, Nike wants a certain sales volume and market share in each market.

Conflict can also arise when channel members fail to fulfill expectations of other channel members—for example, when a franchisee does not follow the rules set down by the franchiser, or when communications channels break down between channel members. As another example, if a manufacturer reduces the length of warranty coverage and fails to communicate this change to dealers, then conflict may occur when dealers make repairs with the expectation that they will be reimbursed by the manufacturer. Furthermore, ideological differences and different perceptions of reality can cause conflict among channel members. For instance, retailers may believe "the customer is always right" and offer very liberal return policies. Wholesalers and manufacturers may feel that people "try to get something for nothing" or don't follow product instructions carefully. These differing views of allowable returns will undoubtedly cause some conflict.

ON LINE 

RadioShack

How does RadioShack use its website to promote its exclusive distribution of the products listed on this page? Do Sprint, HP Compaq, RCA, and others reciprocate? Explain what you discover.

http://www.radioshack.com

http://www.sprint.com

http://www.hp.com

http://www.rca.com

Conflict within a channel can be either horizontal or vertical. **Horizontal conflict** occurs among channel members on the same level, such as two or more different wholesalers or two or more different retailers that handle the same manufacturer's brands. This type of channel conflict is found most often when manufacturers practise dual or multiple distribution strategies. For instance, there was considerable channel conflict after computer manufacturers began distributing their computers beyond the traditional computer resellers, through discount stores, department stores, warehouse clubs, and giant electronics superstores such as Future Shop. Horizontal conflict can also occur when channel members on the same level feel they are being treated unfairly, or differently, by the manufacturer.

horizontal conflict
A channel conflict that occurs among channel members on the same level.

Many regard horizontal conflict as healthy competition. Much more serious is **vertical conflict**, which occurs between different levels in a marketing channel, most typically between the manufacturer and wholesaler or the manufacturer and retailer. Producer-versus-wholesaler conflict occurs when the producer chooses to bypass the wholesaler and deal directly with the consumer or retailer. For example, conflict arose when several producers agreed to Wal-Mart's request to deal with it directly, bypassing intermediaries altogether.

vertical conflict
A channel conflict that occurs between different levels in a marketing channel, most typically between the manufacturer and wholesaler or between the manufacturer and retailer.

Dual distribution strategies can also cause vertical conflict in the channel. For example, high-end fashion designers have traditionally sold their products through luxury retailers. Interested in increasing sales and gaining additional presentation control, many designers such as Giorgio Armani, Donna Karan, and Louis Vuitton have begun opening their own boutiques in the same shopping centres with specialty retailers carrying their products. Similarly, manufacturers that are experimenting with selling to customers directly over the Internet are creating conflict with their traditional retailing intermediaries. For example, Baby Jogger worked closely with retailers to build a business with $15 million in sales. But, when numerous look-alike products began appearing on the market, the company decided to try to increase sales by selling directly to consumers on the Internet. Angry retailers responded by promoting other brands. Recognizing how important the retailers were to its success, Baby Jogger halted Internet sales.[15]

Producers and retailers may also disagree over the terms of the sale or other aspects of the business relationship. When Procter & Gamble introduced "everyday low pricing" to its retail channel members, a strategy designed to standardize wholesale prices and eliminate most trade promotions, many retailers retaliated. Some cut the variety of P&G sizes they carried or eliminated marginal brands. Others moved P&G brands from prime shelf space to less visible shelves.

Channel Partnering

Regardless of the locus of power, channel members rely heavily on one another. Even the most powerful manufacturers depend on dealers to sell their products; even the most powerful retailers require the products provided by suppliers. In sharp contrast to the adversarial relationships of the past between buyers and sellers, contemporary management thought emphasizes the development of close working partnerships among channel members. **Channel partnering**, or **channel cooperation**, is the joint effort of all channel members to create a supply chain that serves customers and creates a competitive advantage. Channel partnering is vital if each member is to gain something from other members.

channel partnering (channel cooperation)
The joint effort of all channel members to create a supply chain that serves customers and creates a competitive advantage.

Channel alliances and partnerships help supply chain managers create the parallel flow of materials and information required to leverage the supply chains' intellectual, material, and marketing resources. The rapid growth in channel partnering is due to new enabling technology and the need to lower costs. A comparison between companies that approach the marketplace unilaterally and those that engage in channel cooperation and form partnerships is detailed in Exhibit 11.6.

6 Describe the logistical components of the supply chain

>> MANAGING THE LOGISTICAL COMPONENTS OF THE SUPPLY CHAIN

Now that you are familiar with the structure and strategy of marketing channels and the role of supply chain management, it is important to also understand the physical means by which products move through the supply chain. As indicated, supply chain management coordinates and integrates all of the activities performed by supply chain members into a seamless process. The supply chain consists of several interrelated and integrated logistical components: (1) sourcing and procurement of raw materials and supplies, (2) production scheduling, (3) order processing, (4) inventory control, (5) warehousing and materials-handling, and (6) transportation. These components are shown in Exhibit 11.7.

Integrating and linking all of the logistics components of the supply chain is the **logistics information system.** Today's supply chain logisticians are at the forefront of information technology, which is not just a functional affiliate of supply chain management. Rather it is the enabler, the facilitator, the linkage that connects the various components and partners of the supply chain into an integrated whole. Electronic data interchange, on-board computers, satellite and cellular communications systems, materials-handling and warehouse-management software, enterprisewide systems solutions, and the Internet are among the information enablers of successful supply chain management.

logistics information system
Information technology that integrates and links all of the logistics functions of the supply chain.

The **supply chain team,** in concert with the logistics information system, orchestrates the movement of goods, services, and information from the source to the consumer. Supply chain teams typically cut across organizational boundaries, embracing all parties who participate in moving the product to market. The best supply chain teams

supply chain team
An entire group of individuals who orchestrate the movement of goods, services, and information from the source to the consumer.

EXHIBIT 11.6
Transaction-Based versus Partnership-Based Firms

	TRANSACTION-BASED	PARTNERSHIP-BASED
Relationships between manufacturer and supplier	• Short-term • Adversarial • Independent • Price more important	• Long-term • Cooperative • Dependent • Value-added services more important
Number of suppliers	Many	Few
Level of information sharing	Minimal	High
Investment required	Minimal	High

SOURCE: *Creating Market-Winning Strategies Through Supply Chain Partnerships* (New York: Chapman & Hall, 1998), 61. Reprinted with permission.

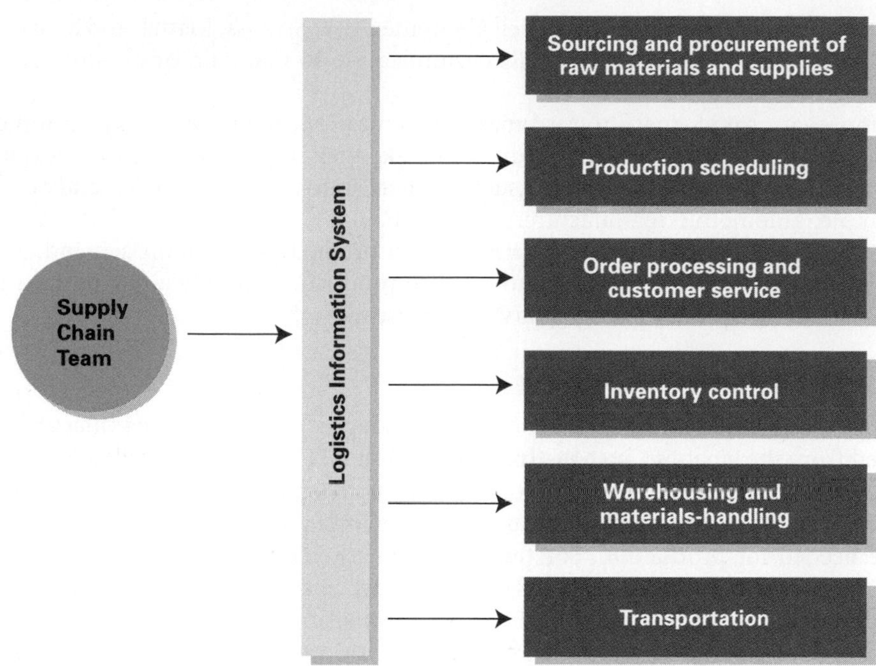

EXHIBIT 11.7

Integrated Logistical Components of the Supply Chain

also move beyond the organization to include the external participants in the chain, such as suppliers, transportation carriers, and third-party logistics suppliers. Members of the supply chain communicate, coordinate, and cooperate extensively.

Sourcing and Procurement

One of the most important links in the supply chain is the one between the manufacturer and the supplier. Purchasing professionals are on the front lines of supply chain management. Purchasing departments plan purchasing strategies, develop specifications, select suppliers, and negotiate price and service levels.

The goal of most sourcing and procurement activities is to reduce the costs of raw materials and supplies. Purchasing professionals have traditionally relied on tough negotiations to get the lowest price possible from suppliers. Perhaps the biggest contribution purchasing can make to supply chain management, however, is in the area of vendor relations. Companies can use the purchasing function to strategically manage suppliers in order to reduce the total cost of materials and services. Through enhanced vendor relations, buyers and sellers can develop cooperative relationships that reduce costs and improve efficiency with the aim of lowering prices and enhancing profits.

Production Scheduling

In traditional mass-market manufacturing, production begins when forecasts call for additional products to be made or inventory control systems signal low inventory levels. The firm then makes a product and transports the finished goods to its own warehouses or those of intermediaries, where the goods wait to be ordered by retailers or customers. Production scheduling based on pushing a product down to the consumer obviously has its disadvantages, the most notable being that companies risk making products that may become obsolete or that consumers don't want.

In a customer "pull" manufacturing environment, which is growing in popularity, production of goods or services is not scheduled until an order is placed by the customer specifying the desired configuration. This process, known as **mass customization,** or **build-to-order,** uniquely tailors mass-market goods and services to the needs of the individuals who buy

mass customization (build-to-order)
A production method whereby products are not made until an order is placed by the customer, and products are made according to customer specifications.

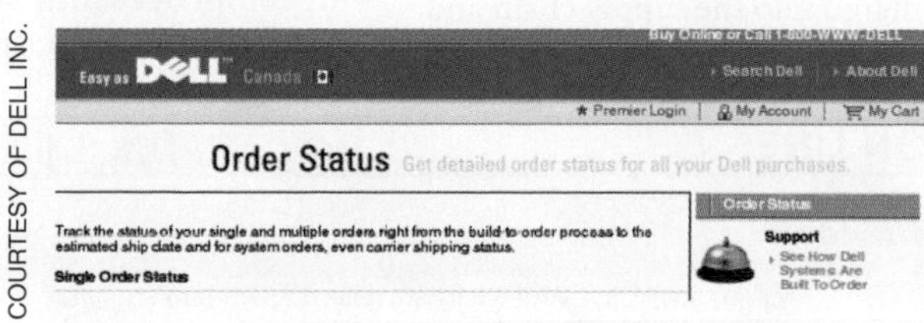

COURTESY OF DELL INC.

Thanks to the direct selling model of Dell Computer, build-to-order computers are more than commonplace today. Dell allows customers to track their orders throughout manufacturing and shipping.

them. Companies as diverse as BMW, Dell Computer, Levi Strauss, Mattel, and a slew of Web-based businesses are adopting mass customization to maintain or obtain a competitive edge.

As more companies move toward mass customization, the need to stay on top of consumer demand is forcing manufacturers to make their supply chains more flexible. Flexibility is critical to a manufacturer's success when dramatic swings in demand occur. For example, automobile manufacturers such as Honda and Toyota have been modifying their assembly plants to make it easier to shift production based on demand. As a result, the companies can move new models into production in only a few months to keep up with the frequently changing tastes of consumers.[16]

Just-in-Time Manufacturing

just-in-time production (JIT)
A process that redefines and simplifies manufacturing by reducing inventory levels and delivering raw materials just when they are needed on the production line.

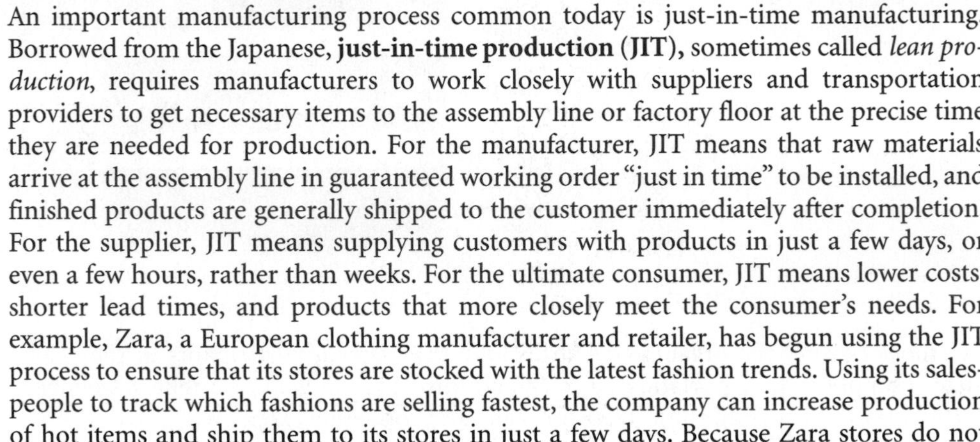

An important manufacturing process common today is just-in-time manufacturing. Borrowed from the Japanese, **just-in-time production (JIT),** sometimes called *lean production,* requires manufacturers to work closely with suppliers and transportation providers to get necessary items to the assembly line or factory floor at the precise time they are needed for production. For the manufacturer, JIT means that raw materials arrive at the assembly line in guaranteed working order "just in time" to be installed, and finished products are generally shipped to the customer immediately after completion. For the supplier, JIT means supplying customers with products in just a few days, or even a few hours, rather than weeks. For the ultimate consumer, JIT means lower costs, shorter lead times, and products that more closely meet the consumer's needs. For example, Zara, a European clothing manufacturer and retailer, has begun using the JIT process to ensure that its stores are stocked with the latest fashion trends. Using its salespeople to track which fashions are selling fastest, the company can increase production of hot items and ship them to its stores in just a few days. Because Zara stores do not maintain large inventories, they can respond quickly to fashion trends and offer their products for less.[17]

JIT benefits manufacturers most by reducing their raw materials inventories. For example, at a typical Dell Computer plant, computer components are delivered just minutes before they are needed. Chips, boards, and drives are kept in trucks backed into bays located very close to the production line. On average, Dell takes only about a week from buying parts to selling them as a finished product. Similarly, Customized Transportation, Inc., works with General Motors to coordinate delivery of interior door panels at the moment they are needed for production.[18]

Additionally, JIT shortens lead times—the time it takes to get parts from a supplier after an order has been placed. Manufacturers also enjoy better relationships with suppliers and can decrease their production and storeroom costs. Because there is little safety stock, and therefore no margin for error, the manufacturer cannot afford to make a mistake. As a result, a manufacturer using JIT must be sure it receives high-quality parts from all vendors, be confident that the supplier will meet all delivery commitments, and have a crisis management plan to handle any disruptions.

Order Processing

order processing system
A system whereby orders are entered into the supply chain and filled.

The order is often the catalyst that sets the supply chain in motion, especially in the build-to-order environments of leading computer manufacturers such as Dell. The **order processing system** processes the requirements of the customer and sends the information into the supply chain via the logistics information system. The order goes to the manufacturer's warehouse. If the order is in stock, the order is filled and arrangements are made to ship it. If the order is not in stock, it triggers a replenishment request that finds its way to the factory floor.

The role of proper order processing in providing good service cannot be overemphasized. As an order enters the system, management must monitor two flows: the flow of goods and the flow of information.

ON LINE

Wal-Mart

Is EDI a requirement for Wal-Mart suppliers? Go to Wal-Mart's website and read the "Supplier Information" pages. Does selling to Wal-Mart seem worth the effort? Why or why not?

http://www.walmartstores.com

Often the best-laid plans of marketers can get entangled in the order processing system. Obviously, good communication among sales representatives, office personnel, and warehouse and shipping personnel is essential to correct order processing. Shipping incorrect merchandise or partially filled orders can create just as much dissatisfaction as stockouts or slow deliveries.

Order processing is becoming more automated through the use of computer technology known as **electronic data interchange (EDI)**. The basic idea of EDI is to replace the paper documents that usually accompany business transactions, such as purchase orders and invoices, with electronic transmission of the needed information. A typical EDI message includes all the information that would traditionally be included on a paper invoice such as product code, quantity, and transportation details. The information is usually sent via private networks, which are more secure and reliable than the networks used for standard e-mail messages. Most importantly, the information can be read and processed by computers, significantly reducing costs and increasing efficiency. Companies that use EDI can reduce inventory levels, improve cash flow, streamline operations, and increase the speed and accuracy of information transmission.

electronic data interchange (EDI)
Information technology that replaces the paper documents that usually accompany business transactions, such as purchase orders and invoices, with electronic transmission of the needed information to reduce inventory levels, improve cash flow, streamline operations, and increase the speed and accuracy of information transmission.

It should not be surprising that retailers have become major users of EDI. For Wal-Mart, Canadian Tire, and the like, logistics speed and accuracy are crucial competitive tools. Many big retailers are helping their suppliers acquire EDI technology so that they can be linked into the system. EDI works hand in hand with retailers' *efficient consumer response* programs, which are designed to have the right products on the shelf, in the right styles and colours, through improved inventory, ordering, and distribution techniques.

Inventory Control

Closely interrelated with the procurement, manufacturing, and ordering processes is the **inventory control system**—a method that develops and maintains an adequate assortment of materials or products to meet a manufacturer's or a customer's demands.

inventory control system
A method of developing and maintaining an adequate assortment of materials or products to meet a manufacturer's or a customer's demand.

Inventory decisions, for both raw materials and finished goods, have a big impact on supply chain costs and the level of service provided. If too many products are kept in inventory, costs increase—as do risks of obsolescence, theft, and damage. If too few products are kept on hand, then the company risks product shortages and angry customers, and ultimately lost sales. For example, many car dealers were left short of product due to a CN strike in February and March 2004.[19] The goal of inventory management, therefore, is to keep inventory levels as low as possible while maintaining an adequate supply of goods to meet customer demand.

Managing inventory from the supplier to the manufacturer is called **materials requirement planning (MRP)**, or **materials management.** This system also encompasses the sourcing and procurement operations, signalling purchasing when raw materials, supplies, or components will need to be replenished. The system that manages the finished goods inventory from manufacturer to end user is commonly referred to as **distribution resource planning (DRP).** Both inventory systems use various inputs, such as sales forecasts, available inventory, outstanding orders, lead times, and mode of transportation to be used, to determine what actions must be taken to replenish goods at all points in the supply chain. With the use of electronic data interchange, the information can be transmitted much faster to meet the quick-response needs of today's competitive marketplace.[20] Exhibit 11.8 provides an example of inventory replenishment using DRP from the retailer to the manufacturer.

materials requirement planning (MRP) (materials management)
An inventory control system that manages the replenishment of raw materials, supplies, and components from the supplier to the manufacturer.

distribution resource planning (DRP)
An inventory control system that manages the replenishment of goods from the manufacturer to the final consumer.

Just-in-time manufacturing processes have had a significant impact on reducing inventory levels. Since JIT requires supplies to be delivered at the time they are needed on the factory floor, little inventory is needed. With JIT the purchasing firm can reduce the amount of raw materials and parts it keeps on hand by ordering more often and in smaller amounts. And lower inventory levels due to JIT can give firms a competitive edge through the flexibility to halt production of existing products in favour of those gaining popularity with consumers. Savings also come from having less capital tied up in inventory and from the reduced need for storage facilities.

EXHIBIT 11.8

Inventory Replenishment Example

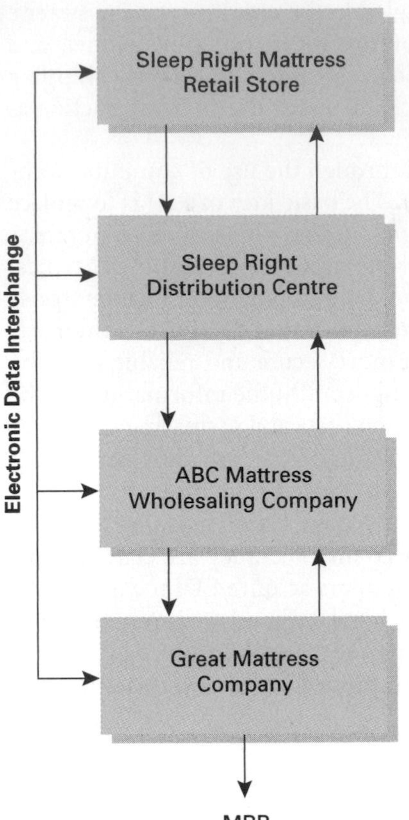

Sleep Right is planning a promotion on the Great Mattress Company's Gentle Rest mattress. Sales forecast is for 50 units to be sold. Sleep Right has 10 open Gentle Rest orders with its distribution centre. New mattresses must be delivered in two weeks in time for the promotion.

Sleep Right's Distribution Centre is electronically notified of the order of 50 new Gentle Rest mattresses. It currently has 20 Gentle Rest mattresses in inventory and begins putting together the transportation plans to deliver these to the Sleep Right Store. Delivery takes one day. It orders 40 new mattresses from its mattress wholesaler to make up the difference.

ABC Mattress Wholesaling Company is electronically notified of Sleep Right DC's order of 40 new Gentle Rest mattresses. It currently does not have any of these in stock but electronically orders 40 from the Great Mattress Company's factory. Once it receives the new mattresses, it can have them delivered to the Sleep Right DC in two days.

The Great Mattress Company electronically receives ABC's order and forwards it to the factory floor. Production of a new mattress takes 20 minutes. The total order of 40 mattresses can be ready to be shipped to ABC in two days. Delivery takes one day. Raw material supplies for this order are electronically requested from Great Mattress's supply partners, who deliver the needed materials just-in-time to its stitching machines.

Warehousing and Materials-Handling Systems

Supply chain logisticians oversee the constant flow of raw materials from suppliers to manufacturer and finished goods from the manufacturer to the ultimate consumer. Although JIT manufacturing processes may eliminate the need to warehouse many raw materials, manufacturers may often keep some safety stock on hand in the event of an emergency, such as a strike at a supplier's plant or a catastrophic event that temporarily stops the flow of raw materials to the production line. Likewise, the final user may not need or want the goods at the same time the manufacturer produces and wants to sell them. Products like grain and corn are produced seasonally, but consumers demand them year-round. Other products, such as Christmas ornaments and turkeys, are produced year-round, but consumers do not want them until autumn or winter. Therefore, management must have a storage system to hold these products until they are shipped.

Storage is what helps manufacturers manage supply and demand, or production and consumption. It provides time utility to buyers and sellers, which means that the seller stores the product until the buyer wants or needs it. Even when products are used regularly, not seasonally, many manufacturers store excess products in case the demand surpasses the amount produced at a given time. Storing additional product does have disadvantages, however, including the costs of insurance on the stored product, taxes, obsolescence or spoilage, theft, and warehouse operating costs. Another drawback is opportunity costs—that is, the opportunities lost because money is tied up in stored product instead of being used for something else.

Because businesses are focusing on cutting supply chain costs, the warehousing industry is also changing to better serve its customers. For example, many warehouses are placing greater emphasis on more efficient unloading and reloading layouts and on customized services that move merchandise through the warehouse faster. They also are investing in services that use sophisticated tracking technology such as materials-handling systems.[21]

A **materials-handling system** moves inventory into, within, and out of the warehouse. Materials-handling includes these functions:

materials-handling system A method of moving inventory into, within, and out of the warehouse.

- Receiving goods into the warehouse or distribution centre
- Identifying, sorting, and labelling the goods
- Dispatching the goods to a temporary storage area
- Recalling, selecting, or picking the goods for shipment (may include packaging the product in a protective container for shipping)

The goal of the materials-handling system is to move items quickly with minimal handling. With a manual, nonautomated materials-handling system, a product may be handled more than a dozen times. Each time it is handled, cost and the risk of damage increase. Consequently, most manufacturers today have moved to automated systems. Scanners quickly identify goods entering and leaving a warehouse through bar-coded labels affixed to the packaging. Automatic storage and retrieval systems store and pick goods in the warehouse or distribution centre. Automated materials-handling systems decrease product handling, ensure accurate placement of product, and improve the accuracy of order picking and the rates of on-time shipment.

Transportation

Transportation typically accounts for 5 to 10 percent of the price of goods.[22] Supply chain logisticians must decide which mode of transportation to use to move products from supplier to producer and from producer to buyer. These decisions are, of course, related to all other logistics decisions. The five major modes of transportation are railways, motor carriers, pipelines, water transportation, and airways. Supply chain managers generally choose a mode of transportation on the basis of several criteria:

- *Cost:* The total amount a specific carrier charges to move the product from the point of origin to the destination
- *Transit time:* The total time a carrier has possession of goods, including the time required for pickup and delivery, handling, and movement between the point of origin and the destination
- *Reliability:* The consistency with which the carrier delivers goods on time and in acceptable condition
- *Capability:* The ability of the carrier to provide the appropriate equipment and conditions for moving specific kinds of goods, such as those that must be transported in a controlled environment (for example, under refrigeration)
- *Accessibility:* A carrier's ability to move goods over a specific route or network
- *Traceability:* The relative ease with which a shipment can be located and transferred

The mode of transportation used depends on the needs of the shipper, as they relate to these six criteria. Exhibit 11.9 compares the basic modes of transportation on these criteria.

In many cases, especially in a JIT manufacturing environment, the transportation network replaces the warehouse or eliminates the expense of storing inventories, since goods are timed to arrive the moment they're needed on the assembly line or for shipment to customers. In fact, Toyota is so committed to JIT that it has no parts warehouses in Canada or the United States. Instead, it works closely with its suppliers to make sure that parts will be delivered on time.

>> TRENDS IN SUPPLY CHAIN MANAGEMENT

7 Discuss new technology and emerging trends in supply chain management

Several technological advances and business trends are affecting the job of the supply chain manager today. Three of the most outstanding trends are advanced computer technology, outsourcing of logistics functions, and electronic distribution.

EXHIBIT 11.9
Criteria for Ranking Modes of Transportation

	HIGHEST				LOWEST
Relative cost	Air	Truck	Rail	Pipe	Water
Transit time	Water	Rail	Pipe	Truck	Air
Reliability	Pipe	Truck	Rail	Air	Water
Capability	Water	Rail	Truck	Air	Pipe
Accessibility	Truck	Rail	Air	Water	Pipe
Traceability	Air	Truck	Rail	Water	Pipe

Advanced Computer Technology

Advanced computer technology has boosted the efficiency of logistics dramatically with tools such as automatic identification systems (auto ID) using bar coding and radio frequency technology, communications technology, and supply chain software systems that help synchronize the flow of goods and information with customer demand. Amazon.com's state-of-the-art distribution centres, for instance, use sophisticated order-picking systems that utilize computer terminals to guide workers through the picking and packing process. Radio frequency technology, which uses radio signals that work with scanned bar codes identifying products, directs Amazon's workers to the precise locations in the warehouse where the product is stored. Warehouse management software examines pick rates, location, and picking and storage patterns, and builds combinations of customer orders for shipping. After installing these supply chain technology tools, Amazon saw a 70 percent improvement in operational efficiency.[23]

outsourcing (contract logistics)
A manufacturer's or supplier's use of an independent third party to manage an entire function of the logistics system, such as transportation, warehousing, or order processing.

One of the major goals of technology is to bring up-to-date information to the supply chain manager's desk. The transportation system has long been referred to as a "black hole," where products and materials fall out of sight until they reappear some time later in a plant, store, or warehouse. Now carriers have systems that track freight, monitor the speed and location of carriers, and make routing decisions on the spur of the moment. For instance, Roadway Express handles more than 60,000 shipments a day, many for large retailers like Wal-Mart and Home Depot. New computer technology allows each package to be tracked from the minute it is received at one of Roadway's terminals until it is delivered. Anxious customers can check on the progress of their shipment anytime by checking with the Roadway Express call centre or by using the company's password-protected website.[24] And Swedish-based communications giant Ericsson, whose operations span the globe, uses specialized supply chain software to gain visibility over the 50,000 outbound shipments it makes each year. As products leave its manufacturing facilities, transportation providers transmit status information at specified intervals to Ericsson's information system, which is accessible to management using a standard Web browser.[25]

© DAVID SAMUEL ROBBINS/CORBIS SYGMA

Matt Spangler and others are pictured here picking orders from the media cage at one of Amazon.com's distribution centres. Amazon's command of the supply chain has translated into increased sales and customer satisfaction.

Outsourcing Logistics Functions

External partners are becoming increasingly important in the efficient deployment of supply chain management. **Outsourcing,** or **contract logistics,** is a rapidly growing segment of the distribution industry in which a manufacturer or supplier turns over the entire function of buying and managing transportation or another function of the supply chain, such as warehousing, to an independent third party. Many manufacturers are turning to outside partners for their logistics expertise in an effort to focus on their core competencies. Partners create and manage entire solutions for getting products where they need to be, when they need to be there. Logistics partners offer staff, an infrastructure, and services that reach consumers virtually anywhere in the world. Because a logistics provider is focused, clients receive service in a timely, efficient manner, thereby increasing customers' level of satisfaction and boosting their perception of the company's offerings. The trend is so strong that the supply chain outsourcing industry is expected to generate almost $1.8 billion in revenue by 2005.[26]

Electronic distribution has become a viable channel for many products, from financial services to postage to software. The Canada Revenue Agency is also realizing gains by accepting tax returns on-line.

Third-party contract logistics allow companies to cut inventories, locate stock at fewer plants and distribution centres, and still provide the same service level or even better. Companies then can refocus investment on their core business. The Ford Motor Company uses third-party logistics provider UPS Worldwide Logistics to manage the delivery of Ford, Lincoln, and Mercury cars and trucks in Canada, the United States, and Mexico. The companies say they expect the alliance will reduce the time it takes to move vehicles from Ford's plants to dealers and customers by up to 40 percent. The alliance will also provide Web-based information systems that allow Ford and its dealers to track individual vehicle status from production through final delivery.[27]

Many firms are taking outsourcing one step further by allowing business partners to take over the final assembly of their product or its packaging in an effort to reduce inventory costs, speed up delivery, or meet customer requirements better. Ryder Truck Lines assembles and packages 22 different combinations of shrink-wrapped boxes that contain the ice trays, drawers, shelves, doors, and other accessories for the various refrigerator models Whirlpool sells. Similarly, the outsourcing firm StarTek, Inc., packages and ships products for Microsoft.[28]

Electronic Distribution

Electronic distribution is the most recent development in the logistics arena. Broadly defined, **electronic distribution** includes any kind of product or service that can be distributed electronically, whether over traditional forms such as fibre-optic cable or through satellite transmission of electronic signals. For instance, instead of buying and installing software from stores, computer users increasingly can purchase software over the Internet and download it electronically to their personal computers or rent the same software from Internet services that have the program available for use on their servers. For example, Intuit, Inc., allows people to fill out their tax returns on its website rather than buying its TurboTax software.[29] Similarly, on-line ticket companies and movie theatres have recently developed the technology to sell tickets to sporting events, concerts, and movies via the Internet; consumers can print the tickets at home on a standard computer printer.[30]

electronic distribution
A distribution technique that includes any kind of product or service that can be distributed electronically, whether over traditional forms such as fibre-optic cable or through satellite transmission of electronic signals

Hollywood movie studios are getting ready to deliver their products directly to consumers through digital pipelines. Consumers can already download digital files of their favourite music, movies, and television shows to be played on their computers, portable players, and televisions, often without paying for the file. This controversial form of electronic distribution is discussed in the "Ethics in Marketing" box.

>> CHANNELS AND DISTRIBUTION DECISIONS FOR GLOBAL MARKETS

8 Discuss channels and distribution decisions in global markets

With the surging popularity of free-trade agreements and treaties over the past decade, such as the European Union and the North American Free Trade Agreement (NAFTA), global marketing channels and management of the supply chain have become increasingly important to Canadian corporations that export their products or manufacture abroad.

Developing Global Marketing Channels

Executives should recognize the unique cultural, economic, institutional, and legal aspects of each market before trying to design marketing channels in foreign countries. Manufacturers introducing products in global markets face a tough decision: what type of channel structure to use. Specifically, should the product be marketed directly, mostly by company salespeople, or through independent foreign intermediaries, such as agents and distributors? Using company salespeople generally provides more control and is less risky than using foreign intermediaries. However, setting up a sales force in a foreign country also entails a greater commitment, both financially and organizationally.

Marketers should be aware that channel structures and types abroad might differ from those in Canada. For instance, the more highly developed a nation is economically, the more specialized its channel types. Therefore, a marketer wishing to sell in

ETHICS IN MARKETING

Video Piracy

As discussed, new Internet and computer technology has been largely responsible for advances in supply chain management. However, the new technology and the Internet are also creating serious supply-chain problems for the entertainment industry. For example, the invention of MP3 music files, which can be swapped on the Internet and burned onto compact discs, had a dramatic effect on traditional music sales. The music industry was forced to sue Napster, the leading music file swapping website, which eventually filed for bankruptcy, for copyright infringement, and to develop both new distribution channels and new technologies to prevent music swapping.

Similarly, new technology now allows consumers to make and swap digital copies of television shows and movies. For instance, digital video recorders (DVRs) allow consumers to record their favourite television shows and movies via traditional cable, broadcast, satellite, and Internet connections. With DVRs, consumers can watch their favourite programs when it is convenient and even pause live programming. As adoption of the technology increases, DVRs could have an impact on television advertising sales and program scheduling. The industry is more concerned, however, about SonicBlue's introduction of ReplayTV 4000, which not only enables consumers to automatically skip commercials but also allows them to send copies over the Internet to other Replay users.

Consumers can also obtain copies of their favourite movies and television shows by going on-line with one of two popular software programs that make it easy to swap video files on the Internet—Morpheus and Kazaa. With more than 40 million users between the two across Canada and the U.S., experts say that more than 1 million users are downloading copies of their favourite television shows and movies at any given time. Available downloads include every *Simpsons* episode ever recorded, film classics such as *Breakfast at Tiffany's*, and episodes of HBO's *The Sopranos* and *Sex and the City*. Finally, digital video cameras with FireWire are even making it easy to share copies of movies currently being shown in theatres.

All of these new technologies are leading to a dramatic increase in video piracy. Movie theatres around the globe are reporting heavy losses as a result. In fact, the Motion Picture Association claims that consumers illegally copy 350,000 films a day on the Internet. Other piracy experts put the number closer to a million a day. What's more, experts predict the trend will grow as technology improves and Internet speed increases.

To protect its product, the television industry has sued SonicBlue, claiming that ReplayTV 4000 illegally jeopardizes the industry's two main revenue sources: advertising and subscription fees. SonicBlue claims that copyright laws give consumers a "fair use" right to share—an argument the courts rejected in the Napster trial. Further, the company contends that it is creating innovative products that give consumers more control over how they use entertainment. The film industry has also sued StreamCast Networks, the distributor of Morpheus, for copyright infringement. StreamCast argues that its software enables people to share home movies and films that are in the public domain.

Regardless of the outcome of these lawsuits, the entertainment industry is examining the future of its distribution channels. Television studios are looking for a way to use electronic tags within a broadcast to prevent copying and are asking the government to require that all television sets, receivers, and computers be capable of reading the tags. For the tags to be effective, the studios would have to cease all nondigital broadcasts—a move that could eliminate free television, forcing consumers to use a cable or satellite company for program access.

In contrast, in an effort to satisfy consumers, MGM, Sony, Paramount, Universal, and Warner Brothers studios have started a joint venture called Moviefly to provide consumers with a secure, reliable way to "rent" movies on the Internet. Of course, if successful, the joint venture would eliminate cable and satellite companies from the pay-per-view distribution channel.[31]

What other distribution options does the entertainment industry have? Will new technology give the industry a way to protect its products, or will the industry be forced to reinvent the way it operates? How do you think television programs and movies will be distributed in the future? What is your view of being able to copy, free, any movie, television show, or piece of music that you would like?

Germany or Japan will have several channel types to choose from. Conversely, developing countries like India, Ethiopia, and Venezuela have limited channel types available; there are typically few mail-order channels, vending machines, or specialized retailers and wholesalers.

Marketers must also be aware that many foreign countries have "grey" marketing channels, in which products are distributed through unauthorized channel intermediaries. It is estimated that sales of counterfeit luxury items like Prada handbags and Big Bertha golf clubs have reached almost $2 billion a year. The new fakes are harder to detect and hit the market almost instantly. For instance, a fake Christian Dior saddlebag was available just weeks after the original arrived on retailers' shelves. Similarly, Chinese companies are producing so many knockoffs of Yamaha, Honda, and Suzuki motorcycles that the Japanese companies are seeing a drop in sales. What's more, many companies are getting so good at design piracy that they are beginning to launch their own new products.[32] The "Global Perspectives" box provides more details on the impact of supply chain globalization.

The Internet has also proved to be a way for pirates to circumvent authorized distribution channels, especially in the case of popular prescription drugs. In recent years, millions of dollars worth of prescription drugs, most of which were purchased from foreign Internet sites, have been seized. Some were seized because they had not been approved for use, others because they did not comply with Canadian labelling laws. Most sites offer just a handful of the most popular drugs, such as Viagra and the diet drug Xenical; consumers can get the drugs after obtaining the approval of a doctor who is affiliated with the site and who never sees the patient.

GLOBAL **PERSPECTIVES**

Challenges and Opportunities in China

Thanks to the Internet, new technology, and international trade agreements, global supply chains are bringing the world's businesses closer together. Today, large multinational corporations and small businesses alike look to markets around the world for their sourcing and procurement needs. Critics argue that this trend is widening the gap between the nations that have and those that do not. Proponents counter that globalization has brought education and economic development to developing nations and lower prices to the world's markets. Either way, both sides agree that globalization is here to stay. One development that global supply chain managers are watching closely is China's admission into the World Trade Organization (WTO).

For the many companies hoping to market their products to the world's largest market, opportunities abound. So do challenges for supply chain managers since China does not function as a single market but as hundreds, each with its own unique trade barriers. For example, each province and municipality has its own tariffs and trade restrictions. Transportation is particularly difficult. Not only is infrastructure questionable outside urban areas but many provinces also have their own government-controlled transportation companies and outside transportation companies are not welcome. As a result, cargo must be unloaded and reloaded at each border crossing within the country. In fact, current supply chain costs in China are typically 30 to 40 percent of wholesale prices, compared to less than 20 percent in Canada.

On the other hand, China's participation in the WTO will secure the opening of additional markets to Chinese exports. With the greater availability of cheap Chinese goods, companies everywhere, including those already doing business with Chinese companies, may see lower sourcing and procurement costs. This drop should be good for consumers, but for emerging economies like India and Thailand, the competition could be deadly. Therefore, many companies are tightening up operations and focusing on quality to improve their ability to compete against the cheaper Chinese products. One such company is Bajaj Auto, a motorcycle manufacturer in New Delhi. Bajaj has expanded operations to take advantage of economies of scale, invested heavily in R&D to stay on the cutting edge, and put its finances in order so that it can take advantage of future growth opportunities.

Supply chain managers will have to manage relationships with their Chinese supply chain partners closely to protect company interests from design piracy. For example, one of Black & Decker's Chinese sources turned around and competed head-to-head with Black & Decker in Germany using Black & Decker's own design. The Japanese motorcycle manufacturers Yamaha, Honda, and Suzuki have also had problems with Chinese companies stealing their designs.

In the end, experts agree that China's participation in world markets will make the global economy more competitive, ultimately benefiting consumers. In the meantime, global supply chain managers will have to monitor developments around the world, particularly in Asia.[33]

What other global supply chain challenges and opportunities do you see in working with China? Will China's participation in world markets strengthen globalization, or will it have a negative impact?

ON LINE

World Trade Organization

Learn more about how globalization affects supply chain management as well as other aspects of business at the World Trade Organization website.

http://www.wto.org

Global Logistics and Supply Chain Management

As global trade becomes a more decisive factor in success or failure for firms of all sizes, a well-thought-out global logistics strategy becomes more important.

One of the most critical global logistical issues for importers of any size is coping with the legalities of trade in other countries. Shippers and distributors must be aware of the permits, licences, and registrations they may need to acquire and, depending on the type of product they are importing, the tariffs, quotas, and other regulations that apply in each country. This multitude of different rules is why multinational companies like Eastman Kodak are committed to working through the World Trade Organization to develop a global set of rules and to encourage countries to participate. Other goals for these companies include reducing trade barriers. As these barriers fall, the flow of merchandise across borders is increasing. For instance, a Kodak camera sold in France may have been assembled there, but the camera mechanism probably came from China and the film from North America.[34]

The presence of different rules hasn't slowed the spread of supply chain globalization, however. In spite of the added costs associated with importing and exporting goods, many companies are looking to other countries for their sourcing and procurement needs. For example, Applica, a maker of small appliances, is committed to using technology to improve its relationships with suppliers in Mexico. The company has linked its suppliers directly to sales data from Wal-Mart stores to help manage production and inventory costs.[35]

Transportation can also be a major issue for companies dealing with global supply chains. Uncertainty regarding shipping usually tops the list of reasons why companies, especially smaller ones, resist international markets. Even companies that have scored overseas successes often are vulnerable to logistical problems. Large companies have the capital to create global logistics systems, but smaller companies often must rely on the services of carriers and freight forwarders to get their products to overseas markets.

In some instances, poor infrastructure makes transportation dangerous and unreliable. And the process of moving goods across borders can still be complicated by government regulations. For example, NAFTA was supposed to improve the flow of goods across the continent, but moving goods across the border still requires approvals from dozens of government agencies, broker intervention, and hours spent at border checks. Shipping companies, like many located near the Ambassador Bridge in Windsor, are working to make the process easier. Automated border crossings technology similar to that of an E-Z pass is in use. The new systems send and receive short-range radio signals containing information on the load to toll booths, weigh stations, and border crossings. If the cargo meets requirements, the truck or train receives a green light to go ahead.[36]

9 Identify the special problems and opportunities associated with distribution in service organizations

>> CHANNELS AND DISTRIBUTION DECISIONS FOR SERVICES

The fastest-growing part of our economy is the service sector. Although distribution in the service sector is difficult to visualize, the same skills, techniques, and strategies used to manage inventory can also be used to manage service inventory—for instance, hospital beds, bank accounts, or airline seats. The quality of the planning and execution of distribution can have a major impact on costs and customer satisfaction.

ON LINE

Does your bank deliver any of its services on-line? Visit its website to find out. Which on-line services would you be inclined to use? Are there any that you would definitely *not* use? Why not?

One thing that sets service distribution apart from manufacturing distribution is that, in a service environment, production and consumption are simultaneous. In manufacturing, a production setback can

often be remedied by using safety stock or a faster mode of transportation. Such substitution is not possible with a service. The benefits of a service are also intangible—that is, you can't normally see the benefits of a service, such as a doctor's physical exam. But a consumer can see the benefits provided by a product—for example, a vacuum cleaner removing dirt from the carpet.

Because service industries are so customer oriented, customer service is a priority. Service distribution focuses on three main areas:

AP/WIDE WORLD PHOTOS

Modelled after successful programs like ExxonMobil's Speedpass, McDonald's is testing a program to minimize the time customers spend at the register. Customers run a small wand over the electronic reader to pay for food they order. People can load the wand electronically with dollars by using a credit or debit card. Reduced time paying for food means that McDonald's can sell hamburgers almost as fast as customers can order them.

- *Minimizing wait times:* Minimizing the amount of time customers wait in line to deposit a cheque, wait for food at a restaurant, or wait in a doctor's office for an appointment is a key factor in maintaining the quality of service. People tend to overestimate the amount of time they spend waiting in line, researchers report, and unexplained waiting seems longer than explained waits. To reduce anxiety among waiting customers, some restaurants give patrons pagers that allow them to roam around or go to the bar. Banks sometimes install electronic boards displaying stock quotes or sports scores. Car rental companies reward repeat customers by eliminating their waits altogether.[37] Airports have designed comfortable sitting areas with televisions and children's play areas for those waiting to board planes. Many hotels are experimenting with electronic check-in kiosks. Travellers can insert their credit cards to check in upon arrival to receive their room key, get directions and print maps to area restaurants and attractions, and print out their hotel bills.[38]
- *Managing service capacity:* For product manufacturers, inventory acts as a buffer, enabling them to provide the product during periods of peak demand without extraordinary efforts. Service firms don't have this luxury. If they don't have the capacity to meet demand, they must either turn down some prospective customers, let service levels slip, or expand capacity. For instance, at tax time a tax preparation firm may have so many customers desiring its services that it has to either turn business away or add temporary offices or preparers. Popular restaurants risk losing business when seating is unavailable or the wait is too long.
- *Improving service delivery:* Like manufacturers, service firms are now experimenting with different distribution channels for their services. Choosing the right distribution channel can increase the times that services are available (such as using the Internet to disseminate information and services 24/7) or add to customer convenience (like pizza delivery, walk-in medical clinics, or a dry cleaner located in a supermarket). The airline industry has found that using the Internet for ticket sales both reduces distribution costs and raises the level of customer service by making it easier for customers to plan their own travel. Air Canada, for example, has recently extended its Internet fare service to its U.S. flights.[39]

The Internet is fast becoming an alternative channel for delivering services. Consumers can now purchase plane tickets, plan a vacation cruise, reserve a hotel room, pay bills, purchase mutual funds, and receive electronic newspapers in cyberspace. Insurance giant Allstate Canada sells auto and home insurance directly to consumers in some provinces through the Internet in addition to its traditional network of agents. The effort reduces costs so that Allstate can stay competitive with rival insurance companies. Similarly, several new residential real estate websites are making it easier for customers to shop for a new home on the Web. Traditionally, the only way for customers to gain access to realtors' listings was to work through a real estate agent, who would search the listings and then show customers homes that met their requirements. The new companies offer direct access to the listings, enabling customers to review properties for sale on their own, and choose which ones they would like to visit.[40]

>> CONNECT IT

As you complete this chapter, you should be able to see how marketing channels operate and how supply chain management is necessary to move goods from the manufacturer to the final consumer. Companies can choose from several different marketing channels to sell their products. For example, as the opening story discussed, Grocery Gateway is using supply chain concepts and technology to compete successfully with giant bricks-and-mortar outlets like Wal-Mart. This strategy has led to sales of over $70 million in just seven years from the company's founding. With growing Internet sales and with many other product line expansion opportunities, Grocery Gateway is just beginning.

REVIEW IT

1 **Explain what a marketing channel is and why intermediaries are needed.** A marketing channel is a business structure of interdependent organizations that reach from the point of product origin to the consumer with the purpose of physically moving products to their final consumption destination, representing "place" in the marketing mix and encompassing the processes involved in getting the right product to the right place at the right time. Members of a marketing channel create a continuous and seamless supply chain that performs or supports the marketing channel functions. Channel members provide economies to the distribution process in the form of specialization and division of labour; overcoming discrepancies in quantity, assortment, time, and space; and providing contact efficiency.

1.1 Your family runs a specialty ice cream parlour that manufactures its own ice cream in small batches and sells it only in small 750 mL containers. Recently, someone not affiliated with your company sent six containers of your ice cream to Oprah Winfrey, who proclaimed on her national TV show that it was the best ice cream she had ever eaten. Immediately after the broadcast, orders came flooding in, overwhelming your small-batch production schedule and your rudimentary distribution system. Your company's shipping manager thinks she can handle it, but you disagree. List the reasons why you need to restructure your supply chain.

2 **Describe the channel structures for consumer and business-to-business products and discuss alternative channel arrangements.** Marketing channels for consumer and business-to-business products vary in degree of complexity. The simplest consumer-product channel involves direct selling from producers to consumers. Businesses may sell directly to business or government buyers. Marketing channels grow more complex as intermediaries become involved. Consumer-product channel intermediaries include agents, brokers, wholesalers, and retailers. Business-product channel intermediaries include agents, brokers, and industrial distributors. Marketers often use alternative channel arrangements to move their products to the consumer. With dual distribution or multiple distribution, they choose two or more different channels to distribute the same product. Nontraditional channels help differentiate a firm's product from the competitor's or provide a manufacturer with another avenue for sales. Finally, strategic channel alliances are arrangements that use another manufacturer's already established channel.

2.1 Describe the most likely marketing channel structure for each of these consumer products: candy bars, Tupperware products, nonfiction books, new automobiles, farmers' market produce, and stereo equipment. Now, construct alternative channels for these same products.

2.2  • Dell Computer successfully uses a direct channel to sell computers and equipment to consumers over the telephone and Internet. How has Dell affected traditional computer retailers with bricks-and-mortar buildings? How have other computer manufacturers, such as Compaq and IBM, countered Dell's competitive advantage in its direct channel? Use InfoTrac® College Edition (**http://infotrac.thomsonlearning.com**) to search for articles on this topic. You may also need to consult your campus library to search for this information.

2.3 

You have been hired to design an alternative marketing channel for a firm specializing in the manufacturing and marketing of novelties for college and university student organizations. In a memo to the president of the firm, describe how the channel operates.

2.4 

Building on question 1.1, determine a new channel structure for the ice cream parlour. Write a proposal to present to your key managers.

3 Define supply chain management and discuss its benefits. Supply chain management coordinates and integrates all of the activities performed by supply chain members into a seamless process from the source to the point of consumption. The responsibilities of a supply chain manager include developing channel design strategies, managing the relationships of supply chain members, sourcing and procurement of raw materials, scheduling production, processing orders, managing inventory and storing product, and selecting transportation modes. The supply chain manager is also responsible for managing customer service and the information that flows through the supply chain. The benefits of supply chain management include reduced costs in inventory management, transportation, warehousing, and packaging; improved service through techniques like time-based delivery and make-to-order; and enhanced revenues, which result from such supply chain–related achievements as higher product availability and more customized products.

3.1 Discuss the benefits of supply chain management. How does the implementation of supply chain management result in enhanced customer value?

4 Discuss the issues that influence channel strategy. When determining marketing channel strategy, the supply chain manager must determine what market, product, and producer factors will influence the choice of channel. The manager must also determine the appropriate level of distribution intensity. Intensive distribution is distribution aimed at maximum market coverage. Selective distribution is achieved by screening dealers to eliminate all but a few in any single area. The most restrictive form of market coverage is exclusive distribution, which entails only one or a few dealers within a given area.

4.1 Decide which distribution intensity level—intensive, selective, or exclusive—is used for each of the following products, and explain why: Rolex watches, Land Rover sport utility vehicles, M&Ms, special edition Barbie dolls, and Crest toothpaste.

4.2 TEAM Now that you have a basic channel structure for the ice cream parlour (from question 2.4), form a team of three to four students and list the market, product, and producer factors that will affect your final channel structure.

5 Explain channel leadership, conflict, and partnering. Power, control, leadership, conflict, and partnering are the main social dimensions of marketing channel relationships. Channel power refers to the capacity of one channel member to control or influence other channel members. Channel control occurs when one channel member intentionally affects another member's behaviour. Channel leadership is the exercise of authority and power. Channel conflict occurs when there is a clash of goals and methods among the members of a distribution channel. Channel conflict can be either horizontal, among channel members at the same level, or vertical, among channel members at different levels of the channel. Channel partnering is the joint effort of all channel members to create a supply chain that serves customers and creates a competitive advantage. Collaborating channel partners meet the needs of consumers more effectively by ensuring that the right products reach shelves at the right time and at a lower cost, boosting sales and profits.

5.1 Procter & Gamble and Wal-Mart are key partners in a shared supply chain. P&G is one of Wal-Mart's biggest suppliers, and Wal-Mart provides extremely detailed scanner data about customer purchases of P&G products. Wal-Mart recently began selling its own brand of Sam's Choice laundry detergent in bright orange bottles alongside P&G's Tide but for a greatly reduced price. What do you think will be the impact of this new product on what has been a stable channel relationship?

6 **Describe the logistical components of the supply chain.** The logistics supply chain consists of several interrelated and integrated logistical components: (1) sourcing and procurement of raw materials and supplies, (2) production scheduling, (3) order processing, (4) inventory control, (5) warehousing and materials-handling systems, and (6) transportation. Integrating and linking all of the logistics functions of the supply chain is the logistics information system. Information technology connects the various components and partners of the supply chain into an integrated whole. The supply chain team, in concert with the logistics information system, orchestrates the movement of goods, services, and information from the source to the consumer. Supply chain teams typically cut across organizational boundaries, embracing all parties who participate in moving product to market. Procurement deals with the purchase of raw materials, supplies, and components according to production scheduling. Order processing monitors the flow of goods and information (order entry and order handling). Inventory control systems regulate when and how much to buy (order timing and order quantity). Warehousing provides storage of goods until needed by the customer while the materials-handling system moves inventory into, within, and out of the warehouse. Finally, the major modes of transportation include railways, motor carriers, pipelines, waterways, and airways.

6.1 Discuss the impact of just-in-time production on the entire supply chain. Specifically, how does JIT affect suppliers, procurement planning, inventory levels, mode of transportation selected, and warehousing? What are the benefits of JIT to the end consumer?

6.2 Assume that you are the supply chain manager for a producer of expensive, high-tech computer components. Identify the most suitable method(s) of transporting your product in terms of cost, transit time, reliability, capability, accessibility, and traceability. Now, assume you are the supply chain manager for a producer of milk. How does this assumption change your choice of transportation?

7 **Discuss new technology and emerging trends in supply chain management.** Several trends are emerging that affect the job of today's supply chain manager. Technology and automation are bringing up-to-date distribution information to the decision maker's desk. Technology is also linking suppliers, buyers, and carriers for joint decision making, and it has created a new electronic distribution channel. Many companies are saving money and time by outsourcing third-party carriers to handle some or all aspects of the distribution process.

7.1 ON LINE Visit the website of Menlo Worldwide Logistics at http://www.menloworldwide.com. What logistics functions can this third-party logistics supplier provide? How does its mission fit in with the supply chain management philosophy?

7.2   Use InfoTrac® College Edition (http://infotrac.thomsonlearning.com) to locate the following article in the June 12, 2000, issue of *Computerworld* magazine: "Filling Orders a Hot E-Business: Companies Race to Offer Logistics Services" by Julia King. Read the article and write a summary of the implications of Internet commerce for the transportation and logistics industries.

8 **Discuss channels and distribution decisions in global markets.** Global marketing channels are becoming more important to companies seeking growth abroad. Manufacturers introducing products in foreign countries must decide what type of channel structure to use—in particular, whether the product should be marketed through direct channels or through foreign intermediaries. Marketers should be aware that channel structures in foreign markets might be very different from those they are accustomed to in Canada. Global distribution expertise is emerging as an important skill for supply chain managers now that many countries are removing trade barriers.

8.1 How are transportation and logistics issues handled around the world? To find out, consult the *Transportation Journal* using InfoTrac® College Edition (http://infotrac.thomsonlearning.com). Create a grid comparing at least two countries according to standard procedures, particular challenges faced, and creative solutions to problems they have encountered.

9 **Identify the special problems and opportunities associated with distribution in service organizations.** Managers in service industries use the same skills, techniques, and strategies to manage logistics functions as managers in goods-producing industries. The distribution of services focuses on three main areas: minimizing wait times, managing service capacity, and improving service delivery.

9.1 Assume that you are the marketing manager of a hospital. Write a report indicating the distribution functions that concern you. Discuss the similarities and dissimilarities of distribution for services and for goods.

DEFINE IT

channel conflict 318
channel control 318
channel leader (channel captain) 318
channel members 308
channel partnering (channel cooperation) 320
channel power 318
direct channel 310
discrepancy of assortment 308
discrepancy of quantity 308
distribution resource planning (DRP) 323
dual distribution (multiple distribution) 312
electronic data interchange (EDI) 323
electronic distribution 327
exclusive distribution 318
horizontal conflict 319
intensive distribution 317
inventory control system 323
just-in-time production (JIT) 322
logistics information system 320
marketing channel (channel of distribution) 308
mass customization (build-to-order) 321
materials-handling system 325
materials requirement planning (MRP) (materials management) 323
order processing system 322
outsourcing (contract logistics) 326
selective distribution 317
spatial discrepancy 309
strategic channel alliance 313
supply chain 308
supply chain management 313
supply chain team 320
temporal discrepancy 309
vertical conflict 319

APPLY IT

Boudreaux has owned and operated a small spice-manufacturing business in Montreal for about 10 years. Boudreaux has also experimented with preparing and selling several sauces, mostly for meats and salads. For the most part, the firm has sold its products locally, but on occasion, distributors have signed contracts to sell Boudreaux's products province-wide.

Boudreaux's most recent product—a spicy Cajun mayonnaise—has been a huge success locally, and several inquiries have come from large distributors about the possibilities of selling the mayonnaise regionally and perhaps nationally. No research has been conducted to determine the level or scope of demand for the mayonnaise. Also, it has been packaged and sold only in 340-gram bottles. The red-and-white label just says "Boudreaux's Cajun Mayonnaise" and lists the major ingredients.

QUESTIONS

1. What should Boudreaux do to help the firm decide how best to market the new Cajun mayonnaise?
2. Should Boudreaux sign a contract with one of the distributors to sell the Cajun mayonnaise, or should his firm try to sell the product directly to one or more of the major supermarket chains?

THINK ABOUT IT

Wholesome Snacks Inc., the maker of a variety of cookies and crackers, has just created a new vitamin-packed cookie. The new cookie has the potential to combat many of the health issues caused by malnutrition in children throughout poverty-stricken parts of the world. To date, however, many of the larger Third World markets have resisted opening distribution channels to Wholesome's products. Wholesome realizes that its new cookie could also help open the door for the company to sell its less nutritious products in these markets. Therefore, the company is offering the new cookie at a low cost to government relief programs in exchange for long sought after distribution channels. The company feels the deal is good for business, but the countries feel it is corporate bullying.

QUESTIONS

1. What do you think about Wholesome's idea for opening a new distribution channel?
2. Does the CMA Code of Ethics address this issue? Go to **http://www.the-cma.org** and review the code.

TRY IT

AP/WIDE WORLD PHOTOS

ON LINE

CarsDirect.com: Driving Car Buyers to the Internet

CarsDirect.com is heating up the new car industry. The first direct broker of cars on the Internet has sent automakers, on-line-buying services, and dealer groups scrambling to control the growing number of customers going on-line to shortcut the traditional process of shopping for new and used vehicles. The Internet startup sparked a growth of copycat websites dedicated to the direct-to-consumer purchase of cars, such as http://www.DriveOff.com, and http://www.autos.com.

Backed by Michael Dell's personal investment firm, CarsDirect.com was conceived by Bill Gross, chairman of Idealab, a venture incubator that has also launched other Internet businesses, such as eToys, Tickets.com, and Cooking.com. After becoming frustrated with his own efforts at buying an auto on-line, Gross realized that current Internet options for car buying not only were inadequate but also did nothing to leverage available technology on behalf of the consumer. At the time of his search, on-line car sites functioned only as lead generators for local dealers, requiring him to close the sale of the car the old-fashioned way: haggling at the dealership.

His vision, CarsDirect.com, sells cars entirely through the Internet, allowing consumers to bypass traditional car dealers in their negotiations. As a car broker, CarsDirect.com offers Web buyers a car at a fixed price based on recent average selling prices. Then, CarsDirect.com works through its network of existing dealers to get the car at that price. Since CarsDirect.com doesn't hold franchise agreements with any car manufacturers, consumers enjoy an impartial and unbiased shopping experience as well as an unrivalled selection. In contrast, buying cars the old-fashioned way makes consumers travel from car dealer to car dealer looking for the models they are interested in or the best price.

Car buyers visiting CarsDirect.com can research a car by searching the site's extensive database, which provides objective information on price, performance, and options for more than 2,500 different makes and models—virtually every production vehicle available. CarsDirect.com's research tools let buyers compare the features of vehicles and see in seconds the manufacturer's suggested retail price, the invoice, and, most importantly, the price CarsDirect.com can get for them. If a consumer wants to buy, payment is arranged completely on-line to close the deal. Financing options are provided through CarsDirect.com's financial partner, a major automotive lender. Then, the buyer can arrange for delivery of the vehicle at home or the office or pick it up from a local automotive retailer.

With on-line auto sales expected to exceed 5 percent of total sales soon, there are still big hurdles ahead for car brokers like CarsDirect.com. General Motors, for instance, recently warned its dealers to cease and desist from using on-line car-buying sites like CarsDirect.com. The largest obstacle, however, is the myriad of franchise laws that protect car dealers and restrict direct sales of automobiles. Car brokers have found that franchise laws are often arcane or impractical. As a result, car brokers have had to redesign their direct-sales model. Often, instead of trying to bypass dealers, Internet car brokers are forming alliances with dealers or reworking their strategies to become more dealer-friendly to comply with various franchise laws.

QUESTIONS

1. Explain how CarsDirect.com fits into the channel structure for car retailing to consumers.
2. How has CarsDirect.com's selling model caused channel conflict?
3. Visit CarsDirect.com's website at **http://www.carsdirect.com.** Give examples of how its website simplifies the car-buying process for consumers.

FLIP IT

Flip to Chapter 11 in your *Grademaker Study Guide* for more review opportunities, including the pretest, vocabulary review, Internet activities, study test questions, and an application exercise based on marketing channel concepts. Can you close your book and diagram the various channel structures discussed in the book? Do you know the issues that marketers must consider when determining a channel strategy? If not, then pick up your *Grademaker* and review.

CLICK IT

The *Marketing* website is rich with materials to help you review and master marketing concepts. Check your knowledge with the free quizzes, practise key terms using the crossword puzzles, or review key concepts using the Microsoft® PowerPoint® slides. Also on the website are updated weblinks to companies mentioned in this chapter, Internet exercises, career marketing information, and much much more! Go to http://www.lamb3e.nelson.com, read the material, and follow the convenient links.

WATCH IT

Cargojet: Canada's Leading Cargo Airline

At a time when the passenger side of the airline industry is experiencing considerable difficulty, the largest passenger air carrier in Canada (Air Canada) is just coming out of bankruptcy protection, and the largest passenger air carrier in the U.S. (American Airlines) is still under bankruptcy protection, the cargo end of the industry is doing quite well. Cargojet moves over 450,000 pounds of cargo every day and is generating over $100 million per year in revenue.

Cargojet itself is partially the result of a bankruptcy in the passenger airline business. Ajay Virmani, the President and CEO of Cargojet, had invested $10 million in Canada 3000 to operate the cargo end of the passenger airline. Shortly after Mr. Virmani's investment came the infamous 9/11 disaster in the U.S., and passenger bookings on Canada 3000 dropped by over 70 percent. Canada 3000 went into bankruptcy and never re-emerged as a passenger carrier. Ajay Virmani, however, invested additional funds in the cargo end of the business, and Cargojet has become a leader in the cargo end of the airline business in Canada.

In the months after 9/11, Ajay Virmani was able to buy a number of now-unneeded passenger planes for very low prices and convert them into cargo planes. Mr. Virmani was also able to hire hundreds of laid-off Canada 3000 employees to give Cargojet an experienced workforce.

As opposed to passenger transportation, which takes place mostly during the day, Cargojet's busy time is at night. Cargojet loads its planes from 10:00 P.M. to 12:30 A.M. each night to ensure delivery of its cargo to its destination by 8:00 A.M. As a tribute to its efficiency in doing this, Cargojet has set on-time performance records in the airline cargo business with 99 percent on-time deliveries.

Might you be interested in a career in the transportation industry? Visit Cargojet's website (http://www.cargojet.com) and look under "Careers." Want to see how easy it is to ship something? Check under "Request a Quote" or "Flight Schedule" on the website. Want to see how easy it is for a shipper or customer to track a shipment? Check under "Cargo Tracking" on the website.

Cargojet states that its mission is "to be the dominant, most reliable air cargo company in Canada." Let's watch Cargojet in action and see how it is accomplishing this mission.

QUESTIONS

1. What do you think of the cargo end of the airline business? Does it match your perceptions of it? How is it different?
2. Why has Cargojet succeeded when Canada 3000 failed?
3. What are your views of the future of the airline cargo industry in Canada?

SUGGESTED INFORMATION SOURCES

CBC, *Venture*, "Cargojet," Broadcast: February 15, 2004.
http://www.cargojet.com

chapter 12

Retailing and Wholesaling

>> LEARNING OBJECTIVES

1. Discuss the importance of retailing in the Canadian economy
2. Describe the nature of retail operations
3. List the major tasks involved in developing a retail marketing strategy
4. Discuss the challenges of expanding retailing operations into global markets
5. Describe future trends in retailing
6. Discuss the importance of wholesaling in the Canadian economy
7. Identify the major types of wholesalers
8. List the major functions that wholesalers perform
9. Describe future trends in wholesaling

>> Canada has been targeted for invasion and Canadians are actually looking forward to it! Who are these invaders and why are Canadian consumers welcoming them? They are U.S. retailers, like electronics superstore Best Buy, who come with already established brand names and reputations. They bring a wider selection of goods and services to Canada and are combining this with lower prices to boot! Canada is a natural "target" for U.S. retailers. The majority of the Canadian population lives within 200 kilometres of the U.S. border and is condensed into a few population centres, the dominant ones being Vancouver, Toronto, and Montreal. The majority of the population speaks English, the nation is democratic and was founded by similar ancestors as those of Americans, the people are thoroughly acquainted with American products and services because of spillover advertising and promotion from U.S. media, and, finally, Canada is a G7 member, which means the economy is strong and represents a substantial market for American goods.

Considering that annual retail sales for Canada in 2002 were $339 billion, it appears that Canada is a great place to develop a market. However, Wal-Mart, the world's largest retailer, had revenues of US$246 billion in 2002, a value that equals the entire Canadian retail market! In 1985 there were about 10 major U.S. retail chains operating in Canada; currently there are over 100. When Wal-Mart entered Canada in 1994 by purchasing 122 Woolco department store sites, there were some strong predictions about the impact on Canadian retailing tempered with the notion that Wal-Mart was really not adding to the scene immediately, since it was taking over established stores. Currently, Wal-Mart is Canada's leading department store, holding 31.2 percent of the $18.2 billion department store market in 2001, followed closely by Sears Canada with 29.7 percent, Zellers with 25 percent, and The Bay with 14.2 percent. The trend for all of the followers is not positive, as all three lost market share to Wal-Mart. Even though it is Canada's leading department store retailer, Wal-Mart Canada only contributes about $5 billion to the total of $262 billion in Wal-Mart's worldwide sales.

The impact of Wal-Mart's entry into Canada has been great, as was expected. The strength of formerly established Canadian-market department store retailers like Sears Canada, The Bay, and Zellers has diminished, while K Mart Canada succumbed entirely and Eaton's collapsed—a surprise, given that it was not really positioned against Wal-Mart at all. The fall of Eaton's was partially a domino effect caused by the need of Sears and The Bay to shift more of their efforts upscale to avoid the impact of Wal-Mart. Aside from impacting established Canadian retailers, Wal-Mart also blunted the expansion plans of some other U.S. retailers. For example, U.S.-based Target stores initially decided against Canadian expansion in light of Wal-Mart's first-mover advantage and the realization that the market was too "crowded" for it to achieve the market position it would need to make the effort worthwhile. However, there has been some further discussion that The Bay and Zellers stores might be takeover possibilities for Target, allowing Target to enter the market while avoiding "overcrowding" an already highly competitive market.

More recent U.S. invaders include Minneapolis-based Best Buy, which acquired Burnaby B.C.-based Future Shop. Best Buy had plans to convert all of the Future Shop stores to "Best Buy" stores but so far has elected to maintain separate brand identities in many markets. The entry of The Gap and its latest retail extension, Old Navy, has all but annihilated the clothing retail offerings of Canada's Dylex Ltd. leaving only the Fairweather stores with a slim chance of survival.

However, Canadians need not despair entirely; some Canadian retailers have initiated a counterinvasion of the U.S. For example, Roots, Bata Shoes, Danier Leather, Aldo Shoes, and West 49 have all expanded into the United States. In addition, Wendy's, which acquired Tim Hortons, is taking the doughnut chain's successful retail concept south to overwhelm Dunkin' Donuts. Canadian retailers have strong evidence that they can be successful with their counterinvasion. For example, of 54 Canadian retail chains that have entered into the U.S. since the 1980s, 26 are still operating successfully.[1]

So what's next? How many more U.S. invaders will consider entering Canada given an increasingly tight market? Will Target stores or some other U.S. retail giant acquire The Bay and Zellers and remove the last "large" Canadian department store retailer from the scene? Will successful Canadian retailers look to the U.S. for expansion? What can retailers do to stand out from competitors? How does a retailer's target market determine its merchandise selection? What factors are involved in developing a store's atmosphere? This chapter seeks to answer these questions and many more by discussing retailers' important role in moving products and services to the ultimate consumer. We begin with a discussion of the role of retailing and the ways in which retail operations can be classified, followed by a description of the decisions involved in developing a retail marketing strategy.

ON LINE

International Council of Shopping Centers

What information does the International Council of Shopping Centers provide? How can this information help Canadian retailers make marketing decisions?

http://www.icsc.org

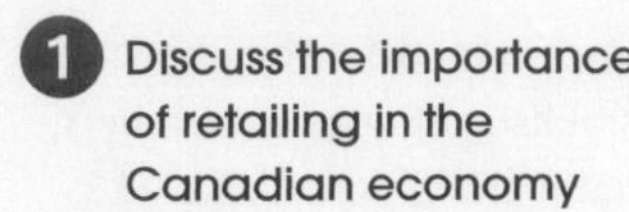
Discuss the importance of retailing in the Canadian economy

>> THE ROLE OF RETAILING

retailing
All the activities directly related to the sale of goods and services to the ultimate consumer for personal, nonbusiness use.

Retailing—all the activities directly related to the sale of goods and services to the ultimate consumer for personal, nonbusiness use—has enhanced the quality of our daily lives. When we shop for groceries, hairstyling, clothes, books, and many other products and services, we are involved in retailing. The millions of goods and services provided by retailers mirror the needs and styles of Canadian society.

Retailing affects all of us directly or indirectly. The retailing industry is one of the largest employers; over 240,000 Canadian retail establishments employ more than 1.46 million people, which accounts for 12 percent of total Canadian employment. At the store level, retailing is still considered a mom-and-pop business. Almost seven out of 10 retail establishments employ fewer than four employees and, according to Statistics Canada, 97 percent of all retail establishments employ less than 50 employees.[2]

The Canadian economy is heavily dependent on retailing. Retailers ring up over $339 billion in sales annually, a little over 30 percent of the gross domestic product (GDP).[3] Although most retailers are quite small, a few large retail chains tend to dominate their categories. Who are these dominant retailers? Exhibit 12.1 lists some Canadian retailing categories and a number of the dominant organizations.

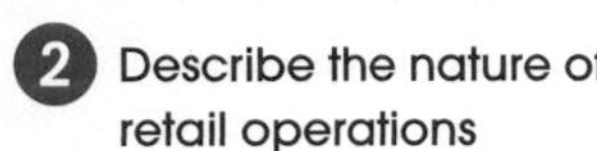
Describe the nature of retail operations

>> THE NATURE OF RETAIL OPERATIONS

A retail establishment can be classified according to its ownership, level of service, product assortment, and price. Specifically, retailers use the latter three variables to position themselves in the marketplace. (As noted in Chapter 6, positioning is the strategy used to influence how consumers perceive one product in relation to all competing products.) These three variables can be combined in several ways to create distinctly different retail operations. Exhibit 12.2 lists the major types of retail stores discussed in this chapter and classifies them by level of service, product assortment, price, and gross margin.

Ownership

independent retailers
Retailers owned by a single person or partnership and not operated as part of a larger retail institution.

chain stores
Stores owned and operated as a group by a single organization.

franchise
The right to operate a business or to sell a product.

Retailers can be broadly classified by form of ownership: independent, part of a chain, or franchise outlet. Retailers owned by a single person or partnership and not operated as part of a larger retail institution are **independent retailers.** Around the world, most retailers are independent, operating one or a few stores in their community. Local florists, shoe stores, and ethnic food markets typically fit this classification.

Chain stores are owned and operated as a group by a single organization. Under this form of ownership, the home office handles many administrative tasks for the entire chain. The home office also buys most of the merchandise sold in the stores.

Franchises are owned and operated by individuals but are licensed by a larger supporting organization. Franchising combines the advantages of independent ownership with those of the chain store organization. Franchising is discussed in more detail later in the chapter.

Level of Service

The level of service that retailers provide can be classified along a continuum, from full service to self-service. Some retailers, such as exclusive clothing stores, offer high levels of service. They provide alterations, credit, delivery, consulting, liberal return policies, layaway, gift wrapping, and personal shopping. Discount stores usually offer fewer services. Retailers like factory outlets and warehouse clubs offer virtually no services.

Product Assortment

The third basis for positioning or classifying stores is by the breadth and depth of their product line. Specialty stores—for example, Laura Secord, Aldo Shoes, and Harvey's Hamburgers—have the most concentrated product assortments, usually carrying single

EXHIBIT 12.1

Dominant Canadian Retailers By Retail Category

RETAIL CATEGORY	2000 RANK	COMPANY	2000 EST. REVENUES (IN MILLIONS)	2000 EST. MARKET SHARE
Grocery	1	Loblaws	20,615	29.2
	2	Sobeys	8,754	12.4
	3	Safeway	5,365	7.6
	4	A&P	4,801	6.8
Coffee shops	1	TDL Group—Tim Hortons	1,898	67.8
	2	The Second Cup	160	5.7
	3	Coffee Time Donuts	146	5.2
	4	Starbucks Coffee	132	4.7
Fast food	1	McDonald's	2,096	28.4
	2	Cara—Harvey's, Swiss Chalet	1,601	21.7
	3	Tricon—KFC, Pizza Hut, Taco Bell	1,200	14.9
	4	Subway	531	7.2
RETAIL CATEGORY	**2001 RANK**	**COMPANY**	**2001 EST. REVENUES (IN MILLIONS)**	**2001 EST. MARKET SHARE**
Hardware	1	Canadian Tire	5,287	19.8
	2	RONA & Réno-Dépôt	3,391	12.7
	3	Home Depot	3,365	12.6
	4	Home Hardware	3,204	12.0
Department stores	1	Wal-Mart	5,834	31.2
	2	Sears	5,554	29.7
	3	Zellers	4,675	25.0
	4	The Bay	2,655	14.2

SOURCES: "Report on Market Shares," *Marketing Magazine*, June 4, 2001; "Report on Market Shares," *Marketing Magazine*, May 27, 2002.

or narrow product lines but in considerable depth. On the other end of the spectrum, full-line discounters typically carry broad assortments of merchandise with limited depth. For example, Zellers carries automotive supplies, household cleaning products, and pet food. However, Zellers may carry only four or five brands of canned dog food; a Loblaws supermarket may carry as many as 20.

Other retailers, such as factory outlet stores, may carry only part of a single line. Nike, a major manufacturer of sporting goods and clothing, sells only certain items of its own brand in its many outlet stores. Discount specialty stores like RONA or Toys "R" Us carry a broad assortment in concentrated product lines, such as building and home supplies or toys.

Price

Price is a fourth way to position retail stores. Traditional department stores and specialty stores typically charge the full "suggested retail price." In contrast, discounters, factory outlets, and off-price retailers use low prices as a major lure for shoppers.

The last column in Exhibit 12.2 shows the typical **gross margin**—how much the retailer makes as a percentage of sales after the cost of goods sold is subtracted. The level of gross margin and the price level generally match. For example, a traditional jewellery store has high prices and high gross margins. A factory outlet has low prices and low gross margins. Markdowns on merchandise during sale periods and price wars among competitors, in which stores lower prices on certain items in an effort to win customers,

gross margin
The amount of money the retailer makes as a percentage of sales after the cost of goods sold is subtracted.

EXHIBIT 12.2

Types of Stores and Their Characteristics

TYPE OF RETAILER	LEVEL OF SERVICE	PRODUCT ASSORTMENT	PRICE	GROSS MARGIN
Department store	Moderately high to high	Broad	Moderate to high	Moderately high
Specialty store	High	Narrow	Moderate to high	High
Supermarket	Low	Broad	Moderate	Low
Convenience store	Low	Medium to narrow	Moderately high	Moderately high
Drugstore	Low to moderate	Medium	Moderate	Low
Full-line discount store	Moderate to low	Medium to broad	Moderately low	Moderately low
Discount specialty store	Moderate to low	Medium to broad	Moderately low to low	Moderately low
Warehouse clubs	Low	Broad	Low to very low	Low
Off-price retailer	Low	Medium to narrow	Low	Low
Restaurant	Low to high	Narrow	Low to high	Low to high

cause gross margins to decline. When Wal-Mart entered the pharmacy business in Newfoundland, a fierce price war ensued between it and Shoppers Drug Mart. By the time the price war was in full swing, the dispensing fee for a prescription had plummeted to zero, a price at which no pharmacist could claim value added for the service and no pharmacy retailer could make a profit on its prescription business.

>> MAJOR TYPES OF RETAIL OPERATIONS

Traditionally, there have been several distinct types of retail stores, with each offering a different product assortment, type of service, and price level, according to its customers' shopping preferences.

In a recent trend, however, retailers are experimenting with alternative formats that make it harder to classify them. For instance, supermarkets are expanding their nonfood items and services, discounters are adding groceries, drugstores are becoming more like convenience stores, and department stores are experimenting with smaller stores.[4] Nevertheless, many stores still fall into the basic types.

Department Stores

department store
A store housing several departments under one roof.

buyer
A department head who selects the merchandise for his or her department and who may also be responsible for promotion and personnel.

Housing several departments under one roof, a **department store** carries a wide variety of shopping and specialty goods, including apparel, cosmetics, housewares, electronics, and sometimes furniture. Purchases are generally made within each department rather than at one central checkout area. Each department is treated as a separate buying centre to achieve economies in promotion, buying, service, and control. Each department is usually headed by a **buyer,** a department head who not only selects the merchandise for his or her department but may also be responsible for promotion and for personnel. For a consistent, uniform store image, central management sets broad policies about the types of merchandise carried and price ranges. Central management is also responsible for the overall advertising program, credit policies, store expansion, customer service, and so on.

Large independent department stores such as Honest Ed's in downtown Toronto and the S&R Department Store in Kingston are rare in Canada. There are a few regional chains such as the three Winnipeg-based chains, The North West Company, V&S Department stores, and SAAN (Surplus Army, Airforce & Navy) department stores, and the Quebec-based Hart Stores/Bargain Giant Department Stores that operate in Quebec and the Maritimes.[5] However, the majority of department store sales are made by national chains. Canada's department store market is dominated by three main department store chains: Wal-Mart, Sears, and the combination of Zellers and The Bay.

In recent years, consumers have become more cost conscious and value oriented. Specialty retailers like The Gap, discounters, catalogue outlets, and even on-line Internet shopping alternatives are offering superior merchandise selection and presentation, sharper pricing, and greater convenience to take sales away from department stores. They have also been quicker to adopt new technologies and invest in labour-saving strategies. In addition, their leaner cost structure translates into lower prices for the customer. Meanwhile, manufacturers like Columbia Sportswear, Nike, Liz Claiborne, Bass, Calvin Klein, and Polo Ralph Lauren have opened outlet stores of their own and more discount stores, such as Wal-Mart and Zellers have upgraded their apparel assortments, taking more sales away from the traditional department stores.

Department store managers are using several strategies to preserve their market share. One is to reposition department stores as specialty outlets. They are dividing departments into miniboutiques, each featuring a distinct fashion taste, as specialty stores do. For example, many upscale department stores feature Donna Karan and Liz Claiborne boutiques within their stores. Department stores are also enhancing customer service to shift the focus away from price. Services include complimentary alterations, longer store hours, personalized attention, after-sale followup, and personal wardrobe planning. Finally, department stores are expanding, remodelling, and revitalizing to show off new merchandising directions and to reflect the growth in their marketing areas.

Specialty Stores

Specialty store formats allow retailers to refine their segmentation strategies and tailor their merchandise to specific target markets. A **specialty store** is not only a type of store but also a method of retail operation—namely, specializing in a given type of merchandise. Examples include children's clothing, men's clothing, candy, baked goods, gourmet coffee, sporting goods, and pet supplies. A typical specialty store carries a deeper but narrower assortment of specialty merchandise than does a department store. Generally, specialty stores' knowledgeable sales clerks offer more attentive customer service. The format has become very powerful in the apparel market and other areas. In fact, according to recent studies, consumers buy more clothing from specialty stores than from any other type of retailer.[6] The Mountain Equipment Co-op, Athletes World, Aldo Shoes, Tim Hortons, and M&M Meat Shops are examples of successful chain specialty retailers.

specialty store
A retail store specializing in a given type of merchandise.

Consumers usually consider price to be secondary in specialty outlets. Instead, the distinctive merchandise, the store's physical appearance, and the calibre of the staff determine its popularity. For example, Moores, a national retail chain, has grown quickly by offering a large selection of quality men's clothing while making the patriotic appeal "When you think Canadian, think Moores." Moores offers shoppers "on-premise tailoring" in its stores with a promise of "while you wait hemming." Moores' retail strategy is summed up in the following company statement: "Everyday low prices, fine quality, great selection, superior service and a guarantee he or she can trust."[7] Because small specialty stores such as Moores pay attention to the customer and offer limited product lines, manufacturers often favour introducing new products in small specialty stores before moving on to larger retail and department stores.

Small specialty stores also provide a low-risk testing ground for many new products. Nike, for instance, often uses athletic footwear retailer Foot Locker as its venue for new shoe introductions. As an example, Nike introduced its $130 Tuned Air running shoe exclusively at Foot Locker shoe outlets. While the arrangement protected Foot Locker from price competition from other retailers, allowing it to charge full retail price, it also created an image of exclusivity for Nike.[8]

© ALAN LEVENSON/GETTY IMAGES/STONE

Recent trends in retailing are making it increasingly difficult to classify retailers, as stores are crossing into one another's domains. This woman is purchasing computer software in her grocery store.

MARK RICHARDS/PHOTOEDIT

U.S.-based Sephora is a specialty cosmetics store that supplements its boutique format with in-store kiosks where customers can consult the company's website for items not in the store. Check out Sephora's Canadian shopping policies at http://www.sephora.com/canada.

Supermarkets

Canadian consumers make 11.25 percent of their total expenditures on food, and food was estimated to represent about 70 percent of the estimated $70.6 billion in sales made by Canadian grocery retailers in 2002. Most of these sales were made in **supermarkets**—large, departmentalized, self-service retailers that specialize in food and some nonfood items.[9]

supermarket
A large, departmentalized, self-service retailer that specializes in food and nonfood items.

A decade ago, industry experts predicted the decline of the supermarket industry, whose slim profit margins of just 1 to 2 percent of sales left it vulnerable. These experts originally felt that supermarkets would merely need an ever-growing customer base to sustain volume and compensate for low margins. Although the population continued to grow, albeit at less than 1 percent a year on average, supermarkets still experienced declining sales. As a result, experts were forced to examine not only population trends but also demographic and lifestyle changes of consumers. They discovered several trends affecting the supermarket industry.

For example, there are more dual-income and single-parent families than ever before; as a result, consumers are eating out more or are too busy to prepare meals at home. According to a recent report from Statistics Canada, Canadians spent 65 percent of their food money in retail grocery stores, compared with 35 percent spent for food away from home. In comparison, Canadians spent over 80 percent of their food money in grocery stores in 1961.[10] The growth in the away-from-home food market has been driven by the entry of more women into the workforce and their need for convenience and time-saving products. Working couples need one-stop shopping, and the increasing numbers of affluent customers are willing to pay for specialty and prepared foods.

As stores seek to meet consumer demand for one-stop shopping, conventional supermarkets are being replaced by bigger *superstores*, which are usually twice the size of supermarkets. Superstores meet the needs of today's customers for convenience, variety, and service. Superstores offer one-stop shopping for many food and nonfood needs, as well as many services—including pharmacies, flower shops, salad bars, in-store bakeries, take-out food sections, sit-down restaurants, health food sections, video rentals, dry-cleaning services, shoe repair, photo processing, and banking. Some even offer family dentistry or optical shops. This tendency to offer a wide variety of nontraditional goods and services under one roof is called **scrambled merchandising.** Canada's largest supermarket chain, Loblaws, exemplifies this trend: along with a dry-cleaner, a liquor store, a coffee shop, a pharmacy, and a banking centre, it offers video-game and cell phone sales outlets, and leases space to a clothing chain and a fitness club complete with a sauna, tanning salon, and daycare centre. Loblaws' ancillary services aim to attract today's time-strapped customers by providing one-stop shopping.[11]

scrambled merchandising
The tendency to offer a wide variety of nontraditional goods and services under one roof.

A recent trend in supermarket diversification is the addition of store-owned gas stations. The gas stations not only are a new revenue source for the supermarkets and a convenience for customers, but also attract customers to the location by offering lower prices than can usually be found at a traditional gas station. Experts expect the trend will continue and that by the year 2005 supermarkets will account for 15 percent of overall gasoline sales.[12]

Another demographic trend affecting supermarkets is expanding ethnicity. During the 1990s over 1.8 million immigrants arrived in Canada, with the majority settling in urban areas such as Montreal, Ottawa-Hull, Toronto, Hamilton, Calgary, Edmonton, and Vancouver. These demographic changes promise to have a vast impact on supermarket retailers. For example, immigrants perceive Canada as a multicultural society and expect to find ethnic foods in the stores. Grocery retailers are aware of the market opportunity that ethnic groups represent so they stock many ethnic products such as basmati rice, curry powders, and egg noodles. However, it is not enough to simply stock ethnic foods; signage in the language of important ethnic groups and employment of multilingual employees to assist customers are also important considerations for supermarket retailers.[13]

Many supermarket chains are tailoring marketing strategies to appeal to specific consumer segments to help them stand out in an increasingly competitive marketplace. Most notable is the shift toward *loyalty marketing programs* that reward loyal customers carrying frequent-shopper cards with discounts or gifts. Once scanned at the checkout, frequent-shopper cards help supermarket retailers electronically track shoppers' buying habits.

Drugstores

Drugstores stock pharmacy-related products and services as their main draw. Consumers are most often attracted to a drugstore by its pharmacy or pharmacist, its convenience, or because it honours a third-party prescription drug plan. Drugstores also carry an extensive selection of over-the-counter (OTC) medications, cosmetics, health and beauty aids, seasonal merchandise, specialty items such as greeting cards and a limited selection of toys, and some nonrefrigerated convenience foods. As competition has increased from mass merchandisers and supermarkets with their own pharmacies, as well as from direct-mail prescription services, drugstores have been adding value-added services such as 24-hour operations and drive-through pharmacies.

drugstore
A retail store that stocks pharmacy-related products and services as its main draw.

Demographic trends in Canada look favourable for the drugstore industry. As members of the baby-boom population continues to age, they will spend an increasing percentage of their disposable income on health care and wellness. This fact is good news for the drugstore industry, as the average 60-year-old purchases 15 prescriptions per year, nearly twice as many as the average 30-year-old. Because baby boomers are attentive to their health and keenly sensitive about their looks, the increased traffic at the pharmacy counter in the future should also spur sales in other traditionally strong drugstore merchandise categories, most notably over-the-counter drugs, vitamins, and health and beauty aids.[14]

Convenience Stores

A **convenience store** can be defined as a miniature supermarket, carrying only a limited line of high-turnover convenience goods. These self-service stores are typically located near residential areas and are open 24/7. Convenience stores offer exactly what their name implies: convenient location, long hours, and fast service. However, prices are almost always higher at a convenience store than at a supermarket. Thus, the customer pays for the convenience.

convenience store
A miniature supermarket, carrying only a limited line of high-turnover convenience goods.

From the mid-1970s to the mid-1980s, hundreds of new convenience stores opened, many with self-service gas pumps. Full-service gas stations fought back by closing service bays and opening miniature stores of their own, selling convenience items like cigarettes, sodas, and snacks. Supermarkets and discount stores also wooed customers with one-stop shopping and quick checkout. To combat the gas stations' and supermarkets' competition, convenience store operators have changed their strategy. They have expanded their offerings of nonfood items with video rentals, health and beauty aids, upscale sandwich and salad lines, and more fresh produce. Some convenience stores are even selling hot foods like pizzas, tacos, and hot dogs that are prepared in the store.

The Canadian market is dominated by chain-store competitors, including North America's market leader, 7-Eleven, and Montreal-based Couche-Tard, which "employs about 17,800 people and operates in Canada under trade names such as Couche-Tard, Provi-Soir, Winks, Sept Jours, Mac's, Mike's Mart, and Becker's." Couche-Tard recently acquired the U.S.-based Circle K convenience store chain to become the fourth-largest convenience store operator in North America, producing $1.79 billion in sales from a network of 4,886 stores in Canada and the United States.[15]

discount store
A retailer that competes on the basis of low prices, high turnover, and high volume.

Discount Stores

A **discount store** is a retailer that competes on the basis of low prices, high turnover, and high volume. Discounters can be classified into four major categories: full-line discount stores, discount specialty stores, warehouse clubs, and off-price discount retailers.

ON LINE

Shoppers Drug Mart

Do you think drugstore websites add value for the consumer? What services on Shoppers Drug Mart's site would you be most likely to use? Would Internet selling be a factor in your choice of a pharmacy? The next time you need to go to the drugstore, try ordering over the Internet and compare the ease and value of buying on-line to a trip around the corner.

http://www.shoppersdrugmart.ca

full-line discount store
A retailer that offers consumers very limited service and carries a broad assortment of well-known, nationally branded "hard goods."

mass merchandising
A retailing strategy using moderate to low prices on large quantities of merchandise and lower service to stimulate high turnover of products.

Full-Line Discount Stores

Compared to traditional department stores, **full-line discount stores** offer consumers very limited service and carry a much broader assortment of well-known, nationally branded "hard goods," including housewares, toys, automotive parts, hardware, sporting goods, and garden items, as well as clothing, bedding, and linens. Some even carry limited nonperishable food items, such as soft drinks, canned goods, and potato chips. As with department stores, national chains dominate the discounters. Full-line discounters are often called mass merchandisers. **Mass merchandising** is the retailing strategy whereby retailers use moderate to low prices on large quantities of merchandise and lower service to stimulate high turnover of products.

U.S.-based Wal-Mart is the largest full-line discount organization in terms of sales. With over 4,000 stores, including 213 in Canada, Wal-Mart has expanded rapidly by locating on the outskirts of small towns and absorbing business for miles around. Much of Wal-Mart's success has been attributed to its merchandising foresight, cost consciousness, efficient communication and distribution systems, and involved, motivated employees. Wal-Mart is credited with pioneering the retail strategy of "everyday low pricing," a strategy now widely copied by retailers the world over. Besides expanding throughout the United States and Puerto Rico, Wal-Mart has expanded globally into Mexico, Canada, Brazil, Argentina, China, Germany, Korea, and the United Kingdom.[16] Wal-Mart has also become a formidable retailing giant in on-line shopping, concentrating on toys and electronics. Wal-Mart is expected to introduce millions of customers to on-line shopping through in-store kiosks linking to the site that have the ability to handle returns and exchanges from Internet sales.[17]

In an attempt to compete against Wal-Mart's expansion into Canada, Zellers has been aggressively positioning its chain of over 330 stores as the Canadian full-line discounter. Owned and operated by the Hudson's Bay Company, Zellers has developed some proprietary labels and has the sole distribution rights for a number of other product labels, including Levi's Orange Tab and Mossimo. Zellers has also taken on a number of celebrity labels, including Gloria Vanderbilt's "wear-to-work," and Delta Burke's line of clothing for plus-sized women.[18]

hypermarket
A retail store that combines a supermarket and full-line discount store in a space ranging from 200,000 to 300,000 square feet.

A hybrid of the full-line discounter is the hypermarket, a concept adapted from the Europeans. The flashy **hypermarket** format combines a supermarket with a full-line discount store in a space ranging from 200,000 to 300,000 square feet. Although they have enjoyed widespread success in Europe, where consumers have fewer retailing choices, hypermarkets have been much less successful in both Canada and the United States. Most Europeans still need to visit several small stores just for their food needs, which makes hypermarkets a good alternative. Canadians, on the other hand, can easily pick among a host of stores that offer large selections of merchandise. According to retailing executives and analysts, North American customers have found hypermarkets to be too big. For example, in the United States, Wal-Mart's Hypermart USA and Kmart's American Fare hypermarket never got beyond the experimental stage.

supercentre
A retail store that combines groceries and general merchandise goods with a wide range of services.

Similar to a hypermarket, but only half the size, is the **supercentre**, which combines groceries and general merchandise with a wide range of services including pharmacy, dry-cleaning, portrait studios, photofinishing, hair salons, optical shops, and restaurants—all in one location. For supercentre operators like Wal-Mart, food is a customer magnet that sharply increases the store's overall volume, while taking customers away from traditional supermarkets. Though it has yet to do so in Canada, Wal-Mart does operate over 900 supercentres and plans to keep opening them at a rate of more than 150 a year for the near future. Loblaws operates supercentres across Canada under names such as The Real Canadian Superstore and Atlantic Superstore. Over and above their full line of President's Choice convenience products, the Loblaws superstores provide photolabs, dry-cleaners, garden centres, and various other value-added services.[19]

Supercentres are threatening to push Europe's traditional small and medium-sized food stores into extinction. Old-fashioned corner stores and family businesses are giving way to larger chains that offer food, drugs, services, and general merchandise all in one place. Many European countries are passing legislation to make it more difficult for supercentres to open. In France, for example, laws have been passed that ban authorizations for new supercentres over 1,000 square metres. Belgium and Portugal have passed similar bans. In Britain and the Netherlands, areas outside towns and cities are off limits to superstores. By imposing planning and building restrictions for large stores, these countries are trying to accommodate environmental concerns, movements to revive city centres, and the worries of small shopkeepers.

An increasingly popular variation of off-price retailing at full-line discount stores is *extreme-value retailing,* the most notable examples being the Great Canadian Dollar Store and Buck or Two. Extreme-value retailers have grown in popularity as major discounters continue to shift toward the supercentre format, broadening their customer base and increasing their offerings of higher-priced goods aimed at higher-income consumers. This situation has created an opening for extreme-value retailers to entice shoppers from the low-income segment. Low- and fixed-income customers are drawn to extreme-value retailers, whose stores are located within their communities. Extreme-value retailers also build smaller stores (a typical store is about the size of one department in a Loblaws superstore) with a narrower selection of merchandise that emphasizes day-to-day necessities. Rock-bottom prices are also key to their success. With the average transaction under $10, extreme-value retailers have found low price to be far more critical to building traffic and loyalty than it is for any other retailing format.[20]

Specialty Discount Stores

Another discount niche is the single-line **specialty discount stores**—for example, stores selling sporting goods, electronics, auto parts, office supplies, and toys. These stores offer a nearly complete selection of single-line merchandise and use self-service, discount prices, high volume, and high turnover to their advantage. Specialty discount stores are often termed **category killers** because they so heavily dominate their narrow merchandise segment. Examples include Toys "R" Us in toys, Future Shop and Best Buy in electronics, Staples and Office Depot in office supplies, RONA and Home Depot in home improvement supplies, IKEA in home furnishings, and Bed Bath & Beyond in kitchen and bath accessories.

specialty discount store
A retail store that offers a nearly complete selection of single-line merchandise and uses self-service, discount prices, high volume, and high turnover.

category killers
Specialty discount stores that heavily dominate their narrow merchandise segment.

Toys "R" Us was the first category killer, offering a giant selection of toys—usually over 15,000 different items per store—at prices usually 10 to 15 percent less than competitors'. When Toys "R" Us came on the retail scene, department stores were generally limiting their toy assortments to the Christmas season. Toys "R" Us offered a broad assortment of inventory all year long. Additionally, the playing field was scattered with many small toy chains or mom-and-pop stores. With its bright warehouse-style stores, Toys "R" Us gobbled up market share; as a result, many small toy stores failed and department stores eliminated their toy departments. The Toys "R" Us chain—currently an $11.3 billion company with more than 1,500 stores worldwide—now commands about one-quarter of the U.S. retail toy business. Toys "R" Us first went international in 1984—initially in Canada, then in Europe, Hong Kong, and Singapore. Since then, the company has opened over 492 stores in more than two dozen foreign countries, the most recent being Japan. Toys "R" Us has also expanded its category-killer retailing concept to include over 200 Kids "R" Us children's clothing stores and 148 Babies "R" Us product stores. In addition, the company's website garnered more than $180 million in sales last year thanks in part to an alliance with Amazon.com. The company plans to build on its momentum by enhancing its websites for Babies "R" Us and Imaginarium.com.[21]

Other specialty segments have followed the lead of Toys "R" Us, hoping to build similar retailing empires in highly fragmented mom-and-pop markets. For instance, the home improvement industry was once dominated by professional builders and small hardware stores that offered basic staple products. Similarly, prior to the creation of pet supplies chains like Petcetera of Nanaimo, B.C., Pet Valu, and PetsMart, the pet industry was dominated by thousands of independent neighbourhood pet stores. Another industry that was very fragmented was the office products industry. As more people began to work from home, replacing their typewriters with personal computers and purchasing fax machines, the local stationery store, with its limited selection of paper and writing materials, quickly became obsolete. The industry is now dominated by Office Depot, Staples, and OfficeMax, each stocking almost 7,000 different types of products. Category-dominant retailers like these serve their customers by offering a large selection of merchandise, stores that make shopping easy, and low prices every day, which eliminates the need for time-consuming comparison shopping.

Warehouse Membership Clubs

warehouse membership clubs
A limited-service merchant wholesaler that sells a limited selection of brand-name appliances, household items, and groceries on a cash-and-carry basis to members, usually small businesses and groups.

Warehouse membership clubs sell a limited selection of brand-name appliances, household items, and groceries. These are usually sold in bulk from warehouse outlets on a cash-and-carry basis to members only. Individual members of warehouse clubs are charged low or no membership fees. Currently, Costco dominates the Canadian market in this category, but Wal-Mart has plans to enter the Canadian market with its own retailing version known as Sam's Club.

Warehouse clubs have had a major impact on supermarkets. With 90,000 square feet or more, warehouse clubs offer 60 to 70 percent general merchandise and health- and beauty-care products, with grocery-related items making up the difference. Warehouse club members tend to be more educated and more affluent and to have larger households than regular supermarket shoppers. These core customers use warehouse clubs to stock up on staples; then they go to specialty outlets or food stores for perishables.

In the U.S., fierce competition has occurred between Costco and Sam's Club in the warehouse club industry. Common practices include price slashing, selling below cost, locating outlets to compete directly with each other, and sometimes hiring away rivals' employees to get an edge in local markets. In one recent battle, Sam's Club has been targeting Costco's more affluent clientele. Costco, with annual revenues more than twice those of Sam's Club, dedicates approximately 25 percent of its inventory to high-end products like TaylorMade golf clubs and Coach handbags to attract wealthier customers who tend to spend more per visit. In an effort to beat Costco at its own game, Sam's Club not only has expanded its selection of fresh food, wine, and branded products, but also has begun holding promotional diamond and fine jewellery sales to draw customers. These "battles" are likely to be repeated in Canada as Sam's Club enters the market here.[22]

Off-Price Retailers

off-price retailer
A retailer that sells at prices 25 percent or more below traditional department store prices because it pays cash for its stock and usually doesn't ask for return privileges.

An **off-price retailer** sells at prices 25 percent or more below traditional department store prices because it pays cash for its stock and usually doesn't ask for return privileges. Off-price retailers buy manufacturers' overruns at cost or even less. They also absorb goods from bankrupt stores, irregular merchandise, and unsold end-of-season output. Nevertheless, much off-price retailer merchandise is first-quality, current goods. Because buyers for off-price retailers purchase only what is available or what they can get a good deal on, merchandise styles and brands often change monthly. Today there are dozens of off-price retailers, one of the best known being Winners.

factory outlet
An off-price retailer that is owned and operated by a manufacturer.

Factory outlets are an interesting variation on the off-price concept. A **factory outlet** is an off-price retailer that is owned and operated by a manufacturer. Thus, it carries one line of merchandise—its own. Each season, from 5 to 10 percent of a manufacturer's output does not sell through regular distribution channels because it consists of closeouts (merchandise being discontinued), factory seconds, and cancelled orders. With factory outlets, manufacturers can regulate where their surplus is sold, and they can realize higher profit margins than they would by disposing of the goods through independent wholesalers and retailers. Factory outlet malls typically locate in out-of-the-way rural areas or near vacation destinations. Most are situated at least 50 kilometres from urban or suburban shopping areas so that manufacturers don't alienate their department store accounts by selling the same goods virtually next door at a discount.

Several manufacturers reaping the benefits of outlet mall popularity include Roots, Danier Leather, Liz Claiborne, and Nike (apparel); Cambridge (towels); Oneida (silversmiths); and Dansk (kitchenwares). Sears has opened a series of outlet centres to make final attempts to move merchandise that failed to sell in the department stores. The

Windsor Crossing Premium Outlets located near Canada's busiest border crossing in Windsor, Ontario, boasts over 40 stores, including Adidas, Danier Leather, Hugo Boss, Kodiak, La Senza, Reitmans, Liz Claiborne, Nike, and Tommy Hilfiger.

As outlet malls have gained in popularity, however, they are beginning to act less and less like traditional outlets, in which manufacturers sold surplus or damaged goods. For instance, some manufacturers such as The Gap, Brooks Brothers, Ann Taylor, and Donna Karan now make lower-quality lines specifically for their outlet stores. Outlet store centres are also becoming less sensitive toward department stores that carry their brands at full retail price and are choosing to compete with regional malls by adding high-end amenities and entertainment to draw customers. [23]

Restaurants

Restaurants straddle the line between retailing establishments and service establishments. Restaurants do sell tangible products—food and drink—but they also provide a valuable service for consumers in the form of food preparation and food service. Most restaurants could even fall into the definition of a specialty retailer, given that most concentrate their menu offerings on a distinctive type of cuisine—for example, TacoTime Mexican food, Tim Hortons doughnuts, Swiss Chalet chicken, and Pizza Hut pizza.

As a retailing institution, restaurants must deal with many of the same issues as a more traditional retailer, such as personnel, distribution, inventory management, promotion, pricing, and location. Restaurants and food-service retailers run the spectrum from those offering limited service and inexpensive food, such as fast-food chains or the local snack bar or coffeehouse, to those that offer sit-down service and moderate to high prices, such as the Keg Steakhouse and Bar chain or a local trendy Italian bistro.

Eating out is an important part of Canadians' daily activities and is growing in popularity. According to Statistics Canada, the number of eating establishments increased from 16.5 per 10,000 Canadians in 1989 to 20.7 per 10,000 Canadians in 1998. The food service industry employs just over 1 million Canadians and has annual sales of about $43 billion annually. This means that Canadians spend an average of $27 per person on commercially prepared meals each week. As might be expected, lower-income families represent 12 percent of the population but account for only 8 percent of the restaurant market, whereas upper-income Canadians represent 25 percent of the population and account for 34 percent of the restaurant market. The trend toward eating out has been fuelled by the increase in working mothers and dual-income families, who have more money to eat out and less time to prepare meals at home. Money spent on food away from home represents about 30 percent of household food budgets, and this percentage is expected to grow.[24]

The restaurant industry is one of the most entrepreneurial of businesses and one of the most competitive. Because barriers to entering the restaurant industry are low, the opportunity appeals to many people. The risks, however, are great. About 50 percent of all new restaurants fail within the first year of operation. Restaurants face competition not only from other restaurants but also from the consumer, who can easily choose to cook at home. Competition has fostered innovation in the restaurant industry, such as Pizza Hut's introduction of The Edge pizza and the ever-changing menus at fast-food restaurants. Seeking out and targeting underserved distribution niches is another way restaurants are competing with one another to reach consumers. Fast-food operators are increasingly looking to provide service at locations such as hospitals, airports, schools, and highway rest stops. Companies like Subway, Tim Hortons, and Church's Chicken also are partnering with branded service stations to offer customers one-stop shopping. These partnerships save money on leases, lure more customers, and foster innovation.

More restaurants are now competing directly with supermarkets by offering takeout and delivery. This is an effort to capture more of the home meal replacement market. Swiss Chalet Restaurants have offered both a full-restaurant dining experience and fast and convenient take-out service for years. Similarly, Chinese food restaurants have long thrived on offering the combination of eat-in, take-out, and delivery. In the United States, Eatzi's Market & Bakery is trying a new approach. Eatzi's is a cross between a gourmet grocery store and an upscale delicatessen; chefs behind counters cook, bake, and prepare meals. Eatzi's now has markets in Dallas, Houston, Atlanta, and Rockville, Maryland, where its chefs prepare over 100 ready-to-go entrees, 75 cheeses, 50 breads, and 125 desserts, and even fresh sushi. Consumers can even purchase wine, flowers, and cigars to complement their prepared meal.[25]

>> NONSTORE RETAILING

nonstore retailing
Shopping without visiting a store.

The retailing methods discussed so far have been in-store methods—in other words, customers must physically shop at stores. In contrast, **nonstore retailing** is shopping without visiting a store. Because consumers demand convenience, nonstore retailing is currently growing faster than in-store retailing. The major forms of nonstore retailing are automatic vending, direct retailing, direct marketing, and electronic retailing.

Automatic Vending

automatic vending
The use of machines to offer goods for sale.

A low-profile yet important form of retailing is **automatic vending**, the use of machines to offer goods for sale—for example, the cola, candy, or snack vending machines found in college and university cafeterias and office buildings. In Canada, vending machine and coffee retailers produce annual sales of about $700 million, with the majority of sales coming from food and beverages. Vending machine operators typically have gross margins in the 50 percent range; recently, however, high operating costs have made this form of retailing a breakeven operation in Canada. Margins are high, but due to the convenience, consumers are willing to pay higher prices for products from a vending machine than for the same products in traditional retail settings.[26]

Retailers are constantly seeking new opportunities to sell via vending. For example, in an attempt to expand its distribution beyond supermarkets, convenience stores, and delicatessens, Snapple has developed a glass-front vending machine capable of offering 54 different flavours simultaneously. Many vending machines today also sell nontraditional kinds of merchandise, such as videos, toys, stickers, and sports cards. Vending machines in college and university libraries sell computer media, pens and highlighters, and other office-type supplies. Tourists can purchase film and disposable cameras from vending machines in many popular destinations. And Joe Boxer underwear can be purchased with a credit card from vending machines in selected department stores.

direct retailing
The selling of products by representatives who work door-to-door, office-to-office, or at home parties.

Of course, vending machines are also an important tool in the ongoing cola wars between Coca-Cola and Pepsi. Both companies are constantly looking for new ways to improve vending machine sales. For example, Pepsi recently introduced new vending machines that allow customers to pay with a credit card for a soft drink. Coca-Cola is working on a new vending machine for workplaces. By using radio frequency identification to bill customers directly for their purchases, the machines would eventually allow Coca-Cola to offer loyalty awards to its vending machine customers.[27]

AP/WIDE WORLD PHOTOS

Automatic vending is being used to sell everything from hot French fries to prescription medication. In Australia, you can even order a Coke from a vending machine using your mobile phone.

Direct Retailing

In **direct retailing,** representatives sell products door-to-door, office-to-office, or at home sales parties. Companies like Avon, Mary Kay, Tupperware, Discovery Toys, and the Pampered Chef depend on these techniques. Even personal computers are now being sold this way.

Most direct retailers seem to favour party plans these days in lieu of door-to-door canvassing. Party plans call for one person, the host, to gather as many prospective buyers as possible. The parties are generally part social gathering, part shopping, and part entertainment. For instance, at a Pampered Chef kitchen show, the party starts with a cooking demonstration that is designed to showcase many of the products offered for sale. Following the demonstration, the guests are treated to food and refreshments while they visit with one another and make their purchases.[28] Similarly, when young mothers shop for their children at house parties held by Discovery Toys, the chance to meet and talk with other young mothers is as much a part of the agenda as the purchases.

ON LINE

Avon

What advantages do you think the Avon site has over a visit from an Avon representative? Can you get the same amount of product information from each? Does Avon offer any products that you would prefer to order from a representative?

http://www.avon.com

The sales of direct retailers have suffered as women have entered the workforce. Working women are not home during the day and have little time to attend selling parties. Although most direct sellers like Avon and Tupperware still advocate the party plan method, the realities of the marketplace have forced them to be more creative in reaching their target customers. Direct sales representatives now hold parties in offices, parks, and even parking lots. Others hold informal gatherings where shoppers can drop in at their convenience or offer self-improvement classes. Many direct retailers are also turning to direct mail, telephone, or more traditional retailing venues to find new channels to their customers and increase sales. Avon, for instance, has begun opening cosmetic kiosks, called Avon Beauty Centres, in malls and strip centres. Direct retailers are also experimenting with the Internet to reach more buyers and increase sales. Amway recently launched an entirely new on-line spin-off, called Quixtar.com. Customers access the site using referral numbers unique to each of the Amway reps; this process ensures that the reps earn commissions. Avon, Tupperware, and Mary Kay have followed Amway's lead by setting up Internet retail sites. At Avon's site, individual reps have created home pages that link from Avon's home page so that the sale will still go through them.[29]

In response to the decline in Canadian and U.S. sales growth, many direct retailers are exploring opportunities in other countries. For example, Mary Kay, Avon, and Amway have started successful operations in China by adapting their business models to China's laws. Mary Kay agents in China do not purchase and resell the products but are paid a sales commission instead. The company also changed its slogan from "God First, Family Second, Career Third," to "Faith First, Family Second, Career Third."[30]

Direct Marketing

Direct marketing, sometimes called **direct-response marketing,** refers to the techniques used to get consumers to make a purchase from their home, office, or other nonretail setting. Those techniques include direct mail, catalogue and mail order, telemarketing, and electronic retailing. Shoppers using these methods are less bound by traditional shopping situations. Time-strapped consumers and those who live in rural or suburban areas are most likely to be direct-response shoppers because they value the convenience and flexibility that direct marketing provides.

direct marketing (direct-response marketing)
Techniques used to get consumers to make a purchase from their home, office, or other nonretail setting.

Many retailers employ a direct selling business model as part of a multichannel distribution approach involving electronic retailing, catalogue retailing, and bricks-and-mortar locations. For example, clothing retailer Justwhiteshirts.com recently opened a retail store in Toronto to support its catalogue and e-tailing efforts. This is the opposite of the usual trend of bricks-and-mortar retailers who offer catalogues and who have begun establishing "e-tailing" sites. The multichannel approach has changed the way marketers employ direct marketing techniques. One recent study found that marketers are planning to shift their marketing budgets away from the established direct marketing approaches of catalogue selling (−13 percent), direct mail (−7 percent), and telemarketing (−7 percent) in favour of electronic retailing appoaches such as the following: direct response television (+18 percent), e-mail (+17 percent), and on-line marketing (+9 percent).[31]

Direct Mail

Direct mail can be the most efficient or the least efficient retailing method, depending on the quality of the mailing list and the effectiveness of the mailing piece. According to estimates based on data from the Canadian Marketing Association, direct mail generated $16 billion in revenue in 2001.[32] By using direct mail, marketers can precisely target their customers according to demographics, geographics, and even psychographics. Good mailing lists come from an internal database or are available from list brokers for about $35 to $150 per 1,000 names. For example, a Halifax-based pharmaceutical salesperson may buy a list of all the physicians in the area. The pharmaceutical representative may then design a direct-mail piece explaining the benefits of some of the products the representative sells and send the piece to each physician. Today, direct mailers are even using videos in place of letters and brochures to deliver their sales message to consumers.

Direct mailers are becoming more sophisticated in targeting the "right" customers. Using statistical methods to analyze census data, lifestyle and financial information, and past-purchase and credit history, direct mailers can pick out those most likely to buy their products. For example, a direct marketer like Dell Computer might use this technique to target 500,000 people with the right spending patterns, demographics, and preferences. Without it, Dell could easily mail millions of solicitations annually. Some solicitations may be targeted to only 10,000 of the best prospects, saving the company millions in postage while still preserving sales.

Catalogues and Mail Order

Canadian consumers spend over $2.2 billion every year on catalogue shopping and they can buy just about anything, from the mundane, like books, music, and polo shirts, to the outlandish, such as the $5-million diamond-and-ruby-studded bra available through the Victoria's Secret catalogue. Although women make up the bulk of catalogue shoppers, the percentage of male catalogue shoppers has recently soared. As changing demographics have shifted more of the shopping responsibility to men, they are viewing shopping via catalogue, mail order, and the Internet as more sensible than a trip to the mall.

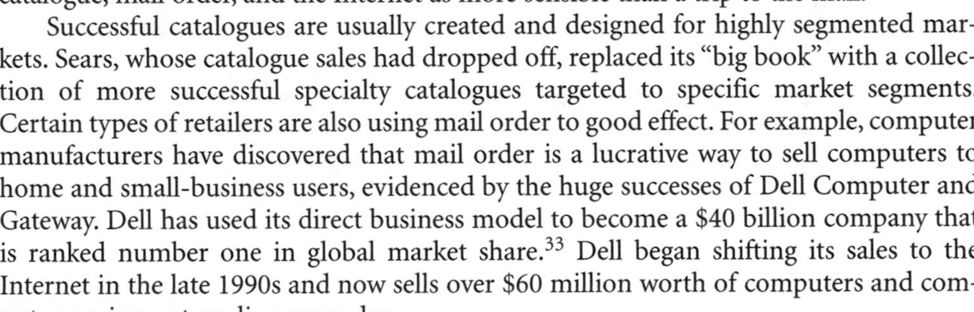

Successful catalogues are usually created and designed for highly segmented markets. Sears, whose catalogue sales had dropped off, replaced its "big book" with a collection of more successful specialty catalogues targeted to specific market segments. Certain types of retailers are also using mail order to good effect. For example, computer manufacturers have discovered that mail order is a lucrative way to sell computers to home and small-business users, evidenced by the huge successes of Dell Computer and Gateway. Dell has used its direct business model to become a $40 billion company that is ranked number one in global market share.[33] Dell began shifting its sales to the Internet in the late 1990s and now sells over $60 million worth of computers and computer equipment on-line every day.

Improved customer service and quick delivery policies have boosted consumer confidence in ordering from home. L.L. Bean and Lands' End are two catalogue companies known for their excellent customer service. Shoppers may order 24 hours a day and return any merchandise for any reason for a full refund. Successful Canadian mail-order catalogues—including IKEA, Mountain Equipment Co-op, and Regal Greetings and Gifts—target hardworking, home-oriented baby boomers who don't have time to visit or would rather not visit a retail store. To remain competitive and save time for customers, catalogue companies are building computer databases containing customer information so that people do not have to repeatedly give their addresses, credit card information, and so on. They also are working with overnight shippers such as UPS and FedEx to speed up deliveries. Indeed, some products can be ordered as late at 12:30 A.M. and still arrive the same day by 10:30 A.M.

Telemarketing

telemarketing
The use of the telephone to sell directly to consumers.

Telemarketing is the use of the telephone to sell directly to consumers. It consists of outbound sales calls, usually unsolicited, and inbound calls—that is, orders through toll-free 800 numbers or fee-based 900 numbers. According to the Canadian Marketing

Association, in 2001 Canadian telemarketing operations employed 300,000 people and produced $17 billion in sales.

Outbound telemarketing is an attractive direct-marketing technique because of rising postage rates and decreasing long-distance phone rates. Skyrocketing field sales costs have also put pressure on marketing managers to use outbound telemarketing. Searching for ways to keep costs under control, marketing managers are discovering how to pinpoint prospects quickly, zero in on serious buyers, and keep in close touch with regular customers. Meanwhile, they are reserving expensive, time-consuming, in-person calls for closing sales. Outbound telemarketing is an industry that is facing decline. Consumers have call display features and answering machines to screen "unwanted calls." In addition, the large number of outbound telemarketing calls has led the CRTC (Canadian Radio-television and Telecommunications Commission) to establish regulations for telemarketing: telemarketers must maintain "do not call/fax lists" and respect these lists; telemarketers are restricted to fax times between 9:00 A.M. and 9:30 P.M. during weekdays and 10:00 A.M. to 6:00 P.M. on weekends (there are no time restrictions on live calls); sequential dialling is not allowed; automatic dialling and announcing devices (ADADs) are not allowed for the purpose of solicitation; random dialling and calls to non-published numbers are not allowed; telemarketers must identify the sponsoring organization they represent and must provide contact information to callers upon request.[34]

ON LINE 

The CRTC (Canadian Radio-television and Telecommunications Commission) regulates telemarketing in Canada. Recall some of your experiences with telemarketers. Were they favourable or unfavourable? Write down a number of rules you believe telemarketers are subject to. Write down some of the rules you think they should be subject to. Now go to the CRTC website and review the current telemarketing rules. Evaluate your knowledge of Canadian telemarketing regulation.

http://www.crtc.gc.ca

In compliance with the CRTC regulations, the Canadian Marketing Association has set up a "do not contact" registry that is shared by all members. However, many telemarketers are not CMA members, so consumers who have contacted the CMA may still receive telemarketing solicitations. In these cases, consumers have to contact individual firms to be removed from some lists. Some in the industry insist that these lists help them by eliminating nonbuyers; however, this trend could have a long-term effect on telemarketing sales.

Inbound telemarketing programs, which use 800 and 900 numbers, are mainly used to take orders, generate leads, and provide customer service. Inbound 800 telemarketing has successfully supplemented direct-response TV, radio, and print advertising for more than 25 years. The more recently introduced 900 numbers, which customers pay to call, are gaining popularity as a cost-effective way for companies to target customers. One of the major benefits of 900 numbers is that they allow marketers to generate qualified responses. Although the charge may reduce the total volume of calls, the calls that do come are from customers who have a true interest in the product.

Electronic Retailing

Electronic retailing includes the 24-hour, shop-at-home television networks and on-line retailing.

Shop-at-Home Networks

The shop-at-home television networks are specialized forms of direct-response marketing. These shows display merchandise, with the retail price, to home viewers. Viewers can phone in their orders directly on a toll-free line and shop with a credit card. The shop-at-home industry has quickly grown into a billion-dollar business with a loyal customer following. Shop-at-home networks have the capability of reaching nearly every home that has a television set.

Most TV shopping networks have converged their services with the Internet to provide a comprehensive and interactive shopping experience for consumers. The Shopping Channel, based in Toronto, has taken this convergence even further by combining its on-air promotional solicitations with its interactive e-commerce website, http://www.theshoppingchannel.com, and with a catalogue and a retail store located in Toronto. This means that customers can purchase items they have seen on television or in the catalogue through The Shopping Channel's website or at the Toronto store location. Aside from merchandise, the website also ties in with the television broadcasts by providing daily broadcast schedules. The actual shows can even be viewed through streaming video players.

Home shopping networks attract a broad audience through diverse programming and product offerings and are now adding new products to appeal to more affluent audiences. For instance, on The Shopping Channel, cooking programs attract both men and women, fashion programs attract mostly women, and electronics and coin shows attract primarily men. Since it began broadcasting, the channel has sold everything from Sharp electronics to space savers to gems and coins.[35]

On-line Retailing

on-line retailing
A type of shopping available to consumers with personal computers and access to the Internet.

For years, shopping at home meant looking through catalogues and then placing an order over the telephone. For many people today, however, it now means turning on a computer, surfing retail websites, and selecting and ordering products on-line with the click of a mouse. **On-line retailing,** or *e-tailing,* is a type of shopping available to consumers with personal computers and access to the Internet. According to the Media Digest prepared by the Canadian Media Directors' Council, 75 percent of all Canadians are on-line and 63 percent of them access it from home. Canadians enjoy the highest penetration of broadband Internet usage, with 54 percent of Canadians using broadband Internet connections, and this percentage is expected to rise.[36]

On-line retailing has exploded in the past several years; consumers have found this type of shopping convenient and often less costly. Consumers can shop without leaving home, choose from a wide selection of merchants, use shopping comparison services to search the Web for the best price, and then have the items delivered to their doorsteps. As a result, on-line shopping continues to grow at a rapid pace. In fact, according to Statistics Canada, in 2002, Canadian e-retailers' sales were $1.7 billion, which represented a 16-percent increase over 2001.[37] On-line retailing is also increasing in popularity outside of Canada. Read more about e-tailing worldwide in the "Global Perspectives" box.

Original Web-based retailers, like Amazon.com and CDNow, pioneered on-line retailing, selling merchandise more cheaply and conveniently than their bricks-and-mortar competition. Both companies have continued to grow and prosper by offering outstanding customer service. Today, CDNow offers customers more than 500,000 CDs, videos, DVDs, and digital music downloads with 48-hour delivery.[38] Similarly, Amazon.com, which opened for business in 1995 with a mission to transform book buying into the fastest, easiest, and most enjoyable shopping experience possible, has grown into a $3.12 billion company selling a combination of new and used items ranging from books and electronics to toys and hardware. Amazon has customers in more than 220 countries around the world.[39]

Most traditional retailers have jumped on the Internet bandwagon, allowing shoppers to purchase the same merchandise found in their stores from their website. On-line retailing also fits well with traditional catalogue companies, such as the former "Winnipeg Fur Exchange," now known as "Winnipeg Outfitters." The firm started as a "fur brokerage" business in 1970, but the development of a large, Winnipeg-based store along with a catalogue retailing operation in 1978 took the firm away from its basic business. The advent of e-tailing, combined with the issue of "animal rights" associated with furs, prompted the firm to change its name to "Winnipeg Outfitters" in order to overcome the negative image of the fur business; this change also fit its merchandise mix more appropriately.[40] In a drastic turnabout in its retail strategy, computer software retailer Egghead has recently closed all of its bricks-and-mortar stores,

ON LINE

Sears Canada

The Shopping Channel

Do you think that making the transition to successful e-tailing is harder for a retailer that began selling primarily through catalogues and bricks-and-mortar outlets (like Sears Canada) or one that began selling primarily through direct response television (like The Shopping Channel)? Check out the two websites and compare how they present their products, their site functionality, and the integration of all their retail venues.

http://www.sears.ca

http://www.theshoppingchannel.com

moved its entire business onto the Web, and added ".com" to the end of its name. Software purchased at the company's site, http://www.egghead.com, can be downloaded directly to the purchaser's computer.

As the popularity of on-line retailing grows, it is becoming critical that retailers be on-line and that their stores, websites, and catalogues be integrated. Customers expect to find the same brands, products, and prices whether they purchase on-line, on the phone, or in a store. Therefore, retailers are increasingly using in-store kiosks to help tie the channels together for greater customer service. Edmonton-based PharmaPlus Drug Mart is offering Internet-enabled touch-screen kiosks in a number of its stores. The kiosks are multifunctional in that they present television commercials, point-of-sale advertising, and contests, but also present information that allows customers to go on-line to access Web portals to get information and even shop. Kiosks are highly useful to pharmacy retailers because they occupy customers who are waiting for their prescriptions. Famous Players Theatres sells tickets through in-theatre kiosks, through its on-line website http://www.famousplayers.com, and of course through its in-theatre box offices. All three ticket venues are linked in order to manage the number of tickets being ordered for a particular showtime in relation to the seating capacity of the theatre. In addition, advanced ticket sales via the Internet enable managers of multi-screen venues to make adjustments to the number of screens and its scheduling for a particular show based on demand. The linking of information from the websites and kiosks enables Famous Players to conduct data mining; it also provides other management information.[41]

A relatively new phenomenon in on-line retailing is the success of auctions run by Internet companies like eBay.ca and Amazon.ca. With close to 2 million items for sale each day, ranging from antique clocks to car stereos, eBay leads the trend in cyberspace auctions. Internet auction services like eBay run the Web service and collect a token listing fee, plus a commission of 1 to 5 percent when a sale is completed. Recently, eBay

GLOBAL PERSPECTIVES

On-Line Retailing Growing Worldwide

Consumers around the world are embracing on-line retailing. In fact, in 2001 about 54 percent of Internet users worldwide used the Internet to gather information about products and services, and 27 percent purchased on-line. What's more, analysts predict that the number of on-line shoppers will double in the next few years.

According to a recent survey, the items most commonly purchased on-line are books, CDs, videos, and computer games. Books are the number one best-seller everywhere except Canada and Brazil, where music tops the list. British and French shoppers like to purchase food and beverages on-line, and flowers are popular purchases in Switzerland. Swiss and Spanish shoppers purchase more financial services on-line than customers in other foreign countries.

Almost 60 percent of on-line shoppers have purchased from an on-line retailer in another country. The main reason they do so is that the product is not available in their country, but finding a product at a lower price in another country also persuades some shoppers to go international.

So what should a retailer know about global on-line retailing? First, having a multichannel approach to retailing is important. Customers worldwide want the option of shopping on-line. Second, contrary to the belief that on-line shoppers are a unique audience, given Internet access, the same customers who shop in stores are buying on-line. Third, consumers expect the same product selection and customer service on-line that they receive in stores. And finally, customers will push retailers to make their website work the way they want it to work.

In addition, retailers interested in global on-line retailing can learn by studying the success of global on-line retailers like Amazon.com. Amazon.com is the most popular place to shop on-line in Canada, the United States, the United Kingdom, Italy, and Australia. In 2001, company sales in the United Kingdom, Germany, France, and Japan grew 81 percent, and more than 29 percent of total company sales were to international customers. The top reasons given for shopping at Amazon.com by customers everywhere are product selection, competitive prices, ease of use, product availability, and delivery speed.[42]

As Internet usage around the world increases, so will the number of on-line shoppers. How do you think that will affect traditional retailers? Will they learn to operate in the cyberworld, or will they try to compete against their on-line counterparts? Do you think the Internet will create a truly global retail marketplace?

announced a new joint venture with Sotheby's to offer fine art, rare coins, sports collectibles, jewellery, and antiques on-line. Each item carries a stamp of authenticity from Sotheby's or one of the 2,800 art and antiques dealers worldwide that have signed exclusive agreements with Sotheby's. The deal is a boost to eBay's fine arts and antiques division and will allow Sotheby's to continue on-line sales without the overhead expense of managing its own site.[43]

ON LINE 

Sylvan Learning Center

What do you need to do to become a Sylvan Learning franchiser? Visit the Web page to find out. Does anything surprise you?

http://www.sylvanlearning.com

>> FRANCHISING

franchiser
The originator of a trade name, product, methods of operation, and so on, that grants operating rights to another party to sell its product.

franchisee
An individual or business that is granted the right to sell another party's product.

A *franchise* is a continuing relationship in which a franchiser grants to a franchisee the business rights to operate or sell a product. The **franchiser** originates the trade name, product, methods of operation, and so on. The **franchisee,** in return, pays the franchiser for the right to use its name, product, or business methods. A franchise agreement between the two parties usually lasts 10 to 20 years, at which time the agreement can be renewed if both parties are agreeable.

To be granted the rights to a franchise, a franchisee usually pays an initial, one-time franchise fee. The amount of this fee depends solely on the individual franchiser, but it generally ranges from $5,000 to $150,000. In addition to this initial franchise fee, the franchisee is expected to pay weekly, biweekly, or monthly royalty fees, usually in the range of 3 to 7 percent of gross revenues. The franchisee may also be expected to pay advertising fees, which usually cover the cost of promotional materials and, if the franchise organization is large enough, regional or national advertising. A McDonald's franchise, for example, costs an initial $45,000 per store plus a monthly fee based on the restaurant's sales performance and base rent. In addition, a new McDonald's franchisee can expect startup costs for equipment and preopening expenses to range from $600,000 to $800,000. The size of the restaurant facility, area of the country, inventory, selection of kitchen equipment, signage, and style of decor and landscaping affect new restaurant costs. While the dollar amount will vary depending on the type of franchise, fees such as these are typical for all major Canadian franchisers, including Apple Auto Glass, Mmmarvelous Mmmuffins, Great Canadian Bagel, and Jani-King Canada.[44]

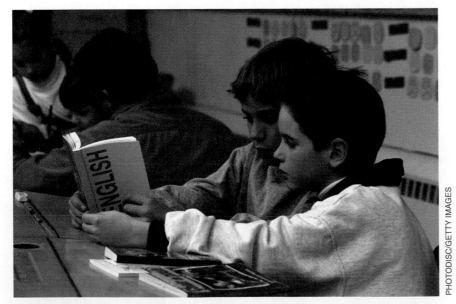

PHOTODISC/GETTY IMAGES

Franchising is most thought of with respect to restaurants, but some of the most successful franchises of late are not food related. Sylvan Learning Center involves an investment of between $110,000 and $250,000 to start up. To learn more about Sylvan, do the On Line activity at the top of this page.

Franchising is not new. General Motors has used this approach since 1898, and Rexall drugstores since 1901. Today, there are about 1,300 franchiser head offices in Canada operating 76,000 franchised establishments, which employ 1 million Canadians and produce sales of $90 billion or about 30 percent of all retail trade. Although franchised restaurants represent 26 percent of all franchise outlets and attract a lot of those dollars, hundreds of retail and service franchises, such as Beachcomber Hot Tubs, Canadian Home Inspection Services, and Sylvan Learning Center, also are thriving. The Canadian Franchise Association identifies 48 different franchise industries, and the Canadian Franchise Directory reports Canadian franchise growth to be over 20 percent since 1993. Industries expected to see real growth in franchising include home repair, business support services, automotive repairs, hair salons, children's services, and telecommunications.[45] Exhibit 12.3 lists some facts about some of the best-known Canadian franchisers.

Two basic forms of franchises are used today: product and trade name franchising and business format franchising. In *product and trade name franchising*, a dealer agrees to sell certain products provided by a manufacturer or a wholesaler. This approach has been used most widely in the auto and truck, soft drink bottling, tire, and gasoline service industries. For example, a local tire retailer may hold a franchise to sell Michelin tires. Likewise, the Coca-Cola bottler in a particular area is a product and trade name franchisee licensed to bottle and sell Coca-Cola's soft drinks.

Business format franchising is an ongoing business relationship between a franchiser and a franchisee. Typically, a franchiser "sells" a franchisee the rights to use the franchiser's format or approach to doing business. This form of franchising has expanded rapidly since the 1950s through retailing, restaurant, food-service, hotel and motel, printing, and real estate franchises. Fast-food restaurants like McDonald's, Wendy's, and Burger King use this kind of franchising, as do other companies such as Kumon Math & Reading Centres, Supercuts, and Valpak of Canada Ltd. To be eligible to be a Domino's Pizza franchisee, you must have worked in a Domino's pizza store for at least one year. The company believes that after working in an existing location, you will have a better understanding of the company and its values and standards. Then potential franchisees must participate in a series of career development, franchise orientation, presentation skills, and franchise development programs.[46]

Like other retailers, franchisers are seeking new growth abroad. U.S.-based franchisers have been particularly successful at international expansion and are actively looking for foreign franchisees to open new locations. KFC operates approximately 5,000 restaurants in the United States and another 6,000 in more than 80 countries around the world including Canada, Japan, Australia, China, Indonesia, and Saudi Arabia. An additional 1,000 overseas locations are planned for the near future. KFC's parent company attributes the franchise's success to its ability to adapt to local cultures

EXHIBIT 12.3

Well-Known Canadian Franchisers

FRANCHISER	TYPE OF BUSINESS	TOTAL UNITS	INITIAL INVESTMENT
Tim Hortons Oakville, Ontario	Coffee and doughnuts	Franchised units: 2,100 Company-owned units: 102	$178,000
Shoppers Drug Mart North York, Ontario	Pharmacy	Franchised units: 825 Company-owned units: 0	Nil
Mr. Sub Toronto, Ontario	Submarine sandwiches	Franchised units: 520 Company-owned units: 1	$50,000–$70,000
Canadian Tire Corporation Toronto, Ontario	Hardware retailing	Franchised units: 450 Company-owned units: 0	$140,000
Second Cup Coffee Ltd. Mississauga, Ontario	Coffee retailer	Franchised units: 400 Company-owned units: 0	$100,000–$140,000
Harvey's Restaurants Mississauga, Ontario	Fast food	Franchised units: 337 Company-owned units: 36	$550,000
M&M Meat Shops Kitchener, Ontario	Frozen food	Franchised units: 357 Company-owned units: 5	$300,000
Apple Auto Glass Concord, Ontario	Glass repair and replacement	Franchised units: 121 Company-owned units: 4	$70,000–$95,000
Mr. Transmission Richmond Hill, Ontario	Auto transmission repair	Franchised units: 85 Company-owned units: 0	$125,000–$150,000
Keg Restaurants Richmond, B.C.	Steakhouse	Franchised units: 33 Company-owned units: 56	$600,000–$1,400,000

SOURCE: Canadian Franchise Association, http://www.cfa.ca.

and tastes without losing control of quality and brand image.[47] The International Franchise Association now lists over 50 national franchise organizations in countries from Argentina to Zimbabwe.

Franchisers usually allow franchisees to alter their business format slightly in foreign markets. For example, some McDonald's franchisees in Germany sell beer, and in Japan they offer food items that appeal to Japanese tastes, such as steamed dumplings, curry with rice, and roast pork cutlet burgers with melted cheese. McDonald's franchisees in India serve mutton instead of beef because most Indians are Hindu, a religion whose followers believe cows are a sacred symbol of the source of life. The menu also features rice-based vegetable burgers made with peas, carrots, red pepper, beans, and Indian spices as well as vegetable McNuggets. But, in spite of menu differences, McDonald's foreign franchisees still maintain the company's standards of service and cleanliness.

3 List the major tasks involved in developing a retail marketing strategy

>> RETAIL MARKETING STRATEGY

Retailers must develop marketing strategies based on overall goals and strategic plans. Retailing goals might include more traffic, higher sales of a specific item, a more upscale image, or heightened public awareness of the retail operation. The strategies that retailers use to obtain their goals might include a sale, an updated decor, or a new advertisement. The key tasks in strategic retailing are defining and selecting a target market and developing the retailing mix to successfully meet the needs of the chosen target market.

Defining a Target Market

The first and foremost task in developing a retail strategy is to define the target market. This process begins with market segmentation, the topic of Chapter 6. Successful retailing has always been based on knowing the customer. Sometimes retailing chains founder when management loses sight of the customers the stores should be serving. For example, during the 1990s The Gap built a retail empire by offering updated, casual classics like white shirts and khaki pants that appealed to everyone from high school through middle age. But the company began losing customers in 1999 when it shifted toward trendier fashions with a limited appeal. Analysts blame the chain's problems on losing focus and touch with its customers.[48]

Target markets in retailing are often defined by demographics, geographics, and psychographics. For instance, Quebec-based Croteau has stores everywhere throughout its home province except for Montreal. The firm is focusing its marketing effort on "one target segment: moms with young kids and/or teenagers, within the regions where Croteau has stores." Croteau has studied the shopping habits of its customers and determined that for its offerings, family purchasing is important. It recognizes that Mom is the key purchaser and that children can be key influencers.[49]

Determining a target market is a prerequisite to creating the retailing mix. For example, in an approach to target suburban couples, Adults Only Video (AOV), Canada's largest adult video rental chain, has developed a concept store called "Magic Moments," the first North American mall-based adult store. Up to now, virtually all of AOV's 40 video stores across Canada have depended mainly on customers making planned purchases, have been located in lower-traffic plazas, have sold and rented "hard core" videos, and have focused on "sex" as their product offering. The first "Magic Moments" store opened in the Bramalea City Centre in Brampton, Ontario, in 2002 with a product mix that did not include "hard core" videos but instead featured "such items as lotions and literature, as well as a line of adult-related products, including instructional and educational videos, marital aids and gag gifts." The fundamental notion behind "Magic Moments," according to Randy Jorgenson, CEO of AOV, is to have a more accessible location in a high customer traffic area that can appeal to suburban couples by "selling romance instead of just sex."[50]

Choosing the Retailing Mix

Retailers combine the elements of the retailing mix to come up with a single retailing method to attract the target market. The **retailing mix** consists of six Ps: the four Ps of the marketing mix (product, place, promotion, and price) plus presentation and personnel (see Exhibit 12.4).

retailing mix
A combination of the six Ps—product, place, promotion, price, presentation, and personnel—to sell goods and services to the ultimate consumer.

The combination of the six Ps projects a store's image, which influences consumers' perceptions. Using these impressions of stores, shoppers position one store against another. A retail marketing manager must make sure that the store's positioning is compatible with the target customers' expectations. As discussed at the beginning of the chapter, retail stores can be positioned on three broad dimensions: service provided by store personnel, product assortment, and price. Management should use everything else—place, presentation, and promotion—to fine-tune the basic positioning of the store.

The Product Offering

The first element in the retailing mix is the **product offering,** also called the *product assortment* or *merchandise mix.* Retailers decide what to sell on the basis of what their target market wants to buy. They can base their decision on market research, past sales, fashion trends, customer requests, and other sources. A new technology, called *analytics,* uses complex mathematical models to help retailers make better product mix decisions. In Canada, The Bay department store uses this technology to analyze its Hbc Rewards customer database, which has 8.5 million members. An example of the power of analytics comes from David Strickland, senior VP of marketing at Zellers in Brampton, Ontario, who says, "When someone's buying kids' clothing at either The Bay or at Zellers, we now have the data to tell us that." Using the SKU (stock keeping unit) number within that data, "we actually know what size they're buying, which effectively tells us the sex and age of their kids."[51]

product offering
The mix of products offered to the consumer by the retailer; also called the *product assortment* or *merchandise mix.*

Developing a product offering is essentially a question of the width and depth of the product assortment. *Width* refers to the assortment of products offered; *depth* refers to the number of different brands offered within each assortment. Price, store design, displays, and service are important to consumers in determining where to shop, but the most critical factor is merchandise selection. This reasoning also holds true for on-line

EXHIBIT 12.4
The Retailing Mix

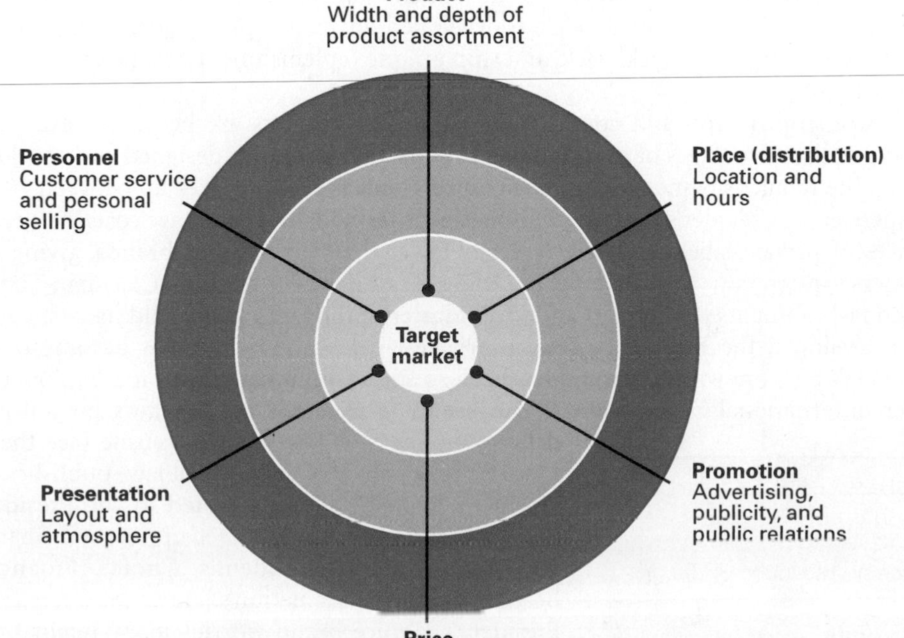

retailers. Amazon.com, for instance, has ambitious plans to build the world's biggest on-line department store so that shoppers can get whatever they want with one click of the Web browser. Like a traditional department store or mass merchandiser, Amazon.ca offers considerable width in its product assortment, with millions of different items, including books, music, toys, videos, tools and hardware, health and beauty aids, electronics, and software. Conversely, on-line specialty retailers, such as Bear St. Canada, Rugman.com, and EntertainMe.ca, focus on a single category of merchandise, hoping to attract loyal customers with a greater depth of products at lower prices and better customer service. Many on-line retailers purposely focus on single product line niches that could never garner enough foot traffic to support a traditional bricks-and-mortar store. For instance, Fridgedoor.com sells 1,500 different types of refrigerator magnets to collectors.[52]

After determining which products will satisfy target customers' desires, retailers must find sources of supply and evaluate the products. When the right products are found, the retail buyer negotiates a purchase contract. The buying function can either be performed in-house or be delegated to an outside firm. The goods must then be moved from the seller to the retailer, which means shipping, storing, and stocking the inventory. The trick is to manage the inventory by cutting prices to move slow goods and by keeping adequate supplies of hot-selling items in stock. As in all good systems, the final step is to evaluate the entire process to seek more efficient methods and eliminate problems and bottlenecks.

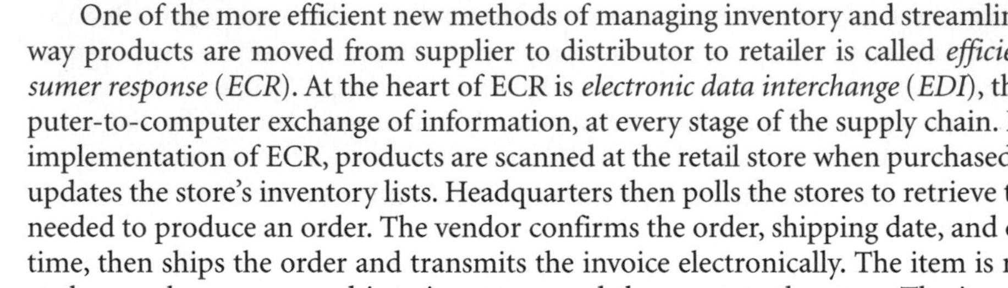

One of the more efficient new methods of managing inventory and streamlining the way products are moved from supplier to distributor to retailer is called *efficient consumer response* (*ECR*). At the heart of ECR is *electronic data interchange* (*EDI*), the computer-to-computer exchange of information, at every stage of the supply chain. In a full implementation of ECR, products are scanned at the retail store when purchased, which updates the store's inventory lists. Headquarters then polls the stores to retrieve the data needed to produce an order. The vendor confirms the order, shipping date, and delivery time, then ships the order and transmits the invoice electronically. The item is received at the warehouse, scanned into inventory, and then sent to the store. The invoice and receiving data are reconciled, after which payment via an electronic transfer of funds completes the process.

Many retailers are experimenting with or have successfully implemented ECR and EDI. Calendar Club, a mall-based kiosk retailer of calendars that operates in Canada, the U.S., England, New Zealand, and Australia, uses ECR and EDI to get the right products at its kiosks, some of which sell more than 1,000 calendars a day for the 120 days a year they are open. Calendar Club developed an ECR replenishment solution that allows the company to pick, pack, and ship unique replenishment orders for each kiosk every night.[53]

private-label brands
Brands that are designed and developed using the retailer's name.

As margins drop and competition intensifies, retailers are becoming ever more aware of the advantages of **private-label brands**, that is, brands designed and developed using the retailer's name. Because the cost of goods typically makes up between 70 and 85 percent of a retailer's expenses, eliminating intermediaries can shave costs. As a result, prices of private-label goods are typically lower than for national brands, giving customers greater value. Private-label branding is not new. For decades, Canadian Tire has been fashioning its Mastercraft and MotoMaster brands into household names. Loblaw has developed the President's Choice private-label brand, which has become one of Canada's best-known brands and has been so successful it has taken on a "national and even international brand status." The brand is plastered on Loblaw's own fleet of delivery trucks, and has its own website (see the On Line exercise on this page). Loblaw publishes the "Insider's Report," a flyer devoted to the President's Choice brand, and has even set up its own financial services, labelled "President's Choice Financial." Because Loblaw is the nation's largest food retailer, its President's Choice brand worries many major brand

ON LINE

Loblaws

How extensive is Loblaws' President's Choice private-label brand? Visit its website to find out.

http://www.presidentschoice.ca/en

marketers, including international giants such as Coca-Cola and PepsiCo. Loblaw was once just an extremely important customer for both Coca-Cola Canada and PepsiCo Canada. With the introduction of President's Choice Cola and President's Choice Diet Cola, Canada's largest food retailer has transformed itself into an equal competitor to both Coca-Cola and PepsiCo in the Canadian market. And although President's Choice will not be sending popular brands like Coke and Pepsi to the sidelines anytime soon, in the long run smaller second- and third-tier brands that don't bring consumers to the shelves may have a difficult time surviving.[54]

Promotion Strategy

Retail promotion strategy includes advertising, public relations and publicity, and sales promotion. The goal is to help position the store in consumers' minds. Retailers design intriguing ads, stage special events, and develop promotions aimed at their target markets. For example, today's grand openings are a carefully orchestrated blend of advertising, merchandising, goodwill, and glitter. All the elements of an opening—press coverage, special events, media advertising, and store displays—are carefully planned.

Retailers' advertising is carried out mostly at the local level, although major Canadian retailers like Zellers and Canadian Tire can advertise nationally. Local advertising by retailers usually provides specific information about their stores, such as location, merchandise, hours, prices, and special sales. In contrast, national retail advertising generally focuses on image. For example, Sears Canada used its "Softer Side of Sears" advertising campaign to help reposition the firm as a low-priced but fashion-conscious apparel retailer. An accompanying campaign featuring the slogan "Come See the Many Sides of Sears" was used to promote the retailer's nonapparel merchandise, such as tools, paint, and car parts.

Many retailers combine their advertising campaigns with those of brand-name manufacturers, a popular retail advertising practice known as cooperative advertising. Traditionally, marketers would pay retailers to feature their products in store mailers, or a marketer would develop a TV campaign for the product and simply tack on several retailers' names at the end. But more and more retailers are making use of cooperative advertising by integrating brand-name products into their campaigns. For example, ads linking Nike and Athletes World, a Canadian athletic clothing and footwear chain, let everyone know that the latter sells the former's latest styles. In turn, these ads expand the reach of Nike's advertising. Another common form of cooperative advertising involves promotion of exclusive products. For instance, the Martha Stewart product line was exclusive to Zellers when it first came to Canada, and the advertising campaign accomplished the dual role of promoting the products and attracting customers to the store. Now Sears Canada has acquired the distribution rights for the Martha Stewart line and will have to establish a new store relationship for this brand in the minds of Canadian customers. The linking of a store's image to a brand's image in promotion is something that both retailers and manufacturers have to consider when they seek retail distribution. See the accompanying Ethics in Marketing box about British retailer French Connection U.K.

Many retailers are reducing or even forgoing media advertising these days in favour of direct-mail or frequent-shopper programs. Direct-mail and catalogue programs are luring many retailers who hope the programs will prove to be a cost-effective means of increasing brand loyalty and spending by core customers. Each quarter, Greenhawk Harness and Equestrian mails a catalogue to the equestrian community across the country. Hardware outlets such as Canadian Tire and Home Hardware have also used direct mail, often around holidays, when people have time off to complete needed repairs. Restaurants and small retailers have successfully used frequent-diner or frequent-shopper programs for years. Now many retail chains, like The Gap, Victoria's Secret, and Eddie Bauer, are offering frequent-shopper programs with perks ranging from gift certificates to special "members only" sale prices. For example, customers with a Victoria's Secret Angel credit card are offered monthly specials on store merchandise, including items that generally are not put on sale to the public.

ETHICS IN MARKETING

Retailing a Controversial Brand

As discussed in the chapter, retailers often like to have their stores associated with new, well-known national brands to create customer loyalty and to develop new customer relationships. But what if your current customers actually turn out to be "repelled" by the new brands and even "organize" against you?

British retailer French Connection U.K. has developed a unique customer franchise in Europe for its fragrance products with a controversial brand name supported by edgy advertising that focuses on the firm's initials, F.C.U.K. It is clear that the usual "promise of benefit" of fragrance products is "attraction" of the opposite sex, but the symbolism of French Connection U.K.'s brand name carries the promise to its most "base" result. The acceptance of any brand name has a cultural bias, and the acceptance of F.C.U.K. in the United States encountered a strong negative reaction by consumer groups, who were aroused by an advertising campaign and responded to it by taking action against retailers who had adopted this "exclusive" brand.

French Connection U.K. developed an advertising campaign with two new fragrance brands labelled FCUK Him and FCUK Her. Print ads were placed in magazines such as *Cosmopolitan, Marie Claire, Maxim, Seventeen,* and *Teen People.* These ads featured sexually suggestive photos of a scantily clad couple and used the logo "Scent to Bed." Parental complaints were made to *Seventeen* and *Teen People*, and these magazines immediately dropped the ads. A spokesperson for French Connection U.K.'s distributor in the U.S. stated that she didn't realize the audience for these two magazines was so young.

A more serious problem for French Connection U.K. went beyond the response to its advertising efforts. Three lobby groups, Concerned Women for America, the Catholic Parents Online, and the American Family Association responded first to the advertising, but the American Family Association went further and pressured U.S.-based Federated Department Stores to remove F.C.U.K.'s merchandize from its chain of 400 stores, which includes the well-known Macy's and Bloomingdale's retail stores. In addition, Kaufman's and Marshall Field's stores are also reviewing their association with the brand. With the loss of the Federated chain and the risk of loss of distribution in two other major retailers, F.C.U.K. faces a tremendous loss of sales revenue and market position in the United States.

In Canada, the brand has not achieved the same notoriety, and F.C.U.K. has demonstrated social responsibility with its brand promotion as well with a Canadian campaign that involved the promotion of safe sex and a promise that 2 percent of all sales in Canada would be donated to the Canadian Foundation for Aids Research.[55]

What do you think F.C.U.K. should do? How can it maintain its current retail distribution? What kinds of "retailers" should the brand pursue to replace the loss of the Federated Department stores? How should it handle the negative publicity it has? Should it scrap the "name"?

The Proper Location

The retailing axiom "location, location, location" has long emphasized the importance of place to the retail mix. The location decision is important first because the retailer is making a large, semipermanent commitment of resources that can reduce its future flexibility. Second, the location will affect the store's future growth and profitability.

Site location begins by choosing a community. Important factors to consider are the area's economic growth potential, the amount of competition, and geography. For instance, retailers like Winners, Wal-Mart, and Toys "R" Us build stores in areas where the population is growing. Often these large retailers build stores in new communities that are still under development. On the other hand, while population growth is an important consideration for fast-food restaurants, most also look for an area with other fast-food restaurants because clusters draw customers for each restaurant. Finally, for many retailers geography remains the most important factor in choosing a community. While many retailers, including Starbucks, look for densely populated urban communities for their stores, the North West Company, the historic firm associated with Canada's fur trade, has located in small and remote northern Canadian communities stretching from British Columbia to Labrador.

After settling on a geographic region or community, retailers must choose a specific site. In addition to growth potential, the important factors are neighbourhood socioeconomic characteristics, traffic flows, land costs, zoning regulations, and public transportation. A particular site's visibility, parking, entrance and exit locations, and accessibility, and safety and security issues, are other variables contributing to site selection. Additionally, a retailer should consider how its store would fit into the surrounding environment. Retail decision makers probably would not want to locate a Great Canadian Dollar store next door to a Les Ailes de la Mode department store.

One final decision about location faces retailers: whether to have a freestanding unit or to become a tenant in a shopping centre or mall.

Freestanding Stores An isolated, freestanding location can be used by large retailers such as Wal-Mart, Shoppers Drug Mart, and Canadian Tire, and by firms that sell shopping goods like furniture and cars, because these are "destination" stores—that is, stores consumers seek out and then purposely plan to visit. An isolated store location may have the advantages of low site cost or rent and no nearby competitors. On the other hand, it may be hard to attract customers to a freestanding location, and there are no other retailers around with which to share costs.

Freestanding units are increasing in popularity as retailers strive to make their stores more convenient to access, more enticing to shop in, and more profitable. Freestanding sites are being developed at an increasing rate as more and more retailers are deciding not to locate in pedestrian malls. Perhaps the biggest reason for developing a freestanding site is greater visibility. Retailers often feel they get lost in huge centres and malls; freestanding units can help stores develop an identity with shoppers. The ability to grow at faster rates through freestanding buildings has also propelled the surge toward standalone units. Retailers like Leon's, IKEA, and Future Shop often choose to be freestanding in order to achieve their expansion objectives. An aggressive expansion plan may not allow time to wait for shopping centres to be built.

Shopping Centres The tremendous boom in shopping centres began after World War II, as the population started migrating to the suburbs. The first shopping centres were *strip centres,* typically located along a busy street. They usually included a supermarket, a variety store, and perhaps a few specialty stores. Essentially unplanned business districts, these strip centres remain popular.

Next, the small *community shopping centres* emerged, with one or two small department store branches, more specialty shops, one or two restaurants, and several apparel stores. These centres offer a broader variety of shopping, specialty, and convenience goods, provide large off-street parking lots, and usually include 7,000 to 28,000 square metres of retail space.

Finally, along came the huge *regional malls,* generally offering 38,000 to 75,000 square metres of shopping space. Regional malls are either entirely enclosed or roofed to allow shopping in any weather. Many are landscaped with trees, fountains, sculptures, and the like to enhance the shopping environment. They have hectares of free parking. The *anchor stores* or *generator stores* (e.g., The Bay, Sears, or Zellers) are usually located at opposite ends of the mall to create heavy foot traffic. The West Edmonton Mall in Edmonton, Alberta, has six anchor stores including The Bay, Sears, Zellers, The Brick, Winners, and London Drugs.[56]

According to shopping centre developers, *lifestyle centres* are now emerging as the newest generation of shopping centres offering time-pressed consumers a more convenient alternative to malls. These new, open-air shopping centres are targeted to upper-income shoppers with an aversion for "the mall" and seek to create an atmosphere that is part neighbourhood park and part urban shopping centre. Lifestyle centres generally feature approximately 300,000 square feet of upscale retail space occupied by trendy restaurants and specialty retailers. Other attractions include expensive landscaping and convenient parking. Developers expect that there will be more than 50 lifestyle centres established in North America by 2004.[57]

Locating in a community shopping centre or regional mall offers several advantages. First, the facilities are designed to attract shoppers. Second, the shopping environment, anchor stores, and "village square" activities draw customers. Third, ample parking is available. Fourth, the centre or mall projects a unified image. Fifth, tenants share the expenses of the mall's common area and promotions for the whole mall. Finally, malls can target different demographic groups. Some malls are considered upscale; others are aimed at people shopping for bargains.

ON LINE

Ivanhoe Cambridge Shopping Centres

Does it make sense for a shopping mall developer to have an Internet site? What would you expect to find there? Go to the Ivanhoe Cambridge site and evaluate the on-line shopping centre information. Search the Web to see if a mall near you has a website. If so, where would you shop?

http://www.ivanhoecambridge.com

Locating in a shopping centre or mall does have disadvantages. These include expensive leases, the chance that common promotion efforts will not attract customers to a particular store, lease restrictions on merchandise carried and hours of operation, the anchor stores' domination of the tenants' association, and the possibility of having direct competitors within the same facility. Consumers have also become more pressed for time in recent years and have decreased the number of visits and the time they spend in malls in favour of more convenient standalone stores and neighbourhood centres. Faced with this trend, mall developers have improved the layout of many malls to make it more convenient for customers to shop.

Retail Prices

Another important element in the retailing mix is price. It is important to understand that retailing's ultimate goal is to sell products to consumers and that the right price is critical in ensuring sales. Because retail prices are usually based on the cost of the merchandise, an essential part of pricing is efficient and timely buying.

Price is also a key element in a retail store's positioning strategy and classification. Higher prices often indicate a level of quality and help reinforce the prestigious image of retailers, as they do for Lord & Taylor, Saks Fifth Avenue, Gucci, Cartier, and Neiman Marcus. On the other hand, discounters and off-price retailers, such as Zellers and Winners, offer good value for the money. There are even stores, such as Dollar Tree, where everything costs shoppers one dollar. Dollar Tree's single-price-point strategy is aimed at getting higher-income customers to make impulse purchases through what analysts call the "wow factor"—the excitement of discovering that an item costs only a dollar.[58]

A pricing trend among North American retailers that seems to be here to stay is *everyday low pricing,* or EDLP. Introduced to the retail industry by Wal-Mart, EDLP offers consumers low prices all the time instead of holding periodic sales on merchandise. The Gap reduced prices on denim jeans, denim shirts, socks, and other items to protect and broaden the company's share of the casual clothes market. Supermarket chains such as Loblaws and Sobeys are also featuring EDLP.

Presentation of the Retail Store

The presentation of a retail store helps determine the store's image; it also positions the retail store in consumers' minds. For instance, a retailer that wants to position itself as an upscale store would use a lavish or sophisticated presentation.

atmosphere
The overall impression conveyed by a store's physical layout, decor, and surroundings.

The main element of a store's presentation is its **atmosphere,** the overall impression conveyed by its physical layout, decor, and surroundings. The atmosphere might create a relaxed or a busy feeling, a sense of luxury or of efficiency, a friendly or a cold attitude, a sense of organization or of clutter, or a fun or a serious mood. For example, the look at Disney stores is designed to make children feel they are actually in an amusement park. HMV music stores have a recording studio feel, with areas for private listening. Roots clothing stores, with their log walls, project a sense of the rustic outdoors. Many Chapters stores have a Starbucks coffee outlet inside so that people can have a coffee and relax while they read.

More often these days, retailers are adding an element of entertainment to their store atmosphere. The Niketown store in Chicago looks more like a museum than a traditional retail store. The three-storey space displays products amid life-sized Michael Jordan statues and glassed-in relics such as baseball legend Nolan Ryan's shoes. A History of Air exhibit explains the pockets of air on the bottom of some Nike shoes. A video theatre plays Nike commercials and short films featuring Nike gear.

ON LINE 

How can a company create an atmosphere on its website? Visit the pages of some of your favourite retailers to see if they have been able to recreate the store atmosphere on the Internet.

The layout of retail stores is a key factor in their success. Layout is planned so that all space in the store is used effectively, including aisles, fixtures, merchandise displays, and nonselling areas. Effective store layout ensures the customer's shopping ease and convenience, but it also has a powerful influence on customer traffic patterns and purchasing behaviour.

Layout includes where products are placed in the store. Many technologically advanced retailers are using a technique called *market-basket analysis* to analyze the huge amounts of data collected through their point-of-purchase scanning equipment. The analysis looks for products that are commonly purchased together to help retailers remerchandise their stores to place products in the right places. Wal-Mart uses market-basket analysis to determine where in the store to stock products for customer convenience. Bananas are placed not only in the produce section but also in the cereal aisle. Kleenex tissues are in the paper-goods aisle and also mixed in with the cold medicines. Measuring spoons are in the housewares and also hanging next to Crisco shortening. During October, flashlights are not only in the hardware aisle but also with the Halloween costumes.[59]

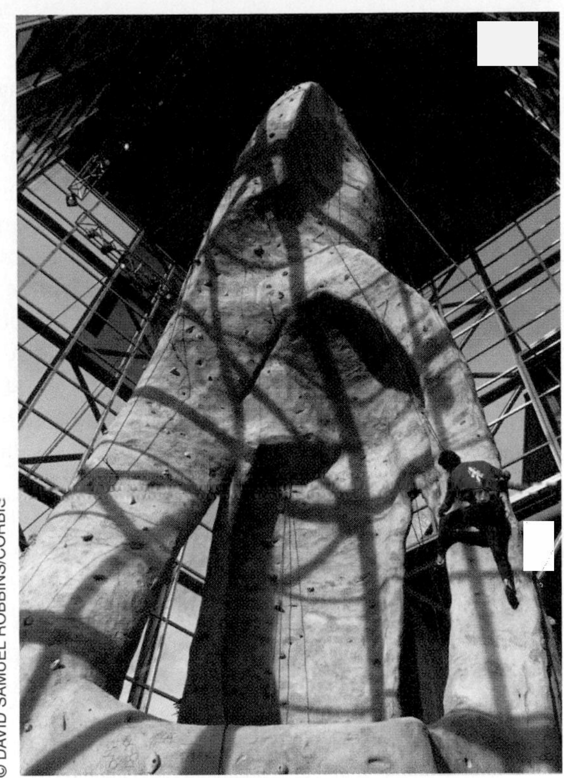

Retailers use the physical space of the store to entice customers to buy merchandise. REI encourages customers to try out the rock climbing wall at its flagship Seattle, Washington, store.

These are the most influential factors in creating a store's atmosphere:

- *Employee type and density:* Employee type refers to an employee's general characteristics—for instance, neat, friendly, knowledgeable, or service oriented. Density is the number of employees per 100 square metres of selling space. A discounter like Zellers has a low employee density that creates a "do-it-yourself," casual atmosphere. In contrast, Holt Renfrew's density is much higher, denoting readiness to serve the customer's every whim. Too many employees and not enough customers, however, can convey an air of desperation and intimidate customers.
- *Merchandise type and density:* The type of merchandise carried and how it is displayed add to the atmosphere the retailer is trying to create. A prestigious retailer like Les Ailes de la Mode in Montreal carries the top brand names and displays them in a neat, uncluttered arrangement. Discounters and off-price retailers may sell some well-known brands, but many carry seconds or out-of-season goods. Their merchandise may be stacked so high that it falls into the aisles, helping create the impression that "We've got so much stuff, we're practically giving it away."
- *Fixture type and density:* Fixtures can be elegant (rich woods), or trendy (chrome and smoked glass), or consist of old, beat-up tables, as in an antiques store. The fixtures should be consistent with the general atmosphere the store is trying to create. The Gap creates a relaxed and uncluttered atmosphere by displaying its merchandise on tables and shelves, rather than on traditional pipe racks; this practice allows customers to see and touch the merchandise more easily. Adding technology as a fixture is a recent successful trend in coffee shops and lounges. The most popular examples include adding PCs to provide Internet access to customers and ultimately get them to remain in the store longer.
- *Sound:* Sound can be pleasant or unpleasant for a customer. Classical music at a nice Italian restaurant helps create ambience, just as country-and-western music does at a truck stop. Music can entice customers to stay in the store longer and buy more, or it can encourage them to eat quickly and leave a table for others. For instance, rapid music tends to make people eat more, chew less, and take bigger bites, whereas slow music prompts people to dine more slowly and eat less. Retailers can tailor their musical atmosphere to their shoppers' demographics and the merchandise they are selling. Music can control the pace of the store traffic, create an image, and attract or direct the shopper's attention. For example, Les Ailes de la Mode in Quebec features piano music by live pianists in the entrances to its stores. Coffee

shops are also getting into the music business, as are theme restaurants like Hard Rock Cafe, Planet Hollywood, Harley-Davidson Cafe, and Rainforest Cafe, which turn eating a hamburger and fries into an experience. Starbucks and Victoria's Secret sell copies of their background music, hoping that the music will remind consumers of the feeling of being in their stores.

- *Odours:* Smell can either stimulate or detract from sales. The wonderful smell of pastries and breads entices bakery customers. Conversely, customers can be repulsed by bad odours such as cigarette smoke, musty smells, antiseptic odours, and overly powerful room deodorizers. When a grocery store pumps in the smell of baked goods, sales in that department increase threefold. Department stores have pumped in fragrances that are pleasing to their target market, and the response has been favourable. Not surprisingly, retailers are increasingly using fragrance as a key design element, as important as layout, lighting, and background music. Research suggests that people evaluate merchandise more positively, spend more time shopping, and are generally in a better mood when an agreeable odour is present. Retailers use fragrances as an extension of their retail strategy. The Rainforest Cafe, for instance, pumps fresh-flower extracts into its retail sections.[60]
- *Visual factors:* Colours can create a mood or focus attention and therefore are an important factor in atmosphere. Red, yellow, and orange are considered warm colours and are used when a feeling of warmth and closeness is desired. Cool colours like blue, green, and violet are used to open up closed-in places and create an air of elegance and cleanliness. Some colours are better for display. For instance, diamonds appear most striking against black or dark blue velvet. The lighting can also have an important effect on store atmosphere. Jewellery is best displayed under high-intensity spotlights and cosmetics under more natural lighting. Many retailers have found that natural lighting, either from windows or skylights, can lead to increased sales. Outdoor lighting can also affect consumer patronage. Consumers often are afraid to shop after dark in many areas and prefer strong lighting for safety. The outdoor facade of the store also adds to its ambience. It can help create favourable first impressions among shoppers, and help establish a visual identity for the store. Canadian book retailer Chapters has developed stores with unique designs, colours, and facades that identify them to customers at a distance even before customers are close enough for their eyes to read the signage.

Personnel and Customer Service

People are a unique aspect of retailing. Most retail sales involve a customer–salesperson relationship, if only briefly. When customers shop at a grocery store, the cashiers check and bag their groceries. When customers shop at a prestigious clothier, the salesclerks may help select the styles, sizes, and colours. They may also assist in the fitting process, offer alteration services, wrap purchases, and even offer a glass of champagne. Sales personnel provide their customers with the amount of service prescribed in the retail strategy of the store.

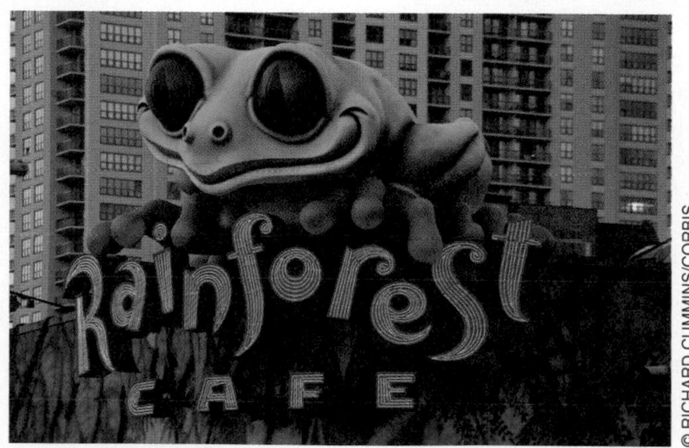

© RICHARD CUMMINS/CORBIS

This enormous frog sculpture crowns the entrance to the Rainforest Cafe. Coupled with the giant toadstools that flank the doors, the sculptures that decorate the outside of the restaurant create an impression of fun and whimsy.

Retail salespeople serve another important selling function: they persuade shoppers to buy. They must therefore be able to persuade customers that what they are selling is what the customer needs. Salespeople are trained in two common selling techniques: trading up and suggestion selling. Trading up means persuading customers to buy a higher-priced item than they originally intended to buy. To avoid selling customers something they do not need or want, however, salespeople should take care when practising trading-up techniques. Suggestion selling, a common practice among most retailers, seeks to broaden customers' original purchases with related items. For example, McDonald's cashiers may ask customers whether they would like a hot apple pie with their hamburger and fries. Suggestion selling and trading up should always help shoppers recognize true needs rather than load them with unwanted merchandise.

Providing great customer service is one of the most challenging elements in the retail mix because customer expectations for service are so varied. What customers expect in a department store is very different from their expectations for a discount store. Customer expectations also change. Ten years ago, shoppers wanted personal one-on-one attention. Today, most customers are happy to help themselves as long as they can easily find what they need. For example, Home Depot has always had a reputation for great customer service. Shoppers enjoy talking to the store's knowledgeable staff in the busy, do-it-yourself warehouse atmosphere. But as store sales increased, the company began receiving customer feedback that the salespeople seemed too busy to help and that the stores were too cluttered. To meet customers' new expectations, the company has recently changed its store policy to free up staff to help customers and has eliminated merchandise displays from the aisles.[61]

Customer service is also critical for on-line retailers. On-line shoppers expect a retailer's website to be easy to use, products to be available, and returns to be simple. The Canadian Online Shopping Mall promotes the following virtues of on-line shopping: dependability, always open 24/7 shopping, privacy and security, immediate access to consumer information, comparative shopping with the use of "shopping agents," clean environment, time savings, access to virtual storefronts of "bricks-and-mortar" retailers, easy gift buying and shipping, and cross-border shopping. Many on-line retailers have begun including a return envelope with all orders to make returns easier for the customer.[62]

>> GLOBAL RETAILING

Discuss the challenges of expanding retailing operations into global markets

The opening vignette described the invasion of Canada by U.S. retailers and how both Canadian and U.S. retailers are now testing their store concepts on a global basis. With the battle for market share among domestic retailers showing no signs of abating and growth prospects dismal, mature retailers are looking for growth opportunities in the growing consumer economies of other countries. American retailers have made quite an impact on the global market, as Exhibit 12.5 indicates. Six of the top 10 global retailers are from the United States, with Wal-Mart holding the top spot with sales about four times that of its nearest competitors.

Several events have made expansion across national borders more feasible. First, the spread of communication networks and mass media has homogenized tastes and product preferences to some extent around the world. As a result, the casual American lifestyle and the products that symbolize it, such as Levi's jeans and Nike sportswear, have become more appealing. Second, the lowering of trade barriers and tariffs has facilitated the expansion of American retailers to Canada, Mexico, and Europe. Last, high growth potential in underserved markets is luring U.S. retailers abroad into Latin America and Asia. China contains one-quarter of the world's population and has only recently opened its markets to outside concerns. Although most Chinese still lack adequate consumer spending power, projections call for the country's economy to eclipse all others in the next 25 years.

The soundest advice retailers can heed before taking the plunge into the international retailing arena is to do their homework (see Exhibit 12.6). Analysts from consulting firm Ernst & Young count among the prerequisites for going global a secure and profitable position domestically, a long-term perspective (because many foreign operations take a long time to set up and even longer to turn a profit), and a global strategy that meshes with the retailer's overall corporate strategy. Retailers should first determine what their core competency is, whether it is low prices, a distinctive fashion look, or excellent customer service, and determine whether this differentiation is what the local market wants. For instance, The Gap's international success is attributable to its allegiance to the "American casual" formula that made it so successful in its home

EXHIBIT 12.5

Ranking of Global Retailers

RANK	RETAILER	COUNTRY OF ORIGIN	FORMAT	2002 RETAIL SALES (US$ MILLIONS)
1	Wal-Mart	U.S.	Discount/Warehouse	229,617
2	Carrefour	France	Cash & Carry/Convenience/ Discount/ Hypermarket/ Supermarket	65,011
3	Home Depot	U.S.	DIY/Specialty	58,247
4	Kroger	U.S.	Convenience/Department/ Discount/Drug/Supermarket	51,760
5	Metro	Germany	Department/DIY/Hypermarket/ Specialty/Supermarket/ Warehouse/Mail Order	48,349
6	Target	U.S.	Department/Discount	42,722
7	Ahold	Netherlands	Cash & Carry/Convenience/ Discount/Drug/Hypermarket	40,755
8	Tesco	U.K.	Convenience, Department Hypermarket/Supermarket	40,071
9	Costco	U.S.	Warehouse	37,993
10	Sears, Roebuck	U.S.	Department/Mail Order/Specialty	35,698

SOURCE: Updated from Nation Retail Federation, "Top 200 Global Retailers 2001," Stores.org.

EXHIBIT 12.6

Factors Used to Analyze Global Retail Markets

- **Market size and economics**: Analyzing factors such as population and demographic trends, economics (including gross domestic product and consumer spending), and political trends that could make or break the success of a retailer in a foreign country. For instance, in China the central government has been urging middle-income Chinese to become homeowners. For retailers, this means plenty of new apartments and homes to fill with more electronics, bigger refrigerators and kitchens for edibles, and roomier closets.
- **Infrastructure and distribution**: Building global supply chains and securing qualified labour can be particularly challenging in emerging markets. Expansion to the U.S. and Mexico is simpler logistically for Canadian retailers than transporting their stores across oceans. In many developing countries such as China, underdeveloped transportation infrastructures as well as few logistics providers pose daunting distribution challenges to retailers trying to stock products in stores.
- **Competition**: Assessing the current competitive landscape and how the retailer could bring innovations to the market. Mexico, for instance, is considered a grossly understored country with less than 50 square metres of food and apparel stores per 1,000 people. In comparison, the United States has tremendous retail development with 1,900 square metres per thousand people. Similarly, Europe has a higher percentage of independent, mom-and-pop operations. The highly fragmented European market appears ripe for well-capitalized Canadian and U.S. big-box retailers.
- **Operations**: Assessing how operational concerns, such as real estate, labour, and inventory, will affect the success of an overseas unit. For instance, labour laws vary drastically from country to country. Cultural differences also affect holidays, number of vacation days for employees, and hours of operation. Canadian and U.S. retail stores are open an average of 70 hours a week whereas retail stores in Greece are open only about 46 hours a week.
- **Financial and tax reporting**: Addressing issues such as currency fluctuations, the hedging of risks, and how a region's tax regime and incentives would fit into a retailer's overall tax strategy. A lot of retailers are entering Brazil and Chile because their markets are open and their business economies and financial systems are more "Western-like."
- **Merchandise acceptability**: Conducting research to understand local consumer needs, preferences, and buying habits, and then reinventing the assortment to match the culture of the region. For instance, back-to-school sales occur in April in Japan, and August in Europe is a traditionally slow retailing month because most Europeans are on vacation. When IKEA came to Canada and the United States, it learned that it needed to offer larger beds, furniture with larger drawers, and different assortments of kitchen utensils.
- **Partnering capability**: Considering the availability of suitable partners in a desired country or region. Starbucks coffee typically picks distribution and supply partners before it decides on a country or region because poor strategic alliances or logistics partnering can make or break a retail operation.

SOURCE: From "Global Retailing '97," Ernst & Young special report for *Chain Store Age*, December 1997. Reprinted by permission of Chain Store Age. Copyright Lebhar-Friedman, Inc., 425 Park Avenue, NY, NY 10022.

market, including The Gap name. Similarly, wherever shoppers travel, they can reasonably expect to experience Wal-Mart's friendliness and the quality, service, and cleanliness of McDonald's.

Besides keeping their core strengths when going global, retailers need to understand the cultural differences of new markets because these differences can affect almost every area of the retail mix. Differences in colour, style, and taste preferences can affect a company's product choices. For example, lime-green is a popular colour on the sunny beaches of St. Tropez, but customers in northern Europe feel it leaves them looking sickly. Tight skirts are popular in France but not in countries like Holland, where women often bicycle to work. Cultural differences also should be considered for all location, presentation, and promotion decisions. For instance, Canadian retailer Pop Shoppes failed in the United States because most U.S. consumers don't call soft drinks "pop" and therefore failed to understand what the store sold. Differences in supply chain, real estate, and employment costs can undermine a retailer's price strategy. And, as always, great customer service depends on a retailer's understanding of customer expectations.[63]

ON LINE

Wal-Mart

Read Wal-Mart's 2001 Annual Report. What is "Retailtainment," and what is its intended goal? (Follow the Investor Relations links to the Annual Reports.)

http://www.walmartstores.com

>> TRENDS IN RETAILING

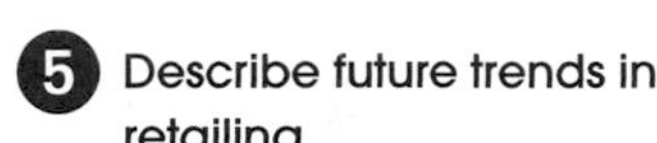

Predicting the future is always risky, but the use of entertainment to lure customers, a shift toward providing greater convenience to receive the patronage of today's precision shoppers, and the emergence of customer management programs to foster loyalty and enhance communications with a retailer's best customers are three of the more important trends for retailing's future.

Entertainment

Adding entertainment to the retail environment is one of the most popular strategies in retailing in recent years. Small retailers as well as national chains are using entertainment to set themselves apart from the competition.

Entertainment is not limited to music, videos, fashion shows, or guest appearances by soap opera stars or book authors. Entertainment includes anything that makes shoppers have a good time, that stimulates their senses or emotions, and that gets them into a store, keeps them there, and encourages them to buy and to keep coming back. The quiet, comfortable couches and cafés of Chapters bookstores are one example. The use of videos in Cinema One and Blockbuster video stores captures the attention of consumers and promotes products at the same time. Many stores use video screens and loud, energetic music to capture the attention of many younger consumers. In the fall of 2003, Holt Renfrew sponsored a promotion called "Flick"—a month-long series of "in-store" events celebrating the links between films and fashions. The event was timed to coincide with Holt's sponsorship of the Toronto International Film Festival and involved an opening gala at the Toronto flagship store featuring Graydon Carter, editor of *Vanity Fair,* combined with the world premiere of a short film by BMW Canada, created by Cundari Integrated Advertising. Holt Renfrew arranged for its attendees to enter the store using a red carpet on Bloor Street, which was shut down from Yonge Street to Bay Street.[64]

Convenience and Efficiency

Today's consumer is increasingly looking for ways to shop more quickly and efficiently. This trend not only reflects the increase in women working full- or part-time but also can be attributed to all consumers being more stretched for time. Consumers are visiting malls only about half as often as they used to, and the number of stores they visit when they get there is down substantially. According to a recent survey, 61 percent of shoppers said that convenience was the most important factor in deciding where to

© BARBARA ALPER/STOCK, BOSTON, INC./PICTUREQUEST

Entertainment in the retail environment is at its pinnacle in this Donna Karan boutique. Customers sit at a coffee bar while a grid of televisions provides the single screen for a fashion show broadcast.

shop. Shoppers in the same study also indicated that they are shopping in only 1.9 stores per week, compared to 2.9 the year before.[65] Therefore, retailers must make sure that customers have a positive experience every time they shop.

Retailers must also learn to better manage the patronage experience. Consumers are no longer satisfied when a store merely meets their expectations. They desire delightful experiences brought about by retailers who anticipate consumers' expectations and go the extra mile to exceed them on a regular basis. Dimensions in which retailers can far exceed expectations include shopping assistance, the buying process, delivery and installation of the product, service after the sale, and disposal and renewal of the product.

Examples of ways this can be done include offering amenities such as pickup service for shoppers who do not want to fight traffic, babysitting services, free drinks and refreshments during shopping, and preferred shopper parking spaces. In trying to exceed customer expectations, Canada's Shoppers Drug Mart chain has developed HealthWatch services, a customer record system that includes computerized prescription tracking and medication information printouts; disease-specific initiatives to help patients effectively manage conditions such as heart disease and diabetes; and breast cancer self-exam cards for women.[66] In addition, retailers that maintain records of consumers' preferences in product features are able to offer individualized attention to consumers during product selection. Sales associates can preselect items that are most likely to be preferred by the customer. For example, the store's records may indicate that a consumer prefers a particular style of suit, leading the sales associate to show the consumer the new suits for the season in that style.

To improve customer service, many retailers are implementing multichannel strategies. Retailers like Eddie Bauer and Talbots women's wear are using their catalogues and websites to familiarize customers with their merchandise selection and then offering special in-store incentives designed to entice customers into the store. Once inside, customers have access to catalogues and websites for purchasing items out-of-stock at the time of their visit.[67] Retailers that successfully integrate multiple channels are finding that doing so increases sales in each channel.

Experts predict that in the future, retailers—especially supermarkets—will become true marketers rather than marketers that act as distribution centres. For instance, packaged goods and staples won't be sold in supermarkets. Instead, they will be delivered directly to consumers at home, within 15 minutes of an order's placement, freeing shoppers to visit stores for things they enjoy buying—fresh produce, meats, and the fixings for a dinner party. Consumers who need staples will use hand scanners to record products' bar codes and update electronic shopping lists. Magazine ads will carry bar codes so that consumers can scan pages to put new products on their lists. Already, Frigidaire has produced a concept model refrigerator that comes complete with a video screen and bar-code scanner, which consumers can use to reorder products by scanning their used-up containers across the door. The scanner picks up the UPC and automatically reorders a fresh supply. The video screen also connects to the Internet, allowing consumers to check e-mail, pay bills, check their bank account, and shop on-line.[68]

Customer Management

Today, prime locations and unique merchandise are not the primary indicators of success they once were in the retail environment. Instead, retailers are recognizing that customer equity is one of the only ways to sustain true competitive advantage. Through customer management strategies, leading retailers are intensifying their efforts to identify, satisfy, retain, and maximize the value of their best customers. Enabled by database technology, these forward-focused retailers are employing strategies designed to capture customers' share of mind, wallet, and time. Using database technology to manage customer relationships is the topic of Chapter 18.

Emerging customer management strategies that retailers are embracing include customer relationship marketing, loyalty programs, and clienteling. Regardless of the strategy used, the intent is the same—to foster loyalty and develop an ongoing dialogue with a retailer's best customers. *Customer relationship marketing (CRM)* originated out of the need to more accurately target a fragmented customer base that was becoming increasingly more difficult to reach through mass advertising vehicles like television and newspapers. CRM is also discussed in Chapter 18.

Armed with richer customer databases and the technology to gather and analyze customer and sales data, retailers are now taking active measures to develop loyalty programs that identify and reward their best customers. Sears' KidVantage program, for example, provides savings to members with young children. Similarly, Shoppers Drug Mart uses data from its Optimum Card program to understand what customers are purchasing, when they are purchasing, and the types of sales events they prefer. In addition to percentage discount savings on purchases, Optimum Card carriers, currently 6 million strong, are notified of special sales events and can earn extra incentive points on certain types of sale merchandize. Shoppers Drug Mart has also launched a cobranded Optimum-CIBC Visa Card that provides five optimum points for every dollar of purchases made with this VISA card.[69]

Another approach to managing and building long-term relationships with best customers is *clienteling.* Saks Fifth Avenue, for example, strongly emphasizes personal contact with customers on the part of managers and sales associates. Associates collect and maintain detailed electronic client profiles that can be used to provide enhanced service. Sales associates are encouraged to service clients across all departments so that the associates, already familiar with size and style preferences, can address clients' complete wardrobe needs as opposed to merely selling merchandise from their assigned departments.

>> WHOLESALING

6 Discuss the importance of wholesaling in the Canadian economy

Along with retailers, wholesalers are important intermediaries in the marketing and distribution of goods and services. Retailers sell most of their goods and services to final consumers; wholesalers sell very few goods and services to final consumers. As presented in Chapter 5, in 2002 the Canadian wholesale sector carried inventories valued at nearly $44 billion and produced $419 billion in sales of goods and services, which were distributed through approximately 123,000 outlets. In 2002 the sales revenues of wholesalers were split up among their customers in the following proportions: retailers (34 percent), industry (30 percent), other wholesalers (17 percent), exporters (11 percent), farmers (4 percent), household consumers (4 percent).[70]

Wholesale revenues are higher than retail revenues because wholesalers sell to industry and farmers but also to other wholesalers, who in turn resell. This means that a product may move through multiple levels of intermediaries before reaching the final end user. Thus, wholesalers can have a major impact on prices in the marketplace. Wholesalers have to undertake all of the marketing and distribution functions that manufacturers/producers undertake. Wholesalers' costs and profits are closely tied to inventory turnover, the dollar value of the products and services they handle, the functions they perform, their efficiency of operations, and the activities of their competitors.

Types of Wholesalers

7 Identify the major types of wholesalers

Merchant wholesalers are organizations that facilitate the movement of products and services from the manufacturer to producers, resellers, governments, institutions, and retailers. All merchant wholesalers take title to the goods they sell, and most of them

merchant wholesaler
Institution that buys goods from manufacturers and resells them to businesses, government agencies, and other wholesalers or retailers and that receives and takes title to goods, stores them in its own warehouses, and later ships them.

agents and brokers
Wholesaling intermediaries who do not take title to a product but facilitate its sale from producer to end user by representing retailers, wholesalers, or manufacturers.

operate one or more warehouses, where they receive goods, store them, and later reship them. Customers are mostly small- or moderate-sized retailers, but merchant wholesalers also market to manufacturers and institutional clients.

Other intermediaries do not take title to goods and services they market but do facilitate the exchange of ownership between sellers and buyers. **Agents and brokers** simply facilitate the sale of a product from producer to end user by representing retailers, wholesalers, or manufacturers. Title reflects ownership, and ownership usually implies control. Unlike wholesalers, agents or brokers only facilitate sales and generally have little input into the terms of the sale. They do, however, get a fee or commission based on sales volume.

Variations in channel structures are due in large part to variations in the numbers and types of wholesaling intermediaries. Generally, product characteristics, buyer considerations, and market conditions determine the type of intermediary the manufacturer should use. Product characteristics that may dictate a certain type of wholesaling intermediary include whether the product is standardized or customized, the complexity of the product, and the gross margin of the product. Buyer considerations affecting wholesaler choice include how often the product is purchased and how long the buyer is willing to wait to receive the product. Market characteristics determining the wholesaler type include how many buyers are in the market and whether they are concentrated in a general location or are widely dispersed. Exhibit 12.7 shows these determining factors. For example, a manufacturer that produces only a few natural gas turbines a year for use in non-utility generating power plants will probably use an agent or broker to sell its product. In addition, the handful of customers that need the product are most likely concentrated near major industrial cities, again making an agent or broker more practical. On the other hand, a book publisher that prints thousands of books and has many widely dispersed customers with year-round demand for its product will probably use a merchant wholesaler.

8 List the major functions that wholesalers perform

Channel Functions Performed by Intermediaries

Retailing and wholesaling intermediaries in marketing channels perform several essential functions that make the flow of goods between producer and buyer possible. The three basic functions that intermediaries perform are summarized in Exhibit 12.8.

Transactional functions involve contacting and communicating with prospective buyers to make them aware of existing products and to explain their features, advantages, and benefits. Intermediaries in the supply chain also provide *logistical* functions. **Logistics** is a term borrowed from the military that describes the process of strategically managing the efficient flow and storage of raw materials, in-process inventory, and finished goods from point of origin to point of consumption. Logistical functions include transporting, storing, sorting out, accumulating, allocating, and assorting products into either homogeneous or heterogeneous collections. For example, grading

logistics
The process of strategically managing the efficient flow and storage of raw materials, in-process inventory, and finished goods from point of origin to point of consumption.

EXHIBIT 12.7
Wholesaling Intermediary to Use

FACTORS	SUGGESTING TYPE OF WHOLESALING	INTERMEDIARY TO USE
Nature of product	Standard	Nonstandard, custom
Technicality of product	Complex	Simple
Product's gross margin	High	Low
Frequency of ordering	Frequent	Infrequent
Time between order and receipt of shipment	Buyer desires shorter lead time	Buyer satisfied with long lead time
Number of customers	Many	Few
Concentration of customers	Dispersed	Concentrated

SOURCE: Reprinted from *Industrial Marketing Management*, February 1989, Donald M. Jackson and Michael F. D'Amico, "Products and Markets Served by Distributors and Agents," 27-33. Copyright 1989, with permission from Elsevier.

EXHIBIT 12.8

Marketing Channel Functions Performed by Intermediaries

TYPES OF FUNCTION	DESCRIPTION
Transactional function	**Contacting and promoting**: Contacting potential customers, promoting products, and soliciting orders **Negotiating**: Determining how many goods or services to buy and sell, type of transportation to use, when to deliver, and method and timing of payment **Risk taking**: Assuming the risk of owning inventory
Logistical functions	**Physically distributing**: Transporting and sorting goods to overcome temporal and spatial discrepancies **Storing**: Maintaining inventories and protecting goods **Sorting**: Overcoming discrepancies of quantity and assortment by *Sorting out*: Breaking down a heterogeneous supply into separate homogeneous stocks *Accumulation*: Combining similar stocks into a larger homogeneous supply *Allocation*: Breaking a homogeneous supply into smaller and smaller lots ("breaking bulk") *Assortment*: Combining products into collections or assortments that buyers want available at one place
Facilitating function	**Researching**: Gathering information about other channel members and consumers **Financing**: Extending credit and other financial services to facilitate the flow of goods through the channel to the final consumer

agricultural products typifies the sorting-out process, whereas consolidation of many lots of grade A eggs from different sources into one lot illustrates the accumulation process. Supermarkets or other retailers perform the assorting function by assembling thousands of different items that match their customers' desires. Similarly, while large companies typically have direct channels, many small companies depend on wholesalers to champion and distribute their products. For example, small beverage manufacturers like Jones Soda, Honest Tea, and Energy Brands depend on wholesalers to distribute their products in a marketplace dominated by large competitors like Coca-Cola and Pepsi.[71]

The third basic channel function, *facilitating*, includes research and financing. Research provides information about channel members and consumers by getting answers to key questions: Who are the buyers? Where are they located? Why do they buy? Financing ensures that channel members have the money to keep products moving through the channel to the ultimate consumer.

A single company may provide one, two, or all three functions. Consider Dominion Citrus Limited, a fresh produce and food processing distributor located in Markham, Ontario. Dominion provides transactional, logistical, and facilitating channel functions as it procures, processes, repacks, warehouses, and distributes fresh produce to large grocery chains and large independent grocers who operate in Ontario and Quebec.[72]

It is important to remember that retailers and wholesalers are noteworthy channel member institutions that can be utilized or bypassed by marketing managers in setting up a distribution system. Marketing managers need to realize that although individual members can be added to or deleted from a channel, someone must still perform these essential functions. They can be performed by producers, end users, or consumers, by channel intermediaries such as wholesalers and retailers, and sometimes by nonmember channel participants. For example, if a manufacturer decides to eliminate its private fleet of trucks, it must still have a way to move the goods to the wholesaler. This task may be accomplished by the wholesaler, which may have its own fleet of trucks, or by a nonmember channel participant, such as an independent trucking firm. Nonmembers also provide many other essential functions that may at one time have been provided by a channel member. For example, research firms may perform the research function; advertising agencies, the promotion function; transportation and storage firms, the physical distribution function; and banks, the financing function.

9 Describe future trends in wholesaling

Future Trends in Wholesaling

Wholesaling has been undergoing major changes over the past decade, and this state of change promises to continue. Some of the key trends are a focus on improving productivity of operations, improving customer service, seizing international opportunities, and integrating forward from wholesale operations into retail operations.

A focus on productivity is an absolute necessity for any wholesale operation because the profit margins in the wholesale market are very small. Consider that food wholesalers have profit margins in the range of 1.5 percent of sales whereas general merchandise wholesalers operate with profit margins of 3 percent or less. Many wholesalers are employing technology to make productivity improvements. For example, Gentec International, a Canadian distributor of photo, cellular, and electronics accessories, purchased a specialized demand forecasting module to streamline operating efficiencies in its warehouse and distribution centre. Produced by Radio Beacon Inc., a developer of warehouse management software, this module uses a company's sales-order history to automatically identify optimal safety stock levels and the appropriate reorder points and reorder quantities for every product in the warehouse.[73]

Improving customer service is critical to maintaining competitive position in the wholesale industry. The wholesale industry tends toward an oligopolistic market structure, with a few competitors who offer very similar products, and wholesalers usually do not sell to many customers, so the competition is very intense. Good customer service is one way for wholesalers to maintain and even grow their business. For example, Core-Mark International is a wholesale supplier to convenience stores, drug stores, gas stations, and supermarkets all across North America. Core-Mark is differentiating itself from other wholesale competitors by offering its customers access to unique business intelligence software supplied by Cognos, Inc. According to Amin Noormohamed, director of e-business, Core-Mark International, "With Cognos we have given our customers unprecedented insight into their purchase data and the ability to perform analysis quickly and easily over the Web."[74]

Seizing international opportunities is another trend for successful wholesalers. Recently, Taiga Forest Products Ltd., Canada's largest wholesale distributor of structural building materials, purchased a large building products distribution centre in Rocklin, California, from Louisiana-Pacific Corporation. Although Taiga has 15 distribution centres across Canada, the firm felt that in order to grow it needed to undertake international expansion. Arkadi Bykhovsky, president and CEO of Taiga, described the acquisition as follows: "It strengthens our relationship with LP, offers us greater product and market diversification, and provides Taiga with a foothold in the key U.S. market."[75]

Forward integration by wholesalers into retail operations is a strong trend in the marketplace for both large and small wholesalers. Many entrepreneurs start out as small wholesale operations selling their products to independent retailers and then evolve their own retail operations when their brands take hold. For example, Jeanne Lottie is the best-known brand of Canadian handbags in the world. Jane Ip and her sister, Charlotte, formed the brand and company. They started out working as wholesale commission agents for a Hong Kong manufacturer selling to retailers. They developed a rapport with the retail businesses, and then Jane Ip started designing and selling her own handbags, which her Hong Kong connection manufactured under the Jeanne Lottie label. Now Jane Ip operates her own store, but she still "wholesales" the brand to other specialty boutiques and a number of chain stores across Canada.[76]

>> CONNECT IT

Think back now to the opening story about the U.S. retailing invasion and the counter-invasion of Canadian firms. Every element in the retailing mix of the firms involved, from merchandise assortment to price levels, service levels, atmosphere, and location, must be carefully considered to provide customers with the products and shopping experience they are looking for. This is no easy feat for retailers, but finding the right combination can mean the difference between success and failure. Clearly, many Canadian and American retailers have found success.

REVIEW IT

1 **Discuss the importance of retailing in the Canadian economy.** Retailing plays a vital role in the Canadian economy for two main reasons. First, retail businesses contribute to our high standard of living by providing a vast number and diversity of goods and services. Second, retailing employs a large part of the Canadian working population—1.46 million people.

1.1 

In order to fully appreciate the role that retailing plays in the Canadian economy, it may be helpful to visit the website of the Retail Council of Canada, the key trade association representing this vital economic sector. Visit http://www.retailcouncil.org and search for articles and information pertaining to retailing in Canada. Read a selection of articles, and report your findings to the class.

2 **Describe the nature of retail operations.** Many different kinds of retailers exist. A retail establishment can be classified according to its ownership, level of service, product assortment, and price. On the basis of ownership, retailers can be broadly differentiated as independent retailers, chain stores, or franchise outlets. The level of service retailers provide can be classified along a continuum of high to low. Retailers also classify themselves by the breadth and depth of their product assortments; some retailers have concentrated product assortments, whereas others have extensive product assortments. Last, general price levels also classify a store, from discounters offering low prices to exclusive specialty stores where high prices are the norm. Retailers use these latter three variables to position themselves in the marketplace.

The major types of retail stores are department stores, specialty retailers, supermarkets, drugstores, convenience stores, discount stores, and restaurants. Department stores carry a wide assortment of shopping and specialty goods, are organized into relatively independent departments, and offset higher prices by emphasizing customer service and decor. Specialty retailers typically carry a narrower but deeper assortment of merchandise, emphasizing distinctive products and a high level of customer service. Supermarkets are large self-service retailers that offer a wide variety of food products and some nonfood items. Drugstores are retail formats that sell mostly prescription and over-the-counter medications, health and beauty aids, cosmetics, and specialty items. Convenience stores carry a limited line of high-turnover convenience goods. Discount stores offer low-priced general merchandise and consist of four types: full-line discounters, discount specialty retailers, warehouse clubs, and off-price retailers. Finally, restaurants straddle the line between the retailing and services industries; whereas restaurants sell a product, food and drink, to final consumers, they can also be considered service marketers because they provide consumers with the service of preparing food and providing table service.

Nonstore retailing, which is shopping outside a store setting, has three major categories. Automatic vending uses machines to offer products for sale. In direct retailing, the sales transaction occurs in a home setting, typically through door-to-door sales or party plan selling. Direct marketing refers to the techniques used to get consumers to buy from their homes or place of business. Those techniques include direct mail, catalogues and mail order, telemarketing, and electronic retailing, such as home shopping channels and on-line retailing using the Internet. Franchising is a continuing relationship in which a franchiser grants to a franchisee the business rights to operate or to sell a product. Modern franchising takes two basic forms. In product and trade name franchising, a dealer agrees to buy or sell certain products or product lines from a particular manufacturer or wholesaler. Business format franchising is an ongoing business relationship in which a franchisee uses a franchiser's name, format, or method of business in return for several types of fees.

2.1 

Form a team of three classmates to identify different retail stores in your city where pet supplies are sold. Include nonstore forms of retailing as well, such as catalogues, the Internet, or the local veterinarian. Team members should divide up and visit all the different retailing outlets for pet supplies. Prepare a report describing the differences in brands and products sold at each of the retailing formats and the differences in store characteristics and service levels. For example, which brands are sold via mass merchandiser, independent specialty store, or other type of retailer? Suggest why different products and brands are distributed through different types of stores.

2.2 Explain the function of warehouse clubs. Why are they classified as both wholesalers and retailers?

2.3 ON LINE Why should retailers market their printed catalogues on-line? Look at http://catalogsite.catalogcity.com.

2.4 What advantages does franchising provide to franchisers as well as franchisees?

3 **List the major tasks involved in developing a retail marketing strategy.** Retail management begins with defining the target market, typically on the basis of demographic, geographic, or psychographic characteristics. After determining the target market, retail managers must develop the six variables of the retailing mix: product, promotion, place, price, presentation, and personnel.

3.1 Identify a successful retail business in your community. What marketing strategies have led to its success?

3.2 WRITING You want to convince your boss, the owner of a retail store, of the importance of store atmosphere. Write a memo citing specific examples of how store atmosphere affects your own shopping behaviour.

4 **Discuss the challenges of expanding retailing operations into global markets.** With increased competition and slow domestic growth, mature retailers are looking for growth opportunities in the developing consumer economies of other countries. The homogenization of tastes and product preferences around the world, the lowering of trade barriers, and the emergence of underserved markets have made the prospects of expanding across national borders more feasible for many retailers. Retailers wanting to expand globally should first determine what their core competency is and determine whether this differentiation is what the local market wants. Retailers also need to skillfully make adjustments in product mix to meet local demands.

4.1 Your retail clothing company is considering expanding into Mexico. What information about the country and its customs should you collect before opening a store in Mexico?

5 **Describe future trends in retailing.** Three major trends are evident in retailing today. First, adding entertainment to the retail environment is one of the most popular strategies in retailing in recent years. Small retailers as well as national chains are using entertainment to set themselves apart from the competition. Second, retailers of the future will offer more convenience and efficiency to consumers as consumers become more precise on their shopping trips. Staples won't be sold in stores but instead will be delivered directly to the consumer, freeing shoppers to visit stores for products they enjoy buying. Advances in technology will make it easier for consumers to obtain the products they want. Last, more and more retailers are using the information they collect about their customers at the point of sale to develop customer management programs, including customer relationship marketing, loyalty programs, and clienteling.

5.1 WRITING You have been asked to write a brief article about the way consumer demand for convenience and efficiency is influencing the future of retailing. Write the outline for your article. Once you have written your outline, use InfoTrac® College Edition (http://infrotrac.thomsonlearning.com) to locate the article in *Business Credit* magazine titled, "Electronic Retailing: A Threat to Brick and Mortar Retailers?" by Keith Ackerman. How does your article differ? Is Ackerman's article still relevant?

6 **Discuss the importance of wholesaling in the Canadian economy.** Along with retailers, wholesalers are important intermediaries in the marketing and distribution of goods and services. Whereas retailers sell the majority of their goods and services to final consumers, wholesalers sell very few goods and services to final consumers. In 2002 the Canadian wholesale sector had $419 billion in sales revenue, which was split up among its customers in the following proportions: retailers (34 percent), industry (30 percent), other wholesalers (17 percent), exporters (11 percent), farmers (4 percent), and finally retail sales to household consumers of 4 percent. Wholesalers have to undertake all of the marketing and distribution functions that manufacturers/producers undertake. Consequently, wholesalers can have a major impact on prices in the marketplace.

6.1 Compare the total value of wholesale dollar sales in Canada versus retail dollar sales. Who sells more, retailers or wholesalers? What accounts for the difference in sales levels between these institutions?

6.2 Identify the key factors that affect wholesaler prices? What advice would you give to a wholesaler to help it compete more effectively on price?

7 **Identify the major types of wholesalers.** Merchant wholesalers are those organizations that facilitate the movement of products and services from the manufacturer to producers, resellers, governments, institutions, and retailers. Agents and brokers do not take title to the goods and services they market, but do facilitate the exchange of ownership between sellers and buyers.

7.1 Identify the various types of wholesalers presented in the chapter. How are they different, and how are they similar? Research these wholesaler types on the Internet. What did you find? Discuss your results.

8 **List the major functions that wholesalers perform.** Wholesalers perform three basic types of functions. Transactional functions include contacting and promoting, negotiating, and risk taking. Logistical functions performed by channel members include physical distribution, storing, and sorting functions. Finally, channel members may perform facilitating functions, such as researching and financing.

8.1 Discuss the reasons intermediaries are important to the distribution of most goods. What important functions do they provide?

9 **Describe future trends in wholesaling.** Wholesaling has been undergoing major changes over the last decade, and this state of change promises to continue. Some of the key trends are a focus on improving productivity of operations, improving customer service, seizing international opportunities, and integrating forward from wholesale operations into retail operations.

9.1 Discuss the reasons why wholesalers would integrate their business operations forward into retailing. Research the recent business press or Internet sources and see if you can find an example of a Canadian retail firm that started out as a wholesaling venture. Based on the information you have uncovered, what were the reasons this firm "integrated" forward?

DEFINE IT

agents and brokers 374
atmosphere 366
automatic vending 352
buyer 344
category killers 349
chain stores 342
convenience store 347
department store 344
direct marketing (direct-response marketing) 353
direct retailing 352
discount store 347
drugstore 347
factory outlet 350
franchise 342
franchisee 358
franchiser 358
full-line discount store 348
gross margin 343
hypermarket 348
independent retailers 342
logistics 374
mass merchandising 348
merchant wholesaler 373–374
nonstore retailing 352
off-price retailer 350
on-line retailing 356
private-label brands 362
product offering 361
retailing 342
retailing mix 361
scrambled merchandising 346
specialty discount store 349
specialty store 345
supercentre 348
supermarket 346
telemarketing 354
warehouse membership clubs 350

APPLY IT

Ron Johnson is developing a retail strategy to open up his new athletic shoe and sports equipment store. He has decided to carry Nike and Brooks as his two lines of athletic shoes. This will give him top-of-the-line merchandise (Nike) and a lower-priced, high-quality alternative (Brooks). He obtained permission from one of his former professors to hold brainstorming sessions in a couple of his classes. From these sessions, he identified the following evaluative criteria customers might use in selecting a particular athletic shoe to purchase: (1) attractiveness/style/colour, (2) brand name, (3) comfort, (4) price, (5) endorsement, and (6) quality. He also determined that location, a friend's recommendation, brands carried, and store atmosphere are important in selecting a place to purchase athletic shoes.

QUESTIONS

1. What type of retailing strategy should Ron use?
2. Which elements of the retailing mix are relatively more important?
3. Should Ron incorporate a website into his retail strategy? Why or why not?

THINK ABOUT IT

A–Z Grocery Company is well known for offering quality grocery products at the lowest prices in the market. When the company applied for a zoning change to build a new store in a middle-class neighbourhood, several city councillors objected because the company has no stores in low-income neighbourhoods, where they argue the low prices are needed most. The company contends they cannot operate profitably in these neighbourhoods because of higher security and operating costs.

QUESTIONS

1. Should low-cost retailers be required to locate near low-income customers? Why or why not?
2. Does the CMA Code of Ethics address this issue? Go to **http://www.the-cma.org** and review the code. Then write a brief paragraph on how the CMA Code of Ethics relates to retailing locations.

TRY IT

dELiA*s Retails to Teens

American entrepreneur Stephen Kahn knew he had a good idea for a new direct retailing business: sell funky clothes and accessories targeted to Sabrina-wannabe girls between the ages of 10 and 24. The problem was convincing financial backers that his idea was more than good—it was very lucrative. When he first presented his idea to venture capitalists, they scoffed at his business plan and refused to lend him money. Teens, they said, are an elusive group with limited financial resources and no access to credit cards. Moreover, teens are fickle, and the pace in teen fashion trends is often too fast for retailers to keep up.

Convinced that this overlooked niche had potential, Kahn, a former leveraged-buyout specialist and recent Yale grad, put up $100,000 of his own money and turned to family and friends for the other $1 million startup capital he needed to print and mass-mail his first catalogue, called dELiA*s. Launched from a Brooklyn, New York, garage in 1993, dELiA*s startled Wall Street with its success, quickly becoming America's leading direct retailer of teen fashion.

Kahn's hunch about preteen and teenage girls, it turns out, was right on target. According to Teenage Research Unlimited, a consulting firm specializing in the U.S. teen market, young Americans between the ages of 12 and 19 spend an estimated $153 billion a year, or roughly $90 a week. Parents provide over half of their teens' incomes on an as-needed basis, with the rest coming from odd jobs, gifts, and allowances. Further, teens increasingly have access to their parents' credit cards and, in a growing number of cases, are acquiring their own credit cards with an adult sponsor. Parents are also setting up "digital on-line credit accounts" for their teens' on-line spending funded by their own credit cards. Not obligated to pay rent or other household expenses, most teens are free to spend their money on whatever they choose—accessories, CDs, and, most importantly, apparel. Additionally, buying decisions in teen apparel are being made at increasingly younger ages.

One of the most significant reasons for dELiA*s phenomenal success is that it makes funky fashion accessible and affordable to preteen and teenage girls across the United States and will even ship to Canada and other international locations. For young girls in rural and remote areas that lack options to buy cool clothes, dELiA*s serves as an equalizer of teen fashion. Now, teens in small towns in the U.S. or who live in other countries have the same fashion choices as their counterparts living in Los Angeles or New York. In schools all across the U.S., critiquing the latest dELiA*s catalogue has become a lunchtime ritual.

After some fairly harrowing experiences with several suppliers early on, Kahn and partner Christopher Edgar, his ex–Yale University roommate, developed more of their own private-label merchandise in order to offer dELiA*s target market more unique clothing and accessories. More recent catalogues also attempt to target a slightly older demographic, aiming to be aspirational to preteens while not turning off older girls. The duo also weeded out suppliers that couldn't make consistent product and on-time shipments and opened their own warehousing facility to better control the fulfillment process and improve quality. These measures paid off for dELiA*s: revenue hit US$215 million in 2000, and its mailing list numbers more than 11 million. Not bad for a company that had sales of US$150,000 just five years earlier.

dELiA*s has taken a multichannel approach to retailing. In addition to its successful direct-mail catalogue, the company has opened some two-dozen retail stores, operates several e-commerce sites, and will undertake international shipping. With virtually no advertising, the on-line store attracts more than 100,000 on-line buyers and more than 5,000 catalogue requests each day.

QUESTIONS

1. What type of retailer is dELiA*s?
2. Describe dELiA*s retailing strategy as best as you can in terms of product, price, place, promotion, people, and presentation.
3. Visit dELiA*s website at **http://www.delias.com.** How does it entertain and involve young girls in its brand? What is the focal point of the website?
4. Examine dELiA*s international shipping policy to Canada. Do you think it can be competitive with Canadian retailers?

FLIP IT

GRADEMAKER

Flip to Chapter 12 in your *Grademaker Study Guide* for more review opportunities, including the pretest, vocabulary review, Internet activities, study test questions, and an application exercise based on retailing concepts. Can you close your book and describe the major types of retail operations? Can you clearly explain to a friend who's not in the class how to classify retailers? Do you know the tasks involved in developing a retailing strategy? If not, then pick up your *Grademaker* and review.

CLICK IT

The *Marketing* website is rich with materials to help you review and master marketing concepts. Check your knowledge with the free quizzes, practise key terms using the crossword puzzles, or review key concepts using the Microsoft® PowerPoint® slides. Also on the website are updated weblinks to companies mentioned in this chapter, Internet exercises, career marketing information, and much much more! Go to http://www.lamb3e.nelson.com, read the material, and follow the convenient links.

WATCH IT

Organics to You

Retailing is a very demanding business and especially hard for new start-up ventures. Many estimates put the failure rate of new retail start-up firms at well over 75 percent. Retailers are always looking for innovative ways to serve consumers and make money in the process. However, before they can flourish, they must first fight the battle for survival. Consider the situation of British Columbia-based Organics To You (OTY), which bills itself as "Vancouver's first and biggest organic produce home delivery service."

OTY is a small company that specializes in putting together bins of organic produce and delivering them fresh to customers. Its business goal is to get good, fresh, organic food to people at a reasonable cost. Its owner-operator, Andrew Capeau, is hoping to capitalize on the organic retail market, which Agriculture Canada estimates to be worth nearly $1 billion in Canada and which has an estimated growth rate between 15 and 20 percent each year. However, Andrew is not alone in trying to tap into this potential market. His business model has been copied by no less than 20 other competitors in Vancouver. For example, Organics@Home competes directly with OTY and has duplicated virtually everything that OTY does except that Organics@Home uses the Internet to take customer orders and make contact. Aside from direct competitors, OTY has to deal with the fact that grocery stores have begun offering more and more organic produce to tap into this market. The firm viewed itself as the market leader, but the truth is that with only 1,400 customers out of a market of millions of residents, OTY's lead is really slim.

To keeps its leading position in the organic produce business, OTY knew it needed to allow its clients to place custom orders so they could select specific fruits and vegetables to be delivered to their homes. This ability would allow OTY to take a lead on the competition and reduce some of the impact of grocery store offerings as well. The problem for OTY was how to develop a communications system whose ordering, invoicing, inventory, and telephone systems would allow customer orders and fulfillment to happen seamlessly.

Because OTY's current system was unable to pass muster, the company needed to reorganize it to stay competitive. OTY needed a technology makeover fast—a new touch-tone phone order system and reliable voicemail system. The company approached a number of consultants who specialized in the kinds of logistics management and ordering systems OTY needed, but the cost was far too high for a firm the size of OTY. Andrew Capeau and his assistant manager, Marion Brulot, decided they had to take on the task themselves. In particular, Marion took the lead on systems development. She battled for a period of 18 months to find technology suppliers and to piece together a computer inventory system tied to the telephone system. The task was extremely difficult, and Marion became so frustrated that she tendered her resignation.

Because OTY was a small retail business, Marion was the only one who understood the automated order system; thus she had become invaluable to the organization. Andrew realized this and offered her a partnership to return to the business. Starting fresh, OTY hired consultants to install an integrated communications program that allowed phone, Internet, and catalogue orders, along with an inventory system that worked. It was expensive, but it allowed OTY to introduce custom orders and stay competitive. With the important order-processing system in place, Andrew Capeau is now free to focus on his plans to fight the competition and grow his retail business.

QUESTIONS

1. Do you think Organics To You will be able to beat the odds and be a successful retail operation? Why or why not?
2. If you were going to get involved in organic produce distribution and retailing, what forms of retailing might you reasonably consider? Compare and contrast the advantages and disadvantages of these various forms of retailing.
3. Organics To You was initially viable without a computerized ordering system. Why do you think it was so important for the firm to develop this system to support its retail operation?
4. Evaluate the six Ps of the retailing mix of Organics To You. Which of the six Ps are most important to its retail operation? Which of the six Ps are least important? Explain your reasoning.

SUGGESTED INFORMATION SOURCES

CBC, *Venture*, "Organics to You," Broadcast: August 15, 2000.

Geary, John. "Going Organic a Growing Concern in Alberta," **http://www.bearlair.ca/orgfood.htm**

"Organic Food Sales Cross Retail Threshold," **http://www.statpub.com/open/22672.html**

http://www.organicsathome.com

http://www.spud.ca

MARKETING MISCUES

Making a Small Fortune in the Airline Business

How do you make a small fortune in the airline business? You start with a large one. A joke? Yes, but Canadian airline operators have been falling for it in the hardest of ways and quite often. It is not the least bit funny when you consider the millions of dollars of financial investments along with human costs in the form of lost jobs and family-life disruptions. The list of failed Canadian air carriers over the last decade is long: Nationair, City Express, Intair, Astoria Airlines, Greyhound Air, Vistajet, Roots Air (yes, named after Roots clothing that had an interest), and most recently Canada 3000 airlines, which really came up short, only making it to the year 2003!!

The airline industry is one of the most brutally competitive industries in the world. Very few airlines are profitable to begin with, and those that are have unique niches or market positions to sustain them. Consider WestJet Airlines, the "darling" of the Canadian airline industry. It is based in Calgary with the majority of its operations in Western Canada, where it connects the major Western cities together. WestJet also connects to a number of major Eastern Canadian cities, but its focus remains in Western Canada. It has adopted a business model similar to that of one of the most successful U.S. air carriers, discount airline Southwest Airlines. The secret to success for WestJet has been owning its own aircraft, using "ticketless" travel and non-unionized labour, and offering no in-flight meal service on short hauls and no connecting baggage handling. With this model, WestJet has been very successful as a low-price and no-frills airline.

In contrast, Roots Air attempted to go after a different market than "price sensitive" flyers. It was after high-paying business customers, and it offered stylish amenities and presented fares that slightly underpriced Air Canada's. The problem for Roots Air was that it only had four planes serving three cities. This offering just did not fulfill the needs of business travellers, who want to be able to fly at their convenience and get directly to their destinations. Roots could not provide the kind of scheduling that business travellers were seeking. The result: Roots Air had a scant six-week lifetime, shattering the previous record for failure of 109 days, held by Vistajet!

Most recently, Air Canada filed for bankruptcy protection and began a reorganization that involved major cost-cutting measures, including layoffs of employees and wage concessions from those who remained employed. As Canada's largest and most "storied" airline, it would appear to be in the national interest for the federal government to intervene and support Air Canada. At one time, Air Canada was owned by the Canadian government as a Crown corporation. In a bid to privatize the industry and bring competition to Canada, the airline was sold off. Now, in the face of the failure of Canada's "own" airline, in addition to the track record of most of the other airline firms in Canada, the federal government must consider the links between Air Canada's survival, the national interest, and the preservation of the free-market economy.

What does the airline industry need to remain viable? WestJet president Clive Beddoe provides the following commentary to answer this question: "Demand a rational business model. The country needs a transportation policy that encourages people to travel. The industry has been whacked by taxes and surcharges and the government needs to back off. The government should let the market work and not bail out airlines like Air Canada. I see two charter carriers and two scheduled carriers. That's all the market will likely sustain. I see more of the domestic market going to us, with Air Canada concentrating on the longer haul and the higher end. They have to differentiate their product."

Clive Beddoe was asked what would happen if WestJet were to have a monopoly. What would stop it from gouging its customers? In response, he provided the following reply: "Nothing would prevent us, but that's not part of our philosophy or what makes us work. The market is very elastic. If you start putting up airfares unreasonably, people won't fly. In Abbotsford (British Columbia), before Air Canada came in, we had a monopoly market. We didn't hike fares. Why? Because we need low fares to stimulate people to fly."

Questions

1. You have been approached by an entrepreneur who wants to start up "Canuck" Airlines in Eastern Canada. What strategy would you recommend to this entrepreneur?
2. Do you think Canada's airline market is big enough to support "competition," or is it a "natural monopoly"?
3. Examine Clive Beddoe's comments about the Canadian airline industry. What role, if any, should the government play in the airline industry? Consider whether the government should once again operate Air Canada. Discuss Beddoe's comments and provide your own thoughts on what you think the industry needs to do to remain "viable"?
4. Thinking broadly, identify the kinds of competitors airline industry firms must face. What advantages and disadvantages do these competitors have versus the airlines?

Source: Clive Beddoe, "How Much is Enough?" *Maclean's* magazine, April 28, 2003, 40. Reprinted with permission.

CRITICAL THINKING CASE

Canada: The Haven of P2P Distribution

In the last few years, music distribution has been undergoing a revolution with the advent of downloadable music files that are stored and played as computer files (MP3 or Windows Media Player format) or burned onto compact discs. Interestingly, the trend toward music downloading is not being driven by the music industry but rather by peer-to-peer (P2P) file-sharing services, one of the most notable being Napster. Founded by Shawn Fanning in May 1999, Napster claimed to be the world's leading file-sharing community. Although Napster was the market leader and an innovator in P2P file sharing, successful copyright infringement lawsuits by the music industry in the U.S. led to the downfall of the firm's business model. In contrast to the U.S. market, the Copyright Board of Canada ruled in December 2003, that downloading copyright music from peer-to-peer networks is legal if it is for personal use. However, uploading music is not legal. To understand the ruling, it has to be appreciated that unlike in the United States, copyright holders in Canada have been compensated via special taxes that the Canadian government levies on blank media, including audio cassettes (29 cents) and CD-R audio (59 cents). This ruling seems to all but ensure the continued existence of P2P firms in Canada.

However, the music industry in Canada decided to go to court to force Internet service providers to turn over their customer lists so the industry could identify and shut down a number of individuals who were known to be major "illegal uploaders" from which the rest of Canadians were able to "legally" download. In early 2004, the Supreme Court of Canada supported the Copyright Board and refused to force Internet service providers to turn their customer lists over to the music industry. Although the Canadian music industry did not prevail, before appealing it should consider that even in the U.S. the successful lawsuits did not lead to the overall demise of the practice of distributing media products via the Internet. In less than a year, over 60 million people downloaded Morpheus, a file-sharing program that enables users to distribute music and video over the Internet. Perhaps the industry needs to adapt to P2P distribution instead of fighting it through the court system. After all, the Internet is international and P2P firms could set up distribution in almost any international location. The balance of free speech and a nation's rights to self-determination versus censorship and intellectual property rights will be hard to maintain in this instance.

Peer-to-Peer File Sharing

File sharing using personal computers has been around for many years. Historically, one person would download a file onto a disk and hand deliver the file to another person or another computer. The emergence of e-mail changed this delivery process. Using e-mail attachments, users could share files by e-mailing the files to one another. The file-sharing revolution took on a whole new dimension, however, with the advent of video games such as *Diablo* (by Blizzard Entertainment) and companies like Napster. Suddenly, by stretching the capabilities of the Internet, a gamer could play *Diablo* against an unknown gamer and/or download music provided by an unknown person.

Unfortunately for these file sharers, the real world has not been as open to file sharing as they might have liked. In the U.S., lawsuits charged that Napster had violated copyright laws by allowing users to use its centralized server to download and copy music. *Diablo* users, however, do not violate copyright laws because they have to buy the game from the manufacturer before playing on-line. With Napster, the file-sharing recipient used a centralized system, Napster, to obtain music without paying for it; with *Diablo*, the file-sharing recipient has paid for the right to play on-line by purchasing the game from Blizzard Entertainment.

The editors at the O'Reilly Network put together a directory of players in the P2P marketplace. Since the nature of P2P distribution is ill defined, the directory is divided into 19 categories: (1) agents as peers, (2) collaboration, (3) development frameworks, (4) devices as peers, (5) distributed computation, (6) distributed objects, (7) distributed search engines, (8) file sharing, (9) gaming, (10) infrastructure, (11) Internet operating system, (12) licensed media distribution, (13) messaging frameworks, (14) metadata, (15) reputation and asset management, (16) security, (17) servers/services as peers, (18) superdistribution, and (19) the writeable Web. The large number of categories appears to be indicative of the evolving nature of this new method of distribution. Clearly, the P2P model is a continually evolving distribution network.

StreamCast Networks, Inc.

According to the company's website (**http://www.streamcastnetworks.com**), StreamCast Networks, Inc., "is a leading global communications technology company that is revolutionizing Internet digital media distribution and communications via a unique software-driven solution that enables users to communicate with one another more efficiently on an unprecedented scale." The company offers two products: Morpheus and MusicCity.com. Morpheus is a P2P file-sharing program that allows users access to media content without utilizing a central server. The program is distributed free to users. MusicCity.com is a website that allows independent artists to showcase their music directly to the customer. Using the Morpheus P2P technology, users can listen to music and then have the option of purchasing it. StreamCast Networks, which is based in Tennessee, has two divisions. The Content Division is home to the company's two products. The Technology Division serves as the research and development arm of the company.

Competing With P2P Distribution

In order to compete with P2P distributors like Morpheus and Kazaa, another P2P file-sharing company, the entertainment industry has developed a number of commercial music distribution sites designed to sell music via the Internet. In Canada Puretracks.com bills itself as "Canada's first legal, digital music download site." Unlike similar American services such as iTunes, which have legal rights to prevent P2P music downloads, Puretracks.com must compete in an environment where P2P downloads are legal.

In 2004, **http://www.Puretracks.com** claimed to have over 175,000 music tracks, deliverable directly to any Internet-connected computer. The site emphasized the fact that the music was legally available and that purchasers could download as many as three copies of any music files they purchased to ensure a quality download. Still, P2P firms offer a wide variety of music for the price of a "guilty conscience" alone. Puretracks has taken on this challenge by advertising aggressive prices of on average 99 cents a download. Puretracks.com promotes its music files as having the highest quality possible for downloading. It presents claims such as: "The music files are taken directly from the master recording." Most of Puretracks' music files are encoded in Windows Media Audio at 192Kbps stereo. The music files are encoded at normalized volume levels and feature complete information about the artist and recording. In addition, Puretracks promises no spyware on its website, unlike P2P sharing. Finally, Puretracks.com advertises its service to parents by communicating the fact that many P2P sites provide pornographic offerings while Puretracks.com does not.

Can Puretracks.com and other "pay-for-download" music firms in Canada succeed against the "free downloads" of P2P firms? Will Canadian legislators change their approach and mirror the activities of their American counterparts, or will Canada remain a haven for P2P users?

Questions

1. Describe the traditional models of distribution. Does P2P fit logically within the traditional framework?
2. What is the basis for the channel conflict?
3. What is the major difference between Morpheus and Napster?
4. Do you think Puretracks.com is delivering enough "value" to entice consumers to "pay-for-downloads" when consumers can acquire the music for "free"?
5. Aside from lobbying legislators to mirror what has happened in the U.S. is there anything else that Puretracks.com and its music suppliers can do to inhibit P2P sharing in Canada?

Sources: http://www.puretracks.com; and Declan McCullagh, "Cyberpiracy North of the Border," *CNET News.com*, last modified: October 27, 2003.

>> Promotion Decisions

part 5

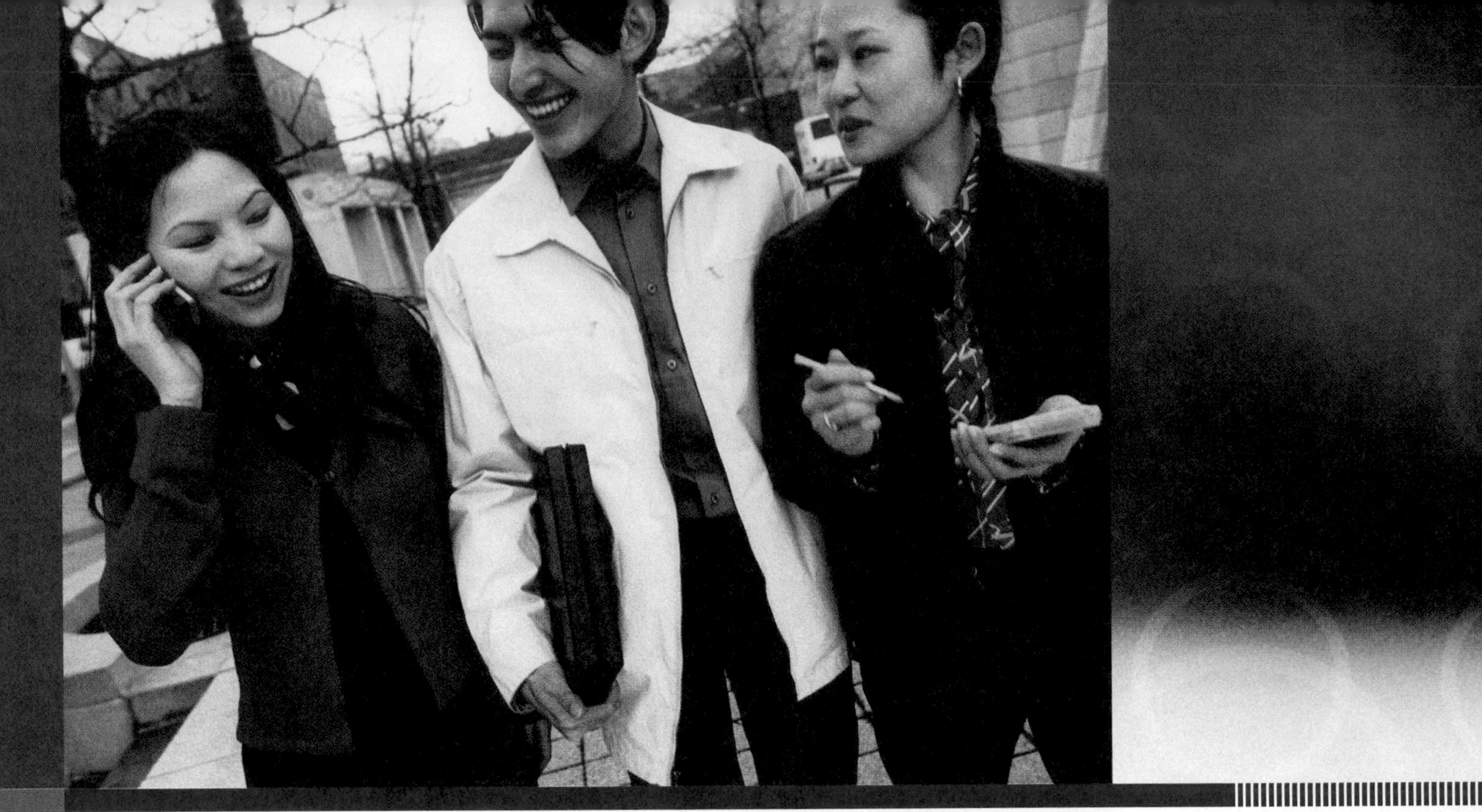

chapter 13

Marketing Communication and Personal Selling

>> LEARNING OBJECTIVES

1. Discuss the role of promotion in the marketing mix
2. Discuss the elements of the promotional mix
3. Describe the communication process
4. Explain the goals and tasks of promotion and the AIDA concept
5. Describe the factors that affect the promotional mix
6. Discuss the concept of integrated marketing communications
7. Describe personal selling
8. Discuss the key differences between relationship selling and traditional selling
9. List the steps in the selling process
10. Describe the functions of sales management

>> Marketing communication these days can be summed up with a paraphrase of the opening to Charles Dickens's book, *A Tale of Two Cities*: "it is the best of times, it is the worst of times." It is the best of times for marketing communicators because they have a plethora of media choices and media vehicles (programs) to select from. It is the worst of times because the audiences for all of the media choices available are smaller and more fragmented than they used to be. And they are being inundated with advertising clutter so they are becoming less responsive to promotional efforts as well. How do Canadians feel about marketing communications and how can marketers reach out to them?

Some marketers are considering using "new media" comprised of digital mobile devices like cell phones, PDAs, and mobile notebook computers to bust through the clutter. In particular, cell phone users with "colour" displays might be quite willing to "accept" advertising if they believe that their calling charges will be subsidized in some fashion by their acceptance of advertising. However, these marketers need to take heed of the results of a survey of 1,800 Canadians undertaken in 2003 by *Marketing Magazine* and Léger Marketing on the acceptability of advertising in various media types that indicated that only 25 percent of Canadians believe that ads on cell phone displays would be acceptable. The poll looked at the acceptability of advertising in a wide variety of media available to Canadians and reported the following results: 81 percent believed advertising was acceptable for print ads in newspapers, 77 percent for radio ads, 75 percent for posters on buses and subways, 72 percent for television advertising, 63 percent for billboards along roads, 46 percent for washrooms, 34 percent for the Internet, 32 percent for ads placed on personal property such as baby carriages, 25 percent for ads on cell phone displays as mentioned before, 20 percent for celebrities who promote prescription drugs on talks shows, and, finally, 17 percent for pop-up ads on the Internet. It's remarkable that advertising on bus and subway posters is seen as more acceptable to Canadians than television advertising when you consider that television was conceived as a "commercial" medium while a bus or a subway is a "mode of transportation" by function rather than a "medium."

Canadians recognize the pervasive nature of promotion, with 73 percent of them reporting that they feel they are always exposed to advertising; in contrast, only 7 percent felt they were seldom or never exposed to promotion. The reality is that virtually 100 percent of the population is actually exposed to promotional messages on a daily basis. The finding that only 73 percent of Canadians seem to be aware of the constant exposure is a strong indicator that a lot of promotional messages, although present, are just not being perceived. In terms of their attitudes to promotional exposure, only 55 percent of Canadians felt it was acceptable while 30 percent felt it was unacceptable. The remaining 15 percent of Canadians were either neutral or unsure about the acceptability of the amount of promotional exposure they faced. What's a marketer to do in the face of all the promotional clutter and the fact that Canadians are not taking as much notice of promotion as they used to?

Marketers are realizing that a broad media targeting approach is no longer viable in an overcommunicated society with fragmented media audiences. One of the approaches that marketers are considering to reach out to consumers is mixing program content and promotional messages together. For example, Quebec-based home renovation chain RONA undertook sponsorship of a reality show entitled *Ma Maison RONA*. The show, a French-Canadian version of *Home Improvement* meets *Family Feud*, involved two families who competed against each other to renovate and decorate a home. The prize for the winning family is the home! Along with the program title identifying RONA as the sponsor, there were a number of other promotional ties including three 30-second commercials run during the show, RONA's name on the opening and closing program credits, and a number of minutes of programming exposure that included exposure of supplier brands. Finally, the contestants were dressed in RONA's blue and yellow colours. The show was so successful that RONA decided to air an English-language version of the show entitled *The RONA Dream House*.

Along with unique approaches like this, Canadian marketers are also looking for other unique ways to communicate their messages. For example, motion pictures, such as Disney's *Pirates of the Caribbean,* which was based on one of its theme park rides, communicate product links. Another unique approach involves Internet movies such as those developed by clothier DKNY, which demonstrates its products in short movie stories, e.g., the film *New York Stories,* which featured Michele Hicks, an actress who performed in the film *Mulholland Drive*. In addition, the website has a second short film entitled *Road Stories* (**http://www.dkny.com**). Magazines are including large advertising sections that look like content and contain interesting information or features that draw the reader in and get them interested before they realize they are actually reading advertising. Consider how TIME Canada included a supplement featuring an eight-page spread devoted to coin sets from the Royal Canadian Mint. The promotion industry has always drawn upon some of the most creative people in the world to develop its communications messages and strategies—fortunately the industry is well represented with creative people to design new messages and new approaches to using media to cut through the clutter.[1]

Promotion is a critical component of a firm's marketing mix. What types of promotional tools are available to companies, and what factors influence the choice of tool? Why is consistent integrated marketing important to the promotional plan? These questions, and others, will be answered as you read this chapter.

ON LINE 

DKNY

How does clothier DKNY use its website as part of its integrated marketing communications strategy? Are there references to any other advertising or promotions activities? How is the site a database marketing tool?

http://www.dkny.com

1 Discuss the role of promotion in the marketing mix

>> THE ROLE OF PROMOTION IN THE MARKETING MIX

promotion
Communication by marketers that informs, persuades, and reminds potential buyers of a product in order to influence an opinion or elicit a response.

promotional strategy
A plan for the optimal use of the elements of promotion: advertising, public relations, personal selling, and sales promotion.

differential advantage
One or more unique aspects of an organization that cause target consumers to patronize that firm rather than competitors.

Few goods or services, no matter how well developed, priced, or distributed, can survive in the marketplace without effective **promotion**—communication by marketers that informs, persuades, and reminds potential buyers of a product in order to influence their opinion or elicit a response.

Promotional strategy is a plan for the optimal use of the elements of promotion: advertising, public relations, personal selling, and sales promotion. As Exhibit 13.1 shows, the marketing manager determines the goals of the company's promotional strategy in light of the firm's overall goals for the marketing mix—product, place (distribution), promotion, and price. Using these overall goals, marketers combine the elements of the promotional strategy (the promotional mix) into a coordinated plan. The promotion plan then becomes an integral part of the marketing strategy for reaching the target market.

The main function of a marketer's promotional strategy is to convince target customers that the goods and services offered provide a **differential advantage** over the competition. A differential advantage is the set of unique features of a company and its products that are perceived by the target market as significant and superior to the competition. Such features can include high product quality, rapid delivery, low prices, excellent service, or a feature not offered by the competition. For example, Revlon ColorStay Lipcolor promises unsmeared lipstick all day long. By effectively communicating this differential advantage through advertising featuring model Cindy Crawford, Revlon can stimulate demand for its smudge-free line of makeup. Promotion is therefore a vital part of the marketing mix, informing consumers of a product's benefits and thereby positioning the product in the marketplace.

EXHIBIT 13.1
Role of Promotion in the Marketing Mix

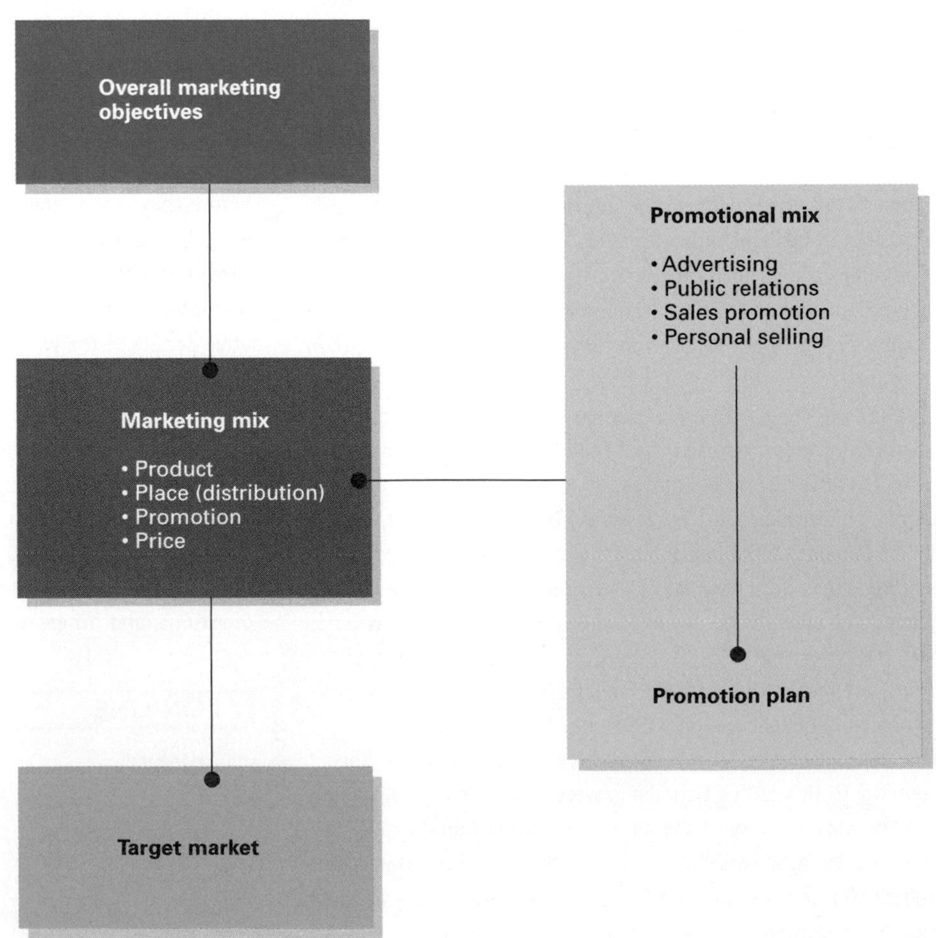

>> THE PROMOTIONAL MIX

Most promotional strategies use several ingredients, including advertising, public relations, sales promotion, and personal selling, to reach a target market. That combination is called the **promotional mix**. The proper promotional mix is the one that management believes will meet the needs of the target market and fulfill the organization's overall goals. The more funds allocated to each promotional ingredient and the more managerial emphasis placed on each technique, the more important that element is thought to be in the overall mix.

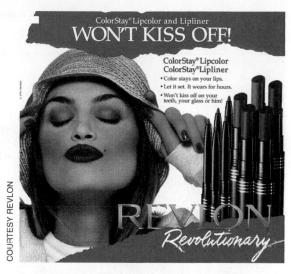

COURTESY REVLON

Revlon ColorStay Lipcolor promises unsmeared lipstick all day long. By effectively communicating this differential advantage through advertising, Revlon can stimulate demand for its smudge-free line of makeup.

Discuss the elements of the promotional mix

promotional mix
The combination of promotional tools, including advertising, public relations, personal selling, and sales promotion, used to reach the target market and fulfill the organization's overall goals.

advertising
Impersonal, one-way mass communication about a product or organization that is paid for by a marketer.

Advertising

Almost all companies selling a good or a service use some form of advertising, whether it be in the form of a multimillion-dollar campaign or a simple classified ad in a newspaper. **Advertising** is any form of paid communication in which the sponsor or company is identified. Traditional media, such as television, radio, newspapers, magazines, books, direct mail, billboards, and transit cards (advertisements on buses and taxis and at bus stops), are most commonly used to transmit advertisements to consumers. With the increasing fragmentation of traditional media choices, marketers are sending their advertisements to consumers in many new and innovative ways, such as with interactive video technology located in department stores and supermarkets and through Internet websites and electronic mail.

One of the primary benefits of advertising is its ability to communicate to a large number of people at one time. Cost per contact, therefore, is typically very low. Advertising has the advantage of being able to reach the masses (for instance, through national television networks), but it can also be microtargeted to small groups of potential customers, such as with television ads on a targeted cable network or through print advertising in a trade magazine.

Although the cost per contact in advertising is very low, the total cost to advertise is typically very high. This hurdle tends to restrict advertising on a national basis to only those companies that are financially able to do so. For instance, Allstream launched a $20 to $25 million campaign to inform Canadians about its identity change from AT&T Canada to Allstream in 2003.[2] Few small companies can match this level of spending for a national campaign. Chapter 14 examines advertising in greater detail.

Many companies are including Internet advertising as a vital component in their marketing mix. Banner ads, viral marketing, and interactive promotions are all ways that marketers utilize the Internet to try and reach their target audience. But some consumers and lawmakers feel that privacy issues are being violated. Read about this issue in the "Ethics in Marketing" box.

Public Relations

Concerned about how they are perceived by their target markets, organizations often spend large sums to build a positive public image. **Public relations** is the marketing function that evaluates public attitudes, identifies areas within the organization the public may be interested in, and executes a program of action to earn public understanding and acceptance. Public relations helps an organization communicate with customers, suppliers, stockholders, government officials, employees, and the community in which it operates. Marketers use public relations not only to maintain a positive image but also to educate the public about the company's goals and objectives, introduce new products, and help support the sales effort.

public relations
The marketing function that evaluates public attitudes, identifies areas within the organization that the public may be interested in, and executes a program of action to earn public understanding and acceptance.

Cisco Systems Canada has used public relations to support its selling efforts. Cisco issues a biweekly newsletter entitled *Cisco MediaFusion* to organizations that would have an interest in IP telephony technology and solutions. This newsletter contains news articles, case studies, and industry research that Cisco has developed or has acquired

ETHICS IN MARKETING

You've Got UCEM (unsolicited commercial electronic mail, a.k.a. spam)

Turn the computer on, check your e-mail, and more than likely you're bombarded with messages like: "You can lose 20 pounds by the summer!" "Save 50 percent on prescription drugs!" and "Click here to find out how you can take the dream vacation of a lifetime!" Welcome to the Internet! You've got unsolicited commercial electronic mail (spam)—now how do you get rid of it?

Some marketers have been making money by sending unwanted e-mail for years. It seems like the perfect way to reach thousands, maybe even millions, with your marketing message. The latest research reports indicate that each day 15 billion spam messages are sent over the Internet. For the multitude of "spam haters" this seems like very bad news. However, there is some good news: the majority of spam messages are now being intercepted and not reaching the e-mail addresses of many users. AOL and MSN are two of the world's largest Internet service providers. They indicate that their services block around 2.4 billion spam messages on a daily basis and that spam comprises about 80 percent of their incoming e-mail messages. Research firm Gartner, Inc., estimates that 60 percent of all the messages on the Internet will be due to spam as early as 2004. Unsolicited commercial electronic mail—spamming—annoys most consumers and has been the subject of legislative treatment from many governments.

Just how do marketers get your e-mail address in the first place? Chat rooms, message boards, Internet directories, Web pages, and on-line shopping are prime "harvesting" sites for spammers. Other companies may sell their customer data lists.

As mentioned earlier, America Online and MSN have been making privacy a competitive advantage by blocking mail from known spammers. However, electronic blocking is not a complete solution to the problem. As such, in March 2004, the major North American Internet service providers (ISPs)—Microsoft, America Online, Yahoo!, and EarthLink—combined together and filed lawsuits against Canadian and U.S.-based organizations and individuals they had identified as being "major spammers" to force them to stop the practice. According to these lawsuits, the four ISPs put a cost price of $10 billion in lost productivity, network upgrades, and destroyed or lost data due to spam. In a press conference, reporters were told that viability of e-mail was being threatened by spam.

A Canadian company, Kitchener-based Gold Disk Canada, was named in one of the lawsuits filed by Yahoo! Gold Disk was alleged to have harvested millions of e-mail addresses that were then sold to other companies. Yahoo! claims that Gold Disk inserted random text into its spam messages to defeat spam blockers and disguise their identity.

Aside from the activities of ISP providers to reduce spam, many countries around the world have enacted legislation to protect Internet customers from spam. An anti-spam law became official in the U.K. in early December 2003. In a vote of 97 to 0 the United States Senate also passed a federal law in 2003 to limit unsolicited mass commercial e-mail in an attempt to protect computer users from unwanted intrusions. Under this law, which was also ratified by the U.S. Congress, e-mailers are prohibited from disguising their identify, using misleading headlines, and using false return addresses. The e-mails should also include the physical addresses of companies, must clearly identify themselves as advertisements, and must contain opt-out instructions. In Canada, similar legislation was introduced in 2003 as a private member's bill but as of the first quarter of 2004, Canada had not passed any anti-spam laws.

Unsolicited e-mail is a huge inconvenience to consumers and as indicated in their lawsuits, very costly to ISP providers. Canadian companies that employ this practice must be prepared to face a consumer backlash and lawsuits from ISP providers; in the future, they could well face criminal investigation. Canadian marketers have an ethical and may very soon also have a legal obligation to keep consumers and their privacy concerns in mind.[3]

Is e-mail an effective marketing tool to use with college and university students? When does e-mail as a marketing tool become spamming?

publicity
Public information about a company, good, or service appearing in the mass media as a news item.

from the public domain. The newsletter is tied in to Cisco Systems Canada's communications campaign, which involves media education, customer success stories, and the use of other promotional media along with personal selling efforts.[4]

A solid public relations program can generate favourable **publicity**—public information about a company, good, or service appearing in the mass media as a news item. The organization generally is not identified as the source of the information. The soy industry in North America received favourable publicity and an increase in sales after the U.S. Food and Drug Administration (FDA) approved a health claim for food labelling suggesting a link between soy protein and the reduced risk of coronary heart disease.[5] This incident underscores a peculiar reality of marketing: no matter how many millions are spent on advertising, nothing sells a product better than free publicity.

ON LINE

Wal-Mart and the Juno Beach Centre

Visit the Juno Beach Centre website and the Wal-Mart Canada website. Can you find a Wal-Mart presence on the Juno Beach website? How is Wal-Mart represented here? (Hint: Do a donor search.) Go to the Wal-Mart website. Look at the kinds of public relations activities it supports. Does the Juno Beach Centre fit into the usual activities that Wal-Mart supports?

http://www.junobeach.org/centre

http://www.walmart.com

Although an organization does not pay for this kind of mass-media exposure, publicity should not be viewed as free. Preparing news releases, staging special events, and persuading media personnel to print or broadcast them costs money. In 2003, Wal-Mart Canada decided to support Garth Webb, a Canadian D-Day veteran who was trying to build a museum on the shores of Juno Beach in France that would be dedicated to Canadian soldiers who fought and died in Europe during World War II. Webb was having trouble finding a corporate sponsor until Wal-Mart Canada stepped in and supported his efforts by raising $1.5 million itself along with providing an additional $2 million in publicity support.[6] Public relations and publicity are examined further in Chapter 15.

Sales Promotion

Sales promotion consists of all marketing activities, other than personal selling, advertising, and public relations, that stimulate consumer purchasing and dealer effectiveness. Sales promotion is generally a short-run tool used to stimulate immediate increases in demand. Sales promotion can be aimed at end consumers, trade customers, or a company's employees. Sales promotions include free samples, contests, premiums, trade shows, vacation giveaways, and coupons. A major promotional campaign might use several of these sales promotion tools. For example, Motorola, a sponsor of a mountain bike event called "24 Hours of Adrenalin," teamed up recently with Canada's Future Shop to debut the Motorola Gear Grab. This promotion gave 10 people 24 seconds to grab as much Motorola gear as they could in a Future Shop store. Contestants worked in pairs and used Motorola two-way radios so that one partner could provide the other with the name, description, and location of a Motorola product, including cell phones and messaging devices, within the store. Contestants were also eligible for a grand prize of various Motorola and mountain biking gear. Besides the Gear Grab, Motorola sponsored several mini-Gear Grabs during mountain bike event weekends in different cities.[7]

sales promotion
Marketing activities, other than personal selling, advertising, and public relations, which stimulate consumer buying and dealer effectiveness.

Often marketers use sales promotion to improve the effectiveness of other ingredients in the promotional mix, especially advertising and personal selling. Research shows that sales promotion complements advertising by yielding faster sales responses. Lever 2000 recently shifted some of its marketing dollars to focus more on sampling instead of traditional advertising. The company literally took to the streets to launch its Pure Rain body wash. Unilever employed samplers dressed in shower costumes and handing out product samples to consumers in different cities. During the program, consumers also were surveyed on shower-related questions such as: "Which famous person would you most like to shower with?" Along with sampling, two transit stops were converted into shower stalls. In cities where ordinances prevented such conversions, tents were set up.[8] Sales promotion is discussed in more detail in Chapter 14.

Personal Selling

Personal selling is a purchase situation in which two people communicate in an attempt to influence each other. In this dyad, both the buyer and the seller have specific objectives they wish to accomplish. The buyer may need to minimize cost or ensure a quality product, for instance, while the salesperson may need to maximize revenue and profits.[9]

personal selling
A purchase situation in which two people communicate in an attempt to influence each other.

Traditional methods of personal selling include a planned presentation to one or more prospective buyers for the purpose of making a sale. Whether it takes place face-to-face or over the phone, personal selling attempts to persuade the buyer to accept a point of view or convince the buyer to take some action. For example, a car salesperson may try to persuade a car buyer that a particular model is superior to a competing model in certain features, such as fuel economy, roominess, and interior styling. Once the buyer is somewhat convinced, then the salesperson may attempt to elicit some action from the buyer, such as a test drive or a purchase. Frequently, in this traditional view of personal selling, the objectives of the salesperson are at the expense of the buyer, creating a win–lose outcome.

More current notions on the subject of personal selling emphasize the relationship that develops between a salesperson and a buyer. This concept is more typical with business- and industrial-type goods, such as heavy machinery or computer systems, than with consumer goods. Relationship selling emphasizes a win–win outcome and the accomplishment of mutual objectives that benefits both buyer and salesperson in the long term. Rather than focusing on a quick sale, relationship selling attempts to create a long-term, committed relationship based on trust, increased customer loyalty, and a continuation of the relationship between the salesperson and the customer.[10] Personal selling and relationship selling are discussed later on in this chapter.

3 Describe the communication process

>> MARKETING COMMUNICATION

communication
The process by which we exchange or share meanings through a common set of symbols.

Promotional strategy is closely related to the process of communication. As humans, we assign meaning to feelings, ideas, facts, attitudes, and emotions. **Communication** is the process by which we exchange or share meanings through a common set of symbols. When a company develops a new product, changes an old one, or simply tries to increase sales of an existing good or service, it must communicate its selling message to potential customers. Marketers communicate information about the firm and its products to the target market and various segments of the public through its promotion programs. Pepsi-Cola Canada Ltd. has developed the strongest market in North America for Pepsi in Quebec, where it claims Pepsi outsells Coca-Cola at a ratio of nearly two to one! The secret to Pepsi's success in Quebec is strongly related to its use of one of the longest-running promotional campaigns in North America. The campaign, begun in 1984, features comedian Claude Meunier who writes and performs in the television commercials and lends his voice to the radio commercials. In one recent Christmas campaign, Meunier appeared as "Santa Claude," wearing, of course, a blue Santa suit à la Pepsi, rather than the traditional red. Over the years Meunier has been able to develop new ideas to sustain the campaign because he is completely plugged into the culture in Quebec and has a creative flair and personality that is strongly appealing and has not worn out the audience.[11]

interpersonal communication
Direct, face-to-face communication between two or more people.

Communication can be divided into two major categories: interpersonal communication and mass communication. **Interpersonal communication** is direct, face-to-face communication between two or more people. When communicating face to face, people see the other person's reaction and can respond almost immediately. A salesperson speaking directly with a client is an example of marketing communication that is interpersonal.

mass communication
The communication of a concept or message to large audiences.

Mass communication refers to communicating a concept or message to large audiences. A great deal of marketing communication is directed to consumers as a whole, usually through a mass medium such as television or newspapers. When a company advertises, it generally does not personally know the people with whom it is trying to communicate. Furthermore, the company is unable to respond immediately to consumers' reactions to its message. Instead, the marketing manager must wait to see whether people are reacting positively or negatively to the mass-communicated promotion. Any clutter from competitors' messages or other distractions in the environment can reduce the effectiveness of the mass communication effort.

The Communication Process

ON LINE 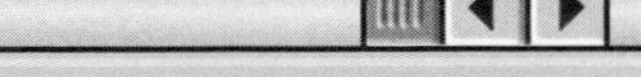

Marketing Magazine

Marketing Magazine is focused on the Canadian advertising and promotion industry. Explore its website and examine the kinds of information the website has to offer. How might you use the kinds of information this website provides to help make promotional decisions?

http://www.marketingmag.ca

Marketers are both senders and receivers of messages. As senders, marketers attempt to inform, persuade, and remind the target market to adopt courses of action compatible with the need to promote the purchase of goods and services. As receivers, marketers attune themselves to the target market in order to develop the appropriate messages, adapt existing messages, and spot new communication opportunities. In this way, marketing communication is a two-way rather than one-way process.[12] The two-way nature of the communication process is shown in Exhibit 13.2.

The Sender and Encoding

The **sender** is the originator of the message in the communication process. In an interpersonal conversation, the sender may be a parent, a friend, or a salesperson. For an advertisement or press release, the sender is the company or organization itself.

Encoding is the conversion of the sender's ideas and thoughts into a message, usually in the form of words or signs.

A basic principle of encoding is that what matters is not what the source says but what the receiver hears. One way of conveying a message that the receiver will hear properly is to use concrete words and pictures. For example, Molson's long running "I Am Canadian!" campaign has undergone a number of variations of presentation, from its storied beginning entitled the "rant," in which a young man stands up and describes what it is to be Canadian, right up until a recent campaign where a Canadian astronaut shoots pucks on the moon and hits an American astronaut on the face plate. Later they sit down to share a Molson Canadian beer in a couple of lawn chairs. No matter what the presentation, these commercials always end with the receivers hearing an ending tag line shouted out—"I Am Canadian!"—while the Molson Canadian logo is displayed.

sender
The originator of the message in the communication process.

encoding
The conversion of the sender's ideas and thoughts into a message, usually in the form of words or signs.

Message Transmission

Transmission of a message requires a **channel**—a voice, radio, newspaper, or other communication medium. A facial expression or gesture can also serve as a channel.

Reception occurs when the message is detected by the receiver and enters his or her frame of reference. In a two-way conversation such as a sales pitch given by a sales representative to a potential client, reception is normally high. In contrast, the desired receivers may or may not detect the message when it is mass communicated because most media are cluttered with **noise**—anything that interferes with, distorts, or slows down the transmission of information. In some media overcrowded with advertisers, such as newspapers and television, the noise level is high and the reception level is low. For example, competing network advertisements and other programming on the network itself can hamper reception of Molson's television ads. Transmission can also be hindered by situational factors such as physical surroundings like light, sound,

channel
A medium of communication, such as a voice, radio, or newspaper, for transmitting a message.

noise
Anything that interferes with, distorts, or slows down the transmission of information.

EXHIBIT 13.2
Communication Process

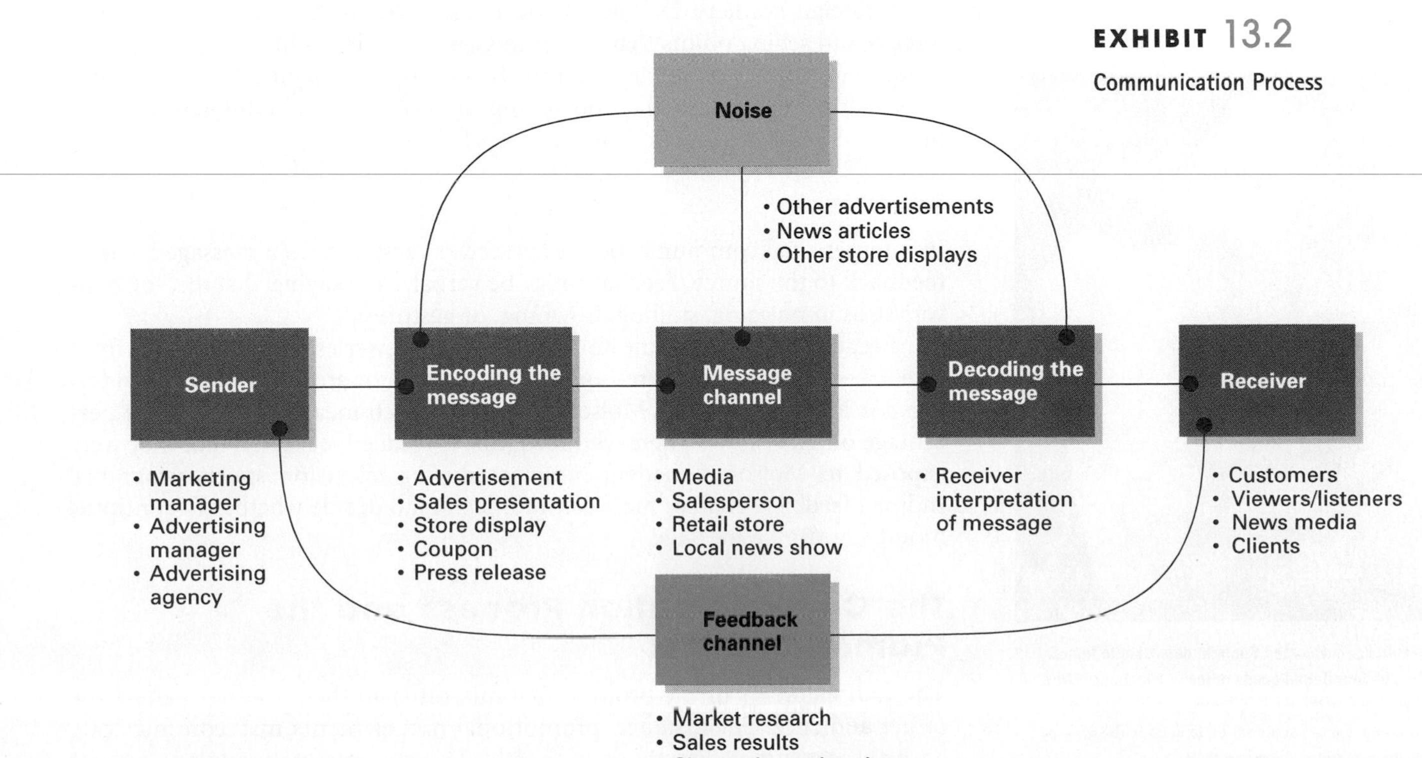

location, and weather; by the presence of other people; or by the temporary moods consumers might bring to the situation. Mass communication may not even reach all the right consumers. Some members of the target audience may have been watching television when advertisements for Molson Canadian were shown, but others may not have been.

The Receiver and Decoding

receiver
The person who decodes a message.

decoding
Interpretation of the language and symbols sent by the source through a channel.

Marketers communicate their message through a channel to customers, or **receivers**, who will decode the message. **Decoding** is the interpretation of the language and symbols sent by the source through a channel. Common understanding between two communicators, or a common frame of reference, is required for effective communication. Therefore, marketing managers must ensure a proper match between the message to be conveyed and the target market's attitudes and ideas.

Even though a message has been received, it will not necessarily be properly decoded—or even seen, viewed, or heard—because of selective exposure, distortion, and retention (refer to Chapter 4).[13] Even when people receive a message, they tend to manipulate, alter, and modify it to reflect their own biases, needs, knowledge, and culture. Factors that can lead to miscommunication include differences in age, social class, education, culture, and ethnicity. Further, because people don't always listen or read carefully, they can easily misinterpret what is said or written. In fact, researchers have found that consumers misunderstand a large proportion of both printed and televised communications. Bright colours and bold graphics have been shown to increase consumers' comprehension of marketing communication. Even these techniques are not foolproof, however. A classic example of miscommunication occurred when Lever Brothers mailed out samples of its then new dishwashing liquid, Sunlight, which contains real lemon juice. The package clearly stated that Sunlight was a household cleaning product. However, many people saw the word sunlight, the large picture of lemons, and the phrase "with real lemon juice" and thought the product was lemon juice.

Marketers targeting consumers in foreign countries must also worry about the translation and possible miscommunication of their promotional messages by other cultures. An important issue for global marketers is whether to standardize or customize the message for each global market in which they sell. For instance, when advertising the PT Cruiser in foreign markets, DaimlerChrysler might choose to use the same commercials and selling points that it uses in Canada, or it might decide to develop unique ads for each country or culture. Read about how some global marketers have adapted their marketing mix to appeal to consumers in different cultures in the "Global Perspectives" box on page 416.

feedback
The receiver's response to a message.

Feedback

In interpersonal communication, the receiver's response to a message is direct **feedback** to the source. Feedback may be verbal, as in saying "I agree," or nonverbal, as in nodding, smiling, frowning, or gesturing.

Because mass communicators like Molson Breweries are often cut off from direct feedback, they must rely on market research or analysis of television ratings for indirect feedback. Molson's might use such measurements as the percentage of television viewers who recognized, recalled, or stated that they were exposed to Molson Canadian messages during television sports programs. Indirect feedback enables mass communicators to decide whether to continue, modify, or drop a message.

© KRISTIINA PAUL

Would you have used Sunlight detergent to lemon flavour your baked goods or make lemonade? When it first came on the market showing lemons on the package, some people failed to decode the message on the product and did just that!

The Communication Process and the Promotional Mix

The four elements of the promotional mix differ in their ability to affect the target audience. For instance, promotional mix elements may communicate with the consumer directly or indirectly. The message may flow one way or two ways. Feedback may be fast or slow, a little or a lot. Likewise, the communicator may have varying degrees of control over message delivery, content, and flexibility. Exhibit 13.3 outlines differences among the promotional mix elements with respect to mode of communication, marketer's control over the communication process, amount and speed of feedback, direction of message flow, marketer's control over the message, identification of the sender, speed in reaching large audiences, and message flexibility.

From Exhibit 13.3, you can see that most elements of the promotional mix are indirect and impersonal when used to communicate with a target market, providing only one direction of message flow. For example, advertising, public relations, and sales promotion are generally impersonal, one-way means of mass communication. Because they provide no opportunity for direct feedback, they cannot easily adapt to consumers' changing preferences, individual differences, and personal goals.

Personal selling, on the other hand, is personal, two-way communication. The salesperson is able to receive immediate feedback from the consumer and adjust the message in response. Personal selling, however, is very slow in dispersing the marketer's message to large audiences. Because a salesperson can only communicate to one person or a small group of people at one time, it is a poor choice if the marketer wants to send a message to many potential buyers.

>> THE GOALS AND TASKS OF PROMOTION AND THE AIDA CONCEPT

4 Explain the goals and tasks of promotion and the AIDA concept

People communicate with one another for many reasons. They seek amusement, ask for help, give assistance or instructions, provide information, and express ideas and thoughts. Promotion, on the other hand, seeks to modify behaviour and thoughts in some way. For example, promoters may try to persuade consumers to eat at Harvey's rather than at McDonald's. Promotion also strives to reinforce existing behaviour—for instance, getting consumers to continue to dine at Harvey's once they have switched. The source (the seller) hopes to project a favourable image or to motivate purchase of the company's goods and services.

EXHIBIT 13.3

Characteristics of the Elements in the Promotional Mix

	ADVERTISING	PUBLIC RELATIONS	SALES PROMOTION	PERSONAL SELLING
Mode of communication	Indirect and nonpersonal	Usually indirect and nonpersonal	Usually indirect and nonpersonal	Direct and face-to-face
Communicator control over situation	Low	Moderate to low	Moderate to low	High
Amount of feedback	Little	Little	Little to moderate	Much
Speed of feedback	Delayed	Delayed	Varies	Immediate
Direction of message flow	One-way	One-way	Mostly one-way	Two-way
Control over message content	Yes	No	Yes	Yes
Identification of sponsor	Yes	No	Yes	Yes
Speed in reaching large audience	Fast	Usually fast	Fast	Slow
Message flexibility	Same message to all audiences	Usually no direct control over message	Same message to varied target audiences	Tailored to prospective buyer

Promotion can perform one or more of three tasks: inform the target audience, persuade the target audience, or remind the target audience. Often a marketer will try to accomplish two or more of these tasks at the same time. Exhibit 13.4 lists the three tasks of promotion and some examples of each.

Informing

Informative promotion may seek to convert an existing need into a want or to stimulate interest in a new product. It is generally more prevalent during the early stages of the product life cycle. People typically will not buy a product service or support a nonprofit organization until they know its purpose and its benefits to them. Informative messages are important for promoting complex and technical products such as automobiles, computers, and investment services. Informative promotion is also important for a "new" brand being introduced into an "old" product class. For example, Ristorante pizza, a new brand of frozen pizza that entered the Canadian frozen pizza industry in 2003, launched with a $2.8 million advertising campaign so it could carve out a slice of a market that is currently dominated by well-known brands like McCain's frozen pizza and Kraft's Delissio pizza. This new Ristorante pizza brand cannot establish itself against more mature brands unless potential buyers are aware of it, understand its benefits, and understand its positioning in the marketplace.[14]

Persuading

Persuasive promotion is designed to stimulate a purchase or an action, for example, to eat more McCain frozen French fries or to use the banking services of the Royal Bank of Canada. Persuasion normally becomes the main promotion goal when the product enters the growth stage of its life cycle. By this time, the target market should have general product awareness and some knowledge of how the product can fulfill its wants. Therefore, the promotional task switches from informing consumers about the product category to persuading them to buy the company's brand rather than the competitor's. At this time, the promotional message emphasizes the product's real and perceived differential advantages, often appealing to emotional needs such as love, belonging, self-esteem, and ego satisfaction.

Persuasion can also be an important goal for very competitive mature product categories such as household items, soft drinks, beer, and banking services. In a marketplace characterized by many competitors, the promotional message often encourages brand switching and aims to convert some buyers into loyal users. For example, to persuade new customers to switch their chequing accounts, a bank's marketing manager may offer a year's worth of free cheques with no fees.

Critics believe that some promotional messages and techniques can be too persuasive, causing consumers to buy products and services they really don't need.

EXHIBIT 13.4

Promotion Tasks and Examples

- **Informative promotion**
  Increasing the awareness of a new brand, product class, or product attribute
  Explaining how the product works
  Suggesting new uses for a product
  Building a company image
- **Persuasive promotion**
  Encouraging brand switching
  Changing customers' perceptions of product attributes
  Influencing customers to buy now
  Persuading customers to call
- **Reminder promotion**
  Reminding consumers that the product may be needed in the near future
  Reminding consumers where to buy the product
  Maintaining consumer awareness

Reminding

Reminder promotion is used to keep the product and brand name in the public's mind. This type of promotion prevails during the maturity stage of the life cycle. It assumes that the target market has already been persuaded of the good's or service's merits. Its purpose is simply to trigger a memory. Crest toothpaste, Tide laundry detergent, Cadbury Caramilk chocolate bars, and many other consumer products often use reminder promotion.

ON LINE

Tide

Consider Tide detergent's website as a promotional tool. Visit the site and decide whether you think the main goal of the site is informing, persuading, or reminding. Explain your choice.

http://www.tide.com

>> PROMOTIONAL GOALS AND THE AIDA CONCEPT

The ultimate goal of any promotion is to get someone to buy a good or service or, in the case of nonprofit organizations, to take some action (for instance, donate blood). A classic model for reaching promotional goals is called the **AIDA concept.**[15] The acronym stands for attention, interest, desire, and action—the stages of consumer involvement with a promotional message.

AIDA concept
A model that outlines the process for achieving promotional goals in terms of stages of consumer involvement with the message; the acronym stands for *attention, interest, desire,* and *action.*

This model proposes that consumers respond to marketing messages in a cognitive (thinking), affective (feeling), and conative (doing) sequence. First, the promotion manager attracts a person's attention by (in personal selling) a greeting and approach or (in advertising and sales promotion) loud volume, unusual contrasts, bold headlines, movement, bright colours, and so on. Next, a good sales presentation, demonstration, or advertisement stimulates interest in the product and then, by illustrating how the product's features will satisfy the consumer's needs, arouses desire. Finally, a special offer or a strong closing sales pitch may be used to obtain purchase action.

The AIDA concept assumes that promotion propels consumers along the following four steps in the purchase-decision process:

1. *Attention*: The advertiser must first gain the attention of the target market. A firm cannot sell something if the market does not know that the good or service exists. When Proctor & Gamble first introduced the Swiffer Sweeper, it advertised heavily on TV and in magazines; it also conducted live demonstrations at malls.
2. *Interest*: Simple awareness of a brand seldom leads to a sale. The next step is to create interest in the product. A print ad or TV commercial can't actually tell people to go and buy the product. Proctor & Gamble had to make clear how the Swiffer would benefit users. Live promotions helped accomplish this.
3. *Desire*: Potential customers may not see a given product as having any advantage over competing brands, especially if customers are loyal to existing brands. Therefore, Proctor & Gamble had to create brand preference for the Swiffer by explaining its differential advantage over the competition. The Swiffer was shown to clean floors better and more efficiently than other floor-cleaning tools. At this stage Proctor & Gamble can offer other reasons to purchase the product such as the ease of disposal of used Swiffer mop heads and replacement with new mop heads.

ON LINE

What role can the Internet play in the AIDA concept? Consider Exhibit 13.5. Recreate the table by deciding how effective you think the Internet would be as an advertising tool to create attention, interest, desire, and action. Continue to evaluate the Internet as a public relations tool, sales promotion tool, and personal selling tool.

4. *Action*: Some members of the target market may now be convinced to buy a Swiffer mop even though they have yet to make the purchase. Displays in grocery stores, coupons, premiums, and trial-size packages can often push the complacent shopper into making a purchase.

Most buyers involved in high-involvement purchase situations pass through the four stages of the AIDA model on the way to making a purchase. The promoter's task is to determine where on the purchase ladder most of the target consumers are located and design a promotion plan to meet their needs. For instance, if Proctor & Gamble has determined that about half its buyers are in the preference or conviction stage but have not bought the Swiffer for some reason, the company may mail cents-off coupons to homeowners to prompt them to buy.

The AIDA concept does not explain how all promotions influence purchase decisions. The model suggests that promotional effectiveness can be measured in terms of consumers progressing from one stage to the next. However, the order of stages in the model, as well as whether consumers go through all steps, has been much debated. For example, a purchase can occur without interest or desire, perhaps when a low-involvement product is bought on impulse. Regardless of the order of the stages or consumers' progression through these stages, the AIDA concept helps marketers by suggesting which promotional strategy will be most effective.[16]

AIDA and the Promotional Mix

Exhibit 13.5 depicts the relationship between the promotional mix and the AIDA model. It shows that although advertising does have an impact in the later stages, it is most useful in gaining attention for goods or services. In contrast, personal selling reaches fewer people at first. Salespeople are more effective at creating customer interest for merchandise or a service and at creating desire. For example, advertising may help a potential computer purchaser gain knowledge and information about competing brands, but the salesperson in an electronics store may be the one who actually encourages the buyer to decide a particular brand is the best choice. The salesperson also has the advantage of having the computer physically there to demonstrate its capabilities to the buyer.

Sales promotion's greatest strength is in creating strong desire and purchase intent. Coupons and other price-off promotions are techniques used to persuade customers to buy new products. Frequent-buyer sales promotion programs, popular among retailers, allow consumers to accumulate points or dollars that can later be redeemed for goods. Frequent-buyer programs tend to increase purchase intent and loyalty and encourage repeat purchases. Canadian Tire stores reward loyal shoppers with Canadian Tire money for cash purchases at its stores. Canadian Tire customers who use the Canadian Tire Options MasterCard will also earn Canadian Tire money on their cards that can be used for purchases at Canadian Tire Stores.

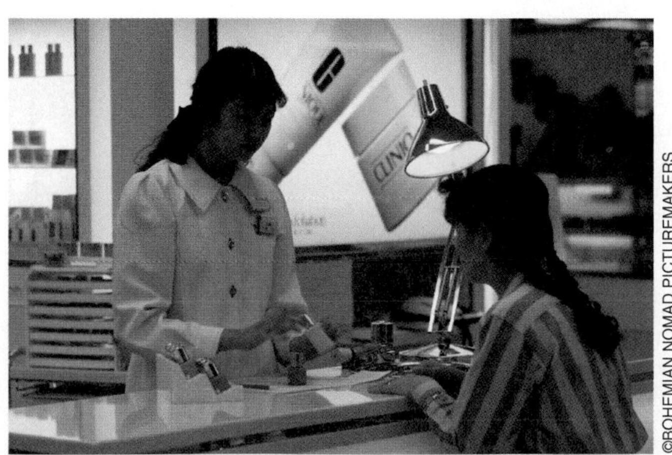

©BOHEMIAN NOMAD PICTUREMAKERS

This cosmetics saleswoman at Clinique can create desire for her line of products by showing her potential customer how wonderful she looks after using them. Salespeople are very effective at arousing desire, particularly in this type of situation.

Public relations has its greatest impact in gaining attention for a company, good, or service. Many companies can attract attention and build goodwill by sponsoring community events that benefit a worthy cause. An example is the Wal-Mart sponsorship of the Juno Beach Centre discussed earlier. Such sponsorships project a positive image of the firm and its products in the minds of consumers and potential consumers. Good publicity can also help develop consumer desire for a product. Book publishers push to get their titles on the bestseller lists of major publications, such as the *National Post.* Book authors also make appearances on talk shows and at bookstores to personally sign books and speak to fans. Similarly, movie marketers use prerelease publicity to raise the profile of their movies and to increase

	ATTENTION	INTEREST	DESIRE	ACTION
Advertising	Very effective	Very effective	Somewhat effective	Not effective
Public relations	Very effective	Very effective	Very effective	Not effective
Sales promotion	Somewhat effective	Somewhat effective	Very effective	Somewhat effective
Personal selling	Somewhat effective	Very effective	Very effective	Very effective

EXHIBIT 13.5

When the Elements of Promotion Are Most Useful

initial box-office sales. For example, most major motion picture studios have their own websites with multimedia clips and publicity photos of their current movies to attract viewers. Furthermore, movie promoters will include publicity gained from reviewers' quotes and Academy Award nominations in their advertising.

>> FACTORS AFFECTING THE PROMOTIONAL MIX

5 Describe the factors that affect the promotional mix

Promotional mixes vary a great deal from one product and one industry to the next. Normally, advertising and personal selling are used to promote goods and services, supported and supplemented by sales promotion. Public relations helps develop a positive image for the organization and the product line. However, a firm may choose not to use all four promotional elements in its promotional mix, or it may choose to use them in varying degrees. The particular promotional mix chosen by a firm for a product or service depends on several factors: the nature of the product, the stage in the product life cycle, target market characteristics, the type of buying decision, funds available for promotion, and whether a push or a pull strategy will be used.

Nature of the Product

Characteristics of the product itself can influence the promotional mix. For instance, a product can be classified as either a business product or a consumer product (refer to Chapter 8). As business products are often custom-tailored to the buyer's exact specifications, they are often not well suited to mass promotion. Therefore, producers of most business goods, such as computer systems or industrial machinery, rely more heavily on personal selling than on advertising. Informative personal selling is common for industrial installations, accessories, and component parts and materials. Advertising, however, still serves a purpose in promoting business goods. Advertisements in trade media may be used to create general buyer awareness and interest. Moreover, advertising can help locate potential customers for the sales force. For example, print media advertising often includes coupons soliciting the potential customer to "fill this out for more detailed information."

In contrast, because consumer products generally are not custom-made, they do not require the selling efforts of a company representative who can tailor them to the user's needs. Thus, consumer goods are promoted mainly through advertising to create brand familiarity. Broadcast advertising, newspapers,

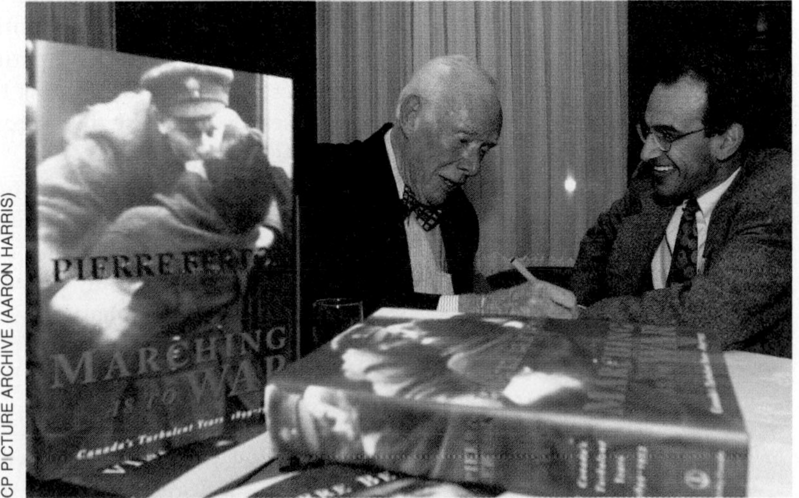

CP PICTURE ARCHIVE (AARON HARRIS)

Pierre Berton signs a copy of his book *Marching As To War* for fellow author and friend Ted Barris. This is but one of a string of stops Mr. Berton made to promote his book.

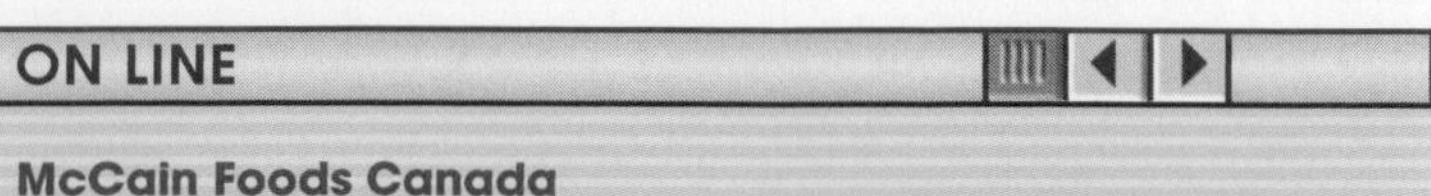

McCain Foods Canada

Go to the McCain Foods (Canada) website and click on the products link and then go to Contests and Promotions. What kinds of promotional relationships has McCain Foods established? Do you think these relationships will help McCain sell its foods? Will the relationship with McCain help the promotional partner make any sales as well? Explain why or why not.

http://www.mccain.ca

and consumer-oriented magazines are used extensively to promote consumer goods, especially nondurables. Sales promotion, the brand name, and the product's packaging are about twice as important for consumer goods as for business products. Persuasive personal selling is important at the retail level for shopping goods such as automobiles and appliances.

The costs and risks associated with a product also influence the promotional mix. As a general rule, when the costs or risks of using a product increase, personal selling becomes more important. Items that are a small part of a firm's budget (supply items) or of a consumer's budget (convenience products) do not require a salesperson to close the sale. In fact, inexpensive items cannot support the cost of a salesperson's time and effort unless the potential volume is high. On the other hand, expensive and complex machinery, new buildings, cars, and new homes represent a considerable investment. A salesperson must assure buyers that they are spending their money wisely and not taking an undue financial risk.

Social risk is an issue as well. Many consumer goods are not products of great social importance because they do not reflect social position. People do not experience much social risk in buying a loaf of bread or a candy bar. However, buying some shopping products and many specialty products such as jewellery and clothing does involve a social risk. Many consumers depend on sales personnel for guidance and advice in making the "proper" choice.

Stage in the Product Life Cycle

The product's stage in its life cycle is a big factor in designing a promotional mix (see Exhibit 13.6). During the *introduction stage*, the basic goal of promotion is to inform the target audience that the product is available. Initially, the emphasis is on the general product class, for example, cell phone service providers. This emphasis gradually changes to gaining attention for a specific brand, such as Telus, Bell Mobility, or Fido. Typically, both extensive advertising and public relations inform the target audience of the product class or brand and heighten awareness levels. Sales promotion encourages early trial of the product, and personal selling gets retailers to carry the product.

When the product reaches the *growth stage* of the life cycle, the promotion blend may shift. Often a change is necessary because different types of potential buyers are targeted. Although advertising and public relations continue to be major elements of the promotional mix, sales promotion can be reduced because consumers need fewer incentives to purchase. The promotional strategy is to emphasize the product's differential advantage over the competition. Persuasive promotion is used to build and maintain brand loyalty to support the product during the growth stage. By this stage, personal selling has usually succeeded in getting adequate distribution for the product.

As the product reaches the *maturity stage* of its life cycle, competition becomes fiercer, and thus persuasive and reminder advertising is more strongly emphasized. Sales promotion comes back into focus as product sellers try to increase their market share.

All promotion, especially advertising, is reduced as the product enters the decline stage. Nevertheless, personal selling and sales promotion efforts may be maintained, particularly at the retail level.

Target Market Characteristics

A target market characterized by widely scattered potential customers, highly informed buyers, and brand-loyal repeat purchasers generally requires a promotional mix with more advertising and sales promotion and less personal selling. Sometimes, however, personal selling is required even when buyers are well informed and geographically dis-

EXHIBIT 13.6

Product Life Cycle and the Promotional Mix

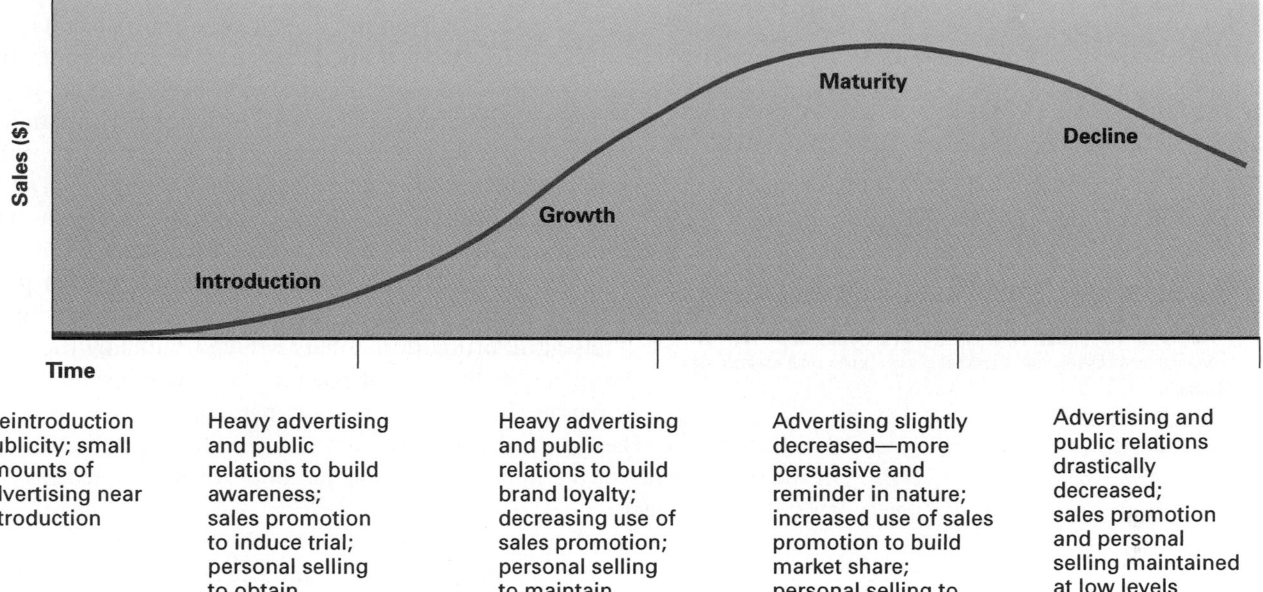
Sales ($)
Time
Introduction
Growth
Maturity
Decline
Preintroduction publicity; small amounts of advertising near introduction
Heavy advertising and public relations to build awareness; sales promotion to induce trial; personal selling to obtain distribution
Heavy advertising and public relations to build brand loyalty; decreasing use of sales promotion; personal selling to maintain distribution
Advertising slightly decreased—more persuasive and reminder in nature; increased use of sales promotion to build market share; personal selling to maintain distribution
Advertising and public relations drastically decreased; sales promotion and personal selling maintained at low levels

persed. Although industrial installations and component parts may be sold to extremely competent people with extensive education and work experience, salespeople must still be present to explain the product and work out the details of the purchase agreement.

Often firms sell goods and services in markets where potential customers are hard to locate. Print advertising can be used to find them. The reader is invited to call for more information or to mail in a reply card for a detailed brochure. As the calls or cards are received, salespeople are sent to visit the potential customers.

Type of Buying Decision

The promotional mix also depends on the type of buying decision, for example, is it a routine decision or a complex decision? For routine consumer decisions like buying toothpaste or soft drinks, the most effective promotion calls attention to the brand or reminds the consumer about the brand. Advertising and, especially, sales promotion are the most productive promotion tools for routine decisions.

If the decision is neither routine nor complex, advertising and public relations help establish awareness for the good or service. Suppose a single and childless person is looking for a baby gift for some expectant friends. As a single and childless person he is not familiar with the needs of an expectant married couple, yet he has seen advertising for retailer "Please Mum" and has also read an article in a business magazine about "Please Mum" retail stores. He may be more likely to shop at this retailer because he is already aware of it.

In contrast, consumers making complex buying decisions are more extensively involved. They rely on large amounts of information to help them reach a purchase decision. Personal selling is most effective in helping these consumers decide. For example, consumers thinking about buying a car usually depend on a salesperson to provide the information they need to reach a decision. Print advertising may also be used for high-involvement purchase decisions because it can often provide a large amount of information to the consumer.

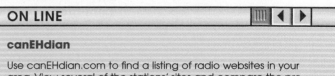

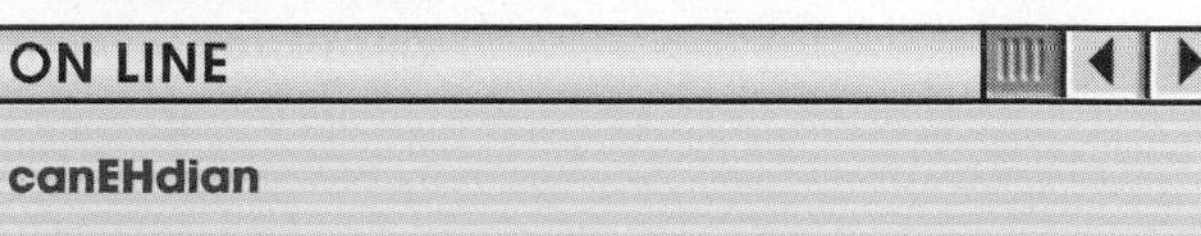
ON LINE

canEHdian

Use canEHdian.com to find a listing of radio websites in your area. View several of the stations' sites and compare the promotions featured. What conclusions can you draw about the target market of each station based on the types of promotions they are currently running? Would any of the promotions entice you to tune to a station that you normally wouldn't listen to?

http://www.canehdian.com

Consumers making complex buying decisions often depend on the salesperson to provide important product information. Purchasing a car is one such example. Can you think of others?

Available Funds

Money, or the lack of it, may easily be the most important factor in determining the promotional mix. A small, undercapitalized manufacturer may rely heavily on free publicity if its product is unique. If the situation warrants a sales force, a financially strained firm may turn to manufacturers' agents, who work on a commission basis with no advances or expense accounts. Even well-capitalized organizations may not be able to afford the advertising rates of publications like *Maclean's* magazine, *Reader's Digest*, and *The Globe and Mail*. The price of a high-profile advertisement in these media could support a salesperson for a year.

When funds are available to permit a mix of promotional elements, a firm will generally try to optimize its return on promotion dollars while minimizing the cost per contact, or the cost of reaching one member of the target market. In general, the cost per contact is very high for personal selling, public relations, and sales promotions like sampling and demonstrations. On the other hand, for the number of people national advertising reaches, it has a very low cost per contact.

Usually, there is a trade-off among the funds available, the number of people in the target market, the quality of communication needed, and the relative costs of the promotional elements. A company may have to forgo a full-page colour advertisement in *Canadian Business* in order to pay for a personal selling effort. Although the magazine ad will reach more people than personal selling, the high cost of the magazine space is a problem.

Push and Pull Strategies

The last factor that affects the promotional mix is whether a push or a pull promotional strategy will be used. Manufacturers may use aggressive personal selling and trade advertising to convince a wholesaler or a retailer to carry and sell their merchandise. This approach is known as a **push strategy** (see Exhibit 13.7). The wholesaler, in turn, must often push the merchandise forward by persuading the retailer to handle the goods. The retailer then uses advertising, displays, and other forms of promotion to convince the consumer to buy the "pushed" products. This concept also applies to services. For example, the Jamaican Tourism Board targets promotions to travel agencies, which, in turn, tell their customers about the benefits of vacationing in Jamaica.

push strategy
A marketing strategy that uses aggressive personal selling and trade advertising to convince a wholesaler or a retailer to carry and sell particular merchandise.

pull strategy
A marketing strategy that stimulates consumer demand to obtain product distribution.

At the other extreme is a **pull strategy**, which stimulates consumer demand to obtain product distribution. Rather than trying to sell to the wholesaler, the manufacturer using a pull strategy focuses its promotional efforts on end consumers or opinion leaders. As consumers begin demanding the product, the retailer orders the merchandise from the wholesaler. The wholesaler, confronted with rising demand, then places an order for the "pulled" merchandise from the manufacturer. Consumer demand pulls the product through the channel of distribution (see Exhibit 13.7). Heavy sampling, introductory consumer advertising, cents-off campaigns, and couponing are frequent parts of a pull strategy for consumer products.

Arguably, the most successful example of a pull strategy is Intel Corporation's "Intel Inside" campaign, which established a brand identity for the Pentium microprocessor, one of the least visible components of a personal computer. It is truly remarkable, when one considers all of the critical components that go into a computer and the brand images of the computer manufacturers themselves, that many people are not only fully aware of the processors that go into their computers, but also even insistent that their computers have Intel Pentium processors. Intel's pull strategy has been so effective that computer retailers and manufacturers cannot even advertise their computers without identifying the processor component. Before this situation developed, computer manufacturers had a customer franchise and could sell their products based on the brand name of the computer.

EXHIBIT 13.7

Push Strategy versus Pull Strategy

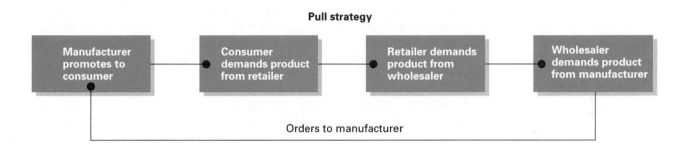

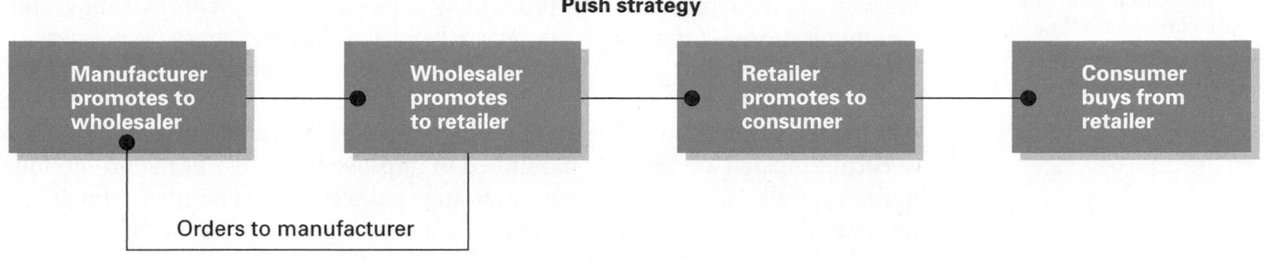

Pull strategy

Manufacturer promotes to consumer

Consumer demands product from retailer

Retailer demands product from wholesaler

Wholesaler demands product from manufacturer

Orders to manufacturer

The computer brands put their choice of microprocessor in the computers and would negotiate for price concessions from a number of microprocessor suppliers. Intel wanted to strengthen its position as a supplier and decided to use a pull strategy. The result: Intel has developed such a strong customer franchise that it now holds almost a monopoly power over both computer manufacturers and retailers as a microprocessor supplier.

Rarely does a company use a pull or a push strategy exclusively. Instead, the mix will emphasize one of these strategies. For example, pharmaceutical companies generally use a push strategy, through personal selling and trade advertising, to promote their drugs and therapies to physicians. Sales presentations and advertisements in medical journals give physicians the detailed information they need to prescribe medication to their patients. Most pharmaceutical companies supplement their push promotional strategy with a pull strategy targeted directly to potential patients through advertisements in consumer magazines and on television.

>> INTEGRATED MARKETING COMMUNICATIONS

6 Discuss the concept of integrated marketing communications

Ideally, marketing communications from each promotional mix element (personal selling, advertising, sales promotion, and public relations) should be integrated—that is, the message reaching the consumer should be the same regardless of whether it is from an advertisement, a salesperson in the field, a magazine article, or a coupon in a newspaper insert.

From the consumer's standpoint, a company's communications are already integrated. Consumers do not think in terms of the four elements of promotion: advertising, sales promotion, public relations, and personal selling. Instead, everything is an "ad." The only people who recognize the distinctions among these communications elements are the marketers themselves. Unfortunately, many marketers neglect this fact when planning promotional messages and fail to integrate their communication efforts from one element to the next. The most common rift typically occurs between personal selling and the other elements of the promotional mix.

integrated marketing communications (IMC)
The careful coordination of all promotional messages for a product or a service to assure the consistency of messages at every contact point where a company meets the consumer.

This unintegrated, disjointed approach to promotion has propelled many companies to adopt the concept of **integrated marketing communications (IMC).** IMC is the careful coordination of all promotional messages—traditional advertising, direct marketing, interactive, public relations, sales promotion, personal selling, event marketing, and other communications—for a product or service to ensure the consistency of messages at every contact point where a company meets the consumer.[17] Following the concept of IMC, marketing managers carefully work out the roles that various promotional elements will play in the marketing mix. Timing of promotional activities is coordinated, and the results of each campaign are carefully monitored to improve future use of the promotional mix tools. Typically, a marketing communications director is appointed who has overall responsibility for integrating the company's marketing communications.

Movie marketing campaigns benefit greatly from an IMC approach. Those campaigns that are most integrated generally have more impact and make a deeper impression on potential moviegoers, leading to higher box-office sales. New Line Cinema used an integrated marketing approach when it released the first installment of *The Lord of the Rings: The Fellowship of the Ring*. Excitement about the release of the film gathered momentum a full year in advance as the trailer was shown on the Internet (the trailer received 62 million hits the first week on-line). A partnership with Burger King gave consumers the opportunity to buy *The Fellowship of the Ring* glass goblets with the purchase of a Whopper sandwich value meal. Consumers could also buy a Burger King Big Kids Meal to receive one of 19 premiums featuring characters from the movie. One hundred selected bookstores in North America sponsored lunchtime events featuring a 20-minute video that included never-before-seen interviews, behind-the-scenes footage, and conversations with director Peter Jackson and various stars from the movie. The bookstores were also given in-store event kits to supplement the showing with a trivia contest, in-store readings by fans of favourite scenes, and other activities. Cobranded DVD players and VCR packages loaded with movie trailers, behind-the-scenes footage, and stickers hit shelves a couple of months before the movie premiered. Through an agreement with the New York Times Company, both the Times and NYTimes.com promoted the film. Praised by critics and audiences alike, *The Fellowship of the Ring* surpassed the $100 million mark on its opening weekend and was named the top movie of the year by *Entertainment Weekly* and *Rolling Stone*.[18]

The IMC concept has been growing in popularity for several reasons. First, the proliferation of thousands of media choices beyond traditional television has made promotion a more complicated task. Instead of promoting a product just through mass-media options, like television and magazines, promotional messages today can appear in many varied sources. Furthermore, the mass market has fragmented—more selectively segmented markets and an increase in niche marketing have replaced the traditional broad market groups that marketers promoted to in years past. For instance, there are a large number of ethnic media choices in Canada to cater to our country's diverse multicultural population. Consider that Canadian marketers can select from 190 newspapers and magazines to reach 43 different ethnic groups.[19] Finally, marketers have slashed their advertising spending in favour of promotional techniques that generate immediate sales responses and those that are more easily measured, such as direct marketing. Thus, the interest in IMC is largely a reaction to the scrutiny that marketing communications has come under and, particularly, to suggestions that uncoordinated promotional activity leads to a strategy that is wasteful and inefficient.[20]

AP/WIDE WORLD PHOTOS

Movies are often very successful at implementing integrated marketing campaigns. *The Lord of the Rings, Spider-Man,* and others were able to parlay huge box-office successes into merchandising successes—not to mention great anticipation for sequels.

>> PERSONAL SELLING

7 Describe personal selling

Personal selling is direct communication between a sales representative and one or more prospective buyers in an attempt to influence each other in a purchase situation.

In a sense, all businesspeople are salespeople. An individual may become a plant manager, a chemist, an engineer, or a member of any profession and yet still have to sell. During a job search, applicants must "sell" themselves to prospective employers in an interview. To reach the top in most organizations, individuals need to sell ideas to peers, superiors, and subordinates. Most important, people must sell themselves and their ideas to just about everyone with whom they have a continuing relationship and to many other people they see only once or twice. Chances are that students majoring in business or marketing will start their professional careers in sales. Even students in non-business majors may pursue a sales career.

Personal selling offers several advantages over other forms of promotion:

- Personal selling provides a detailed explanation or demonstration of the product. This capability is especially needed for complex or new goods and services.
- The sales message can be varied according to the motivations and interests of each prospective customer. Moreover, when the prospect has questions or raises objections, the salesperson is there to provide explanations. In contrast, advertising and sales promotion can only respond to the objections the copywriter thinks are important to customers.
- Personal selling can be directed only to qualified prospects. Other forms of promotion include some unavoidable waste because many people in the audience are not prospective customers.
- Personal selling costs can be controlled by adjusting the size of the sales force (and resulting expenses) in one-person increments. On the other hand, advertising and sales promotion must often be purchased in fairly large amounts.
- Perhaps the most important advantage is that personal selling is considerably more effective than other forms of promotion in obtaining a sale and gaining a satisfied customer.

Given certain customer and product characteristics, personal selling might work better than other forms of promotion. Generally speaking, personal selling becomes more important as the number of potential customers decreases, as the complexity of the product increases, and as the value of the product grows (see Exhibit 13.8). When there are relatively few potential customers and the value of the good or service is relatively sufficient, the time and travel costs of personally visiting each prospect are justifiable. For highly complex goods, such as business jets or private communication systems, a salesperson is needed to determine the prospective customer's needs, explain the product's basic advantages, and propose the exact features and accessories that will meet the client's needs.

EXHIBIT 13.8

Comparison of Personal Selling and Advertising/Sales Promotion

PERSONAL SELLING IS MORE IMPORTANT IF...	ADVERTISING AND SALES PROMOTION ARE MORE IMPORTANT IF...
The product has a high value.	The product has a low value.
It is a custom-made product.	It is a standardized product.
There are few customers.	There are many customers.
The product is technically complex.	The product is easy to understand.
Customers are concentrated.	Customers are geographically dispersed.
Examples: insurance policies, custom windows, airplane engines	Examples: soap, magazine subscriptions, cotton T-shirts

8 Discuss the key differences between relationship selling and traditional selling

Relationship Selling

Until recently, marketing theory and practice concerning personal selling focused almost entirely on a planned presentation to prospective customers for the sole purpose of making the sale. Marketers were most concerned with making a one-time sale and then moving on to the next prospect. Whether the presentation took place face-to-face during a personal sales call or over the telephone (telemarketing), traditional personal selling methods attempted to persuade the buyer to accept a point of view or convince the buyer to take some action. Once the customer was somewhat convinced, the salesperson used a variety of techniques in an attempt to elicit a purchase. Frequently, the objectives of the salesperson were at the expense of the buyer, creating a win–lose outcome. Although this type of sales approach has not disappeared entirely, it is being used less and less often by professional salespeople.

relationship selling (consultative selling)
A sales practice that involves building, maintaining, and enhancing interactions with customers in order to develop long-term satisfaction through mutually beneficial partnerships.

In contrast, modern views of personal selling emphasize the relationship that develops between a salesperson and a buyer. **Relationship selling,** or **consultative selling,** is a multistage process that emphasizes personalization and empathy as key ingredients in identifying prospects and developing them as long-term, satisfied customers. The old way was to sell a product, but with relationship selling, the objective is to build long-term branded relationships with consumers/buyers.[21] Thus, the focus is on building mutual trust between the buyer and seller through the delivery of anticipated, long-term, value-added benefits to the buyer. Relationship or consultative salespeople, therefore, become consultants, partners, and problem solvers for their customers. They strive to build long-term relationships with key accounts by developing trust over time. The emphasis shifts from a one-time sale to a long-term relationship in which the salesperson works with the customer to develop solutions for enhancing the customer's bottom line. Moreover, research has shown that a positive customer–salesperson relationship contributes to trust, increased customer loyalty, and the intent to continue the relationship with the salesperson.[22] Thus, relationship selling promotes a win–win situation for both buyer and seller.

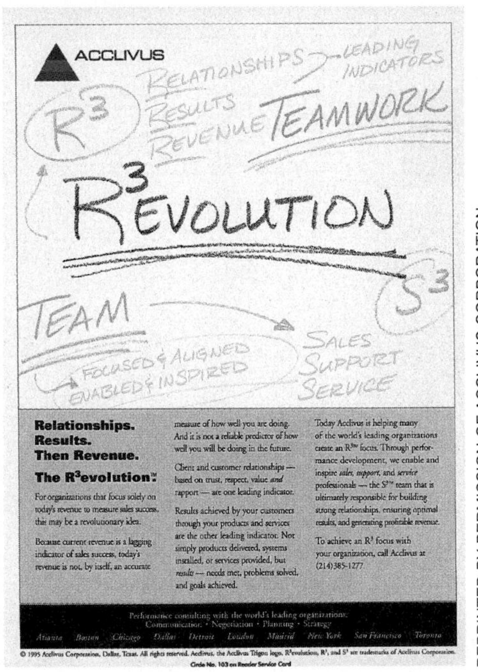

A multistage process focusing on developing trust over time, relationship selling emphasizes a win–win outcome.

The end result of relationship selling tends to be loyal customers who purchase from the company time after time. A relationship-selling strategy focused on retaining customers costs a company less than if it were constantly prospecting and selling to new customers. Companies that focus on customer retention through high customer service gain 6 percent market share per year, while companies that offer low customer service lose 2 percent market share per year.[23] In fact, it costs businesses six times more to gain a new customer than to retain a current one.[24]

Relationship selling is more typical with selling situations for industrial-type goods, such as heavy machinery or computer systems, and services, such as airlines and insurance, than for consumer goods.

Exhibit 13.9 lists the key differences between traditional personal selling and relationship or consultative selling. These differences will become more apparent as we explore the personal selling process later in the chapter.

9 List the steps in the selling process

>> STEPS IN THE SELLING PROCESS

sales process (sales cycle)
The set of steps a salesperson goes through in a particular organization to sell a particular product or service.

Although personal selling may sound like a relatively simple task, completing a sale actually requires several steps. The **sales process,** or **sales cycle,** is simply the set of steps a salesperson goes through to sell a particular product or service. The sales process or cycle can be unique for each product or service, depending on the features of the product or service, characteristics of customer segments, and internal processes in place within the firm, such as how leads are gathered.

Some sales take only a few minutes, but others may take months or years to complete, especially when selling customized goods or services. The typical sale for Eastman Kodak's line of high-speed motion analysis cameras takes anywhere from nine to

EXHIBIT 13.9

Key Differences between Traditional Selling and Relationship Selling

TRADITIONAL PERSONAL SELLING	RELATIONSHIP OR CONSULTATIVE SELLING
Sell products (goods and services)	Sell advice, assistance, and counsel
Focus on closing sales	Focus on improving the customer's bottom line
Limited sales planning	Consider sales planning as top priority
Spend most contact time telling customers about product	Spend most contact time attempting to build a problem-solving environment with the customer
Conduct "product-specific" needs assessment	Conduct discovery in the full scope of the customer's operations
"Lone wolf" approach to the account	Team approach to the account
Proposals and presentations based on pricing and product features	Proposals and presentations based on profit-impact and strategic benefits to the customer
Sales follow-up is short term, focused on product delivery	Sales followup is long term, focused on long-term relationship enhancement

SOURCE: Robert M. Peterson, Patrick L. Schul, and George H. Lucas, Jr., "Consultative Selling: Walking the Walk in the New Selling Environment," National Conference on Sales Management, Proceedings, March 1996.

18 months to close.[25] On the other end of the spectrum, sales of its more basic cameras to retailers are generally more routine and may take only a few days. Whether a salesperson spends a few minutes or a few years on a sale, these are the seven basic steps in the personal-selling process:

1. Generating leads
2. Qualifying leads
3. Approaching the customer and probing needs
4. Developing and proposing solutions
5. Handling objections
6. Closing the sale
7. Following up

Like other forms of promotion, these steps of selling follow the AIDA concept discussed earlier. Once a salesperson has located a prospect with the authority to buy, he or she tries to get the prospect's attention. A thorough needs assessment turned into an effective sales proposal and presentation should generate interest. After developing the customer's initial desire (preferably during the presentation of the sales proposal), the salesperson seeks action in the close by trying to get an agreement to buy. Followup after the sale, the final step in the selling process, not only lowers cognitive dissonance (refer to Chapter 4) but also may open up opportunities to discuss future sales. Effective followup will also lead to repeat business in which the process may start all over again at the needs assessment step.

Traditional selling and relationship selling follow the same basic steps. What is different between the two selling methods is the relative importance placed on key steps in the process. Traditional selling efforts are transaction oriented, focusing on generating as many leads as possible, making as many presentations as possible, and closing as many sales as possible. Minimal effort is placed on asking questions to identify customer needs and wants or matching these needs and wants to the benefits of the product or service. In contrast, the salesperson practising relationship selling emphasizes an upfront investment in the time and effort needed to uncover each customer's specific needs and wants and matching to them, as closely as possible, the product or service offering. By doing the homework up front, the salesperson creates the conditions necessary for a relatively straightforward close.[26] Let's look at each step of the selling process individually.

ON LINE

InfoCANADA

Can personal selling translate into the Internet space? Go to InfoCANADA to find out. How does this company's suggested way of generating and qualifying leads compare to the information you read in the text? Try a free demonstration. Do you get enough information to determine whether the monthly subscription fee is worth it?

http://www.infocanada.ca

lead generation (prospecting)
Identification of those firms and people most likely to buy the seller's offerings.

Generating Leads

Initial groundwork must precede communication between the potential buyer and the salesperson. **Lead generation,** or **prospecting,** is the identification of those firms and people most likely to buy the seller's offerings. These firms or people become "sales leads" or "prospects."

Sales leads can be secured in several different ways, most notably through advertising, trade shows and conventions, or direct-mail and telemarketing programs. Favourable publicity also helps create leads. Company records of past client purchases are another excellent source of leads. Many sales professionals are also securing valuable leads from their firm's Internet website. For example, Ford Motor Company's drive to reach consumers on-line is paying off. Recently, the company's combination of websites and other on-line ventures sent an estimated half-million leads to its dealers throughout the world.[27] In the future, more than half of all sales leads likely will come from the Internet.

referral
A recommendation to a salesperson from a customer or business associate.

Another way to gather a lead is through a **referral**—a recommendation from a customer or business associate. The advantages of referrals over other forms of prospecting include highly qualified leads, higher closing rates, larger initial transactions, and shorter sales cycles. Simply put, the salesperson and the company can earn more money in less time when prospecting using referrals. To increase the number of referrals they receive, some companies even pay or send small gifts to customers or suppliers who provide referrals. Research has suggested that one referral is as valuable as up to 12 cold calls. However, although 80 percent of clients would be willing to give referrals, only 20 percent are ever asked.[28]

networking
A process of finding out about potential clients from friends, business contacts, coworkers, acquaintances, and fellow members in professional and civic organizations.

Networking is the related method of using friends, business contacts, coworkers, acquaintances, and fellow members in professional and civic organizations to find out about potential clients. Indeed, a number of national networking clubs have recently been started for the sole purpose of generating leads and providing valuable business advice. The networking clubs usually have between 15 and 30 members in noncompeting business categories. During weekly breakfast or lunch meetings, each member is allowed to talk about the company he or she represents for an allotted period of time. Then members exchange lead cards. Research suggests that, on average, chapter members see an increase in business volume of between 16 and 25 percent after they've been with their group for three to six months.[29]

cold calling
A form of lead generation in which the salesperson approaches potential buyers without any prior knowledge of the prospects' needs or financial status.

Before the advent of more sophisticated methods of lead generation, such as direct mail and telemarketing, most prospecting was done through **cold calling**—a form of lead generation in which the salesperson approaches potential buyers without any prior knowledge of the prospects' needs or financial status. Although this method is still used, many sales managers have realized the inefficiencies of having their top salespeople use their valuable selling time searching for the proverbial "needle in a haystack." Passing the job of cold calling to a lower-cost employee, typically an internal sales support person, allows salespeople to spend more time and use their relationship-building skills on prospects who have already been identified. Sales experts note that the days of cold calls and unannounced office visits have given way to referral-based and relationship selling.[30]

Qualifying Leads

When a prospect shows interest in learning more about a product, the salesperson has the opportunity to follow up, or qualify, the lead. Personally visiting unqualified prospects wastes valuable salesperson time and company resources. Often many leads go unanswered because salespeople are given no indication as to how qualified the leads are in terms of interest and ability to purchase. One study that surveyed 400 marketers whose companies advertise in trade publications found that almost 40 percent of the leads generated went completely unanswered, most likely due to the fact that they were unqualified.[31]

lead qualification
Determination of a sales prospect's (1) recognized need, (2) buying power, and (3) receptivity and accessibility.

Lead qualification consists of determining whether the prospect has three things:[32]

- *A recognized need:* The most basic criterion for determining whether someone is a prospect for a product is a need that is not being satisfied. The salesperson should first consider prospects who are aware of a need but should not discount prospects who have not yet recognized that they have one. With a little more information about the product, they may decide they do have a need for it. Preliminary interviews and questioning can often provide the salesperson with enough information to determine whether there is a need.
- *Buying power:* Buying power involves both authority to make the purchase decision and access to funds to pay for it. To avoid wasting time and money, the salesperson needs to identify the purchasing authority and the ability to pay before making a presentation. Organizational charts and information about a firm's credit standing can provide valuable clues.
- *Receptivity and accessibility:* The prospect must be willing to see the salesperson and be accessible to the salesperson. Some prospects simply refuse to see salespeople. Others, because of their stature in their organization, will see only a salesperson or sales manager with similar stature.

Often the task of lead qualification is handled by a telemarketing group or a sales support person who prequalifies the lead for the salesperson. Prequalification systems free sales representatives from the time-consuming task of following up on leads to determine need, buying power, and receptiveness. Prequalification systems may even set up initial appointments with the prospect for the salesperson. The result is more time for the sales force to spend in front of interested customers. Protocol Marketing Group, an integrated direct marketing services company, helps clients with followup by loading lead information into a high-yield database. Protocol contacts trade show attendees and qualifies them using a scripting process based on input from the company for which it is working. After qualification, Protocol distributes A- and B-level leads to the client.[33]

With more and more companies setting up websites on the Internet, qualifying online leads has also received some attention. The objective of a company's website should be to get visitors to register, indicate what products they are interested in, and offer up some information on their time frame and resources. Leads from the Internet can then be prioritized (those indicating a short time frame, for instance, given a higher priority) and then transferred to salespeople. Often website visitors can be enticed to answer questions with offers of free merchandise or information. Enticing visitors to register also allows companies to customize future electronic interactions, for example, by giving prospects who visit the website their choice from a menu of products tailored specifically to their needs.[34]

Approaching the Customer and Probing Needs

Prior to approaching the customer, the salesperson should learn as much as possible about the prospect's organization and its buyers. This process, called the **preapproach,** describes the "homework" that must be done by the salesperson before contacting the prospect. This may include consulting standard reference sources, such as Frasers Canadian Trade Directory, the Canadian Trade Index, or D&B Canada (formerly Dun & Bradstreet Canada), or contacting acquaintances or others who may have information about the prospect. Another preapproach task is to determine whether the actual approach should be a personal visit, a phone call, a letter, or some other form of communication.

preapproach
A process that describes the "homework" that must be done by the salesperson before he or she contacts a prospect.

During the sales approach, the salesperson either talks to the prospect or secures an appointment for a future time in which to probe the prospect further as to his or her needs. Relationship selling theorists suggest that salespeople should begin developing mutual trust with their prospect during the approach. Salespeople should use the approach as a way of introducing themselves and their company and products. They must sell themselves before they can sell the product. Small talk that introduces sincerity and some suggestion of friendship is encouraged to build rapport with the prospect, but remarks that could be construed as insincere should be avoided.[35]

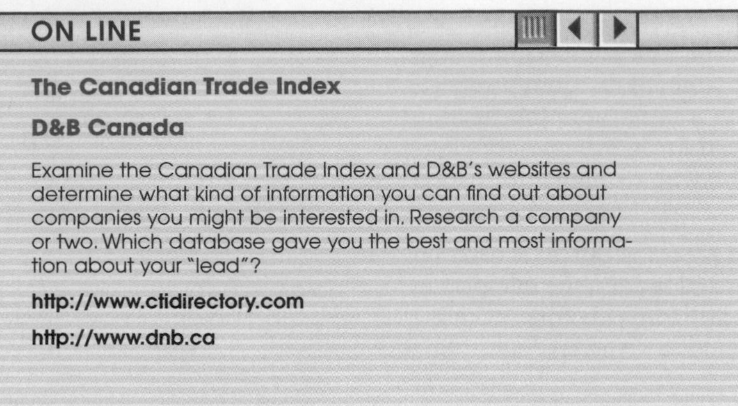
ON LINE

The Canadian Trade Index

D&B Canada

Examine the Canadian Trade Index and D&B's websites and determine what kind of information you can find out about companies you might be interested in. Research a company or two. Which database gave you the best and most information about your "lead"?

http://www.ctidirectory.com

http://www.dnb.ca

The salesperson's ultimate goal during the approach is to conduct a needs assessment to find out as much as possible about the prospect's situation. This involves interviewing the customer to determine his or her specific needs and wants and the range of options the customer has for satisfying them. The salesperson should be determining how to maximize the fit between what he or she can offer and what the prospective customer wants. As part of the **needs assessment**, the consultative salesperson must know everything there is to know about the following:[36]

needs assessment
A determination of the customer's specific needs and wants and the range of options the customer has for satisfying them.

- *The product or service:* Product knowledge is the cornerstone for conducting a successful needs analysis. The consultative salesperson must be an expert on his or her product or service, including technical specifications, the product's features and benefits, pricing and billing procedures, warranty and service support, performance comparisons with the competition, other customers' experiences with the product, and current advertising and promotional campaign messages.
- *Customers and their needs:* The salesperson should know more about customers than they know about themselves. That's the secret to relationship and consultative selling, where the salesperson acts not only as a supplier of products and services but also as a trusted consultant and adviser. The professional salesperson doesn't just sell products; he or she brings to each client business-building ideas and solutions to problems. For the customer, consulting a professional salesperson is like having another vital person on the team at no cost.
- *The competition:* The salesperson must know as much about the competitor's company and products as he or she knows about his or her own company. Competitive intelligence includes many factors: who the competitors are and what is known about them; how their products and services compare; advantages and disadvantages; and strengths and weaknesses.
- *The industry:* Knowing the industry involves active research on the part of the salesperson. This means attending industry and trade association meetings, reading articles published in industry and trade journals, keeping track of legislation and regulations that affect the industry, awareness of product alternatives and innovations from domestic and foreign competition, and having a feel for economic and financial conditions that may affect the industry.

Creating a *customer profile* during the approach helps salespeople optimize their time and resources. This profile is then used to help develop an intelligent analysis of the prospect's needs in preparation for the next step, developing and proposing solutions. Customer profile information is typically stored and manipulated using sales force automation software packages designed for use on laptop computers. Sales force automation software provides sales reps with a computerized and efficient method of collecting customer information for use during the entire sales process. Furthermore, customer and sales data stored in a computer database can be easily shared among sales team members. The information can be appended with industry statistics, sales or meeting notes, billing data, and other information that may be pertinent to the prospect or the prospect's company. The more salespeople know about their prospects, the better they can meet their needs.

Salespeople should wrap up their sales approach and need-probing mission by summarizing the prospect's need, problem, and interest. The salesperson should also get a commitment from the customer to some kind of action, whether it's reading promotional material or agreeing to a demonstration. This commitment helps qualify the prospect further and justify additional time invested by the salesperson. The salesperson should reiterate the action he or she promises to take, such as sending information or calling back to provide answers to questions. The date and time of the next call should be set at the conclusion of the sales approach as well as an agenda for the next call in terms of what the salesperson hopes to accomplish, such as providing a demonstration or presenting a solution.[37]

Developing and Proposing Solutions

Once the salesperson has gathered the appropriate information about the client's needs and wants, the next step is to determine whether his or her company's products or services match the needs of the prospective customer. The salesperson then develops a solution, or possibly several solutions, in which the salesperson's product or service solves the client's problems or meets a specific need.

sales proposal
A formal written document or professional presentation that outlines how the salesperson's product or service will meet or exceed the prospect's needs.

sales presentation
A formal meeting in which the salesperson presents a sales proposal to a prospective buyer.

These solutions are typically presented to the client in the form of a **sales proposal** presented at a **sales presentation.** A sales proposal is a written document or professional presentation that outlines how the company's product or service will meet or exceed the client's needs. The sales presentation is the formal meeting in which the salesperson has the opportunity to present the sales proposal. The presentation should be explicitly tied to the prospect's expressed needs. Also, the prospect should be involved in the presentation by being encouraged to participate in demonstrations or by exposure to computer exercises, slides, video or audio, flipcharts, photographs, and so on.[38]

Technology has become an important part of presenting solutions for many salespeople. Pen manufacturer BIC utilized the Internet to connect with its wholesale and convenience store customers. Before launching http://www.BIClink.com, BIC received 80 percent of its order volume by fax. Processing these orders was time-consuming, and the orders often were filled with errors. BIClink.com has eliminated the potential for errors and made it easier and faster to validate purchase order numbers, ship dates, case quantities, and pricing. When customers sign on (through a secure, password-protected system), the welcome screen is personalized with their company's name and the name of their BIC rep. On placing an order, customers receive both a hard copy and e-mail confirmation statement with the salesperson's name and contact information including e-mail, voice mail, phone, and fax numbers. The site has proved to be a success—in its first six weeks of operation, more than 50 percent of customers who previously ordered by fax began ordering on-line.[39]

Because the salesperson often has only one opportunity to present solutions, the quality of both the sales proposal and presentation can make or break the sale. Salespeople must be able to present the proposal and handle any customer objections confidently and professionally. For a powerful presentation, salespeople must be well prepared, use direct eye contact, ask open-ended questions, be poised, use hand gestures and voice inflection, focus on the customer's needs, incorporate visual elements that impart valuable information, know how to operate the audio/visual or computer equipment being used for the presentation, make sure the equipment works, and practise, practise, practise.[40] Nothing dies faster than a boring presentation. If the salesperson doesn't have a convincing and confident manner, then the prospect will very often forget the information. Prospects take in body language, voice patterns, dress, and body type. Often customers are more likely to remember how salespeople present themselves than what salespeople say.

Handling Objections

Rarely does a prospect say, "I'll buy it" right after a presentation. Instead, the prospect often raises objections or asks questions about the proposal and the product. The potential buyer may insist that the price is too high, that he or she does not have enough information to make a decision, or that the good or service will not satisfy the present need. The buyer may also lack confidence in the seller's organization or product.

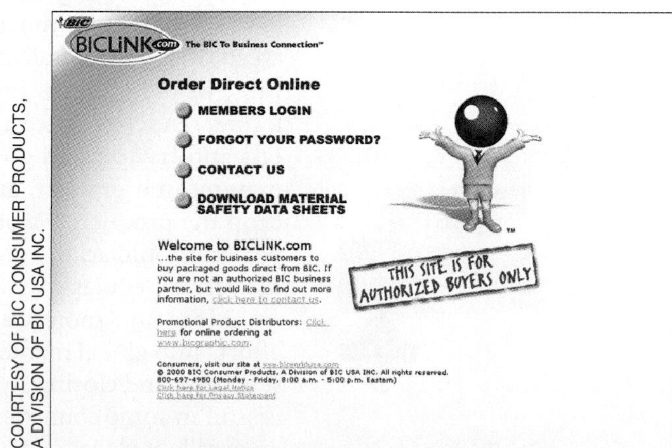

COURTESY OF BIC CONSUMER PRODUCTS, A DIVISION OF BIC USA INC.

Part of the selling process involves proposing solutions to resolve difficulties customers are having. BIC utilized the Internet to streamline the order process for its wholesale and convenience store customers. The result was BIClink.com.

One of the first lessons that every salesperson learns is that objections to the product should not be taken personally as confrontations or insults. Rather, a salesperson should view objections as requests for information. A good salesperson considers objections a legitimate part of the purchase decision. To handle objections effectively, the salesperson should anticipate specific objections such as concerns about price, fully investigate the objection with the customer, be wary of what the competition is offering, and, above all, stay calm. Before a crucial sales presentation with an important prospect, for example, Dell Computer salespeople anticipated that the customer would have doubts as to whether Dell's direct selling model would provide the same level of service and dedication as a reseller would. Being prepared helped Dell win the contract.[41]

Often the salesperson can use the objection to close the sale. If the customer tries to pit suppliers against one another to drive down the price, the salesperson should be prepared to point out weaknesses in the competitor's offer and stand by the quality in his or her own proposal.[42]

Closing the Sale

At the end of the presentation, the salesperson should ask the customer how he or she would like to proceed. If the customer exhibits signs that he or she is ready to purchase and all questions have been answered and objections have been met, then the salesperson can try to close the sale. Customers often give signals during or after the presentation that they are ready to buy or are not interested. Examples include changes in facial expressions, gestures, and questions asked. The salesperson should look for these signals and respond appropriately.

Closing requires courage and skill. Naturally, the salesperson wants to avoid rejection, and asking for a sale carries with it the risk of a negative answer. A salesperson should keep an open mind when asking for the sale and be prepared for either a "yes" or a "no" answer. Rarely is a sale closed on the first call. In fact, the typical salesperson averages about 765 sales calls a year, many of which are repeat calls to the same client in an attempt to make the sale.[43] Some salespeople may negotiate with large accounts for several years before closing a sale. As you can see, building a good relationship with the customer is very important. Often, if the salesperson has developed a strong relationship with the customer, only minimal efforts are needed to close a sale.

negotiation
The process during which both the salesperson and the prospect offer special concessions in an attempt to arrive at a sales agreement.

Negotiation often plays a key role in the closing of the sale. Negotiation is the process during which both the salesperson and the prospect offer special concessions in an attempt to arrive at a sales agreement. For example, the salesperson may offer a price cut, free installation, free service, or a trial order. Effective negotiators, however, avoid using price as a negotiation tool because cutting price directly affects a company's profitability. Because companies spend millions on advertising and product development to create value, when salespeople give in to price negotiations too quickly, it decreases the value of the product. Instead, effective salespeople should emphasize value to the customer, rendering price a nonissue. Salespeople should also be prepared to ask for tradeoffs and try to avoid giving unilateral concessions. If you're making only a 50-percent margin on a product, and you need at least a 60-percent margin, raise your prices or drop the product.[44] Moreover, if the customer asks for a 5-percent discount, the salesperson should ask for something in return, such as higher volume or more flexibility in delivery schedules.

More and more Canadian companies are expanding their marketing and selling efforts into global markets. Salespeople selling in foreign markets should tailor their presentation and closing styles to each market. Different personalities and skills will be successful in some countries and absolute failures in others. For instance, if a salesperson is an excellent closer and always focuses on the next sale, doing business in Latin America may be difficult—Latin Americans want to take a long time building a personal relationship with their suppliers.[45] Read about other global dos and don'ts of selling in the "Global Perspectives" box.

Following Up

Unfortunately, many salespeople hold the attitude that making the sale is all that's important. Once the sale is made, they can forget about their customers. They are wrong. Salespeople's responsibilities do not end with making the sales and placing the orders. One of the most important aspects of their jobs is **followup**—the final step in the delivery process, in which they must ensure that delivery schedules are met, that the goods or services perform as promised, and that the buyers' employees are properly trained to use the products.

followup
The final step of the selling process, in which the salesperson ensures that delivery schedules are met, that the goods or services perform as promised, and that the buyers' employees are properly trained to use the products.

Whereas the traditional sales approach's extent of followup with the customer is generally limited to successful product delivery and performance, a basic goal of relationship selling is to motivate customers to come back, again and again, by developing and nurturing long-term relationships. Most businesses depend on repeat sales, and repeat sales depend on thorough and continued followup by the salesperson. Finding a new customer is far more expensive than retaining an existing customer. When customers feel abandoned, cognitive dissonance arises and repeat sales decline. Today, this issue is more pertinent than ever because customers are far less loyal to brands and vendors. Buyers are more inclined to look for the best deal, especially in the case of poor after-the-sale followup. More and more buyers favour building a relationship with sellers.

Automated e-mail followup marketing—a combination of sales automation and Internet technology—is enhancing customer satisfaction as well as bringing in more business for some marketers. Here's how it works: After the initial contact with a prospect, a software program automatically sends a series of personalized e-mails over a period of time. CollegeRecruiter.com is a U.S.-based Internet company taking advantage of this technology. The company posts ads for businesses recruiting recent college graduates on its website and has seen phenomenal results from autoresponse marketing. Prospects start receiving a series of e-mails once they have visited the site and requested advertising rates. The first message goes out immediately. The next two go out in four to 11 days. From there, e-mails go out monthly. The average sale for CollegeRecruiter.com is $375, and the company gets $4,000 to $5,000 in additional sales from new customers each month just from the automated followups.[46]

>> SALES MANAGEMENT

10 Describe the functions of sales management

There is an old adage in business that nothing happens until a sale is made. Without sales there is no need for accountants, production workers, or even a company president. Sales provide the fuel that keeps the corporate engines humming. Companies like Bombardier, Magna Corporation, and Cisco Systems Canada, and hundreds of other large Canadian manufacturers, would cease to exist without successful salespeople. Even companies like Procter & Gamble Canada and Kraft General Foods Canada, which mainly sell consumer goods and use extensive advertising campaigns, still rely on salespeople to move products through the channel of distribution. Thus, sales management is one of marketing's most critical specialties. Effective sales management stems from a highly success-oriented sales force that accomplishes its mission economically and efficiently. Poor sales management can lead to unmet profit objectives or even to the downfall of the corporation.

Just as selling is a personal relationship, so is sales management. Although the sales manager's basic job is to maximize sales at a reasonable cost while also maximizing profits, he or she also has many other important responsibilities and decisions:

1. Defining sales goals and the sales process
2. Determining the sales force structure
3. Recruiting and training the sales force
4. Compensating and motivating the sales force
5. Evaluating the sales force

GLOBAL PERSPECTIVES

Global Dos and Don'ts in Selling

Most large companies with operations on foreign soil are employing locals to sell their products. Most selling skills that are successful in North America will also work overseas. However, knowing how to act in certain cultures can be the difference between closing the deal and losing a customer. Some things that North Americans take for granted could easily cost them a deal overseas. A simple thumbs-up sign that we give everyday could offend a customer in another country. Here, from many international business experts, are some things to watch out for in various countries and regions around the world.

- Arab countries: Don't use your left hand to hold, offer, or receive materials because Arabs use their left hand to touch toilet paper. If you must use your left hand to write, apologize for doing so. Handshakes in Arab countries are a bit limp and last longer than typical North American handshakes.
- China: Never talk business on the first meeting—it's disrespectful. Don't refuse tea during a business discussion. Always drink it, even if you're offered a dozen cups a day. Never begin to eat or drink before your host does. Also, printed materials presented to Chinese business leaders should be in black and white, because colours have great significance for the Chinese. The Chinese tend to be extremely meticulous, looking to create long-term relationships with a supplier before agreeing to buy anything. Chinese are more intradependent and tend to include more people in on a deal. Most deals in China are finalized in a social setting, over either drinks or dinner. Additionally, getting to know the businessperson's family will personalize and strengthen the relationship.
- European countries: Western and Eastern Europeans reshake hands whenever they're apart for even a short period of time, for example, lunch.
- France: Don't schedule a breakfast meeting—the French tend not to meet until after 10 a.m. Since the French knowledge of wine is far greater than that of most North Americans, avoid giving wine or wine-related gifts to French clients. The French also prefer gifts that are of French origin.
- Germany: Don't address a business associate by his or her first name, even if you've known each other for years. Always wait for an invitation to do so. Also, breakfast meetings are unheard of here, too. Salespeople should expect a sobre, rigid business climate and negotiations that lack flexibility and compromise.
- Central and South America: People here don't take the clock too seriously—scheduling more than two appointments in one day can prove disastrous. Latin Americans also tend to use a lighter, lingering handshake. Negotiations with Central and South American customers typically include a great deal of bargaining. Personal relationships are also important in Central and South America, so salespeople should make face-to-face contact with their clients during meetings and presentations.
- Japan: Don't bring up business on the golf course—always wait for your host to take the initiative. Don't cross your legs in Japan—showing the bottom of the foot is insulting. Japanese businesspeople shake hands with one firm gesture combined with a slight bow, which should be returned. Japanese prefer gifts from well-known American stores, such as Tiffany's or Saks Fifth Avenue. Also, the higher the position of the recipient, the more elaborately wrapped the gift should be.
- Mexico: Don't send a bouquet of red or yellow flowers as a gift—Mexicans associate those colours with evil spirits and death. Instead, send a box of premium chocolates. Including a small gift for the client's children creates a positive impression.
- Vietnam: When meeting a Vietnamese woman, wait for her to extend a hand first—she may simply nod or bow slightly, the most common form of greeting in Vietnam. Vietnamese do not like to be touched or patted on the back or shoulders in social situations.
- Miscellaneous: The thumbs-up gesture is considered offensive in the Middle East, rude in Australia, and a sign of "OK" in France. It's rude to cross your arms while facing someone in Turkey. In the Middle East don't ask: "How's the family?"—it's considered too personal. In most Asian countries, staring directly into a person's eyes is considered discourteous.[47]

Defining Sales Goals and the Sales Process

Effective sales management begins with a determination of sales goals. Without goals to achieve, a salesperson's performance will be mediocre at best, and the company will likely fail. Like any marketing objective, sales goals should be stated in clear, precise, and measurable terms and should always specify a time frame for their fulfillment. Overall sales force goals are usually stated in terms of desired dollar sales volume, market share, or profit level. For example, a life insurance company may have a goal to sell $50 million in life insurance policies annually, to attain a 12 percent market share, or to achieve $1 million in profits. Individual salespeople are also assigned goals in the form of quotas. A **quota** is simply a statement of the salesperson's sales goals, usually based on sales volume alone but sometimes including key accounts (those with greatest potential), new accounts, repeat sales, and specific products.

quota
A statement of the individual salesperson's sales objectives, usually based on sales volume alone but sometimes including key accounts (those with greatest potential), new accounts, repeat sales, and specific products.

Great sales managers focus not only on sales goals but also on the entire process that drives their sales organizations to reach those goals. Without a keen understanding of the sales process, a manager will never be successful—no matter how defined the sales goals or how great the sales reps. An important responsibility of the sales manager, therefore, is to determine the most effective and efficient sales process to follow in selling each different product and service. Although the basic steps of the sales process are the same as discussed earlier in the chapter (i.e., lead generation and qualification, approach and needs assessment, proposal creation and presentation, handling objections, closing, and followup), a manager must formally define the specific procedures salespeople go through to do their jobs—for example, where to generate leads, how to qualify them, how best to approach potential clients, and what terms can be negotiated during closing. General Electric is a multinational company that operates in Canada through its wholly-owned subsidiary, GE Canada. GE focuses on attracting, hiring, and keeping the right salespeople through continuous training and the development of an effective sales process for its global sales force. GE has an excellent performance management program that gives an employee concrete goals to meet in order to receive a promotion. The company performs formal reviews three or four times a year and also provides an extensive product- and skills-training program that can last anywhere from one to two years. Salespeople are also rotated through up to five assignments before being placed in a permanent position to see what best suits the individual sales rep. When a GE Canada rep finally makes a call, he or she is completely knowledgeable about the product being sold.[48]

Determining the Sales Force Structure

Because personal selling is so costly, no sales department can afford to be disorganized. Proper design helps the sales manager organize and delegate sales duties and provide direction for salespeople. Sales departments are most commonly organized by geographic regions, by product line, by marketing function performed (such as account development or account maintenance), by market or industry, or by individual client or account. The sales force for IBM could be organized into sales territories covering the Maritimes, Quebec, Ontario, and Western Canada or could be organized into distinct groups selling personal computer systems and networked computer systems. IBM salespeople may also be assigned to a specific industry or market, for example, the telecommunications industry, or to key clients such as Air Canada or Bombardier.

Market- or industry-based structures and key account structures are gaining popularity in today's competitive selling environment, especially with the emphasis on relationship selling. Being familiar with one industry or market allows sales reps to become experts in their fields and thereby offer better solutions and service. And by organizing the sales force around specific customers, many companies hope to improve customer service, encourage collaboration with other arms of the company, and unite salespeople in customer-focused sales teams.

Recruiting and Training the Sales Force

Sales force recruitment should be based on an accurate, detailed description of the sales task as defined by the sales manager. Aside from the usual characteristics such as level of experience or education, what traits should sales managers look for in applicants? One of the most important traits of top performers is ego strength, or having a strong, healthy self-esteem and the ability to bounce back from rejection. Great salespeople also have a sense of urgency and competitiveness that pushes their sales to completion. Moreover, they have a desire to persuade people and close the sale. Effective salespeople are also assertive; they have the ability to be firm in one-to-one negotiations, to lead the sales process, and to get their point across confidently, without being overbearing or aggressive. They are sociable, willing to take risks, and capable of understanding complex concepts and ideas. Additionally, great salespeople are creative in developing client solutions, and they possess empathy—the ability to place oneself in someone else's shoes. Not surprisingly, in a recent study of top salespeople, almost 95 percent claim their sales style is relationship oriented rather than transaction oriented.[49]

After the sales recruit has been hired and given a brief orientation, training begins. A new salesperson generally receives instruction in company policies and practices, selling techniques, product knowledge, industry and customer characteristics, and

AP/WIDE WORLD PHOTOS

Motivating the sales force is one of the sales managers' toughest jobs. At Wal-Mart, associates attend sales meetings that bring executives, management, and associates together in an informal setting.

nonselling duties such as filling out sales and market information reports or using a sales automation computer program. Firms that sell complex products generally offer the most extensive training programs. Pharmaceutical giant Merck Frosst, for example, takes a highly scientific approach to its market and trains its reps to understand the science of the medicine it sells so that they can maintain a peer-to-peer discussion with the physicians they call upon.[50]

Most successful sales organizations have learned that training is not just for newly hired salespeople. Instead, training is offered to all salespeople in an ongoing effort to hone selling skills and relationship building. In pursuit of solid salesperson–client relationships, training programs now seek to improve salespeople's consultative selling and listening skills and to broaden their product and customer knowledge. In addition, training programs stress the interpersonal skills needed to become the contact person for customers. Because negotiation is increasingly important in closing a sale, salespeople are also trained to negotiate effectively without risking profits. A recent international study predicts the corporate on-line learning market will soon surpass the $7 billion mark as more companies reevaluate the high cost of sending one or two employees to a central training classroom. Ottawa's Corel Corporation started an on-line training program to educate its own salespeople. The on-line training has been so successful that it recently was expanded to include customers using Corel products.[51]

Compensating and Motivating the Sales Force

Compensation planning is one of the sales manager's toughest jobs. Only good planning will ensure that compensation attracts, motivates, and retains good salespeople. Generally, companies and industries with lower levels of compensation suffer higher turnover rates, which increase costs and decrease effectiveness. Therefore, compensation needs to be competitive enough to attract and motivate the best salespeople. Firms sometimes take profit into account when developing their compensation plans. Instead of paying salespeople on overall volume, they pay according to the profitability achieved from selling each product. Still other companies tie a part of the salesperson's total compensation to customer satisfaction assessed through periodic customer surveys.

straight commission
A method of compensation in which the salesperson is paid some percentage when a sale is made.

straight salary
A method of compensation in which the salesperson receives a salary regardless of sales productivity.

The three basic compensation methods for salespeople are commission, salary, and combination plans. A typical commission plan gives salespeople a specified percentage of their sales revenue. A **straight commission** system compensates the salesperson only when a sale is made. On the other end of the spectrum, a **straight salary** system compensates a salesperson with a stated salary regardless of sales productivity. Most companies, however, offer a compromise between straight commission and straight salary plans. A *combination system* offers a base salary plus an incentive—usually a commission or a bonus. Combination systems have benefits for both the sales manager and the salesperson. The salary portion of the plan helps the manager control the sales force; the incentive provides motivation. For the salesperson, a combination plan offers an incentive to excel while minimizing the extremely wide swings in earnings that may occur when the economy surges or contracts too much.

As the emphasis on relationship selling increases, many sales managers feel that tying a portion of a salesperson's compensation to a client's satisfaction

ON LINE

Canadian Professional Sales Association

What can you find out about selling in Canada and careers in sales? Visit the Canadian Professional Sales Association website and explore some of the resources that salespeople and sales managers can tap into. What did you learn about a career in "professional selling"?

http://www.cpsa.com

with the salesperson and the company encourages relationship building. To determine this, sales managers can survey clients on a salesperson's ability to create realistic expectations and his or her responsiveness to customer needs.[52] At PeopleSoft, structure, culture, and strategies are built around customer satisfaction. Sales force compensation is tied to both sales quotas and a satisfaction metric that allows clients to voice their opinions on the service given.[53]

Although the compensation plan motivates a salesperson to sell, sometimes it is not enough to produce the volume of sales or the profit margin required by sales management. Sales managers, therefore, often offer rewards or incentives, such as recognition at ceremonies, plaques, vacations, merchandise, and pay raises or cash bonuses. The most popular incentives are cash rewards, used by 64 percent of sales organizations polled in a recent survey.[54] Rewards may help increase overall sales volume, add new accounts, improve morale and goodwill, move slow items, and bolster slow sales. They can be used to achieve long-term or short-term objectives, such as unloading overstocked inventory and meeting a monthly or quarterly sales goal.

Motivation also takes the form of effective sales leadership on the part of the sales manager. An effective sales manager is inspirational to his or her salespeople, encouraging them to achieve their goals through clear and enthusiastic communications. He or she has a clear vision and commitment to the mission of the organization and the ability to instill pride and earn the respect of employees. Effective sales leaders continuously increase their knowledge and skill base while also encouraging others to do so. A recent study that assessed the attributes of sales leaders found that the best sales leaders share a number of key personality traits, such as assertiveness, a sense of urgency, an ability to handle rejection, drive, openness to new ideas, empathy toward customers, and a willingness to take risks. These traits separate motivational sales leaders from mere sales managers.[55]

Evaluating the Sales Force

The final task of sales managers is evaluating the effectiveness and performance of the sales force. To evaluate the sales force, the sales manager needs feedback, that is, regular information from salespeople. Typical performance measures include sales volume, contribution to profit, calls per order, sales or profits per call, and percentage of calls achieving specific goals such as sales of products that the firm is heavily promoting.

Performance information helps the sales manager monitor a salesperson's progress through the sales cycle and pinpoint where breakdowns may be occurring. For example, by knowing the number of prospects an individual salesperson has at each step of the sales cycle process and determining where prospects are falling out of the sales cycle, a manager can determine how effective a salesperson may be at the lead generation, needs assessment, proposal generation, presenting, closing, and followup stages. This information can then tell a manager what sales skills may need to be reassessed or retrained. For example, if a sales manager notices that a sales rep seems to be letting too many prospects slip away after presenting proposals, it may mean he or she needs help with developing proposals, handling objections, or closing sales.

The Impact of Technology on Personal Selling

Will the increasingly sophisticated technology now available at marketers' fingertips eliminate the need for salespeople? Experts agree that a relationship between the salesperson and customer will always be necessary. Technology, however, can certainly help improve that relationship.[56] Cell phones, laptops, pagers, e-mail, and electronic organizers allow salespeople to be more accessible to both clients and the company. Moreover, the Internet provides salespeople with vast resources of information on clients, competitors, and the industry. In fact, many companies are utilizing technology to stay more in touch with their own employees. For instance, IBM invited 320,000 employees to an electronic brainstorming session. A total of 52,600 employees logged on to the event to discuss issues of employee retention, work efficiency, quality, and teamwork.[57]

E-business, or buying, selling, marketing, collaborating with partners, and servicing customers electronically using the Internet, is also having a significant impact on personal selling. In 2002, almost 100 percent of large companies, more than 80 percent of medium-sized companies, and almost 50 percent of small companies were engaged in e-commerce.[58] Additionally, 85 percent of business respondents regard e-business as vital to their company's success.[59] For customers, the Web has become a powerful tool for getting accurate and up-to-date information on products, pricing, and order status. The Internet also cost-effectively processes orders and services requests. Although on the surface the Internet might look like a threat to the job security of salespeople, the Web is actually freeing sales reps from tedious administrative tasks, such as shipping catalogues, placing routine orders, and tracking orders. This leaves them more time to focus on the needs of their clients. At Carlson Wagonlit Travel, for instance, shifting sales of routine products like short-haul shuttle flights to the Web is freeing up travel agents to do more outbound selling to high-potential customers.[60]

>> CONNECT IT

Canadian marketers can employ many different elements of the promotional mix to reach out to customers. However, with so many marketers and so many communication channels being used, Canadian consumers seem to be overwhelmed by promotions. The use of new and innovative approaches to communication combined with good targeting efforts are ways for Canadian marketers to cut through the clutter and communicate their messages effectively. Personal selling is one of four key promotional elements that marketers can use to communicate to customers and avoid "clutter." Although personal selling is the most comprehensive and most flexible promotional tool available to marketers, it is also the most expensive communication tool on a cost per contact basis. As you read the next chapter, keep in mind that marketers try to choose the mix of promotional elements that will best promote their good or service in an economical fashion. Rarely will a marketer rely on just one method of promotion.

REVIEW IT

1 Discuss the role of promotion in the marketing mix. Promotion is communication by marketers that informs, persuades, and reminds potential buyers of a product in order to influence an opinion or elicit a response. Promotional strategy is the plan for using the elements of promotion—advertising, public relations, sales promotion, and personal selling—to meet the firm's overall objectives and marketing goals. Based on these objectives, the elements of the promotional strategy become a coordinated promotion plan. The promotion plan then becomes an integral part of the total marketing strategy for reaching the target market along with product, distribution, and price.

1.1 What is a promotional strategy? Explain the concept of a differential advantage in relation to promotional strategy.

2 Discuss the elements of the promotional mix. The elements of the promotional mix include advertising, public relations, sales promotion, and personal selling. Advertising is a form of impersonal, one-way mass communication paid for by the source. Public relations is the function of promotion concerned with a firm's public image. Firms can't buy good publicity, but they can take steps to create a positive company image. Sales promotion is typically used to back up other components of the promotional mix by stimulating immediate demand. Finally, personal selling typically involves direct communication, in person or by telephone; the seller tries to initiate a purchase by informing and persuading one or more potential buyers.

2.1 WRITING As the promotional manager for a new line of cosmetics targeted to preteen girls, you have been assigned the task of deciding which promotional mix elements—advertising, public relations, sales promotion, and personal selling—should be used in promoting it. Your budget for promoting the preteen cosmetics line is limited. Write a promotional plan explaining your choice of promotional mix elements given the nature of the product, the stage in the product life cycle, the target market characteristics, the type of buying decision, available funds, and the use of a pull or push strategy.

3 **Describe the communication process.** The communication process has several steps. When an individual or organization has a message it wishes to convey to a target audience, it encodes that message using language and symbols familiar to the intended receiver and sends the message through a channel of communication. Noise in the transmission channel distorts the source's intended message. Reception occurs if the message falls within the receiver's frame of reference. The receiver decodes the message and usually provides feedback to the source. Normally, feedback is direct for interpersonal communication and indirect for mass communication.

3.1 Why is understanding the target market a crucial aspect of the communication process?

4 **Explain the goals and tasks of promotion and the AIDA concept.** The fundamental goals of promotion are to induce, modify, or reinforce behaviour by informing, persuading, and reminding. Informative promotion explains a good's or service's purpose and benefits. Promotion that informs the consumer is typically used to increase demand for a general product category or to introduce a new good or service. Persuasive promotion is designed to stimulate a purchase or an action. Promotion that persuades the consumer to buy is essential during the growth stage of the product life cycle, when competition becomes fierce. Reminder promotion is used to keep the product and brand name in the public's mind. Promotions that remind are generally used during the maturity stage of the product life cycle.

The AIDA model outlines the four basic stages in the purchase decision-making process, which are initiated and propelled by promotional activities: (1) attention, (2) interest, (3) desire, and (4) action. The components of the promotional mix have varying levels of influence at each stage of the AIDA model. Advertising and public relations are good tools for increasing awareness and knowledge of a good or service. Sales promotion is effective when consumers are at the purchase stage of the decision-making process. Personal selling is most effective in developing customer interest and desire.

4.1 Why might a marketing manager choose to promote his or her product using persuasion? Give some current examples of persuasive promotion.

4.2 Discuss the AIDA concept. How do these different stages of consumer involvement affect the promotional mix?

5 **Describe the factors that affect the promotional mix.** Promotion managers consider many factors when creating promotional mixes. These factors include the nature of the product, product life-cycle stage, target market characteristics, the type of buying decision involved, availability of funds, and feasibility of push or pull strategies. Because most business products tend to be custom-tailored to the buyer's exact specifications, the marketing manager may choose a promotional mix that relies more heavily on personal selling. On the other hand, consumer products are generally mass produced and lend themselves more to mass promotional efforts such as advertising and sales promotion. As products move through different stages of the product life cycle, marketers will choose to use different promotional elements. For example, advertising is emphasized more in the introductory stage of the product life cycle than in the decline stage. Characteristics of the target market, such as geographic location of potential buyers and brand loyalty, influence the promotional mix as does whether the buying decision is complex or routine. The amount of funds a firm has to allocate to promotion may also help determine the promotional mix. Small firms with limited

funds may rely more heavily on public relations, whereas larger firms may be able to afford broadcast or print advertising. Last, if a firm uses a push strategy to promote the product or service, the marketing manager may choose to use aggressive advertising and personal selling to wholesalers and retailers. If a pull strategy is chosen, then the manager often relies on aggressive mass promotion, such as advertising and sales promotion, to stimulate consumer demand.

5.1 Explain the difference between a "pull" and a "push" promotional strategy. Under what conditions should each strategy be used?

5.2 

Choose two companies, one a consumer-products company and the other an on-line retailer. Conduct some research on these two companies in terms of their promotional practices by observation (such as looking in magazines, the newspaper, television, website, etc.) and searching at your campus library. You may also use InfoTrac® College Edition (**http://infotrac.thomsonlearning.com**) to locate any articles written on the promotional activities of the companies you select. Describe some of the types of promotions that these companies have engaged in during the last year, for example, ran television ads, sponsored an event, held a sweepstakes, or expanded their sales force. To the best of your abilities, determine the objective of each promotion in relation to the AIDA model. For example, the objective of a magazine ad might be to gain attention or to create interest, while the objective of a coupon might be to stimulate the action of purchase. Also note if the companies' promotions are integrated or not.

6 **Discuss the concept of integrated marketing communications.** Integrated marketing communications is the careful coordination of all promotional messages for a product or service to assure the consistency of messages at every contact point where a company meets the consumer—advertising, sales promotion, personal selling, and public relations, as well as direct marketing, packaging, and other forms of communication. Marketing managers carefully coordinate all promotional activities to ensure that consumers see and hear one message. Integrated marketing communications has received more attention in recent years due to the proliferation of media choices, the fragmentation of mass markets into more segmented niches, and the decrease in advertising spending in favour of promotional techniques that generate an immediate sales response.

6.1 Discuss the importance of integrated marketing communications. Give some current examples of companies that are and are not practising IMC.

7 **Describe personal selling.** Personal selling is direct communication between a sales representative and one or more prospective buyers in an attempt to influence one another in a purchase situation. Broadly speaking, all businesspeople use personal selling to promote themselves and their ideas. Personal selling offers several advantages over other forms of promotion. Personal selling allows salespeople to thoroughly explain and demonstrate a product. Salespeople have the flexibility to tailor a sales proposal to the needs and preferences of individual customers. Personal selling is more efficient than other forms of promotion because salespeople target qualified prospects and avoid wasting efforts on unlikely buyers. Personal selling affords greater managerial control over promotion costs. Finally, personal selling is the most effective method of closing a sale and producing satisfied customers.

7.1 Discuss the role of personal selling in promoting products. What advantages does personal selling offer over other forms of promotion?

8 **Discuss the key differences between relationship selling and traditional selling.** Relationship selling is the practice of building, maintaining, and enhancing interactions with customers in order to develop long-term satisfaction

through mutually beneficial partnerships. Traditional selling, on the other hand, is transaction focused. That is, the salesperson is most concerned with making one-time sales and moving on to the next prospect. Salespeople practising relationship selling spend more time understanding a prospect's needs and developing solutions to meet those needs.

8.1 What are the key differences between relationship selling and traditional methods of selling? What types of products or services do you think would be conducive to relationship selling?

9 **List the steps in the selling process.** The selling process is composed of seven basic steps: (1) generating leads, (2) qualifying leads, (3) assessing approach and needs, (4) developing and proposing solutions, (5) handling objections, (6) closing the sale, and (7) following up.

9.1 WRITING You are a new salesperson for a well-known medical software company, and one of your clients is a large group of physicians. You have just arranged an initial meeting with the office manager. Develop a list of questions you might ask at this meeting to uncover the group's specific needs.

9.2 What does sales followup entail? Why is it an essential step in the selling process, particularly from the perspective of relationship selling? How does it relate to cognitive dissonance?

10 **Describe the functions of sales management.** Sales management is a critical area of marketing that performs several important functions. Sales managers set overall company sales goals and define the sales process most effective for achieving those goals. They determine sales force structure based on geographic, product, functional, or customer variables. Managers develop the sales force through recruiting and training. Sales management motivates the sales force through compensation planning, motivational tools, and effective sales leadership. Finally, sales managers evaluate the sales force through salesperson feedback and other methods of determining their performance.

10.1 ON LINE Managing a sales force in today's e-business environment can be difficult, especially with the Internet perceived as a threat to job security. Use InfoTrac® College Edition (**http://infotrac.thomsonlearning.com**) to locate an article in Electronic News titled, "Creating a Web-Savvy Sales Force" by Wally York. Read the article and list elements York considers key. How does this tie in with what you read in the chapter?

10.2 Without revenue, a company cannot survive, and sales is the means to that end. How important is the effectiveness of a company's sales force? Use InfoTrac® College Edition (**http://infotrac.thomsonlearning.com**) to run keyword searches for "sales force" and "sales force automation." Skim six to ten articles and write down all the automation tools (software and hardware) that you discover.

DEFINE IT

advertising 391
AIDA concept 399
channel 395
cold calling 410
communication 394
decoding 396
differential advantage 390
encoding 395
feedback 396
followup 415
integrated marketing communications (IMC) 406
interpersonal communication 394
lead generation (prospecting) 410
lead qualification 410
mass communication 394
needs assessment 412
negotiation 414
networking 410
noise 395
personal selling 393
preapproach 411
promotion 390
promotional mix 391

APPLY IT

Be Safe is a small, independent business that markets childproofing services to parents with small children and to daycare centres and home daycare providers. For a small fee, Jill Sherman, the owner, will visit the customer's home or facility and point out areas that might be dangerous to small children, such as exposed electrical outlets, poisonous products and plants, and falling hazards. Jill also sells and installs safety items in homes and facilities to make them safer for children. Currently, most of her business comes through referrals or the Yellow Pages, but she would like to increase her business through some form of promotion, although her budget to do so will be small. She has noticed that many of her clients, especially new parents, don't know much about child safety in the home or about the products that can help prevent child injuries. Other clients, especially daycare centres, know about child safety but often install the wrong products or don't maintain a safe environment at all times, exposing children to danger.

QUESTIONS

1. What goals should Be Safe's promotional efforts try to achieve? How will these goals differ by target market?
2. How might the type of buying decision and the nature of this service influence the promotional mix?
3. Given Be Safe's small budget, what types of promotional methods would you suggest?

THINK ABOUT IT

Integrated Marketing Solutions is a small public relations firm managed by Jane Brown. The firm has received numerous contracts from government-owned corporations over the years and has a good relationship with these organizations. The firm's staff have often "subcontracted" work out to other firms when they themselves have determined they are unable to do the work. In these instances, Integrated Marketing Solutions takes a 15 percent commission on the total contract, which is an industry standard practice. Integrated Marketing Solutions has been asked by a government-owned corporation to engage in an unusual transaction. Integrated Marketing Solutions will be paid $5 million and will bill the corporation for $5 million for public relations services. Integrated Marketing Solutions will then transfer a cheque worth $4.25 million to ABC Promotions, keeping $750,000, which is equivalent to a standard 15-percent commission for services rendered. Integrated Marketing Solutions will not actually perform any public relations services for this contract but will still be paid as if it has. The transaction will look no different from those involving a subcontract. Jane has been told that the transaction involves the national interest. Jane must decide whether to accept this offer or not.

QUESTIONS

1. What should Jane do?
2. Go to **http://www.the-cma.org/consumer/ethics.cfm** and review the CMA Code of Ethics and write a brief paragraph describing how it relates to this issue.

TRY IT

Will Virtual Promotions Lead to Virtual Salespeople?

The Internet is often described as a convergent medium because it has the ability to provide all of the functions of every other medium that currently exists; also, it can provide interactivity. The promotional elements of advertising, publicity and public relations, and sales promotion can be duplicated extremely well on the Internet. But what about "personal selling"? Can the convergent medium handle this?

In 2003, Saturn Canada launched its new Ion model automobile in Canada with an Internet-based campaign on its SaturnCanada.com website. The campaign featured four short films, such as one of a young man driving a new Ion on a deserted highway. A UFO appears in his rear view mirror and starts to chase him. He calmly steps on the accelerator and leaves the alien spaceship behind.

Eric LeBlanc, advertising and promotions manager at Saturn Canada, states that the launch campaign for the new Ion "wouldn't be complete without the Internet." In addition to the Internet film presentation, the campaign includes promotions using media such as television, direct mail, outdoor, cinema, and newspaper. However, in the Ion campaign, the Internet is being used as a primary medium. This makes sense according to Daniel Taras, vice-president, i-business and sector specialist of business intelligence company iPerceptions, who notes that automotive websites have the highest frequency of repeat visitors compared with the sites of other industries. Taras notes that Canadian consumers undertake purchase research on the Web and he states Canadian data show that 45 percent of all visitors to primary automotive sites have already visited the site at least six times before in the previous six months (just 20 percent of visitors are first timers).

"Our target markets are the largest users of the Internet in the automotive industry, so as part of a launch campaign we need to keep the Web front and centre," says LeBlanc, who adds that up to 75 percent of Saturn's drivers surf the Web. "Consumers arm themselves with so much information from the on-line medium before they go into a retail facility. It isn't like in the past when they shopped from dealership to dealership." The demographic profile of the Ion's target market is single urban dwellers between 18 and 40 with a university education and an average household income of $35,000 and over. Saturn also knows that this demographic also matches people who are heavy users of the Internet.

In selling the Ion, Saturn is depending on its website to identify, qualify, and encourage customers to visit showrooms to deal with salespeople in person. However, marketers are considering the possibility of having this final step occur immediately and on-line with the idea of a "virtual salesperson." Previously the stuff of science fiction, the Internet will soon offer marketers the ability to make sales with "realistic, three-dimensional 'bots' [that] will help make the on-line experience of tomorrow far closer to real life." The Internet will be "personified" with characters having "faces created from real photographs, and personalities based on psychological questionnaires answered by real people. For instance, people are already hard at work devising ways to program bots so that they can, much like pushy real-life salespeople, suggest products to accompany those that a customer has already picked out." In essence, these virtual salespeople will take us through some of the most important steps of the personal selling process from probing our needs, developing and proposing solutions, handling objections, closing the sale, and even following up!

Based on Chris Daniels, "Saturn Sets a Virtual Scene," *Marketing Magazine*, April 21, 2003; and Recommended Reading, "Shopping with the Bots," *Marketing Magazine*, April 2, 2001.

QUESTIONS

1. Evaluate Saturn's use of the Internet in the promotional campaign for the Saturn Ion. Do you think that it would work as an Internet campaign alone? Why or why not?
2. What do you think were some of Saturn's promotional goals in designing this campaign?
3. All promotional campaigns run their course eventually and need to be replaced or followed up. How might Saturn follow up the campaign for the Ion. Would you recommend staying with the Internet focus or would you suggest emphasis on some other form of promotion?
4. On the subject of virtual salespeople, based on what you read, will virtual promotions lead to virtual salespeople? Why or why not? Discuss the selling steps in your answer and compare and contrast what a "live" person can bring to the selling situation versus what a "virtual person" would have to offer.
5. Review your answer to question 4 and consider a number of different kinds of products. Are there any products that you can think of that could probably be sold just as well by a virtual salesperson as by a "real" salesperson? State your reasoning.

FLIP IT

Flip to Chapter 13 in your *Grademaker Study Guide* for more review opportunities, including the pretest, vocabulary review, Internet activities, study test questions, and an application exercise based on IMC concepts. What is the role of promotion in the marketing mix? Can you close your book and diagram the communication process? What about describing the difference between push and pull strategies? If not, then pick up your *Grademaker* and review.

CLICK IT

The *Marketing* website is rich with materials to help you review and master marketing concepts. Check your knowledge with the free quizzes, practise key terms using the crossword puzzles, or review key concepts using the Microsoft® PowerPoint® slides. Also on the website are updated weblinks to companies mentioned in this chapter, Internet exercises, career marketing information, and much much more! Go to http://www.lamb3e.nelson.com, read the material, and follow the convenient links.

WATCH IT

Quebecor's Move into the World of Media Convergence

Media convergence or media cross-ownership is believed to be a key to survival for media companies in Canada these days. "Convergence" refers to multimedia ownership, which includes newspapers, television broadcasting, radio broadcasting, magazine publishing, and Internet portals. By combining different media, firms can leverage their content. Doing so can reduce costs; at the same time, the owners are able to acquire more advertising revenues. A number of Canadian firms have embraced the concept of convergence: Astral Media, Bell Globemedia, CanWest Global Communications, CHUM Limited, Corus Entertainment, Hollinger Canadian Publishing, Pattison Group, Rogers Media, Slaight Communications, Torstar Corporation, Transcontinental Media, and Quebecor Communications.

Quebecor is a media giant and the world's largest commercial printer. The firm decided that in order to protect itself in a world moving toward more electronic communication, it needed to have an interest in this business. Therefore, when Vidéotron, Quebec's dominant cable television firm, was available for purchase, Quebecor decided it had to have it. Vidéotron was highly profitable and offered Internet service as well as cable television programming. Quebecor saw Vidéotron as the means by which it could pursue a convergence media strategy with electronic communication. The problem was that Vidéotron had another suitor interested in buying it: Rogers Media. In fact, Rogers went so far as to publicly announce it had made a deal to purchase Vidéotron.

Quebecor felt compelled to acquire Vidéotron, so it partnered with the Caisse de dépôt et placement du Québec, which had the funds from Quebec's Provincial Public Pension Fund along with a mandate to invest in provincial businesses and also to serve the provincial interest. Together, they outbid Rogers Media and paid a whopping $5 billion cash for Vidéotron. A number of financial analysts felt that Quebecor had "overpaid" for Vidéotron, and when the bubble burst on tech stocks and the economy slowed down, the deal had a negative impact on Quebecor's stock prices.

A second problem for Quebecor in making this acquisition was a corporate culture clash between the two organizations. Vidéotron was used to operating as a near-monopoly and was not focused on cost management. Conversely, Quebecor had a philosophy of cutting costs and managing efficiently. Quebecor began its management tenure at Vidéotron by asking employees to make pay concessions, to work longer hours, and to cut costs. Naturally the employees were highly resistant to giving up the wage levels and working conditions that they were used to, and they went on strike in 2002. The problem for Quebecor was that in order to benefit from convergence, it had to make Vidéotron work more efficiently and market more effectively. The current operational approach was forcing Quebecor to subsidize the Vidéotron operations from its print business.

According to York University economist Fred Lazar, convergence deals are not efficient. It is his opinion that Quebecor's purchase of Vidéotron was a foolish strategy that would "suck the company dry." Lazar was able to point to a number of convergence deals that did not work: AOL-Time Warner, Vivendi Universal, and Bell Canada, which backed off from its convergence approach with Bell Globemedia.

With the acquisition of Vidéotron, Quebecor became the owner and operator of a television network, nine television stations, four specialty stations, 16 consumer magazines, 10 trade publications, 16 daily newspapers, and 13 websites—ranking it as one of the largest media convergence firms in Canada. Quebecor believed it had to make convergence work; consequently, it settled the strike at Vidéotron and got down to business. As a result, in 2003 Quebecor moved from being a financial loser to making money, and now it is being viewed as a model of successful convergence rather than a failure.

QUESTIONS

1. Media convergence seems to be the way to go. The case lists a dozen Canadian firms that have embraced cross-media ownership. Why do you think so many firms have pursued this strategy?
2. In assessing Quebecor's convergence approach, what do you think were the main difficulties the firm encountered? How might you have handled these issues if you had been in charge?
3. Why do you think economist Fred Lazar was so skeptical about the concept of convergence? Do you agree or disagree with him? Explain your reasoning.
4. It turns out that Quebecor was successful despite its difficulties. Were you surprised, given the situation described in the case and the video? Discuss your impressions and evaluate what you learned about the firm through the case and the video. Did you notice any indications of what may have contributed to Quebecor's success?

SUGGESTED INFORMATION SOURCES

Canadian Media Directors Council, "Media Cross-Ownership," *Media Digest*, 03–04, 11.
CBC, *Venture*, "Media Mess," Broadcast: December 15, 2002.
Kucharsky, Danny, "Convergence Redeemers," *Marketing Magazine*, January 26, 2004.

chapter 14

Advertising, Sales Promotion, and Public Relations

>> LEARNING OBJECTIVES

1. Discuss the effects of advertising on market share and consumers
2. Identify the major types of advertising
3. Discuss the creative decisions in developing an advertising campaign
4. Describe media evaluation and selection techniques
5. Define and state the objectives of sales promotion
6. Discuss the most common forms of consumer sales promotion
7. List the most common forms of trade sales promotion
8. Discuss the role of public relations in the promotional mix
9. Describe the major types of public relations activities

>> One of North America's largest sports and entertainment companies and indeed, one of the world's largest, is found in the heart of Toronto. Maple Leaf Sports & Entertainment Ltd., is privately owned and is the owner-operator of the Toronto Maple Leafs of the NHL, the Toronto Raptors of the NBA, and the Air Canada Centre, where the Leafs and Raptors play, and also the owner of Leafs TV and Raptors NBA TV. Sports and entertainment properties are unique in the world of marketing because they are a product and medium combined. The value of the product will influence its value as a medium, and the fortunes of sports properties usually rise and fall with the records of the teams they are bound up with. This seems to ring true everywhere but not for hockey in Toronto. The memories of people who last witnessed a Stanley Cup victory by the Toronto Maple Leafs in 1967 are growing dim, and the real skeptics wonder if they will have to wait until 2067 before they witness another one. Despite this, the Toronto Maple Leafs remain a jewel among the NHL franchises, many of which are struggling to remain viable in a sport that probably has too many teams for its lack of national television exposure in the United States.

The lifeblood of sports and entertainment companies is the sponsorships they can acquire. The payroll costs of operating professional sports franchises in the NHL and the NBA are massive, and the operating costs of venues are not small change either. Simply filling venues and earning revenues on ticket and concession sales will not pay the bills these days. What profit there is to be had depends on the sale of sponsorships. What do sports entertainment companies like Maple Leaf Sports & Entertainment have to offer that attracts other marketers to sponsor them and seek association with them?

According to Keith McIntyre, a Toronto-based sports marketing professional, the key basis for selecting a sports sponsorship is a clear definition and understanding of the target market you are seeking and the relationship that can be established between your brand and the sports property you are sponsoring.

Sports properties are generally highly engaging and involving for their audience. Sponsors can take advantage of this to connect with a target audience through their entertainment. Sponsorships can take many forms from league sponsorship to full team sponsorship, event sponsorship, athletic sponsorship, organizational sponsorship, stadium sponsorship, and broadcast rights sponsorship. There are almost no limits to which sponsorship can be arranged but there is some question as to the value of each sponsorship. For example, the naming of the Air Canada Centre represents a major sponsorship expense for Air Canada and holds tremendous value because the venue is mentioned every time an event is promoted and held there. In contrast, how many people are aware that Philishave is the official electric shaver of the Toronto Maple Leafs and Toronto Raptors?

How can marketers ensure that they get the most value possible out of their sports sponsorship efforts? McIntyre offers the following guidelines:

1. *Devise a game plan.* Team up with a specialty organization that focuses on sports promotion and has excellent contacts. Be sure that you have considered your objectives in undertaking the sponsorship so you know how to evaluate the return on your sponsorship investment. In particular, make sure your brand positioning is clear and fits with the sports property you are tying into. Sponsorships do not stand alone; they must be part of the total marketing mix. Their strength is the ability to cut through promotional clutter.
2. *Invest in talent.* You have to realize that the total investment will exceed the sponsorship rights by two to three times. As such, if you are going to spend $500,000 on a sponsorship be prepared to spend at least an additional $1 million on supporting communications. This means involving the whole organization from top to bottom in understanding and supporting the sponsorship and the message it will be sending.
3. *Player negotiation.* A sponsorship does not bring everything with it. Rather, sports sponsorships often bring more limitations than flexibility. Becoming the official chewing gum of the Toronto Maple Leafs does not mean that you can promote your gum through all of the Maple Leaf players or all the NHL players and personnel. The menu is very limited and totally a la carte! In addition, there may be geographic limitations associated with a sponsorship so that you can only promote in a certain area. This allows the sports property to subdivide the rights among a number of different parties.
4. *Team play.* The sport property itself has an image to maintain and there must be a fit between sponsor and property. Some sponsors might not be a desirable fit for a particular sport. For example, the sponsorship of Junior A hockey by breweries, wineries, and spirits makers is controversial because it is an amateur sport whose players are not of legal drinking age. Conversely, hockey has a rough and tough image and is a male oriented sport so a women's fashion retailer would probably not benefit from a sponsorship.
5. *Star players.* The value of the sponsorship will shift up and down with the value and popularity of the sport. In the early 1990s when the Toronto Blue Jays were winning World Series titles, the value of their properties was very high and tickets to games were hard to come by. In recent times the Jays have not been contenders and tickets have been plentiful. The value of their sponsorships to marketers has declined. As such, marketers need to negotiate some flexibility into the

ON LINE

The Air Canada Centre and Maple Leaf Sports & Entertainment

Find out about Maple Leaf Sports & Entertainment. What kinds of sponsorship opportunities are evident? Do some searches and find as many sponsorship links between either the Toronto Maple Leafs or the Toronto Raptors and other marketing companies as you can. How many did you find?

http://www.theaircanadacentre.com

sponsorship deals and tie costs to performance. It would be best to try and identify up-and-coming sports or athletes and ride their success upwards. For example, sponsors who tied themselves to 2003 Masters Golf Champion Mike Weir have received a great amount of exposure as a result of his success. Sometimes underrated sports can perform better than expected. The Canadian Football League has had many ups and downs but has been resurgent in recent years, especially with its weekly telecasts on TSN, which have provided the league with tremendous television exposure.[1]

How do marketers decide what type of advertising message should be conveyed to prospective consumers? How do marketers decide which media to use? How do public relations and publicity benefit a marketer's promotional plan? Answers to these questions and many more will be found as you read through this chapter.

1 Discuss the effects of advertising on market share and consumers

>> THE EFFECTS OF ADVERTISING

Advertising is defined in Chapter 13 as any form of impersonal, paid communication in which the sponsor or company is identified. It is a popular form of promotion, especially for consumer packaged goods and services. Advertising spending increases annually, with estimated Canadian expenditures at approximately $10 billion per year. This level of expenditure is allocated to the Canadian media in the following proportions: 26 percent to television, 17 percent to daily newspapers, 15 percent to direct mail, 12 percent to "other" print, 11 percent to radio, 10 percent to the Yellow Pages, 5 percent to consumer magazines, 3 percent to outdoor and transit, and 1 percent to the Internet. Although the Internet is the smallest in terms of percentage, it has been experiencing annual growth rates of 100 times the previous year's expenditures![2]

Total advertising expenditures seem large, yet the industry itself is very small. Only about 54,000 people are employed in the advertising industry in Canada.[3] The Canadian industry is composed of both Canadian firms and U.S. multinationals. For example, in 2001, Cossette Communication Group (http://www.cossette.com) from Quebec City was Canada's largest domestic advertising agency, employing 1,243 people with total Canadian revenues of $128.8 million. The next-largest agency was a U.S. multinational, MacLaren McCann Canada, with 2001 Canadian reveunes of $93 million. A listing of Canada's top 10 marketing communications companies and their Canadian billings is provided in Exhibit 14.1.

Spending on advertising varies by industry. For example, the game and toy industry has one of the highest ratios of advertising dollars to sales. For every $1.00 of merchandise sold in the toy industry, about 12¢ to 15¢ is spent on advertising the toy to consumers. Book publishers spend roughly 27¢ on advertising for every $1.00 of book revenue. Other consumer goods manufacturers that spend heavily on advertising in relation to total sales include sugar and confectionery products manufacturers, leather manufacturers, watchmakers, perfume and cosmetics manufacturers, detergent makers, and wine and liquor companies.[4]

Advertising and Market Share

Today's most successful brands of consumer goods in Canada, like Molson Canadian and Coca-Cola, were built by heavy advertising and marketing investments long ago. Most companies spend their advertising dollars to maintain brand awareness and market share.

New brands with a small market share tend to spend proportionately more for advertising and sales promotion than those with a large market share, typically for two reasons. First, beyond a certain level of spending for advertising and sales promotion, diminishing returns set in. That is, sales or market share begins to decrease no matter how much is spent on advertising and sales promotion. This phenomenon is called the **advertising response function**. Understanding the advertising response function helps marketers use budgets wisely. A market leader like Johnson & Johnson's Neutrogena typically spends proportionately less on advertising than a newcomer like Jergens' Naturally Smooth Shave Minimizing Moisturizer brand. Jergens spends more on its brand to gain

advertising response function
A phenomenon in which spending for advertising and sales promotion increases sales or market share up to a certain level but then produces diminishing returns.

RANK	AGENCY	TOTAL CANADIAN REVENUES 2000 (IN MILLIONS)	NUMBER OF EMPLOYEES IN 2001
1	Cossette Communications, Quebec City	$128.86	1,236
2	MacLaren McCann, Global	92.99	675
3	Young & Rubicam, Global	71.67	694
4	BBDO, Global	70.52	501
5	Maxxcom, Toronto	69.12	400
6	DDB Group, Global	59.82	358
7	Publicis, Global	53.44	375
8	DraftWorldwide, Global	47.68	280
9	Maritz, Mississauga	45.09	350
10	Ogilvy & Mather, Global	44.26	236

SOURCE: Data obtained from "The Rankings, Canada's Top Marketing Communications Services Companies," *Marketing Magazine*, June 24, 2002, 12–14.

EXHIBIT 14.1

Top 10 Marketing Communications Service Companies in Canada

attention and increase market share. Neutrogena, on the other hand, spends only as much as is needed to maintain market share; anything more would produce diminishing benefits. Neutrogena has already captured the attention of the majority of its target market. It only needs to remind customers of its product.

The second reason that new brands tend to require higher spending for advertising and sales promotion is that a certain minimum level of exposure is needed to measurably affect purchase habits. If Jergens advertised Naturally Smooth Shave Minimizing Moisturizer in only one or two publications and bought only one or two television spots, it certainly would not achieve the exposure needed to penetrate consumers' perceptual defences, gain attention, and ultimately affect purchase intentions. Instead, Naturally Smooth Shave Minimizing Moisturizer was advertised in many different media for a sustained time.

The Effects of Advertising on Consumers

Advertising affects consumers' daily lives, informing them about products and services and influencing their attitudes, beliefs, and ultimately their purchases. The average Canadian resident is exposed to hundreds of advertisements a day from all types of advertising media. In the television medium alone, the average Canadian viewer watches about 21.5 hours of television a week, and typically 25 percent of that time involves commercials. In addition, that person is probably exposed to countless print ads and promotional messages seen in other places.[5] Advertising affects the TV programs people watch, the content of the newspapers they read, the politicians they elect, the medicines they take, and the toys their children play with. Consequently, the influence of advertising on the Canadian socioeconomic system has been the subject of extensive debate among economists, marketers, sociologists, psychologists, politicians, consumerists, and many others.

While advertising cannot change consumers' deeply rooted values and attitudes, it may succeed in transforming a person's negative attitude toward a product into a positive one. For instance, serious or dramatic advertisements are more effective at changing consumers' negative attitudes. Humourous ads, on the other hand, have been shown to be more effective at shaping attitudes when consumers already have a positive image of the advertised brand.[6] For this reason, beer marketers often use humourous ads to communicate with their core market of young adults.

Advertising also reinforces positive attitudes toward brands. When consumers have a neutral or favourable frame of reference toward a product or brand, advertising often positively influences them. To see the

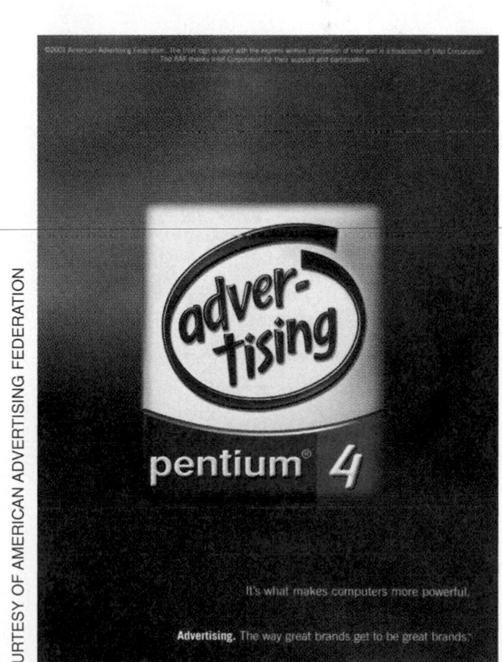

COURTESY OF AMERICAN ADVERTISING FEDERATION

Advertising investments undeniably help build a brand. The Advertising Industry has developed an institutional campaign called "Great Brands" to remind companies of this fact. Intel Corporation gave permission to modify its logo for use in this campaign.

impact of culture on a consumer's frame of reference, read the Global Perspectives box on managing international brand advertising. When consumers are already highly loyal to a brand, they may buy more of it when advertising and promotion for that brand increase.[8] This is why market leaders like Loblaw, General Motors, and Procter & Gamble spend in the hundreds of millions of dollars in Canada every year to remind their loyal customers about the benefits of their stores, cars, and household products.

Further, advertising can affect the way consumers rank a brand's attributes, such as colour, taste, smell, and texture. For example, in years past, car ads emphasized such brand attributes as roominess, speed, and low maintenance. Today, however, car marketers have added safety to the list. Safety features like antilock brakes, power door locks, and air bags are now a standard part of the message in many carmakers' ads.

2 Identify the major types of advertising

>> MAJOR TYPES OF ADVERTISING

institutional advertising
A form of advertising designed to enhance a company's image rather than promote a particular product.

product advertising
A form of advertising that touts the benefits of a specific good or service.

The firm's promotional objectives determine the type of advertising it uses. If the goal of the promotion plan is to build up the image of the company or the industry, **institutional advertising** may be used. In contrast, if the advertiser wants to enhance the sales of a specific good or service, **product advertising** is used.

Institutional Advertising

advocacy advertising
A form of advertising in which an organization expresses its views on controversial issues or responds to media attacks.

Advertising in Canada has historically been product oriented. However, modern corporations market multiple products and need a different type of advertising. Institutional advertising, or corporate advertising, promotes the corporation as a whole and is designed to establish, change, or maintain the corporation's identity. It usually does not ask the audience to do anything but maintain a favourable attitude toward the advertiser and its goods and services. Shell Canada wants to improve its perception in the eyes of influential Canadians such as business and industry leaders, academics, media people, and elected officials. The firm wants people to be aware of its commitment to sustainable development. It wants people to perceive Shell Canada as a responsible company, a company with strong ethics, and a company that listens to people. It has been running an image campaign with promotional messages such as "Living Our Values" and "Profits. Principles. or Both?" In order to evaluate the effectiveness of the campaign Shell surveyed Canadians and asked them how they perceived the company. The campaign results demonstrated an improved perception for Shell Canada.[9]

A form of institutional advertising called **advocacy advertising** is typically used to safeguard against negative consumer attitudes and to enhance the company's credibility among consumers who already favour its position. Often corporations use advocacy advertising to express their views on controversial issues. At other times, firms' advocacy campaigns react to criticism or blame, some in direct response to criticism by the media. Other advocacy campaigns may try to ward off increased regulation, damaging legislation, or an unfavourable outcome in a lawsuit. The Liquor Control Board of Ontario (LCBO) and Mothers Against Drunk Driving (MADD) have combined for six different promotional campaigns over the years. The focus of all of their campaigns has been to discourage "drinking and driving." The interest of MADD is very clear; the LCBO is clearly trying to advocate moderation to reduce the negative social effects of the products it markets: alcoholic beverages.[10]

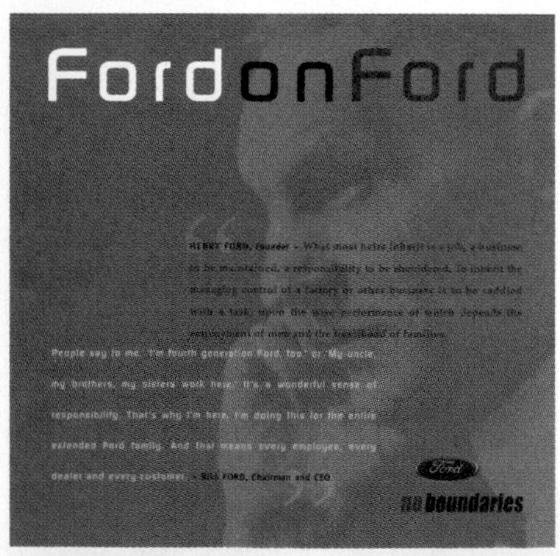

COURTESY OF FORD MOTOR COMPANY

In one of the most compelling institutional ad campaigns of recent memory, Ford Chairman and CEO Bill Ford appears in several TV spots that communicate both the heritage and the vision of Ford. These ads are critical in the wake of several crises that befell the company under Jacques Nasser's tenure.

Product Advertising

Unlike institutional advertising, product advertising promotes the benefits of a specific good or service. The product's stage in its life cycle often determines which type of product advertising is used: pioneering advertising, competitive advertising, or comparative advertising.

GLOBAL **PERSPECTIVES**

Managing International Brand Advertising

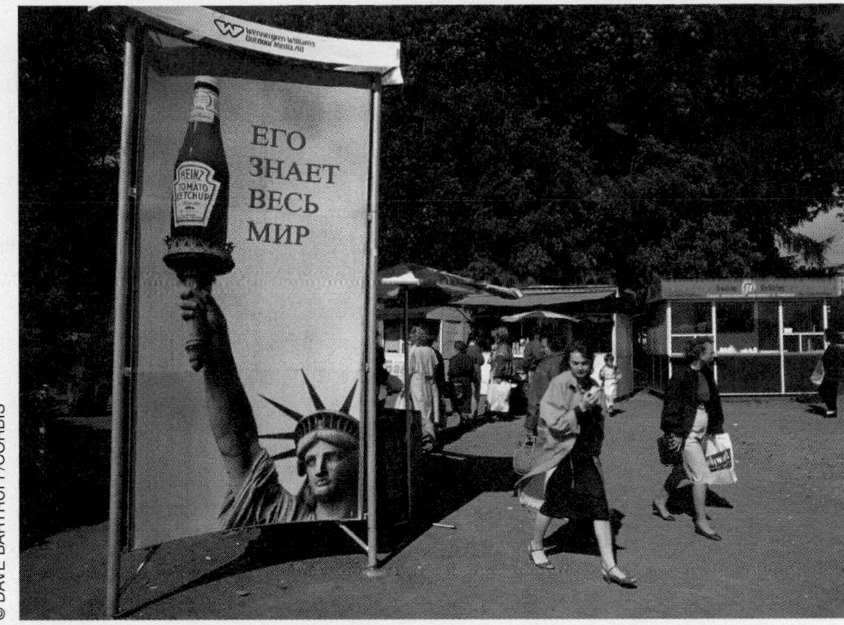

© DAVE BARTRUFF/CORBIS

Global marketers must pay attention to cultural differences, linguistic differences, and the attitudes of consumers in the given market. Heinz, however, was able to use a generally standardized approach because it discovered that teens around the world were more alike in their use of ketchup than they were different.

Global marketing—being able to sell your products or services worldwide—is a huge undertaking. Marketing products or services overseas requires both cultural sensitivity and an understanding of the consumers in the market. In particular, communication strategies and brand name advertising as part of promotion have to be carefully scrutinized. For example, brand names in English may have a totally different meaning in other countries. American Motors once offered a model named Matador, evoking the glamourous image of a bullfighter—but the word also means "killer" in Spanish. Likewise, General Motors' Chevy Nova, which conjures the image of an exploding star in English, literally translates to "No Go" for Spanish speakers in Mexico and Latin America! When another North American company wanted to market a cosmetic product called "Mist Stick" in Europe, it found that the name would have been a bad idea in German-language countries. The name looks and sounds like the German equivalent of "piece of manure." Finally, popular French orange soda brand "Pschitt!" would have to undergo a name change before being launched in Canada! The key to avoiding these kinds of problems is to pay close attention to basic language translation.

For example, multinational chemical giant, Dow Chemical Company has located its global translation department in Westmount, Quebec. All of Dow's promotional literature as well as company operating documents such as training manuals and technical brochures are handled by the global translation department, which translates into 16 different languages and processes an annual volume of 3.5 million words! The goal of Dow's translation department is to see that translations appear original to the readers and are appropriate to the purpose of the document and acceptable to the culture. For example, French words used in Quebec can differ in context and meaning from how they are used in France. Dow's translation department goes beyond simple language translation by seeking to find words that convey the intended message and have the same meaning in both cultures.

The issue of translation is just part of one of the hottest debates among global marketing professionals—whether to customize or standardize promotional messages. Some believe the message should be tailored to each country or region to be most effective since different cultures perceive and react to promotional messages differently. Kodak, for example, favours a customized approach to advertising in China because consumer tastes and values vary between mainland China and the more progressive Taiwan and Hong Kong areas. Others believe marketers should develop one message, translate it into the language of each country, and deliver it to all target markets. They say consumers everywhere have the same basic needs and desires and can therefore be persuaded by universal appeals. For example, Heinz concluded from its research that teens around the world are really more alike in their use of ketchup than they are different. As a result, it rolled out a $50 million global advertising campaign to 75 countries with only minor creative tweaks in the food the teens were pouring the ketchup over. Probably the best answer to this dilemma is to use a mixture of standardization and customization—standardize the message but pay attention to local differences when executing it. For example, Coca-Cola uses a standardized appeal when promoting cola, but it tailors the message to regional and international markets. All ads include the tagline "Coca-Cola. Enjoy," but the campaign's "Enjoy" melody has 19 different versions in genres as varied as reggae, techno, hip-hop, and country depending on demographic and regional preferences.[7]

So what can marketers do as they enter new cultural markets? Taking time to research and define customer needs and learn how the market operates can go a long way in helping companies to promote their products. What other types of promotional research could marketers utilize when entering new countries? Can you think of any barriers, other than language, that could hinder a company's promotional efforts in a new country?

ON LINE 

MADD Canada: Mothers Against Drunk Driving

How does MADD advocate against drinking and driving? What kinds of information does its website provide? Are there any corporate sponsors or partners associated with this website? (Hint: Click on the donate link.) Who are they and why do you think they have an interest in MADD?

http://www.madd.ca

Pioneering Advertising

Pioneering advertising is intended to stimulate primary demand for a new product or product category. Heavily used during the introductory stage of the product life cycle, pioneering advertising offers consumers in-depth information about the benefits of the product class. Pioneering advertising also seeks to create interest. Microsoft used pioneering advertising to introduce its new Windows and Office software products. In a move to reposition the products as more "user-friendly," the software giant renamed its flagship products by adding "XP"—short for "Experience"—to the Windows and Office upgrades.[11] Microsoft's $200 million four-month North American launch phase kicked off with two 15-second TV teaser spots, plus one 60-second and two 30-second TV spots that featured the Madonna song "Ray of Light." The print, outdoor, TV, and on-line campaign carries the tagline "Yes, you can" and features XP's signature look—blue skies with white clouds over a green field. The goal of Microsoft's pioneering campaign was to convince PC users to buy the upgrade because of the more intuitive interfaces and abilities to work seamlessly and easily with digital photographs, music files, and video.[12]

pioneering advertising
A form of advertising designed to stimulate primary demand for a new product or product category.

Competitive Advertising

Firms use competitive or brand advertising when a product enters the growth phase of the product life cycle and other companies begin to enter the marketplace. Instead of building demand for the product category, the goal of **competitive advertising** is to influence demand for a specific brand. Often promotion becomes less informative and appeals more to emotions during this phase. Advertisements may begin to stress subtle differences between brands, with heavy emphasis on building recall of a brand name and creating a favourable attitude toward the brand. Automobile advertising has long used very competitive messages, drawing distinctions based on such factors as quality, performance, and image.

competitive advertising
A form of advertising designed to influence demand for a specific brand.

Comparative Advertising

Comparative advertising directly or indirectly compares two or more competing brands on one or more specific attributes. Some advertisers even use comparative advertising against their own brands. Products experiencing sluggish growth or those entering the marketplace against strong competitors are more likely to employ comparative claims in their advertising. For instance, Canadian credit unions have developed a number of campaigns to lure customers from traditional banks. In one advertising approach, First Calgary Savings decided to compare itself with the banks using the theme "Megabank. The 'Great Escape.'" This "TV spot is seen from the vantage point of a security camera. The ad shows an empty bank, then a pen slithering snake-like across the marble floor. It then cuts to a note saying: "Gone to First Calgary Savings. Never coming back. The Pen" and then the tag line: "Bigger where it counts, looking after you."[13]

comparative advertising
A form of advertising that compares two or more specifically named or shown competing brands on one or more specific attributes.

Comparative advertising can lead to litigation if a company feels its product has been misrepresented or displayed inappropriately. The federal Competition Act prohibits advertisers from falsely describing competitors' products and allows competitors to sue if ads show their products or mention their brand names in an incorrect or false manner. For instance, Shaw Communications, Inc. of Calgary launched a $1 million lawsuit against Telus Corporation for misleading advertising. Telus was running ads for its ADSL Internet service and made the claim that cable services were slower because they used shared lines. Shaw claimed that it was losing customers to Telus as a result of misleading advertising. Shaw later suspended its lawsuit as market conditions changed.[14]

Companies must be careful with comparative advertising approaches in other countries as well. Germany, Italy, Belgium, and France, for example, do not permit advertisers to claim that their products are the best or better than competitors' products, which are common claims acceptable in Canada. In the Netherlands, car manufacturers cannot make claims in their advertising about the fuel consumption or environmental aspects of the car. In Italy, Seagram's brand Absolut ran an ad claiming that it was the only vodka made from grain, which is perceived to produce a higher-quality vodka than that made from potatoes. Rival distributor Aosta Company, noting that two of its products were made from grain, filed a complaint against Absolut's Italian distributor, Seagram Italia. Although comparative advertising has been legal in Italy since 1999, ads cannot make unsubstantiated claims. So authorities ordered the campaign stopped and Seagram Italia had to pull all ads.[15]

In other countries, hard-hitting comparative advertising will not be effective because it offends cultural values. For example, Arabic culture generally encourages people not to compete with one another, and the sharing of wealth is common practice. Therefore, comparative advertising is not consistent with social values in these countries.[16] Japanese advertisers are also reluctant to use comparative advertising because it is considered confrontational and doesn't promote the respectful treatment of consumers or portray a company in a respectful light. Nevertheless, although the Japanese have traditionally favoured soft-sell advertising approaches, consumers are witnessing a trend toward comparative ads.

>> CREATIVE DECISIONS IN ADVERTISING

3 Discuss the creative decisions in developing an advertising campaign

Advertisements that are seen on television, in magazines, and on the Internet are typically the result of an **advertising campaign**—a series of related advertisements focusing on a common theme, slogan, and set of advertising appeals. It is a specific advertising effort for a particular product that extends for a defined period of time. For example, Puretracks.com, a new Canadian digital music download website, developed an introductory advertising campaign around the themes "High Quality, Virus Free Music Downloads." Puretracks is trying to persuade consumers to pay $0.99 a song and $9.99 an album instead of using free peer-to-peer services like Morpheus and Kazaa. The Puretracks promotional campaign involves a multimedia approach that includes Web ads, television, posters, billboards, transit ads, and radio ads in major cities across Canada. Puretracks has also partnered with Zellers to sell prepaid music credit cards that can be redeemed on Puretracks.com to download songs. Puretracks recognizes that it must establish itself quickly with its promotional campaign because it faces competition not only from "free" peer-to-peer services but also from a new Canadian Internet distributor, Quebecor Media's Archambault Group, Inc., which has launched the first French-language music download site in Canada, ArchambaultZik.ca.[17]

advertising campaign
A series of related advertisements focusing on a common theme, slogan, and set of advertising appeals.

Before any creative work can begin on an advertising campaign, it is important to determine what goals or objectives the advertising should achieve. An **advertising objective** identifies the specific communication task that a campaign should accomplish for a specified target audience during a specified period. The objectives of a specific advertising campaign often depend on the overall corporate objectives and the product being advertised. For instance, Puretracks.com's main campaign objective was to establish itself as Canada's first Internet music download service and to establish the quality of its service, which is a key to its branding strategy of "Puretracks." In its first four months of operations, Puretracks sold 1 million songs in Canada. By comparison, Apple i-Tunes sold 1 million songs in the first week of operation in the U.S. but then the sales rate slowed down, with 10 million songs being sold over the first five months.[18]

advertising objective
A specific communication task that a campaign should accomplish for a specified target audience during a specified period.

The DAGMAR approach (Defining Advertising Goals for Measured Advertising Results) is one method of setting objectives. According to this method, all advertising objectives should precisely define the target audience, the desired percentage change in some specified measure of effectiveness, and the time frame in which that change is to occur. For example, the objectives for an advertising campaign for Telus Mobility cell phones might be to convert 20 percent of current competitor Fido subscribers living in Ontario over to a new Telus Mobility plan within six months.

Once objectives are defined, creative work can begin on the advertising campaign. Advertising campaigns often follow the AIDA model, which was discussed in Chapter 13. Depending on where consumers are in the AIDA process, the creative development of an advertising campaign might focus on creating attention, arousing interest, stimulating desire, or ultimately leading to the action of buying the product. Specifically, creative decisions relate to identifying product benefits, developing and evaluating advertising appeals, executing the message, and evaluating the effectiveness of the campaign.

Identifying Product Benefits

A well-known rule of thumb in the advertising industry is, "Sell the sizzle, not the steak"—that is, in advertising the goal is to sell the benefits of the product, not its attributes. An attribute is simply a feature of the product such as its easy-open package or special formulation. A benefit is what consumers will receive or achieve by using the product. A benefit should answer the consumer's question: "What's in it for me?" Benefits might be such things as convenience, pleasure, savings, or relief. A quick test to determine whether you are offering attributes or benefits in your advertising is to ask: "So?" Consider this example:

Attribute: "Bring in your active Fido™ phone (including SIM card, charger, and battery), Fido invoice—and choose a cool phone. You can keep your FIDO rate plan or get a better Telus Mobility rate plan." "So... ?"

Benefit: "Get a better phone, save money, and get six times better digital coverage than Fido offers."

Marketing research and intuition are usually used to unearth the perceived benefits of a product and to rank consumers' preferences for these benefits. Telus's rival, Fido, has its own wireless communications offerings, and positions itself as a leader in providing subscribers with international roaming capabilities. Fido is countering the efforts of Telus and other Canadian wireless competitors to switch its customers with a "rewards" program that will allow customers to upgrade their handsets and save money on their services.[19]

Developing and Evaluating Advertising Appeals

advertising appeal
A reason for a person to buy a product.

An **advertising appeal** identifies a reason for a person to buy a product. Developing advertising appeals, a challenging task, is typically the responsibility of the creative people in the advertising agency. Advertising appeals typically play off consumers' emotions, such as fear or love, or address some need or want the consumer has, such as a need for convenience or the desire to save money.

Advertising campaigns can focus on one or more advertising appeals. Often the appeals are quite general, thus allowing the firm to develop a number of subthemes or minicampaigns using both advertising and sales promotion. Several possible advertising appeals are listed in Exhibit 14.2.

Choosing the best appeal from those developed normally requires market research. Criteria for evaluation include desirability, exclusiveness, and believability. The appeal first must make a positive impression on and be desirable to the target market. It must also be exclusive or unique; consumers must be able to distinguish the advertiser's message from competitors' messages. Most important, the appeal should be believable. An appeal that makes extravagant claims not only wastes promotional dollars but also creates ill will for the advertiser.

ON LINE

The kinds of promotional executions in advertising can lead to complaints and even lawsuits if the advertising offends people or misrepresents the products being advertised. Advertising Standards Canada (ASC) provides a set of guidelines to assist advertisers so they do not develop offensive or misleading advertising. Visit the Advertising Standards website and review the Canadian Code of Advertising Standards. Think about some of the most recent television ads you have seen or some recent radio ads you remember hearing. Were they all in compliance with the code? Why or why not?

http://www.adstandards.com

EXHIBIT 14.2
Common Advertising Appeals

Profit	Lets consumers know whether the product will save them money, make them money, or keep them from losing money
Health	Appeals to those who are body-conscious or who want to be healthy
Love or romance	Is used often in selling cosmetics and perfumes
Fear	Can centre around social embarrassment, growing old, or losing one's health; because of its power, requires advertiser to exercise care in execution
Admiration	Is the reason that celebrity spokespeople are used so often in advertising
Convenience	Is often used for fast-food restaurants and microwave foods
Fun and pleasure	Are the key to advertising vacations, beer, amusement parks, and more
Vanity and egotism	Are used most often for expensive or conspicuous items such as cars and clothing
Environmental consciousness	Centres around protecting the environment and being considerate of others in the community

The advertising appeal selected for the campaign becomes what advertisers call its **unique selling proposition.** The unique selling proposition usually becomes the campaign's slogan. Telus Mobility's advertising campaign aimed at switching Fido subscribers carries the slogan: "It's never been easier to switch." Telus Mobility's unique selling proposition is "future friendly," which is the firm's "commitment to innovation, fresh thinking and technological progress."[20]

unique selling proposition
A desirable, exclusive, and believable advertising appeal selected as the theme for a campaign.

Effective slogans often become so ingrained that consumers can immediately conjure up images of the product just by hearing the slogan. For example, most consumers can easily name the companies and products behind these memorable slogans or even hum the jingle that goes along with some of them: "Have it your way," "Tastes great, less filling," "Ring around the collar," and "Tum te Tum Tum." Advertisers often revive old slogans or jingles in the hope that the nostalgia will create good feelings with consumers. Automaker Isuzu brought back Joe Isuzu after an 11-year absence because research showed that during the initial four-year campaign the brand's awareness was at an all-time high. Maytag Corporation refreshed its campaign featuring its appliance pitchman by changing the actor who plays him—the second change since the ads originated in 1967. And Hershey Foods' Kit Kat bar's 10-year-old jingle "Gimme a Break" is so etched in consumers' minds that recently the agency hired a film crew to walk around and ask people on the street to sing the jingle for use in future spots.[21]

Executing the Message

Message execution is the way an advertisement portrays its information. In general, the AIDA plan (see Chapter 13) is a good blueprint for executing an advertising message. Any ad should immediately draw the reader's, viewer's, or listener's attention. The advertiser must then use the message to hold consumers' interest, create desire for the good or service, and ultimately motivate action—a purchase.

The style in which the message is executed is one of the most creative elements of an advertisement. Exhibit 14.3 lists some examples of executional styles used by advertisers. Executional styles often dictate what type of media is to be employed to convey the message. Scientific executional styles lend themselves well to print advertising, where more information can be conveyed. On the other hand, demonstration and musical styles are more likely found in broadcast advertising.

Injecting humour into an advertisement is a popular and effective executional style. Humourous executional styles are more often used in radio and television advertising than in print or magazine advertising, where humour is less easily communicated. Humourous ads are typically used for lower-risk, routine purchases such as candy, snackfoods, and soft drinks than for higher-

COURTESY OF THE DIAL CORPORATION

Although there are numerous appeals that could be successfully used to advertise laundry detergent, Purex has chosen the profit appeal in this print ad.

EXHIBIT 14.3

10 Common Executional Styles for Advertising

Slice-of-life	Depicts people in normal settings, such as at the dinner table or in their cars. McDonald's often uses slice-of-life styles showing youngsters munching French fries and Happy Meals on family outings.
Lifestyle	Shows how well the product will fit in with the consumer's lifestyle. As their Mitsubishi Lancer moves through the streets of Toronto, the Gen-X drivers plug in a techno music CD and marvel at how the rhythms of the world mimic the ambient vibe inside their vehicle.
Spokesperson/ testimonial	Can feature a celebrity, company official, or typical consumer making a testimonial or endorsing a product. Sarah Michelle Gellar, star of Buffy the Vampire Slayer, endorses Maybelline cosmetics while country singer Shania Twain introduced Revlon's ColorStay Liquid Lip. Dell Computer founder Michael Dell touts his vision of the customer experience via Dell in television ads.
Fantasy	Creates a fantasy for the viewer built around use of the product. Carmakers often use this style to let viewers fantasize about how they would feel speeding around tight corners or down long country roads in their cars.
Humourous	Advertisers often use humour in their ads, such as Snickers' "Not Going Anywhere for a While" campaign featuring hundreds of souls waiting, sometimes impatiently, to get into heaven.
Real/animated product symbols	Creates a character that represents the product in advertisements, such as the Energizer bunny, or General Mills' longtime icon, Betty Crocker, redesigned for the new millennium.
Mood or image	Builds a mood or image around the product, such as peace, love, or beauty. De Beers ads depicting shadowy silhouettes wearing diamond engagement rings and diamond necklaces portray passion and intimacy while extolling that a "diamond is forever."
Demonstration	Shows consumers the expected benefit. Many consumer products use this technique. Laundry-detergent spots are famous for demonstrating how their product will clean clothes whiter and brighter.
Musical	Conveys the message of the advertisement through song. For example, GM's long-running "Like A Rock" campaign that features rocker Bob Seger's hit song.
Scientific	Uses research or scientific evidence to give a brand superiority over competitors. Pain relievers like Advil, Bayer, and Tylenol use scientific evidence in their ads.

risk purchases or those that are expensive, durable, or flamboyant.[22] W.K. Buckley's consistent humourous approach to its cough syrup campaign features the line: "It tastes awful. And it works." Buckley's has run this campaign in Canada for over 18 years now. When the campaign began, Buckley's had a 2 percent market share and sales of $2 million per year. The campaign has enabled Buckley's to attain a 15 percent market share in the $70 million Canadian cough syrup market. This translates into annual sales of $10.5 million for Buckley's. The humourous approach has been very efficient—the company has supported this sales level using a mass media budget of less than $500,000![23]

Executional styles for foreign advertising are often quite different from those we are accustomed to in Canada. Sometimes they are sexually oriented or aesthetically imaginative. For example, European advertising avoids the direct-sell approaches common in Canadian ads and instead is more indirect, more symbolic, and, above all, more visual. Nike, known in North America for "in-your-face" advertising and irreverent slogans such as "Just Do It," discovered that its brash advertising did not appeal to Europeans. A television commercial of Satan and his demons playing soccer against a team of Nike endorsers was a hit in North America. Many European stations refused to run it, however, saying it was too scary and offensive to show in prime time, when kids were watching.[24]

Postcampaign Evaluation

Evaluating an advertising campaign can be the most demanding task facing advertisers. How do advertisers know whether the campaign led to an increase in sales or market share or elevated awareness of the product? Most advertising campaigns aim to create an image for the good or service instead of asking for action, so their real effect is unknown. So many variables shape the effectiveness of an ad that in many cases advertisers must guess whether their money has been well spent. Despite this grey area, marketers spend a considerable amount of time studying advertising effectiveness and its probable impact on sales, market share, or awareness.

AP/WIDE WORLD PHOTOS

Using a spokesperson is a common executional style (recall the Bill Ford ad on page 432. The Lonely Maytag Repair Man, the long-running symbol of reliability for Maytag appliances, is one of the most well-known spokespeople in the world.

Testing ad effectiveness can be done either before or after the campaign. Before a campaign is released, marketing managers use pretests to determine the best advertising appeal, layout, and media vehicle. After advertisers implement a campaign, they often conduct tests to measure its effectiveness. Several monitoring techniques can be used to determine whether the campaign has met its original goals. Even if a campaign has been highly successful, advertisers still typically do a post-campaign analysis. They assess how the campaign might have been more efficient and which factors contributed to its success. Every year, the Institute of Communications and Advertising (ICA), along with the Association of Quebec Advertising Agencies and Le Publicité Club de Montreal combine to present The Cassies Awards to honour Canadian advertising campaigns. The Cassies were created to recognize, reward, and improve the effectiveness of advertising. Cassie awards involve a thorough case history of advertising success, and the campaigns are published as exemplars for Canadian businesses to learn from. For a sample of award winning efforts by Canadian advertisers as judged by the industry itself, visit http://www.cassies.ca.

>> MEDIA DECISIONS IN ADVERTISING

4 Describe media evaluation and selection techniques

A major decision for advertisers is the choice of **medium**—the channel used to convey a message to a target market. **Media planning,** therefore, is the series of decisions advertisers make regarding the selection and use of media, allowing the marketer to optimally and cost-effectively communicate the message to the target audience.[25] Specifically, advertisers must determine which types of media will best communicate the benefits of their product or service to the target audience and when and for how long the advertisement will run.

medium
The channel used to convey a message to a target market.

media planning
The series of decisions advertisers make regarding the selection and use of media, allowing the marketer to optimally and cost-effectively communicate the message to the target audience.

Promotional objectives and the appeal and executional style of the advertising strongly affect the selection of media. It is important to understand that both creative and media decisions are made at the same time. Creative work cannot be completed without knowing which medium will be used to convey the message to the target market. For instance, creative planning will likely differ for an ad to be displayed on an outdoor billboard versus one placed in a print medium, such as a newspaper or magazine. In many cases, the advertising objectives dictate the medium and the creative approach to be used. For example, if the objective is to demonstrate how fast a product operates, a TV commercial that shows this action may be the best choice.

As mentioned at the beginning of this chapter, Canadian advertisers spend almost $10 billion on media advertising annually. About 61 percent, or $6.1 billion, is spent in daily and weekly newspapers, radio, and television, and $3.1 billion or roughly 50 percent of this amount is spent on nationally distributed vehicles. This means that local advertisers spend nearly $3 billion on local daily or weekly newspapers, and local radio and television

ON LINE 

Canadian Advertising Rates and Data service (CARD) is the most complete single reference source of the media available to Canadian advertisers. Find a unique medium to advertise your favourite product or service. Visit the Canadian Advertising Rates and Data service (CARD) website at **http://www.cardmedia.com** and view samples of the kinds of information that are available to Canadian advertisers. What is the subscription rate to CARD? Do you think it is worth it to a large business? a medium business? a small business?

stations![26] Exhibit 14.4 breaks down the $10 billion spent in monitored advertising by media type. As you can see, about 26 percent of every dollar spent in monitored media goes toward purchasing time for TV ads. The largest advertisers spend even more on television advertising—about 63¢ of every $1.00 spent in monitored media.[27]

Media Types

Advertising media are channels that advertisers use in mass communication. The seven major advertising media are newspapers, magazines, radio, television, outdoor media, Yellow Pages, and the Internet. Exhibit 14.5 summarizes the advantages and disadvantages of these major channels. In recent years, however, alternative media vehicles have emerged that give advertisers innovative ways to reach their target audience and avoid advertising clutter. The most comprehensive source of information on the available Canadian media types, media vehicles, their markets, and media costs is available from a single source, Canadian Advertising Rates and Data (CARD), at http://www.cardmedia.com.

Newspapers

The advantages of newspaper advertising include geographic flexibility and timeliness. Because copywriters can usually prepare newspaper ads quickly and at a reasonable cost, local merchants can reach their target market almost daily. Because newspapers are generally a mass-market medium, however, they may not be the best vehicle for marketers trying to reach a very narrow market. For example, local newspapers are not the best media vehicles for reaching purchasers of specialty steel products or even tropical fish. These target consumers make up very small, specialized markets. Newspaper advertising also encounters a lot of distractions from competing ads and news stories; thus, one company's ad may not be particularly visible.

cooperative advertising
An arrangement in which the manufacturer and the retailer split the costs of advertising the manufacturer's brand.

The main sources of newspaper ad revenue are local retailers, classified ads, and cooperative advertising. In **cooperative advertising,** the manufacturer and the retailer split the costs of advertising the manufacturer's brand. One reason manufacturers use cooperative advertising is the impracticality of listing all their dealers in national advertising. Also, co-op advertising encourages retailers to devote more effort to the manufacturer's lines.

Magazines

Compared to the cost of other media, the cost per contact in magazine advertising is usually high. The cost per potential customer may be much lower, however, because magazines are often targeted to specialized audiences and thus reach more potential cus-

EXHIBIT 14.4

Domestic Advertising Spending in Monitored Media for 2001

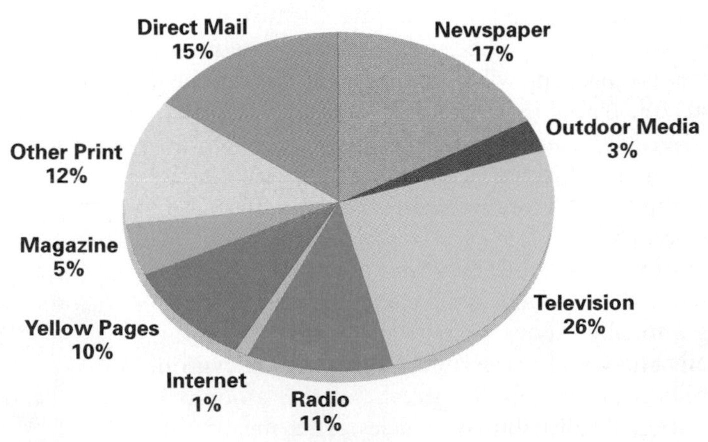

SOURCE: Canadian Media Directors Council, "Components of Net Advertising Revenue by Medium," *Media Digest 03–04,* 10. Reprinted with permission.

MEDIUM	ADVANTAGES	DISADVANTAGES
Newspapers	Geographic selectivity and flexibility; short-term advertiser commitments; news value and immediacy; year-round readership; high individual market coverage; co-op and local tie-in; availability; short lead time	Little demographic selectivity; limited colour capabilities; low pass-along rate; may be expensive
Magazines	Good reproduction, especially for colour; demographic selectivity; regional selectivity; local market selectivity; relatively long advertising life; high pass-along rate	Long-term advertiser commitments; slow audience buildup; limited demonstration capabilities; lack of urgency; long lead time
Radio	Low cost; immediacy of message; can be scheduled on short notice; relatively no seasonal change in audience; highly portable; short-term advertiser commitments; entertainment carryover	No visual treatment; short advertising life of message; high frequency required to generate comprehension and retention; distractions from background sound; commercial clutter
Television	Ability to reach a wide, diverse audience; low cost per thousand; creative opportunities for demonstration; immediacy of messages; entertainment carryover; demographic selectivity with cable stations	Short life of message; some consumer skepticism about claims; high campaign cost; little demographic selectivity with network stations; long-term advertiser commitments; long lead times required for production; commercial clutter
Outdoor media	Repetition; moderate cost; flexibility; geographic selectivity	Short message; lack of demographic selectivity; high "noise" level distracting audience
Internet	Fastest-growing medium; ability to reach a narrow target audience; relatively short lead time required for creating Web-based advertising; moderate cost	Difficult to measure ad effectiveness and return on investment; ad exposure relies on "clickthrough" from banner ads; not all consumers have access to the Internet

EXHIBIT 14.5

Advantages and Disadvantages of Major Advertising Media

tomers. The types of products most frequently advertised in magazines include automobiles, apparel, computers, and personal care products.

One of the main advantages of magazine advertising is its market selectivity. Magazines are published for virtually every market segment. For instance, *Maclean's* is a leading current events publication; *Fifty Plus* targets one of the fastest-growing consumer segments; *Golf Canada* has one of the highest reported circulations (148,501) for a Canadian distributed sporting publication; *Marketing Magazine* is a trade magazine for marketing and advertising professionals; and *Urban Male Magazine* is a niche publication geared to young male urbanites.[28]

Radio

Radio has several strengths as an advertising medium: selectivity and audience segmentation, a large out-of-home audience, low unit and production costs, timeliness, and geographic flexibility. Local advertisers are the most frequent users of radio advertising, contributing over three-quarters of all radio ad revenues. Like newspapers, radio also lends itself well to cooperative advertising.

Radio advertising has been enjoying a resurgence in popularity. As Canadians become more mobile and pressed for

Bureau of Broadcast Measurement Canada

What kind of information does the Bureau of Broadcast Measurement provide for advertisers? Look at some of the press releases provided by the BBM. What did you learn about its media measurement services from these press releases? How would the information provided by the BBM help you buy television and radio advertising in Canada?

http://www.bbm.ca

time, other media such as network television and newspapers struggle to retain viewers and readers. Radio listening, however, has grown in step with population increases mainly because its immediate, portable nature meshes so well with a fast-paced lifestyle. The ability to target specific demographic groups is also a major selling point for radio stations; this ability attracts advertisers who are pursuing narrowly defined audiences that are more likely to respond to certain kinds of ads and products. Moreover, radio listeners tend to listen habitually and at predictable times, with the most popular being "drive time," when commuters form a vast captive audience.[29]

Television

Because television is an audiovisual medium, it provides advertisers with many creative opportunities. Television broadcasters include network television, independent stations, cable television, and a relative newcomer, direct broadcast satellite television. CBC and CTV are the only national networks in Canada, both claiming to have 99 percent of coverage of Canada's English-speaking population. Radio-Canada (French CBC) and TVA are also national networks that broadcast in French. Conversely, regional networks provide excellent coverage of many of Canada's larger population centres. The Global Television Network covers 97 percent of Ontario, while NewNet covers Southern Ontario and Ottawa with stations in Barrie, London, Wingham, Windsor, and Ottawa/Pembroke. CHTV is owned by CanWest Global; it operates through seven rebroadcast transmitters and covers 90 percent of Ontario's population. Subscription television services through cable television systems in Canada (Shaw Cable, Rogers Cable), and also delivered via satellite television systems (Bell ExpressVu and Star Choice), are among the most highly developed in the world. Both systems are able to distribute the signals of virtually all of the commercial television networks; they also offer Pay TV and specialty channels. The cable television system has also been able to piggyback high-speed Internet access along many of its lines. Specialty networks abound in Canada, with a multitude of channels devoted exclusively to particular audiences—for example, women, children, aboriginal peoples, diverse ethnic groups, nature lovers, food lovers, senior citizens, religious groups, sports fans, music lovers, and fitness enthusiasts.[30] Because of its targeted channels, cable and satellite subscription television is often characterized as "narrowcasting" by media buyers. Canadian businesses routinely include cable and satellite buys in their marketing mixes.

Advertising time on television can be very expensive, especially for network stations and popular cable stations. First-run prime-time shows and special events command the highest rates. The average price of a 30-second ad on the CBC full network is $6,500, but depending on the program and the time of day, this cost can range from a low of $100 to a maximum of $52,000. The specialty network MuchMusic has an average price of $2,025 an ad, with a range of $1,050 to $3,000. The CTV network is among the priciest, with an average rate of $12,000 per 30-second ad and a range of $2,500 to $80,000! The most expensive television advertising in the world is a national ad on the U.S. broadcast of the Super Bowl. A 30-second spot on the 2003 Super Bowl cost US$2.2 million and delivered an audience of 138.9 million people. In contrast, the CFL's 2003 Grey Cup commanded $57,000 for a 30-second ad and delivered an audience estimated at 4 million viewers.[31]

infomercial
A 30-minute or longer advertisement that looks more like a TV talk show than a sales pitch.

A relatively new form of television advertising is the **infomercial,** a 30-minute or longer advertisement. Infomercials are an attractive advertising vehicle for many marketers because of the cheap air time and the relatively small production cost. Although they are considered cheap, a well-designed infomercial can still cost between $150,000 and $250,000 to produce. Advertisers say the infomercial is an ideal way to present complicated information to potential customers, which other advertising vehicles typically don't allow time to do. Infomercials are rapidly gaining favour

ON LINE

CTV Network

CBC Network

What kind of advertising is done on the CTV network's website? Compare it with the site for CBC. What differences do you notice? Why do you think a television network would choose not to sell ad space on its website?

http://www.ctv.ca

http://www.cbc.ca

with some of the more mainstream marketers. Canadian firms using Direct Response TV in their marketing programs include the Royal Bank, Bell Canada, Liberty Health, and ING Direct.[32]

Outdoor Media

Outdoor or out-of-home advertising is a flexible, low-cost medium that may take a variety of forms. Examples include billboards, skywriting, giant inflatables, minibillboards in malls and on bus stop shelters, signs in sports arenas, lighted moving signs in bus terminals and airports, and ads painted on the sides of cars, trucks, buses, or even water towers. Marketers have even begun utilizing the plywood scaffolding that often rings downtown construction sites.[33]

Outdoor advertising reaches a broad and diverse market and is, therefore, ideal for promoting convenience products and services as well as directing consumers to local businesses. One of outdoor's main advantages over other media is that its exposure frequency is very high, yet the amount of clutter from competing ads is very low. Outdoor advertising also has the ability to be customized to local marketing needs. For these reasons, local business establishments, such as local services and amusements, retailers, public transportation, and hotels and restaurants, are the leading outdoor advertisers.[34]

Outdoor advertising can be very expensive. For example, for a one-month exposure of 25 gross rating points in the top 10 markets in Canada it would cost $286,000 for 171 front-illuminated panels. Outdoor advertising categories on the rise include telecommunications with a heavy emphasis on wireless services, financial services, and packaged goods. Canadian advertisers interested in outdoor advertising can join the Outdoor Marketing Association of Canada. The Canadian Outdoor Measurement Bureau (COMB at http://www.comb.org) provides comprehensive, up-to-date, and accurate traffic and audience data for major out-of-home products. The audience data is location-specific, full coverage, and in-market in nature.[35]

The Internet

The World Wide Web and the Internet have undoubtedly shaken up the advertising world. Canadian ad revenues were $116 million in 2001, but with a growth rate of revenues in triple digits, the Internet is quickly establishing itself as a solid advertising medium.[36] On-line advertising has made significant gains since the early 1990s and is making up an ever-larger portion of companies' total advertising budgets. By 2005, Internet advertising is expected to represent close to 10 percent of total media spending. Popular Internet sites and search engines, such as Netscape and Yahoo!, as well as on-line service providers like America Online, generally sell advertising space, called "banners," to marketers to promote their goods and services. Internet surfers click on these banners to be linked to more information about the advertised product or service.

Advertising executives and academicians have hotly debated the effectiveness of banner ads. Early research indicated that banner ads were generating response rates as high as 30 percent.[37] But other industry observers feel that banner ads have been largely ineffective, with low click-through rates and recall. Consumers today are more Web savvy and often ignore banner advertising, to the point that the click-through rate is less than 1 percent. Marketers are recognizing, however, that banner ads can build brand awareness, so banners are being produced that don't actually link to anything.

AP/WIDE WORLD PHOTOS

Outdoor advertising is becoming increasingly innovative and three-dimensional. Delta's living billboard is an example of how far you can go with outdoor media.

Initial studies indicate that brand awareness increases by 5 percent and that the association between the brand and its tagline increases by an average of 16 percent with banner advertising.[38] With over 75 percent of the Canadian population on-line, 63 percent of them from home, and over 54 percent with broadband services, marketers are looking for new approaches to on-line advertising.[39] Some marketers are offering a variety of content-sponsorship deals, video ads that pop up in another window, and on-line and off-line cross-promotions. They are also developing new ad formats with big, hard-to-miss shapes. The new formats include the *skyscraper,* a tall, skinny oblong at the side of a Web page, and the *rectangle,* a box much larger than a banner. These new formats are large enough for marketers to include their entire message so that users don't have to click through to another site.[40]

Marketing on the Internet and World Wide Web is discussed in more detail in Chapter 17.

Alternative Media

To cut through the clutter of traditional advertising media, advertisers are creating new media vehicles to advertise their products, some ordinary and others quite innovative. Alternative media vehicles can include shopping carts in grocery stores, computer screen savers, CD-ROMs, interactive kiosks in department stores, aerial ads, washroom posters, and advertisements run before movies at the cinema and on rented DVDs and videocassettes. In fact, just about anything can become a vehicle for displaying advertising. For instance, supermarkets are now testing "flooranimation," ads on supermarket floors that will be animated with graphics and sounds. Unanimated floor ads are already in use in a number of Canadian convenience stores, and research shows that static floor ads increase sales 15 percent to 30 percent. Marketers are hoping that with animation and sound, sales will increase even more.[41] Video Venue recently unveiled plans to install 10-inch, wireless, high-resolution screens at gas pumps to run six-minute cycles of full-motion video and sound ads. Marketers are hoping to capitalize on the four to six minutes it takes for consumers to pump gas and will advertise products available right there in the store.[42] Marketers are also looking for more innovative ways to reach captive and often bored commuters. For instance, subway systems are now showing ads via lighted boxes installed along tunnel walls. As a train passes through the tunnel, the passengers view the illuminated boxes, which create the same kind of illusion as a child's flip book, in which the images appear to move as the pages are flipped rapidly.[43]

media mix
The combination of media to be used for a promotional campaign.

cost per contact
The cost of reaching one member of the target market.

Media Selection Considerations

An important element in any advertising campaign is the **media mix,** the combination of media to be used. Media mix decisions are typically based on several factors: cost per contact, reach, frequency, target audience considerations, flexibility of the medium, noise level, and the life span of the medium.

AP/WIDE WORLD PHOTOS

Lunch hour elevator passengers follow the stock market through a wireless Internet device installed by the elevator door. Otis Elevator and Captivate are two firms offering this alternative media space and bringing weather, news, sports, and stock market data to elevator riders in large office towers in most of Canada's largest cities.

Cost per contact is the cost of reaching one member of the target market. Naturally, as the size of the audience increases, so does the total cost. Cost per contact enables an advertiser to compare media vehicles, such as television versus radio or magazine versus newspaper, or more specifically *Canadian Family* versus *Today's Parent.* An advertiser debating whether to spend local advertising dollars for TV spots or radio spots could consider the cost per contact of each. The advertiser might then pick the vehicle with the lowest cost per contact to maximize advertising punch for the money spent.

Reach is the number of different target consumers who are exposed to a commercial at least once during a specific period, usually four weeks. Media plans for product introductions and attempts at increasing brand awareness usually emphasize reach. For example, an advertiser might try to reach 70 percent of the target audience during the first three months of the campaign. Reach is related to media ratings, generally referred to in the industry as *gross ratings points*, or GRP. A television program with a higher GRP means that more people are tuning in to the show and the reach is higher. Accordingly, as GRP increases for a particular medium, so does cost per contact.

reach
The number of target consumers exposed to a commercial at least once during a specific period, usually four weeks.

Because the typical ad is short-lived and because often only a small portion of an ad may be perceived at one time, advertisers repeat their ads so that consumers will remember the message. **Frequency** is the number of times an individual is exposed to a message during a specific period. Advertisers use average frequency to measure the intensity of a specific medium's coverage. For example, Telus Mobility might want an average exposure frequency of five for its television ads featuring its new cameraphones. That means that each of the television viewers who saw the ad saw it an average of five times.

frequency
The number of times an individual is exposed to a given message during a specific period.

Media selection is also a matter of matching the advertising medium with the product's target market. If marketers are trying to reach expectant mothers, they could select either of *Baby & Child Care Encylopedia* magazine or *Expecting's Labour & Birth Guide* magazine. If they are trying to reach consumers over 50 years old, they may choose *Fifty Plus* magazine. The ability of a medium to reach a precisely defined market is its **audience selectivity.** Some media vehicles, such as general newspapers and network television, appeal to a wide cross section of the population. Others, such as *Ski Canada, Ontario Snowmobiler,* Leafs TV, Telelatino, and CHIN AM and FM radio stations, appeal to very specific groups. Viewer profiles for a sampling of popular cable networks are presented in Exhibit 14.6.

audience selectivity
The ability of an advertising medium to reach a precisely defined market.

The *flexibility* of a medium can be extremely important to an advertiser. In the past, because of printing timetables, pasteup requirements, and so on, some magazines required final ad copy several months before publication. Therefore, magazine advertising traditionally could not adapt as rapidly to changing market conditions. While this situation is changing quickly due to computer technology that creates electronic ad images and layouts, the lead time for magazine advertising is still considerably longer. Radio and Internet advertising, on the other hand, provide maximum flexibility. Usually, the advertiser can change a radio ad on the day it is aired, if necessary. Similarly, advertisements on the Internet can be changed in minutes with the click of a few buttons.

Noise level is the level of distraction to the target audience in a medium. For example, to understand a televised promotional message, viewers must watch and listen carefully. But they often watch television with others, who may well provide distractions. Noise can also be created by competing ads, as when a street is lined with billboards or when a television program is cluttered with competing ads. About two-thirds of a newspaper's pages are now filled with advertising. Even more space is dedicated to ads in magazines. For example, 85 percent of the space in the February/March issue of *Brides* magazine is typically devoted to advertisements. In contrast, direct mail is a private medium with a low noise level. Typically, no other advertising media or news stories compete for direct-mail readers' attention.

Media have either a short or long life span. *Life span* means that messages can either quickly fade or persist as tangible copy to be carefully studied. For example, a radio commercial may last less than a minute. Listeners can't replay the commercial unless they have recorded the program. One way advertisers overcome this problem is by repeating radio ads often. In contrast, a magazine has a relatively long life span. A person may read several articles, put the magazine down, and pick it up a week later to continue reading. In addition, magazines often have a high pass-along rate. That is, one person will read the publication and then give it to someone else to read.

Media planners have traditionally relied on the above factors for selecting an effective media mix, with reach, frequency, and cost often the overriding criteria. Some recent studies, however, question the reliance media planners have traditionally placed on reach and frequency. For instance, one recent study suggests that well-established brands with familiar messages may need fewer exposures to be effective, while newer brands or brands with unfamiliar messages may need more exposures to become familiar.[44]

EXHIBIT 14.6

Selected Canadian Specialty Television Network Profiles

APTN	Aboriginal Peoples Television Network is available to 8 million Canadian Households. It provides documentaries, newsmagazines, dramas, and other programs illustrating the lives of indigenous peoples in Canada and throughout the world. The content is broadcast in English (60 percent) and French (15 percent) and in aboriginal languages (25 percent).
Bravo!	Bravo! is available to an audience of 5.2 million households and is targeted at the 35–54 age bracket. It is an English-language network whose programming is focused on literature visual arts, drama, dance, music, opera, and documentary.
CLT	Canadian Learning Television is targeted at people 18 years and older and is distributed to 2.3 million homes in Canada. The programming is linked to universities and colleges across Canada. The website (**http://www.clt.ca**) is tied into the learning objectives of the programming. Film and media studies, careers, sciences, management studies, computer studies, personal development, and books and literature are all part of the programming themes.
Canal Z	Targeted at men, ages 18–49 this French-language station offers programming devoted to science and technology, multimedia and computers, and science fiction.
CMT	Country Music Television is available to 7.8 million Canadian households and operates 24/7. The station is devoted to country music videos but also includes programs and spotlights on the lives of country music artists and on concerts by country music performers.
MuchMusic	Originating in Canada, this service is targeted at the 12–34 year old age group and is available to 6.8 million Canadian homes but is also distributed to 13 million homes in the United States. The music programming involves music industry news, information, international music guests, and many of the latest music videos of popular artists.
YTV	YTV Canada (Youth Television) is targeted to children and teens and is available to 8 million Canadian households. The programming is blocked to appeal to specific age groups throughout the day. Early morning programs focus on elementary school children, a block of commercial-free daytime programming on preschoolers, and lunchtime on elementary school age. Afternoon returns to preschool, and then, after school and in the evening, programming shifts demographics again.

SOURCE: Canadian Media Directors Council, "Specialty Networks," *Media Digest 04–04*, 18–22. Reprinted with permission.

Additionally, media planners have hundreds more media options today than they had 40 years ago when network television reigned. For instance, Canada has 43 television markets and 144 commercial television stations to cover them. The nation has 941 radio stations, 274 AM and 667 FM, offering a wide variety of formats. There are 105 daily newspapers in Canada with daily circulation numbers of 4.7 million copies. The number of unique magazine titles is impressive, with 1,600 magazines listed, of which 550 are targeted to consumers.[45] Satellite television can now bring hundreds of channels into viewers' homes. The Internet provides media planners with even more targeted choices in which to send their messages. Alternative media choices are popping up in some very unlikely places. *Media fragmentation* is forcing media planners to pay as much attention to where they place their advertising as to how often the advertisement is repeated. New research suggests evaluating reach along with frequency in assessing the effectiveness of advertising. That is, it may be more important to reach as many consumers in as many media vehicles as possible than to achieve a certain number of exposures in any one particular medium.[46] In evaluating reach versus frequency, therefore, the media planner ultimately must select an approach that is most likely to result in the ad being understood and remembered when a purchase decision is being made.

Advertising researchers are also discussing the qualitative factors that should be present during media selection. These qualitative factors include such things as attention to the commercial and the program, involvement, program liking, lack of distractions, and other audience behaviours that affect the likelihood that a commercial message is being seen and, hopefully, absorbed. While advertisers can advertise their product in as many media as possible and repeat the ad as many times as they like, the ad still may not be effective if the audience is not paying attention.[47] Recent research into audience attentiveness for television, for example, shows that the longer viewers

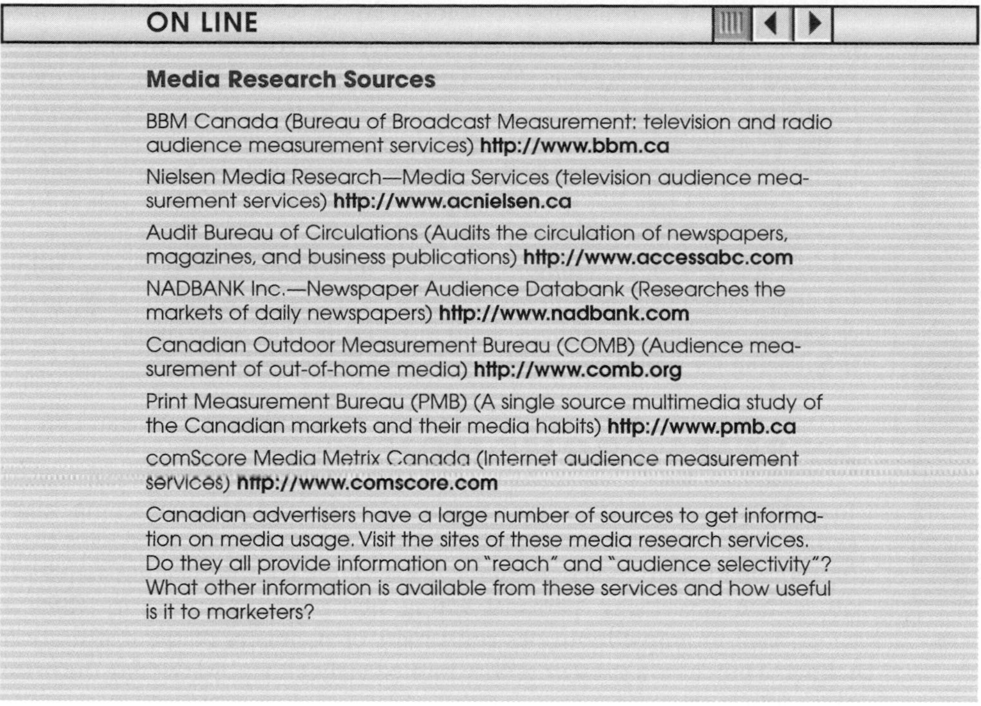

ON LINE

Media Research Sources

BBM Canada (Bureau of Broadcast Measurement: television and radio audience measurement services) **http://www.bbm.ca**

Nielsen Media Research—Media Services (television audience measurement services) **http://www.acnielsen.ca**

Audit Bureau of Circulations (Audits the circulation of newspapers, magazines, and business publications) **http://www.accessabc.com**

NADBANK Inc.—Newspaper Audience Databank (Researches the markets of daily newspapers) **http://www.nadbank.com**

Canadian Outdoor Measurement Bureau (COMB) (Audience measurement of out-of-home media) **http://www.comb.org**

Print Measurement Bureau (PMB) (A single source multimedia study of the Canadian markets and their media habits) **http://www.pmb.ca**

comScore Media Metrix Canada (Internet audience measurement services) **http://www.comscore.com**

Canadian advertisers have a large number of sources to get information on media usage. Visit the sites of these media research services. Do they all provide information on "reach" and "audience selectivity"? What other information is available from these services and how useful is it to marketers?

stay tuned to a particular program, the more memorable they find the commercials. The study suggests that "holding power," is more important than ratings (the number of people tuning in to any part of the program) when selecting media vehicles; this challenges the long-held assumption that the higher the rating of a program, the higher the cost to advertise during the program.

Media Scheduling

After choosing the media for the advertising campaign, advertisers must schedule the ads. A **media schedule** designates the medium or media to be used (such as magazines, television, or radio), the specific vehicles (such as *The Hockey News* magazine, *Hockey Night in Canada* TV broadcasts, or sports talk radio stations), and the insertion dates of the advertising.

media schedule
Designation of the media, the specific publications or programs, and the insertion dates of advertising.

There are three basic types of media schedules:

- Products in the latter stages of the product life cycle, which are advertised on a reminder basis, use a **continuous media schedule.** A continuous schedule allows the advertising to run steadily throughout the advertising period. Examples include President's Choice, Molson Canadian, and The Bay.
- With a **flighted media schedule,** the advertiser may schedule the ads heavily every other month or every two weeks to achieve a greater impact with an increased frequency and reach at those times. Movie studios might schedule television advertising on Wednesday and Thursday nights, when moviegoers are deciding which films to see that weekend. A variation is the **pulsing media schedule,** which combines continuous scheduling with flighting. Continuous advertising is simply heavier during the best sale periods. A retail department store may advertise on a year-round basis but place more advertising during certain sale periods such as spring and summer, Christmas, and back-to-school.
- Certain times of the year call for a **seasonal media schedule.** Products like Contac cold tablets and Coppertone suntan lotion, which are used more during certain times of the year, tend to follow a seasonal strategy. Advertising for champagne is concentrated during the weeks of Christmas and New Year's, whereas health clubs concentrate their advertising in January to take advantage of New Year's resolutions.

continuous media schedule
A media scheduling strategy in which advertising is run steadily throughout the advertising period; used for products in the latter stages of the product life cycle.

flighted media schedule
A media scheduling strategy in which ads are run heavily every other month or every two weeks, to achieve a greater impact with an increased frequency and reach at those times.

pulsing media schedule
A media scheduling strategy that uses continuous scheduling throughout the year coupled with a flighted schedule during the best sales periods.

seasonal media schedule
A media scheduling strategy that runs advertising only during times of the year when the product is most likely to be used.

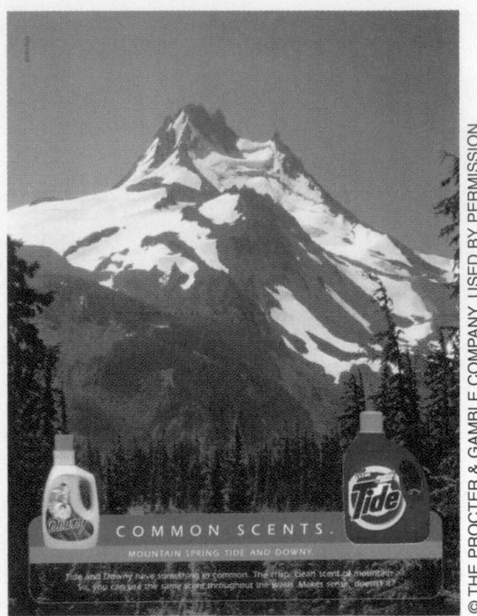

Laundry detergent is a product in the mature stage of the product life cycle. As such, companies like Procter & Gamble use a continuous media schedule to remind consumers to chose Tide over the competition. Compare this ad for Tide with the ad for Purex on page 437. Which do you find more compelling? Why?

New research comparing continuous media schedules to flighted ones finds that continuous schedules for television advertisements are more effective than flighting in driving sales. The research suggests that it may be more important to get exposure as close as possible to the time when someone is going to make a purchase. For example, if a consumer shops on a weekly basis, the best time to reach that person is right before he or she shops. Therefore, the advertiser should maintain a continuous schedule over as long a period of time as possible.[48] Often called *recency planning*, this new theory of scheduling is now commonly used for scheduling television advertising for frequently purchased products, such as Molson Canadian or Sunlight detergent. Recency planning's main premise is that advertising works by influencing the brand choice of people who are ready to buy.[49]

>> SALES PROMOTION

In addition to using advertising, public relations, and personal selling, marketing managers can use sales promotion to increase the effectiveness of their promotional efforts. *Sales promotion* is marketing communication activities, other than advertising, personal selling, and public relations, in which a short-term incentive motivates consumers or members of the distribution channel to purchase a good or service immediately, either by lowering the price or by adding value.

Advertising offers the consumer a reason to buy; sales promotion offers an incentive to buy. Both are important, but sales promotion is usually cheaper than advertising and easier to measure. A major Canadian national TV advertising campaign may cost over $2 million to create, produce, and place. In contrast, a newspaper coupon campaign or promotional contest may cost only about half as much. It is also hard to calculate exactly how many people buy a product as a result of seeing a TV ad. With sales promotion, however, marketers know the precise number of coupons redeemed or the number of contest entries.

 Define and state the objectives of sales promotion

consumer sales promotion
Sales promotion activities targeting the ultimate consumer.

trade sales promotion
Sales promotion activities targeting a channel member, such as a wholesaler or retailer.

Sales promotion is usually targeted toward either of two distinctly different markets. **Consumer sales promotion** is targeted to the ultimate consumer market. **Trade sales promotion** is directed to members of the marketing channel, such as wholesalers and retailers. Sales promotion has become an important element in a marketer's integrated marketing communications program (see Chapter 13). Sales promotion expenditures have been steadily increasing over the last several years as a result of increased competition, the ever-expanding array of available media choices, consumers and retailers demanding more deals from manufacturers, and the continued reliance on accountable and measurable marketing strategies. In addition, product and service marketers that have traditionally ignored sales promotion activities, such as power companies and restaurants, have discovered the marketing power of sales promotion. In fact, *PROMO Magazine* estimates that promotion marketing in North America exceeds $100 billion a year.[50]

The Objectives of Sales Promotion

Sales promotion usually has more effect on behaviour than on attitudes. Immediate purchase is the goal of sales promotion, regardless of the form it takes. Therefore, it seems to make more sense when planning a sales promotion campaign to target customers according to their general behaviour. For instance, is the consumer loyal to your product or to your competitor's? Does the consumer switch brands readily in favour of the best deal? Does the consumer buy only the least expensive product, no matter what? Does the consumer buy any products in your category at all?

The objectives of a promotion depend on the general behaviour of target consumers (see Exhibit 14.7). For example, marketers who are targeting loyal users of their product actually don't want to change behaviour. Instead, they need to reinforce existing behaviour or increase product usage. An effective tool for strengthening brand loyalty is the *frequent-buyer program* that rewards consumers for repeat purchases. Other types of promotions are more effective with customers prone to brand switching or with those who are loyal to a competitor's product. A cents-off coupon, free sample, or eye-catching display in a store will often entice shoppers to try a different brand. Consumers who do not use the product may be enticed to try it through the distribution of free samples.

Once marketers understand the dynamics occurring within their product category and have determined the particular consumers and consumer behaviours they want to influence, they can then go about selecting promotional tools to achieve these goals.

ON LINE

Save.ca versus Coupons.com

Would you be willing to register at an on-line coupon site in order to get information on discounts? Compare what information you can get easily from Save.ca versus what you can get at Coupons.com. Which would you be more inclined to use? If you want to find other on-line coupon sites, type "online coupons" into the AltaVista search engine.

http://www.save.ca

http://www.coupons.com

Tools for Consumer Sales Promotion

6 Discuss the most common forms of consumer sales promotion

Marketing managers must decide which consumer sales promotion devices to use in a specific campaign. The methods chosen must suit the objectives to ensure success of the overall promotion plan. Popular tools for consumer sales promotion are coupons and rebates, premiums, loyalty marketing programs, contests and sweepstakes, sampling, and point-of-purchase promotion. Consumer sales promotion tools have also been easily transferred to on-line versions to entice Internet users to visit sites, purchase products, or use services on the Web.

Coupons and Rebates

A **coupon** is a certificate that entitles consumers to an immediate price reduction when they buy the product. Coupons are a particularly good way to encourage product trial and repurchase. They are also likely to increase the amount of a product bought.

coupon
A certificate that entitles consumers to an immediate price reduction when they buy the product.

EXHIBIT 14.7

Types of Consumers and Sales Promotion Goals

TYPE OF BUYER	DESIRED RESULTS	SALES PROMOTION EXAMPLES
Loyal customers People who buy your product most or all of the time	Reinforce behaviour, increase consumption, change purchase timing	• Loyalty marketing programs, such as frequent-buyer cards or frequent-shopper clubs • Bonus packs that give loyal consumers an incentive to stock up or premiums offered in return for proofs of purchase
Competitor's customers People who buy a competitor's product most or all of the time	Break loyalty, persuade to switch to your brand	• Sampling to introduce your product's superior qualities compared to their brand • Sweepstakes, contests, or premiums that create interest in the product
Brand switchers People who buy a variety of products in the category	Persuade to buy your brand more often	• Any promotion that lowers the price of the product, such as coupons, price-off packages, and bonus packs • Trade deals that help make the product more readily available than competing products
Price buyers People who consistently buy the least expensive brand	Appeal with low prices or supply added value that makes price less important	• Coupons, price-off packages, refunds, or trade deals that reduce the price of the brand to match that of the brand that would have been purchased

SOURCE: From *Sales Promotion Essentials*, 2nd ed., by Don E. Schultz, William A. Robinson, and Lisa A. Petrison. Reprinted with permission of The McGraw-Hill Companies.

Although coupons are a high-cost promotion alternative, they are still an important incentive. Since coupons tend to be redeemed by customers who would have bought the product anyway, a coupon site like Save.ca is an efficient way to distribute coupons. It also allows marketers to get information on coupon users. Can you argue that coupons are really more of a loyalty marketing program? Why or why not?

Coupon distribution has been steadily declining in recent years as packaged-goods marketers attempt to wean consumers off coupon clipping. Although approximately 2.67 billion coupons were distributed in Canada in 2001, the redemption rate was only 4.6 percent, with 122 million actually redeemed by consumers and with an average value of $1.05 per coupon. This means that consumers saved $128 million![51] Part of the problem is that coupons are often wasted on consumers who have no interest in the product, such as with pet food or feminine products coupons that reach the petless or men. This is due mainly to the typical distribution of coupons in mass-media newspaper inserts. Additionally, coupons are more likely to encourage repeat purchase by regular users, customers who would have purchased the product regardless, than to stimulate product trial by nonusers.

Because of their high cost and disappointing redemption rates, many marketers are reevaluating their use of coupons. By shortening the time the coupon can be redeemed, some marketers have increased redemption rates by creating a greater sense of urgency to redeem the coupon. Other marketers are de-emphasizing their use of coupons in favour of everyday low pricing, while others are distributing single, all-purpose coupons that can be redeemed for several brands. In-store coupons are becoming more popular as they have proved more likely to affect customer buying decisions.

Instant coupons on product packages, coupons distributed from on-shelf coupon-dispensing machines, and electronic coupons issued at the checkout counter are achieving much higher redemption rates. Indeed, instant coupons are redeemed more than 15 times more frequently than traditional newspaper coupons, indicating that consumers are making more in-store purchase decisions. As marketing tactics grow more sophisticated, coupons are no longer being viewed as a stand-alone tactic, but as an integral component of a larger promotional campaign. For example, Dr Pepper/Seven Up kicked off its sponsorship of the Grammys with a "Sit On Your Can at the Grammys" under-the-cap game and included a 55¢-coupon on-pack to encourage buying the brand.[52]

rebate
A cash refund given for the purchase of a product during a specific period.

Rebates are similar to coupons in that they offer the purchaser a price reduction; however, because the purchaser must mail in a rebate form and usually some proof of purchase, the reward is not as immediate. Traditionally used by food and car manufacturers, rebates now appear on all types of products, from computers and software to film and baby seats. Electronics retailer Future Shop routinely promotes products with rebates and often quotes "prices after savings" in its flyers. It is almost a standard practice to offer cell phone handsets for "free" after rebates with an agreement to sign a two-year service plan!

Manufacturers prefer rebates for several reasons. Rebates allow manufacturers to offer price cuts to consumers directly. Manufacturers have more control over rebate promotions because they can be rolled out and shut off quickly. Further, because buyers must fill out forms with their names, addresses, and other data, manufacturers use rebate programs to build customer databases. Perhaps the best reason of all to offer rebates is that although rebates are particularly good at enticing purchase, most consumers never bother to redeem them. Studies have found that as few as 2 percent of consumers eligible for rebates apply for them.[53]

Premiums

premium
An extra item offered to the consumer, usually in exchange for some proof of purchase of the promoted product.

A **premium** is an extra item offered to the consumer, usually in exchange for some proof that the promoted product has been purchased. Premiums reinforce the consumer's purchase decision, increase consumption, and persuade nonusers to switch brands. Premiums like telephones, tote bags, and umbrellas are available when consumers buy cosmetics, magazines, bank services, rental cars, and so on. Probably the best example of the use of premiums is the McDonald's Happy Meal, which rewards children with a small toy in the meal. The fast-food marketer's lucrative pacts with Ty, Inc., marketer of Beanie Babies, and Disney have resulted in MacDonald's Happy Meals having high demand among children. And recently, McDonald's teamed up with Toys "R" Us for a holiday program that made the most of cross-promotion for both companies. During the Christmas holidays, Happy Meals featured one of eight miniature premiums based on Paramus, the Toys "R" Us private-label plush line. The toys were polybagged with a miniature 20-page version of the Big Toy Book, the chain's annual holiday megacircular. The minibooks contained $100 in Toys "R" Us coupons for McDonald's customers. The campaign marks the first time McDonald's has let a retailer tie into Happy Meals on such a grand scale.[54]

Premiums can also involve more product for the regular price, such as two-for-the-price-of-one bonus packs or packages that include more of the product. Kellogg's, for instance, added two more pastries and waffles to its Pop-Tarts and Eggo waffles packages without increasing the price in an effort to boost market share lost to private-label brands and new competitors. The promotion was so successful the company decided to keep the additional product in its regular packaging.

Loyalty Marketing Programs

Loyalty marketing programs, or **frequent-buyer programs,** reward loyal consumers for making multiple purchases. One of the longest-running loyalty programs in Canada was instituted by Canadian Tire Corporation in 1958 when it introduced Canadian Tire Money into its gasoline retail outlets as a redemption for cash purchases. It quickly spread the program into its retail stores and the program has remained highly popular ever since. According to current company information, over 90 percent of Canadians shop at Canadian Tire every year and 40 percent of Canadians shop there weekly. In Canada, Canadian Tire money is arguably the most popular discount program in use because it has an over 90-percent redemption rate![55] Loyalty marketing enables companies to strategically invest sales promotion dollars in activities designed to capture greater profits from customers already loyal to the product or company.[56] One study concluded that if a company retains an additional 5 percent of its customers each year, profits will increase by at least 25 percent. What's more, improving customer retention by a mere 2 percent can decrease costs by as much as 10 percent.[57]

loyalty marketing programs
A promotional program designed to build long-term, mutually beneficial relationships between a company and its key customers.

frequent-buyer program
A loyalty program in which loyal consumers are rewarded for making multiple purchases of a particular good or service.

The objective of loyalty marketing programs is to build long-term, mutually beneficial relationships between a company and its key customers. Through loyalty programs, shoppers receive discounts, alerts on new products, and other types of enticing offers. In exchange, retailers are able to build customer databases that help them better understand customer preferences. A recent survey of Canadians indicates that loyalty programs may be becoming overused. For example, two-thirds of Canadians have at least one loyalty card from a supermarket or retailer. However, only 27 percent said they really liked these programs and that the programs influenced their behaviour. In contrast, 26 percent indicated they disliked the programs and would not use them at all. An additional 41 percent said they used loyalty programs but didn't like them. The remaining 6 percent of people surveyed refused to answer.[58]

Contests and Sweepstakes

Contests and sweepstakes are generally designed to create interest in a good or service, often to encourage brand switching. *Contests* are promotions in which participants use some skill or ability to compete for prizes. A consumer contest usually requires entrants to answer questions, complete sentences, or write a paragraph about the product and submit proof of purchase. Winning a *sweepstakes,* on the other hand, depends on chance or luck, and participation is free. Sweepstakes usually draw about 10 times more entries than contests do.

AP/WIDE WORLD PHOTOS

Although it seems that loyalty marketing programs are a recent trend, they actually date back quite a while. Canadian Tire Money seems old at 46 years but General Mills' Betty Crocker coupon program is entering its seventh decade and is among the longest-running loyalty marketing programs in North America. Customers collect points from the packaging of General Mills products and then redeem the accumulated points for various products.

ON LINE

Sweepstakes Online

How do on-line sweepstakes sites compare to the kinds of sweepstakes entries you receive in the mail? Visit the SomewhereInCanada.com site to find contests and links to sites with contests that are open to Canadians. Do any of the contests interest you? Do you think the pitches on-line are ethical? Why or why not?

http://www.somewhereincanada.com

While contests and sweepstakes may draw considerable interest and publicity, generally they are not effective tools for generating long-term sales. To increase their effectiveness, sales promotion managers must make certain the award will appeal to the target market.[59] For example, Frito-Lay (formerly Hostess Frito-Lay) has one of the most successful promotional contests in recent times with its "Pick the Final Survivor Contest" promotion. Frito-Lay felt it could create an exciting promotion by associating its Doritos brand chips with the CBS network hit show *Survivor.* The contest was promoted with prominent in-store displays. Survivor torches and bandanas were also provided as premiums for Doritos purchasers. People were asked to log on to a website once a week during the run of the show and enter the contest. The prize was $100,000 for the person who could pick the winner of *Survivor.* The contest produced 22,000 on-line entries and another 6,000 mail entries from Canada alone. The contest was a tremendous success, producing the largest sales volume of Doritos ever for Frito-Lay.[60]

The effectiveness of a promotion can often be increased by offering several smaller prizes to many winners instead of one huge prize to just one person. A recent trend in sweepstakes is to combine on-pack with on-line promotions such as Kraft Foods' Game of Life (get the game piece on the packaging and check on-line to see if you're a winner). Such sweepstakes not only drive site traffic, but also save money on postage, seeding packages with game pieces, and security. On-line sweepstakes can also require consumers to divulge information before entering—a plus for databases. And companies are offering extra entries as perks for supplying information.[61]

Sampling

sampling
A promotional program that allows the consumer the opportunity to try a product or service for free.

Consumers generally perceive a certain amount of risk in trying new products. Many are afraid of trying something they will not like (such as a new food item) or spending too much money and getting little reward. **Sampling** allows the customer to try a product risk-free. Sampling can increase retail sales by as much as 40 percent.[62] It comes as no surprise, therefore, that product sampling has increased 8.2 percent annually in recent years and that spending on sampling in North America is projected to reach $1.8 billion by 2005.[63]

Sampling can be accomplished by directly mailing the sample to the customer, delivering the sample door-to-door, packaging the sample with another product, or demonstrating or sampling the product at a retail store. Before Krispy Kreme donuts opened its first Canadian store in Toronto in 2001, it undertook an introductory sampling campaign. "KremeKo handed out 2,500-dozen doughnuts in strategic locations throughout Mississauga and the Greater Toronto Area, including the Union Station transportation hub, the Yonge and Dundas shopping district, the King and Bay financial district, the Canadian National Exhibition, shopping centres, selected large employers, and hospitals. In the weeks leading up to the December 11, 2001, Mississauga opening, another several thousand-dozen were offered at places like the Air Canada Centre and community centres."[64]

© JEFF GREENBERG/PHOTOEDIT

Distributing samples can often mitigate the risks consumers perceive in trying a new product. Here, a Hispanic sales representative for Starbucks offers Bahamians smoothie samples at the Goombay Festival.

Sampling at special events is a popular, effective, and high-profile distribution method that permits marketers to piggyback onto fun-based consumer activities, including sporting events, campus fests, fairs, festivals, beach events, and chili cook-offs. Wrigley Canada signed a sponsorship deal to make Juicy Fruit the "official gum" of the NBA in Canada. The company tied this relationship to the sponsorship of the NBA's summertime Hoop-It-Up three-on-three basketball tournament, which takes place in cities all across Canada. Wrigley's sent representatives to each of the cities where the tournament was held to hand out samples of Juicy Fruit Gums. In addition, it sponsored a side competition called the "Juicy Fruit Passing Challenge."[65]

Distributing samples to specific location types where consumers regularly meet for a common objective or interest, such as health clubs, churches, or doctors' offices, is one of the most efficient methods of sampling. What better way to get consumers to try a product than to offer a sample exactly when it is needed most? Marketers agree that companies must be much more precise in what, where, and how samples are delivered. If someone visits a health club regularly, chances are he or she is a good prospect for a health-food product or vitamin supplement. Health club instructors are handing out not only these products but also body wash, deodorant, and face cloths to sweating participants at the end of class, and makers of stain removers and hand cleansers are giving away samples in mall food courts and petting zoos. This method of distributing samples is working. In fact, one recent study found that sampling events produced an average 36 percent increase in sales soon afterward.[66]

Likewise, pharmaceutical companies offer free samples of new and expensive drugs as a tactic to entice doctors and consumers to become loyal to a product. Marketing practices for the pharmaceutical industry as a whole, however, are coming under increased scrutiny. Read about this issue in the "Ethics in Marketing" box.

Point-of-Purchase Promotion

Point-of-purchase (P-O-P) promotion includes any promotional display set up at the retailer's location to build traffic, advertise the product, or induce impulse buying. Point-of-purchase promotions include shelf "talkers" (signs attached to store shelves), shelf extenders (attachments that extend shelves so products stand out), ads on grocery carts and bags, end-aisle and floor-stand displays, television monitors at supermarket checkout counters, in-store audio messages, and audiovisual displays. One big advantage of P-O-P promotion is that it offers manufacturers a captive audience in retail stores. Another advantage is that between 70 and 80 percent of all retail purchase decisions are made in-store, so P-O-P promotions can be very effective. A recent study found that properly displayed P-O-P promotions boosted sales anywhere from 2 to 65 percent, depending on the brand and P-O-P mix. Signs such as header or riser cards increased weekly store sales 6 percent for one brand; base or case wraps boosted total sales 12 percent; standees, 2 percent; inflatable or mobile displays, 40 percent; and signs that advertised a brand's sports, movie, or charity tie-in, 65 percent.[67]

point-of-purchase display
A promotional display set up at the retailer's location to build traffic, advertise the product, or induce impulse buying.

Companies are cashing in on in-store purchasing decisions through more sophisticated P-O-P promotions. For example, Flora Manufacturing and Distributing of Vancouver has introduced BIJA Healing Teas to the Canadian market and is promoting the line through extensive in-store promotions and displays. Larger health food stores have been taking a 1.5-metre-high revolving mahogany stand display that contains 120 boxes of teas. A smaller cardboard mahogany replica display containing 54 tea boxes is available for stores with more limited space. In addition to these sales displays, Flora Distributing sent out a special offer for a counter-top sampler display to 1,500 health food stores to encourage them to try out the teas with their customers. Flora was hoping the health food stores would like to give a "free offer" to their customers and in turn, the customers would enjoy the tea and ask the stores to carry the product. As further encouragement to retailers, Flora is running a special contest that is open to both the trade and consumers. The contest is being promoted both in stores and on-line. One consumer and one trade winner will get a 10-day trip for two to Cape Town, South Africa.[68]

On-Line Sales Promotion

On-line sales promotions have been booming in recent years due to the overwhelming popularity of the Internet. In North America, marketers funnelled some $926 million into on-line sales promotions in 1999 and close to $2 billion in 2000. Sales promotion on the Internet has proved to be effective and cost-efficient, generating response rates that are three to five times higher than their off-line counterparts. According to a recent survey of marketers, the most effective types of on-line sales promotions are free merchandise, sweepstakes, free shipping with purchases, and coupons.

ETHICS IN MARKETING

Pharmaceutical Sales—Just What the Doctor Ordered?

With free trips, expensive dinners, promotional gadgets, and hundreds of free drug samples, drug companies are waging an increasingly sophisticated campaign to win over doctors and patients, while keeping a $120 billion-a-year business in North America growing. In recent years, the pharmaceutical industry has been highly criticized for its sales and marketing practices, and many physicians are concerned that the increasingly lavish spending on the part of drug companies is undermining the integrity of the profession. Of course, other doctors reject the idea that receiving gifts ranging from pens and note cards to free meals and travel would affect their prescribing habits.

Either way, pharmaceutical selling is quickly becoming a daily exercise in ethical judgment. Why? There's a fine line between the common practice of buying a prospect's time with a free meal and bribing doctors to prescribe a manufacturer's drug. Although some supporters of incentives and samples may feel bribery is too strong a word, a recent industry estimate shows that pharmaceutical promotional spending has reached nearly $14 billion. Add to this figure the fact that the collective pharmaceutical sales force has grown to more than 56,000 people and that equals one sales rep and approximately $100,000 for every 11 practising physicians in North America. The explosion in the number of salespeople in the field—and the amount of funding used to promote their products—forces close examination of the pressures and influences drug reps may exert on doctors and the relationships between them.

While most physicians agree that pharmaceutical reps provide much-needed information and education through brochures, article reprints, and presentations, the sales push rarely stops there. Office visits are often followed by meals at expensive restaurants, meetings in exotic locales, and a deluge of promotional specialty items. Pfizer alone spends an estimated $85.7 million annually on promotional products like pens, coffee mugs, shirts, and umbrellas for reps to leave behind.

This is not a new phenomenon. Drugmakers have been "wining and dining" physicians for years—and this practice has aroused enough controversy to bring about periodic reviews by Congress and the American Medical Association (AMA) in the United States and the Health Products and Food Branch and the Canadian Medical Association in Canada. According to current guidelines, doctors are supposed to limit gifts they receive from pharmaceutical companies to $100. However, both drug manufacturers and physicians can easily get around these guidelines. Doctors are allowed to receive honoraria for "advising" drug companies for just a couple of hours. Training seminars held at vacation destinations, dinner parties with featured guest lecturers, and golf excursions are all ways to buy time with doctors. In fact, recent figures show that in North America, physicians received invitations to 225,000 pharmaceutical events in one year.

Although many doctors deny that the marketing practices employed by the pharmaceutical industry influence their prescription decisions, research shows the contrary. Studies have shown that after doctors participate in industry-sponsored events, they write more prescriptions and are more likely to prescribe expensive, brand-name medications than generic drugs.[69]

In the end, the fact remains that drug companies have every right to make a profit and will continue to find ways to increase sales. But at what price? Patients are the ones who are really paying—in the form of skyrocketing prescription costs—for every promotional item that's handed out, every honorarium given, and every dinner bought.

Should pharmaceutical companies be able to spend so much to entertain and provide gifts to physicians? How much is too much to spend on physicians in an attempt to market a particular drug?

Eager to boost traffic, Internet retailers have been busy giving away free services or equipment to lure consumers not only to their own website but also to the Internet in general. For example, Ford of Mexico has developed "the world's largest on-line auto dealership that today accounts for more than 3 percent of all Ford vehicles sold in Mexico." In order to stimulate sales, Ford ran a special promotion that involved giving customers who bought vehicles during the month of December a Palm Pilot personal organizer. Ford of Mexico estimated that the offer of a $200 Palm Pilot helped it to sell 300 extra cars during the month.[70]

ChumCity Interactive of Toronto approached Sears Canada and Esteé Lauder, Inc. to run a special promotion entitled "Spin For Great Skin" that would tie in with Clinique's annual three-step skin care promotion program, which it runs jointly with Sears Canada. The idea was for Clinique to reach out to the younger teenage market with its brand. Television viewers were directed to CHUM's MuchMusic or MusiquePlus websites with a 30-second advertisement that ran on stations MuchMusic and MusiquePlus. Website visitors would spin a contest wheel that would transition into the Clinique logo. A message would appear telling the

ON LINE

uPromote.com

How can uPromote.com help you with your sales promotions efforts? What kind of marketing budget would you need to take advantage of its services? What kind of company would be best served by uPromote.com?

http://www.upromote.com

visitor whether he or she was an instant winner of a Clinique three-step program gift pack or suggesting, "try again." After spinning, both winners and losers were presented with an on-line entry form to win a grand prize of $1,000 in Clinique merchandize and diamond stud earrings from Sears. In addition, contest spinners could print off a coupon for a Clinique sample and a free skin-care consultation at Sears. The month-long "digital campaign resulted in more than 25,000 spins of the wheel and a click-through rate of 84 percent for visits versus spins."[71]

On-line versions of loyalty programs are also popular. For example, Canadian Tire developed a campaign built around its Canadian Tire Money program entitled the "Big Spender Giveaway" contest. Customers could enter a contest to win three grand prizes of $50,000 in Canadian Tire Money with ballots acquired in stores or on-line. The on-line approach involved a scavenger hunt game that was tied in with Sympatico-Lycos and The Marketing Store Worldwide, which built and operated the contest website. Canadian Tire chose Sympatico as its business partner because it knew that http://www.sympatico.ca had more than 7 million visits each month! The contest ran for a month and included daily prizes of $1,000 in Canadian Tire Money and draws for smaller amounts of Canadian Tire Money. Canadian Tire assessed the contest as a hit with its customers and pronounced it to be "one of the most successful integrated retail and on-line promotions ever run in Canada."[72]

Tools for Trade Sales Promotion

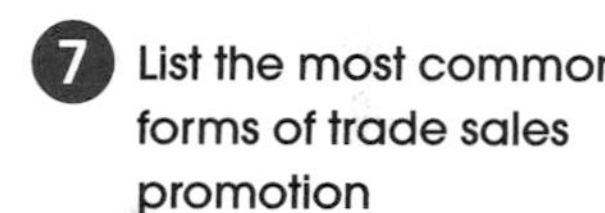

7 List the most common forms of trade sales promotion

Whereas consumer promotions *pull* a product through the channel by creating demand, trade promotions *push* a product through the distribution channel (see Chapter 11). When selling to members of the distribution channel, manufacturers use many of the same sales promotion tools used in consumer promotions—such as sales contests, premiums, and point-of-purchase displays. Several tools, however, are unique to manufacturers and intermediaries:

- *Trade allowances:* A **trade allowance** is a price reduction offered by manufacturers to intermediaries such as wholesalers and retailers. The price reduction or rebate is given in exchange for doing something specific, such as allocating space for a new product or buying something during special periods. For example, a local dealer could receive a special discount for running its own promotion on Telus Mobility cellular phones.

trade allowance
A price reduction offered by manufacturers to intermediaries, such as wholesalers and retailers.

- *Push money:* Intermediaries receive **push money** as a bonus for pushing the manufacturer's brand through the distribution channel. Often the push money is directed toward a retailer's salespeople. LinoColor, the leading high-end scanner company, produces a Picture Perfect Rewards catalogue filled with merchandise that retailers can purchase with points accrued for every LinoColor scanner they sell. The cover of the catalogue features a wave runner that was brought to three industry trade shows and given away in a sweepstakes to one of the dealers who had visited all the product displays and passed a quiz. The program resulted in a 26 percent increase in LinoColor sales, and the manufacturer recruited 32 new dealers to carry the product line.[73]

push money
Money offered to channel intermediaries to encourage them to "push" products, that is, to encourage other members of the channel to sell the products.

- *Training:* Sometimes a manufacturer will train an intermediary's personnel if the product is rather complex—as frequently occurs in the computer and telecommunication industries. For example, if a large department store purchases an NCR computerized cash register system, NCR may provide free training so the salespeople can learn how to use the new system.
- *Free merchandise:* Often a manufacturer offers retailers free merchandise in lieu of quantity discounts. For example, a breakfast cereal manufacturer may throw in one case of free cereal for every 20 cases ordered by the retailer. Occasionally, free merchandise is used as payment for trade allowances normally provided through other sales promotions. Instead of giving a retailer a price reduction for buying a certain quantity of merchandise, the manufacturer may throw in extra merchandise "free" (that is, at a cost that would equal the price reduction).

- *Instore demonstrations:* Manufacturers can also arrange with retailers to perform an in-store demonstration. Food manufacturers often send representatives to grocery stores and supermarkets to let customers sample a product while shopping. Cosmetics companies also send their representatives to department stores to promote their beauty aids by performing facials and makeovers for customers.
- *Business meetings, conventions, and trade shows:* Trade association meetings, conferences, and conventions are an important aspect of sales promotion and a growing, multibillion-dollar market in North America. At these shows, manufacturers, distributors, and other vendors have the chance to display their goods or describe their services to customers and potential customers. A recent study reported that, on average, it costs 56 percent less to close a lead generated at an exhibition than a lead generated in the field—$625 versus $1,117.[74] Trade shows have been uniquely effective in introducing new products; they can establish products in the marketplace more quickly than can advertising, direct marketing, or sales calls. Companies participate in trade shows to attract and identify new prospects, serve current customers, introduce new products, enhance corporate image, test the market response to new products, enhance corporate morale, and gather competitive product information.

Trade promotions are popular among manufacturers for many reasons. Trade sales promotion tools help manufacturers gain new distributors for their products, obtain wholesaler and retailer support for consumer sales promotions, build or reduce dealer inventories, and improve trade relations. Car manufacturers annually sponsor dozens of auto shows for consumers. Many of the displays feature interactive computer stations where consumers enter vehicle specifications and get a printout of prices and local dealer names. In return, the local car dealers get the names of good prospects. The shows attract millions of consumers, providing dealers with increased store traffic as well as good leads.

8 Discuss the role of public relations in the promotional mix

>> PUBLIC RELATIONS

Public relations is the element in the promotional mix that evaluates public attitudes, identifies issues that may elicit public concern, and executes programs to gain public understanding and acceptance. Like advertising and sales promotion, public relations is a vital link in a progressive company's marketing communication mix. Marketing managers plan solid public relations campaigns that fit into overall marketing plans and focus on targeted audiences. These campaigns strive to maintain a positive image of the corporation in the eyes of the public. Before launching public relations programs, managers evaluate public attitudes and company actions. Then they create programs to capitalize on the factors that enhance the firm's image and minimize the factors that could generate a negative image. Because of a number of recent corporate scandals such as the Enron accounting affair, the Martha Stewart insider trading trial, and the federal government investigation into improprieties in Crown corporation–Quebec advertising agencies sponsorship dealings, Canadian organizations are highly aware that they must undertake more transparent and more accountable business practices. It is not enough to simply develop and undertake these activities in-house; rather, Canadian business firms need to promote these practices to actually make them transparent and to regain public trust. Because of the public emphasis on the importance of corporate governance and the need to undertake transparent business practices, public relations is likely to play a more central role in the promotional mix of business firms in the future.

ON LINE

Many people associate public relations with publicity. *Publicity* is the effort to capture media attention, for example, through articles or editorials in publications or through human-interest stories on radio or television programs. Corporations usually initiate publicity through a press release that furthers their public relations plans. A company about to introduce a new product or open a new store may send press releases to the media in the hope that the story will be published or broadcast. Savvy publicity can often create overnight sensations. Artisan Entertainment hoped its independent film, *The Blair Witch Project,* would be its summer 1999 hit, but couldn't spend big-studio advertising dollars to advertise it. So Artisan turned to a public relations strategy to build excitement and curiosity about the film. The cornerstone of its strategy proved to be the film's website, which showed outtakes from unused footage, faked official documents, and interviews that suggested a police coverup to build the legend of the Blair Witch. At the height of the campaign, the site was getting 3 million hits a day. Artisan also used "street" teams to distribute missing person fliers and stick figures. It also held film screenings on 40 college and university campuses across the country. When the film finally opened after weeks of builtup suspense, it quickly became a hit, breaking attendance records and topping opening weekend numbers for such heavyweights as *Star Wars: The Phantom Menace.*[75]

Corporate donations and sponsorships can also create favourable publicity. Roots Clothing Canada hit an absolute publicity home run with its clothing sponsorship of the Canadian, American, and British Olympic teams for the 2002 Winter Olympics. For starters, all of the Winter Olympic viewers were exposed to Roots clothing when the Olympic athletes paraded into the Olympic Stadium; this exposure was further enhanced by the fact that President George W. Bush was present among the American athletes, all of them wearing blue Roots jackets and berets. However, the ultimate in exposure for Roots occurred because of the controversy over the pairs figure skating competition judging. Skaters Jamie Sale and David Pelletier were fan favourites and clear performance winners in the pairs competition but were denied the gold medal. When allegations of judging impropriety were raised, a sustained media circus ensued in which Sale and Pelletier, dressed in their Roots Canadian Olympic Team clothing, gave a massive number of interviews that were aired all over the world. In addition, the Roots-clad couple became hot celebrity guests, appearing on all the major American talk shows, including *The Tonight Show with Jay Leno* and *Rosie O'Donnell.*[76]

Public relations departments may perform any or all of the following functions:

- *Press relations:* placing positive, newsworthy information in the news media to attract attention to a product, a service, or a person associated with the firm or institution.
- *Product publicity:* publicizing specific products or services.
- *Corporate communication:* creating internal and external messages to promote a positive image of the firm or institution.
- *Public affairs:* building and maintaining national or local community relations.
- *Lobbying:* influencing legislators and government officials to promote or defeat legislation and regulation.
- *Employee and investor relations:* maintaining positive relationships with employees, shareholders, and others in the financial community.
- *Crisis management:* responding to unfavourable publicity or a negative event.

Major Public Relations Tools

9 Describe the major types of public relations activities

Public relations professionals commonly use several tools, including new-product publicity, product placement, consumer education, event sponsorship, and issue sponsorship. A relatively new tool public relations professionals are using in increasing numbers is a website on the Internet. Although many of these tools require an active role on the part of the public relations professional, such as writing press releases and engaging in proactive media relations, many of these techniques create their own publicity.

New-Product Publicity

Publicity is instrumental in introducing new products and services. Publicity can help advertisers explain what's different about their new product by prompting free news stories or positive word of mouth about it. During the introductory period, an especially innovative new product often needs more exposure than conventional, paid advertising

ON LINE

BMW FILMS

Find out more about BMW films starring Clive Owen. Do these films, directed by award-winning directors, do a good job promoting BMW cars?

http://www.bmwfilms.com

affords. Public relations professionals write press releases or develop videos in an effort to generate news about their new product. They also jockey for exposure of their product or service at major events, on popular television and news shows, and in the hands of influential people. Coincident with the campaign to introduce the new Windows XP operating system discussed earlier in the chapter, Microsoft founder Bill Gates made a guest appearance on the television show, *Frasier,* which aired on Canada's Global Television Network. Gates was cast as himself; he was taking part in a radio show hosted by the program's lead character, Frasier. The show included a scene in which a caller to Frasier's radio show asked Gates to help him configure the new Microsoft XP operating system. The first commercial break after this scene featured a paid commercial for the Microsoft XP operating system.[77]

Product Placement

By making sure their products appear at special events or in movies or television shows, companies can reap invaluable product exposure through product placement, usually at a fraction of the cost of paid-for advertising. Often the fee for exposure is in merchandise. Fashion designer Giorgio Armani, for example, uses celebrities to burnish his brand in the eyes of the public. Armani clothed Samuel L. Jackson for his role in the movie *Shaft.* The designer then marketed a line of *Shaft*-inspired clothes and featured Jackson in fashion shows in Milan, Italy. Armani also provides select Hollywood stars and celebrities like Ricky Martin and Lauryn Hill with free gowns and tuxedos for personal appearances.[78]

Consumer Education

Some major firms believe that educated consumers are better, more loyal customers. Financial planning firms often sponsor free educational seminars on money management, retirement planning, and investing in the hope that the seminar participants will choose the sponsoring organization for their future financial needs. Likewise, computer hardware and software firms, realizing that many consumers feel intimidated by new technology and recognizing the strong relationship between learning and purchasing patterns, sponsor computer seminars and free in-store demonstrations. BMW Canada, for example, sponsors instructional driving schools in major cities across Canada. Drivers receive a special training session in driving techniques, accident avoidance skills, and traction aid tricks from a professional driver.

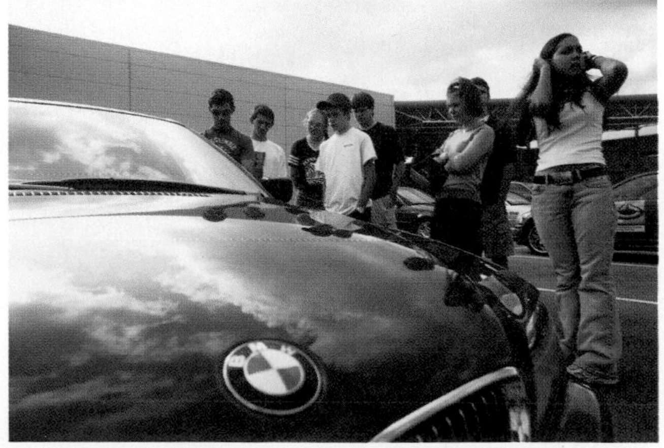

© MARK PETERSON/CORBIS

Consumer education cannot only influence the buying decision but can result in better, more loyal customers. BMW's instructional driving tour is a way to show off its cars' capabilities to prospective purchasers and current owners without mounting expensive advertising campaigns.

Event Sponsorship

Public relations managers can sponsor events or community activities that are sufficiently newsworthy to achieve press coverage; at the same time, these events reinforce brand identification. Sporting, music, and arts events remain the most popular choices of event sponsors, although many are now turning to more specialized events such as tie-ins with schools, charities, and other community service organizations. Bell Canada is the title sponsor of the Royal Canadian Golf Association's (RGCA) Canadian Open tournament and recently negotiated to remain the title sponsor until 2007. In a bid to broaden the appeal of the Bell Canadian Open, Bell Canada asked the RCGA to move the tournament from its established venue at the Glen Abbey Golf Club in Oakville, Ontario, to other places around the country. The tournament was held in

Hamilton, Ontario, in 2003 and at Glen Abbey in 2004. However, the RCGA agreed to hold the tournament at the Shaughnessy Golf and Country Club in Vancouver, B.C., in 2005 and in Quebec in 2006.[79]

Marketers can also create their own events tied around their product. L'Oréal wanted to reach out to Canadian teenage consumers in a high-impact way. It developed a national video dance party program that would bring dance parties into Canadian high schools. The firm recently launched a new line of hairstyling products branded as L'Oréal's Special FX Studio Line. The launch was tied in directly to the video dance program, with a styling contest held during the dance so that L'Oréal could demonstrate that the products could deliver the promised results. The contest was judged by the dance participants. L'Oreal estimated that the sponsorship of the dance party program provided interactive brand exposure to more than 180,000 Canadian teens.[80]

Issue Sponsorship

Corporations can build public awareness and loyalty by supporting their customers' favourite issues. Education, health care, and social programs get the largest share of corporate funding. Firms often donate a percentage of sales or profits to a worthy cause that their target market is likely to favour. For example, The Gap hoped to break through the holiday advertising clutter by focusing on a simple theme of "Give your gift," reinforced by corporate donations. The company made donations to charities on behalf of the celebrities appearing in the commercials and print ads, including the singers Sheryl Crow and Alanis Morissette and the cast of *The Producers*.[81]

"Green marketing" has also become an important way for companies to build awareness and loyalty by promoting a popular issue. By positioning their brands as ecologically sound, marketers can convey concern for the environment and society as a whole. Burger King and McDonald's no longer use styrofoam cartons to package their burgers in an effort to decrease waste in landfills. In a similar effort, Toyota is working with the Japanese government to implement a program where people purchase "transportation" without owning a car. Consumers can buy access to Toyota's electronic fleet of automobiles to travel for short distances. Thus, Toyota is both establishing itself as the leader in electronic-combustion automobiles and reducing a negative environmental impact.[82]

Websites

Public relations professionals are increasingly using their websites as a vehicle to post news releases on products, product enhancements, strategic relationships, and financial earnings. Corporate press releases, technical papers and articles, and product news help inform the press, customers, prospects, industry analysts, stockholders, and others of the firm's products and services and their applications. The website can also be an open forum for new-product ideas, product improvements, and customer feedback. On-line reviews from opinion leaders and other consumers also help marketers sway shopping decisions in their favour. When Sony redesigned PlayStation.com, it incorporated message boards where its game-playing community could post notes. Players discuss techie topics like "Desperately Seeking PlayStation2," review and exchange tips on games, and even vote on lifestyle issues such as music and personal taste.[83]

Several marketers also use the Web to try new products and gather more consumer data. Through research, Volkswagen knew that 60 percent of its customers use the Internet. So when the company wanted to attract a different, "funkier" audience for its new Beetle and test out new car colours, it employed a special on-line marketing promotion. Volkswagen made a limited-edition model of its Beetle available exclusively on-line, in two limited-edition colours: Vapour Blue and Reflex Yellow. The company got the word out about the promotion through traditional advertising methods. After experiencing print, TV, or radio advertisements, consumers signed up to learn more via e-mail. On being admitted to a special section of the VW site, consumers learned more about the car, viewed photos, checked the availability, picked a dealer, and considered financing and a purchase date. The on-line promotion was a huge success, and Volkswagen sold out of all 4,000 limited-edition Beetles.[84]

Managing Unfavourable Publicity

Although the majority of marketers try to avoid unpleasant situations, crises do happen. Intel faced this reality after consumers became aware of an obscure flaw in its Pentium chip. In our free-press environment, publicity is not easily controlled, especially in a crisis. **Crisis management** is the coordinated effort to handle the effects of unfavourable publicity, ensuring fast and accurate communication in times of emergency.

crisis management
A coordinated effort to handle the effects of unfavourable publicity or of another unexpected, unfavourable event.

A good public relations staff is perhaps more important in bad times than in good. Companies must have a communication policy firmly in hand before a disaster occurs, because timing is uncontrollable. When a promotional game scandal rocked McDonald's, the company found out just how important crisis management is. An employee of the agency that had handled promotion for McDonald's for over 25 years was arrested for stealing winning game pieces from McDonald's popular *Monopoly* and *Who Wants to Be a Millionaire* games and giving them to family and friends to redeem. Although McDonald's employees had no knowledge of the fraud and none were implicated in the scandal, several class-action lawsuits were filed against the company. McDonald's immediately initiated a recovery plan to minimize damage among its customer base. This plan included mass distribution of a letter, a newspaper ad, a TV ad, and a five-day instant win game in which McDonald's awarded $10 million in prizes to customers to make up for the prizes that had been wrongfully awarded.[85]

>> CONNECT IT

As you finish reading this chapter, think back to the opening story about how Maple Leaf Sports & Entertainment exemplifies the unique combination of being both a product offering and a medium. Maple Leaf Sports & Entertainment employs all of the promotional tools to market its two main product offerings, the Toronto Maple Leafs and the Toronto Raptors. However, the profits of the company depend very heavily on its ability to leverage the value of its sports properties through sales of sponsorships that other businesses use as part of their promotional strategies. Although Maple Leaf Sports & Entertainment uses advertising, sales promotion, and even personal selling in its marketing mix, unlike the products of most other marketers, publicity and public relations is actually the most powerful promotional tool available to Maple Leaf Sports & Entertainment.

REVIEW IT

1 Discuss the effects of advertising on market share and consumers. Advertising helps marketers increase or maintain brand awareness and, subsequently, market share. Typically, more is spent to advertise new brands with a small market share than to advertise older brands. Brands with a large market share use advertising mainly to maintain their share of the market. Advertising affects consumers' daily lives as well as their purchases. Although advertising can seldom change strongly held consumer attitudes and values, it may transform a consumer's negative attitude toward a product into a positive one. Additionally, when consumers are highly loyal to a brand, they may buy more of that brand when advertising is increased. Last, advertising can also change the importance of a brand's attributes to consumers. By emphasizing different brand attributes, advertisers can change their appeal in response to consumers' changing needs or try to achieve an advantage over competing brands.

1.1 Discuss the reasons why new brands with a smaller market share spend proportionately more on advertising than brands with a larger market share.

1.2 TEAM Form a three-person team. Divide the responsibility for getting newspaper advertisements and menus for several local restaurants. While you are at the restaurants to obtain copies of their menus, observe the atmosphere and interview the manager to determine what he or she believes are the primary reasons people choose to dine there. Pool your information and develop a table comparing the restaurants in terms of convenience of location, value for the money, food variety and quality, atmosphere, and so on. Rank the restaurants in terms of their appeal to college and university students. Explain the basis of your rankings. What other market segments would be attracted to the restaurants and why? Do the newspaper advertisements emphasize the most effective appeal for a particular restaurant? Explain.

2 **Identify the major types of advertising.** Advertising is any form of nonpersonal, paid communication in which the sponsor or company is identified. The two major types of advertising are institutional advertising and product advertising. Institutional advertising is not product oriented; rather, its purpose is to foster a positive company image among the general public, investment community, customers, and employees. Product advertising is designed mainly to promote goods and services; it is classified into three main categories: pioneering, competitive, and comparative. A product's place in the product life cycle is a major determinant of the type of advertising used to promote it.

2.1 At what stage in a product's life cycle are pioneering, competitive, and comparative advertising most likely to occur? Give a current example of each type of advertising.

3 **Discuss the creative decisions in developing an advertising campaign.** Before any creative work can begin on an advertising campaign, it is important to determine what goals or objectives the advertising should achieve. The objectives of a specific advertising campaign often depend on the overall corporate objectives and the product being advertised. Once objectives are defined, creative work can begin on the advertising campaign. Creative decisions include identifying the product's benefits, developing possible advertising appeals, evaluating and selecting the advertising appeals, executing the advertising message, and evaluating the effectiveness of the campaign.

3.1 What is an advertising appeal? Give some examples of advertising appeals you have observed recently in the media.

3.2 WRITING Design a full-page magazine advertisement for a new brand of soft drink. The name of the new drink, as well as package design, is at your discretion. On a separate sheet, specify the benefits stressed or appeals made in the advertisement.

4 **Describe media evaluation and selection techniques.** Media evaluation and selection make up a crucial step in the advertising campaign process. Major types of advertising media include newspapers, magazines, radio, television, outdoor advertising such as billboards and bus panels, and the Internet. Recent trends in advertising media include fax, video shopping carts, computer screen savers, and cinema and video advertising. Promotion managers choose the advertising campaign's media mix on the basis of the following variables: cost per contact, reach, frequency, characteristics of the target audience, flexibility of the medium, noise level, and the life span of the medium. After choosing the media mix, a media schedule designates when the advertisement will appear and the specific vehicles it will appear in.

4.1 What are the advantages of radio advertising? Why is radio expanding as an advertising medium?

4.2 You are the advertising manager of a sailing magazine, and one of your biggest potential advertisers has questioned your rates. Write the firm a letter explaining why you believe your audience selectivity is worth the extra expense for advertisers.

4.3 Identify an appropriate media mix for the following products:
  - **a.** Chewing gum
  - **b.** *Maclean's* magazine
  - **c.** Weed-Eaters
  - **d.** Foot odour killers
  - **e.** "Drink responsibly" campaigns by beer brewers

5 **Define and state the objectives of sales promotion.** Sales promotion consists of those marketing communication activities, other than advertising, personal selling, and public relations, in which a short-term incentive motivates consumers or members of the distribution channel to purchase a good or service immediately, either by lowering the price or by adding value. The main objectives of sales promotion are to increase trial purchases, consumer inventories, and repeat purchases. Sales promotion is also used to encourage brand switching and to build brand loyalty. Sales promotion supports advertising activities.

5.1 You have recently been assigned the task of developing promotional techniques to introduce your company's new product, a Cajun chicken sandwich. Advertising spending is limited, so the introduction will include only some low-budget sales promotion techniques. Write a sales promotion plan that will increase awareness of your new sandwich and allow your customer base to try it risk-free.

6 **Discuss the most common forms of consumer sales promotion.** Consumer forms of sales promotion include coupons and rebates, premiums, loyalty marketing programs, contests and sweepstakes, sampling, and point-of-purchase displays. Coupons are certificates entitling consumers to an immediate price reduction when they purchase a product or service. Coupons are a particularly good way to encourage product trial and brand switching. Similar to coupons, rebates provide purchasers with a price reduction, although it is not immediate. To receive a rebate, consumers generally must mail in a rebate form with a proof of purchase. Premiums offer an extra item or incentive to the consumer for buying a product or service. Premiums reinforce the consumer's purchase decision, increase consumption, and persuade nonusers to switch brands. Rewarding loyal customers is the basis of loyalty marketing programs. Loyalty programs are extremely effective at building long-term, mutually beneficial relationships between a company and its key customers. Contests and sweepstakes are generally designed to create interest, often to encourage brand switching. Because consumers perceive risk in trying new products, sampling is an effective method for gaining new customers. Finally, point-of-purchase displays set up at the retailer's location build traffic, advertise the product, and induce impulse buying.

6.1 Discuss how different forms of sales promotion can erode or build brand loyalty. If a company's objective is to enhance customer loyalty to its products, what sales promotion techniques will be most appropriate?

6.2 What forms of consumer sales promotion might induce impulse purchases? What forms of sales promotion are more effective at persuading consumers to switch brands?

6.3 Form a three-person team. Go to the local grocery store and write down all of the forms of sales promotion you see, including company name, product being promoted, form of promotion, and objective. Also, make a note of the sales promotion's message or offer, such as "two-for-one" or "cents off." Create a table that lists this information; then rate the effectiveness of each one, in your opinion, on a scale from 1 to 5 where 1 is "poor" and 5 is "excellent." Present a summary of your findings to the class. What kind of conclusions can you draw about product type and promotion?

6.4 ON LINE Not everyone thinks supermarket shopper cards are a bargain. Go to http://www.nocards.org and read several pages. Is the information on the site compelling? What do you think of shopper cards? You may want to use the Internet to research shopper cards in more detail before forming an opinion.

7 **List the most common forms of trade sales promotion.** Manufacturers use many of the same sales promotion tools used in consumer promotions, such as sales contests, premiums, and point-of-purchase displays. In addition, manufacturers and channel intermediaries use several unique promotional strategies: trade allowances, push money, training programs, free merchandise, store demonstrations, and meetings, conventions, and trade shows.

7.1 How does trade sales promotion differ from consumer sales promotion? How is it the same?

7.2 TEAM Form a team of three to five students. As marketing managers, you are in charge of selling Dixie Cups. Design a consumer sales promotion plan and trade sales promotion plan for your product. Incorporate at least three different promotion tools into each plan. Share your results with the other teams in the class.

8 **Discuss the role of public relations in the promotional mix.** Public relations is a vital part of a firm's promotional mix. A company fosters good publicity to enhance its image and promote its products.

8.1 How can advertising and publicity work together? Give an example.

9 **Describe the major types of public relations activities.** Popular public relations tools include new-product publicity, product placement, consumer education, event sponsorship, issue sponsorship, and websites. An equally important aspect of public relations is managing unfavourable publicity in a way that is least damaging to a firm's image.

9.1 WRITING As the new public relations director for a sportswear company, you have been asked to set public relations objectives for a new line of athletic shoes to be introduced to the teen market. Draft a memo outlining the objectives you propose for the shoe's introduction and your reasons for them.

9.2 WRITING The Ford/Firestone tire recall of 2000 was one of the biggest public relations nightmares of recent memory. How well did the companies handle the situation? Use InfoTrac® College Edition (http://infotrac.thomsonlearning.com) to run a keyword search on "Ford public relations." Read a selection of the articles, and then write an analysis of CEO Jacques Nasser's performance in the face of this crisis. What did he do well? What could he have done better? Evaluate his solution to the problem. Has Ford recovered from the recall? What about Firestone?

DEFINE IT

APPLY IT

Quality of service is increasingly the basis for deciding where to do business. Customers are five times more likely to return to a particular business if they perceive that it is providing higher-quality service than the competition.

The Student Copy Centre is a local business competing with a couple of other franchise copy centres. Its owner, Mack Bayles, just attended a workshop on customer service offered by the local Chamber of Commerce. He learned that when people say they expect good customer service, they most often mean they want prompt and accurate service from friendly, knowledgeable, and courteous employees. The presenter also emphasized that all market segments, even the most price conscious, expect good customer service. Mack wants to use this knowledge to develop an effective advertising campaign.

Mack has no idea what his customers think about either his copy business or that of his competitors. He decides, therefore, to ask his customers to complete a brief survey while in his store. From his survey he learns that Student Copy Centre is considered friendlier and more courteous than the major competitors but is rated lower on speed of service.

QUESTIONS

1. What should Mack do before developing his advertising campaign?
2. Should Mack use comparative ads? Explain your choice.
3. What advertising appeal would be most effective for Mack? Why?
4. Should Mack consider Internet advertising? If so, what kind?

THINK ABOUT IT

Creative Advertising Agency has been asked to help its largest client improve its corporate image after a highly publicized product recall. The client requests a television advertisement highlighting the company's generous donation of products to low-income families. The only such donation the company has made, however, is a donation of the recalled products. The account executive fears that promoting the donation could cause further consumer backlash, but the client continues to press for the spot.

QUESTIONS

1. Should Creative Advertising meet the client's expectations (i.e., create the promotional spot) or risk losing the account? Explain your reasoning.
2. What does Canadian Code of Advertising Standards say about truth in advertising? Go to **http://www.adstandards.com** and review the code. Then write a brief paragraph describing how the Canadian Code of Advertising Standards relates to this issue.

TRY IT

The Move from TV to TiVo

In the late 1990s, Silicon Graphics, Inc., employees Mike Ramsay and Jim Barton were working together on the *Full-Service Network Project* in Orlando, Florida, a joint venture between then Time Warner and Silicon Graphics to create the first large-scale interactive television system, when they hit upon an idea. They could build a system that would give viewers control over their television programming and their time, but with far greater intelligence and ease-of-use than anything previously designed and at a price the average customer could afford.

Their idea was the genesis of TiVo, a revolutionary new service that puts viewers in control of their television-viewing experience in a way never before possible. TiVo's service uses an electronic device called a digital video recorder (DVR). Its newest set-top box, the Series2, can digitally save up to 60 hours of television programs to its hard disk. But instead of punching in times and channels one at a time to record a show on a video cassette tape, as with a VCR, the DVR uses a telephone connection to download television program schedules that pop up on the TV screen. TiVo subscribers then click on any shows they want to select and digitally record them. What's more, the Series2 has the ability to deliver digital music and photo files, video party games, Internet radio, and broadband video.

With TiVo, viewers get more control than ever over what they want to watch on television. Subscribers can digitally record their favourite shows, creating and organizing their own programming schedule to watch when they want, not bound by the timetable of any network schedule. Some of TiVo's television network partners even allow subscribers to select shows as they are advertised in televised promotions. For instance, if a subscriber sees a promo for an upcoming show to be aired on Showtime, she can click the remote when a small icon appears in the corner of her television screen during the promo to automatically record it when the program is aired. No longer do viewers have to remember when the desired show will come on in order to watch it—TiVo records properly even if the network changes its schedule! TiVo can also automatically record subscribers' favourite shows every week or suggest other shows that they might want to see based on what they've recorded in the past.

Ranging in cost from $299 for the 40-hour version available for AT&T Broadband customers to $399 for the 60-hour version, the digital video recorders provide several features that are superior to a conventional VCR with its limited recording capabilities. During live programs, for example, viewers can pause during a broadcast while the DVR keeps recording. DVRs can also provide instant replay and slow motion features so avid sports fans will never miss a play again. Additionally, TiVo DVRs include a fast-forward button so that viewers can bypass television commercials or catch up with live programming that they have paused.

TiVo, based in Alviso, California, currently has over 422,000 subscribers, with projections of continued growth. While analysts expect DVRs to take several years to reach the market penetration of the ubiquitous VCR, DVRs are projected to be in 14 million homes by 2005, possibly making them the fastest-growing consumer electronics product in history. If this prediction pans out, the impact on television from DVRs and TiVo-like services could be enormous. For instance, since TiVo subscribers can create their own programming schedules, prime time could become increasingly irrelevant as more shows get recorded for later viewing. Additionally, viewers armed with the ability to fast-forward through commercials will see fewer of them; analysts are estimating that the viewing of commercials will decrease by 50 percent by 2009 with increased market penetration of DVRs.

Not surprisingly, TiVo and DVRs have most advertising and television executives watching carefully to see how the technology emerges. TiVo believes its technology is actually an opportunity for advertisers to target their audiences more directly. Best Buy was the first consumer electronics retailer to work with TiVo to deliver customized advertising to TiVo subscribers. As an extension of its national "Go Mobile" advertising campaign, Best Buy provided an electronic tag for commercials that appeared to TiVo subscribers. Simply clicking their remote control while the ads were on their television screen transported TiVo subscribers to a "Video Showcase" area where they could view innovative Best Buy branded entertainment.

For the TiVo portion of this campaign, Best Buy filmed an exclusive "behind the scenes" jam session with artist Sheryl Crow featuring two singles from her latest album. In addition to the Sheryl Crow content, TiVo viewers also saw branded entertainment vignettes that offered fun, tongue-in-cheek tips for achieving "Electronic Feng Shui" with Best Buy's mobile products. While viewers watched the Best Buy branded advertainment, TiVo paused the program they were watching so they could return immediately to the programming, whether live or recorded, without missing a moment of their show.

Another feature Best Buy took advantage of was TiVo's lead generation and request-for-information capabilities. To test this feature, Best Buy gave TiVo subscribers a chance to receive a free Sheryl Crow CD. Using their remote control, the first 2,000 TiVo subscribers to opt in received the CD from Best Buy.

Lastly, but perhaps most importantly, the feature that advertisers may look forward to the most is the ability to measure audience exposure in real time. For the first time ever, companies can accurately track their return on advertising. TiVo can provide deep information on how anonymous users interacted with the entertainment, including when it was viewed and how often, giving brand marketers new tools for maximizing the effectiveness of their television campaigns.

For now, many in the entertainment industry have decided it's better to join than oppose digital video recording services. Entertainment giants like AOL Time Warner, DIRECTV, AT&T, RealNetworks, Blockbuster, Cox Communications, Showtime Networks, Home Box Office, and others have partnered with TiVo to develop programming and advertising solutions. Additionally, entertainment companies including Interscope Geffen A&M, New Line Cinema, Sony Pictures, and PBS have partnered with TiVo to produce entertainment showcases similar to the Best Buy campaign that will extend their advertising campaigns and appeal to the entertainment enthusiasts within TiVo's subscriber base.

QUESTIONS

1. If the majority of TiVo viewers fast-forward through commercials, advertisers will be essentially wasting the millions of dollars they spend on them. What solutions might you suggest to advertisers as TiVo gains in popularity?
2. How might TiVo and DVRs affect traditional television networks that rely on advertising revenue to support original programming?
3. How might the popularity of TiVo's service affect traditional media selection criteria like reach and frequency?

FLIP IT

Flip to Chapter 14 in your *Grademaker Study Guide* for more review opportunities, including the pretest, vocabulary review, Internet activities, study test questions, and an application exercise based on advertising concepts. What are the major types of advertising? How do you decide where to advertise your message? Can you close your book and list several advertising appeals and executional styles? If not, then pick up your *Grademaker* and review.

CLICK IT

The *Marketing* website is rich with materials to help you review and master marketing concepts. Check your knowledge with the free quizzes, practise key terms using the crossword puzzles, or review key concepts using the Microsoft® PowerPoint® slides. Also on the Website are updated weblinks to companies mentioned in this chapter, Internet exercises, career marketing information, and much much more! Go to http://www.lamb3e.nelson.com, read the material, and follow the convenient links.

WATCH IT

When Sex Appeal Doesn't Sell

Marketers have long known that tying products to powerful human emotions can facilitate product acceptance and rapid sales. Consider the highly successful and long-running Michelin tires advertising campaign of "Who is riding on your tires?" This campaign features a cute and cuddly baby and ties Michelin tires to one of the most powerful human emotions, parental love. Of course, sexual attraction is the powerful human emotion that ultimately gives rise to "parental love" and marketers often tie their products to this emotion as well. The issue is: what ground rules should marketers follow when they tie these powerful emotions to their products?

Marketing executives of Canadian industrial work boot maker, Terra, were forced to deal with this issue in the fall of 2003. In conception, the campaign must have seemed to be a sure thing. The product is work boots, the kinds of boots that have been worn by industrial and construction workers for years and years. The basic need is filled by providing comfortable and safe work boots. Work boots are not inherently exciting or interesting; after all, you wear them for work, not play. The target market was male blue-collar industrial and construction workers who comprise a large majority of the industrial and construction work force. The stereotype is well established in people's minds: hard working, hard drinking, tough macho men.

The problem for Terra was basic. Work boots are in the maturity stage of the product life cycle so it is hard to make any major market share gains. The company wanted to appeal to industrial and construction workers and make them aware of the Terra brand as well as to liven up an otherwise dull product while improving the company's market position. The approach must have seemed obvious: tie Terra work boots to the sexual attraction of males for females. Terra dressed up, or rather, undressed a number of attractive models, featuring them in lingerie but wearing Terra work boots on their feet. As a campaign to increase sales or change the image of work boots, it is working right here. The potential to "cross over" work boots from work wear to everyday wear was possible. Work boots in the boudoir, work boots that can be worn "after" work, and so on. However, Terra was focused on its target market—male industrial and construction workers.

Terra had the models pose in sexually suggestive positions. Aside from the work boots, the models would hold work tools placed in sexually provocative positions. A tape measure here, a compressor hose there, let the imagination take hold and you have a powerful "sex" appeal. A website was developed for a tie-in to the campaign featuring a video of one of the models leaving work in her work clothes and her Terra work boots. She goes to a bar after work, presumably to have a drink, but instead she is going to her night job, which turns out to be "stripper," wherein she takes everything off but the work boots. Most companies that tie their products to sex appeal do so in lighthearted or subtler ways. Sex appeal is certainly natural and clearly so is attraction. Canadian society is very accepting of appeals in this fashion. However, most Canadians do not consider a complete striptease in a promotional video as being either lighthearted or subtle. In the least, it is erotica, and at its worst it could be viewed as pornography.

At this point, any marketing manager would need to pause and think about the image being developed and whether the firm wanted to go with something this provocative and potentially controversial in the Canadian market. With the decision to go forward made, the execution of the campaign was undertaken, and controversy was ignited. The firm decided to target the workers with a billboard campaign featuring the models in lingerie and including the Web address. The billboards were simple. They showed the models, put Terra's brand name in bold letters, and then asked the question: "Want to see more?" to which the answer was a URL for a website devoted to Terra boots. When you got to the website you were warned that you needed to be 18 or older to view the video.

Many female industrial and construction workers noticed the campaign right away. The billboards were certainly eye-catching but they were not "overly sexy." If the campaign had been restricted to the billboard promotions, it might not have drawn as much ire. Many people simply thought the billboards were promoting lingerie. A number of people thought they were promoting building tools. A third group received them as intended. On this level, a campaign is not working if it is misunderstood by a large group of people. However, female members of the Canadian Auto Workers (CAW) received the message clearly and did not accept the campaign well at all. They were greatly offended by the blatant sexual appeals, in particular the website video that was viewed as particularly demeaning. The video was designed to appeal to working men by turning working women into "sex" objects in a most base way; after work they became "strippers."

Offended strongly, the women of the CAW decided to act. They developed their own campaign against Terra. They began, of course, with Terra itself and complained to the company and asked it to withdraw its promotion. Terra had invested $750,000 in the campaign and it would all be lost if the company withdrew it as requested. Because Terra didn't fully understand the depth and strength of the complaints and it had invested so much money, it refused. A person who has complained to a firm and hasn't been satisfied can lodge a complaint with Advertising Standards Canada. This ability is part of the self-regulation mechanism developed by the industry. However, the women of the CAW were not aware of this process so they proceeded with a process they were more familiar with: dealing through their employers. They put pressure on all the industrial firms that employed them to delist Terra as a supplier on the grounds of conducting an unethical campaign. They also went public with the controversy, and now Terra was in the court of public opinion. Terra boots and Terra ads made news all across Canada and in the United States. The controversy was presented in the press, and commentary was requested from women's groups, men's groups, promotional experts, the women of the CAW, and finally, Terra itself. Although very extensive, the publicity was entirely negative for Terra.

Even with negative publicity, Terra accomplished two campaign objectives: it did establish its brand name in the minds of a lot of people, and it certainly changed the image of work boots. To its credit, Terra now realized the depth of emotion and feeling about the campaign, and responded very quickly. Terra removed the billboard posters, shut down its website video, and apologized publicly. However, the company still has to deal with the fallout of the campaign and any long-term implications.

QUESTIONS

1. On common sense alone, you have to wonder how Terra could develop and implement such an ill-advised campaign. And yet it is not the first company to make this kind of mistake, and it very likely won't be the last. Discuss reasons why companies and their promotional agencies might miss the mark on campaigns of this sort.
2. What kinds of steps should a company undertake in its promotional message design to avoid making the kind of error that Terra made?
3. Upon realizing the depth of response to the campaign, in your opinion, did Terra respond appropriately? What should the company have done that it didn't do?
4. Some commentators believe that people took this campaign far too seriously and that Terra really didn't do anything all that bad. Other commentators felt Terra should have been subject to criminal investigation and that the firm got off too lightly. Discuss your views of this campaign. What do you think?
5. Finally, Terra ran this campaign in Europe with success and continues to do so. Europeans seem completely nonplussed about the approach. Discuss some of the reasons why you think the campaign was more accepted in Europe as opposed to Canada.

SUGGESTED INFORMATION SOURCES

Deborah Barretto "Terra Boots Keep Walking," *Marketing Magazine*, February 9, 2004.
CBC, *Marketplace* "Sexed-up Ads," Broadcast: January 27, 2004.
Mark Etting "Given the Boot," *Marketing Magazine*, December 08/15, 2003.
Shari Graydon "Putting the Boots to Terra," *Marketing Magazine*, November 17, 2003.
David Menzies "It's Only Advertising," *Marketing Magazine*, January 12, 2004.

MARKETING MISCUES

Duracell's Duck Is Turned Off

The Duracell division of The Gillette Company is a worldwide leader in the manufacturing and marketing of high-performance alkaline batteries; its Duracell CopperTop battery is one of the most popular alkaline batteries in the world. In June 2001, Duracell introduced an improved line of Duracell CopperTop alkaline batteries. In November 2001, the company announced the debut of "Mr. Quackers" as the star of a new television advertising campaign. By early 2002, however, the company had to stop running the ad. Battery competitor Energizer had accused Duracell of false and misleading advertising.

Founded in 1901, Gillette is a world-renowned consumer-products company. It operates in three major consumer businesses: grooming, portable power, and oral care. Skillful marketing and superior technology are hallmarks of Gillette's success. The company's vision focuses on building its brands by delivering consumer value faster and better than its competition. The company's success at achieving its vision is reflected in the fact that more than 1 billion people around the world use one or more Gillette products daily. All three of the company's major businesses within Gillette are world leaders in their markets.

With the proliferation of portable electronic devices, the premium battery market in North America had become a $2.5-billion segment by 2001. The two market leaders were Duracell and Energizer. Though Energizer, long known for its Energizer bunny, held a sizable share of this premium segment, Duracell was, by far, the market share leader with almost 50 percent share of the important U.S. alkaline battery market. Nevertheless, 75 percent of the world's battery consumers still used the less costly zinc carbon battery, a lower-performing battery. Hence, a huge market opportunity existed if consumers could be persuaded to switch from zinc carbon to alkaline batteries.

Recognizing this vast market potential, both Duracell and Energizer decided to refocus their 2001 promotional efforts on their flagship brands. For Duracell, this meant focusing on the new and improved version of its flagship CopperTop brand, which incorporated the company's revolutionary M3 technology—more fuel, more efficiency, and more power. The battery line consisted of AA, AAA, C, D, and 9-volt sizes. Additionally, Duracell offered a line of specialty batteries for use in items such as cameras, hearing aids, and watches.

New York-based BBDO created "Mr. Quackers" to star in Duracell's new television advertising campaign for the improved battery. Mr. Quackers was a cute little robotic duck whose alkaline power outlasted that of three remote-controlled villains (Dr. Shred, The Incinerator, and The Black Widow), who were powered by heavy-duty batteries. The ad closed with the claim that Duracell CopperTop batteries lasted up to three times longer than heavy-duty or super heavy-duty batteries. The commercial, part of a $100-million global ad and marketing campaign, was targeted to air during prime-time, daytime, late-night, syndicated, cable, and Hispanic programming in North America.

With such an unassuming star in the ad, Gillette, Duracell, and BBDO were surprised when Energizer filed a lawsuit alleging false and misleading advertising. Gillette's ad touted the durability of its Duracell CopperTop battery over zinc. Energizer felt that the commercials led consumers to believe that only Duracell alkaline batteries were more durable than zinc batteries, when, in fact, all alkaline batteries (including those made by Energizer) outperform zinc batteries.

Questions

1. What were the goals of the "Mr. Quackers" ad?
2. Why was Duracell using this form of comparative advertising?
3. Do you think that Engergizer's complaint about Duracell's advertising was substantive or was it just a "nuisance" complaint? Why or why not?
4. What could Duracell do with the Mr. Quackers' ads that could get the point across but not be misleading? Suggest some changes that might be acceptable.

CRITICAL THINKING CASE

Using Automobiles as Promotional "Vehicles"

Automobiles are often used in promotional campaigns as part of sales promotion activities or as public relation tools that are supported by advertising and personal selling efforts. Simply designing a promotion around the latest and hottest assembly-line vehicle is not enough. To really have campaign impact, the car must become "one" with the product. Combine a custom paint and decoration job with a current interesting or unique production car and you are literally ready to "drive" a promotional campaign.

Recent car models like the new Volkswagen Beetle, the Chrysler PT Cruiser, and GM's Hummer have hit the road with a distinctive flair. Given the high amount of promotional clutter, these cars represent an opportunity to break through the clutter and get attention. Marketers want to make an emotional connection with their consumers, and if they can make a link between their brand and the image of a vehicle that appeals to their consumers and combine this with an event that appeals to their consumers, they will have a winning promotion. Tony Chapman, president of marketing promotion company Capital C in Toronto says, "You want to choose a vehicle that has a natural fit, if it's a men's shaver, consider a Porsche because it is clean, sleek, and has sex appeal. If it's Levi's, consider a motorcycle. If it's Mountain Dew, use a Jeep. Travel insurance? Look to a Winnebago."

Consider how Pepsi-Cola Canada introduced Mug root beer with a promotion tied to Volkswagen's new Beetle launch in 1998. Pepsi was targeting teens with Mug and the company felt the Beetle was a perfect fit because teens perceived it as a cool car. As part of the promotion Pepsi had a number of new Beetles wrapped with Mug logos. Pepsi also decorated and refurbished 25 air-cooled engine powered vintage Beetles as well. A Pepsi spokesperson summed up the whole effort as follows: "We wanted to get around to as many events as possible and we were trying to extend the (Mug) brand's persona, which made sampling all the more effective. I think the car promotion was the cornerstone of the whole launch. It was old-fashioned, and had a retro, authentic iconic image that fit well with our Mug's formulation."

Shoppers Drug Mart decided to support the Optimum loyalty card program using two "never-seen-before-in-Canada" stretch Hummers. The Hummer is a military vehicle that gained fame and notoriety during the Persian Gulf War in the 1990s. Shoppers Drug Mart felt that the use of these vehicles would create a "military aura" to the campaign as the Hummers swept in to take over Canadian cities. The physical entry of the vehicles was complicated by their size, over 9 metres long, so Shoppers had to plan its "invasions" carefully. A Shoppers' spokesperson quoted the success of the effort in the following terms: The Hummers attracted enormous publicity, providing press coverage estimated to be worth one hour of TV news. The promotion "made the front page of at least 20 major daily newspapers. It paid for itself more than 10 times over."

As attractive as "hot cars" can be, some marketers have been successful with "old fashion" approaches. In assessing its "Go Ahead, Get Dirty" campaign for Sunlight detergent, Unilever discovered that the market share of the product in Western Canada was lagging behind the rest of the nation. Unilever wanted to reach out to Western Canada in a different way to improve its sales. The firm decided that a more "grassroots" appeal was needed for Sunlight Detergent so it decided to get involved in the sponsorship of a series of Western Canadian rodeos and cycling races held in the provinces of Manitoba, Saskatchewan, Alberta, and B.C.

Unilever visited these events with a trailer and set of vans decorated with giant detailed wrappings that depicted cowboys and cyclists who are all dirty as a result of their competitions. Unilever felt that by physically demonstrating its "Go Ahead and Get Dirty" positioning, it could heighten the message impact. In assessing the campaign, Unilever considered it successful because the firm selected appropriate events and because of the strong visual images on its vehicles. The firm decided to continue the sponsorships and planned to extend the effort to "soccer" tournaments to reach out to families across Canada.

Interestingly, not all automakers are ready to jump into these promotional relationships. When a car is new and about to be launched, automakers are more than willing to take part in promotions that expand their exposure. However, if a vehicle is already extremely popular and established, auto manufacturers aren't as motivated to undertake cross-promotions. For example, DaimlerChrysler Canada was not marketing its popular PT Cruiser for this use. Consequently, marketers interested in a cross-promotional tie-in had to purchase the vehicles from dealerships in order to use them in promotions. Auto marketers welcome co-promotional opportunities when they feel they need to add some excitement to their vehicles.

The use of "wrapped" automobiles and trailers as part of a sponsorship or sales promotion effort needs to amount to being more than just a billboard in motion. There has to be an emotional attachment to the vehicles and/or the event or the impact will not be worth the effort. The whole idea is to break through the normal promotional clutter that one sees every day.

Based on: Lesley Young, "Promo Vehicles," *Marketing Magazine*, January 15, 2001.

Questions

1. What other brands do you associate with automobiles?
2. What are the possible positive and negative effects of associating a packaged consumer good with a brand of automobile? Can you think of any examples you are familiar with that you thought were successful associations? unsuccessful associations?
3. How would you design a promotional campaign to include an automobile (restriction: it can't be only a contest prize)?
4. The case presents a number of assessments of the success for these promotional campaigns. How would you go about assessing the success of the campaigns. How could they be compared to the choices of other "media" available to you as a marketing manager?

>> Pricing Decisions

part 6

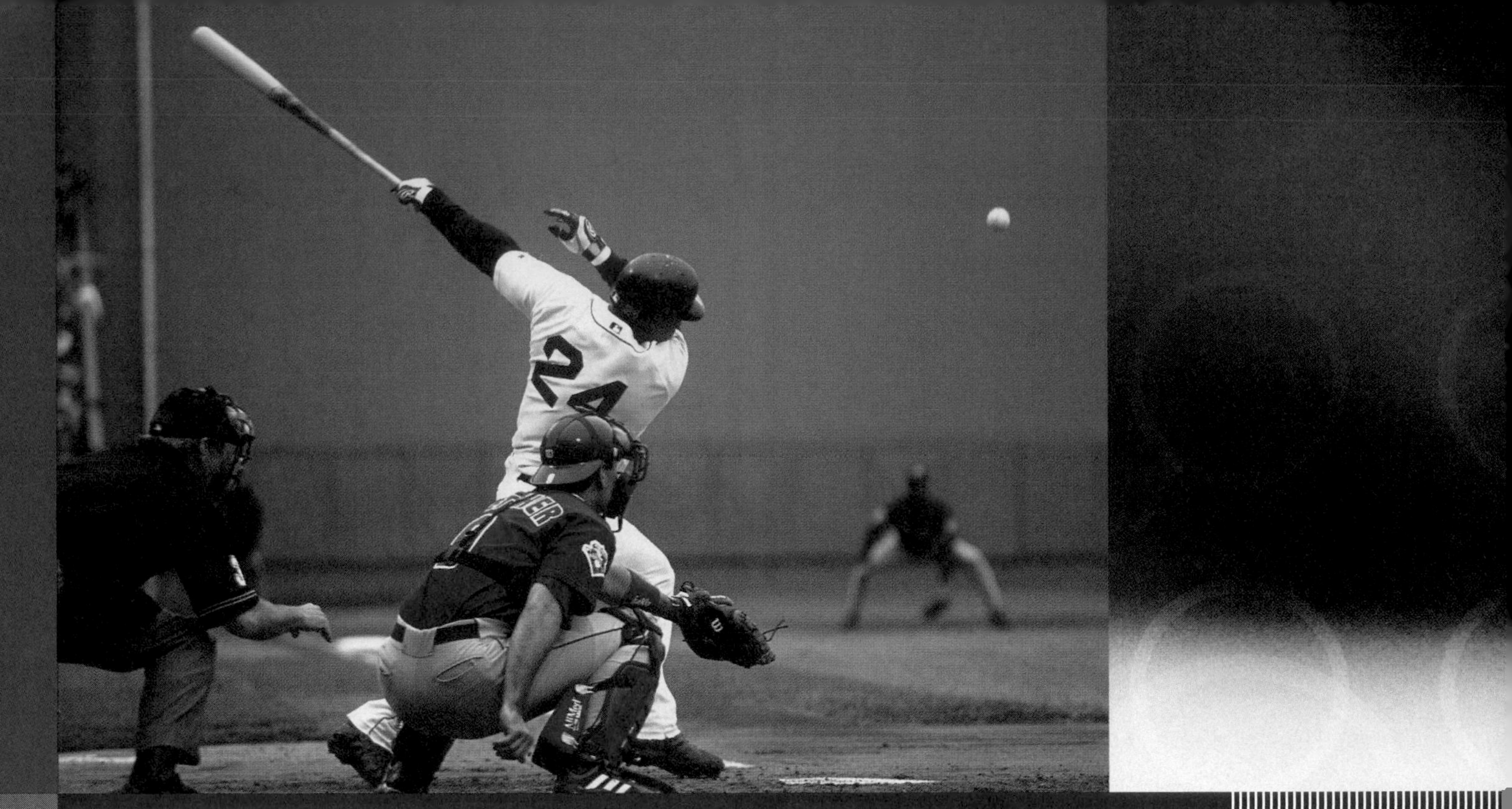

chapter 15

Pricing Concepts

>> LEARNING OBJECTIVES

1. Discuss the importance of pricing decisions to the economy and to the individual firm
2. List and explain a variety of pricing objectives
3. Explain the role of demand in price determination
4. Understand the concept of yield management systems
5. Describe cost-oriented pricing strategies
6. Demonstrate how the product life cycle, competition, distribution and promotion strategies, customer demands, the Internet and extranets, and perceptions of quality can affect price

>> Major League Baseball is banking on fan loyalty in a new way. It is charging fees for searchable video highlights and live radio feeds of games broadcast over the Internet.

The Internet arm of Major League Baseball is streaming video highlights of nearly all games over the Net. The video is available on **http://MLB.com** and on individual team sites (see, for example, the Toronto Blue Jays at **http://toronto.bluejays.mlb.com** or the 2004 World Series Champion Boston Red Sox at **http://www.redsox.com**) an hour after each game. Major League Baseball Advanced Media is using Virage, Inc.'s video-serving technology, which breaks up video clips pitch-by-pitch and makes them searchable. Fans can download the clips at 56 Kbps or 300 Kbps. Major League Baseball officials hope such capabilities will persuade fans to log on, even though they'll have to pay a small monthly fee, less than $10, for the video clip-search service.

Virage CEO Paul Lego says the service is worth the price. "It's the biggest video product on the Web today," he says. "There's no reason Internet content shouldn't be able to command the same types of deals as TV content."

That philosophy is extending to Internet radio broadcasts as well. Baseball has cut a deal with RealNetworks, Inc., that ends free Internet radio broadcasts of major league games. The broadcasts cost $10 per year, though subscribers get a $10 gift certificate from MLB.com's on-line store.

Ultimately, Major League Baseball wants to show live videocasts of games over the Net, says Bob Bowman, CEO of MLB Advanced Media, a company jointly owned by the 30 major league franchises, though he declined to predict a date. Baseball is prevented from televising local games on the Net under existing TV contracts. "Sports helped make the cable industry," Bowman says. "They're going to help make the Internet as well."[1]

If, like many baseball, hockey, and other sports fans, you would like to attend games live rather than watch videos after the game has been played, what kind of discount ticket prices can you find on the Internet? Check out sites like **http://www.theseats.com** and **http://www.anytickets.com** to find out. What other types of sporting and entertainment events can you find tickets for on these sites? What other Internet sources can you locate to search for discount sports and entertainment tickets?

Major League Baseball is counting on significant demand for its Internet video highlights. How are demand, costs, and profits related? Will the Internet have a major impact on pricing in general? What role are yield management systems playing in increased profitability? Can price influence the perceived quality of a product?

ON LINE

Major League Baseball

Is Major League Baseball playing up its new streaming video highlights on its website? How successful do you think the feature will be in generating revenue, particularly since people have been conditioned by dot.coms to get Internet content for free?

http://mlb.com

http://toronto.bluejays.mlb.com

http://www.redsox.com

1 Discuss the importance of pricing decisions to the economy and to the individual firm

>> THE IMPORTANCE OF PRICE

Price means one thing to the consumer and something else to the seller. To the consumer, it is the cost of something. To the seller, price is revenue, the primary source of profits. In the broadest sense, price allocates resources in a free-market economy. With so many ways of looking at price, it's no wonder that marketing managers find the task of setting prices a challenge.

What Is Price?

price
That which is given up in an exchange to acquire a good or service.

Price is that which is given up in an exchange to acquire a good or service. Price is typically the money exchanged for the good or service. It may also be time lost while waiting to acquire the good or service. Standing in long lines at the airport first to check in and then to get through the new security checkpoint procedures is a cost. In fact, these delays are one reason more people are selecting alternative modes of transportation for relatively short trips. Price might also include "lost dignity" for individuals who lose their jobs and must rely on charity to obtain food and clothing.

Consumers are interested in obtaining a "reasonable price." "Reasonable price" really means "perceived reasonable value" at the time of the transaction. One of the authors of this textbook bought a fancy European-designed toaster for about $45. The toaster's wide mouth made it possible to toast a bagel, warm a muffin, and, with a special $15 attachment, make a grilled sandwich. The author felt that a toaster with all these features surely must be worth the total price of $60. But after three months of using the device, toast burned around the edges and raw in the middle lost its appeal. The disappointed buyer put the toaster in the attic. Why didn't he return it to the retailer? Because the boutique had gone out of business, and no other local retailer carried the brand. Also, there was no local service centre. Remember, the price paid is based on the satisfaction consumers *expect* to receive from a product and not necessarily the satisfaction they *actually* receive.

Price can relate to anything with perceived value, not just money. When goods and services are exchanged, the trade is called *barter*. For example, if you exchange this book for a chemistry book at the end of the term, you have engaged in barter. The price you paid for the chemistry book was this textbook.

The Importance of Price to Marketing Managers

revenue
The price charged to customers multiplied by the number of units sold.

profit
Revenue minus expenses.

Prices are the key to revenues, which in turn are the key to profits for an organization. **Revenue** is the price charged to customers multiplied by the number of units sold. Revenue is what pays for every activity of the company: production, finance, sales, distribution, and so on. What's left over (if anything) is **profit.** Managers usually strive to charge a price that will earn a fair profit.

To earn a profit, managers must choose a price that is not too high or too low, a price that equals the perceived value to target consumers. If, in consumers' minds, a price is set too high, the perceived value will be less than the cost, and sales opportunities will be lost. Many mainstream purchasers of cars, sporting goods, CDs, tools, wedding gowns, and computers arc buying "used or preowned" items to get a better deal. Pricing a new product too high may give some shoppers an incentive to go to a "preowned" or consignment retailer.

Lost sales mean lost revenue. Conversely, if a price is too low, it may be perceived as a great value for the consumer, but the firm loses revenue it could have earned. Setting prices too low may not even attract as many buyers as managers might think. Retailers that place too much emphasis on discounts may not be able to meet the service expectations of full-price customers.

Trying to set the right price is one of the most stressful and pressure-filled tasks of the marketing manager, as trends in the consumer market attest:

- Confronting a flood of new products, potential buyers carefully evaluate the price of each one against the value of existing products.

- The increased availability of bargain-priced private and generic brands has put downward pressure on overall prices.
- Many firms are trying to maintain or regain their market share by cutting prices. For example, Dell has gained PC market share by aggressively cutting prices, and General Motors has been holding sales by offering zero percent financing and rebates averaging over $4,000 on new GM light vehicles.
- With the slow economy in 2002 and 2003, some consumers have become more reluctant to spend.

In the organizational market, where customers include both governments and businesses, buyers are also becoming more price sensitive and better informed. In the consumer market, consumers are using the Internet to make wiser purchasing decisions. Computerized information systems enable the organizational buyer to compare price and performance with great ease and accuracy. Improved communication and the increased use of telemarketing and computer-aided selling have also opened up many markets to new competitors. Finally, competition in general is increasing, so some installations, accessories, and component parts are being marketed like indistinguishable commodities.

>> PRICING OBJECTIVES

2 List and explain a variety of pricing objectives

To survive in today's highly competitive marketplace, companies need pricing objectives that are specific, attainable, and measurable. Realistic pricing goals then require periodic monitoring to determine the effectiveness of the company's strategy. For convenience, pricing objectives can be divided into three categories: profit oriented, sales oriented, and status quo.

Profit-Oriented Pricing Objectives

Profit-oriented objectives include profit maximization, satisfactory profits, and target return on investment. A brief discussion of each of these objectives follows.

Profit Maximization

Profit maximization means setting prices so that total revenue is as large as possible relative to total costs. Profit maximization does not always signify unreasonably high prices, however. Both price and profits depend on the type of competitive environment a firm faces, such as whether it is in a monopoly position (being the only seller, as with Canada Post) or in a much more competitive situation. Also, remember that a firm cannot charge a price higher than the product's perceived value. Many firms do not have the accounting data they need for maximizing profits. It is easy to say that a company should keep producing and selling goods or services as long as revenues exceed costs. Yet it is often hard to set up an accounting system that can accurately determine the point of profit maximization.

Satisfactory Profits

Satisfactory profits are a reasonable level of profits. Rather than maximizing profits, many organizations strive for profits that are satisfactory to the stockholders and management, in other words, a level of profits consistent with the level of risk an organization faces. In a risky industry, a satisfactory profit may be 35 percent. In a low-risk

Setting the right price on a product is extremely critical and so is a source of much stress for the marketing manager. Part of the reason is the continuous flood of new products that encourages shoppers to carefully compare prices.

industry, it might be 7 percent. To maximize profits, a small-business owner might have to keep his or her store open seven days a week. However, the owner might not want to work that hard and might be satisfied with less profit.

Target Return on Investment

return on investment (ROI)
Net profit after taxes divided by total assets.

The most common profit objective is a target **return on investment (ROI),** sometimes called the firm's return on total assets. ROI measures management's overall effectiveness in generating profits with the available assets. The higher the firm's return on investment, the better off the firm is. Many companies, including DuPont Canada, General Motors, Navistar International, ExxonMobil, and Magna, use target return on investment as their main pricing goal.

Return on investment is calculated as follows:

$$\text{Return on investment} = \frac{\text{Net profits after taxes}}{\text{Total assets}}$$

Assume that in 2005 Johnson Controls had assets of $4.5 million, net profits of $550,000, and a target ROI of 10 percent. This was the actual ROI:

$$\text{ROI} = \frac{550{,}000}{4{,}500{,}000}$$

$$= 12.2 \text{ percent}$$

As you can see, the ROI for Johnson Controls exceeded its target, which indicates that the company prospered in 2005.

Comparing the 12.2 percent ROI of Johnson Controls with the industry average provides a more meaningful picture. Any ROI needs to be evaluated in terms of the competitive environment, risks in the industry, and economic conditions. Generally speaking, firms seek ROIs in the 10 to 30 percent range. For example, General Electric seeks a 25 percent ROI, whereas Alcoa, Rubbermaid, and most major pharmaceutical companies strive for a 20 percent ROI. In some industries, such as the grocery industry, a return of less than 5 percent is common and acceptable.

A company with a target ROI can predetermine its desired level of profitability. The marketing manager can use the standard, such as 10 percent ROI, to determine whether a particular price and marketing mix are feasible.

Sales-Oriented Pricing Objectives

Sales-oriented pricing objectives are based either on market share or on dollar or unit sales. The effective marketing manager should be familiar with these pricing objectives.

Market Share

market share
A company's product sales as a percentage of total sales for that industry.

Market share is a company's product sales as a percentage of total sales for that industry. Sales can be reported in dollars or in units of product. It is very important to know whether market share is expressed in revenue or units because the results may be different. Consider four companies competing in an industry with 2,000,000 total unit sales and total industry revenue of $4 million (see Exhibit 15.1). Company A has the largest unit market share at 50 percent, but it has only 25 percent of the revenue market share. In contrast, company D has only a 15 percent unit share but the largest revenue share: 30 percent. Market share may be expressed in terms of revenue or units.

Many companies believe that maintaining or increasing market share is an indicator of the effectiveness of their marketing mix. Larger market shares have indeed often meant higher profits, thanks to greater economies of scale, market power, and ability to compensate top-quality management. Conventional wisdom also says that market share and return on investment are strongly related. For the most part they are; however, many companies with low market share survive and even prosper.

COMPANY	UNITS SOLD	UNIT PRICE	TOTAL REVENUE	UNIT MARKET SHARE	REVENUE MARKET SHARE
A	1,000,000	$1.00	$1,000,000	50%	25%
B	200,000	4.00	800,000	10	20
C	500,000	2.00	1,000,000	25	25
D	300,000	4.00	1,200,000	15	30
Total	2,000,000		$4,000,000		

EXHIBIT 15.1

Two Ways to Measure Market Share (Units and Revenue)

The late 1990s and early 2000s proved that the conventional wisdom about market share and profitability isn't always reliable. Because of extreme competition in some industries, many market share leaders either did not reach their target ROI or actually lost money. Air Canada, with nearly 60 percent of Canada's airline passenger market, lost nearly $2 billion in 2003. To try to get back to profitability, Air Canada is slashing jobs and asking for wage concessions from its employees.[2] Procter & Gamble switched from market share to ROI objectives after realizing that profits don't automatically follow from a large market share. PepsiCo says its new Pepsi challenge is to be No. 1 in share of industry profit, not in share of sales volume.

Still, the struggle for market share can be all-consuming for some companies. For over a decade, Maxwell House and Folgers, the biggest coffee brands, have been locked in a struggle to dominate the market. Their weapons have been advertising, perpetual rounds of price-cutting, and millions upon millions of cents-off coupons. At this point, Maxwell House, a unit of Kraft Foods, has regained a few drops of market share that it had lost to Folgers, a unit of Procter & Gamble, earlier in the war. Maxwell House's strategy has been to advertise heavily and to introduce new products that lure consumers with taste rather than price. Examples include ready-made coffee in refrigerator cartons and coffee syrup, both designed for consumers to pour and microwave as needed.

Research organizations like ACNielsen and Information Resources, Inc., provide excellent market share reports for many different industries. These reports enable companies to track their performance in various product categories over time.

Sales Maximization

Rather than strive for market share, sometimes companies try to maximize sales. A firm with the objective of maximizing sales ignores profits, competition, and the marketing environment as long as sales are rising.

If a company is strapped for funds or faces an uncertain future, it may try to generate a maximum amount of cash in the short run. Management's task when using this objective is to calculate which price–quantity relationship generates the greatest cash revenue. Sales maximization can also be used effectively on a temporary basis to sell off excess inventory. It is not uncommon to find Christmas cards, ornaments, and so on discounted at 50 to 70 percent off retail prices after the holiday season. In addition, management can use sales maximization for year-end sales to clear out old models before introducing the new ones.

Status Quo Pricing Objectives

Status quo pricing seeks to maintain existing prices or to meet the competition's prices. This third category of pricing objectives has the major advantage of requiring little planning. It is essentially a passive policy.

status quo pricing
A pricing objective that maintains existing prices or meets the competition's prices.

ON LINE

Canadian Tire

Wal-Mart

Zellers

Shop for some kind of electronic device (DVD player, digital camera, MP3 player, etc.) on the Canadian Tire, Wal-Mart, and Zellers websites. How do the prices for the same product compare at the three retailers? Do they all even carry the same product? Compare the price on the Web with the price offered at the physical store and explain any discrepancies.

http://www.canadiantire.ca

http://www.walmart.com

http://www.hbc.com/zellers

Often firms competing in an industry with an established price leader simply meet the competition's prices. These industries typically have fewer price wars than those with direct price competition. In other cases, managers regularly shop competitors' stores to ensure that their prices are comparable. Fast-food chains regularly monitor one another's prices. In response to MCI WorldCom's claims that its long-distance service is overpriced, AT&T struck back with advertisements showing that its rates are essentially equal to competitors'. AT&T was attempting to convince target consumers that it follows a status quo pricing strategy.

3 Explain the role of demand in price determination

>> THE DEMAND DETERMINANT OF PRICE

After marketing managers establish pricing goals, they must set specific prices to reach those goals. The price they set for each product depends mostly on two factors: the demand for the good or service and the cost to the seller for that good or service. When pricing goals are mainly sales oriented, demand considerations usually dominate. Other factors, such as distribution and promotion strategies, perceived quality, demands of large customers, the Internet, and stage of the product life cycle, can also influence price.

The Nature of Demand

demand
The quantity of a product that will be sold in the market at various prices for a specified period.

Demand is the quantity of a product that will be sold in the market at various prices for a specified period. The quantity of a product that people will buy depends on its price. The higher the price, the fewer goods or services consumers will demand. Conversely, the lower the price, the more goods or services they will demand.

This trend is illustrated in Exhibit 15.2(a), which graphs the demand per week for gourmet popcorn at various prices. This graph is called a *demand curve.* The vertical axis of the graph shows different prices of gourmet popcorn, measured in dollars per package. The horizontal axis measures the quantity of gourmet popcorn that will be demanded per week at each price. For example, at a price of $2.50, 50 packages will be sold per week; at $1.00, consumers will demand 120 packages, as the *demand schedule* in Exhibit 15.2(b) shows.

The demand curve in Exhibit 15.2 slopes downward and to the right, which indicates that more gourmet popcorn is demanded as the price is lowered. One reason more is sold at lower prices than at higher prices is that lower prices bring in new buyers. This fact might not be so obvious with gourmet popcorn, but consider the example of steak. As the price of steak drops lower and lower, some people who have not been eating steak will probably start buying it rather than hamburger. With each reduction in price, existing customers may also buy extra amounts. Similarly, if the price of gourmet popcorn falls low enough, some people will buy more than they have bought in the past.

supply
The quantity of a product that will be offered to the market by a supplier at various prices for a specified period.

Supply is the quantity of a product that will be offered to the market by a supplier or suppliers at various prices for a specified period. Exhibit 15.3(a) illustrates the resulting *supply curve* for gourmet popcorn. Unlike the falling demand curve, the supply curve for gourmet popcorn slopes upward and to the right. At higher prices, gourmet popcorn manufacturers will obtain more resources (popcorn, flavourings, salt) and produce more gourmet popcorn. If the price consumers are willing to pay for gourmet popcorn increases, producers can afford to buy more ingredients.

Output tends to increase at higher prices because manufacturers can sell more packages of gourmet popcorn and earn greater profits. The *supply schedule* in Exhibit 15.3(b) shows that at $2.00 suppliers are willing to place 110 packages of gourmet popcorn on the market, but they will offer 140 packages at a price of $3.00.

How Demand and Supply Establish Prices

At this point, let's combine the concepts of demand and supply to see how market prices are determined. So far, the premise is that if the price is X, then consumers will purchase Y amount of gourmet popcorn. How high or low will prices actually go? How many packages of gourmet popcorn will be produced? How many packages will be consumed?

EXHIBIT 15.2

Demand Curve and Demand Schedule for Gourmet Popcorn

(a) Demand curve

(b) Demand schedule

Price per package of gourmet popcorn ($)	Packages of gourmet popcorn demanded per week
3.00	35
2.50	50
2.00	65
1.50	85
1.00	120

The demand curve cannot predict consumption, nor can the supply curve alone forecast production. Instead, we need to look at what happens when supply and demand interact, as shown in Exhibit 15.4.

At a price of $3.00, the public would demand only 35 packages of gourmet popcorn. However, suppliers stand ready to place 140 packages on the market at this price (data from the demand and supply schedules). If 140 packages were supplied, this would create a surplus of 105 packages of gourmet popcorn. How does a merchant eliminate a surplus? The merchant lowers the price.

At a price of $1.00, 120 packages of popcorn would be demanded, but only 25 would be placed on the market. A shortage of 95 units would be created. If a product is in short supply and consumers want it, how do they entice the seller to provide more? They offer more money, that is, pay a higher price.

Now let's examine a price of $1.50. At this price, 85 packages are demanded and 85 are supplied. When demand and supply are equal, a state called **price equilibrium** is achieved. A temporary price below equilibrium, say, $1.00, results in a shortage because at that price the demand for gourmet popcorn is greater than the available supply. Shortages put upward pressure on price. Similarly, a price above equilibrium puts a downward pressure on price. At equilibrium, there is no inclination for prices to rise or fall.

An equilibrium price may not be reached all at once. Prices may fluctuate during a trial-and-error period as the market for a good or service moves toward equilibrium. Sooner or later, however, demand and supply will settle into proper balance.

price equilibrium
The price at which demand and supply are equal.

elasticity of demand
Consumers' responsiveness or sensitivity to changes in price.

elastic demand
A situation in which consumer demand is sensitive to changes in price.

inelastic demand
A situation in which an increase or a decrease in price will not significantly affect demand for the product.

Elasticity of Demand

To appreciate demand analysis, you should understand the concept of elasticity. **Elasticity of demand** refers to consumers' responsiveness or sensitivity to changes in price. **Elastic demand** occurs when consumers buy more or less of a product when the price changes. Conversely, **inelastic demand** means that an increase or a decrease in price will not significantly affect demand for the product.

Elasticity over the range of a demand curve can be measured by using the formula on page 483:

ON LINE 

uBid

See how demand and supply establish prices by checking out the offerings at uBid.com. Click on a variety of products and identify the price and the number of items in the lot. Can you see a correlation between the price and the number of, say, printers uBid has on hand?

http://www.uBid.com

EXHIBIT 15.3

Supply Curve and Supply Schedule for Gourmet Popcorn

(a) Supply curve

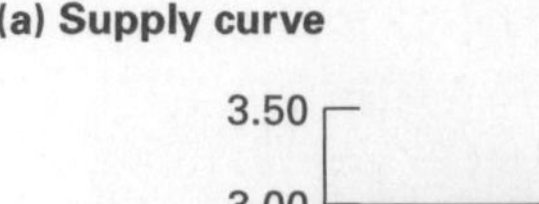

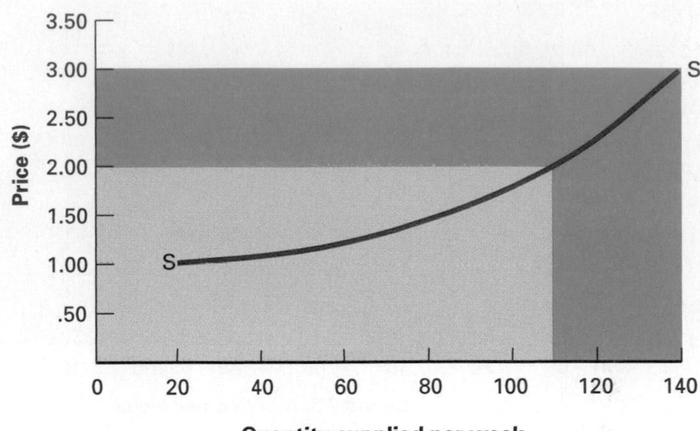

(b) Supply schedule

Price per package of gourmet popcorn ($)	Packages of gourmet popcorn supplied per week
3.00	140
2.50	130
2.00	110
1.50	85
1.00	25

ON LINE

Columbia House

How can Columbia House offer so many CDs, videos, or DVDs for one cent? Go to the website to see what kind of deals Columbia House is offering right now. Compare the introductory offers to the pricing for subsequent purchases. What conclusions can you draw about Columbia House and about the elasticity of demand for CDs (or videos or DVDs) based on the posted pricing for the initial signup and for subsequent purchases?

http://www.columbiahousecanada.com

EXHIBIT 15.4

Equilibrium Price for Gourmet Popcorn

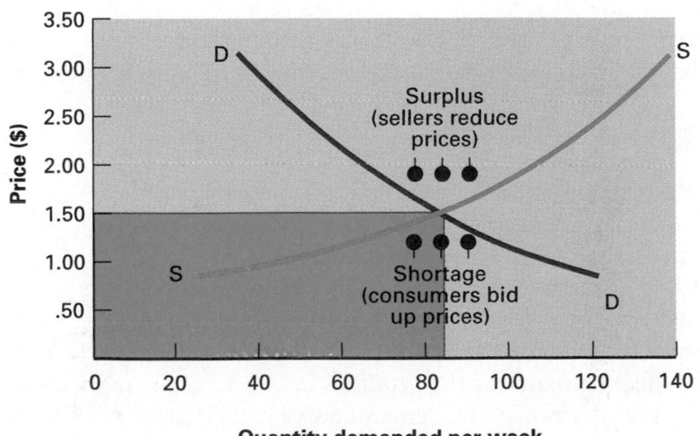

$$\text{Elasticity } (E) = \frac{\text{Percentage change in quantity demanded of good A}}{\text{Percentage change in price of good A}}$$

If E is greater than 1, demand is elastic.
If E is less than 1, demand is inelastic.
If E is equal to 1, demand is unitary.

Unitary elasticity means that an increase in sales exactly offsets a decrease in prices, so total revenue remains the same.

unitary elasticity
A situation in which total revenue remains the same when prices change.

Elasticity can be measured by observing these changes in total revenue:

If price goes down and revenue goes up, demand is elastic.
If price goes down and revenue goes down, demand is inelastic.
If price goes up and revenue goes up, demand is inelastic.
If price goes up and revenue goes down, demand is elastic.
If price goes up or down and revenue stays the same, elasticity is unitary.

Exhibit 15.5(a) shows a very elastic demand curve. Decreasing the price of a Sony VCR from \$300 to \$200 increases sales from 18,000 units to 59,000 units. Revenue increases from \$5.4 million (\$300 × 18,000) to \$11.8 million (\$200 × 59,000). The price decrease results in a large increase in unit sales and revenue.

Exhibit 15.5(b) shows a completely inelastic demand curve. Let's assume that Ontario dropped its vehicle emission inspection fee from \$35 to \$25. There is no change in the number of vehicle emission inspections in Ontario. Decreasing the price (inspection fee) did not cause people to increase the number of inspections. Demand is completely inelastic for inspection fees, which are required by law. Thus, it also follows that Ontario could double the original fee to \$70 and double the province's inspection revenues.

Exhibit 15.6 presents the demand curve and demand schedule for bottles of Spring Break suntan lotion. Let's follow the demand curve from the highest price to the lowest and examine what happens to elasticity as the price decreases.

Inelastic Demand

The initial decrease in the price of Spring Break suntan lotion, from \$5.00 to \$2.25, results in a decrease in total revenue of \$969 (\$5,075 – \$4,106). When price and total revenue fall, demand is inelastic. The decrease in price is much greater than the increase in suntan lotion sales (810 bottles). Demand is therefore not very flexible in the price range \$5.00 to \$2.25. When demand is inelastic, sellers can raise prices and increase total revenue. Often items that are relatively inexpensive but convenient tend to have inelastic demand.

EXHIBIT 15.5

Elasticity of Demand for Sony VCRs and Vehicle Emission Inspections

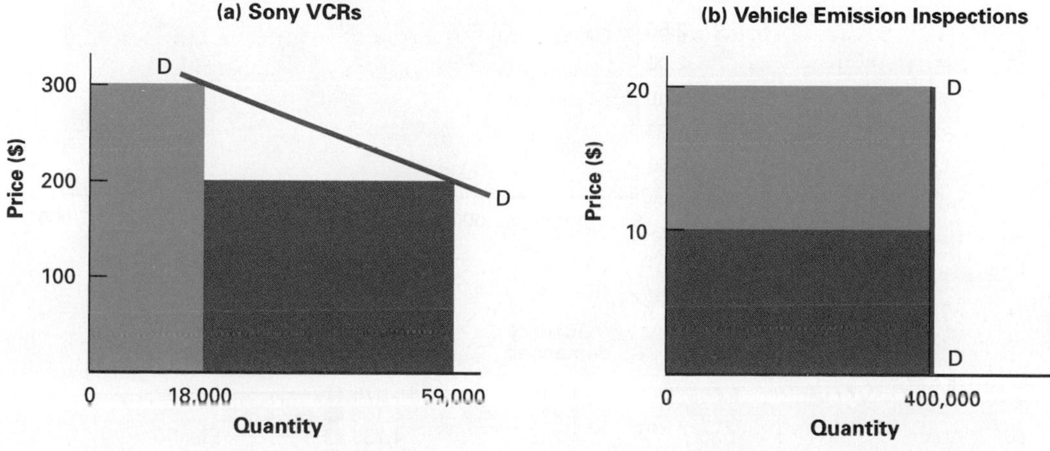

Elastic Demand

In the example of Spring Break suntan lotion, shown in Exhibit 15.6, when the price is dropped from \$2.25 to \$1.00, total revenue increases by \$679 (\$4,785 – \$4,106). An increase in total revenue when price falls indicates that demand is elastic. Let's measure Spring Break's elasticity of demand when the price drops from \$2.25 to \$1.00 by applying the formula presented earlier:

$$E = \frac{\text{Change in quantity/(Sum of quantities/2)}}{\text{Change in price/(Sum of prices/2)}}$$

$$= \frac{(4{,}785 - 1{,}825)/[(1{,}825 + 4{,}785)/2]}{(2.25 - 1)/[(2.25 + 1.00)/2]}$$

$$= \frac{2{,}690/3{,}305}{1.25/1.63}$$

$$= \frac{.896}{.767}$$

$$= 1.17$$

Because E is greater than 1, demand is elastic.

Factors That Affect Elasticity

Several factors affect elasticity of demand, including the following:

- *Availability of substitutes:* When many substitute products are available, the consumer can easily switch from one product to another, making demand elastic. The same is true in reverse: A person with complete renal failure will pay whatever is charged for a kidney transplant because there is no substitute.
- *Price relative to purchasing power:* If a price is so low that it is an inconsequential part of an individual's budget, demand will be inelastic. For example, if the price of salt doubles, consumers will not stop putting salt and pepper on their eggs, because salt is cheap anyway.

EXHIBIT 15.6

Demand for Bottles of Spring Break Suntan Lotion

(a) Demand curve

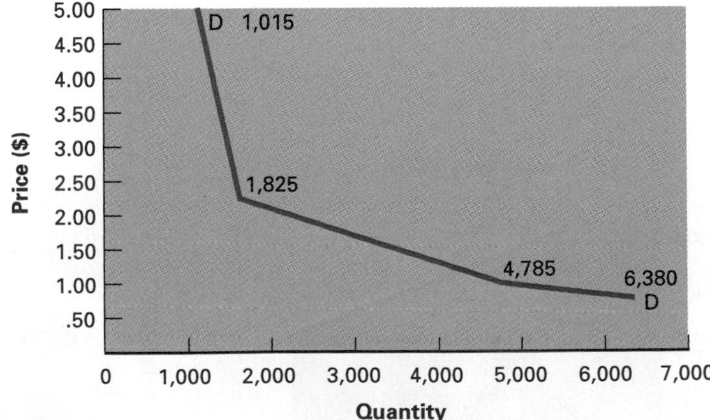

(b) Demand schedule

Price (\$)	Quantity demanded	Total revenue (price X quantity)	Elasticity
5.00	1,015	\$5,075	Inelastic
2.25	1,825	4,106	
1.00	4,785	4,785	Elastic
0.75	6,380	4,785	Unitary

- *Product durability:* Consumers often have the option of repairing durable products rather than replacing them, thus prolonging their useful life. If a person had planned to buy a new car and prices suddenly began to rise, he or she might elect to fix the old car and drive it for another year. In other words, people are sensitive to the price increase, and demand is elastic.
- *A product's other uses:* The greater the number of different uses for a product, the more elastic demand tends to be. If a product has only one use, as may be true of a new medicine, the quantity purchased probably will not vary as price varies. A person will consume only the prescribed quantity, regardless of price. On the other hand, a product like steel has many possible applications. As its price falls, steel becomes more economically feasible in a wider variety of applications, thereby making demand relatively elastic.

Examples of both elastic and inelastic demand abound in everyday life. For example, as the cell phone rate in India fell from 16.8 rupees per minute to 4.5 rupees per minute, the number of cell phone subscribers rose from 1.7 million to 4.5 million.[3] Does this indicate elastic or inelastic demand for cell phone service? When car manufacturers began offering zero percent financing, sales of new vehicles jumped 35 percent over the same period a year earlier. Sales of so many new cars resulted in a huge surplus of used vehicles. When demand remains constant and supply increases, prices fall. In this case, the price of a used Lexus fell 12 percent from the price for a comparable vehicle a year earlier; the price of a used Chevrolet Tahoe fell 14 percent, and the price of a used Ford F-series pickup truck fell 11 percent.[4] This is simply supply and demand at work.

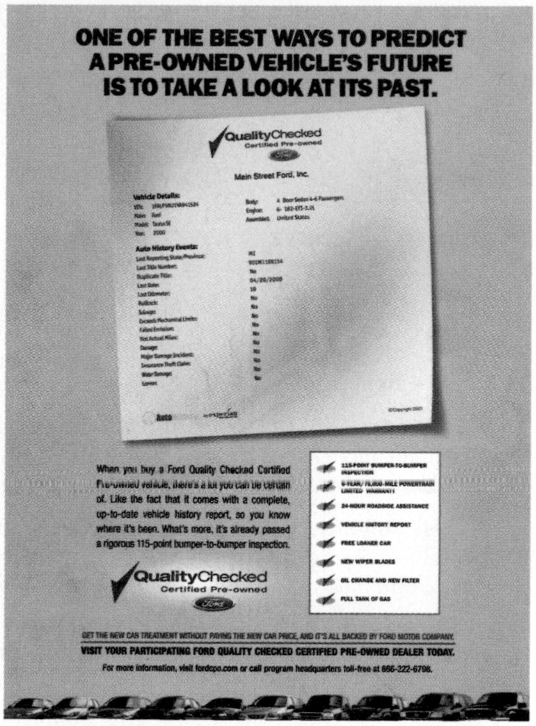

COURTESY OF FORD MOTOR COMPANY

The new- and used-car industries have an inverse relationship to supply and demand. As the demand for new cars rises (such as with the zero percent financing deals), demand for new cars increases, and supplies shrink. At the same time, when this occurs, the demand for used cars decreases, and used-car inventories swell. This situation puts manufacturers and their dealers (who often stock both new and used automobiles) in a delicate relationship.

The Power of Yield Management Systems

4 Understand the concept of yield management systems

When competitive pressures are high, a company must know when it can raise prices to maximize its revenues. More and more companies are turning to yield management systems to help adjust prices. First developed in the airline industry, **yield management systems (YMS)** use complex mathematical software to profitably fill unused capacity. The software employs techniques such as discounting early purchases, limiting early sales at these discounted prices, and overbooking capacity. YMSs now are appearing in other services such as lodging, other transportation forms, rental firms, and even hospitals.[5]

yield management systems (YMS)
A technique for adjusting prices that uses complex mathematical software to profitably fill unused capacity by discounting early purchases, limiting early sales at these discounted prices, and overbooking capacity.

Yield management systems are spreading beyond service industries as their popularity increases. The lessons of airlines and hotels aren't entirely applicable to other industries, however, because plane seats and hotel rooms are perishable—if they go empty, the revenue opportunity is lost forever. So it makes sense to slash prices to move toward capacity if it's possible to do so without reducing the prices that other customers pay. Cars and steel aren't so perishable. Still, the capacity to make these goods is perishable. An underused factory or mill is a lost revenue opportunity. So it makes sense to cut prices to use up capacity if it's possible to do so while getting other customers to pay full price.

ProfitLogic has helped customers such as Gymboree, Ann Taylor, and The Gap determine the best markdown price. The software has boosted profit margins from 5 to 18 percent. Khimetrics, used by Buy.com and others, analyzes dozens of factors such as a product's life cycle, competitors' prices, and past sales data at various price points before churning out a list of possible prices and calculating the best ones. New sales data are fed back into the formulae daily to refine the process. Systems such as this aren't cheap, however, costing from $200,000 to $500,000.[6]

Some companies, such as Omni Hotels, are creating their own YMS software. Omni CHARM (Centralized Hotel Automated Revenue Management), created by Omni Hotels, predicts demand and indicates when to discount rooms and when to charge the maximum. Marriott Hotels & Resorts, with a similar system, earns an additional estimated $400 million per year.[7]

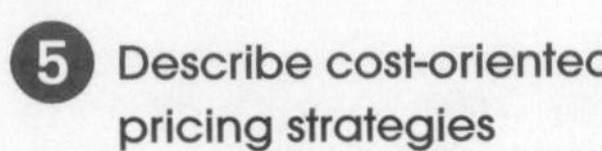

5 Describe cost-oriented pricing strategies

THE COST DETERMINANT OF PRICE

Sometimes companies minimize or ignore the importance of demand and decide to price their products largely or solely on the basis of costs. Prices determined strictly on the basis of costs may be too high for the target market, thereby reducing or eliminating sales. On the other hand, cost-based prices may be too low, causing the firm to earn a lower return than it should. Nevertheless, costs should generally be part of any price determination, if only as a floor below which a good or service must not be priced in the long run.

The idea of cost may seem simple, but it is actually a multifaceted concept, especially for producers of goods and services. A **variable cost** is a cost that varies with changes in the level of output; an example of a variable cost is the cost of materials. In contrast, a **fixed cost** does not change as output is increased or decreased. Examples include rent and executives' salaries.

variable cost
A cost that varies with changes in the level of output.

fixed cost
A cost that does not change as output is increased or decreased.

To compare the cost of production to the selling price of a product, it is helpful to calculate costs per unit, or average costs. **Average variable cost (AVC)** equals total variable costs divided by quantity of output. **Average total cost (ATC)** equals total costs divided by output. As the graph in Exhibit 15.7(a) shows, AVC and ATC are basically U-shaped curves. In contrast, average fixed costs (AFC) decline continually as output increases because total fixed costs are constant.

average variable cost (AVC)
Total variable costs divided by quantity of output.

average total cost (ATC)
Total costs divided by quantity of output.

Marginal cost (MC) is the change in total costs associated with a one-unit change in output. Exhibit 15.7(b) shows that when output rises from seven to eight units, the change in total cost is from \$640 to \$750; therefore, marginal cost is \$110.

marginal cost (MC)
The change in total costs associated with a one-unit change in output.

All the curves illustrated in Exhibit 15.7(a) have definite relationships:

- AVC plus AFC equals ATC.
- MC falls for a while and then turns upward, in this case after the fourth unit. At that point diminishing returns set in, meaning that less output is produced for every additional dollar spent on variable input.
- MC intersects both AVC and ATC at their lowest possible points.
- When MC is less than AVC or ATC, the incremental cost will continue to pull the averages down. Conversely, when MC is greater than AVC or ATC, it pulls the averages up, and ATC and AVC begin to rise.
- The minimum point on the ATC curve is the least cost point for a fixed-capacity firm, although it is not necessarily the most profitable point.

Costs can be used to set prices in a variety of ways. The first two methods discussed here, markup pricing and formula pricing, are relatively simple. The other three—profit maximization pricing, break-even pricing, and target-return pricing—make use of the more complicated concepts of cost.

markup pricing
The cost of buying the product from the producer plus amounts for profit and for expenses not otherwise accounted for.

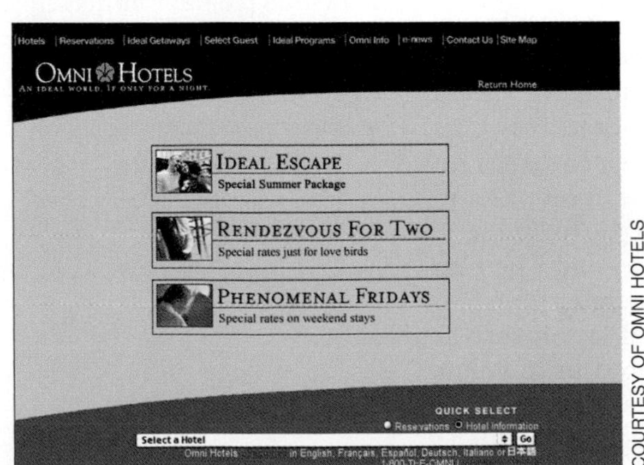

COURTESY OF OMNI HOTELS

Although yield management is being implemented across diverse and multiple industries, it continues to be the hallmark of the travel industry. Often hotels like Omni offer different weekend specials each week to encourage the kind of spontaneous travel that will maximize company revenues.

Markup Pricing

Markup pricing, the most popular method used by wholesalers and retailers to establish a selling price, does not directly analyze the costs of production. Instead, **markup pricing** uses the cost of buying the product from the producer, plus amounts for profit and for expenses not otherwise accounted for. The total determines the selling price.

A retailer, for example, adds a certain percentage to the cost of the merchandise received to arrive at the retail price. An item that costs the retailer \$1.80 and is sold for \$2.20 carries a markup of 40¢, which is a markup of 22 percent of the cost (40¢/\$1.80). Retailers, however, tend to discuss markup in terms of its percentage of the retail price—in this example, 18 percent (40¢/\$2.20). The difference between the retailer's cost and the selling price (40¢) is the gross margin.

EXHIBIT 15.7

Hypothetical Set of Cost Curves and a Cost Schedule

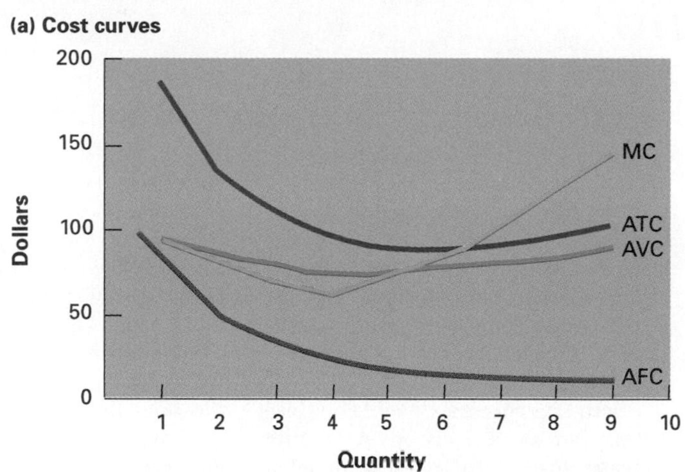

(b) Cost schedule

Total-cost data, per week				Average-cost data, per week			
(1) Total product (Q)	(2) Total fixed cost (TFC)	(3) Total variable cost (TVC)	(4) Total cost (TC)	(5) Average fixed cost (AFC)	(6) Average variable cost (AVC)	(7) Average total cost (ATC)	(8) Marginal cost (MC)
			TC = TFC + TVC	$AFC = \frac{TFC}{Q}$	$AVC = \frac{TVC}{Q}$	$ATC = \frac{TC}{Q}$	$(MC) = \frac{\text{change in TC}}{\text{change in Q}}$
0	$100	$ 0	$ 100	—	—	—	—
1	100	90	190	$100.00	$90.00	$190.00	$ 90
2	100	170	270	50.00	85.00	135.00	80
3	100	240	340	33.33	80.00	113.33	70
4	100	300	400	25.00	75.00	100.00	60
5	100	370	470	20.00	74.00	94.00	70
6	100	450	550	16.67	75.00	91.67	80
7	100	540	640	14.29	77.14	91.43	90
8	100	650	750	12.50	81.25	93.75	110
9	100	780	880	11.11	86.67	97.78	130
10	100	930	1,030	10.00	93.00	103.00	150

Markups are often based on experience. For example, many small retailers mark up merchandise 100 percent over cost. In other words, they double the cost. This tactic is called **keystoning.** Some other factors that influence markups are the merchandise's appeal to customers, past response to the markup (an implicit demand consideration), the item's promotional value, the seasonality of the goods, their fashion appeal, the product's traditional selling price, and competition. Most retailers avoid any set markup because of such considerations as promotional value and seasonality.

keystoning
The practice of marking up prices by 100 percent, or doubling the cost.

The biggest advantage of markup pricing is its simplicity. The primary disadvantage is that it ignores demand and may result in overpricing or underpricing the merchandise.

High profits from unhealthy products such as cigarettes can raise ethical questions. So can governments' addictions to cigarette revenue, as discussed in the "Ethics in Marketing" box.

ETHICS IN MARKETING

Many Governments Are Hooked on Tobacco Revenue

Four million people will die this year from lung cancer and other smoking-related diseases, according to the World Health Organization. By 2030, the agency predicts, the annual loss of life will more than double, making cigarettes the leading cause of premature death around the globe, outstripping malaria, AIDS, and other scourges.

Yet, some countries make more money from a pack of smokes than do the tobacco companies. More than 70 percent of the average retail price of cigarettes in the European Union goes into governments' pockets. In Brazil, the government's take is about 65 percent. Tobacco taxes account for about 6 percent of federal government tax revenue in Germany. For the roughly two dozen governments that still manufacture cigarettes, dependence on tobacco revenue can be even higher. China, whose government is the world's largest cigarette maker, derives about 13 percent of its annual income from tobacco sales and taxes.

All that can make governments reluctant to take aggressive action against smoking. In Japan, where the government owns two-thirds of the country's largest cigarette maker, Japan Tobacco, Inc., the Health Ministry dropped plans for specific targets to reduce tobacco use after complaints from tobacco interests.

Because smokers are hooked on cigarettes, they are less responsive to price increases than consumers of many other goods. That means that in the short to medium term, tax revenue would increase as consumption declines. Experience in Canada shows that a 10 percent increase in cigarette prices translates into a 4 percent drop in consumption. In developing countries, where people have less disposable income, the World Bank estimates that a 10 percent price increase would reduce consumption by about 8 percent, on average.

A study by Teh-wei Hu, a health economist, of the University of California–Berkeley, and Zhengzhong Mao, of the West China University of Medical Sciences, concludes that a 25 percent cigarette-tax increase in China would reduce consumption there by 4.57 billion packs and boost central-government revenue by 24.74 billion yuan.

Worldwide, the public-health benefits of tax increases would be significant, the World Bank says. A recent bank report estimates that a sustained 10 percent increase in the real price of cigarettes around the globe would prompt 40 million people to quit and deter many others from starting to smoke, saving about 10 million lives while, at the same time, boosting government revenue by an average of 7 percent.[8]

Should governments get out of the tobacco business? Why or why not? Do you think that the Canadian government should increase taxes on cigarettes 100 percent or more to reduce usage and increase tax revenue? Why or why not? A more direct alternative is to ban smoking altogether. Is this goal feasible?

Profit Maximization Pricing

profit maximization
A method of setting prices that occurs when marginal revenue equals marginal cost.

marginal revenue (MR)
The extra revenue associated with selling an extra unit of output or the change in total revenue with a one-unit change in output.

Producers tend to use more complicated methods of setting prices than distributors use. One is **profit maximization,** which occurs when marginal revenue equals marginal cost. You learned earlier that marginal cost is the change in total costs associated with a one-unit change in output. Similarly, **marginal revenue (MR)** is the extra revenue associated with selling an extra unit of output. As long as the revenue of the last unit produced and sold is greater than the cost of the last unit produced and sold, the firm should continue manufacturing and selling the product.

Exhibit 15.8 shows the marginal revenues and marginal costs for a hypothetical firm, using the cost data from Exhibit 15.7(b). The profit-maximizing quantity, where MR = MC, is six units. You might say, "If profit is zero, why produce the sixth unit? Why not stop at five?" In fact, you would be right. The firm, however, would not know that the sixth unit would produce zero profits until it determined that profits were no longer increasing. Economists suggest producing up to the point where MR = MC. If marginal revenue is just one penny greater than marginal costs, it will still increase total profits.

Break-Even Pricing

break-even analysis
A method of determining what sales volume must be reached before total revenue equals total costs.

Now let's take a closer look at the relationship between sales and cost. **Break-even analysis** determines what sales volume must be reached before the company breaks even (its total revenue equals total costs).

The typical break-even model assumes a given fixed cost and a constant average variable cost. Suppose that Universal Sportswear, a hypothetical firm, has fixed costs of $2,000 and that the cost of labour and materials for each unit produced is 50¢. Assume that it can sell up to 6,000 units of its product at $1.00 without having to lower its price.

EXHIBIT 15.8

Point of Profit Maximization

QUANTITY	MARGINAL REVENUE (MR)	MARGINAL COST (MC)	CUMULATIVE TOTAL PROFIT
0	–	–	–
1	$140	$ 90	$ 50
2	130	80	100
3	105	70	135
4	95	60	170
5	85	70	185
*6	80	80	185
7	75	90	170
8	60	110	120
9	50	130	40
10	40	150	(70)

*Profit maximization

Exhibit 15.9(a) illustrates Universal Sportswear's break-even point. As Exhibit 15.9(b) indicates, Universal Sportswear's total variable costs increase by 50¢ every time a new unit is produced, and total fixed costs remain constant at $2,000 regardless of the level of output. Therefore, for 4,000 units of output, Universal Sportswear has $2,000 in fixed costs and $2,000 in total variable costs (4,000 units × 50¢), or $4,000 in total costs.

Revenue is also $4,000 (4,000 units × $1.00), giving a net profit of zero dollars at the break-even point of 4,000 units. Notice that once the firm gets past the break-even point, the gap between total revenue and total costs gets wider and wider because both functions are assumed to be linear.

The formula for calculating break-even quantities is simple:

$$\text{Break-even quantity} = \frac{\text{Total fixed costs}}{\text{Fixed cost contribution}}$$

Fixed cost contribution is the price minus the average variable cost. Therefore, for Universal Sportswear,

$$\text{Break-even quantity} = \frac{\$2{,}000}{(\$1.00 - 50¢)} = \frac{\$2{,}000}{50¢}$$

$$= 4{,}000 \text{ units}$$

The advantage of break-even analysis is that it provides a quick estimate of how much the firm must sell to break even and how much profit can be earned if a higher sales volume is obtained. If a firm is operating close to the break-even point, it may want to see what can be done to reduce costs or increase sales.

Break-even analysis is not without several important limitations. Sometimes it is hard to know whether a cost is fixed or variable. If labour wins a tough guaranteed-employment contract, are the resulting expenses a fixed cost? Are middle-level executives' salaries fixed costs? More important than cost determination is the fact that simple break-even analysis ignores demand. How does Universal Sportswear know it can sell 4,000 units at $1.00? Could it sell the same 4,000 units at $2.00 or even $5.00? Obviously, this information would profoundly affect the firm's pricing decisions.

Price competition was turned on its head with the introduction of the euro in 2002. Now consumers across the European Union can compare prices as never before, as explained in the "Global Perspectives" box.

EXHIBIT 15.9

Costs, Revenues, and Break-Even Point for Universal Sportswear

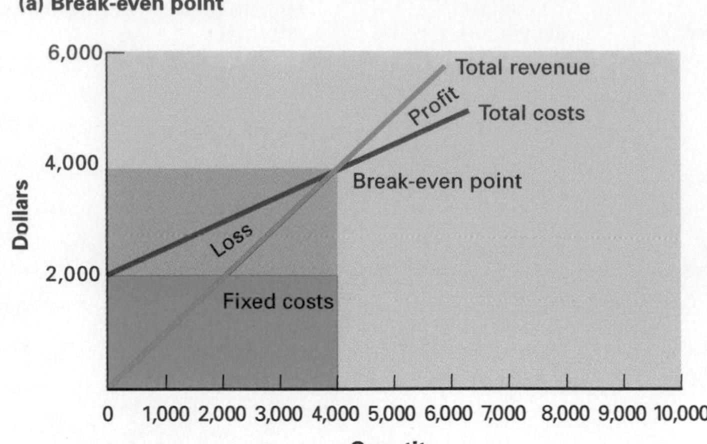

(b) Costs and revenues

Output	Total fixed costs	Average variable costs	Total variable costs	Average total costs	Average revenue (price)	Total revenue	Total costs	Profit or loss
500	$2,000	$0.50	$ 250	$4.50	$1.00	$ 500	$2,250	($1,750)
1,000	2,000	0.50	500	2.50	1.00	1,000	2,500	(1,500)
1,500	2,000	0.50	750	1.83	1.00	1,500	2,750	(1,250)
2,000	2,000	0.50	1,000	1.50	1.00	2,000	3,000	(1,000)
2,500	2,000	0.50	1,250	1.30	1.00	2,500	3,250	(750)
3,000	2,000	0.50	1,500	1.17	1.00	3,000	3,500	(500)
3,500	2,000	0.50	1,750	1.07	1.00	3,500	3,750	(250)
*4,000	2,000	0.50	2,000	1.00	1.00	4,000	4,000	(0)
4,500	2,000	0.50	2,250	.94	1.00	4,500	4,250	250
5,000	2,000	0.50	2,500	.90	1.00	5,000	4,500	500
5,500	2,000	0.50	2,750	.86	1.00	5,500	4,750	750
6,000	2,000	0.50	3,000	.83	1.00	6,000	5,000	1,000

*Break-even point

6 Demonstrate how the product life cycle, competition, distribution and promotion strategies, customer demands, the Internet and extranets, and perceptions of quality can affect price

>> OTHER DETERMINANTS OF PRICE

Other factors besides demand and costs can influence price. For example, the stages in the product life cycle, competition, the product distribution strategy, promotion strategy, and perceived quality can all affect pricing.

Stages in the Product Life Cycle

As a product moves through its life cycle, the demand for the product and the competitive conditions tend to change:

- *Introductory stage:* Management usually sets prices high during the introductory stage. One reason is that it hopes to recover its development costs quickly. In addition, demand originates in the core of the market (the customers whose needs ideally match the product's attributes) and thus is relatively inelastic. On the other hand, if the target market is highly price sensitive, management often finds it better to price the product at the market level or lower. For example, when Kraft Foods brought out Country Time lemonade, it was priced like similar products in the highly competitive beverage market because the market was price sensitive.

GLOBAL **PERSPECTIVES**

The Euro Shines a Bright Light on Price Differentials across Europe

On the front page of the European edition of *The Guardian*, a British newspaper, is a small table showing the price of the newspaper in both dollars and euros (€) for over thirty countries, from Albania ($2.00) to Ukraine ($3.50). It comes as a surprise that readers in Greece and Portugal pay €1.67, in France €2.13, and in Finland and the Netherlands as much as €2.61. Before euro prices, such price differentials were hard to spot. Now they are glaring.

The price information on the front of *The Economist*, a British journal, tells a different story, with prices bunched closely around €4.30. In some markets that means a small price cut, in others an increase. The only euro-zone country where the price remains out of line is Greece, which joined the European Union's monetary union later than the other members and has relatively low prices for newspapers and magazines.

The Economist's managers decided as long as three years ago to equalize European prices as far as possible, believing that it was better to send a consistent price signal to customers than to price by market. Since then, the price has been capped in the more expensive markets and steadily increased in the cheaper ones to achieve the necessary convergence. The eventual common newsstand price of €4.35 was not aligned to the lowest euro-zone price because that would have been too costly; nor was it set to match the highest one because that would have risked losing sales in cheaper markets. Like businesses all over Europe, *The Economist* had to make a judgment based on its knowledge of its customers and markets.

Such judgments are necessary because the greater transparency the single currency brings to prices will make a big difference to the way business is conducted. Simple economic theory suggests that savvy consumers now look across European markets and note where the price of a good or service is lowest. They then either purchase the good or service there, or they use the information to prevail upon their more expensive local provider to bring the price down. The overall effect across dozens of sectors is deflationary. In the face of relentless downward pressure on prices, some businesses are struggling to maintain their profitability.

This deflationary pressure is applied not only by consumers but also by businesses to their own suppliers, thus reinforcing the trend. Big retailers are increasingly seeking to buy from manufacturers at a single euro price, whereas in the past they typically bought locally in each country where they trade. Manufacturers had been able to maintain price differentials because their customers found it difficult to compare prices. With the euro, it is now much easier.

Examples of big price differentials abound. Recently, a 10-kilometre taxi ride in Lisbon was a quarter of the price of a similar journey in Luxembourg. A kilo of beef cost €15 in Paris, €21 in Amsterdam, and €9.90 in Madrid. A visit to the cinema in Dublin or Brussels cost €8, but in Athens moviegoers paid only €5.90 to see the same film. A 5-kilogram jumbo pack of laundry detergent cost €9.80 in Brussels, but an extortionate €24.30 in Helsinki. And a packet of proprietary aspirin cost €3.70 in Athens, but €12.90 in Rome and Berlin.

How can such differences be justified? Some companies continue to cling to traditional explanations involving different local tax rates, varying transport costs, and so on. The truth is that until now manufacturers and retailers alike have deliberately exploited the fact that consumers found it hard to make price comparisons. They have also used sophisticated ways of disguising their true prices from one another.[9]

If you were a manufacturer in the European Union, how would you handle different prices in different euro-zone countries? Do you think that the euro will be beneficial for European Union consumers? Why or why not? Do customs, such as the French preference for side-loading washing machines and the German preference for top-loaders, have any impact on pricing strategy?

- *Growth stage:* As the product enters the growth stage, prices generally begin to stabilize for several reasons. First, competitors have entered the market, increasing the available supply. Second, the product has begun to appeal to a broader market, often lower income groups. Finally, economies of scale are lowering costs, and the savings can be passed on to the consumer in the form of lower prices.
- *Maturity stage:* Maturity usually brings further price decreases as competition increases and inefficient, high-cost firms are eliminated. Distribution channels become a significant cost factor, however, because of the need to offer wide product lines for highly segmented markets, extensive service requirements, and the sheer number of dealers necessary to absorb high-volume production. The manufacturers that remain in the market toward the end of the maturity stage typically offer similar prices. Usually, only the most efficient remain, and they have comparable costs. At this stage, price increases are usually cost initiated, not demand initiated. Nor do price reductions in the late phase of maturity stimulate much demand. Because

ON LINE 

FragranceNet

Compare the effect of product life cycle on pricing. Compare FragranceNet's prices for White Shoulders (introduced in 1935) and Cool Water (introduced in 1996). Do the prices surprise you? What can you conclude about the product life cycle of each fragrance? Does the cycle even apply to perfumes?

http://www.fragrancenet.com

demand is limited and producers have similar cost structures, the remaining competitors will probably match price reductions.

- *Decline stage:* The final stage of the life cycle may see further price decreases as the few remaining competitors try to salvage the last vestiges of demand. When only one firm is left in the market, prices begin to stabilize. In fact, prices may eventually rise dramatically if the product survives and moves into the specialty goods category, as horse-drawn carriages and vinyl records have.

The Competition

Competition varies during the product life cycle so, at times, it may affect pricing decisions. Although a firm may not have any competition at first, the high prices it charges may eventually induce another firm to enter the market. Several Internet auto sellers, such as Autobytel.com, have sprung up in response to the perceived high profit margins earned by car dealers.

On the other hand, intense competition can sometimes lead to price wars. What pulls companies into such self-defeating price wars? Often they make the mistake of measuring their success by market share rather than by profitability—but something more is at play. Michael Marn, a partner at McKinsey & Company, the worldwide management consulting company, who heads its pricing practice worldwide, says that price wars are often caused by companies misreading or misunderstanding competitors. Marn tells of one McKinsey client, a company that dominated the market for adhesive labels nationwide. After a small competitor built a tiny factory with no prospects for further expansion, the company reacted with a price cut of 15 to 20 percent and, says Marn, "gave away profitability for two years." Typically, concludes Marn, price wars are "overreactions to threats that either aren't there at all or are not as big as they seem."[10]

selling against the brand
Stocking well-known branded items at high prices in order to sell store brands at discounted prices.

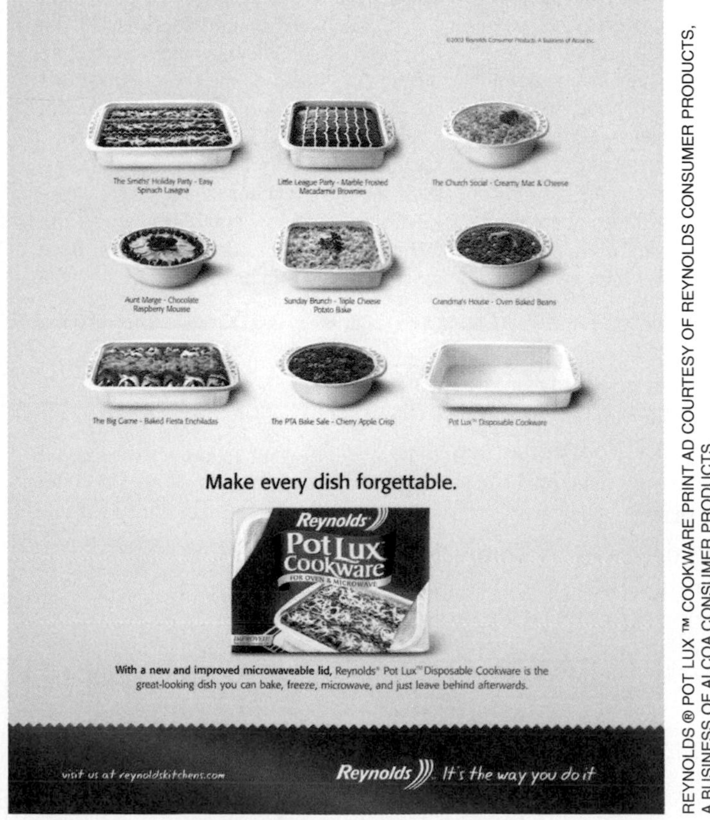

Make every dish forgettable.
Reynolds
Pot Lux
Cookware
With a new and improved microwaveable lid, Reynolds® Pot Lux™ Disposable Cookware is the great-looking dish you can bake, freeze, microwave, and just leave behind afterwards.
visit us at reynoldskitchens.com
Reynolds It's the way you do it

REYNOLDS ® POT LUX ™ COOKWARE PRINT AD COURTESY OF REYNOLDS CONSUMER PRODUCTS, A BUSINESS OF ALCOA CONSUMER PRODUCTS.

Management usually sets prices higher during the introductory stage of the product life cycle. Still, it must be careful not to set the price so high that it turns customers off. With a product innovation like Reynold's PotLux disposable cookware, how do you think marketing managers decide on a base price?

Distribution Strategy

An effective distribution network can often overcome minor flaws in the marketing mix.[11] For example, although consumers may perceive a price as being higher than normal, they may buy the product anyway if it is being sold at a convenient retail outlet.

Adequate distribution for a new product can often be attained by offering a larger-than-usual profit margin to distributors. A variation on this strategy is to give dealers a large trade allowance to help offset the costs of promotion and further stimulate demand at the retail level.

Manufacturers have gradually been losing control within the distribution channel to wholesalers and retailers, which often adopt pricing strategies that serve their own purposes. For instance, some distributors are **selling against the brand:** they place well-known brands on the shelves at high prices while offering other brands—typically, their private-label brands, such as Craftsman tools, Mastercraft auto parts, or Life Brand cosmetics—at lower prices. Of course, sales of the higher-priced brands decline.

Manufacturers can regain some control over price by using an exclusive distribution system, by franchising, or by avoiding doing business with price-cutting discounters. Manufacturers can also package merchandise with the selling price marked on it or place goods on consignment. The best way for manufacturers to control prices, however, is to develop brand loyalty in consumers by delivering quality and value.

The Impact of the Internet and Extranets

AP/WIDE WORLD PHOTOS

Competition can be a significant factor in pricing. Microsoft's Xbox and Sony's PlayStation are continuing to go head-to-head, much like Coke and Pepsi. Such intense competition has a definite impact on pricing.

The Internet, corporate networks, and wireless setups are linking people, machines, and companies around the globe—and connecting sellers and buyers as never before. This link is enabling buyers to quickly and easily compare products and prices, putting them in a better bargaining position. At the same time, the technology allows sellers to collect detailed data about customers' buying habits, preferences, and even spending limits so that they can tailor their products and prices. For a time, these developments raised hopes of a more efficient marketplace.

Unfortunately, the promise of pricing efficiencies for Internet retailers and lower costs for consumers has run headlong into reality. Flawed pricing strategies have taken much of the blame for the continuing implosion of dot.coms. Too many merchants offered deep discounts that made profits all but impossible to achieve. Other e-retailers have felt the consumer backlash against price discrimination, as the Internet has given shoppers the ability to better detect price discrepancies and bargains. The dot.com survivors must now figure out if it is even possible to take advantage of the Internet's unique capabilities to set dynamic prices, which would better reflect a customer's willingness to pay more under different circumstances.

"Before the Internet existed, retail was a very competitive, difficult, low-margin business," says economist Austan Goolsbee. "With the advent of Internet retailers, there was a brief moment in which they and others believed they had broken the iron chain of low margins and high competition in retail by introducing the Internet. Now, retail on-line is starting to look like retail off-line—very competitive, profit margins squeezed. In all, a very tough place to be."[12]

Setting prices on the Internet was expected to offer retailers a number of advantages. To begin with, it would be far easier to raise or lower prices in response to demand, without the need for a clerk to run through a store with a pricing gun. On-line prices could be changed in smaller increments—even by just a penny or two—as frequently as a merchant desired, making it possible to fine-tune pricing strategies.

But the real payoff was supposed to be better information on exactly how price-conscious customers are. For instance, knowing that customer A doesn't care whether an Oscar-nominated DVD in her shopping basket costs $24.95 or $29.95 would leave an enterprising merchant free to charge the higher price on the spot. In contrast, knowing that customer B is going to put author John le Carré's latest thriller back on the shelf unless it's priced at $20, instead of $28, would open an opportunity for a bookseller to make the sale by cutting the price in real time.

The idea was to charge exactly what the market will bear. But putting this into practice on-line has turned out to be exceptionally difficult, in part because the Internet has also empowered consumers to compare prices to find out if other merchants are offering a better deal or if other consumers are getting a bigger break. And the Internet has also made it easier for consumers to complain. For example, Amazon.com faced a problem when customers learned they had paid different prices for the same DVD movies as a result of a marketing test in which the retailer varied prices to gauge the effect on demand. After complaints from irate consumers, who learned from on-line chat boards that they had paid higher prices, Amazon announced it would refund the difference between the highest and lowest prices in the test.

While the Internet helps drive down prices by making it easier for consumers to shop for the best bargain, it also makes it possible for on-line merchants to monitor each other's prices—whether higher or lower—and to adjust them in concert without overtly colluding. As long as the number of retailers in a given market is relatively small, it is now much simpler for merchants to signal each other by changing prices for short periods—long enough for their competitors to notice, but not so long that consumers do. Airlines have long used on-line reservation systems to signal fare changes to one another.

Recent research has supported the notion that on-line merchants can find ways to raise prices. One study looked at the on-line pricing of books at Amazon.com and its closest competitors such as chapters.indigo.ca. The researchers found that for over half the items studied, all of the Internet booksellers charged virtually the same price, differing at most by five cents.[13]

On-line price-comparison engines, known as shopbots, were supposed to make it easy for consumers to find the lowest prices for any goods. But making effective use of competitive price information has been more difficult for consumers than originally thought. For one thing, price comparisons, which must include a range of shipping options and fees, taxes, and any special offers from individual merchants, are far from straightforward. And the time it takes to look up the best prices for a collection of items—say, books or DVDs—can outweigh price savings of a dollar or two.

"Shopbots are tedious to use," says Karen Clay, an economist, who notes that consumers also tend to be willing to pay more for goods from familiar on-line retailers. Since trying a new retailer always involves uncertainty as to whether goods will arrive on time, whether customer service is satisfactory, and even whether the merchant has honestly posted its prices, Clay says, "uncertainty can easily outweigh what you could save by shopping somewhere else."[14]

One area where the Internet is having a major impact on pricing is the bargaining power between buyers and sellers. For example, a group of 40-plus retailers, with nearly three and a half times the buying power of Wal-Mart, have formed the WorldWide Retail Exchange. On the manufacturing side, Procter & Gamble, Kraft Foods, and others have invested more than $250 million to build the business-to-business (B2B) megamarket Transora. With these types of developments, suppliers will be facing a world in which there are no weak customers. Every buyer will wield Wal-Mart's bargaining power.[15]

extranet
A private electronic network that links a company with its suppliers and customers.

As bargaining power evens out, companies are reaching price agreements more quickly and disseminating this information throughout the channel of distribution. Manufacturers are creating private networks, or **extranets,** that link them with their suppliers and customers. These systems make it possible to get a precise handle on inventory, costs, and demand and, after bargaining with suppliers, adjust prices instantly. In the past, communicating price changes took time. For a company with a large product line, it could take months for price adjustments to filter down to distributors, retailers, and salespeople. Streamlined networks reduce cost and time to near zero.

Internet Auctions

The Internet auction business is huge. Part of the lure of buying on-line is that shoppers don't have to go to a flea market or use up a coveted weekend day or worry about the weather. Plus, bidding itself can be fun and exciting. A few of the most popular consumer auction sites are the following:

- http://www.auctions.amazon.com: Links to Sotheby's for qualified sellers of high-end items.
- http://www.ebay.ca: The most popular auction site.
- http://www.auctions.yahoo.com: Free listings and numerous selling categories, including international auctions.

Even though consumers are spending billions on Internet auctions, B2B auctions are likely to be the dominant form in the future. FreeMarkets, Inc., a publicly traded B2B exchange, has hosted on-line reverse auctions, in which suppliers bid for a factory's component order, involving $5.4 billion of transactions. Among the companies using FreeMarkets are Owens

ON LINE

BotSpot

Want to find out more about shopping (and other) bots? Go to BotSpot and click on the list of bots. Under "Shopping Bots," you'll find dozens of interesting bots that drag the Internet for the lowest prices on everything from computers to brokers and prescriptions to flowers. Shop for something you need using a bot and see how satisfied you are with the shopping and pricing functions.

http://www.botspot.com

Corning, GlaxoSmithKline PLC, and Magna, the largest auto-parts company in Canada.[16] As an example of the benefits of using FreeMarkets.com, one company paid $175,000 for its last batch of plastic auto parts—before turning to auctions. This time, after 33 minutes of frenzied bidding by 25 competing suppliers, the price came down to $118,000.[17]

FreeMarkets has quickly moved beyond selling metal and plastic parts and is auctioning tax preparation services, relocation services, temporary help, and other services. And it's just getting started: retailers have created the Worldwide Retail Exchange and GlobalNetXchange, and dozens of similar services are running or in the works.

Recently, Whirlpool began holding on-line auctions. Participants bid on the price of the items that they would supply to Whirlpool, but with a twist: they had to include the date when Whirlpool would have to pay for the items. The company wanted to see which suppliers would offer the longest grace period before requiring payment. Five auctions held over five months helped Whirlpool uncover savings of close to $2 million and more than doubled the grace period. Whirlpool's success is a sign that the B2B auction world is shifting from haggling over prices to niggling over parameters of the deal. Warranties, delivery dates, transportation methods, customer support, financing options, and quality have all become bargaining chips. "Price-only auctions are dead," says Sarah Pfaff, co-founder and executive vice president of eBreviate, a subsidiary of EDS. "Businesses can't afford to rely only on the lowest price."[18]

Promotion Strategy

Price is often used as a promotional tool to increase consumer interest. The weekly flyers sent out by grocery stores, for instance, advertise many products with special low prices. Crested Butte Ski Resort in Colorado tried a unique twist on price promotions. It made the unusual offer of free skiing between Thanksgiving and Christmas. Its only revenues were voluntary contributions from lodging and restaurant owners who benefited from the droves of skiers taking advantage of the promotion. Lodging during the slack period is now booked solid, and on the busiest days 9,000 skiers jam slopes designed for about 6,500.

Pricing can be a tool for trade promotions as well. For example, Levi's Dockers (casual men's pants) are very popular with men between 25 and 45. Sensing an opportunity, rival pants maker Bugle Boy began offering similar pants at cheaper wholesale prices, which gave retailers a bigger gross margin than they were getting with Dockers. Levi Strauss had to either lower prices or risk its $400 million annual Docker sales. Although Levi Strauss intended its cheapest Dockers to retail for $35, it started selling Dockers to retailers for $18 a pair. Retailers could then advertise Dockers at a very attractive retail price of $25.

Demands of Large Customers

Large customers of manufacturers such as Wal-Mart, Zellers, Canadian Tire, and others often make specific pricing demands. Large retailers are making greater-than-ever demands on their suppliers to cover the heavy discounts and markdowns on their own selling floors. They want suppliers to guarantee their stores' profit margins, and they insist on cash rebates if the guarantee isn't met. They are also exacting fines for violations of ticketing, packing, and shipping rules. Cumulatively, the demands are nearly wiping out profits for all but the very biggest suppliers.

In the past when a garment maker sold to a store, the two parties would agree on a retail price, and at the end of the season, the supplier would rebate some of the cost of markdowns. Discounts and markdowns were far rarer then than they are today: department stores could afford plenty of sales help to push products. As stores cut labour costs, however, they came to rely on promotional markdowns and sales to move goods—with suppliers covering profit-margin shortfalls.

The Relationship of Price to Quality

When a purchase decision involves great uncertainty, consumers tend to rely on a high price as a predictor of good quality. Reliance on price as an indicator of quality seems to occur for all products, but it reveals itself more strongly for some items than for

COURTESY OF TIGI

Hair-care products benefit from the customer perception that higher prices mean higher quality. Salon products, like Bed Head and Paul Mitchell, convey the message of quality through high prices and exclusive distribution. In fact, customers may assume that the products are better because of the expertise of the hairdresser in whose salon the products are sold.

others.[19] Among the products that benefit from this phenomenon are coffee, stockings, aspirin, salt, floor wax, shampoo, clothing, furniture, perfume, whiskey, and many services. If the consumer obtains additional information, for instance, about the brand or the store, then reliance on price as an indicator of quality decreases.[20] In the absence of other information, people typically assume that prices are higher because the products contain better materials, because they are made more carefully, or, in the case of professional services, because the provider has more expertise.[21] Knowledgeable merchants take these consumer attitudes into account when devising their pricing strategies. **Prestige pricing** is charging a high price to help promote a high-quality image. A successful prestige pricing strategy requires a retail price that is reasonably consistent with consumers' expectations. No one goes shopping at Gucci in Toronto and expects to pay $9.95 for a pair of loafers. In fact, demand would fall drastically at such a low price. A new mustard packaged in a crockery jar was not successful until its price was doubled.

Consumers also expect private or store brands to be cheaper than national brands. However, if the price difference between a private brand and a nationally distributed manufacturer's brand is *too* great, consumers tend to believe that the private brand is inferior. On the other hand, if the savings aren't big enough, there is little incentive to buy the private brand. One study of scanner data found that if the price difference between the national brand and the private brand was less than 10 percent, people tended not to buy the private brand. If the price difference was greater than 20 percent, consumers perceived the private brand to be inferior.[22]

prestige pricing
Charging a high price to help promote a high-quality image.

ON LINE

De Beers

Rolex

How comfortable would you be buying a high-ticket item via the Internet? Check out some premium brands and decide whether you would take the plunge without seeing or holding the merchandise. Compare what you find at De Beers and Rolex. What do their Internet selling strategies say about their brands?

http://www.debeers.com

http://www.rolex.com

>> CONNECT IT

Look back at the story at the beginning of this chapter on how Major League Baseball is charging fees for Internet video clips. Costs, revenues, and profits are directly related. Revenue minus costs equals profits. Increasing revenues, lowering costs, or both, can increase profits. The Internet is already having a major impact on pricing. Consumers are finding better deals and making better decisions by comparing prices. Old-line manufacturers face the dilemma of competing directly with their channel members if the manufacturer sells through its own website.

Yield management systems will help boost revenues of not only service businesses but also old-line manufacturers. This in turn will mean increased profits for the organization.

Price can have an impact on perceived quality, depending on a number of issues, such as the type of product, advertising, and the consumer's personality. For durable goods, price plays a key role in determining quality if consumers are focusing on prestige and/or durability as determinants of quality.

REVIEW IT

1 **Discuss the importance of pricing decisions to the economy and to the individual firm.** Pricing plays an integral role in the Canadian economy by allocating goods and services among consumers, governments, and businesses. Pricing is essential in business because it creates revenue, which is the basis of all business activity. In setting prices, marketing managers strive to find a level high enough to produce a satisfactory profit.

1.1 Why is pricing so important to the marketing manager?

2 **List and explain a variety of pricing objectives.** Establishing realistic and measurable pricing objectives is a critical part of any firm's marketing strategy. Pricing objectives are commonly classified into three categories: profit oriented, sales oriented, and status quo. Profit-oriented pricing is based on profit maximization, a satisfactory level of profit, or a target return on investment. The goal of profit maximization is to generate as much revenue as possible in relation to cost. Often, a more practical approach than profit maximization is setting prices to produce profits that will satisfy management and stockholders. The most common profit-oriented strategy is pricing for a specific return on investment relative to a firm's assets. The second type of pricing objective is sales oriented, and focuses on either maintaining a percentage share of the market or maximizing dollar or unit sales. The third type of pricing objective aims to maintain the status quo by matching competitors' prices.

2.1 Give an example of each major type of pricing objective.

3 **Explain the role of demand in price determination.** Demand is a key determinant of price. When establishing prices, a firm must first determine demand for its product. A typical demand schedule shows an inverse relationship between quantity demanded and price: When price is lowered, sales increase; when price is increased, the quantity demanded falls. For prestige products, however, there may be a direct relationship between demand and price: The quantity demanded would increase as price increases.

Marketing managers must also consider demand elasticity when setting prices. Elasticity of demand is the degree to which the quantity demanded fluctuates with changes in price. If consumers are sensitive to changes in price, demand is elastic; if they are insensitive to price changes, demand is inelastic. Thus, an increase in price will result in lower sales for an elastic product and little or no loss in sales for an inelastic product.

3.1 Explain the role of supply and demand in determining price.

3.2 If a firm can increase its total revenue by raising its price, shouldn't it do so?

3.3 Explain the concepts of elastic and inelastic demand. Why should managers understand these concepts?

4 **Understand the concept of yield management systems.** Yield management systems use complex mathematical software to profitably fill unused capacity. The software uses techniques such as discounting early purchases, limiting early sales at these discounted prices, and overbooking capacity. These systems are primarily used in service businesses and are substantially raising revenues.

4.1 Why are so many companies adopting yield management systems?

4.2 • How is yield management helping companies achieve competitive advantage? Use InfoTrac® College Edition to find out (http://infotrac.thomsonlearning.com). Run a keyword search for "yield management" and read through the headlines to see what industries are profiled most often. Then read the article from *Computerworld* titled "Software Fills Trucks, Maximizes Revenue: Sitton Motor Lines Takes Lead in Applying Analysis Tool Outside the Travel Industry" by Matthew Schwartz. Answer the following questions:

- How is Sitton Motor Lines using yield management principles and software?
- Describe the implementation of the new software.
- What other industries are cited as good candidates for yield management?

5 **Describe cost-oriented pricing strategies.** The other major determinant of price is cost. Marketers use several cost-oriented pricing strategies. To cover their own expenses and obtain a profit, wholesalers and retailers commonly use markup pricing: They tack an extra amount onto the manufacturer's original price. Another pricing technique is to maximize profits by setting price where marginal revenue equals marginal cost. Still another pricing strategy determines how much a firm must sell to break even and uses this amount as a reference point for adjusting price.

5.1 WRITING Your firm has based its pricing strictly on cost in the past. As the newly hired marketing manager, you believe this policy should change. Write the president a memo explaining your reasons.

5.2 Why is it important for managers to understand the concept of break-even points? Are there any drawbacks?

6 **Demonstrate how the product life cycle, competition, distribution and promotion strategies, customer demands, the Internet and extranets, and perceptions of quality can affect price.** The price of a product normally changes as it moves through the life cycle and as demand for the product and competitive conditions change. Management often sets a high price at the introductory stage, and the high price tends to attract competition. The competition usually drives prices down because individual competitors lower prices to gain market share.

Adequate distribution for a new product can sometimes be obtained by offering a larger-than-usual profit margin to wholesalers and retailers. The Internet enables consumers to compare products and prices quickly and efficiently. Extranets help control costs and lower prices. Price is also used as a promotional tool to attract customers. Special low prices often attract new customers and entice existing customers to buy more. Demands of large customers can squeeze the profit margins of suppliers.

Perceptions of quality can also influence pricing strategies. A firm trying to project a prestigious image often charges a premium price for a product. Consumers tend to equate high prices with high quality.

6.1 TEAM Divide the class into teams of five. Each team will be assigned a different grocery store from a different chain. (An independent is fine.) Appoint a group leader. The group leaders should meet as a group and pick 15 nationally branded grocery items. Each item should be specifically described as to brand name and size of the package. Each team will then proceed to its assigned store and collect price data on the 15 items. The team should also gather price data on 15 similar store brands and 15 generics, if possible.

Each team should present its results to the class and discuss why there are price variations between stores, national brands, store brands, and generics.

As a next step, go back to your assigned store and share the overall results with the store manager. Bring back the manager's comments and share them with the class.

6.2 How does the stage of a product's life cycle affect price? Give some examples.

6.3 ON LINE Go to http://www.priceline.com. Can you research a ticket's price before purchasing it? What products and services are available for purchasing? How comfortable are you with naming your own price? Relate the supply and demand curves to customer-determined pricing.

Go to one of the Internet auction sites listed in this chapter. Report to the class on how the auction process works and the items being auctioned.

6.4 How important is pricing when a company is entering new markets? The article "Is the Price Right?" by Peter Meyer in *Across the Board* can tell you. Print out the article using InfoTrac® College Edition (http://infotrac.thomsonlearning.com) and then underline all of the chapter concepts that it discusses. What issues does the article address that the chapter does not? What issues does the chapter address that are not included in the article?

DEFINE IT

average total cost (ATC) 486
average variable cost (AVC) 486
break-even analysis 488
demand 480
elastic demand 481
elasticity of demand 481
extranet 494
fixed cost 486
inelastic demand 481
keystoning 487
marginal cost (MC) 486
marginal revenue (MR) 488
market share 478
markup pricing 486
prestige pricing 496
price 476
price equilibrium 481
profit 476
profit maximization 488
return on investment (ROI) 478
revenue 476
selling against the brand 492
status quo pricing 479
supply 480
unitary elasticity 483
variable cost 486
yield management systems (YMS) 485

APPLY IT

Bernie Opinal has decided to wash windows in his neighbourhood during spring break. Bernie lives with his parents in a neighbourhood with homes in the 280- to 325-square-metre range. Bernie plans to hire his little brother, Butch, to help him. His plan is to clean every window inside and out, plus replace any missing caulking or weatherstripping at no extra charge. His estimated demand and associated costs are as follows:

OUTPUT	P	AR	MR	MC	AVC	ATC
0				–	–	–
1	$140.00			$31.00	$31.00	$54.00
2	130.00			28.00	29.50	41.00
3	120.00			31.00	30.00	37.67
4	110.00			34.00	31.00	36.75
5	100.00			37.00	32.20	36.80
6	90.00			40.00	33.50	37.33
7	80.00			43.00	34.86	38.14
8	70.00			46.00	36.25	39.13
9	60.00			49.00	37.67	40.22
10	50.00			52.00	39.10	41.40

QUESTIONS

1. What are the marginal revenue and average revenue at each price?
2. How many houses should Bernie contract with to maximize profits?
3. What is the total profit at profit maximization?

THINK ABOUT IT

Advanced Bio Medics (ABM) has invented a new stem cell-based drug that will arrest even advanced forms of lung cancer. Development costs were actually quite low because the drug was an accidental discovery by scientists working on a different project. To stop the disease requires a regimen of taking one pill per week for 20 weeks. There is no substitute offered by competitors. ABM is thinking that it could maximize its profits by charging $10,000 per pill. Of course, many will die because they can't afford the medicine at this price.

QUESTIONS

1. Should ABM maximize its profits?
2. Does the CMA Code of Ethics address this issue? Go to **http://www.the-cma.org/consumer/ethics.cfm** and review the code. Then write a brief paragraph on what the CMA Code of Ethics contains that relates to ABM's dilemma.

TRY IT

© INDEX STOCK IMAGERY/ZEPHYR PICTURE

A Taste of Class

In 1991, JoAnn James left her job at a popular Calgary restaurant to start her own catering company, A Taste of Class (ATOC). Soon she found a partner, Ernie Block, and the company quickly grew to annual revenues of $250,000. Specializing in traditional Canadian food, ATOC is an off-premise catering company that serves both the business and consumer markets.

JoAnn's son, Mark, joined the business while still in high school and worked there through university. He eventually bought out his mother's partner in 2001. Mark's first concern was to make sure that he did not alienate his customer base by implementing any changes to the basic formula that had made ATOC successful. But Mark had a goal of reaching $1 million in sales by his fifth year of partnership in the company, so he knew that continuing to operate out of the existing location—a moderate-sized kitchen with no office space—would not work in the long run.

By 2005, four years into his plan, he was still $250,000 away from his goal. Although Mark has made great strides and has been very creative in growing the business by following commonsense marketing techniques, he has not implemented any formal marketing plan. About one-third of his business comes from corporate clients, one-third from weddings, and one-third from other special occasions.

ATOC has a traditional product mix: hot buffet, cold buffet, hot sit-down, breakfast buffet, box lunches, and dropoffs (hot and cold meals). The company can serve parties of 25 to several thousand, all with only six full-time employees (i.e., cooks) and a small army of contract servers. On any given week, ATOC will have four to five caterings a day, with 20 to 25 each weekend day.

Mark's menus are very straightforward (roast beef and gravy, green beans, lasagna, lemon chicken, etc.). He thinks that they may be too simplistic. In fact, some employees want to incorporate more exotic, gourmet dishes into the company's offerings. Mark wants to stick to the company's core business, but he admits that the *language* used to describe his menus could be a bit more interesting. Mark knows that his best-value menu is his gourmet buffet (carved meat, sides, salads, and desserts), his best-selling food items are on his hot buffet (roast beef and gravy, mashed potatoes, and green beans), and that his best return on investment is on hot buffet dropoffs (where he drops the food off at the client, who then returns ATOC's catering equipment). In fact, he knows that he makes a better return in general on parties for which ATOC does not provide the personnel.

Mark currently uses variable pricing: he tries to match his prices to what his prospective customers expect to pay. He has a base price for his standard menus. The base price is designed to attract the largest number of customers. He used to have tiered pricing, where an increase in the number of people to be served resulted in a per person reduction in the price of the meal. Printed menus indicated different prices for different sized groups. For example, a dinner for 10 to 20 people was priced more expensively than the same dinner for a party of 110. When the tiered prices were printed on the menu, Mark had limited flexibility in his pricing strategy. But after doing some competitive research, he discovered that it was mostly lower-end caterers that were using this pricing strategy. Mark still varies the price charged according to party size. He now does it at the bidding end, however, not on the printed menu. This change gives him greater flexibility to achieve desired profit margins. When Mark first took over the daily operations of the business, he did not raise prices. In fact, the company saw its first price increases in nearly a decade in 2002. Still, ATOC's prices are about 5 to 10 percent below the market.

QUESTIONS

1. How can Mark keep prices low without communicating a low-end, average product?
2. How can he raise prices without alienating customers who have been trained over the years to expect a deal from ATOC?
3. If A Taste of Class was using an activity-based costing method of accounting, determine which specific business activities—areas such as accounting, food costs, food preparation, marketing, and administrative activities—would contribute to the cost of each individual sale.
4. Does a yield management system make sense for A Taste of Class? If so, how would it work?

FLIP IT

Flip to Chapter 15 in your *Grademaker Study Guide* for more review opportunities, including the pretest, vocabulary review, Internet activities, study test questions, and an application exercise based on pricing concepts. How does demand determine product pricing? Can you describe cost-oriented pricing strategies? How do various elements like the PLC, competition, and others affect the pricing of an offering? If you're a bit shaky, then pick up your *Grademaker* and review.

CLICK IT

The *Marketing* website is rich with materials to help you review and master marketing concepts. Check your knowledge with the free quizzes, practise key terms using the crossword puzzles, or review key concepts using the Microsoft® PowerPoint® slides. Also on the website are updated weblinks to companies mentioned in this chapter, Internet exercises, career marketing information, and much much more! Go to http://www.lamb3e.nelson.com, read the material, and follow the convenient links.

WATCH IT

Toronto Blue Jays: Ballpark Pricing

The Toronto Blue Jays officially came into existence on June 18, 1976, when a group consisting of Imperial Trust, Ltd., Labatt's Breweries, and the Canadian Imperial Bank of Commerce paid a franchise fee of US$7 million to major league baseball. The first Blue Jays game was played at Exhibition Stadium on a very cold April 7, 1977, and 44,649 fans showed up to watch the Blue Jays defeat the Chicago White Sox 9 to 5. In its first full year, the Blue Jays set an attendance record for a new first-year major league baseball team, having sold 1,701,052 tickets.

The Blue Jays have now completed their 28th season in the American League. Over this period, the Blue Jays have lost more games than they have won. The Blue Jays now play in the SkyDome, the world's most advanced retractable-roof stadium, with a seating capacity of 50,516.

While the Blue Jays were mired in last place during the 2004 season, tickets to their games were priced in the range of $9 to $62. This pricing structure is based on the perceived value of the entertainment offered. Every season the Blue Jays have to balance two key economic factors when determining their ticket prices: the demand for seats and the skyrocketing costs of running a major league baseball club.

The Jays management does not expect consumers to be highly sensitive to ticket price fluctuations. They expect to sell a good number of tickets even as prices increase each year. This inelastic demand for baseball tickets is based on the fact that loyal baseball fans want to watch major league baseball. Loyal Blue Jays fans, moreover, are willing to pay a price to support their team. Another reason for the inelastic demand is the fact that there is no locally available substitute. While there are other sports and entertainment events available, the Blue Jays are the only major league baseball team in town (and now the only one in Canada).

Ticket prices provide a large portion of the Blue Jays revenue. Merchandising contributes as well. Blue Jays souvenirs and gifts are sold at the SkyDome, at Blue Jays Bullpen souvenir stores, at many other retail stores across Canada, through catalogues, and through the Blue Jays website. The Blue Jays merchandising managers use a prestige pricing strategy —that is, they charge high prices. For example, Blue Jays home jerseys are priced at $139.99, caps at up to $24.99, and sweatshirts at $109.99. Consumers seem to be willing to pay a high price for official, authentic merchandise that has been approved by the Blue Jays.

QUESTIONS

1. What considerations are included in the Jays ticket pricing?
2. Why is demand for Blue Jays tickets inelastic?
3. How do the Jays use price as a promotional tool?
4. What pricing strategy is used for Blue Jays merchandise?

SUGGESTED INFORMATION SOURCES

http://toronto.bluejays.mlb.com

chapter 16

Setting the Right Price

>> LEARNING OBJECTIVES

1. Describe the procedure for setting the right price
2. Identify the legal and ethical constraints on pricing decisions
3. Explain how discounts, geographic pricing, and other special pricing tactics can be used to fine-tune the base price
4. Discuss product line pricing
5. Describe the role of pricing during periods of inflation and recession

>>The personal-computer industry is indeed in the doghouse. Worldwide growth is slowing from its once-guaranteed run of 20 percent-plus a year to somewhere closer to 10 to 15 percent a year. And while the state of the economy is always mentioned as a contributor to dropping demand, analysts seem worried about something greater: saturation.

If this were not enough, Dell Computer, the investment community's perennial favourite, has launched an aggressive price war. Speaking to reporters about the current price battle, IBM's former CEO Lou Gerstner noted, "Price wars in a commodity business are really dumb." All of this raises the question: Is this a commodity business? Or has Michael Dell become smitten with a strategy that, in Gerstner's words, is less than smart?

If a commodity is a product for which no one can establish a competitive advantage, then it follows that a commodity business is one in which no participant can obtain a competitive business advantage. However, even in tough times, Dell's business model stands head and shoulders above its competitors'. Dell's competitive advantage comes not from building better boxes per se, but from building them smarter and faster, and consuming fewer resources in the process.

Much has been written about Dell's direct model, which removes the intermediaries, along with their margins, from the sales process. And others have noted that Dell's incredible five days of inventories allow it to pass on component price declines faster than anyone else in the industry. But perhaps the unique aspect of Dell's business advantage is its negative cash conversion cycle. Because it keeps only five days of inventories, manages receivables to 30 days, and pushes payables out to 59 days, the Dell model will generate cash—even if the company were to report no profit whatsoever.

Dell is clearly the low-cost leader when it comes to looking solely at the income statement. The company has continued to generate a substantial profit margin even as other vendors have struggled. For instance, IBM's personal and printing systems division is barely able to break even. However, Dell's balance-sheet advantage is the added kicker here. Even in an environment where a price war eliminates all profitability—including that of Dell—the company will remain cash-flow positive. No wonder then that Dell would be willing to start a price war, and no wonder that IBM would find it "dumb."

By pushing for market share gains through a price war, Dell has presented its competitors with a true lose–lose dilemma. On the one hand, you can try to maintain market share by pricing against Dell. The problem is that because of its business model advantage, Dell can stand in the deep end of the pool forever. A competitor wading down there will likely run out of oxygen before too long. Currently, Gateway is the only player that has followed this path, and understandably so. As the only other large player with a completely direct strategy, Gateway is best equipped to ride out the war.

The other possible response, and the one that has been chosen by IBM and Hewlett-Packard, is to declare the price war "irrational." The problem here is that along the way they will lose market share, while Dell continues the tear that led it to become the No. 1 maker of PCs in the world. Sitting out the war is as dangerous as entering it, which is why Dell's decision to push the pedal during these tough times is so remarkably shrewd.[1]

What type of basic price strategy is Dell following? What are some ways to fine-tune that strategy? What kinds of discounts can Dell offer?

ON LINE 

Dell

IBM

Hewlett-Packard

Apple

At the moment, how serious is the price war among the major PC manufacturers? Visit each company's website and look for evidence of price-cutting. How does the price war among the PC manufacturers seem to be affecting Apple?

http://www.dell.ca

http://www.ibm.ca

http://www.hp.com

http://www.apple.ca

1 Describe the procedure for setting the right price

>> HOW TO SET A PRICE ON A PRODUCT

Setting the right price on a product is a four-step process (see Exhibit 16.1):

1. Establish pricing goals.
2. Estimate demand, costs, and profits.
3. Choose a price strategy to help determine a base price.
4. Fine-tune the base price with pricing tactics.

Establish Pricing Goals

The first step in setting the right price is to establish pricing goals. Recall from Chapter 15 that pricing objectives fall into three categories: profit oriented, sales oriented, and status quo. These goals are derived from the firm's overall objectives.

A good understanding of the marketplace and of the consumer can sometimes tell a manager very quickly whether a goal is realistic. For example, if firm A has an objective of a 20 percent target return on investment (ROI), and its product development and implementation costs are $5 million, the market must be rather large or must support the price required to earn a 20 percent ROI. Assume that company B has a pricing objective that all new products must reach at least 15 percent market share within three years after their introduction. A thorough study of the environment may convince the marketing manager that the competition is too strong and the market share goal can't be met.

All pricing objectives have tradeoffs that managers must weigh. A profit maximization objective may require a bigger initial investment than the firm can commit or wants to commit. Reaching the desired market share often means sacrificing short-term profit because without careful management, long-term profit goals may not be met. Meeting the competition is the easiest pricing goal to implement. But can managers really afford to ignore demand and costs, the life-cycle stage, and other considerations? When creating pricing objectives, managers must consider these tradeoffs in light of the target customer and the environment.

EXHIBIT 16.1

Steps in Setting the Right Price on a Product

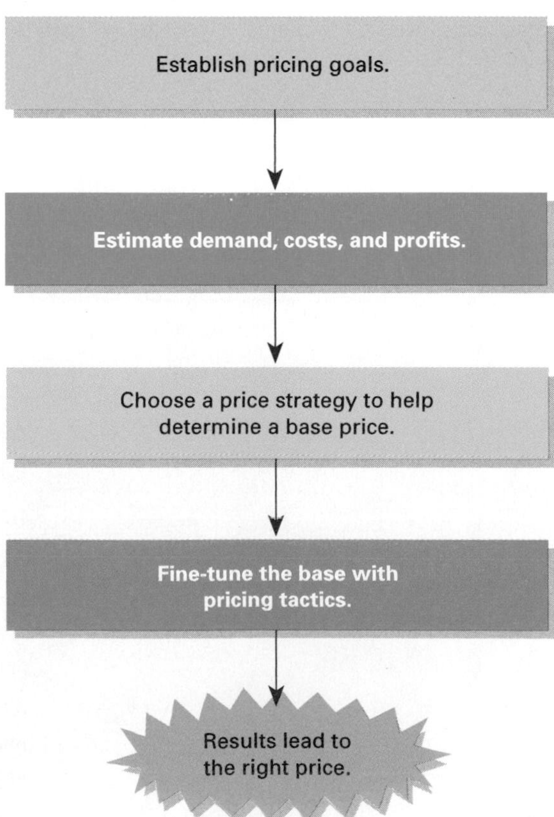

Estimate Demand, Costs, and Profits

Chapter 15 explained that total revenue is a function of price and quantity demanded and that quantity demanded depends on elasticity. After establishing pricing goals, managers should estimate total revenue at a variety of prices. Next, they should determine corresponding costs for each price. They are then ready to estimate how much profit, if any, and how much market share can be earned at each possible price. Managers can study the pricing options in light of revenues, costs, and profits. In turn, this information can help determine which price can best meet the firm's pricing goals.

Choose a Price Strategy

The basic, long-term pricing framework for a good or service should be a logical extension of the pricing objectives. The marketing manager's chosen **price strategy** defines the initial price and gives direction for price movements over the product life cycle.

price strategy
A basic, long-term pricing framework, which establishes the initial price for a product and the intended direction for price movements over the product life cycle.

The price strategy sets a competitive price in a specific market segment, based on a well-defined positioning strategy. Changing a price level from premium to superpremium may require a change in the product itself, the target customers served, the promotional strategy, or the distribution channels. Thus, changing a price strategy can require dramatic alterations in the marketing mix. A carmaker cannot successfully compete in the superpremium category if the car looks and drives like an economy car.

A company's freedom in pricing a new product and devising a price strategy depends on the market conditions and the other elements of the marketing mix. If a firm launches a new item resembling several others already on the market, its pricing freedom will be restricted. To succeed, the company will probably have to charge a price close to the average market price. In contrast, a firm that introduces a totally new product with no close substitutes will have considerable pricing freedom.

price skimming
A pricing policy whereby a firm charges a high introductory price, often coupled with heavy promotion.

Most companies do not undertake adequate research into their price strategy. McKinsey & Company's Pricing Benchmark Survey estimated that only about 15 percent of companies do serious pricing research. A Coopers & Lybrand study found that 87 percent of the surveyed companies had changed prices in the previous year. Only 13 percent of the price changes, however, came after a review of pricing strategy.[2]

These numbers indicate that strategic pricing decisions tend to be made without an understanding of the likely buyer or the competitive response. Further, the research shows that managers often make tactical pricing decisions without reviewing how they may fit into the firm's overall pricing or marketing strategy. The data suggest that many companies make pricing decisions and changes without an existing process for managing the pricing activity.

Companies that do serious planning for creating a price strategy can select from three basic approaches: price skimming, penetration pricing, and status quo pricing.

ceiva
Internet-connected digital
PICTURE FRAME
SEND THE KIDS TO
YOUR
ROOM!

Introducing Ceiva. The digital picture frame that lets you share photos over the internet. It's easy to set up. Easy to use. You don't even need a computer to receive photos. And anyone you want can send photos to your Ceiva frame from just about anywhere. Set your sights on one. And get one for your parents. So you can send the kids to their house whenever you want.
SHAREphotos EVERYDAY
ceiva.com

COURTESY OF CEIVA LOGIC, INC.

Companies with new products with no close substitutes are less restricted in the pricing strategies they can pursue. How do you think Ceiva will price this Internet-connected digital picture frame? Keep in mind that other factors besides novelty may affect the pricing strategy.

Price Skimming

Price skimming is sometimes called a "market-plus" approach to pricing because it denotes a high price relative to the prices of competing products. Radius Corporation produces unique oval-headed toothbrushes made of black neoprene that look like a scuba-diving accessory. Radius uses a skimming policy, pricing the toothbrushes at $9.95, compared to around $2.95 for a regular toothbrush.[3]

The term **price skimming** is derived from the phrase "skimming the cream off the top." Companies often use this strategy for new products when the product is perceived by the target market as having unique advantages. For example, Caterpillar sets premium prices on its construction equipment to support and capture its high-perceived value. Genzyme Corporation introduced Ceredase as the first effective treatment for Gaucher's disease. The pill allows patients to avoid years of painful physical deterioration and lead normal lives. A year's supply for one patient can exceed $300,000.

As a product progresses through its life cycle, the firm may lower its price to successfully reach larger market segments. Economists have described this type of pricing as "sliding down the demand curve." Not all companies slide down the curve. Genentech's TPA, a drug that clears blood clots, was still priced at $2,200 a dose four years after its introduction, despite competition from a much lower-priced competitor.

Price skimming works best when the market is willing to buy the product even though it carries an above-average price. If, for example, some purchasing agents feel that Caterpillar equipment is far superior to competitors' products, then Caterpillar can charge premium prices successfully. Firms can also effectively use price skimming when a product is well protected legally, when it represents a technological breakthrough, or when it has in some other way blocked the entry of competitors. Managers may follow a skimming strategy when production cannot be expanded rapidly because of technological difficulties, shortages, or constraints imposed by the skill and time required to produce a product. As long as demand is greater than supply, skimming is an attainable strategy.

A successful skimming strategy enables management to recover its product development or "educational" costs quickly. Even if the market perceives an introductory price as too high, managers can easily correct the problem by lowering the price. Firms often feel it is better to test the market at a high price and then lower the price if sales are too slow. They are tacitly saying, "If there are any premium-price buyers in the market, let's reach them first and maximize our revenue per unit." Successful skimming strategies are not limited to products. Well-known athletes, entertainers, lawyers, and hairstylists are experts at price skimming.[4] Naturally, a skimming strategy will encourage competitors to enter the market.

Penetration Pricing

penetration pricing
A pricing policy whereby a firm charges a relatively low price for a product initially as a way to reach the mass market.

Penetration pricing is at the opposite end of the spectrum from skimming. **Penetration pricing** means charging a relatively low price for a product as a way to reach the mass market. The low price is designed to capture a large share of a substantial market, resulting in lower production costs. If a marketing manager has made obtaining a large market share the firm's pricing objective, penetration pricing is a logical choice.

Penetration pricing does mean lower profit per unit. Therefore, to reach the break-even point, it requires a higher volume of sales than would a skimming policy. If reaching a high volume of sales takes a long time, then the recovery of product development costs will also be slow. As you might expect, penetration pricing tends to discourage competition.

A penetration strategy tends to be effective in a price-sensitive market. Price should decline more rapidly when demand is elastic because the market can be expanded through a lower price. Also, price sensitivity and greater competitive pressure should lead to a lower initial price and a relatively slow decline in the price later. WestJet's success is based on penetration pricing. By flying primarily Boeing 737s, it realizes efficiencies in stocking parts and training pilots and mechanics. It also saves by avoiding a costly computer reservation system and by not serving meals.

If a firm has a fixed cost structure and each sale provides a large contribution to those fixed costs, penetration pricing can boost sales and provide large increases to profits—but only if the market size grows or if competitors choose not to respond. Low prices can draw additional buyers to enter the market. The increased sales can justify production expansion or the adoption of new technologies, both of which can reduce costs. And, if firms have excess capacity, even low-priced business can provide incremental dollars toward fixed costs.

WestJet

It's no secret that WestJet has continuously attempted to underprice Air Canada. But just how much cheaper are WestJet fares? The next time you travel, take the time to compare WestJet's prices with Air Canada's. Has Air Canada met the challenge of WestJet's penetration pricing strategy? If so, how?

http://www.westjet.ca

http://www.aircanada.ca

Penetration pricing can also be effective if an experience curve will cause costs per unit to drop significantly. The experience curve proposes that per-unit costs will go down as a firm's production experience increases. On average, for each doubling of production, a firm can expect per-unit costs to decline by roughly 20 percent. Cost declines can be significant in the early stages of production. Manufacturers that fail to take advantage of these effects will find themselves at a competitive cost disadvantage relative to others that are further along the curve.

The big advantage of penetration pricing is that it typically discourages or blocks competition from entering a market. The disadvantage is that penetration means gearing up for mass production to sell a large volume at a low price. What if the volume fails to materialize? The company will face huge losses from building or converting a factory to produce the failed product. Skimming, in contrast, lets a firm "stick its toe in the water" and see if limited demand exists at the high price. If not, the firm can simply lower the price. Skimming lets a company start out with a small production facility and expand it gradually as price falls and demand increases.

Penetration pricing can also prove disastrous for a prestige brand that adopts the strategy in an effort to gain market share and fails. When Omega—once a more prestigious brand than Rolex—was trying to improve the market share of its watches, it adopted a penetration pricing strategy that succeeded in destroying the watches' brand image by flooding the market with lower-priced products. Omega never gained sufficient share on its lower-priced/lower-image competitors to justify destroying its brand image and high-priced position with upscale buyers. The Cadillac Cimarron and Lacoste clothing experienced similar outcomes from a penetration pricing strategy.

Sometimes marketers in other countries see the success of Canadian companies' price strategies and decide to emulate them. Such was the case of Ryanair, as explained in the "Global Perspectives" box.

Status Quo Pricing

The third basic price strategy a firm may choose is status quo pricing, or meeting the competition. It means charging a price identical to or very close to the competition's price. Although status quo pricing has the advantage of simplicity, its disadvantage is that the strategy may ignore demand or cost or both. If the firm is comparatively small, however, meeting the competition may be the safest route to long-term survival.

>> THE LEGALITY AND ETHICS OF PRICE STRATEGY

2 Identify the legal and ethical constraints on pricing decisions

As we mentioned in Chapter 3, some pricing decisions are subject to government regulation. Before marketing managers establish any price strategy, they should know the laws that limit their decision making. Among the laws that fall into this category are the ones relating to resale price maintenance, price fixing, price discrimination, and predatory pricing.

Resale Price Maintenance

Most producers would like to be able to control the price of their products on retail store shelves. However, **resale price maintenance**, as this practice is called, is illegal in Canada. Section 50 of the Competition Act prohibits a manufacturer from requiring a retailer to sell a product at a particular price or below a particular price. The act allows a manufacturer to set a *suggested retail price* as long as it is clear that the retailer will not be discriminated against if it does not maintain that suggested price.

resale price maintenance
Laws that prohibit manufacturers from controlling prices at the retail level.

Price Fixing

Price fixing is an agreement between two or more firms on the price they will charge for a product. Suppose two or more executives from competing firms meet to decide how much to charge for a product or to decide which of them will submit the lowest bid on

price fixing
An agreement between two or more firms on the price they will charge for a product.

GLOBAL PERSPECTIVES

Irish Airline Flies High Just Like WestJet

Europe's grand old airlines have hit a rough patch of air these days and Michael O'Leary is proud to be a big part of their problem. The chief executive of Ryanair Holdings didn't set out to rattle the once cozy world of European aviation, but he has.

Ten years ago, when he was financial adviser to Irish tycoon Tony Ryan, he was asked by Ryan for some thoughts on fixing the struggling family-owned carrier. O'Leary's advice: "Shut the bloody thing down."

Instead, Ryan persuaded O'Leary to visit several low-fare airlines and learn how low-cost carriers make a big profit. Based on his visits, O'Leary found cut-price religion. He agreed to run Ryanair, in the process taking on some of the biggest names in aviation.

Today, Ryanair stands foremost among a handful of European budget airlines, rewriting the rules and battering venerable flag carriers. Passengers grumble that flying Ryanair is like riding a bus, but they are doing it by the busload. Ryanair carries 7 million passengers in 11 countries each year—Britain, France, and Italy, among them—ranking its traffic volume above that of Ireland's state-owned Aer Lingus. That makes Ryanair Europe's first start-up to surpass a national carrier.

Ryanair's rise from Irish puddle-jumper to continental contender is more than one airline's growth story. The Gaelic upstart and its followers such as London-based EasyJet are fundamentally shifting the economics of flying around Europe. While some promotional Ryanair fares are as cheap as £1 ($2.40) to fly from one European city to another, the majority of the carrier's tickets are in the same price range as old-line carriers' bargain fares. But while major airlines make most of their money from premium travellers and offer discounts mainly to fill unsold seats, Ryanair is able to turn a profit at discount-fare levels.

The carrier, which today bases most of its flights in London, can make money on bargain fares because it pares costs to the bone and then keeps cutting. Frequent-flyer plan? Forget about it. Want a snack or drink on board? You buy it. And Ryanair won't serve peanuts, because prying them out from between the seat cushions takes too long (and hence, costs too much money). In its no-frills fervor, Ryanair even refuses to use those extendable boarding corridors at airports because it's quicker to park a plane at the gate, roll stairs up to the front and back doors, and let passengers hustle across the tarmac. The result: Ryanair can break even with its planes almost half empty—although its average flight is 75 percent full, better than most major European carriers.[5]

What type of pricing strategy is Ryanair following? What might Europe's traditional airlines, like British Airways and Lufthansa, do to counteract Ryanair's success? What other problems might Ryanair face in following this pricing strategy?

a certain contract. Such practices are illegal under the Competition Act. Offenders have received fines and sometimes prison terms. Canada's three largest flour milling companies—Robin Hood Multifoods, Maple Leaf Foods, and Ogilvie Mills—were fined $1 million each for rigging bids to supply flour to the federal government.

Price Discrimination

The Competition Act prohibits any firm from selling to two or more different buyers, within a reasonably short time, commodities (not services) of like grade and quality at different prices where the result would be to substantially lessen competition. The act also makes it illegal for a seller to offer two buyers different supplementary services and for buyers to use their purchasing power to force sellers into granting discriminatory prices or services. Note that not all price differences represent price discrimination. For example, children and senior citizens pay lower prices for movie tickets.

Six elements are needed for price discrimination to occur:

- There must be price discrimination; that is, the seller must charge different prices to different customers for the same product.
- The two customers must be competitors.
- The seller must discriminate by price among two or more purchasers; that is, the seller must make two or more actual sales within a reasonably short time.
- The products sold must be commodities or other tangible goods.

ON LINE

Price Fixing

To find out more about current price-fixing cases, type "price fixing" into the AltaVista or Yahoo! Internet search engine. Compare the information you find there with some of the companies' own Web pages. How do companies deal with this type of scandal on their websites? Does this surprise you?

http://www.altavista.ca

http://www.yahoo.ca

- The products sold must be of like grade and quality, not necessarily identical. If the goods are truly interchangeable and substitutable, then they are of like grade and quality.
- The act of discrimination must be part of an ongoing practice of discrimination.

AP/WIDE WORLD PHOTOS

In a scandal that rocked the art world, Sotheby's and Christie's, two of the industry's most venerable auction houses, were caught in a price-fixing scheme. The CEOs of both companies received substantial fines and prison time.

Predatory Pricing

Predatory pricing is the practice of charging a very low price for a product with the intent of driving competitors out of business or out of a market. Once competitors have been driven out, the firm raises its prices. This practice is illegal under section 34(b) of the Competition Act. Proving the use of the practice is difficult, however. It must be shown that the predator, the destructive company, explicitly tried to ruin a competitor and that the predatory price was below the predator's average variable cost. Some provinces, such as British Columbia, Alberta, and Manitoba, have provincial legislation that prohibits companies from selling below cost plus some reasonable markup, such as 5 percent.

predatory pricing
The practice of charging a very low price for a product with the intent of driving competitors out of business or out of a market.

Proving predatory pricing is often very difficult. Under the Competition Act, pricing below cost to sell off excess inventory is not considered predatory, but pricing below cost to drive a competitor out of business *is*. Within the past year, both WestJet and Hawkair (a discount B.C. airline) have accused Air Canada of predatory pricing.[6] In the case of Hawkair, Air Canada lowered fares between Terrace, B.C., and Vancouver to \$126. The Hawkair price over this route is \$149. Yet Air Canada charges \$275 for a flight from Sandpit, B.C., to Vancouver (a comparable distance but a route not covered by Hawkair). In the case of WestJet, after WestJet moved many of its flights from Hamilton to Toronto Pearson International Airport, Air Canada lowered one-way fares from Toronto to Ottawa to \$12. Are these cases of selling off excess inventory (empty seats) or predatory pricing?

>> TACTICS FOR FINE-TUNING THE BASE PRICE

3 Explain how discounts, geographic pricing, and other special pricing tactics can be used to fine-tune the base price

After managers understand both the legal and the marketing consequences of price strategies, they should set a **base price,** the general price level at which the company expects to sell the good or service. The general price level is correlated with the pricing policy: above the market (price skimming), at the market (status quo pricing), or below the market (penetration pricing). The final step, then, is to fine-tune the base price.

base price
The general price level at which the company expects to sell the good or service.

Fine-tuning techniques are short-run approaches that do not change the general price level. They do, however, result in changes within a general price level. These pricing tactics allow the firm to adjust for competition in certain markets, meet ever-changing government regulations, take advantage of unique demand situations, and meet promotional and positioning goals. Fine-tuning pricing tactics include various sorts of discounts, geographic pricing, and special pricing tactics.

Discounts, Allowances, Rebates, and Value-Based Pricing

A base price can be lowered through the use of discounts and the related tactics of allowances, rebates, low or zero percent financing, and value-based pricing. Managers use the various forms of discounts to encourage customers to do what they would not ordinarily do, such as paying cash rather than using credit, taking delivery out of season, or performing certain functions within a distribution channel. The following are the most common tactics:

ON LINE

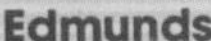

Edmunds

Which automakers are currently offering rebates? Go to Edmunds' advice page and check out the new car incentives, rebates, and leases to find out. What effect do you think rebates and incentives have on operating costs and company financial performance?

http://www.edmunds.com/advice

- *Quantity discounts:* When buyers get a lower price for buying in multiple units or above a specified dollar amount, they are receiving a **quantity discount.** A **cumulative quantity discount** is a deduction from list price that applies to the buyer's total purchases made during a specific period; it is intended to encourage customer loyalty. In contrast, a **noncumulative quantity discount** is a deduction from list price that applies to a single order rather than to the total volume of orders placed during a certain period. It is intended to encourage orders in large quantities.
- *Cash discounts:* A **cash discount** is a price reduction offered to a consumer, an industrial user, or a marketing intermediary in return for prompt payment of a bill. Prompt payment saves the seller carrying charges and billing expenses and allows the seller to avoid bad debt.
- *Functional discounts:* When distribution channel intermediaries, such as wholesalers or retailers, perform a service or function for the manufacturer, they must be compensated. This compensation, typically a percentage discount from the base price, is called a **functional discount** (or **trade discount**). Functional discounts vary greatly from channel to channel, depending on the tasks performed by the intermediary.
- *Seasonal discounts:* A **seasonal discount** is a price reduction for buying merchandise out of season. It shifts the storage function to the purchaser. Seasonal discounts also enable manufacturers to maintain a steady production schedule year-round.
- *Promotional allowances:* A **promotional allowance** (also known as a **trade allowance**) is a payment to a dealer for promoting the manufacturer's products. It is both a pricing tool and a promotional device. As a pricing tool, a promotional allowance is like a functional discount. If, for example, a retailer runs an ad for a manufacturer's product, the manufacturer may pay half the cost. If a retailer sets up a special display, the manufacturer may include a certain quantity of free goods in the retailer's next order.
- *Rebates:* A **rebate** is a cash refund given for the purchase of a product during a specific period. The advantage of a rebate over a simple price reduction for stimulating demand is that a rebate is a temporary inducement that can be taken away without altering the basic price structure. A manufacturer that uses a simple price reduction for a short time may meet resistance when trying to restore the price to its original, higher level.
- *Zero percent financing:* After the terrorist attacks in the U.S. on September 11, 2001, new-car sales in both Canada and the U.S. plummeted. To get people back into the automobile showrooms, manufacturers offered zero percent financing, which enabled purchasers to borrow money to pay for new cars with no interest charges. The tactic created a huge increase in sales but not without a cost to the manufacturers. A five-year interest-free car loan represented a cost of over $3,000 on a typical vehicle sold with zero percent financing. And automakers were still offering such incentives over three years later!

quantity discount
A price reduction offered for buying in multiple units or above a specified dollar amount.

cumulative quantity discount
A deduction from list price that applies to the buyer's total purchases made during a specific time period.

noncumulative quantity discount
A deduction from list price that applies to a single order rather than to the total volume of orders placed during a certain period.

cash discount
A price reduction offered to a consumer, an industrial user, or a marketing intermediary in return for prompt payment of a bill.

functional discount (trade discount)
A discount to wholesalers and retailers for performing channel functions.

seasonal discount
A price reduction for buying merchandise out of season.

promotional allowance (trade allowance)
A payment to a dealer for promoting the manufacturer's products.

rebate
A cash refund given for the purchase of a product during a specific period.

Value-Based Pricing

value-based pricing
Setting the price at a level that seems to the customer to be a good price compared to the prices of other options.

Value-based pricing (also called *value pricing*) is a pricing strategy that has grown out of the quality movement. Instead of figuring prices based on costs or competitors' prices, it starts with the customer, considers the competition, and then determines the appropriate price. The basic assumption is that the firm is customer driven, seeking to understand the attributes customers want in the goods and services they buy and the value of that bundle of attributes to customers. Because very few firms operate in a pure monopoly, however, a marketer using value-based pricing must also determine the value of competitive offerings to customers. Customers determine the value of a product (not just its price) relative to the value of alternatives. In value-based pricing, therefore, the price of the product is set at a level that seems to the customer to be a good price compared with the prices of other options.

Procter & Gamble instituted a form of value pricing in 1992. In an effort to reduce operating costs and strengthen brand loyalty, it coupled value prices with increased advertising but a reduction in coupons, product displays, and other forms of sales promotion. The introduction of value pricing meant that average P&G prices fell across 24 product categories. Yet as costs rose during the 1990s, there was a corresponding increase in the prices of P&G's products. P&G's change in pricing tactics, sales promotion, and advertising strategies resulted in an average 18 percent loss in market share across the 24 categories during the 1990s. Researchers, using sophisticated analytical models, found that most of the loss in market share was due to the severe cuts in coupons and sales promotion deals.[7] Because competitors' prices also rose during the decade, P&G's price increases played a lesser role in the loss of market share. P&G had hoped that increased advertising would strengthen brand loyalty and therefore increase sales, but it did not. As P&G's experience demonstrates, value pricing alone does not guarantee increased market share or profitability.

Pricing Products Too Low

Sometimes managers price their products too low, thereby reducing company profits.[8] This seems to happen for two reasons. First, managers attempt to buy market share through aggressive pricing. Usually, however, competitors quickly meet these price cuts. Thus, any gain in market share is short-lived, and overall industry profits end up falling. Second, managers have a natural tendency to want to make decisions that can be justified objectively. The problem is that companies often lack hard data on the complex determinants of profitability, such as the relationship between price changes and sales volumes, the link between demand levels and costs, and the likely responses of competitors to price changes. In contrast, companies usually have rich, unambiguous information on costs, sales, market share, and competitors' prices. As a result, managers tend to make pricing decisions based on current costs, projected short-term share gains, or current competitor prices rather than on long-term profitability.

FOB origin pricing
A price tactic that requires the buyer to absorb the freight costs from the shipping point ("free on board").

Occasionally, underpricing occurs by mistake. When this happens, what are the company's obligations to its customers? The "Ethics in Marketing" box explores this issue.

COURTESY OF EBATES

You read in Chapter 15 how the Internet is affecting pricing strategies, and that extends to the world of coupons and rebates. Many sites, like ebates.com, catalogue rebate opportunities and pass information along to consumers who are willing to sign up.

Geographic Pricing

Because many sellers ship their wares to a nationwide or even a worldwide market, the cost of freight can greatly affect the total cost of a product. Sellers may use several different geographic pricing tactics to moderate the impact of freight costs on distant customers. The following methods of geographic pricing are the most common:

- *FOB origin pricing:* **FOB origin pricing,** also called FOB factory or FOB shipping point, is a price tactic that requires the buyer to absorb the freight costs from the shipping point ("free on board"). The farther buyers are from sellers, the more they pay, because transportation costs generally increase with the distance merchandise is shipped.

ETHICS IN MARKETING

Less Than $30 to Paris? United Airlines Says "Oops"

Eric Bescher almost flew to Paris for less than $30. Bescher visited United's website to search for a low fare to Europe. The deal he found was a lot better than he'd bargained for—passage to France for less than the price of a bottle of good burgundy. A technical glitch at the site listed the round-trip fare to Paris as just $27.98. "I snapped it up right away," he says.

Bescher wasn't alone in his good fortune. United Airlines says it inadvertently sold 143 tickets to destinations such as Hong Kong at *really* rock bottom prices via its website during a 55-minute period.

United says a computer bug "zeroed out" the fare on a number of international flights so that the amounts shown reflected only a portion of the taxes and miscellaneous fees. In fact, fares were in a free-for-all: one minute a round-trip fare to Paris was $85.42; seconds later that same ticket sold for $24.98.

United spokesman Chris Brathwaite says the airline won't honour any tickets sold at those prices. He likens the situation to a bank error when the teller inadvertently credits a customer's account with $1,000 instead of $100. "It's clearly a mistake: everyone knows you don't fly first class to Paris for $29," he says. "You don't get something for nothing." As a consolation, United did waive any cancellation fees should passengers not wish to pay the correct fare.

Some travellers are fuming nonetheless. One super discount purchaser says United even sent an e-mail confirmation of his purchase of two tickets to Paris for $85 each and now refuses to honour that price. The customer believes the airline has a responsibility to honour the tickets because its own website was responsible for the error.

Moments after purchasing his ticket to Paris, Bescher also received an e-mail confirmation of the $27.98 fare. But days later, United charged his credit card $573—which he assumes is the price he would have been quoted for the ticket had ual.com been working correctly. Bescher immediately contacted United's customer service office about what he viewed as an unauthorized charge. "If they don't come through with a goodwill gesture," he says, "I'm going to dispute it."[9]

Should United honour the very low fares? Wouldn't United receive great publicity for doing so? It could write off the cost as a promotional expense. Or were the mistakes like bank errors, so that customers should not expect United to honour the fares?

uniform delivered pricing
A price tactic in which the seller pays the actual freight charges and bills every purchaser an identical, flat freight charge.

zone pricing
A modification of uniform delivered pricing that divides the country (or the total market) into segments or zones and charges a flat freight rate to all customers in a given zone.

freight absorption pricing
A price tactic in which the seller pays all or part of the actual freight charges and does not pass them on to the buyer.

basing-point pricing
A price tactic that charges freight from a given (basing) point, regardless of the city from which the goods are shipped.

- *Uniform delivered pricing:* If the marketing manager wants total costs, including freight, to be equal for all purchasers of identical products, the firm will adopt uniform delivered pricing, or "postage stamp" pricing. With **uniform delivered pricing,** the seller pays the actual freight charges and bills every purchaser an identical, flat freight charge.
- *Zone pricing:* A marketing manager who wants to equalize total costs among buyers within large geographic areas—but not necessarily all of the seller's market area—may modify the base price with a zone-pricing tactic. **Zone pricing** is a modification of uniform delivered pricing. Rather than placing the entire country (or its total market) under a uniform freight rate, the firm divides the market into segments or zones and charges a flat freight rate to all customers in a given zone.
- *Freight absorption pricing:* In **freight absorption pricing,** the seller pays all or part of the actual freight charges and does not pass them on to the buyer. This tactic might be used in intensely competitive areas or as a way to break into new market areas.
- *Basing-point pricing:* With **basing-point pricing,** the seller designates a location as a basing point and charges all buyers the freight cost from that point, regardless of the city from which the goods are shipped.

Special Pricing Tactics

single-price tactic
A price tactic that offers all goods and services at the same price (or perhaps two or three prices).

Unlike geographic pricing, special pricing tactics are unique and defy neat categorization. Managers use these tactics for various reasons—for example, to stimulate demand for specific products, to increase store patronage, and to offer a wider variety of merchandise at a specific price point. Special pricing tactics include a single-price tactic, flexible pricing, professional services pricing, price lining, leader pricing, bait pricing, odd–even pricing, price bundling, and two-part pricing. A brief overview of each of these tactics follows, along with a manager's reasons for using that tactic or a combination of tactics to change the base price.

Single-Price Tactic

A merchant using a **single-price tactic** offers all goods and services at the same price (or perhaps two or three prices). Retailers using this tactic include Buck or Two, Dollar Plus Stores, Dre$$ to the Nine$, Your $10 Store, and Fashions $9.99. One Dollar Stores, located in malls across Canada, sell all products at a price of one or two dollars.

Single-price selling removes price comparisons from the buyer's decision-making process. The consumer just looks for suitability and the highest perceived quality. The retailer enjoys the benefits of a simplified pricing system and minimal clerical errors. However, continually rising costs are a headache for retailers following this strategy.

ON LINE

Canada Post

Go to Canada Post's website and do a quick cost comparison on sending the same package to a friend in town and to a friend out-of-province. Does the difference in cost surprise you? Do you think it is justified? Why or why not?

http://www.canadapost.ca

Flexible Pricing

Flexible pricing (or **variable pricing**) means that different customers pay different prices for essentially the same merchandise bought in equal quantities. This tactic is often found in the sale of shopping goods, specialty merchandise, and most industrial goods except supply items. Car dealers, many appliance retailers, and manufacturers of industrial installations, accessories, and component parts commonly follow the practice. It allows the seller to adjust for competition by meeting another seller's price. Thus, a marketing manager with a status quo pricing objective might readily adopt the tactic. Flexible pricing also enables the seller to close a sale with price-conscious consumers. If buyers show promise of becoming large-volume shoppers, flexible pricing can be used to lure their business.

flexible pricing (variable pricing)
A price tactic in which different customers pay different prices for essentially the same merchandise bought in equal quantities.

The obvious disadvantages of flexible pricing are the lack of consistent profit margins, the potential ill will of high-paying purchasers, the tendency for salespeople to automatically lower the price to make a sale, and the possibility of a price war among sellers. The disadvantages of flexible pricing have led the automobile industry to experiment with one price for all buyers. General Motors uses a one-price tactic for some of its models, including the Saturn and the Buick Regal.

Professional Services Pricing

Professional services pricing is used by people with lengthy experience, training, and often certification by a licensing board—for example, lawyers, physicians, and family counsellors. Professionals sometimes charge customers at an hourly rate, but sometimes fees are based on the solution of a problem or performance of an act (such as an eye examination) rather than on the actual time involved. A lawyer may charge $2,000 for completing a divorce but only $200 for handling a traffic violation.

Price Lining

When a seller establishes a series of prices for a type of merchandise, it creates a price line. **Price lining** is the practice of offering a product line with several items at specific price points. For example, HON, an office furniture manufacturer, may offer its

price lining
The practice of offering a product line with several items at specific price points.

ON LINE

Ford Motor Company

Using the "Build and Price" function on Ford's website, compare MSRP and options pricing on a Ford Focus with those of a more upscale model, such as the Crown Victoria or Taurus. What are the differences? Can you determine the pricing strategy adopted by Ford for its Ford line of vehicles?

http://www.fordvehicles.com

four-drawer file cabinets at $125, $250, and $400. Limited Brands may offer women's dresses at $40, $70, and $100, with no merchandise marked at prices between those figures. Instead of a normal demand curve running from $40 to $100, The Limited has three demand points (prices).

Price lining reduces confusion for both the salesperson and the consumer. The buyer may be offered a wider variety of merchandise at each established price. Price lines may also enable a seller to reach several market segments. For buyers, the question of price may be quite simple: All they have to do is find a suitable product at the predetermined price. Moreover, price lining is a valuable tactic for the marketing manager, because the firm may be able to carry a smaller total inventory than it could without price lines. The results may include fewer markdowns, simplified purchasing, and lower inventory carrying charges.

Price lines also present drawbacks, especially if costs are continually rising. Sellers can offset rising costs in three ways. First, they can begin stocking lower-quality merchandise at each price point. Second, sellers can change the prices, although frequent price line changes confuse buyers. Third, sellers can accept lower profit margins and hold quality and prices constant. This third alternative has short-run benefits, but its long-run handicaps may drive sellers out of business.

Leader Pricing

leader pricing (loss-leader pricing)
A price tactic in which a product is sold near or even below cost in the hope that shoppers will buy other items once they are in the store.

Leader pricing (or **loss-leader pricing**) is an attempt by the marketing manager to attract customers by selling a product near or even below cost in the hope that shoppers will buy other items once they are in the store. This type of pricing appears weekly in the newspaper advertising of supermarkets, specialty stores, and department stores. Leader pricing is normally used on well-known items that consumers can easily recognize as bargains at the special price. The goal is not necessarily to sell large quantities of leader items, but to try to appeal to customers who might shop elsewhere.

Leader pricing is not limited to products. Health clubs offer a one-month free trial as a loss leader. Lawyers give a free initial consultation. Restaurants may distribute two-for-one coupons. When Krispy Kreme opened its first outlet in Windsor, it gave away thousands of free doughnuts.

Bait Pricing

bait pricing
A price tactic that tries to get consumers into a store through false or misleading price advertising and then uses high-pressure selling to persuade consumers to buy more expensive merchandise.

In contrast to leader pricing, which is a genuine attempt to give the consumer a reduced price, bait pricing is deceptive. **Bait pricing** tries to get the consumer into a store through false or misleading price advertising and then uses high-pressure selling to persuade the consumer to buy more expensive merchandise. You may have seen this ad or a similar one:

> REPOSSESSED ... Singer slant-needle sewing machine ... take over 8 payments of $5.10 per month ... ABC Sewing Centre.

This is the bait. When a customer goes in to see the machine, a salesperson says that it has just been sold or else shows the prospective buyer a piece of junk no one would buy. Then the salesperson says, "But I've got a really good deal on this fine new model." This is the switch that may cause a susceptible consumer to walk out with a $400 machine. Bait pricing may be illegal if the seller has no intention of providing the advertised item or is unable to provide the advertised item.

Odd–Even Pricing

odd–even pricing (psychological pricing)
A price tactic that uses odd-numbered prices to connote bargains and even-numbered prices to imply quality.

Odd–even pricing (or **psychological pricing**) means pricing at odd-numbered prices to connote a bargain and pricing at even-numbered prices to imply quality. For years, many retailers have priced their products in odd numbers—for example, $99.95 or $49.95—to make consumers feel they are paying a lower price for the product.

Some retailers favour odd-numbered prices because they believe that $9.99 sounds much less imposing to customers than $10.00. Other retailers believe that an odd-numbered price signals to consumers that the price is at the lowest level possible, thereby encouraging them to buy more units. Neither theory has ever been conclusively proved, although one study found that consumers perceive odd-priced products as being on sale.[10] The most recent research shows that consumers do purchase more at odd prices.[11]

Even-numbered pricing is sometimes used to denote quality. Examples include a fine perfume at $100 a bottle, a good watch at $500, or a mink coat at $3,000. The demand curve for such items would also be sawtoothed, except that the outside edges would represent even-numbered prices and, therefore, elastic demand.

Price Bundling

Price bundling involves marketing two or more products in a single package for a special price. Examples include the sale of maintenance contracts with computer hardware and other office equipment, packages of stereo equipment, packages of options on cars, weekend hotel packages that include a room and several meals, and airline vacation packages. Microsoft offers "suites" of software that bundle spreadsheets, word processing, graphics, electronic mail, Internet access, and groupware for networks of micro computers. Price bundling can stimulate demand for the bundled items if the target market perceives the price as a good value.[12]

price bundling
Marketing two or more products in a single package for a special price.

Services like hotels and airlines sell a perishable commodity (hotel rooms and airline seats) with relatively constant fixed costs. Bundling can be an important income stream for these businesses because the variable cost tends to be low—for instance, the cost of cleaning a hotel room or putting one more passenger on an airplane. Therefore, the added revenue can help cover fixed costs and generate profits.

The automobile industry has a different motive for bundling. People buy cars only every three to five years. Thus, selling options is a somewhat rare opportunity for the car dealer. Price bundling can help the dealer sell a maximum number of options.

Bundling has also been used in the telecommunications industry. Companies offer local service, long distance, DSL Internet service, wireless, and even cable TV in various menus of bundling. Such bundling is not necessarily consumer focused. Telecom companies use bundling as a way to protect their market share and fight off competition by locking customers into a group of services. For consumers, comparison shopping may be difficult since they may not be able to determine how much they are really paying for each component of the bundle.[13]

unbundling
Reducing the bundle of services that comes with the basic product.

A related price tactic is **unbundling,** or reducing the bundle of services that comes with the basic product. Rather than raise the price of hotel rooms, some hotel chains have started charging registered guests for parking. To help hold the line on costs, some stores require customers to pay for gift wrapping.

Some of the latest research has focused on how people consume certain bundled services. Studies show that when people buy season tickets to a concert series, sporting event, or other activity, the sunk costs (price of the bundle) and the pending benefit (going to see an event) become decoupled, which reduces the likelihood of consumption of the event over time. For example, researchers found that theatregoers who purchased tickets to four plays were only 84 percent likely to use their first-play tickets and only 78 percent likely to use any given ticket across the four plays.[14] In contrast, theatregoers who purchased tickets to a single play were almost certain to use those tickets.

In practice, these findings mean that a theatre manager might expect a no-show rate of 20 percent when the percentage of season ticket holders is high, but a no-show rate of only 5 percent when the percentage of season ticket holders is low. With a high number of season ticket holders, a manager could oversell performances and maximize the revenue for the theatre. Airlines routinely overbook in anticipation of a predictable percentage of no-shows.

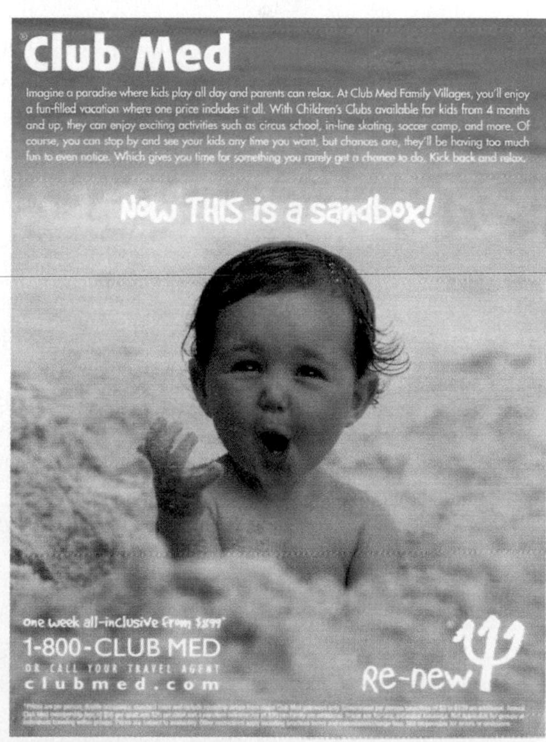

COURTESY OF CLUB MED

Club Med advertises an all-inclusive vacation for one from $899 in this humourous ad. Included in the price are the airfare, room, meals, sports, and children's clubs. However, several contingencies are placed on this bundled vacation—listed in the ad's fine print.

AP/WIDE WORLD PHOTOS

In order to maximize revenue, managers could oversell tickets to an event for which season ticket subscriptions are high. This is because people who buy season tickets for an event are less likely to use all the tickets they purchase.

Price bundling of services can result in a lower rate of total consumption of that service. The same is not necessarily true, however, for products. Consider the purchase of an expensive bottle of wine, which can be inventoried until needed. When the wine is purchased as a single unit, its cost and eventual benefit are tightly coupled. As a result, the cost of the wine will be quite important, and a person will likely reserve that wine for a special occasion. When purchased as part of a bundle (e.g., as part of a case of wine), however, the cost and benefit of that individual bottle of wine will likely become decoupled, reducing the impact of the cost on eventual consumption. As a result, a person will likely find the wine appropriate for many more (not-so-special) occasions. Thus, in contrast to the price bundling of services, the price bundling of physical goods could lead to an increase in product consumption.

Two-Part Pricing

two-part pricing
A price tactic that charges two separate amounts to consume a single good or service.

Two-part pricing means establishing two separate charges to consume a single good or service. Tennis clubs and health clubs charge a membership fee and a flat fee each time a person uses certain equipment or facilities. In other cases they charge a base rate for a certain level of usage, such as 10 racquetball games per month, and a surcharge for anything over that amount.[15]

Consumers sometimes prefer two-part pricing because they are uncertain about the number and the types of activities they might use at places like an amusement park. Also, the people who use a service most often pay a higher total price. Two-part pricing can increase a seller's revenue by attracting consumers who would not pay a high fee even for unlimited use. For example, a health club might be able to sell only 100 memberships at $700 annually with unlimited use of facilities, for total revenue of $70,000. However, perhaps it could sell 900 memberships at $200 with a guarantee of using the racquetball courts 10 times a month. Every use over 10 would require the member to pay a $5 fee. Thus, membership revenue would provide a base of $180,000, with some additional usage fees coming in throughout the year.

Consumer Penalties

consumer penalty
An extra fee paid by the consumer for violating the terms of the purchase agreement.

More and more businesses are adopting **consumer penalties**—extra fees paid by consumers for violating the terms of a purchase agreement (see Exhibit 16.2 on page 520).

Businesses will impose consumer penalties for two reasons: they will allegedly (1) suffer an irrevocable revenue loss and/or (2) incur significant additional transaction costs should customers be unable or unwilling to complete their purchase obligations. For the company, these customer payments are part of doing business in a highly competitive marketplace. With profit margins in many companies increasingly coming under pressure, organizations are looking to stem losses resulting from customers not meeting their obligations. However, the perceived unfairness of a penalty may affect some consumers' willingness to patronize a business in the future.

One study found that most consumers (53 percent) had paid a price penalty in the past year. A "fair" penalty exists when consumers believe that they are reimbursing the seller for actual lost revenue and not simply enabling the seller to make extra profit.[16]

ON LINE

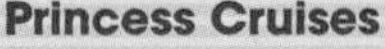

Princess Cruises

Carnival Cruises

How upfront are companies about their pricing penalties? Compare what you find out at Princess Cruises' Web page (type "penalties" into the search box) with what you find on Carnival Cruises' page. From a marketing standpoint, do you think it is better to hide penalties in the fine print or to clearly let the customer know in advance?

http://www.princess.com

http://www.carnival.com

>> PRODUCT LINE PRICING

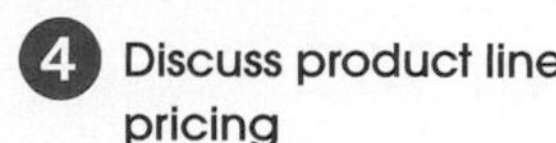

Product line pricing is setting prices for an entire line of products. Compared to setting the right price on a single product, product line pricing encompasses broader concerns. In product line pricing, the marketing manager tries to achieve maximum profits or other goals for the entire line rather than for a single component of the line.

product line pricing
Setting prices for an entire line of products.

Relationships among Products

The manager must first determine the type of relationship that exists among the various products in the line:

- If items are *complementary,* an increase in the sale of one good causes an increase in demand for the complementary product, and vice versa. For example, the sale of ski poles depends on the demand for skis, making these two items complementary.
- Two products in a line can also be *substitutes* for each other. If buyers buy one item in the line, they are less likely to buy a second item in the line. For example, if someone goes to an automotive supply store and buys paste Turtle Wax for a car, it is very unlikely that he or she will buy liquid Turtle Wax in the near future.
- A *neutral* relationship can also exist between two products. In other words, demand for one of the products is unrelated to demand for the other. For instance, Ralston Purina sells chicken feed and Wheat Chex, but the sale of one of these products has no known impact on demand for the other.

© INDEX STOCK IMAGERY/TOM STILLO

The demand curve is influenced by the relationship between products. For example, the demand for bindings depends on the demand for skis. This kind of relationship is described as complementary.

Joint Costs

Joint costs are costs that are shared in the manufacturing and marketing of several products in a product line. These costs pose a unique problem in product pricing. In oil refining, for example, fuel oil, gasoline, kerosene, naphtha, paraffin, and lubricating oils are all derived from a common production process. Another example is the production of compact discs that combine photos and music.

joint costs
Costs that are shared in the manufacturing and marketing of several products in a product line.

Any assignment of joint costs must be somewhat subjective because costs are actually shared. Suppose a company produces two products, X and Y, in a common production process, with joint costs allocated on a weight basis. Product X weighs 100 kilograms and product Y weighs 50 kilograms. Thus, costs are allocated on the basis of $2 for X for every $1 for Y. Gross margins (sales less the cost of goods sold) might then be as follows:

	Product X	Product Y	Total
Sales	$20,000	$6,000	$26,000
Less: cost of goods sold	15,000	7,500	22,500
Gross margin	$ 5,000	($1,500)	$ 3,500

ON LINE

Beauty.com

Does Beauty.com use a product line pricing strategy? Choose a brand and view the product list and pricing sheet. What evidence do you see of product line pricing? Of other pricing strategies?

http://www.beauty.com

EXHIBIT 16.2

Common Consumer Penalties

1. **Airlines**
   - Most airlines charge a penalty for changing reservations on discount tickets.
   - A lost ticket can result in the traveller paying full price for a new ticket, with a possible refund later, but usually with an administration penalty fee added.
   - Some travel agents charge an additional $10 to $20 penalty for cancelled tickets.
2. **Automobiles**
   - Penalties are imposed for early terminations of car leases. In some cases, deposits on cancelled leases can be subject to penalties.
   - Car owners in England pay penalties, administration fees, and commissions if they cancel an insurance policy early.
3. **Banks**
   - Penalties are often associated with early withdrawal of certificates of deposit.
   - Some banks charge penalties for too many withdrawals in a month.
   - Some have monthly penalties of $5 to $10 if a client's balance falls below a minimum level.
   - Banks can charge late fees, in addition to interest, for tardy payments.
   - Banks might charge penalty fees to ATM users who are customers of another bank.
4. **Car Rentals**
   - Rental companies often have $25 to $100 penalties for no-shows for specialty vehicles. Budget, National, and Dollar Thrifty are experimenting with no-show fees on all rentals.
5. **Child Day Care**
   - Many daycare centres charge a penalty of up to $5 a minute when parents are late in picking up their children.
6. **Cellular Phones**
   - Companies have cancellation penalties, often in the small print on the back of a contract, which can run as high as $525.
7. **Credit and Debit Cards**
   - Some vendors now charge late fees (beyond normal interest).
   - GE Rewards MasterCard charges $25 a year for those who pay their bill each month, in full, on time. Advanta credit card company may charge $25 for six-month inactivity on an account and $25 to close an account.
8. **Cruises**
   - If a cruise is sailing, even though there are hurricane warnings, some cruise lines will assess penalties if a passenger cancels.
   - Even trip cancellation insurance will not ensure a refund if the traveller has embarked on the trip.
   - Britain is trying to crack down on executive cancellation penalties on package holidays.
   - The Carnival *Paradise* will disembark passengers found smoking.
9. **Hotels**
   - Some hotels require 72 hours' cancellation notice, or the client must pay a penalty of one day's room cost.
   - Most hotels have high charges for using in-room long-distance service.
   - Hilton, Hyatt, and Westin have early departure fees ranging from $25 to $50.
10. **Restaurants**
    - Some now charge up to $50 per person for no-show parties.
11. **Retail Stores**
    - Some retailers are charging a 15-percent restocking fee on certain items. A restocking fee is for putting a returned item back in inventory.
12. **Trains**
    - Via Rail Canada has a penalty for a returned ticket and charges a fee for changing a ticket.
13. **Universities**
    - Universities will give only a partial tuition refund after a course begins.

SOURCE: Eugene Fram and Michael McCarthy, "The True Price of Penalties," *Marketing Management*, Fall 1999, 51.

This statement reveals a loss of $1,500 on product Y. Is that important? Yes, any loss is important. However, the firm must realize that overall it earned a $3,500 profit on the two items in the line. Also, weight may not be the right way to allocate the joint costs. Instead, the firm might use other bases, such as market value or quantity sold.

5 Describe the role of pricing during periods of inflation and recession

>> PRICING DURING DIFFICULT ECONOMIC TIMES

Pricing is always an important aspect of marketing, but it is especially crucial in times of inflation and recession. The firm that does not adjust to economic trends may lose ground that it can never make up.

Inflation

When the economy is characterized by high inflation, special pricing tactics are often necessary. They can be subdivided into cost-oriented and demand-oriented tactics.

Cost-Oriented Tactics

One popular cost-oriented tactic is *culling products with a low profit margin* from the product line. However, this tactic may backfire for three reasons:

- A high volume of sales on an item with a low profit margin may still make the item highly profitable.
- Eliminating a product from a product line may reduce economies of scale, thereby lowering the margins on other items.
- Eliminating the product may affect the price–quality image of the entire line.

Another popular cost-oriented tactic is **delayed-quotation pricing,** which is used for industrial installations and many accessory items. Price is not set on the product until the item is either finished or delivered. Long production lead times force many firms to adopt this policy during periods of inflation. Builders of nuclear power plants, ships, airports, and office towers sometimes use delayed-quotation tactics.

delayed-quotation pricing
A price tactic used for industrial installations and many accessory items, in which a firm price is not set until the item is either finished or delivered.

Escalator pricing is similar to delayed-quotation pricing in that the final selling price reflects cost increases incurred between the time an order is placed and the time delivery is made. An escalator clause allows for price increases (usually across the board) based on the cost-of-living index or some other formula. As with any price increase, management's ability to implement such a policy is based on inelastic demand for the product. About a third of all industrial product manufacturers now use escalator clauses. Many companies do not apply the clause in every sale, however. Often it is used only for extremely complex products that take a long time to produce or with new customers.

escalator pricing
A price tactic in which the final selling price reflects cost increases incurred between the time the order is placed and the time delivery is made.

Any cost-oriented pricing policy that tries to maintain a fixed gross margin under all conditions can lead to a vicious circle. For example, a price increase will result in decreased demand, which in turn will increase production costs (because of lost economies of scale). Increased production costs require a further price increase, leading to further diminished demand, and so on.

Demand-Oriented Tactics

Demand-oriented pricing tactics use price to reflect changing patterns of demand caused by inflation or high interest rates. Cost changes are considered, of course, but mostly in the context of how increased prices will affect demand.

Price shading is the use of discounts by salespeople to increase demand for one or more products in a line. Often shading becomes habitual and is done routinely without much forethought. Ducommun Incorporated, a metals producer, is among the major companies that have succeeded in eliminating the practice. Ducommun has told its salespeople not to deviate from book price without management authorization.

price shading
The use of discounts by salespeople to increase demand for one or more products in a line.

To make the demand for a good or service more inelastic and to create buyer dependency, a company can use several strategies:

- *Cultivate selected demand:* Marketing managers can target prosperous customers who will pay extra for convenience or service. Harry Rosen, for example, stresses quality and service. As a result, the luxury retailer is more lenient with suppliers and their price increases than are discount retailers. In cultivating close relationships with affluent organizational customers, marketing managers should avoid putting themselves at the mercy of a dominant firm. They can more easily raise prices when an account is readily replaceable. Finally, in companies where engineers exert more influence than purchasing departments do, performance is favoured over price. Often a preferred vendor's pricing range expands if other suppliers prove technically unsatisfactory.

- *Create unique offerings:* Marketing managers should study buyers' needs. If the seller can design distinctive goods or services uniquely fitting buyers' activities, equipment, and procedures, a mutually beneficial relationship will evolve. Buyers would incur high changeover costs in switching to another supplier. By satisfying targeted buyers in a superior way, marketing managers can make them dependent. Cereal manufacturers have skirted around passing on costs by marketing unique value-added or multi-ingredient cereals, increasing the perceived quality of cereals, and allowing companies to raise prices. These cereals include General Mills' Basic 4, Honey Nut Clusters, and Oatmeal Crisp; Post's Banana Nut Crunch and Blueberry Morning; and Kellogg's Mueslix and Nutri-Grain.
- *Change the package design:* Another way companies pass on higher costs is to shrink product sizes but keep prices the same. Scott Paper Company reduced the number of sheets in the smallest roll of Scott paper towels from 96 to 60 and actually lowered the price by 10¢ a roll. The increases in costs for paper towels were tied to a 50 to 60 percent increase in the cost of pulp paper.
- *Heighten buyer dependence:* Owens-Corning Fiberglas supplies an integrated insulation service (from feasibility studies to installation) that includes commercial and scientific training for distributors and seminars for end users. This practice freezes out competition and supports higher prices.

Recession

A recession is a period of reduced economic activity. Reduced demand for goods and services, along with higher rates of unemployment, is a common trait of a recession. Yet astute marketers can often find opportunities during recessions. A recession is an excellent time to build market share because competitors are struggling to make ends meet.

Two effective pricing tactics to hold or build market share during a recession are value-based pricing and bundling. *Value-based pricing,* discussed earlier in the chapter, stresses to customers that they are getting a good value for their money. Charles of the Ritz, usually known for its pricey products, introduced the Express Bar during a recession. A collection of affordable cosmetics and skin treatment products, the Express Bar sold alongside regular Ritz products in department stores. Although lower-priced products offer lower profit margins, Ritz found that increases in volume could offset slimmer margins. For example, the company found that consumers would buy two to three Express Bar lipsticks at a time. "The consumer is very conscious of how she spends her income and is looking for value and quality that she can find elsewhere in department stores," said Holly Mercer, vice president of marketing for Ritz.[17]

Bundling or *unbundling* can also stimulate demand during a recession. If features are added to a bundle, consumers may perceive the offering as having greater value. For example, suppose that Hyatt offers a "great escape" weekend for $119. The package includes two nights' lodging and a continental breakfast. Hyatt could add a massage and a dinner for two to create more value for this price. Conversely, companies can unbundle offerings and reduce base prices to stimulate demand. A furniture store, for example, could start charging separately for design consultation, delivery, credit, setup, and hauling away old furniture.

Recessions are a good time for marketing managers to study the demand for individual items in a product line and the revenue they produce. Pruning unprofitable items can save resources to be better used elsewhere. Borden, for example, found that it made about 3,200 sizes, brands, types, and flavours of snacks—but got 95 percent of its revenues from just half of them.

Retailers also use recessions to drop or reduce shelf space for manufacturers' brands and introduce more store brands. Consumers increase their consumption of store brands during recessions because

ON LINE

Loblaw

How does Loblaw's website promote its store brands? Is the site designed more to promote the store or its brands?

http://www.loblaw.com

these products are typically less expensive. During the recession of the early 2000s, one out of every five items purchased at supermarkets, drugstores, and mass merchandisers such as Wal-Mart was a store brand.[18]

Prices often fall during a recession as competitors try desperately to maintain demand for their wares. Even if demand remains constant, falling prices mean lower profits or no profits. Falling prices, therefore, are a natural incentive to lower costs. During the last recession, companies implemented new technologies to improve efficiency and then slashed payrolls. They also discovered that suppliers were an excellent source of cost savings; the cost of purchased materials accounts for slightly more than half of most manufacturers' expenses. General Electric's appliance division told 300 key suppliers that they had to reduce prices 10 percent or risk losing GE's business. The automobile assemblers have been demanding price reductions of 5 percent each year from their suppliers. Specific strategies that companies use with suppliers include the following:

- *Renegotiating contracts:* Sending suppliers letters demanding price cuts of 5 percent or more; putting out for rebid the contracts of those that refuse to cut costs.
- *Offering help:* Dispatching teams of experts to suppliers' plants to help them reorganize and suggest other productivity-boosting changes; working with suppliers to make parts simpler and cheaper to produce.
- *Keeping the pressure on:* To make sure that improvements continue, setting annual, across-the-board cost-reduction targets, often of 5 percent or more a year.
- *Paring down suppliers:* To improve economies of scale, slashing the overall number of suppliers, sometimes by up to 80 percent, and boosting purchases from those that remain.

Tough tactics like these help keep companies afloat during economic downturns.

>> CONNECT IT

Dell Computer, as described at the beginning of the chapter, is using a penetration pricing strategy. The company can fine-tune the base price with discounts, FOB pricing or other geographic pricing tactics, price bundling, rebates, and leader pricing. Dell can offer a number of discounts. These include cash, cumulative quantity, noncumulative quantity, and seasonal discounts.

REVIEW IT

1 **Describe the procedure for setting the right price.** The process of setting the right price on a product involves four major steps: (1) establishing pricing goals; (2) estimating demand, costs, and profits; (3) choosing a price policy to help determine a base price; and (4) fine-tuning the base price with pricing tactics.

A price strategy establishes a long-term pricing framework for a good or service. The three main types of price policies are price skimming, penetration pricing, and status quo pricing. A price-skimming policy charges a high introductory price, often followed by a gradual reduction. Penetration pricing offers a low introductory price to capture a large market share and attain economies of scale. Finally, status quo pricing strives to match competitors' prices.

1.1 A manufacturer of office furniture decides to produce antique-style rolltop desks reconfigured to accommodate personal computers. The desks will have built-in surge protectors, a platform for raising or lowering the monitor, and a number of other features. The quality, solid-oak desks will be priced far below comparable products. The marketing manager says, "We'll charge a low price and plan on a high volume to reduce our risks." Comment.

1.2 Janet Oliver, owner of a mid-priced dress shop, notes, "My pricing objectives are simple: I just charge what my competitors charge. I'm happy because I'm making money." React to Janet's statement.

1.3 What is the difference between a price policy and a price tactic? Give an example.

1.4 TEAM Divide into teams of four persons. Each team should choose one of the following topics: skimming, penetration pricing, status quo pricing, price fixing, geographic pricing, adopting a single-price tactic, flexible pricing, or professional services pricing. Each team should then pick a retailer that it feels most closely follows the team's chosen pricing strategy. Go to the store and write down examples of the strategy. Interview the store manager and get his or her views on the advantages and disadvantages of the strategy. Each team should then make an oral report in class.

2 **Identify the legal and ethical constraints on pricing decisions.** Government regulation helps monitor four major areas of pricing: resale price maintenance, price fixing, predatory pricing, and price discrimination. Some provinces have enacted unfair trade practice acts that protect small businesses from large firms that operate efficiently on extremely thin profit margins; the acts prohibit charging below-cost prices. The Competition Act prohibits price fixing, which is an agreement between two or more firms on a particular price, and predatory pricing, in which a firm undercuts its competitors with extremely low prices to drive them out of business; and makes it illegal for firms to discriminate between two or more buyers in terms of price.

2.1 What sorts of factors can push a respectable firm to enter a price-fixing arrangement with a competitor? Using InfoTrac® College Edition (http://www.infotrac-thomsonlearning.com), read about the price-fixing scandals that rocked the art auction industry or the Hollywood movie studios and Blockbuster Video during 2001 and 2002. If there are more current scandals, read a selection of articles on a particular industry. Then compile a list of business practices and pricing issues that are present in the reports of each scandal. Is each scandal unique, or are there overlapping characteristics? What conclusion can you draw about price fixing from the articles you read?

3 **Explain how discounts, geographic pricing, and other special pricing tactics can be used to fine-tune the base price.** Several techniques enable marketing managers to adjust prices within a general range in response to changes in competition, government regulation, consumer demand, and promotional and positioning goals. Techniques for fine-tuning a price can be divided into three main categories: discounts, allowances, rebates, and value-based pricing; geographic pricing; and special pricing tactics.

The first type of tactic gives lower prices to those that pay promptly, order a large quantity, or perform some function for the manufacturer. Value-based pricing starts with the customer, considers the competition and costs, and then determines a price. Other tactics in this category include seasonal discounts, promotion allowances, and rebates (cash refunds).

Geographic pricing tactics, such as FOB origin pricing, uniform delivered pricing, zone pricing, freight absorption pricing, and basing-point pricing, are ways of moderating the impact of shipping costs on distant customers.

A variety of special pricing tactics stimulate demand for certain products, increase store patronage, and offer more merchandise at specific prices.

More and more customers are paying price penalties, which are extra fees for violating the terms of a purchase contract. The perceived fairness or unfairness of a penalty may affect some consumers' willingness to patronize a business in the future.

3.1 WRITING You are contemplating a price change for an established product sold by your firm. Write a memo analyzing the factors you need to consider in your decision.

3.2 Columnist Dave Barry jokes that federal law requires this message under the sticker price of new cars: "Warning to stupid people: Do not pay this amount." Discuss why the sticker price is generally higher than the actual selling price of a car. Tell how you think car dealers set the actual prices of the cars they sell.

3.3 Explain the difference between freight absorption pricing and uniform delivered pricing. When would it be appropriate to use each?

3.4 Canada Post regularly raises the price of a first-class stamp but continues to operate in the red year after year. Is uniform delivered pricing the best choice for first-class mail? Explain your reasoning.

3.5 How is the "information age" changing the nature of pricing?

3.6 Have you ever paid a price penalty? How did it affect your attitude toward that company?

4 **Discuss product line pricing.** Product line pricing maximizes profits for an entire product line. When setting product line prices, marketing managers determine what type of relationship exists among the products in the line: complementary, substitute, or neutral. Managers also consider joint (shared) costs among products in the same line.

4.1 Develop a price line strategy for each of these firms:
a. a university bookstore
b. a restaurant
c. a video-rental store

5 **Describe the role of pricing during periods of inflation and recession.** Marketing managers employ cost-oriented and demand-oriented tactics during periods of economic inflation. Cost-oriented tactics include dropping products with a low profit margin, delayed-quotation pricing, and escalator pricing. Demand-oriented pricing methods include price shading and increasing demand through cultivating selected customers, creating unique offerings, changing the package size, and heightening buyer dependence.

To stimulate demand during a recession, marketers use value-based pricing, bundling, and unbundling. Recessions are also a good time to prune unprofitable items from product lines. Managers strive to cut costs during recessions in order to maintain profits as revenues decline. Implementing new technology, cutting payrolls, and pressuring suppliers for reduced prices are common techniques used to cut costs.

5.1 During a recession, what pricing strategies would you consider using to gain or maintain market share? Explain your answer.

5.2 ON LINE After a decade of growth and prosperity, Canadians were challenged by the economic downturn of 2000 and 2001. As a result, pricing became an issue for many consumers looking to pinch pennies. This was also true in areas where penny-pinching isn't a common occurrence, like high-end retailers. Search *The Globe and Mail*'s on-line archives (http://www.theglobeandmail.com) to find articles on price-cutting. Make a list of pricing tactics that are illustrated in the articles.

5.3 ON LINE WRITING Search for the following articles in *The Wall Street Journal*'s on-line archives (http://www.online.wsj.com): Pamela Druckerman, "Argentina's Middle Class Makes Do: In a Crisis, Barter Clubs and Discount Hunting," May 1, 2002, and Michelle Wallin, "Argentines Hone Art of Shopping in a Crisis," May 28, 2002. Read both articles and list the topics from the chapter that appear in each. How are Argentine consumers coping with serious economic difficulties? How are Argentine businesses changing their pricing to stay afloat? Write a brief summary of what you discover.

DEFINE IT

bait pricing 516
base price 511
basing-point pricing 514
cash discount 512
consumer penalty 518
cumulative quantity discount 512
delayed-quotation pricing 521
escalator pricing 521
flexible pricing (variable pricing) 515
FOB origin pricing 513
freight absorption pricing 514
functional discount (trade discount) 512
joint costs 519
leader pricing (loss-leader pricing) 516
noncumulative quantity discount 512
odd–even pricing (psychological pricing) 516
penetration pricing 508
predatory pricing 511
price bundling 517
price fixing 509
price lining 515
price shading 521
price skimming 507
price strategy 507
product line pricing 519
promotional allowance (trade allowance) 512
quantity discount 512
rebate 512
resale price maintenance 509
seasonal discount 512
single-price tactic 514–515
two-part pricing 518
unbundling 517
uniform delivered pricing 514
value-based pricing 512
zone pricing 514

APPLY IT

RoseAnn decided that time is, indeed, money. So she opened a Chinese buffet in Kingston, Ontario. The new twist is that you pay by the minute. The restaurant, known as Rose's Chinese Buffet, is all-you-can-eat-by-the-minute.* The buffet table is piled with delectable seafood and steaming stir-fried dishes. Diners rush to their tables and wolf down spring rolls, fried noodles, fried rice, and other goodies. RoseAnn allows only the first 30 customers at lunch and dinner to pay by the minute. The rest must order from a traditional menu or pay the normal buffet price. By-the-minute lunch customers pay 30¢ a minute.

*Such restaurants do exist in Japan.

QUESTIONS

1. RoseAnn concedes that she only breaks even on her by-the-minute customers. Should she drop the concept?
2. What pricing tactics is she using?
3. Would such a restaurant be successful in your community?

THINK ABOUT IT

People feel better when they think that they are getting a great bargain when they shop. Knowing this, some retailers mark up items above the traditional retail price and then offer a 60-percent discount. If they had simply discounted the normal retail price by 20 percent the resulting "sale price" would have been the same. One retailer says that he is just making shoppers happy that they got a great deal when he inflates the retail price before discounting.

QUESTIONS

1. What do you think?
2. Does the CMA Code of Ethics address this issue? Go to **http://the-cma.org/consumer/ethics.cfm** and review the code. Then write a brief paragraph summarizing what the CMA Code of Ethics contains that relates to retail pricing.

TRY IT

Setting the Right Price for a Special ISP

With only 2,000 residents, Boblo Island is small enough to avoid recognition as a major market for anything. The affluent community, however, is situated on a small strip of land in the Detroit River between Canada and the U.S. near Amherstburg, Ontario. That means the community has normal market needs. A group of ambitious entrepreneurs want to provide the island's Internet service.

A high school information-technology teacher, John Davis, heads a team of students seeking to become the island's sole Internet service provider. He and his band of students call their nonprofit company IslanderISP, and together they trust that the profits from the business will fund the high school's technology needs.

© JIM LOTT/SEATTLE TIMES

The group hopes to prove that it isn't necessary to have hundreds of thousands or millions of dollars in seed money from a venture capitalist to start a successful technology company. Having worked for IBM and Hewlett-Packard, Davis has the experience to lead his youthful partners. He sees the start-up as a means to developing more mature, experienced, and job-ready students in an increasingly competitive world. He plans to bolster his time-strapped staff by recruiting retired teachers to work for them.

After incorporating as a nonprofit, staff members approached school officials about locating headquarters on high school property. They also contacted Qwest, which will provide them with connectivity to the Internet and advice on modem quantities and server locations. Qwest will also house IslanderISP's e-mail and Web servers, an arrangement that will give IslanderISP an advantage over most dial-up services by greatly reducing the time it will take for its customers to dial into the information superhighway.

At the high school, the young entrepreneurs are generating a buzz through word of mouth and by handing out brochures at school sporting events. David Booth, a senior and public relations officer for the company, is pushing local radio stations and the local newspapers for exposure.

A subscription costs $32.50 per month. Customers who pay in full and upfront for the year receive one month free and pay only $357.50 for 12 months of service. Those who sign for a three-year subscription pay just $975, a discount equalling six months of free service at the introductory price. If it achieves 100-percent market penetration, IslanderISP projects a $50,000 annual profit.

QUESTIONS

1. Did IslanderISP thoroughly follow the procedure for setting the right price? Explain and critique.
2. What type of pricing strategy do you think would work best for IslanderISP?
3. Explain the special pricing tactics IslanderISP used in fine-tuning its base price.

FLIP IT

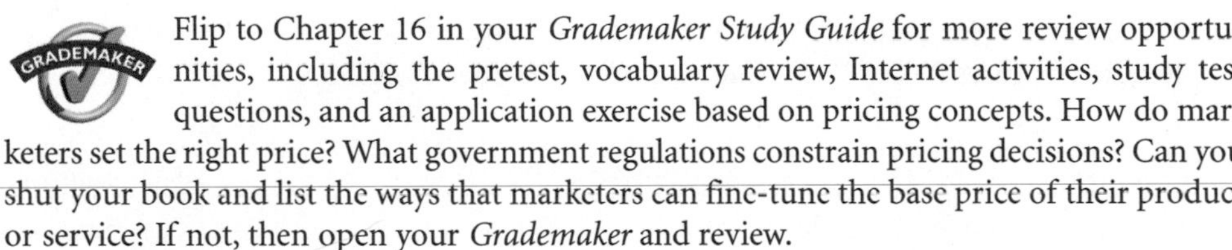

Flip to Chapter 16 in your *Grademaker Study Guide* for more review opportunities, including the pretest, vocabulary review, Internet activities, study test questions, and an application exercise based on pricing concepts. How do marketers set the right price? What government regulations constrain pricing decisions? Can you shut your book and list the ways that marketers can fine-tune the base price of their product or service? If not, then open your *Grademaker* and review.

CLICK IT

The *Marketing* website is rich with materials to help you review and master marketing concepts. Check your knowledge with the free quizzes, practise key terms using the crossword puzzles, or review key concepts using the Microsoft® PowerPoint® slides. Also on the website are updated weblinks to companies mentioned in this chapter, Internet exercises, career marketing information, and much much more! Go to http://www.lamb3e.nelson.com, read the material, and follow the convenient links.

WATCH IT

Air Wars: Air Canada's Pricing Woes

Since its establishment as a Crown Corporation by an act of the Parliament of Canada in 1937, Air Canada has been Canada's largest airline. After being privatized and taking over Canadian Airlines, Air Canada controlled over 90 percent of airline passenger travel in Canada. In 2004, Air Canada served over

700 destinations, in 128 countries, and generated nearly $9 billion in revenue. Sound good to you? Well, being large can bring on many different types of problems. Among them, how would you like to have every move you make closely watched by the government?

While many aspects of Air Canada's operations are closely scrutinized to ensure that the company is in compliance with all federal legislation, one of the areas most closely monitored by the government is Air Canada's pricing. Because Air Canada is Canada's largest air passenger carrier, the government wants to ensure that Air Canada charges "fair" prices to Canadian air travellers. Generally, of course, Air Canada would like to comply with the wishes of the government. What do you do, however, when different government agencies send different signals?

Let's watch as Air Canada and its President and CEO, Robert Milton, battle with two government departments over Air Canada's prices. On the one hand, the Ministry of Transport has accused Air Canada of charging monopoly prices on some of its routes and wants Air Canada to lower its fares. On the other hand, the Competition Bureau of Industry Canada has accused Air Canada of charging predatory prices, making it difficult for other air carriers to compete with Air Canada. The Competition Bureau wants Air Canada to raise its fares. What's a company to do?

QUESTIONS

1. How would you handle Air Canada's pricing problems if you were in Robert Milton's shoes?
2. Is the current level of government regulation of business good or bad for consumers? What is too much government regulation?
3. What sort of pricing policy do you feel Air Canada is following?

SUGGESTED INFORMATION SOURCES

http://www.aircanada.ca

CBC, *Venture*, "Air Wars," Broadcast: January 27, 2002.

Michael Janigan, "The Airline Ticket Pricing Game," Public Interest Advocacy Centre (**http://www.piac.ca**), January 29, 2001.

"Roots Air charges Air Canada with predatory pricing," CBC News (**http://cbc.ca**), March 8, 2001.

"Small B.C. Airline Accuses Insolvent Air Canada of Predatory Pricing," *Canadian Press NewsWire*, April 16, 2003.

Nicolas Van Praet, "Profitable WestJet Accuses Air Canada of Using Court-Protection to Reduce Air Fares Below Cost," *CanWest News*, October 20, 2003, 1.

MARKETING MISCUES

Apple's Futuristic Cube Is Already a Thing of the Past

Apple Computer has been at the forefront in innovative computer design. The company ignited the computer revolution in the 1970s with the Apple II and then reenergized the personal computer market in the 1980s with the Macintosh. In an attempt to bring the PC market into the twenty-first century, Apple introduced its Cube in July 2000. Although Cube owners loved their Cubes, not enough customers were willing to pay the price for the futuristic box.

Price appears to have been a major factor in the Cube's market failure. At $1,799, it was one of the higher-priced PCs in the marketplace. For this higher price, consumers got a PC that took up very little desk space. The Cube's features included the following:

- 64 MB of RAM
- 20 GB hard drive
- Mac OS 9.0.4
- DVD-ROM drive
- A silvery cube, 203 mm on each side, inside a clear plastic column, 254 mm high
- A power-on/off light indicator (requiring merely tapping to power up or down)
- Two baseball-shaped Harmon Kardon speakers
- A fan-free liquid cooling system (resulting in quieter running)
- A ball-free, buttonless optical mouse
- Reduced cable clutter

Although these features, particularly the product's futuristic design, were lauded by those closest to the system (Apple employees), the Cube failed to meet computer users' expectations on various fronts:

- A monitor was not included.
- The Cube lacked removable storage devices (e.g., Zip drive).
- The on/off switch was in a sensitive area on the case top, resulting in accidental touches.
- There was no floppy drive.
- There were no expansion slots.

Apple's share of the North American PC market was around 7 percent in the first half of 2000. Its worldwide market share was almost 4 percent. Apple aspired to increase its market share one to two percentage points per year, with each point worth around $1.3 billion in revenue. With average industry growth of 15 percent, Apple expected to grow at a rate of 34 percent. The Cube was to play a key role in meeting the company's growth targets. Sales forecasts for the cool-looking Cube were around 800,000 units in year one.

Unfortunately, the Cube failed to lead Apple in the right direction. The computer's liabilities apparently outweighed its assets. Several industry experts complained that the Cube's price was high in relation to the value it gave the user. Although it offered a new design, some questioned why anyone would pay the price for a computer so lacking in new, innovative technology. While the computer had been touted as a work of art, its pricey aesthetics failed to compensate for its unimpressive internal mechanics.

While competitors courted the multibillion-dollar corporate computer market, Apple's brand of individualism had led the company to target niche markets. Consumers in many of these niche markets have generally sought fun, easy-to-use computer systems. Unfortunately for Apple, consumers in its niche markets were not cool enough to pay the desired price for the Cube, and production was suspended only a year after it was introduced. In hindsight, the price was too high for the market, and the product had a low price–quality relationship.

Questions

1. Were Apple's pricing objectives profit oriented, sales oriented, or status quo oriented?
2. How could Apple have done a better job of setting the right price for the Cube?

CRITICAL THINKING CASE

Nokia's $20,000 Cellular Phone

Nokia's luxury-edition cell phone has it all—platinum or 18-karat gold housing, crystal screen, soft leather casings, upgradeable internal components—all for only $21,240 (in Europe 24,000 euros)! Why such a high-priced cell phone? Will anyone buy it?

The Mobile Phone Industry

The mobile phone industry has burgeoned in the past few years. By 2005, cellular penetration is expected to be over 80 percent in many European countries and well over 30 percent in North America. Product innovation and pricing appear to be the drivers for this level of market penetration. Price-sensitive consumers are expected to purchase the low-end cell phones, while price-insensitive consumers will demand the latest and greatest in cellular technology.

By 2000, the mobile phone industry was thought to be the world's largest consumer electronics industry in terms of unit sales. Although overall market penetration has been phenomenal, such growth levels are not expected to continue. Rather, experts predict only modest growth in the mid to late 2000s. Since first-time users accounted for over half of mobile phone purchases at the start of 2000, replacement sales are expected to comprise around 75 percent of sales in later years.

The mobile phone industry is dominated by major competitors including Ericsson (Sony), Motorola, Nokia, Qualcomm, Samsung, and Sanyo. Each of these companies offers cellular phones with numerous product options and various price ranges. Consumers' wants vary, but prevailing wisdom suggests that important phone features include size (the smaller the better), ease of use, and technological advances. Interestingly, cellphones may have a sexual connotation as well. One study suggests that men use their cellphones to attract women.

Nokia

Nokia (**http://www.nokia.com**) has annual worldwide sales of $28 billion. A world leader in mobile communications, Nokia comprises two business groups: Nokia Networks and Nokia Mobile Phones.

With around 40 percent of the worldwide market for cellular phones, Nokia is the global leader in the development, manufacturing, and sales of mobile phones. In one recent year alone, Nokia introduced 22 new cell phones. The company has been called the fifth most valuable brand in the world.

Attempting to differentiate its product offerings while building on its branding efforts, Nokia has founded the world's first luxury mobile phone company. This new, independent subsidiary, Vertu, started operations in 2002 and will cater to very wealthy consumers. A senior vice president in Nokia's Asia-Pacific division, Nigel Litchfield, will serve as president of London-based Vertu, Ltd.

Historically, Nokia has been known for marketing well-designed, user-friendly phones that are popular with the everyday phone user. The new Vertu phones, however, focus on the phone as a status symbol of the very wealthy and take Nokia into a niche market. Selling under the Vertu brand, the company's most expensive product carries a hefty price tag of $21,240. For this premium price, the rich and discerning customer gets a cellular phone that makes a fashion statement. In addition to its platinum handset and crystal display screen, this limited-edition luxury phone features evolutionary technology that will allow the phone's internal mechanisms to be upgraded while keeping the outside casing intact. The lower end of this elite product will feature similar internal technology inside a stainless steel casing. The low-end price is expected to be around $5,300. These luxury phones will be available by private showing only in the most distinguished shopping areas of Paris, London, Los Angeles, New York, Toronto, and Hong Kong.

Nokia is not the only company offering limited-edition, high-end cellular phones. For many years, Ericsson has made gold-plated phones, and Motorola has an 18-karat gold, diamond-studded phone. Priced in the tens of thousands of dollars, both companies' phones have been particularly popular with oil sheiks in the Middle East. The London-based jeweller, de Grisogono, also provides diamond casings for mobile phone units. Reportedly, one celebrity paid $90 million for a diamond-studded phone. Although Nokia will be competing with these companies for the high-end market, the Vertu phone has the internal sophistication to allow it to stand alone in the marketplace—whatever and wherever that marketplace may be.

Questions

1. What are the determinants of Vertu's pricing strategy?
2. What pricing strategy is being followed?
3. Does Vertu's pricing strategy fit within Nokia's broader product line pricing strategy?
4. Why might Nokia have entered what appears to be a relatively small niche market?

>> # Managing Marketing-Created Relationships

part 7

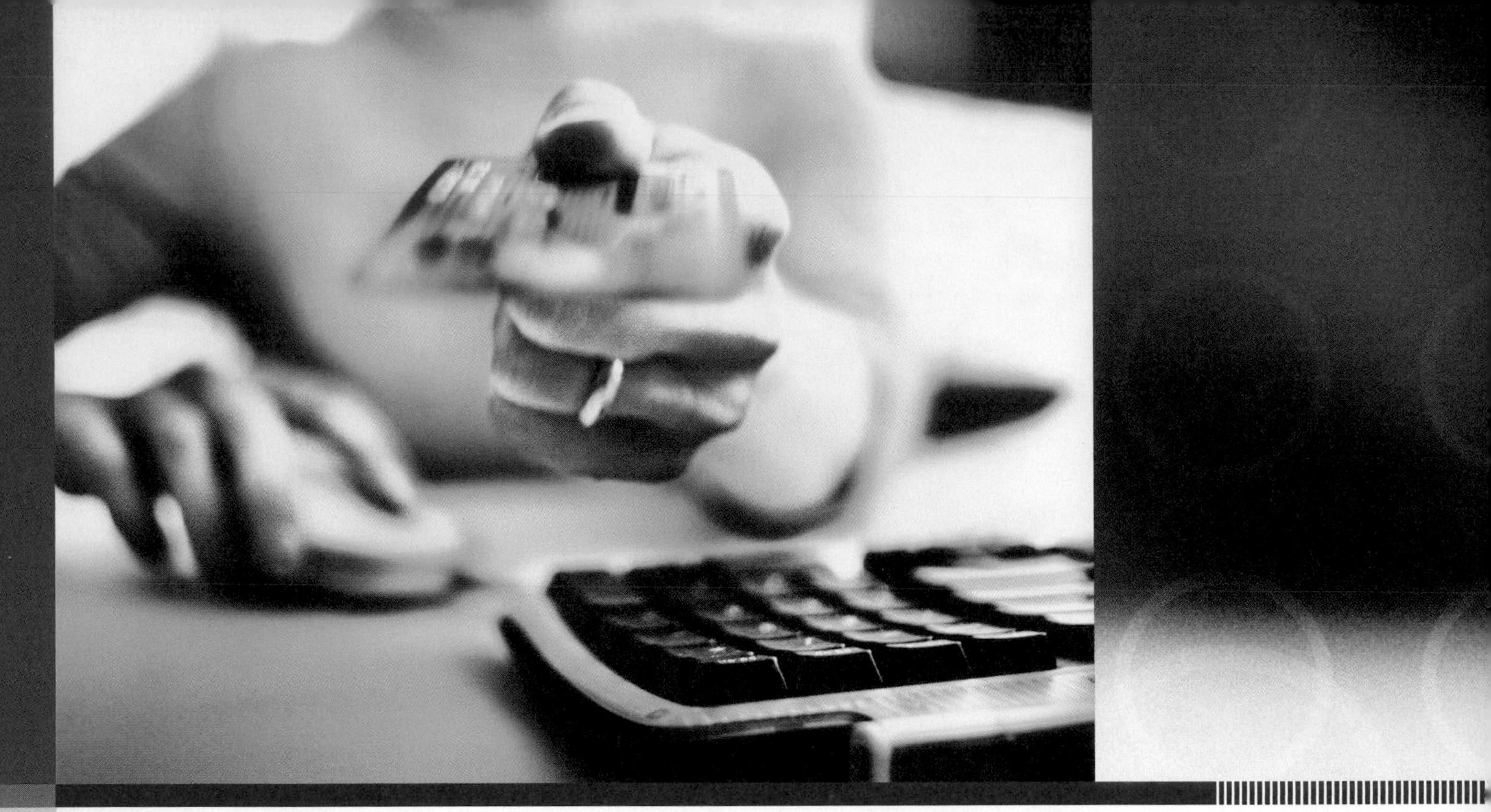

chapter 17

One-to-One and Internet Marketing

>> LEARNING OBJECTIVES

1. Define one-to-one marketing and discuss its dependence on database technology
2. Discuss the forces that have influenced the emergence of one-to-one marketing
3. Compare the one-to-one marketing communications process with the traditional mass-marketing communications process
4. List eight common one-to-one marketing applications
5. Discuss the basics of one-to-one marketing database technology
6. Describe the impact of the Internet on business practices
7. Describe the current Internet marketing environment
8. Discuss on-line business strategies
9. Discuss Internet marketing objectives and strategies
10. Describe one-to-one marketing using the Internet
11. Discuss privacy issues related to one-to-one marketing and Internet marketing

>> Amazon.com is an e-tailer that sells books, CDs, videos, electronic equipment, and more to over 38 million customers in 220 countries around the world including Canada (through Amazon.ca). Its customers say they enjoy shopping at Amazon because of the product selection, convenience, and customer service. Company president Jeff Bezos says Amazon's success is due to the company's relentless commitment to its customers.

When Bezos started the company in 1995, his mission was to use the Internet to transform book buying into the fastest, easiest, and most enjoyable shopping experience possible. Since then, the company has grown to offer Earth's Biggest Selection, where customers can find anything they might want to buy on-line.

Everything Amazon does is based on exceeding customers' expectations. For instance, the website is designed to be easy to navigate, product selection is comprehensive, and fulfillment centres are spread around the globe to ensure prompt order delivery. All of these things contribute to the company's success. A large part of Amazon's $3.12 billion in sales, however, is due to the company's one-to-one marketing expertise.

The first time customers visit Amazon they are encouraged to register. From that point on, anytime they log on from their own computer, they can expect to be greeted by name. When customers make a purchase, they immediately receive an order confirmation with a purchase tracking number via e-mail. When their order is shipped, they are again notified by e-mail.

Additionally, from the time a customer registers with Amazon, the company tracks the customer's browsing and purchasing behaviour in order to learn about the customer's preferences. The company then uses that information to make product recommendations based on the customer's interest. For example, if a customer purchased *The One to One Future: Building Relationships One Customer at a Time* by Don Peppers and Martha Wang, the next time that customer visits Amazon, he or she may receive a recommendation for *Strategic Database Marketing* by Rob Jackson and Paul Wang. To improve the value of its recommendations, Amazon encourages customers to provide additional information about their likes and dislikes by rating the recommended items. Eventually, clients who shop and communicate with Amazon regularly find that Amazon makes valuable recommendations based on their individual preferences. As a result, customers find themselves looking forward to the recommendations and making more purchases.[1]

So how does Amazon market its products and communicate individually with 38 million customers? It does so by developing, maintaining, and implementing a successful database system of one-to-one marketing via the Internet. In this chapter, you will learn more about the advantages of one-to-one marketing and the technology that makes it possible. You will also learn about the Internet and how marketers can use this new medium to engage in marketing activities such as one-to-one marketing.

ON LINE 

Amazon

Test the accuracy of Amazon's recommendations by registering at the site and tweaking your profile over several purchases. Do you find the items recommended to you appealing? Enough to purchase them? How successful has Amazon been in identifying products that match your tastes and interests?

http://www.amazon.ca

1 Define one-to-one marketing and discuss its dependence on database technology

>> WHAT IS "ONE-TO-ONE MARKETING"?

One-to-one marketing is the ultimate goal of a new trend in marketing that focuses on understanding customers as individuals instead of as part of a group. To this end, contemporary marketers are making their communications more customer-specific, like the personalized marketing efforts being initiated by Amazon.com.

Most businesses today use a mass-marketing approach designed to increase their *market share* by selling their products to the greatest number of people. For many businesses, however, it is more efficient and profitable to use one-to-one marketing to increase *share of customer*—in other words, to sell more products to each customer. **One-to-one marketing** is an individualized marketing method that utilizes customer information to build long-term, personalized, and profitable relationships with each customer. The goal is to reduce costs through customer retention and increase revenue through customer loyalty.[2] Customer relationship management (CRM), a related marketing strategy that takes a broader approach than one-to-one marketing, will be presented in Chapter 18.

one-to-one marketing
An individualized marketing method that utilizes customer information to build long-term, personalized, and profitable relationships with each customer.

The difference between one-to-one marketing and the traditional mass-marketing approach can be compared to shooting a rifle and a shotgun. If you have good aim, a rifle is the most efficient weapon to use. A shotgun, on the other hand, increases your odds of hitting the target when it is more difficult to focus. Instead of scattering messages far and wide across the spectrum of mass media (the shotgun approach), one-to-one marketers are now homing in on ways to communicate with each individual customer (the rifle approach).

The Evolution of One-to-One Marketing

It may surprise many readers—especially those who grew up to the sound of advertising jingles on television and the sight of billboards dotting the landscape—that one-to-one marketing is not at all new. In fact, before the Industrial Revolution introduced mass advertising, businesses understood that their success depended on their ability to build relationships with their customers. Merchants built their businesses by tracking customer purchases and making recommendations based on past purchases and the customer's interests. Moreover, products often were custom produced or modified to fit the customer's needs.

The Industrial Revolution brought about mass production and led to volume buying and mass advertising. Companies grew and prospered by manufacturing large quantities of the same product, advertising it through mass media, and profiting from sales volume.

As a result, marketers developed a different view of the customer. No longer viewed as unique, all customers were perceived as having the same needs and as being reachable through the same channels with the same message. As Henry Ford said it, "We'll give you any color you want, as long as it's black."

Today, however, customers demand more choices; they seek to buy precisely what meets their needs and wants, and they expect individualized attention. Technology now makes it possible for companies to interact with these customers in new ways, by creating databases that pull data from, and feed information to, those interactions. Companies are using technology that makes it possible to tailor products, services, and communications to meet those expectations.

© REUTERS NEWMEDIA INC./CORBIS

How serious are companies about giving customers individualized attention? Levi Strauss, based in San Francisco, California, and famous for manufacturing jeans, has a shrink tub in its San Francisco megastore. Customers can sit in the tub and shrink their jeans to fit. After the shrink tub, they pass through the human dryer before leaving the store.

ON LINE 

www.pooch.ca

www.pluscious.com

Pet lovers can find information on over 200 different breeds of dogs and then locate sources that can provide a dog of that breed. Food and pet supplies to suit your dog are also readily available. Go to the Pooch.ca website and find a breed of dog that fits your personality and lifestyle. Now go to Pluscious.com and find a bed for your potential new friend. Were you able to find a bed that would suit your pet and the decor of your bedroom? Were you able to adjust the bed to suit the size of your new pet? Can you think of any important aspect of customization for purchasing a pet or pet supplies that is missing from these services?

http://www.pooch.ca

http://www.pluscious.com

As a result of one-to-one marketing and the benefits of technology, companies are increasingly shifting from a product-driven orientation to a customer-driven emphasis. Early visionaries of this change were Stan Rapp and Tom Collins, who cowrote the 1987 book *Maxi-Marketing*, which summarized the new direction emerging at the time:[3]

> Every established norm in advertising and promotion is being transformed.... We are living through a shift from selling virtually everyone the same thing a generation ago to fulfilling the individual needs and tastes of better-educated consumers by supplying them with customized products and services. The shift [is] from a "get a sale now at any cost" to building and managing customer databases to track the lifetime value of your relationship with each customer. As the cost of accumulating and accessing data drops, the ability to talk directly with prospects and customers, building one-to-one relationships with them, will grow.
>
> As one-to-one marketing takes hold, it is no longer enough to understand customers and prospects by aggregate profiles. The one-to-one future requires that marketers understand their customers and collaborate with them, rather than use them as targets. In fact, many early one-to-one marketing efforts failed because marketers bombarded customers with irrelevant, one-to-one communications before making an effort to understand the customers. The fundamental challenge of one-to-one marketing today is to combine the customer information gleaned from database technology with compelling marketing communications.[4]

The one-to-one future is still a goal, not a reality, for most companies. But progress toward one-to-one marketing is evident in the increase in personalized communications and product customization. The battle for customers will be won by marketers who understand why and how their customers buy their products and who win them over one customer at a time.

New technology allows businesses to personalize messages to their customers. For example, a user of My Yahoo.com is greeted by name and presented with information in which the user has expressed interest. Similarly, RedEnvelope.com helps customers keep track of special occasions and offers personalized gift recommendations. The best-known example of one-to-one product customization is Dell Computer.

Why One-to-One Marketing Needs Database Technology

How can marketers really communicate with their customers one at a time? How can huge corporations like Bombardier and Canadian Tire communicate with each and every one of their thousands or millions of customers on a personal level?

The answer lies in *database technology*. Fundamentally, one-to-one marketing is no more than the relationship cultivated by a salesperson with the customer. A successful salesperson builds a relationship over time, constantly thinks about what the customer needs and wants, and is mindful of the trends and patterns in the customer's purchase history. A good salesperson often knows what the customer needs even before the customer knows. The salesperson may also inform, educate, and instruct the customer about new products, technologies, or applications in anticipation of the customer's future needs or requirements.

This kind of thoughtful attention is the basis of one-to-one marketing. Database technology provides the tools marketers need to "get to know" their customers on a personal basis. Moreover, today's databases are capable of storing information about a company's customers, their purchasing history, and their preferences and then presenting it in a meaningful format that marketers can use to assess, analyze, and anticipate customer needs.

ON LINE 

Search Systems.net

Search Systems.net provides access to free databases in Canada, the U.S., and internationally. The service provides access to both free and paid information and is organized by country and then individual state or province. Go to the public records directory and find Canada by province. Click on Ontario and find out how many licensed podiatrists and chiropodists are available to look after the feet of Ontario citizens. What other healthcare professionals can you find? Look at the other provinces and see what kinds of healthcare professional databases they have available. Compare the various databases available from province to province. What did you find?

http://www.searchsystems.net/

With the help of database technology, one-to-one marketers can track their customers as individuals, even if they number in the millions. Database technology enables marketers to sift through the millions of pieces of data to target the right customers, to develop the right communication based on these customers' needs, and to monitor the ongoing relationship, making adjustments in message strategy as needed.

The number of consumer and business names in many databases and the variety of these databases is astounding—for example http://www.searchsystems.net/ promises access to the largest directory of links to free public record databases on the Internet. The site offers information on "businesses, corporate filings, property records, unclaimed property, professional licences, offenders, inmates, criminal and civil court filings, and much more."[5] The Bay has 500,000 names of Canadian Hbc Rewards and credit card holders; and Mead Johnson, maker of Enfamil baby formula, has 5 million names of expectant or new mothers in North America.[6] The data some companies collect can take up huge amounts of computer memory. Wal-Mart's database, considered second in size only to that of the U.S. Department of Defense, contains over 200 terabytes (trillions of characters) of past customer transaction data. Wal-Mart uses its massive database to help each of its stores adapt its merchandising mix to local neighbourhood preferences.[7]

Amazingly, many companies fail to use the information in their databases. Instead, they treat returning customers like first-time customers and continue to ask for the same information over and over again, thereby missing the opportunity to build a relationship. For instance, some hotel chains fail to track customers' room preferences, and many catalogue companies require customers to provide their address and credit card information every time they place an order.[8]

Although developing databases for one-to-one marketing efforts can be expensive, the return on investment can be huge. For example, Rocky Mountaineer Railtours, a Western Canadian firm, invested in a direct-mail campaign in 2002. The firm had a mailing list of 32,000 names developed from past brochure inquiries, referrals, and past customers. Rocky Mountaineer targeted these people with a full-colour postcard that offered them a chance to win their trip if they booked a tour. In addition, the firm set up a toll-free number tied to the campaign and also provided a special air travel offer to encourage people to fly then ride the rails. The result: the firm recorded $1.3 million in bookings from the promotion, which amounted to a return of 58 times the cost of the campaign![9]

2 Discuss the forces that have influenced the emergence of one-to-one marketing

>> FORCES INFLUENCING ONE-TO-ONE MARKETING

Several forces have helped shape this new one-to-one focus on customers. They include a more diverse society, more demanding and time-poor consumers, a decline in brand loyalty, the explosion of new media alternatives, and demand for marketing accountability.[10]

Increasing Diversity

In the 1950s and 1960s, Canadians strove for the TV family ideal of the perfect lifestyle like the one epitomized on shows such as *Leave It to Beaver*. The ideal family was Caucasian and lived in a comfortable suburban house; the father worked to support the family, and mom stayed home to keep a tidy house and raise the children. Life was simple. Dad came home from work at 5 P.M., the family ate dinner together, and later they gathered around the one television set to watch the *Wayne and Shuster Comedy Hour.* Although not everyone of that era lived this lifestyle, nearly everybody agreed that it was the ideal.

Today, less than 7 percent of households fit this profile. Modern families are split into many smaller segments, such as unmarried couples living together, fathers or mothers heading households alone, married couples without children, homosexual couples, singles living alone or with roommates, older "empty nesters," and many other permutations. Even more important than the diversity of today's household, however, is society's acceptance of that diversity. Today, people acknowledge and accept diversity, and our definition of what is acceptable has changed as the family has changed.

More Demanding, Time- and Cash-Poor Consumers

Consumers today are more strapped for time than any previous generation. Canadian families are spending less time together, having fewer births, and as a consequence living in smaller households. These smaller families are composed of one-child couples and single parents but also include more childless couples and lone homeowners than ever before. Along with this trend, adult children are staying at home longer, and multigenerational family units are growing too. The smaller families are time-poor—that is, they work long hours to earn money. Also, multigenerational families tend to be cash-poor—that is, their money is spread thin. Canadian consumers have less and less time to spend on anything but the most pressing details of their lives. This is having a profound impact on consumers' buying behaviour. Consumers are becoming more demanding, more impatient, and much less likely to spend time agonizing over small purchases or driving across town to the mall. This situation is evident in the statistics showing that 43 percent of Canadians have made at least one purchase on-line since they began using the Net. In addition, over 16 percent of Canadians report that they bank mainly on-line, while another one-third of Canadians report they do some on-line banking.[11]

Decreasing Brand Loyalty

In a 1975 survey of male and female heads of households, over three-quarters agreed with this statement: "I try to stick to well-known brand names." Ten years later, only a little over half agreed with the same statement. This trend has continued through the 1990s and into the new century. Consumers are now more likely to experiment with generics or switch back and forth between major brands in a category. They are also more likely to shop for discounts, and if presented with two comparable brands, will likely choose based on price.

The decline in brand loyalty can be attributed in part to the excessive couponing, trade deals, and deep price promotions by manufacturers and retailers; these practices have accustomed consumers to look for the best deal. Brand loyalty has also wavered due to the proliferation of brands available, with thousands more being introduced annually. With so many product choices, consumers often become confused about product differentiation or lack the time to learn about each new brand. As a result, consumers often resort to basing their purchases on price.

The decrease in brand loyalty can also be attributed to the increasing power of many retailers today. Retailers are increasingly taking control of their relationships with brand marketers, dictating level and type of in-store promotions, placement of product, and price. These retailers are also more sophisticated at developing their own customer communications programs, which include multicoupon direct-mail and relationship-oriented marketing programs. As a result, consumers are building more of a relationship with a particular retailer than with a brand. For example, consumers may drive 50 or more kilometres to a Wal-Mart store to shop even though they can get the same brands at relatively the same prices in their own neighbourhood.

Emergence of New Media Alternatives

Three decades ago, most Canadians spent their evenings in front of their television sets, watching cable television programming with a limited choice of channels—CBC, CTV, and Global television along with the major American networks, NBC, CBS, and ABC.

They were also more likely to read the newspaper and subscribe to a general newsmagazine such as *Maclean's*. Marketers reached consumers by blanketing mass media with image advertising.

Today's busy consumers are not at all likely to be found spending their evenings watching the latest sitcom on network television. Instead, they are probably surfing the hundreds of channels available through their digital cable or direct satellite system, watching a rented movie, or visiting their favourite game or news site on the Internet. Newspapers and general-interest magazines have given way to an abundance of specialty publications that cater to a wide range of interests.

With the emergence of new and varied media alternatives, mass-media advertising will never be the same. Marketers must increasingly divvy up their marketing dollars among the various media available, concentrating on those that will bring them the most bang for their buck. Although mass-media advertising on network television or through general-interest magazines will continue to play an important role in communicating brand messages, it will never again be the dominant force it once was.

Demand for Accountability

The impact of mass-media advertising on sales has always been difficult to measure. Generations of marketers have quoted the comment of John Wanamaker, a late-nineteenth-century American merchant: "I know half of my advertising is wasted. I just don't know which half." Historically, the results of a newspaper or television advertising expenditure could be measured only through future sales of the advertised offering, its increase in market share, or the increase in store traffic. Even sales promotional tactics, which provide more measurability than mass-media efforts, have come under attack. For instance, coupons distributed through the freestanding inserts found in the weekend paper are just as much a form of mass-media advertising as a full-page image ad in the same paper and, therefore, largely unaccountable. Manufacturers today are under pressure to maintain growth and profits for stockholders. It is no longer acceptable to say that sales increased after an advertising campaign. Management now wants proof that monies spent on advertising and marketing will deliver results.

How Have These Trends Influenced One-to-One Marketing?

What are these forces telling marketers? How are they pushing forward the customer-focused philosophy of one-to-one marketing?

For starters, a more diverse society has ruled that the one-size-fits-all marketing of yesteryear no longer fits. Consumers do not want to be treated like the masses. Instead, they want to be treated as the individuals they are, with their own unique sets of needs and wants. By its personalized nature, one-to-one marketing can fulfill this desire.

Second, more direct and personal marketing efforts will continue to grow to meet the needs of consumers who no longer have the time to spend shopping and making purchase decisions. With the personal and targeted nature of one-to-one marketing, consumers can spend less time making purchase decisions and more time doing the things that are important.

Third, consumers will be loyal only to those companies and brands that have earned their loyalty and reinforced it at every purchase occasion. One-to-one marketing techniques focus on finding a firm's best customers, rewarding them for their loyalty, and thanking them for their business.

Fourth, mass-media approaches will decline in importance as advances in market research and database technology allow marketers to collect detailed information on their customers, not just the approximations offered by demographics but the specific

ON LINE

CBC

Visit CBC's website and sign on to become a member. How does CBC personalize its content? Can this action be considered one-to-one marketing? Why or why not?

http://www.cbc.ca

names and addresses. One-to-one marketing will increase in importance and offer marketers a more cost-effective avenue to reach customers. Finally, the demand for accountability will drive the growth of one-to-one marketing and justify its continued existence.

One-to-one marketing is a huge commitment and often requires a 180-degree turnaround for marketers who spent the last half of the twentieth century thick in mass-marketing efforts. Although mass marketing will probably always be part of the promotional mix, especially to create brand awareness or to remind consumers of a product, the advantages of one-to-one marketing cannot be ignored. Today, the new commandment of marketing's future rings loudly in every marketer's ears: "Know thy customer and communicate with him or her based on what you know."[12]

>> A REVISED MARKETING COMMUNICATIONS PROCESS

3 Compare the one-to-one marketing communications process with the traditional mass-marketing communications process

The traditional mass-marketing communications process, introduced in Chapter 13, in which everyone receives the same message through the same channel, no longer holds true in a one-to-one marketing environment. Recall that the mass-marketing communications process presented in Exhibit 13.2 depicts an advertiser or marketer sending a promotional message through some type of mass-marketing channel, such as a television ad or an outdoor billboard, to the target audience. Noise from competing advertisements affects the encoding and decoding of the message. Feedback on the effectiveness of the communication comes through market research and changes in sales levels or market share.

Now compare this process with Exhibit 17.1, which depicts marketing communications using one-to-one marketing and database technology. The revised **one-to-one marketing communications process** flows as follows: (1) the one-to-one marketer, the *sender*, encodes individualized messages for customers and prospects identified from the database; (2) the message is then sent through a direct communications channel, such as direct mail, a salesperson, a telemarketer, or the Internet; (3) the customer or prospect, the *receiver*, interprets the personalized message; (4) the customer or prospect responds to the communication through a response, a purchase, or other communication; (5) the one-to-one marketer captures this response, feeding it back into the marketing database, where it will help shape the next marketing communication.

one-to-one marketing communications process
A revised marketing communications process that depicts the individualized communication between the one-to-one marketer and the customer; characterized by the use of personalized communication, the lack of interfering noise, and the ability to capture the response of the customer.

Although the flow of the communications process is still basically the same, from marketer to customer, there are a few significant differences. First, the encoded message is *personalized* to the individual. A personalized, one-to-one communication is sent to relatively few individuals who are known to be interested, in contrast to a mass communication, in which the same message is sent to a large group of potential respondents who may or may not be interested.

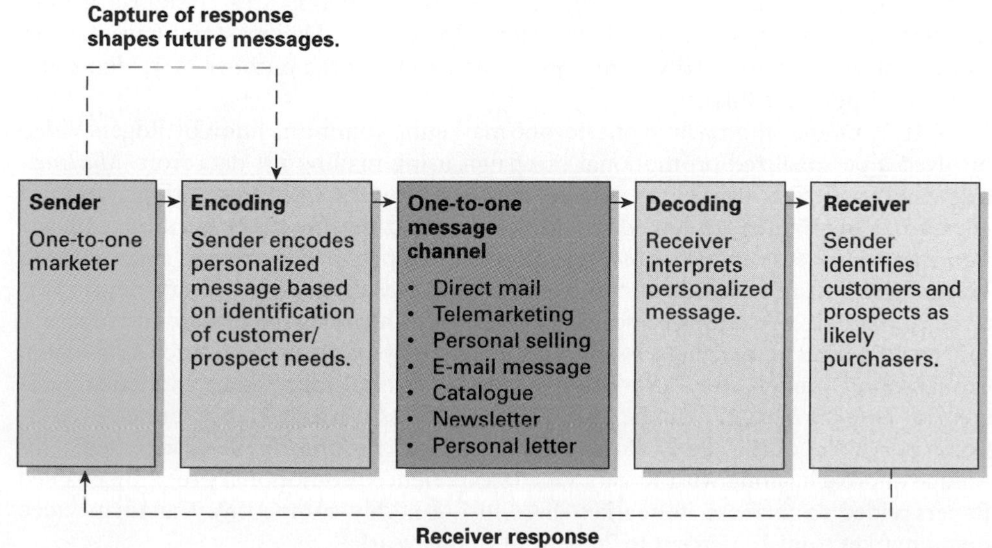

EXHIBIT 17.1
One-to-One Marketing Communications Process

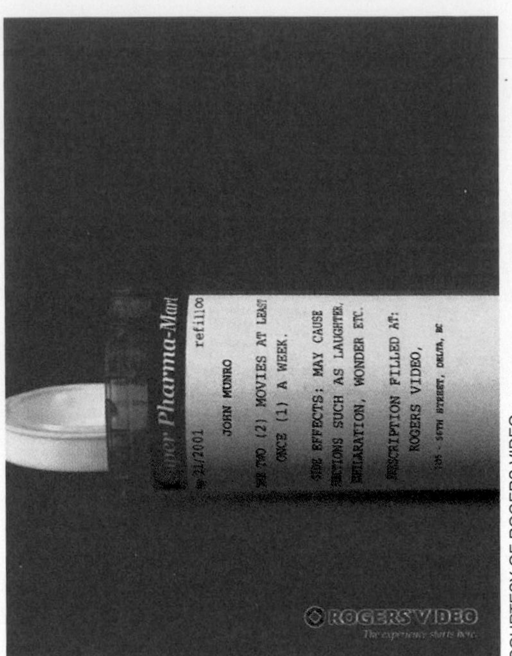

COURTESY OF ROGERS VIDEO

Using one-to-one marketing as part of its strategy, Rogers Video accomplished a market share increase from 16 percent to 26 percent in one year! Rogers Video was able to access the *Maclean's* magazine subscription database from its parent firm, Rogers Communications of Toronto, to implement a highly targeted promotional strategy. Each *Maclean's* subscriber received a magazine that included an ad for Rogers Video, which was personalized with their name and the location of their closest Rogers Video store.

Second, the channel used to send the message is a *direct* channel rather than a mass-media channel. With mass-media channels such as television or newspapers, marketers do not personally know the people with whom they are trying to communicate. With a direct one-to-one channel, the marketer has some information about each individual customer. Further, with mass-media channels, the company is unable to respond immediately to customers' reactions to its message. Instead, it must wait to see whether people are reacting positively or negatively by conducting research or by monitoring sales and market share. With a direct one-to-one channel, marketers can capture individual customer responses and use this information to shape future communications.

Third, notice that *noise*, or interference from competing advertisements, news articles, or other competing store displays, is not present in the one-to-one marketing communications process. This is because the communication occurs directly from the marketer to the customer or prospect, with minimal interference from competing messages. Although no communications environment is completely free of interfering noise—the dog may be barking, the children interrupting, or the telephone ringing—the one-to-one communications process comes as close as possible to being noise-free. With less interference, the receiver of the one-to-one marketing message is more likely to receive and interpret the communication correctly.

Last, in the one-to-one communications process the response of the individual can be captured, allowing the marketer to use the response to update the customer record, tailor the next marketing effort, and provide accountability for marketing dollars spent. John Munro, vice president of marketing for Rogers Video in Richmond, B.C., understands the one-to-one communications process very well. His firm researched consumer buying behaviour for video rentals. Rogers discovered that video renters considered watching videos an experience. Based on this research, Munro oversaw the development of a humourous television advertising campaign built around the themes of some key movies. For example, one commercial shows a renter's car blowing up in the parking lot as he returns the movie *The Godfather*. Another ad has a woman flying out of the door of a moving bus, rolling on the ground, and then coming to her feet in front of a Rogers Video store. She dusts herself and returns the movie *Speed*. In addition to a more focused advertising approach, store managers were given the freedom to act independently to select the kinds of movies and products that would fit their neighbourhoods. For example, Vancouver's West End contains one of Canada's largest concentrations of gays and lesbians. Rogers Video stores in this area contain a greater selection of films with gay and lesbian themes. In contrast, Halifax stores have a larger concentration of sports and war movies to cater to the large number of students and sailors who populate this city.

A truly unique approach to one-to-one marketing communication by Rogers Video involved a personalized promotional campaign using mailing list data from *Maclean's* magazine, which is owned by parent company Rogers Communications, Inc., of Toronto. Rogers Video combined the *Maclean's* magazine subscriber database with the information on its store locations and with high-tech print technology to create custom Rogers Video ads for each distinct subscriber to *Maclean's* magazine. Every single magazine contained an ad with a prescription bottle with the following printed instructions: "Take two movies at least once a week. Side effects: may cause reactions such as laughter, exhilaration, wonder, etc. Prescription filled at: Rogers Video." Each individual subscriber's name was printed on the prescription in the issue mailed to him or her. In addition, the address of the closest Rogers Video store to the subscriber was included! This unique approach, along with Rogers Video's experience promotional program, enabled Rogers Video to increase its market share in the highly competitive Canadian video rental market from 16 percent to 26 percent in one year![13]

>> ONE-TO-ONE MARKETING APPLICATIONS

4 List eight common one-to-one marketing applications

As mentioned earlier, a marketing database is not an end in and of itself but rather a *tool* that helps marketers reach customers and prospects with one-to-one marketing communications. The information contained in marketing databases helps marketers know and understand their customers on an individual level. By analyzing and manipulating the information, marketers can identify sales opportunities and drive the communications process to address these opportunities. Several one-to-one applications for marketing databases are presented in Exhibit 17.2 and discussed in the text that follows.

Identifying the Best Customers

Smart marketers have found that not all customers are created equal; that is, a majority of sales will come from a minority of customers. When companies examine closely where their sales are coming from, most find that the 80/20 principle applies: 20 percent of the customer base accounts for 80 percent of sales. If a company can identify these customers and develop a relationship with them, chances are it will enjoy enormous profitability. Thus, one of the most important uses of a one-to-one marketing database is to track the 10 or 20 percent of customers who account for the majority of the sales. Grouse Mountain, a North Vancouver Ski Resort, has tracked its customer base for over a decade. Stuart McLaughlin, president of Grouse Mountain Resorts Ltd., states that over time the

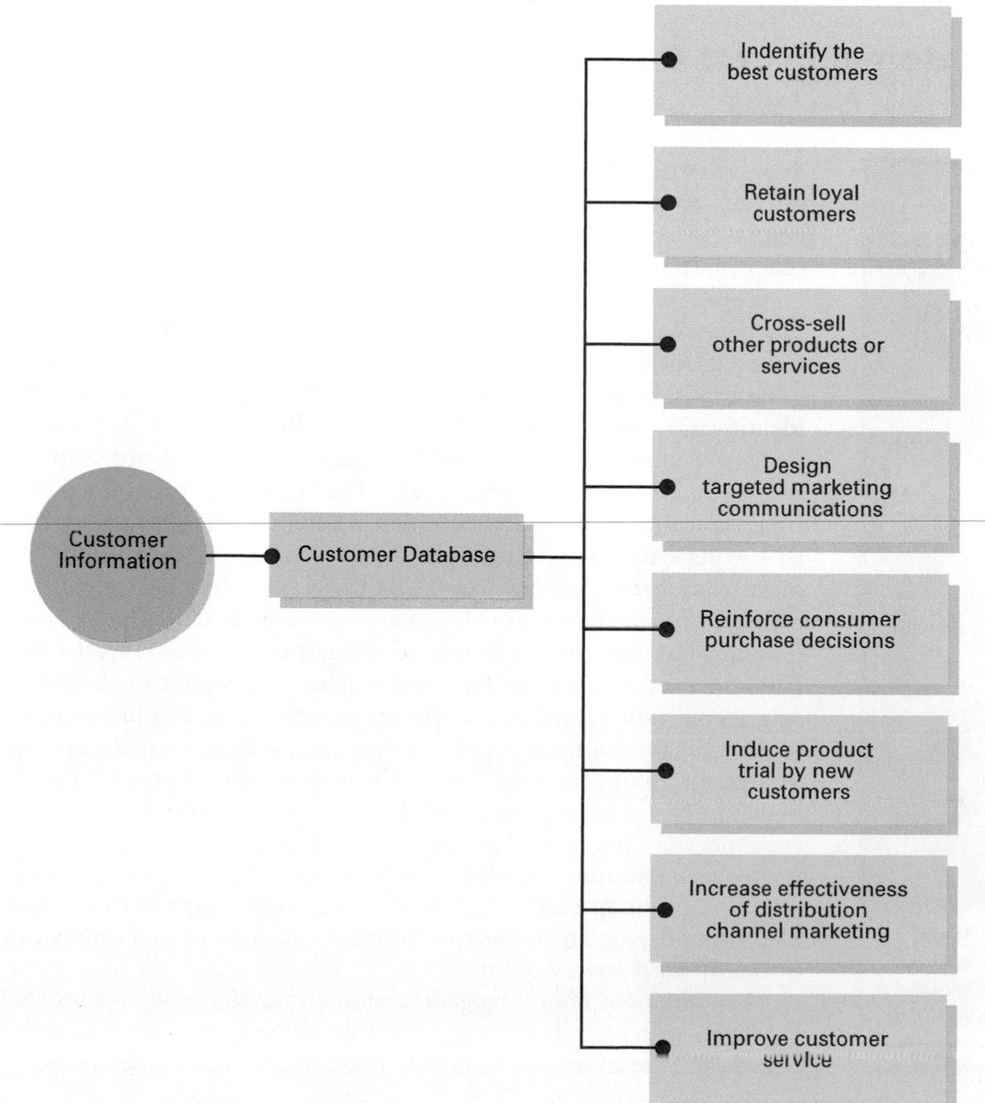

EXHIBIT 17.2
Eight Common One-to-One Marketing Applications

> **ON LINE**
>
> **Movies For Me**
>
> **Thunder DVD.Com**
>
> Can you build a customer profile at Movies For Me or at ThunderDVD.com without purchasing anything? Go to their websites to find out. Explain what you discover.
>
> **http://www.moviesforme.ca**
>
> **http://www.thunderdvd.com**

customer base of the resort has changed dramatically. In 1990, over 75 percent of the customers came to the resort during the winter. In 1996, that number had dropped to 30 percent. In 1990 the majority of customers came from British Columbia's Lower Mainland, but by 1996, 70 percent of the customers were tourists. From his database, McLaughlin was able to understand why Grouse Mountain was losing money: local skiers, the lifeblood of the resort, were not coming to Grouse Mountain. In response, Grouse Mountain designed a special Y2Play pass to coincide with the turn of the millennium and offered an incredibly low price that led to an incredible market response. Grouse Mountain sold 13,700 passes, of which 89 percent were to new customers, many of whom had not skied for 3 to 10 years. The resort experienced a 192 percent increase in snow visits, a 40 percent increase in rental equipment, a 29 percent increase in snow school programs, and finally, a 54 percent increase in food and beverage sales. In total, Grouse Mountain experienced a 63 percent increase in ski revenues. Using the database of Y2Play subscribers, a direct-mail and telephone campaign enabled Grouse Mountain to attain a 70 percent repurchase rate for the next year; this increase translated into a second jump in revenues that was 40 percent greater than the year when Y2Play was introduced![14]

Retaining Loyal Customers

It follows, then, that if a company knows who its best customers are, it should make every effort to maintain and increase their loyalty to retain their business. One study concluded that if a company retains an additional 5 percent of its customers each year, profits will increase by at least 25 percent. What's more, improving customer retention by a mere 2 percent can decrease costs by as much as 10 percent.[15]

Loyalty programs reward loyal consumers for making multiple purchases with the objective of building long-term, mutually beneficial relationships between a company and its key customers. Loyalty programs take advantage of database technology built around the identification of a firm's best customers. Quebec-based Laurentian Bank of Canada has developed the "Passport" reward program for holders of its VISA Gold credit card. The "Passport" program differs from typical reward programs in that it offers its members personalized experiences. It is promoted as a way to use reward points "to make your dreams come true." The program offers typical reward merchandise, of course, but also offers the exotic as well. The Passport program has four different reward categories, entitled Travel Chic, Outdoor Passions, Techno Fun, and À la carte. People can choose an African safari or a week of spa relaxation in the Alps. In addition, customers can add a unique activity to their trip, such as "cruising around in a Lamborghini for a weekend." Customers have freedom to combine points and money as part of their packages as well. For example, customers can use reward points to get a digital camera that they can use to commemorate a weekend vacation acquired with other rewards points. Laurentian Bank wants to position itself uniquely from other banks by offering an innovative difference in how its customers can use credit card reward points.[16]

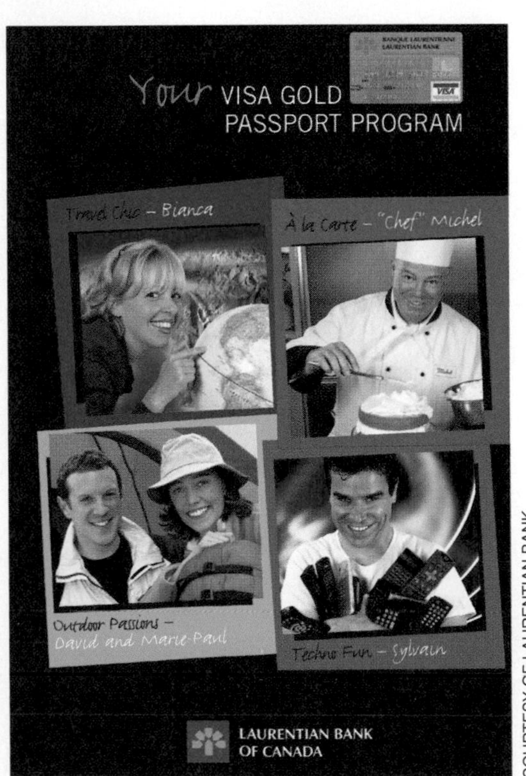

COURTESY OF LAURENTIAN BANK

The Laurentian Bank of Canada is building customer loyalty through its innovative Passport rewards program for customers who use its Gold Visa Card. The Passport program's four different reward categories of Travel Chic, Outdoor Passions, Techno Fun, and À la carte provide Laurentian Bank customers with the ability to choose an African safari or a week of spa relaxation in the Alps.

In addition to rewarding good customers, loyalty programs provide businesses with a wealth of information about their customers and shopping trends; these data can be used to make future business decisions.

Cross-Selling Other Products or Services

One-to-one marketing provides tremendous opportunities for cross-selling related products. A database allows marketers to match product profiles and consumer profiles to cross-sell customers other products that match their demographic, lifestyle, or behavioural characteristics. The Hudson's Bay Company is a Canadian retail leader in cross-selling. As early as 2001, Hbc united its Zellers and Bay credit cards and its Bay and Zellers Club Z loyalty programs under one banner, Hbc Rewards, to produce a database of 500,000 Canadians. The power of the Hbc database was tested with the launch of the Mossimo fashion line. Zellers used the Hbc database to target customers who bought fashions goods at The Bay but not at Zellers. These customers were sent direct-mail pieces based on the database of their past purchasing behaviour. Zellers noted an increase in fashion purchases in its stores among the members of this customer group![17] Marketers rely a great deal on related purchase behaviour to stimulate future purchases. For instance, past purchase behaviour may show that subscribers of *Golf Canada* may also be interested in business magazines such as *Canadian Business* or *Profit Magazine*. Similarly, the Internet music retailer Puretracks.com develops profiles of music buyers who have purchased similar selections. When a buyer searches or purchases music titles that match a profile, he or she can then be presented with titles that other buyers in the profile have bought.

Designing Targeted Marketing Communications

Using transaction and purchase data, a database allows marketers to track customers' relationships to the company's products and services and modify the marketing message accordingly. For instance, a company may segment its customers as infrequent users, moderate users, and heavy users. It may then devise a segmented communications strategy based on the group in which the customer falls. Marketing communications to infrequent users might encourage or stimulate a repeat purchase through a direct incentive such as a limited-time price discount for ordering again. Communications to moderate users may use fewer incentives and more reinforcement of past purchase decisions. Targeted communications to heavy users would be designed around loyalty and reinforcement of the purchase rather than price promotions.

Shoppers Drug Mart, working with Schering Canada, mined its 8 million-customer Optimum Card database to identify allergy sufferers, who were then targeted with a specific promotion for the antihistamine Claritin. By looking at information on past purchasing behaviour for antihistamines in the Optimum database, Shoppers Drug Mart identified 180,000 potential buyers. These buyers were sent a direct-mail communication with an outdoor theme containing information about allergies as well as a special offer of 3,000 Optimum bonus points, which would be awarded for a purchase of Claritin. Schering Canada believes that targeting consumers who have demonstrated a specific need for its products, and then providing them with a bonus like Optimum points, will give it a competitive advantage. Franco Di Clemente, senior brand manager for Claritin, made the following comments on the promotional effort: "As we move forward on this brand it is these kinds of programs that will help us grow."[18]

Reinforcing Consumer Purchase Decisions

As you learned in Chapter 4, *cognitive dissonance* is the feeling consumers get when they recognize an inconsistency between their values and opinions and their behaviour. In other words, they begin to doubt the soundness of their purchase decision. A database offers marketers an excellent opportunity to reach out to customers to reinforce the purchase decision. By thanking customers for their purchase and letting them know that they are important to the business, marketers can help cement a long-term and profitable relationship. A survey of business travellers who stay frequently at Canada's Fairmont Hotels & Resorts (formerly Canadian Pacific Hotels) revealed that rather than extra stays in a Fairmont hotel for being loyal, they actually preferred to receive special recognition of their individual preferences, extraordinary efforts to make their stays more pleasant, and more flexible check-in and check-out times. Fairmont Hotels responded by developing a frequent-guest club that was committed to satisfying customers with extraordinary efforts. For example, if customers preferred a twin versus a king-sized bed they would get it. Likewise, if they wanted Mountain Dew to drink instead of Pepsi, the staff would provide it. The value of reinforcing consumer purchases was significant for Fairmont Hotels; the chain saw its share of the market among Canadian business travellers increase by 16 percent.[19]

Updating customers periodically about the status of their order also reinforces purchase decisions. For example, minutes after customers order merchandise from Chapters' Indigo.ca website, they receive an e-mail acknowledging their order. Every few days thereafter, customers receive updates that allow them to track the shipment of the order, from ship date to receipt.

Inducing Product Trial by New Customers

Although a significant portion of one-to-one marketing effort is expended on encouraging repeat purchases by a firm's best customers or market segments, a marketing database can also be used to identify new customers. Because a firm using a marketing database already has a profile of its best customers, it can easily find new customers who fit that profile.

One-to-one marketers generally use demographic and behavioural data overlaid on existing customer data to develop a detailed customer profile that is a powerful tool for evaluating lists of prospects. For instance, if a firm's best customers are 35 to 50 years of age, live in suburban areas, own luxury cars, like to eat at Thai restaurants, and enjoy mountain climbing, then the company can find prospects already in its database or customers who currently are identified as using a competitor's product who match this profile. In order to market its new Whiskas Flavor-Lock pouch and Temptations treats to Canadian cat owners, Effem, Inc., decided to employ a database-specific sampling program. Effem acquired cat owner data from two consumer promotion companies, Tann Selective Communications and ICOM Information & Communications, to target known cat owners with direct-mail samples. The firm also commissioned a website, http://www.whiskas.ca, to allow cat owners to request Whiskas mail samples that would be sent directly to their homes. The campaign produced 250,000 sample requests, with the website accounting for 50,000 sample requests, and a database of cat owners who agreed to be contacted in the future by Effem. In addition, the website encouraged customers to refer a friend who owned a cat and who might like to receive a sample; those referrals resulted in another 10,000 contact names. The impact of the total campaign was a 1.5 percent increase in market share for Whiskas wet pouch and a 7 percent market share increase for Temptations treats.[20]

Increasing the Effectiveness of Distribution Channel Marketing

In Chapter 11 you learned that a *marketing channel* is a business structure consisting of interdependent organizations, such as wholesalers and retailers, which move a product from producer to ultimate consumers. Most marketers rely on heavily layered, indirect channels to move their products to the end user. Thus, marketers often lose touch with the customer as an individual since the relationship is really between the retailer and the consumer. Marketers in this predicament tend to view their customers as aggregate statistics because specific customer information is hard to gather.

AXA Insurance wanted to increase its market share among women in Quebec who were the principal drivers of their cars and in the age bracket of 30 to 49. The firm began by designing an appealing product offering for this group, which was branded as

ON LINE

Whiskas Canada

What kind of information on cat food is available on the Whiskas cat food website? Request a cat food sample and find out how the company implements its one-to-one marketing plan through its website.

http://www.whiskas.ca

Assurelle and contained the key feature of a 24/7 roadside assistance program that was valid in both Canada and the United States. The firm's customer research indicated that this kind of offering was very appealing to women in this age group, and AXA had experience in offering this kind of product with its auto insurance. AXA used a two-pronged direct marketing strategy to launch the product. In order to develop a prospect database, AXA reached out to its current customers with a personalized direct-mail piece containing information on the Assurelle product and a roadside assistance card. In addition, an invitation to participate in the "AXA treats you right contest" was included. The contest featured a three-day getaway trip to a spa and required the contestants to submit the name of a friend with whom they would like to share the prize.

The second prong of the direct marketing approach involved direct response marketing to the independent brokers who represent AXA's auto insurance, among other companies. AXA wanted its brokers to recognize the business opportunity that a product like Assurelle would provide them so that these brokers would support the product. To this end, two communications were sent to the brokers: the first explained the product's features and benefits and explained the contest, and the second provided details of the Assurelle Insurance program and a breakdown of AXA's media strategy that was being targeted at the current customer base and the new target market. In evaluating the results of this one-to-one campaign, AXA found an increase in brand awareness, an increase in the number of new customers, and a higher retention of current clients. Finally, AXA's brokers were both more loyal and more motivated to sell AXA products.[21]

With one-to-one marketing databases, manufacturers now have a tool to gain insight into who is buying their products. Instead of simply unloading product into the distribution channel and leaving marketing and relationship-building to dealers, auto manufacturers today are taking a more active role in learning about their customers. Carmakers now keep in touch with owners and prospects, learning their life stages and hobbies, understanding their vehicle needs, and developing relationships in the hope that these consumers will reward them with brand loyalty in the future. Car manufacturers then pass on the information they collect to their dealers, so that they can better understand their customers and tailor their dealerships to better meet customers' needs.

Improving Customer Service

One-to-one marketing techniques are increasingly being used to improve the customer service experience for customers. Rogers Communications undertakes one-to-one marketing to improve customer service with its shared call centre for its cable, wireless, and Web customers. The idea is to allow customers to have multichannel contact with the firm via toll-free numbers, e-mail, Web-chat, and fax machines. In addition, the firm is offering a single point of contact to handle questions and issues for three different products: cable television, Rogers Yahoo! Internet service, and wireless telephone customers, which are often used by the same customers. This approach is designed to allow Rogers to improve customer service with new technology and to focus the skills of its employees while also lowering costs. However, staff turnover among call centre employees is generally very high—typically 20 percent or more—which adds to the difficulty of maintaining consistent and excellent customer service. In order to deliver good customer service, the staff are trained to provide "just in time" service. The representatives are trained to use all of the communication equipment, and telephone calls are recorded and computer screen interactions are photographed in order to monitor service quality and allow for continuous training. The call centre is staffed by representatives with different skill levels in handling inbound and outbound calls, as well as by specialists in handling specific service type calls. Such variety enables Rogers to route its calls on a skill basis so that customers talk with representatives who have the knowledge to deal with their problems. In order to reduce staff turnover, and thereby field experienced agents and reduce training costs, Rogers is trying to shake the image that call centres are dead-end jobs for the poorly educated. The firm offers career paths to other areas of the organization that are based on experience within the call centre.[22]

Discuss the basics of one-to-one marketing database technology

>> THE BASICS OF MARKETING DATABASE TECHNOLOGY

In almost all cases, one-to-one marketing is characterized by the creation of a large computerized file of customers' and potential customers' profiles and purchase patterns; this information is then used to direct marketing communications. One-to-one marketing using technology is commonly referred to as **data-driven marketing.** That is, by gathering, enhancing, and analyzing information about customers and prospects, marketers will be able to implement more efficient and effective marketing communications and perform precise marketing. With data, technology, and statistical techniques, one-to-one marketers communicate to individuals, not to mass-market segments.

data-driven marketing
The process of gathering, maintaining, and analyzing information about customers and prospects to implement more efficient and effective marketing communications; another term for one-to-one marketing.

database
A collection of data, especially one that can be accessed and manipulated by computer software.

marketing database
The compilation of names, addresses, and other pieces of pertinent information about individual customers and prospects that affects what and how marketers sell to them.

At the very core of one-to-one marketing is, of course, a database. As defined by *Random House Webster's Dictionary*, a **database** is "a collection of data, especially one that can be accessed and manipulated by computer software." More specifically, a **marketing database** is the compilation of names, addresses, and other pieces of pertinent information about individual customers and prospects that affect what and how marketers sell to them.

A database can store almost any kind of information about consumers. In its most basic form, database marketing relies on transactional processing systems that record the details of individual purchase transactions. For example, when a consumer makes a purchase using a credit card, a database records the store name, the store location, the date of the purchase, and the purchase price, among other things. Over time a transaction history is produced for every customer. This basic transactional system provides critical information about purchasing patterns and preferences that is valuable in creating new products or sales offers. Transaction data can be further enhanced with additional information about individual customers such as age and income level, interests, or something that reflects lifestyles or attitudes. Exhibit 17.3 shows several different types of basic information that marketers could collect on their customers and prospects, divided by whether they are consumers or business-to-business customers.

In many cases, a database gives marketing decision makers access to the vast amounts of customer information traditionally stored in separate computer systems throughout a company. Data kept for other purposes, such as financial data kept by the billing department or customer service data kept by the service area, are merged together into a data warehouse to provide a complete picture of the customer. Instead of the days, weeks, or months it traditionally took to create reports from data stored in different computer systems, a data warehouse allows today's managers to answer questions in seconds. Marketing decision makers can now ask a "what if" question such as "What if we sent the last offer only to the top 20 percent of our customers instead of the top 50 percent?" When decision makers can go from one question to the next in seconds rather than days or weeks, they ask not only more but also better questions, and, ideally, the right questions.[23]

Marketers should remember, though, that having a marketing database is not a process in and of itself. Instead, the database is the *tool* used to achieve the full potential of one-to-one data-driven marketing. Any marketer can have a database of customer information, but if the right data are not collected and effectively manipulated to provide answers and insights, or if the data are not properly maintained to ensure their integrity, the marketer has not fully achieved one-to-one marketing.

Last quarter you had 1000 customers.
This quarter you have 1000 customers.
How many customers *did you lose?*
Where did they go? Why? Are the customers you gained as profitable as the ones you lost? Don't know the answers? Then you should know Business Objects. Our customer intelligence software mines the customer data that's scattered across your various systems – sales, marketing, customer support and finance – to give you an integrated 360° view of each and every customer. Then you, like the Global 1000 companies who use our software every day, will have the intelligence you need to grow your customer relationships. Instead of losing them. Call **1-800-527-0580** ext. 33 or visit **businessobjects.com/customer** and register for our free online "Customer Intelligence" seminar.
BUSINESS INTELLIGENCE. IF YOU HAVE IT, YOU KNOW.
BUSINESS OBJECTS
The Business Objects logo is a registered trademark of Business Objects SA. ©2001 Business Objects SA. All rights reserved.

COURTESY OF BUSINESS OBJECTS

Marketing databases are critical for companies operating in fiercely competitive industries. Business Objects is a global firm with offices in five Canadian cities. It promotes itself with an ad that raises the issue that it is important to know who your customers are and whether they are planning on defecting (if they haven't already).

Building a Marketing Database

As database marketing experts Rob Jackson and Paul Wang state in their book *Strategic Database Marketing*, "A database is only as powerful as the information it houses."[24] Data form the cornerstone of data-driven, one-to-one marketing. A company can have the most elaborate and expensive database system available and a staff of statistical professionals and marketing experts, but if the right data are not collected, then the other building blocks will never be used to their potential.

Many firms make it a point to gather customer information at the time of purchase at the same time transaction data are gathered. Future Shop salespeople and cashiers routinely ask for a phone number when the customer is purchasing or checks out. This number brings up information on the current transaction that is being processed as well as the customer's contact information. Virtually all appliances and electric tools include product registration cards to be sent in after purchasing. Marketers often provide an incentive in exchange for customer information. Many retailers run promotional contests that require customers to provide name and address information, which can then be used undertake promotional contacts later on. In all these cases, customers must either sign or check off some statement giving the marketer permission to use the information to contact them later on.

Data gathering can be overt or covert. Members of frequent-shopper clubs generally understand that the retailer is collecting information about their purchases in exchange for discounts or gifts. For instance, Virgin Entertainment Group offers free Internet appliances to customers who are willing to part with their personal information. The Internet devices allow users to surf the Internet and send e-mail in exchange for answering questions about shopping preferences, music, and entertainment interests, where and how customers generally get on-line, and how they spend their time once they get on the Web. In accepting the Internet appliances, customers give Virgin the right to track their movements on the Web and also agree to receive targeted advertising and e-mails from Virgin and other marketers.[25] The data gathering in the Fairmont (CP) Hotels & Resorts chain, which was discussed under reinforcing consumer purchase behaviour, is generally invisible to consumers but can create a special relationship over time. The hotel chain keeps track of guests' predilections and provides them with individualized service. The data gathering is very subtle—many guests aren't aware that their preferences are recorded in a database.[26]

Often the beginning of a marketing database is right under the marketer's nose in the form of a response list. A **response list** includes the names and addresses of individuals at home or in the workplace who have responded to an offer of some kind either by mail, telephone, direct-response television, product rebates, contests or sweepstakes, or billing inserts, to name a few.[27] Response lists tend to be especially actionable because past behaviour is a strong predictor of future behaviour. For instance, food products manufacturers often have the names of many people who

response list
A customer list that includes the names and addresses of individuals who have responded to an offer of some kind, such as by mail, telephone, direct-response television, product rebates, contests or sweepstakes, or billing inserts.

EXHIBIT 17.3

Basic Consumer and Business-to-Business Data

CONSUMER DATA	BUSINESS-TO-BUSINESS DATA
• Name, address, telephone number, e-mail address • Demographic data: age, income, gender, ethnicity, household size, etc. • Lifestyle and leisure interests • Financial characteristics such as credit history and rating • Recency, frequency, and monetary transaction history by date, dollar amount of purchase, and products purchased • Source of order, inquiry, or referral • Promotional response data	• Name, genderization (e.g., Mr./Mrs./Ms.), title of buyer, direct telephone number, e-mail address • Company name, address, and telephone number • Company demographics: NAICS code, number of employees, sales volume, number of branches, key contacts • Recency, frequency, and monetary transaction history by date, dollar amount of purchase, and products purchased • Financial characteristics such as credit history and rating • Predictive complementary product information (purchase behaviour that indicates a propensity to purchase a complementary product) • Industry surveys • Assigned salesperson

responded to past offers of recipes using their products. These people are a good place to start a database; they have already shown significant interest in the product and are therefore more prone to purchase.

compiled list
A customer list that was developed by gathering names and addresses from telephone directories and membership rosters, usually enhanced with information from public records, such as census data, auto registrations, birth announcements, business start-ups, or bankruptcies.

Other firms can get a jump-start on building a customer database by purchasing a compiled list. A **compiled list** generally includes names and addresses gleaned from telephone directories or membership rosters. A great many companies offer compilations. They range from Business Information Group (http://www.businessinformationgroup.ca), CLB Media Inc. (http://www.clbmedia.ca), Scott's Directories (http://www.scottsinfo.com), and The D&B Companies of Canada Ltd. (http://www.dnb.ca), for business-to-business data; to ICOM Information & Communications Inc. (http://www.i-com.com), Communications Real Laforte (Montreal), and Watt (http://www.wattgroup.com) for consumer lists; to *info*Canada, which has both business and consumer lists. Finally, small groups or associations are willing to sell their membership lists. [28] Data compiled by large data-gathering companies can be very accurate. For instance, *info*Canada consults thousands of independent data sources and makes over 1.6 million phone calls each year to verify the data on the 1.2 million Canadian businesses in its mailing list. These businesses are categorized by type of business, size, geographic location, and credit rating. The company also has a list of over 12 million Canadian consumers who can be selected according to age, income, gender, median home value, lifestyle, ethnicity, postal code, and mail order response history.[29]

Multinational companies building worldwide databases often face difficult problems when pulling together internal data about their customers. Differences in language, computer systems, and data collection methods can be huge obstacles. In spite of the challenges, many global companies are committed to building databases. Unilever has begun using the Internet not only to educate consumers about the brand but also to develop relationships with its customers by providing helpful information. Visitors to the Persil.com UK website can get information about removing stubborn stains. Customers also receive a discount on their next purchase in exchange for completing an on-line questionnaire. To date, the company has collected information on more than 30 million loyal customers.[30]

Enhancing Customer Data

database enhancement
The overlay of information to customer or prospect records for the purpose of better describing or better determining the responsiveness of customers or prospects.

A customer database becomes even more useful to one-to-one marketers when it is *enhanced* to include more than simply a customer's or prospect's name, address, telephone number, and transaction history. **Database enhancement** is the overlay of information to customer or prospect records for the purpose of better describing or better determining the responsiveness of customers or prospects. Types of enhancement data typically include demographic, lifestyle, or behavioural information about a customer.

There are three primary reasons to enhance a database with outside sources of information. First, marketers use database enhancement to learn more about customers or prospects. By overlaying demographic, lifestyle, and behavioural data onto customer records, marketers can gain a fuller picture of customers and their relative value to the company. For instance, a marketer of athletic equipment will find it valuable to know which of its customers are its best customers based on past transaction data. However, if that same marketer also knows that these customers have incomes over $50,000, enjoy outdoor recreation activities, especially biking and mountain climbing, and are also recent purchasers of mountain bikes, then the company will have a better understanding of who the customers really are.

Customer profiles allow marketers to distinguish different customer groupings by more than product purchases. For instance, Shoppers Drug Mart Optimum Card database described earlier contains information, on age, sex, address, home and business telephone numbers, e-mail addresses language preference, and number of children for those who are enrolled in the program. A related Shoppers Optimum Visa Card collects far more detailed personal information, including income and credit history. This information can be combined with the actual shopping behaviour of customers to identify market segments for both Shoppers Drug Mart and client companies that wish to participate in Shoppers Drug Mart's Vendor Marketing Program.[31]

Second, database enhancement can increase the effectiveness of customer marketing programs. By learning more about the best and most profitable customers, marketers can understand how to maximize marketing communications and cross-selling opportunities. The same athletic equipment company, for example, now armed with a profile of its best customers, can tailor communications to these customers that showcase its line of mountain bike gear, such as helmets, protective pads, and clothing.

Finally, by understanding the profiles of their best customers, marketers can find prospects that match the profile and thereby can increase the success rate of future marketing communications and business expansions. For example, CS CO-OP, an Ottawa-based credit union, had an existing database of 149,000 customers in Ontario. CS CO-OP wanted to understand its members needs better in order to develop a segmentation scheme that would serve as the basis for a customer relationship management strategy. The database that CS CO-OP had available contained two types of information. The first type involved the history and pattern of the transaction activities of customers. The second type involved customer demographics and purchasing behaviour. CS CO-OP hired Generation 5, a Toronto-based agency that specializes in data-centric consumer marketing, to set up its database so it could develop a segmentation scheme. Generation 5 combined the two types of information and set up a database based on postal codes to allow CS CO-OP to map its target market. "Using mathematical technologies such as Very Important Variable Analysis (ViVa), the segmentation system lets CS CO-OP predict, and therefore target, customer behaviour. For example, comparing transaction history and products held to the postal code data, the institution might find that a member is an ideal prospect for loan or mortgage products." In addition to identifying customers, CS CO-OP can also map out neighbourhoods where it might open new branches. The database will allow the credit union to predict the level of service and kinds of products that potential members might prefer; on this basis, the credit union can decide the size of the branch, its hours of service, and the nature of its equipment. Finally, the database will allow CS CO-OP management to identify high-value and low-value customers and pursue different marketing and customer service strategies for these different segments.[32]

Compiled lists, mentioned earlier, are often enhanced with information gathered from public records (such as Statistics Canada census data), auto registrations, birth announcements, business start-ups, and bankruptcies. Thus, compiled data can indicate several key attributes about consumers that may suggest their financial status, demographics, buying preferences, lifestyle, or attitude patterns.

Another form of enhancement data is modelled data. **Modelled data** include information that has already been sorted into distinct groups or clusters of consumers or businesses based on census, household, or business-level data. Several organizations specialize in collecting these types of data to develop models of consumer purchase behaviour based on the theory of *geographic behavioural patterns*—that is, people who live near one another will have similar characteristics and will behave similarly. These systems have the added advantage of being able to work within geographic areas at the postal code level. These companies have conducted a great amount of research analyzing demographics, psychographics, and sometimes response patterns to determine these geographic "pockets" of similar decision makers.

modelled data
Enhancement information that has already been sorted into distinct groups or clusters of consumers or businesses based on census, household, or business-level data.

In Canada, MapInfo offers the PSYTE™-Automotive database. PSYTE™ is a segmentation system that categorizes Canadian neighbourhoods into one of 60 distinct clusters based on over 250 demographic and consumer behaviour variables. The variables are integrated from a variety of sources such as Statistics Canada census information, consumer surveys, and R.L. Polk Canada, Inc., auto data.[33]

Marketers often have specific data enhancement elements on their wish lists that cannot be collected via internal or external sources. Acquiring this information may require the marketers to use a little creativity to develop their own custom, primary sources of enhancement data. Sources of **custom data** could include such things as customer surveys, customer participation programs, product registration, warranty cards, or loyalty marketing programs. The ultimate approach to custom data could well be Montreal-based Blitz Direct, Data & Promotions' approach to marketing via cell phones. Blitz has partnered with Profilium, a wireless advertising company, to develop a system

custom data
Enhancement information acquired by the marketer, including customer surveys, customer participation programs, product registration, warranty cards, or loyalty marketing programs.

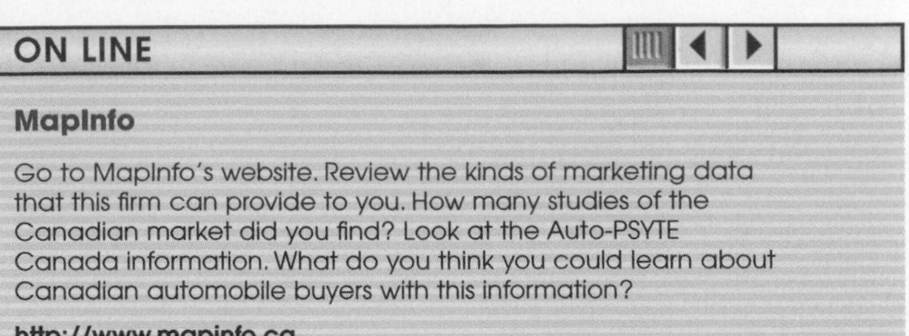

that will allow marketers to send ads to the cell phones of profiled customers when they are near the point of purchase of an advertiser's product. The system will enable "a car company to tell a passerby to come into the dealership to check out the latest model. An art patron can receive a gallery discount pass when in the vicinity. Someone passing The Gap might want to know that T-shirts are on sale." Patrons will be recruited into the database with the offer of discounted or free service cell phone plans provided that they accept a number of unpredictable promotional contacts. In order to encourage people to continue to participate in the program, Profilium has set a limit on the number of times a cell phone "profile" can be tapped.[34]

Finding Answers by Analyzing Customer Data

One of the most important aspects of one-to-one marketing is not the names and addresses stored but the ability to go beyond creating mere mailing lists to manipulating the data to profile the best customers or segments of customers, analyze their lifetime value, and, ultimately, predict their purchasing behaviour through statistical modelling. Database marketing expert James R. Rosenfield's comments on database marketing sum it up: "Marketers confuse a marketing database, which can simply be stored information about customers, with database marketing, which is a dynamic approach to managing customers. You can't do database marketing without modelling and profiling—that's what it's all about."[35]

The real value of one-to-one marketing, therefore, is not in the data. Actually, large quantities of data can remove value from one-to-one marketing by making the exercise confusing and complex. That is not to say that data are not necessary, only that to be valuable, data must be turned into marketing information in the form of customer profiles, scores, and predictions. The data must be transformed from operational bits and bytes into the information that marketers need for successful marketing communication.

Common data analysis techniques for marketing databases include (1) customer segmentation, (2) recency–frequency–monetary analysis (RFM), (3) lifetime value analysis, (4) predictive modelling, and (5) data mining. Although other statistical and modelling techniques are available and widely used, these five types of data analysis are used quite often by one-to-one marketers. Most companies with customer databases should be able to conduct the first three data analysis techniques easily, if transaction data and enhancement data have been collected. Predictive modelling and data mining are more sophisticated techniques and generally require more data and expertise in statistical analysis. Predictive modelling provides an excellent means for marketers to ask "what if" questions, whereas data mining uses a variety of tools to uncover subtle patterns in consumer purchasing behaviour.

Customer Segmentation

Customer segmentation is the process of breaking large groups of customers into smaller, more homogenous groups. One-to-one marketers use this analysis to paint a picture of what customers look like, in particular the best customers. By identifying a segment of customers in the database by any means, such as by survey, purchase data, response, or word of mouth, a firm then can find a way to compare the identified customer segment with the rest of its customers. These segmentations can be based on such characteristics as demographics, geographic location, previous purchase behaviour, or psychographic variables. Some examples of these variables are shown in Exhibit 17.4. Refer back to Chapter 6 for more information about segmentation.

recency–frequency–monetary analysis (RFM)
A data manipulation technique that determines the firm's best customers by identifying those customers who have purchased most recently, most frequently, and who have spent the most money.

Recency-Frequency-Monetary Analysis (RFM)

Research has shown that customers who purchase most recently and more often and who spend more money are more likely to purchase again. **Recency–frequency–monetary analysis (RFM)** identifies those customers most likely to purchase again because they

EXHIBIT 17.4

Four Major Groups of Segmentation Variables

GEOGRAPHIC	DEMOGRAPHIC	BEHAVIOURAL	PSYCHOGRAPHIC
• Country • Region • Province • County • Metropolitan type (urban, suburban, rural, etc.) • Metropolitan statistical area • Census tract • Retail trading area • Postal code • Telephone area code • Climate • Seasons	• Age • Gender • Height/weight • Marital status • Family size • Family life cycle • Ages of children • Race • Ethnicity • Nationality • Country of birth • First language • Religion • Education • Occupation • Industry • Income • Mobility • Dwelling type • Dwelling size • Autos registered	• Purchase occasion • Recent purchases • Benefits sought • User status (e.g., active or inactive) • Usage rate • Loyalty status (e.g., loyal users, frequent users, switchers, price buyers) • Readiness stage (i.e., is the customer ready to purchase now, in 12 months, in 24 months?) • Attitude toward the product • Charities contributed to • Political affiliation	• Attitudes • Interests • Opinions • Activities • Lifestyle • Social class • Personality type • Conspicuous consumption (e.g., mean current auto value, home value)

have bought most recently, bought most frequently, or spent a specified amount of money with the firm. With these data a firm can build a simple equation to identify the "best customers" by assigning a score to customer records in the database based on how often, how recently, and how much they have spent. These customers are then ranked to determine which customers rise to the top of the list and which ones fall to the bottom. This ranking provides the basis for maximizing profits because it enables the firm to use the information in its customer database to select those persons who have proved to be good sources of revenue. As an example of RFM analysis, refer to Exhibit 17.5, which depicts the breakdown of customers in categories that describe their value at a hypothetical company.

Many marketers take RFM analysis one step further by introducing *profitability* into the equation. For instance, based on the monetary value of purchases, a customer may float to the top of the RFM list. If this customer only buys items on sale, however, then he or she is less profitable for the firm than a customer who buys the same dollar amount in nonsale items.

Lifetime Value Analysis (LTV)

Recency, frequency, and monetary data can also be used to create a lifetime value model on customers in the database. Whereas RFM looks at how valuable a customer is currently to a company, **lifetime value analysis (LTV)** projects the future value of the customer over a period of years. One of the basic assumptions in any lifetime value calculation is that marketing to repeat customers is more profitable than marketing to first-time buyers. It costs more to find a new customer in terms of promotion and gaining trust than to sell more to a customer who is already loyal.

lifetime value analysis (LTV) A data manipulation technique that projects the future value of the customer over a period of years using the assumption that marketing to repeat customers is more profitable than marketing to first-time buyers.

Customer lifetime value has a number of uses: (1) It shows marketers how much they can spend to *acquire* a new customer, (2) it provides a level of profitable spending to *retain* a customer, and (3) it provides a basis for targeting new customers who look like a company's most profitable customers.[36] Lifetime value analysis allows a marketer to identify its

EXHIBIT 17.5

RFM Analysis: All Customers Are Not Created Equal

BEST CUSTOMERS N = 1,200 (10%)	NEXT-BEST CUSTOMERS N = 2,400 (20%)	AVERAGE CUSTOMERS N = 3,600 (30%)	POOR CUSTOMERS N = 4,800 (40%)
• High profit • Spent > $1,000 • Multiple purchases • Purchased in last six months • LTV: High • Total annual sales = $1,200,000	• Good profit • Spent approx. $500 • Multiple purchases • Purchased in last 12 months • LTV: Good • Total annual sales = $1,200,000	• Average profit • Spent $250 • One purchase • Purchased in last 18 months • LTV: Average • Total annual sales = $900,000	• Low profit • Spent < $100 • One purchase • Purchased in last 24 months • LTV: Low • Total annual sales = $504,000

LTV = Lifetime value

N = Number of customers in category

Total annual sales = $3,804,000

Total number of customers: 12,000

Total number of orders per year: 20,000

Average order value: $190.20

SOURCE: Reprinted from ***Desktop Database Marketing*** by Jack Schmid and Alan Weber. © 1998. Used with permission of The McGraw-Hill Companies.

most valuable customers and profit from them over the long term by building relationships. Cadillac has calculated the lifetime value of its top customers at $332,000. Similarly, Pizza Hut figures its customers are worth $8,000 in bottom-line lifetime value.[37]

Predictive Modelling

predictive modelling
A data manipulation technique in which marketers try to determine, based on some past set of occurrences, what the odds are that some other occurrence, such as a response or purchase, will take place in the future.

The ability to reasonably predict future customer behaviour gives marketers a significant competitive advantage. Through **predictive modelling,** marketers try to determine, based on some past set of occurrences, what the odds are that some other occurrence, such as a response or purchase, will take place in the future. The occurrence a marketer is trying to predict through predictive modelling is described by the *dependent variable*, typically the likelihood of a response, making a sale, the amount of the sale, or all three. The *independent variables*, or predictor variables, are the things that affect the dependent variable. Past buying behaviour, age, income, family size, and the neighbourhood in which one lives could all be independent variables that affect purchase behaviour, the dependent variable. Toronto-based Tener Solutions Group specializes in database marketing and customer relationship management. The firm offers predictive modelling as well as behavioural segmentation, customer profiling, and lifetime value analysis to find patterns in its clients' database information that will allow its clients to better understand customer behaviour. Michelle Edgar, the database marketing manager of Compaq Canada, provides the following comments: "Tener Solutions Group performed an in-depth audit of Compaq Canada's marketing database. Leveraging TSG's knowledge and expertise about data and database marketing strategy, Compaq was able to ensure that its database supported its customer relationship marketing objectives. TSG's recommendations helped Compaq to exceed customer expectations and satisfaction objectives, turn information into knowledge and provide the company with the tools to better manage and analyze our most valuable asset: our customer information."[38]

data mining
The process of using statistical analysis to detect relevant purchasing behaviour patterns in a database.

ON LINE

Tener Solutions Group

How can Tener Solutions Group help marketers with predictive modelling? Review some of the articles under the News Button, Articles link of this website. What were you able to learn about "predictive modelling" and its use in database marketing?

http:// www.tenersolutions.com

Data Mining

Data mining, a relatively new and sophisticated modelling technique, will be described in more detail in Chapter 18, where customer relationship management is presented. **Data mining** is the automated discovery of "interesting," nonobvious patterns hidden in a database that have a high potential for contributing to the bottom line. The discovery process often involves sifting through massive quantities of data such as electronic point-of-sale transactions, inventory records, and on-line customer orders matched with demographics.[39] Data-mining software accesses the data in the database and offers analysis tools such as decision trees, cluster analysis, neural networks, and regression analysis. Data mining can create customer profiles; help determine the reason for customer loyalty; analyze the potential return for pricing, promotion, and direct-mail strategies; and even help forecast sales.[40]

>> THE IMPACT OF THE INTERNET ON BUSINESS PRACTICES

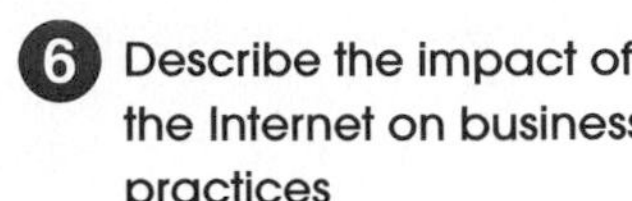

The Internet, and especially the World Wide Web, exploded onto the world scene in just a few short years. Companies like Chapters.Indigo.ca, Puretracks.com, eBay.ca, Amazon.com, MapQuest.com, and Canada.com did not exist 10 years ago. These companies saw opportunities based on innovative ways of running their businesses. Looking back at what they did, we can see some of the characteristics of successful Internet businesses and describe marketing's role on the Internet. Because the Internet has become widespread in a relatively short period of time, marketers must recognize the profound impact it has on business practices, particularly in the areas of marketing channels, finance, marketing research, marketing communications, and marketing strategy.

Electronic Marketing Channel

For even the most experienced Web surfers, the amount and variety of material available on the Web can be overwhelming. In addition to information overload, it is often hard to find what you want in the maze of the Web, especially when banner and pop-up ads distract your attention as well. For marketers, however, the Web is much more than a way to grab customers' attention through advertising. It represents a new, electronic channel to conduct all sorts of marketing activities, including advertising, customer service, marketing research, transactions, and even distribution and new-product development. Think of it as a new business franchise—one that is open 24/7.

One profound advantage the Internet has, as an electronic marketing channel, is the excellent opportunities it provides for customer relationship management (CRM). Web-based companies can build a personalized rapport with customers, much like a salesperson does with his or her clientele. By capturing information about the purchases of individual customers, a Web merchant can build profiles of their likes and dislikes. When the company stocks a new product that matches an individual's profile, the merchant can automatically e-mail the customer to let him or her know about the product's availability. When was the last time your local bookstore set up a "book gift registry" so that your friends and family could buy books for you? Chapters.Indigo.ca has a "Wish List" feature that allows you do indicate which books you would like and allows you to authorize access to your friends and families so they can order a book for you! You will read more about CRM in Chapter 18.

Financial Implications of the Internet

When a new technology revolutionizes traditional marketing practices, it makes sense to discuss how it will affect the bottom line. A single development can set off a chain of events that have a profound effect on individuals, companies, industries, and nations. Probably the best historical example is the invention of printing by Johannes Gutenberg in 1452. Prior to Gutenberg's invention, books were luxury items owned mainly by royalty and the very wealthy. Few things, if any, in the modern world are similar in status and exclusivity to the book prior to 1452.

Clearly, the invention of the printing press created a completely new industry and established financial (and consumption) opportunities where there had been none. Publishing and printing sectors were added to the fifteenth-century economy, and a new

Chapters.Indigo.ca

Visit the Chapters.Indigo.ca website and examine the wish list feature. Would you ever use this feature? What kinds of information would you have to provide Chapters.Indigo to enable the Wish List feature? What kinds of privacy concerns does the wish list bring into play that would be different from simply ordering merchandise on your own?

http://www.chapters.indigo.ca

breed of manufacturers and component producers emerged to satisfy corporate demand for the new technology—a situation not unlike the recent effect of developments in Internet technology.

Companies that embrace Internet technology can gain an advantage over their competitors that do not. In the mid-1990s, Chapters was driving many independent bookstores out of business by offering greater in-store selection, lower prices, and an inviting ambience. In 1998, Internet technology allowed Amazon.com to capture a significant share of the bookseller market by providing its customers with more convenience and even lower prices than its bricks-and-mortar competition. Indigo.ca was a Canadian Internet bookseller start-up company that tried to duplicate Amazon.com's approach in Canada. Chapters was faced with the strongest competition it had seen in a long time. As such, it had to develop a Web presence that could counter Amazon.com and equal Indigo.ca. The result was an alliance with Indigo to form Chapters.Indigo.ca.

It is not only the large players that have benefited financially from Internet technology. Innumerable small businesses have started and blossomed from Internet technology. Creating an Internet storefront or launching Internet operations often does not require the same intensive financial investment needed to open a bricks-and-mortar company. Expenses for facilities and equipment can be nonexistent. Reduced expenses and start-up costs can mean a quicker and more substantial return on investment for entrepreneurs. At the same time, these reduced start-up costs translate into low barriers to entry, which has created a crowded field of on-line competitors in many industries. For established companies, the impact of the Internet on expenses also can be great. Consider the on-line purchase of airline tickets. If electronic ticketing is used, the airline can save on the expenses of the ticketing agent, travel agent commission, data entry, ticket printing, and ticket delivery, as well as the office supplies, payroll, and time required for each step. Because all of these savings result in a reduction of the cost of goods sold, they can translate into increased profitability for the company.

Another financial implication of implementing Internet technology in some industries is reduced inventory and its associated holding costs. A good example is the printing industry. On-demand printing is currently available and will likely expand. Trafford Publishing, a privately held company based in Victoria, B.C., started operations in 1995 and claims to be the first company in the world to offer "true" on-demand publishing. The firm identifies its mission as "helping creative people publish their books and other products." Trafford describes its start-up situation as follows:

> "People thought we were nuts: Print-on-Demand was an industry term for printing short runs of 300 to 500 books and no one, even the equipment manufacturers, thought anyone could viably operate a service printing runs of ONE copy. We proposed to sell the books on the Internet, accepting payment with credit cards, and programmed an elaborate website that would display the books and even take orders. There were very few e-commerce sites (except pornographers) at the time, and book industry people quickly dismissed the idea that anyone would ever use the Internet to look for books and scoffed at the idea that people would use credit cards for Internet payments. We were stubborn and kept developing our service—and steadily gathered a clientele of dedicated authors, first at a rate of one or two per month. By early 2002, we had over 100 authors joining on each month. Now there are a dozen or so companies offering variations on our original innovative service—yet we believe ours is still the best suited for most authors' needs. We are providing a unique publishing service, taking full advantage of the latest advances in Internet communications and print technologies."[41]

Clearly this kind of on-demand production does not work in all industries, but where it does, reducing inventory holding costs amounts to another positive stroke for corporate financial health.

Although the financial implications of Internet technology on the overall economy seem to be great, it will take time to see how *significant* their impact will be. How many new industries will actually be created because of Internet technology and marketing? New jobs? New businesses? How tightly will companies be able to link increased consumer spending to increased savings generated through Internet pressure on prices? These questions have yet to be definitively answered.

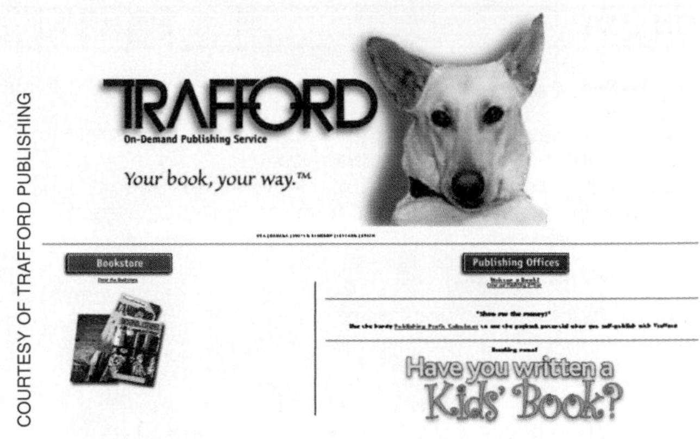

COURTESY OF TRAFFORD PUBLISHING

B.C.'s Trafford Publishing is a global pioneer in on-demand book publishing services for both book buyers and book authors. Using the Internet, Trafford has created a marketplace where any budding writer can afford to get a book "published" and let the marketplace decide whether the book will be a bestseller or not!

Marketing Research through the Web

The Internet is having an electrifying effect on the ways we conduct research. Prior generations of college and university graduates can recall spending many hours in the library searching out information for a project or term paper. The Internet, however, puts a vast amount of information on a wide variety of topics at your fingertips. Numerous organizations, including *The Globe and Mail, Marketing Magazine, Canadian Business, The Financial Post, Consumer Reports, Fortune,* the Canada Revenue Agency, and the CBC, now offer their publications on-line as well as in print

Some organizations provide marketing research information on Canada over the Internet at no cost, such as the Strategis Database, Statistics Canada, and the Government of Canada. There are a number of U.S. sources that contain data on markets of interest to Canadian firms, including American Demographics, CyberAtlas, Survey.Net, the U.S. Census Bureau, and the U.S. Department of Commerce. Other organizations sell their information, including *info*Canada, the Conference Board of Canada, Canadian Advertising Rates & Data, and Ipsos-Reid.

Accessing secondary data electronically offers many advantages over print media:

- Easier access to information from around the world
- Information content that is more current
- The ability to make complex searches
- Incorporation of multimedia
- Lower publication costs

The Internet is also revolutionizing primary research techniques. For example, even organizations without a Web presence can use e-mail to conduct surveys. It is easier, faster, and less expensive for people to participate in an e-mail-based survey than in conventional mail surveys. Furthermore, the response rate is typically higher. Web-based surveys are even better! A greater variety of questions can be posed on a Web page than is possible through e-mail. Graphics and multimedia may be used to expand or enhance the survey tool. Response data are immediately available once the respondent completes the survey.

Focus groups are also moving on-line. Saskatoon-based ITracks.com enables an organization to conduct live graphical and interactive meetings with anyone on the Internet. A company can present materials on-line to a live audience and gather feedback in real time. Information can be shown to participants in a variety of formats, including white board, text slides, polling slides, Web slides, SnapShot, and LiveDemo. Presenters can ask people in the audience to evaluate or vote on any number of issues, such as product features, colours, appearance, and price.[42]

The Internet is proving to be a valuable tool for competitive intelligence activities as well. Organizations can collect information about their competitors by directly observing product, pricing, and promotion decisions executed by key competitors at their websites. Organizations also can use an intelligent agent, a digital robot known as a "bot," to explore a range of competitive Internet offerings. For example, Shopping.com is a popular shopping bot that conducts comparison shopping for products at thousands of on-line stores.

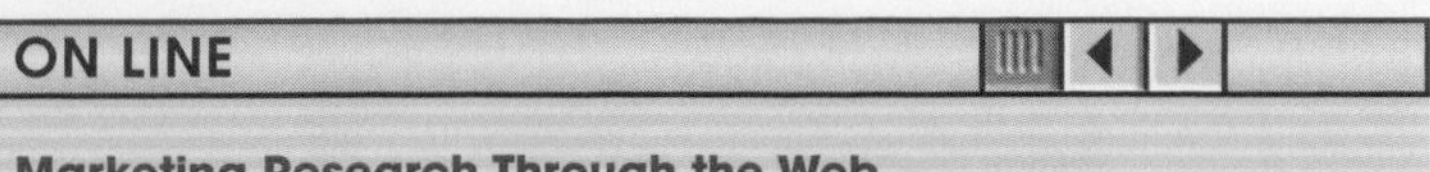

Marketing Research Through the Web

Can companies cull marketing research data through the Web without compromising consumer privacy? Visit the MapInfo site and then read the article "A Little ZIP Goes a Long Way in Targeted Marketing" from the April 2, 2001, issue of *Information Week.*

http://www.mapinfo.ca

http://www.informationweek.com

Although most shopping bots currently limit their assessments to price offerings, evolving software will allow more complex assessments of the overall value of competitive offerings. Gomez.com currently uses an algorithmic and data-driven process to rate on-line stores by various standards, including overall cost, ease of use, customer confidence, and relationship services. Of course, these on-line services make competitive information easily available to consumers and competitors alike.

Integrating Conventional and Internet Marketing Strategies

Companies like Amazon.com, Trafford Publishing.com, and Travelocity began on the Internet, and their business continues to be almost entirely Web-based. These companies are the exception rather than the rule. For most companies, Internet marketing is used to complement and augment existing marketing programs. This is particularly important in light of evidence suggesting that many on-line customers use the Internet to shop but ultimately make their purchases off-line.[43]

Taking advantage of cross-channel synergies can lead to enhanced customer satisfaction *and* increased sales and profits. For example, major retailers that offer multiple channels (store, Internet, and catalogue) can integrate these channels and cross-promote them to customers. Research studies that considered the value of a customer have indicated that multichannel buyers spend from two to three times as much as retail customers alone and 10 times as much as Internet buyers alone. A recent study, "Measuring the Impact of the Internet on Shopping Centers," by T. Hernandez, R. Gomez-Insausti, and M. Biasiotto from Ryerson University in Toronto, indicated that Canadian bricks-and-mortar retailers who provide on-line sales opportunities could produce more off-line sales. The survey of "nearly 2,000 consumers at three major shopping malls in the Greater Toronto Area" revealed the relationship between on-line and off-line shopping: "In-store sales generated by Web browsing compared to on-line sales are as high as $8.84 to $1 for consumer electronics and $4.38 to $1 for clothing. Over 34 percent check the Internet for product information, while 25 percent check it for store and mall information."[44]

One way to encourage cross-channel awareness and loyalty is through an integrated marketing communications strategy. An organization's Internet promotion efforts should project a consistent and coherent presence. Every venue where consumers encounter the company—whether broadcast, print, or Internet media—should reinforce past experiences. Consistency in slogans, appearance, and other cues serves to strengthen consumer familiarity with the company. When customers have to resolve differences between messages, it weakens their confidence in the company.

In implementing integrated, cross-channel strategies, the Internet should be used to enhance marketing programs that are already working—not to replace them. If a marketing program is not working, implementing a flashy new Internet promotion will succeed only in making the marketing program fail faster. It is better to find out what is wrong with a marketing program before taking corrective action.

Planning is important, both in one's personal and professional life, yet sometimes people undertake a task without sufficient forethought. As tasks become more complex or difficult, however, the odds for successfully completing them without proper planning diminish. Regardless of your vocation—the arts, business, engineering, or science—you will be involved in planning. Most plans have similar elements. At a minimum, an Internet marketing plan should include the following elements:

- An analysis of the Internet marketing environment
- A statement of the company's on-line business strategy
- Specific Internet marketing objectives and strategies

The proliferation of Internet marketers has slowed a bit since massive dot.com failures resulting from a failure in marketing strategy. Firms quick to launch an Internet program without considering the full implications of doing so had failed consistently by 2000 and 2001. Only firms with well-developed, realistic strategies were able to survive the dot.com bust.

>> THE INTERNET MARKETING ENVIRONMENT

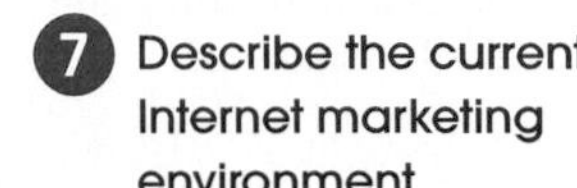

The Internet and the ways it is used are perpetually changing, and the Internet environment will continue to be turbulent for many years to come. Because of this, no single person can claim to be an expert about the entire Internet. Nevertheless, people who are well informed about Internet marketing can often cope with its dynamics better than people who are less informed. Individuals who can combine diverse information in innovative ways can discover and develop new business opportunities.

As the twentieth century came to a close, there was much clamour about electronic commerce. Television, radio, newspapers, magazines, and even billboards saturated us with news, articles and advertisements about e-tailers such as Chapters.Indigo.ca, Amazon.com, eBay, and Toys "R" Us. But there were other winners and losers that went unnoticed. Intermediaries were eliminated from the distribution chain as manufacturers and suppliers shipped products directly to customers. The inconspicuous winners included delivery services such as Canada Post, Purolator Courier, Federal Express, and United Parcel Service, which provided just-in-time product delivery to millions of Canadians.

At the beginning of the twenty-first century, we are witnessing the most dramatic and rapid changes in the history of humanity. This situation is largely due to the development of the Internet and the creation of the World Wide Web. What makes these innovations even more exciting (or scary) is that the Internet and its uses are only in their infancy. Even bigger changes are about to take place as products make the transition from atoms to bits.[45] We are accustomed to processing and delivering tangible goods and services. For a business to grow in a physical world, it must expand its production, storage, transportation, and other tangible resources. Even Amazon, the foremost Internet retailer, has numerous large warehouses and an expansive distribution system.

But as we move into the information age, non-physical product features will increase in value. Video, sound, and computer data captured as digital bits increase in value as they are combined, enhanced, and manipulated. Development of these intangible products will still require physical resources and people, but even now the marketing, sales, and distribution of these items no longer rely on physical mechanisms. The Internet is ideally suited to perform these functions, and this ability will eliminate the need for their physical counterparts. Some examples include insurance, financial services, and software purchases. Unless they want to, customers no longer have to visit a store to buy these items. It can all occur on-line.

Futurists foresee a day when today's diverse electronic technologies will converge and combine into a single high-speed communication and distribution channel. This channel will carry broadband content to telephones, televisions, and computers. This integrated channel will feature multimedia content and the inherent advantage that the Internet currently offers over broadcast media, such as radio or television—that is, the ability to hold a conversation on-line. With broadcast media, a message originates from a source and is sent to one or more recipients, but the converse is not true. Using the Internet, messages can be sent back and forth among participants.

It is difficult to predict what will happen in the foreseeable future, let alone in the long term. What can we say about the Internet marketing environment, knowing that these statements may be outdated by the time you read them? It should be safe to say that marketing will employ new technologies to improve the exchange process in order to satisfy individual and organizational goals. And we can make useful general observations about the current Internet marketing environment.

ON LINE

Integrating Conventional and Internet Marketing Strategies

What elements of Mountain Dew's website have you seen echoed in its recent conventional marketing programs? Rate its message consistency, describe its on-line business strategy, and identify at least two marketing objectives.

http://www.mountaindew.com

Basic Forms of Virtual Business

business-to-consumer (B2C) electronic commerce
Using the Internet to conduct business between an organization and individual consumers.

Internet marketing to consumers has received much attention in the media. This form of marketing is referred to as **business-to-consumer ("B-to-C" or "B2C") electronic commerce.** For many consumers the Internet has altered the way they make purchase decisions. Once a person recognizes the need for a product or service, information about it can be readily obtained through the Internet. Manufacturers, suppliers, and retailers are anxious to provide information that can influence purchase decisions in their favour. Consumers are not only more informed but have more alternatives to choose from. In some instances, the Internet makes the actual purchase easier and more convenient. A customer can shop for many items 24/7 without leaving home—and have the items delivered as well. Even financing for expensive purchases such as automobiles and houses can be arranged for over the Internet.

business-to-business (B2B) electronic commerce
Using the Internet to conduct business between two or more organizations.

The use of the Internet to facilitate activities between companies is called **business-to-business ("B-to-B" or "B2B") electronic commerce.** In 2002, B2B e-commerce totalled $823 billion worldwide, and these revenues are expected to grow nearly 200 percent by 2004.[46] The products or services a company buys from another company may be the same as those bought by individual consumers. Recall from Chapter 5: One basic difference between consumer and company purchases relates to the intended use of the products. Another difference between consumer-targeted and company-oriented business involves the relationships established between the parties. For consumers, the Internet makes it easier to do comparative shopping and to switch between retailers. In a business situation, relationship marketing redefines the fundamental roles of buyers and sellers by establishing ongoing partnerships among participating companies. The Internet can be used to improve relationships between companies and help to build strategic alliances. As a result, business markets are becoming more and more competitive.

Internet Demographics and Trends

A vast amount of information exists on and about the Internet: the number and growth rates of websites on the Internet; traffic rates of individual websites; the number of Internet users and their demographic characteristics; the scope of Internet businesses and their products or services, and so on. Similar information may be derived from multiple sources, each offering its results in a different way. It should be no surprise to find sizable differences in future projections for Internet markets.

Almost two-thirds of Canadian users access the Internet from home on weekly basis. When combined with people who have access at work and at school, essentially 75 percent of Canadians access the Internet regularly, and the percentage with broadband access is 54 percent and growing. Internet access used to be higher among better-educated, higher-income households, but this "digital divide" has narrowed. The use among Canadian men and women is about equal, but the growth potential for use among women is higher. In the United States, the number of women on-line exceeds the number of men on-line. Outside Canada and the U.S., men still represent the majority of users of the Internet.[47]

In *Now or Never—How Companies Must Change Today to Win the Battle for Internet Consumers*, Mary Modahl of Forrester Research discusses the fallacies of using historical data to make projections about future Internet markets.[48] Forrester identifies three factors that influence a consumer's on-line buying behaviour:

1. Attitude toward technology
2. Income
3. Motivation to use technology

Using these three factors, buyers fit into one of three broad categories. *Early adopters* are aggressive consumers who are eager to try new technology, enjoy benefiting from the convenience it brings them, and have the means to acquire and use it. People in the *mainstream* take a more conservative approach and may wait a year or two before going on-line, either because of pessimism about new technology or because of a lack of resources to support it. *Laggards* are both pessimistic and low-income. These people are genuine "have-nots": they are averse to change and can't afford to change. Many laggards may never go on-line.

For high-velocity developments like the Internet, using historical data for making projections is problematic. For example, Internet grocery stores have had a very poor reception even though they have developed solutions to their critical logistical problem, which is grocery delivery. Although they have reached out to a large number of consumers, they have only been able to convert 30 percent of first-time triers to regular customers.[49]

In fact, the potential consumer base for every company is a combination of all three categories of adopters. The most important determinant for a company is the proportion of its customer base that corresponds to each of the three categories. Once this is known, the company can devise a targeting strategy that reflects that customer base. Well-placed magazine advertisements may be more effective for targeting early adopters. Broadcast media may be more effective for targeting a mainstream audience.

The Global Village

One of the best opportunities for company expansion and growth is in the international arena. The 6 billion people on the earth live in about 1 billion households. More than half of those do not have a telephone, let alone a personal computer. In 2004, it was estimated that more than 940 million individuals had access to the Internet and only 280 million of them were English speakers.[50]

As business and commerce expand into the global arena, the Internet is helping overcome the physical distance that separates peoples of the world. Numerous factors will contribute to greater diversity and sophistication in the marketing environment. Conflict between social, cultural, economic, political, demographic, resource, infrastructure, and legal factors may increase due to the accelerating rate at which these factors interact. The effect the Internet will have on this changing environment is unknown, but certainly the Internet is serving as a catalyst in this change. In order to survive and prosper, organizations will need to develop a vision that strikes a balance between local and global factors.

Although technology makes communication between distant people possible, language differences complicate interaction. There is no such thing as a universal language translator. The most straightforward translations can break down if not carefully handled. Geographic and regional variations further muddy the waters. For example, although many words may be similar, Canadian French and Parisian French are not the same, and Louisiana French, with its many different dialects, differs too. The same situation is found with any language.

Even though demographic and growth trends are favourable in Europe, care must be exercised when entering into this arena. Europe is economically unified, but as far as Internet commerce is concerned, it is still very diverse. The richness in the different languages, cultures, and societies in Europe complicates Internet marketing on that continent. Religious, social, and ethnic considerations span time and transcend nationalities. Like any business strategy, investment in European Internet marketing should be targeted, and the objectives should be well defined.

But what can the Internet do for those areas in the world that have had limited access to communication technologies? Much larger long-term opportunities exist in Asia, Africa, and South America. The economies and infrastructures of many countries in these regions lag behind those of the more industrialized nations in North America and Europe. The Internet can broaden and enhance access in developing nations because it offers a relatively cheap, versatile, and technically efficient service. Furthermore, it can allow businesses from developing countries to "leapfrog" into the development

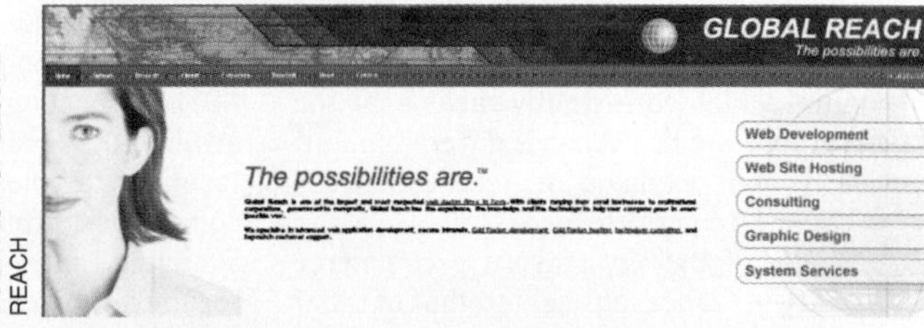

COURTESY OF GLOBAL REACH

The Internet brings the world very close together, and successful marketers on the Internet will need to be more culturally aware. Global Reach provides statistics on Internet usage around the world, including the languages spoken by Internet users. Global Reach offers a multilingual website with eight different language versions currently available.

mainstream because electronic commerce allows them to sell their products and services directly to customers around the world. The Internet can level the playing field by eliminating disadvantages in developing countries, such as distance from markets, underinvestment in basic infrastructure, and underutilized capacity.[51]

GLOBAL PERSPECTIVES

Internet Access and E-Commerce around the World

Although current statistics indicate that Canada has a very high participation rate (75 percent of the population can access the Internet) and has wide broadband usage (over 54 percent) the United States still represents the world's largest e-commerce market, although its dominance will decrease rapidly over the next few years. In discussing global trends in e-commerce, it is easier to group countries into regions—for example, trends in Western Europe, North America, or Asia-Pacific regions. But doing so draws attention away from specific national differences that can play a large role in e-commerce development.

It is easy to point to differences between the most and least developed countries, but significant differences also exist among countries recognized as the most developed economically. Consider, for example, the differences that exist among the Group of Seven (G7) countries, which are recognized as being seven of the most industrialized countries in the world. As indicated in the accompanying chart, activity in these seven countries represented 88 percent of global e-commerce activity in 2001. Although that percentage will decline in the coming years, it is nevertheless expected to account for 77 percent of e-commerce activity during 2004.

What is interesting, though, are the differences between some of these industrialized countries. Consider the differences between Canada and the United States, which both consistently rank at the top of this list in terms of e-commerce activity as a percentage of revenues, and France, which consistently ranks near the bottom of the list. What is different about France that explains its relatively weak e-commerce performance?

One of the key reasons e-commerce activity in France lags behind that of other industrialized countries has to do with limited access—less than 20 percent of French homes were connected to the Internet at the end of 2001 compared to more than 50 percent in the United States and 45 percent in Canada. Why? French telecommunications have long been controlled by a monopoly, France Telecom, with little or no competition. Although recent legislation calls for France Telecom to unbundle its lines to allow Internet service provider competition, little competition has occurred so far. France Telecom dial-up users are subject to metered rates that result in surcharges for extra minutes spent on-line, and lower overall usage times for the French who do have Internet connections.

	2001 % OF THE POPULATION WITH INTERNET ACCESS	2001 E-COMMERCE REVENUES ($B)	2004 E-COMMERCE REVENUES (PROJECTED) ($B)	E-COMMERCE REVENUES AS A % OF TOTAL 2004 REVENUES (PROJECTED)
Total	10.0%	$1,233.60	$6,789.80	8.60%
United States	53.6	864.10	3,189.00	13.30
Canada	44.9	38.00	160.30	9.20
Japan	17.4	64.40	880.30	8.40
Germany	31.3	46.40	386.50	6.50
United Kingdom	55.4	38.50	288.80	7.10
France	18.3	22.10	206.40	5.00
Italy	19.1	15.60	142.40	4.30

Another factor limiting e-commerce activity in France is limited access to broadband connections—particularly ADSL and cable, which make up the lion's share of broadband access. In France, only 2 percent of homes have broadband connections compared with more than 54 percent of Canadian homes. The low number of ADSL connections in France can again be attributed to France Telecom's reluctance to unbundle lines and open up access to competitive offers. As a result, ADSL is available only in major markets and requires significant start-up costs.

The situation with cable is different but equally pessimistic. Although there are several French cable operators currently vying to offer complete packages of interactive video, voice, and data, the infrastructure is not in place to reach a majority of the French population. Consider that in Canada and the United States, cable passes nearly 97 percent of all homes, with 70 percent of those homes opting for basic cable packages or more. In France, cable passes only 36 percent of all homes, with some 30 percent opting for a cable subscription. With research indicating that broadband users are two to three times more active on-line than dial-up users, the lack of broadband access promises to constrain e-commerce activity in France for the foreseeable future.

Finally, there also are consumer behaviour differences that will constrain e-commerce development in France. A key difference is the lower use of credit cards, which are the most popular method of on-line payment. Whereas the average North American holds 2.8 credit or debit cards, the average for the French is less than 1 per person. Thus, a large percentage of the French population has no way to charge for on-line purchases, even if they did have Internet access. An international e-commerce business should fully understand these differences before launching an Internet marketing plan targeting customers in France—or any other country.[52]

>> ON-LINE BUSINESS STRATEGIES

8 Discuss on-line business strategies

You don't have to start big to make it big on the Internet. Although it's becoming increasingly difficult for small-business websites to compete with the heavily funded sites of large companies, it is nevertheless possible for small firms to do a very credible job. The market is so big and growing so fast that operating even a small piece of it can produce substantial income for a small business. The opportunities are limitless—many of the successful Web-based businesses of today didn't even exist 10 years ago!

The business environment and climate on the Web are changing so rapidly that to stay profitable, companies must be agile and prepared to grasp new opportunities. In fact, the high number of dot.com failures attests to the increased need for solid business plans that are flexible enough for a rapidly changing environment. Small businesses hold a definite advantage over large companies in this regard. It can take months, if not years, for a large company to change a strategy that isn't working—it's like turning an aircraft carrier. Small businesses are more like speedboats—they can turn quickly and dart in a promising direction.

Building a business on the Internet involves more than putting up a website and expecting the world to beat a path to your URL. Achieving success in this arena requires the same basic ingredients as starting any small business. Only some 20 percent of all small businesses survive beyond five years, and the life expectancy for Web businesses is proving comparable. But consumers are wary of unproven websites. What does it take for a company to survive and prosper on the Web?

- Offer products that fulfill customer needs, wants, or desires.
- Sell your products at a fair price to customers.
- Use promotions to make potential customers aware of your products and website and to drive site traffic.
- Make your products available to customers when and where they want them.

Many advantages exist to building a small business on the Internet. The financial investment for a Web-based business can be smaller than for a bricks-and-mortar store. The time invested by owners, however, can be considerably more for electronic businesses. Successful Web-based companies must be competent with the technologies they employ, but they also need sound business and marketing strategies. Customers don't visit a site because they heard it has great Java running.

Internet Goals

All good strategies start with a clear statement of purpose or with a recognizable goal. An Internet strategy should start with a meaningful goal—for example, to optimize organizational performance—and consider ways the Internet can be used to achieve that goal. For example, the Internet can

- Increase or enhance company exposure
- Improve customer service
- Provide new products or services
- Add value to existing products or services
- Lower overall costs for the company
- Create one-to-one relationships with customers

Many other possibilities could be added to this list. Careful consideration of one or more of these options should lead to achievable Internet goals that are stated in general terms. These goals guide the design of the Internet presence. General goals should then be refined into more precise statements later used to define objectives that can be evaluated or measured. For example, if an organization sets a goal to

ON LINE 

On-line Business Strategies

What's the difference between a successful Internet marketing program and an unsuccessful one? Use the Internet to find out. Scan the DotCom Flop Tracker at DotComDoom.com to find a dot bomb you like. Compare your dot bomb to a successful dot.com. Make a list of at least five differences and any similarities. Compare your dot bomb against the four bullet points under "On-line Business Strategies." On which point(s) did your company fail? You may want to use InfoTrac® College Edition as well as your favourite search engine to help you research your companies.

http://www.dotcomdoom.com

http://infotrac.thomsonlearning.com

improve customer service, it could target a low number of customer complaints as a measurable objective. Viable Internet strategies can be devised to achieve this goal. Because of the Internet's ability for two-way communications, it provides an excellent means for interaction between a company and its customers. Consumers can contact the company to complain about faulty products, ask product support questions, or suggest new products. The company can respond to these complaints and concerns and announce the availability of new products. The key is to clearly identify the role of the Internet in attaining the goal.

Internet Presence

Well-executed websites can be persuasive marketing tools. To achieve that, it is a good idea to formally state the desired on-line positioning. On-line positioning statements identify the most important target market or markets, each market's most vital on-line need, how the company's Internet presence can meet that need, and how the on-line presence can be better than the competition. To appeal to consumers, a website should be intuitive and easy to use. Well-designed programs can be deceptively difficult to develop and run. Despite the availability of low to moderately priced templates, establishing an Internet presence can be a daunting task that takes more time and money than some people might think.

Besides incurring many of the same costs as conventional marketing programs, Internet marketing also can entail significant technological costs. Because costs can easily spiral out of control, it is essential to delineate major cost elements and approximate those costs. A few short paragraphs can provide enough information to estimate the significant costs associated with establishing an Internet presence. Each of the following factors must be considered:

- Prior experience in developing and running an Internet marketing program
- Degree of program sophistication
- Magnitude of the program
- Dynamics of the program

A good place to start when developing a website is to review other successful websites. Organizations that are implementing Internet-based marketing programs for the first time should seek assistance from companies in that line of business. Business-oriented aspects of the program can remain in-house, but the technical aspects should be delegated to a company with more experience in that area. Organizations that already have considerable in-house experience in developing and running websites can undertake the technical aspects of an Internet marketing program. There also should be people within the company who are familiar with operational budgeting and other practical aspects necessary for a program's success.

Marketing on the Internet can employ a variety of techniques ranging from simple e-mail to a full-service electronic commerce website. E-mail is the least sophisticated and can be readily accomplished using a third-party organization such as an Internet service provider (ISP).

The most basic type of website—sometimes referred to as a corporate website—provides consumers with basic information about the company and its product line but little or no opportunity to communicate with the organization. **Corporate websites** can be run internally or by a third-party organization. The amount of content and how often it changes will affect the size of the Internet program. Common information found on corporate websites includes company history, product descriptions, investor information, and contact information.

corporate website
A website that provides consumers with information but provides little or no opportunity to communicate with the organization.

Websites that permit two-way communication between an organization and its customers are sometimes referred to as **interactive** or **transactional websites.** Most e-commerce efforts require the use of interactive website technology. This type of website can be very powerful and sophisticated but also expensive to develop and operate. Even though an organization may have sufficient internal resources to develop and operate an electronic commerce website, many choose not to do so due to the difficulty

interactive/transactional website
A website that permits two-way communication between an organization and its customers.

in attracting and retaining qualified technical staff. People are needed to develop, manage, and update the content throughout the life of the program—which may be indefinitely!

Interactive websites allow complex interactions that go beyond one-way communication. They can be used to execute transactions, deliver electronic products and services, and collect detailed demographic and behaviouristic information about customers. This complex set of interactions can lead to a variety of on-line business models, including direct selling models, Internet retailing models, and Internet marketplaces.

Direct Selling

The Internet direct selling model can be very appealing for manufacturers that wish to increase direct contact with their customers and intensify their focus on service. Because this model can mean the elimination of complex distribution networks, many companies are hesitant to convert to Internet selling for fear of angering distributors and dealers. Nonetheless, manufacturers sometimes must offer a direct selling channel or lose market share.

The obvious advantage of selling directly to customers is that it eliminates intermediaries who mark up prices before the product reaches the buyer. This advantage can turn into a disadvantage, however, if the manufacturer cannot successfully manage all of the activities that the intermediaries in the channel typically perform. These activities include promotion, transaction and delivery services, and after-sale customer service.

Dell Computer is an example of a manufacturer that has successfully used the Internet to manage nearly all of the channel activities. Dell Computer is committed to building excellent relationships with its customers, and this focus has translated into high revenues and solid profitability. Dell doesn't use any retail stores or distributors; all sales are made directly to its customers. Dell is responsible for taking and fulfilling orders, and it controls shipping and customer service.

Easy as DELL Canada

COURTESY OF DELL INC.

Dell is frequently described as the world's most successful direct marketing company. Dell Canada's website is a model for how a website should be designed and laid out for the specific purpose of creating an immediate sales transaction.

Dell's website simplifies order placement; it also provides a wealth of helpful information. Once orders are placed, customers can view their status through Dell's website. After receiving their computers, customers can get assistance for their setup over the phone. Should a computer fail during its warranty period, customers can use Dell's website to diagnose and solve the problem. If this doesn't work, they can get individualized help over the phone from a technician. And if the diagnosis reveals a defective component or part, Dell will have a replacement shipped express to the customer the next working day.

Using the Internet as the foundation of its direct selling model has enabled Dell to become the market leader in PCs. Not only that, but it has the highest cash flow in the industry. Savings from its streamlined electronic business practices have accrued to the point where Dell is cash-rich and so able to shape industry marketing activities almost single-handedly.

The direct selling model is particularly well-suited to digital product producers, who can use a variety of revenue models. Puretracks.com sells music downloads directly on-line. Computer software manufacturers like Adobe sell their products directly online. Informational product producers like *Marketing Magazine* sell and distribute information via the Web using a subscription revenue model. Other information and entertainment producers, such as *Canoe*, use advertising revenue models, providing free on-line news directly to consumers, who in turn act as audiences for advertising messages provided and paid for by other on-line businesses.

Internet Retailing

Why is there so much interest in retailing on the Web, or **e-tailing**? On-line purchasing didn't even exist several years ago, yet worldwide e-commerce revenues from the Internet for 2004 are predicted to exceed $7 trillion. In Canada, on-line transactions were valued at $13.7 billion in 2002—a growth rate of 46 percent over 2001. Of this amount, $4 billion were retail sales.[53] That's worth paying attention to!

e-tailing
Using the Internet to sell retail products and services.

The consumer sees three basic differences between shopping on the Internet and purchasing items in a bricks-and-mortar store:

For many people it is more convenient to shop on-line than in a store. The convenience of purchasing through the Web has translated into increased levels of on-line retail purchases. Buyers don't need to drive to the store during normal business hours because they can shop 24/7 from home. It is easy to window-shop by moving from one retailer to another on the Web. Consumers can compare prices more easily over the Internet than in bricks-and-mortar stores. Purchased items can be delivered directly to customers' homes at a time convenient to them.

Unlike buying in a store, you can't actually feel or touch products you purchase over the Internet. Physical interaction with the product is severely limited over the Internet. Items like music, baseball highlights, and books, and some services, such as tax preparation and e-courses, allow customers to interact with the product directly over the Internet. If the product cannot be created electronically, however, the consumer will not be able to interact with it. Sometimes this problem can be mitigated by the ability of the consumer to view the product at a traditional retail outlet before purchasing the item on-line. For example, someone wanting a printer could shop at Future Shop to see and test the product, and then order the product from an on-line retailer, circumventing Future Shop altogether.

Neither lavish surroundings and strolling crowds nor salespeople exist on e-tailing sites. For some people, store-hopping is an entertaining and social experience. Others may welcome the pure functionality of shopping on the Internet. The relative lack of tactile and social interaction during an on-line purchase is a major challenge facing e-tailers. Many people like the experience of going to the mall to shop, even if they don't buy anything. There's a social experience and personal attention that you can't quite get sitting in front of your computer. What does the fabric of a suit feel like? Can a computer compliment you on how the colour of your eyes is enhanced by the colour of the jacket you chose? By building an individual rapport with their customers, merchants add value that increases customer satisfaction. Relationship marketing seeks to create long-term partnerships between companies and their customers. In return the company can gain repeat sales and referrals from its customers.

On the other hand, Internet retailing can provide a level of attention to detail that conventional stores may not be able to match. Products can be tailored on-line to suit the preferences of individual customers. E-tailers like Dell Canada, Future Shop, Canada Flowers, and Chapters.Indigo already provide customers with an impressive level of attention through "mass customization," that is, the use of programs and features to tailor the site for any individual. These companies have learned how to satisfy customers by giving them exactly what they want even though no two customers are the same.

Marketers also face differences between traditional retail and e-tail. One example is in the area of fulfillment. Some e-retailers implement virtual operations that allow them to take orders from customers and rely on manufacturers or wholesalers for product fulfillment. This way, the e-retailer doesn't incur inventory and warehousing costs. This is the approach used by Armenager.com, a European e-tailer that offers a huge assortment of household appliances from a wide variety of manufacturers to consumers throughout the European Union. However, when something goes wrong, customer service often cannot handle the problem, and customer satisfaction suffers. Many e-tailers have created their own bricks-and-mortar warehouses to resolve these fulfillment challenges.

Internet Marketplaces

The Internet has fostered the creation of on-line marketplaces, sometimes referred to as e-marketplaces. An **e-marketplace** acts as a channel intermediary bringing together buyers and sellers to form a virtual exchange community. At the minimum, the creator of the e-marketplace works as an agent or broker, and charges a fee for each transaction and provides efficiencies associated with search and procurement costs. The e-market producer also may provide value-added services ranging from logistics and delivery guarantees to complete supply chain management services that streamline and consolidate ordering, bidding, delivery, and inventory management.

e-marketplace
A channel intermediary bringing together buyers and sellers to form a virtual exchange community.

The term e-marketplace often denotes a B2B marketplace. Some of these business-oriented communities and marketplaces, such as BellZinc.ca, cater to specialized segments of the business marketplace and bring together information seekers, prospects, and buyers. Others, such as http://www.cbsc.org, http://sbinfocanada.about.com, http://www.microsoft.com/canada/smallbiz, and http://strategis.ic.gc.ca, target more general small business interests.

There are several variations of e-marketplaces in B2C and consumer-to-consumer ("C-to-C" or "C2C") contexts as well. For example, Travelocity is a B2C e-marketplace. The on-line community of travel companies, which includes airlines, hotels, and car rental agencies, offers travel information and services to consumers who share an interest in travel. eBay is a largely C2C e-marketplace that brings together individual sellers and buyers in an auction format that parallels an old-fashioned flea market. And usedcars.autonet.ca provides a marketplace for individual consumers to buy and sell used cars.

Other e-marketplaces include financial services sites like eTrade Canada, employment agency sites like www.workopolis.com, and portals like Canada.com or Canoe.ca that act as shopping and entertainment destinations. For example, Canada.com offers the following: an on-line mall that brings together e-tailers at one location so that consumers can conduct one-stop shopping; chat rooms for topics ranging from politics to movies; and on-line clubs with interests ranging from business and finance to sex and romance.

Portals like Canada.com and Canoe.ca have created broad-based e-marketplaces. Other **virtual communities** have created e-marketplaces based on common interests such as a hobby, sport, or other avocation, where participants interact with one another through the Internet. Using bulletin boards, chat rooms, newsletters, or discussion lists, individuals contribute content to the communal website, which over time may build a deep reservoir of information. Loyal members who visit the site frequently can develop a sense of ownership and trust through their involvement in the community. Such people may be more comfortable making a purchase within their virtual community than someplace less known; this creates enhanced advertising opportunities for the virtual community operator. For example, iVillage.com maintains a virtual community dedicated to women, who can find information as well as engage in bulletin boards or chats about a variety of women's issues. iVillage.com participants are exposed to a variety of advertisements specifically targeting a female audience.

virtual community
People with a common interest who interact on and contribute content to a communal website.

>> INTERNET MARKETING OBJECTIVES AND STRATEGIES

9 Discuss Internet marketing objectives and strategies

A company's Internet marketing program will depend in large part on its Internet business strategy—that is, the type of website it has created (corporate or transactional) and the type of Internet business model it is implementing. Internet marketing plans will include some objectives that are similar to standard marketing plans. Objectives related to on-line market share, sales level, repeat purchase, and fulfillment are appropriate for transactional websites. Objectives related to market positioning, image, and brand awareness or recognition might be appropriate for all websites. In each case, it is important to identify quantifiable objectives that later can be compared to measured performance levels.

Some marketing objectives are particularly appropriate for the Internet. A key success factor for most Internet businesses is traffic, traffic, and more traffic. Objectives related to generating and building traffic should be included in any Internet marketing plan. Traffic can be quantified, however, in a variety of ways. There is traffic that you drive to your website, and then there is traffic that you keep and drive deeper into the website. Longer visits, deeper exploration of the site, and return visits to the site are signals of stronger relational ties. The overall goals for the website should determine which types of traffic objectives are most important. For a better idea of how these objectives might be articulated, visit Nielsen//NetRatings (http://www.nielsen-netratings.com) for a listing of the world's highest-traffic Internet sites. These ratings are based on the number of unique visitors to a site and the average amount of time each visitor spends at the site.

Most Internet marketing plans also should include objectives targeting specific responses from visitors to the website. Corporate websites can include objectives related to e-mail or telephone contacts generated by the website. Interactive websites can include objectives related to converting incoming traffic into active website participation. These conversion objectives can address a variety of activities that serve to deepen the on-line relationship. For example, objectives can be associated with converting incoming traffic into new members through on-line registration, or identifying potential new prospects by allowing them to request followup information, or converting traffic into actual customers through on-line transactions. Again, these objectives may vary depending on the Internet business model, but Internet marketing plans should include objectives that identify desired customer response behaviours.

Internet marketing strategies should be designed to directly support the Internet marketing objectives. In developing these strategies, all four elements of the marketing mix—product, place, promotion, and price—must be carefully considered and balanced with one another for an Internet marketing program to succeed. Futureshop, Puretracks.com, Amazon.ca, Dell Computer, and The Shopping Channel have mastered blending all four elements in the marketing mix on the Internet. They are able to promote and offer products consumers want at affordable prices through a convenient distribution channel.

Product Strategies on the Web

One of the biggest differences between the Internet and conventional retail channels is in the physical contact consumers have with actual products. Some items are well suited for marketing and sales on the Internet. Many people feel comfortable purchasing books, golf balls, vitamins, airline tickets, or video movies over the Web. These items are near-commodity, physically small, and relatively inexpensive, so consumers are generally indifferent about the channel they use to purchase them. They could just as easily buy these items in a store, through the mail, or on the Internet. For many customers, the Internet may offer greater convenience.

Certain products require direct sensory experience to fully appreciate them. This kind of contact with the product cannot be achieved in the virtual space of the Internet. For example, many people may be reluctant to buy a car, a diamond ring, a new perfume, or a suit through the Web. One way to overcome this shortcoming is to provide personalized service and virtual product trials on-line. In some cases, this can be accomplished by increasing the audio and visual sensory experience that customers encounter at the website. For example, Puretracks.com allows customers to listen to audio clips from CDs.

Branding is another powerful tool that on-line companies can use to reassure reluctant consumers and to distinguish their products from those of their competitors. The brand identity customers associate with a company's products can be more important than the utility gained from using the products themselves. Because the Internet involves two-way communication, each consumer actively participates in a dialogue that may build a stronger relationship with the company. For example, Canoe applies its brand name to virtually all of its products to reinforce and enhance brand identity. Canoe Mortgages, Canoe Money, Canoe Travel, and Shop.Canoe all contribute to making Canoe a widely recognized on-line brand name.

On-Line Distribution Options

Internet-based businesses often use different distribution channels than conventional businesses. Many variations of the supply chain are possible, and they can be very complex and require a substantial amount of time for products to reach the retail stores. As the complexity of a channel increases, so do its costs, which are passed along to the consumer in the purchase price of the product.

For traditional retailers, the distribution channel has several steps. Products for sale in retail stores are purchased in large quantities from suppliers and delivered to a central warehouse. The products are then divided into smaller quantities, which are sent to geographically dispersed warehouses. These warehouses are close to retail stores. When product stock in a store runs low, store managers order more of the product from the closest distributor. Only after the product arrives in a retail store can the consumer purchase it.

When a consumer buys a product over the Internet, many steps in the traditional retail channel can be modified or eliminated. Internet retailers like Sears.ca arrange for customer orders to be filled from a central warehouse and shipped directly to the customer. Some intermediaries may be eliminated from the supply chain, whereas direct shippers like Purolator, United Parcel Service, and Canada Post are added. Sears.ca has leveraged its warehouse and distribution competency by sharing its information with its traditional bricks-and-mortar outlets. As a result, customers can order silverware online and pick it up at their local Sears store in order to save on shipping costs.[54]

Fulfilling customer orders can become rather complex as the number of low-price shipments increases. Making timely, low-price, low-volume deliveries is one of the greatest challenges facing on-line grocers. Ontario-based Grocery Gateway has spent millions of dollars to establish "a fleet of over 140 trucks with nifty climate zone compartments, a 26,500-square metre market centre in Downsview, and an operations office in Mississauga" to support its independent distribution system in the Greater Toronto Area.[55] Another early Canadian on-line grocer, Peachtree.com, began in 1998 with a different approach. Peachtree opted to take a brokerage approach by developing relationships with local grocery retailers and distributing orders through them. However, Peachtree was unable to make the grocery business profitable and filed for bankruptcy protection in 2001.[56] In contrast, Loblaw has opted to try a very unique logistics approach with logistics firm eBox.com. Toronto-based eBox.com offers an overnight delivery service through which parcels and packages can be delivered when customers are away from home or even asleep! At no cost, eBox installs a secure lock box outside the home through which it can deliver products. Its clients include Canadian Tire, Sears, Canada Post, and now Loblaw.[57] These trends suggest that successful on-line grocers in the future will utilize clicks and bricks synergies and limit distribution to high-density, urban areas.

As products become more digital, direct on-line distribution will become more prevalent. The direct on-line channel may eliminate many traditional distribution challenges, but will also create new ones. For example, one of the biggest challenges facing digital entertainment producers is how to control postsale mass distribution of their digital products in peer-to-peer (P2P) networks such as Kazaa and Morpheus. (Read more about Morpheus in the "Critical Thinking Case" at the end of Part 4.)

On-Line Promotion

One might think that by simply putting up a website, an organization will attract potential customers—that is, "If you build it they will come." Nothing could be further from the truth. Promotion on the Internet differs from promotion through conventional channels in the basic way consumers encounter promotions and in the substance of those promotions. Recall from Chapter 14 that conventional media, such as television, radio, and print, gain greater reach by *pushing* their message out to the general public. For the most part, the Internet relies on potential customers actively seeking out and *pulling* information about products or services. And whereas broadcast and print media can be used for reaching diverse or highly targeted audiences, the Internet is particularly well suited for providing information-rich content and enabling two-way interactions between a company and its individual customers. Because the Internet enables a two-way exchange, customers actually play an active role in the promotion.

The "instantaneous nature" of the Internet enables firms to undertake unique promotional approaches that some marketers have referred to as "brand buzz." For example, Burger King wanted to promote its new Spicy TenderCrisp Chicken Sandwich using a "brand buzz" approach. The firm commissioned the creation of a unique website called the Subservient Chicken (http://www.subservientchicken.com).

ON LINE 

On-Line Retail Distribution Options

Review the eBox website and list all of the strategies the company is using to help Internet-based businesses effectively and efficiently "physically distribute" their products. Look up the way the website describes how the company developed its lock box approach to help clients like Sears, Canadian Tire, and Loblaw.

http://www.ebox.com

The site features a person dressed in a raunchy chicken suit who will do your bidding. The chicken will flap wings, dance around, stand on its head, play dead, clap hands, waggle its rear end at you, and do almost any other actions you can think of. If you make an obscene request the chicken will give a no-no gesture and often will give the Webcam a gentle smack. A link at the bottom of the screen displays "BK TenderCrisp." The impact of this approach went far beyond any of Burger King's expectations. Visits to the site were primed by its two programmers, who sent out 20 e-mails to their friends with instructions to pass on the link. In the first week of operations the site had 46 million hits![58]

Companies use promotion to build brand awareness and recognition and to drive traffic to a website. More and more, we see companies implementing integrated marketing communications strategies that use conventional media to make customers aware of the company's on-line business channel. They then use a mix of on-line promotion tactics to further build awareness and drive traffic to the website. These tactics include on-line advertising, newsletters, e-mail, and publicity. Expedia.com is an example. Expedia uses television advertisements to gain attention for and drive traffic to its travel services website.

banner advertisement
A paid advertisement that runs the entire width of the Web page, usually placed near the top or bottom of the page.

Banner advertisements have been the mainstay of Internet advertising since their inception. A full banner ad is rectangular and runs the entire width of the Web page, typically positioned at the top or bottom of the page. A popular variation is the half-banner ad. The ad is usually "clickable" to drive visitors to a Web location designated by the advertiser.

button advertisement
A paid advertisement that is smaller than a banner ad, appearing in medium, micro, short, and tall size variations.

Although banner ads remain the industry standard for on-line advertising, **button advertisements** are becoming increasingly popular. Buttons are smaller than banners and come in medium, micro, short, and tall variations. The different sizes make it easy to place button ads in a variety of locations, including the bottom of a Web page or on the left or right margin.

interstitial advertisement
An advertisement that appears in a separate browser window—also referred to as a "pop-up" ad.

Interstitial advertisements appear in separate browser windows while you wait for the main Web page to appear. These small windows, known as "pop-up" ads, may use sophisticated graphics or other special media effects to attract your attention. Users are more inclined to click on interstitials than on banner ads, but they also can be irritating to users.

Affiliate marketing is a form of advertising that is widely used on the Internet. Unlike traditional advertising messages, where fees are typically based on display time or number of impressions, affiliate marketing programs use a pay-for-performance incentive structure. Affiliates place ads or hyperlinked text messages on their site and earn referral fees when visitors click through and purchase products from the referred site.

According to JupiterResearch, spending on e-mail promotions in North America will grow from \$164 million in 1999 to \$7.3 billion in 2005.[59] The key reasons for this growth are the high response rates and the cost effectiveness associated with e-mail campaigns. E-mail marketing falls into two general categories—untargeted e-mail marketing (spam) and targeted e-mail marketing.

untargeted e-mail marketing
A mass e-mailing sent to unqualified e-mail addresses.

E-mail promotions continue to be the stalwart of Internet customer communications. **Untargeted e-mail marketing** on the Internet usually takes the form of unsolicited bulk e-mails sent to unqualified addresses (that is, to people who have not asked for such information). This "on-line junk mail" is often called spam and is considered poor netiquette. It is tempting to use this type of promotion because it has little or no cost. Although the thought of sending an ad to thousands of recipients for free is appealing, mass e-mailing is usually as ineffective as conventional junk mail. Furthermore, unsuspecting recipients may complain to the Internet provider from which the e-mail was sent, and reputable providers will discontinue the account of an offender.

targeted e-mail marketing
E-mail sent to qualified recipients, those who have expressed interest in receiving e-mail on a specific topic.

On the opposite end of the spectrum from massive junk e-mailing is **targeted e-mail marketing**. This practice is often referred to as permission-based marketing because recipients of targeted e-mails have been "qualified"; they have indicated their willingness to receive the e-mail before it is actually sent. Just like using mailing lists to target conventional mail, you can rent e-mail lists of people who are interested in specific topics. These are referred to as "opt-in" e-mail lists. Besides qualifying themselves on topics of interest, these people have preapproved e-mail on those topics. Companies that provide these lists typically charge 15 to 30 cents per address and will even send the e-mails for you. Targeted e-mail marketing services are available from a number of firms, including Vancouver-based Radiant Communications, 24/7 Canada, and HTMail; emailaddresses.com also provides information and resources on using e-mail promotion and communications.

Electronic magazines—**e-zines**—are in concept similar to paper newsletters: they are focused on a particular subject area or topic of interest; they provide a means to stay in touch with clientele; and they can inform current and potential customers of new products and services. CanadaOne provides information for Canadian small business operators with sections like Biz-Briefs, which has articles such as "Statscan Study Finds Small Business Closing Technology Gap," Ask-an-Expert, which answers specific questions such as "starting a business in Leduc, Alberta," and Locate Biz Events (e.g., the "Canadian business events calendar"). E-zines can also be used to generate income by selling advertising space! Dozens of marketing and electronic commerce e-zines can be found at Wilson Internet Services' marketing periodicals and e-zines.

e-zine
Abbreviation for electronic magazine—an on-line publication similar in concept to a printed magazine.

Canadian businesses spent an estimated $116 million on Web promotion in 2001, but on-line marketers rank search engine registration—which is usually free—as the most effective form of on-line promotion.[60] Reviewing search engine registration and submission tips provided at sites like Search Engine Watch can improve the likelihood that your site will be found when key word searches are conducted through the top on-line search engines. And that will drive traffic to your site.

Pricing on the Internet

The Internet has increased the pressure on prices of a wide variety of products and services. It is easier to engage in price comparison shopping on the Web than off-line, and that goes for customers and competitors. With the help of shopping bots, price comparisons of multiple sellers can be conducted simultaneously. It is also easier to change prices on the Internet. On-line airline reservation systems such as Air Canada's (http://www.aircanada.ca) make thousands of ticket price changes daily to optimize flight loads and airfares. On-line auction sites like eBay create the option for sellers to be price takers rather than price setters.

The extent to which on-line businesses will implement flexible pricing is a hot topic among Internet observers. Some analysts have predicted that the technical ability to implement flexible pricing on the Internet will lead to the widespread use of this pricing strategy. To date, however, on-line flexible pricing strategies have been limited to industries and contexts that tend to feature flexible pricing off-line as well—to industries with perishable inventories like airlines and hotels, and to the auctioning of unique or used items that might be found off-line at an auction house or flea market.

As with off-line pricing decisions, the on-line pricing strategy must support the company's overall business strategy and objectives. In many cases, flexible pricing may not be the best pricing strategy. A recent study by Cap Gemini Ernst & Young (CGE&Y) suggests that on-line consumers are far more interested in finding "honest prices" than they are in finding the lowest price.[61]

Companies that conduct business both off-line and on-line face another consideration when setting prices: whether on-line and off-line prices should be the same or different. Generally speaking, charging different prices for different channels can be effective provided that (1) channel use behaviour is an effective means to segment the market, and/or (2) the company benefits by encouraging the use of one channel rather than the other. For example, banks may charge lower prices for on-line services to encourage customers to bank on-line rather than using bank branches, which are more expensive to build and staff.

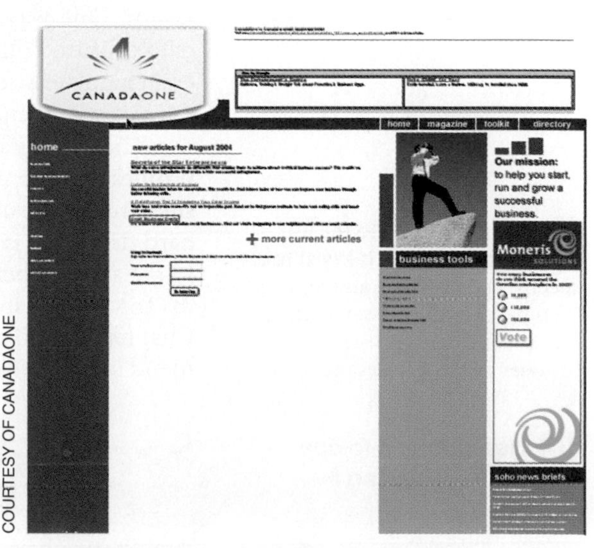

COURTESY OF CANADAONE

The CanadaOne website is an e-zine targeted to small business operators in Canada. Aside from an informational magazine, the website has a small business tool kit and a directory of Canadian businesses.

ON LINE 

Pricing Strategies on the Internet

How consistent are retailers with their on-line and off-line pricing? Choose a company that sells in multiple channels, like Future Shop, Chapters, or HMV. Visit a retail location for that store and select three products for price comparison. Then visit the company's website and compare the on-line and off-line prices of the items you selected. How can you explain what you find? (You may want to divide into teams and select different types of products. You can then compare how different products or industries deal with the issue of on-line versus off-line pricing.)

Evaluating the Outcome

Once the Internet marketing program is underway, how do you know if you are accomplishing what you originally set out to do? You compare the results achieved to your Internet goals and marketing objectives. Deviations from objectives signal that changes to marketing strategies may be necessary.

A variety of techniques are available for obtaining detailed information that allows you to compare results to objectives. Regardless of the technology deployed for an Internet marketing program, the Web server used to run the site can tabulate a wealth of data. Unfortunately, the quality of the information can vary widely.[62]

Traffic coming to a site can be quantified as hits, as page views, or as unique visitors. A **hit** is a record that a file was requested from a website. But since one page can be composed of multiple files, tracking hits can be somewhat misleading. For example, a single page with four pictures embedded will yield five hits since each picture is a separate file.

hit
A record that a file was requested from a website.

page view
A single page requested from a website.

A better statistic to capture is a **page view,** which is a single page requested from a website. Page-view statistics allow you to identify more and less successful pages. Infrequently visited pages can be reevaluated and revamped or removed from the website. Web pages that exceed expected hit counts can be analyzed to determine why they are successful.

When a visitor arrives at a site, his or her clickstream can be followed to identify which pages are viewed, the sequence in which they are viewed, and the duration of the entire visit. Combining page-view statistics with clickstream sequencing information helps identify possible design and flow problems in the website. That knowledge can be applied to improve website design and the overall performance of the Internet marketing program.

A tally of hits or page views shows the activity level of a website. It is simply a count or quantitative measure. But counts are only part of the story; they don't address other important questions such as these:

- Is the site reaching the target audience?
- Who is actually visiting the website?
- Can visitors easily move around the website?
- Are the visitors getting what they want from the website?

Answering these questions requires more detailed information about each unique visitor. One way to accomplish this is by encouraging site registration. Demographic data captured during the initial site registration can be analyzed to determine the general characteristics of people visiting the site. These characteristics reveal whether or not the target audience is responding to the Internet marketing program.

The demographic information also can be matched with clickstream data to generate profiles for each unique visitor. These profiles can be developed over multiple visits to the site through the use of cookie technology. A **cookie** is a digital tag written to the user's local hard drive that is keyed to a specific server (for example, a Web page) and is passed back to the server when the user's browser again accesses the server. This electronic ID is used to track clickstream or purchase behaviour over multiple visits. For example, Chapters.Indigo.ca combines collaborative software with cookie technology to recommend books to frequent buyers once they have established a purchase preference pattern.

cookie
A digital tag written to the user's local hard drive that is keyed to a specific server (for example, a Web page) and is passed back to the server when the user's browser again accesses the server.

 10 Describe one-to-one marketing using the Internet

>> ONE-TO-ONE MARKETING USING THE INTERNET

One of the most important trends in the field of one-to-one marketing is the emergence of one-to-one marketing over the Internet. As previously discussed, marketers have overwhelmingly adopted the Internet and World Wide Web as a new channel for promotions and commerce, and one-to-one marketers are capitalizing on the Web's full set of interactive marketing capabilities. Internet companies are learning more about their customers and using this information to fine-tune their marketing efforts and build relationships with each customer on a more individual level.

One advantage of on-line one-to-one marketing is the ability to deliver personalized promotional messages to each customer visiting a company's website. Past customer transaction history, clickstream data, and survey responses are used to identify buying patterns and interests. Based on information known about the customer visiting its site, such as colour and brand preferences, geographic location, and past customer transaction data, the marketer can develop a targeted and personalized on-line promotion or custom catalogue.

When used in conjunction with on-line ad-serving technology, one-to-one marketing has the power to make the Internet an effective and cost-efficient advertising vehicle. On-line database marketing helps advertisers improve their return on investment by directing their banner ads to the consumers most likely to have an interest in their products or services. It also benefits consumers since they don't have to view ads that are of no interest to them.[63] Internet ad server specialists like MaxOnline and 24/7 Canada are building huge databases filled with anonymous profiles about consumers' activities on the Web with the goal of delivering ads that will home in on a Web surfer's interests. By profiling Web visitors, marketers can send banner ads and messages to just those who are likely to be interested instead of wasting money on sending advertisements to those who are not. The technology can also be used to capture the attention of target groups.

AP/WIDE WORLD PHOTOS

As technology develops, marketers are finding new media to convey their messages. 3G technology may become a powerful, mobile vehicle for targeted marketing messages. A Japanese woman, pictured here, tests a new 3G mobile phone relaying a live colour image of her smiling face.

Increasingly, more and more companies are realizing that e-mail is the ideal one-to-one medium, capable of establishing and building enduring customer relationships with highly targeted lists of prospects. This technique works much the same way as off-line one-to-one marketing campaigns: companies build databases of e-mail addresses by enticing customers to register on a site in exchange for information or access to a special offer.[64] One-to-one e-mail campaigns are proving more effective than banner advertising on the Internet. Click-through rates for e-mail campaigns average 10 to 15 percent, compared to banner ad click rates that average around 1 percent, and traditional direct mail that averages between 0.5 and 2 percent.[65]

One-to-one e-mail marketing should be strictly permission based. That is, consumers should "opt-in" or give their permission to receive e-mail messages from a marketer. Chapters.Indigo.ca and other on-line booksellers ask customers to provide them with additional information about their likes and dislikes so that they can receive future book recommendations. But customers can indicate that they do not wish to receive recommendations. Similarly, Palm One, the maker of the Palm Pilot, sends messages to some 400,000 customers who have opted in through Palm's website or registration cards to receive e-mail. The personalized messages include the recipient's name and contain information relevant to the product and model the person owns as well as tips on using it better.[66]

>> PRIVACY CONCERNS WITH ONE-TO-ONE AND INTERNET MARKETING

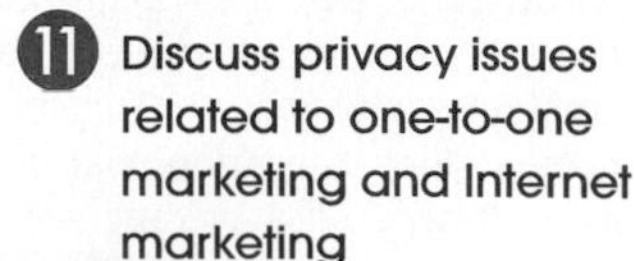

11 Discuss privacy issues related to one-to-one marketing and Internet marketing

Before rushing out to invest in computer hardware and software to build a database, marketers should heed consumer reaction to the growing use of databases. One-to-one marketing concerns many Canadians because of the potential for invasion of privacy, specifically the sheer volume of information that is aggregated in databases and the vulnerability of this information to unauthorized access and use. A fundamental aspect of one-to-one marketing is providing valuable services to customers based on knowledge of what customers really value. However, it is critical that marketers remember that these relationships should be built on trust. While database

ON LINE 

Privacy Commissioner of Canada

Visit the Privacy Commissioner of Canada website. What resources have been made available to marketers and business people to help them comply with Canadian privacy laws? Take the privacy quiz to see how well you know your privacy rights. How did you do?

http://www.privcom.gc.ca

technology allows marketers to compile ever-richer information about their customers to build and manage relationships, if these customers feel their privacy is being violated, then the relationship becomes a liability.[67]

The popularity of the Internet for direct marketing, for consumer data collection, and as a repository of sensitive consumer data has alarmed privacy-minded consumers. On-line users have complained of being "spammed"—the Internet's equivalent of junk mail. Web surfers, including children who are using the Internet, are routinely asked to divulge personal information in order to access certain screens or purchase goods or services on-line. Internet users who once felt fairly anonymous when using the Web are now disturbed by the amount of information marketers collect on them as they visit various sites in cyberspace.

Most consumers are unaware of how personal information is collected, used, and distributed, and they are unaware of how technology helps in collecting personal data. Further, there is widespread misunderstanding among consumers about existing privacy laws and regulations. Frustrated by their lack of control, consumers want more opportunities to determine how their personal information will be used.

ETHICS IN MARKETING

Collecting Customers' Data While Maintaining Their Privacy

One-to-one marketing and customer relationship management are two of the hottest concepts in business today. However, a key component of both these concepts is often overlooked: privacy. To remain competitive and to be in compliance with the law, businesses must include privacy relationship management as part of their business practices.

The capture of personal data for marketing purposes is a longstanding practice in Canadian business. Today, however, policies and laws that govern what businesses can do with customer information are changing. In Canada, Bill C-6, the Personal Information Protection and Electronic Documents Act, came into force on January 1, 2004. The PIPED Act requires all businesses across Canada to follow rules that are designed to protect the personal information of both their employees and their customers. For businesses, the legislation will require the appointment of a privacy specialist and will require them to have systems that insure their customer information is gathered with the consent of their customers and once gathered, that the information is secure, accurate, and not used beyond the stated purpose for which it was collected and stored. The adjustment is expected to be most difficult for small businesses. For example, a survey conducted for the Canadian Chamber of Commerce in 2003 found that "81 percent of small and mid-sized businesses were nearly clueless about the need to comply with new privacy legislation." In addition to the federal PIPED Act, provincial privacy legislation had been passed in British Columbia, Alberta, and Quebec prior to January 1, 2004.[68]

In other parts of the world, policies and laws regarding the use of customer data for marketing purposes are becoming increasingly restrictive. For example, at the Direct Marketing Association/Internet Alliance 2001 Government Affairs Conference, it was reported that 465 privacy-related bills were introduced in 46 U.S. states in 2001. Argentina now has the strictest information protection law in Latin America. In Europe, each member of the European Union (EU) has agreed to abide by the Data Protection Directive of 1998, which is a formal set of strict privacy practices; the directive bars transmission of personal data to countries that don't have parallel privacy safeguards. One consequence has been that the amounts and types of data flowing from the EU to Canada and the United States are severely restricted. Canada responded by developing and implementing Bill C-6, the PIPED Act, which brings Canada into compliance with the EU. With respect to American firms, the U.S. Department of Commerce and the European Commission negotiated the "Safe Harbor," which was approved in July 2000. The Safe Harbor allows U.S. companies to voluntarily self-certify to the Department of Commerce that they will adhere to certain privacy principles as stated by the European Commission. In this way, U.S. companies can avoid experiencing interruptions in their business dealings with the EU or facing prosecution by European authorities under European privacy laws. Adhering to the Safe Harbor will ensure that U.S. businesses will provide adequate privacy protection as defined by the directive. Respectively, if these firms are in compliance with the EU's privacy laws, they will most likely be in compliance with Canada's PIPED Act as well.[69]

How can a company create a privacy management program that will make customers and prospects feel comfortable when they provide personal data? What should a company with international markets, especially in Europe, be doing regarding privacy?

On-line privacy concerns were addressed recently in a 2003 privacy case finding under Canada's PIPED Act with respect to the use of "cookies" on a Canadian airline's website. A customer complained that the airline's website would not allow him access because his Web browser was set up to disable "cookies." In addition, the individual complained that this website was collecting his and other visitors' information without their knowledge and consent because permanent "cookies" were being placed on their hard drives. The airline responded by saying that the access denial to users who had disabled "cookies" was an unintentional computer glitch that was corrected. The use of permanent cookies was designed to collect information on the language of the visitor and their chosen country (Canada or the U.S.) so that on future visits they would be greeted with a Web page configured to their language and nationality. The airline did not state in its privacy policy how it used or applied cookies as part of its website. However, the airline did indicate that it would develop and publish this policy in the future. Canada's privacy commissioner ruled that information stored in cookies fell under the jurisdiction of the PIPED Act. The actions of the airline to deny access to its website unless cookies were enabled and the failure to inform website visitors that cookies were being collected and stored, and how they were used, caused the airline to be in violation of the act. The corrective actions of the airline to enable people to visit the website while not accepting cookies, and the establishment of an information policy, would bring the airline into compliance. This case is an example of the published rulings of the Privacy Commission, which in keeping with its mission to protect privacy, rarely identifies the complainants or respondents in legal cases.[70] Canadian marketers operating on the Web must deal not only with federal legislation in the form of the Personal Information Protection and Electronic Documents Act (PIPED Act) but also with the provincial privacy legislation that has been enacted by the provinces of Quebec, Alberta, and British Columbia. Marketing firms using e-mail are advised to consider the guidelines presented in Exhibit 17.6 if they want to be in compliance with Canada's federal and provincial privacy legislation.[71]

While all Canadian business firms must conduct their business in accordance with the Personal Information Protection and Electronic Documents Act, database marketers venturing into new data territories need to be aware of foreign privacy laws. As discussed in the "Ethics in Marketing" box, in the U.S., privacy policies have been mostly voluntary for Canada's largest trading partner. In contrast, in 1998 the European Union passed the European Data Protection Directive, which requires that any business that trades with a European organization must comply with the EU's rules for handling information about individuals, or risk prosecution. This directive prohibits the export of personal data to countries not doing enough to protect privacy.[72]

EXHIBIT 17.6

Some Privacy Guidelines for E-Mail Marketers

- Provide customers with an explicit reason for collecting their personal information.
- Ask only for what is relevant to the identified purpose.
- Provide a clearly worded sign-up form or opt-in page to confirm consent.
- Link the opt-in page to the company's privacy policy.
- Disclose any third parties, such as a marketing firm, involved in e-mail promotions and campaigns; link to the third party's privacy policy as well.
- Maintain accurate records of customer sign-ups and ensure individuals have access to their records on request.
- Use personal information only for its stated purpose; gain additional consent if that purpose changes.
- Do not make information collection a condition of an offer.
- Destroy personal information records after they've been used for the permitted purpose.
- Visit the Privacy Commissioner of Canada website at **http://www.privcom.gc.ca** for a PIPED Act e-kit for businesses. For more on PIPA, visit the B.C. Office of the Information and Privacy Commissioner at **http://www.oipcbc.org.**

SOURCE: Carrie Harrison, "E-mail Marketing in a Private World," *Marketing Magazine*, March 8, 2004.

More than 50 nations have, or are developing, privacy legislation. Outside of Canada, Europe has the strictest legislation regarding the collection and use of consumer data, and other countries look to that legislation when formulating their policies. Australia, for instance, recently introduced legislation that would require private companies to follow a set of guidelines regarding the collection, storage, use, and transfer of personal information about individuals. Common privacy rules include obtaining data fairly and lawfully, using the information only for the original purpose specified, making sure it is accurate and up to date, and destroying data after the purpose for collection is completed. The EU requires that consumers be presented with an opt-out provision at the point of data collection.

>> CONNECT IT

As you recall from the opening story, Amazon.ca, like many other marketers today, has embraced one-to-one marketing using the Internet as an alternative to mass-media marketing. Using the Internet to reach out and get to know customers on an individual basis with the help of database technology provides an efficient and effective means of providing customers with the individualized attention that they demand. Amazon.ca uses its database of past customer transaction data to develop personalized service and promotional offers and to cross-sell other merchandise. Amazon.ca demonstrates the fundamentals that must be undertaken to create a successful Internet marketing program. It requires that you use promotion to make potential customers aware of your website and ultimately to drive traffic to your site. Once customers reach your site, you must provide them with content or products that fulfill their needs, wants, or desires. Ideally, these offerings should make customers want to return to the site. Amazon.ca represents the "model" that other Internet marketers try to copy.

REVIEW IT

1 **Define one-to-one marketing and discuss its dependence on database technology.** One-to-one marketing is an individualized marketing method that utilizes customer information to build long-term, personalized, and profitable relationships with each customer. Database technology makes it possible for companies to interact with customers on a personal, one-to-one basis. A database stores pertinent information about a company's customers and contacts and makes it readily available to the sales and marketing staff for assessing, analyzing, and anticipating customers' needs. Database technology allows marketers to sift through the millions of pieces of data to target the right customers, to develop the right communication based on these customer needs, and to monitor the ongoing relationship, making adjustments in message strategy as needed.

1.1 Explain why one-to-one marketing today would not be possible without database technology.

2 **Discuss the forces that have influenced the emergence of one-to-one marketing.** Forces that have helped shape one-to-one marketing include a more diverse society, more demanding and time-poor consumers, a decline in brand loyalty, the explosion of new media alternatives, changing channels of distribution, and demand for marketing accountability. Consumers no longer want to be treated like the masses. One-to-one marketing allows consumers to be treated as individuals with their own unique sets of needs and wants. Consumers today also have less time to spend shopping for the products they need. Through its targeted nature, one-to-one marketing can decrease the time consumers need to make purchase decisions. Further, consumers are less brand loyal than they once were. One-to-one marketing techniques increase brand loyalty by focusing on finding a firm's best customers, rewarding them for their loyalty, and thanking them for their business. As mass-media approaches become less important, one-to-one marketing will increase in importance and offer marketers a more cost-effective avenue for reaching customers. Finally, the demand for marketing accountability will drive the growth of one-to-one marketing and justify its continued existence.

2.1 List several local businesses that you feel would benefit from one-to-one marketing. Choose one business and develop a one-to-one marketing plan, outlining the one-to-one applications that could be utilized, identifying what data should be collected about customers, and recommending data analysis methods. Also identify how the company could perform some of its one-to-one marketing using the Internet. Present your findings to the class.

3 **Compare the one-to-one marketing communications process with the traditional mass-marketing communications process.** The marketing communications process follows the flow of a marketing message from the marketer to the consumer. In the more traditional, mass-media version, an advertiser or marketer sends a promotional message through a mass-marketing channel to its target audience. Noise from competing advertisements affects the encoding and decoding of the message. Feedback on the effectiveness of the communication comes through market research and changes in sales levels or market share. In the one-to-one marketing communications process, the flow is similar; however, the message encoded by the marketer is personalized, there is relatively little noise to affect encoding and decoding, and the marketer has the ability to capture the response from the consumer and feed this information back into the marketing database for future use.

3.1 Explain the differences between traditional mass-media marketing communications and targeted one-to-one marketing communications. Why are these differences important to the success of one-to-one marketing?

4 **List eight common one-to-one marketing applications.** Common marketing applications of customer databases include (1) identifying the best customers, (2) retaining loyal customers, (3) cross-selling other products or services, (4) designing targeted marketing communications, (5) reinforcing consumer purchase decisions, (6) inducing product trial by new customers, (7) increasing the effectiveness of distribution channel marketing, and (8) improving customer service.

4.1 As the marketing manager of a local retailing chain, you have just analyzed your database of customers and determined that your best customers constitute 12 percent of your customer database and provide nearly 80 percent of your sales. Additionally, you have discovered that about 50 percent of the customers in your database have not purchased in over two years. What can you do with this knowledge?

4.2 ON LINE WRITING As marketing director for a regional chain of restaurants with a country gift shop theme, you have been assigned the task of developing a loyalty marketing program. Use the Internet to find a company that can help you. Once you select a provider, write a brief memo describing what the provider can do for your company. Identify in your memo which of the eight common one-to-one marketing applications your chosen provider can help you implement and how (see Exhibit 17.2). Also identify what tools your chosen provider has to help you with your segmentation, RFM analysis, LTV analysis, and predictive modelling.

5 **Discuss the basics of one-to-one marketing database technology.** One-to-one marketing is characterized by the creation of a large computerized database of customers' and potential customers' profiles and purchase patterns, which are then used to direct marketing communications. A marketing database is the compilation of names, addresses, and other pieces of pertinent information about individual customers and prospects that affect what and how marketers sell to them. In its most basic form, database marketing relies on transactional processing systems that record the

details of individual purchase transactions. These data can then be enhanced using external sources of modelled data or custom data. Marketers can analyze customer data using segmentation, recency–frequency–monetary analysis, lifetime value analysis, predictive modelling, or data-mining techniques.

5.1 Explain the statement "A database is only as powerful as the information it houses."

5.2 Define the two different types of database enhancement and give examples of each.

5.3 Explain the concept of lifetime value. Why is this type of data manipulation so important to one-to-one marketers?

6 **Describe the impact of the Internet on business practices.** The Internet represents a new electronic channel to conduct a wide variety of marketing activities. Companies that embrace Internet technology can gain advantages associated with lower infrastructure, inventory, and transaction costs. The Internet also provides excellent opportunities for conducting marketing research. Tremendous amounts of secondary data are readily available, and the Internet allows for relatively easy collection of primary data in the form of e-mail surveys, Web-based surveys with graphics and multimedia, and on-line focus groups. Additional information related to the purchases of individual customers can be used to build profiles of customer preferences, and competitor information can be collected from direct observation or through shopping bots. By using the Internet, consumers can access a greater variety of information before a purchase decision is made. For businesses, the Internet provides a tool for building better relationships with suppliers and customers. Every company must address the issue of whether or not it should have an Internet presence. For most companies, Internet marketing can be used to augment existing marketing programs. Planning the Internet marketing program involves analyzing the Internet marketing environment, articulating the company's on-line business strategy, and setting specific Internet marketing objectives and strategies.

6.1 The Internet is revolutionizing how primary marketing research is being conducted. Describe how you could utilize the Internet to conduct a marketing research project. What are some advantages and disadvantages of conducting marketing research over the Internet?

6.2 Explain why it is important for a company to convey a consistent message and appearance in all the media forms it uses in its marketing endeavours. Identify a specific company that employs broadcast, print, and Internet media in its marketing efforts. Discuss their effectiveness in projecting a consistent message and appearance in all these media forms.

7 **Describe the current Internet marketing environment.** Most Internet business activity can be distinguished as either business-to-consumer (B2C) electronic commerce or business-to-business (B2B) electronic commerce. In either case, knowing the on-line habits of the target market is essential. On-line buyers can be characterized as early adopters, the mainstream, and laggards. One way to identify and target specific markets is through virtual communities, which include members who have a common interest, such as a hobby, sport, or other avocation. These virtual communities use bulletin boards, chat rooms, newsletters, or discussion lists to build social relationships and exchange information. By overcoming the physical distance that separates markets around the world, the Internet also facilitates targeting international markets. To be successful, organizations need to develop a global vision that recognizes social, cultural, economic, political, demographic, resource, infrastructural, and legal differences. As communications and products become more digitized, diverse electronic technologies will converge and combine into a single high-speed communication and distribution channel that will carry broadband content to telephones, televisions, and computers. These technological advances will create new marketing opportunities.

7.1 On-line privacy is a primary concern for some consumers, but many people do not fully understand on-line tracking technology. To better understand how on-line companies track your movements across the Internet, let's look at how DoubleClick.com does it.

a. Look at your own cookie file. If you are running Windows, choose the "Start Search File or Folders . . ." option from the menu bar. Look in the computer's hard drive (usually C:) for a file named "cookies." Doubleclick on the cookies text file that is located in your Internet browser folder. Then do a search for "doubleclick." You will probably find an entry that looks like: .doubleclick.net TRUE / FALSE 1920499140 id 99999996452b115. (On a Mac, under the File menu choose Find, search the hard drive for "cookies," and doubleclick on the configuration manager file. Scroll through the cookie settings to "doubleclick.net" and hit View.)

b. Now that you know what a cookie file looks like, go to the DoubleClick website and click over to the privacy policy statement. What happens if you choose the adserving cookie opt-out option? How will your cookie file change? How will that change the on-line advertisements you see in the future? Did you opt-out? Why?

7.2 The Global Perspectives box identified several key factors constraining growth of electronic commerce in France. Choose another country and conduct a similar analysis, i.e., identify current levels of e-commerce activity, likely near-term growth in e-commerce activity, and key factors either constraining or contributing to e-commerce growth.

8 **Discuss on-line business strategies.** To be successful, Web-based companies must develop sound business and marketing strategies. The Internet business strategy should start with a high-level goal and consider ways the Internet can be used to achieve that goal. This goal will determine the sophistication of the Internet presence and the desired level of interactivity, which can range from a purely informational corporate website to a fully interactive or transactional website. Transactional websites are capable of implementing complex on-line business models. Three basic business models include direct selling models, Internet retailing models, and Internet marketplaces. Direct sellers can be product manufacturers such as Dell that use the Internet to sell directly to consumers. Producers of digital products including software, music, and information can use the Internet to both sell and distribute products directly to consumers. Internet retailers and e-marketplaces provide the added convenience of a wide variety of products with easy access to price-comparison information. Despite these conveniences, however, drawbacks include lack of direct contact with the merchandise, reduced social interaction, and some difficulties resolving customer service complaints.

8.1 The Internet provides new opportunities for companies to operate their businesses. Some products and services are well suited for on-line marketing while others are currently less appropriate for the Internet.

a. Suggest a product or service that is ideally suited for marketing over the Internet. Describe why on-line marketing of this product or service is superior to more traditional marketing approaches.

b. Suggest a product or service that is now inappropriate for marketing over the Internet. Describe why more traditional marketing approaches of this product or service are better than on-line marketing.

8.2 On-line shopping bots represent one manifestation of an e-marketplace. Intelligent shopping bots allow buyers to conduct on-line searches using a variety of criteria, including specific product availability, price, or even overall value. To test these services, start by going to BotSpot, a site that groups a multitude of bots under various categories such as Commerce Bots, Search Bots, Stock Bots, and the like.

a. Observe the different product categories that are represented. Are all product categories represented? Can you categorize the products as mostly convenience, shopping, or specialty products?

b. Choose a category and scan through the list to choose two or three different bots to test drive. Choose a specific product and use these bots to compare availability and prices. Which bot is better and why?

c. How valuable do you think these shopping bots are to buyers and sellers?

8.3 E-marketplaces are frequently set up as on-line agents that create a marketplace for buyers and sellers. Exactly how the on-line agent generates revenue is not always clear. Let's see how Monster.com generates its revenue. Start by reading About Monster.com. Then go to the Employers page and get the Monster Products information page. What are some of Monster's products and who pays for them?

9 **Discuss Internet marketing objectives and strategies.** A company's Internet marketing program should include marketing objectives that are directly relevant to the website. These include objectives for generating and building traffic to the website and objectives targeting specific responses from visitors to the website. Firms should track page views and clickstream data to monitor users' on-line behaviour. Corporate websites can encourage users to respond with e-mail or telephone calls, and interactive websites can encourage on-line registration or actual transactions. On-line companies can offer personalized service and virtual product trials to build relationships with their customers and partially overcome the sensory and tactile limitations of the electronic channel. Although the Internet facilitates flexible pricing tactics, on-line companies need to evaluate whether a strategy of charging different prices for different customers or for different channels (on-line versus off-line) is consistent with the overall business strategy. On-line promotion takes various forms. Sending targeted e-mails to recipients who have indicated a willingness to receive marketing messages is more effective than sending untargeted e-mails. Newsletters and discussion lists provide other options for targeted Internet marketing. Advertising on the Internet takes the form of banner ads, button ads, and interstitial advertisements (pop-up ads). Search engine registration provides the equivalent of free publicity. Direct on-line distribution of digital products and services promises to be an exciting direction for electronic commerce. For tangible goods, on-line businesses typically rely on direct shippers to deliver products to their customers. Fulfillment of on-line orders has proven more problematic than initially envisioned by many on-line entrepreneurs. Using demographic information, clickstream data, and cookie technology, on-line businesses can offer better service to their customers. However, these data collection methods raise concerns about on-line privacy. Ultimately, consumers, public policy officials, and on-line businesses must determine whether the benefits outweigh the privacy concerns.

9.1 Harvey's has successfully employed brand recognition to build relationships with its customers for many decades without using the Internet. Visit the Harvey's website and comment on how well it integrates and reinforces the brand identity the company has built into its conventional marketing channels.

9.2 The Internet can have a significant impact on product distribution. Many steps in the product "supply chain" can be eliminated, thus reducing both delivery time and price for the consumer. What types of organizations and industries could be adversely affected by the Internet? What are some of the potential negative impacts on individual companies and industries that have been eliminated from the supply chain?

9.3 Portals like Canada.com and Canoe.ca generate much of their revenue from advertising. It would be logical for these companies to have marketing objectives to increase (1) the length of time each visitor spends at the site and (2) the frequency of return visits.

a. What types of services do these sites provide that encourage customers to increase the length of each visit?

b. What types of services do these sites provide that create a dynamic marketplace that encourages consumers to keep coming back?

9.4 Choose a product that you might like to buy. Then do price/quality comparisons across a variety of sites, including an on-line mall (e.g., Canada.com/shopping), an e-tailer (e.g., Chapters.Indigo.ca), and an on-line broker/auction (e.g., eBay). Then go to an on-line shopping bot (e.g., mySimon) and search for the same product. What are the differences in prices, product assortment, and quality across sites? Are the differences similar to price/assortment/quality variations you find in traditional stores?

10 **Describe one-to-one marketing using the Internet.** Marketers have recently capitalized on the Internet's interactive capabilities as a one-to-one marketing tool. By collecting past customer transaction data and studying a user's movements on the Web, the on-line one-to-one marketer gains the ability to create a personalized experience for each customer who visits its site. Additionally, banner advertising can be more efficiently targeted to just those Internet users who would be interested. An on-line marketer can also send personalized e-mail messages to those customers who give their permission.

10.1 ON LINE Visit the site developed by one-to-one marketing experts Don Peppers and Martha Rogers at http://www.1to1.com to read success stories of companies that have made one-to-one marketing strategies work for them. Select one of the articles at the "Publications" link (http://www.1to1.com/issues.aspx) and present a summary to the rest of the class.

11 **Discuss privacy issues related to one-to-one marketing and Internet marketing.** One-to-one marketing concerns many Canadians because of the potential for invasion of privacy, specifically the sheer volume of information that is aggregated in databases and the vulnerability of this information to unauthorized access and use. Most consumers are unaware of how personal information is collected, used, and distributed, and they are unaware of how technology helps in collecting personal data. Additionally, there is widespread misunderstanding among consumers about existing privacy laws and regulations. Frustrated by their lack of control, consumers want more opportunities to determine how their personal information will be used. The popularity of the Internet for direct marketing, for consumer data collection, and as a repository of sensitive consumer data has also alarmed privacy-minded consumers.

11.1 ETHICS Visit the Privacy Commissioner of Canada's website (http://www.privcom.gc.ca). Look for findings of the Commissioner under PIPEDA. Read up on several recent cases that the commissioner has judged. Discuss some of the implications of the findings of these cases for Canadian companies that do business with electronic communications.

DEFINE IT

APPLY IT

Molly's Flowers is a small flower shop located in a medium-sized metropolitan area. The proprietor, Molly Edwards, has always measured the success of her business based on market share, which she estimates at roughly 10 percent. This estimate is based on a report published by the local chamber of commerce that provides total flower sales from area flower shops in her city but does not include flowers purchased at grocery stores.

Molly has used traditional mass-marketing approaches in an attempt to increase her market share, such as advertising heavily during holidays like Valentine's Day and Mother's Day and offering discounts during the low periods in between. These measures have increased sales, she believes, but she is not totally sure to what extent. Additionally, the ads cost money and the discounts eat into her profits. She knows that grocery stores cut into her business by offering lower prices on lower-quality flowers and arrangements, but she is not sure how to counter this pricing because lowering her prices across the board would be devastating to her profits.

Molly knows that she has a number of customers who order from her time and again, but she has never thought much about how to take advantage of this loyal customer base. Shuffling through a stack of flower orders on her desk from the past year, she begins to look closely at the information that she actually does collect about her customers. Each order form contains the customer's name, address, telephone number, date of order, date flowers are to be delivered, type of flower arrangement requested, total price, to whom the flowers were sent, and what was to be printed on the card. Additionally, about 9 out of 10 orders were purchased over the phone with a credit card.

QUESTIONS

1. Suggest a one-to-one marketing plan in which Molly can use the customer information she collects to (1) identify her best customers, (2) increase sales from her best customers, and (3) reinforce their purchase decision.
2. Through credit card records, Molly can overlay data onto her customer database to provide more information about her customers. What additional enhancement data would you suggest she overlay?
3. What can Molly do to determine how much business her customers give to floral departments in grocery stores? With this information, what one-to-one marketing techniques could influence her customers to choose Molly's Flowers more often?

THINK ABOUT IT

Rani Pharmaceuticals is the maker of several popular drugs used to treat high blood pressure and arthritis. Over time, the company has developed a positive relationship with many of the patients who use its medications through a weekly e-zine that offers all the latest information on new medical research findings and general health and fitness articles. The company has just been acquired by a group of investors who also own Soothing Waters Hot Tubs and Spas. The marketing director for Soothing Waters would like to use Rani's e-zine list for an e-mail promotion.

QUESTIONS

1. What should Rani Pharmaceuticals do?
2. Does the CMA Code of Ethics address using customer information by multiple divisions of the same company in its Code of Ethics? Go to **http://www.the-cma.org/consumer/ethics.cfm** and review the code. Then write a brief paragraph on how the CMA Code of Ethics relates to Rani Pharmaceutical's dilemma.

TRY IT

HMV: Staying On-Line

"With over 75 years of music retailing history, 346 stores worldwide and 100 stores in Canada, HMV is the world's premier retailer of music. HMV has proven itself as an innovative leader in Canada since 1986 and has been named Canadian Music Retailer of the Year for the past 15 years." In 1999, HMV worldwide decided it needed to establish an on-line venture. The firm believed that an e-mail and Internet presence would be absolute necessities for music retailers, especially in light of near stagnant sales many music retailers were experiencing through their bricks-and-mortar retail stores. HMV was hoping to seize upon the power of one-to-one marketing methods to turn its fortunes around.

The firm chose Canada as the country in which it would establish its first retail website because at the time Canada had a 38 percent Internet penetration among its population. HMV.com wanted to see if on-line distribution of its retail products would be feasible. The firm hired Sara Ross as its Internet marketing manager, established a Web page, and began developing a customer list and a database of e-mail addresses of customers who said they were interested in receiving information on offers via e-mail. Using this list, in 1999, HMV conducted a permission-based e-mail campaign to support a cross-selling promotion for DVDs and videocassettes featuring Canadian artist Sarah McLachlan. According to Sara Ross, "music fans are very responsive to permission-based-email" but "Don't go [out of bounds] by extending offers or content that has not been invited or you risk losing the subscriber from your list."

Ross developed a number of innovative initiatives to create and drive traffic to HMV.com. For example, in 2000, she set up an on-line concert (Webcast) featuring the Red Hot Chili Peppers. The result was record Internet traffic numbers for an on-line event. In addition, she developed a special tracks feature to promote new album releases. At the time, e-commerce banners, sound on banners, and permission-based e-mail were relatively new concepts, which Ross applied to HMV.com. For example, by permission, HMV would send out the HMV.communique to 70,000 registered users on a weekly basis. This e-mail contained special offers, as well as event and contest information. HMV also developed a special free Internet access CD that was sold through its retail stores for $9.95 but included a $10.00 HMV.com coupon. When installed, the CD would make HMV.com the home page of the user and allow them to redeem their $10.00 coupon.

However, the most significant promotions for HMV.com have been Web promotions such as the ability for HMV.com users to download the reissued album *Aladdin Sane* by David Bowie, which sold more on-line than through the retail outlets. Still, a survey of HMV retail store customers indicated that only 9 percent of them were buying on-line although 22 percent of them did browse the HMV.com site to help them shop. In addition, many of them acquired Web coupons to make their in-store purchases. In this respect, the site has shown more impact as a promotional vehicle as opposed to an additional retail distribution outlet. In the year 2000, even though HMV's website sales ranked it fifth behind four other Canadian retail stores, it was not profitable.

A number of other music retailers went on-line alongside HMV.com and like HMV online, they were able to generate sales but struggled to generate profits. For example the e-tail arm of Sam the Record Man, SamsCD.com, generated $800,000 sales in a nine-month period during the year 2000, but this figure was badly offset by operating losses of $3.6 million during the same time. Canadian on-line music e-tailer mymusic.ca began operations in September 1999 and during Christmas 1999 the firm had trouble filling its orders. In 2000, mymusic.ca was able to boast sales in the million-dollar neighbourhood but was struggling to make a profit, and its owner was talking about having to stay in for the long run.

With all the competition and a limited market on-line, it became difficult for all the players to make money. Despite all of its efforts and activities, HMV.com found it hard to be profitable in the Canadian market. Therefore, in the spring of 2003, HMV.com made a bold move. It linked up with Amazon.ca to relaunch its site as a co-branded distribution site of HMV and Amazon.com. In essence, the site is being operated by Amazon.ca, which will provide inventory and customer service and manage the site's content. Amazon.ca's current partner, Assured Logistics, will fill the orders. HMV's presence will be limited to promotional content such as HMV store locations, in-store events, and career opportunities. It seems that the Christmas season of 2000 was a harbinger for many on-line retailers. The score as of 2004 was SamsCD.com ceased operations, mymusic.ca keeps rolling along, and HMV.com is a co-branded partner of Amazon.ca.

Sources: Stephen D. Wise, "No Longer Net Bad Boys," *Marketing Magazine*, November 22, 1999; Chris Daniels, "Fumbling Towards Digital Ecstasy," *Marketing Magazine*, November 20, 2000; Derek Mellon,

"Holiday E-tail Season Only Booms for Some On-line Merchants," *Silicon Valley North* (GTA Edition), December, 2000, 38; and Press Release, "Amazon.ca and HMV Announce Relaunch of the HMV.com Website, Now Powered by Amazon.ca," *Canada Newswire*, April 29, 2003, 1.

QUESTIONS

1. It seemed like HMV.com was well managed and very innovative in its efforts, yet the venture struggled. Why do you think it is so difficult for on-line retailers like HMV.com to be profitable in Canada?
2. How do you think HMV benefits from its co-branding link with Amazon.ca? How does Amazon.ca benefit?
3. Will HMV be able to maintain the same one-to-one marketing relationship with its customers now that Amazon.ca is part of the relationship? Why or why not?
4. What do think HMV.com's marketing strategy and objectives were when the firm first started the website? How might these objectives and strategies have changed to lead HMV.com to an alliance with Amazon.ca? Discuss HMV.com's objectives, then and now.

FLIP IT

Flip to Chapter 17 in your *Grademaker Study Guide* for more review opportunities, including the pretest, vocabulary review, Internet activities, study test questions, and an application exercise based on direct marketing concepts. What forces influence one-to-one marketing? Can you describe the basics of database technology? What about shutting your book and listing the eight one-to-one marketing applications? If not, then flip open your *Grademaker* and review.

CLICK IT

The *Marketing* website is rich with materials to help you review and master marketing concepts. Check your knowledge with the free quizzes, practise key terms using the crossword puzzles, or review key concepts using the Microsoft® PowerPoint® slides. Also on the website are updated weblinks to companies mentioned in this chapter, Internet exercises, career marketing information, and much much more! Go to http://www.lamb3e.nelson.com, read the material, and follow the convenient links.

WATCH IT

Marketing Gone Bad: Attack of the Spammers

One of the greatest communication opportunities available for marketers has emerged in the form of the Internet. The Internet is a convergence medium that combines the media characteristics of television, radio, print, and direct mail with instant-response communication by consumers, who can choose to respond with telecommunications, voice communication, or, most commonly, via e-mail. However, this great opportunity has also spawned a great problem that puts the viability of this medium at risk. The problem is unsolicited electronic communications, or, as it is more commonly known, spam.

The term "spam" comes from a skit created many years ago by the classic British comedy troupe Monty Python. In the skit, a male and female couple is in a restaurant ordering food and the male orders spam, whereupon the female member announces "I don't like spam." A restaurant chorus starts repeating "spam, spam, spam, spam" in unison. Hence the name "spam" was transferred from a packaged food to mean something that is repeated over and over again; the term was then used to describe unwanted Internet communications. The quote "I don't like spam" is a very mild expression of the feelings that many people have about spam today.

For businesspeople, spam is a time robber operating 24/7 as it sends hundreds of e-mails to business networks every day. Laurie Guttman is a direct mail business marketer whose small business is being overwhelmed by spam. He is just one of many of the world's victims who are on the receiving end of the 9 billion junk e-mails sent every day. The legitimate e-mail volume is dwarfed in comparison, and e-mail users spend an average of 4.5 seconds per e-mail to get rid of the unwanted junk. It is estimated that for businesses that communicate electronically with computers—virtually all businesses these days—the costs of deleting spam average $1,000 per year in wasted time per employee. Some estimates put the cost of lost productivity in the tens of billions of dollars!

According to Chris Kraft, manager of Internet security firm Sophos Canada, "the viability of e-mail is at risk." He comments that e-mail inboxes are being ruined, and his firm has been growing tremendously as it develops software tools to fight off the spammers. Spammers are described as "marketers gone bad." For $50 they can acquire 20 million e-mail addresses, and with a further investment of $400 to $500 they can begin a spam campaign from their home computers. Statistical research indicates that about 8 percent of computer users respond to spam and that this response rate far exceeds what most spammers need to break even on their small investment.

As such, it is a business opportunity that is paying off. Many spammers are legitimate (an oxymoron, it would appear), since they are simply small business people trying to make a living. Others are scammer spammers, like the perpetrators of what is known as the "Nigerian letter scam." In this spam scam, an e-mail is sent out from a person who identifies himself as a Nigerian civil servant who needs help in managing some international government contracts. The civil servant needs to undertake some foreign exchange transactions with which only "you" can help. If you agree to help, you will get a large percentage of the proceeds of millions of dollars. All that is required is a small investment from you and access to your personal banking information. Of course, your small investment is never repaid and the scammer spammer cleans out your bank account. You never meet your "business" partner, who is usually operating outside of Canada and thus is beyond not only your reach but also the reach of the authorities.

As if "legitimate spammers" and "scammer spammers" are not bothersome enough, there are also cyberterrorists to contend with. David McMahon, a cyberterrorism expert, describes spam as a critical threat as it can spread computer viruses, Trojan viruses, and malicious code. He describes how the SOBIG virus was spread through spam, infected 30 percent of small companies, and cost businesses an estimated $3 billion.

The question for Laurie Guttman and all businesses is how to deal with the attack of the spammers. A number of responses are possible. The simplest approach is to hit the "delete" key, which has been Laurie's approach up to now. This practice may work well for the individual consumer who is receiving e-mail at home. However, the loss of business productivity for businesses as each employee spends time sifting through hundreds of messages is just too high, and Laurie Guttman is reaching his limit. As such, businesses have been lobbying government for antispam legislation that will force "legitimate spammers" to reduce or even desist in their efforts. Industry Canada set up an antispam task force in 2004 to study how the government can best address the problem. Existing legislation such as the *Personal Information Protection and Electronic Documents Act* (PIPEDA) requires all commercial e-mail to be permission-based. Recipients have to have agreed to receive solicitations in the first place and must also have agreed to any reselling of their information to other parties for purposes of communications. The Competition Act does not address unsolicited e-mail practices but does have provisions regarding deceptive and misleading advertising. Forged identification on spam communications and the sending of malware programs fall under the Criminal Code. The problem is that the legislation is enforced by different bodies and is not unified under one jurisdiction. Also, enforcement of these laws on perpetrators who are located outside Canada is highly problematic.

The most feasible and direct solution will come from software systems that will defeat spam. Sophos Canada and other companies are developing interception tools to filter spam and defeat viruses before they get to employees' computers. This software accounts for the 400 percent growth rate in these companies, which have become a $1.5 billion industry on their own. However, the solution systems are expensive and will still be vulnerable to large spammers, who will develop systems to stay ahead. This battle will continue, and although employee productivity may go up, information technology costs will go up as well. In addition, the amount of spam flowing on the information highway may remain unaffected. The solution is going to be expensive. What is needed are controlled access information highways, which spammers cannot penetrate easily, but they will come at a high cost to Internet service providers; these costs will in turn be passed on to the users of these highways.

It is likely that some kind of international cyberpolice force with multinational jurisdiction will have to be set up to police the activity on the information highway. It promises to be an interesting future as the commercial use of the Internet grows along with the accompanying growth pains in the form of spam, scams, and malware!

QUESTIONS

1. Small business people like Laurie Guttman and individual consumers are able to buy antispam software packages and the like. How effective do you think they are? Do you think they are the solution to spam? Why or why not?
2. Consider legitimate marketers who want to communicate responsibly on the Internet. When does a message cross the line from being legitimate to being spam? Come up with your own definition of spam.
3. Spam is an international problem. Do you think legislation will ever be able to deal with it effectively? Explain your answer.
4. Consider the various solutions to spam proposed in the case. Go on-line and research the current situation on the Internet. Do you think the problem is getting better or worse? If you had the power to affect the situation, what solution(s) would you propose?

SUGGESTED INFORMATION SOURCES

CBC, *Venture*, "Life of the Spammed"; Broadcast: January 18, 2004.

Industry Canada, "An Anti-Spam Action Plan for Canada," *A Report*, May 2004.

"Nigerian Letter Scam Cracked," *Leader Post*, [Final Edition], Regina, Saskatchewan, July 11, 2001, A12.

chapter 18

Customer Relationship Management

>> LEARNING OBJECTIVES

1. Define customer relationship management
2. Explain how to establish customer relationships within the organization
3. Explain how to establish and manage interactions with the current customer base
4. Outline the process of acquiring and capturing customer data
5. Describe the use of technology to store and integrate customer data
6. Describe how to analyze data for profitable and unprofitable segments
7. Explain the process of leveraging and disseminating customer information throughout the organization

>> Marketers are realizing that they must contend and adapt to the new wireless and mobile world of their customers. In Japan, the mobile Internet has been adopted faster than any other major electronic innovation in the nation's history, including radio, television, and personal computers. As early as 1999, there were 43 million mobile Internet subscribers in Japan! Consider the situation in Sweden, where three-quarters of the population use mobile phones and 90 percent of Swedes between 15 and 25 are mobile phone users. Krista, a suburb of Stockholm, is called the "wireless valley," because of the high use of mobile services such as phones, palm pilots, and mobile computers that have Internet access.

But how do you establish relationships with people who are always on the move? And it's not just a matter of simply finding out their mobile addresses or phone numbers. You see, Japan, Sweden, and other European countries, and most recently Canada, have enacted privacy laws to protect mobile users from being contacted without their permission. After all, unlike your home phone, for which you do not pay for in-bound calls, mobile airtime is paid no matter who initiates the connection. This means that marketers have to find ways to encourage the mobile consumers to make the first contact and then convince these consumers to give the marketers permission to initiate future contacts. A challenge, you might say, but marketers and the creative people they employ are up to the challenge of creating relationships and managing them. The following are some examples of how marketers are "relating" to today's young mobile consumers.

TeliaSonera, Sweden's largest telecom operator, has developed a unique customer relationship management approach to encourage its customers to interact with one another through its short message service (SMS). TeliaSonera introduced a game called BotFighters, which is a position-based game in which mobile phones are used as laser weapons and radar devices to find competitors. Players need to physically locate their competitors, and they do this by navigating and "firing their lasers" through the SMS, which are addressed to a phone number. As people play this game they begin to identify very closely with the mobile phone service they are using. TeliaSonera benefits by encouraging users to employ their service and pay for it while also encouraging nonusers to adopt the service so that they can play and socialize with their friends.

Nokia also has an SMS-based game, in which people are given "missions" via the SMS service. The people who play may have to solve a puzzle or problem or may even have to go and meet someone in a particular place. All this message traffic adds up to income for the service provider and provides it with database information on its users.

However, it's not just service providers who are reaching out to the mobile market. One Swedish beer marketer, Pripps, developed a fun SMS promotion for its Bla (Blue) brand of beer. Bla drinkers who sent an SMS with the message "Bla" to Pripps were sent a return message in the form of a pickup line. In the first few weeks of the promotion, which was supported by television commercials and a website, over 45,000 messages were sent out.

Tsutaya, a leading video, book, and CD retailer in Japan, has been able to recruit 2.5 million members to its i-mobile Tsutaya Online website. The site tracks the purchase and use behaviour of its subscribers. If, for example, a person buys a CD of a particular artist, in the future the website will send out an e-mail in the form of a digital music clip to announce any new music releases by that artist. The firm has developed a "recommendation" engine that considers the rental history of customers and then matches it with relevant new movie releases. The information is then sent out to the mobile phone or PC of the subscriber. This strategy has led to sales for Tsutaya as well with subscribers purchasing 14 percent more goods a month than nonsubscribers. In addition, the Tsutaya website is ranked as one of the top 10 in Japan and is visited an average of 11 times a month by customers.

Finally, marketers have developed mobile "commerce" systems that allow people to make purchases of retail goods and services with their mobile phones. For example, in Finland, some Coke machines are outfitted to allow you to make a purchase with your mobile phone. Stockholm, Sweden, is developing a system that will allow people to pay for parking via their mobile phones. Also in Sweden, a company called Mint has developed a system to allow payment for pizzas and convenience foods via mobile phones. How are these miracles accomplished? Quite simply, the purchases are added to your phone bill.

The use of customer relationship management and innovative marketing approaches has elevated the use of mobile devices far beyond "mere" communications.[1]

Can you think of other ways in which marketers can use mobile commerce to establish or maintain customer relationships? How does a company go about setting up a CRM program? And once such a program is in place, how does the company use the information it collects to its advantage? We will answer these questions and more in this chapter.

ON LINE 

Tsutaya

Visit the Tsutaya Company website. How is the website presented? Can you figure out how to sign up? How is it different from Blockbuster Canada's Video's website?

http://www.tsutaya.co.jp

http://www.blockbuster.ca

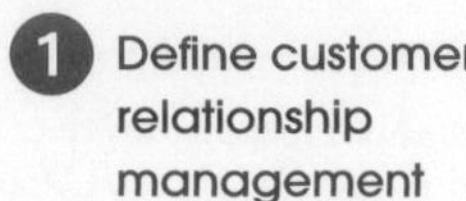

1 Define customer relationship management

>> WHAT IS CUSTOMER RELATIONSHIP MANAGEMENT?

customer relationship management (CRM)
A company-wide business strategy designed to optimize profitability, revenue, and customer satisfaction by focusing on highly defined and precise customer groups.

Customer relationship management (CRM) is a company-wide business strategy designed to optimize profitability, revenue, and customer satisfaction by focusing on highly defined and precise customer groups. This is accomplished by organizing the company around customer segments, encouraging and tracking customer interaction with the company, fostering customer-satisfying behaviours, and linking all processes of the company from its customers through to its suppliers. Canadian mobile phone companies such as Telus, Bell Canada, and Rogers Communications have recognized the market potential of mobile services and they want to become the single source communications provider for their customers. The phone companies believe that if they "bundle" their services appropriately, their customers will buy everything in one place. And if they don't bundle their products, their customers will turn to those firms that do! However, bundling may not work effectively unless customers who bundle receive special consideration such as quicker customer service and single-billing. In order to be successful at this, the phone companies know they must concentrate on upgrading their customer relationship management abilities. For example, as early as 2001 Bell Canada announced plans to invest $200 million to develop a single-bill system for all of its services. Rogers Communications, a Toronto-based cable, Internet, and wireless company, has been competing with bundles such as the "VIP discount program." The problem with a one-bill approach is "sticker" shock for customers. They are used to receiving three or four bills for $50, and when they receive only one bill of $150, they are surprised. However, having one contact and payment point for all of these services is still an attractive feature for customers and can reduce transaction management for the marketer as well. Surveys have shown that only 50 percent of customers are actually interested in a single-billing approach and that only 6 percent of customers would consider bundling to receive a single bill. Rather, 33 percent of customers would want to receive a discount for bundling their services and giving one provider an "exclusive" on their business. With all the market potential available to mobile phone providers, it seems certain that the firms that will lead this market will be the ones that most effectively use the information they have to increase customer service and satisfaction.[2]

CRM is a strategy designed to optimize business performance by focusing on highly defined customer groups. This Surado ad for SCM SQL is a perfect example of what CRM systems seek to know: The real customer.

The Customer Relationship Management Cycle

On the surface, CRM may appear to be a rather simplistic customer service strategy. But while customer service is part of the CRM process, it is only a small part of a totally integrated, holistic approach to building customer relationships. CRM is often described as a closed-looped system that builds relationships with customers. Exhibit 18.1 illustrates this closed-looped system, one that is continuous and circular with no predefined starting or end point.[3]

To initiate the CRM cycle, a company must first *establish customer relationships within the organization.* This may simply entail learning who the customers are or where they are located, or it may require more complex information on the products and services they are using. For example, a bank may find it very beneficial to determine all the services a customer is using, such as loans, savings accounts, investment instruments, and so forth. Once the company identifies its customers and its popular products and services, it then *determines the level of interaction each customer has with the company.* The bank, for example, would determine how frequently each customer interacts with the bank and the channel used for the interaction (branch location, telephone call centre,

Web, etc.). Based on its knowledge of the customer and his or her interaction with the company, the company can then *acquire and capture all relevant information about the customer,* including measures of satisfaction, response to targeted promotions, changes in account activity, and even movement of assets. One industry that has acquired and captured relevant data about its customers is the digital cable industry. Through ongoing telephone surveys of more than 24,500 households conducted semiannually, industry monitors have discovered that digital cable subscribers, compared with direct broadcast satellite (DBS) subscribers, are less likely to own their own home and are more likely to be single. They are as a group younger and better educated than DBS subscribers.[4]

Technology plays a major role in any CRM system. It is used not only to enhance the collection of customer data, as will be discussed later in this chapter, but also to store and integrate customer data throughout the company. Customer data are the actual firsthand responses that are obtained from customers through investigation or asking direct questions. These initial data, which might include individual responses on questionnaires, responses on warranty cards, or lists of purchases recorded by electronic cash registers, have not yet been analyzed or interpreted. A critical component of a CRM system is the *use of the appropriate technology to store and integrate customer data.* The value of customer data depends on the system that stores the data and the consistency and accuracy of the data captured. Companies like General Motors and Amazon.com have taken great strides to improve their data collection processes by using "data cleansing" and accuracy software such as "Validity Integrity Software."[5] Data-cleansing software checks for inconsistencies and extracts them. It then organizes and streamlines the data. Obtaining high-quality, actionable data from various but complementary sources is a key element in a CRM system.

Every customer wants to be a company's main priority, yet not all customers are equally important in the eyes of a business. Some customers occupy segments that are simply more profitable for the company than others. Consequently, the company conducts data mining to *determine its profitable and unprofitable customer segments.* Data mining is an analytical process that compiles personal, pertinent, actionable data about the purchase habits of a firm's current and potential customers. (We will discuss data mining in greater detail later in the chapter.) Essentially, data mining transforms customer data into customer information, which consists of data that have been

EXHIBIT 18.1

A Simple Flow Model of the Customer Relationship Management System

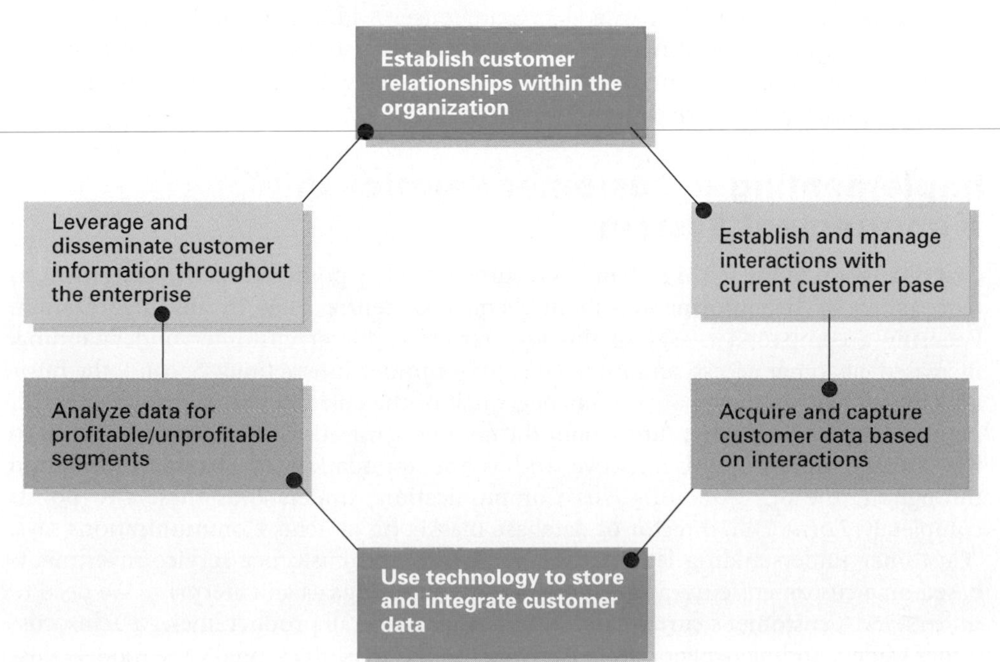

SOURCE: Joseph Hair, Robert Bush, and David Ortinau, *Marketing Research: Within a Changing Information Environment,* 2nd ed. (Burr Ridge, Ill.: McGraw-Hill/Irwin, 2002). Reproduced with permission of The McGraw-Hill Companies.

interpreted and to which narrative meaning has been attached. The data are subjected to a pattern-building procedure that profiles customers on variables such as profitability and risk. Customers may be categorized as highly profitable, unprofitable, high risk, or low risk; these categories may depend on the customer's affiliation with the business. For example, the bank might categorize its customers as long-time customers, commercial clients, customers with little money in the bank, or customers with several accounts. Once the customer data are analyzed, they are assigned interpretative meaning (transformed into information) and *disseminated throughout the entire organization.* A primary objective of the CRM system is to spread customer information across all functional areas of the business. This is because the customer does not interact with only one function of the business (e.g., sales or marketing), but rather with all functions (e.g., operations, production, accounting). A company using a CRM system must view its customers comprehensively, understanding that they interact, either directly or indirectly, with all components of the internal business system from suppliers and manufacturers to wholesalers and retailers.

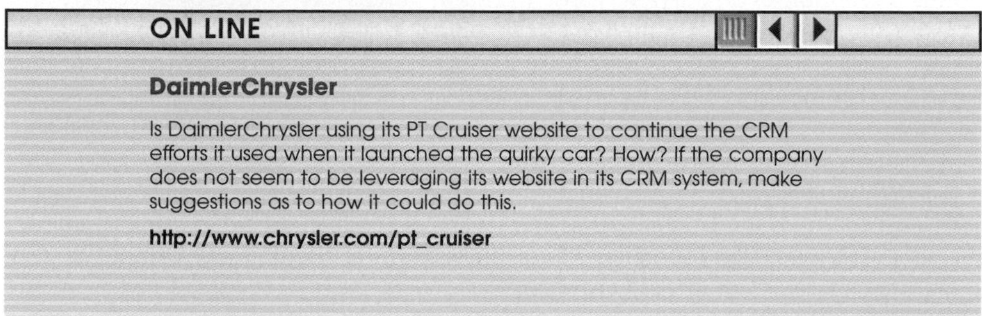

Although many would consider the retail industry to be at the forefront of CRM (think of Amazon.com and your supermarket shopper card), a Blue Martini Software survey conducted in 2002 revealed that the majority of retailers are not using CRM. The company conducted an e-mail poll of registered attendees at the 2002 National Retail Federation show. The survey's questions focused on retailers' ability to identify customers at the point of sale, access data about those customers in real-time, and "act on that information" to increase sales—all key steps in a CRM system. Results of the survey showed that only 45 percent of survey participants have technology to collect, aggregate, and analyze transaction data in a data warehouse. Additionally, only 41 percent of retailers surveyed can identify their "most profitable" customers and use that information for personalized promotions. And a paltry 10 percent of retailers are using individual customer data to drive promotional activities.[6]

Implementing a Customer Relationship Management System

Our discussion of the CRM system has assumed two key points. First, the customers, as represented by the information about them, take centre stage in any organization. Focusing a company's energy in this way results in better customer understanding, increased customer access, and more efficient customer interactions. Second, the business must focus on the day-to-day management of the customer relationship across all points of customer contact throughout the entire organization. This factor is critical to the success of any CRM initiative and is the foundation of shared information throughout the organization. Telus Communications understands these two points completely. Lorne Hill, director of database marketing at Telus Communications says: "Customer understanding lets us vary marketing and customer service investments based on a customer's current and potential value to Telus as an enterprise. We need to understand a customer's current and future value across all product lines. At Telus, customer understanding depends on customer and market profiles, predictive models, customer segmentation, campaign tracking and "ask the customer" data."[7]

Keeping these two points in mind, let's now look at how a CRM system is implemented. We will follow the progression depicted in Exhibit 18.1 as we explain each step in greater detail.

>> ESTABLISHING CUSTOMER RELATIONSHIPS WITHIN THE ORGANIZATION

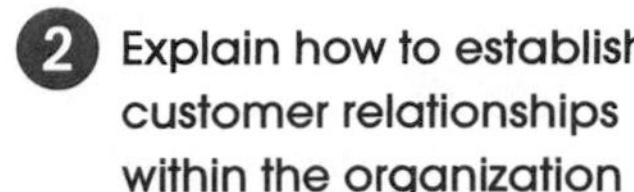
2 Explain how to establish customer relationships within the organization

Companies that implement a CRM system adhere to a **customer-centric** focus or model. Customer-centric is an internal management philosophy similar to the marketing concept discussed in Chapter 1. Under this philosophy, the company customizes its product and service offering based on data generated through interactions between the customer and the company. This philosophy transcends all functional areas of the business (production, operations, accounting, etc.), producing an internal system where all decisions and actions of the company are a direct result of customer information. A customer-centric company builds its system on what satisfies and retains valuable customers, while learning those factors that build long-lasting relationships with those customers. For example, before launching its PT Cruiser, DaimlerChrysler amassed a database of 450,000 interested customers. In addition to potential customer contact information, the database contained information on those features, options, and styling characteristics consumers wanted built into the vehicle.[8] Not only was this *information* important for the success of the PT Cruiser, but the *direct interaction* between customers and company engineers was equally important in shaping the product. The PT Cruiser development team was customer-centric.

customer-centric
Under this philosophy, the company customizes its product and service offering based on data generated through interactions between the customer and the company.

Customer-centric organizations establish relationships with customers similar to those of the artisans of bygone years. Artisans sought to understand their customers' needs and expectations and negotiated with them a mutually satisfying commitment for product and service delivery. Artisans knew they could make flexible commitments to customers because they alone, not tens or hundreds of delegated representatives, were accountable for fulfilling their end of the bargain. This, in turn, allowed artisans to develop lasting relationships with customers, learn more about them, and generate repeat business. Similar to the artisans' approach, though expanded in scope, CRM is a company-wide process that focuses on learning, managing customer knowledge, and empowerment. It differs from one-to-one marketing, which we discussed in Chapter 17, in a very important way: One-to-one marketing is an individualized marketing method that utilizes customer information to build a long-term, personalized, and profitable relationship with each customer. CRM is broad and systemic, whereas one-to-one marketing is focused and individualized.

learning (CRM)
An informal process of collecting customer data through customer comments and feedback on product or service performance.

Learning

A customer-centric company and its representatives continually learn from customers about ways to enhance its product and service offerings. **Learning** in a CRM environment is normally an informal process of collecting customer information through customer comments and feedback on product or service performance. Dell Computer, for example, learned from its customers that they were experiencing difficulties unpacking its computers. The packaging was so strong that the customers were damaging the computers while removing them from the box. Dell responded with a simpler, more efficient packaging design that allowed customers to disassemble the packaging material in one easy procedure.[9] Likewise, Apple Computer learned from its customers that assembling the computer hardware devices was difficult. Apple's response was to produce a computer that required no assembly whatsoever.[10]

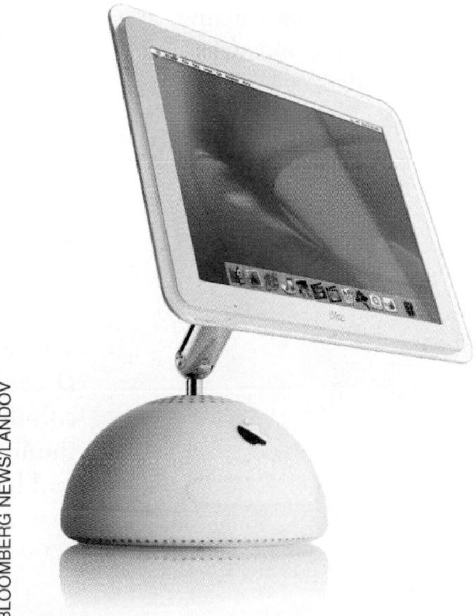

BLOOMBERG NEWS/LANDOV

Learning about customers' preferences can help a company maximize sales through product offerings that better match what customers actually want. Apple did just that when it designed the iMac computer that needs no assembly.

Knowledge Management

Each functional unit of a business usually has its own way of recording what it learns and perhaps even its own customer information system. The disparate interests of departments make it difficult to pull together learned customer information into one place using a common format. To overcome this disparity, companies operating in a CRM mode use knowledge management. **Knowledge management** is a process by which learned information from customers is centralized and shared in order to enhance the relationship between customers and the organization. The information collected includes experiential observations, comments, learned lessons, conclusions, and qualitative facts about the customer. All of these are formatted so that the information can be disseminated and shared throughout the entire organization.

knowledge management
The process by which learned information from customers is centralized and shared in order to enhance the relationship between customers and the organization.

A good example of knowledge management comes from General Electric's Appliances Division, where the GE Answer Centre has provided service to GE appliance customers (and frequently to customers of other GE divisions) since the early 1980s. In the late 1980s, the GE Answer Centre also became the GE Appliance Customer Knowledge Centre, although it was never given that formal name. Each service representative records customer comments about appliances, dealers, or other relevant issues in a central system. This information is then reviewed by marketing, dealer relations, customer service, and, perhaps most important, manufacturing and new-product development managers. The service-based customer knowledge is also used to rapidly identify appliance problems in the field, such as an improper installation approach, that can be addressed with product or documentation changes, saving vast amounts in field dispatch costs.[11]

Empowerment

As Chapter 1 explained, empowerment involves delegating authority to solve customers' problems. In other words, **empowerment** refers to the latitude organizations bestow on their representatives to negotiate mutually satisfying commitments with customers. Organizational representatives make commitments during interactions with customers (via phone, fax, e-mail, or Web communication, or face-to-face). An **interaction** is a point at which a customer and a company representative exchange information and develop learning relationships. In a CRM system, where the organization adheres to a customer-centric focus, the customer, not the organization, defines the terms of the interaction. The organizational response is to design products and services around the customer's desired experience.

empowerment
Delegation of authority to solve customers' problems quickly—usually by the first person the customer notifies regarding the problem.

interaction
The point at which a customer and a company representative exchange information and develop learning relationships.

Customers define the terms at the time of the interaction. For example, customer A may want a Whirlpool washing machine just as it is. Customer B may want a Whirlpool washing machine in a special colour. Customer C may want a Whirlpool washing machine in a special colour and delivered the next day. Customer D may want a price discount from the company because he or she is purchasing a Whirlpool washing machine, dryer, dishwasher, and refrigerator.

With a CRM system, the organization's representative becomes a knowledge worker and has the latitude to make on-the-spot decisions that affect the outcomes of the interaction. In the above example, the representative may determine that customers A, B, and D can be accommodated, but that customer C cannot be helped because the special-colour washing machine is out of stock and cannot be delivered tomorrow. Thus, during the interaction, the organizational representative focuses on each individual customer and his or her requests; the representative is also concerned with achieving negotiations that will result in a mutually satisfying commitment and with learning from each interaction to create profitable, lasting relationships.

The success of CRM—building lasting and profitable relationships—can be directly measured by the effectiveness of the interaction between the customer and the organization. In fact, what further differentiates CRM from other strategic initiatives, such as one-to-one marketing and market development, is the organization's ability to establish and manage interactions with its current customer base. The more latitude (empowerment) a company gives its representatives, the more likely the interaction will conclude in a way that satisfies the customer.

>> ESTABLISHING AND MANAGING INTERACTIONS WITH THE CURRENT CUSTOMER BASE

3 Explain how to establish and manage interactions with the current customer base

The interaction between the customer and the organization is the foundation on which a CRM system is built. Only through effective interactions can organizations learn about the expectations of their customers, generate and manage knowledge about them, negotiate mutually satisfying commitments, and build long-term relationships.

Exhibit 18.2 illustrates the customer-centric approach for managing customer interactions. Following a consumer-centric approach, an interaction can occur through a formal communication channel, such as a phone, PC, or salesperson; through a previous relationship a customer has had with the organization, such as a past purchase or a response to a marketing research request; or through some current transaction by the customer, such as an actual product purchase, a request for repair service, or a response to a coupon offer. In short, any activity a customer has with an organization, either directly or indirectly, constitutes an interaction.

Companies that effectively manage customer interactions recognize that customers provide data to the organization that affect a wide variety of internal and external company touch points. In a CRM system, **touch points** are those areas of a business where customer data are gathered and used to guide and direct the decision making within that business unit. Touch points can be both internal and external to the company. External touch points might include a customer registering for some particular service, a customer communicating with customer service for product information, a customer completing and returning the warranty information card for a product, or a customer talking with salespeople, delivery personnel, and product installers. Data gathered at these external touch points, once interpreted, provide information that affects internal touch points. For example, when a customer purchases a new Sony TV from The Bay, the point-of-sale interaction is an external touch point for Sony. If the customer purchases an extended warranty, the customer data obtained from that warranty application (an additional interaction) are then directed to an internal touch point, the repair and service department. Even though the repair and service department did not directly interact with the customer, it has an indirect interaction based on the information obtained from the warranty application. This information can be used to schedule routine and problematic repairs. In addition, customer information of this type can be directed to multiple internal touch points—marketing research, for developing profiles of extended warranty purchasers; production, for analyzing recurring problem and repair components; and accounting, for establishing cost-control models for repair service calls. This simple example illustrates one of the most compelling aspects of CRM: a single external customer interaction can generate multiple indirect interactions across multiple internal touch points within any given company.

touch point
All possible areas of a business where customers communicate with that business.

An extremely common and almost standard touch point is the knowledge centre. A **knowledge centre** (call centre) is an organization's internal operational component that manages and fulfills customer requests. It is the logistical system that reacts to, monitors, and controls the interaction between the customer and the organization. As seen in the earlier General Electric example, the knowledge centre is responsible for obtaining customer information, evaluating the information, and directing the information to the appropriate department (touch point) within the company.

knowledge centre
An organization's internal operational component that manages and fulfills customer requests; the logistical system that reacts to, monitors, and controls the interaction between the customer and the organization.

A knowledge centre is a passive means of managing customer interactions because the customer must call to initiate the interaction. Companies themselves must also generate customer interactions, but doing so is becoming increasingly difficult. Consumers are often bombarded with unsolicited mailers and surveys that are sometimes viewed as intrusive. In these cases, consumers are more likely to refuse an opportunity for interaction than to accept. As the "Ethics in Marketing" box illustrates, rising privacy concerns are forcing companies to rethink their approaches to generating customer interactions. In a CRM system, the objective is to obtain this information in a nonintrusive manner and to allow customers to freely relay information when they want to

EXHIBIT 18.2

Customer-Centric Approach for Managing Customer Interactions

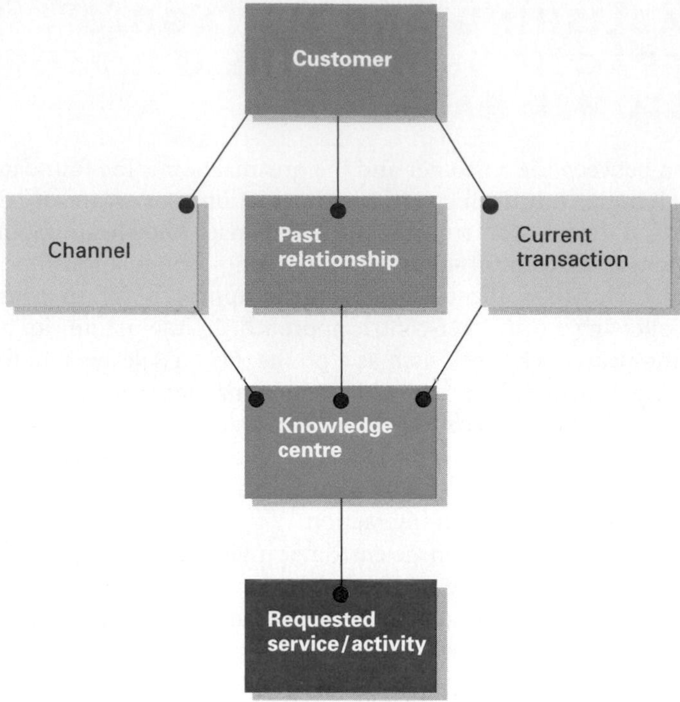

communicate it, not when the company wants it. Customer-centric organizations are implementing new and unique interactions specifically for this purpose, such as Web-based interactions, point-of-sale interactions, and transaction-based interactions.

Web-Based Interactions

E-mail addresses and websites are allowing customers to communicate with companies on their own terms. Instead of wasting time with phone numbers and mail surveys, companies are beginning to publicize their websites as the first touch point for customer interactions. Web users can purchase products, make reservations, input preferential data, and comment on the organization's services. The data from these **Web-based interactions** are then captured at the knowledge centre, compiled, and used to segment customers, refine marketing efforts, develop new products, and deliver a degree of individual customization to improve customer relationships.

Web-based interactions
Communications between customers and organizations using Web vehicles.

Mars, Inc., maker of Pedigree brand dog food and Whiskas brand cat food, has designed a global multilingual website called mypetstop.com. Targeted at the world's pet lovers, the site provides an on-line collection of pet content, and combines this with personalized information and tools, and merchandize offers that are both relevant and timely for the individual pet owners. The dog owner portion of the site features a "pet lifecycle map" that is divided up according to pet lifestages such as the following: prospective puppy decision-making stage, new first-time puppy owner stage, and aging-dog stage. Visitors select the stage that interests them, and their choice becomes an initial segmentation step, after which further segmentation occurs according to type of dog, location, and type of relationship with the pet. The site is designed to convey the notion that Mars understands the needs of pet owners throughout their pets' lifecyles. Through the website, Mars has been able to gather detailed information to determine the preferences of its customers in each global market. In turn, the firm has been able to design more effective marketing strategies for each market. Mars has noted that as a result, stronger relationships have developed with its channel partners and with its consumers, who have become more loyal to its brands.[12]

ON LINE

Canadian Marketing Association

Visit the Canadian Marketing Association's website. What resources have been made available to consumers to let them opt out of direct-mail, telephone, and fax solicitations? Does the site address the issue of unwanted e-mail solicitations? What advice does the site provide?

http://www.the-cma.org

ETHICS IN MARKETING

CRM: Issues of Opting In and Opting Out

Amidst rising consumer privacy concerns, Gartner research predicts that the amount of personal data collected will increase thirty-fold between 2001 and 2004 as more and more firms desire to undertake customer relationship management programs. Canada's PIPED Act gives consumers a say in the collection and use of their personal data, but only in Canada. There is widespread debate, however, as to how consumers' rights to privacy can be protected. To a large extent, this debate revolves around opt-in/opt-out options.

When a consumer chooses to opt in at a site, he or she explicitly agrees to supply information to a company with the understanding that the company can use that information for research and marketing. In off-line retailing, opt-in agreements are widespread in the supermarket sector, where consumers apply for and use company "discount cards." These discount cards, which use names like VIP cards, MVP cards, VIC cards, allow the customer to receive advertised discounts on a variety of products. In exchange, the retailer receives personal information regarding individual consumers' purchase behaviour, which can be coupled with demographic data submitted during the application process. In short, the retailer has rich personal data on each of its opt-in, discount card users, which it can use for targeted promotions or which it can sell to other companies for promotional purposes. But the retailer does not have the same level of detailed personal information about customers who choose not to apply for or use the discount cards.

Canadian e-marketers are required to explicitly state the reasons why they are collecting customer information and how they plan to use this information. When customers fill out a sign-in form (referred to as an opt-in page), the marketer is bound to use the information collected only for the originally stated purpose and no other unless they obtain a further consent. One issue that arises revolves around what constitutes "consent"? Canada's privacy laws provide customers the right to request copies of their files. Marketing firms need to be able to demonstrate that the customer did, in fact, opt in by providing information on the date and location where the customer signed up. In addition, a stated privacy policy must be linked to the opt-in page. Further, marketing firms that are operating as third parties to gather information or build databases for other marketers must disclose this fact as well. Many marketers rely on firms that are specialists in customer relationship management to assist them, but unless they have told their customers that these third parties will have access to their personal data, the marketers will be in violation of the PIPED Act if they share this information.[13]

Canadians who visit U.S.-based websites need to be aware that unlike Canada, the United States currently does not have a federally mandated privacy policy that applies for on-line exchange relationships, and privacy policies can vary from company to company. The majority of on-line sites that collect information, however, do so without unambiguous consent; as a result, it is a climate of "browser beware." On-line sites place cookies on visitors' hard drives without user consent, and personal information is routinely collected and shared by companies for a variety of purposes. As discussed in Chapter 17, this activity is illegal under Canada's PIPED Act, but this only applies in Canada, while many Canadians like to visit international websites. Canadian browsers can safeguard their privacy with a technical solution (for example, set their browser software preferences to deny all cookies) or submit an opt-out request, which U.S. companies are not required to process or accept. Thus, Canadians need to realize that on-line companies operating in the United States are not required to solicit explicit opt-in consent, although many do provide an opt-out opportunity that diligent and aware consumers can use.[14]

Growing technical threats to privacy underscore the importance of the opt-in/opt-out debate. Although the threat to privacy posed by cookie technology has been ruled on under the PIPED Act, the privacy threat posed by more sophisticated Web bugs that track users' whereabouts in cyberspace is less recognized. As mobile commerce becomes more prevalent, privacy concerns associated with location tracking will grow. Canadian marketers must remain diligent in ensuring that in all of their electronic commerce activities, they acknowledge the consumer's right to be notified prior to data collection and to unambiguously opt in or opt out of data collection activities.

What would you say or do for customers to encourage them to opt in to a CRM database that you were managing?

Point-of-Sale Interactions

Another method of generating customer interactions is through **point-of-sale interaction** in stores or at informational kiosks. Many point-of-sale software packages now allow customers to willingly reveal information about themselves without feeling violated. The information is then used in two ways: for marketing and merchandising activities, and for accurately identifying the store's best customers and the types of inventory they buy. The data collected at point-of-sale interactions are also used to increase customer satisfaction through the development of in-store services and customer recognition promotions.

point-of-sale interactions Communications between customers and organizations that occur at the point of sale, normally in a store.

Consumers in Quebec have demonstrated a preference for instant gratification, and this preference encourages point-of-sale interactions. However, it also creates a dilemma for retailers trying to establish loyalty programs as part of their customer

AP/WIDE WORLD PHOTOS

At the University Village Starbucks, customers can listen to the latest music on CDs at kiosks installed at the store. This kind of innovative point-of-sale interaction will help the company further tailor its product lines to match the lifestyles of customers who want to relax.

relationship management strategies in this province. One firm that has been successful at dealing with this dilemma is the Montreal-based Les Boutiques San Francisco, Inc., which owns more than 185 stores, including Les Ailes de la Mode, San Francisco, Bikini Village, and West Coast. The firm has combined data collection with instant rebates at the point-of-sale. For example, under Les Ailes MasterCard, San Francisco, Inc., allows customers to collect points anywhere they make purchases on the card. In addition, the card contains an electronic chip that grants a $10 rebate every month. The firm has found that about 50 percent of its 100,000 subscribers regularly redeem their rebate monthly and get "instant gratification." However, San Francisco has also found that the points program has not worked as quickly as the firm hoped. Lyne Martinoli, San Francisco's relationship marketing director, comments: "We know that there are a lot of cardholders not using their points, but they may be waiting to get enough points to get their dream trip or something else."[15]

Transaction-Based Interactions

transaction-based interactions The exchange of information that occurs between the customer and the company at the point of the actual transaction.

Transaction-based interactions differ from other interactions in that they focus on the exchange of information at the point of the actual transaction. Through the use of optical scanning technology and product bar codes, in conjunction with the payment method used by the customer (credit card or cheque), retailers can create parallel streams of information on each individual customer.

Once a credit card is swiped (or a cheque is processed for bank approval), two major streams of information are produced. First, optical scanning and bar coding allow retailers to capture information about which products the customer purchased and in what quantity. Second, by swiping a credit card or processing a bank cheque, the retailer can obtain all information contained in the customer's credit card file or chequing account file. Thus, the retailer obtains information on both the customer's purchases and the customer's profile. These two streams of information can then be merged at the point of transaction and used in the retailer's knowledge centre. To boost their data collection capabilities, many retailers are offering customers a Visa or MasterCard brand credit card positioned as a source of convenience for the customer. The stores also benefit, however. For example, Canadian Tire's Options Mastercard generates additional income for the retailer while capturing customer-specific data at the point of transaction.

4 Outline the process of acquiring and capturing customer data

>> ACQUIRING AND CAPTURING CUSTOMER DATA

Vast amounts of data can be obtained from the interactions between an organization and its customers. Therefore, in a CRM system, the issue is not how much data can be obtained, but rather what types of data should be acquired and how they can be used effectively for relationship enhancement. Thus, before discussing the types of data to collect, we must understand how the data will be used in the CRM system. The guidelines for a CRM system include several ground rules regarding customer data:

1. The customer, as represented by the information obtained via the interaction, takes centre stage in the organization.

2. Customer information must be centralized so that a single definitive source is established, typically within the knowledge centre.
3. Information is retained beyond the initial contact with the customer and accumulated over the customer's entire life span with the organization.
4. Information must define the product and services the customer desires, and the customer's preferences for future products and services, as well as contact methods for future interaction.

These CRM guidelines suggest that specific data about customers be collected via interactions and then, once collected, be used in a capacity that will foster future relationships throughout the entire organization. Exhibit 18.3 illustrates how these guidelines operate regarding the collection of customer data. The channel, the transaction, and the product or service purchased all constitute external touch points between a customer and an organization that provide the opportunity for acquiring data from the customer.

As discussed in Chapter 17, once customer data have been collected, the question of who owns those collected data becomes extremely salient. In its privacy statement, Internet retailer Toysmart.com declared that it would never sell information registered at the site, including children's names and birthdates, to a third party. When the company filed for bankruptcy protection, it proclaimed that the information collected constituted a company asset that needed to be sold off to pay creditors.[16] Despite the very vocal customer outrage at this announcement, many dot.com companies closing their doors found that they had little in the way of assets and followed Toysmart's lead. In the U.S., the attorney general of Delaware filed suit against MySeasons.com, a garden products seller, for selling its customer list despite promises to keep that information confidential.[17]

Channel

The traditional approach for acquiring data from customers is through channels. A **channel** is a medium of communication through which the customer interacts with a business at an external touch point. Channels include store visits, conversations with salespeople, interactions via the Web, traditional phone conversations, and wireless communications, such as cell phone conversations and satellite communications. What is important is the method of communication used by the customer, not the data that can be collected from the channel. For example, a particular customer may develop a pattern of calling his or her bank every other Friday at 10 A.M. to check on account balances. This channel contact is an interaction, and, indirectly, customer information is exchanged. From this contact, the bank may realize that this particular customer calls every other Friday at 10 A.M.; it can then use this pattern to communicate back to the customer. To create a nonintrusive interaction with this customer, the bank might call the customer at

channel (CRM)
A medium of communication through which the customer interacts with a business at an external touch point; the traditional approach for acquiring information from customers.

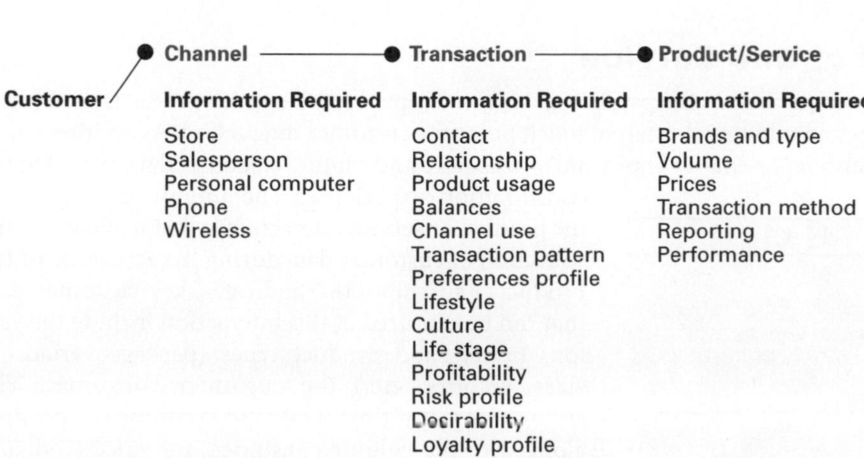

EXHIBIT 18.3
Key External Touch Points and Customer Information Requirements in the CRM System

or around 10 A.M. on Fridays to communicate new services or introduce special promotions. Likewise, it realizes that a certain group of customers visits a particular Bay location every Saturday afternoon; it can use this information to establish in-store promotions on Saturday afternoons appealing specifically to this customer group. In a CRM system, channel interactions are viewed as prime information sources based on the channel selected to initiate the interaction, rather than on the data acquired.

Transaction

transaction
An interaction between a company and a customer involving an exchange of information as well as an exchange of products or services.

A **transaction,** when viewed as an interaction between the company and the customer, presents the opportunity to collect vast amounts of data about the customer. The company can obtain not only simple contact information (name, address, phone number), but also data pertaining to the customer's current relationship with the organization—past purchase history, quantity and frequency of purchases, average amount spent on purchases, sensitivity to promotional activities, and so forth.

From the transaction, product usage information can be obtained, along with the customer's preferred channel of contact with the company and preferred transaction pattern—payment by cheque, cash, credit card, or debit card. Many companies utilizing a CRM system also view the transaction as an opportunity to collect behavioural data on customers. A recent study of Canadian consumers indicated that nearly 25 percent of them would be willing to transact on-line with insurance companies as long as these companies would provide sufficient company information and also provide on-line "price" quotes. The study estimated that the potential for on-line insurance sales was as high as $10 billion per year. However, realizing this potential is going to be hard, because only 18 percent of Canadian insurance company websites are able to provide on-line quotes in real time.[18]

By examining patterns or historical data relating to a customer's transaction, the company can also obtain information about the customer's profitability, risk, desirability, and loyalty. Profitability is the actual dollar amount a particular customer spends on a company's products over a specific time period. Risk refers to the amount of investment required to retain a customer. The higher the investment required to retain a customer, the higher the risk. For example, customers who buy General Motors cars only if GM is offering cash incentives can be considered high risk. Without cash incentives, the probability of these customers purchasing GM cars is reduced. These customers are high risk for GM because the company must offer incentives (higher investment) to win their business. In contrast, low-risk customers will periodically buy a GM vehicle regardless of the incentive.[19] Customers who, based on a pattern of current and past transactions, exhibit low risk and high profitability to the organization are highly desirable, as are customers who demonstrate high levels of loyalty by purchasing the same brand consistently over time. The company will seek to retain these customers but may choose not to make an effort to retain less desirable customers who exhibit high risk and low profitability.

Product and Service

The physical, as well as the psychological, consumption of the firm's products or services constitutes an additional external touch point for customer interaction. As an interaction point, it also represents an opportunity to acquire and capture customer data related to the consumption experience. The unique dimension of the product or service interaction is that it allows for the collection of customer data during the actual use of the product. As Exhibit 18.3 indicates, key customer data that can be captured at this interaction include the various brands and product types (package variations, sizes, colours, etc.) the customer consumes. The average length of time it takes to consume the product along with the volume consumed, the price paid, and the preferred transaction method can also be obtained.

ON LINE

TD Canada Trust Insurance

How comfortable are you completing the information form for an on-line rate quote at TD Canada Trust Insurance? Would you be more comfortable talking with a representative on the phone? How effective is the Web as a channel for this type of customer interaction?

http://www.tdcanadatrust.com

Even more important are data related to the performance of the product and the method customers use to report performance-related issues. Because the customer typically initiates the interaction, these data are extremely valuable for the organization. Customers may call in to a company's knowledge centre requesting information on product warranties, optional features, repair services, or installation requirements. Once these data are gathered and stored by the knowledge centre, they can be translated into critical information and disseminated across all areas of the company, as we saw in the earlier example for General Electric's Appliances division.

It should be obvious at this point that a voluminous amount of information can be captured from one individual customer across several external touch points. Multiply this by the thousands of customers across all of the touch points (both internal and external) within the organization, and the volume of data can rapidly become unmanageable for company personnel. The large volumes of data resulting from a CRM initiative can be managed effectively only through the use of technology.

>> USE OF TECHNOLOGY TO STORE AND INTEGRATE CUSTOMER DATA

5 Describe the use of technology to store and integrate customer data

As previously mentioned, customer data are only as valuable as the system in which the data are stored and the consistency and accuracy of the data captured. Customer data gathering is further complicated by the fact that the data needed by one unit of the organization, such as sales and marketing, often are generated by another area of the business or even a third-party supplier, such as an independent marketing research firm. Lack of a standard structure and interface forces organizations to rely on technology to capture, store, and integrate strategically important customer information. This process of centralizing data in a CRM system is referred to as data warehousing.

A **data warehouse** (or *informational warehouse*) is a central repository of customer data collected by an organization. The data warehouse contains data from various functional areas of the organization that are stored and inventoried on a centralized computer system so that the resulting information can be shared across all functional departments of the business. The end result of the data warehouse is to provide the company with a system driven toward shared information. In a CRM environment, all customer data collected through customer interactions are stored in the data warehouse. Data pertaining to the channel, the transaction, and the product or service consumed by the customer are structured and categorized in the warehouse and made available to all internal touch points in the organization. To accomplish this task, the data warehouse contains three operational components: an information access component, a system management component, and a customer-initiated component.

data warehouse
A central repository for data from various functional areas of the organization that are stored and inventoried on a centralized computer system so that the information can be shared across all functional departments of the business.

The information access component provides for the classification of customer data and enables any department of the business to access the data for any specific purpose. The system management component defines and interprets the data in a longitudinal manner, allowing for the storage and structure of all data beginning with the initial contact made by the customer. The customer-initiated component stores and categorizes data initiated by the customer through various channel contacts.

Decibel Credit Union of Winnipeg has signed on with NCR of Canada for a new service that will allow it to improve the capabilities of its ATM machines. NCR has developed new software known as "APTRA Promote" that will help financial institutions create and manage promotional campaigns delivered through ATM networks. Instead of the dull static, mono-colour appearance of a typical ATM, Canadians will be faced with full-motion colour video screens that will carry advertisements. For ATMs located in convenience stores, the ads could be for soft drinks or snack foods. However, the machines will be capable of drawing on the database warehouse of the banking organization associated with the ATM; consequently, it will be possible to customize the advertisements

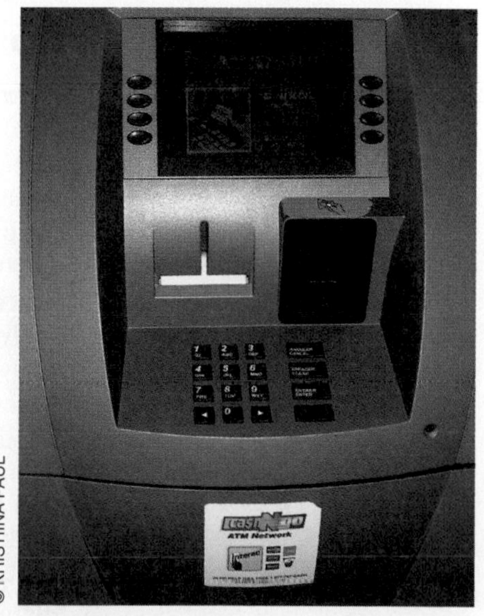

© KRISTIINA PAUL

By using data warehousing, an ATM could use a bank's database information to deliver a targeted message to an individual consumer while that person waits to receive cash.

shown on these screens to the specific user. In addition, the ATMs will be able to dispense coupons for use in an immediate purchase. Nicholas Hames, vice president of NCR Canada's Financial Solutions Division in Toronto, describes the system as follows: "It allows us to do a targeted and relevant message or advertising right down to the individual consumer level."[20]

Data warehouses such as the one developed by NCR enable companies to better customize their products and services according to their customers' needs and wants. Such attention to customer preferences helps forge long-term relationships that benefit both customer and company. By combining the wealth of data collected through customer interactions, companies like Decibel Credit Union can target highly specific customer groups and offer them finely tuned products or services. More importantly, organizations can use their data warehouses to monitor important financial aspects of the relationship, such as the current and potential value the customer represents to the organization. Through various predictive modelling techniques, data warehouses can generate customer profiles that categorize customers as either profitable or unprofitable to the business. The organization can then use this information to determine the amount of time and dollars required to build relationships with certain customers and to assess whether this investment will produce profitable relationships for the company.

6 Describe how to analyze data for profitable and unprofitable segments

>> ANALYZING DATA FOR PROFITABLE AND UNPROFITABLE SEGMENTS

As a process strategy, CRM attempts to manage the interactions between a company and its customers. To be successful, organizations must identify customers who yield high profits or potential profits. To accomplish this task, significant amounts of data must be gathered from customers, stored and integrated in the data warehouse, and then analyzed and interpreted for commonalities that can produce distinct homogeneous segments that are different from other customer segments. Because all customers are not the same, organizations need to develop interactions that target *individual* customer needs and wants. Likewise, all customers do not contribute the same or generate the same revenue for the company. Recall from Chapter 6 that 80 percent of a company's revenue is generated by 20 percent of its customers (the 80/20 principle). Therefore, the question becomes: How do we identify the 20 percent of our customer base that contributes 80 percent to our revenue? In a CRM framework, the answer is data mining.

Data Mining

data mining
A data analysis procedure that identifies significant patterns of variables and characteristics that pertain to particular customers or customer groups.

Data mining is the process of finding hidden patterns and relationships in the customer data stored in the data warehouse. It is a data analysis procedure that identifies significant patterns of variables and characteristics that pertain to particular customers or customer groups. Although businesses have been conducting such analyses for many years, the procedures were normally performed on small data sets containing as few as 500 to 1,000 customer respondent records. Today, with the development of sophisticated data warehouses, thousands and even hundreds of thousands of respondent records can be analyzed. Special data-mining tools have been developed for the specific purpose of analyzing customer patterns and characteristic relationships found in these extremely large data sets.

The Bank of Montreal has been implementing a CRM strategy that has involved data mining of its massive transaction databases, which record the more than 100 million transactions a month that occur at the bank. In addition to the transactions, the bank's databases contain other data such as personal information, liability, income, and net assets for 5.6 million customers. The bank's CRM software undertakes calculations that determine the fees and costs of all those transactions per customer. Based on these calculations, one-third of the bank's customers were identified as "valuable" or profitable customers, and as such, were chosen to become the focus of the firm's marketing efforts. This group was analyzed and divided into segments of customers with similar profiles. These segments were targeted with direct communications. According to David Moxley, VP customer knowledge management for the Bank of Montreal, the effort has "produced response rates north of 20 percent. It's not unlikely our return on investment is in excess of 1,000 percent."[21]

Data-mining tools analyze significant relationships simultaneously among several customer dimensions within vast data warehouses. This procedure is conducted when the decision maker has limited knowledge of a particular subject. For example, the management of a casino may wish to identify the attributes of the gaming customers who had the largest gambling budgets in the casino in the previous year. Data-mining techniques would search the data warehouse, capture the relevant data, categorize the significant attributes, and form a profile of the high-budget gambler.

Two major capabilities associated with data mining are the automated prediction of trends and behaviours and the automated discovery of previously unknown patterns. Data mining automates the process of finding predictive customer information in large data warehouses. Questions that traditionally required extensive hands-on analysis can now be answered directly from the data. A typical example of a predictive problem relates to the targeting of certain customer groups. Data mining uses information on past customer behaviours to identify those customers most likely to maximize the return on investment from future marketing campaigns. Data-mining tools also sweep through data warehouses to identify previously hidden patterns of behaviour that normally would not be recognized.

Many businesses operating in a CRM environment are turning to data-mining techniques to build and enhance relationships with highly profitable customer groups. For example, Carrier Corporation is using data mining to profile on-line customers and offer them customized packages on air conditioners and related products. Carrier began selling air conditioners, air purifiers, and related products to customers via its website (http://www.roomair.carrier.com) in 1999, but initially its sales were low largely because it did not know exactly who its customers were and what they wanted. Carrier therefore initiated a program to raise awareness of its Web store and to convert Internet traffic to sales. Using a combination of on-line sales data, data obtained from customer registrations for a sweepstakes contest, and demographic data provided by a third-party research firm, Carrier initiated a data-mining program to identify customers who were also high users of on-line shopping. The procedure matches customer profiles to postal codes, so that when customers visit the Carrier website and type in their postal code, it is matched to their profile. Automatically, a pop-up window is displayed, offering customized products to specific customer groups, such as multiroom air conditioners to suburbanites and compact models to apartment dwellers. These techniques have enabled Carrier to turn more Web visitors into buyers, thereby increasing per-visit revenues from $1.47 to $37.42.[22] Data mining also revealed that Carrier's use of radio advertising to promote its Web store was not very effective. Profiles showed that Carrier's customers used public transportation, which suggested that subway advertising would be more effective.

The Data-Mining Process

Data mining works through a process known as modelling. **Modelling** is simply the act of building a model in a situation where the answer is known and then applying the model to another situation where the answer is unknown. If the necessary information exists in the data warehouse, the data-mining process can model virtually any customer activity. The key is to find relevant patterns. Typical unknown situations that our data mining could address for a business include the following: "Which customers are most likely to suspend our cell phone service?" "What is the probability a customer will purchase $100 of merchandise from a particular store location?" and "Which potential customers are most likely to respond to a particular coupon?" Data mining builds models to answer such questions by using existing information from a data warehouse to predict future customer behaviour. This behaviour might be attrition at the end of a magazine subscription, purchasing of complementary

modelling
The act of building a model in a situation where the answer is known and then applying the model to another situation where the answer is unknown.

score
A numerical value assigned to each record in a data warehouse that indicates the likelihood that the customer whose record has been scored will exhibit the behaviour in question.

products, willingness to use a debit card over a cheque, and so forth. The data-mining model assigns each prediction a score. The **score,** a numerical value that is assigned to each record in the data warehouse, indicates the likelihood that the customer whose record has been scored will exhibit the behaviour in question. For example, if a model predicts customer attrition, a high score indicates that a customer is likely to leave, whereas a low score indicates the opposite. After a set of customers is scored, the numerical values are used to selectively target individual customers for a new marketing campaign.

A wide range of companies have deployed data-mining applications successfully. For instance, the Royal Bank of Canada reorganized itself from product and service based departments into a customer management team focusing on 14 different customer-based segments such as builders and borrowers, medium-sized businesses, and agriculture and agribusiness.[23] After using data-mining techniques, U.S. retailer Camelot Media discovered that a large number of senior citizens were purchasing rap and alternative music. When managers investigated further, they discovered seniors were buying the music as gifts for their grandchildren.[24] Data-mining technology is applicable to most companies looking to leverage a large data warehouse to better manage their customer relationships. The two critical factors for success with data mining are (1) a large, well-integrated data warehouse and (2) a well-defined understanding of how the end result of the mining activities will be used and leveraged throughout the organization.

7 Explain the process of leveraging and disseminating customer information throughout the organization

>> LEVERAGING AND DISSEMINATING CUSTOMER INFORMATION THROUGHOUT THE ORGANIZATION

Data mining identifies the most important (profitable) customers and prospects. Managers can then design tailored marketing strategies to best penetrate the identified segments. In CRM this is commonly referred to as leveraging and disseminating customer information throughout the organization to facilitate development of enhanced relationships among customers.

For example, Bayer Pharmaceuticals analyzed its recent sales force activities to improve its targeting of high-value physicians and to determine which marketing activities would be most effective. Data in this analysis included competitor market activity and information about community healthcare systems. Results of the analysis were distributed to the sales force via a wide area network; this information enabled the sales representatives to learn the key attributes used by physicians in selecting pharmaceutical vendors.[25] Ongoing analysis of the data warehouse enabled the best practices from throughout the organization to be applied in specific sales situations.

Another good example of leveraging customer information comes from Canada Post's SmartMoves program. Originally designed to help Canada Post manage one of its most important customer services—change of address information—Canada Post SmartMoves has been developed into an integrated program whereby Canadian marketers can access a database of Canadians moving into new homes via a website, a booklet, and a sweepstakes contest. Canada Post has turned the program into a moneymaker by selling sponsorships in the program. For example, Larry Westbrook, national marketing manager at Discount Car & Truck Rental in Toronto, says his firm took on the title sponsorship at a cost of $52,000 because "SmartMoves offered an opportunity and dovetailed with our desire to grow the truck business in the home relocation area. It's very targeted at an area of our truck strategy we want

ON LINE

Smartmoves.ca

Visit the Smartmoves.ca website and examine the kinds of CRM initiatives that companies could undertake with people who visit this site. Look at some of the site's sponsors. How do the products and services of these sponsors tie in with "moving"? Read through the various information services available on the site. Do they provide useful advice for movers? Can you think of any other markets that the site could target with this information?

http://www.smartmoves.ca

to build." SmartMoves provides its database through the sweepstakes program and gives marketers information on the names, addresses, phone numbers, and moving dates of the contestants. Discount Car & Truck Rental has focused on placing print ads in the SmartMoves booklets while maintaining a presence on the SmartMoves website.[26]

In an effort to increase the activity of its direct sales force, Federal Express applied data-mining techniques to identify the best prospects for its new ground delivery service. Using data mining to analyze its current customer base, FedEx discovered a unique segment of high-value business prospects. Information associated with this segment was then applied to a business database provided by D&B Canada, yielding a prioritized list of business customers across several regions in North America.[27]

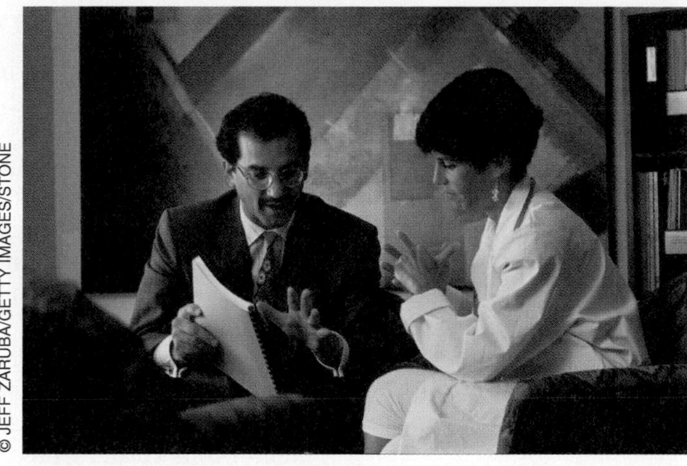

© JEFF ZARUBA/GETTY IMAGES/STONE

Collecting information is a wasted effort unless the company disseminates it throughout the organization. Bayer Pharmaceuticals does just that. As a result, the company's sales force can increase efficiency by targeting high-value physicians.

These examples have a clear common denominator. In each case, the organization applied various data-mining techniques to leverage knowledge about its customers contained in a data warehouse. The information was then disseminated throughout the appropriate channels of the organizational structure. Indeed, one of the benefits of a CRM system is this capacity to share information throughout the organization.

Through campaign management, all functional areas of an organization participate in the development of programs targeted to its customers. **Campaign management** involves concentrating on outbound communications to customers designed to sell a company's product or service. The design of the campaign is based directly on data obtained from customers through various interactions. Campaign management includes monitoring the success of the communications based on customer reactions through sales, orders, callbacks to the company, and the like. If a campaign appears unsuccessful, it must be evaluated and possibly changed in order to achieve the company's desired objective. Consider Reader's Digest Association (Canada), for example. The firm has been operating successfully in Canada for over 54 years. Today, Reader's Digest provides Canada's most popular magazine, with a readership of 3.1 million Canadians and a total database of 4.1 million Canadians. Although it is considered the flagship, *Reader's Digest* magazine accounts for only 25 percent of the company's revenue and profit; the remainder comes from books, music, and videos. Reader's Digest Association wants to double its influence in Canadian homes from a measured 15 percent to 30 percent with new products. The firm has decided to target its database of customers to sell home, car, and life insurance that will be cobranded with its new partners BELAIRdirect, ING Direct, and Manulife Financial. In addition, Reader's Digest is planning to sell vitamins as well!

campaign management
Developing product or service offerings customized for the appropriate customer segment and then pricing and communicating these offerings for the purpose of enhancing customer relationships.

Reader's Digest is aware that it will have to deal through different channels to reach out to those Canadians who are not currently part of its database. It plans to integrate a promotional strategy with a direct marketing philosophy. Telemarketing and the Internet will be employed to sell the insurance and vitamin products, along with direct mail. However, Reader's Digest will rely on in-bound calls that build relationships, as opposed to out-bound cold calling, which often upsets customers. The firm plans to use its Internet contacts to create commerce and to manage customer relationships; e-mail contacts will be another channel designed to foster relationships.

In describing the management approach behind the campaign, Pierre Dion, president of Reader's Digest has stated: "We have learned a lesson. Whatever we do, even if we get into more products, more channels, all the good best practices in direct marketing will apply. It's a question of offering the right product, the right price through the right channel to the right people."[28]

Product and Service Customization

Using information stored in the data warehouse, highly customized, even personalized, products and services can be developed for customers. For example, eDiets personalizes diet plans for its subscribers. Approximately 40,000 customers sign up for eDiets' newsletter at a cost of $45 for a three-month subscription. The subscription entitles members to weekly fitness and meal plans personalized according to their eating habits, dietary preferences, medical condition, and emotional and weight-loss needs.[29] eDiets relies on both customer and meal plan databases connected via software. The software extracts information from both databases to produce a customized diet plan for each individual member.

Similar to eDiets, Reflect.com developed technology to customize skin-care, hair-care, and cosmetic products for women. When a customer visits Reflect.com and interacts with the company, she is prompted to fill out a questionnaire that will help Reflect.com create a product specifically for her. The customer might indicate, for example, that she gets dark circles or puffiness under her eyes, that she would like the skin under her eyes to be smoother, that she has laugh lines she wants reduced, or that her eyes are sensitive. The information is then transmitted to the product development centre, which determines which ingredients should be included in the product, given the customer's information.[30] Once the product is developed, the information from the customer is stored for use in future interactions.

Pricing

Shared information from customer interactions can also be used to develop an individualized pricing plan for each customer. PSS/World Medical supplies health care organizations with more than 56,000 products ranging from bandages and syringes to test tubes and petri dishes to diagnostic imaging equipment and X-ray technology. After physicians register with PSS/World Medical, they can choose to see only products that are relevant to their practice. Once they begin placing orders, PSS maintains a real-time listing of all the products each physician ordered during the previous 18 months, ranked in descending order by quantity and frequency of purchase.[31] Items purchased most frequently by physicians are given a priority pricing policy, allowing deep price discounts if the physician continues to purchase the item frequently.

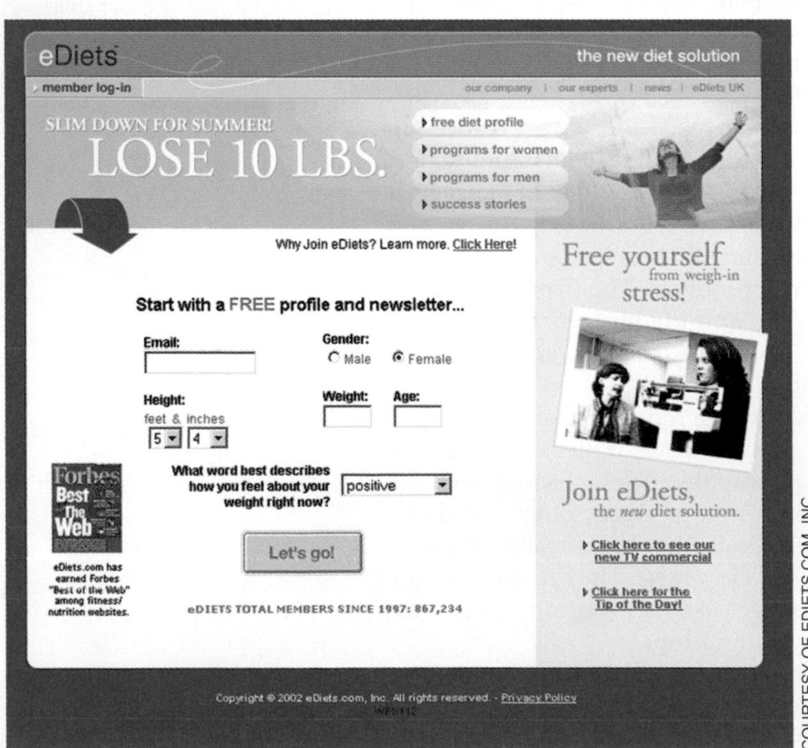

COURTESY OF EDIETS.COM, INC.

One of the major benefits of CRM is the ability to customize product and service offerings for each customer. eDiets uses the information it collects from each of its customers to create a customized diet and/or fitness plan based on his or her individual needs.

Communication

Communication means interacting in a manner that is most effective and nonintrusive for the customer. For example, eDiets' survival is based on customers returning to its website on a weekly basis and renewing their subscriptions every three months. To encourage this behaviour, eDiets uses the same technology it uses to personalize diets. For instance, if the system finds that a member hasn't logged on to the website for several weeks, it will automatically send that individual an e-mail encouraging him or her to stay on the plan. Unfortunately, this method of communication is not very effective when it comes to weight loss. With online weigh-ins, people have less motivation to stay on the program than they do with a face-to-face encounter as at Weight Watchers. To combat this problem, eDiets supports chat rooms and bulletin boards, as well as toll-free phone numbers that members can call for help or support.[32] If a member calls and reports problems maintaining the diet because of being hungry all the time, eDiets can access that member's information in its database, review the meal plan the customer is currently using, and adjust it as needed.

ON LINE 

KidsDadsMoms

Would you be comfortable building a profile about your child at KidsDadsMoms.com? Why or why not? What are the advantages of giving complete information? Are there any disadvantages? Can you use the highly customized site without building a learning profile for a child?

http://www.kidsdadsmoms.com

KidsDadsMoms (KDM) is another company that customizes products for its members. The company's mission is to help children learn and develop by enabling parents to identify the individual learning preferences of their children. Parents can build a profile about their child's strengths, weaknesses, and inclinations. KDM then suggests tools and toys that complement the child's unique learning style and preferences. KDM recommends appropriate items for each child; also, the company's website enables parents to modify their children's profiles as they grow.[33]

European companies have been somewhat slow to adapt campaign management and other CRM techniques. Nevertheless, as the "Global Perspectives" box describes, one European company is successfully implementing CRM.

GLOBAL PERSPECTIVES

CRM in Europe

Canadians ordering a meal at a restaurant in many southern European cities may wonder whether customer relationship management is a foreign concept in Europe. Compared to Canada, waiters are frequently less responsive to their customers. Certainly, European companies have been slow to adopt CRM. One reason for this reluctance has been the cultural differences between countries. In Spain, for example, sales cycles are longer than in many other European countries because Spanish customers are less inclined to move quickly on purchases. This means that a company has to take time nurturing its customers to develop relationships with them.

The adoption of CRM has also been slowed by political and geographic differences. While Canadian companies can sell primarily to Canadians and Americans, European companies must often sell in multiple countries, each with its own language and political structure. Such differences make CRM initiatives more complicated. Customer information has to be shared across borders, and transactions must be converted into different currencies. (Not all European Union countries have embraced the euro.) Due to the inconsistencies of information, modelling and data mining are more difficult.

Europe's widespread wireless infrastructure presents another complication. Many European companies already allow customers to access and change account information using wireless applications. Similarly, many European service organizations use wireless technology to handle field sales calls. Differences in wireless technology not only lead to disparities in the information obtained, but also make it more difficult to build data warehouses for capturing critical customer information.

Nevertheless, despite these difficulties, some European companies are adopting CRM as they look for ways to better understand and serve their customers. For example, Heineken Ireland recently implemented a CRM approach driven by a clear need to track its customers. In its traditional channel, the brewer sells beer directly to pubs or hotels through the pub owner. The company had little information about these customers and was not even tracking how much a pub purchased or when an order was due for replenishment. This lack of information meant that Heineken treated all customers the same with no attempt to distinguish between the top customers and less profitable ones.

A knowledge centre and sales force automation became the foundations of Heineken's CRM initiative. The company restructured its sales organization and customer interaction processes so that it could track each customer's buying patterns and the marketing resources devoted to that customer. In addition, the knowledge centre collected and managed this information, which was then shared throughout the marketing and sales divisions. Heineken can now see into its customer data, and its managers are able to predict customers' reactions and respond appropriately to them. The system allows Heineken to classify all customers in terms of importance to the company. High-value customers get weekly calls and visits from a dedicated salesperson, while lower value customers are contacted by direct methods through the knowledge centre. As it developed its CRM program, Heineken had to keep Irish culture in mind; it therefore emphasized face-to-face contact and building friendships with its customers.[34]

>> CONNECT IT

The opening vignette described how the world's consumers are using mobile communications devices. Customer relationship management is critical to the success of marketers who wish to operate in the fast-growing world of mobile commerce. Successful mobile commerce marketers create interactions with their markets such as the BotFighter game created by Sweden's TeliaSonera Corporation for its short message service. The creation of highly customized products and service offerings is one strategy that mobile marketers can pursue. A few of the approaches to getting customers to provide information about themselves so that mobile commerce marketers can develop data warehouses and undertake data mining were presented—for example, Bla Beer's promotion to provide "pickup" lines to its customers. Data mining allows firms to target their product offerings to specific customers. For example, Japanese video retailer Tsutaya could make video recommendations based on a customer's past rental activity. Finally, campaign management techniques will be critical to companies like Sweden's Mint, which has developed a system to allow payment for pizzas and convenience foods via mobile phones. People will need encouragement on many fronts to adopt mobile technology and then to employ it to make routine purchases. It may not be too long before you hear: "We don't take cash, will that be debit, credit card or cell phone"?

REVIEW IT

1 Define customer relationship management. Customer relationship management (CRM) is a company-wide business strategy designed to optimize revenue, profitability, and customer satisfaction by focusing on highly defined and precise customer groups. This is accomplished by organizing the company around customer segments, encouraging and tracking customer interaction with the company, fostering customer-satisfying behaviours, and linking all processes of a company from customers through suppliers.

1.1 Identify the six components of the CRM process.

1.2 TEAM Form a team and identify several local businesses that would benefit from a CRM strategy. Select one business and outline a plan for implementing a CRM strategy for that business. You may want to visit the company and interview managers about their current initiatives. When you have completed your CRM plan, share it with the class—and the company.

1.3 ON LINE WRITING General Motors recently began installing the "On Star" system in many of its vehicles. On Star is a location, information, and communication system available to drivers who wish to subscribe to the service. Go to the On Star website, http://www.onstar.com, and read about some of the services that are offered to consumers. Based on your discovery, write a short report describing the various ways that On Star can be used as a CRM tool, specifically in the context of creating interactions, gathering customer data, and customizing service offerings to customers.

2 Explain how to establish customer relationships within the organization. Companies that implement a CRM system adhere to a customer-centric focus or model. A customer-centric company builds its system on what satisfies and retains valuable customers, while learning the factors that build long-lasting relationships with those customers. Building relationships through CRM is a strategic process that focuses on learning, managing customer knowledge, and empowerment.

2.1 Briefly explain the concept of a customer-centric focus. Why is this so important in a CRM process?

2.2 What is meant by knowledge management? Why is it so important in a CRM system?

3 Explain how to establish and manage interactions with the current customer base. The interaction between the customer and the organization is the foundation on which a CRM system is built. Only through effective interactions can organizations learn about the expectations of their customers, generate and manage knowledge about them, negotiate mutually satisfying commitments, and build long-term relationships. Effective management of customer interactions recognizes that customers provide information to organizations across a wide variety of touch points. Customer-centric organizations are implementing new and unique approaches for establishing interactions specifically for this purpose. They include Web-based interactions, point-of-sale interactions, and transaction-based interactions.

3.1 Develop a plan for establishing and managing interactions with a business's customers. In this plan, identify the key touch points for customers, explain how the knowledge centre would be designed, and indicate the main interaction methods that would be promoted to the customer.

4 Outline the process of acquiring and capturing customer data. Based on the interaction between the organization and its customers, vast amounts of information can be obtained. In a CRM system, the issue is not how much data can be obtained, but rather the type of data acquired and how the data can effectively be used for relationship enhancement. The channel, the transaction, and the product or service consumed all constitute touch points between a customer and the organization. These touch points represent possible areas within a business where customer interactions can take place and, hence, present opportunities for acquiring data from the customer.

4.1 WRITING Assume you are the manager for Casino Windsor. Your boss has asked you to evaluate how the company is using its website to gather customer data. Go to the website for Casino Windsor (http://www.casinowindsor.com) and provide a detailed critique on how the site is used for capturing customer data. Comment on the types of customer data the website is designed to capture, and explain how those data would benefit Casino Windsor's operation.

5 Describe the use of technology to store and integrate customer data. Customer data gathering is complicated because information needed by one unit of the organization (e.g., sales and marketing) is often generated by another area of the business or even a third-party supplier (e.g., an independent marketing research firm). Because of the lack of a standard structure and interface, organizations are relying on technology to capture, store, and integrate strategically important customer information. The process of centralizing data in a CRM system is referred to as data warehousing. A data warehouse is a central repository of customer information collected by an organization.

5.1 WRITING Briefly explain the concept of a data warehouse. In the context of a CRM framework, why is a data warehouse such an important tool?

5.2 What is being written about customer data in today's periodicals? Search the InfoTrac® College Edition database of articles at http://infotrac.thomsonlearning.com using keywords like "customer data" and "data warehousing." Are certain industries better represented in the citation list generated by your search? Are certain issues more prevalent? Read a selection of at least three to four articles, and write a brief analysis of what is being discussed in the press regarding these CRM topics.

6 Describe how to analyze data for profitable and unprofitable segments. Customer relationship management, as a process strategy, attempts to manage the interactions between a company and its customers. To be successful, organizations must identify customers who yield high profits or potential profits. To accomplish this task, significant amounts of information must be gathered from customers, stored and integrated in the data warehouse, and then analyzed for commonalities that can produce segments that are highly similar, yet different from other customer segments. Data-mining tools identify significant relationships among several customer dimensions within vast data warehouses.

6.1 Explain the concept of data mining. Provide five examples of companies that are currently using data mining, and explain why each is using it.

Explain the process of leveraging and disseminating customer information throughout the organization. One of the benefits of a CRM system is the capacity to share information throughout the organization. This ability allows all functional areas of the organization to interact and develop programs targeted for their customers. This process is commonly referred to as campaign management. Campaign management involves developing customized product or service offerings for the appropriate customer segment and then pricing and communicating these offerings for the purpose of enhancing customer relationships.

7.1 Campaign management is a benefit derived by an organization's ability to leverage and disseminate information throughout the company. Briefly define campaign management and explain how a business may apply it to its daily operations. In your answer, select a particular business as an example of effective campaign management.

DEFINE IT

campaign management 605
channel (CRM) 599
customer-centric 593
customer relationship management (CRM) 590
data mining 602
data warehouse 601
empowerment 594
interaction 594
knowledge centre 595
knowledge management 594
learning (CRM) 593
modelling 603
point-of-sale interactions 597
score 604
touch point 595
transaction 600
transaction-based interactions 598
Web-based interactions 596

APPLY IT

Tunnel Bar-B-Q (TBQ), a downtown Windsor, Ontario, restaurant, was established in the 1950s. Located near the exit of the Detroit Windsor Tunnel, the establishment has flourished as one of the most popular attractions in the downtown area, where it caters to the local business crowd and tourists. TBQ is particularly noteworthy for its famous barbecue ribs. In an attempt to grow the business, TBQ opened a new location in a suburban part of Windsor, known as South Windsor. This community is a highly affluent, upwardly mobile market, consisting mainly of businesspeople and professionals. It also houses one of the campuses of St. Clair College, so it is, in some respects, a college community.

To date, the South Windsor restaurant has not experienced the same success as the downtown TBQ. As a result, TBQ management has begun to develop a CRM approach to increase traffic at the South Windsor location. TBQ is attempting to establish interactions with patrons in the area and to use the information gathered through these interactions to adjust its current business practices.

QUESTIONS

1. Conceptually design a CRM approach TBQ can implement at its South Windsor location. Specifically, design a program that will foster interactions between TBQ and the community. Identify the customer information requirements that are critical in developing these relationships, and explain what channels of interaction would be best suited for this market.
2. What type(s) of customer data should TBQ consider gathering from this process? Identify the key data requirements, and explain how they would assist TBQ management in designing future offerings (menu items, store atmosphere, prices, hours of operation, etc.) for this market.
3. Based on your answers to questions 1 and 2, design a campaign management approach that TBQ can implement at the South Windsor location. Be sure to explore the demographic makeup of the South Windsor market before developing your campaign.

THINK ABOUT IT

By combining several of its databases about parental purchasing behaviour and the results of its market research, Maxwell Inc. believes it has the tools to launch one-to-one marketing messages for the 6- to 9-year-old fans of its JoyMax educational toy products without violating the law. In spite of potential parental backlash, the company believes the approach will help customize new children's products and increase the company's share of these profitable young customers.

QUESTIONS

1. What do you think? Should Maxwell use one-to-one marketing tools to communicate with children?
2. Does the CMA Code of Ethics address marketing to children in its Code of Ethics? Go to **http://www.the-cma.org/consumer/ethics.cfm** and review the code. Then write a brief paragraph on how the CMA Code of Ethics relates to Maxwell's dilemma.

United Way of Greater Toronto

TRY IT

COURTESY OF UNITED WAY OF GREATER TORONTO

Nonprofit organizations do not typically come to mind when one thinks of entrepreneurs, but, in reality, most are entrepreneurs—even the well-known and firmly established United Way. Each city's branch of the United Way functions, in part, as its own entrepreneurial venture and is responsible for raising funds from local public and private donors. Those donors are, in effect, United Way's customers.

Philip King, vice president of e-business for the United Way of Greater Toronto (UWGT), realized that United Way could probably increase donations at his branch by implementing the type of CRM solutions commonly used by big businesses to establish more personal relationships with their customers. Because UWGT could not afford one of those systems on its own merit, United Way raised $2.3 million from major local businesses to fund the project.

Before its CRM program, UWGT, like most other philanthropic organizations, was able to reach its many diverse customers only by mass-mailing generic solicitations. Now the branch has the ability to draw from its previously built customer database to target solicitation messages to specific individuals or businesses. Dubbed UnitedWay@Work, the system's primary focus is on increasing contact with corporate donors by reaching employees who chair United Way giving campaigns within businesses.

UWGT piloted UnitedWay@Work by sending 8,600 customized and personalized e-mails to 16 different companies with regular histories of donating to United Way campaigns. Sent to companies based on identity and past donation levels, those e-mails gave employees HTML links to a personalized Web page with information on an individual's personal contributions and related United Way campaigns.

The Web page shows real-time updates on the amount of money raised by particular charitable campaigns, specific details on how those funds are being used in the community, and comparisons of the donation levels across departments within that employee's company. Individual contributors can also make donations on-line with credit cards or through payroll deductions, calculate tax implications, and elect to receive e-mail updates detailing exactly how their gifts are being applied throughout the year.

The personalization strategy is working. Almost 40 percent of those solicited returned $1.5 million in gifts—a $300,000 increase over the previous year—and 85 percent of those targeted by the new e-mail system pledged on-line. Combined with an estimated $200,000 savings in paper, data entry, administrative, and mailing costs, the new CRM program contributed $500,000 to the UWGT's charitable causes in its first year.

Important to note, too, is how the system affected the behaviour of individual contributors. First-time donors who gave on-line offered, on average, $100 more than first-time off-line givers, and returning givers who made donations on-line parted with 5 percent more than returning givers who paid off-line. UWGT combines what it learns from individuals acting on e-mail and website links with information in its existing database; then, together with the CRM system, it analyzes that information for use in developing future customer communications.

King points out that the change in customer behaviour is incremental but still noteworthy. The eventual impact on the individual lives of those the United Way helps could be huge—and that, of course, is the ultimate goal. Following its successful pilot, UWGT plans to make UnitedWay@Work available to 60 more companies in and around Toronto. It also plans to share the system with its partners in the United States. Six city branches are slated to pilot the system immediately, with the hope that all United Way branches will adopt it eventually.

QUESTIONS

1. Identify the six components of the CRM process, and explain which one the UnitedWay@Work system employs.
2. Explain how the UnitedWay@Work program establishes and manages interactions with its customers.
3. Describe how UWGT collects and integrates customer data. How has the use of these data affected it business?

FLIP IT

Flip to Chapter 18 in your *Grademaker Study Guide* for more review opportunities, including the pretest, vocabulary review, Internet activities, study test questions, and an application exercise based on CRM concepts. What is the process for acquiring and capturing customer data? What do companies need to do to leverage the customer data they collect? If you don't know, flip open your *Grademaker* and review.

CLICK IT

The *Marketing* website is rich with materials to help you review and master marketing concepts. Check your knowledge with the free quizzes, practise key terms using the crossword puzzles, or review key concepts using the Microsoft® PowerPoint® slides. Also on the Website are updated weblinks to companies mentioned in this chapter, Internet exercises, career marketing information, and much much more! Go to http://www.lamb3e.nelson.com, read the material, and follow the convenient links.

WATCH IT

Toronto Blue Jays: One Fan at a Time

The Toronto Blue Jays score high marks with local baseball fans through their one-to-one marketing program, a customer-based, information-intensive method that focuses on one baseball lover at a time. By using database technology, the Jays can make a pitch to each fan and cultivate long-term relationships. The team's database is carefully planned to gather pertinent information about customers and contacts so that the sales and marketing staff can analyze it and use it to provide better customer service.

The need for one-to-one marketing results from today's more demanding and very busy sports enthusiasts. Baseball fans are more strapped for time now than in any previous generation. They demand better, faster service, are more impatient, and don't want to get stuck in line waiting to buy tickets. In today's ballgame, people prefer to order tickets and merchandise by phone, mail, or e-mail.

How do the Blue Jays create their database? A compilation of bits of key information about customers, the database stems from several sources: season ticket subscribers; group season ticket subscribers; single ticket holders who purchase by telephone or mail; and community programs such as "K for Kids," a fundraiser that relies on phone-in pledges. Tickets are sold at the SkyDome, at the Bullpen Souvenir Store, over the "SportLine," or toll free at 1-888-OKGOJAYS. Tickets are also available on-line at the Jays website.

The Blue Jays season ticket form asks for the subscriber's name, address, phone number, zip or postal code, and e-mail address. The sales staff regularly uses this information, which is stored in a database along with seating options (e.g., several price ranges from preferred to general), to design all sorts of marketing initiatives. The zip or postal code indicates a subscriber's neighbourhood, which often pinpoints subculture, social class, income level, and lifestyle. This kind of geographic information can help direct further marketing efforts. For example, if enough subscribers live in a postal code that has a large Asian community, the Blue Jays may consider advertising in Asian-language neighbourhood publications. The database also helps identify fans who purchase high-end seats; they can then be rewarded with special perks.

A space for questions and comments on the ticket form provides additional information to help staff hone in on the right mix of products and services to offer. If a fan indicates that she or he is hard of hearing, the Jays can provide free of charge a hearing aid, called Phonic Ear, that amplifies sound levels and makes the game far more enjoyable. Amateur coaches, players, and parents of little leaguers seeking assistance in fundamental baseball skills can receive information about an inexpensive instructional video titled "A Coaching Clinic."

The e-mail address on the subscription form allows the Jays to communicate easily with individual subscribers. By contacting subscribers one at a time rather than hitting the entire community with direct mail, the Jays reach those who live and breathe baseball, rather than waste valuable marketing dollars on those who don't. E-mail is also a fast way to provide season ticket holders with particulars about ordering postseason tickets over the Internet.

The season ticket form is not the only method the Jays use to collect crucial information. On group ticket sales forms, the staff ask for detailed information. This information enables them to offer group benefits to businesses and other organizations. Through preferred group seating, promotional posters, and announcements of group names on the Jumbotron, the group sales staff really step up to the plate to help businesses and organizations promote themselves.

Database technology enables the Jays to cross-sell their many products and services. Staff marketers match products to consumer profiles to cross-sell products that match demographic, lifestyle, or behavioural characteristics. At the Blue Jays Baseball Camp, an intense, skill-oriented program for boys and girls between 11 and 19, registration information (including age) is stored in the database. This gives the Jays the opportunity to mail the campers merchandise information about youth jackets, jerseys, and caps, or Blue Jays Kids Stuff—a youth batting glove, school kit, helmet bank, or MVP bear. These items may be available at retail outlets around Toronto; however, the Jays database has made it possible to explore selling through direct mail.

Database marketing also helps the Jays retain loyal fans. By tracking season ticket holders, they can offer them special benefits. Loyalty is strengthened by identifying longstanding fans who have generated the most revenue, by creating different messages for new and long-term subscribers, and by finding out exactly what the fans want.

A database this extensive takes time to build, but the investment has paid off for the Toronto Blue Jays. With one-to-one marketing, the Jays hit a home run with the fans every time.

QUESTIONS

1. Why do the Toronto Blue Jays use one-to-one marketing?
2. Why is one-to-one marketing timely?
3. What are the sources of the Toronto Blue Jays database?
4. Describe some of the ways the Toronto Blue Jays use database technology.

MARKETING MISCUES

Air Canada Brochure Runs Afoul of Privacy Act

On January 1, 2001 the first provisions of the PIPED Act came into force in Canada. Shortly thereafter, George Radwanski, who was serving as Canada's privacy commissioner, announced publicly that Air Canada was under investigation by his office for potential violations to individual privacy rights that occurred as a result of a process by which the firm was collecting customers' personal information. It was one of the few times that the name of a company was revealed during an investigation by the privacy commissioner's office. At that time, Air Canada was the largest company ever investigated.

In a letter to Air Canada headquarters in Montreal that was later published, George Radwanski asked Air Canada to respond to complaints about a brochure entitled "All About Your Privacy," which had been sent to members of Air Canada's Aeroplan loyalty program. The brochure contained a description of five instances where Aeroplan would collect and/or disclose personal information and indicated that the initiative to opt out was the responsibility of the members of the program. Although all five situations were of note, the privacy commissioner was investigating only two circumstances described in the brochure—specifically, collecting, using, and disclosing personal information to third parties, and doing so without the opt-in consent of participants.

According to the PIPED Act, particularly sensitive types of customer information such as health and financial information cannot be disclosed without opt-in consent. Companies need to contact their customers to get permission to disclose this information. The allegation against Air Canada was a bit of a surprise given that Air Canada is a member of the Canadian Marketing Association, which has a clear privacy code. All CMA members must agree to abide by the CMA's Code of Ethics, and this includes the CMA's privacy code. In addition, John Gustavson, president and CEO of the Canadian Marketing Association in Toronto, provided the following comment: "Air Canada and Aeroplan members have attended our privacy compliance seminars and they are sensitive to this. They have very carefully complied with our own privacy code since 1993. Air Canada has a pretty good track record on this issue. So this slip is a surprise."

A mailing that went out to its 60,000 Aeroplan members that was intended as information about how Air Canada was planning to comply with the new privacy legislation triggered the issue. Almost half of the members contacted were sent an additional questionnaire using an opt-out format and requesting financial information. According to Air Canada, the mailing was not intended to collect and use information but as a test to find out how the members felt about being asked sensitive information with an opt-out option. Air Canada was trying to comply with the privacy legislation, not circumvent it, when it sent out this brochure. Instead, it ended up triggering an action under the Privacy Act!

Source: Lesley Young, "Brochure Flies in Face of Privacy Act," *Marketing Magazine*, July 30, 2001.

Questions

1. The privacy commissioner does not usually name the firms that have come under investigation, especially not before a decision has been rendered. Why do you think the commissioner made an exception in this case?
2. Air Canada is a member of the Canadian Marketing Association; this requires the company to comply with the CMA's Code of Ethics. Review the CMA's Code of Ethics and Privacy Guidelines at **http://www.the-cma.org/consumer/ethics.cfm**. What would you advise the CMA do about this apparent violation by one of its members?
3. What can Air Canada do to rectify the situation and comply with the Privacy Act, and at the same time reassure all of its Aeroplan customers?

CRITICAL THINKING CASE

How Kraft Canada Gets Close to Customers

With all of the technology available, sometimes marketers lose sight of what is most important—fulfilling the needs of their customers better than their competitors. Kraft Canada is a firm that has avoided this pitfall by keeping its purpose front and centre, using technology to get close to customers and then offering simple food solutions.

Kraft Canada accomplishes its purpose with a number of tools. The first tool is "Kraft Kitchens," which consumers can reach via a toll-free number or through the Kraft Canada website (**http://www.kraftcanada.com**) and ask questions about food offerings and recipes. It is not just the name of a contact centre either. It is a real kitchen where, for a fee, Canadians can take cooking lessons or attend workshops. Kraft Kitchens publishes *What's Cooking* magazine, which is mailed to nearly 1 million Canadians. Kraft Canada believes in using all of the available communication technology. Kraft Kitchens uses the telephone and the mail, and provides on-line assistance to its cooks with thousands of food recipes on its website. The firm also sends out recipes via weekly e-mails.

All of this effort is part of Kraft's strategy to develop a one-to-one relationship with its customers, to understand them better, and to support their needs as they buy Kraft brands such as Miracle Whip, Philadelphia Cream Cheese, Shake 'n Bake, and, of course, Kraft Dinner Macaroni and Cheese (a.k.a. KD). The development of a direct customer relationship management program with so many customers is not usually considered financially feasible, but Kraft Canada decided that the current technology would give it the means. The number of Canadian households with access to the Web and e-mail, and the availability of CRM tools and technology, convinced Kraft Canada's marketing people that it wasn't a matter of whether they could afford to reach out to customers—they couldn't afford not to.

Kraft perceived its customers as wanting a closer relationship as much as Kraft did, and consequently it has always offered service solutions. As far back as the 1970s, the firm ran Canadian television commercials that demonstrated how to prepare recipes. With today's technology, Kraft can go one better than a television demonstration, to the point of offering individual solutions. In order to provide these solutions, Kraft has a variety of content, including recipes, food and entertainment ideas, and basic cooking skills. The theme of Kraft's CRM program is "Family. Food. Simple." In addition, Kraft is interested in helping its consumers, so its service offerings focus on a few simple steps, a few dishes, and recipes requiring products that are currently in the kitchen whether they are Kraft brands or not.

Kraft's direct marketing campaign begins by sending out *What's Cooking* magazine in both English and French versions with coverage to 900,000 Canadians. Every three months Kraft mails hundreds of thousands of direct-mail pieces, which are targeted in Canada's official languages but also include ethnic languages such as Mandarin. Kraft Canada sends out weekly e-mails to its customers who have opted into its e-mail list; this communication is combined with asking people to visit **http://www.kraftcanada.com**, the firm's website. People are responding. Kraft's website is ranked number one in Canada among packaged foods manufacturers. The website has a couple of key personalized features such as, "My Recipe Box" and "My Profile," which allow users to customize the site.

Consumers who sign into Kraft Kitchens' cooking classes and workshops are greeted by cooking experts who know their subject and who have featured roles in Kraft's promotional communications. Many consumers feel they already know these people and are delighted to discover that they are "real-life," down-to-earth people, not just "models, actors, or professional talking heads." The personal and helpful approach is the objective of the program, and as such, the Kraft brand presence is not overdone in the cooking classes or the *What's Cooking* magazine.

As much as possible, Kraft Canada personalizes all its communications. Along with the website data collection, surveys are conducted in *What's Cooking* magazine, in the direct-mail pieces, and in the e-mails to discover needs and wants, preferences, key demographics like family size, and product usage rates. However, Kraft is careful to use the information to design communications focused on responding to customer needs rather than on making a "hard sell pitch."

One of the prime reasons that Kraft has been successful with this approach is the breadth and width of its product line. Packaged goods products are usually low purchase involvement, low margin, and high turnover products. These kinds of products are usually not conducive to CRM programs. However, given Kraft's wide product line combined with its ability to build loyalty and cross-sell its products, the weekly purchase value in Kraft products can easily approach $10 to $20 per week, an amount that will lower the costs of a CRM program.

Given that food is something people need to survive, something that is consumed daily, and given that meals represent an important social process, establishing a strong relationship by providing food solutions seems to make a lot of sense. Kraft Canada recognizes its role in serving its customers with the following statement: "Consumers don't get up in the morning thinking about how they want to use Miracle Whip. Consumers get up worried about what they are going to put on the table for breakfast, lunch, and dinner."

Based on: Kraft Canada website, www.kraftcanada.com; and Lesley Young, "One Bite at a Time," *Marketing Magazine*, November 5, 2001.

Questions

1. How does Kraft Canada's CRM approach differ from many of the CRM approaches that you have read about so far in this textbook? With reference to some of these other programs you have encountered, do you have any suggestions that might improve Kraft's CRM program?
2. Kraft's CRM program is relatively new and, as described, fairly expensive. Often companies start these programs without being sure where they will lead or how much they will cost. Usually when these evaluations are finally made, a lot of customers have become involved with the program. What are some of the negative impacts that a firm like Kraft might face if it had to close down its CRM program because of expense?
3. Describe how you think Kraft's perspective on its customers' needs has guided the development of its CRM program.

>> GLOSSARY

(Numbers in parentheses refer to the chapter(s) containing the main discussion of the term.)

A

accessory equipment Goods, such as portable tools and office equipment, that are less expensive and shorter-lived than major equipment. (5)

adopter A consumer who was happy enough with his or her trial experience with a product to use it again. (9)

advertising Impersonal, one-way mass communication about a product or organization that is paid for by a marketer. (13)

advertising appeal A reason for a person to buy a product. (14)

advertising campaign A series of related advertisements focusing on a common theme, slogan, and set of advertising appeals. (14)

advertising objective A specific communication task that a campaign should accomplish for a specified target audience during a specified period. (14)

advertising response function A phenomenon in which spending for advertising and sales promotion increases sales or market share up to a certain level but then produces diminishing returns. (14)

advocacy advertising A form of advertising in which an organization expresses its views on controversial issues or responds to media attacks. (14)

agents and brokers Wholesaling intermediaries who do not take title to a product but facilitate its sale from producer to end user by representing retailers, wholesalers, or manufacturers. (12)

AIDA concept A model that outlines the process for achieving promotional goals in terms of stages of consumer involvement with the message; the acronym stands for *attention, interest, desire,* and *action.* (13)

applied research An attempt to develop new or improved products. (3)

aspirational reference group A group that someone would like to join. (4)

assurance The knowledge and courtesy of employees and their ability to convey trust. (10)

ATC. *See* average total cost.

atmosphere The overall impression conveyed by a store's physical layout, decor, and surroundings. (12)

attitude A learned tendency to respond consistently toward a given object. (4)

audience selectivity The ability of an advertising medium to reach a precisely defined market. (14)

automatic vending The use of machines to offer goods for sale. (12)

AVC. *See* average variable cost.

average total cost (ATC) Total costs divided by quantity of output. (15)

average variable cost (AVC) Total variable costs divided by quantity of output. (15)

B

baby boomers People born between 1946 and 1964. (3)

bait pricing A price tactic that tries to get consumers into a store through false or misleading price advertising and then uses high-pressure selling to persuade consumers to buy more expensive merchandise. (16)

banner advertisement A paid advertisement that runs the entire width of the Web page, usually placed near the top or bottom of the page. (17)

base price The general price level at which the company expects to sell the good or service. (16)

basic research Pure research that aims to confirm an existing theory or to learn more about a concept or phenomenon. (3)

basing-point pricing A price tactic that charges freight from a given (basing) point, regardless of the city from which the goods are shipped. (16)

BehaviorScan A scanner-based research program that tracks the purchases of 3,000 households through store scanners. (7)

belief An organized pattern of knowledge that an individual holds as true about his or her world. (4)

benefit segmentation The process of grouping customers into market segments according to the benefits they seek from the product. (6)

brainstorming The process of getting a group to think of unlimited ways to vary a product or solve a problem. (9)

brand A name, term, symbol, design, or combination thereof that identifies a seller's products and differentiates them from competitors' products. (8)

brand equity The value of company and brand names. (8)

brand loyalty A consistent preference for one brand over all others. (8)

brand mark The elements of a brand that cannot be spoken. (8)

brand name That part of a brand that can be spoken, including letters, words, and numbers. (8)

break-even analysis A method of determining what sales volume must be reached before total revenue equals total costs. (15)

business analysis The second stage of the screening process, where preliminary figures for demand, cost, sales, and profitability are calculated. (9)

business marketing The marketing of goods and services to individuals and organizations for purposes other than personal consumption. Often referred to as B2B. (5)

business product (industrial product) A product used to manufacture other goods or services, to facilitate an organization's operations, or to resell to other customers. (8)

business services Expense items that do not become part of a final product. (5)

business-to-business (B2B) electronic commerce Using the Internet to conduct business between two or more organizations. (17)

business-to-consumer (B2C) electronic commerce Using the Internet to conduct business between an organization and individual consumers. (17)

button advertisement A paid advertisement that is smaller than a banner ad, appearing in medium, micro, short, and tall size variations. (17)

buyer A department head who selects the merchandise for his or her department and who may also be responsible for promotion and personnel. (12)

buying centre All those persons in an organization who become involved in the purchase decision. (5)

C

campaign management Developing product or service offerings customized for the appropriate customer segment and then pricing and communicating these offerings for the purpose of enhancing customer relationships. (18)

cannibalization A situation that occurs when sales of a new product cut into sales of a firm's existing products. (6)

cash cow In the portfolio matrix, a business unit that usually generates more cash than it needs to maintain its market share. (2)

cash discount A price reduction offered to a consumer, an industrial user, or a marketing intermediary in return for prompt payment of a bill. (16)

category killers Specialty discount stores that heavily dominate their narrow merchandise segment. (12)

central-location telephone (CLT) facility A specially designed phone room used to conduct telephone interviewing. (7)

chain stores Stores owned and operated as a group by a single organization. (12)

channel A medium of communication, such as a voice, radio, or newspaper, for transmitting a message. (13)

channel (CRM) A medium of communication through which the customer interacts with a business at an external touch point; the traditional approach for acquiring information from customers. (18)

channel conflict A clash of goals and methods between distribution channel members. (11)

channel control A situation that occurs when one marketing channel member intentionally affects another member's behaviour. (11)

channel leader (channel captain) A member of a marketing channel that exercises authority and power over the activities of other channel members. (11)

channel members All parties in the marketing channel that negotiate with one another, buy and sell products, and facilitate the change of ownership between buyer and seller in the course of moving the product from the manufacturer into the hands of the final consumer. (11)

channel partnering (channel cooperation) The joint effort of all channel members to create a supply chain that serves customers and creates a competitive advantage. (11)

channel power The capacity of a particular marketing channel member to control or influence the behaviour of other channel members. (11)

CLT. *See* central-location telephone facility.

closed-ended question An interview question that asks the respondent to make a selection from a limited list of responses. (7)

cobranding Placing two or more brand names on a product or its package. (8)

code of ethics A guideline to help marketing managers and other employees make better decisions. (3)

cognitive dissonance Inner tension that a consumer experiences after recognizing an inconsistency between behaviour and values or opinions. (4)

cold calling A form of lead generation in which the salesperson approaches potential buyers without any prior knowledge of the prospects' needs or financial status. (13)

commercialization The decision to market a product. (9)

communication The process by which we exchange or share meanings through a common set of symbols. (13)

comparative advertising A form of advertising that compares two or more specifically named or shown competing brands on one or more specific attributes. (14)

Competition Bureau The federal department charged with administering most marketplace laws. (3)

competitive advantage The set of unique features of a company and its products that are perceived by the target market as significant and superior to the competition. (2)

competitive advertising A form of advertising designed to influence demand for a specific brand. (14)

competitive intelligence (CI) An intelligence system that helps managers assess their competition and vendors in order to become more efficient and effective competitors. (7)

compiled list A customer list that was developed by gathering names and addresses from telephone directories and membership rosters, usually enhanced with information from public records, such as census data, auto registrations, birth announcements, business start-ups, or bankruptcies. (17)

component lifestyles The practice of choosing goods and services that meet one's diverse needs and interests rather than conforming to a single, traditional lifestyle. (3)

component parts Either finished items ready for assembly or products that need very little processing before becoming part of some other product. (5)

computer-assisted personal interviewing An interviewing method in which the interviewer reads the questions from a computer screen and enters the respondent's data directly into the computer. (7)

computer-assisted self-interviewing An interviewing method in which a mall interviewer intercepts and directs willing respondents to nearby computers where the respondent reads questions off a computer screen and directly keys his or her answers into the computer. (7)

concentrated targeting strategy A strategy used to select one segment of a market for targeting marketing efforts. (6)

concept test A test to evaluate a new-product idea, usually before any prototype has been created. (9)

consumer behaviour Processes a consumer uses to make purchase decisions, as well as to use and dispose of purchased goods or services; also includes factors that influence purchase decisions and product use. (4)

consumer decision-making process A five-step process used by consumers when buying goods or services. (4)

consumer penalty An extra fee paid by the consumer for violating the terms of the purchase agreement. (16)

consumer product A product bought to satisfy an individual's personal wants. (8)

consumer sales promotion Sales promotion activities targeting the ultimate consumer. (14)

continuous media schedule A media scheduling strategy in which advertising is run steadily throughout the advertising period; used for products in the latter stages of the product life cycle. (14)

control Provides the mechanisms for evaluating marketing results in light of the plan's goals and for correcting actions that do not help the organization reach those goals within budget guidelines. (2)

convenience product A relatively inexpensive item that merits little shopping effort. (8)

convenience sample A form of nonprobability sample using respondents who are convenient or readily accessible to the researcher—for example, employees, friends, or relatives. (7)

convenience store A miniature supermarket, carrying only a limited line of high-turnover convenience goods. (12)

cookie A digital tag written to the user's local hard drive that is keyed to a specific server (for example, a Web page) and is passed back to the server when the user's browser again accesses the server. (17)

cooperative advertising An arrangement in which the manufacturer and the retailer split the costs of advertising the manufacturer's brand. (14)

core service The most basic benefit the consumer is buying. (10)

corporate social responsibility Business's concern for society's welfare. (3)

corporate website A website that provides consumers with information but provides little or no opportunity to communicate with the organization. (17)

cost competitive advantage Being the low-cost competitor in an industry while maintaining satisfactory profit margins. (2)

cost per contact The cost of reaching one member of the target market. (14)

coupon A certificate that entitles consumers to an immediate price reduction when they buy the product. (14)

credence quality A characteristic that consumers may have difficulty assessing even after purchase because they do not have the necessary knowledge or experience. (10)

crisis management A coordinated effort to handle the effects of unfavourable publicity or of another unexpected, unfavourable event. (14)

CRM *See* customer relationship management

cross-tabulation A method of analyzing data that lets the analyst look at the responses to one question in relation to the responses to one or more other questions. (7)

culture The set of values, norms, attitudes, and other meaningful symbols that shape human behaviour and the artifacts, or products, of that behaviour as they are transmitted from one generation to the next. (4)

cumulative quantity discount A deduction from list price that applies to the buyer's total purchases made during a specific time period. (16)

custom data Enhancement information acquired by the marketer, including customer surveys, customer participation programs, product registration, warranty cards, or loyalty marketing programs. (17)

customer-centric Under this philosophy, the company customizes its product and service offering based on data generated through interactions between the customer and the company. (18)

customer relationship management (CRM) A company-wide business strategy designed to optimize profitability, revenue, and customer satisfaction by focusing on highly defined and precise customer groups. (18)

customer satisfaction The feeling that a product has met or exceeded the customer's expectations. (1)

customer value The ratio of benefits to the sacrifice necessary to obtain those benefits. (1)

D

data-driven marketing The process of gathering, maintaining, and analyzing information about customers and prospects to implement more efficient and effective marketing communications; another term for one-to-one marketing. (17)

data mining The process of using statistical analysis to detect relevant purchasing behaviour patterns in a database; a data analysis procedure that identifies significant patterns of variables and characteristics that pertain to particular customers or customer groups. (17, 18)

data warehouse A central repository for data from various functional areas of the organization that are stored and inventoried on a centralized computer system so that the information can be shared across all functional departments of the business. (18)

database A collection of data, especially one that can be accessed and manipulated by computer software. (17)

database enhancement The overlay of information to customer or prospect records for the purpose of better describing or better determining the responsiveness of customers or prospects. (17)

database marketing The creation of a large computerized file of customers' and potential customers' profiles and purchase patterns. (7)

decision support system (DSS) An interactive, flexible computerized information system that enables managers to obtain and manipulate information as they are making decisions. (7)

decline stage A long-run drop in sales. (9)

decoding Interpretation of the language and symbols sent by the source through a channel. (13)

delayed-quotation pricing A price tactic used for industrial installations and many accessory items, in which a firm price is not set until the item is either finished or delivered. (16)

demand The quantity of a product that will be sold in the market at various prices for a specified period. (15)

demographic segmentation Segmenting markets by age, gender, income, ethnic background, and family life cycle. (6)

demography The study of people's vital statistics, such as their age, race and ethnicity, and location. (3)

department store A store housing several departments under one roof. (12)

derived demand The demand for business products. (5)

development The stage in the product development process in which a prototype is developed and a marketing strategy is outlined. (9)

differential advantage One or more unique aspects of an organization that cause target consumers to patronize that firm rather than competitors. (13)

diffusion The process by which the adoption of an innovation spreads. (9)

direct channel A distribution channel in which producers sell directly to consumers. (11)

direct marketing (direct-response marketing) Techniques used to get consumers to make a purchase from their home, office, or other nonretail setting. (12)

direct retailing The selling of products by representatives who work door-to-door, office-to-office, or at home parties. (12)

discount store A retailer that competes on the basis of low prices, high turnover, and high volume. (12)

discrepancy of assortment The lack of all the items a customer needs to receive full satisfaction from a product or products. (11)

discrepancy of quantity The difference between the amount of product produced and the amount an end user wants to buy. (11)

distribution resource planning (DRP) An inventory control system that manages the replenishment of goods from the manufacturer to the final consumer. (11)

diversification A strategy of increasing sales by introducing new products into new markets. (2)

dog In the portfolio matrix, a business unit that has low growth potential and a small market share. (2)

DRP. *See* distribution resource planning.

drugstore A retail store that stocks pharmacy-related products and services as its main draw. (12)

DSS. *See* decision support system.

dual distribution (multiple distribution) The use of two or more channels to distribute the same product to target markets. (11)

E

e-marketplace A channel intermediary bringing together buyers and sellers to form a virtual exchange community. (17)

e-tailing Using the Internet to sell retail products and services. (17)

e-zine Abbreviation for electronic magazine—an on-line publication similar in concept to a printed magazine. (17)

EDI. *See* electronic data interchange.

80/20 principle A principle holding that 20 percent of all customers generate 80 percent of the demand. (6)

elastic demand A situation in which consumer demand is sensitive to changes in price. (15)

elasticity of demand Consumers' responsiveness or sensitivity to changes in price. (15)

electronic data interchange (EDI) Information technology that replaces the paper documents that usually accompany business transactions, such as purchase orders and invoices, with electronic transmission of the needed information to reduce inventory levels, improve cash flow, streamline operations, and increase the speed and accuracy of information transmission. (11)

electronic distribution A distribution technique that includes any kind of product or service that can be distributed electronically, whether over traditional forms such as fibre-optic cable or through satellite transmission of electronic signals. (11)

empathy Caring, individualized attention to customers. (10)

empowerment Delegation of authority to solve customers' problems quickly—usually by the first person the customer notifies regarding the problem. (1, 18)

encoding The conversion of the sender's ideas and thoughts into a message, usually in the form of words or signs. (13)

environmental management When a company implements strategies that attempt to shape the external environment within which it operates. (3)

environmental scanning Collection and interpretation of information about forces, events, and relationships in the external environment that may affect the future of the organization or the implementation of the marketing plan. (2)

escalator pricing A price tactic in which the final selling price reflects cost increases incurred between the time the order is placed and the time delivery is made. (16)

ethics The moral principles or values that generally govern the conduct of an individual. (3)

evaluation Gauging the extent to which the marketing objectives have been achieved during the specified time period. (2)

evoked set (consideration set) Group of brands, resulting from an information search, from which a buyer can choose. (4)

exchange The idea that people give up something to receive something they would rather have. (1)

exclusive distribution A form of distribution that establishes one or a few dealers within a given area. (11)

executive interviews A type of survey that involves interviewing businesspeople at their offices concerning industrial products or services. (7)

experience curves Curves that show costs declining at a predictable rate as experience with a product increases. (2)

experience quality A characteristic that can be assessed only after use. (10)

experiment A method a researcher uses to gather primary data. (7)

express warranty A written guarantee. (8)

extensive decision making The most complex type of consumer decision making, used when buying an unfamiliar, expensive product or an infrequently bought item; requires use of several criteria for evaluating options and much time for seeking information. (4)

external information search The process of seeking information in the outside environment. (4)

extranet A private electronic network that links a company with its suppliers and customers. (15)

F

factory outlet An off-price retailer that is owned and operated by a manufacturer. (12)

family brand Marketing several different products under the same brand name. (8)

family life cycle (FLC) A series of stages determined by a combination of age, marital status, and the presence or absence of children. (6)

feedback The receiver's response to a message. (13)

field service firm A firm that specializes in interviewing respondents on a subcontracted basis. (7)

fixed cost A cost that does not change as output is increased or decreased. (15)

FLC. *See* family life cycle.

flexible pricing (variable pricing) A price tactic in which different customers pay different prices for essentially the same merchandise bought in equal quantities. (16)

flighted media schedule A media scheduling strategy in which ads are run heavily every other month or every two weeks, to achieve a greater impact with an increased frequency and reach at those times. (14)

FOB origin pricing A price tactic that requires the buyer to absorb the freight costs from the shipping point ("free on board"). (16)

focus group Seven to ten people who participate in a group discussion led by a moderator. (7)

followup The final step of the selling process, in which the salesperson ensures that delivery schedules are met, that the goods or services perform as promised, and that the buyers' employees are properly trained to use the products. (13)

four Ps Product, place, promotion, and price, which together make up the marketing mix. (2)

frame error An error that occurs when a sample drawn from a population differs from the target population. (7)

franchise The right to operate a business or to sell a product. (12)

franchisee An individual or business that is granted the right to sell another party's product. (12)

franchiser The originator of a trade name, product, methods of operation, and so on, that grants operating rights to another party to sell its product. (12)

freight absorption pricing A price tactic in which the seller pays all or part of the actual freight charges and does not pass them on to the buyer. (16)

frequency The number of times an individual is exposed to a given message during a specific period. (14)

frequent-buyer program A loyalty program in which loyal consumers are rewarded for making multiple purchases of a particular good or service. (14)

full-line discount store A retailer that offers consumers very limited service and carries a broad assortment of well-known, nationally branded "hard goods." (12)

functional discount (trade discount) A discount to wholesalers and retailers for performing channel functions. (16)

G

gap model A model identifying five gaps that can cause problems in service delivery and influence customer evaluations of service quality. (10)

Generation X People born between 1965 and 1978. (3)

Generation Y People born between 1979 and 1994. (3)

generic product A no-frills, no-brand-name, low-cost product that is simply identified by its product category. (8)

generic product name Identifies a product by class or type and cannot be trademarked. (8)

geodemographic segmentation Segmenting potential customers into neighbourhood lifestyle categories. (6)

geographic segmentation Segmenting markets by region of a country or the world, market size, market density, or climate. (6)

global brand A brand where at least 20 percent of the product is sold outside its home country or region. (8)

gross margin The amount of money the retailer makes as a percentage of sales after the cost of goods sold is subtracted. (12)

group dynamics Group interaction essential to the success of focus-group research. (7)

growth stage The second stage of the product life cycle, when sales typically grow at an increasing rate, many competitors enter the market, large companies may start acquiring small pioneering firms, and profits are healthy. (9)

H

hit A record that a file was requested from a website. (17)

horizontal conflict A channel conflict that occurs among channel members on the same level. (11)

hypermarket A retail store that combines a supermarket and full-line discount store in a space ranging from 200,000 to 300,000 square feet. (12)

I

ideal self-image The way an individual would like to be. (4)

IMC. *See* integrated marketing communications.

implementation The process that turns marketing plans into action assignments and ensures that these assignments are executed in a way that accomplishes the plan's objectives. (2)

implied warranty An unwritten guarantee that the good or service is fit for the purpose for which it was sold. (8)

independent retailers Retailers owned by a single person or partnership and not operated as part of a larger retail institution. (12)

individual branding Using different brand names for different products. (8)

inelastic demand A situation in which an increase or a decrease in price will not significantly affect demand for the product. (15)

inflation A general rise in prices without a corresponding increase in wages that results in decreased purchasing power. (3)

infomercial A 30-minute or longer advertisement that looks more like a TV talk show than a sales pitch. (14)

informational labelling A type of package labelling designed to help consumers make proper product selections and lower their cognitive dissonance after the purchase. (8)

InfoScan A scanner-based sales-tracking service for the consumer packaged-goods industry. (7)

innovation A product perceived as new by a potential adopter. (9)

institutional advertising A form of advertising designed to enhance a company's image rather than promote a particular product. (14)

intangibility The inability of services to be touched, seen, tasted, heard, or felt in the same manner that goods can be sensed. (10)

integrated marketing communications (IMC) The careful coordination of all promotional messages for a product or a service to assure the consistency of messages at every contact point where a company meets the consumer. (13)

intensive distribution A form of distribution aimed at having a product available in every outlet where target customers might want to buy it. (11)

interaction The point at which a customer and a company representative exchange information and develop learning relationships. (18)

interactive/transactional website A website that permits two-way communication between an organization and its customers. (17)

internal information search The process of recalling past information stored in the memory. (4)

internal marketing Treating employees as customers and developing systems and benefits that satisfy their needs. (10)

interpersonal communication Direct, face-to-face communication between two or more people. (13)

interstitial advertisement An advertisement that appears in a separate browser window—also referred to as a "pop-up" ad. (17)

introductory stage The full-scale launch of a new product into the marketplace. (9)

inventory control system A method of developing and maintaining an adequate assortment of materials or products to meet a manufacturer's or a customer's demand. (11)

involvement The amount of time and effort a buyer invests in the search, evaluation, and decision processes of consumer behaviour. (4)

J

JIT. *See* just-in-time production.

joint costs Costs that are shared in the manufacturing and marketing of several products in a product line. (16)

joint demand The demand for two or more items used together in a final product. (5)

just-in-time production (JIT) A process that redefines and simplifies manufacturing by reducing inventory levels and delivering raw materials just when they are needed on the production line. (11)

K

keiretsu A network of interlocking corporate affiliates. (5)

keystoning The practice of marking up prices by 100 percent, or doubling the cost. (15)

knowledge centre An organization's internal operational component that manages and fulfills customer requests; the logistical system that reacts to, monitors, and controls the interaction between the customer and the organization. (18)

knowledge management The process by which learned information from customers is centralized and shared in order to enhance the relationship between customers and the organization. (18)

L

lead generation (prospecting) Identification of those firms and people most likely to buy the seller's offerings. (13)

lead qualification Determination of a sales prospect's (1) recognized need, (2) buying power, and (3) receptivity and accessibility. (13)

leader pricing (loss-leader pricing) A price tactic in which a product is sold near or even below cost in the hope that shoppers will buy other items once they are in the store. (16)

learning A process that creates changes in behaviour, immediate or expected, through experience and practice. (4)

learning (CRM) An informal process of collecting customer data through customer comments and feedback on product or service performance. (18)

lifestyle A mode of living as identified by a person's activities, interests, and opinions. (4)

lifetime value analysis (LTV) A data manipulation technique that projects the future value of the customer over a period of years using the assumption that marketing to repeat customers is more profitable than marketing to first-time buyers. (17)

limited decision making The type of decision making that requires a moderate amount of time for gathering information and deliberating about an unfamiliar brand in a familiar product category. (4)

logistics The process of strategically managing the efficient flow and storage of raw materials, in-process inventory, and finished goods from point of origin to point of consumption. (12)

logistics information system Information technology that integrates and links all of the logistics functions of the supply chain. (11)

loyalty marketing programs A promotional program designed to build long-term, mutually beneficial relationships between a company and its key customers. (14)

LTV. *See* lifetime value analysis.

M

major equipment (installations) Capital goods such as large or expensive machines, mainframe computers, blast furnaces, generators, airplanes, and buildings. (5)

mall intercept interview A survey research method that involves interviewing people in the common areas of shopping malls. (7)

management decision problem A broad-based problem that requires marketing research in order for managers to take proper actions. (7)

manufacturer's brand The brand name of a manufacturer. (8)

marginal cost (MC) The change in total costs associated with a one-unit change in output. (15)

marginal revenue (MR) The extra revenue associated with selling an extra unit of output or the change in total revenue with a one-unit change in output. (15)

market People or organizations with needs or wants and the ability and willingness to buy. (6)

market development A marketing strategy that entails attracting new customers to existing products. (2)

market opportunity analysis (MOA) The description and estimation of the size and sales potential of market segments that are of interest to the firm and the assessment of key competitors in these market segments. (2)

market orientation A philosophy that assumes that a sale does not depend on an aggressive sales force but rather on a customer's decision to purchase a product. (1)

market penetration A marketing strategy that tries to increase market share among existing customers. (2)

market segment A subgroup of people or organizations sharing one or more characteristics that cause them to have similar product needs. (6)

market segmentation The process of dividing a market into meaningful, relatively similar, and identifiable segments or groups. (6)

market share A company's product sales as a percentage of total sales for that industry. (15)

marketing The process of planning and executing the conception, pricing, promotion, and distribution of ideas, goods, and services to create exchanges that satisfy individual and organizational goals. (1)

marketing audit A thorough, systematic, periodic evaluation of the goals, strategies, structure, and performance of the marketing organization. (2)

marketing channel (channel of distribution) A set of interdependent organizations that ease the transfer of ownership as products move from producer to business user or consumer. (11)

marketing concept The idea that the social and economic justification for an organization's existence is the satisfaction of customer wants and needs while meeting organizational objectives. (1)

marketing-controlled information source A product information source that originates with marketers promoting the product. (4)

marketing database The compilation of names, addresses, and other pieces of pertinent information about individual customers and prospects that affects what and how marketers sell to them. (17)

marketing information Everyday information about developments in the marketing environment that managers use to prepare and adjust marketing plans. (7)

marketing mix A unique blend of product, distribution, promotion, and pricing strate gies designed to produce mutually satisfying exchanges with a target market. (2)

marketing myopia Defining a business in terms of goods and services rather than in terms of the benefits that customers seek. (2)

marketing objective A statement of what is to be accomplished through marketing activities. (2)

marketing plan A written document that acts as a guidebook of marketing activities for the marketing manager. (2)

marketing planning Designing activities relating to marketing objectives and the changing marketing environment. (2)

marketing research The process of planning, collecting, and analyzing data relevant to a marketing decision. (7)

marketing research objective The specific information needed to solve a marketing research problem; the objective should be to provide insightful decision-making information. (7)

marketing research problem Determining what information is needed and how that information can be obtained efficiently and effectively. (7)

marketing strategy The activities of selecting and describing one or more target markets and developing and maintaining a marketing mix that will produce mutually satisfying exchanges with target markets. (2)

markup pricing The cost of buying the product from the producer plus amounts for profit and for expenses not otherwise accounted for. (15)

Maslow's hierarchy of needs A method of classifying human needs and motivations into five categories in ascending order of importance: physiological, safety, social, esteem, and self-actualization. (4)

mass communication The communication of a concept or message to large audiences. (13)

mass customization (build-to-order) A strategy that uses technology to deliver customized services on a mass basis; a production method whereby products are not made until an order is placed by the customer, and products are made according to customer specifications. (10, 11)

mass merchandising A retailing strategy using moderate to low prices on large quantities of merchandise and lower service to stimulate high turnover of products. (12)

materials-handling system A method of moving inventory into, within, and out of the warehouse. (11)

materials requirement planning (MRP) (materials management) An inventory control system that manages the replenishment of raw materials, supplies, and components from the supplier to the manufacturer. (11)

maturity stage A period during which sales increase at a decreasing rate. (9)

MC. *See* marginal cost.

measurement error An error that occurs when there is a difference between the information desired by the researcher and the information provided by the measurement process. (7)

media mix The combination of media to be used for a promotional campaign. (14)

media planning The series of decisions advertisers make regarding the selection and use of media, allowing the marketer to optimally and cost-effectively communicate the message to the target audience. (14)

media schedule Designation of the media, the specific publications or programs, and the insertion dates of advertising. (14)

medium The channel used to convey a message to a target market. (14)

merchant wholesaler Institution that buys goods from manufacturers and resells them to businesses, government agencies, and other wholesalers or retailers and that receives and takes title to goods, stores them in its own warehouses, and later ships them. (12)

mission statement The firm's long-term vision based on a careful analysis of benefits sought by present and potential customers and analysis of existing and anticipated environmental conditions. (2)

modelled data Enhancement information that has already been sorted into distinct groups or clusters of consumers or businesses based on census, household, or business-level data. (17)

modelling The act of building a model in a situation where the answer is known and then applying the model to another situation where the answer is unknown. (18)

modified rebuy A situation where the purchaser wants some change in the original good or service. (5)

morals The rules people develop as a result of cultural values and norms. (3)

motive A driving force that causes a person to take action to satisfy specific needs. (4)

MR. *See* marginal revenue.

MRP. *See* materials requirement planning.

multiculturalism When all major ethnic groups in an area—such as a city, county, or census metropolitan area—are roughly equally represented. (3)

multiplier effect (accelerator principle) Phenomenon in which a small increase or decrease in consumer demand can produce a much larger change in demand for the facilities and equipment needed to make the consumer product. (5)

multisegment targeting strategy A strategy that chooses two or more well-defined market segments and develops a distinct marketing mix for each. (6)

mystery shoppers Researchers posing as customers who gather observational data about a store. (7)

N

need recognition Result of an imbalance between actual and desired states. (4)

needs assessment A determination of the customer's specific needs and wants and the range of options the customer has for satisfying them. (13)

negotiation The process during which both the salesperson and the prospect offer special concessions in an attempt to arrive at a sales agreement. (13)

networking A process of finding out about potential clients from friends, business contacts, coworkers, acquaintances, and fellow members in professional and civic organizations. (13)

new buy A situation requiring the purchase of a product for the first time. (5)

new-product strategy A plan that links the new-product development process with the objectives of the marketing department, the business unit, and the corporation. (9)

new product A product new to the world, the market, the producer, the seller, or some combination of these. (9)

newsgroups Function like bulletin boards on the Internet. They are established to focus on a particular topic. (7)

niche One segment of a market. (6)

niche competitive advantage The advantage achieved when a firm seeks to target and effectively serve a small segment of the market. (2)

noise Anything that interferes with, distorts, or slows down the transmission of information. (13)

nonaspirational reference group A group with which an individual does not want to associate. (4)

noncumulative quantity discount A deduction from list price that applies to a single order rather than to the total volume of orders placed during a certain period. (16)

nonmarketing-controlled information source A product information source that is not associated with advertising or promotion. (4)

nonprobability sample Any sample in which little or no attempt is made to get a representative cross section of the population. (7)

nonprofit organization An organization that exists to achieve some goal other than the usual business goals of profit, market share, or return on investment. (10)

nonprofit organization marketing The effort by nonprofit organizations to bring about mutually satisfying exchanges with target markets. (10)

nonresponse error An error that occurs when the sample that responds is different from the sample that was selected. (7)

nonstore retailing Shopping without visiting a store. (12)

norm A value or attitude deemed acceptable by a group. (4)

North American Free Trade Agreement (NAFTA) An agreement among Canada, the United States, and Mexico that created the world's largest free trade zone. (3)

North American Industry Classification System (NAICS) A detailed numbering system developed by Canada, the United States, and Mexico to classify North American business establishments by their main production processes. (5)

O

observation research A research method that relies on three types of observation: people watching people, people watching an activity, and machines watching people. (7)

odd–even pricing (psychological pricing) A price tactic that uses odd-numbered prices to connote bargains and even-numbered prices to imply quality. (16)

OEM The acronym OEM stands for original equipment manufacturer. OEMs buy business goods, which they incorporate into the products they produce for eventual sale to other producers or to consumers. (5)

off-price retailer A retailer that sells at prices 25 percent or more below traditional department store prices because it pays cash for its stock and usually doesn't ask for return privileges. (12)

on-line retailing A type of shopping available to consumers with personal computers and access to the Internet. (12)

one-to-one marketing An individualized marketing method that utilizes customer information to build long-term, personalized, and profitable relationships with each customer. (17)

one-to-one marketing communications process A revised marketing communications process that depicts the individualized communication between the one-to-one marketer and the customer; characterized by the use of personalized communication, the lack of interfering noise, and the ability to capture the response of the customer. (17)

open-ended question An interview question that encourages an answer phrased in the respondent's own words. (7)

opinion leader An individual who influences the opinions of others. (4)

optimizers Business customers who consider numerous suppliers, both familiar and unfamiliar, solicit bids, and study all proposals carefully before selecting one. (6)

order processing system A system whereby orders are entered into the supply chain and filled. (11)

outsourcing (contract logistics) A manufacturer's or supplier's use of an independent third party to manage an entire function of the logistics system, such as transportation, warehousing, or order processing. (11)

P

page view A single page requested from a website. (17)

penetration pricing A pricing policy whereby a firm charges a relatively low price for a product initially as a way to reach the mass market. (16)

perception The process by which people select, organize, and interpret stimuli into a meaningful and coherent picture. (4)

perceptual mapping A means of displaying or graphing, in two or more dimensions, the location of products, brands, or groups of products in customers' minds. (6)

personal selling A purchase situation in which two people communicate in an attempt to influence each other. (13)

personality A way of organizing and grouping the consistencies of an individual's reactions to situations. (4)

personalized economy Delivering customized goods and services at a good value on demand. (3)

persuasive labelling A type of package labelling that focuses on a promotional theme or logo; consumer information is secondary. (8)

pioneering advertising A form of advertising designed to stimulate primary demand for a new product or product category. (14)

planned obsolescence The practice of modifying products so those that have already been sold become obsolete before they actually need replacement. (8)

planning The process of anticipating future events and determining strategies to achieve organizational objectives in the future. (2)

PLC. *See* product life cycle.

point-of-purchase display A promotional display set up at the retailer's location to build traffic, advertise the product, or induce impulse buying. (14)

point-of-sale interactions Communications between customers and organizations that occur at the point of sale, normally in a store. (18)

portfolio matrix A tool for allocating resources among products or strategic business units on the basis of relative market share and market growth rate. (2)

position The place a product, brand, or group of products occupies in consumers' minds relative to competing offerings. (6)

positioning Developing a specific marketing mix to influence potential customers' overall perception of a brand, product line, or organization in general. (6)

poverty of time A lack of time to do anything but work, commute to work, handle family situations, do housework, shop, sleep, and eat. (3)

preapproach A process that describes the "homework" that must be done by the salesperson before he or she contacts a prospect. (13)

predatory pricing The practice of charging a very low price for a product with the intent of driving competitors out of business or out of a market. (16)

predictive modelling A data manipulation technique in which marketers try to determine, based on some past set of occurrences, what the odds are that some other occurrence, such as a response or purchase, will take place in the future. (17)

premium An extra item offered to the consumer, usually in exchange for some proof of purchase of the promoted product. (14)

prestige pricing Charging a high price to help promote a high-quality image. (15)

price That which is given up in an exchange to acquire a good or service. (15)

price bundling Marketing two or more products in a single package for a special price. (16)

price equilibrium The price at which demand and supply are equal. (15)

price fixing An agreement between two or more firms on the price they will charge for a product. (16)

price lining The practice of offering a product line with several items at specific price points. (16)

price shading The use of discounts by salespeople to increase demand for one or more products in a line. (16)

price skimming A pricing policy whereby a firm charges a high introductory price, often coupled with heavy promotion. (16)

price strategy A basic, long-term pricing framework, which establishes the initial price for a product and the intended direction for price movements over the product life cycle. (16)

primary data Information collected for the first time. Can be used for solving the particular problem under investigation. (7)

primary membership group A reference group with which people interact regularly in an in-formal, face-to-face manner, such as family, friends, or fellow employees. (4)

private brand A brand name owned by a wholesaler or a retailer. (8)

private-label brands Brands that are designed and developed using the retailer's name. (12)

probability sample A sample in which every element in the population has a known statistical likelihood of being selected. (7)

problem child (question mark) In the portfolio matrix, a business unit that shows rapid growth but poor profit margins. (2)

processed materials Products used directly in manufacturing other products. (5)

product Everything, both favourable and unfavourable, that a person receives in an exchange. (8)

product advertising A form of advertising that touts the benefits of a specific good or service. (14)

product category All brands that satisfy a particular type of need. (9)

product development A marketing strategy that entails the creation of marketable new products; the process of converting applications for new technologies into marketable products. (2, 9)

product differentiation A positioning strategy that some firms use to distinguish their products from those of competitors. (6)

product item A specific version of a product that can be designated as a distinct offering among an organization's products. (8)

product life cycle (PLC) A concept that provides a way to trace the stages of a product's acceptance, from its introduction (birth) to its decline (death). (9)

product line A group of closely related product items. (8)

product line depth The number of product items in a product line. (8)

product line extension Adding additional products to an existing product line in order to compete more broadly in the industry. (8)

product line pricing Setting prices for an entire line of products. (16)

product mix All products that an organization sells. (8)

product mix width The number of product lines an organization offers. (8)

product modification Changing one or more of a product's characteristics. (8)

product offering The mix of products offered to the consumer by the retailer; also called the *product assortment* or *merchandise mix*. (12)

product/service differentiation The provision of something that is unique and valuable to buyers beyond simply offering a lower price than the competition's. (2)

production orientation A philosophy that focuses on the internal capabilities of the firm rather than on the desires and needs of the marketplace. (1)

profit Revenue minus expenses. (15)

profit maximization A method of setting prices that occurs when marginal revenue equals marginal cost. (15)

promotion Communication by marketers that informs, persuades, and reminds potential buyers of a product in order to influence an opinion or elicit a response. (13)

promotional allowance (trade allowance) A payment to a dealer for promoting the manufacturer's products. (16)

promotional mix The combination of promotional tools, including advertising, public relations, personal selling, and sales promotion, used to reach the target market and fulfill the organization's overall goals. (13)

promotional strategy A plan for the optimal use of the elements of promotion: advertising, public relations, personal selling, and sales promotion. (13)

PSA. *See* public service advertisement.

psychographic segmentation Market segmentation on the basis of personality, motives, lifestyles, and geodemographics. (6)

public relations The marketing function that evaluates public attitudes, identifies areas within the organization that the public may be interested in, and executes a program of action to earn public understanding and acceptance. (13)

public service advertisement (PSA) An announcement that promotes a program of a federal, provincial, or local government or of a nonprofit organization. (10)

publicity Public information about a company, good, or service appearing in the mass media as a news item. (13)

pull strategy A marketing strategy that stimulates consumer demand to obtain product distribution. (13)

pulsing media schedule A media scheduling strategy that uses continuous scheduling throughout the year coupled with a flighted schedule during the best sales periods. (14)

push money Money offered to channel intermediaries to encourage them to "push" products, that is, to encourage other members of the channel to sell the products. (14)

push strategy A marketing strategy that uses aggressive personal selling and trade advertising to convince a wholesaler or a retailer to carry and sell particular merchandise. (13)

pyramid of corporate social responsibility A model that suggests that corporate social responsibility is composed of economic, legal, ethical, and philanthropic responsibilities and that the firm's economic performance supports the entire structure. (3)

Q

quantity discount A price reduction offered for buying in multiple units or above a specified dollar amount. (16)

quota A statement of the individual salesperson's sales objectives, usually based on sales volume alone but sometimes including key accounts (those with greatest potential), new accounts, repeat sales, and specific products. (13)

R

random error An error that occurs when the selected sample is an imperfect representation of the overall population. (7)

random sample A sample arranged in such a way that every element of the population has an equal chance of being selected as part of the sample. (7)

raw materials Unprocessed extractive or agricultural products, such as mineral ore, lumber, wheat, corn, fruits, vegetables, and fish. (5)

reach The number of target consumers exposed to a commercial at least once during a specific period, usually four weeks. (14)

real self-image The way an individual actually perceives himself or herself. (4)

rebate A cash refund given for the purchase of a product during a specific period. (14, 16)

receiver The person who decodes a message. (13)

recency–frequency–monetary analysis (RFM) A data manipulation technique that determines the firm's best customers by identifying those customers who have purchased most recently, most frequently, and who have spent the most money. (17)

recession A period of economic activity when income, production, and employment tend to fall—all of which reduce demand for goods and services. (3)

reciprocity A practice where business purchasers choose to buy from their own customers. (5)

recruited Internet sample A sample in which respondents are prerecruited and must qualify to participate. They are then e-mailed a questionnaire or directed to a secure website. (7)

reference group A group in society that influences an individual's purchasing behaviour. (4)

referral A recommendation to a salesperson from a customer or business associate. (13)

relationship marketing A strategy that entails forging long-term partnerships with customers. (1)

relationship selling (consultative selling) A sales practice that involves building, maintaining, and enhancing interactions with customers in order to develop long-term satisfaction through mutually beneficial partnerships. (13)

reliability The ability to perform a service dependably, accurately, and consistently. (10)

repositioning Changing consumers' perceptions of a brand in relation to competing brands. (6)

resale price maintenance Laws that prohibit manufacturers from controlling prices at the retail level. (16)

research design Specifies which research questions must be answered, how and when the data will be gathered, and how the data will be analyzed. (7)

response list A customer list that includes the names and addresses of individuals who have responded to an offer of some kind, such as by mail, telephone, direct-response television, product rebates, contests or sweepstakes, or billing inserts. (17)

responsiveness The ability to provide prompt service. (10)

retailing All the activities directly related to the sale of goods and services to the ultimate consumer for personal, nonbusiness use. (12)

retailing mix A combination of the six Ps—product, place, promotion, price, presentation, and personnel—to sell goods and services to the ultimate consumer. (12)

return on investment (ROI) Net profit after taxes divided by total assets. (15)

revenue The price charged to customers multiplied by the number of units sold. (15)

RFM. *See* recency–frequency–monetary analysis.

ROI. *See* return on investment.

routine response behaviour The type of decision making exhibited by consumers buying frequently purchased, low-cost goods and services; requires little search and decision time. (4)

S

sales orientation The idea that people will buy more goods and services if aggressive sales techniques are used and that high sales result in high profits. (1)

sales presentation A formal meeting in which the salesperson presents a sales proposal to a prospective buyer. (13)

sales process (sales cycle) The set of steps a salesperson goes through in a particular organization to sell a particular product or service. (13)

sales promotion Marketing activities, other than personal selling, advertising, and public relations, which stimulate consumer buying and dealer effectiveness. (13)

sales proposal A formal written document or professional presentation that outlines how the salesperson's product or service will meet or exceed the prospect's needs. (13)

sample A subset from a large population. (7)

sampling A promotional program that allows the consumer the opportunity to try a product or service for free. (14)

sampling error An error that occurs when a sample somehow does not represent the target population. (7)

satisficers Business customers who place an order with the first familiar supplier to satisfy product and delivery requirements. (6)

scaled-response question A closed-ended question designed to measure the intensity of a respondent's answer. (7)

scanner-based research A system for gathering information from a single group of respondents by continuously monitoring the advertising, promotion, and pricing they are exposed to and the things they buy. (7)

score A numerical value assigned to each record in a data warehouse that indicates the likelihood that the customer whose record has been scored will exhibit the behaviour in question. (18)

scrambled merchandising The tendency to offer a wide variety of nontraditional goods and services under one roof. (12)

screened Internet sample An Internet sample with quotas based on desired sample characteristics. (7)

screening The first filter in the product development process; it eliminates ideas that are inconsistent with the organization's new-product strategy or are obviously inappropriate for some other reason. (9)

search quality A characteristic that can be easily assessed before purchase. (10)

seasonal discount A price reduction for buying merchandise out of season. (16)

seasonal media schedule A media scheduling strategy that runs advertising only during times of the year when the product is most likely to be used. (14)

secondary data Data previously collected for any purpose other than the one at hand. (7)

secondary membership group A reference group with which people associate less consistently and more formally than a primary membership group, such as a club, professional group, or religious group. (4)

segmentation bases (variables) Characteristics of individuals, groups, or organizations. (6)

selective distortion A process whereby a consumer changes or distorts information that conflicts with his or her feelings or beliefs. (4)

selective distribution A form of distribution achieved by screening dealers to eliminate all but a few in any single area. (11)

selective exposure The process whereby a consumer notices certain stimuli and ignores others. (4)

selective retention A process whereby a consumer remembers only that information which supports his or her personal beliefs. (4)

self-concept How consumers perceive themselves in terms of attitudes, perceptions, beliefs, and self-evaluations. (4)

self-regulation Programs voluntarily adopted by business groups to regulate the activities of their members. (3)

selling against the brand Stocking well-known branded items at high prices in order to sell store brands at discounted prices. (15)

sender The originator of the message in the communication process. (13)

service The result of applying human or mechanical efforts to people or objects. (10)

service mark A trademark for a service. (8)

shopping product A product that requires comparison shopping because it is usually more expensive than a convenience product and is found in fewer stores. (8)

simulated (laboratory) market testing The presentation of advertising and other promotion materials for several products, including a test product, to members of the product's target market. (9)

simultaneous product development A team-oriented approach to new-product development. (9)

single-price tactic A price tactic that offers all goods and services at the same price (or perhaps two or three prices). (16)

social class A group of people in a society who are considered nearly equal in status or community esteem, who regularly socialize among themselves both formally and informally, and who share behavioural norms. (4)

socialization process How cultural values and norms are passed down to children. (4)

societal marketing orientation The idea that an organization exists not only to satisfy customer wants and needs and to meet organizational objectives but also to preserve or enhance individuals' and society's long-term best interests. (1)

spatial discrepancy The difference between the location of the producer and the location of widely scattered markets. (11)

specialty discount store A retail store that offers a nearly complete selection of single-line merchandise and uses self-service, discount prices, high volume, and high turnover. (12)

specialty product A particular item for which consumers search extensively and for which they are very reluctant to accept substitutes. (8)

specialty store A retail store specializing in a given type of merchandise. (12)

star In the portfolio matrix, a business unit that is a fast-growing market leader. (2)

status quo pricing A pricing objective that maintains existing prices or meets the competition's prices. (15)

stimulus Any unit of input affecting one or more of the five senses: sight, smell, taste, touch, hearing. (4)

stimulus discrimination A learned ability to differentiate among similar products. (4)

stimulus generalization A form of learning that occurs when one response is extended to a second stimulus similar to the first. (4)

straight commission A method of compensation in which the salesperson is paid some percentage when a sale is made. (13)

straight rebuy A situation in which the purchaser reorders the same goods or services without looking for new information or investigating other suppliers. (5)

straight salary A method of compensation in which the salesperson receives a salary regardless of sales productivity. (13)

strategic alliance (strategic partnership) A cooperative agreement between business firms. (5)

strategic business unit (SBU) A subgroup of a single business or collection of related businesses within the larger organization. (2)

strategic channel alliance A cooperative agreement between business firms to use the other's already established distribution channel. (11)

strategic planning The managerial process of creating and maintaining a fit between the organization's objectives and resources and evolving market opportunities. (2)

subculture A homogeneous group of people who share elements of the overall culture as well as unique elements of their own group. (4)

supercentre A retail store that combines groceries and general merchandise goods with a wide range of services. (12)

supermarket A large, departmentalized, self-service retailer that specializes in food and nonfood items. (12)

supplementary services A group of services that support or enhance the core service. (10)

supplies Consumable items that do not become part of the final product. (5)

supply The quantity of a product that will be offered to the market by a supplier at various prices for a specified period. (15)

supply chain The connected chain of all of the business entities, both internal and external to the company, that perform or support the logistics function. (11)

supply chain management A management system that coordinates and integrates all of the activities performed by supply chain members into a seamless process, from the source to the point of consumption, resulting in enhanced customer and economic value. (11)

supply chain team An entire group of individuals who orchestrate the movement of goods, services, and information from the source to the consumer. (11)

survey research The most popular technique for gathering primary data. A researcher interacts with people to obtain facts, opinions, and attitudes. (7)

sustainable competitive advantage An advantage that cannot be copied by the competition. (2)

SWOT analysis Identifying internal strengths (S) and weaknesses (W) and also examining external opportunities (O) and threats (T). (2)

T

tangibles The physical evidence of a service, including the physical facilities, tools, and equipment used to provide the service. (10)

target market A defined group most likely to buy a firm's products; a group of people or organizations for which an organization designs, implements, and maintains a marketing mix intended to meet the needs of that group, resulting in mutually satisfying exchanges. (3, 6)

targeted e-mail marketing E-mail sent to qualified recipients, those who have expressed interest in receiving e-mail on a specific topic. (17)

teamwork Collaborative efforts of people to accomplish common objectives. (1)

telemarketing The use of the telephone to sell directly to consumers. (12)

temporal discrepancy A situation that occurs when a product is produced but a customer is not ready to buy it. (11)

test marketing The limited introduction of a product and a marketing program to determine the reactions of potential customers in a market situation. (9)

touch point All possible areas of a business where customers communicate with that business. (18)

trade allowance A price reduction offered by manufacturers to intermediaries, such as wholesalers and retailers. (14)

trade sales promotion Sales promotion activities targeting a channel member, such as a wholesaler or retailer. (14)

trademark The exclusive right to use a brand or part of a brand. (8)

transaction An interaction between a company and a customer involving an exchange of information as well as an exchange of products or services. (18)

transaction-based interactions The exchange of information that occurs between the customer and the company at the point of the actual transaction. (18)

two-part pricing A price tactic that charges two separate amounts to consume a single good or service. (16)

U

unbundling Reducing the bundle of services that comes with the basic product. (16)

undifferentiated targeting strategy Marketing approach that views the market as one big market with no individual segments and thus requires a single marketing mix. (6)

uniform delivered pricing A price tactic in which the seller pays the actual freight charges and bills every purchaser an identical, flat freight charge. (16)

unique selling proposition A desirable, exclusive, and believable advertising appeal selected as the theme for a campaign. (14)

unitary elasticity A situation in which total revenue remains the same when prices change. (15)

universal product codes (UPCs) Series of thick and thin vertical lines (bar codes), readable by computerized optical scanners, which represent numbers used to track products. (8)

universe The population from which a sample will be drawn. (7)

unrestricted Internet sample A sample in which anyone with a computer and modem can fill out the questionnaire. (7)

unsought product A product unknown to the potential buyer or a known product that the buyer does not actively seek. (8)

untargeted e-mail marketing A mass e-mailing sent to unqualified e-mail addresses. (17)

UPCs. *See* universal product codes.

usage-rate segmentation Dividing a market by the amount of product bought or consumed. (6)

V

value The enduring belief that a specific mode of conduct is personally or socially preferable to another mode of conduct. (4)

value-based pricing Setting the price at a level that seems to the customer to be a good price compared to the prices of other options. (16)

variable cost A cost that varies with changes in the level of output. (15)

vertical conflict A channel conflict that occurs between different levels in a marketing channel, most typically between the manufacturer and wholesaler or between the manufacturer and retailer. (11)

virtual community People with a common interest who interact on and contribute content to a communal website. (17)

W

want Recognition of an unfulfilled need and a product that will satisfy it. (4)

warehouse membership clubs A limited-service merchant wholesaler that sells a limited selection of brand-name appliances, household items, and groceries on a cash-and-carry basis to members, usually small businesses and groups. (12)

warranty A confirmation of the quality or performance of a good or service. (8)

Web-based interactions Communications between customers and organizations using Web vehicles. (18)

Y

yield management systems (YMS) A technique for adjusting prices that uses complex mathematical software to profitably fill unused capacity by discounting early purchases, limiting early sales at these discounted prices, and overbooking capacity. (15)

Z

zone pricing A modification of uniform delivered pricing that divides the country (or the total market) into segments or zones and charges a flat freight rate to all customers in a given zone. (16)

ENDNOTES

Chapter 1

1. Geoff Kirbyson, "City Candy Firm Signs National Retail Deals: Clodhoppers to Appear in Video Outlets," *Winnipeg Free Press*, March 21, 2003, B1; www.kraves.com; www.profitguide.com/sales/articles.jsp?content=1064; *Manitoba Business Magazine*, January/February 2002, 5; Brent Sedo, "Krave Something Sweet," *Realm Magazine*, Winter 1998–99, 17–18; www.cbc.ca/business/programs/venture/onventure/120799.html.
2. "About Us," www.marketingpower.com/index, January 2004.
3. Philip Kotler, *Marketing Management*, millennium ed. (Upper Saddle River, N.J.: Prentice-Hall, 2000), 12.
4. Nora Isaacs, "Crash & Burn," www.upsidetoday.com, March 2001, 186–92.
5. Rekha Balu, "Listen Up," *Fast Company*, May 2000, 304–16.
6. Lucy McCauley, "Unit of One," *Fast Company*, March 2000, 94.
7. Ibid.
8. David W. Cravens, Charles W. Lamb, Jr., and Victoria L. Crittenden, *Strategic Marketing Management Cases*, 7th ed. (New York: McGraw-Hill Irwin, 2002), 2.
9. Balu, 312.
10. Cravens, Lamb, and Crittenden, 3.
11. Isaacs, 190.
12. Joann Muller, "It Doesn't Get Any Bigger Than This," *Business Week*, September 4, 2000, 84.
13. Sandra Dolbow, "Kmart May Be Down, But Don't Count It Out," *Brandweek*, January 28, 2002, 5.
14. Ed Garsten, "Toyota Aims for Custom, Fast Delivery," *The Windsor Star*, August 8, 2003, C1.
15. www.mtdcanada.com/home.asp.
16. "Top 10 Things That Irked Holiday Shoppers," *Business Week*, February 7, 2000, EB12.
17. Tony Pachi, "Sublime Service," *Customer Relationship Management*, October 2001, 25–26.
18. "Return to Sender," *Marketing News*, June 18, 2001, 3.
19. Scott Thurm, "How to Drive an Express Train," *Wall Street Journal*, June 1, 2000, B1.
20. Robert Bibb and Eric Gehm, "The 360-Degree View," *Customer Relationship Management*, June 2001, 23–24.
21. "Ask Yourself, What the Hell Really Works Here?" *Fast Company*, May 2001, 82.
22. Dana Jones, "Respondez-Vous, B-to-B," *Marketing News*, May 22, 2000, 1, 9, 10.
23. Robert Levering and Milton Moskowitz, "The 100 Best Companies to Work For," *Fortune*, January 10, 2000, 81–110.
24. Alessandra Galloni, "Coke to Launch Powerade Drink across Europe," *Wall Street Journal*, October 16, 2001, B11E. Used with permission.
25. Veronique Mandel, "Ontario to Help Boost Casino Take," *The Windsor Star*, January 27, 2004, A1, A4.
26. Kotler, 22.

Chapter 2

1. Jordan Heath-Rawlings, "Pet Valu Seeks to Mark its Territory," *The Globe and Mail*, August 4, 2003, B1, B4; www.petvalu.com/canada/aboutus.html.
2. Chris Reidy, "Lands' End to Join Sears Family for $1.9 Billion," *Knight Ridder Tribune Business News*, May 14, 2002, 1.
3. Bertrand Marotte, "Bombardier Experiencing a Different Kind of Jet Lag," *The Globe and Mail*, April 10, 2004, B6.
4. Norma Ramage, "WestJet Revels in Rival's Shadow," *Marketing Magazine* (Online Edition), May 6, 2002.
5. John Heinzl, "Molson Offers Beer Cans Sporting Cherry's Colours," *The Globe and Mail*, April 2, 2003, B4.
6. www.norco.com/profile/index.htm.
7. "Technology Brief—Hewlett-Packard Co.: Officials Don't Get Bonuses Because of Failed Objectives," *Wall Street Journal*, January 30, 2002, B5.
8. Andrew Park and Peter Burrows, "Dell, The Conqueror," *Business Week*, September 24, 2001, 92–102.
9. John Heinzl, "Labatt Enticing Customers with Free Long-Distance Phone Calls," *The Globe and Mail*, July 11, 2002, B4.
10. Khanh T. L. Tran, "Nike Puts Its Swoosh on MP3 Players, Walkie-Talkies, Heart Monitors," *Wall Street Journal*, May 10, 2000, B1, B4.
11. "Designing Products around Customer Needs," *Fortune*, Special Advertising Section, July 23, 2001, S18.
12. Jim Wilson, "Airbag Shield Foils Terrorists," *Popular Mechanics*, June 2000, 17.
13. Sandra I. Irwin, "Smart Armor Shield Deploys Like Air Bag to Stop Bullets," *National Defense*, May 2000, 23. Reprinted from *National Defense* with permission.
14. Ibid.
15. "Britney Show Too Sexy for a Few in Toronto," *The Windsor Star*, April 5, 2004, C3.
16. Marina Strauss, "Sporting Life Puts Game Plan to Test," *The Globe and Mail*, August 22, 2003, B7.

Chapter 3

1. Wendy Warburtan, "Bottom-Line-Conscious Consumers," *CanWest News*, March 15, 2004, 1; "Levi Strauss & Co. Energizes Canadian Retail Industry with Launch of Levi Strauss Brand at Wal-Mart Canada," *Canada NewsWire*, November 5, 2003, 1; Shirley Won, "Levi's to Shut Three Remaining Plants in Canada," *The Globe and Mail*, September 26, 2003, B1; Sarah Ellison, "Levi Strauss, Losing Ground to Rivals, Is Set to Iron Wrinkles Out of Jeans Sales," *Wall Street Journal*, February 12, 2001, A23B.
2. The "Coming of Age" material is adapted from Charles Schewe, Geoffrey Meredith, and Stephanie Noble, "Defining Moments: Segmenting by Cohorts," *Marketing Management*, Fall 2000, 47–53.
3. "Leisure Squeeze," *Roper Reports*, January 1999, 1.
4. Ibid.
5. "For Harried Workers in the Twenty-First Century, Six Trends to Watch," *Wall Street Journal*, December 29, 1999, B1. Used with permission.
6. Gerry Myers, "Selling to Women," *American Demographics*, April 1996, 36–42.
7. Norma Ramage, "Mark's Keeps an Eye on the Ladies," *Marketing Magazine*, February 10, 2003, 2.
8. Ibid.

9. "Food Irradiation," *Canadian Food Inspection Agency Fact Sheet*, Canadian Food Inspection Agency, November 2003; Ray Klassen, "Status of Food Irradiation in Canada," *First World Congress on Food Irradiation*, Health Canada (www.hc-sc.gc.ca); "Food and Drugs Amendments," *Food Program*, Health Canada, November 23, 2003; Douglas Powell, "Food Irradiation in Canada," *The Food Safety Network*, November 27, 2002 (www.foodsafetynetwork.ca).
10. "Generation Y Has Its Sights Firmly Fixed on Home Ownership," *Canada NewsWire*, Ottawa, June 18, 2003, 1.
11. "Hotels Target Generation X; Young Travelers Demand High-Tech Services, Amenities," *USA Today*, February 10, 2000, 1B.
12. "Harley-Davidson's New 'Buell Blast' Roars into 18–34 Year-Old Novice Market," *PR Newswire*, March 16, 2000.
13. "Survey Sheds Light on Typical Boomer," *Marketing News*, January 31, 1994, 2.
14. "Baby Boomers Are Driving into the Sunset Behind the Wheel of a 40-Foot Diesel Van with Flat-Screen Television and a Queen-Sized Bed," *Canada NewsWire*, Don Mills, Ontario, October 6, 2003, 1.
15. Howard Willens and Leslie Harris, "The Mature Market … Is It for Real?" *Quirk's Marketing Research Review*, May 2001, 40–43. Reprinted with permission.
16. Canadian Statistics, *Visible Minority Population by Age*, www.statcan.ca.
17. Bob Meyer, "Local Supermarket Caters to the World," *The Windsor Star*, April 19, 2004, C9.
18. "Diversity in the Main Stream," *Marketing News*, May 21, 2001, 1, 13.
19. Andre Mayer, "New Magazine will Focus on Asian Women," *The Globe and Mail*, August 6, 2003, B9.
20. "The Web Goes Multicultural," *Advertising Age*, November 29, 1999, 51, 54.
21. "Creating the Digital Dividend," *Business2.com*, March 6, 2001, 60.
22. Canadian Statistics, *Economic Indicators—Canada*, www.statcan.ca.
23. Ibid.
24. Ibid.
25. Ibid.
26. "Masters of Innovation," *Business Week 50*, Spring 2001, 162.
27. Stacy Perman, "Automate or Die," www.ecompany.com, July 2001, 60–67.
28. Peter Landers, "Electronics E-Commerce in Japan Held Back by Retail Traditions," *Wall Street Journal*, March 30, 2000, A22. Used with permission.
29. Marina Strauss, "Retailers Brace to Battle Sam's Club," *The Globe and Mail*, October 27, 2003, B3.
30. The Tide story is from Katrina Brooker, "A Game of Inches," *Fortune*, February 5, 2001, 98–100.
31. Based on Edward Stevens, *Business Ethics* (New York: Paulist Press, 1979). Reprinted with permission. Used with permission of Paulist Press.
32. Anusorn Singhapakdi, Skott Vitell, and Kenneth Kraft, "Moral Intensity and Ethical Decisionmaking of Marketing Professionals," *Journal of Business Research* 36, March 1996, 245–55; Ishmael Akaah and Edward Riordan, "Judgments of Marketing Professionals about Ethical Issues in Marketing Research: A Replication and Extension," *Journal of Marketing Research*, February 1989, 112–20. See also Shelby Hung, Lawrence Chonko, and James Wilcox, "Ethical Problems of Marketing Researchers," *Journal of Marketing Research*, August 1984, 309–24; Kenneth Andrews, "Ethics in Practice," *Harvard Business Review*, September–October 1989, 99–104; Thomas Dunfee, Craig Smith, and William T. Ross, Jr., "Social Contracts and Marketing Ethics," *Journal of Marketing*, July 1999, 14–32; and Jay Handleman and Stephen Arnold, "The Role of Marketing Actions with a Social Dimension: Appeals to the Institutional Environment," *Journal of Marketing*, July 1999, 33–48.
33. O. C. Ferrell, Debbie Thorne, and Linda Ferrell, "Legal Pressure for Ethical Compliance in Marketing," *Proceedings of the American Marketing Association*, Summer 1995, 412–13.
34. "Ethics Programs Aren't Stemming Employee Misconduct," *Wall Street Journal*, May 11, 2000, A1. Used with permission.
35. This section is adapted from Archie B. Carroll, "The Pyramid of Corporate Social Responsibility: Toward the Moral Management of Organizational Stakeholders," *Business Horizons*, July–August 1991, 39–48; see also Kirk Davidson, "Marketers Must Accept Greater Responsibilities," *Marketing News*, February 2, 1998, 6.
36. "The Best Corporate Reputations in America," *Wall Street Journal*, September 23, 1999, B1, B20.
37. Madelaine Drohan, "Corporations Add Values," *The Globe and Mail*, February 24, 2000, B14.
38. Amy Borrus, "Commerce Reweaves the Social Fabric," *Business Week*, August 28, 2000, 187–89.
39. Rashanda Williams, "Burger King to Aid Storm Victims," *The Windsor Star*, November 20, 1998, B1.
40. "Survey Rates Companies' Reputations, And Many Are Found Wanting," *Wall Street Journal*, February 7, 2001, B1, B6.
41. Sankar Sen and C. B. Bhattacharya, "Does Doing Good Always Lead to Doing Better? Consumer Reactions to Corporate Responsibility," *Journal of Marketing Research*, May 2001, 225–43.
42. "N.S. Government Spent $98,000 Researching Sunday Shopping Issue," *Canadian Press NewsWire*, November 4, 2003; "Stores in Truro, N.S., Say They May Have to Open Sundays to Keep Market Share," *Canadian Press NewsWirek*, October 29, 2003; "N.S. Opens Doors to Sunday Shopping for Six Weeks Prior to Christmas," *Canadian Press NewsWire*, October 28, 2003; "The Last Sunday Holdout," *Canadian HR Reporter*, October 6, 2003, 4; "Amherst, N.S., Does Brisk Trade in Cross-Border Sunday Shopping," *Canadian Press NewsWire*, November 16, 2003.

Chapter 4

1. Lesley Young, "In The Fat Seat," *Marketing Magazine*, August 11/18, 2003, 8–11; Lesley Young, "Harvey's Keeps an Eye on the Grill," *Marketing Magazine*, September 29, 2003, 3; World Health Organization, "Obesity and Other Diet-Related Chronic Diseases," www.who.int/health_topics/obesity/en/; Statistics Canada, *The Daily*, Friday, October 18, 2002, www.statcan.ca/daily.
2. Michael Totty, "Information, Please," *Wall Street Journal*, October 29, 2001, R6.
3. Emily Nelson, "P&G Checks Out Real Life," *Wall Street Journal*, May 17, 2001, B1.
4. Jean-Pierre Tremblay, "Got 'em . . . Need 'em . . . " *Marketing Magazine*, September 2, 2002, P14.
5. "A Leg Up," *Continental*, November 2001, 22; Lee Gomes, "Download, Downshift and Go: MP3 Takes to the Road," *Wall Street Journal*, February 27, 2001, B1.
6. Suzanne Bidlake, "P&G to Roll Laundry Tablet in Europe," *Advertising Age*, March 1, 1999, 18.

7. Nancy Shepherdson, "New Kids on the Lot," *American Demographics,* January 2000.
8. Jean-Marc Leger and Dave Scholz, "Advertising Avalanche," *Marketing Magazine,* November 11, 2002, 25–26.
9. Ronald Alsop, "Survey Rates Companies' Reputations, and Many Are Found Wanting," *Wall Street Journal,* February 7, 2001, B1. See also Gordon Fairclough, "Philip Morris Seeks to Mold Its Image into an Altria State," *Wall Street Journal,* November 16, 2001, A3.
10. Thomas E. Weber, "To Get Expert Advice about Digital Cameras, Check Out These Sites," *Wall Street Journal,* November 5, 2001, B1.
11. Ernest Beck, "Boosting Diageo's Sprits," *Wall Street Journal,* February 23, 2001, B1.
12. David P. Hamilton, "Not an Easy Sell: TiVo, ReplayTV and Other 'PVRs' Don't Take Off," *Wall Street Journal,* February 7, 2001, B1.
13. "2003 Buyers' Guide," *Carguide,* 32:1, February 2003; Emily Nelson, "Too Many Choices," *Wall Street Journal,* April 20, 2001, B1.
14. Ronald Alsop, "The Best Corporate Reputations in America: Johnson & Johnson (Think Babies!) Turns Up Tops," *Wall Street Journal,* September 23, 1999, B1. See also Alsop, "Survey Rates Companies' Reputations, and Many Are Found Wanting."
15. Princeton Research Survey Associates, "Consumer Behavior, Experiences and Attitudes: A Comparison by Age Groups," *AARP,* March 1999.
16. Press Release, "Hyundai Sets Gold Standard With Best Warranty In Canada,"*Canada NewsWire,* April 1, 2004.
17. Michael Totty, "Making the Sale," *Wall Street Journal,* September 24, 2001, R6.
18. Stephanie Thompson, "Marketers Embrace Latest Health Claims," *Advertising Age,* February 28, 2000, 20–22.
19. Ibid.; Judy Waytiuk, "Good Eats," *Marketing Magazine,* June 30/July 7, 2003, 11–12.
20. Jo Marney, "Counting Ethnic Canadians In," *Marketing Magazine,* June 4, 2001; Astid Van Den Broek, "A Toast to More Colour in Beer Ads," *Marketing Magazine,* June 4, 2001.
21. Graham Watt, "History and the Canadian Way," *Marketing Magazine,* May 1, 1995, 8.
22. Bill Stoneman, "Beyond Rocking the Ages: An Interview with J. Walker Smith," *American Demographics,* May 1998, 44–49.
23. Pamela Paul, "Getting Inside Gen Y," *American Demographics,* September 2001, 42–49. See also Pooja Bhatia, "Look Who's Reading," *Wall Street Journal,* November 9, 2001, W1.
24. Elliott Ettenberg, "Les Blokes Canadiens," *Marketing Magazine,* March 13, 1995, 8; "A Common Border Does Not Mean Shared Values," *Marketing Magazine,* January 25, 1993, 3.
25. Miriam Jordon, "Global Craze for Diet Drugs," *Wall Street Journal,* August 24, 2001, B1. See also Leslie Chang, "Bring Science to Weight Loss in China," *Wall Street Journal,* August 24, 2001, B1.
26. Bill Spindle, "Cowboys and Samurai: The Japanizing of Universal," *Wall Street Journal,* March 22, 2001, B1.
27. Bob Riel, "Profiles in Culture—A Snapshot Look at the Canadian People," *Relocation Journal & Real Estate News,* 1996, www.relojournal.com/nov96/culture.htm, accessed October 23, 2003.
28. Jo Marney, "Counting Ethnic Canadians In," *Marketing Magazine,* June 4, 2001.
29. Erla Zwingle, "A World Together," *National Geographic,* August 1999, 10–33; Hillary Mayell, "Death of the Mother Tongue," nationalgeographic.com/NEWS, February 25, 1999; Oliver Burkeman and Emma Brockes, "Trouble Brewing," *The Guardian,* December 3, 1999; "'Americanization' Fears Seem Misplaced," *Canberra Times,* October 24, 1999, 19; Swaminathan S. Ankleesaria Aiyar, "Does Globalisation Threaten Indian Culture?" *Economic Times,* December 22, 1999; Naomi Klein, "The Tyranny of Brands," *Australian Financial Review,* February 11, 2000, 1; Sally Beatty and Carol Hymowitz, "How MTV Stays Tuned Into Teens," *Wall Street Journal,* March 21, 2000, B1, B4.
30. Eve Lazarus, "VanCity Makes Bold Play for Gays," *Marketing Magazine,* August 19, 2002, 3.
31. Patrick Lejtenyi, "Underlying Differences," *Marketing Magazine,* June 5, 2000; Canadian Media Directors' Council, "*Media Digest,* 2003–04," *Marketing Magazine.*
32. Rebecca Piirto Heath, "Life on Easy Street," *American Demographics,* April 1997.
33. Elia Kacapyr, "Are You Middle Class?" *American Demographics,* October 1996.
34. Rebecca Piirto Heath, "The New Working Class," *American Demographics,* January 1998, 51–55.
35. Suein L. Hwang, "Dot-Coms Head Down-Market for Dollars," *Wall Street Journal,* July 16, 2001, B1.
36. Michelle Warren, "Sick Kids' Direct Drama" *Marketing Magazine,* February 10, 2003, 19–20.
37. Bhatia, "Look Who's Reading."
38. Doug Stewart, "Britney 101," *Marketing Magazine,* August 6, 2001, 14.
39. Norihiko Shirouzu, "Japan's High-School Girls Excel in Art of Setting Trends," *Wall Street Journal,* April 24, 1998, B1, B6.
40. Matt Haig, "Teenage Clicks," *The Guardian,* October 25, 2001, 46.
41. Angela Scardillo, "Making Milk COOL," *Marketing Magazine,* August 11/18, 2003, 26.
42. Statistics Canada, *The Daily,* Friday, October 18, 2002, www.statcan.ca/daily; Greg Winter, "States Try to Limit Sales of Junk Food in School Buildings," *New York Times,* September 9, 2001, 1; Betsy McKay, "Coke Finds Its Exclusive School Contracts Aren't So Easily Given Up," *Wall Street Journal,* June 26, 2001, B1; Randy Southerland, "Schools' Soda Deals Losing Fizz? Challenges Mount over Issues of Nutrition, Commercialization," *Atlanta Journal-Constitution,* September 26, 2001, JA1.
43. John Gaffney, "The Kids Are Doing It. Should You?" *Business 2.0,* November 2001, 141.
44. Astrid Van Den Broek, "Athletic Endorsements with Equity," *Marketing Magazine,* March 29, 1999.
45. Jonathan Eig, "Edible Entertainment," *Wall Street Journal,* October 24, 2001, B1.
46. Diane Crispell, "Fruit of the Boom," *Marketing Tools,* April 1998.
47. Matthew Klein, "He Shops, She Shops," *American Demographics,* March 1998, 34–35.
48. Wendy Bounds and Rebecca Quick, "Men Who Shop: Retailers Target Male Shoppers as Santa's New Helpers; Gift-Wrapping Tips for Guys," *Wall Street Journal,* November 12, 1999, W1, W4; Find Gift.com website, www.findgift.com/, accessed October 25, 2003.
49. Khanh T. L. Tran, "Women Assert Computer Games Aren't Male Preserve," *Wall Street Journal,* February 26, 2001, B1. See also Meeyoung Song, "Credit-Card Companies Cater to Korean Women," *Wall Street Journal,* June 6, 2001, B4.
50. Emily Nelson, "Forget Super-Models—Revlon's New Face Gets Lipstick on Her Teeth," *Wall Street Journal,* March 30, 2001, B1.

51. www.owlkids.com, accessed October 26, 2003; Janice Rosenberg, "Tweens Mesh Latest Fads, Moms & Dads," *Advertising Age*, February 14, 2000, 40.
52. Nancy Shepherdson, "New Kids on the Lot," *American Demographics*, January 2000.
53. Statistics Canada, "Census Families by Number of Children at Home," *2001 Census*, www.statcan.ca; Laura Pratt, "Not Like the Other," *Marketing Magazine*, December 9, 2002, 25.
54. Anita Lienert, "A More Visible Altima," *Detroit News*, September 26, 2001, 01.
55. Nora J. Rifon and Molly Catherine Ziske, "Using Weight Loss Products: The Roles of Involvement, Self-Efficacy and Body Image," in *1995 AMA Educators' Proceedings*, ed. Barbara B. Stern and George M. Zinkhan (Chicago: American Marketing Association, 1995), 90–98.
56. Lisa Vickery, Kelly Greene, Shelly Branch, and Emily Nelson, "Marketers Tweak Strategies as Age Groups Realign," *Wall Street Journal*, May 15, 2001, B1; 2001 Cassies, "Les Rotisseries St-Hubert," *Marketing Magazine*, November 19, 2001, Cassies 10.
57. Amy Merrick, "Counting on the Census," *Wall Street Journal*, February 14, 2001, B1; Astrid van den Broek, "GM's Carefree Ads," *Marketing Magazine*, September 21, 1998.
58. Sarah Hall, "What Color Is Your Cart?" *Self*, September 1999, 150.
59. Joshua Rosenbaum, "Guitar Maker Looks for a New Key," *Wall Street Journal*, February 11, 1998, B1, B5.
60. Elizabeth J. Wilson, "Using the Dollarmetric Scale to Establish the Just Meaningful Difference in Price," in *1987 AMA Educators' Proceedings*, ed. Susan Douglas et al. (Chicago: American Marketing Association, 1987), 107.
61. Cassies Awards, "Listerine Mouthwash and PocketPaks," *Marketing Magazine*, November 18, 2002, Cassies 9.
62. Mike Sundell, "Snow Job," *Marketing Magazine*, December 9, 2002, 13.
63. Michelle Warren, "Standing Shoulder to Shoulder," *Marketing Magazine*, October 6/13, 2003, 22.
64. Kelly Lynne Aston, "Wise to the Game," *Marketing Magazine*, August 11/18, 2003, 22.
65. Lara Mills, "Body Shop Boldly Redefines Beauty," *Marketing Magazine*, September 8, 1997.
66. Deborah Ball, "Despite Downturn, Japanese Are Still Having Fits for Luxury Goods," *Wall Street Journal*, April 24, 2001, B1.
67. Eryn Brown, "Just Another Product Launch," *Fortune*, November 12, 2001, 102.
68. Chris Gaither, "Microsoft Explores a New Territory: Fun," *New York Times* on-line, November 4, 2001.
69. "Woolly Bully," *Canadian Business*, February 1996, 22.
70. Steven Lipin, Brian Coleman, and Jeremy Mark, "Pick a Card: Visa, American Express, and MasterCard Vie in Overseas Strategies," *Wall Street Journal*, February 15, 1994, A1, A5.
71. Tracey Arial, "BRAs with Attitude," *Marketing Magazine*, February 3, 2003, 7.
72. Cassies, "Bank of Montreal, Quebec," *Marketing Magazine*, November 18, 2002, Cassies 6.
73. Jack Neff, "James River Puts Muscle Behind Dixie Paper Brand," *Advertising Age*, June 16, 1997, 22.
74. Miriam Jordan, "Debut of Rival Diet Colas in India Leaves a Bitter Taste," *Wall Street Journal*, July 21, 1999, B1, B4.

Chapter 5

1. Canada Post On-line Business website, www.canadapost.ca/business/obc; Press Release, "Canada Post and Purolator Courier Ltd. Deliver for Bell's New Portal BellZinc.ca—'B2B from sea to sea—and beyond'," *Canada NewsWire*, February 26, 2001.
2. For a more thorough discussion of marketing on the Internet, see Chapter 17.
3. Ward Hanson, *Internet Marketing* (Cincinnati, OH: South-Western, 2000), 6.
4. "E-Procurement Could Save Trillions," *eMarketer*, December 18, 2001, on-line; Margaret Nearing, "What's Next for the Next Economy," *Marketing Magazine*, February 19, 2001, Digital Insert 2; Andrew Bartels, Ryan Hudson, and Tom Pohlmann, "ISM/Forrester Report on Technology in Supply Management: Q3 2003," *Forrester Research website*, www.forrester.com, accessed October 29, 2003; Statistics Canada, "Electronic Commerce and Technology," *The Daily*, Wednesday, April 2, 2003.
5. Statistics Canada, "Electronic Commerce and Technology," *The Daily*, Wednesday, April 2, 2003; Statistics Canada, *The Daily*, June 6, 2002.
6. Paul C. Judge, "How I Saved $100 Million on the Web," *Fast Company*, February 2001, 174–81.
7. Ibid.
8. Ibid.
9. James Careless, "Cornering the B2B Markets," *Marketing Magazine*, June 18, 2001, Digital Marketing 10; Bellzinc website, www.bellzinc.ca, accessed October 29, 2003.
10. Ibid.
11. David Sims, "Bringing Online Help to the B2B World," *Customer Relationship Management*, August 2001, 32–36.
12. Statistics Canada, "Electronic Commerce and Technology," *The Daily*, Wednesday, April 2, 2003; Statistics Canada, *The Daily*, June 6, 2002.
13. *Canada NewsWire*, "Quebec Bakery to Deploy Integrated System from IFS," September 22, 2003, 1.
14. Press Release, "EPOST Names Derivion as New E-Business Solution Partner," *Canada NewsWire*, January 9, 2001.
15. Karen L. Lundegaard, "Online Exchange of Auto's Big Three Clears Final Hurdle," *Wall Street Journal*, September 27, 2000, B10.
16. Jocelyn Parker, "As Covisint Auto Market Materializes, Concerns Arise over Smaller Suppliers," *Wall Street Journal*, September 18, 2000, B18H.
17. "Business Watch," *Plant*, September, 22, 2003, 14.
18. *Statistics Canada*, "Manufacturing and Construction," Canadian Statistics, www.statcan.ca, accessed October 31, 2003; "The Global 500," *Fortune Magazine*, July 21, 2003, 106–12.
19. Karby Leggett, "In Rural China, GM Sees a Frugal but Huge Market," *Wall Street Journal*, January 16, 2001, A1. Used with permission.
20. Statistics Canada, "The Economy," Canadian Statistics, www.statcan.ca, accessed November 3, 2003; *Canada NewsWire*, "Industry Pays Tribute To Retail Leaders," June 3, 2003, 1; Sarah Smith, "Checking Out the New Loblaws," *Marketing Magazine*, April 29, 2002, 10–11; Holly Quan, "Grocery Programs Take Flight," *Marketing Magazine*, July 8, 2002, 12; and "Lanzarotta Wholesale Grocers: The Tradition Continues," *Canadian Grocer*, March 2000, Insert.
21. *Paul Emanuelli*, "Understanding Government Procurement Policy in the Era of Globalization," *Purchasing B2B*, December 2002, 36.
22. Ibid.; *Laura Eggertson* and *Marja Hughes*, "Unlocking Procurement Barriers," *Summit*, March 2003, 12; Statistics Canada, "Public Sector Statistics," Canadian Statistics, www.statcan.ca, accessed November 3, 2003.

23. Charity Village, "Frequently Asked Questions," www.charityvillage.com, accessed November 3, 2003.
24. *Statistics Canada*, "North American Industry Classification System (NAICS)—Canada 2002," www.statcan.ca.
25. Mark Tatge, "Caterpillar's Truck Engine Sales May Skid Amid High Inventories," *Wall Street Journal Interactive Edition*, March 13, 2000, on-line.
26. *Nicolas Van Praet*, "Investors Dump Shares After CAE Loses Contract," *CanWest News*, September 26, 2003, 1; "Former Diplomat Steers CAE Inc. to New Heights in Flight Simulator Business," *Canadian Press NewsWire*, May 19, 2002.
27. "Integrating Purchasing and Accounts Payable: The Right Medicine for Improving Services at London's University Hospital," *Modern Purchasing*, September 1996, 14.
28. "Amex Canada Sees Travel Turnaround: Buying Pros Help Control Costs," *Purchasing B2B*, April 2002.
29. Purchasing Management Association of Canada, "PMAC Code of Ethics," www.pmac.ca, accessed November 3, 2003.
30. "Customer Adoption Rates Beat Industry Norms," *Canada NewsWire*, November 20, 2002; James W. Taylor, *The Marketing Strategy & Planning Workbook* (South Nyack, NY: Wellington Press, 2000), 9.
31. "Why Speed Counts," *Marketing Magazine*, May 28, 2001, 30.

Chapter 6

1. Beth Hitchcock, "Thank Heaven for Little Girls," *Marketing Magazine*, January 1/8, 2001, 14–15; Stephanie Whittaker, "Tweens and Teens Lobby for High-Speed Access," *Marketing Magazine*, May 2001, 5; Doug Stewart, "Britney 101," *Marketing Magazine*, August 6, 2001, 14; Andrea Zoe Aster, "Back to School," *Marketing Magazine*, August 11/18, 2003, 20–21; "Kid Power [Tweens an Important Market]," *Canadian Grocer*, November, 1999, 9; "Tween Scene," *Marketing Magazine*, December 1, 1997; Lori Smith, "The New & Young Uber-Consumers," *Gifts & Tablewares*, June 2000; "Television Viewing," *The Daily*, Monday, December 2, 2002.
2. Kathleen Martin, "The Next 20%," *Marketing Magazine*, April 2, 2001, 15.
3. Leslie Chang, "Bringing Science to Weight Loss in China," *Wall Street Journal*, August 21, 2001, B1, B7. Used with permission.
4. Eve Lazarus, "Kokanee Brews Up Fans in the U.S.," *Marketing Magazine*, March 29, 1999.
5. All population numbers in this section sourced from Statistics Canada, "Population by Sex and Age Group," *Canadian Statistics: The People*, www.statcan.ca, accessed November 7, 2003.
6. Nichole L. Torres, "It's Child's Play," *Entrepreneur*, December 2001, 24–26.
7. Lesley Daw, "Schaefer Takes on YTV Marketing Job," *Marketing Magazine*, July 5, 1999.
8. Lori Smith, "The New & Young Uber-Consumers," *Gifts & Tablewares*, June 2000.
9. Torres, "It's Child's Play."
10. Andrea Zoe Aster, "Back to School," *Marketing Magazine*, August 11/18, 2003, 20–21.
11. Tracey Arial, "Cover Girls," *Marketing Magazine*, September 23, 2002, 13–14; Canadian Media Directors' Council, *Media Digest*, 2003–04.
12. Lisa Vickery, Kelly Greene, Shelly Branch, and Emily Nelson, "Marketers Tweak Strategies as Age Groups Realign," *Wall Street Journal*, May 15, 2001, B1.
13. Eve Lazarus, "Carving a Slice Out of KFC," *Marketing Magazine*, September 9, 2002, 16.
14. Newsline, "Dentures Get Sexed Up," *Marketing Magazine*, April 9, 2001.
15. Statistics Canada, "Population by Sex and Age Group," *Canadian Statistics: The People*, www.statcan.ca, accessed November 7, 2003.
16. Danny Kucharsky, "AskMen—Online Help for Clueless Men," *Marketing Magazine*, June 17, 2002, 20.
17. Khanh T. L. Tran, "Women Assert Computer Games Aren't Male Preserve," *Wall Street Journal*, February 26, 2001, B1, B8.
18. Emily Nelson, "Beauty Makers Now Go Where the Boys Are," *Wall Street Journal*, August 10, 2000, B1, B4.
19. Statistics Canada, "Population by Sex and Age Group," *Canadian Statistics, Families, Households and Housing*, www.statcan.ca, accessed November 7, 2003.
20. Anne Faircloth, "Value Retailers Go Dollar for Dollar," *Fortune*, July 6, 1998, 164–166; Ann Zimmerman, "Taking Aim at Costco, Sam's Club, Marshals, Diamonds, and Pearls," *Wall Street Journal*, August 9, 2001, A1, A4.
21. Statistics Canada, "Population by Home Language, Provinces and Territories," *Canadian Statistics, Population, Languages*, www.statcan.ca, accessed November 8, 2003.
22. Loretta Lam, "Music to Ethnic Ears," *Marketing Magazine*, May 19, 2003, 10–11.
23. Statistics Canada, "Census Families by Number of Children at Home," *2001 Census*, www.statcan.ca; Statistics Canada, "Type of Dwelling and Population by Type of Dwelling," *Canadian Statistics: families, households and housing*, www.statcan.ca, accessed November 7, 2003.
24. Bonnie Elgie, "Making a Day of Child's Play," *Marketing Magazine*, September 2, 2002, P8.
25. Alex Taylor III, "Porsche Slices Up Its Buyers," *Fortune*, January 16, 1995, 24.
26. Karen Benezra, "The Fragging of the American Mind," *Superbrands*, June 15, 1998, S12–19.
27. Ken Mison, "Cutting Back on Wasted Mail," *Marketing Magazine*, February 11, 2002, 18.
28. Ken Jones and Michael Pearce, "The Geography of Markets: Spatial Analysis for Retailers," *Ivey Business Journal*, March/April 1999, 66–70.
29. Ryan Bigge, "Lifestyles of the Not So Rich and Famous," *Marketing Magazine*, October 15, 2001, 8; Amy Merrick, "The 2000 Count: Counting on the Census—New Data Will Let Starbucks Plan Store Openings, Help Blockbuster Stock Its Videos," *Wall Street Journal*, February 14, 2001, B1.
30. Bryan Tenenhouse and Steve Murray, "Direct Mail Goes Big," *Marketing Magazine*, April 16, 2001.
31. Canadian Press, "Federal Burger Study Offers Food for Thought (Environment Canada)," *Canadian Press NewsWire*, January 5, 1997.
32. David Armstrong, "Here's to the Net," *Wall Street Journal*, April 23, 2001, R30. Used with permission; Averil Joseph, "Marketing's Guide to Liquor Advertising Regulations," *Marketing Magazine*, August 20, 2001; Labatt website, www.labatt.com; Labatt Blue website, www.labattblue.ca; Bud Light Institute website, www.budlight.ca; Molson website, www.molson.com; and The Molson Canadian website, www.iam.ca.

33. Ginger Cooper, "Centricity," *Customer Relationship Management*, December 2001, 35–40.
34. Dennis J. Chapman, "Clients, Customers and Buyers," *Customer Relationship Management*, March 2001, 65–71.
35. Anick Jesdanun, "AOL Gambit Works A-OK," *Fort Worth Star Telegram*, January 3, 2001, 1C, 3C.
36. Tricia Bisoux, "Niche Marketing Makes Its Mark," *Biz Ed*, November/December 2001, 45–47.
37. Lisa Bannon, "Let's Play Makeover Barbie," *Wall Street Journal*, February 17, 2000, B1, B4.
38. Ryan Bigge, "One Beer, Two Solitudes," *Marketing Magazine*, May 5, 2003, 12–13.
39. "Can Levi's Be Cool Again?" *Business Week*, March 13, 2000, 144, 148.
40. Danny Kucharsky, "Mega Bloks Target Kids at Retail," *Marketing Magazine*, November 12, 2001, 4.
41. D'Arcy Jenish, "Up in the Air," *Macleans*, April 2, 2001.
42. Patrice Carle, "Shelving a Tired Image," *Marketing Magazine*, September 16, 2002, 13.
43. Ian Johnson, "Herbal Remedies Aimed at East and West," *Wall Street Journal*, January 31, 2000, A26.

Chapter 7

1. Mark David Campbell, "No More Blind Ducks," *Marketing Magazine*, September 27, 1999.
2. "Fantastic Voyage," *Fast Company*, March 2000, 178–200.
3. Ingrid Button, "Turning the Export Ship Around," *Marketing Magazine*, August 27, 2001, 23.
4. "Why Some Customers Are More Equal Than Others," *Fortune*, September 19, 1994, 215–24.
5. Kendra Parker, "Got Questions? All You Have to Do Is Ask," *American Demographics*, November 1999, 36–39.
6. Canadian Press, "Winesicles Starts as Joke, Could Be Big Business," *Canadian Press NewsWire*, November 19, 1997.
7. Eve Lazarus, "Asking for Their Number," *Marketing Magazine*, August 5, 2002, 15.
8. www.casro.org, October 29, 2001.
9. Eileen Moran, "Managing the Minefields of Global Product Development," *Quirk's Marketing Research Review*, November 2000, 24–28. Used with permission.
10. Molly Williams, "Monkey See," *Wall Street Journal*, April 23, 2001, R32. Used with permission.
11. Dana James, "The Future of Online Research," *Marketing News*, January 3, 2000, 1, 11.
12. Chris Yalonis, "The Revolution in E-research," *CASRO Journal*, 1999, 131–34.
13. Ibid.
14. Canadian Media Directors' Council, "*Media Digest*, 2003–04," published in *Marketing Magazine*, 55–59; Dana James, "Precision Decision," *Marketing News*, September 27, 1999, 23–24.
15. This section was adapted from James Watt, "Using the Internet for Quantitative Survey Research," *Quirk's Marketing Research Review*, June/July 1997, 67–71.
16. Carl McDaniel and Roger Gates, *Contemporary Marketing Research*, 5th ed. (Cincinnati: International Thomson Publishing, 2002).
17. Phone conversation between Kevin Bender, Information Resources, Inc., and Carl McDaniel on April 17, 2000.
18. David Menzies, "Four First Class Flops," *Marketing Magazine*, April 23, 2001.
19. Michael McCullough, "Truth Is Out There," *Marketing Magazine*, September 28, 1998.
20. Sheena Sharp, "New Techniques for Corporate Foresight," *Research Conference Report*, May 1998, 7–8.

Chapter 8

1. Shirley Won, "Toy Maker Plays a Different Game," *The Globe and Mail*, January 3, 2004, B1, B4; Marina Strauss, "Hot Mexican Bean Toy Gets Retailers Jumping for More," *The Globe and Mail*, September 19, 2003, B1, B2; www.spinmaster.com; www.mightybeanz.com.
2. Shawna Richer, "Guitars for Stars," *The Globe and Mail*, October 1, 2003, R1, R2.
3. "Oral-B Unveils Age-Pegged Toothbrushes for Kids," *BusinessWeek Online*, October 4, 2001. www.businessweek.com/reuters_market/8/REUT-8KW.IITM.
4. "GM Isn't Giving Up on the Pontiac Aztec Yet," *WSJ.com*, November 27, 2001, interactive.wsj.com.
5. Teri Agins, "Hilfiger Returns to Preppy Roots, but Sales Slump," *Wall Street Journal*, February 2, 2001, B1, B6.
6. Christine Bittar, "Shiseido Rolls Color, Light and $7M in Major Cosmetic Repositioning," *Brandweek*, October 16, 2000, 6.
7. Sonia Reyes, "Minute Maid Juices Up Calcium Fortified Line," *Brandweek*, March 13, 2000, 323.
8. Mike Beirne, "Hershey Chews on Gum, Mint Plans; Jolly Rancher Eyes Preemptive Strike," *Brandweek*, February 26, 2001, 9.
9. Katrina Brooker, "A Game of Inches," *Fortune*, February 5, 2001, 98–100.
10. Steve Erwin, "Big Harv Aimed at Big Boys," *The Windsor Star*, September 18, 2003, E2.
11. Gerry Khermouch, Stanley Holmes, and Moon Ihlwan, "The Best Global Brands," *Business Week*, August 6, 2001, 50–57.
12. Betsy McKay, "Drinks for Developing Countries," *Wall Street Journal*, November 27, 2001, B1, B6. Used with permission.
13. Brian O'Keefe, "Global Brands," *Fortune*, November 26, 2001, 102–10.
14. Fara Warner, "C'Mon, Get Closer," *Fast Company*, August 2001, 129–39.
15. Matthew Boyle, "Brand Killers," *Fortune*, August 11, 2003, 88–100; Lauren Gold and Michael Gold, "Change the Rules of Private-Label Parkaging," *The Marketing News*, November 22, 1999, 20–21; Susan Bourette, "Private Label Share," *The Globe and Mail*, November 30, 1998, B1, B3.
16. Peter Galuszka and Wendy Zellner, "Soap Opera at Wal-Mart," *Business Week*, August 16, 1999, 44.
17. Marina Strauss, "Zellers Takes Page from Target," *The Globe and Mail*, April 19, 2003, B3.
18. Mike Beirne, "Hey, Partner: Ramada Joins AmEx, Continental in Big Co-Brand Push," *Brandweek*, November 13, 2000, 18.
19. Frederic M. Biddle, "American Express, Lexus in Co-Brand Pact," *Wall Street Journal*, February 9, 2000, B12.
20. Stephanie Thompson, "The Mouse in the Food Aisle," *Advertising Age*, September 10, 2001, 73.
21. Michelle Wirth Fellman, "Ti-Gear: Owning Up to a Name," *Marketing News*, October 26, 1998, 2; www.golfgearin.com; www.iwantgolf.com.
22. Sonia Reyes, "Sunsweet Updates Look, Tells Families: 'Be Good,'" *Brandweek*, February 7, 2000, 10.
23. Jonathan Eig, "Food Companies Grab Kids' Attention by Packaging Products as Toys, Games," *WSJ.com*, October 26, 2001, interactive.wsj.com.
24. Kenneth Hein, "Miracle-Gro Seeds TV, Radio, Print; $20M Push Targets Spring Planters," *Brandweek*, February 12, 2001, 4.

25. Gerry Khermouch, "Guinness Pours It On in Chicago," *Brandweek*, February 28, 2000, 18.
26. Herbert M. Meyers, "The Internet's Threat to Branding," *Brandweek*, December 4, 2000, 30.

Chapter 9

1. Ted Whipp, "Heinz Star Search," *The Windsor Star*, May 21, 2003, B3; www.junkfoodnews.com/purpleketchup.htm; Parija Bhatnagar, "Blue Food Goes Down the Drain," *cnnmoney*, June 20, 2003 at www.money.cnn.com/2003/06/17/news/companies/failed_food; John Heinzl, "Heinz Serves Up Funky Fries As Firms Focus on Fun Foods," *The Globe and Mail*, February 12, 2002, B2.
2. William J. Holstein, "Dump the Cookware," *Business 2.0*, May 1, 2001, 69–72.
3. Gary Strauss, "Squeezing New from Old," *USA Today*, January 4, 2000, B1, B2.
4. Sonia Reyes, "Groove Tube," *Brandweek*, October 16, 2000, M111.
5. David Koenig, "Product Adds Softer Touch to Tissue Issue," *Fort Worth Star-Telegram*, January 17, 2001, C1.
6. Strauss, "Squeezing New from Old," B1.
7. Gerry Khermouch, "Beefeater Gin Sets New Bottle, First Radio Ads on Renewal Drive," *Brandweek*, December 4, 2000, 17.
8. Strauss, "Squeezing New from Old," B2.
9. Ted Whipp, "Food Giants Respond to Low-Carb Craze," *The Windsor Star*, January 7, 2004, B3; John Heinzl, "Canadian Thirst Grows for Imported Beer," *The Globe and Mail*, July 10, 2003, B1, B8; Philip Demont, "Canada Drier," *The Windsor Star*, March 1, 2000, B3, B5.
10. "Acquire a Taste for Lower Cholesterol," *Fort Worth Star-Telegram*, June 25, 2001, 3D.
11. Anna Muoio, "GM Has a New Model for Change," *Fortune*, December 2000, 62–64.
12. Alex Taylor III, "Kellogg Cranks Up Its Idea Machine," *Fortune*, July 5, 1999, 181–82.
13. Reyes, "Groove Tube," M114.
14. "Phytol Products Take Market Test," *Food Ingredients News*, August 2001, on-line.
15. Philip Brasher, "Teens Sample Milk from Vending Machines," *Fort Worth Star-Telegram*, April 5, 2001, 10A.
16. John Gaffney, "How Do You Feel about a $44 Tooth-Bleaching Kit?" *Business 2.0*, October 2001, 125–27.
17. Ibid.
18. Summarized from a catalogue entitled, "Roadtrek: The Motorhome That Drives Like a Van," *Home & Park Motorhomes*, 100 Shirley Avenue, Kitchener, Ontario, N2B 2E1.
19. David W. Cravens, *Strategic Marketing*, 6e (New York: Irwin McGraw-Hill, 2000), 235.
20. Gregory L. White, "How the Chevy Name Landed on SUV Using Russian Technology," *Wall Street Journal*, February 20, 2001, A1, A8.
21. Karby Leggett, "GM Confirms Plans to Produce Less Costly Buick for the Chinese," *Wall Street Journal*, October 24, 2000, A21.
22. Michael Flagg, "Coca-Cola Is Adopting Strategy in Asia of Inventing Drinks Tied to Local Tastes," *Wall Street Journal*, July 30, 2001, B9C.
23. Ibid.
24. Alessandra Galloni, "Coke to Launch Powerade Drink Across Europe," *Wall Street Journal*, October 16, 2001, B11E.
25. A.J. Faria, "Major Automotive Assembler Investment Announcements," *Automotive Parts Manufacturers' Association*, Toronto, Ontario, January 8, 2004; "2003 Global Market Data Book," *Automotive News Europe*, June 16, 2003; Dennis DesRosiers, "New 'Canada-Only' Vehicles," *DesRosiers Automotive Reports*, www.desrosiers.ca, January 15, 2004.
26. James Daly, "Restart, Redo, Recharge," *Business 2.0*, May 1, 2001, 11.

Chapter 10

1. Chuck Salter, "On the Road Again," *Fast Company*, January 2002, 50–58; www.myyellow.com.
2. *Statistics Canada*, www.ic.gc.ca, Canadian Industry Statistics, Trade Data On-Line, CANSIM table 282-0008, January 8, 2004.
3. *Statistics Canada*, www.ic.gc.ca, Canadian Industry Statistics, Employment by Industry (based on NAICS), CANSIM tables 282-0088 and 282-0089, January 8, 2004.
4. Christina Binkley, "From Orange Shag to Pin Stripes: Sheraton Gets a Makeover," *Wall Street Journal*, April 19, 2000, B1, B10.
5. Valarie A Zeithaml and Mary Jo Bitner, *Services Marketing* (New York: McGraw-Hill, 2000).
6. Susan Greco, "Fanatics!" *Inc.*, April 2001, 35–48.
7. Zeithaml and Bitner, *Services Marketing*.
8. Chris Daniels, "A Room for all Seasons," *Marketing*, February 4, 2002, 6, 7.
9. Much of the material in this section is based on Christopher H. Lovelock, *Services Marketing* (Upper Saddle River, NJ: Prentice-Hall, 2001), 39–41.
10. Wendy Perrin, "Bells and Whistles," Special business supplement 2000 to *Conde Nast Traveler*, 21–22.
11. Ibid.
12. Susan Kuchinskas, "Organic San Francisco," *IQnews*, February 14, 2000, 36.
13. Lovelock, *Services Marketing*, 262–65.
14. Lovelock, *Services Marketing*, 149–50.
15. Much of the material in this section is based on Leonard L. Berry and A. Parasuraman, *Marketing Services* (New York: Free Press, 1991), 132–50.
16. Sue Shellenberger, "To Win the Loyalty of Your Employees, Try a Softer Touch," *Wall Street Journal*, January 26, 2000, B1.
17. Berry and Parasuraman, *Marketing Services*, 151–52.
18. Ellen Graham, "Marriott's Bid to Patch the Child-Care Gap Gets a Reality Check," *Wall Street Journal*, February 2, 2000, B1.
19. Richard Bloom, "Canadian CEOs View Their Companies as World Class: Poll," *The Globe and Mail*, January 21, 2004, B1, B5.
20. *Statistics Canada*, CANSIM Catalogue no. 71F0004XCB, January 8, 2004.
21. "Wal-Mart's Famous Service with a Smile? Not in Germany," *National Post*, October 31, 2000, B5.
22. *Canada NewsWire*, "Midnight Movie Marathon at Rainbow Cinemas to Benefit Two Charities," January 21, 2004, 1, www.gateway.proquest.com.
23. A graduate class under the guidance of Professor David Bussiere (bussiere@uwindsor.ca) at the University of Windsor has undertaken a study of this product in the Canadian market.

Chapter 11

1. "Grocery Gateway and STAPLES Business Depot—Bringing Home Office Supplies Home," *Canada NewsWire*, November 18, 2003, 1; Gillian Livingston, "Grocery Gateway Inc.," *Canadian Press NewsWire*, February 2, 2003, 3; "Grocery Gateway—The New Way to Deliver a Gourmet Café Experience to the Office," *Canada NewsWire*, March 19, 2002, 1; Michelle Warren, "Web Grocer Thrives on Partnerships," *Marketing Magazine*, December 9, 2002, 23.

2. "Dell Seizes No. 1 Market Position in U.S. Corporate Desktop PC Sales," September 10, 1997, Dell Computer Corporation press release, www.dell.com.
3. Nicole Harris, " 'Private Exchanges' May Allow B-to-B Commerce to Thrive After All," *Wall Street Journal*, March 16, 2001, B1; Michael Totty, "The Next Phase," *Wall Street Journal*, May 21, 2001, R8.
4. Amy Merrick and Emily Nelson, "Sears Says Stores Won't Sell Makeup, a Setback for Avon's New Line," *Wall Street Journal*, July 11, 2001, B1.
5. Gary McWilliams and Kortney Stringer, "Dell Tries Selling in Kiosks, on TV as PC Sales Drop," *Wall Street Journal*, December 20, 2001, B1.
6. Wade Lambert, "Publisher Puts Story Machines in London Tube," *Wall Street Journal*, February 22, 2001, B1.
7. Matthew Schifrin, "Partner or Perish," *Forbes Best of the Web*, May 21, 2001, 26; Jonathan Eig, "H.J. Heinz, Japan's Kagome Agree to Investments as Part of Alliance," *Wall Street Journal*, July 26, 2001, B11.
8. Jonathan Welsh, "Auto Makers Now 'Slam' Cars Right in the Factory," *Wall Street Journal*, October 30, 2001, B1.
9. Matthew Boyle, "Supply Chains Get Sexy," *Fortune*, December 12, 2001, 272.
10. Owen Keates, "Flow Control," *Management*, March 2001, 28.
11. Rob Wherry, "Ice Cream Wars: Dreyer's Conquered Supermarket Freezers. Now It's Going After the Corner Store," *Forbes*, May 28, 2001, 160.
12. Leigh Muzslay, "Shoes That Morph from Sneakers to Skates Are Flying Out of Stores," *Wall Street Journal*, July 26, 2001, B1.
13. Shelly Branch, "P&G Buys Iams: Will Pet-Food Fight Follow?" *Wall Street Journal*, August 12, 1999, B1, B4.
14. Evan Ramstad, "Inside Radio Shack's Surprising Turnaround," *Wall Street Journal*, June 8, 1999, B1, B16.
15. Ellen Neuborne, "Big Brands (Small Companies)," *Business Week*, August 13, 2001, 12.
16. Norihiko Shirouzu, "Fickle Consumers Force Auto Makers to Be More Flexible," *Wall Street Journal*, September 10, 2001, B8.
17. Carlita Vitzthum, "Just-in-Time Fashion," *Wall Street Journal*, May 18, 2001, B1; Julie Creswell, "Confessions of a Fashion Victim," *Fortune*, December 10, 2001, 48.
18. Thomas A. Foster, "3PL's Serve Up Supply Chain Innovation," *Logistics Management & Distribution Report*, November 1999.
19. Shirley Won, "Fallout from CN Strike Continues," *The Globe and Mail*, February 25, 2004, B4.
20. Ross, *Competing through Supply Chain Management*, 232.
21. Russ Dixon, "Tomorrow's Warehouse," *Snack Food & Wholesale Bakery*, May 2000, TD10.
22. "Transportation and the Economy," Transport Canada, www.tc.gc.ca/pol/en/Report/anre2002/2H_e.htm, 2002.
23. James Aaron Cooke, "Clicks and Mortar," *Logistics Management & Distribution Report*, January 31, 2000.
24. James Aaron Cooke, "Making the Global Connection," *Logistics Management & Distribution Report*, June 1999.
25. Caitlin Kelly, "Rolling Onward," *Supply Chain Management* on-line, September 30, 2001.
26. Renee Boucher Ferguson, "Outsourcing Supply Chains," *eWeek*, April 2, 2001, 17.
27. "Ford Hands Off Vehicle Delivery to Third Party," *Logistics Management & Distribution Report*, March 2000.
28. Michael Selz, "Outsourcing Firms Venture Beyond Primary Functions," *Wall Street Journal*, June 26, 2001, B2.
29. Don Clark, "Canceled Programs: Software Is Becoming an Online Service, Shaking Up an Industry," *Wall Street Journal*, July 21, 1999, A1, A6.
30. Rhonda L. Rundle, "New Battlefield for E-Tickets: Home Printers," *Wall Street Journal*, February 17, 2000, B1, B4; Bruce Orwall, "Six Theater Chains Will Join in Venture to Sell Movie Tickets via Web, Phone," *Wall Street Journal*, March 3, 2000, B4.
31. Nick Wingfield, "Digital Video Recorders Stir Up a New Battle," *Wall Street Journal*, December 17, 2001, B4; Jon Healy, "Studios Spur Measures to Thwart Digital Piracy," *Los Angeles Times*, January 18, 2002, C1; Amy Harmon, "A Wave of Video Piracy," *San Diego Union-Tribune*, February 11, 2002; Scott Wooley, "Steal This Movie," *Forbes*, February 18, 2001, 66.
32. Ken Bensinger, "Can You Spot the Fake?" *Wall Street Journal*, February 16, 2001, W1; Todd Zaun and Karby Leggett, "Motorcycle Makers from Japan Discover Piracy Made in China," *Wall Street Journal*, July 25, 2001, A1.
33. Alejandro Reyes, "Against a World of Giants," *AsiaWeek* wire report, February 2, 2001; Todd Zaun and Karby Leggett, "Motorcycle Makers from Japan Discover Piracy Made in China," *Wall Street Journal*, July 25, 2001, A1; "Meeting of the Minds," *Supply Chain Management Review* on-line, September 30, 2001; Andrew Tanzer, "Chinese Walls," *Forbes*, November 12, 2001, 74.
34. Louis Uchitelle, "Globalization Marches On, as U.S. Eases Up on the Reins," *New York Times* on-line, December 17, 2001.
35. Jon E. Hilsenrath, "Globalization Persists in Precarious New Age," *Wall Street Journal*, December 31, 2001, A1.
36. Kevin Hogan, "Borderline Savings," *Business 2.0*, May 17, 2001, 34. © 2001 Time Inc. All rights reserved.
37. Richard Gibson, "Merchants Mull the Long and the Short of Lines," *Wall Street Journal*, September 3, 1998, B1, B4.
38. Neal Templin, "Electronic Kiosks Check In Guests at More Hotels," *Wall Street Journal*, February 16, 1999, B1, B4.
39. "Air Canada Extends Simplified Internet Fares to U.S. Flights," *The Globe and Mail*, January 27, 2004, B2.
40. Patrick Barta, "Home Rules," *Wall Street Journal*, October 29, 2001, R12.

Chapter 12

1. Susan Thorne, "Canadian Retailers Expanding Around the World," *International Council of Shopping Centers*, May 2002, www.icsc.org; Report on Market Shares, "Market Shares Report: Retail," *Marketing Magazine*, May 27, 2002; Stan Sutter, "Retail Rationalism," *Marketing Magazine*, August 27, 2001, 34; Global 500, *Fortune Magazine*, July 21, 2003, 106; James Pollock, "Canada Tougher Than U.S. Stores Thought," *Marketing Magazine*, July 3–10, 1995, 4.
2. Statistics Canada, "Economic Conditions: Labour Market," *Canadian Statistics*, www.statcan.ca, accessed November 30, 2003.
3. Statistics Canada, "Annual Retail Trade," *The Daily*, April 11, 2003;
4. David Schulz, "The Nation's Biggest Retail Companies," *Stores* on-line, July 1, 2001.
5. V&S Department Stores website, www.truserv.ca; SAAN Stores website, www.saan.ca; The Northwest Company website, www.northwest.ca; Hart Department Stores website, www.hartstores.com.

6. David Schultz, "The Definitive Ranking of the Nation's Biggest Specialty Chains," *Stores* on-line, August 2001.
7. Moores Clothing for Men website, www.mooresclothing.com.
8. Leigh Gallagher, "Rebound," *Forbes*, May 3, 1999, 60.
9. Statistics Canada, "Population by Sex and Age Group," *Canadian Statistics, Families, Households and Housing*, www.statcan.ca, accessed November 7, 2003.
10. Don Little and Leslie Bennett, "Food Services Competition in the 1990s," *Analytical Paper Series: Services Indicators*, Statistics Canada, July 2000.
11. Joel A. Baglole, "Loblaw Supermarkets Add Fitness Clubs to Offerings," *Wall Street Journal*, December 27, 1999, B4.
12. Alexei Barrionuevo and Ann Zimmerman, "Lastest Supermarket Special—Gasoline," *Wall Street Journal*, April 30, 2001, B1.
13. Lisa Rostoks, "The Changing Profile of the Consumer," *Canadian Grocer*, March 2003, 32.
14. Carini, "Retailing," 12.
15. Press Release, "Convenience Store Chain Couche-Tard's Q3 Profit Drops 40%, Stock Falls 14%," *Canadian Press NewsWire*, March 16, 2004; "Couche-Tard Profit Up 27% on Acquisitions: Dairy Mart was Highlight," *National Post*, [National Edition], July 4, 2003, FP.6.
16. Wal-Mart website, www.walmart.com.
17. Emily Nelson, "Overhauling Its Web Site, Wal-Mart Will Push Toys and Electronics," *Wall Street Journal*, October 1, 1999, B1, B4.
18. Jeffrey Arlen, "Zellers: Carving Out a New Niche," *Discount Store News*, 1999, 38/4, 8; and Sarah Dobson, "Zellers Pushes New Mossimo Label," *Marketing Magazine*, March 17, 2003, 4.
19. Schulz, "The Nation's Biggest Retail Companies."
20. Tony Lisanti, "Extreme Segment, Extreme Growth," *Discount Store News*, July 26, 1999, 13.
21. Company News Release, "Toys "R" Us Reports Fourth Quarter and 2000 Fiscal Year Results," March 7, 2001.
22. Ann Zimmerman, "Taking Aim at Costco, Sam's Club, Marshals, Diamonds, and Pearls," *Wall Street Journal*, August 9, 2001, A1.
23. Ray A. Smith, "Outlet Centers Go Upmarket with Amenities," *Wall Street Journal*, June 6, 2001, B12.
24. Don Little and Leslie Bennett, "Food Services Competition in the 1990s," *Analytical Paper Series: Services Indicators*, Statistics Canada, July 2000; Canadian Restaurant and Foodservices Association website, "Research: Canada's Foodservice Industry," www.crfa.ca, accessed December 8, 2003.
25. Eatzi's Market and Bakery website at www.eatzis.com.
26. Rodney Ho, "Vending Machines Make Change," *Wall Street Journal*, July 7, 1999, B1, B4; Statistics Canada, "Non-Store Retailers," *The Daily*, July 25, 2003.
27. Cathleen Egan, "Vending-Machine Technology Matures, Offering Branded Foods, Convenience," *Wall Street Journal*, December 13, 2001, B13; *Dow Jones Newswire*, "Pepsi Plans to Launch New Vending Machines That Take Credit Cards," December 13, 2001.
28. Elizabeth Lee, "Parties That Sell," *Atlanta Journal-Constitution*, September 6, 2001, BE12; Pampered Chef, "Canadian Web site Connection," www.pamperedchef.com, accessed December 10, 2003.
29. Dennis Berman, "Is the Bell Tolling for Door-to-Door Selling? *Business Week*, November 1, 1999. 58–60; Rachel Beck, "Amway Puts Direct Selling Model Online," *Marketing News*, March 29, 1999, 12.
30. Amy Lo, "Selling Dreams the Mary Kay Way," *AsiaWeek*, June 29, 2001.
31. Chris Daniels, "Justwhiteshirts.com to Open Stores," *Marketing Magazine*, January 7, 2002, 2; Marketing Direct: Briefs, "U.S. Marketers to Spend More on DRTV," *Marketing Magazine*, August 19, 2002, 12.
32. Hailey Biback, "Address for Success: Thinking Outside of the (Mail) Box," *Canadian Printer*, February 2001, 24.
33. Dell Computer website, www.dell.com/us/en/gen/corporate.
34. "Telemarketing Fact Sheet," CRTC website, www.crtc.gc.ca.
35. The Shopping Channel website, www.theshoppingchannel.com.
36. Canadian Media Directors' Council, "*Media Digest*, 2003–04," *Marketing Magazine*, 2003, 55–59.
37. Statistics Canada, "Electronic Commerce and Technology," *The Daily*, April 2, 2003.
38. CDNow website, www.CDNow.com.
39. Amazon.com website, www.Amazon.com.
40. Winnipeg Outfitters website, www.outfitters.ca, accessed December 10, 2003.
41. The Online Group of the National Retail Federation website, www.shop.org; Ernst & Young press release, "Despite Dot.com Woes, On-line Retailing Growth in 2000 Confirmed by New Ernst & Young Global Study," *Business Wire*, January 15, 2002; "Amazon.com: The First Global Cyber-Brand," *Ernst & Young Global Online Retail Report* at Stores on-line, January 2000, 24; Amazon.com press release, "Amazon.com Announces 4th Quarter Profit," www.Amazon.com, January 22, 2002.
42. Michelle Warren, "Plugged In," *Marketing Magazine*, November 19, 2001; Chris Daniels, "Keeping Control of Explosive Growth," *Marketing Magazine*, November 17, 2003.
43. Alexandra Peers and Nick Wingfield, "Sotheby's, eBay Team Up to Sell Fine Art Online," *Wall Street Journal*, January 31, 2002, B8.
44. Canadian Franchise Association, "Canadian Franchise Association Members," www.cfa.ca.
45. Canadian Franchise Directory website, www.franchisedirectory.ca; "Canadian Franchise Market," Royal Bank of Canada website, www.royalbank.com/franchise/market_ca.html; International Franchise Association website, www.franchise.org.
46. Domino's Pizza website, www.dominos.com/Franchise.
47. Brian O'Keefe, "Global Brands," *Fortune*, November 26, 2001, 104.
48. Louise Lee, "Gap: Missing That Ol' Mickey Magic," *Business Week*, October 29, 2001, 86–88.
49. Robert Beaudoin And Daniel Charron, "Dressing Up Croteau," *Marketing Magazine*, September 16, 2002.
50. Chris Daniels, "AOV Takes Its Steam to the Suburbs," *Marketing Magazine*, October 2, 2002.
51. Scott Gardiner, "A Truly Awesome Database," *Marketing Magazine*, April 29, 2002.
52. Eleena De Lisser, "Online Retailers Slice and Dice Niches Thinner Than Julienne Fries," *Wall Street Journal*, November 29, 1999, B1, B6.
53. "An Exclusive Club," *Chain Store Age*, October 1998; Calendar Club website, www.calendarclub.com.
54. Canadian Tire web site, www.canadiantire.ca; President's Choice website, www.presidentschoice.ca; Report On Market Shares, "Beverages," *Marketing Magazine*, June 5, 2000, 13.

55. Jennifer Campbell , "FCUK's Risque Ads Get the Boot," *CanWest News*, Don Mills, Ontario, October 20, 2003, 1.
56. West Edmonton Mall website, www.westedmontonmall.com.
57. Dean Starkman, "The Mall, Without the Haul," *Wall Street Journal*, July 25, 2001, B1.
58. Anne Faircloth, "Value Retailers Go Dollar for Dollar," *Fortune*, July 6, 1998, 164–66.
59. Emily Nelson, "Why Wal-Mart Sings, 'Yes, We Have Bananas!'" *Wall Street Journal*, October 6, 1998, B1, B4.
60. Kate Murphy, "A Sales Pitch Right Under Your Nose," *New York Times*, September 13, 1998, 8.
61. Chad Terhune, "Home Depot's Home Improvement," *Wall Street Journal*, March 8, 2001, B1.
62. Canadian Online Shopping Mall, www.homer.ca/shopping; Totty, "Making the Sale," *Wall Street Journal*, November 24, 2001, R6.
63. John C. Koopman, "Successful Global Retailers: A Rare Breed," *Canadian Manager*, Spring 2000, 22.
64. Lesley Young, "Holt's 'Flick' Celebrates Film, Fashion," *Marketing Magazine*, September 8, 2003.
65. "More Consumers Shopping at Super Centers," *Chain Store Age* on-line, February 4, 2002.
66. Jennifer Ralston, "Beyond Pill Pushing," *Marketing Magazine*, March 27, 2000.
67. Susan Reda, "On-line Retail Grows Up," *Stores on-line*, February 2002.
68. Jack Neff, "Dawn of the Online Icebox," *Advertising Age*, March 15, 1999, 7.
69. Newsline, "New Optimum Visa Debuts," *Marketing Magazine*, May 13, 2002; Shoppers Drug Mart website, www.shoppersdrugmart.ca, accessed January 13, 2004.
70. Statistics Canada, "The Economy," Canadian Statistics, www.statcan.ca, accessed November 3, 2003;
71. Jeffery A. Tannenbaum, "Beverage Marketers See Refreshing Distribution Possibilities," *Wall Street Journal*, May 29, 2001, B2. Used with permission.
72. David Cohen, "Dominion Citrus Incorporated," *e-Research*, The Independent Equity Research Corporation, sourced from Dominion Citrus website, www.dominioncitrus.com, accessed January 15, 2004.
73. Ken Mark, "Radio Beacon Launches New Demand Forecasting Module for Its WMS," *Canadian Transportation Logistics*, October 2003, 21.
74. Press Release, "Core-Mark Extends Cognos Extranet to Customers Across North America," *Canada NewsWire*, Ottawa: March 19, 2002.
75. Press Release, "Taiga Forest Products Acquires California Distribution Business," *Canada NewsWire*, Ottawa: November 18, 2002.
76. Doris Montanera, "Jane Ip Has a Firm Handle on Canada's Handbag Market," *CanWest News*, September 8, 2003.

Chapter 13

1. Jean-Marc Leger and Dave Scholz, "Back From the Saturation Brink," *Marketing Magazine*, December 1, 2003, 40–41; Chris Powell, "Where Is Media Heading?" *Marketing Magazine*, December 1, 2003, 33–36; "Four Views of Media's Future," *Marketing Magazine*, December 1, 2003, 37–39.
2. Michelle Warren, "Allstream Speaks with Its Customers," *Marketing Magazine*, October 27, 2003, 3.
3. CBC, "U.S., Canada Debating Anti-Spam Laws," *CBC News Online*, Thursday, October 23, 2003; Robin Rowland, "Spam, Spam, Spam: The Cyberspace Wars," *CBC News Online*, November 24, 2003, updated March 12, 2004; Frank Witsil, "Spam I Am," *Tampa Tribune*, February 9, 2002, 1; Frances Katz, "Putting the Lid on SPAM: Almost Everybody Hates the Kudzu of E-mail, but There's No Magic Formula," *Atlanta Journal and Constitution*, August 5, 2001, Q1; "Privacy Action," *Advertising Age*, October 15, 2001, 14; Donna Gillin, "Privacy Issues Take Center Stage in 2001," *Marketing Research*, Spring 2001, 36; William M. Savino and Stephen J. Smirti, Jr., "Privacy Please!" *Marketing Management*, Winter 2000, 46.
4. Karin Scott, "Beyond Press Coverage," *Marketing Magazine*, June 16, 2003, 14.
5. Stephanie Thompson, "Marketers Embrace Latest Health Claims," *Advertising Age*, February 28, 2000, 20–22.
6. Mark Etting, "Wal-Mart's Spoils," *Marketing Magazine*, June 16, 2003, 23.
7. "Promo Shorts," *Marketing Magazine*, September 3, 2001, P4.
8. "Showering in the Streets," *Marketing Magazine*, May 21, 2001, 1.
9. Frank G. Bingham, Jr., Charles J. Quigley, Jr., and Elaine M. Notarantonio, "The Use of Communication Style in a Buyer–Seller Dyad: Improving Buyer–Seller Relationships," Proceedings: Association of Marketing Theory and Practice, 1996 Annual Meeting, Hilton Head, South Carolina, March 1996, 188–95.
10. Michael Beverland, "Relationship Selling and the Selling Dyad," *Journal of Personal Selling & Sales Management*, Summer 2001, 207.
11. Lara Mills, "Campaigns with Legs," *Marketing Magazine*, May 15, 2000.
12. Philip J. Kitchen, "Marketing Communications Renaissance," *Internal Journal of Advertising* 12 (1993), 367–86.
13. Ibid, 372.
14. Paul-Mark Rendon, "Ristorante Sets Up Shop," *Marketing Magazine*, February 24, 2003, 1.
15. The AIDA concept is based on the classic research of E. K. Strong, Jr., as theorized in *The Psychology of Selling and Advertising* (New York: McGraw-Hill, 1925) and "Theories of Selling," *Journal of Applied Psychology* 9 (1925), 75–86.
16. Thomas E. Barry and Daniel J. Howard, "A Review and Critique of the Hierarchy of Effects in Advertising," *International Journal of Advertising* 9 (1990), 121–35.
17. Bill Adams, "Talking about Integrated Communications," *Public Relations Tactics*, February 2001, 26.
18. Brad Zeller, "Lord of the Rings Redux," *Publishers Weekly*, September 10, 2001, 23, used with permission; J.D. Andrews, "The Lord of the Onion Rings: Burger King Is Offering Magical Premiums to Hungry Fellowship Fans," *Point of Purchase*, December 2001, 6.
19. Canadian Media Directors' Council, "Ethnic Media," *Media Digest*, 2003–04, 66.
20. Lynne Eagle, Philip Kitchen, Ken Hyde, Wina Fourie, and Mani Padisetti, "Perceptions of Integrated Marketing Communications among Marketers and Ad Agency Executives in New Zealand," *International Journal of Advertising*, February 1999, 79–94.
21. Elana Harris, "Standing Tall," *Sales & Marketing Management*, December 2000, 84.
22. Michael Beverland, "Contextual Influences and the Adoption and Practice of Relationship Selling in a Business-to-Business Setting: An Exploratory Study," *Journal of Personal Selling & Sales Management*, Summer 2001, 207.
23. Richard Morrison, "The Business Process of Customer Retention and Loyalty," *Customer Interaction Solutions*, October 2001, 4.

24. "The Right Questions and Attitudes Can Beef Up Your Sales, Improve Customer Retention," *Selling*, June 2001, 3.
25. Erika Rasmusson, "How to Manage Long Term Leads," *Sales & Marketing Management*, January 1998, 77.
26. Roger Brooksbank, "The New Model of Personal Selling: Micro-Marketing," *Journal of Personal Selling & Sales Management*, Spring 1995, 61–66; Donald W. Jackson, Jr., "Relationship Selling: The Personalization of Relationship Marketing," *Asia-Australia Marketing Journal*, August 1994, 45–54.
27. Jean Halliday, "Ford Finds E-Leads Productive," *Advertising Age*, January 22, 2001, 28.
28. Sarah Lorge, "The Best Way to Prospect," *Sales & Marketing Management*, January 1988, 80; Tricia Campbell, "What's a Referral Worth to You?" *Sales & Marketing Management*, September 1997, 103.
29. Alf Nucifora, "Need Leads? Try a Networking Group," *Business News New Jersey*, November 14, 2000, 22.
30. Mike Grebb, "The Customer Connection: Living Up to Your Sales Pitch," www.sammag.com, March 1, 2001.
31. "Leads Are a Terrible Thing to Waste," *Sales & Marketing Management*, August 1997, 108; Center for Strategic Communication.
32. Marvin A. Jolson and Thomas R. Wortruba, "Selling and Sales Management in Action: Prospecting: A New Look at This Old Challenge," *Journal of Personal Selling & Sales Management*, Fall 1992, 59–66.
33. Janelle Rice, "Show and Sell: Filling the Sales Manager's Shoes," *Sales*, www.sammag.com, July 2001.
34. Robyn Griggs, "Qualifying Leads Online," *Sales & Marketing Management*, July 1997, 68.
35. Marvin A. Jolson, "Broadening the Scope of Relationship Selling," *Journal of Personal Selling and Sales Management*, Fall 1997, 75.
36. Adapted from Bob Kimball, *Successful Selling* (Chicago: American Marketing Association, 1994).
37. "Five Steps to Wrapping Up a Sales Call," *Sales & Marketing Management*, January 1998, 75.
38. Jolson, "Broadening the Scope of Relationship Selling."
39. Gina DeLapa, "Something to Write Home About," *Sales & Marketing Management*, December 2000, 33–34.
40. Scott Cressman, "Eight Tips for Highly Effective Presentations," *Sales*, www.sammag.com, May 1, 2001.
41. Colleen Cooper, "Overcoming Last Minute Objections," *Sales & Marketing Management*, March 1997, 32; Sarah Lorge, "How to Close a Deal," *Sales & Marketing Management*, April 1998, 84.
42. Cooper, "Overcoming Last Minute Objections."
43. Michelle Marchetti, "Hey Buddy, Can You Spare $113.25?" *Sales & Marketing Management*, August 1997, 69–77.
44. Cliff Ennico, "Cynical? Insecure? Ruthless? You're Hired. Essential Characteristics for Sales Success," www.sammag.com, May 1, 2001.
45. "Can Your Reps Sell Overseas?" *Sales & Marketing Management*, February 1998, 110.
46. David Garfinkel, "The E-Vangelist: Autoresponse Marketing," *Sales & Marketing Management*, May 2001, 27.
47. Andy Cohen, "Global Dos and Don'ts," *Sales & Marketing Management*, June 1996, 72; Esmond D. Smith, Jr., and Cuong Pham, "Doing Business in Vietnam: A Cultural Guide," *Business Horizons*, May/June 1996, 47–51; "Five Tips for International Handshaking," *Sales & Marketing Management*, July 1997, 90, from Dorothea Johnson, director of The Protocol School of Washington; Tricia Campbell, "What to Give Overseas," *Sales & Marketing Management*, September 1997, 85; "Negotiating: Getting to Yes, Chinese-Style," *Sales & Marketing Management*, July 1996, 44–45; Michelle Marchetti, "Selling in China? Go Slowly," *Sales & Marketing Management*, January 1997, 35–36; Sergey Frank, "Global Negotiating: Vive Les Différences!" *Sales & Marketing Management*, May 1992, 64–69.
48. Andy Cohen, "The Traits of Great Sales Forces," *Sales & Marketing Management*, October 2000, 67–72.
49. Erika Rasmusson, "The 10 Traits of Top Salespeople," *Sales & Marketing Management*, August 1999, 34–37.
50. "America's 25 Best Sales Forces: Best at Sales Training," *Sales & Marketing Management*, July 2000, 68.
51. Gabriel Landriault, "In Class, Online," *Computing Canada*, March 1, 2001, 11.
52. Arun Sharma, Customer Satisfaction-Based Incentive Systems: Some Managerial and Salesperson Considerations," *Journal of Personal Selling & Sales Management*, April 1997, 61.
53. Cohen, "The Traits of Great Sales Forces."
54. Libby Estelle, "Rewarding and Improving Performance Motivate Employees and Customers to Grab the Brass Ring," *Sales & Marketing Management*, October 2001, S1–S4.
55. Geoffrey Brewer, "The 7 Traits of Great Sales Leaders," *Sales & Marketing Management*, July 1997, 38–46.
56. James Champy, "Waiting for Change," *Sales & Marketing Management*, August 2001, 30.
57. Kathleen Cholewka, "E-Market Stats," *Sales & Marketing Management*, September 2001, 21.
58. Brent Keltner, "Just Another Channel?" *Sales & Marketing Management*, January 2000, 23–34.
59. Ginger Conlon, "No Turning Back," *Sales & Marketing Management*, December 1999, 50–55.
60. Keltner, 23–34; Brent Keltner, "Harnessing the Internet's Potential," *Sales & Marketing Management*, February 2000, 29.

Chapter 14

1. Michelle Warren, "The Sporting Life," *Marketing Magazine*, February 23, 2004, 13–16; Air Canada Centre website, www.theaircanadacentre.com.
2. Canadian Media Directors' Council, "Components of Net Advertising Revenue By Medium," *Media Digest*, 2003–04, 10.
3. Statistics Canada, Canadian Statistics, Finance and Services General Indicators for the Year 2000, www.statscan.ca, accessed February 27, 2004.
4. "2000 Advertising-to-Sales Ratios for the 200 Largest Ad Spending Industries," *Advertising Age*, July 24, 2000, 44.
5. Statistics Canada, "Television Viewing," *The Daily*, Friday, November 21, 2003; Lesley Young, "Report Claims TV Clutter Out of Hand," *Marketing Magazine*, August 12, 2002; Tom Reichert, "Sexy Ads Target Young Adults," *USA Today Magazine*, May 2001, 50.
6. Amitava Chattaopadhyay and Kunal Basu, "Humor in Advertising: The Moderating Role of Prior Brand Evaluation," *Journal of Marketing Research*, November 1990, 466–76.
7. Kellie Searle, "The Brown Trucks Are Coming! The Brown Trucks Are Coming! UPS Joins the Global Revolution," *Sales, Advertising &*

Marketing, November 1, 2001, www.sammag.com; Allyson L. Stewart-Allen, "Sense of Identity Crucial for Fast Food Worldwide," *Marketing News*, November 19, 2001, 12; Thomas T. Semon, "Cutting Corners in Language Risky Business," *Marketing News*, 9; Thomas J. Madden, Kelly H. Hewett, and Martin S. Roth, "Managing Images in Different Cultures: A Cross-National Study of Color Meanings and Preferences," *Journal of International MKT*, 8/4, 2000; Yumiko Ono, "U.S. Superstores Find Japanese Are a Hard Sell," *Wall Street Journal*, February 14, 2000, B1, B4; John S. McClenahen, "How Can You Possibly Say That?" *Industry Week*, July 17, 1995, 17; Allyson L Stewart-Allen, "Don't Lose Advertising in the Translation," *Marketing News*, June 5, 2000, 16.

8. Rajiv Grover and V. Srinivasan, "Evaluating the Multiple Effects of Retail Promotions on Brand Loyalty and Brand Switching Segments," *Journal of Marketing Research*, February 1992, 76–89; see also S. P. Raj, "The Effects of Advertising on High and Low Loyalty Consumer Segments," *Journal of Consumer Research*, June 1982, 77–89.
9. Norma Ramage, "Shell Builds a Worldwide Reputation," *Marketing Magazine*, September 15, 2003.
10. Lesley Young, "Men Target of MADD's 'Innuendo," *Marketing Magazine*, June 30, 2003.
11. Tobi Elkin, "Microsoft to Focus on Experience," *Advertising Age*, February 26, 2001, 26.
12. Tobi Elkin, "Window XP's $200 Million Launch Kicks Off," *AdAge.com*, October 11, 2001.
13. Astrid Van Den Broek, "Moving in on Bay Street," *Marketing Magazine*, April 16, 2001.
14. Eve Lazarus, "Shaw Suing Telus over Cable Ads," *Marketing Magazine*, December 10, 2001; Newsline, "Shaw Suspends Telus Lawsuit," *Marketing Magazine*, January 7, 2002.
15. www.adageglobal.com, "Absolut Vodka Must Pull Campaign in Italy," February 2, 2001.
16. Fahad S. Al-Olyan and Kiran Karade, *Journal of Advertising*, Fall 2000, 69.
17. Paul-Mark Rendon, "Puretracks Rocks onto the Web," *Marketing Magazine*, October 20, 2003; "Puretracks Sells One Million Songs," *Canada NewsWire*, February 11, 2004, 1; Danny Kucharsky, "Archambault Readies Download Site," *Marketing Magazine*, January 26, 2004.
18. Tyler Hamilton, "Puretracks.com, Which Offers Legal Music Downloads Over the Internet in Canada, Says It Has Sold More Than One Million Songs after Four Months in Operation," *Canada NewsWire*, February 11, 2004.
19. Telus Mobility website, www.telusmobility.com; and Fido website, www.fido.ca.
20. Telus Mobility website, www.telusmobility.com.
21. Laura Q. Hughes and Wendy Davis, "Revival of the Fittest," *Advertising Age*, March 12, 2001, 18–19.
22. Marc G. Weinberger, Harlan Spotts, Leland Campbell, and Amy L. Parsons, "The Use and Effect of Advertising Media," *Journal of Advertising Research*, May/June, 1995, 44–56.
23. Lara Mills, "Campaigns with Legs," *Marketing Magazine*, May 15, 2000.
24. Roger Thurow, "Shtick Ball: In Global Drive, Nike Finds Its Brash Ways Don't Always Pay Off," *Wall Street Journal*, May 5, 1997, A1, A10.
25. Russell Abratt and Deanna Cowan, "Client Agency Perspectives of Information Needs for Media Planning," *Journal of Advertising Research*, November 1999, 37.
26. Canadian Media Directors' Council, "Components of Net Advertising Revenue By Medium," *Media Digest*, 2003–04, 10; and Canadian Media Directors' Council, "National vs. Local Share of Net Advertising," *Media Digest*, 2003–04, 10.
27. "Domestic Advertising Spending by Media," *Advertising Age*, September 25, 2000, s4.
28. Canadian Media Directors' Council, "Consumer Magazines," *Media Diges*, 2003–04, 44–49.
29. "Radio: No Longer an Advertising Afterthought," *Standard & Poor's Industry Surveys*, July 20, 1995, M36; Rebecca Piirto, "Why Radio Thrives," *American Demographics*, May 1994, 40–46.
30. Canadian Media Directors' Council, "Consumer Magazines," *Media Digest*, 2003–04, 13–29.
31. Ibid.; Rick Westhead, "Grey Cup Advertisers Giving 124 Percent for Telecast: $57,000 for 30 Seconds," *Canada NewsWire*, November 13, 2003; Superbowl website, www.superbowl.com.
32. Jim Edwards, "The Art of the Infomercial," *Brandweek*, September 3, 2001, 14; Ian French, "A Primer on DRTV," *Marketing Magazine*, August 25, 2003.
33. Barbara Martinez, "City Sight: Giant Ads Spring from Holes in the Ground," *Wall Street Journal*, August 18, 1999, B1, B10.
34. "Top 10 Advertising Categories in 2000," Outdoor Advertising Association of America.
35. Canadian Media Directors' Council, "Outdoor," *Media Digest*, 2003–04, 50–52 and 74; Kate Fitzgerald, "Out of Home," *Advertising Age*, July 9, 2001, s1, s4.
36. Canadian Media Directors' Council, "Outdoor," *Media Digest*, 2003–04, 10; "Internet Advertising Revenue Holds Steady As All Ad Sectors Decline," www.iab.com, December 4, 2001.
37. Jennifer Rewick, "Brand Awareness Fuels Strategies for Online Advertisers Next Year," *Wall Street Journal*, December 28, 2000, B2.
38. Ibid.
39. Canadian Media Directors' Council, "The Internet," *Media Digest*, 2003–04, 55–59.
40. Vanessa O'Connell, "Looking Beyond Banners to Revive Web Advertising," *Wall Street Journal*, February 26, 2001, B1, B12.
41. Jack Neff, "Floors in Stores Start Moving," *Advertising Age*, August 20, 2001, 15.
42. Cara Beardi, "Video Venue Joins the Line for Gas-Pump Advertising," *Advertising Age*, April 23, 2001, 8.
43. Suzanne Vranica, "Think Graffiti Is All That's Hanging in Subway Tunnels? Look Again," *Wall Street Journal*, April 4, 2001, B1, B4.
44. Sara Teasdale, "Study Challenges Three-Plus Viewing Rule," *Business Marketing*, December 1995, 5; Hugh M. Cannon and Edward A. Riordan, "Effective Reach and Frequency: Does It Really Make Sense?" *Journal of Advertising Research*, March 1994, 19.
45. Canadian Media Directors Council, *Media Digest*, 2003–04, 13, 32, 34, 44.
46. Cannon and Riordan, "Effective Reach and Frequency," 19; Erwin Ephron, "A New Media-Mix Strategy: As Advertisers Eye Obvious Decline of TV, Agencies Expand Options," *Advertising Age*, February 28, 2000, s10.
47. Kate Lynch and Horst Stripp, "Examination of Qualitative Viewing Factors for Optimal Advertising Strategies," *Journal of Advertising Research*, May 1999, 7.
48. Chuck Ross, "Study Finds Continuity vs. Flights," *Advertising Age*, April 19, 1999, B2.
49. Erwin Ephron, "Recency Planning: A New Media Approach," *Advertising Age*, July 1, 1999, 21. Sales Promotion

50. "2001 Annual Report: Industry Report 2001," *PROMO Magazine.*
51. Promo Shorts, "Coupon Distribution and Redemption Up in 2001," *Marketing Magazine*, May 13, 2002.
52. "2001 Annual Report: Industry Report 2001."
53. Anne Kandra, "Bait and Rebate," *PC World*, September 2001, 45.
54. "Right Up Their Alley; McDonald's, Toys 'R' Us Share a Holiday Happy Meal," *PROMO Magazine*, December 1, 2001, 11.
55. Eymbert Vaandering, "Hey, Big Spender," *Marketing Magazine*, January 14, 2002.
56. Mark Lacek, "Loyalty Marketing No Ad Budget Threat," *Advertising Age*, October 23, 1995, 20.
57. Ginger Conlon, "True Romance," *Sales & Marketing Management*, May 1996, 85–90.
58. Danny Kucharsky, "Consumers Drawn to Loyalty Rewards," *Marketing Magazine*, May 6, 2002.
59. Vincent Alonzo, "Money Isn't Everything," *Sales & Marketing Management*, April 2000, 47–48.
60 Jason Macdonald, "Winning Contests," *Marketing Magazine*, July 9, 2001.
61. "2001 Annual Report: Industry Report 2001."
62. Lafayette Jones, "Ethnic Product Sampling: The Hidden Opportunity," *Retail Merchandiser*, August 2001, 45.
63. Stephanie Fagnani, "A Taste of Success: The Practice of Product Sampling Combines Favorable Location, Product Innovation, Thorough Promotion and Timely Execution," *Supermarket News*, August 27, 2001, 33.
64. Angela Kryhul, "The Krispy Cult," *Marketing Magazine*, January 28, 2002
65. Newsline, "Shoot Hoops, Chew at Same Time," *Marketing Magazine*, May 14, 2001.
66. Geoffrey A. Fowler, "When Free Samples Become Saviors," *Wall Street Journal*, August 14, 2001, B1, B4.
67. "Point-of-Purchase: $17 Billion," *PROMO Magazine*, October 29, 2001, 3.
68. "BIJA Healing Teas Backs Launch by Brewing Up Revolving In-Store Displays," Out of Home Report, *Marketing Magazine*, November 18, 2002.
69. Erin Strout, "Doctoring Sales," *Sales & Marketing Management*, May 2001, 53–60; Joseph P. Shapiro and Stacey Schultz, "Prescriptions: How Your Doctor Makes the Choice," *U.S. News & World Report*, February 19, 2001, 58; Bill Brubaker, "Drug Firms Still Lavish Pricey Gifts on Doctors; Ethics Debated as Freebies Flow," *Washington Post*, January 19, 2002, E01; Ed Susman, "U.S. Doctors Touchy on Topic of Pharmaceutical Gifts," *Medical Post*, July 17, 2001.
70. Trish Wheaton, "Driving Online Sales," *Marketing Magazine*, August 19, 2002.
71. Sarah Smith, "Clinique Gets Customers to Spin for Great Skin," *Marketing Magazine*, February 18, 2002.
72. Eymbert Vaandering, "Hey, Big Spender," *Marketing Magazine*, January 14, 2002.
73. Libby Estell, "Economic Incentives," *Sales & Marketing Management*, October 2001, S2–S4.
74. Ben Chapman, "The Trade Show Must Go On," *Sales & Marketing Management*, June 2001, 22.
75. Nicholas Maiesse, " 'Blair Witch' Casts Its Spell," *Advertising Age*, March 20, 2000, s8; Nancy Coltun Webster "The Marketing 100: 'The Blair Witch Project' Amorette, Jones," *Advertising Age*, June 26, 2000, s22.
76. Stan Sutter, "Indisputably Golden," *Marketing Magazine*, February 25, 2002.
77. Street Talk, "Worlds Collide," *Marketing Magazine*, December 3, 2001.
78. Teri Agins, "Armani Touts Urban Chic with 'Shaft,' " *Wall Street Journal*, June 19, 2000, 16.
79. Eve Lazarus, "Canadian Open Tees Off in Vancouver," *Marketing Magazine*, May 12, 2003.
80. Lauren Sherman, "Dancing into the Hearts of Teens," *Marketing Magazine*, January 20, 2003.
81. "Modernista! Adds Avon, to Unveil Holiday Gap Ads" *Adweek*, November 12, 2001, 32.
82. Michael Jay Polonsky, "Reevaluating Green Marketing: A Strategic Approach," *Business Horizons*, September/October 2001, 21.
83. Kathleen Cholewka, "The 5 Best E-Marketing Campaigns," *Sales & Marketing Management*, January 2001, 53.
84. Ibid.
85. Maxine Lans Retsky, "More Steps to Avoid McDonald's Situation," *Marketing News*, November 19, 2001, 11.

Chapter 15

1. Christopher T. Heun, "Log Me On to the Ball Game—For a Price," *Informationweek.com*, April 2, 2001, 33. Used with permission.
2. Keith McArthur, "Rivals Grab Bigger Piece of Air Canada's Market Share," *The Globe and Mail*, April 4, 2004, B1, B6.
3. "India's Mobile Users Hit 4.5 Million," *CNN.com*, September 19, 2001.
4. "Financing Deals for New Cars Shake Up Market for Used Cars," *Wall Street Journal*, November 16, 2001, B1, B4.
5. Ramarao Desuaju and Steven Shugan, "Strategic Service Pricing and Yield Management," *Journal of Marketing*, January 1999, 44–56.
6. Michael Mendano, "Priced to Perfection," *Business2.com*, March 6, 2001, 40–41.
7. "Your Room Costs $250… No! $200… No," *Wall Street Journal*, May 5, 1999, B1, B16.
8. Gordon Fairclough, "Governments Can Be Addicted to Cigarettes," *Wall Street Journal*, October 2, 2000, A1. Used with permission.
9. "The Common Good," *The Economist*, December 2, 2001. © 2001 The Economist Newspaper Ltd. All rights reserved. Reprinted with permission. Further reproduction prohibited. www.economist.com.
10. David Henderson, "What Are Price Wars Good For? Absolutely Nothing," *Fortune*, May 12, 1997, 156.
11. See Joseph Cannon and Christian Homburg, "Buyer-Supplier Relationships and Customer Firm Costs," *Journal of Marketing*, January 2001, 29–43.
12. Most of this section is taken from: David Hamilton, "The Price Isn't Right," *Wall Street Journal*, February 12, 2001, R8, R10. Used with permission.
13. Ibid.
14. Ibid.
15. Gary Hamel, "Edison's Curse," *Fortune*, March 5, 2001, 175–78. See also Florian Zettlemeyer, "Expanding to the Internet: Pricing and Communications Strategies When Firms Compete on Multiple Channels," *Journal of Marketing Research*, August 2000, 292–308; and Subir Bandyopadhyay, Guang Bo Lin, and Yan Zhong, "Under the Gavel," *Marketing Management*, November/December 2001, 25–28.
16. "Price Buster," *Wall Street Journal*, July 17, 2000, R12.
17. "Value Driven," *Fortune*, May 1, 2000, 74.
18. Cindy Waxer, "When Price Takes a Back Seat," *Business2.com*, June 26, 2001, 37.
19. Praveen Kopalle and Donald Lehmann, "The Effects of Advertised and Observed Quality on Expectations about New Product Quality," *Journal of*

Marketing Research, August 1995, 280–90; Akshay Rao and Kent Monroe, "The Effect of Price, Brand Name, and Store Name on Buyers' Perceptions of Product Quality: An Integrative Review," *Journal of Marketing Research*, August 1989, 351–57; Gerard Tellis and Gary Gaeth, "Best Value, Price-Seeking, and Price Aversion: The Impact of Information and Learning on Consumer Choices," *Journal of Marketing*, April 1990, 34–35; Dawar Niraj and Phillip Parker, "Marketing Universals: Consumers' Use of Brand Name, Price, Physical Appearance, and Retailer Reputation as Signals of Product Quality," *Journal of Marketing*, April 1994, 81–95; and R. Chandrashekaran, "The Implications of Individual Differences in Reference to Price Utilization for Designing Effective Price Communications," *Journal of Business Research*, August 2001, 85–92.

20. William Dodds, Kent Monroe, and Dhruv Grewal, "Effects of Price, Brand, and Store Information on Buyers' Product Evaluations," *Journal of Marketing Research*, August 1991, 307–19. See also Akshay Rao and Wanda Sieben, "The Effect of Prior Knowledge on Price Acceptability and the Type of Information Examined," *Journal of Consumer Research*, September 1992, 256–70; Ajay Kalra and Ronald Goldman, "The Impact of Advertising Positioning Strategies on Consumer Price Sensitivity," *Journal of Marketing Research*, May 1998, 210–24.
21. Donald Lichtenstein and Scott Burton, "The Relationship between Perceived and Objective Price—Quality," *Journal of Marketing Research*, November 1989, 429–43.
22. "Store-Brand Pricing Has to Be Just Right," *The Wall Street Journal*, February 14, 1992, B1. See also George Cressman, Jr., "Snatching Defeat from the Jaws of Victory," *Marketing Management*, Summer 1997, 9–19.

Chapter 16

1. J. William Gurley, "Above the Crowd: Why Dell's War Isn't Dumb," *Fortune*, July 9, 2001, 134–36. © 2001 Time Inc. All rights reserved.
2. Kent Monroe and Jennifer Cox, "Pricing Practices That Endanger Profits," *Marketing Management*, September/October 2001, 42–46.
3. "Building a Better Mousetrap Is No Claptrap," *Business Week*, February 1, 1999, 47.
4. "Take Me Out to the Ballgame, James," *Business Week*, March 13, 2000, 142.
5. Daniel Michaels, "No-Frills Irish Airline Flies High," *The Wall Street Journal*, September 6, 2000, B1, B4. Used with permission.
6. Nicolas Van Praet, "Profitable WestJet Accuses Air Canada of Using Court-Protection to Reduce Fares Below Cost," *CanWest News*, October 20, 2003, 1; "Small B.C. Airline Accuses Insolvent Air Canada of Predatory Pricing," *Canadian Press NewsWire*, April 16, 2003.
7. Kusum L. Ailawadi, Donald Lehmann, and Scott Neslin, "Market Response to a Major Policy Change in the Marketing Mix: Learning from Procter & Gamble's Value Price Strategy," *Journal of Marketing*, January 2001, 44–61. See also Kusum L. Ailawadi, Scott Neslin, and Karen Gedenk, "Pursuing the Value-Conscious Consumer: Store Brands versus National Brand Promotions," *Journal of Marketing*, January 2001, 71–89; Kissan Joseph, "On the Optimality of Delegating Pricing Authority to the Sales Force," *Journal of Marketing*, January 2001, 62–70.
8. Joel Urbany, "Are Your Prices Too Low?" *Harvard Business Review*, October 2001, 26–27.
9. Jane Costello, "$27.98 Airfare to Paris, China? United: 'Oops,'" *The Wall Street Journal*, February 15, 2001, B1, B14. Used with permission.
10. Charles Quigley and Elaine Notarantonio, "An Exploratory Investigation of Perceptions of Odd and Even Pricing," in *Developments in Marketing Science*, ed. Victoria Crittenden (Miami: Academy of Marketing Science, 1992), 306–9.
11. "Nine Cents of Separation," *American Demographics*, May 1998, 41.
12. "Three-for-$3 and Other Numerical Pitches Work Magic in Stores," *The Wall Street Journal*, March 12, 1998, A1. See also Herman Simon and Robert Dolan, "Price Customization," *Marketing Management*, Fall 1998, 11–17; and Margaret Campbell, "Perceptions of Price Unfairness: Antecedents and Consequences," *Journal of Marketing Research*, May 1999, 187–99.
13. "Why Bundling Its Consumer Services Hasn't Benefited AT&T," *The Wall Street Journal*, October 24, 2000, B1, B4.
14. Dilip Soman and John Gourville, "Transaction Decoupling: How Price Bundling Affects the Decision to Consume," *Journal of Marketing Research*, February 2001, 30–44.
15. Vicki Morwitz, Eric Greenleaf, and Eric Johnson, "Divide and Prosper: Consumers' Reactions to Partitioned Prices," *Journal of Marketing Research*, November 1998, 453–63.
16. This material on price penalties is from Eugene Fram and Michael McCarthy, "The True Price of Penalties," *Marketing Management*, Fall 1999, 49–54.
17. "Value Strategy to Battle Recession," *Advertising Age*, January 7, 1991, 1, 44.
18. "Brand X No Longer Plan B for Shoppers," *Dallas Morning News*, July 14, 2001, 3F.

Chapter 17

1. Stewart Alsop, "I'm Betting on Amazon.com," *Fortune* online, April 20, 2001; Alex Frangos, "Here's My Advice...," *The Wall Street Journal*, January 14, 2002, R15; Company press release, "Amazon.com Announces 4th Quarter Profit," Amazon.com, January 22, 2002; company website, Amazon.com/AboutAmazon.com.
2. Susan Fournier, Susan Dobscha, and David Glen Mick, "Preventing the Premature Death of Relationship Marketing," *Harvard Business Review*, January/February 1998, 2–8.
3. Gerri Knilans, "Database Marketing: Fad, Fantasy or Reality?" *Direct Marketing*, May 1997, 48.
4. J. Walker Smith, "Marketing with Attitude," *Marketing Management*, January/February 2002, 48.
5. Search Systems website, www.searchsystems.net/freepub.php.
6. Carol Krol, "Case Study: Mead Johnson Finds Winning Formula for Reaching Moms," *Advertising Age*, April 26, 1999, 25; Lesley Young, "When Three Heads Are Better Than One," *Marketing Magazine*, December 8, 2003.
7. Todd Wasserman, Gerry Khermouch, Jeff Green, "Minding Everyone's Business," *Brandweek*, February 28, 2000, 32.
8. Fournier, Dobscha, and Mick.

9. "Rocky Mountaineer Touts Unprecedented ROI for 2002 Season," *Marketing Magazine*, November 4, 2002, 9.
10. This section based on Rob Jackson and Paul Wang, *Strategic Database Marketing* (Lincolnwood, IL: NTC Business Books, 1997), 4–11; and Frederick Newell, *The New Rules of Marketing: How to Use One-to-One Relationship Marketing to Be the Leader in Your Industry* (New York: McGraw-Hill, 1997), 10–32.
11. Lesley Young, "Portrait of the New Family," *Marketing Magazine*, March 15, 2004; Canadian Media Directors' Council, *Media Digest*, 2003–04, 57.
12. Jackson and Wang, *Strategic Database Marketing*,11.
13. Eve Lazarus, Videos Star," *Marketing Magazine*, September 9, 2002, 12–13.
14. Eve Lazarus, "Not Just a Ski Hill," *Marketing Magazine*, October 9, 2000.
15. Ginger Conlon, "True Romance," *Sales & Marketing Management*, May 1996, 85–90.
16. Laurentian Bank Press Release, "Tailored Rewards for Laurentian Bank VISA Gold Credit Card Holders Through a New 'Passport' Program," *Canada NewsWire*, December 17, 2003, 1; "Your Visa Gold Passport Program," Laurentian Bank website, www.laurentianbank.com.
17. Lesley Young, "When Three Heads Are Better Than One," *Marketing Magazine*, December 8, 2003.
18. Chris Daniels, "Vendor Bender," *Marketing Magazine*, April 5, 2004.
19. Catherine Allen, "Getting the Most Out of loyalty," *Marketing Magazine*, December 1, 1997; and George S. Day, "No Two Customers Are Alike," *National Post*, June 16, 2003, FE.5.
20. Lesley Young, "Smart Sampling Wins Award and New Cat Owners," *Marketing Magazine*, November 3, 2003.
21. Robert Beaudoin and Daniel Charron, "Answering the Needs of Female Drivers," *Marketing Magazine*, June 30, 2003.
22. David Carr, "The Renaissance Rep," *Marketing Magazine*, April 16, 2001.
23. Jack Schmid and Alan Weber, *Desktop Database Marketing* (Lincolnwood, IL: NTC Business Books, 1998), 33–34.
24. Jackson and Wang, 83.
25. Julia Angwin, "Virgin to Trade Web Use for Personal Data," *Wall Street Journal*, April 10, 2000, B16.
26. Op cit.
27. Denny Hatch, "The Business of Business Lists: A Look at This Incredibly, Unbelievably Complex World," *Target Marketing*, January 1997, 65.
28. "The Big Book," Directories, *Marketing Magazine* website, www.marketingmag.ca.
29. *Info*Canada website, www.infocanada.ca.
30. Andrew Fisher, "How IT Underpins Groups Global Business Strategy," *Financial* Times on-line, August 8, 2001.
31. Shoppers Drug Mart website, www.shoppersdrugmart.ca; and Chris Daniels, "Vendor Bender," *Marketing Magazine*, April 5, 2004.
32. Milorad Krneta, "Data Deluge," *Marketing Magazine*, April 7, 2003.
33. MapInfo website, www.mapinfo.ca.
34. Lesley Young, "Cellphone Marketing Put to the Test," *Marketing Magazine*, April 23, 2001.
35. James R. Rosenfield, "The Myth of Database Marketing," *Direct Marketing*, February 1998, 28.
36. Newell, *The New Rules of Marketing*, 82.
37. Heath, "Loyalty for Sale," 40.
38. Tener Solutions Group website, www.tenersolutions.com.
39. Peter R. Peacock, "Data Mining in Marketing: Part 1: The Revolution Is Upon Us, So Choose Your Weapons Carefully," *Marketing Management*, Winter 1998, 9–18.
40. Skip Press, "Fool's Gold?" *Sales & Marketing Management*, June 1998, 58–62.
41. Trafford Publishing website, www.trafford.com.
42. iTracks webSite, www.itracks.com.
43. Staff, "B2B E-commerce Headed for Trillions," *CyberAtlas*, March 6, 2002. cyberatlas.internet.com/markets/b2b/article/0,,10091_986661,00.html.
44. Andrea Zoe Aster, Interview of Leon Goren for article, "What Now for Net Retailing," *Marketing Magazine*, March 19, 2001; and Recommended Reading, "Benefiting Bricks and Mortar," *Marketing Magazine*, June 3, 2002.
45. Nicholas Negroponte, *Being Digital*. Vintage Books, New York, NY, 1996.
46. Staff, "B2B E-commerce Headed for Trillions," *CyberAtlas*, March 6, 2002. cyberatlas.internet.com/markets/b2b/article/0,,10091_986661,00.html.
47. Canadian Media Directors' Council, "The Internet," *Media Digest*, 2003–04, 55–59; Falling through the Net: Toward Digital Inclusion, U.S. Department of Commerce, October 2000. www.ntia.doc.gov/ntiahome/fttn00/Front00.htm; and Michael Pastore, "Internet Remains a Man's Domain." *CyberAtlas*, July 26, 2001. cyberatlas.internet.com/big_picture/demographics/article/0,,5901_809341,00.html.
48. Mary Modahl, *Now or Never—How Companies Must Change Today to Win the Battle for Internet Consumers*. HarperCollins, New York, NY, 2000.
49. Philip Coppard, "Is Your Customer an E-Shopper or an E-Buyer?," *Marketing Magazine*, September 27, 1999.
50. Staff, "Global Internet Statistics by Language," *Global Reach*, March 30, 2004, www.glreach.com/globstats/index.php3.
51. Anonymous, Ready? Net. Go! McConnell International, May 2001. mcconnellinternational.com/ereadiness/report.cfm.
52. Adapted from Michael Pastore, "Europe Remains Behind in Broadband Game," *CyberAtlas*, June 12, 2001; CyberAtlas Staff, "The World's On-line Population," *CyberAtlas*, March 21, 2002; Staff, "Global Internet Statistics," *Global Reach*, September 30, 2002; Owen Wood, "Debit Cards," CBC.ca, October 29, 2001; David Collier, "Broadband Access: Europe's Own Goal," Fibers.org, February 14, 2002. Basic Facts & Indicators, European Commission, 2002; and Media Directors' Council, "The Internet," *Media Digest*, 2003–04, 55–59.
53. Staff, "Projected e-Commerce Statistics by Country," *Global Reach*, March 30, 2004, www.glreach.com/globstats/index.php3; and Statistics Canada, "Electronic Commerce and Technology," *The Daily*, Wednesday, April 2, 2003; Statistics Canada, *The Daily*, June 6, 2002.
54. Sears Canada website, www.sears.ca.
55. Grocery Gateway website, www.grocerygateway.com/.
56. Stephanie Whittaker, "On Special in Web Aisle Nine," *Marketing Magazine*, June 15, 1998, 27; and Bob MacKalski, "Coping After Peachtree Withers," *Canadian Grocer*, February 2002, 10.
57. Logging On, "Ebox to Secure Loblaw Deliveries," *Marketing Magazine*, October 21, 2002; and Ebox website, www.ebox.com

58. Angela Pacienza, "Unusual Ad Campaign Turning Heads: Burger King's Bizarre Website Attracts Millions: [Final Edition], *Telegram*. St. John's, Newfoundland, April 19, 2004, B.3; and Subservient Chicken website, www.subservientchicken.com.
59. Michael Pastore, "E-Mail Marketing Delivering the Message," *CyberAtlas*, May 9, 2000. cyberatlas.internet.com/markets/advertising/article/0,,5941_356791,00.html.
60. Canadian Media Directors' Council, "Components of Net Advertising Revenue By Medium," *Media Digest*, 2003–04, 10.
61. Robyn Greenspan, "Consumers Rank Trust Above Low Prices," *CyberAtlas*, April 23, 2002. cyberatlas.internet.com/markets/retailing/article/0,6061_1014831,00.html.
62. Bill Winett, "Tracking Tutorial," Webmonkey, No Date. hotwired.lycos.com/webmonkey/e-business/tracking/index.html.
63. Don Peppers and Martha Rogers, "Opening the Door to Customers," *Sales & Marketing Management*, October 1998, 22–29.
64. Ira Teinowitz, "Consumers to Be Notified about Profiling," *Advertising Age*, November 15, 1999, 52.
65. Sarah Lorge, "Banner Ads vs. E-Mail Marketing," *Sales & Marketing Management*, August 1999, 15.
66. Kaydo, "As Good As It Gets," 56–57.
67. Jim Costelli, "How to Handle Personal Information," *American Demographics*, March 1996, 50–58.
68. Tyler Hamilton, "New Privacy Watchdog Advises Businesses Not to Panic Over New Legislation," *Canadian Press NewsWire*, December 15, 2003.
69. Privacy Commissioner of Canada, "A Guide To The New Private Sector Data Protection Bill," www.privcom.gc.ca/legislation; An interesting interpretation of the Safe Harbor can be found at www.atw%cv.the-dma.org/library/privacy/safeharbor5.shtml. Additional information on privacy can be found at www.privacy.org and www.privacyexchange.org.
70. PIPED Act Case Summary #162, "Customer Complains About Airline's Use of 'Cookies' on Its Website," Commissioners Findings, 2003, www.privcom.gc.ca/cf-dc/2003/index2-3_e.asp70.
71. Carrie Harrison, "E-mail Marketing In A Private World," *Marketing Magazine*, March 8, 2004.
72. Erika Rasmusson, "The Perils of International Direct Mail," *Sales & Marketing Management*, April 2000, 107; "E-Commerce III: Nations Fall Slowly in Line on Privacy-Protection Laws," *The Globe and Mail*, November 30, 1999, E25; Mark Ward, "Connected: EU Deal with U.S. over Privacy," *Daily Telegraph*, March 23, 2000, 3; Beverley Head, "No Privacy, But at Least Some Control," *Business Review Weekly*, April 20, 2000, 44; Wasserman, Khermouch, and Green, "Minding Everyone's Business"; "U.S., EU Make Safe Harbor Agreement, No Shelter for Financial Institutions," *Retail Delivery News*, March 2000.

Chapter 18

1. Johan Nylander, "Unwired in Sweden," *Digital Marketing*, November 2001, 4–5; David Kilburn, "Top of the Mobile Learning Curve," *Digital Marketing*, November 2001, 4–5.
2. Lesley Young, "Peddling Telecom Bundles," *Marketing Magazine*, May 7, 2001.
3. Joseph Hair, Robert Bush, and David Ortinau, *Marketing Research: Within a Changing Information Environment*, 2nd ed. (Burr Ridge, IL: McGraw-Hill/Irwin, 2002) 128.
4. Louis Chunovic, "Digital Cable, Satellite Studies Target Churn," *Electronic Media*, February 18, 2002, 4.
5. Thomas Hicks, "Establishing and Maintaining Customer Relationships," *SGB*, August 23, 2000, 9.
6. Sara Fraser, "Many Retailers Cannot Identify Most Valuable Customers," *Customer Interface*, March 2002, 17. See also "Blue Martini Software Demonstrates Integration with Point of Sale Devices at National Retail Federation Show," *PR Newswire*, January 14, 2002.
7. Lorne Hill, "As Nimble as the Little Guys," *Marketing Magazine*, February 12, 2001.
8. "Chrysler to Unveil New PT Cruiser," *Associated Press*, On-line, March 27, 2002, www.ptcruiserforum.com/pressrelease/press-03-27-2002.
9. Kenneth Cramer and Jason Dedrick, "Dell Computers: Organization of a Global Production Network," *Center for Research on Information Technology and Organizations*, 2001, www.crito.uci.edu/git/publications/pdf/dell.pdf.
10. Scott Rosenburg, "Brilliant Careers: Steve Jobs," *Salon*, January 5, 1999, www.salon.com/bc/1999/01/cov-05bc.html.
11. Robert Slater, *Jack Welch and the GE Way*, (New York: McGraw-Hill, 1998); Slater, *Get Better or Get Beaten* (New York: McGraw-Hill, 2001).
12. Rob Sandler And Emily Rayson, "Lifecycling in the Right Direction," *Marketing Magazine*, April 29, 2002; www.mypetstop.com.
13. Carrie Harrison, "E-mail Marketing in a Private World, *Marketing Magazine*, March 8, 2004.
14. Adapted from the Electronic Privacy Information Center; Safe Harbor website; Stefanie Olsen "Nearly Undetectable Tracking Device Raises Concern," Cnet.com July 12, 2000; Eric Picard "Wireless: Location Tracking Will Change Everything," Internet.com July 25,2001; Scarlet Pruit <HREF= "http://www.infoworld.com/articles/hn/xml/02/09/27/020927hnamazon.xml "Amazon Agrees to Change Privacy Policy," *InfoWorld*, September 27, 2002.
15. Tracey Arial, "Crazy For Coupons," *Marketing Magazine*, September 16, 2002.
16. Sean Doherty, "Keeping Data Private," *Network Computing*, June 25, 2001, 83.
17. "Attorney General Files Motion to Prevent Bankrupt Company from Selling Customer Information," *M2 Presswire*, December 17, 2001.
18. Logging On, "Online Quotes Key Demand From Insurance Shoppers," *Digital Marketing Report*, April 21, 2003.
19. Larry Stevens, "CRM by the Slice: Running Analytics Is Expensive, So Companies Are Focusing on Areas with Customers," *Internetweek*, April 3, 2001, www.internetweek.com/indepth01/indepth040301.
20. Sarah Smith, "NCR Aims to Arm ATMs with Ads," *Marketing Magazine*, January 7, 2002.
21. Lesley Young, "Cutting Through All the Hype About CRM," *Marketing Magazine*, February 12, 2001.
22. "Carrier Relies on Ascential Data Integration Software to Enhance Product Quality," *Businesswire*, February 4, 2002.
23. Lesley Young, "Cutting Through All the Hype About CRM."

24. Carol Krol, "Data Warehouse Generates Surprise Leads for Camelot," *Advertising Age,* January 4, 1999, 20; Todd Wasserman, Gerry Khermouch, and Jeff Green, "Minding Everyone's Business," *Brandweek,* February 28, 2000, 32.
25. "AvantGo Introduces Mobile Application Built Specifically for Pharmaceutical Sales," *Business Wire,* March 4, 2002.
26. Sarah Dobson, "All the Right Moves," *Marketing Magazine,* February 10, 2003.
27. Curt Hall, "The Move to Real-Time Data Warehousing and Business Intelligence," May 22, 2001, www.cutter.com/consortium/research; "D&B and Netegrity Forge Strategic Alliance to Minimize Risk in E-Business Transactions," Press release: Netegrity, Inc., March 18, 2002.
28. Lesley Young, "All in a Day's Work," *Marketing Magazine,* April 16, 2001.
29. www.Ediets.com/programs.
30. www.Reflect.com.
31. PSS World Medical, Inc. Quarterly Report (SEC Form 10q), February 11, 2002
32. www.Ediets.com/programs.
33. www.kidsdadsmoms.com.
34. Jeff Sweat, "CRM Migration," *InformationWeek,* May 21, 2001, 57–64. Used with permission.

>> BIBLIOGRAPHY

Chapter-opening photo credits:

p. 1: The Image Bank/Getty Images; p. 2: Courtesy of Clodhoppers; pp. 22, 88, 230, and 340: © Kristiina Paul; p. 52: © T. Ozonas/Masterfile; p. 87: Photodisc Green/Getty Images; p. 130: CP Photo/Jeff McIntosh; p. 158: © Graham French/Masterfile; p. 188: Taxi/Getty Images; p. 229: MEIGNEUX/EPA/Landov; p. 254: Copyright © David Young-Wolff/PhotoEdit. All rights reserved; p. 280: ©Walter Hodges/Getty Images; p. 305: © AbleStock/Index Stock Imagery; p. 306: Courtesy of Grocery Gateway; p. 387: Taxi/Getty Images; p. 388: © Leland Bobbé/CORBIS; p. 428: © Ron Stroud/Masterfile; p. 473: The Image Bank/Getty Images; p. 474: © Damian Strohmeyer/ SI/NewSport/Corbis; p. 504: Peter Lynch/Getty Images; p. 533: Photodisc Blue/Getty Images; p. 534: © Gary Buss/Getty Images; p. 586: © Leland Bobbé/Getty Images.

Chapter 1

Try It: Jan Jaben Eilon, "Small Business Entices Marketers," *Bank Technology News*, June 2002, 1.

Chapter 2

Try It: Marina Strauss, "Sporting Life Puts Game Plan to Test," *The Globe and Mail*, August 22, 2003, B7. Reprinted with permission from *The Globe and Mail*.

Chapter 3

Try It: "N.S. Government Spent $98,000 Researching Sunday Shopping Issue," *Canadian Press NewsWire*, November 4, 2003; "Stores in Truro, N.S., Say They May Have to Open Sundays to Keep Market Share," *Canadian Press NewsWire*, October 29, 2003; "N.S. Opens Doors to Sunday Shopping for Six Weeks Prior to Christmas," *Canadian Press NewsWire*, October 28, 2003; "The Last Sunday Holdout," *Canadian HR Reporter*, October 6, 2003; "Amherst, N.S., Does Brisk Trade in Cross-Border Sunday Shopping," *Canadian Press NewsWire*, November 16, 2004.

Marketing Miscues: Keith McArthur, "Rivals Grab Bigger Piece of Air Canada's Market Share," *The Globe and Mail*, April 21, 2004, B1, B6; Keith McArthur, "Air Canada Boosting Reward Seat Program," *The Globe and Mail*, April 23, 2004, B1, B4; Paul Waldie and John Partridge, "Allegations of Espionage, Moles Fly in Air Canada-WestJet Spat," *The Globe and Mail*, April 8, 2004, B1, B24; www.aircanada.ca.

Critical Thinking Case: Brian Milner, "Fiorina Claims Victory in Fight of Her Life," *The Globe and Mail*, March 20, 2002, A1; Sam Omatseye, "HP Serves Up Initiatives for Increasingly Mobile World," *RCR Wireless News*, October 15, 2001; www.hp.com.

Chapter 4

Try It: Kevin Coupe, "A Theme Retailing Failure and Some Views on Restaurant and Pub Trends," *Store Equipment & Design*, January 2001, 24; Danielle Furfaro, "Entrepreneur Opens Family-Centered Restaurant in Albany, N.Y.," *Knight-Ridder Tribune Business News*, February 18, 2002; "McDonald's Launches World's First 'Town Center' Restaurant: New Restaurant Is Second Largest in U.S., Features Family 'Edu-Tainment,'" *PR Newswire*, April 30, 2002; "New Amex Seminars Focus on Consumer Dining Trends," *Nation's Restaurant News*, May 20, 2002, 200. Richard L. Papiernik, "Industry Sales for 2002 Projected to Hit $407 B," *Nation's Restaurant News*, January 7, 2002, 1; Norma Ramage, "TacoTime Dreams Grande," *Marketing Magazine*, March 3, 2003; TacoTime Corporate Website, www.tacotimecanada.ca, accessed October 28, 2003.

Chapter 5

Ethics in Marketing: Purchasing Management Association of Canada. Reprinted with permission.

Try It: Robin Raizel, "Net Gains," *Canadian Business*, October 14–Oct 26, 2003, 107; Mediagrif website, www.mediagrif.com; Press Release, "Mediagrif Announces Acquisition of GovernmentBids.com, a Leading US-Based Government Bid Aggregation Service," *Canada NewsWire*, February 23, 2004, 1; Luis. E Millan, "Over a Barrel: At Some Point, the Bigger Industry Players Have to Twist Some Arms to Get Their Smaller Supply Chain Partners on the E-Commerce Bandwagon," *Business Journal*, March 2002, 15.

Chapter 6

Try It: Kipp Cheng, "eBay Best Viral Marketing," *Adweek*, June 28, 1999, IQ42. eBay website: www.ebay.com/community/aboutebay/overview/index.html; Claire Tristram, "Takin' It to the Street," *MC Technology Marketing Intelligence*, February 1999, 22–28.

Chapter 7

Try It: Youth Culture Group website, www.youthculture.com. Julia Drake, "Teen Purchasing Power [Study]," *Canadian Grocer*, September 2001, G11; Cassandra Szklarski, "Teen Boys Spend More Time, Money on Their Appearance," *Canadian Press NewsWire*, May 23, 2002.

Marketing Miscues: Lesley Young, "Tapping into Youth Wireless Market," *Marketing Magazine*, April 9, 2001; Marlene Milczarek, "Voices Carry," *Marketing Magazine*, August 6, 2001; Press Release, "Rogers AT&T Wireless Equips Canadian Students with Everything They Need to Be Heard," *Canada NewsWire*, August 23, 2001; Lesley Young, "Pitfalls Await Wireless Marketers," *Marketing Magazine*, February 25, 2002.

Critical Thinking Case: "Golf Company Shifts Focus to Women Players," *Marketing to Women: Addressing Women and Women's Sensibilities*, May 2001, 5; Liz Consavage, "Square Two Gains with Women's Lines," *Golf World*, May 18, 2001, S6. www.womensgolfunlimited.com; E. Michael Johnson, "The Total

Package," *Golf World Business*, August 2000, 30; "Women's Business Square Two's Focus," *Golf World*, July 14, 2000, S6; "Women Wanted," *Golf World*, August 10, 2001, S2; Royal Canadian Golf Association website, www.rcga.org; Press Release, "Nancy Lopez Golf Named Official Golf Ball and Clubs of The Canadian Ladies' Golf Association," Oakville, ON (April 23, 2003); Canadian Ladies' Golf Association website www.clga.org; Jazz Golf website, www.jazzgolf.com.

Chapter 8

Ethics in Marketing: Producer Carmel Smyth/CBC.ca *Marketplace*. Reprinted with permission.

Try It: "Topozone Launches Interactive Topographic Map Size, Revolutionizes Topographic Map Industry," *PR Newswire*, November 30, 1999, on-line: www.topozone.com.

Chapter 9

Try It: www.chippery.com.

Chapter 10

Try It: "i.c.stars Addresses Digital Divide and Creates a New Business Model for Not-for-Profits," *PR Newswire*, May 23, 2000, on-line: www.iccapital.com; www.icstars.org.

Marketing Miscues: "Moxi's Fortunes Rely on Middleware," *CED*, February 2002, 10; Richard Cole, "Perlman to Unveil Home-Networking Set-Up," *Cable World*, January 7, 2002, 2; Ben Elgin, Linda Himelstein, and Cliff Edwards, "Jazzy Product, Sizzling Start, Lots of Trouble," *Business Week*, March 4, 2002, 92–94; www.moxi.com.

Critical Thinking Case: "Mystery Project Revealed," *Design Engineering*, January 2002, 7; " 'Ginger' Revealed to Be Electric Scooter," *Electric Vehicle Online Today*, December 4, 2001, on-line; Karl Greenberg, "The 'It' Girl," *Brandweek*, November 12, 2001, 12; John Heileman, "Here 'It' Is: The Inside Story of the Secret Invention That So Many Are Buzzing About," *Time*, December 10, 2001, 76: www.dekaresearch.com; www.segway.com.

Chapter 11

Try It: Maynard M. Gordon, "Battle Lines Forming in the Wild World of the Automotive Web Sites," *Ward's Dealer Business*, June 1, 2000, 12; Chris Knap, "Online Car Sales Will Rise, Analysts Say," *KRTBN Knight-Ridder Tribune Business News*, September 19, 1999; Scott Woolley, "A Car by Any Other Name," *Forbes*, November 29, 1999, 113–16; www.carsdirect.com.

Chapter 12

Try It: Soozhana Choi, "Funky Fashions for Teen-Age Girls," *Gannett News Service*, March 16, 1999; Becky Ebenkamp, "Stephen Kahn," *Brandweek*, November 8, 1999, 32; Laura Keating, "The In Crowd: Retail Rushes to Keep Pace with Generation Y," *Shopping Center World*, May 30, 2000; Melanie Kletter, "Catalogs Lose Teen Appeal," *WWD*, March 2, 2000, 11; Paul Miller, "Apparel: Trends Analysis," *Catalog Age*, March 15, 2000, 65–69; David S. Murphy, "Delia's Next Big Step," *Fortune*, February 15, 1999, 192[C]–192[H]; Vicki M. Young, "Playing the Junior Game," *WWD*, October 27, 1999, 20; "Teen Shopping Heats Up Online," *WWD*, February 3, 2000, 26B.

Marketing Miscues: Clive Beddoe, "How Much Is Enough?" *Maclean's Magazine*, April 28, 2003. 40.

Critical Thinking Case: http://www.oreillynet.com; http://www.streamcastnetworks.com; Dawn Chmielewski, "Movie, Film Groups Sue File-Swapping Services, Alleging Online Piracy," *San Jose Mercury News*, October 4, 2001, on-line; Lisa Rein and David Sims, "O'Reilly P2P Directory," *The O'Reilly Network*, October 20, 2000, on-line; Erick Schonfield, "Goodbye Napster, Hello Morpheus," *ZDNet*, March 18, 2002, on-line; Clay Shirky, "What Is P2P ... and What Isn't," *The O'Reilly Network*, November 24, 2000, on-line; Scott Woolley, "Steal This Movie," *Forbes*, February 18, 2002, 66. Pure Tracks website, www.puretracks.com; Declan McCullagh, "Cyberpiracy North of the Border," *CNET News.com*, last modified: October 27, 2003, 4:00 AM PST.

Chapter 13

Try It: Chris Daniels, "Saturn Sets a Virtual Scene," *Marketing Magazine*, April 21, 2003; "Shopping with the Bots," *Marketing Magazine*, April 2, 2001.

Chapter 14

Try It: Bill Carter, "Will This Machine Change Television?" The *New York Times*, July 5, 1999, 1; Jim Cooper, "Inside the Box," *Brandweek*, May 8, 2000, C32; Marla Matzer Rose, "TV Advertisers Worry About Growth of New PVRs," *Chicago Tribune*, April 14, 2000, 4; Erin Strout, "The End of TV Advertising?" *Sales & Marketing Management*, January 2000, 15; www.tivo.com; "TiVo Signs Showtime," *Advertising Age*, May 16, 2000.

Marketing Miscues: www.gillette.com; "The Gillette Co.," *Drug Store News-Newsfirst*, February 13, 2002, 1; Ann Davin, "Duracell Launches New Advertising for America's Favorite Battery," company press release, November 19, 2001, 1; Daniel Golden and Suzanne Vranica, "Advertising: Duracell's Duck Ad Will Carry Disclaimer," *Wall Street Journal*, February 7, 2002, B7; Jack Neff, "Energizing Their Bases: Duracell and Energizer Focus Ads on Flagships," *Advertising Age*, June 4, 2001, 4.

Critical Thinking Case: Lesley Young, "Promo Vehicles," *Marketing Magazine*, January 15, 2001.

Chapter 15

Try It: Case based on an interview with Mark James, CEO of *A Taste of Class*.

Chapter 16

Try It: Angela Lo, "Young Entrepreneurs' Dream Is to Become Mercer Island's Sole Internet Provider," *Seattle Times*, February 13, 2002; www.mercerislandchamber.org.

Marketing Miscues: "Apple," *Business Week*, July 31, 2000, 102; Jerry Langdon, "Cube on Centre Stage," *Computer Dealer News*, August 11, 2000, 30; Harry McCracken, "Coolness Cubed: Apple's Radical New Mac," *PC World*, November 2000, 106; Josh Quittner, "Apple's New Core," *Time*, January 14, 2002, 46–52; www.apple.com.

Critical Thinking Case: "Could Diamonds Be Nokia's Best Friend?" *Reuters*, January 14, 2002, on-line; Elisa Batista, "The Jewel of Cell Phones," *Wired News*, January 31, 2001, on-line; Aloysius Choong, "Nokia Asia Exec Takes Helm at Vertu," *CNETAsia*, January 25, 2002, on-line; Hillary Smith, "For the Person with Everything, Nokia Offers Jeweled Handset," *RCR Wireless News*, January 28, 2002, on-line; www.nokia.com.

Chapter 17

Try It: Stephen D. Wise, "No Longer Net Bad Boys," *Marketing Magazine*, November 22, 1999; Chris Daniels, "Fumbling Towards Digital Ecstasy," *Marketing Magazine*, November 20, 2000; Derek Mellon, "Holiday E-Tail Season Only Booms for Some Online Merchants," *Silicon Valley North* (GTA Edition), December, 2000, 38; Press Release, "Amazon.ca and HMV Announce Relaunch of the HMV.com Web Site, Now Powered by Amazon.ca," *Canada Newswire*, April 29, 2003, 1.

Chapter 18

Try It: Marion Agnew, "CRM Becomes a Charitable Application," *InformationWeek*, October 16, 2000, 176; Patricia Odell, "The Web Way," *Direct*, May 15, 2001, 63; Susan Stellin, "A Non-Profit Uses Customer-Relationship Management Software to Net $1.5 Million," *ECompany.com*, July 2001.

Marketing Miscues: Lesley Young, "Brochure Flies in Face of Privacy Act," *Marketing Magazine*; PIPED Act Case Summary #162, "Customer Complains about Airline's Use of 'Cookies' on Its Web Site," Commissioners Findings, 2003, http://www.privcom.gc.ca/cf-dc/2003/index2-3_e.asp70. July 30, 2001.

Critical Thinking Case: Kraft Canada website, www.kraftcanada.com; Lesley Young, "One Bite at a Time," *Marketing Magazine*, November 5, 2001.

>> SUBJECT/COMPANY INDEX

(Key terms and the page numbers on which their definitions appear are printed in bold.)

A